DISCOVERING COMPUTERS &
MICROSOFT® OFFICE 365™
OFFICE 2016

A FUNDAMENTAL COMBINED APPROACH

DISCOVERING COMPUTERS & MICROSOFT® OFFICE 365™ OFFICE 2016

A FUNDAMENTAL COMBINED APPROACH

Steven M. Freund
Mary Z. Last
Philip J. Pratt
Susan L. Sebok
Misty E. Vermaat
Jennifer T. Campbell
Mark Frydenberg

CENGAGE
Learning®

SHELLY CASHMAN SERIES®

Australia • Brazil • Japan • Korea • Mexico • Singapore • Spain • United Kingdom • United States

Discovering Computers and Microsoft Office 2016: A Fundamental Combined Approach

Steven M. Freund
Mary Z. Last
Philip J. Pratt
Susan L. Sebok
Misty E. Vermaat
Jennifer T. Campbell
Mark Frydenberg

SVP, GM Skills & Global Product Management: Dawn Gerrain

Product Director: Kathleen McMahon

Senior Product Team Manager: Lauren Murphy

Associate Product Managers: William Guiliani, Amanda Lyons, Melissa Stehler

Senior Director, Development: Marah Bellegarde

Product Development Manager: Leigh Hefferon

Managing Content Developer: Emma F. Newsom

Developmental Editors: Amanda Brodkin, Deb Kaufmann, Lyn Markowicz, Lisa Ruffolo, Karen Stevens

Product Assistant: Erica Chapman, Cara Suriyamongkol

Manuscript Quality Assurance: Jeffrey Schwartz, John Freitas, Serge Palladino, Susan Pedicini, Danielle Shaw, Susan Whalen

Senior Production Director: Wendy Troeger

Production Director: Patty Stephan

Senior Content Project Manager: Matthew Hutchinson

Manufacturing Planner: Julio Esperas

Designer: Diana Graham

Text Design: Joel Sadagursky

Cover Template Designer: Diana Graham

Cover image(s): Mario7/Shutterstock.com; Mrs. Opossum/Shutterstock.com

Compositor: Lumina Datamatics

Vice President, Marketing: Brian Joyner

Marketing Director: Michele McTighe

Marketing Manager: Stephanie Albracht

Mac users: If you're working through this product using a Mac, some of the steps may vary. Additional information for Mac users is included with the data files for this product.

The material in this book was written using Microsoft Office 2016 and was Quality Assurance tested before the publication date. As Microsoft continually updates Office 2016 and Office 365, your software experience may vary slightly from what is seen in the printed text.

For product information and technology assistance, contact us at
Cengage Learning Customer & Sales Support, 1-800-354-9706

For permission to use material from this text or product, submit all requests online at **www.cengage.com/permissions.**

Further permissions questions can be e-mailed to **permissionrequest@cengage.com**

Library of Congress Control Number: 2015958649

ISBN: 978-1-305-87180-9

Cengage Learning
20 Channel Center Street
Boston, MA 02210
USA

Cengage Learning is a leading provider of customized learning solutions with employees residing in nearly 40 different countries and sales in more than 125 countries around the world. Find your local representative at **www.cengage.com.**

Cengage Learning products are represented in Canada by Nelson Education, Ltd.

To learn more about Cengage Learning, visit **www.cengage.com**

Purchase any of our products at your local college store or at our preferred online store **www.cengagebrain.com**

Printed in the United States of America
Print Number: 02   Print Year: 2017

DISCOVERING COMPUTERS &
MICROSOFT® OFFICE 365™ OFFICE 2016

A FUNDAMENTAL COMBINED APPROACH

Contents

Microsoft Office 2016 and Windows 10

Office 2016 and Windows 10: Essential Concepts and Skills

Microsoft **Word 2016**

MODULE ONE
Creating, Formatting, and Editing
a Word Document with a Picture

Microsoft PowerPoint 2016

Microsoft **Excel 2016**

MODULE ONE
Creating a Worksheet and a Chart

MODULE TWO
Formulas, Functions, and Formatting

Microsoft Access 2016

MODULE ONE
Databases and Database Objects: An Introduction

MODULE TWO
Querying a Database

Productivity Apps for School and Work

Corinne Hoisington

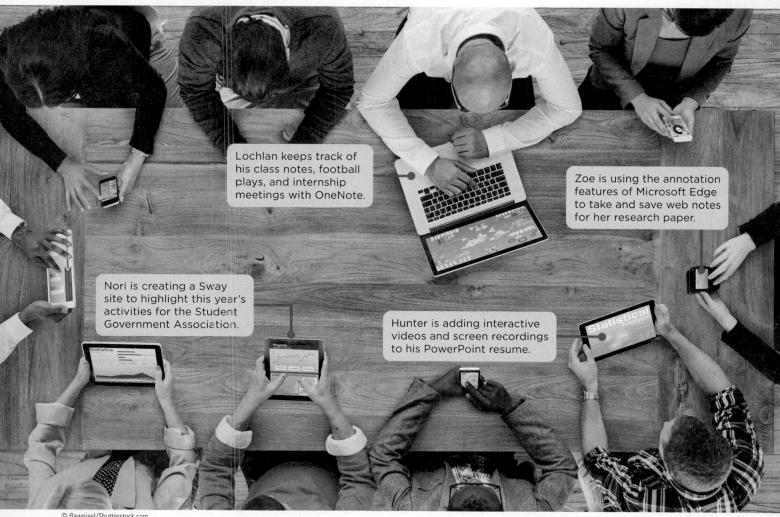

Lochlan keeps track of his class notes, football plays, and internship meetings with OneNote.

Zoe is using the annotation features of Microsoft Edge to take and save web notes for her research paper.

Nori is creating a Sway site to highlight this year's activities for the Student Government Association.

Hunter is adding interactive videos and screen recordings to his PowerPoint resume.

© Rawpixel/Shutterstock.com

Being computer literate no longer means mastery of only Word, Excel, PowerPoint, Outlook, and Access. To become technology power users, Hunter, Nori, Zoe, and Lochlan are exploring Microsoft OneNote, Sway, Mix, and Edge in Office 2016 and Windows 10.

Learn to use productivity apps!
Links to companion **Sways**, featuring **videos** with hands-on instructions, are located on www.cengagebrain.com.

Introduction to OneNote 2016

notebook | section tab | To Do tag | screen clipping | note | template | Microsoft OneNote Mobile app | sync | drawing canvas | inked handwriting | Ink to Text

As you glance around any classroom, you invariably see paper notebooks and notepads on each desk. Because deciphering and sharing handwritten notes can be a challenge, Microsoft OneNote 2016 replaces physical notebooks, binders, and paper notes with a searchable, digital notebook. OneNote captures your ideas and schoolwork on any device so you can stay organized, share notes, and work with others on projects. Whether you are a student taking class notes as shown in **Figure 1** or an employee taking notes in company meetings, OneNote is the one place to keep notes for all of your projects.

Figure 1: OneNote 2016 notebook

Each **notebook** is divided into sections, also called **section tabs**, by subject or topic.

Use **To Do tags**, icons that help you keep track of your assignments and other tasks.

Type on a page to add a **note**, a small window that contains text or other types of information.

Personalize a page with a **template**, or stationery.

Write or draw directly on the page using drawing tools.

Pages can include pictures such as **screen clippings**, images from any part of a computer screen.

Attach files and enter equations so you have everything you need in one place.

Creating a OneNote Notebook

OneNote is divided into sections similar to those in a spiral-bound notebook. Each OneNote notebook contains sections, pages, and other notebooks. You can use OneNote for school, business, and personal projects. Store information for each type of project in different notebooks to keep your tasks separate, or use any other organization that suits you. OneNote is flexible enough to adapt to the way you want to work.

When you create a notebook, it contains a blank page with a plain white background by default, though you can use templates, or stationery, to apply designs in categories such as Academic, Business, Decorative, and Planners. Start typing or use the buttons on the Insert tab to insert notes, which are small resizable windows that can contain text, equations, tables, on-screen writing, images, audio and video recordings, to-do lists, file attachments, and file printouts. Add as many notes as you need to each page.

Syncing a Notebook to the Cloud

OneNote saves your notes every time you make a change in a notebook. To make sure you can access your notebooks with a laptop, tablet, or smartphone wherever you are, OneNote uses cloud-based storage, such as OneDrive or SharePoint. **Microsoft OneNote Mobile app**, a lightweight version of OneNote 2016 shown in **Figure 2**, is available for free in the Windows Store, Google Play for Android devices, and the AppStore for iOS devices.

If you have a Microsoft account, OneNote saves your notes on OneDrive automatically for all your mobile devices and computers, which is called **syncing**. For example, you can use OneNote to take notes on your laptop during class, and then open OneNote on your phone to study later. To use a notebook stored on your computer with your OneNote Mobile app, move the notebook to OneDrive. You can quickly share notebook content with other people using OneDrive.

Figure 2: Microsoft OneNote Mobile app

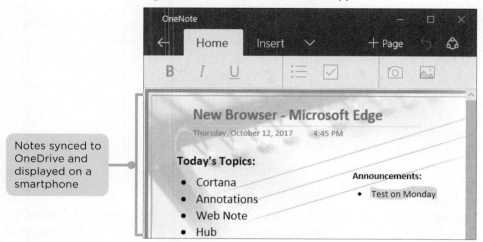

Notes synced to OneDrive and displayed on a smartphone

Taking Notes

Use OneNote pages to organize your notes by class and topic or lecture. Beyond simple typed notes, OneNote stores drawings, converts handwriting to searchable text and mathematical sketches to equations, and records audio and video.

OneNote includes drawing tools that let you sketch freehand drawings such as biological cell diagrams and financial supply-and-demand charts. As shown in **Figure 3**, the Draw tab on the ribbon provides these drawing tools along with shapes so you can insert diagrams and other illustrations to represent your ideas. When you draw on a page, OneNote creates a **drawing canvas**, which is a container for shapes and lines.

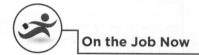

On the Job Now

OneNote is ideal for taking notes during meetings, whether you are recording minutes, documenting a discussion, sketching product diagrams, or listing follow-up items. Use a meeting template to add pages with content appropriate for meetings.

Figure 3: Tools on the Draw tab

Pens and highlighters are in the Tools group.

Insert rectangles and lines from the Shapes group.

Lines and shapes are in the Shapes group.

Make drawings using pens in the Tools group.

Insert text using the Type button in the Tools group.

Converting Handwriting to Text

When you use a pen tool to write on a notebook page, the text you enter is called **inked handwriting**. OneNote can convert inked handwriting to typed text when you use the **Ink to Text** button in the Convert group on the Draw tab, as shown in **Figure 4**. After OneNote converts the handwriting to text, you can use the Search box to find terms in the converted text or any other note in your notebooks.

Figure 4: Converting handwriting to text

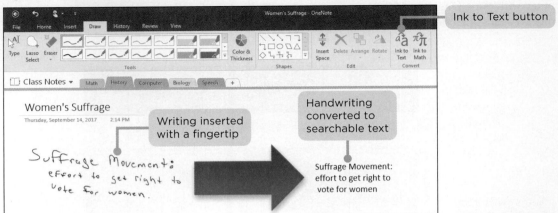

On the Job Now

Use OneNote as a place to brainstorm ongoing work projects. If a notebook contains sensitive material, you can password-protect some or all of the notebook so that only certain people can open it.

Recording a Lecture

If your computer or mobile device has a microphone or camera, OneNote can record the audio or video from a lecture or business meeting as shown in **Figure 5**. When you record a lecture (with your instructor's permission), you can follow along, take regular notes at your own pace, and review the video recording later. You can control the start, pause, and stop motions of the recording when you play back the recording of your notes.

Figure 5: Video inserted in a notebook

Try This Now

Learn to use OneNote!
Links to companion **Sways**, featuring **videos** with hands-on instructions, are located on www.cengagebrain.com.

1: Taking Notes for a Week

As a student, you can get organized by using OneNote to take detailed notes in your classes. Perform the following tasks:

a. Create a new OneNote notebook on your Microsoft OneDrive account (the default location for new notebooks). Name the notebook with your first name followed by "Notes," as in **Caleb Notes**.

b. Create four section tabs, each with a different class name.

c. Take detailed notes in those classes for one week. Be sure to include notes, drawings, and other types of content.

d. Sync your notes with your OneDrive. Submit your assignment in the format specified by your instructor.

2: Using OneNote to Organize a Research Paper

You have a research paper due on the topic of three habits of successful students. Use OneNote to organize your research. Perform the following tasks:

a. Create a new OneNote notebook on your Microsoft OneDrive account. Name the notebook **Success Research**.

b. Create three section tabs with the following names:

- **Take Detailed Notes**
- **Be Respectful in Class**
- **Come to Class Prepared**

c. On the web, research the topics and find three sources for each section. Copy a sentence from each source and paste the sentence into the appropriate section. When you paste the sentence, OneNote inserts it in a note with a link to the source.

d. Sync your notes with your OneDrive. Submit your assignment in the format specified by your instructor.

3: Planning Your Career

Note: This activity requires a webcam or built-in video camera on any type of device.

Consider an occupation that interests you. Using OneNote, examine the responsibilities, education requirements, potential salary, and employment outlook of a specific career. Perform the following tasks:

a. Create a new OneNote notebook on your Microsoft OneDrive account. Name the notebook with your first name followed by a career title, such as **Kara - App Developer**.

b. Create four section tabs with the names **Responsibilities, Education Requirements, Median Salary**, and **Employment Outlook**.

c. Research the responsibilities of your career path. Using OneNote, record a short video (approximately 30 seconds) of yourself explaining the responsibilities of your career path. Place the video in the Responsibilities section.

d. On the web, research the educational requirements for your career path and find two appropriate sources. Copy a paragraph from each source and paste them into the appropriate section. When you paste a paragraph, OneNote inserts it in a note with a link to the source.

e. Research the median salary for a single year for this career. Create a mathematical equation in the Median Salary section that multiplies the amount of the median salary times 20 years to calculate how much you will possibly earn.

f. For the Employment Outlook section, research the outlook for your career path. Take at least four notes about what you find when researching the topic.

g. Sync your notes with your OneDrive. Submit your assignment in the format specified by your instructor.

Introduction to Sway

Sway site | responsive design | Storyline | card | Creative Commons license | animation emphasis effects | Docs.com

Expressing your ideas in a presentation typically means creating PowerPoint slides or a Word document. Microsoft Sway gives you another way to engage an audience. Sway is a free Microsoft tool available at Sway.com or as an app in Office 365. Using Sway, you can combine text, images, videos, and social media in a website called a **Sway site** that you can share and display on any device. To get started, you create a digital story on a web-based canvas without borders, slides, cells, or page breaks. A Sway site organizes the text, images, and video into a **responsive design**, which means your content adapts perfectly to any screen size as shown in **Figure 6**. You store a Sway site in the cloud on OneDrive using a free Microsoft account.

Figure 6: Sway site with responsive design

You can display a Sway presentation in a web browser.

Sway uses responsive design to make sure pages fit perfectly on any device.

Creating a Sway Presentation

You can use Sway to build a digital flyer, a club newsletter, a vacation blog, an informational site, a digital art portfolio, or a new product rollout. After you select your topic and sign into Sway with your Microsoft account, a **Storyline** opens, providing tools and a work area for composing your digital story. See **Figure 7**. Each story can include text, images, and videos. You create a Sway by adding text and media content into a Storyline section, or **card**. To add pictures, videos, or documents, select a card in the left pane and then select the Insert Content button. The first card in a Sway presentation contains a title and background image.

Figure 7: Creating a Sway site

Design and create Sway presentations.

Share and play published Sway sites.

Arrange content in a Storyline, which contains all the text, pictures, videos, and other media in a Sway presentation.

To add content, select a card, which is designed to hold a particular type of information.

After selecting a card, click the Insert Content button to add the content to the Sway presentation.

Adding Content to Build a Story

As you work, Sway searches the Internet to help you find relevant images, videos, tweets, and other content from online sources such as Bing, YouTube, Twitter, and Facebook. You can drag content from the search results right into the Storyline. In addition, you can upload your own images and videos directly in the presentation. For example, if you are creating a Sway presentation about the market for commercial drones, Sway suggests content to incorporate into the presentation by displaying it in the left pane as search results. The search results include drone images tagged with a **Creative Commons license** at online sources as shown in **Figure 8**. A Creative Commons license is a public copyright license that allows the free distribution of an otherwise copyrighted work. In addition, you can specify the source of the media. For example, you can add your own Facebook or OneNote pictures and videos in Sway without leaving the app.

On the Job Now

If you have a Microsoft Word document containing an outline of your business content, drag the outline into Sway to create a card for each topic.

Figure 8: Images in Sway search results

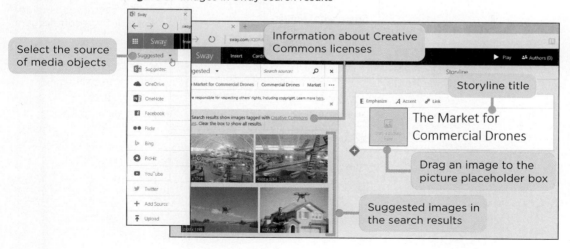

Select the source of media objects

Information about Creative Commons licenses

Storyline title

The Market for Commercial Drones

Drag an image to the picture placeholder box

Suggested images in the search results

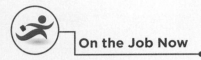

Designing a Sway

Sway professionally designs your Storyline content by resizing background images and fonts to fit your display, and by floating text, animating media, embedding video, and removing images as a page scrolls out of view. Sway also evaluates the images in your Storyline and suggests a color palette based on colors that appear in your photos. Use the Design button to display tools including color palettes, font choices, **animation emphasis effects**, and style templates to provide a personality for a Sway presentation. Instead of creating your own design, you can click the Remix button, which randomly selects unique designs for your Sway site.

Publishing a Sway

Use the Play button to display your finished Sway presentation as a website. The Address bar includes a unique web address where others can view your Sway site. As the author, you can edit a published Sway site by clicking the Edit button (pencil icon) on the Sway toolbar.

Sharing a Sway

When you are ready to share your Sway website, you have several options as shown in **Figure 9**. Use the Share slider button to share the Sway site publically or keep it private. If you add the Sway site to the Microsoft **Docs.com** public gallery, anyone worldwide can use Bing, Google, or other search engines to find, view, and share your Sway site. You can also share your Sway site using Facebook, Twitter, Google+, Yammer, and other social media sites. Link your presentation to any webpage or email the link to your audience. Sway can also generate a code for embedding the link within another webpage.

Figure 9: Sharing a Sway site

Try This Now

Learn to use Sway! PA-9

Links to companion **Sways**, featuring **videos** with hands-on instructions, are located on www.cengagebrain.com.

1: Creating a Sway Resume

Sway is a digital storytelling app. Create a Sway resume to share the skills, job experiences, and achievements you have that match the requirements of a future job interest. Perform the following tasks

    a. Create a new presentation in Sway to use as a digital resume. Title the Sway Storyline with your full name and then select a background image.

    b. Create three separate sections titled **Academic Background, Work Experience**, and **Skills**, and insert text, a picture, and a paragraph or bulleted points in each section. Be sure to include your own picture.

    c. Add a fourth section that includes a video about your school that you find online.

    d. Customize the design of your presentation.

    e. Submit your assignment link in the format specified by your instructor.

2: Creating an Online Sway Newsletter

Newsletters are designed to capture the attention of their target audience. Using Sway, create a newsletter for a club, organization, or your favorite music group. Perform the following tasks:

    a. Create a new presentation in Sway to use as a digital newsletter for a club, organization, or your favorite music group. Provide a title for the Sway Storyline and select an appropriate background image.

    b. Select three separate sections with appropriate titles, such as Upcoming Events. In each section, insert text, a picture, and a paragraph or bulleted points.

    c. Add a fourth section that includes a video about your selected topic.

    d. Customize the design of your presentation.

    e. Submit your assignment link in the format specified by your instructor.

3: Creating and Sharing a Technology Presentation

To place a Sway presentation in the hands of your entire audience, you can share a link to the Sway presentation. Create a Sway presentation on a new technology and share it with your class. Perform the following tasks:

    a. Create a new presentation in Sway about a cutting-edge technology topic. Provide a title for the Sway Storyline and select a background image.

    b. Create four separate sections about your topic, and include text, a picture, and a paragraph in each section.

    c. Add a fifth section that includes a video about your topic.

    d. Customize the design of your presentation.

    e. Share the link to your Sway with your classmates and submit your assignment link in the format specified by your instructor.

Introduction to Office Mix

add-in | clip | slide recording | Slide Notes | screen recording | free-response quiz

To enliven business meetings and lectures, Microsoft adds a new dimension to presentations with a powerful toolset called Office Mix, a free add-in for PowerPoint. (An **add-in** is software that works with an installed app to extend its features.) Using Office Mix, you can record yourself on video, capture still and moving images on your desktop, and insert interactive elements such as quizzes and live webpages directly into PowerPoint slides. When you post the finished presentation to OneDrive, Office Mix provides a link you can share with friends and colleagues. Anyone with an Internet connection and a web browser can watch a published Office Mix presentation, such as the one in **Figure 10**, on a computer or mobile device.

Figure 10: Office Mix presentation

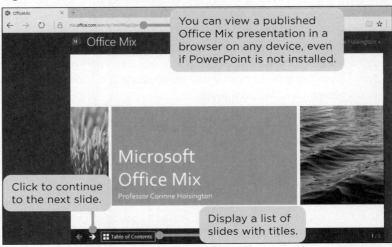

Adding Office Mix to PowerPoint

To get started, you create an Office Mix account at the website mix.office.com using an email address or a Facebook or Google account. Next, you download and install the Office Mix add-in (see **Figure 11**). Office Mix appears as a new tab named Mix on the PowerPoint ribbon in versions of Office 2013 and Office 2016 running on personal computers (PCs).

Figure 11: Getting started with Office Mix

Capturing Video Clips

A **clip** is a short segment of audio, such as music, or video. After finishing the content on a PowerPoint slide, you can use Office Mix to add a video clip to animate or illustrate the content. Office Mix creates video clips in two ways: by recording live action on a webcam and by capturing screen images and movements. If your computer has a webcam, you can record yourself and annotate the slide to create a **slide recording** as shown in **Figure 12**.

Figure 12: Making a slide recording

When you are making a slide recording, you can record your spoken narration at the same time. The **Slide Notes** feature works like a teleprompter to help you focus on your presentation content instead of memorizing your narration. Use the Inking tools to make annotations or add highlighting using different pen types and colors. After finishing a recording, edit the video in PowerPoint to trim the length or set playback options.

The second way to create a video is to capture on-screen images and actions with or without a voiceover. This method is ideal if you want to show how to use your favorite website or demonstrate an app such as OneNote. To share your screen with an audience, select the part of the screen you want to show in the video. Office Mix captures everything that happens in that area to create a **screen recording**, as shown in **Figure 13**. Office Mix inserts the screen recording as a video in the slide.

Figure 13: Making a screen recording

Inserting Quizzes, Live Webpages, and Apps

To enhance and assess audience understanding, make your slides interactive by adding quizzes, live webpages, and apps. Quizzes give immediate feedback to the user as shown in **Figure 14**. Office Mix supports several quiz formats, including a **free-response quiz** similar to a short answer quiz, and true/false, multiple-choice, and multiple-response formats.

Figure 14: Creating an interactive quiz

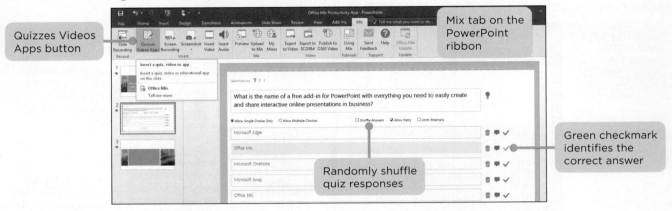

Sharing an Office Mix Presentation

When you complete your work with Office Mix, upload the presentation to your personal Office Mix dashboard as shown in **Figure 15**. Users of PCs, Macs, iOS devices, and Android devices can access and play Office Mix presentations. The Office Mix dashboard displays built-in analytics that include the quiz results and how much time viewers spent on each slide. You can play completed Office Mix presentations online or download them as movies.

Figure 15: Sharing an Office Mix presentation

Try This Now

Learn to use Office Mix!
Links to companion **Sways**, featuring **videos** with hands-on instructions, are located on www.cengagebrain.com.

1: Creating an Office Mix Tutorial for OneNote

Note: This activity requires a microphone on your computer.

Office Mix makes it easy to record screens and their contents. Create PowerPoint slides with an Office Mix screen recording to show OneNote 2016 features. Perform the following tasks:

    a. Create a PowerPoint presentation with the Ion Boardroom template. Create an opening slide with the title **My Favorite OneNote Features** and enter your name in the subtitle.

    b. Create three additional slides, each titled with a new feature of OneNote. Open OneNote and use the Mix tab in PowerPoint to capture three separate screen recordings that teach your favorite features.

    c. Add a fifth slide that quizzes the user with a multiple-choice question about OneNote and includes four responses. Be sure to insert a checkmark indicating the correct response.

    d. Upload the completed presentation to your Office Mix dashboard and share the link with your instructor.

    e. Submit your assignment link in the format specified by your instructor.

2: Teaching Augmented Reality with Office Mix

Note: This activity requires a webcam or built-in video camera on your computer.

A local elementary school has asked you to teach augmented reality to its students using Office Mix. Perform the following tasks:

    a. Research augmented reality using your favorite online search tools.

    b. Create a PowerPoint presentation with the Frame template. Create an opening slide with the title **Augmented Reality** and enter your name in the subtitle.

    c. Create a slide with four bullets summarizing your research of augmented reality. Create a 20-second slide recording of yourself providing a quick overview of augmented reality.

    d. Create another slide with a 30-second screen recording of a video about augmented reality from a site such as YouTube or another video-sharing site.

    e. Add a final slide that quizzes the user with a true/false question about augmented reality. Be sure to insert a checkmark indicating the correct response.

    f. Upload the completed presentation to your Office Mix dashboard and share the link with your instructor.

    g. Submit your assignment link in the format specified by your instructor.

3: Marketing a Travel Destination with Office Mix

Note: This activity requires a webcam or built-in video camera on your computer.

To convince your audience to travel to a particular city, create a slide presentation marketing any city in the world using a slide recording, screen recording, and a quiz. Perform the following tasks:

    a. Create a PowerPoint presentation with any template. Create an opening slide with the title of the city you are marketing as a travel destination and your name in the subtitle.

    b. Create a slide with four bullets about the featured city. Create a 30-second slide recording of yourself explaining why this city is the perfect vacation destination.

    c. Create another slide with a 20-second screen recording of a travel video about the city from a site such as YouTube or another video-sharing site.

    d. Add a final slide that quizzes the user with a multiple-choice question about the featured city with five responses. Be sure to include a checkmark indicating the correct response.

    e. Upload the completed presentation to your Office Mix dashboard and share your link with your instructor.

    f. Submit your assignment link in the format specified by your instructor.

Introduction to Microsoft Edge

Reading view | Hub | Cortana | Web Note | Inking | sandbox

Microsoft Edge is the default web browser developed for the Windows 10 operating system as a replacement for Internet Explorer. Unlike its predecessor, Edge lets you write on webpages, read webpages without advertisements and other distractions, and search for information using a virtual personal assistant. The Edge interface is clean and basic, as shown in **Figure 16**, meaning you can pay more attention to the webpage content.

Figure 16: Microsoft Edge tools

Forward button | New tab button | Web address in the Address bar | Add to favorites or reading list button | Reading view button | More button | Back button | Share Web Note button | Make a Web Note button | Refresh (F5) button | Hub (Favorites, reading list, history, and downloads) button

Browsing the Web with Microsoft Edge

One of the fastest browsers available, Edge allows you to type search text directly in the Address bar. As you view the resulting webpage, you can switch to **Reading view**, which is available for most news and research sites, to eliminate distracting advertisements. For example, if you are catching up on technology news online, the webpage might be difficult to read due to a busy layout cluttered with ads. Switch to Reading view to refresh the page and remove the original page formatting, ads, and menu sidebars to read the article distraction-free.

Consider the **Hub** in Microsoft Edge as providing one-stop access to all the things you collect on the web, such as your favorite websites, reading list, surfing history, and downloaded files.

Locating Information with Cortana

Cortana, the Windows 10 virtual assistant, plays an important role in Microsoft Edge. After you turn on Cortana, it appears as an animated circle in the Address bar when you might need assistance, as shown in the restaurant website in **Figure 17**. When you click the Cortana icon, a pane slides in from the right of the browser window to display detailed information about the restaurant, including maps and reviews. Cortana can also assist you in defining words, finding the weather, suggesting coupons for shopping, updating stock market information, and calculating math.

Figure 17: Cortana providing restaurant information

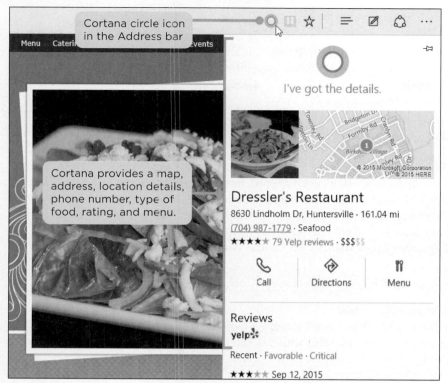

Cortana circle icon in the Address bar

I've got the details.

Cortana provides a map, address, location details, phone number, type of food, rating, and menu.

Dressler's Restaurant
8630 Lindholm Dr, Huntersville · 161.04 mi
(704) 987-1779 · Seafood
★★★★★ 79 Yelp reviews · $$$$$

📞 Call   ◈ Directions   🍴 Menu

Reviews
yelp⁙

Recent · Favorable · Critical
★★★★★ Sep 12, 2015

Annotating Webpages

One of the most impressive Microsoft Edge features are the **Web Note** tools, which you use to write on a webpage or to highlight text. When you click the Make a Web Note button, an **Inking** toolbar appears, as shown in **Figure 18**, that provides writing and drawing tools. These tools include an eraser, a pen, and a highlighter with different colors. You can also insert a typed note and copy a screen image (called a screen clipping). You can draw with a pointing device, fingertip, or stylus using different pen colors. Whether you add notes to a recipe, annotate sources for a research paper, or select a product while shopping online, the Web Note tools can enhance your productivity. After you complete your notes, click the Save button to save the annotations to OneNote, your Favorites list, or your Reading list. You can share the inked page with others using the Share Web Note button.

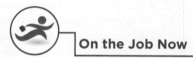

On the Job Now

To enhance security, Microsoft Edge runs in a partial sandbox, an arrangement that prevents attackers from gaining control of your computer. Browsing within the **sandbox** protects computer resources and information from hackers.

Figure 18: Web Note tools in Microsoft Edge

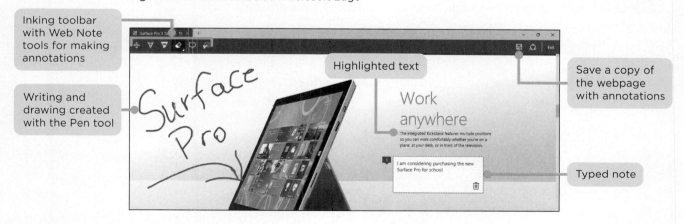

Inking toolbar with Web Note tools for making annotations

Highlighted text

Save a copy of the webpage with annotations

Writing and drawing created with the Pen tool

Work anywhere

The integrated Kickstand features multiple positions so you can work comfortably whether you're on a plane, at your desk, or in front of the television.

I am considering purchasing the new Surface Pro for school

Typed note

Try This Now

1: Using Cortana in Microsoft Edge

Note: This activity requires using Microsoft Edge on a Windows 10 computer.

Cortana can assist you in finding information on a webpage in Microsoft Edge. Perform the following tasks:

a. Create a Word document using the Word Screen Clipping tool to capture the following screenshots.

- Screenshot A—Using Microsoft Edge, open a webpage with a technology news article. Right-click a term in the article and ask Cortana to define it.
- Screenshot B—Using Microsoft Edge, open the website of a fancy restaurant in a city near you. Make sure the Cortana circle icon is displayed in the Address bar. (If it's not displayed, find a different restaurant website.) Click the Cortana circle icon to display a pane with information about the restaurant.
- Screenshot C—Using Microsoft Edge, type **10 USD to Euros** in the Address bar without pressing the Enter key. Cortana converts the U.S. dollars to Euros.
- Screenshot D—Using Microsoft Edge, type **Apple stock** in the Address bar without pressing the Enter key. Cortana displays the current stock quote.

b. Submit your assignment in the format specified by your instructor.

2: Viewing Online News with Reading View

Note: This activity requires using Microsoft Edge on a Windows 10 computer.

Reading view in Microsoft Edge can make a webpage less cluttered with ads and other distractions. Perform the following tasks:

a. Create a Word document using the Word Screen Clipping tool to capture the following screenshots.

- Screenshot A—Using Microsoft Edge, open the website **mashable.com**. Open a technology article. Click the Reading view button to display an ad-free page that uses only basic text formatting.
- Screenshot B—Using Microsoft Edge, open the website **bbc.com**. Open any news article. Click the Reading view button to display an ad-free page that uses only basic text formatting.
- Screenshot C—Make three types of annotations (Pen, Highlighter, and Add a typed note) on the BBC article page displayed in Reading view.

b. Submit your assignment in the format specified by your instructor.

3: Inking with Microsoft Edge

Note: This activity requires using Microsoft Edge on a Windows 10 computer.

Microsoft Edge provides many annotation options to record your ideas. Perform the following tasks:

a. Open the website **wolframalpha.com** in the Microsoft Edge browser. Wolfram Alpha is a well-respected academic search engine. Type **US$100 1965 dollars in 2015** in the Wolfram Alpha search text box and press the Enter key.

b. Click the Make a Web Note button to display the Web Note tools. Using the Pen tool, draw a circle around the result on the webpage. Save the page to OneNote.

c. In the Wolfram Alpha search text box, type the name of the city closest to where you live and press the Enter key. Using the Highlighter tool, highlight at least three interesting results. Add a note and then type a sentence about what you learned about this city. Save the page to OneNote. Share your OneNote notebook with your instructor.

d. Submit your assignment link in the format specified by your instructor.

INTRODUCING TODAY'S TECHNOLOGIES:
Computers, Devices, and the Web

Technology provides access to the digital world around you.

"I use computers, mobile devices, and the web to do homework, look up information, check email, play games, post updates, talk to friends, upload photos, sync music, and so much more! I feel comfortable using technology. What more do I need to know?"

While you may be familiar with some of the content in this module, do you know how to . . .

- Use a touch screen?
- Configure social media privacy settings to prevent others from posting unauthorized photos of you?
- Ease eyestrain while working on a computer or mobile device?
- Protect your hearing when using earbuds or headphones?
- Back up computers and mobile devices?
- Perform a web search?
- Sync computers and mobile devices?
- Protect your computer from viruses and other malware?
- Shop safely online?
- Create a strong password?
- 'Like' the Discovering Computers page on Facebook and 'follow' it on Twitter?
- Connect to a wireless network?

In this module, you will discover how to perform these tasks along with much more information essential to this course.

✓ Objectives

After completing this module, you will be able to:

1   Differentiate among laptops, tablets, desktops, and servers

2   Describe the purpose and uses of smartphones, digital cameras, portable and digital media players, e-book readers, wearable devices, and game devices

3   Describe the relationship between data and information

4   Briefly explain various input options (keyboards, pointing devices, voice and video input, and scanners), output options (printers, displays, and speakers), and storage options (hard disks, solid-state drives, USB flash drives, memory cards, optical discs, and cloud storage)

5   Differentiate the web from the Internet, and describe the relationship among the web, webpages, websites, and web servers

6   Explain the purpose of a browser, a search engine, and an online social network

7   Briefly describe digital security risks associated with viruses and other malware, privacy, your health, and the environment

8   Differentiate between an operating system and applications

9   Differentiate between wired and wireless network technologies, and identify reasons individuals and businesses use networks

10   Discuss how society uses technology in education, government, finance, retail, entertainment, health care, science, travel, publishing, and manufacturing

11   Identify technology used by home users, small/home office users, mobile users, power users, and enterprise users

Today's Technology

In the course of a day, you may . . . complete a homework assignment and watch a streaming video using your laptop, flip through news headlines and make dinner reservations using your tablet, search for directions and the local weather forecast while listening to music on your smartphone, edit a video on a desktop computer, and share photos online from your digital camera with family and friends. These and many other technologies are an integral part of everyday life: at school, at home, and at work (Figure 1-1).

Technology can enable you to more efficiently and effectively access and search for information; share personal ideas, photos, and videos with friends, family, and others; communicate with and meet other people; manage finances; shop for goods and services; play games or access other sources of entertainment; keep your life and activities organized; and complete business activities. People who can accomplish these types of tasks using technology often are said to be tech savvy.

Because technology changes, you must keep up with the changes to remain digitally literate. *Digital literacy* involves having a current knowledge and understanding of computers, mobile devices, the web, and related technologies. This book presents the knowledge you need to be digitally literate today.

As you read this first module, keep in mind it is an overview. Most of the terms and concepts introduced in this module will be discussed in more depth later in the book.

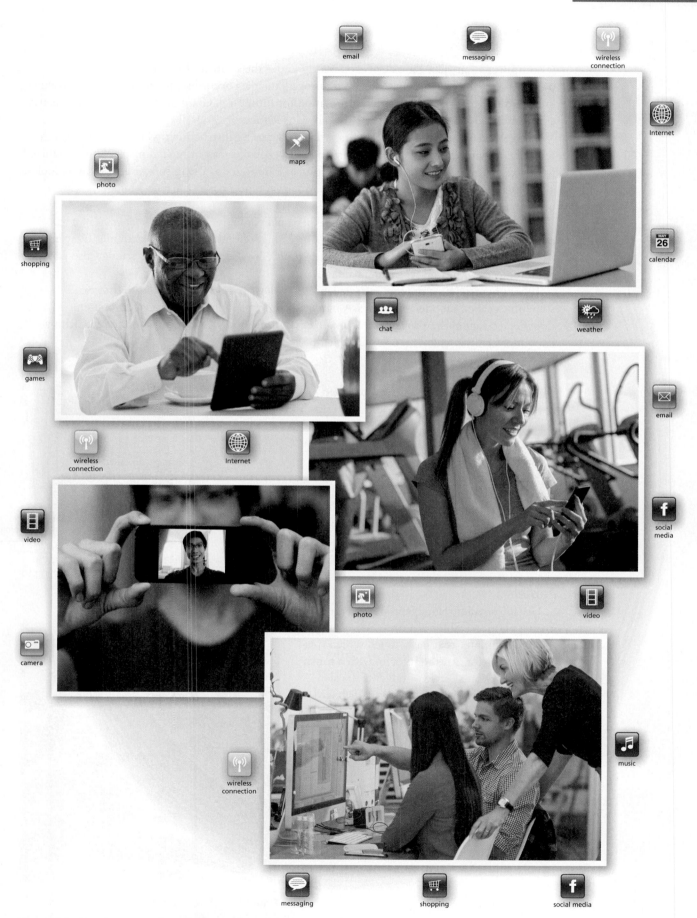

Figure 1-1   People use a variety of computers, mobile devices, and apps everyday.

Computers

A **computer** is an electronic device, operating under the control of instructions stored in its own memory, that can accept data (*input*), process the data according to specified rules, produce information (*output*), and store the information for future use. Computers contain many electric, electronic, and mechanical components known as *hardware*.

Electronic components in computers process data using instructions, which are the steps that tell the computer how to perform a particular task. A collection of related instructions organized for a common purpose is referred to as software or a program. Using software, you can complete a variety of activities, such as search for information, type a paper, balance a budget, create a presentation, or play a game.

One popular category of computer is the personal computer. A *personal computer* (PC) is a computer that can perform all of its input, processing, output, and storage activities by itself and is intended to be used by one person at a time. Most personal computers today also can communicate with other computers and devices.

Types of personal computers include laptops, tablets, and desktops, with the first two sometimes called mobile computers. A *mobile computer* is a portable personal computer, designed so that a user can carry it from place to place. A *user* is anyone who interacts with a computer or mobile device, or utilizes the information it generates.

Laptops

A **laptop**, also called a *notebook computer*, is a thin, lightweight mobile computer with a screen in its lid and a keyboard in its base (Figure 1-2). Designed to fit on your lap and for easy transport, most laptops weigh up to 7 pounds (varying by manufacturer and specifications). A laptop that is less than one inch thick and weighs about three pounds or less sometimes is referred to as an ultrathin laptop. Most laptops can operate on batteries or a power supply or both.

screen

keyboard

hinges

Figure 1-2   A typical laptop has a keyboard in the base and a screen in the lid, with the lid attaching to the base with hinges.
© iStockphoto / Stephen Krow

Tablets

Usually smaller than a laptop but larger than a phone, a **tablet** is a thin, lighter-weight mobile computer that has a touch screen (read How To 1-1 for ways to interact with a touch screen). A popular style of tablet is the slate, which does not contain a physical keyboard (Figure 1-3). Like laptops, tablets run on batteries or a power supply or both; however, batteries in a tablet typically last longer than those in laptops.

Figure 1-3   A slate tablet.
© iStockphoto / franckreporter

HOW TO 1-1

Interact with a Touch Screen

You usually can interact with a touch screen using gestures. A *gesture* is a motion you make on a touch screen with the tip of one or more fingers or your hand. Touch screens are convenient because they do not require a separate device for input. Tablets and smartphones typically have touch screens.

The table below presents common ways to interact with a touch screen.

Touch Screen Gestures

Motion	Description	Common Uses
Tap	Quickly touch and release one finger one time	Activate a link (built-in connection) Press a button Run a program or app
Double-tap	Quickly touch and release one finger two times	Run a program or app Zoom in (show a smaller area on the screen, so that contents appear larger) at the location of the double-tap
Press and hold	Press and hold one finger to cause an action to occur, or until an action occurs	Display a shortcut menu (immediate access to allowable actions) Activate a mode enabling you to move an item with one finger to a new location
Drag, or *slide*	Press and hold one finger on an object and then move the finger to the new location	Move an item around the screen Scroll
Swipe	Press and hold one finger and then move the finger horizontally or vertically on the screen	Scroll Display a bar that contains commands on an edge of the screen
Stretch	Move two fingers apart	Zoom in (show a smaller area on the screen, so that contents appear larger)
Pinch	Move two fingers together	Zoom out (show a larger area on the screen, so that contents appear smaller)

 Consider This: In addition to the motions listed in the table, what other motions do you think a touch screen should support?

© Cengage Learning

 CONSIDER THIS

If a slate tablet has no keyboard, how do you type on it?

You can use your fingers to press keys on a keyboard that appears on the screen, called an *on-screen keyboard*, or you can purchase a separate physical keyboard that attaches to or wirelessly communicates with the tablet. You also may be able to speak into the tablet, and your spoken words will translate to typed text.

Internet Research

What is a virtual keyboard?

Search for: virtual keyboard

BTW

Desktop
The term, desktop, also sometimes is used to refer to an on-screen work area on laptops, tablets, and desktops.

Desktops and All-in-Ones

A **desktop**, or desktop computer, is a personal computer designed to be in a stationary location, where all of its components fit on or under a desk or table. On many desktops, the screen is housed in a display device (or simply display) that is separate from a tower, which is a case that contains the processing circuitry (Figure 1-4a). Another type of desktop called an **all-in-one** does not contain a tower and instead uses the same case to house the display and the processing circuitry (Figure 1-4b). Some desktops and all-in-ones have displays that support touch.

Figure 1-4 Some desktops have a separate tower; all-in-ones do not.
© iStockphoto / Oleksiy Mark; Source: Microsoft; © iStockphoto / hocus-focus; Apple, Inc.

 CONSIDER THIS

Which type of computer — laptop, tablet, or desktop — is best?
It depends on your needs. Because laptops can be as powerful as the average desktop, more people today choose laptops over desktops so that they have the added benefit of portability. Tablets are ideal for those not needing the power of a laptop or for searching for information, communicating with others, and taking notes in lectures, at meetings, conferences, and other forums where a laptop is not practical. Desktops and all-in-ones often have larger displays than laptops or tablets, which make them well suited for developing software, editing large documents, or creating images and videos.

 BTW

Online
When a computer or device connects to a network, it is said to be online.

Figure 1-5 A server provides services to other computers or devices on a network.
© iStockPhoto / GuidoVrola

Servers

A **server** is a computer dedicated to providing one or more services to other computers or devices on a network. A network is a collection of computers and devices connected together, often wirelessly. Services provided by servers include storing content and controlling access to hardware, software, and other resources on a network.

A server can support from two to several thousand connected computers and devices at the same time. Servers are available in a variety of sizes and types for both small and large business applications (Figure 1-5). Smaller applications, such as at home, sometimes use a high-end desktop as a server. Larger corporate, government, and web applications use powerful, expensive servers to support their daily operations.

Mobile and Game Devices

A *mobile device* is a computing device small enough to hold in your hand. Because of their reduced size, the screens on mobile devices are small — often between 3 and 5 inches.

Some mobile devices are Internet capable, meaning that they can connect to the Internet wirelessly. You often can exchange information between the Internet and a mobile device or between a computer or network and a mobile device. Popular types of mobile devices are smartphones, digital cameras, portable and digital media players, e-book readers, and wearable devices.

 CONSIDER THIS

Are mobile devices computers?
The mobile devices discussed in this section can be categorized as computers because they operate under the control of instructions stored in their own memory, can accept data, process the data according to specified rules, produce or display information, and store the information for future use.

Smartphones

A **smartphone** is an Internet-capable phone that usually also includes a calendar, an address book, a calculator, a notepad, games, and several other apps (which are programs on the smartphone). Other apps are available through an app store that typically is associated with the phone.

Smartphones typically communicate wirelessly with other devices or computers. With most smartphone models, you also can listen to music, take photos, and record videos.

Many smartphones have touch screens. Instead of or in addition to a touch screen, some smartphones have a keyboard that slides in and out from behind the phone (Figure 1-6). Others have built-in mini keyboards or keypads that contain both numbers and letters. Some are called a *phablet* because they combine the features of a smartphone with a tablet.

touch screen

slide out keyboard

Figure 1-6
Smartphones may have a touch screen and/or a slide out keyboard.
© iStockphoto / Moncherie;
© iStockPhoto / scanrail

Internet Research
What are some app stores?
Search for: popular app stores

Instead of calling someone's phone to talk, you can send messages to others by pressing images on an on-screen keyboard on the phone, keys on the phone's mini keyboard, or buttons on the phone's keypad. Four popular types of messages that you can send with smartphones include voice messages, text messages, picture messages, and video messages.

- A *voice mail message* is a short audio recording sent to or from a smartphone or other mobile device.
- A *text message* is a short note, typically fewer than 300 characters, sent to or from a smartphone or other mobile device.
- A *picture message* is a photo or other image, sometimes along with sound and text, sent to or from a smartphone or other mobile device.
- A *video message* is a short video clip, usually about 30 seconds, sent to or from a smartphone or other mobile device.

 BTW

Messaging Services
Mobile service providers may charge additional fees for sending text, picture, or video messages, depending on the messaging plan.

Read Ethics & Issues 1-1 to consider whether it should be legal to use a hands-free device, such as a smartphone, while driving.

ETHICS & ISSUES 1-1

Should It Be Legal to Use a Hands-Free Device while Driving?
Your new vehicle includes a sophisticated hands-free system that enables you to connect a mobile device to the vehicle's sound system. In addition to making phone calls without holding your device, you also can use this technology to read and respond to email messages or to update your Facebook status using speech-to-text, which converts your spoken words to text. Is this technology safe to use?

The debate about hands-free device safety elicits different points of view from vehicle insurance companies, consumer safety groups, and the telecommunications industry. AAA (American Automobile

Association) conducted a study to measure the mental effect of using hands-free devices while driving. The conclusions indicated that drivers using hands-free devices are distracted, miss visual clues, and have slower reaction times. The report also stated that 3000 fatalities occur each year due to the use of hands-free devices.

Critics say that using a hands-free device gives people a false sense of security. Others claim that drivers can be just as easily distracted if they are discussing business or emotional matters with passengers in the vehicle. Some states have outlawed any use of mobile phones while driving; others require drivers to use hands-free devices

while driving. Lawmakers are attempting to regulate "distracted driving" caused by using hands-free devices. One issue that remains unclear is whether law enforcement has a right to look at a user's devices to determine whether they were used illegally.

Consider This: Do you think the government should be able to establish rules about hands-free device usage while driving? Why or why not? Do you believe you are distracted if you use hands-free devices while driving? Why or why not? Do you think auto manufacturers should continue to put hands-free device technology in vehicles? Why or why not?

Digital Cameras

A **digital camera** is a device that allows you to take photos and store the photographed images digitally (Figure 1-7). A smart digital camera also can communicate wirelessly with other devices and include apps similar to those on a smartphone. Many mobile computers and devices, such as tablets and smartphones, include at least one integrated digital camera.

Digital cameras typically allow you to review, and sometimes modify, images while they are in the camera. You also can transfer images from a digital camera to a computer or device, so that you can review, modify, share, organize, or print the images. Digital cameras often can connect to or communicate wirelessly with a computer, a Smart TV (discussed later in the module), a printer, or the Internet, enabling you to access the photos on the camera without using a cable. Some also can record videos. Many digital cameras also have built-in GPS (discussed later in this module), giving them the capability to record the exact location where a photo was taken and store these details with the photo.

Figure 1-7 With a digital camera, you can view photographed images immediately through a small screen on the camera to see if the photo is worth keeping.
Source: Samsung

Internet Research

What is a digital SLR camera?

Search for: digital slr camera

Portable and Digital Media Players

A **portable media player** is a mobile device on which you can store, organize, and play or view digital media (Figure 1-8). *Digital media* includes music, photos, and videos. Thus, portable media players enable you to listen to music, view photos, and watch videos, movies, and television shows. With most, you transfer the digital media from a computer or the web, if the device is Internet capable, to the portable media player. Some enable you to play the media while it streams, that is, while it transfers to the player.

Portable media players usually require a set of *earbuds*, which are small speakers that rest inside each ear canal. Some portable media player models have a touch screen, while others have a pad that you operate with a thumb or finger, so that you can navigate through digital media, adjust volume, and customize settings. Some portable media players also offer a calendar, address book, games, and other apps (discussed later in this module).

Portable media players are a mobile type of digital media player. A *digital media player* or *streaming media player* is a device, typically used in a home, that streams digital media from a computer or network to a television, projector, or some other entertainment device.

Internet Research

What are popular digital media players?

Search for: digital media players

Figure 1-8 Portable media players, such as the iPod shown here, typically include a set of earbuds. Digital media players stream media to a home entertainment device.
© iStockphoto / Sebastien Cote; © iStockPhoto / marvinh

E-Book Readers

An **e-book reader** (short for electronic book reader), or *e-reader*, is a mobile device that is used primarily for reading e-books (Figure 1-9). An *e-book*, or digital book, is an electronic version of a printed book, readable on computers and other digital devices. In addition to books, you typically can purchase and read other forms of digital media such as newspapers and magazines.

Most e-book reader models have a touch screen, and some are Internet capable. These devices usually are smaller than tablets but larger than smartphones.

Wearable Devices

A **wearable device** or *wearable* is a small, mobile computing consumer device designed to be worn (Figure 1-10). These devices often communicate with a mobile device or computer.

Wearable devices include activity trackers, smartwatches, and smartglasses. Activity trackers monitor heart rate, measure pulse, count steps, and track sleep patterns. In addition to keeping time, a smartwatch can communicate with a smartphone to make and answer phone calls, read and send messages, access the web, play music, work with apps, such as fitness trackers and GPS, and more. With smartglasses, a user looks into an eyeglass-type device to view information or take photos and videos that are projected to a miniature screen in the user's field of vision.

Figure 1-9 An e-book reader.
© iStockPhoto

Figure 1-10 Activity trackers, smartwatches, and smartglasses are popular types of wearable devices.
© iStockPhoto / MileA;
© iStockPhoto / scanrail;
© iStockPhoto / ferrantraite

Game Devices

A **game console** is a mobile computing device designed for single-player or multiplayer video games. Gamers often connect the game console to a television so that they can view their gameplay on the television's screen (Figure 1-11). Many game console models are Internet capable and also allow you to listen to music and watch movies or view photos. Typically weighing between three and eleven pounds, the compact size of game consoles makes them easy to use at home, in the car, in a hotel, or any location that has an electrical outlet and a television screen.

A handheld game device is small enough to fit in one hand, making it more portable than the game console. Because of their reduced size, the screens are small — similar in size to some smartphone screens. Some handheld game device models are Internet capable and also can communicate wirelessly with other similar devices for multiplayer gaming.

game console

handheld game device

Figure 1-11 Game consoles often connect to a television; handheld game devices contain a built-in screen.
© iStockPhoto / pagadesign; © iStockPhoto / AnthonyRosenberg

❋ **CONSIDER THIS**

Are digital cameras, portable media players, e-book readers, and handheld game devices becoming obsolete because more and more smartphones and tablets include their functionality?

Many smartphones and tablets enable you to take and store photos; store, organize, and play or view your digital media; read e-books; and play games. This trend of computers and devices with technologies that overlap, called **digital device convergence**, means that consumers may need fewer devices for the functionality that they require.

Still, consumers may purchase separate stand-alone devices (i.e., a separate digital camera, portable media player, etc.) for a variety of reasons. The stand-alone device (i.e., a digital camera) may have more features and functionality than the combined device offers (i.e., a smartphone). You might want to be able to use both devices at the same time; for example, you might send text messages on the phone while reading a book on an e-book reader. Or, you might want protection if your combined device (i.e., smartphone) breaks. For example, you still can listen to music on a portable media player if your smartphone becomes nonfunctional.

Mini Feature 1-1: Living Digitally — Gaming and Digital Home

Technology has made homes entertaining, efficient, and safe. Read Mini Feature 1-1 to learn how game devices provide entertainment and education, and home automation offers convenience and significant cost savings.

MINI FEATURE 1-1

Gaming and Digital Home

Academic researchers developed the first video games in the 1950s as part of their studies of artificial intelligence and simulations, and their work was applied and expanded commercially to early home consoles and arcade games. The concept of home automation can be traced back to 1898 when Nikola Tesla invented the first remote control. The following sections describe how these two technologies are used today.

Gaming

Video gamers spend billions of dollars each year making the most of their downtime with game consoles and devices, with an estimated 5 billion people worldwide playing at least 45 hours per week. The popularity is due, in large part, to the social aspect of gathering families and friends to play together as a group or online with each other and those around the world. The wide variety of categories offers a gaming experience for practically everyone in genres such as adventure, education, fitness, puzzles, sports, role-playing, and simulation.

- **Obtaining Games:** Gamers have several options available for locating games. For tablets and smartphones, they can download games from an app store to a mobile computer or device. For game consoles, they can purchase or rent discs or other media that contain games; download or transfer them from online stores; or sign up for cloud services that stream or transfer games on demand.

- **Accessories and Input Techniques:** The more popular game consoles work with a wide variety of accessories and input techniques for directing movements and actions of on-screen players and objects. They include gamepads, voice commands, and fitness accessories, some of which are shown here. Although many games are played using a controller, several systems operate by allowing the player to be the controller.

© iStockphoto / Florea Marius Catalin; © iStockphoto / Brandon Alms; © iStockphoto / Lee Pettet; © iStockphoto / Craig Veltri; © Courtesy of DDR Game

Home Automation

New home builders and existing homeowners are integrating features that automate a wide variety of tasks, save time and money, and enhance the overall at-home environment.

- **Lighting:** Controlling lighting is one of the more common uses of technology in the home. Remotes turn light fixtures on and off, and motion sensors turn on lights when a car or a visitor approaches the driveway or walkway.

- **Thermostats**: Programmable thermostats adjust to seasonal needs and can be set to control temperatures in individual rooms. Homeowners can use their smartphones to monitor heating and cooling systems, adjust temperatures, and manage energy consumption.

- **Appliances**: Smart appliances, such as dishwashers, can be programmed to run at nonpeak electrical times. Coffeemakers can turn on at set times and shut off if an overheating coffeepot has been left on accidentally. Refrigerators can track expiration dates and create shopping lists.

- **Security:** Security systems can detect break-ins at doors and heat from fires, and they can send text and email messages to alert a homeowner when someone has entered or left the home. Surveillance cameras keep a watchful eye on the premises and interior rooms; homeowners can view the images on televisions and computers within the house or on a webpage when they are away from home, as shown in the figure.

© DavidEwingPhotography / Shutterstock.com; © Poulsons Photography / Shutterstock.com; © Anthony Berenyi / Shutterstock.com

- **Remotes:** Many people are turning to using their smartphones and tablets to control all the devices in the room. Users enjoy the convenience of customizing apps to operate their television, DVR, and security system and to perform other functions anywhere in the home.

✹ **Consider This:** How has your life become more efficient, safe, and enjoyable by using home automation and entertainment features? What are the advantages of playing games, and do they outweigh the disadvantages?

© iStockphoto / Christian J. Stewart; © Mmaxer / Shutterstock.com; © iStockphoto / Nastco; © ESPN; © Cengage Learning

Data and Information

Computers process data (input) into information (output) and often store the data and resulting information for future use. *Data* is a collection of unprocessed items, which can include text, numbers, images, audio, and video. *Information* conveys meaning to users. Both business and home users can make well-informed decisions because they have instant access to information from anywhere in the world.

Many daily activities either involve the use of or depend on information from a computer. For example, as shown in Figure 1-12, computers process several data items to print information in the form of a cash register receipt.

Step 1
Cashier scans or enters items purchased and the amount received from the customer. These items are entered into the computer as data.

DATA (input)

2 Medium Sodas	$1.49 each
1 Small Turkey Sub	$3.49 each
1 Caesar Salad	$4.49 each
1 Bag of Chips	$0.99 each
3 Cookies	$0.39 each
Amount Received	$20.00

Step 2
The computer receives the entered data, stores it, processes the data into information (the receipt), and stores the resulting information.

STORAGE and PROCESSES

- Stores entered data.
- Computes each item's total price by multiplying the quantity ordered by the item price (i.e., 2 * 1.49 = 2.98).
- Organizes data.
- Sums all item total prices to determine order total due from customer (13.12).
- Calculates change due to customer by subtracting the order total from amount received (20.00 - 13.12 = 6.88).
- Stores resulting information.

Step 3
The resulting information (the cash register receipt) is printed for the customer.

Arrow Deli
10 Park Street
Maple River, DE 20393
(734) 555-2939

QTY	ITEM	TOTAL
2	Medium Sodas	2.98
1	Small Turkey Sub	3.49
1	Caesar Salad	4.49
1	Bag of Chips	0.99
3	Cookies	1.17
Total Due		13.12
Amount Received		20.00
Change		6.88

Thank You!

INFORMATION (output)

Figure 1-12 A computer processes data into information. In this simplified example, the item ordered, item price, quantity ordered, and amount received all represent data (input). The computer processes the data to produce the cash register receipt (information, or output).
© Cengage Learning; © iStockphoto / Norman Chan; © bikeriderlondon / Shutterstock

 BTW

Mobile Computer Input
If you prefer a full-sized keyboard to a laptop's keyboard or a tablet's on-screen keyboard, you can use a full-sized keyboard with your mobile computer. Likewise, if you prefer using a mouse instead of a touchpad, you can use a mouse with your mobile computer.

✳ **CONSIDER THIS**

Can you give another example of data and its corresponding information?
Your name, address, term, course names, course sections, course grades, and course credits all represent data that is processed to generate your semester grade report. Other information on the grade report includes results of calculations such as total semester hours, grade point average, and total credits.

Input

Users have a variety of input options for entering data into a computer, many of which involve using an input device. An **input device** is any hardware component that allows you to enter data and instructions into a computer or mobile device. The following sections discuss common input methods.

Keyboards A *keyboard* contains keys you press to enter data and instructions into a computer or mobile device (Figure 1-13). All desktop keyboards have a typing area that includes letters of the alphabet, numbers, punctuation marks, and other basic keys. Some users prefer a wireless keyboard because it eliminates the clutter of a cord.

Keyboards for desktops contain more keys than keyboards on mobile computers and devices. To provide the same functionality as a desktop keyboard, many of the keys on mobile computers and devices serve two or three purposes. On a laptop, for example, you often use the same keys to type numbers and to show various areas on a screen, switching a key's purpose by pressing a separate key first.

Instead of a physical keyboard, users also can enter data via an on-screen keyboard or a virtual keyboard, which is a keyboard that projects from a device to a flat surface.

desktop keyboard

laptop keyboard

Figure 1-13 Users have a variety of options for entering typed text.
© skyfotostock / Shutterstock.com;
© Africa Studio / Shutterstock.com;
© iStockphoto /
kycstudio; © iStockphoto /
MorePixels; Courtesy of Virtek, Inc.

on-screen keyboard   mini keyboard   virtual keyboard

Pointing Devices A pointing device is an input device that allows a user to control a small symbol on a screen, called the pointer. Desktops typically use a mouse as their pointing device, and laptops use a touchpad (Figure 1-14).

A *mouse* is a pointing device that fits under the palm of your hand comfortably. With the mouse, you control movement of the pointer and send instructions to the computer or mobile device. Table 1-1 identifies some of the common mouse operations. Like keyboards, some users prefer working with a wireless mouse.

A *touchpad* is a small, flat, rectangular pointing device that is sensitive to pressure and motion. To control the pointer with a touchpad, slide your fingertip across the surface of the pad. On most touchpads, you also can tap the pad's surface to imitate mouse operations, such as clicking.

Figure 1-14 A mouse and a touchpad.
© iStockphoto / PhotoTalk;
© iStockphoto / Michael Bodmann

mouse   touchpad

Table 1-1	Mouse Operations	
Operation	**Description**	**Common Uses**
Point	Move the mouse until the pointer is positioned on the item of choice.	Position the pointer on the screen.
Click	Press and release the primary mouse button, which usually is the left mouse button.	Select or deselect items on the screen or start a program or feature.
Right-click	Press and release the secondary mouse button, which usually is the right mouse button.	Display a shortcut menu.
Double-click	Quickly press and release the primary mouse button twice without moving the mouse.	Start a program or program feature.
Drag	Point to an item, hold down the primary mouse button, move the item to the desired location on the screen, and then release the mouse button.	Move an object from one location to another or draw pictures.

Voice and Video Input Some mobile devices and computers enable you to speak data instructions using voice input and to capture live full-motion images using video input. With your smartphone, for example, you may be able to use your voice to send a text message, schedule an appointment, and dial a phone number. Or, you may opt for video calling instead of a voice phone call, so that you and the person you called can see each other as you chat on a computer or mobile device. As in this example, video input usually works in conjunction with voice input. For voice input, you use a microphone, and for video input you use a webcam (Figure 1-15).

A *microphone* is an input device that enables you to speak into a computer or mobile device. Many computers and most mobile devices contain built-in microphones. You also can talk into a *headset*, which contains both a microphone and a speaker. Many headsets can communicate wirelessly with the computer or mobile device. A *webcam* is a digital video (DV) camera that allows you to capture video and usually audio input for your computer or mobile device.

microphone built into phone

wireless headset

webcam

Figure 1-15 You can speak instructions into a microphone or wireless headset and capture live video on a webcam for a video call.
© iStockphoto / Stephen Krow; © iStockphoto / pierrephoto; © iStockphoto / Suprijono Suharjoto

Figure 1-16 A scanner.
© iStockphoto / Edgaras Marozas

Scanners A *scanner* is a light-sensing input device that converts printed text and images into a form the computer can process (Figure 1-16). A popular type of scanner works in a manner similar to a copy machine, except that instead of creating a paper copy of the document or photo, it stores the scanned document or photo electronically.

Output

Users have a variety of output options to convey text, graphics, audio, and video — many of which involve using an output device. An **output device** is any hardware component that conveys information from a computer or mobile device to one or more people. The following sections discuss common output methods.

Printers A **printer** is an output device that produces text and graphics on a physical medium, such as paper or other material (Figure 1-17). Printed content sometimes is referred to as a *hard copy* or *printout*. Most printers today print text and graphics in both black-and-white and color on a variety of paper types with many capable of printing lab-quality photos. A variety of printers support wireless printing, where a computer or other device communicates wirelessly with the printer.

A *3-D printer* can print solid objects, such as clothing, prosthetics, eyewear, implants, toys, parts, prototypes, and more. 3-D printers use a plastic substance that prints in layers to create a 3-D (three-dimensional) model.

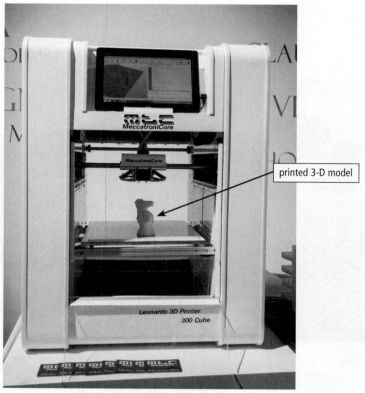

printed 3-D model

printed photo

Figure 1-17 A printer can produce a variety of printed output including photos and 3-D solid objects.
Courtesy of Epson America, Inc.; © iStockPhoto / Stefano Tinti

Displays A display is an output device that visually conveys text, graphics, and video information. Displays consist of a screen and the components that produce the information on the screen. The display for a desktop typically is a monitor, which is a separate, physical device. Mobile computers and devices typically integrate the display in their same physical case (Figure 1-18). Some displays have touch screens.

Home users sometimes use a digital television or a Smart TV as a display. A *Smart TV* is an Internet-enabled high-definition television (HDTV) from which you can use the Internet to watch video, listen to the radio, play games, and communicate with others — all while watching a television show.

smartphone display

digital camera display

tablet display

laptop display

monitor display

Figure 1-18 Displays vary depending on the computer or mobile device.
© iStockphoto / Sebastien Cote; © David Lentz / Photos.com; © Dmitry Rukhlenko / Photos.com; © Mrallen / Dreamstime.com; © Pakhnyushcha / Shutterstock.com

❋ **CONSIDER THIS** ─────────────────────────────

What can you do to ease eyestrain while using a computer or mobile device?
Position the display about 20 degrees below eye level. Clean the screen regularly. Blink your eyes every five seconds. Adjust the room lighting. Face into an open space beyond the screen. Use larger fonts or zoom the display. Take an eye break every 30 minutes. If you wear glasses, ask your doctor about computer glasses.

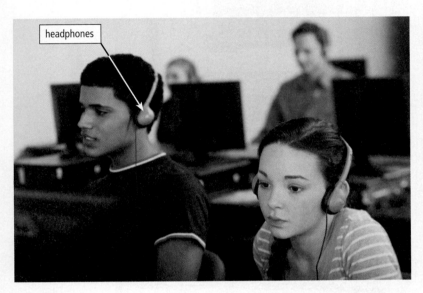

headphones

Figure 1-19 In a crowded environment where speakers are not practical, users can wear headphones to hear music, voice, and other sounds.
© iStockphoto / Photo_Alto

Speakers, Earbuds, and Headphones

Speakers allow you to hear audio, that is, music, voice, and other sounds. Most personal computers and mobile devices have a small internal speaker. Many users attach higher-quality speakers to their computers and mobile devices, including game consoles.

So that only you can hear sound, you can listen through earbuds (shown earlier in this module in Figure 1-8) or headphones, which cover or are placed outside of the ear (Figure 1-19). Both earbuds and headphones usually include noise-cancelling technology to reduce the interference of sounds from the surrounding environment. To eliminate the clutter of cords, users can opt for wireless speakers or wireless headphones. Read How To 1-2 to learn how to protect your hearing when using earbuds or headphones.

❋ **HOW TO 1-2** ───────────────────────────────

Protect Your Hearing when Using Earbuds or Headphones
Using earbuds and headphones improperly can lead to permanent hearing loss. The following tips describe some ways to protect your hearing when using earbuds or headphones:

• If people standing next to you can hear the sound being transmitted through the earbuds or headphones you are wearing, decrease the volume until they no longer can hear it. The quieter the sounds, the less damage you will incur.

• If you intend to listen to music through earbuds or headphones for hours at a time, consider listening at only 30 percent maximum volume. Listening for extended periods of time at a high volume may be unsafe for your ears.

• Consider using a high-quality set of headphones. These headphones reduce your risk of developing hearing loss because the sound quality often is better and does not require you to turn up the volume as loud. Also, their design is better, allowing a closer fit and thus

reducing the necessary volume required for optimal listening.

• Consider using a set of earbuds or headphones that reduce outside noise. When the earbuds or headphones eliminate the external noise effectively, they can reduce the volume level needed. The lower the volume levels, the less potential hearing damage.

❋ **Consider This:** Do you prefer earbuds or headphones? Why? Do you think you turn the volume up too loud while listening to music through earbuds or headphones?

Internet Research
What types of headphones are available?

Search for: headphone reviews

Memory and Storage

Memory consists of electronic components that store instructions waiting to be executed and the data needed by those instructions. Although some forms of memory are permanent, most memory keeps data and instructions temporarily, which means its contents are erased when the computer is shut off.

Storage, by contrast, holds data, instructions, and information for future use. For example, computers can store hundreds or millions of student names and addresses permanently.

A computer keeps data, instructions, and information on **storage media**. Examples of local storage media includes hard disks, solid-state drives, USB (universal serial bus) flash drives, memory cards, and optical discs. The amount of storage for each type of storage media varies, but hard disks, solid-state drives, and optical discs usually hold more than USB flash drives and memory cards. Some storage media are portable, meaning you can remove the medium from one computer and carry it to another computer.

A **storage device** records (writes) and/or retrieves (reads) items to and from storage media. Storage devices often also function as a source of input and output because they transfer items from storage to memory and vice versa. Drives and readers/writers, which are types of storage devices, accept a specific kind of storage media. For example, a DVD drive (storage device) accepts a DVD (storage media).

Hard Disks   A *hard disk* is a storage device that contains one or more inflexible, circular platters that use magnetic particles to store data, instructions, and information. The entire device is enclosed in an airtight, sealed case to protect it from contamination. Laptops and desktops often contain at least one hard disk that is mounted inside the computer's case (Figure 1-20).

hard disk is positioned in base of laptop

Figure 1-20   A hard disk mounted inside a laptop's case.
© iStockphoto / Brian Balster

hard disk contains moving parts

SSD contains no moving parts

Solid-State Drives   A *solid-state drive* (SSD) is a storage device that typically uses flash memory to store data, instructions, and information. Flash memory contains no moving parts, making it more durable and shock resistant than other types of media. For this reason, some manufacturers are using SSDs instead of hard disks in their laptops, tablets, and desktops (Figure 1-21).

Figure 1-21   A solid-state drive (SSD) is about the same size as a laptop hard disk.
© iStockphoto / Ludovit Repko

🌼 **CONSIDER THIS**

What is an external hard drive?
An external hard drive is a separate, portable, freestanding hard disk or SSD that usually connect to the computer with a cable (Figure 1-22). As with an internal hard disk or SSD, the entire external hard drive is enclosed in an airtight, sealed case.

external hard drive connected to laptop

Figure 1-22   A external hard drive is a separate, freestanding storage device.
© iStockphoto / murat sarica

Figure 1-23 You insert a USB flash drive in a USB port on a computer.
© Pakhnyushcha / Shutterstock.com

USB Flash Drives A *USB flash drive* is a portable flash memory storage device that you plug in a USB port, which is a special, easily accessible opening on a computer or mobile device (Figure 1-23). USB flash drives are convenient for mobile users because they are small and lightweight enough to be transported on a keychain or in a pocket.

Memory Cards A *memory card* is removable flash memory, usually no bigger than 1.5 inches in height or width, that you insert in and remove from a slot in a computer, mobile device, or card reader/writer (Figure 1-24). With a card reader/writer, you can transfer the stored items, such as digital photos, from a memory card to a computer or printer that does not have a built-in card slot.

Figure 1-24 Computers and mobile devices use a variety of styles of memory cards to store documents, photos, and other items.
© Verisakeet / Fotolia; © Sonar / Fotolia; Courtesy of Mark Frydenberg; © uwimages / Fotolia

memory card in computer

memory card in digital camera

memory card in phone

memory card in card reader/writer, which is attached to computer

✺ **CONSIDER THIS**

What is the general use for each type of local storage media?
Hard disks and SSDs store software and all types of user files. A *file* is a named collection of stored data, instructions, or information and can contain text, images, audio, and video. Memory cards and USB flash drives store files you intend to transport from one location to another, such as a homework assignment or photos. Optical discs generally store software, photos, movies, and music.

DVD

DVD drive

Figure 1-25 You can insert a DVD in a DVD drive on a computer.
© iStockphoto / Hanquan Chen

Optical Discs An *optical disc* is a type of storage media that consists of a flat, round, portable metal disc made of metal, plastic, and lacquer that is written and read by a laser. CDs (compact discs) and DVDs (digital versatile discs) are two types of optical discs (Figure 1-25).

Cloud Storage Instead of storing data, instructions, and information locally on a hard drive or other media, some users opt for cloud storage. **Cloud storage** is an Internet service that provides remote storage to computer users. For example, Figure 1-26 shows JustCloud, which provides cloud storage solutions to home and business users.

Types of services offered by cloud storage providers vary. Some provide storage for specific types of media, such as photos, whereas others store any content and provide backup services. A **backup** is a duplicate of content on a storage medium that you can use in case the original is lost, damaged, or destroyed. Read Secure IT 1-1 for suggestions for backing up your computers and mobile devices.

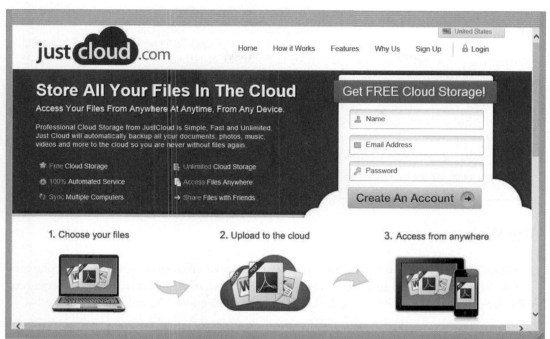

Figure 1-26 JustCloud is an example of a website that provides cloud storage solutions to home and business users.
Source: JustCloud.com

⚙ SECURE IT 1-1

Backing Up Computers and Mobile Devices

Power outages, hardware failure, theft, and many other factors can cause loss of data, instructions, or information on a computer or mobile device. To protect against loss, you should back up the contents of storage media regularly. Backing up can provide peace of mind and save hours of work attempting to recover important material in the event of a mishap.

A backup plan for laptop and desktop computers could include the following:

- Use a backup program, either included with your computer's operating system or one that you purchased separately, to copy the contents of your entire hard drive to a separate device.

- Regularly copy music, photos, videos, documents, and other important items to an external hard drive, a USB flash drive, or a DVD.

- Subscribe to a cloud storage provider.

- Schedule your files to be backed up regularly.

Backup plans for mobile devices are less specific. Apps for backing up your smartphone or tablet's content are available. You also can back up a mobile device to your computer's hard drive using synchronization software that runs on your computer (synchronization software is discussed later in this module). Some mobile device manufacturers, such as Apple, provide cloud storage solutions to owners of their devices. Other services allow subscribers to use another computer as a backup storage location. Overall, the best advice is to back up often using a variety of methods.

⚙ **Consider This:** Do you back up files regularly? If not, why not? What would you do if you had no backup and then discovered that your computer or mobile device had failed?

cloud storage provider

Courtesy of Western Digital Corporation; © iStockphoto / Stephen Krow; © Cengage Learning

NOW YOU SHOULD KNOW

Be sure you understand the material presented in the sections titled Today's Technology, Computers, Mobile and Game Devices, and Data and Information, as it relates to the module objectives.
Now you should know . . .

- Which type of computer might be suited to your needs (Objective 1)
- Why you would use a smartphone, digital camera, portable or digital media player, e-book reader, or wearable device, and which game software/apps you find interesting (Objective 2)
- How to recognize the difference between data and information (Objective 3)
- When you might use the various methods of input, output, and storage (Objective 4)

The Web

The World Wide Web (or web, for short) is a global library of information available to anyone connected to the Internet. The **Internet** is a worldwide collection of computer networks that connects millions of businesses, government agencies, educational institutions, and individuals (Figure 1-27).

✴ **CONSIDER THIS**

How do I access the Internet?
Businesses, called Internet service providers (ISPs), offer users and organizations access to the Internet free or for a fee. By subscribing to an ISP, you can connect to the Internet through your computers and mobile devices.

Figure 1-27 The Internet is the largest computer network, connecting millions of computers and devices around the world.

CONSIDER THIS

Are the web and Internet the same?
No. The Internet provides more than three billion home and business users around the world access to a variety of services. The World Wide Web is one of the widely used services of the Internet. Other popular services include email, instant messaging, VoIP, and FTP (all discussed later in this module).

People around the world access the web to accomplish the following types of online tasks:

- Search for information
- Conduct research
- Communicate with and meet other people
- Share information, photos, and videos with others
- Access news, weather, and sports
- Participate in online training
- Shop for goods and services
- Play games with others
- Download or listen to music
- Watch videos
- Download or read books
- Make reservations

 BTW

Downloading
Downloading is the process of transferring content from a server on the Internet to a computer or mobile device.

The **web** consists of a worldwide collection of electronic documents. Each electronic document on the web is called a **webpage**, which can contain text, graphics, audio, and video (Figure 1-28). A **website** is a collection of related webpages, which are stored on a web server. A **web server** is a computer that delivers requested webpages to your computer or mobile device.

Webpages often contain links. A *link*, short for *hyperlink*, is a built-in connection to other documents, graphics, audio files, videos, webpages, or websites. To activate an item associated with a link, you tap or click the link. In Figure 1-27, for example, tapping or clicking the audio link connects to a live radio show so that you can hear the broadcast. A text link often changes color after you tap or click it to remind you visually that you previously have visited the webpage or downloaded the content associated with the link.

Links allow you to obtain information in a nonlinear way. That is, instead of accessing topics in a specified order, you move directly to a topic of interest. Some people use the phrase *surfing the web* to refer to the activity of using links to explore the web.

A **browser** is software that enables users with an Internet connection to access and view webpages on a computer or mobile device. Some widely used browsers include Internet Explorer, Firefox, Safari, Edge, and Google Chrome.

Figure 1-28 Webpages, such as the one shown here, can display text, graphics, audio, and video on a computer or mobile device. Pointing to a link on the screen typically changes the shape of the pointer to a small hand with a pointing index finger.
Source: WTMJ

Web Searching

A primary reason that people use the web is to search for specific information, including text, photos, music, and videos. The first step in successful searching is to identify the main idea or concept in the topic about which you are seeking information. Determine any synonyms, alternate spellings, or variant word forms for the topic. Then, use a search engine, such as Google, to help you locate the information. A **search engine** is software that finds websites, webpages, images, videos, news, maps, and other information related to a specific topic. Read How To 1-3 for instructions about how to perform a basic web search using a search engine on a computer or mobile device.

⚙ HOW TO 1-3

Perform a Basic Web Search
The following steps describe how to use a search engine on a computer or mobile device to perform a basic web search:

1. Run a browser. (For instructions on running programs and apps, see How To 1-4 later in this module.)
2. Display the search engine's webpage on the screen by entering its web address in the address bar. For example, you could type google.com to access the Google search engine, bing.com to access the

Bing search engine, or yahoo.com to access the Yahoo! search engine.

3. Tap or click the Search box and then type the desired search text in the Search box. The more descriptive the search text, the easier it will be to locate the desired search results. As the figure shows, the search engine may provide search text suggestions as you type search text in the Search box.
4. To display search results based on your typed search text, press the ENTER key or tap or click the Search button. To display search results based on one of the suggestions provided

by the search engine, tap or click the desired search text suggestion.

5. Scroll through the search results and then tap or click a search result to display the corresponding webpage.
6. To return to the search results, tap or click the Back button in your browser or on your mobile device, which typically looks like a left-pointing arrow.

✳ **Consider This:** What search text would you enter to locate the admission criteria for your school?

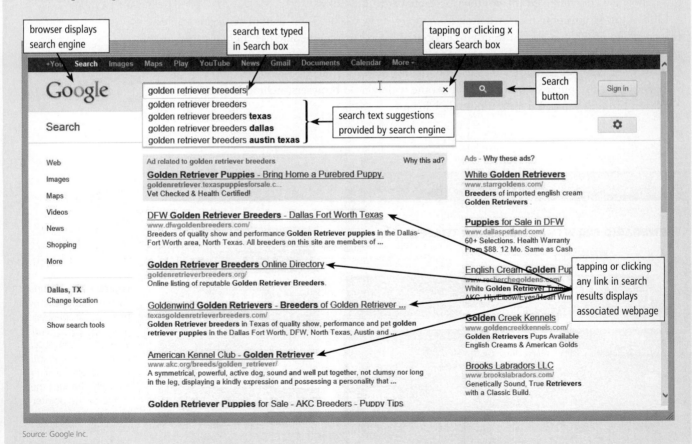

Source: Google Inc.

Online Social Networks

An **online social network**, also called a *social networking site*, is a website that encourages members in its online community to share their interests, ideas, stories, photos, music, and videos with other registered users (Figure 1-29). Popular online social networks include Facebook, Twitter, and LinkedIn.

Some online social networks have no specialized audience; others are more focused. A photo sharing site, for example, is a specific type of online social network that allows users to create an online photo album and store and share their digital photos. Similarly, a video sharing site is a type of online social network that enables users to store and share their personal videos. Read Ethics & Issues 1-2 to consider whether you should be required to obtain permission before posting photos of others.

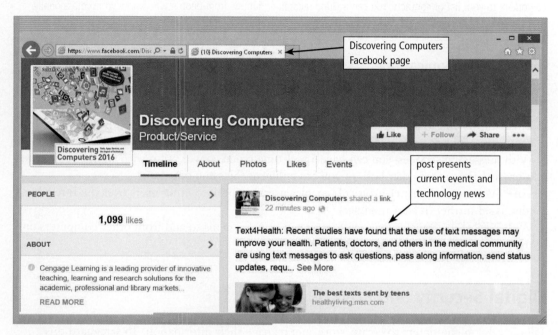

Figure 1-29   When Facebook users 'like' this Discovering Computers Facebook page, posts from the Discovering Computers page will appear on their own personal pages. As a student in this class, you should 'like' the Discovering Computers page so that you easily can keep up to date with relevant technology changes and events in the computing industry. If you do not have a Facebook account, use a search engine to search for the text, discovering computers facebook, to display the page in a browser.
Source: Facebook

 ETHICS & ISSUES 1-2

Should You Be Required to Obtain Permission before Posting Photos of Others?

Your friends and followers on online social networks instantly can view photos you post. If others appear in the photo and you post it without their permission, they might feel you have violated their privacy. Tagging people in a photo may create a link to their social network profiles, exposing their identity. Depending on your privacy settings, your friends' contacts can view a photo you post and/or share the photo without your permission.

You may be able to adjust tagging rules in the privacy settings of your online social network account. For example, you can use Facebook's privacy settings to approve all photos in which others tag you. The person posting the photo still can upload the photo, but your tag will not be associated with the photo until you approve it. Facebook also allows you to report a photo as abusive if you feel it portrays you negatively or if the person who posted it refuses to remove it upon request. Facebook's own Statement of Rights and Responsibilities states that "You will not tag users . . . without their consent."

People may not want photos of themselves posted for a variety reasons. They may have professional contacts as friends on their online social network and do not want to show themselves in a personal setting. Others may not be concerned with personal photos of themselves but do not want their children's

photos shared online. Or, they simply may find the photo unflattering. A poll by Sophos stated that 80 percent of respondents consider asking before posting a photo to be common courtesy. Eight percent of respondents felt that it should be illegal to do so.

Consider This: Is it ever acceptable to post photos of others without permission? Why or why not? Has someone posted or tagged you in a photo that you did not want others to see? How did you handle the situation? If asked to remove a photo or tag, would you respect the person's feelings and honor the request? What restrictions and policies should online social networks have about posting photos of others?

BTW
Blogs
Posts on Twitter also form a blog, because of its journal format with the most recent entry at the top.

 CONSIDER THIS ————————————————————

How do Facebook, Twitter, and LinkedIn differ?
With Facebook, you share messages, interests, activities, events, photos, and other personal information — called posts — with family and friends. You also can 'like' pages of celebrities, companies, products, etc., so that posts from others who like the same items will appear along with your other activities on Facebook. With Twitter, you 'follow' people, companies, and organizations in which you have an interest. Twitter enables you to stay current with the daily activities of those you are following via their Tweets, which are short posts (messages) that Twitter users broadcast for all their followers.

On LinkedIn, you share professional interests, education, and employment history, and add colleagues or coworkers to your list of contacts. You can include recommendations from people who know you professionally. Many employers post jobs using LinkedIn and consider information in your profile as your online resume.

Internet Communications

As mentioned earlier, the web is only one of the services on the Internet. Other services on the Internet facilitate communications among users, including the following:

- Email allows you to send messages to and receive messages and files from other users via a computer network.
- With messaging services, you can have a real-time typed conversation with another connected user (real-time means that both of you are online at the same time).
- VoIP (Voice over Internet Protocol) enables users to speak to other users over the Internet (discussed further in later modules).
- With FTP (File Transfer Protocol), users can transfer items to and from other computers on the Internet (discussed further in later modules).

Digital Security and Privacy

People rely on computers to create, store, and manage their information. To safeguard this information, it is important that users protect their computers and mobile devices. Users also should be aware of health risks and environmental issues associated with using computers and mobile devices.

Viruses and Other Malware

 BTW
Malware
A leading maker of security software claims its software blocked more than five billion malware attacks in a single year.

Malware, short for malicious software, is software that acts without a user's knowledge and deliberately alters the computer's or mobile device's operations. Examples of malware include viruses, worms, trojan horses, rootkits, spyware, adware, and zombies. Each of these types of malware attacks your computer or mobile device differently. Some are harmless pranks that temporarily freeze, play sounds, or display messages on your computer or mobile device. Others destroy or corrupt data, instructions, and information stored on the infected computer or mobile device. If you notice any unusual changes in the performance of your computer or mobile device, it may be infected with malware. Read Secure IT 1-2 for ways to protect computers from viruses and other malware.

Privacy

Nearly every life event is stored in a computer somewhere . . . in medical records, credit reports, tax records, etc. In many instances, where personal and confidential records were not protected properly, individuals have found their privacy violated and identities stolen. Some techniques you can use to protect yourself from identity theft include shredding financial documents before discarding them, never tapping or clicking links in unsolicited email messages, and enrolling in a credit monitoring service.

Adults, teens, and children around the world are using online social networks to share their photos, videos, journals, music, and other personal information publicly. Some of these unsuspecting, innocent computer users have fallen victim to crimes committed by dangerous strangers.

 Internet Research
What are other techniques that deter identity theft?
Search for: prevent identity theft

SECURE IT 1-2

Protection from Viruses and Other Malware

It is impossible to ensure a virus or malware never will attack a computer, but you can take steps to protect your computer by following these practices:

- **Use virus protection software.** Install a reputable antivirus program and then scan the entire computer to be certain it is free of viruses and other malware. Update the antivirus program and the virus signatures (known specific patterns of viruses) regularly.

- **Use a firewall.** Set up a hardware firewall or install a software firewall that protects your network's resources from outside intrusions.

- **Be suspicious of all unsolicited email and text messages.** Never open an email message unless you are expecting it, *and* it is from a trusted source. When in doubt, ask the sender to confirm the message is

legitimate before you open it. Be especially cautious when deciding whether to tap or click links in email and text messages or to open attachments.

- **Disconnect your computer from the Internet.** If you do not need Internet access, disconnect the computer from the Internet. Some security experts recommend disconnecting from the computer network before opening email attachments.

- **Download software with caution.** Download programs or apps only from websites you trust, especially those with music and video sharing software.

- **Close spyware windows.** If you suspect a pop-up window (a rectangular area that suddenly appears on your screen) may be spyware, close the window. Never tap or click an Agree or OK button in a suspicious window.

- **Before using any removable media, scan it for malware.** Follow this procedure even for shrink-wrapped software from major developers. Some commercial software has been infected and distributed to unsuspecting users. Never start a computer with removable media inserted in the computer unless you are certain the media are uninfected.

- **Keep current.** Install the latest updates for your computer software. Stay informed about new virus alerts and virus hoaxes.

- **Back up regularly.** In the event your computer becomes unusable due to a virus attack or other malware, you will be able to restore operations if you have a clean (uninfected) backup.

☀ **Consider This:** What precautions do you take to prevent viruses and other malware from infecting your computer? What new steps will you take to attempt to protect your computer?

Protect yourself and your dependents from these criminals by being cautious in email messages and on websites. For example, do not share information that would allow others to identify or locate you, and do not disclose identification numbers, user names, passwords, or other personal security details. A user name is a unique combination of characters, such as letters of the alphabet or numbers, that identifies one specific user. A password is a private combination of characters associated with a user name. Read Secure IT 1-3 for tips on creating strong passwords.

 SECURE IT 1-3

Creating Strong Passwords

A good password is easy for you to remember but difficult for criminals and password-breaking software to guess. Use these guidelines to create effective, strong passwords:

- **Personal information:** Avoid using any part of your first or last name, your family members' or pets' names, phone number, street address, license plate number, Social Security number, or birth date.

- **Length:** Use at least eight characters.

- **Difficulty:** Use a variety of uppercase and lowercase letters, numbers, punctuation marks, and symbols. Select characters located on different parts of the keyboard, not the ones you commonly use or that are adjacent to each other. Criminals often use software that converts common words to symbols, so their program might generate the passwords

GoToSleep and Go2Sleep as possibilities to guess.

- **Modify:** Change your password frequently, at least every three months.

- **Variation:** Do not use the same password for all websites you access. Once criminals have stolen a password, they attempt to use that password for other accounts they find on your computer or mobile device, especially banking websites.

- **Passphrase:** A passphrase, which is similar to a password, consists of several words separated by spaces. Security experts recommend misspelling a few of the words and adding several numerals. For example, the phrase, "Create a strong password," could become the passphrase, "Creaet a strang password42."

- **Common sequences:** Avoid numbers or letters in easily recognized patterns, such

as "asdfjkl;," "12345678," "09870987," or "abcdefg." Also, do not spell words backwards, use common abbreviations, or repeat strings of letters or numbers.

- **Manage:** Do not keep your passwords in your wallet, on a sheet of paper near your computer, or in a text file on your computer or mobile device. Memorize all of your passwords, or store them securely using a password management app on your computer or mobile device. Additional information about password management software is provided in Secure IT 5-3 in Module 5.

- **Test:** Use online tools to evaluate password strength.

☀ **Consider This:** How strong are your passwords? How will you modify your passwords using some of these guidelines?

Health Concerns

Prolonged or improper computer and mobile device use can lead to injuries or disorders of the hands, wrists, elbows, eyes, neck, and back. Computer and mobile device users can protect themselves from these health risks through proper workplace design, good posture while at the computer, and appropriately spaced work breaks.

With the growing use of earbuds and headphones, some users are experiencing hearing loss. Ways to protect your hearing when using these devices were presented in How To 1-2 earlier in this module.

Two behavioral health risks are technology addiction and technology overload. Technology addiction occurs when someone becomes obsessed with using technology. Individuals suffering from technology overload feel distressed when deprived of computers and mobile devices. Once recognized, both technology addiction and technology overload are treatable disorders.

Environmental Issues

Manufacturing processes for computers and mobile devices along with *e-waste*, or discarded computers and mobile devices, are depleting natural resources and polluting the environment. When computers and mobile devices are stored in basements or other locations, disposed of in landfills, or burned in incinerators, they can release toxic materials and potentially dangerous levels of lead, mercury, and flame retardants.

Green computing involves reducing the electricity consumed and environmental waste generated when using a computer. Strategies that support green computing include recycling, using energy efficient hardware and energy saving features, regulating manufacturing processes, extending the life of computers, and immediately donating or properly disposing of replaced computers. When you purchase a new computer, some retailers offer to dispose of your old computer properly.

 CONSIDER THIS ───────────────────────────────────

How can you contribute to green computing?

Some habits you can alter that will help reduce the environmental impact of computing include the following:

1. Do not leave a computer or device running overnight.
2. Turn off your monitor, printer, and other devices when you are not using them.
3. Use energy efficient hardware.
4. Use paperless methods to communicate.
5. Recycle paper and buy recycled paper.
6. Recycle toner, computers, mobile devices, printers, and other devices.
7. Telecommute.
8. Use videoconferencing and VoIP for meetings.

Programs and Apps

Software, also called a **program**, consists of a series of related instructions, organized for a common purpose, that tells the computer what tasks to perform and how to perform them.

Two categories of software are system software and application software (or applications). System software consists of the programs that control or maintain the operations of the computer and its devices. Operating systems are a widely recognized example of system software. Other types of system software, sometimes called tools, enable you to perform maintenance-type tasks usually related to managing devices, media, and programs used by computers and mobile devices. The next sections discuss operating systems and applications.

Operating Systems

An *operating system* is a set of programs that coordinates all the activities among computer or mobile device hardware. It provides a means for users to communicate with the computer or mobile device and other software. Many of today's computers and mobile devices use a version of Microsoft's Windows, Apple's Mac OS, Apple's iOS, or Google's Android (Figure 1-30).

To use an application, your computer or mobile device must be running an operating system.

Applications

An **application** (or **app** for short) consists of programs designed to make users more productive and/or assist them with personal tasks. Browsers, discussed in an earlier section, are an example of an application that enables users with an Internet connection to access and view webpages. Table 1-2 identifies the categories of applications with samples of ones commonly used in each category.

Figure 1-30 Shown here are the Mac OS and Windows operating systems for laptops and desktops and the Android and iOS operating systems for smartphones. You interact with these operating system interfaces by tapping or clicking their icons or tiles.
Sources: Apple Inc.; Apple Inc.; Google Inc.; Microsoft.

Table 1-2 Categories of Applications

Category	Sample Applications	Sample Uses
Productivity	Word Processing	Create letters, reports, and other documents.
	Presentation	Create visual aids for presentations.
	Schedule and Contact Management	Organize appointments and contact lists.
	Personal Finance	Balance checkbook, pay bills, and track income and expenses.
Graphics and Media	Photo Editing	Modify digital photos, i.e., crop, remove red-eye, etc.
	Video and Audio Editing	Modify recorded movie clips, add music, etc.
	Media Player	View images, listen to audio/music, watch videos.
Personal Interest	Travel, Mapping, and Navigation	View maps, obtain route directions, locate points of interest.
	Reference	Look up material in dictionaries, encyclopedias, etc.
	Educational	Learn through tutors and prepare for tests.
	Entertainment	Receive entertainment news alerts, check movie times and reviews, play games.

(Continued)

Table 1-2 *Continued*

Category	Sample Applications	Sample Uses
Communications	Browser	Access and view webpages.
	Email	Send and receive messages.
	VoIP	Speak to other users over the Internet.
	FTP	Transfer items to and from other computers on the Internet.
Security	Antivirus	Protect a computer against viruses.
	Personal Firewall	Detect and protect against unauthorized intrusions.
	Spyware, Adware, and other Malware Removers	Detect and delete spyware, adware, and other malware.
File, System, and Disk Management	File Manager	Display and organize files on storage media.
	Search	Locate files and other items on storage media.
	Image Viewer	Display, copy, and print contents of graphics files.
	Screen Saver	Shows moving image or blank screen if no keyboard or mouse activity occurs.

© Cengage Learning; Courtesy of NCH Software, Source: Apple Inc.; Source: Google Inc.; Courtesy of AVG Technologies; Source: Microsoft

Applications include programs stored on a computer, as well as those on a mobile device or delivered to your device over the Internet.

- A *desktop app* is an application stored on a computer.
- A *web app* is an application stored on a web server that you access through a browser.
- A *mobile app* is an application you download from a mobile device's app store or other location on the Internet to a smartphone or other mobile device.

Some applications are available as both a web app and a mobile app. In this case, you typically can sync (or match) the data and activity between the web app and the mobile app, which is discussed later in this module.

Installing and Running Programs

Installing a program is the process of setting up the program to work with a computer or mobile device, printer, and/or other hardware. When you buy a computer or mobile device, it usually has some software, such as an operating system, preinstalled on its internal media so that you can use the computer or mobile device the first time you turn it on.

Installed operating systems often include applications such as a browser, media player, and calculator. To use additional desktop apps on a computer, you usually need to install the software. Mobile apps typically install automatically after you transfer the app's files to your mobile device from its website. You usually do not need to install web apps before you can run them.

Once installed, you run a program so that you can interact with it. When you instruct a computer or mobile device to run a program, the computer or mobile device *loads* it, which means the program's instructions are copied from storage to memory. Once in memory, the computer or mobile device can carry out, or execute, the instructions in the program so that you can use it.

You interact with a program through its user interface. The *user interface* controls how you enter data and instructions and how information is displayed on the screen. Often, you work with icons or tiles (shown in Figure 1-30 earlier in the module), which are miniature images that link to programs, media, documents, or other objects. Read How To 1-4 for instructions about locating, installing, and running programs and mobile apps.

 HOW TO 1-4

Locate, Install, and Run Programs and Mobile Apps
The following steps describe how to locate, install, and run programs and mobile apps:

Locate the Program or Mobile App
- Locate the program or mobile app to install. Programs are available from retail stores, websites, and from other online services such as Apple's App Store or Google Play. Mobile apps are available from your device's app store.

Download and/or Install the Program or Mobile App
- If you are installing a program on your computer from physical media such as a CD or DVD, insert the media in your computer. If the installation process does not start automatically, locate the installation program on the media and then double-tap or double-click the installation program.
- If the program or mobile app is available from a website or online store, download the application to your computer or mobile device. Once the download is complete, if the installation process does not start automatically, locate and then double-tap or double-click the downloaded file to begin the installation.

Run the Program or Mobile App
- You have various options for running a program or mobile app:
  - If you are using a computer, tap or click the program's tile or double-tap or double-click the program's icon in the desktop.

- Display a list of all programs and apps on your computer or mobile device and then tap or click the icon representing the program to run (some computers may require you to double-tap or double-click the icon).
- Use the search feature in the operating system to locate the newly installed program or app and then tap or click the search result to run the program or app.

Consider This: After installing a mobile app, where are some locations you might look to find the new app's icon or tile?

 CONSIDER THIS

How do you know if a program will run on your computer?
When you buy a computer, you can find a list of the computer's specifications on the box, the manufacturer's website, or the order summary. Similarly, when you buy software, the box or the product's website will list specifications and minimum requirements for memory, speed, and more. Your computer's specifications should be the same as or greater than the software specifications. Ensure the software will run on your computer before making a purchase, because many retailers will not allow you to return software.

Developing Programs and Apps

A *software developer*, sometimes called a developer or programmer, is someone who develops programs and apps or writes the instructions that direct the computer or mobile device to process data into information. When writing instructions, a developer must be sure the program or app works properly so that the computer or mobile device generates the desired results. Complex programs can require thousands to millions of instructions.

Software developers use a programming language or application development tool to create programs and apps. Popular programming languages include C++, Java, JavaScript, Visual C#, and Visual Basic. Figure 1-31 shows some of the Visual Basic instructions a software developer may write to create a simple payroll program.

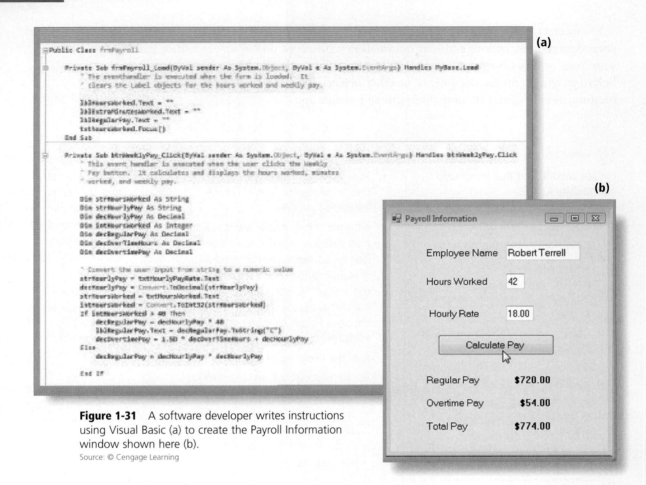

Figure 1-31   A software developer writes instructions using Visual Basic (a) to create the Payroll Information window shown here (b).
Source: © Cengage Learning

 NOW YOU SHOULD KNOW

Be sure you understand the material presented in the sections titled The Web, Digital Security and Privacy, and Programs and Apps, as it relates to the module objectives.
Now you should know . . .

- Why webpages use links (Objective 5)

- How to perform a basic web search (Objective 6)

- What risks you are exposed to as a result of your technology use and how you can minimize those risks (Objective 7)

- How to recognize an operating system and which programs and apps you might find useful (Objective 8)

Communications and Networks

Communications technologies are everywhere. Many require that you subscribe to an Internet service provider. With others, an organization such as a business or school provides communications services to employees, students, or customers.

In the course of a day, it is likely you use, or use information generated by, one or more of the communications technologies in Table 1-3.

Table 1-3   Uses of Communications Technologies

Type	Brief Description
Chat rooms	Real-time typed conversation among two or more people on a computers or mobile devices connected to a network
Email	Transmission of messages and files via a computer network
Fax	Transmission and receipt of documents over telephone lines
FTP	Permits users to transfer files to and from servers on the Internet
GPS	Navigation system that assists users with determining their location, ascertaining directions, and more
Instant messaging	Real-time typed conversation with another connected user where you also can exchange photos, videos, and other content
Internet	Worldwide collection of networks that links millions of businesses, government agencies, educational institutions, and individuals
Newsgroups	Online areas in which users have written discussions about a particular subject
RSS	Specification that enables web content to be distributed to subscribers
Videoconference	Real-time meeting between two or more geographically separated people who use a network to transmit audio and video
Voice mail	Allows users to leave a voice message for one or more people
VoIP	Conversation that takes place over the Internet using a telephone connected to a computer, mobile device, or other device
Wireless Internet access points	Enables users with computers and mobile devices to connect to the Internet wirelessly
Wireless messaging services	Send and receive wireless messages to and from smartphones, mobile phones, handheld game devices, and other mobile devices using text messaging and picture/video messaging

© Cengage Learning

Wired and Wireless Communications

Computer communications describes a process in which two or more computers or devices transfer (send and receive) data, instructions, and information over transmission media via a communications device(s). A **communications device** is hardware capable of transferring items from computers and devices to transmission media and vice versa. Examples of communications devices are modems, wireless access points, and routers. As shown in Figure 1-32, some communications involve cables and wires; others are sent wirelessly through the air.

Wired communications often use some form of telephone wiring, coaxial cable, or fiber-optic cables to send communications signals. The wiring or cables typically are used within buildings or underground between buildings.

Because it is more convenient than installing wires and cables, many users opt for wireless communications, which sends signals through the air or space. Examples of wireless communications technologies include Wi-Fi, Bluetooth, and cellular radio, which are discussed below:

- **Wi-Fi** uses radio signals to provide high-speed Internet and network connections to computers and devices capable of communicating via Wi-Fi. Most computers and many mobile devices, such as smartphones and portable media players, can connect to a Wi-Fi network.

combination modem/router/wireless access point

Internet

modem

Figure 1-32   Modems, wireless access points, and routers are examples of communications devices that enable communications between computers/mobile devices and the Internet. Notice that some computers and devices communicate via wires, and others communicate wirelessly.

© Cengage Learning; © iStockphoto / Petar Chernaev; © iStockphoto / Oleksiy Mark; © Patryk Kosmider / Shutterstock.com.; © Pablo Eder / Shutterstock.com; © iStockphoto / 123render.; Source: Microsoft; © iStockphoto / aquarius83men

- **Bluetooth** uses short-range radio signals to enable Bluetooth-enabled computers and devices to communicate with each other. For example, Bluetooth headsets allow you to connect a Bluetooth-enabled phone to a headset wirelessly.
- Cellular radio uses the cellular network to enable high-speed Internet connections to devices with built-in compatible technology, such as smartphones. Cellular network providers use the categories 3G, 4G, and 5G to denote cellular transmission speeds, with 5G being the fastest.

Wi-Fi and Bluetooth are both hot spot technologies. A *hot spot* is a wireless network that provides Internet connections to mobile computers and devices. Wi-Fi hot spots provide wireless network connections to users in public locations, such as airports and airplanes, train stations, hotels, convention centers, schools, campgrounds, marinas, shopping malls, bookstores, libraries, restaurants, coffee shops, and more. Bluetooth hot spots provide location-based services, such as sending coupons or menus, to users whose Bluetooth-enabled devices enter the coverage range.

Networks

A **network** is a collection of computers and devices connected together, often wirelessly, via communications devices and transmission media. Networks allow computers to share *resources*, such as hardware, software, data, and information. Sharing resources saves time and money. In many networks, one or more computers act as a server. The server controls access to the resources on a network. The other computers on the network, each called a client, request resources from the server (Figure 1-33). The major differences between the server and client computers are that the server typically has more power, more storage space, and expanded communications capabilities.

Many homes and most businesses and schools network their computers and devices. Most allow users to connect their computers wirelessly to the network. Users often are required to sign in to, or log on, a network, which means they enter a user name and password (or other credentials) to access the network and its resources. Read Ethics & Issues 1-3 to consider issues associated with unsecured networks.

Figure 1-33 A server manages the resources on a network, and clients access the resources on the server. This network enables three separate computers to share the same printer, one wirelessly.

client

client

printer

server

✱ ETHICS & ISSUES 1-3

Would You Connect to an Unsecured Network?

If you turn on your laptop and notice that you can connect to a nearby home or business's wireless network and access the Internet without a password, for free, you may find yourself in an ethical dilemma. Because they do not know how to secure a wireless network, many home and business users leave their networks open for use by anybody in their signal's range. Experts estimate that up to 35 percent of wireless connections are unsecured, leaving them open to hackers. (A hacker is someone who accesses a computer or network illegally.)

Criminals sometimes use unsecured wireless networks to cover up technology-related crimes. Others may steal connections to avoid the costs of Internet service. In other cases, a user's laptop or mobile device may connect automatically to an open wireless network, without the user's authorization or knowledge. If you are using an unsecured wireless network, hackers may be able to capture your passwords, hijack your accounts, or send spam or a virus.

The Electronic Communications Privacy Act (ECPA) states that it is not illegal "to intercept or access an electronic communication made through an electronic communication system that is configured so that such electronic communication is readily accessible to the general public." It is unclear whether this law refers to an unsecured home network or whether it pertains only to public hot spots, such as restaurants and libraries. Some lawmakers even support punishing those who leave their networks unsecured.

Consider This: Would you use your neighbor's unsecured wireless home network without permission? Why or why not? What would you do if you found out that someone was using your wireless home network without your permission? How should legal authorities address such abuse? What punishment should violators receive? Should those leaving their networks unsecured receive punishment, too? Why or why not?

Home Networks   Home networks save the home user money and provide many conveniences. Each networked computer or mobile device on a home network has the following capabilities:

- Connect to the Internet at the same time
- Share a single high-speed Internet connection
- Access photos, music, videos, and other content on computers and devices throughout the house
- Share devices such as a printer, scanner, or external hard drive
- Play multiplayer games with players on other computers and mobile devices in the house
- Connect game consoles to the Internet
- Subscribe to and use VoIP
- Interact with other devices in a smart home (such as thermostats, lighting controls, etc.)

Home networks usually are small, existing within a single structure, and use wireless technologies such as those shown previously in Figure 1-30. You do not need extensive knowledge of networks to set up a home network. You will need a communications device, such as a router, which usually includes setup instructions. Most operating systems also provide tools enabling you easily to connect all the computers and devices in your house.

Business Networks   Business and school networks can be small, such as in a room or building, or widespread, connecting computers and devices across a city, country, or the globe. Some reasons that businesses network their computers and devices together include the following:

- **Facilitate communications.** Using a network, employees and customers communicate efficiently and easily via email, messaging services, blogs, online social networks, video calls, online meetings, videoconferencing, VoIP, and more.
- **Share hardware.** In a networked environment, each computer on the network can access the hardware on the network, instead of providing each user with the same piece of hardware. For example, computer and mobile device users can access the laser printer on the network, as they need it.
- **Share data, information, and software.** In a networked environment, any authorized computer user can access data, information, and software stored on other computers on the network. A large company, for example, might have a database of customer information that any authorized user can access.

Mini Feature 1-2: Staying in Sync

If you use multiple computers and mobile devices throughout the day, keeping track of common files may be difficult. Read Mini Feature 1-2 to learn how to keep your computers and devices in sync with each other.

 MINI FEATURE 1-2

Staying in Sync

Assume that each morning you begin the day by checking your appointment calendar on your home or office computer. That same calendar appears on your smartphone, so that you can view your schedule throughout the day. If you add, change, or delete appointments using the smartphone, however, you may need to update the calendar on your computer to reflect these edits. When you **synchronize**, or **sync**, computers and mobile devices, you match the files in two or more locations with each other, as shown in the figure below. Along with appointments, other commonly synced files from a smartphone are photos, email messages, music, apps, contacts, calendars, and ringtones.

Syncing can be a one-way or a two-way process. With a one-way sync, also called mirroring, you add, change, or delete files in a destination location, called the *target*, without altering the same files in the original location, called the *source*. For example, you may have a large collection of music stored on your home computer (the source), and you often copy some of these songs to your mobile device (the target). If you add or delete songs from your computer, you also will want to add or change these songs on your mobile device. If, however, you add or change the songs on your mobile device, you would not want to make these changes on your computer.

In two-way sync, any change made in one location also is made in any other sync location. For example,

you and your friends may be working together to create one document reflecting your combined ideas. This document could be stored on a network or on cloud storage on the Internet. Your collaboration efforts should reflect the latest edits each person has made to the file.

You can use wired or wireless methods to sync. In a wired setup, cables connect one device to another, which allows for reliable data transfer. While wireless syncing offers convenience and automation, possible issues include battery drain and low signal strength when the devices are not close to each other. Strategies for keeping your files in sync include the following:

- **Use a cable and software.** Syncing photos from a camera or a smartphone to a computer frees up memory on the mobile device and creates a backup of these files. You easily can transfer photos using a data sync cable and synchronization software. Be certain not to disconnect the mobile device from the computer until the sync is complete. You also can copy your photos and documents from the computer to a smartphone, an external hard drive, a USB flash drive, or some other portable storage device.

- **Use cloud storage.** Cloud storage can provide a convenient method of syncing files stored on multiple computers and accessing them from most devices with Internet access. Several cloud storage providers offer a small amount of storage space at no cost and additional storage for a nominal fee per month or per year. Each provider has specific features, but most allow users to share files with other users, preview file contents, set passwords, and control who has permission to edit the files.

- **Use web apps.** By using web apps for email, contacts, and calendars, your information is stored online, so that it is accessible anywhere you have an Internet connection and can sync with multiple devices.

 Consider This: Synchronization is an effective method of organizing and sharing common files. What files have you synced, such as photos, music, and email? Which sync method did you use?

© iStockphoto / 123render; Source: Microsoft; © iStockphoto / Moncherie; © iStockphoto / Ivan Stevanovic; Courtesy of Western Digital Corporation

Technology Uses

Technology has changed society today as much as the industrial revolution changed society in the eighteenth and nineteenth centuries. People interact directly with technology in fields such as education, government, finance, retail, entertainment, health care, science, travel, publishing, and manufacturing.

Education/Mini Feature 1-3: Digital School

Educators and teaching institutions use technology to assist with education. Most equip labs and classrooms with laptops or desktops. Some even provide computers or mobile devices to students. Many require students to have a mobile computer or mobile device to access the school's network or Internet wirelessly, or to access digital-only content provided by a textbook publisher. To promote the use of technology in education, vendors often offer substantial student discounts on hardware and software.

Educators may use a course management system, sometimes called a learning management system, which is software that contains tools for class preparation, distribution, and management. For example, through the course management system, students access course materials, grades, assessments, and a variety of collaboration tools.

Many schools offer distance learning classes, where the delivery of education occurs at one place while the learning occurs at other locations. Distance learning courses provide time, distance, and place advantages for students who live far from a campus or work full time. A few schools offer entire degrees online. National and international companies offer distance learning training because it eliminates the costs of airfare, hotels, and meals for centralized training sessions.

Read Mini Feature 1-3 to learn about additional technologies integrated in the classroom.

 BTW

Technology @ Work
For more information about how technology is used in a variety of fields, read the Technology @ Work feature at the end of each module in this book.

 Internet Research

How do educators use iTunes U?

Search for: itunes u

 MINI FEATURE 1-3

Digital School

Technology and education intersect in today's classrooms. Students can use a variety of devices, apps, and websites to collaborate and obtain content while teachers can share information in most content areas to engage students and enhance the learning process. Digital technology offers flexibility and a revised classroom setting.

- **Mobile devices and tablets:** Schools are updating their computer labs by eliminating rows of desktops and allowing students to bring their own devices into the room and also into their classrooms, a practice often referred to as *BYOD* (bring your own device). They connect their laptops and mobile devices to power and data; they then they use educational apps, store and share files, read digital books, and create content without leaving their desks.

- **Virtual field trips:** Virtual tours of museums, ancient sites, and galleries allow audiences to see exhibits, examine paintings, and explore historical objects. After viewing 360-degree panoramas of such places as Colonial Williamsburg and Machu Picchu, students can interact with experts via Twitter and videoconferencing.

- **Games and simulations:** Game design theory can help engage students and reinforce key

concepts. When students master one set of objectives in a particular topic, they can progress to more advanced levels. They can receive instant feedback and recognition for their accomplishments, collaborate with teammates, repeat play to achieve higher scores, and document their experiences. Researchers claim that students are more likely to pursue challenging subject matter when it is offered in a gaming setting.

- **Interactive whiteboards:** Teachers and students can write directly on an interactive display, shown in the figure, which is a touch-sensitive device resembling a dry-erase board. It displays images on a connected computer screen. Touch gestures are used to zoom, erase, and annotate displayed content.

- **Share projects:** Effective movies can bring the words in a textbook to life. Students can create scripts and then use animation software or a video camera to tell stories that apply the concepts they have learned

Used with permission of SMART Technologies ULC (www.smarttech.com). SMART Board and the SMART logo are trademarks of SMART Technologies ULC and may be registered in the European Union, Canada, the United States and other countries.

(continued)

and upload them to media sharing websites. They also can write blogs, design graphics, and conduct interviews to apply and share the concepts they have learned in the classroom.

- **3-D printers:** Low-cost 3-D printers created for the classroom and libraries are becoming popular, especially in science and engineering classes. Geology students can create topography models,

biology students can examine cross sections of organs, architecture students can print prototypes of their designs, and history students can create artifacts.

 Consider This: Which digital technologies have you used in your classrooms? Did they help you learn and retain information presented? If so, how?

Government

Most government offices have websites to provide citizens with up-to-date information. People in the United States access government websites to view census data, file taxes, apply for permits and licenses, pay parking tickets, buy stamps, report crimes, apply for financial aid, and renew vehicle registrations and driver's licenses.

Employees of government agencies use computers as part of their daily routine. North American 911 call centers use computers to dispatch calls for fire, police, and medical assistance. Military and other agency officials use the U.S. Department of Homeland Security's network of information about domestic security threats to help protect against terrorist attacks. Law enforcement officers have online access to the FBI's National Crime Information Center (NCIC) through in-vehicle laptops, fingerprint readers, and mobile devices (Figure 1-34). The NCIC contains more than 15 million missing persons and criminal records, including names, fingerprints, parole/probation records, mug shots, and other information.

Figure 1-34 Law enforcement officials use computers and mobile devices to access emergency, missing person, and criminal records in computer networks in local, state, and federal agencies.
© iStockPhoto / jacomstephens

Finance

Many people and companies use online banking or finance software to pay bills, track personal income and expenses, manage investments, and evaluate financial plans. The difference between using a financial institutions' website versus finance software on your computer is that all your account information is stored on the bank's computer instead of your computer. The advantage is you can access your financial records from anywhere in the world.

Investors often use online investing to buy and sell stocks and bonds — without using a broker. With online investing, the transaction fee for each trade usually is much less than when trading through a broker.

Retail

You can purchase just about any product or service on the web, including groceries, flowers, books, computers and mobile devices, music, movies, airline tickets, and concert tickets. To purchase from an online retailer, a customer visits the business's storefront, which contains product descriptions, images, and a shopping cart. The shopping cart allows the customer to collect purchases. When ready to complete the sale, the customer enters personal data and the method of payment, which should be through a secure Internet connection. Figure 1-35 illustrates the steps involved when a customer purchases from an online retailer.

Many mobile apps make your shopping experience more convenient. Some enable you to manage rewards, use coupons, locate stores, or pay for goods and services directly from your phone or other mobile device. Other mobile apps will check a product's price and availability at stores in your local area or online. Read Secure IT 1-4 for tips about shopping safely online.

SECURE IT 1-4

Shopping Safely Online

Browsing electronic storefronts and making online purchases can be convenient and economical, but the experience can be a disaster if you encounter unscrupulous vendors. These tips can help you enjoy a safe and productive online shopping trip.

- **Read customer reviews.** Shoppers frequently post comments about merchandise quality, pricing, and shipping. Their evaluations may help you decide whether a company is legitimate. Be aware, however, that the Federal Trade Commission has sued companies for posting false positive reviews and that some companies remove negative comments. Make it a habit to rate merchants as often as possible so that others can learn from your experiences.

- **Look for seals of approval.** Online businesses can display seals if they have met rigorous standards. Some unscrupulous merchants, however, will place the seals on their websites even if they have not been approved. To check a seal's legitimacy, tap or click the logo and be certain you are directed to the issuing agency's website to verify the seal is valid.

- **Create a strong password and password questions.** If the merchant requires you to create a user name and password, be certain to develop a long, complex password with at least eight characters that include letters, numbers, and special characters. (Refer to Secure IT 1-3 earlier in this module for guidance on creating a strong password.) The website also may ask for answers to security questions; if so, do not supply information that hackers could locate easily, such as your high school, place of birth, or family members' or pets' names.

- **Check website details.** Locate the business's privacy policy to learn how your information will be stored. Also, look for phone numbers, physical addresses, and email addresses to contact the vendor if questions arise about damaged goods or billing discrepancies.

- **Beware of requests to supply further information.** After you have placed an order, you may receive an email message asking you to confirm the transaction or to supply additional account information. A reputable business will not solicit these requests, so do not reply to the message.

☀ **Consider This:** Have you made online purchases? If so, have you followed the precautions listed here? How will you change your activities the next time you shop online?

Purchasing from an Online Retailer

Step 1
The customer displays the online retailer's storefront.

Step 2
The customer collects purchases in a shopping cart.

Step 3
The customer enters payment information on a secure website. The online retailer sends financial information to a bank.

Step 5
The online retailer's web server sends confirmation to the customer, processes the order, and then sends it to the fulfillment center.

Step 4
The bank performs security checks and sends authorization back to the online retailer.

Step 6
The fulfillment center packages the order, prepares it for shipment, and then sends a report to the server where records are updated.

Step 7
While the order travels to the customer, shipping information is posted on the web.

Step 8
The order is delivered to the customer, who may be required to sign a handheld computer or document to acknowledge receipt.

Figure 1-35 This figure shows the steps involved when a customer purchases from an online retailer.

© Comstock Images / Photos. com; © iStockphoto / Mark Evans; © iStockphoto / AndyL; © iStockphoto / Mlenny Photography; © Oleksiy Mark / Photos.com; © Oleksiy Mark / Shutterstock. com.; © iStockphoto / Ed Hidden; © iStockphoto / Oksana Perkins; © Cengage Learning; © iStockphoto / stevecoleimages

Entertainment

You can use computers and mobile devices to listen to audio clips or live audio; watch video clips, television shows, or live performances and events; read a book, magazine, or newspaper; and play a myriad of games individually or with others. In some cases, you download the media from the web to a computer or mobile device so that you can watch, listen to, view, or play later. Some websites support *streaming*, where you access the media content while it downloads. For example, radio and television broadcasts often use streaming media to broadcast music, interviews, talk shows, sporting events, news, and other segments so that you can listen to the audio or view the video as it downloads to your computer. You also can create videos, take photos, or record audio and upload (transfer) your media content to the web to share with others, such as on an online social network.

 CONSIDER THIS

Can I make copies of songs or other media that I have purchased and downloaded from a legitimate website, such as iTunes?
You typically can make a copy as a personal backup, but you cannot share the copy with others in any format unless you have legal permission from the copyright owner to do so. That is, you cannot give someone a CD copy, nor can you share a digital file by posting it on the web or sending it as an email message.

Health Care

Nearly every area of health care today uses computers. Whether you are visiting a family doctor for a regular checkup, having lab work or an outpatient test, filling a prescription, or being rushed in for emergency surgery, the medical staff around you will be using computers for various purposes:

- Hospitals and doctors use computers and mobile devices to maintain and access patient records (Figure 1-36).
- Computers and mobile devices monitor patients' vital signs in hospital rooms and at home; patients use computers to manage health conditions, such as diabetes.
- Robots deliver medication to nurses' stations in hospitals.
- Computers and computerized devices assist doctors, nurses, and technicians with medical tests.

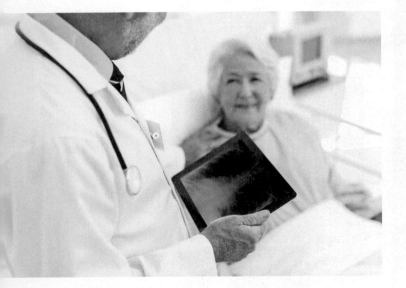

- Doctors use the web and medical software to assist with researching and diagnosing health conditions.
- Doctors use email, text messaging, and other communications services to correspond with patients.
- Patients use computers and mobile devices to refill prescriptions, and pharmacists use computers to file insurance claims and provide customers with vital information about their medications.
- Surgeons implant computerized devices, such as pacemakers, that allow patients to live longer.
- Surgeons use computer-controlled devices to provide them with greater precision during operations, such as for laser eye surgery and robot-assisted heart surgery.
- Medical staff create labels for medicine, hospital ID bracelets, and more, enabling staff to verify dosage and access patient records by scanning the label.

Figure 1-36 Doctors, nurses, technicians, and other medical staff use computers and computerized devices to assist with medical tests.
© iStockPhoto / Neustockimage

Science

All branches of science, from biology to astronomy to meteorology, use computers to assist them with collecting, analyzing, and modeling data. Scientists also use the Internet to communicate with colleagues around the world. Breakthroughs in surgery, medicine, and treatments often result from scientists' use of computers. Tiny computers now imitate functions of the central nervous system, retina of the eye, and cochlea of the ear. A cochlear implant allows a deaf person to distinguish sounds. Electrodes implanted in the brain stop tremors associated with Parkinson's disease.

A *neural network* is a system that attempts to imitate the behavior of the human brain. Scientists create neural networks by connecting thousands of processors together much like the neurons in the brain are connected. The capability of a personal computer to recognize spoken words is a direct result of scientific experimentation with neural networks..

Travel

Whether traveling by car or plane, your goal is to arrive safely at your destination. As you make the journey, you may interact with a navigation system or GPS, which uses satellite signals to determine a geographic location. GPS technology also assists people with creating maps, determining the best route between two points, locating a lost person or stolen object, monitoring a person's or object's movement, determining altitude, calculating speed, and finding points of interest. Vehicles manufactured today typically include some type of onboard navigation system (Figure 1-37). Many mobile devices, such as smartphones, also have built-in navigation systems.

In preparing for a trip, you may need to reserve a car, hotel, or flight. Many websites offer these services to the public where you can search for and compare flights and prices, order airline tickets, or reserve a rental car. You also can print driving directions and maps from the web.

Figure 1-37 Many vehicles include an onboard navigation system.
© kaczor58 / Shutterstock.com

Publishing

Many publishers of books, magazines, newspapers, music, film, and video make their works available online. Organizations and individuals publish their thoughts and ideas using a blog, podcast, or wiki.

- A *blog* is an informal website consisting of time-stamped articles (posts) in a diary or journal format, usually listed in reverse chronological order. Posts can contain text, photos, links, and more. For example, Figure 1-38 shows the Nutrition Blog Network, in which registered

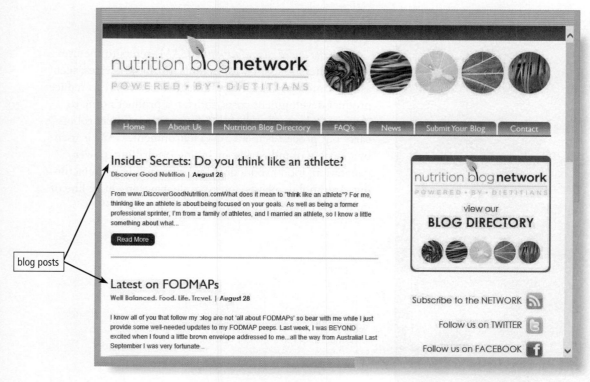

blog posts

Figure 1-38 Any group or individual can create a blog, so that they can share thoughts and ideas.
Source: Nutrition Blog Network

Internet Research

How can you create a blog?

Search for: create a blog

dietitians post articles about nutrition. As others read articles in your blog, you can enable them to reply with their own thoughts. A blog that contains video is called a video blog.

- Podcasts are a popular way to distribute audio or video on the web. A *podcast* is recorded media that users can download or stream to a computer or portable media player. Examples of podcasts include lectures, political messages, radio shows, and commentaries. Podcasters register their podcasts so that subscribers can select content to automatically download when they are connected.

- A *wiki* is a collaborative website that allows users to create, add to, modify, or delete the content via their browser. Many wikis are open to modification by the general public. The difference between a wiki and a blog is that users cannot modify original posts made by a blogger. Read Ethics & Issues 1-4 for an issue related to using wikis as a source for research.

 ETHICS & ISSUES 1-4

Should Wikis Be Allowed as Valid Sources for Academic Research?

As wikis have grown in number, size, and popularity, many educators and librarians have shunned them as valid sources of research. While some wikis are tightly controlled with a limited number of contributors and expert editors, these wikis usually focus on narrowly defined, specialized topics. Most large, multi-topic online wikis, such as Wikipedia, often involve thousands of editors, many of whom remain anonymous.

Critics of wikis cite the lack of certified academic credentials by the editors, as well as potential political or gender bias by contributors. Wikis also are subject to vandalism. Vandals' motives vary; some enter false information to discredit the wiki, and others for humorous results. On occasion, rival political factions have falsified or embellished wiki entries in an attempt to give their candidate an advantage. Some wiki supporters argue that most wikis provide adequate controls to correct false or misleading content quickly and to punish those who submit it. One popular wiki now requires an experienced editor to verify changes made to certain types of articles. Other wiki protection methods include locking articles from editing, creating a list of recently edited articles, enabling readers to report vandalism, and allowing people to be notified about changes to a wiki page that they have edited or that is about them. Some proponents propose that people should use wikis as a starting point for researching a fact, but that they should verify the fact using traditional sources.

Consider This: Should instructors allow wikis as valid sources for academic research? Why or why not? Would you submit a paper to your instructor that cites a wiki as a source? Why or why not? What policies might wikis enforce that could garner more confidence from the public? If a wiki provided verification of the credentials of the author, would you trust the wiki more? Why or why not?

Figure 1-39 Automotive factories use industrial robots to weld car bodies.
© Small Town Studio / Shutterstock.com

Manufacturing

Computer-aided manufacturing (CAM) refers to the use of computers to assist with manufacturing processes, such as fabrication and assembly. Industries use CAM to reduce product development costs, shorten a product's time to market, and stay ahead of the competition. Often, robots carry out processes in a CAM environment. CAM is used by a variety of industries, including oil drilling, power generation, food production, and automobile manufacturing. Automobile plants, for example, have an entire line of industrial robots that assemble a car (Figure 1-39).

Special computers on the shop floor record actual labor, material, machine, and computer time used to manufacture a particular product. The computers process this data and automatically update inventory, production, payroll, and accounting records on the company's network.

Technology Users

Every day, people around the world use various technologies at home, at work, and at school. Depending on the hardware, software, and communications requirements, these users generally can be classified in one of five categories. Keep in mind that a single user may fall into more than one category.

- A *home user* is any person who spends time using technology at home. Parents, children, teenagers, grandparents, singles, couples, etc., are all examples of home users.
- A *small/home office user* includes employees of companies with fewer than 50 employees, as well as the self-employed who work from home. Small offices include local law practices, accounting offices, travel agencies, and florists.
- A *mobile user* includes any person who works with computers or mobile devices while away from a main office, home, or school. Examples of mobile users are sales representatives, real estate agents, insurance agents, meter readers, package delivery people, journalists, consultants, and students.
- A *power user* is a user who requires the capabilities of a powerful computer. Examples of power users include engineers, scientists, architects, desktop publishers, and graphic artists.
- An enterprise has hundreds or thousands of employees or customers who work in or do business with offices across a region, the country, or the world. Each employee or customer who uses computers, mobile devices, and other technology in the enterprise is an *enterprise user*. Read Ethics & Issues 1-5 to consider whether employees should be held accountable for their online social network posts.

✳ ETHICS & ISSUES 1-5

Should Employees Be Held Accountable for Their Online Social Network Posts?
In addition to looking at your resume and scheduling an interview, a potential employer may search the web to find out information about you. A recent Career Builder survey found that 39 percent of employers look at applicants' use of online social networks, and 43 percent of those found information that caused them not to hire the applicant.

Once employed, your manager still may track your online activity. Companies are concerned about damaged reputations, or even lawsuits. Employee actions that worry their employers include discussing company sales activity, griping about their managers or customers, or posting photos that show them taking part in unethical, illegal, or unsavory activities.

Social network-related firings have raised the question of whether companies should monitor employees' online social network activity. Accessing an employee's or a potential employee's social network profile also could have consequences for the company. If a company realizes that a person is a member of a minority group or has a disability, the company could face discrimination charges if it does not hire or later fires the employee. Privacy experts state that your online social network posts are your own business. Debate about what falls under free speech is ongoing. Remember that you cannot delete easily what you post online. Whether or not you currently are searching for employment, online posts you make now can damage your future job prospects.

Consider This: What are the results when you search for yourself online? What steps can you take to clean up and protect your online reputation? Would you share social networking accounts or passwords with an employer or potential employer? Why or why not? Should companies monitor employees' accounts? Why or why not?

Table 1-4 illustrates the range of hardware, programs/apps, and communications forms used in each of these categories.

Table 1-4 Categories of Users

User	Sample Hardware	Sample Desktop Apps	Sample Mobile or Web Apps	Forms of Communications
All Users	– Smartphone – Digital camera – Printer	– Word processing – Schedule and contact management – Browser – Security	– Alarm clock – Calculator – News, weather, sports – Reference – Finance	– Email – Online social networks – Blogs
Home User	– Laptop, tablet, or desktop – Portable media player and earbuds or headphones – Game console – E-book reader – Wearable device – Webcam – Headset	– Personal finance – Photo and video editing – Media player – Educational – Entertainment	– Banking – Travel – Mapping – Navigation – Health and fitness – Retail – Media sharing – Educational	– Messaging – VoIP
Small/Home Office User	– Desktop(s) or laptop(s) – Server – Webcam – Scanner	– Spreadsheet – Database – Accounting	– Travel – Mapping	– Messaging – VoIP – FTP
Mobile User	– Laptop or tablet – Video projector – Wireless headset	– Note taking – Presentation – Educational – Entertainment	– Travel – Mapping – Navigation – Retail – Educational	
Power User	– Desktop – Scanner	– Desktop publishing – Multimedia authoring – Computer-aided design – Photo, audio, video editing		– FTP – Videoconferencing
Enterprise User	– Server – Desktop(s) or laptop(s) – Industry-specific handheld computer – Webcam – Scanner	– Spreadsheet – Database – Accounting	– Travel – Mapping – Navigation	– Messaging – VoIP – FTP – Videoconferencing

NOW YOU SHOULD KNOW

Be sure you understand the material presented in the sections titled Communications and Networks, Technology Uses, and Technology Users, as it relates to the module objectives.
Now you should know . . .

- When you might use wired and wireless communications, and why you would use a network (Objective 9)
- How you would use technology in education, government, finance, retail, entertainment, health care, science, travel, publishing, and manufacturing (Objective 10)
- What types of hardware, software, and communications you couldw at home, school, and work (Objective 11)

Summary

Module 1 introduced you to basic computer concepts. You learned about laptops, tablets, desktops, servers, smartphones, digital cameras, portable media players, e-book readers, and game devices. The module introduced various methods for input, output, memory, and storage. It discussed the Internet, browsing and searching the web, and online social networks. Next, the module introduced digital security and safety risks and precautions, along with various types of programs, applications, communications, and networks. The many different uses of technology applications in society also were presented, along with types of users. This module is an overview. Many of the terms and concepts introduced will be discussed further in later modules.

TECHNOLOGY @ WORK

Health Care

You are out running on a beautiful day, tracking your route and distance using a health and fitness app on a smartphone. While running, you accidentally step on uneven pavement and suffer an injury that requires a trip to an emergency room. Upon check-in, the employee at the front desk uses a tablet to record your personal data and symptoms. She also uses the tablet to verify that your insurance coverage is current and informs you of your co-payment amount. After waiting several minutes, a triage nurse takes your temperature and blood pressure and then asks a series of questions about your symptoms. The nurse also records this data in a tablet and asks you to remain in the waiting room until someone from the radiology department is available to perform a CT scan. The radiology department is located in a different area of the hospital, so the technicians watch a computer screen that displays a list of patients who currently are waiting for their services.

About 30 minutes later, a technician calls your name and escorts you to the radiology department for your CT scan. As she is performing the scan, a computer records the images that later will be reviewed by a physician. When the CT scan is complete, you return to the waiting room until a physician reviews the results. Once she receives the results and reviews them, a hospital employee takes you to a consultation room.

The physician informs you that other than a few bumps and bruises, she believes that you have sustained no permanent damage and prescribes medication to help ease the pain. She then returns to a computer at the nurses' station and adds her diagnosis to the database that stores your medical records. She also sends your prescription electronically to the hospital's pharmacy. Once discharged, you visit the cashier to pay the bill. You then use a tablet to sign an electronic version of your discharge paperwork so that the hospital can store it

electronically. The hospital bills your insurance company electronically. If you owe a balance

© Shutterstock / Image Point Fr

after the insurance company pays its portion, a computer at the hospital will generate a bill that will be mailed to you. After purchasing your medication and leaving the hospital, you realize that despite the hospital being busy, computers decreased the time of your visit by automating processes that otherwise would have been performed manually and reduced possible errors by storing all of your personal information centrally.

Consider This: How else might computers and technology be used in the health care industry?

Study Guide

The Study Guide exercise reinforces material you should know for the module exam.

Instructions: Answer the questions below using the format that helps you remember best or that is required by your instructor. Possible formats may include one or more of these options: write the answers; create a document that contains the answers; record answers as audio or video using a webcam, smartphone, or portable media player; post answers on a blog, wiki, or website; or highlight answers in the book/e-book.

1. Define the term, digital literacy.

2. Define the terms, computer, hardware, and user.

3. Differentiate between a PC and a mobile computer. A laptop also is known as a(n) ___ computer.

4. Describe the characteristics and features of a tablet. List several touch screen gestures.

5. Explain the difference between a desktop and an all-in-one. What additional meaning does the term, desktop, sometimes have?

6. Define the term, server. What services does a server provide?

7. Explain whether or not a mobile device is a computer.

8. List characteristics of a smartphone.

9. Differentiate among voice, text, picture, and video messages.

10. Describe the purpose of these mobile devices: digital cameras, portable and digital media players, e-book readers, wearable devices, and game devices.

11. Describe the trend of digital device convergence and how it applies to mobile devices.

12. Describe uses of technology in home automation.

13. Differentiate between data and information. Give an example of each.

14. Define the terms, input and output. List several types of input devices and output devices.

15. Describe the purpose of a pointing device. Give an example.

16. List the hardware you can use to input and view output for voice and video.

17. Differentiate between memory and storage.

18. A computer keeps data, instructions, and information on ___ media. Give some examples.

19. Define the term, cloud storage. Describe the types of services offered by cloud storage providers.

20. Describe components of a backup plan. How do backup plans for mobile devices and personal computers differ?

21. Describe the Internet. Identify reasons people use the Internet.

22. Differentiate between the web and the Internet.

23. The ___ consists of a worldwide collection of electronic documents. What is each electronic document called?

24. What is a browser? Describe the purpose of a search engine.

25. Explain the purpose of an online social network.

26. Differentiate between the services and uses of Facebook, Twitter, and LinkedIn.

27. List services of the Internet that facilitate communications.

28. Define the term, malware. List ways you can protect yourself from malware.

29. What privacy risks are involved with using technology? List guidelines for creating a strong password.

30. Explain physical and behavioral health risks associated with using computers.

31. Describe strategies that support green computing.

32. Define the term, software. Software also is called a(n) ___.

33. Define the term, operating system. List popular operating systems for computers and mobile devices.

34. Differentiate between desktop, web, and mobile apps.

35. List the steps involved in installing programs.

36. Explain how to locate, install, and run programs. What is the role of a software developer?

37. Define the term, communications device. List examples of wireless communications technologies.

38. Define the term, hot spot. Give two examples and describe how each is used.

39. Describe how homes and businesses use networks.

40. Identify issues surrounding accessing an unsecured network.

41. Explain what occurs when you synchronize computers and mobile devices.

42. List ways that schools use technology to enhance education.

43. Identify how the following industries use technology: government, financial, retail, entertainment, health care, science, travel, publishing, and manufacturing.

44. Describe how you might use blogs, wikis, and podcasts to publish content.

45. Differentiate among the following technology user types: home user, small/home office user, mobile user, power user, and enterprise user.

46. Describe how technology is used in the health care industry.

You should be able to define the Primary Terms and be familiar with the Secondary Terms listed below.

Key Terms

Primary Terms (shown in **bold-black** characters in the module)

all-in-one (6)
app (27)
application (27)
backup (18)
browser (21)
Bluetooth (32)
cloud storage (18)
communications
   device (31)
computer (4)
desktop (6)

digital camera (8)
digital device
   convergence (10)
e-book reader (9)
game console (10)
green computing (26)
hard drive (17)
input device (12)
Internet (20)
laptop (4)
memory (16)

network (32)
online social network (23)
output device (14)
portable media player (8)
printer (14)
program (26)
search engine (22)
server (6)
smartphone (7)
software (26)
storage device (17)

storage media (17)
sync (34)
synchronize (34)
tablet (4)
wearable device (9)
web (21)
web server (21)
webpage (21)
website (21)
Wi-Fi (31)

Secondary Terms (shown in *italic* characters in the module)

3-D printer (15)
blog (39)
BYOD (35)
click (13)
computer-aided manufacturing (40)
data (12)
desktop app (28)
digital literacy (2)
digital media (8)
digital media player (9)
double-click (13)
double-tap (5)
downloading (21)
drag (5, 13)
earbuds (8)
e-book (9)
enterprise user (41)
e-reader (9)
e-waste (26)
file (18)
gesture (5)
hard copy (14)
hard disk (17)
hardware (4)
headset (14)
home user (41)

hot spot (32)
hyperlink (21)
information (12)
input (4)
keyboard (13)
link (21)
loads (28)
malware (24)
memory card (18)
microphone (14)
mobile app (28)
mobile computer (4)
mobile device (7)
mobile user (41)
mouse (13)
neural network (39)
notebook computer (4)
on-screen keyboard (5)
operating system (27)
optical disc (18)
output (4)
personal computer (4)
phablet (7)
picture message (7)
pinch (5)
podcast (40)

point (13)
power user (41)
press and hold (5)
printout (14)
resources (32)
right-click (13)
scanner (14)
slide (5)
small/home office user (41)
Smart TV (15)
social networking site (23)
software developer (29)
solid-state drive (17)
source (34)
streaming (38)
streaming media player (9)

stretch (5)
surfing the web (21)
swipe (5)
tap (5)
target (34)
text message (7)
touchpad (13)
USB flash drive (18)
user (4)
user interface (29)
video message (7)
voice mail message (7)
wearable (9)
web app (28)
webcam (14)
wiki (40)

all-in-one (6)

Checkpoint

The Checkpoint exercises test your knowledge of the module concepts. The page number containing the answer appears in parentheses after each exercise. The Consider This exercises challenge your understanding of module concepts.

True/False   Mark T for True and F for False.

_____ 1. Electronic components in computers process data using instructions, which are the steps that tell the computer how to perform a particular task. (4)

_____ 2. An all-in-one contains a separate tower. (6)

_____ 3. Smartphones typically communicate wirelessly with other devices or computers. (7)

_____ 4. Data conveys meaning to users, and information is a collection of unprocessed items, which can include text, numbers, images, audio, and video. (12)

_____ 5. A headset is a type of input device. (14)

_____ 6. A scanner is a light-sensing output device. (14)

_____ 7. Although some forms of memory are permanent, most memory keeps data and instructions temporarily, meaning its contents are erased when the computer is turned off. (16)

_____ 8. A solid-state drive contains one or more inflexible, circular platters that use magnetic particles to store data, instructions, and information. (17)

_____ 9. The terms, web and Internet, are interchangeable. (21)

_____ 10. One way to protect your computer from malware is to scan any removable media before using it. (25)

_____ 11. Operating systems are a widely recognized example of system software. (26)

_____ 12. You usually do not need to install web apps before you can run them. (28)

Multiple Choice   Select the best answer.

1. A(n) _____ is any hardware component that allows you to enter data and instructions into a computer or mobile device. (12)
   a. output device
   b. communications device
   c. input device
   d. display

2. Which of the following is *not* an example of an output device? (14)
   a. scanner
   b. printer
   c. display
   d. speaker

3. _____ consists of electronic components that store instructions waiting to be executed and the data needed by those instructions. (16)
   a. Storage
   b. Cloud storage
   c. Solid-state drives
   d. Memory

4. _____ is an Internet service that provides remote storage to computer users. (18)
   a. Smart TV
   b. Cloud storage
   c. Solid-state drive (SSD)
   d. Bluetooth

5. A computer that delivers requested webpages to your computer or mobile device is a(n) _____. (21)
   a. VoIP computer
   b. web server
   c. FTP device
   d. hard drive

6. A _____ is software that enables users with an Internet connection to access and view webpages on a computer or mobile device. (21)
   a. search engine
   b. wiki
   c. browser
   d. digital media player

7. _____ uses short-range radio signals to enable computers and devices to communicate with each other. (32)
   a. Cellular radio
   b. Bluetooth
   c. Wi-Fi
   d. A hot spot

8. A(n) _____ is a collaborative website that allows users to create, add to, modify, or delete the content via their browser. (40)
   a. podcast
   b. blog
   c. online social network
   d. wiki

Checkpoint

Matching Match the terms with their definitions.

_____ 1. all-in-one (6)

_____ 2. server (6)

_____ 3. phablet (7)

_____ 4. digital device convergence (1C)

_____ 5. touchpad (13)

_____ 6. storage device (17)

_____ 7. solid-state drive (17)

_____ 8. file (18)

_____ 9. software (26)

_____ 10. operating system (27)

a. term that describes the trend of computers and devices with technologies that overlap

b. mobile device that combines features of a smartphone and a tablet

c. storage device that typically uses flash memory to store data, instructions, and information

d. small, flat, rectangular pointing device that is sensitive to pressure and motion

e. set of programs that coordinates all the activities among computer or mobile device hardware

f. named collection of stored data, instructions, or information

g. type of desktop computer that does not contain a tower and instead uses the same case to house the display and the processing circuitry

h. series of related instructions, organized for a common purpose, that tells the computer what tasks to perform and how to perform them

i. computer that is dedicated to providing one or more services to other computers or devices on a network

j. component that records and/or retrieves items to and from storage media

✳ Consider This Answer the following questions in the format specified by your instructor.

1. Answer the critical thinking questions posed at the end of these elements in this module: Ethics & Issues (8, 23, 33, 40, 41), How To (5, 16, 22, 29), Mini Features (11, 34, 35), Secure IT (19, 25, 25, 37), and Technology @ Work (43).

2. What does it mean to be digitally literate, and why is it important? (2)

3. What are the different touch screen gestures and the actions they may cause to occur? (5)

4. What types of keyboards are available for smartphones and tablets? (5, 7)

5. In addition to books, what other digital media can be read on an e-book reader? (9)

6. In addition to keeping time, how might you use a smartwatch? (9)

7. Why might a consumer purchase separate stand-alone devices, such as smartphones, digital cameras, portable media players? (10)

8. How can you ease eyestrain while using a computer or mobile device? (16)

9. What types of files might you choose to store on a memory card or USB flash drive, rather than on a hard drive? (18)

10. What steps might you include in a backup plan? (19)

11. Why might you choose to use LinkedIn rather than Facebook? (24)

12. How might you know if your computer or mobile device is infected with malware? (24)

13. What types of software protect a computer from viruses and other malware? (25)

14. Why should you use a different password for all websites you access? (25)

15. How might you know if you are addicted to computers or suffer from technology overload? (26)

16. Why is green computing important? (26)

17. What steps can you take to contribute to green computing? (26)

18. What is the difference between system and application software? (26)

19. What are some examples of popular operating systems? (27)

20. How do desktop apps, web apps, and mobile apps differ? (28)

21. Where can you obtain programs or apps? (29)

22. What does a user interface control? (29)

23. What are some popular programming languages? (29)

24. Why might you opt for wireless communications? (31)

25. In a network, what is the major difference between a server and a client? (32)

26. When should you use a one-way sync or a two-way sync? (34)

27. What type of industries use computer-aided manufacturing (CAM)? (40)

✹ Problem Solving

The Problem Solving exercises extend your knowledge of module concepts by seeking solutions to practical problems with technology that you may encounter at home, school, or work. The Collaboration exercise should be completed with a team.

Instructions: You often can solve problems with technology in multiple ways. Determine a solution to the problems in these exercises by using one or more resources available to you (such as a computer or mobile device, articles on the web or in print, blogs, podcasts, videos, television, user guides, other individuals, electronics or computer stores, etc.). Describe your solution, along with the resource(s) used, in the format requested by your instructor (brief report, presentation, discussion, blog post, video, or other means).

Personal

1. **Shopping for Software** You are shopping for software that will assist you with your home's interior design. The package for the program you would like to purchase states that it was designed for the most recent version of Windows, but an older version is installed on your computer. How can you determine whether the program will run on your computer?

2. **Bad Directions** You are driving to your friend's house and are using your smartphone for directions. While approaching your destination, you realize that your smartphone app instructed you to turn the wrong way on your friend's street. How could this have happened?

3. **Bank Account Postings** While reviewing your checking account balance online, you notice that debit card purchases have not posted to your account for the past several days. Because you use online banking to balance your account, you become concerned about your unknown account balance. What steps will you take to correct this situation?

4. **Trial Expired** You have been using an app on your mobile device for a 30-day trial period. Now that the 30 days have expired, the app is requesting that you to pay to continue accessing your data. What are your next steps? What steps could you have taken to preserve your data before the trial period expired?

5. **Problematic Camera** After charging your digital camera battery overnight, you insert the battery and turn on the camera only to find that it is reporting a low battery. Seconds later, the camera shuts off automatically. What might be wrong?

Professional

6. **Discarding Old Computer Equipment** Your company has given you a new laptop to replace your current, outdated desktop. Because of the negative environmental impact of discarding the old computer in the trash, your supervisor asked you to suggest options for its disposal. How will you respond?

7. **Dead Battery** While traveling for business, you realize that you forgot to bring the battery charger for your laptop. Knowing that you need to use the laptop to give a presentation tomorrow, what steps will you take tonight to make sure you have enough battery power?

8. **Cannot Share Photos** You are attempting to send photos of a house for sale in an email message to your real estate partner. Each time you attempt to send the email message, you receive an automatic response stating that the files are too large. What are your next steps?

9. **Incorrect Sign-In Credentials** Upon returning to the office from a well-deserved two-week vacation, you turn on your computer. When you enter your user name and password, an error message appears stating that your password is incorrect. What are your next steps?

10. **Synchronization Error** You added appointments to the calendar on your computer, but these appointments are not synchronizing with your smartphone. Your calendar has synchronized with your smartphone in the past, but it has stopped working without explanation. What are your next steps?

Collaboration

11. **Technology in Health Care** Your primary care physician is moving from a shared office so that he can open his own practice. He mentioned that he would like to use technology in his office that not only will improve the patient experience, but also make his job easier. Form a team of three people to determine the types of technology your doctor can use in his new office. One team member should research ways that technology can help improve patient check-in and billing. Another team member should research the types of technology your doctor can use while he is working with patients, and the third team member should research any additional technology that can be used in the office to improve the patient experience. Compile your findings in a report and submit it to your instructor.

The How To: Your Turn exercises present general guidelines for fundamental skills when using a computer or mobile device and then require that you determine how to apply these general guidelines to a specific program or situation.

How To: Your Turn

Instructions: You often can complete tasks using technology in multiple ways. Figure out how to perform the tasks described in these exercises by using one or more resources available to you (such as a computer or mobile device, articles on the web or in print, online or program help, user guides, blogs, podcasts, videos, other individuals, trial and error, etc.). Summarize your 'how to' steps, along with the resource(s) used, in the format requested by your instructor (brief report, presentation, discussion, blog post, video, or other means).

1 Create a Facebook Account, Find the Discovering Computers Facebook Page, and Like It

The Discovering Computers Facebook page contains links to current events and other technology news, as well as relating the links to content in this book. The following steps guide you through the process of signing up for a Facebook account, navigating to the Discovering Computers Facebook page, and liking the page.

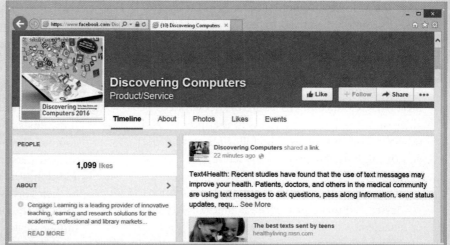

Source: Facebook

a. Run a browser and then navigate to www.facebook.com.

b. Follow the steps on the Facebook webpage to sign up for a new account. If you already have an account, enter your sign-in information and sign in to your Facebook account.

c. Search for the Discovering Computers Facebook page using the search text, Discovering Computers.

d. Select the Discovering Computers Product/Service in the search results.

e. Tap or click the Like button to like the page.

f. If your screen displays a Follow button, tap or click it to see information from the Discovering Computers Facebook page in your news feed.

g. View the posts and tap or click links on the page that are of interest to you.

h. When you are finished, sign out of Facebook.

Exercises

1. Summarize the process you use to sign up for or sign in to your Facebook account.

2. Which links on the Discovering Computers Facebook page are of interest to you? Why?

3. Browse Facebook and find at least three other Facebook pages that are of interest to you. Which pages have you found, and why do you like them?

2 Create a Twitter Account, Find the Discovering Computers Twitter Account, and Follow It

The Discovering Computers Twitter account contains links to current events and other technology news, as well as how it relates to the content in this textbook. The following steps guide you through the process of signing up for a Twitter account, navigating to the Discovering Computers Twitter account, and following it.

a. Run a browser and then navigate to www.twitter.com.

b. Follow the steps on the Twitter webpage to sign up for a new account. If you already have an account, enter your sign-in information and sign in to your Twitter account.

c. Search for the Discovering Computers Twitter account using the search text, DiscoveringComp.

d. Select Shelly Cashman @DiscoveringComp in the search results.

e. Tap or click the Follow button to follow the account.

f. View the posts and tap or click links on the page that are of interest to you.

g. When you are finished, sign out of Twitter.

✳ How To: Your Turn

Exercises

1. Summarize the process you use to sign up for or sign in to your Twitter account.
2. How is the Discovering Computers Twitter account similar to the Discovering Computers Facebook page? How are they different?
3. Browse Twitter and find at least three other Twitter accounts to follow. Which ones have you found, and why do you like them?

③ Connect to a Wireless Network

Wireless networks are available in many homes and businesses. Connecting to a wireless network can provide you with high-speed access to the Internet and other network resources. The following steps guide you through the process of connecting to a wireless network from a computer or mobile device.

a. If necessary, turn on your computer or mobile device and make sure wireless functionality is enabled.
b. Obtain the name of the wireless network to which you want to connect. **Note:** *You should connect only to wireless networks for which you have permission.*
c. On your computer or mobile device, view the list of available wireless networks.
d. Select the wireless network to which you want to connect.

e. If necessary, enter the requested security information, such as an encryption key or a password.
f. Run a browser to test your connection to the wireless network.

Exercises

1. Why should you not connect to a wireless network unless you have permission?
2. What is the name of the wireless network to which you connected?
3. Why might you connect to a wireless network on your smartphone instead of using your mobile data plan?

④ Manage Your Calendar

Individuals are choosing to use calendars on computers and mobile devices to keep track of events in their personal and professional lives more easily. In addition, students might use calendars to keep track of their class schedules. The following steps guide you through the process of managing your computer or mobile device's calendar.

a. Run the calendar app (usually by tapping or clicking its icon or tile on the home screen).
b. To add a new appointment, tap or click the Add or New Appointment button or icon and then enter the title or subject of the appointment, its date, time, location, and other information. Tap or click the Save button or icon on the New Appointment screen to save the information to your calendar.
c. Specify repeating information for appointments that occur at the same time over multiple occurrences, such as a class that meets every Tuesday from 10:00 a.m. to 11:00 a.m.
d. View your appointments on a daily, weekly, or monthly calendar by tapping or clicking the appropriate choice in the calendar app.
e. To edit an appointment, meeting, or event on your calendar, open the item by tapping or clicking it, make the necessary changes and then save the changes.

combination
modem/router/wireless
access point

Internet

modem

f. To delete an appointment, meeting, or event on your calendar, open the item by tapping or clicking it, and then tap or click the button to delete it. If necessary, confirm the deletion. If you are attempting to delete a recurring item on the calendar, the calendar app may ask whether you want to delete the one occurrence, or the entire series of appointments, meetings, or events.

© iStockphoto / Moncherie

How To: Your Turn

Exercises

1. In addition to your class schedule, what other recurring appointments might you add to your calendar?
2. Many calendar apps have a feature that can remind you of upcoming appointments in advance. How far in advance do you think you should be reminded of upcoming appointments?
3. How can you synchronize the calendar on your mobile device with the calendar on your home computer?

⑤ Back Up Photos from a Phone or Tablet

Many individuals take photos using mobile devices such as phones and tablets. Many, however, neglect to realize the importance of backing up these memories. A backup of the photos will be useful if you lose your mobile device, upgrade it to a newer model, or the device becomes damaged. While many mobile devices have built-in capabilities to back up photos to the cloud or to a desktop or laptop, it is important to make sure these features are configured properly. The following steps guide you through the process of backing up photos from a phone or tablet.

Backing Up to the Cloud

a. If necessary, install and sign in to an app on a phone or tablet that can back up photos to the cloud. Make sure the service you use gives you enough storage space for the photos you intend to upload.
b. Follow the instructions in the app and configure it to back up the photos at an interval of your choosing. Some options might include:
   • Back up all photos at certain intervals (such as one time per day or one time per week)
   • Back up photos as you take them
   • Back up photos stored in specific folders
c. If you are using a mobile device with a data plan, consider specifying whether you want the backup to occur only when you are connected to

Wi-Fi. Backing up using your phone or tablet's data plan may result in additional charges if you inadvertently exceed your quota.
d. Verify all photos have been backed up to the cloud service.

Backing Up to a Computer

a. Use the USB cable that came with your phone or tablet to connect it to the computer to which you want to back up the photos.
b. After the computer has recognized that a phone or tablet is connected, navigate to the drive on the computer representing the phone or tablet and then navigate to the folder containing the photos. If your phone or tablet stores pictures on both internal storage and a memory card, remember to back up your photos from both locations.
c. Drag the photos from the location on your phone or tablet to a folder on your computer that will store the backed up files.
d. When the files have finished backing up to the computer, close all open folder windows on the computer and then safely disconnect the phone or tablet from the computer.

© Dmitry Rukhlenko / Photos.com

Exercises

1. How often do you think you should back up your photos? Why?
2. When backing up photos, why might it be better to connect your phone or tablet to the computer using a cable instead of inserting the memory card from the phone or tablet into the computer?
3. Compare and contrast three apps or services that can back up photos from your phone or tablet to the cloud. Which one would you choose, and why?

✳ Internet Research

The Internet Research exercises broaden your understanding of module concepts by requiring that you search for information on the web.

Instructions: Use a search engine or another search tool to locate the information requested or answers to questions presented in the exercises. Describe your findings, along with the search term(s) you used and your web source(s), in the format requested by your instructor (brief report, presentation, discussion, blog post, video, or other means).

❶ Making Use of the Web
Informational and Research

Informational and research websites contain factual information and include reference works such as libraries, encyclopedias, dictionaries, directories, and guides. More than 2.4 billion people worldwide use the Internet, and Google is one of the websites they visit most often. Google reports that people perform more than 100 billion searches every month using its Google Search. In How To 1-3 in this module, you learned how to use a browser to display a webpage on a computer or mobile device and to perform a basic web search using a search engine.

Research This: Using a browser and search engine, find the answers to the following questions. (1) Search for the top five informational websites and top five research websites. What types of information or research does each present? What search text did you use? (2) Visit Google's website and locate the company's early philosophy: "Ten things we know to be true." What are five of these values? What is the goal of the "Made with Code" initiative? (3) Visit the Engadget website and read at least three reviews of tablets. Create a table listing the product name, price, battery life, pros, and cons. (4) Locate articles about using hands-free devices for conversations while driving. Which states have passed legislation to restrict drivers' use of hands-free devices while driving? Describe the features found in the sophisticated hands-free system of one of this year's vehicles.

❷ Social Media

Online social networks are a central communications tool and the primary source of news and information for many people. Historians place the birth of online social networking with the BBS (Bulletin Board System), where users communicated with a central computer and sent messages to other BBS members and also downloaded files and games. The next phase of online social networks evolved when CompuServe, AOL (America Online), and Prodigy were among the services linking people with similar interests. Today's online social networks share many of the same basic principles by allowing members to communicate common interests, play games, and share photos, videos, and music. Some of these online social networks are for personal use, while others are for entrepreneurs, business owners, and professionals to share job-related topics.

Research This: Compare the features of the top personal online social networks, and create a table listing the number of active members in the United States and worldwide, the number of years the sites have existed, the more popular features, and the amount of content, such as photos, news stories, and links, that is shared each month. What types of advertisements are featured in each of these sites? Which sites are marketed toward younger and older users? Then, research the online social networks used for business. How does their content differ from that found on the personal online social networks? How many companies use these sites as a recruiting tool? How many native languages are supported? How are professionals using these websites to find potential clients and business partners?

❸ Search Skills
Selecting Search Terms

Search text that you send to a search engine, such as Google, Bing, or Yahoo!, impacts the quality of your search results. Rather than typing a long question in the search box, you may improve your results if you select the question's most important words as your search text. For example, instead of typing the

Google's mission is to organize the world's information and make it universally accessible and useful.

Products   Company · Management

Internet Research

entire question "How many users currently are on Facebook?" as your search text, type the following as your search text: facebook users current. Many search engines consider common words — such as how, are, and on — as stop words, or words that a search engine ignores when performing a search.

Place the most specific or important word (facebook) first in your search text and then follow it with additional words to narrow the results. To see if rearranging the order of the words yields different results, type current users facebook. Some search results from both queries likely will overlap. Many search engines assist you by automatically completing terms as you type them and will display a list of popular alternatives from which you can select. Sometimes, replacing a search term with a synonym will improve your results. For example, try using the search text, facebook users, followed by the current year instead of the using the word, current. Most search engines are not case sensitive. (They do not distinguish between uppercase and lowercase characters.)

| WEB | IMAGES | VIDEOS | MAPS | NEWS | MORE |

bing | facebook users

facebook users
facebook users 2016
facebook users **statistics**
facebook users **statistics**
facebook users **by country**
facebook users **by age**
facebook users **guide**
facebook users **in the world**

Source: Microsoft

Research This: Create search text using the techniques described above, and type it into a search engine to find answers to these questions. (1) What English words are stop words for Google? (2) What is the largest solid-state drive available? (3) How many hours per day on average do teens spend playing video games? (4) When is the next update to the Android mobile operating system expected to be released?

❹ Security

Secure IT 1-3 in this module offers advice about creating secure passwords when registering for websites. Despite suggestions and constant reminders from security experts to develop and then periodically change passwords, users continue to create weak passwords.

These common passwords are broken easily and, therefore, never should be used. For many years, the most common passwords have been the word, password, and the number sequences 123456 and 12345678.

Research This: Use a search engine to locate at least 2 different companies' lists of the 10 or 20 more common passwords in the past two years. Which passwords appear on both lists? Find a password-strength checking website and type three passwords to determine how easy or difficult they are to crack. Why do consumers continue to use these passwords despite repeated warnings to avoid them? Do you have accounts using one or more of these passwords? What advice is given for developing strong passwords, such as using the lyrics to the first line of a favorite song? How do the companies gather data to determine common passwords?

❺ Cloud Services
Cloud Storage (Iaas)

Cloud storage providers offer online access to hardware for storing files, and web and mobile apps to access, back up, and manage files. Cloud storage is an example of IaaS (infrastructure as a service), a service of cloud computing that allows individuals and businesses to use a vendor's hardware to manage their computing needs.

Cloud storage providers offer both free and paid service plans based on the amount of free storage, and some allow users to earn additional storage by recommending friends to use their services or by participating in promotional campaigns. Many cloud storage providers enable users to synchronize files across multiple devices, access files via mobile or web apps, share files with team members, and maintain previous versions of files. Some provide built-in access to web-based productivity software or integrate with third-party web and mobile apps.

Research This: (1) Use a search engine to find three popular cloud storage providers. Create accounts and try each for a period specified by your instructor. In a table, summarize their features, including amount of free storage available (offered or earned), restrictions on file sizes you can upload, ease of use of web and mobile apps, operating systems or devices supported, cost of paid plans, and additional services provided for a fee. (2) Many cloud storage providers offer several gigabytes of free storage to their users. What is the largest amount of free storage you can find? Who is the provider? Can you identify any drawbacks to using this service?

Critical Thinking

The Critical Thinking exercises challenge your assessment and decision-making skills by presenting real-world situations associated with module concepts. The Collaboration exercise should be completed with a team.

Instructions: Evaluate the situations below, using personal experiences and one or more resources available to you (such as articles on the web or in print, blogs, podcasts, videos, television, user guides, other individuals, electronics or computer stores, etc.). Perform the tasks requested in each exercise and share your deliverables in the format requested by your instructor (brief report, presentation, discussion, blog post, video, or other means).

1. Reactions to Software Problems

People who use computers and mobile devices sometimes experience problems with software, including operating systems, desktop apps, web apps, and mobile apps. Problems range from not being able to install or download the program or app to a computer or mobile device, to a program or an app producing unanticipated results. Depending on the situation, these problems can result in user stress. Many people believe reactions to software problems tend to be more extreme than reactions to problems with other tools.

Do This: Evaluate situations in which you have seen people react to program and app problems on their computers and mobile devices. Discuss how these users can reduce their frustration when dealing with such problems. Have you ever been frustrated by problems with a program or an app? How did you react? What did you do to solve the problem?

2. Energy Efficiency

Increases in energy prices lead many individuals to look at purchasing energy-efficient computers and devices. Energy-efficient models often look and perform similarly to equivalent computers or devices that use more energy.

Do This: Find two computers or devices of identical configuration, where the only difference is energy consumption. How much energy does the energy-efficient model save? Are energy-efficient computers and devices more or less expensive? Will the difference in cost (if any) affect your purchasing decision? How else might you be able to change your settings on your existing computer or device to save energy? Use the web to locate articles that recommend energy-efficient products and that provide tips about additional ways to save energy.

3. Case Study

Amateur Sports League   You are the new manager for a nonprofit amateur soccer league. The previous manager tracked all of the data on paper. You realize that using technology will increase your efficiency and enable you to communicate better with the board of directors, coaches, and players. At the board's next meeting, you will share ideas of how you will use technology.

Do This: To prepare for the meeting, you compile the following: differences between input and output, a list of the types of data you can use as input, and a list of the types of information you can produce as output. You include the types of computers, mobile devices, and other technologies you will use to enter data and produce the information. Incorporate your own experiences and user reviews of the devices. Compile your findings.

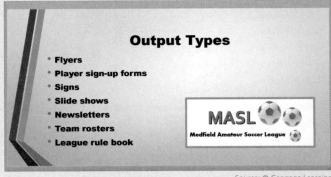

Source: © Cengage Learning

Collaboration

4. Recommending Technology Solutions

People use computers and mobile devices in a variety of fields, including travel, manufacturing, and more. Although the way people use computers and mobile devices varies, each use involves hardware, programs and apps, and some type of communications method, such as the Internet or cellular network.

Do This: Form a three-member team and choose a field in which you all are interested. Assign one member to investigate hardware, another to investigate programs and apps, and the third member to investigate communications methods used in the field. Locate user reviews and articles by industry experts. Each team member should develop a list of related items that may be used. After the investigation, create a hypothetical business or organization in the field. Recommend specific hardware, programs or apps, and communications capabilities that would be best for the network or organization. Include comparisons of specific items, as well as costs. Be sure to summarize your investigations, describe the hypothetical business or organization, and outline and support your recommendations.

CONNECTING AND COMMUNICATING ONLINE: The Internet, Websites, and Media

2

The Internet provides a variety of ways to communicate online.

"I use the Internet and web to shop for bargains, browse Google for all sorts of information, manage my fantasy sports teams, download music, check email on my phone, and so much more! What more could I gain from using the Internet?"

While you may be familiar with some of the content in this module, do you know how to . . .

- Use a public Wi-Fi hot spot safely?
- Register a domain name?
- Identify a cybersquatter?
- Browse the web safely?
- Tag digital content?
- Protect yourself from identity theft?
- Improve search results?
- Publish a website?
- Download digital media from online services?
- Set up a personal VoIP service?
- Combat cyberbullying?
- Determine your IP address?
- Search for a job online?

In this module, you will discover how to perform these tasks along with much more information essential to this course.

Source: © scyther5 / Shutterstock.com; © Kristina Postnikova / Shutterstock.com; Source: Pinterest; © Pablo Eder / Shutterstock.com, © iStockPhoto / pixelfit; © DeiMosz / Shutterstock.com

✔ Objectives

After completing this module, you will be able to:

1 Discuss the evolution of the Internet
2 Briefly describe various broadband Internet connections
3 Describe the purpose of an IP address and its relationship to a domain name
4 Describe features of browsers and identify the components of a web address
5 Describe ways to compose effective search text
6 Explain benefits and risks of using online social networks
7 Describe uses of various types of websites: search engines; online social networks; informational and research; media sharing; bookmarking; news, weather, sports, and other mass media; educational; business, governmental, and organizational; blogs; wikis and collaboration; health and fitness; science; entertainment; banking and finance; travel and tourism; mapping; retail and auctions; careers and employment; e-commerce; portals; content aggregation; and website creation and management
8 Explain how the web uses graphics, animation, audio, video, and virtual reality
9 Explain how email, email lists, Internet messaging, chat rooms, online discussions, VoIP, and FTP work
10 Identify the rules of netiquette

The Internet

One of the major reasons business, home, and other users purchase computers and mobile devices is for Internet access. The **Internet** is a worldwide collection of networks that connects millions of businesses, government agencies, educational institutions, and individuals. Each of the networks on the Internet provides resources that add to the abundance of goods, services, and information accessible via the Internet.

Today, billions of home and business users around the world access a variety of services on the Internet using computers and mobile devices. The web, messaging, and video communications are some of the more widely used Internet services (Figure 2-1). Other Internet services include chat rooms, discussion forums, and file transfer. To enhance your understanding of Internet services, the module begins by discussing the history of the Internet and how the Internet works and then explains each of these services.

Evolution of the Internet

The Internet has its roots in a networking project started by the Pentagon's Advanced Research Projects Agency (ARPA), an agency of the U.S. Department of Defense. ARPA's goal was to build a network that (1) allowed scientists at different physical locations to share information and work together on military and scientific projects and (2) could function even if part of the network were disabled or destroyed by a disaster such as a nuclear attack. That network, called *ARPANET*, became functional in September 1969, linking scientific and academic researchers across the United States.

The original ARPANET consisted of four main computers, one each located at the University of California at Los Angeles, the University of California at Santa Barbara, the Stanford Research Institute, and the University of Utah. Each of these computers served as a host on the network. A *host*, more commonly known today as a server, is any computer that provides services and connections to other computers on a network. Hosts often use high-speed communications to transfer data and messages over a network. By 1984, ARPANET had more than 1,000 individual computers linked as hosts. Today, millions of hosts connect to this network, which now is known as the Internet.

Figure 2-1 People around the world use the Internet in daily activities, such as accessing information, sending or posting messages, and conversing with others from their computers and mobile devices.

The Internet consists of many local, regional, national, and international networks. Both public and private organizations own networks on the Internet. These networks, along with phone companies, cable and satellite companies, and the government, all contribute toward the internal structure of the Internet.

✸ CONSIDER THIS

 Internet Research

Which organizations are members of the World Wide Web Consortium?

Search for: w3c members

Who owns the Internet?
No single person, company, institution, or government agency owns the Internet. Each organization on the Internet is responsible only for maintaining its own network.

The World Wide Web Consortium (*W3C*), however, oversees research and sets standards and guidelines for many areas of the Internet. The mission of the W3C is to ensure the continued growth of the web. Nearly 400 organizations from around the world are members of the W3C, advising, defining standards, and addressing other issues.

Connecting to the Internet

Users can connect their computers and mobile devices to the Internet through wired or wireless technology and then access its services free or for a fee. With wired connections, a computer or device physically attaches via a cable or wire to a communications device, such as a modem, that transmits data and other items over transmission media to the Internet. For wireless connections, many mobile computers and devices include the necessary built-in technology so that they can transmit data and other items wirelessly. Computers without this capability can use a wireless modem or other communications device that enables wireless connectivity. A *wireless modem*, for example, uses a wireless communications technology (such as cellular radio, satellite, or Wi-Fi) to connect to the Internet. Figure 2-2 shows examples of modems. The wireless modem shown in the figure is known as a *dongle*, which is a small device that connects to a computer and enables additional functions when attached.

Today, users often connect to the Internet via *broadband* Internet service because of its fast data transfer speeds and its always-on connection. Through broadband Internet service, users can download webpages quickly, play online games, communicate in real time with others, and more. Table 2-1 shows examples of popular wired and wireless broadband Internet service technologies for home and small business users.

Figure 2-2 Using a modem is one way to connect computers and mobile devices to the Internet.
Courtesy of Zoom Telephonics Inc; © Oleksiy Mark / Shutterstock.com; Source: Microsoft; © Kristina Postnikova / Shutterstock.com; Kristina Postnikova / Shutterstock.com; © Cengage Learning; © DR / Fotolia

Table 2-1   Popular Broadband Internet Service Technologies

	Technology	Description
Wired	Cable Internet service	Provides high-speed Internet access through the cable television network via a cable modem
	DSL (digital subscriber line)	Provides high-speed Internet connections through the telephone network via a DSL modem
	Fiber to the Premises (FTTP)	Uses fiber-optic cable to provide high-speed Internet access via a modem
Wireless	**Wi-Fi** (wireless fidelity)	Uses radio signals to provide high-speed Internet connections to computers and devices with built-in Wi-Fi capability or a communications device that enables Wi-Fi connectivity
	Mobile broadband	Offers high-speed Internet connections over the cellular radio network to computers and devices with built-in compatible technology (such as 3G, 4G, or 5G) or a wireless modem or other communications device
	Fixed wireless	Provides high-speed Internet connections using a dish-shaped antenna on a building, such as a house or business, to communicate with a tower location via radio signals
	Satellite Internet service	Provides high-speed Internet connections via satellite to a satellite dish that communicates with a satellite modem

© Cengage Learning

Many public locations, such as shopping malls, coffee shops, restaurants, schools, airports, hotels, and city parks have Wi-Fi hot spots. Recall that a **hot spot** is a wireless network that provides Internet connections to mobile computers and devices. Although most hot spots enable unrestricted or open access, some require that users agree to terms of service, obtain a password (for example, from the hotel's front desk), or perform some other action in order to connect to the Internet. Read Secure IT 2-1 for ways to use a public Wi-Fi hot spot safely.

⚙ SECURE IT 2-1

Using Public Wi-Fi Hot Spots Safely

Connecting wirelessly to a public hot spot at your local coffee shop or at the airport can be convenient and practical. Using this free service can be risky, however, because cybercriminals may lurk in public Wi-Fi hot spots, hoping to gain access to confidential information on your computer or mobile device. Follow these guidelines for a safer browsing experience:

- **Avoid typing passwords and financial information.** Identity thieves are on the lookout for people who sign in to accounts, enter their credit card account numbers in shopping websites, or conduct online banking transactions. If you must type this personal information, be certain the website's web address begins with "https," signifying a secure connection. If the website's web address changes to "http," indicating an unsecure connection,

sign out to end your Internet session immediately.

- **Sign out of websites.** When finished using an account, sign out of it and close the window.

- **Disable your wireless connection.** If you have finished working online but still need to use the computer, disconnect from the wireless connection.

- **Do not leave your computer or mobile device unattended.** It may seem obvious, but always stay with your computer or mobile device. Turning your back to talk with a friend or to refill your coffee gives thieves a few seconds to steal sensitive information that may be displayed on the screen.

- **Beware of over-the-shoulder snoopers.** The person sitting behind you may be watching or using a camera

phone to record your keystrokes, read your email messages and online social network posts, and view your photos and videos.

⚙ **Consider This:** How will you apply these precautions the next time you use a public Wi-Fi hot spot? Should businesses post signs alerting customers about Wi-Fi security issues?

© DelMosz / Shutterstock.com

Home and small business users can share and provide wireless Internet connections by creating their own Wi-Fi hot spot through a communications device in the home or business that is connected to broadband Internet service. Instead of a stationary Wi-Fi hot spot, some users opt to create mobile hot spots through mobile broadband Internet service via a separate communications device or a tethered Internet-capable device (Figure 2-3). *Tethering* transforms a smartphone or Internet-capable tablet into a portable communications device that shares its Internet access with other computers and devices wirelessly. Users may pay additional fees for mobile hot spot and tethering services.

 Internet Research

What is a MiFi device?

Search for: mifi

Figure 2-3   You can create a mobile hot spot using a communications device or by tethering a smartphone.

Courtesy of Verizon Wireless; © figarro / Can Stock Photo; © iStockphoto / Dane Wirtzfeld; © amfoto / Shutterstock.com; © Alex Staroseltsev / Shutterstock.com; Source: Microsoft; © Cengage Learning

Employees and students typically connect their computers and mobile devices to the Internet wirelessly through a business or school network, which, in turn, usually connects to a high-speed Internet service. When away from the office, home, or school, mobile users often access the Internet using Wi-Fi, mobile hot spots, or tethering services. Hotels and airports often provide wireless Internet connections as a free service to travelers. Many hotels have computers in their lobbies for customers to check email, browse the web, or print travel documents. Customers often bring their laptops or tablets to coffee shops, restaurants, libraries, hotels, and malls that offer free Wi-Fi as a service to their patrons.

✹ **CONSIDER THIS**

Does everyone use broadband Internet?

No. Some home users connect computers and devices to the Internet via slower-speed dial-up access because of its lower cost or because broadband access is not available where they live. Dial-up access takes place when a modem in a computer connects to the Internet via a standard telephone line that transmits data and information using an *analog* (continuous wave pattern) signal.

Internet Service Providers

An **Internet service provider** (**ISP**), sometimes called an Internet access provider, is a business that provides individuals and organizations access to the Internet free or for a fee. ISPs often charge a fixed amount for an Internet connection, offering customers a variety of plans based on desired speeds, bandwidth, and services. In addition to Internet access, ISPs may include additional services, such as email and online storage.

Bandwidth represents the amount of data that travels over a network. A higher bandwidth means more data transmits. Data sizes typically are stated in terms of megabytes and gigabytes. A *megabyte* (**MB**) is equal to approximately one million characters, and a *gigabyte* (**GB**) is equal to approximately one billion characters. Table 2-2 shows approximate data usage for various Internet activities.

⚙️ BTW
Byte
A byte is the basic storage unit on a computer or mobile device and represents a single character.

Table 2-2   Data Usage Examples

Activity	Quantity	Approximate Data Usage
Send and receive email messages (with no attachments)	100 messages	3–6 MB
Post on online social networks (text only)	100 posts	25–50 MB
Upload or download photos	50 photos	50 MB
Send and receive email messages (with attachments)	100 messages	0.75–1 GB
Visit webpages	200 visits	1 GB
Talk with others using VoIP (without video)	1 hour	1.25 GB
Listen to streaming music	1 hour	1–2 GB
Play online games	1 hour	1.75 GB
Watch smaller, standard-quality streaming video	1 hour	2–5 GB
Download apps, games, music, e-books	25 downloads	3 GB
Talk with others using VoIP (with video)	1 hour	5–7.5 GB
Watch HD streaming video	1 hour	5–20 GB

© Cengage Learning

🔍 **Internet Research**
Can I check the speed of my Internet connection?
Search for: internet speed test

✳️ **CONSIDER THIS**

Does the term data have multiple meanings?

In the technology field, as discussed in Module 1, data can refer to unprocessed items that computers often process into information. Data also refers to the content that is stored on media or transmitted over a network. For example, when you select a data plan for your smartphone, the mobile service provider typically limits the amount of data (number of bytes) you can transfer each month depending on the plan you selected.

Wi-Fi networks often provide free Internet access, while some charge a daily or per use fee. Instead of locating a hot spot, some users prefer to subscribe to a mobile service provider, such as Verizon Wireless, so that they can access the Internet wherever they have mobile phone access. A **mobile service provider**, sometimes called a wireless data provider, is an ISP that offers wireless Internet access to computers and mobile devices with the necessary built-in wireless capability (such as Wi-Fi, wireless modems, or other communications devices that enable wireless connectivity. An antenna on or built into the computer or device, wireless modem, or communications device typically sends signals through the airwaves to communicate with a mobile service provider.

How Data Travels the Internet

Computers and devices connected to the Internet work together to transfer data around the world using servers and clients and various wired and wireless transmission media. On the Internet, your computer or device is a client that can access data and services on a variety of servers. Wired transmission media includes phone line, coaxial cable, and fiber-optic cable. Wireless transmission media includes radio waves and satellite signals.

The inner structure of the Internet works much like a transportation system. Just as interstate highways connect major cities and carry the bulk of the automotive traffic across the country, several main transmission media carry the heaviest amount of **traffic**, or communications activity, on the Internet. These major carriers of network traffic are known collectively as the *Internet backbone*.

In the United States, the transmission media that make up the Internet backbone exchange data at several different major cities across the country. That is, they transfer data from one network to another until reaching the final destination (Figure 2-4).

How a Home User's Request for a Webpage Might Travel the Internet Using Cable Internet Service

Step 1
You send a request to the Internet. For example, you enter the web address of a webpage you want to visit in the address bar of your browser.

Step 2
A cable modem transfers the computer's digital signals to the cable television line in your house.

Step 3
Your request (digital signals) travels through cable television lines to a central cable system, which is shared by up to 500 homes in a neighborhood.

Step 4
The central cable system sends your request over high-speed fiber-optic lines to the cable operator, who often also is the ISP.

Step 5
The ISP routes your request through the Internet backbone to the destination server (in this example, the server that contains the requested webpage).

Step 6
The server retrieves the requested webpage and sends it back through the Internet backbone to your computer.

Figure 2-4 This figure shows how a home user's request for eBay's webpage might travel the Internet using cable Internet service.
© romakoma / Shutterstock.com; © Pablo Eder / Shutterstock.com; © dotshock / Shutterstock.com; © TonyV3112 / Shutterstock.com; © iStockPhoto / loops7; © iStockphoto / luismmolina; Source: eBay

IP Addresses and Domain Names

The Internet relies on an addressing system much like the postal service to send data to a computer or device at a specific destination. An **IP address**, short for Internet Protocol address, is a sequence of numbers that uniquely identifies the location of each computer or device connected to the Internet.

The Internet uses two IP addressing schemes: IPv4 and IPv6. Due to the growth of the Internet, the original IPv4 addresses began dwindling in availability. The IPv6 scheme increased the available number of IP addresses exponentially. Because lengthy IP addresses can be difficult to remember, the Internet supports domain names. A **domain name** is a text-based name that corresponds to the IP address of a server that hosts a website (Figure 2-5). A domain name is part of the web address that you type in a browser's address bar to access a website.

IPv4 address ⟶ 74.125.224.72

IPv6 address ⟶ 2001:4860:4860::8844

Domain name ⟶ google.com

top-level domain

Figure 2-5 The IPv4 and IPv6 addresses, along with the domain name for Google's website.
© Cengage Learning

The suffix of the domain name, called the *top-level domain* (*TLD*), identifies the type of organization associated with the domain. In Figure 2-5, for example, the .com is the TLD. Table 2-3 lists some of the original TLDs. New TLDs are being introduced to give individuals and businesses flexibility and creativity when purchasing domain names. For example, .museum, .technology, .name, and .biz have been introduced as TLDs within recent years.

The organization that approves and controls TLDs is called *ICANN* (pronounced EYE-can), which stands for Internet Corporation for Assigned Names and Numbers. For websites outside the United States, the suffix of the domain name may include a country code TLD (*ccTLD*), which is a two-letter country code, such as au for Australia. For example, www.philips.com.au is the domain name for Philips Australia. Read How To 2-1 to learn how to register a domain name.

Table 2-3	Original TLDs
TLD	**Intended Purpose**
.com	Commercial organizations, businesses, and companies
.edu	Educational institutions
.gov	Government agencies
.mil	Military organizations
.net	Network providers or commercial companies
.org	Nonprofit organizations

© Cengage Learning

⚙ HOW TO 2-1

Register a Domain Name
Individuals and companies register domain names so that people can find their websites easily using a browser. You register a domain name through a *registrar*, which is an organization that sells and manages domain names. When creating a website to post online, register a domain name that is easy to remember so that visitors can navigate to your website quickly. The following steps describe how to register a domain name.

1. Run a browser.
2. Use a search engine to locate a domain name registrar and then navigate to the

website. You may want to evaluate several domain name registrars before deciding which one to use. Domain name registrars often offer various pricing models for registering domain names.

3. Perform a search on the domain name registrar's website for the domain name you wish to register. If the domain name is not available or costs too much, continue searching for a domain name that is available and within your price range, or explore various TLDs. For example, if the domain name you wish to register is not available or too expensive with the

".com" TLD, consider using another TLD such as ".net" or ".org."

4. Follow the steps on the domain name registrar's website to select and complete the purchase and registration of the desired domain name.

☀ **Consider This:** What domain name based on your name would you register for your personal website? If your preferred domain name is not available, what are three alternative domain names you would consider?

The *domain name system* (*DNS*) is the method that the Internet uses to store domain names and their corresponding IP addresses. When you enter a domain name (i.e., google.com) in a browser, a DNS server translates the domain name to its associated IP address so that the request can be routed to the correct computer (Figure 2-6). A *DNS server* is a server on the Internet that usually is associated with an ISP. Read Ethics & Issues 2-1 to consider issues related those who purchase unused or lapsed domain names for nefarious purposes.

How a Browser Displays a Requested Webpage

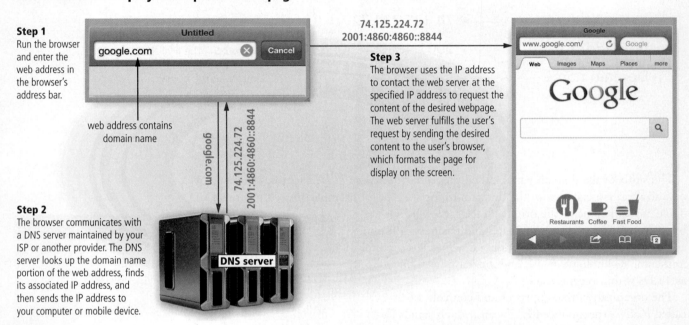

Step 1
Run the browser and enter the web address in the browser's address bar.

web address contains domain name

google.com

74.125.224.72
2001:4860:4860::8844

Step 3
The browser uses the IP address to contact the web server at the specified IP address to request the content of the desired webpage. The web server fulfills the user's request by sending the desired content to the user's browser, which formats the page for display on the screen.

Step 2
The browser communicates with a DNS server maintained by your ISP or another provider. The DNS server looks up the domain name portion of the web address, finds its associated IP address, and then sends the IP address to your computer or mobile device.

DNS server

Figure 2-6 This figure shows how a user's entered domain name (google.com) uses a DNS server to display a webpage (Google, in this case).
Apple Inc.; © Cengage Learning; © Cengage Learning; © Sashkin / Shutterstock.com; Source: Google Inc.

✷ ETHICS & ISSUES 2-1

Should Cybersquatters Be Prosecuted?
You learn from a registrar that a domain name containing your company name is not available. When you enter the web address in a browser, a webpage appears that contains ads, false content, or a notice that the domain is available for purchase, likely by a cyber-squatter. Cybersquatters purchase unused or lapsed domain names so that they can profit from selling them. Cybersquatters sometimes will sell you the domain name, but some take advantage of people trying to reach a more popular website to promote their own busi-ness or needs. One example is when a politi-cian registered several domain names that included his opponent's names and redirected them to his own campaign website.

Website owners periodically must renew domain names. Cybersquatters look for out-of-date registrations and buy them so that the original website owner must buy them back. Cybersquatters often purchase domain names with common words, alternate spellings of trademarked terms, or celebrity names. With the constant increase of new TLDs, cybersquatting cases are on the rise. Experts recommend purchasing your domain name with as many TLDs as you can afford, as well as to register your own name and that of your children.

More than 15 years ago, lawmakers enacted the *Anticybersquatting Consumer Protection Act* (ACPA). The ACPA's goal is to protect trademark owners from having

to pay a cybersquatter for a domain name that includes their trademark. To win a case against a cybersquatter, the owners must prove that the cybersquatters acted in bad faith, meaning they tried knowingly to profit from purchasing a domain name with a trademarked term, or a common misspelling or nickname of a trademarked term. Critics say that the ACPA prohibits free speech and free market.

Consider This: Should cybersquatting be illegal? Why or why not? Is it ethical to profit from cybersquatting? Why or why not? How should companies protect their brands when registering for domain names?

The World Wide Web

While the Internet was developed in the late 1960s, the World Wide Web emerged in the early 1990s as an easier way to access online information using a browser. Since then, it has grown phenomenally to become one of the more widely used services on the Internet.

As discussed in Module 1, the **World Wide Web** (**WWW**), or **web**, consists of a worldwide collection of electronic documents. Each electronic document on the web is called a **webpage**, which can contain text, graphics, animation, audio, and video. Some webpages are static (fixed); others are dynamic (changing). Visitors to a *static webpage* all see the same content each time they view the webpage. With a *dynamic webpage*, by contrast, the content of the webpage generates each time a user displays it. Dynamic webpages may contain customized content, such as the current date and time of day, desired stock quotes, weather for a region, or ticket availability for flights. The time required to download a webpage varies depending on the speed of your Internet connection and the amount of graphics and other media involved.

A **website** is a collection of related webpages and associated items, such as documents and photos, stored on a web server. A **web server** is a computer that delivers requested webpages to your computer or mobile device. The same web server can store multiple websites.

As web technologies matured in the mid-2000s, industry experts introduced the term *Web 2.0* to refer to websites that provide a means for users to share personal information (such as online social networks), allow users to modify website content (such as wikis), and provide applications through a browser (such as web apps).

Navigating the Web

Recall from Module 1 that a **browser** is an application that enables users with an Internet connection to access and view webpages on a computer or mobile device. Internet-capable mobile devices such as smartphones use a special type of browser, called a *mobile browser*, which is designed for their smaller screens and limited computing power. Many websites can detect if you are accessing their content on a mobile device (Figure 2-7).

> **BTW**
> **Web vs. Internet**
> Recall that the terms web and Internet should not be used interchangeably. The World Wide Web is a service of the Internet.

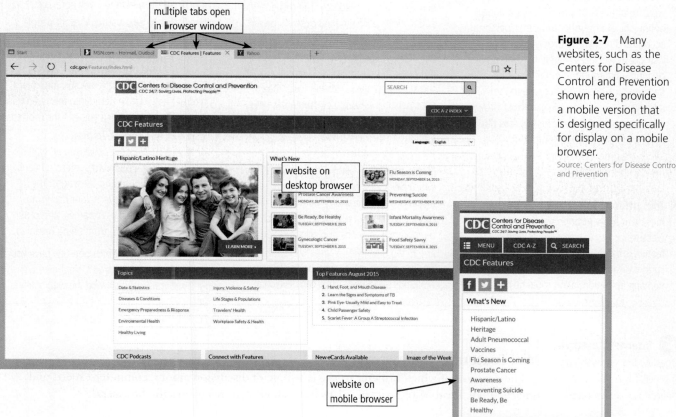

multiple tabs open in browser window

website on desktop browser

website on mobile browser

Figure 2-7 Many websites, such as the Centers for Disease Control and Prevention shown here, provide a mobile version that is designed specifically for display on a mobile browser.
Source: Centers for Disease Control and Prevention

When you run a browser, it may retrieve and display a starting webpage, sometimes called a home page. The initial home page that is displayed is specified in the browser. You can change your browser's home page at any time through its settings, options, or similar commands.

Internet Research

How do I change my browser's home page?

Search for: change browser home page

Another use of the term, **home page**, refers to the first page that is displayed on a website. Similar to a book cover or a table of contents, a website's home page provides information about its purpose and content. Many websites allow you to personalize the home page so that it contains areas of interest to you.

Current browsers typically support **tabbed browsing**, where the top of the browser shows a tab (similar to a file folder tab) for each webpage you display (shown in Figure 2-7). To move from one displayed webpage to another, you tap or click the tab in the browser. Tabbed browsing allows users to have multiple home pages that automatically are displayed when the browser runs. You also can organize tabs in a group, called a tab group, and save the group as a favorite, so that at any time you can display all tabs at once.

Because some websites attempt to track your browsing habits or gather personal information, current browsers usually include a feature that allows you to disable and/or more tightly control the dissemination of your browsing habits and personal information. Read Secure IT 2-2 for safe browsing tips.

 SECURE IT 2-2

Safe Browsing Techniques

Browsing the web is similar to crossing a busy street: you need to exercise caution and look carefully for unexpected traffic. Cybercriminals are on the lookout to prey upon unsuspecting users, so you should follow these guidelines when browsing:

- **Verify the website is safe.** Type the website address of your email, banking, online social network, and other personal accounts directly in a browser; never visit these websites merely by tapping or clicking links found in email messages. Before you sign in, double-check the web address to verify it is correct. Most browsers change the color of the address bar to verify the website is legitimate. Also, check that the web address begins with https instead of the less secure http, and look for a closed padlock symbol beside it.

- **Turn off location sharing.** At times, you may want allow *location sharing*, which gives websites access to your current location. This feature is handy when you want to obtain current weather conditions or use a navigation app. This information could be misused

by dishonest individuals, however, so it is recommended you turn off location sharing.

- **Clear your browsing history.** A copy of every website you visit is stored in the browser's *cache* (pronounced cash) folder. If you perform online banking or view your credit card transactions, the cache could contain personal information, such as passwords and account numbers. You can specify to clear cache automatically each time you close a browser.

- **Never store passwords.** Many browsers can store your passwords so that you do not need to type them each time you visit the same websites. Although you may consider this feature a convenience, keep in mind that anyone who accesses your computer can view these secure websites easily using your account information.

- **Use a phishing filter.** *Phishing* is a scam in which a perpetrator attempts to obtain your personal and/or financial information. Many browsers include a *phishing filter*, which is a program that warns or blocks you from potentially fraudulent or suspicious websites.

- **Enable a pop-up or pop-under blocker.** Malicious software creators can develop a

pop-up ad or pop-under ad, which are Internet advertisements that suddenly appear in a new window on top of or behind a webpage displayed in a browser. A **pop-up blocker** is a filtering program that stops pop-up ads from displaying on webpages; similarly a **pop-under blocker** stops pop-under ads. Many browsers include these blockers. You also can download them from the web at no cost.

- **Use private browsing.** Prevent people using your computer or mobile device from seeing the websites you viewed or searches you conducted by using *private browsing*. The browser discards passwords, temporary Internet files, data entered into forms, and other information when you exit the browser.

- **Use a proxy server.** To protect your online identity, use a *proxy server*, which is another computer that screens all your incoming and outgoing messages. The proxy server will prevent your browsing history, passwords, user names, and other personal information from being revealed.

✳ **Consider This:** Which pop-ups have you encountered while browsing? What new techniques will you use to browse the web safely?

Internet Research

Does the browser war have a winner?

Search for: browser wars

Mini Feature 2-1: Browsers

The decision of which browser to use is a topic of discussion among computer experts and novices alike. Read Mini Feature 2-1 to learn about features of specific browsers.

MINI FEATURE 2-1

Browsers

All browsers can retrieve and display webpages, but their features and ease of use vary. Many factors can affect the decision to choose the browser that best fits your needs.

Configuring Options

Users can customize some settings to improve their browsing experience, such as those listed below.

- **Favorites**, also called *bookmarks*, are links to preferred websites. When you add a website to the list of favorites, you can visit that website simply by tapping or clicking its name in a list instead of typing its web address. Favorites can be organized into folders, alphabetized, and sorted by date or how frequently you view the websites.

- Security features, such as filters and secure connections, help protect you from fraudulent and malicious websites that might attempt to steal your identity and personal information. These features also can block websites you do not want to be displayed and can instruct the browser to save passwords.

- Privacy features help prevent thieves from accessing information about your browsing history, such as websites you have visited, data about your browsing session, and content you have seen on specific webpages.

Obtaining Browsers

A browser often is included in the operating system of a computer or mobile device. For example, many computer manufacturers include Edge or Internet Explorer when they install Windows and include Safari when they install Mac OS. Use a search engine to locate the browser you want to install, and visit its website to download the most recent version. Most browsers are available for download at no cost. Keep your browser up to date to prevent security holes. You can set your browser to perform updates automatically.

Making a Decision

Selecting the best browser for you needs involves some careful thought. You may decide to install several and then use each one for specific needs. Perform some research to compare browsers and then consider the following factors:

- How old is your computer or mobile device? A newer browser may not work properly on older hardware.

- How much memory is in your computer or mobile device? Some browsers work best with a lot of memory.

- Which operating system are you using? Some browsers are available for specific operating systems.

- What do you want the browser to do? Some browsers are best suited for performing simple searches, while others excel when running websites containing media.

Specific Browsers

- **Chrome:** Google's Chrome was first released in 2008. This free browser is available for Windows and Mac OS and must be downloaded and installed. Chrome has independent tabbed browsing; if one tab develops a problem, the other tabs continue to function.

- **Firefox:** Developed by the Mozilla Corporation for Windows, Mac OS, and Linux, Firefox is known for its extensive array of plug-ins. This free browser was first released in 2004 and must be downloaded and installed. It has enhanced privacy and security features, a spelling checker, tabbed browsing, and a password manager.

- **Internet Explorer:** Internet Explorer is a free browser available primarily for Microsoft Windows and comes preinstalled. First released in 1995, it features protection against phishing and malware, and settings to delete information about searches performed and webpages visited.

- **Edge:** Edge is a Microsoft web browser included in the Windows 10 operating system. It is the default browser for Windows 10 on most devices, and is not compatible with prior versions of Windows. Features include integration with Cortana and OneDrive, along with annotation and reading tools.

- **Opera:** This second-oldest browser is free, fast, and small. Used on both computers and mobile devices, Opera must be downloaded and installed. It began as a research project in Norway in 1994 and introduced several features found on most of today's browsers.

- **Safari:** Preinstalled on Apple computers and devices, Safari has been the default browser for Mac OS since 2003 and is relatively new to Windows. The browser has built-in sharing with online social networks, fast performance, parental controls, and ease of use.

Mobile Browsers

Many browsers are included by default with some mobile devices and smartphones. Their features vary greatly. Some allow users to zoom and use keyboard shortcuts with most websites, while others display only websites optimized for mobile devices. The more popular mobile browsers are Chrome, Firefox, Internet Explorer, Edge, Safari, and Opera Mini.

 Consider This: Which browser or browsers have you used? Would you consider using another browser? Why or why not? When browsers were first invented, their only function was to browse the web.

Chrome

Firefox

Internet Explorer

Edge

Opera

Safari

Google Inc; Mozilla Foundation; Microsoft; Opera Software; Apple Inc

 Internet Research

What is the Silk browser?

Search for: silk browser

Web Addresses

A webpage has a unique address, called a **web address** or *URL* (Uniform Resource Locator). For example, the web address of http://www.nps.gov identifies the U.S. Department of the Interior National Park Service home page. A browser retrieves a webpage using its web address.

If you know the web address of a webpage, you can type it in the address bar of the browser. For example, if you type the address http://www.nps.gov/history/places.htm in the address bar and then press the ENTER key or tap or click the Search, Go, or similar button, the browser downloads and displays the associated webpage (Figure 2-8). The path, history/places.htm, in this web address identifies a webpage that is specified in a file named places.htm, which is located in a folder named history on the server that hosts the nps.gov website. When you enter this web address, after obtaining the IP address for the nps.gov domain name, the browser sends a request to the web server to retrieve the webpage named places.htm, and delivers it to your browser to be displayed.

 CONSIDER THIS

Although you entered the web address correctly, your screen does not match Figure 2-8. Why?
Organizations may update or redesign their websites, which may cause your screens to look different from those shown in this book.

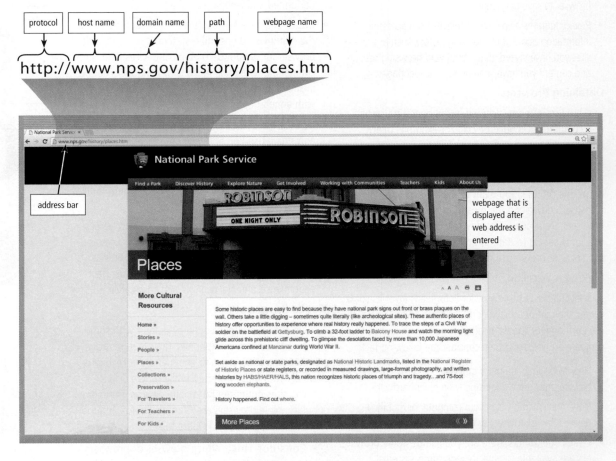

Figure 2-8   After entering http://www.nps.gov/history/places.htm in the address bar and then pressing the ENTER key or tapping or clicking the Search, Go, or similar button in a browser, the U.S. Department of the Interior National Park Service home page is displayed.
Source: National Park Service U.S. Department of the Interior

A web address consists of a protocol, domain name, and sometimes the host name, path to a specific webpage, or file name of the webpage. The *http*, which stands for Hypertext Transfer Protocol, is a set of rules that defines how webpages transfer on the Internet. Many web addresses begin with http // as the protocol. The text between the protocol and the domain name, called the host name, identifies the type of Internet server or the name of the web server. The www, for example, indicates a web server.

 CONSIDER THIS ————————————————————————

Do you need to type the protocol and host name in a web address?
Many browsers and websites do not require that you enter the http:// or the host name www in the web address. For example, you could enter nps.gov instead of http://www.nps.gov. As you begin typing a web address or if you enter an incorrect web address, browsers often display a list of similar addresses or related websites from which you can select. If, however, the host name is not www, you will need to type the host name as part of the web address. For example, the web address of schools.nyc.gov for the New York City schools website does not contain a www and thus requires entry of the entire web address.

When you enter a web address in a browser, you request, or pull, information from a web server. Another way users can pull content is by subscribing to a *web feed*, which contains content that has changed on a website. Mass media, blogs, and online social networks often provide web feeds, saving users the time spent checking the websites for updated content. Most browsers contain the capability to read web feeds.

Internet Research
How do I read web feeds?
Search for: rss reader

Web Apps and Mobile Apps

Recall from Module 1 that a *web app* is an application stored on a web server that you access through a browser. Users typically interact with web apps directly on a website, sometimes referred to as the host. Web app hosts usually provide storage for users' data and information on their servers, known as *cloud storage*.

Many web app hosts provide free access to their software. Others offer part of their web app free and charge for access to a more comprehensive program. Many include advertisements in the free version and charge for an advertisement-free version. Some allow you to use the web app free and pay a fee when a certain action occurs. For example, you can prepare your tax return for free, but if you elect to print it or file it electronically, you pay a minimal fee.

A *mobile app* is an application you download from a mobile device's app store or other location on the Internet to a smartphone or other mobile device. Mobile apps often take advantage of features of the device, such as touch screens, digital cameras, microphones, and embedded GPS receivers, to enable you to enter and capture data.

 CONSIDER THIS ————————————————————————

What are GPS receivers?
GPS (global positioning system) is a navigation system that consists of one or more earth-based receivers that accept and analyze signals sent by satellites in order to determine the receiver's geographic location. A **GPS receiver** is a handheld, mountable, or embedded device that contains an antenna, a radio receiver, and a processor. Most smartphones include embedded GPS receivers so that users can determine their location, obtain directions, and locate points of interest. Read Ethics & Issues 2-2 to consider issues related to apps that track your location.

GPS receivers determine their location on Earth by analyzing at least 3 separate satellite signals from 24 satellites in orbit.

Should Apps Be Allowed to Track Your Location?

When you install an app on your smartphone, you unintentionally may be allowing the app to send personal data. Apps can transmit your location, as well as the time you spend using the app. Apps also can collect personal information, including gender and birth year, if you access the app through an online social network profile. Although apps often present an option to review their security policies, some track user data without permission, or require you to enable tracking before you can use the app. You may see the results of tracking in the ads you see when browsing the web or using an app. Other

apps may track your location without your knowledge, such as apps that parents use to pinpoint a child's whereabouts.

If you search for driving directions, coupons, or restaurant tips based on your current location or past activities, you might be using apps that openly use this type of tracking. For example, a check-in app posts your location to online social networks, and another app enables you to locate friends by tracking their Bluetooth signals. Even when you opt to share data, use of these types of apps is not without risk. When people use location-tracking apps, for instance, they run the risk of someone stalking or robbing them. One positive use of location-tracking apps is with emergency

services. Lawmakers have struggled with whether law enforcement officials can use location-tracking without a user's knowledge. The U.S. Supreme Court recently ruled that police must get a warrant before searching a user's phone or reading text messages.

Consider This: Should app makers be able to require you to enable tracking or track your activity without your knowledge? Why or why not? Should the police be able to track GPS data without warrants? Why or why not? Would you use apps that post your location to your online social network profile or otherwise alert others of your whereabouts? Why or why not?

⚡ **Internet Research**

What are popular mobile apps?

Search for: top mobile apps

Web apps and mobile apps often work together (Figure 2-9). You might access your cloud storage website from a laptop or desktop. The cloud storage website hosts web apps to upload, download, browse, organize, and view files. The website also may provide a mobile app that you install on a smartphone so that you can access the same information or perform the same tasks from a mobile device. Because the data and information for each app is stored on cloud storage, all data is synchronized and accessible from anywhere you have an Internet connection, regardless of the computer or device used. The functionality of the app across computers and devices generally is the same, although the mobile app sometimes has fewer features. Some tasks may be easier to accomplish on one device or the other. For example, if a lot of typing is required, you may opt to use the web app on a laptop so that you can use a standard keyboard.

web app on Smart TV

web app on browser window

mobile app on tablet

mobile app on smartphone

Figure 2-9 Web and mobile apps often work together, enabling you to access your content from a variety of computers and devices.

Courtesy of Microsoft Corporation

Be sure you understand the material presented in the sections titled The Internet, Connecting to the Internet, and The World Wide Web, as it relates to the module objectives.
Now you should know...

- Why you interact with hosts and networks on the Internet (Objective 1)

- Which broadband Internet service and ISP is best suited to your needs (Objective 2)

- How a browser works with domain names and IP addresses when you enter a web address (Objectives 3 and 4)

- Which browser(s) you would use and why (Objective 4)

Types of Websites

The web contains several types of websites: search engines; online social networks; informational and research; media sharing; bookmarking; news, weather, sports, and other mass media; educational; business, governmental, and organizational; blogs; wikis and collaboration; health and fitness; science; entertainment; banking and finance; travel and tourism; mapping; retail and auctions; careers and employment; e-commerce; portals; content aggregation; and website creation and management. Many websites fall into more than one of these types. All of these websites can be accessed from computers or mobile devices but often are formatted differently and may have fewer features on mobile devices.

Search Engines

A web **search engine** is software that finds websites, webpages, images, videos, news, maps, and other information related to a specific topic. You also can use a search engine to solve mathematical equations, define words, and more.

Thousands of search engines are available. Some search engines, such as Bing, Google, and Yahoo!, are helpful in locating information on the web for which you do not know an exact web address or are not seeking a specific website. Those that work with GPS devices or services are location based, meaning they display results related to the device's current geographical position. For example, your smartphone may be able to display all gas stations within a certain distance of your current location. Some search engines restrict searches to a specific type of information, such as jobs or recipes.

Search engines typically allow you to search for one or more of the following items:

- Images: photos, diagrams, and drawings
- Videos: home videos, music videos, television programs, and movie clips
- Maps: maps of a business or address, or driving directions to a destination
- Audio: music, songs, recordings, and sounds
- Publications: news articles, journals, and books
- People or Businesses: addresses and phone numbers
- Blogs: specific opinions and ideas of others

Search engines require that you enter a word or phrase, called *search text*, to describe the item you want to find. Search text can be broad, such as spring break destinations, or more specific, such as walt disney world. If you misspell search text, search engines typically correct the misspelling or identify alternative search text. Some also provide suggested search text, links, and/or images as you type your search text.

Depending on your search text, search engines may respond with thousands to billions of search results, sometimes called *hits*. The content of the search results varies depending on the type of information you are seeking and your search text. Some search results contain links to webpages or articles; others are media, such as images or videos. Most search engines sequence the search results based on how close the words in the search text are to one another in the titles and descriptions of the results. Thus, the first few links probably contain more relevant information.

If you enter a phrase with spaces between the words in search text, most search engines display results that include all of the keywords. Because keywords describe content, search

Internet Research
What is a natural language search engine?
Search for: natural language search

Internet Research
What is a search engine spider?
Search for: search engine spider

results exclude articles, conjunctions, and other similar words (e.g., to, the, and). Table 2-4 lists some operators you can use in search text to refine searches. Instead of working with operators to refine search text, many search engines provide an advanced search feature or search tools that assist with limiting search results based on items such as date, TLD, language, etc.

Table 2-4 Search Engine Operators

Operator	Description	Examples	Explanation
Space or +	Display search results that include specific words.	art + music art music	Results have both words, art and music, in any order,
OR	Display search results that include only one word from a list.	dog OR puppy	Results have either the word, dog, or the word, puppy.
		dog OR puppy OR canine	Results have the word, dog, or the word, puppy, or the word, canine.
( )	Combine search results that include specific words with those that include only one word from a list.	Kalamazoo Michigan (pizza OR subs)	Results include both words, Kalamazoo Michigan, and either the word, pizza, or the word, subs.
–	Exclude a word from search results.	automobile-convertible	Results include the word, automobile, but do not include the word, convertible.
" "	Search for an exact phrase in a certain order.	"19th century literature"	Results include the exact phrase, 19th century literature.
*	Substitute characters in place of the asterisk.	writer*	Results include any word that begins with the text, writer (e.g., writer, writers, writer's)

© Cengage Learning

 CONSIDER THIS

How can you improve search results?
You may find that many items listed in the search results have little or no bearing on the item you are seeking. You can eliminate superfluous items in search results by carefully crafting search text and use search operators to limit search results. Other techniques you can use to improve your searches include the following:
- Use specific nouns.
- Put the most important terms first in the search text.
- List all possible spellings, for example, email, e-mail.
- Before using a search engine, read its Help information.
- If the search is unsuccessful with one search engine, try another.

Subject Directories   A *subject directory* classifies webpages in an organized set of categories, such as sports or shopping, and related subcategories. A subject directory provides categorized lists of links arranged by subject. Using a subject directory, you locate a particular topic by tapping or clicking links through different levels, moving from the general to the specific. A disadvantage with a subject directory is that users sometimes have difficulty deciding which categories to choose as they work through the menus of links presented.

Mini-Feature 2-2: Online Social Networks

Recall from Module 1 that an **online social network**, or *social networking site*, is a website that encourages members in its online community to share their interests, ideas, stories, photos, music, and videos with other registered users. Some online social networks also enable users to communicate through text, voice, and video chat, and play games together online. You interact with an online social network through a browser or mobile app on your computer or mobile device. Read Mini Feature 2-2 for features and uses of popular online social networks.

⊕ **MINI FEATURE 2-2**

Online Social Networks

People you know through personal and professional circles form your social network. You share common interests, work or spend leisure time together, and know many of one another's friends. Online social networks allow you to manage your social networks online.

Your account on an online social network includes profile information, such as your name, location, photos, and personal and professional interests. You might create accounts on several online social networks to separate your personal and professional activities. Online social networks allow you to view the profiles of other users and designate them as your *friends* or contacts. Some sites, such as Facebook and LinkedIn, require friends to confirm a friendship, while others, such as Twitter and Google+, allow users to follow one another without confirmation.

You can expand your online social network by viewing your friends' friends and then, in turn, designating some of them as your friends. Friends of your friends and their friends form your *extended contacts*.

- Extended contacts on a personal online social network such as Facebook can introduce you to others at your college or from your hometown, connect you with long-distance friends or relatives, or enable you to stay in touch with those who have interests similar to yours.

© iStockphoto / temizyurek

- Extended contacts on a professional online social network such as LinkedIn can introduce you to people who work at companies where you might be seeking employment. You can share employment history and skills in your profile, enabling potential employers who look at your profile to learn about your specific skills.

Read Secure IT 2-3 for tips about securing your privacy when using online social networks.

Personal Uses

Personal uses of online social networks include sharing photos and videos, greetings, or status updates. A *status update* informs friends about what you are doing. You can *like*, or show appreciation for, online content such as photos or videos

© iStockphoto / Lentz Photography

on online social networks such as Facebook and Google+. When you do, people who see the same content will know that you liked it, and the person who posted it is notified. All of your updates, likes, posts, and events appear in the activity stream associated with your account. Activity updates from friends may appear on a separate page associated with your account, often called a *news feed*.

On many online social networks, updates can include hashtags to identify their topics. A *hashtag* is a word(s) preceded by a # symbol that describes or categorizes a post. Users can search for posts on a topic by searching for a hashtag. Some online social networks list trending topics based on popular hashtags. Many television broadcasts, advertisements, and businesses post hashtags to encourage viewers and customers to share comments on Twitter or Facebook.

When accessing an online social network with a GPS-enabled mobile device, the location where you check in may be revealed as part of a status update. An online social network's mobile app can share your location with friends, find others nearby, and alert you to promotional deals from local businesses.

Business Uses

Businesses use online social networks to connect with their customers, provide promotional offers, and offer targeted advertising. For example, users who recommend online content about travel services may see travel-related advertising on their online social network's webpage.

Businesses also use data from online social networks to better connect with and understand customers. They can review comments from customers about their experiences using companies' products or services. Monitoring these feeds continuously gives companies immediate feedback from customers.

Nonprofit organizations use online social networks to promote activities and causes, accept donations, and allow volunteers to contact one another online.

⊛ **Consider This:** How can businesses and individuals use online social networks to bring people together in support of a common goal? What benefits and risks are involved when using online social networks?

Follow button

© iStockphoto / hocus-focus

SECURE IT 2-3

Privacy and Security Risks with Online Social Networks

Online social networks can be excellent places to share messages, photos, and videos. They can, however, be risky places to divulge personal information. Follow these tips to help protect against thieves who are following the network traffic and attempting to invade private facets of your life.

- **Register with caution.** During the registration process, provide only necessary information. Do not disclose your birthdate, age, place of birth, or the city where you currently are living. If an email address is required, consider using a new address so that the online social network cannot access your email address book. Online social networks occasionally ask users to enter their email address and password to determine if their friends also are members of the network. In turn, the network obtains access to contacts in your address book and can send spam (unsolicited email messages) to your friends.

- **Manage your profile.** Check for privacy settings, usually found on the Settings or Options tabs, to set permissions so that you

can control who can review your profile and photos, determine how people can search for you and make comments, and if desired, block certain people from viewing your page. Be aware that online social networks may change privacy settings. Periodically check your settings to ensure you have the most up-to-date settings.

- **Choose friends carefully.** You may receive a friend request that appears to be from someone you know. In reality, this message may originate from an identity thief who created a fake profile in an attempt to obtain your personal information. Confirm with the sender that the request is legitimate.

- **Limit friends.** While many online social networks encourage the practice, do not try to gather too many friends in your social network. Some experts believe that a functional online social network should not exceed 150 people. Occasionally review what your friends are posting about you.

- **Divulge only relevant information.** Write details about yourself that are relevant to the reasons you are participating in an online social network. When posting

information, be aware that the message may be accessible publicly and associated with your identity permanently. Do not post anything you would not want to be made public.

- **Be leery of urgent requests for help.** Avoid responding to emergency pleas for financial assistance from alleged family members. In addition, do not reply to messages concerning lotteries you did not enter and fabulous deals that sound too good to be true.

- **Read the privacy policy.** Evaluate the website's privacy policy, which describes how it uses your personal information. For example, if you watch a video while signed in to your account, an external website or app may have access to this information and post this activity as an entry in both your activity stream and your friends' news feeds.

⊛ **Consider This:** Should online social networks do a better job of telling their users what information is safe or unsafe to share? What role should parents play in overseeing their child's involvement in online social networks?

Informational and Research

An informational and research website contains factual information. Examples include libraries, encyclopedias, dictionaries, directories, guides (Figure 2-10), and other types of reference. You can find guides on numerous topics, such as health and medicine, research paper documentation styles, and grammar rules. Many of the other types of websites identified in this section also are used to research information.

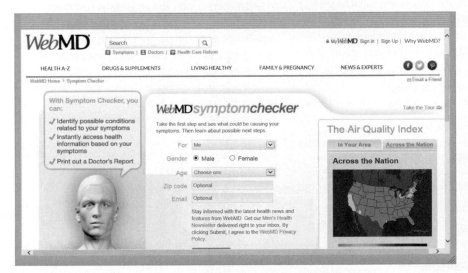

Figure 2-10   You can research health conditions from your symptoms on a medical website, such as WebMD.
Source: WebMD, LLC

Media Sharing

A *media sharing site* is a website that enables members to manage and share media such as photos, videos, and music. These websites are sometimes called photo sharing sites, video sharing sites (Figure 2-11), and music sharing sites, respectively. Media sharing sites, which may be free or charge a fee, provide a quick and efficient way to upload, organize, store, share, and download media.

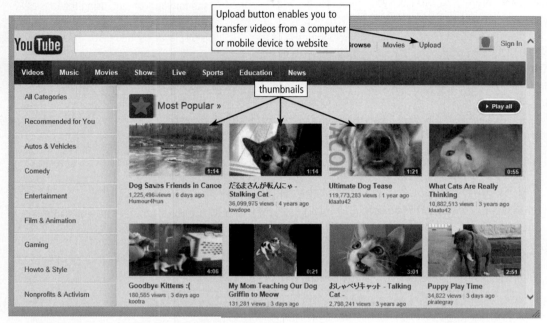

Figure 2-11 YouTube is an example of a video sharing site. You tap or click the thumbnail to view the video.
Source: YouTube, Inc.

✺ CONSIDER THIS

Why would you use a media sharing site instead of an online social network?
Although the lines between media sharing sites and online social networks are becoming blurred, some users chose a traditional media sharing site if they simply want to post photos, videos, or music to share with others and do not require the full functionality of an online social network. Before you allow someone to take your photo or record video of you, however, remember that the photo or video may be posted on a media sharing site. These photos or videos may be accessible publicly and associated with your identity for a long time. Also, once posted, you may be giving up certain rights to the media. Further, do not post photos or videos that are protected by copyright.

Bookmarking

A *bookmarking site* is a website that enables members to organize, tag, and share links to media and other online content (Figure 2-12). A **tag** is a short descriptive label that you assign to webpages, photos, videos blog posts, email messages, and other digital content so that it is easier locate at a later time. Many websites and web apps support tagging, which enables users to organize their online content. Read How To 2-2 to learn how to tag digital content.

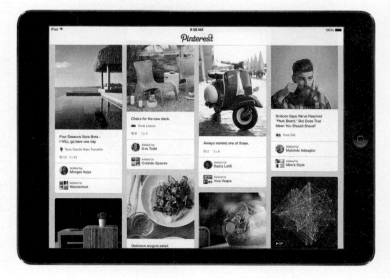

Figure 2-12 Pinterest is an example of a bookmarking site.

⚙ **HOW TO 2-2**

Tag Digital Content

When you post digital content online, it is a good idea to tag the content so that it is easy for you and others to locate and organize. After you have uploaded digital content to a media sharing site, follow the instructions on the website to apply tags to the digital content you uploaded. Consider the following suggestions when tagging digital content:

- Apply tags to all digital media, such as photos, music, and videos.

- If you are using multiple tags to identify one file, separate each tag with a separator. The website to which you are posting will inform you how to separate multiple tags (such as a space, comma, or semicolon).

- Choose tags that are descriptive of the content you are posting. For example, if you are posting a photo from a recent family vacation to Hammonasset Beach State Park, you might choose

"Hammonasset" and "vacation" as two of your tags for this photo.

- After you have tagged the digital content, perform a search on the media sharing site for your content, using the tags as your search criteria, to verify your content is displayed as intended.

✳ **Consider This:** Why else is it important to tag digital content? What tags might you assign to your favorite song in your music library?

✳ **CONSIDER THIS**

What are the various kinds of social media?

Social media consists of content that users create and share online, such as photos, videos, music, links, blog posts, Tweets, wiki entries, podcasts, and status updates. Social media websites facilitate the creation or publishing of social media online and include media sharing sites (for photo, video, and audio files), bookmarking sites, blogs and microblogs, wikis, podcasts, online social networks, and online gaming sites.

News, Weather, Sports, and Other Mass Media

News, weather, sports, and other mass media websites contain newsworthy material, including stories and articles relating to current events, life, money, politics, weather (Figure 2-13), and sports. You often can customize these websites so that you can receive local news or news about specific topics. Some provide a means to send you alerts, such as weather updates or sporting event scores, via text or email messages.

News on the web is not replacing the newspaper but enhancing it and reaching different populations. Although some exist solely online, many magazines and newspapers sponsor websites that provide summaries of printed articles, as well as articles not included in the printed versions. Newspapers, magazines, and television and radio stations often have corresponding news, weather, or sports websites and mobile apps. Read Ethics & Issues 2-3 to consider the issues related to using fake names on websites.

Figure 2-13 Forecasts, radar, and other weather conditions are available on the WEATHER webpage on USA TODAY's website.

Source: Gannett

Is It Ethical to Use a Fake Name or ID on a Website?

You are signing up for an account on an online social network, an online dating website, or a news website that enables you to post comments. Should you use your real name?

Many argue that it is harmless to protect your anonymity by using a fake name but believe that it is not right to create a fake profile to mislead others or leave malicious comments on a website. The latter has become so prevalent that terms have emerged to describe this behavior. For example, *catfishing* is when someone creates a fake online social network or online dating profile and forms relationships with unsuspecting users. A *troll* is a user who posts negative, inflammatory comments on a blog post or article with the intent of inciting other users.

One website creates very thorough, but completely fake, personas, which include email addresses, Social Security numbers, phone numbers, and more. Although law enforcement has raised concerns over the potential misuses of fake profiles, it technically is legal, even though the names and personas are not real. Legitimate uses for fake name generators include testers of large databases, such as ones for hospitals.

Facebook currently requires members to use their real names. Twitter's policy is that anyone can create a fake account, but it has a verification process to identify the official account of a celebrity or public figure. Most fake Twitter accounts are harmless, and often are flattering. Although some argue that creating a fake account constitutes identity theft, unless the intent is to harm or embarrass the real person, it is not unethical or illegal. When a journalist created a fake account for a politician and posted discriminatory quotes and Tweets in the politician's name, many considered it an ethics violation, because journalists are supposed to report the truth.

Consider This: Is it ever acceptable to use a fake name online? Why or why not? Is it unethical to create fake personas for others to use? Why or why not? Should websites require you to use a real name, or have a verification process? Why or why not?

Educational

An educational website offers exciting, challenging avenues for formal and informal teaching and learning. The web contains thousands of tutorials from learning how to fly airplanes to learning how to cook a meal. For a more structured learning experience, companies provide online training to employees, and colleges offer online classes and degrees. Instructors often use the web to enhance classroom teaching by publishing course materials, grades, and other pertinent class information.

Business, Governmental, and Organizational

A business website contains content that increases brand awareness, provides company background or other information, and/or promotes or sells products or services. Nearly every enterprise has a business website. Examples include Allstate Insurance Company, Apple Inc., General Motors Corporation, Kraft Foods Inc., and Walt Disney Company.

Most United States government agencies have websites providing citizens with information, such as census data, or assistance, such as filing taxes (Figure 2-14). Many other types of organizations use the web for a variety of reasons. For example, nonprofit organizations raise funds for a cause and advocacy groups present their views or opinions.

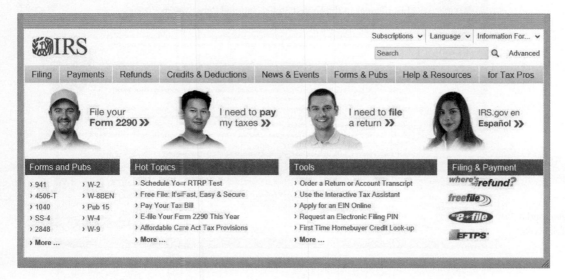

Figure 2-14
Government agencies, such as the IRS webpage shown here, have websites providing assistance and information to citizens.
Source: IRS

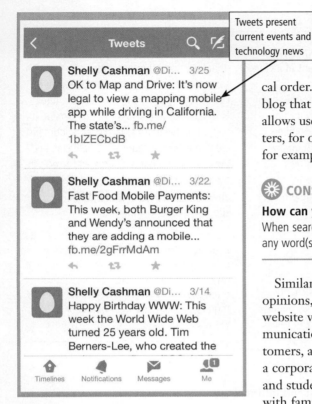

Tweets present current events and technology news

Figure 2-15 When you 'follow' @DiscoveringComp on Twitter, you will see Tweets such as those shown here posted by the Discovering Computers user "Shelly Cashman", in your account's timeline, along with Tweets from others whom you are following. As a student in this class, you should 'follow' @DiscoveringComp so that you easily can keep current with relevant technology changes and events in the computing industry.
Source: Twitter

Blogs

As described in Module 1, a **blog** (short for weblog) is an informal website consisting of time-stamped articles, or posts, in a diary or journal format, usually listed in reverse chronological order. The term *blogosphere* refers to the worldwide collection of blogs. A blog that contains video sometimes is called a video blog, or vlog. A *microblog* allows users to publish short messages usually between 100 and 200 characters, for others to read. The collection of a user's Tweets, or posts on Twitter, for example, forms a microblog (Figure 2-15).

✷ CONSIDER THIS

How can you locate Tweets about certain topics?
When searching Twitter, you can use hashtags to find related posts. Similarly, you can tag any word(s) in your Tweets by typing it as a hashtag, such as #election.

Similar to an editorial section in a newspaper, blogs reflect the interests, opinions, and personalities of the author, called the **blogger**, and sometimes website visitors. Blogs have become an important means of worldwide communications. Businesses create blogs to communicate with employees, customers, and vendors. They may post announcements of new information on a corporate blog. Teachers create blogs to collaborate with other teachers and students. Home users create blogs to share aspects of their personal lives with family, friends, and others.

Wikis and Collaboration

Whereas blogs are a tool for publishing and sharing messages, wikis enable users to organize, edit, and share information. A **wiki** is a type of collaborative website that allows users to create, add, modify, or delete the website content via a browser. Wikis can include articles, documents, photos, or videos. Some wikis are public, accessible to everyone (Figure 2-16). Others are private so that content is accessible only to certain individuals or groups.

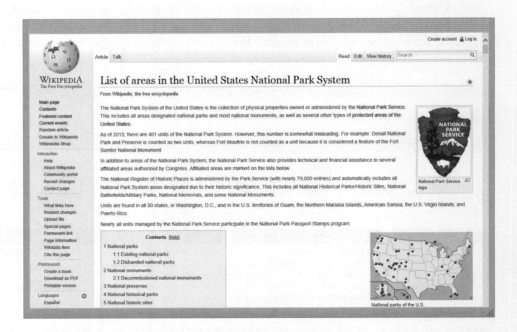

Figure 2-16 Wikipedia is a popular public wiki.
Source: Wikimedia Foundation

Many companies, for example, set up wikis as an intranet for employees to collaborate on projects or access information, procedures, and documents. (An *intranet* is an internal network that uses Internet technologies.)

Contributors to a wiki typically must register before they can edit content or add comments. Wikis usually hold edits on a webpage until an editor or website manager can review them for accuracy. Unregistered users typically can review the content but cannot edit it or add comments.

Other types of collaboration sites enable users to share and edit any type of project — including documents, photos, videos, designs, prototypes, schedules, and more, often at the same time. On these websites, comments or edits are seen by other connected users. Most of these websites also enable users to communicate via chat windows, and some provide a whiteboard.

⚡ Internet Research

Have errors been found in Wikipedia?

Search for: wikipedia factual errors

Health and Fitness

Many websites provide up-to-date medical, fitness, nutrition, or exercise information for public access. Some offer users the capability of listening to health-related seminars and discussions. Consumers, however, should verify the online information they read with a personal physician. Health service organizations store your personal health history, including prescriptions, lab test results, doctor visits, allergies, and immunizations. Doctors use the web to assist with researching and diagnosing health conditions.

Science

Several websites contain information about space exploration, astronomy, physics, earth sciences, microgravity, robotics, and other branches of science. Scientists use online social networks to collaborate on the web. Nonprofit science organizations use the web to seek public donations to support research.

Entertainment

An entertainment website offers music, videos, shows, performances, events, sports, games, and more in an interactive and engaging environment. Many entertainment websites support streaming media. **Streaming** is the process of transferring data in a continuous and even flow, which allows users to access and use a file while it is transmitting. You can listen to streaming audio or watch streaming video, such as a live performance or broadcast, as it downloads to your computer, mobile device, or an Internet-connected television.

Sophisticated entertainment websites often partner with other technologies. For example, you can cast your vote on a television show via your phone or online social network account.

Banking and Finance

Online banking and online trading enable users to access their financial records from anywhere in the world, as long as they have an Internet connection. Using online banking, users can access accounts, pay bills, transfer funds, calculate mortgage payments, and manage other financial activities from their computer or mobile device (Figure 2-17). With online trading, users can invest in stocks, options, bonds, treasuries, certificates of deposit,

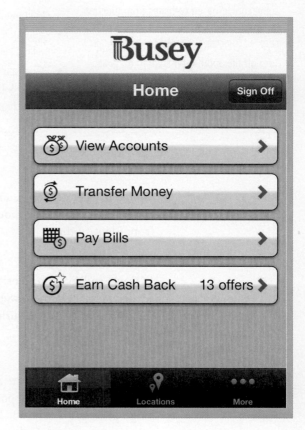

Figure 2-17   Many banks, such as Busey shown here, provide mobile versions of their online banking website so that users can manage financial accounts from their smartphones.

Source: First Busey Corporation

SECURE IT 2-4

Protecting Yourself from Identity Theft

The fastest growing crime in the United States is identity theft. More than nine million people fall victim each year, with the unauthorized use of an existing credit card accounting for much of the problem. The National Crime Victimization Survey reports that household identity theft losses amount to more than $13 billion each year, and that figure does not account for the aggravation and time required to repair the accounts. Practice these techniques to thwart attempts to steal your personal data:

- Do not tap or click links in or reply to spam for any reason.

- Install a personal firewall (software that protects network resources from outside intrusions).

- Clear or disable web cookies (small text files that web servers store on a computer) in your browser. This action might prevent some cookie-based websites from functioning, but you will be able to decide which cookies to accept or reject.

- Turn off file and printer sharing on your Internet connection.

- Set up a free email account. Use this email address for merchant forms.

- Sign up for email filtering through your ISP or use an anti-spam program.

- Shred financial documents before you discard them.

- Provide only the required information on website forms.

- Avoid checking your email or performing banking activities on public computers. These computers are notorious for running *keyloggers*, which record keystrokes in a hidden file, and other tracking software. If you must use a public computer for critical activities, be certain to sign out of any password-protected website and to clear the browser's cache.

- Request a free copy of your medical records each year from the Medical Information Bureau.

- Obtain your credit report once a year from each of the three major credit reporting agencies and correct any errors. Enroll in a credit monitoring service.

- Request, in writing, to be removed from mailing lists.

- Place your phone number on the National Do Not Call Registry.

- Avoid shopping club and buyer cards.

- Do not write your phone number on charge or credit receipts. Ask merchants not to write this number or any other personal information, especially your Social Security number and driver's license number, on the back of your personal checks.

- Do not preprint your phone number or Social Security number on personal checks.

- Fill in only the required information on rebate, warranty, and registration forms.

- Learn how to block your phone number from displaying on the receiver's system.

If your identity has been stolen, immediately change any passwords that may have been compromised. If you have disclosed your debit or credit card numbers, contact your financial institutions. You also should visit the Federal Trade Commission website or call the FTC help line.

Consider This: Do you know anyone who has been a victim of identity theft? What steps will you take to protect your identity using some of these guidelines?

---

money market accounts, annuities, mutual funds, and so on, without using a broker. Read Secure IT 2-4 for tips about protecting your bank accounts and other personal information from identity theft.

Travel and Tourism

Travel and tourism websites enable users to research travel options and make travel arrangements. On these websites, you typically can read travel reviews, search for and compare flights and prices, order airline tickets, book a room, or reserve a rental car.

Mapping

Several mapping website and web apps exist that enable you to display up-to-date maps by searching for an address, postal code, phone number, or point of interest (such as an airport, lodging, or historical site). The maps can be displayed in a variety of views, including terrain, aerial, maps, streets, buildings, traffic, and weather. These websites also provide directions when a user enters a starting and destination point (Figure 2-18). Many work with GPS to determine where a user is located, eliminating the need for a user to enter the starting point and enabling the website to recommend nearby points of interest.

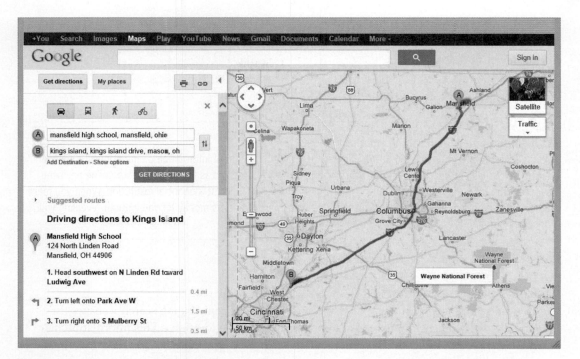

Figure 2-18 Using mapping web apps, such as Google Maps shown here, you can obtain driving directions from one destination to another.
Source: Google Inc.

Retail and Auctions

You can purchase just about any product or service on the web, a process that sometimes is called *e-retail* (short for electronic retail). To purchase online, the customer visits the business's *electronic storefront*, which contains product descriptions, images, and a shopping cart (Figure 2-19). The *shopping cart* allows the customer to collect purchases. When ready to complete the sale, the customer enters personal data and the method of payment, which should be through a secure Internet connection.

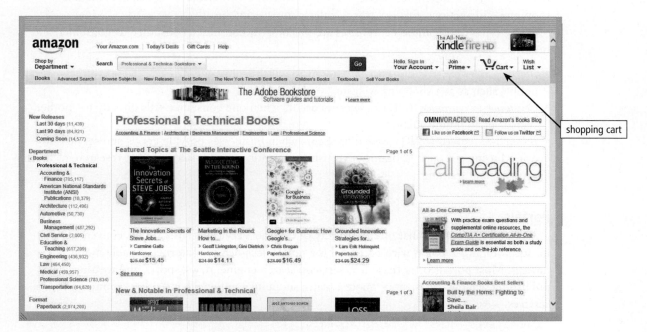

Figure 2-19 Shown here is Amazon's storefront for Professional and Technical Books.
Source: Amazon.com, Inc.

With an **online auction**, users bid on an item being sold by someone else. The highest bidder at the end of the bidding period purchases the item. eBay is one of the more popular online auction websites.

 CONSIDER THIS

Is it safe to enter financial information online?
As an alternative to entering credit card, bank account, or other financial information online, some shopping and auction websites allow consumers to use an online payment service such as PayPal. To use an online payment service, you create an account that is linked to your credit card or funds at a financial institution. When you make a purchase, you use your online payment service account, which transfers money for you without revealing your financial information.

Careers and Employment

You can search the web for career information and job openings. Job search websites list thousands of openings in hundreds of fields, companies, and locations. This information may include required training and education, salary data, working conditions, job descriptions, and more. In addition, many organizations advertise careers on their websites.

When a company contacts you for an interview, learn as much about the company and the industry as possible before the interview. Many have websites with detailed company profiles.

E-Commerce

E-commerce, short for electronic commerce, is a business transaction that occurs over an electronic network, such as the Internet. Anyone with access to a computer or mobile device, an Internet connection, and a means to pay for purchased goods or services can participate in e-commerce. Some people use the term *m-commerce* (mobile commerce) to identify e-commerce that takes place using mobile devices. Popular uses of e-commerce by consumers include shopping and auctions, finance, travel, entertainment, and health.

Three types of e-commerce websites are business-to-consumer, consumer-to-consumer, and business-to-business.

- *Business-to-consumer (B2C) e-commerce* consists of the sale of goods and services to the general public, such as at a shopping website.
- *Consumer-to-consumer (C2C) e-commerce* occurs when one consumer sells directly to another, such as in an online auction.
- *Business-to-business (B2B) e-commerce* occurs when businesses provide goods and services to other businesses, such as online advertising, recruiting, credit, sales, market research, technical support, and training.

Portals

A **portal** is a website that offers a variety of Internet services from a single, convenient location (Figure 2-20). A wireless portal is a portal designed for Internet-capable mobile devices. Most portals offer these free services: search engine; news, sports, and weather; web publishing; yellow pages; stock quotes; maps; shopping; and email and other communications services.

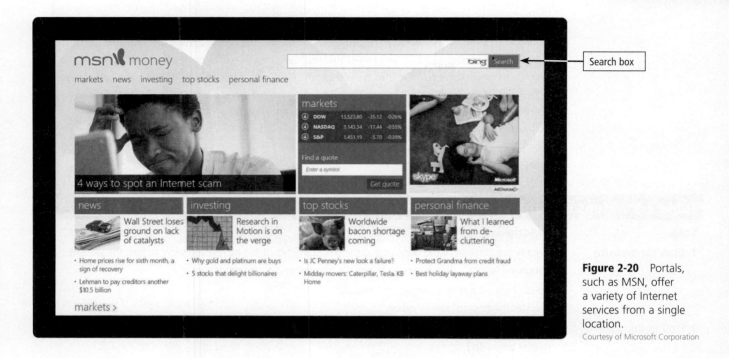

Search box

Figure 2-20   Portals, such as MSN, offer a variety of Internet services from a single location.
Courtesy of Microsoft Corporation

Content Aggregation

A **content aggregation** website or web app, sometimes called a *curation website*, allows users to collect and compile content from a variety of websites about a particular topic or theme (Figure 2-21). Types of content that may be compiled includes news, reviews, images, videos, podcasts (discussed later in this module), and blogs. Content aggregation websites save users time because they need to visit only one website (the content aggregation website) instead of visiting multiple websites to obtain information.

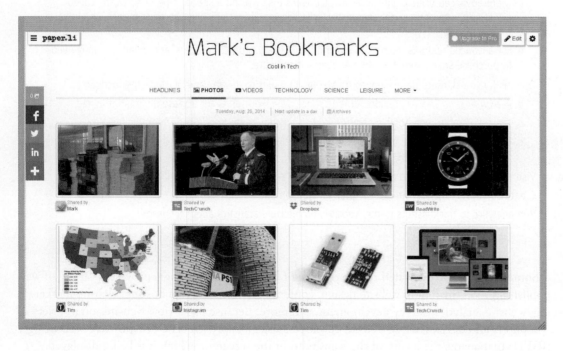

Figure 2-21   A content aggregation web app that compiles news from a variety of online sources.
Source: SmallRivers

Website Creation and Management

By creating their own websites, businesses and individuals can convey information to billions of people. The content of the webpages ranges from news stories to product information to blogs to surveys. Web creation and management sites provide tools that support the steps in **web publishing**, which is the creation and maintenance of websites. To create a website, you do not have to be a computer programmer. For the small business or home user, web publishing is fairly easy as long as you have the proper tools. Table 2-5 outlines the five main steps in web publishing.

Table 2-5   Steps in Web Publishing

Step	Description
1. Plan the website.	Identify the purpose of the website and the characteristics of the people you want to visit the website. Determine ways to differentiate your website from other similar ones. Decide how visitors will navigate the website. Register the desired domain name.
2. Design the website.	Design the appearance and layout of elements on the website. Decide colors and formats. Determine content for links, text, graphics, animation, audio, video, virtual reality, and blogs. You may need specific hardware, such as a digital camera, webcam, video camera, scanner, and/or audio recorder. You also may need software that enables you to create images or edit photos, audio, and video.
3. Create the website.	To create a website, you have several options: a. Use the features of a word processing program that enable you to create basic webpages from documents containing text and graphics. b. Use a *content management system*, which is a tool that assists users with creating, editing, and hosting content on a website. c. Use website authoring software to create more sophisticated websites that include text, graphics, animation, audio, video, special effects, and links. d. More advanced users create sophisticated websites by using a special type of software, called a text editor, to enter codes that instruct the browser how to display the text, images, and links on a webpage. e. For advanced features, such as managing users, passwords, chat rooms, and email, you may need to purchase specialized website management software.
4. Host the website.	Options for transferring the webpages from your computer to a web server include the following: a. A *web hosting service* provides storage space on a web server for a reasonable monthly fee. b. Many ISPs offer web hosting services to their customers for free or for a monthly fee. c. Online content management systems usually include hosting services for free or for a fee, depending on features and amount of storage used.
5. Maintain the website.	Visit the website regularly to ensure its contents are current and all links work properly. Create surveys on the website to test user satisfaction and solicit feedback. Run analytics to track visitors to the website and measure statistics about its usage.

Some websites are dedicated to one portion of web publishing; others provide a variety of web publishing tools, including website design, content management, web hosting, website marketing, website analytics, survey development, and more. Because users view websites on a variety of computers and devices, many website developers use an approach called **responsive web design** (RWD) that adapts the layout of the website to fit the screen on which it is being displayed.

✸ CONSIDER THIS ─────────────────────────────

Can you assume that content on a website is correct and accurate?

No. Any person, company, or organization can publish a webpage on the Internet. No one oversees the content of these webpages.

Use the criteria below to evaluate a website or webpage before relying on its content.

- Affiliation: A reputable institution should support the website without bias in the information.
- Audience: The website should be written at an appropriate level.
- Authority: The website should list the author and the appropriate credentials.
- Content: The website should be well organized and the links should work.
- Currency: The information on the webpage should be current.
- Design: The pages at the website should download quickly, be visually pleasing, and be easy to navigate.
- Objectivity: The website should contain little advertising and be free of bias.

🗸 NOW YOU SHOULD KNOW ─────────────────────────────

Be sure you understand the material presented in the section titled Types of Websites as it relates to the module objectives. *Now you should know ...*

- How to enter search text and improve your search results (Objective 5)
- How you can benefit from online social networks (Objective 6)
- When you would use specific types of websites (Objective 7)
- How you can publish your own website (Objective 7)

Digital Media on the Web

Most webpages include *multimedia*, which refers to any application that combines text with media. Media includes graphics, animation, audio, video, and/or virtual reality. The sections that follow discuss how the web uses these types of media.

Graphics

A **graphic** is a visual representation of nontext information, such as a drawing, chart, or photo. Many webpages use colorful graphics to convey messages (Figure 2-22). As shown in the figure, some websites use thumbnails on their pages because larger graphics can be time-consuming to display. A *thumbnail* is a small version of a larger image. You usually can tap or click a thumbnail to display the image in full size.

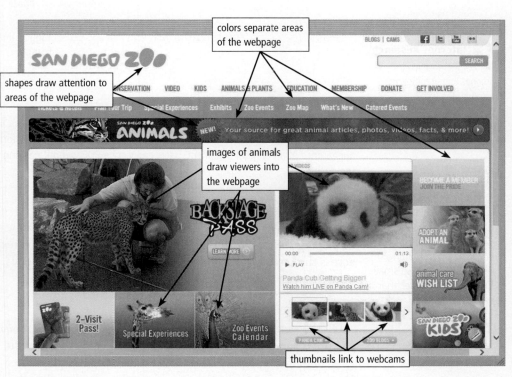

Figure 2-22 Many webpages use colorful graphics to convey messages. For example, the variety of colors, images, shapes, and thumbnails on the San Diego Zoo webpage visually separate and draw attention to areas of the webpage, making the webpage more dynamic and enticing.
Source: Zoological Society of San Diego

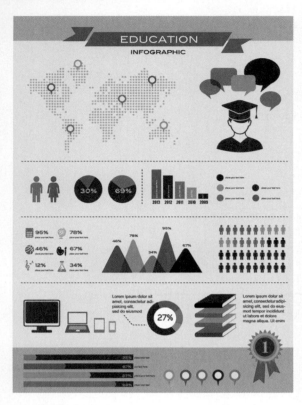

Figure 2-23 An infographic presents complex concepts at a glance.
© Marish / Shutterstock

The web often uses infographics to present concepts, products, and news. An *infographic* (short for information graphic) is a visual representation of data or information, designed to communicate quickly, simplify complex concepts, or present patterns or trends (Figure 2-23). Many forms of infographics exist: maps, signs, charts, and diagrams.

Of the graphics formats for displaying images on the web (Table 2-6), the JPEG and PNG formats are more common. *JPEG* (pronounced JAY-peg) is a compressed graphics format that attempts to reach a balance between image quality and file size. With JPG files, the more compressed the file, the smaller the image and the lower the quality. *PNG* (pronounced ping) is a patent-free compressed graphics format that restores all image details when the file is viewed. That is, the PNG format does not lose image quality during compression.

Table 2-6	Graphics Formats Used on the Web	
Abbreviation	**Name**	**Uses**
BMP	Bitmap	Desktop backgrounds Scanned images
GIF	Graphics Interchange Format	Images with few colors Simple diagrams Shapes
JPEG	Joint Photographic Experts Group	Digital camera photos Game screenshots Movie still shots
PNG	Portable Network Graphics	Comic-style drawings Line art Web graphics
TIFF	Tagged Image File Format	Photos used in printing industry

© Cengage Learning

 Internet Research
What other formats for images and graphics are used on the web?

Search for: web image formats

 CONSIDER THIS

What is a PDF file?
PDF, which stands for Portable Document Format, is an electronic image format by Adobe Systems that mirrors the appearance of an original document. Users can view a PDF without needing the software that originally created the document.

 BTW

Compressed Files
Compressed files take up less storage space. Smaller file sizes result in faster downloading of webpages because small files transmit faster than large files.

Animation Many webpages use *animation*, which is the appearance of motion created by displaying a series of still images in sequence. For example, text that animates by scrolling across the screen can serve as a ticker to display stock updates, news, sports scores, weather, or other information. Web-based games often use animation.

Audio

 Internet Research
How do you subscribe to an iTunes podcast?

Search for: subscribe itunes podcast

On the web, you can listen to audio clips and live audio. *Audio* includes music, speech, or any other sound. Simple applications consist of individual audio files available for download to a computer or device. Once downloaded, you can play (listen to) the content of these files. Read How To 2-3 for instructions about downloading digital media from online services. Other applications use streaming audio so that you can listen to the audio while it downloads.

✷ HOW TO 2-3

Download Digital Media from Online Services

Online services make various forms of digital media available, such as books, music, movies, and apps. You typically can use a program, such as iTunes, or an app, such as the Google Play Store, to access digital media. Digital media also may be available from these services' websites. The following steps describe how to download digital media from online services when you know the name or keyword(s) for the digital media you want to find.

1. On a computer or mobile device, run the program or app from which the digital media is available. If a program or app is not accessible easily, navigate to the online service using a browser.

2. Enter the name or keyword(s) in the Search box.

3. Tap or click the Search button to perform the search.

4. Navigate through the search results and then tap or click the search result for the item you want to download.

5. Locate and then tap or click the Download button or link to download the digital media to your computer or mobile device.

The following steps describe how to browse for and download digital media.

1. On your computer or mobile device, run the program or app from which the digital media is available. If a program or app is not accessible easily, navigate to the online service using a browser.

2. Tap or click the category corresponding to the type of digital media you want to browse. Common categories include music, movies, books, and apps.

3. Browse the items in the category.

4. When you find an item you want to download, tap or click the item to display additional information.

5. Look for and then tap or click the Download button or link to download the digital media to your computer or mobile device.

✷ **Consider This:** In addition to the online services listed in this box, what are three additional resources from which you can download digital media?

Audio files are compressed to reduce their file sizes. For example, the *MP3* format reduces an audio file to about one-tenth its original size, while preserving much of the original quality of the sound.

To listen to an audio file on your computer, you need special software called a *media player*. Most current operating systems contain a media player; for example, the Windows operating system includes Windows Media Player (Figure 2-24). Some audio files, however, might require you to download a media player. Media players available for download include iTunes and RealPlayer. You can download media players free from the web.

Video

On the web, you can view video clips or watch live video. *Video* consists of images displayed in motion. Most video also has accompanying audio. You also can upload, share, or view video clips at a video sharing site. Educators, politicians, and businesses use video blogs and video podcasts to engage students, voters, and consumers.

Simple video applications on the web consist of individual video files, such as movie or television clips, that you must download completely before you can play them on a computer or mobile device. Video files often are compressed because they are quite large in size. Videos posted to the web often are short in length, usually less than 10 minutes, because they can take a long time to download. As with streaming audio files, streaming video files allows you to view longer or live videos by playing them as they download to your computer.

Virtual Reality Virtual reality (VR) is the use of computers to simulate a real or imagined environment that appears as a three-dimensional (3-D) space. VR involves the display of 3-D images that users explore and manipulate interactively. Using special VR software, a developer

Figure 2-24 Windows Media Player is a popular media player, through which you can listen to music and watch video.
Source: Microsoft Corporation

 Internet Research

What is a Smart TV?

Search for: smart tv

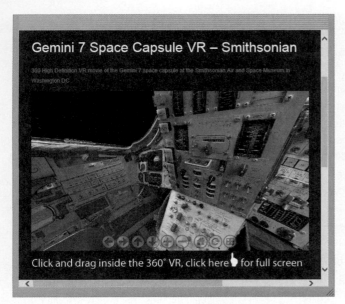

Gemini 7 Space Capsule VR – Smithsonian

360 High Definition VR movie of the Gemini 7 space capsule at the Smithsonian Air and Space Museum in Washington DC

Click and drag inside the 360° VR, click here for full screen

Figure 2-25   Users can explore a VR world using a touch screen or their input device. For example, users can explore the inside of the Gemini 7 space capsule, located at the Smithsonian Air and Space Museum in Washington, D.C., from their computer or mobile device.
Source: World VR

 Internet Research

What is HTML5?

Search for: html5

creates an entire 3-D environment that contains infinite space and depth, called a VR world (Figure 2-25). A VR world on the web, for example, might show a house for sale where potential buyers walk through rooms in the VR house by sliding their finger on a touch screen or moving an input device forward, backward, or to the side.

In addition to games and simulations, many practical applications of VR also exist. Science educators create VR models of molecules, organisms, and other structures for students to examine. Companies use VR to showcase products or create advertisements. Architects create VR models of buildings and rooms so that clients can see how a completed construction project will look before it is built.

Plug-Ins

Most browsers have the capability of displaying basic multimedia elements on a webpage. Sometimes, however, a browser requires an additional program, called a plug-in, to display multimedia. A *plug-in*, or add-on, is a program that extends the capability of a browser. For example, your browser may require Adobe Reader to view and print PDF files. You typically can download plug-ins at no cost from various websites. Some plug-ins run on all sizes of computers and mobile devices; others have special versions for mobile devices.

Some mobile devices and browsers, however, do not support plug-ins. For this reason, web designers are using newer technologies to create websites that display correctly in both desktop and mobile browsers; these technologies generally do not require the use of plug-ins to display media.

Other Internet Services

As previously mentioned, the web is only one of the many services on the Internet. Other Internet services include the following: email, email lists, Internet messaging, chat rooms, online discussions, VoIP (Voice over IP), and FTP (File Transfer Protocol).

Email

Email (short for electronic mail) is the transmission of messages and files via a computer network. Email was one of the original services on the Internet, enabling scientists and researchers working on government-sponsored projects to communicate with colleagues at other locations.

You use an **email program** to create, send, receive, forward, store, print, and delete email messages. Email programs are available as desktop apps, web apps, and mobile apps. An email message can be simple text or can include an attachment such as a document, a graphic, an audio clip, or a video clip.

Just as you address a letter when using the postal system, you address an email message with the email address of your intended recipient. Likewise, when someone sends you a message, he or she must have your email address.

An *email address* is a combination of a user name and a domain name that identifies a user so that he or she can receive Internet email. A **user name** is a unique combination of characters, such as letters of the alphabet and/or numbers, that identifies a specific user. Your user name must be different from the other user names in the same domain. For example, a user named Rick Claremont whose server has a domain name of esite.com might want to select rclaremont as his user name. If esite.com already has an rclaremont (for Rita Claremont) user name, then Rick will have to select a different user name, such as rick.claremont or rclaremont2.

Sometimes, organizations decide the format of user names for new users so that the user names are consistent across the company. In many cases, however, users select their own user names, often selecting a nickname or any other combination of characters for their user name. Many users select a combination of their first and last names so that others can remember it easily.

In an Internet email address, an @ (pronounced at) symbol separates the user name from the domain name. Your service provider supplies the domain name. A possible email address for Rick Claremont would be rclaremont@esite.com, which would be read as follows: R Claremont at e site dot com. Most email programs allow you to create a *contacts folder*, which contains a list of names, addresses, phone numbers, email addresses, and other details about people with whom you communicate.

Figure 2-26 illustrates how an email message may travel from a sender to a receiver. When you send an email message, an outgoing mail server determines how to route the message through the Internet and then sends the message. As you receive email messages, an incoming mail server holds the messages in your mailbox until you use your email program to retrieve them. Most email programs have a mail notification alert that informs you via a message and/or sound when you receive a new email message(s).

 CONSIDER THIS

What are good practices to follow when using email?

1. Keep messages brief.
2. Respond to messages promptly.
3. Use proper grammar, spelling, and punctuation.
4. Never respond to unsolicited messages.
5. Use meaningful subject lines.
6. Read the message before you send it.
7. Use email when you want a permanent record of a communication.

How an Email Message May Travel from a Sender to a Receiver

Step 1
Using an email program, you create and send a message on a computer or mobile device.

Step 2
Your email program contacts software on the outgoing mail server.

Step 3
Software on the outgoing mail server determines the best route for the data and sends the message, which travels along Internet routers to the recipient's incoming mail server.

Internet router

incoming mail server

Step 4
When the recipient uses an email program to check for email messages, the message transfers from the incoming mail server to the recipient's computer or mobile device.

Internet router

Figure 2-26 This figure shows how an email message may travel from a sender to a receiver.

© Oleksiy Mark / Shutterstock.com; © iStockphoto / luismmolina; Courtesy of Juniper Networks; © iStockphoto / hocus-focus; © Cengage Learning; © Cengage Learning

Email Lists

An **email list**, or electronic mailing list, is a group of email addresses used for mass distribution of a message. When a message is sent to an email list, each person on the list receives a copy of the message in his or her mailbox. You *subscribe* to an email list by adding your email address to the mailing list, which is stored on a list server. To remove your name, you *unsubscribe* from the mailing list.

The original use of email lists, such as *LISTSERV*, allowed any subscriber to send a message, which created a discussion-type forum among all subscribers via email. Many mailing lists today, such as in Figure 2-27, however, are one-way communications and do not allow subscribers to send messages.

Figure 2-27 When you subscribe to a mailing list, you and all others in the list receive messages from the website. Shown here is a user who receives newsletters and alerts from FoxNews.com.

Source: FOX News Network, LLC

Figure 2-28 With Internet messaging services, you and the person(s) with whom you are conversing are online at the same time. The conversation appears on all parties' screens at the same time. Shown here is Facebook messenger.

© iStockphoto / Petar Chernaev; © Cengage Learning; © iStockphoto / Oleksiy Mark; © Cengage Learning

Internet Messaging

Internet messaging services, which often occur in real-time, are communications services that notify you when one or more of your established contacts are online and then allows you to exchange messages or files or join a private chat room with them (Figure 2-28). *Real time* means that you and the people with whom you are conversing are online at the same time. Some Internet messaging services support voice and video conversations, allow you to send photos or other documents to a recipient, listen to streaming music, and play games with another online contact.

For real-time Internet messaging to work, both parties must be online at the same time. Also, the receiver of a message must be willing to accept messages. To use an Internet messaging service, you may have to install messenger software or an app on the computer or mobile device, such as a smartphone, you plan to use.

Many online social networks include a messaging feature. To ensure successful communications, all individuals on the friend list need to use the same or a compatible messenger.

Chat Rooms

A **chat** is a real-time typed conversation that takes place on a computer or mobile device with many other online users. A **chat room** is a website or application that permits users to chat with others who are online at the same time. A server echoes the user's message to everyone in the chat room. Anyone in the chat room can participate in the conversation, which usually is specific to a particular topic. Businesses sometimes use chat rooms to communicate with customers.

As you type on your keyboard, others connected to the same chat room server also see what you have typed (Figure 2-29). Some chat rooms support voice chats and video chats, in which people hear or see each other as they chat. Most browsers today include the capability to connect to a chat server.

Figure 2-29 As you type, others in the same chat room see what you have typed.
Attribution: © ARENA Creative / Shutterstock.com; © Cengage Learning; © topseller / Shutterstock.com; © Alex Staroseltsev / Shutterstock.com; © Oleksiy Mark / Shutterstock.com; © Oleksiy Mark / Shutterstock.com; © Tom Wang / Shutterstock.com; © vlad_star / Shutterstock.com; © artjazz / Shutterstock.com

Online Discussions

An **online discussion**, or *discussion forum*, is an online area in which users have written discussions about a particular subject (Figure 2-30). To participate in a discussion, a user posts a message, called an article, and other users read and reply to the message. A *thread*, or threaded discussion, consists of the original article and all subsequent related replies.

Some discussion forums require that you enter a user name and password to participate in the discussion. For example, an online discussion for students taking a college course may require a user name and password to access the discussion. This ensures that only students in the course participate in the discussion. Posts in an online discussion usually are stored for a certain amount of time, such as a semester, in this example.

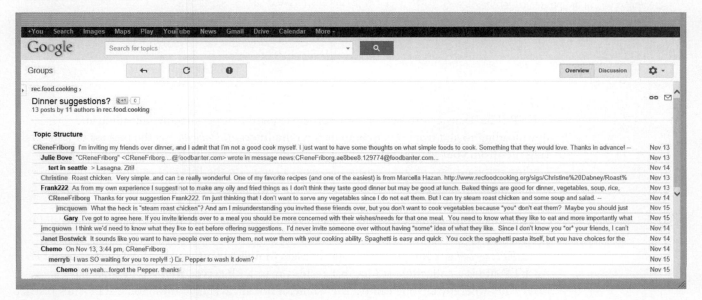

Figure 2-30 Users in an online discussion read and reply to other users' messages.
Source: Google Inc.

VoIP

VoIP, short for Voice over IP (Internet Protocol), enables users to speak to other users via their Internet connection. That is, VoIP uses the Internet (instead of the public switched telephone network) to connect a calling party to one or more local or long-distance called parties.

To place an Internet phone call, you need a broadband Internet connection, a microphone and speaker, both of which are included with a standard computer or mobile device, and VoIP software, such as Skype. Some VoIP services require that you purchase a separate phone and VoIP router, and subscribe to their service. Others offer certain services free and require a subscription for additional services. Read How To 2-4 for instructions about how to set up a personal VoIP service and make a call.

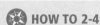

BTW

VoIP Microphone
You also can use a headset connected to or that communicates with your computer or mobile device.

 HOW TO 2-4 ───────────────────────────────

Set Up a Personal VoIP Service and Make a Call

VoIP services enable you to make free video or voice calls to others around the world. In many cases, the person you are calling also must use the same VoIP service. The following steps describe how to set up a VoIP service and make a call.

1. If you do not know the VoIP service you want to use, search for a program or app that enables you to place and receive VoIP calls.

2. If necessary, download the program or app for the VoIP service you will use.

3. Most VoIP services require you to have an account with their service before you can place or receive a call. When you start the VoIP program or app, search for the button or link to create a new account.

Follow the steps in the program or app to finish creating the account.

4. Once the account has been created, if necessary, sign in to the VoIP service with your user name and password.

5. Make sure the person you are calling also has an account with the same VoIP service. You should know at least one person using this service to successfully place a call. VoIP services typically allow you to locate and call someone by entering their user name or adding them to your list of contacts. If necessary, add the person you want to call to your list of contacts.

6. On the list of contacts, select the person you want to call and then tap or click the appropriate button to place the call.

7. When the other person answers, you can start your voice or video call.

8. When you are ready to end the call, tap or click the button to end the call.

9. When you are finished using the VoIP service, you should sign out of and exit the VoIP program or app.

✸ **Consider This:** Survey your friends and family to see if they use a VoIP service. If so, which service is the most popular among them?

Source: Microsoft

FTP

FTP (File Transfer Protocol) is an Internet standard that permits file uploading and downloading to and from other computers on the Internet. *Uploading* is the process of transferring files from your computer or mobile device to a server on the Internet. Recall that downloading is the process of transferring files from a server on the Internet to your computer or mobile device. Webpage developers, for example, often use FTP to upload their webpages to a web server.

Many operating systems include FTP capabilities. If yours does not, you can download FTP programs from the web, usually for a small fee.

An *FTP server* is a computer that allows users to upload and/or download files using FTP. An FTP site is a collection of files that reside on an FTP server. Many FTP sites have *anonymous FTP*, whereby anyone can transfer some, if not all, available files. Some FTP sites restrict file transfers to those who have authorized accounts (user names and passwords) on the FTP server.

Mini Feature 2-3: Digital Communications

Home users, small/home office users, mobile users, power users, and enterprise users interact with technology for many reasons, including communication, productivity, and information. Read Mini Feature 2-3 for examples of how a home user might interact with digital communications.

 MINI FEATURE 2-3

Digital Communications

This scenario, which assumes you are a home user with a busy family, presents situations and questions regarding technology use during a single day.

7:30 a.m. You notice a leaky pipe under the kitchen sink. Your regular plumber recently has retired. On your smartphone, you run an app that enables you to use search criteria, GPS, and user reviews. You find a local plumber who has many positive reviews and tap the phone number on the smartphone touch screen to place the call. You leave a message explaining the problem and asking the plumber to call you back.
✸ How can you evaluate reviews for authenticity and bias? How might an app provider use your location information in ways you have not authorized?

8:45 a.m. The plumber calls you back to schedule an appointment time. You open your laptop and use the electronic calendar web app your entire family uses to keep track of appointments. You find a time that works for both of you and update the electronic calendar.
✸ What features enable multiple people, such as a family or small business, to use an electronic calendar? What issues may occur from using a shared calendar?

10:00 a.m. You have a freelance job blogging for a local florist. You are required to post twice weekly to the florist's blog about agreed-upon topics. You use a wiki to confirm the symbolic meaning of different types of roses so that you can include that in your next blog post. You sign in to the blog's content management system and submit your post to the blog.
✸ What responsibility do bloggers have to post accurate, verified information? Should users rely on wikis to verify content?

 11:00 a.m. While you are driving to a doctor's appointment, you receive several text messages on your smartphone. You use your Bluetooth headset and your smartphone's speech-to-text feature to respond to the text messages without taking your eyes off of the road.
✸ Is it legal in your state to use hands-free devices while driving? What, if any, are the consequences of noncompliance?

1:00 p.m. Back at home, you flip through today's mail. You received a bill for your monthly mortgage payment.

Using your laptop, you navigate to your bank's website and schedule a recurring payment for the mortgage to ensure you never will be late on a payment.
✸ What precautions should you take when accessing financial information and authorizing payments on the web?

 5:30 p.m. Unsure of what to make for dinner, you use your tablet to view recipes you bookmarked on a bookmarking site. You verify that you have the ingredients on hand and follow the recipe on your tablet as you prepare dinner.
✸ Who owns the content posted to social networking or bookmarking sites? What risks are involved with using these types of websites?

8:30 p.m. While helping your daughter with her math homework, you discover a website that includes the answers to questions asked in her textbook. You have a discussion with your daughter about ethical issues surrounding posting and using that type of content.
✸ Should students receive punishment for using answers they find on a website?

9:00 p.m. You sit down to watch your favorite vocal competition reality show, streaming live through your Smart TV. The show enables you to send a text message to vote for your favorite contestant. You debate between two popular singers, then finally send your vote via text message.
✸ How else do TV, movie, and other entertainment websites use the Internet to interact with viewers or listeners?

10:30 p.m. You use the calendar app on your smartphone to confirm your schedule for tomorrow and then head to bed.
✸ How does technology enhance the daily life of a home user?

Netiquette

Netiquette, which is short for Internet etiquette, is the code of acceptable behaviors users should follow while on the Internet; that is, it is the conduct expected of individuals while online. Netiquette includes rules for all aspects of the Internet, including the web, social media, Internet messaging, chat rooms, online discussions, and FTP. Figure 2-31 outlines some of the rules of netiquette, with respect to online communications. Read Ethics & Issues 2-4 to consider issues related to an extreme misuse of online communications — online bullying.

Netiquette Guidelines for Online Communications
Golden Rule: Treat others as you would like them to treat you.

Be polite. Avoid offensive language.

Avoid sending or posting *flames*, which are abusive or insulting messages. Do not participate in *flame wars*, which are exchanges of flames.

Be careful when using sarcasm and humor, as it might be misinterpreted.

Do not use all capital letters, which is the equivalent of SHOUTING!

Use **emoticons** to express emotion. Popular emoticons include:

:) Smile   :| Indifference   :o Surprised   :(Frown   :\ Undecided   ;) Wink

Use abbreviations and acronyms for phrases:

BTW	by the way	IMHO	in my humble opinion	FWIW	for what it's worth
FYI	for your information	TTFN	ta ta for now	TYVM	thank you very much

Clearly identify a *spoiler*, which is a message that reveals an outcome to a game or ending to a movie or program.

Be forgiving of other's mistakes.

Read the *FAQ* (frequently asked questions), if one exists.

Figure 2-31 Some of the rules of netiquette, with respect to online communications.
© Cengage Learning

✳ ETHICS & ISSUES 2-4

Who Is Responsible for Monitoring Cyberbullying?

Sending or forwarding threatening text messages, posting embarrassing or altered pictures of someone without his or her permission, or setting up a fake online social network page where others make cruel comments and spread rumors about someone all are examples of cyberbullying. *Cyberbullying* is harassment using technology, often involving teens and preteens. Unlike verbal bullying, the perpetrators can hide behind the anonymity of the Internet and can reach a wide audience quickly. Victims cannot just walk away or ignore bullying that comes in the form of text messages, email, or online social network posts.

Cyberbullying often takes place outside of school hours on personal devices or computers not owned or monitored by a school. Yet the ramifications affect the victim at school. Schools struggle to come up with policies. Many schools are adopting policies that include consequences for any form of student-to-student bullying, even using nonschool resources, if it contributes to a hostile environment for any student or group of students. Some schools specify that students who retaliate against anyone who reports instances of bullying or cyberbullying will receive punishment.

Anti-bullying laws vary from state to state and often do not include specific language about cyberbullying. One argument against

criminalizing cyberbullying is the protection of free speech. Awareness campaigns, school policies, and parent monitoring of technology use are some ways to attempt to prevent cyberbullying. These methods are not always effective. The impact on the victim can lead to poor grades, health issues, mental health concerns, and even suicide.

Consider This: Should schools be responsible for punishing students who cyberbully other students outside of school? Why or why not? What role can parents play in reducing cyberbullying? What are the positive and negative aspects of the freedom to be anonymous on the Internet?

NOW YOU SHOULD KNOW

Be sure you understand the material presented in the sections titled Digital Media on the Web, Other Internet Services, and Netiquette as it relates to the module objectives.
Now you should know …

- Why you use media on the web (Objective 8)
- How you can benefit from using email, email lists, Internet messaging, chat rooms, discussion forums, VoIP, and FTP (Objective 9)
- What rules you should follow in online communications (Objective 10)

 # Summary

This module presented the evolution of the Internet, along with various ways to connect to the Internet, how data travels the Internet, and how the Internet works with domain names and IP addresses. It discussed the web at length, including topics such as browsing, navigating, web addresses, web apps and mobile apps, searching, and online social networks. It presented various types of websites and media on the web. It also introduced other services available on the Internet, such as email, email lists, Internet messaging, chat rooms, online discussions, VoIP, and FTP. Finally, the module listed rules of netiquette.

 TECHNOLOGY @ WORK

Transportation

What is transportation like without computers and mobile devices? Delivery drivers use clipboards to hold their records. Human navigators use paper maps to track routes for pilots. Ship captains rely solely on experience to navigate through shallow waters. Today, the transportation industry relies heavily on computer and mobile device usage.

Many vehicles include onboard navigation systems to help you navigate from one location to another. Some of these systems provide other services, such as dispatching roadside assistance, unlocking the driver's side door if you lock the keys in your vehicle, and tracking the vehicle if it is stolen.

The shipping and travel industries identify items during transport using bar codes, which are identification codes that consist of lines and spaces of different lengths. When you ship a package, the shipping company, such as UPS or FedEx, places a bar code on the package to indicate its destination to a computer. Because a package might travel to its destination by way of several trucks, trains, and airplanes,

computers automatically route the package as efficiently as possible. You are able to visit a website or sign up for text message notifications to track a package's progress during shipment.

When you travel by airplane, baggage handling systems ensure that your luggage reaches its destination on time. When you check in your baggage at the airport, a bar code identifies the airplane on which the bags should be placed. If you change planes, automated baggage handling systems route your bags to connecting flights with very little, if any, human intervention. When the bags reach their destination, they are routed automatically to the baggage carousel in the airport's terminal building.

Pilots of high-technology commercial, military, and space aircraft today work in a glass cockpit, which features computerized instrumentation, navigation, communications, weather reports, and an autopilot. The electronic flight information shown on high-resolution displays is designed to reduce pilot workload, decrease fatigue, and enable pilots to concentrate on flying safely.

Boats and ships also are equipped with computers that include detailed electronic maps, which help the captain navigate, as well as calculate the water depth and provide a layout of the underwater surface so that the captain can avoid obstructions.

As you travel the roadways, airways, and waterways, bear in mind that computers often are responsible for helping you to reach your destination as quickly and safely as possible.

Consider This: In what other ways do computers and technology play a role in the transportation industry?

Digital Vision / Getty Images

Study Guide

The Study Guide exercise reinforces material you should know for the module exam.

Instructions: Answer the questions below using the format that helps you remember best or that is required by your instructor. Possible formats may include one or more of these options: write the answers; create a document that contains the answers; record answers as audio or video using a webcam, smartphone, or portable media player; post answers on a blog, wiki, or website; or highlight answers in the book/e-book.

1. Explain how ARPANET contributed to the growth of the Internet.
2. Describe the role of a host on a network.
3. Identify the role of the W3C.
4. Define the terms, dongle and broadband. List popular wired and wireless broadband Internet services.
5. State the purpose of a hot spot, and list tips for using hot spots safely.
6. ISP stands for _____.
7. Briefly describe how data and information travel the Internet.
8. Describe the purpose and composition of an IP address. Differentiate between IPv4 and IPv6.
9. Define the term, domain name. List general steps to register for a domain name.
10. Identify the purpose of several generic TLDs. Identify ICANN's role with TLDs.
11. Describe how and why cybersquatters register domain names.
12. State the purpose of a DNS server.
13. Differentiate between static and dynamic webpages.
14. Distinguish among the web, a webpage, a website, and a web server.
15. Explain the purpose of a browser. Describe the function of tabbed browsing.
16. List ways you can browse safely.
17. Name examples of popular browsers for personal computers and mobile devices.
18. Define the term, web address. Name a synonym.
19. Name and give examples of the components of a web address.
20. Describe the purpose of a web feed.
21. Explain the relationship between web and mobile apps.
22. Describe the purpose of GPS receivers, and why manufacturers embed them in smartphones.
23. Explain the risks and concerns involved in letting apps track your location. List any benefits.
24. Describe how to use a search engine. What are some ways you can refine a search?
25. Besides webpages, identify other items a search engine can find.
26. Differentiate between a search engine and a subject directory.
27. Explain how to use an online social network for personal or business use.
28. List ways to use online social networks securely.
29. Describe the purpose of these types of websites: informational and research; media sharing; bookmarking; news, weather, sports, and other mass media; educational; business, governmental, and organizational; blogs; wikis and collaboration; health and fitness; science; entertainment; banking and finance; travel and tourism; mapping; retail and auctions; careers and employment; e-commerce; portals; content aggregation; and website creation and management.
30. Is it ethical to use a fake name online? Why or why not? List techniques to protect yourself from identity theft.
31. Describe the uses of tags. List steps to tag digital content.
32. Define the term, e-commerce. Differentiate among B2C, C2C, and B2B e-commerce.
33. List uses and benefits of content aggregation websites and apps.
34. Identify and briefly describe the steps in web publishing.
35. The _____ web design approach adapts the layout of the website to fit the screen on which it is displayed.
36. List the seven criteria for evaluating a website's content.
37. _____ refers to any application that combines text with media.
38. Explain how webpages use graphics, animation, audio, video, virtual reality, and plug-ins.
39. Define the terms, thumbnail and infographic.
40. Name the types of graphics formats used on the web and how they use compression.
41. List general steps to download digital media.
42. Describe the purpose of these Internet services and explain how each works: email, email lists, messaging, chat rooms, online discussions, VoIP, and FTP.
43. Describe the components of an email address.
44. _____ refers to Internet communications in which both parties communicate at the same time.
45. List steps to set up a personal VoIP service and make a call.
46. Describe how a home user interacts with digital communications.
47. Define the term, netiquette.
48. Describe cyberbullying, and explain why it is difficult to catch the perpetrators.
49. Describe how the transportation industry uses technology.

You should be able to define the Primary Terms and be familiar with the Secondary Terms listed below.

Key Terms

Primary Terms (shown in **bold-black** characters in the module)

blog (78)
blogger (78)
browser (65)
chat (91)
chat room (91)
Chrome (67)
content
  aggregation (83)
domain name (63)
e-commerce (82)
Edge (67)
email (88)
email list (90)
email program (88)
emoticons (94)
favorites (67)

Firefox (67)
FTP (92)
GB (61)
GPS (70)
GPS receiver (70)
graphic (85)
home page (66)
hot spot (59)
Internet (56)
Internet
  Explorer (67)
Internet
  messaging (90)
Internet service
  provider (ISP) (61)
IP address (62)

MB (61)
mobile service
  provider (61)
netiquette (94)
online auction (82)
online discussion (91)
online social network (72)
Opera (67)
PDF (86)
pop-up blocker (66)
pop-under blocker (66)
portal (82)
responsive web design (84)
Safari (67)
search engine (71)
social media (76)

streaming (79)
tabbed browsing (66)
tag (75)
traffic (62)
user name (88)
virtual reality (87)
VoIP (92)
web (65)
web address (68)
web publishing (84)
web server (65)
webpage (65)
website (65)
wiki (78)
World Wide Web
  (WWW) (65)

Secondary Terms (shown in *italic* characters in the module)

analog (60)
animation (86)
anonymous FTP (92)
Anticybersquatting Consumer
  Protection Act (64)
ARPANET (56)
audio (86)
bandwidth (61)
blogosphere (78)
bookmarks (67)
bookmarking site (75)
broadband (58)
business-to-business (B2B)
  e-commerce (82)
business-to-consumer (B2C)
  e-commerce (82)
cable Internet service (59)
cache (66)
catfishing (77)
ccTLD (63)
cloud storage (69)
consumer-to-consumer (C2C)
  e-commerce (82)
contacts folder (89)
content management system (84)
curation website (83)
cyberbullying (94)
discussion forum (91)
DNS server (64)
domain name system (DNS) (64)
dongle (58)

DSL (59)
dynamic webpage (65)
electronic storefront (81)
e-retail (81)
email address (88)
extended contacts (73)
FAQ (94)
Fiber to the Premises (FTTP) (59)
fixed wireless (59)
flames (94)
flame wars (94)
friends (73)
FTP server (92)
gigabyte (61)
hashtag (73)
hits (71)
host (56)
http (69)
ICANN (63)
infographic (86)
Internet backbone (62)
intranet (78)
JPEG (86)
keyloggers (80)
like (73)
LISTSERV (90)
location sharing (66)
m-commerce (82)
media player (87)
media sharing site (75)
megabyte (61)

microblog (78)
mobile app (69)
mobile broadband (59)
mobile browser (65)
MP3 (87)
multimedia (85)
news feed (73)
phishing (66)
phishing filter (66)
plug-in (88)
PNG (86)
pop-up ad (66)
pop-under ad (66)
private browsing (66)
proxy server (66)
real time (90)
registrar (63)
satellite Internet service (59)
search text (71)
shopping cart (81)
social networking site (72)

spoiler (94)
static webpage (65)
status update (73)
subscribe (90)
subject directory (72)
tethering (60)
thread (91)
thumbnail (85)
top-level domain (TLD) (63)
troll (77)
unsubscribe (90)
uploading (93)
URL (68)
video (87)
W3C (58)
Web 2.0 (65)
web app (69)
web feed (69)
web hosting service (64)
Wi-Fi (59)
wireless modem (58)

wiki (78)

Checkpoint

The Checkpoint exercises test your knowledge of the module concepts. The page number containing the answer appears in parentheses after each exercise. The Consider This exercises challenge your understanding of module concepts.

True/False   Mark T for True and F for False.

_____ 1. No single person or government agency controls or owns the Internet. (58)

_____ 2. The W3C is responsible for maintaining all networks and content on the Internet. (58)

_____ 3. Users typically pay additional fees for mobile hot spot and tethering services. (60)

_____ 4. A gigabyte (GB) is the basic storage unit on a computer or mobile device and represents a single character. (61)

_____ 5. A dynamic webpage's contents generate each time a user displays the page. (65)

_____ 6. Most browsers are available for download at no cost. (67)

_____ 7. Mobile apps sometimes have fewer features than a web app. (69)

_____ 8. A subject directory is software that finds websites, webpages, images, videos, maps, and other information related to a specific topic. (71)

_____ 9. When you post digital content online, it is a good idea to tag it so that it is easy to locate and organize. (76)

_____ 10. The term, blogosphere, refers to the worldwide collection of blogs. (78)

_____ 11. Tethering is the process of transferring data in a continuous and even flow, which allows users to access and use a file while it is transmitting. (79)

_____ 12. One way to protect yourself from identity theft online is to retain all your cookies in your browser. (80)

Multiple Choice   Select the best answer.

1. A(n) _____ is any computer that provides services and connections to other computers on a network. (56)
   a. host
   b. client
   c. FTP site
   d. subject directory

2. A(n) _____ is a sequence of numbers that uniquely identifies the location of each computer or device connected to the Internet. (62)
   a. Internet backbone
   b. domain name
   c. IP address
   d. ccTLD

3. You register a domain name through _____, which is an organization that sells and manages domain names. (63)
   a. a cybersquatter
   b. a registrar
   c. ICANN
   d. an ISP

4. The _____ is the method the Internet uses to store domain names and their corresponding IP addresses. (64)
   a. domain name system (DNS)
   b. top-level domain (TLD)
   c. File Transfer Protocol (FTP)
   d. W3C

5. One way to protect your identity while browsing is to use a(n) _____, which is another computer that screens all your incoming and outgoing messages. (66)
   a. password
   b. anonymous FTP
   c. phishing filter
   d. proxy server

6. _____ is a set of rules that defines how webpages transfer on the Internet. (69)
   a. Top-level domain
   b. Hypertext Transfer Protocol
   c. IPv4
   d. Web 2.0

7. A(n) _____ website contains factual material, such as libraries, encyclopedias, dictionaries, directories, guides, and other types of reference. (74)
   a. wikis and collaboration
   b. media sharing
   c. business
   d. informational and research

8. A _____ is a website that offers a variety of Internet services from a single, convenient location. (82)
   a. LISTSERV
   b. microblog
   c. portal
   d. cache

Checkpoint

Matching   Match the terms with their definitions.

_____ 1. tethering (60)

_____ 2. Internet backbone (62)

_____ 3. domain name (63)

_____ 4. web server (65)

_____ 5. tag (75)

_____ 6. catfishing (77)

_____ 7. wiki (78)

_____ 8. curation website (83)

_____ 9. chat (91)

_____ 10. cyberbullying (94)

a. text-based name that corresponds to the IP address of a server that hosts a website

b. website or web app that allows users to collect and compile content from a variety of websites about a particular topic or theme

c. harassment, often involving teens and preteens, using technology

d. collaborative website that allows users to create, add, modify, or delete website content via a browser

e. technique that transforms a smartphone or Internet-capable tablet into a portable communications device that shares its Internet access with other computers and devices wirelessly

f. real-time typed conversation that takes place on a computer or mobile device with many other online users

g. computer that delivers requested webpages to your computer or mobile device

h. online practice of creating a fake profile to form relationships with unsuspecting users

i. term used to refer to the major carriers of network traffic

j. short descriptive label that you assign to digital content so that it is easier to locate at a later time

✳ **Consider This**   Answer the following questions in the format specified by your instructor.

1. Answer the critical thinking questions posed at the end of these elements in this module: Ethics & Issues (64, 70, 77, 94), How To (63, 76, 87, 92), Mini Features (67, 73, 93), Secure IT (59, 66, 74, 80), and Technology @ Work (95).

2. What were ARPA's original goals? (56)

3. What are the advantages of using a broadband Internet service? (58)

4. What is the relationship between domain names and IP addresses? (62)

5. Is cybersquatting ethical? Why or why not? (64)

6. What is a cybersquatter? (64) What is the goal of the Anticybersquatting Consumer Protection Act (ACPA)? (64)

7. How does a static webpage differ from a dynamic webpage? (65)

8. How does using a proxy server help protect your online identity? (66)

9. What are some safe browsing techniques? (66)

10. What are some popular mobile browsers? (67)

11. How do GPS receivers track their location on earth? (70)

12. What are the advantages and risks associated with allowing an app to track your location? (70)

13. What techniques can you use to improve search results? (72)

14. What precautions can you take to minimize privacy and security risks associated with online social networks? (74)

15. Would you use a public computer to check email or do online banking? Why or why not? What are the risks? (80)

16. How do e-commerce and m-commerce differ? (82)

17. What should you determine during the planning stage of a website? (84)

18. What steps are involved in web publishing? (84)

19. What are some criteria you can use to evaluate a website or webpage before relying on its content? (85)

20. How do JPEG and PNG formats differ? (86)

21. What are some practical applications of virtual reality? (88)

22. Where can you obtain plug-ins? (88)

23. Besides the web, what other Internet services are available? (88)

24. What are some good practices to follow when using email? (89)

25. What elements do you need to place an Internet phone call? (92)

26. What is anonymous FTP? (92)

27. What activities might be considered cyberbullying? (94)

❋ Problem Solving

The Problem Solving exercises extend your knowledge of module concepts by seeking solutions to practical problems with technology that you may encounter at home, school, work, or with nonprofit organizations. The Collaboration exercise should be completed with a team.

Instructions: You often can solve problems with technology in multiple ways. Determine a solution to the problems in these exercises by using one or more resources available to you (such as a computer or mobile device, articles on the web or in print, blogs, podcasts, videos, television, user guides, other individuals, electronics or computer stores, etc.). Describe your solution, along with the resource(s) used, in the format requested by your instructor (brief report, presentation, discussion, blog post, video, or other means).

Personal

1. **Cyberbullying Message**   While reviewing the email messages in your email account, you notice one that you interpret as cyberbullying. You do not recognize the sender of the email message, but still take it seriously. What are your next steps?

2. **Unsolicited Friend Requests**   You recently signed up for an account on the Facebook online social network. When you log in periodically, you find that people you do not know are requesting to be your friend. How should you respond?

3. **Unexpected Search Engine**   A class project requires that you conduct research on the web. After typing the web address for Google's home page and pressing the ENTER key, your browser redirects you to a different search engine. What could be wrong?

4. **Images Do Not Appear**   When you navigate to a webpage, you notice that no images are appearing. You successfully have viewed webpages with images in the past and are not sure why images suddenly are not appearing. What steps will you take to show the images?

5. **Social Media Password**   Your social media password has been saved on your computer for quite some time and the browser has been signing you in automatically. After deleting your browsing history and saved information from your browser, the online social network began prompting you again for your password, which you have forgotten. What are your next steps?

Source: Twitter

Professional

6. **Suspicious Website Visits**   The director of your company's information technology department sent you an email message stating that you have been spending an excessive amount of time viewing websites not related to your job. You periodically visit websites not related to work, but only on breaks, which the company allows. How does he know your web browsing habits? How will you respond to this claim?

7. **Automatic Response**   When you return from vacation, a colleague informs you that when she sent email messages to your email address, she would not always receive your automatic response stating that you were out of the office. Why might your email program not respond automatically to every email message received?

8. **Email Message Formatting**   A friend sent an email message containing a photo to your email account at work. Upon receiving the email message, the photo does not appear. You also notice that email messages never show any formatting, such as different fonts, font sizes, and font colors. What might be causing this?

9. **Mobile Hot Spot Not Found**   Your supervisor gave you a mobile hot spot to use while you are traveling to a conference in another state. When you attempt to connect to the hot spot with your computer, tablet, and phone, none of the devices is able to find any wireless networks. What might be the problem, and what are your next steps?

10. **Sporadic Email Message Delivery**   The email program on your computer has been displaying new messages only every hour, on the hour. Historically, new email messages would arrive and be displayed immediately upon being sent by the sender. Furthermore, your coworkers claim that they sometimes do not receive your email messages until hours after you send them. What might be the problem?

Collaboration

11. **Technology in Transportation**   Your project team has been assigned to present a business proposal to a group of potential investors. Because the presentation will take place in Kansas City, Missouri, you will need to transport people and ship some materials to that location. Form a team of three people and determine how to use technology to ship materials and how to make travel arrangements. One team member should research the steps required to use a website to make flight reservations, one team member should determine the steps necessary to print a package shipping label from his or her computer and track the package while it is en route, and another team member should find directions from Kansas City International Airport to a nearby hotel.

The How To: Your Turn exercises present general guidelines for fundamental skills when using a computer or mobile device and then require that you determine how to apply these general guidelines to a specific program or situation.

How To: Your Turn ✸

Instructions: You often can complete tasks using technology in multiple ways. Figure out how to perform the tasks described in these exercises by using one or more resources available to you (such as a computer or mobile device, articles on the web or in print, online or program help, user guides, blogs, podcasts, videos, other individuals, trial and error, etc.). Summarize your 'how to' steps, along with the resource(s) used, in the format requested by your instructor (brief report, presentation, discussion, blog post, video, or other means).

❶ Determine Your IP (Internet Protocol) Address

Knowing a computer or mobile device's IP address can help you identify it on a network and can help you troubleshoot any problems you may experience connecting to the Internet or other computers and devices on your network. The following steps guide you through the process of determining your IP address.

a. Run a browser and then navigate to a search engine of your choice.

b. Search for a website that can determine your IP address and then navigate to one of these websites.

c. Your IP address should be displayed upon navigating to the website. If it does not, return to the search results and navigate to a different site.

or

a. Run a browser and then navigate to a search engine of your choice.

b. Search for a website that explains how to determine the IP address for your specific operating system and version.

c. View the search results and then navigate to the website that provides you with the best guidance.

d. Follow the instructions on your computer or mobile device to determine the IP address.

Source: Microsoft Corporation

Exercises

1. Summarize the process you used to determine your IP address.
2. What is your IP address?
3. Is it possible for a computer to have more than one IP address at the same time? Why or why not?

❷ Participate in an Online Auction

Online auctions allow consumers to bid on products that other people are selling. If you are the highest bidder at the end of the bidding period, you often can arrange payment through the online auction. The following steps guide you through the process of participating in an online auction. **WARNING: Do not purchase or bid on an item if you do not intend to purchase it. If you win the auction, you legally may be obligated to provide payment for the item.**

a. Run a browser and then navigate to www.ebay.com.

b. Tap or click the link to register for a new account.

c. Enter the requested information to create the account.

d. Search for an item on which you would like to bid. If you want to browse items in a specific category instead, tap or click the link to browse for items by category.

e. When the search results appear, tap or click an item that interests you to see more details about the item.

f. Review the item details to determine whether you would like to bid on this item. If the item does not interest you, return to the search results and select another item.

g. The seller may have a "Buy It Now" option that allows you to purchase the item immediately at a predetermined price. Alternatively, you can bid on the item by making an offer. The highest bidder at the end of the auction will win the item. **Remember: If you bid on and win an item, you are obligated to provide payment.**

h. You will be notified if you are the winning bidder when the auction closes. At that time, follow the instructions to arrange to pay the seller.

i. When you are finished, sign out of eBay.

✳ How To: Your Turn

Exercises

1. What item(s) did you view? If the buyer had the "Buy It Now" option available, do you think the asking price was fair?
2. Would you purchase an item from an online auction? Why or why not?
3. What items might you post for sale on an online auction?

Source: eBay

➌ View and Manage Data Usage

Many people have limited data plans, so it is important to know how to view the amount of data you have used on your phone or tablet when you are not connected to the Internet using a Wi-Fi connection. If you are using a phone or tablet where Wi-Fi is available, you should strongly consider using the Wi-Fi connection not only to limit data plan usage, but also to experience faster speed. If you find that your data usage is high each month, you may be able to see which apps are using the most data and adjust usage of those apps accordingly. The following steps guide you through the process of viewing and managing data usage.

a. Display the settings on your mobile device.
b. Select the option to view data usage.
c. If necessary, tap the option to display a list of apps and how much data each app uses. If necessary, select the time period for which you want to see the data usage.
d. If you notice an app using a large amount of data, tap the app to see details for that app. If necessary, disable background data transfer for the app. Background data transfer is data the app downloads and uploads even while you are not actively using the app.
e. If you want your mobile device to notify you when you are approaching your monthly data limit, set the necessary notification option and select a value under your monthly data limit in the appropriate area.

f. If you want your mobile device to turn off data (this does not include Wi-Fi) when you reach a certain limit, set the necessary option and then select a value that is just less than your monthly data limit to ensure you never reach or exceed the limit.
g. Save all changes.

Exercises

1. Do you have a data limit on your mobile data plan? If so, what is it?
2. When you enter an area with Wi-Fi, do you configure your mobile device to connect to the Wi-Fi? Why or why not?
3. Review the mobile data usage on your mobile device. Which app uses the most data? Which app uses the least data?

Source: Google Inc.

➍ Search for a Job Online

If you know the company for which you would like to work, you may be able to visit that company's website and search for a webpage with current job postings. If you would like to search for openings in multiple companies, consider using a job search website. The following steps guide you through the process of searching for a job online.

a. Run a browser.
b. Use a search engine to locate a job search website and then navigate to the website.
c. Many job search websites allow you to search for jobs by criteria, such as keyword, category or location. If

How To: Your Turn ✷

you are searching for a job in a specific field, enter relevant keyword(s) (i.e., software developer) or select an appropriate category (i.e., technology). To limit your search results to a specific geographical area, specify a location (i.e., Atlanta).

d. Some websites allow you to search for jobs based on additional criteria, such as company, salary, job type, education, and experience. Specify these additional criteria by performing an advanced search.

e. After entering the job search criteria, start the search.

f. When the search results appear, scroll through the results. To find out more about a particular job, tap or click the job listing.

g. If desired, follow the instructions in the job listing to apply for the job.

Exercises

1. Review three job search websites. Which one did you like the best? Why?

2. Which keywords would you use on a job search website to search for a job in your desired field?

3. Before completing this exercise, have you ever searched for a job online? Do you think it is better to search for a job using a job search website, or by vising company websites directly and viewing their job postings? Justify your answer.

⑤ Send Email Messages Using Various Email Programs and Web Apps

The process required to send an email message using a computer or mobile device from various email programs and web apps is very similar. The following steps guide you through the process of sending email messages using various email programs and web apps.

a. Run the email program or navigate to the email web app on your computer or mobile device.

b. Locate and then tap or click the button to compose a new email message.

c. Type the recipient's email address in the To text box. If you are sending the email message to multiple recipients, separate each email address with a semicolon (;).

d. If you would like to send a carbon copy of the email message to one or

more people, type their email address(es) in the Cc text box (which stands for carbon copy).

e. To send a copy of the email message to someone while hiding his or her email address from the other recipients, enter his or her email address in the Bcc text box (which stands for blind carbon copy). The email recipients listed in the To or Cc text boxes will not be able to see the recipients you specified in the Bcc text box.

f. Enter a descriptive subject in the Subject text box. It is not good practice to leave the subject blank when you send an email message because the recipient's email server may place messages without a subject in a spam or junk mail folder.

g. Type the body of the email message in the appropriate area.

h. If your email program supports it, check the spelling of your email message and correct any errors found.

i. Tap or click the Send button, which sends the email message to everyone listed in the To, Cc, and Bcc text boxes.

Exercises

1. Under what circumstances might you want to send a blind carbon copy of an email message to one or more people?

2. Send an email message to your instructor and put your email address in the Cc text box. Use an appropriate subject and tell your instructor you have successfully completed this exercise.

3. Search for and evaluate three web apps that can send and receive email. Which one is your favorite, and why?

How an Email Message May Travel from a Sender to a Receiver

Step 1
Using an email program, you create and send a message on a computer or mobile device.

Step 2
Your email program contacts software on the outgoing mail server.

Step 3
Software on the outgoing mail server determines the best route for the data and sends the message, which travels along Internet routers to the recipient's incoming mail server.

incoming mail server

Internet router

Step 4
When the recipient uses an email program to check for email messages, the message transfers from the incoming mail server to the recipient's computer or mobile device.

Internet router

© Oleksiy Mark / Shutterstock.com; © iStockphoto / luismmolina; Courtesy of Juniper Networks; © iStockphoto / hocus-focus; © Cengage Learning; © Cengage Learning

✳ Internet Research

The Internet Research exercises broaden your understanding of module concepts by requiring that you search for information on the web.

Instructions: Use a search engine or another search tool to locate the information requested or answers to questions presented in the exercises. Describe your findings, along with the search term(s) you used and your web source(s), in the format requested by your instructor (brief report, presentation, discussion, blog post, video, or other means).

❶ Making Use of the Web
Online Social Networks and Media Sharing

Every second, an average of 5,700 Tweets and 41,000 Facebook posts are created. With these impressive numbers, it is no wonder that online social media have become ubiquitous throughout the world. Twitter, Facebook, and other online social networks, especially those featured in Mini Feature 2-2 in this module, are popular among users of all ages. Likewise, media sharing sites, such as YouTube, which is shown in Figure 2-11 in this module, are popular means of managing and sharing photos, videos, and music.

Research This: Visit two of the websites discussed in Mini Feature 2-2 or other online social networks and create a profile if you do not currently have one. What personal information is required to join? Does either website ask for personal information that you are uncomfortable sharing? How does the content of these two websites differ? Which features are beneficial for casual users, and which are targeted toward business or professional users? Then, visit two social media sites. What personal information is required to join? Are these websites supported by advertisements? Locate the instructions for posting media. Are these instructions straightforward? Do these websites impose a limit on the number and/or size of media files a user can post?

Source: Facebook

❷ Social Media

Most social media companies have invested millions of dollars to develop and maintain their websites. Unlike other commercial media, such as television, radio, and

newspapers, advertisements generally are not used to fund the majority of operating costs, nor are users required to pay monthly or annual fees for basic services that they receive at no cost. One method that social media sites use to generate start-up and ongoing subsidies is through venture capitalists' funding. These investors scrutinize business plans and market trends in an effort to locate Internet start-up companies with the potential to generate substantial returns. Once the businesses are running, additional monies are needed to maintain and improve the websites. At this point, some websites display advertisements. The charge for companies to place an advertisement generally increases as the number of subscribers grows. Another method of generating income is to charge users for accessing premium content. Online dating services use this tactic successfully, for they allow people to browse online profiles free of charge but require them to pay to contact a potential dating match.

Research This: Locate venture capitalists who are seeking Internet start-up companies. Which criteria do they use to make investment decisions? Who are the successful venture capitalists, and which companies have they funded? Which types of advertisements are displayed on specific social media and online social networks? How does the content of these ads pertain to the demographics and interests of users?

❸ Search Skills
Understand Search Results

Search results display the most relevant results first. Search results may include links to websites, news stories, images, videos, maps, and information from Wikipedia and other online databases. Results also may show links to similar searches, related people, or posts from online social networks or social media sites.

Because many search engines rely on advertising for revenue, some search results are paid advertisements. Companies and organizations may pay search providers to display links to their websites prominently in the

Internet Research ☀

search results when search text contains words relevant to their products and services. Paid ads often appear at the top or along the side of a search results page. A search results page may display an icon or use shading to specify that the search result is an advertisement.

When evaluating the reliability of search results, consider the sources of the information provided. Specialized information such as medical advice or stock performance should come from recognizable sources in those areas, while you might rely on reviews from customers when selecting a restaurant or purchasing a smartphone.

Source: Google Inc.

Research This: Type each search text phrase listed in the paragraph below into the search boxes in Bing, Google, and Yahoo! and then take a screenshot of the first page of search results from each. Compare them, identifying ads, news, images, videos, social media results, information from online databases, search tools, and common links that both search engines returned. Which search engine's results do you find more useful in each case? Why?

Type the following search text: (1) internet service providers, (2) google corporate headquarters, (3) flights from boston to los angeles, and (4) identity theft.

❹ Security

Cybercriminals may lurk in public Wi-Fi hot spots, as you learned in Secure IT 2-1 in this module. These thieves also may be on the lookout for customers entering their PIN at keypads near cash registers

or at ATMs. Body heat from fingers touching the keys remains for a short time, and a device with infrared-scanning capabilities can detect which keys are warmer than others. This device, which is readily available for purchase at cell phone accessories stores, snaps on the back of cell phones. It captures the thermal heat signatures, with the most recently touched keys glowing red and the cooler keys glowing light green. The thief, therefore, knows which keys comprise the PIN and the sequence of numbers by looking at the intensity of colors on the infrared scan.

Research This: How much does a thermal imaging cell phone case cost? Which brand of phone is more commonly used to capture thermal imaging? What steps can consumers take to thwart thieves using infrared scanning? Which key materials are less apt to retain the thermal signatures: metal, rubber, or plastic? Researchers from which university published a paper discussing thermal camera-based attacks?

❺ Cloud Services

Collaboration and Productivity (SaaS)

Microsoft's Office Online and Google Docs are online productivity suites for creating documents, presentations, spreadsheets, and other projects. Microsoft and Google offer these apps as part of their respective cloud storage services. Because documents are stored on the cloud, you can access them from any computer or device connected to the Internet.

These are examples of SaaS (software as a service), a service of cloud computing that allows access to software using a browser, without the need to install software on a computer or device. As providers update their software, users receive the latest version upon signing in. SaaS apps often allow users to collaborate and share their work with other users. Many providers offer SaaS titles at no cost; others require users to purchase a subscription or pay a fee for the features they use.

Research This: (1) Sign up for accounts on Microsoft OneDrive and Google Drive to create and store documents with Office Online and Google Docs. With each app, create a document, share it with another user, and edit it simultaneously. What is an advantage of sharing documents over sending the files by email to collaborators? (2) How do Microsoft Office Online and Google Docs compare with Microsoft Office installed on your computer? What features are available on the cloud that are not possible on a desktop version?

✳ Critical Thinking

The Critical Thinking exercises challenge your assessment and decision-making skills by presenting real-world situations associated with module concepts. The Collaboration exercise should be completed with a team.

Instructions: Evaluate the situations below, using personal experiences and one or more resources available to you (such as articles on the web or in print, blogs, podcasts, videos, television, user guides, other individuals, electronics or computer stores, etc.). Perform the tasks requested in each exercise and share your deliverables in the format requested by your instructor (brief report, presentation, discussion, blog post, video, or other means).

1. Mobile Browser Comparison

Although most mobile devices include a mobile browser, users have the option of downloading and installing other browsers.

Source: Google, Inc.

Do This: Evaluate and compare reviews of at least four mobile browsers, such as Android, Firefox, Opera, Safari, or Silk. Discuss the major differences among the browsers you researched, including number and types of features, which devices are compatible, how they display webpages, security features, and the speed at which they perform. Discuss any experiences you or your classmates have had with various browsers. Include in your discussion which mobile browser you would recommend and why.

2. Acceptable Use Policy

Most businesses provide Wi-Fi and Internet access, as well as compatible computers or devices, to employees while they are at work. While the intention is for employees to use the Internet for work-related purposes, employees often find it easy to become distracted with other activities on the Internet, such as social media, checking personal email messages, playing games, or visiting websites for entertainment. These activities can degrade Internet access for others or lead to poor performance, as well as expose the company to malware or other risks. Many businesses create an acceptable use policy (AUP) that outlines how employees should use the Internet. It also may outline consequences for unauthorized Internet use.

Do This: Locate two AUPs published online. Compare the two policies and then create a policy you believe would be fair to employees of a small business. Include guidelines for Internet use during breaks, use of smartphones, and restrictions for using social media.

3. Case Study

Amateur Sports League You are the new manager for a nonprofit amateur soccer league. The league needs a website. You prepare information about the website to present to the board of directors.

Do This: First, you plan the website by determining its purpose and audience. Use a search engine to locate two sports league websites, and print their home pages. Identify what you like and do not like about each. Think about the design of your website, and select the colors you would recommend. Describe the types of media you would include on the webpage and give specific examples, such as a logo, photos or a slide show, or links to videos. Make a sketch of the home page layout, including navigation, media, and text. Research content management systems. Evaluate whether you could use a preformatted template to meet your needs, and find what types of customization options are available. Determine whether you need a separate ISP for hosting the website, and calculate the costs. List ways you will maintain and update the site content. Compile your findings.

Collaboration

4. Website Evaluation
You and three teammates want to open a new chain of fast food sandwich shops. You envision a website that includes a menu, nutritional options, and allergy information, and that has regular promotions and special offers.

Do This: With your teammates, evaluate existing fast food and sandwich websites by comparing the advantages and disadvantages of each. Assign each member the task of evaluating one chain. Team members should print the home page of the assigned website and evaluate each restaurants' website. Pay particular attention to the following areas: (1) design, (2) ease of use, (3) menu, (4) nutritional information, (5) allergy information, (6) special offers, (7) location information and directions, and (8) hours and contact information. Summarize your evaluations and rank the websites in terms of their effectiveness. Be sure to include brief explanations supporting your rankings.

People use or interact with a variety of computers or mobile devices every day.

"I use my laptop at home and school and an all-in-one at work. I send messages and access the Internet on my smartphone, take photos with my digital camera, and read books on my e-book reader. What more do I need to know about computers and mobile devices?"

While you may be familiar with some of the content in this module, do you know how to ...

- Protect computers and devices from malware infections?
- Determine which mobile computer, desktop, or mobile device to purchase?
- Safely use an ATM?
- Rent a movie using a DVD kiosk?
- Help eliminate e-waste?
- Use a mobile device safely in a public area?
- Identify a DisplayPort or an HDMI port?
- Pair Bluetooth devices?
- Connect your phone to a Wi-Fi network to save data charges?
- Protect your hardware from theft, vandalism, and failure?
- Prevent technology-related tendonitis or CTS?
- Tell if you are addicted to technology?
- Manage power for your computers and mobile devices

In this module, you will discover how to perform these tasks along with much more information essential to this course.

© iStockPhoto / German

✔ Objectives

After completing this module, you will be able to:

1　Describe the characteristics and uses of laptops, tablets, desktops, and all-in-ones

2　Describe the characteristics and types of servers

3　Differentiate among POS terminals, ATMs, and self-service kiosks

4　Describe cloud computing and identify its uses

5　Describe the characteristics and uses of smartphones, digital cameras, portable and digital media players, e-book readers, and wearable devices

6　Describe the characteristics of and ways to interact with game devices, including gamepads, joysticks and wheels, dance pads, and motion-sensing controllers

7　Identify uses of embedded computers

8　Differentiate a port from a connector, identify various ports and connectors, and differentiate among Bluetooth, Wi-Fi, and NFC wireless device connections

9　Identify safeguards against hardware theft and vandalism and hardware failure

10　Discuss ways to prevent health-related injuries and disorders caused from technology use, and describe ways to design a workplace ergonomically

Computers and Mobile Devices

As Module 1 discussed, a **computer** is an electronic device, operating under the control of instructions stored in its own memory, that can accept data (input), process the data according to specified rules, produce information (output), and store the information for future use. A **mobile device** is a computing device small enough to hold in your hand. Types of computers and mobiles devices include laptops, tablets, and desktops; servers and terminals; smartphones, digital cameras, e-book readers, portable and digital media players, and wearable devices; game devices; and embedded computers. Figure 3-1 shows a variety of computers and mobile devices.

In addition to discussing features, functions, and purchasing guidelines of computers and mobile devices, this module also presents ways to connect peripheral devices, protect computers and mobile devices from theft and failure, and minimize your health risks while using computers and mobile devices.

Mobile Computers and Desktops

A **mobile computer** is a portable personal computer, such as a laptop or tablet, designed so that a user easily can carry it from place to place, whereas a desktop is designed to be in a stationary location. A *personal computer* (PC) is a mobile computer or desktop that can perform all of its input, processing, output, and storage activities by itself and is intended to be used by one person at a time. Personal computers often are differentiated by the type of operating system they use, with Windows and Mac operating systems leading the market share. Companies such as Acer, Dell, Lenovo, HP (Hewlett-Packard), and Samsung sell personal computers that use the Windows operating system, and Apple sells personal computers that use the Mac operating system. Other operating systems for personal computers include Linux and Chrome OS.

Read Secure IT 3-1 for suggestions about how to avoid malware infections on your computers and mobile devices.

 BTW
Peripheral Devices
A *peripheral device* is a device you connect to a computer or mobile device to expand its capabilities. Examples include a keyboard, mouse, microphone, monitor, printer, scanner, external hard drive, webcam, and speakers.

 BTW
The term PC sometimes is used to describe a computer that runs a Windows operating system.

Computers and Mobile Devices

Figure 3-1 Computers and mobile devices are available in a variety of shapes and sizes.

SECURE IT 3-1

Avoid Malware Infections

Some websites contain tempting offers to download free games and music, install toolbars that offer convenience, enter contests, and receive coupons on your computers or mobile devices. Danger, however, may lurk in those files, for they secretly could install malware with effects ranging from a mild annoyance to a severe problem such as identity theft. Recall that malware is malicious software that acts without your knowledge and deliberately alters operations of your computer or mobile device. As a general rule, do not install or download unfamiliar software. Follow these guidelines to minimize the chance of your computer or mobile device becoming infected with malware:

- **Social media:** Malware authors often focus on social media, with the goal of stealing personal information, such as passwords, profiles, contact lists, and credit card account details. Their websites urge unsuspecting users to take surveys, tap or click links to obtain free merchandise and games, and download antivirus programs. Ignore these deceitful tactics.

- **Email:** Spam (unsolicited email messages) can be loaded with malware, but even email messages from friends can be a

culprit. If the message does not contain a subject line or contains links or an attachment, exercise caution. One option is to save the attachment to your computer so that antivirus software can scan the file for possible malware before you open it. Your best practice is to avoid opening suspicious messages at all costs.

- **Flash memory storage:** Colleagues and friends may hand you a USB flash drive or memory card with software, photos, and other files. Scan these media with security software before opening any files.

- **Pop-up windows:** At times, a window may open suddenly (called a pop-up window), with a warning that your computer is infected with a virus or that a security breach has occurred, and then make an urgent request to download free software to scan your computer or mobile device and correct the alleged problem. Beware. Many of these offers actually are rogue security software that will infect a computer.

- **Websites:** Websites you visit or pop-up windows may present instructions to download new software or update current programs installed on a computer or mobile device. If you are uncertain of their legitimacy, exit and research the software

by reading reviews online before you decide to install it.

- **Software:** Occasionally, some seemingly safe software attempts to install malware. Even worse, some software touted as offering malware protection actually installs more malware. Always obtain software from reputable sources and, if possible, update software directly from manufacturers' websites. Consider using the custom installation option to ensure that only the desired software is installed. Read the permissions dialog boxes that are displayed on your screen before tapping or clicking the OK or Agree buttons. If you are uncertain about the messages you are viewing, cancel the installation.

- **Smartphones:** Malware creators are targeting smartphones, particularly those using the Android operating system. While an estimated 80 percent of all smartphones are unprotected now, savvy users are obtaining protection from malware attacks. Read reviews before downloading antimalware apps from trusted sources.

✹ **Consider This:** What online activities might cause malware to be installed on your computer? Which specific websites provide reputable antimalware apps for mobile devices? What new techniques will you use to avoid malware?

✹ CONSIDER THIS

What is inside a personal computer?

The electronic components and circuitry of a personal computer usually are part of or are connected to a motherboard (Figure 3-2). A *motherboard*, sometimes called a system board, is the main circuit board of the personal computer. Many electronic components attach to the motherboard; others are built into it. Two main components on the motherboard are the processor and memory. Many motherboards also integrate sound, video, and networking capabilities. A *processor*, also called a *CPU* (central processing unit), is the electronic component that interprets and carries out the basic instructions that operate a computer. Memory consists of electronic components that store instructions waiting to be executed and data needed by those instructions.

 Internet Research

What is a computer chip?

Search for: computer chip

Figure 3-2 Shown here is a partial motherboard in a laptop.
© rawgroup / Fotolia

Laptops, Tablets, and Other Mobile Computers

A **laptop**, also called a *notebook computer*, is a thin, lightweight mobile computer with a screen in its lid and a keyboard in its base (Figure 3-3). Designed to fit on your lap and for easy transport, most laptops weigh up to 7 pounds (varying by manufacturer and specifications) and can be as powerful as the average desktop.

Laptops have input devices, such as a keyboard, touchpad, and webcam; output devices, such as a screen and speakers; a storage device(s), such as a hard drive and maybe an optical disc drive; and usually built-in wireless communications capability. Some laptops have touch screens. Most can operate on batteries or a power supply or both. Read Ethics & Issues 3-1 to consider issues related to laptops and other devices with cameras.

traditional laptop

ultrathin laptop

Figure 3-3   Traditional laptops weigh more than ultrathin laptops.
© Sergey Peterman / Shutterstock.com; © iStockphoto / Skip Odonnell; Microsoft; Apple, Inc.

✳ ETHICS & ISSUES 3-1

What Punishment for Webcam Spying Is Appropriate?

Microphones, digital cameras, and webcams have many practical and harmless uses. These technologies also can leave you open to spying. For example, one school district used software, which was supposed to track the school-distributed laptops in case of theft, to take photos and screen captures of students. In another instance, a person noticed that when she gave a customer service rep access to her computer, he turned on her webcam without asking for her permission.

Cybercriminals can use spy tools that take photos, or record video or audio, without turning on a light or other notification that indicates your camera or microphone is in use. The Flame virus is one way for spy tools to infect your computer. Security experts recommend using a sticker to cover your webcam, and inserting a dummy plug in the microphone port when you are not using it. These technologies also allow people to take photos or videos in a public setting and share them without your knowledge. A director at the American Civil Liberties Union stated that when you are in a public place, people have the right to photograph you. Privacy advocates criticize *Google Street View*, however, which takes images captured using moving vehicles equipped with GPS and cameras and then creates a panoramic view of an area, including people entering and exiting buildings or relaxing on a beach.

Many states' laws do not cover these types of acts. Massachusetts, however, recently passed a law that made secretly taking photos or videos that focused on people's private body parts a criminal offense. Lawmakers continue to debate and expand current laws, as well as pass new ones.

Consider This: Should webcam spying punishments be comparable to other types of spying? Why or why not? What kind of privacy should you expect when you are in a public place?

Ultrathin laptops weigh less than traditional laptops, usually have a longer battery life, and generally run the Windows operating system. In order to minimize their thickness, many ultrathin laptops have fewer ports than traditional laptops, do not include an optical disc drive, and often require the use of special dongles to attach cables that connect to external displays or a network. (Recall that a dongle is a small device that connects to a computer and enables additional functions when attached.)

 BTW
Ultrabooks
An ultrathin laptop that uses a low-power Intel processor often is called an *ultrabook*.

Tablets Usually smaller than a laptop but larger than a phone, a **tablet** is a thin, lighter-weight mobile computer that has a touch screen.

Two popular form factors (shapes and sizes) of tablets are the slate and convertible (Figure 3-4). Resembling a letter-sized pad, a *slate tablet* is a type of tablet that does not contain a physical keyboard. A *convertible tablet* is a tablet that has a screen it its lid and a keyboard in its base, with the lid and base connected by a swivel-type hinge. You can use a convertible tablet like a traditional laptop, or you can rotate the display and fold it down over the keyboard so that it looks like a slate tablet. As with laptops, tablets run on batteries or a power supply or both; however, batteries in a tablet typically last longer than those in laptops.

Some tablets include a *stylus*, which looks like a small ink pen, that you can use instead of a fingertip to enter data, make selections, or draw on a touch screen. A stylus may include buttons you can press to simulate clicking a mouse. As an alternative to interacting with the touch screen, some users prefer to purchase a separate physical keyboard that attaches to or wirelessly communicates with the tablet (shown with the slate tablet in Figure 3-4).

Tablets are useful especially for taking notes in class, at meetings, at conferences, and in other forums where the standard laptop is not practical. Because slate tablets can have a more durable construction, they often are used in the medical field and other areas where exposure to germs, heat, humidity, dust, and other contaminants is greater.

 BTW

Pens
Some tablet manufacturers refer to a stylus as a pen.

magnetic keyboard cover

slate tablet in stand

convertible tablet

stylus

Figure 3-4 Examples of slate and convertible tablets.
Courtesy of Microsoft; © iStockPhoto / rasslava

 CONSIDER THIS

What is a phablet?
Some manufacturers use the term, *phablet*, to refer to a device that combines features of a smartphone with a tablet (Figure 3-5). These devices are larger than smartphones but smaller than full-sized tablets. The screen on a phablet usually measures five to seven inches diagonally. Some include a stylus.

Figure 3-5 A phablet combines features of a smartphone and a tablet.
© iStockPhoto / Krystian Nawrocki

Handheld Computers

A *handheld computer* is a computer small enough to fit in one hand. Many handheld computers communicate wirelessly with other devices or computers. Some handheld computers have miniature or specialized keyboards. Others have a touch screen and also include a stylus for input.

Many handheld computers are industry-specific and serve the needs of mobile employees, such as parcel delivery people or warehouse employees (Figure 3-6), whose jobs require them to move from place to place. Handheld computers often send data wirelessly to central office computers.

Figure 3-6 This handheld computer is a lightweight computer that enables warehouse employees to take inventory and check supplies.
© iStockphoto / Ermin Gutenberger

Mini Feature 3-1: Mobile Computer Buyer's Guide

If you need computing capability while traveling and during lectures or meetings, you may find a laptop or tablet to be an appropriate choice. Read Mini Feature 3-1 for tips to consider when purchasing a mobile computer.

 MINI FEATURE 3-1

Mobile Computer Buyer's Guide

With the abundance of mobile computer manufacturers, research each before making a purchase. The following are purchasing considerations unique to mobile computers.

© iStockPhoto / vtls

1. **Determine which mobile computer form factor fits your needs.** Consider a tablet or ultrathin laptop if you require a lightweight device and the most mobility. If you require additional ports or want the computer's capabilities to be more comparable to a desktop, consider purchasing a traditional laptop.

2. **Consider a mobile computer with a sufficiently large screen.** Laptops and tablets are available with various screen sizes. For example, most traditional and ultrathin laptop screens range in size from 11 to 18 inches, while most tablet screens range in size from 7 to 12 inches.

3. **Experiment with different keyboards and pointing devices.** Mobile computers often vary in size, and for that reason have different keyboard layouts. Familiarize yourself with the keyboard layout of the computer you want to purchase, and make sure it is right for you. If you have large fingers, for example, you should not purchase a computer with a small, condensed keyboard. Laptops typically include a touchpad to control the pointer. Tablets have a touch screen and an on-screen keyboard.

4. **Consider processor, memory, and storage upgrades at the time of purchase.** As with a desktop, upgrading a mobile computer's memory and internal storage may be less expensive at the time of initial purchase. Some internal storage is custom designed for mobile computer manufacturers, meaning an upgrade might not be available in the future.

5. **The availability of built-in ports and slots is important.** Determine which ports and slots (discussed later in this module) you require on the mobile computer. If you plan to transfer photos from a digital camera using a memory card, consider a mobile computer with a built-in card slot compatible with your digital camera's memory card. If you plan to connect devices such as a printer or USB flash drive to your mobile computer, consider purchasing one with a sufficient number of USB ports. In addition, evaluate mobile computers with ports enabling you to connect an external monitor.

6. **If you plan to use your mobile computer for a long time without access to an electrical outlet, or if the battery life for the mobile computer you want to purchase is not sufficient, consider purchasing a second battery.** Some mobile computers, such as most tablets and ultrathin laptops, have built-in batteries that can be replaced only by a qualified technician. In that case, you might look into options for external battery packs or power sources.

7. **Purchase a well-padded and well-designed carrying case that is comfortable and ergonomic.** An amply padded carrying case will protect your mobile computer from the bumps it may receive while traveling. A well-designed carrying case will have room for accessories such as USB flash drives, pens, and paperwork. Although a mobile computer may be small enough to fit in a handbag, make sure that the bag has sufficient padding to protect the computer. Test the carrying case with the laptop inside to ensure it is comfortable and ergonomic.

8. **If you plan to connect your mobile computer to a video projector, make sure the mobile computer is compatible with the video projector.** You should check, for example, to be sure that your mobile computer will allow you to display an image on the screen and projection device at the same time. Also, ensure that the mobile computer has the ports required or that you have the necessary dongle and cables to connect to the video projector.

☀ **Consider This:** Based on your current computing needs, should you purchase a traditional laptop, ultrathin laptop, or tablet? What are the specifications of the mobile computer you would purchase?

Desktops and All-in-Ones

A **desktop**, or desktop computer, is a personal computer designed to be in a stationary location, where all of its components fit on or under a desk or table (Figure 3-7). Components that typically occupy space outside of a desktop include peripheral devices such as a keyboard, mouse, and webcam (input devices); speakers and printer (output devices); external hard drive (storage device); and possibly a router and/or modem (communications devices). Depending on the form factor of the desktop, it may also require an external monitor.

Some people use the term, *system unit*, to refer to the case that contains and protects the motherboard, internal hard drive, memory, and other electronic components of the computer from damage. A desktop may have a system unit tower that is a separate device from a monitor. A *tower*, which is made of metal or plastic, is a frame that houses the system unit on a desktop. Towers are available in a variety of form factors. Although they can range in height from 12 inches to 30 inches or more, the trend is toward smaller desktop tower form factors. An **all-in-one** (AIO) or *all-in-one desktop*, by contrast, does not have a tower and instead houses the display, system unit, and possibly an optical drive, in the same case.

BTW
Monitor Speakers
Many monitors have integrated speakers.

Figure 3-7   The desktop with a tower shown in this figure is a Windows computer, and the all-in-one is a Mac computer.
© George Dolgikh / Shutterstock.com; © iStockphoto / Skip Odonnell; © iStockphoto / Evgeny Kuklev; © Cengage Learning; Microsoft; Apple, Inc.

CONSIDER THIS

Who uses desktops?
Home and business users who do not require the portability of a mobile computer may work with desktops for their everyday computing needs. Gaming enthusiasts often choose a *gaming desktop*, which offers high-quality audio, video, and graphics with optimal performance for sophisticated single-user and networked or Internet multiplayer games. Power users may work with a high-end desktop, sometimes called a *workstation*, that is designed to handle intense calculations and sophisticated graphics. For example, architects use powerful desktops to design buildings and homes, and graphic artists use them to create computer-animated special effects for full-length motion pictures and video games. Some users configure a desktop to function as a server on a network (servers are discussed later in this module).

Internet Research
Which movies use computer animation?
Search for: movies using computer animation

Mini Feature 3-2: Desktop Buyer's Guide

Desktops are a suitable option if you work mostly in one place and have plenty of space in a work area. Read Mini Feature 3-2 for tips to consider when purchasing a desktop.

 MINI FEATURE 3-2

Desktop Buyer's Guide

Today, desktop manufacturers emphasize desktop style by offering bright colors, trendy displays, and theme-based towers so that the computer looks attractive if it is in an area of high visibility. If you have decided that a desktop is most suited to your technology needs, the next step is to determine specific software, hardware, peripheral devices, and services to purchase, as well as where to buy the computer. The following considerations will help you determine the appropriate desktop to purchase.

© Alexey Salo / Photos.com

1. **Determine the specific software to use on the desktop.** Decide which software contains the features necessary for the tasks you want to perform. Your hardware requirements depend on the minimum requirements of the software you plan to use on the desktop.

2. **Know the system requirements of the operating system.** Determine the operating system you want to use because this also dictates hardware requirements. If, however, you purchase a new desktop, chances are it will include the latest version of your preferred operating system (Windows, Mac OS, or Linux).

3. **Look for bundled software.** Purchasing software at the same time you purchase a desktop may be less expensive than purchasing the software at a later date.

4. **Avoid purchasing the least powerful desktop available.** Technology changes rapidly, which means a desktop that seems powerful enough today may not serve your computing needs in the future. Purchasing a desktop with the most memory, largest hard drive capacity, and fastest processor you can afford will help delay obsolescence.

5. **Consider upgrades to the keyboard, mouse, monitor, printer, microphone, and speakers.** You use these peripheral devices to interact with the desktop, so make sure they meet your standards.

6. **Consider a touch screen monitor.** A touch screen monitor will enable you to interact with the latest operating systems and apps using touch input.

7. **Evaluate all-in-ones, which may be less expensive than purchasing a tower and monitor separately.** In addition, all-in-ones take up less space and often look more attractive than desktops with separate towers.

8. **If you are buying a new desktop, you have several purchasing options:** buy directly from a school bookstore, a local computer dealer, or a large retail store, or order from a vendor by mail, phone, or the web. Each purchasing option has its advantages. Explore each option to find the best combination of price and service.

9. **Be aware of additional costs.** Along with the desktop itself, you also may need to make extra purchases. For example, you might purchase computer furniture, an uninterruptable power supply (UPS) or surge protector (discussed later in the module), an external hard drive, a printer, a router, or a USB flash drive.

10. **If you use your computer for business or require fast resolution of major computer problems, consider purchasing an extended warranty or a service plan through a local dealer or third-party company.** Most extended warranties cover the repair and replacement of computer components beyond the standard warranty.

☀ **Consider This:** Shop around for a desktop that meets your current needs. Which desktop would you purchase? Why?

Table 3-1 Dedicated Servers

Type	Main Service Provided
Application server	Stores and runs apps
Backup server	Backs up and restores files, folders, and media
Database server	Stores and provides access to a database
Domain name server	Stores domain names and their corresponding IP addresses
File server (or *storage server*)	Stores and manages files
FTP server	Stores files for user upload or download via FTP
Game server	Provides a central location for online gaming
Home server	Provides storage, Internet connections, or other services to computers and devices in a household
List server	Stores and manages email lists
Mail server	Stores and delivers email messages
Network server	Manages network traffic
Print server	Manages printers and documents being printed
Web server	Stores and delivers requested webpages to a computer via a browser

© Cengage Learning

Servers

A **server** is a computer dedicated to providing one or more services to other computers or devices on a network. Services provided by servers include storing content and controlling access to hardware, software, and other resources on a network. In many cases, a server accesses data, information, and programs on another server. In other cases, personal computers, devices, or terminals (discussed in the next section) access data, information, and programs on a server. Servers can support from two to several thousand connected computers or devices at the same time.

Some servers, called dedicated servers, perform a specific service and can be placed with other dedicated servers to perform multiple services (Table 3-1). Each type of dedicated server uses software designed specifically to manage its service. Dedicated servers typically require a faster processor, more memory, and additional storage.

Servers typically include a processor, memory, storage, and network connections. Depending on its function, a server may or may not require a monitor or an input device. Some servers are controlled from remote computers. Form factors for servers include rack server, blade server, and tower server, which are shown in Figure 3-8 and briefly described below.

rack server

blade server

rack

blade server chassis

tower server

Figure 3-8 Shown here are a rack server, blade server, and tower server.
© iStockphoto / Godfried Edelman; © iStockphoto / luismmolina; © iStockphoto / evirgen;
© iStockphoto / Alexander Shirokov; © iStockphoto / luismmolina

- A *rack server*, sometimes called a rack-mounted server, is a server that is housed in a slot (bay) on a metal frame (rack). A rack can contain multiple servers, each in a different bay. The rack is fastened in place to a flat surface.
- A *blade server* is a server in the form of a single circuit board, or blade. The individual blades insert in a blade server chassis that can hold many blades. Like a rack server, the chassis is fastened in place to a flat surface.
- A *tower server* is a server built into an upright cabinet (tower) that stands alone. The tower can be similar in size and shape to a desktop tower or larger.

✺ CONSIDER THIS ————————

Which server should you use?

Home or small business users and organizations with ample floor space often choose tower servers. (Some home users even use a desktop tower or powerful laptop to act as a home server.) Data centers and other organizations looking to conserve floor space often choose rack servers or blade servers. Organizations that require a large quantity of servers usually opt for blade servers.

Some organizations use virtualization to improve utilization of technology. *Virtualization* is the practice of sharing or pooling computing resources, such as servers and storage devices. *Server virtualization* uses software to enable a physical server to emulate the hardware and computing capabilities of one or more servers, known as virtual servers. Users can use software to configure the storage, processing power, memory, operating system, and other characteristics of virtual servers. From the end user's point of view, a virtual server behaves just like a physical server. The advantages are that a virtual server can be created and configured quickly, does not require a new physical server, and is easier to manage. Cloud computing, discussed later in this module, uses server virtualization.

Major corporations use server farms, mainframes, or other types of servers for business activities to process everyday transactions (Figure 3-9). A *server farm* is a network of several servers together in a single location. Server farms make it possible to combine the power of multiple servers. A *mainframe* is a large, expensive, powerful server that can handle hundreds or thousands of connected users simultaneously. Enterprises use server farms, mainframes, or other large servers to bill millions of customers, prepare payroll for thousands of employees, and manage millions of items in inventory.

Figure 3-9   Server farms and mainframes can handle thousands of connected computers and process millions of instructions per second.
© Sashkin / Shutterstock.com

Terminals

A *terminal* is a computer, usually with limited processing power, that enables users to send data to and/or receive information from a server, or host computer. The host computer processes the data and then, if necessary, sends information (output) back to the terminal. Terminals may include a monitor and/or touch screen, keyboard, and memory.

A *thin client* is a terminal that looks like a desktop but has limited capabilities and components. Because thin clients typically do not contain a hard drive, they run programs and access data on a network or the Internet. Public locations, such as libraries and schools, and enterprises sometimes use thin clients because they cost less, are easier to maintain, last longer, use less power, and are less susceptible to malware attacks than desktops.

Special-purpose terminals perform specific tasks and contain features uniquely designed for use in a particular industry. Three widely used special-purpose terminals are point-of-sale (POS) terminals, ATMs, and self-service kiosks.

Point-of-Sale Terminals

The location in a retail or grocery store where a consumer pays for goods or services is the point of sale (POS). Most retail stores use a *POS terminal* to record purchases, process credit or debit cards, and update inventory.

touch screen

bar code reader scans bar code on item being purchased

Figure 3-10   Many grocery stores offer self-service checkouts, where consumers use POS terminals to scan purchases, scan their store or saver card and coupons, and then pay for the goods.
© Valentyna Chukhlyebova / Shutterstock; © iStockPhoto / 00one

In a grocery store, the POS terminal is a combination of an electronic cash register, bar code reader, and printer (Figure 3-10). A *bar code reader* is an input device that uses laser beams to read bar codes on products. When the checkout clerk or customer scans the bar code on the grocery item, the computer uses the manufacturer name and item numbers to look up the price of the item and the complete product name. Then, the price of the item shows on the display device, the name of the item and its price print on a receipt, and the item being sold is recorded so that the inventory can be updated. Thus, the output from a POS terminal serves as input to other computers to maintain sales records, update inventory, verify credit, and perform other activities associated with the sales transactions that are critical to running the business. Some POS terminals are Internet capable, which allows updates to inventory at geographically separate locations.

Many POS terminals handle credit card or debit card payments. After swiping your card through the reader, the POS terminal connects to a system that authenticates the purchase. Once the transaction is approved, the terminal prints a receipt for the customer.

ATMs

An *ATM* (automated teller machine) is a self-service banking terminal that connects to a host computer through a network (Figure 3-11). Banks place ATMs in public locations, including grocery stores, convenience stores, retail outlets, shopping malls, sports and concert venues, and gas stations, so that customers can access their bank accounts conveniently.

Using an ATM, people withdraw and deposit money, transfer funds, or inquire about an account balance. Some ATMs have a touch screen; others have special buttons or keypads for entering data. To access a bank account, you insert a plastic bank card in the ATM's card reader. The ATM asks you to enter a numeric password, called a *PIN* (personal identification number), which verifies that you are the holder of the bank card. When your transaction is complete, the ATM prints a receipt for your records. Read Secure IT 3-2 for ATM safety tips.

Figure 3-11   An ATM is a self-service banking terminal that allows customers to access their bank accounts.
© bankerwin / Fotolia

SECURE IT 3-2

ATM Safety

Visiting an ATM to withdraw or deposit money is convenient, but it also is ripe with potential for criminal activity. Avoid being a victim by exercising common sense and following these guidelines.

- **Location:** Choose an ATM in a well-lit public area away from bushes and dividers and near the entrance of a building. If using a drive-up ATM, keep the engine running and doors locked, roll windows up while waiting for the ATM to process your request, and leave adequate room to maneuver between your vehicle and the one in the lane in front of you. Observe your surroundings and be suspicious of people sitting in vehicles or loitering nearby.

- **ATM card and PIN:** Handle the ATM card like cash by keeping it in a safe location and storing it in a protective sleeve. Do not write the PIN on the back of the card or store it in a text file on your smartphone; instead, memorize the numbers. (For information about password manager apps, read Secure IT 5-3 in Module 5.) Report a lost or stolen card immediately.

- **Transaction:** Minimize time by having the ATM card ready as you approach the machine. Do not allow people to watch your activity. Cover the keypad or screen with one hand as you enter the PIN, and use your body to block as much of the area as possible. If the ATM screen appears different, behaves unusually, or offers options with which you are unfamiliar or uncomfortable, cancel the transaction and leave the area.

- **Be suspicious of skimmers:** Thieves can capture a credit card number and PIN by placing a *skimmer* on an ATM (shown in the figure) or on other self-service stations, such as gas pumps, where users swipe their credit cards for payment. Sophisticated skimmers are Bluetooth enabled or are entire panels placed directly on top of the ATM faces and are virtually undetectable. Less-technical devices are false card readers secured to the card slot with double-sided tape and a hidden camera or an overlay on the keypad. Many ATMs have security stickers informing customers to notify attendants if the seal is broken.

- **Valuables:** Expensive clothes and jewelry can be incentives to potential assailants. Dress modestly and leave jewels at home.

- **Exiting:** Do not count cash in public; immediately put it in your pocket or fold it in your hand. If you receive a receipt, take

skimmer

© photobeginner / Shutterstock

it with you and do not discard it in a trash can near the area. As you leave, be certain you are not being followed. If you suspect someone is tracking you, immediately walk to a populated area or business, or drive to a police or fire station.

- **Statements:** Review your balances and bank statements frequently. Be certain all deposits and withdrawals are listed, and look for unusual or unfamiliar activity.

☀ **Consider This:** Which of these tips do you follow, and how will you change your behavior the next time you visit an ATM or other self-service stations? Which ATMs in your neighborhood appear to be in safe locations?

Self-Service Kiosks

A self-service *kiosk* is a freestanding terminal that usually has a touch screen for user interaction. Table 3-2 identifies several widely used self-service kiosks. Because users interact with self-service kiosks independently, without a salesperson nearby, it is important the kiosk is simple and easy to use. In many cases, a web app or mobile app can extend or enhance the capability of the kiosk. For example, you can reserve an item via the app on a computer or mobile device and then use the kiosk to finalize the transaction.

Internet Research

What is a mobile boarding pass?

Search for: mobile boarding pass

Table 3-2 Self-Service Kiosks

Type	Typical Services Provided
Financial kiosk	Pay bills, add minutes to phone plans, add money to prepaid cards, and perform other financial activities.
Photo kiosk	Print photos from digital images. Some allow editing of digital photos. Users may print directly at the kiosk or may send an order to a photo lab to be printed.
Ticket kiosk	Print tickets. Located in airports, amusement parks, movie theaters, rental companies, and train stations.
Vending kiosk	Dispense item after payment is received. Examples include DVD rentals and license plate renewals.
Visitor kiosk	Manage and track visitors upon check-in. Located in businesses, schools, hospitals, and other areas where access is controlled or registration is required.

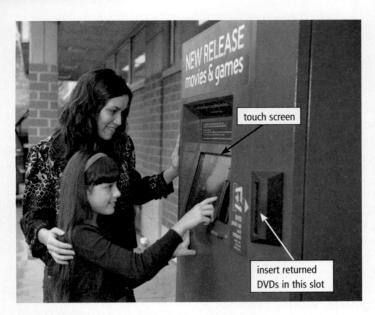

touch screen

insert returned
DVDs in this slot

Figure 3-12 A DVD kiosk is a self-service DVD rental terminal.
Courtesy of Redbox

A *DVD kiosk*, for example, is a self-service DVD rental machine that connects to a host computer through a network (Figure 3-12). DVD kiosks are associated with a particular vendor. To rent a movie online, for example, a customer establishes an account or connects to an existing account on the vendor's website, selects the desired movie, and then chooses a nearby DVD kiosk where the movie will be picked up. Customers also usually can select movies directly at the DVD kiosk via a touch screen or some other input device on the kiosk. After presenting identifying information and swiping a credit card through the reader, the DVD kiosk dispenses the rented movie to the customer. The customer returns it to any of the vendor's nationwide DVD kiosks, at which time the customer's account is charged a fee based on the time elapsed.

Supercomputers

A *supercomputer* is the fastest, most powerful computer — and the most expensive (Figure 3-13). Supercomputers are capable of processing many trillions of instructions in a single second. With weights that exceed 100 tons, these computers can store more than 20,000 times the data and information of an average desktop.

Applications requiring complex, sophisticated mathematical calculations use supercomputers. For example, large-scale simulations and applications in medicine, aerospace, automotive design, online banking, weather forecasting, nuclear energy research, and petroleum exploration use a supercomputer.

Internet Research

How is the fastest supercomputer used?

Search for: fastest supercomputer

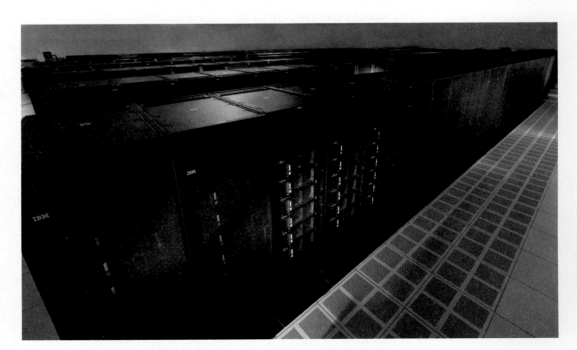

Figure 3-13 Supercomputers can process more than one quadrillion instructions in a single second.
Los Alamos National Laboratory

NOW YOU SHOULD KNOW ———————————————————————————

Be sure you understand the material presented in the sections titled Computers and Mobile Devices, Mobile Computers and Desktops, Servers, Terminals, and Supercomputers, as it relates to the module objectives.
Now you should know . . .

- What you should consider when purchasing a desktop or mobile computer (Objective 1)
- When you would use specific types of servers (Objective 2)
- How you use a POS terminal, ATM, and self-service kiosk (Objective 3)

Cloud Computing

Cloud computing refers to an environment that provides resources and services accessed via the Internet (Figure 3-14). Resources include email messages, schedules, music, photos, videos, games, websites, programs, web apps, servers, storage, and more. Services include accessing software, storing files online, and configuring an environment of servers for optimal performance. That is, instead of accessing these resources and services locally, you access them on the cloud. For example, you use cloud computing capabilities when you store or access documents, photos, videos, and other media online; use programs and apps online (i.e., email, productivity, games, etc.); and share ideas, opinions, and content with others online (i.e., online social networks).

⚙ **BTW**
The Cloud
The cloud-shaped symbol, which today universally represents cloud computing, stems from early diagrams that visually portrayed the Internet as a cloud, intangible and widespread.

Figure 3-14   Users access resources on the cloud through their Internet connections.

Businesses use cloud computing to more efficiently manage resources, such as servers and programs, by shifting usage and consumption of these resources from a local environment to the Internet. For example, an employee working during the day in California could use computing resources located in an office in Paris that is closed for the evening. When the company uses the computing resources, it pays a fee that is based on the amount of computing time and other resources it consumes, much in the way that consumers pay utility companies for the amount of electricity used.

Cloud computing allows a company to diversify its network and server infrastructure. Some cloud computing services automatically add more network and server capacity to a company's website as demand for services of the website increases. The network and server capacity may be duplicated around the world so that, for example, an outage of a single server does not affect the company's operations.

 Internet Research

How secure is the cloud?

Search for: cloud privacy issues

 CONSIDER THIS ——————————————————————————

Are all cloud services available to everyone?
Some cloud services are public and others are private. A public cloud is made available free or for a fee to the general public or a large group, usually by a cloud service provider. A private cloud is dedicated to a single organization. Some cloud services are hybrid, combining two or more cloud types.

Mobile Devices

A mobile device is a computing device small enough to hold in your hand. Because of their reduced size, the screens on mobile devices are small — often between 3 and 5 inches. Popular types of mobile devices are smartphones, digital cameras, portable and digital media players, e-book readers, and wearable devices. Read Ethics & Issues 3-2 to consider issues related to recycling computers and mobile devices.

ETHICS & ISSUES 3-2 ——————————————————————————

Should Recycling of Electronics Be Made Easier?
As technology advances and prices fall, many people think of computers and mobile devices as disposable. Worldwide, consumers generate an estimated 20 to 50 million tons of e-waste annually. (Recall that e-waste consists of discarded computers and mobile devices.) E-waste releases lead, mercury, barium, and other elements into soil and water.

Electronics recycling is known as eCycling. Only about 12 percent of e-waste is eCycled. Electronics recycling can take several forms: reusing parts; creating new products from old products; or melting down or reducing parts to basic elements or materials.

Many not-for-profit organizations, retail websites, mobile service providers, and big box retailers offer reselling and eCycling options. Several electronics companies allow you to trade your device for a gift certificate. The Sustainable Materials Management (SMM) Electronics Challenge promotes eCycling by certifying recycling businesses that meet or pass qualification guidelines. Other companies focus exclusively on eCycling. One business has developed automated kiosks that tell you what your device is worth, connect you to a buyer, take your device, and dispense cash back on the spot. The U.S. Environmental Protection Agency (EPA) lists eCycling, reselling, and donation resources on its website.

A large amount of e-waste pollutes developing countries that may accept the materials for profit. A proposed federal bill, supported by many electronics manufacturers and resellers, makes it illegal for companies to export e-waste to developing countries. Currently, several states have laws that mandate eCycling.

Consider This: Should the government, manufacturers, or users be responsible for recycling of obsolete equipment? Why? What impact does exporting toxic waste have on developing nations? Should the state or federal government mandate an eCycling program for electronics? Why or why not?

Smartphones

A **smartphone** is an Internet-capable phone that usually also includes a calendar, an address book, a calculator, a notepad, games, browser, and numerous other apps. In addition to basic phone capabilities, many smartphones include these features:

- Send and receive email messages and access the web — via Wi-Fi or a mobile data plan
- Communicate wirelessly with other devices or computers
- Function as a portable media player
- Include a built-in digital camera
- Talk directly into the smartphone's microphone or into a Bluetooth headset that wirelessly communicates with the phone
- Conduct live video calls, where the parties can see each other as they speak
- Receive GPS signals to determine a user's current location
- Synchronize data and information with a computer or another mobile device
- Support voice control so that you can speak instructions to the phone and it speaks responses back to you
- Connect to external devices wirelessly, such as via BlueTooth
- Serve as a wireless access point

Many smartphones have touch screens. Instead of or in addition to an on-screen keyboard, some have a built-in mini keyboard on the front of the phone or a keyboard that slides in and out from behind the phone. Others have keypads that contain both numbers and letters. Some also include a stylus.

 CONSIDER THIS

How do you type text messages on a phone that has only a numeric keypad and no touch screen?
Each key on the keypad represents multiple characters, which are identified on the key. For example, the 2 key on the phone's keypad displays the letters a, b, and c on the key's face. On many phones, you cycle through the number, letters, and other symbols associated with a particular key by pressing a key on the keypad multiple times. To type the word, hi, for instance, you would press the 4 key (labeled with the letters g, h, and i) twice to display the letter h, pause momentarily to advance the cursor, and then press the 4 key three times to display the letter i.

A variety of options are available for typing on a smartphone (Figure 3-15). Many can display an *on-screen keyboard*, where you press keys on the screen using your fingertip or a stylus. Some phones support a *swipe keyboard app*, on which users enter words by tracing a path on an on-screen keyboard with their fingertip or stylus from one letter to the next in a continuous motion. With other phones, you press letters on the phone's keyboard or keypad. Some phones use *predictive text*, where you press one key on the keyboard or keypad for each letter in a word, and software on the phone predicts the word you want. Swipe keyboard apps and predictive text save users time when entering text on the phone.

on-screen keyboard swipe keyboard app mini keyboard keypad

slide out keyboard portable keyboard virtual keyboard speech to text

Figure 3-15 A variety of options for typing on a smartphone.

© iStockphoto / TommL; Courtesy of Nuance; © FreezeFrameStudio / Photos.com; © iStockphoto / webphotographeer; Courtesy of Jorno; © Italianestro / dreamstime .com; © iStockPhoto / Giorgio Magini; © Oleksiy Mark / Fotolia; Courtesy of Blackberry

Instead of typing on a phone's keyboard or keypad, users can enter text via a *portable keyboard*, which is a full-sized keyboard that communicates with a smartphone via a dock, cables, or wirelessly. Some portable keyboards physically attach to and remove from the device; others are wireless. Another option is a *virtual keyboard* that projects an image of a keyboard on a flat surface. Finally, some phones work with apps that convert your spoken word to text.

Messaging Services With messaging services, users can send and receive messages to and from smartphones, mobile phones, handheld game devices, other mobile devices, and computers. The type of messages you send depends primarily on the services offered by the mobile service provider that works with the phone or other mobile device you select. Many users have unlimited wireless messaging plans, while others pay a fee per message sent or received. Messaging services include text and picture/video.

With text messaging service, or *SMS* (*short message service*), users can send and receive short text messages, typically fewer than 300 characters, on a phone or other mobile device or computer. Text message services typically provide users with several options for sending and receiving messages, including:

- Mobile to mobile: Send a message from your mobile device to another mobile device.
- Mobile to email: Send a message from your mobile device to any email address.
- Mobile to provider: Send a message by entering a *common short code* (*CSC*), which is a four- or five-digit number assigned to a specific content or mobile service provider, sometimes followed by the message, for example, to a vote for a television program contestant or donate to a charity.
- Web to mobile: Send a message from a website to a mobile device or notification from a website to a mobile device with messages of breaking news and other updates, such as sports scores, stock prices, weather forecasts, incoming email messages, game notifications, and more.

 CONSIDER THIS ──────────────────────────────

What is the difference between push and pull notifications?
A *push notification*, sometimes called a server push, is a message that initiates from the sending location (such as a server) without a request from the receiver. With a *pull notification*, by contrast, receiver requests information from the sending location.

──────────────────────────────

With picture messaging service, users can send photos and audio files, as well as short text messages, to a phone or other mobile device or computer. With video messaging services, users can send short video clips, usually about 30 seconds in length, in addition to all picture messaging services. Smartphones and other mobile devices with picture/video messaging services, also called *MMS* (*multimedia message service*), typically have a digital camera built into the device. Users who expect to receive numerous picture/video messages should verify the phone has sufficient memory. Picture/video message services typically provide users these options for sending and receiving messages:

- Mobile to mobile: Send the picture/video from your mobile device to another mobile device.
- Mobile to email: Send the picture/video from your mobile device to any email address.

Internet Research

What messaging apps are recommended?

Search for: best messaging apps

If you send a picture message to a phone that does not have picture/video messaging capability, the phone usually displays a text message directing the user to a webpage that contains the picture/video message. Some online social networks allow you to send a picture/video message directly to your online profile.

 CONSIDER THIS ──────────────────────────────

Do you need a messaging service to send a text or picture/video message?
Instead of using a messaging plan from your mobile service provider, you can use a mobile messaging app to send and receive text, picture, and other message from users. Many messaging apps also provide group chat capabilities. Most messaging apps can be downloaded to your mobile device at no cost.

──────────────────────────────

Voice mail, which functions much like an answering machine, allows someone to leave a voice message for one or more people. Unlike answering machines, however, a computer in the voice mail system converts an analog voice message into digital form. Once digitized, the message is stored in a voice mailbox. A voice mailbox is a storage location on a hard drive in the voice mail system. To help users manage voice mail messages, some systems offer visual voice mail. With *visual voice mail*, users can view message details, such as the length of calls and, in some cases, read message contents instead of listening to them. Some voice mail systems can convert a voice mail message to a text message for display on a computer or mobile device, such as a smartphone, which you then can manage like any other text message.

Messaging services and voice mail systems also may be able to send messages to groups of phone numbers or email addresses. Read Secure IT 3-3 for tips about safely using smartphones and other mobile devices in public.

 BTW

Analog vs. Digital
Human speech is analog because it uses continuous (wave form) signals that vary in strength and quality. Most computers and electronic devices are digital, which use only two discrete states: on and off.

 SECURE IT 3-3 ————————————————

Safe Mobile Device Use in Public Areas

Sending a text message, updating a Facebook status, posting a Tweet, selecting a new playlist, and checking email messages are tasks you may perform using a mobile device many times each day. They all require some concentration as you focus on the device, usually while looking downward, and they distract you from events occurring around you. Using technology responsibly and safely can prevent theft and injuries.

One common method of thwarting a smartphone thief is to avoid using the phone to check the time. Potential thieves randomly ask people for the correct time. If a person stops and takes a phone out of a pocket or purse, the thief glances at the make and model and decides if it is worth snatching.

Bus stops and train stations are common places for mobile device theft. People in these locations tend to use their smartphones to check schedules, send text messages, and make phone calls. Headphones and earbuds are giveaways that you are using a mobile device and may not be focused on your surroundings. Recent studies show that more than 100 mobile phones are stolen every minute in the United States. Thieves are likely to snatch the devices while the doors are closing just before the train or bus departs from a station so that the victim is unable to pursue the thief. To decrease the chance of theft or pickpocketing, keep your mobile device(s) in a front pocket or in a zippered backpack. Keep your head up and stay aware of your surroundings. If possible, when in public, avoid using accessories that

indicate the type of device to which they are connected.

Cognitive psychologists have studied the effects of inattentional blindness, which occurs when a person's attention is diverted while performing a natural activity, such as walking. The researchers have determined that diverted attention is particularly pronounced when people are talking on a mobile phone and, to a lesser extent, using a portable media player. Emergency room reports indicate that distracted walking accidents are on the rise, especially when people trip over cracks in sidewalks or run into fixed objects, such as parked cars and telephone poles.

Consider This: Do you know anyone who has had a mobile device stolen? If so, how did the theft occur? Have you ever experienced inattentional blindness or distracted walking?

Digital Cameras

A **digital camera** is a mobile device that allows users to take photos and store the photographed images digitally. A *smart digital camera* also can communicate wirelessly with other devices and can include apps similar to those on a smartphone. Mobile computers and devices, such as smartphones and tablets, often include at least one integrated digital camera.

 CONSIDER THIS ————————————————

Do you need a digital camera if you have a camera built into your mobile phone?

If you use a camera only for posts on social media sites, then you may choose to use your mobile phone's built-in camera. If, however, you want increased zoom capabilities, more powerful flash, image stabilization, manual control of settings, and to reduce the drain on your phone's battery, then you may want to opt for a separate digital camera.

In addition to cameras built into phones and other devices, types of digital cameras include point-and-shoot cameras and SLR cameras (Figure 3-16). A *point-and-shoot camera* is an affordable and lightweight digital camera with lenses built into it and a screen that displays an approximation of the image to be photographed. Point-and-shoot cameras, which range in size and features, provide acceptable quality photographic images for the home or small office user. An *SLR camera* (single-lens reflex camera), by contrast, is a high-end digital camera that has interchangeable lenses and uses a mirror to display on its screen an exact replica of the image to be photographed. SLR cameras are much heavier and larger than point-and-shoot cameras. They also can be quite expensive, with a variety of available lens sizes and other attachments.

Figure 3-16 SLR digital cameras have lenses and other attachments, whereas the lenses on point-and-shoot cameras are built into the device. Many smartphones also have built-in digital cameras.
© iStockphoto / andrew-thief;
© Pawel Gaul / Photos.com;
© iStockphoto / Stephen Krow;
Courtesy of Samsung

Most point-and-shoot cameras include zoom and autofocus capability, use a built-in flash, store images on memory cards, and enable you to view and sometimes edit images directly on the camera. Many can take video in addition to still photos. Some are equipped with GPS, giving them the capability to record the exact location where a photo was taken and then store these details with the photo. Others are waterproof. Figure 3-17 illustrates how a point-and-shoot digital camera might work.

Internet Research

What is an SD card?

Search for: sd card information

How a Digital Camera Might Work

Step 1
Point to the image to photograph and take the photo. Light passes into the lens of the camera.

Step 2
The image is focused on a chip called a *charge-coupled device (CCD)*.

Step 3
The CCD generates an analog signal that represents the image.

Step 4
The analog signal is converted to a digital signal by an analog-to-digital converter (ADC).

Step 5
A processor in the camera adjusts the quality of the image and usually stores the digital photo on media inserted in the camera.

Figure 3-17 This figure shows how a point-and-shoot digital camera might work.
© iStockphoto / David Birkbeck;
© iStockphoto / David Birkbeck;
© Johan Larson / Shutterstock.com;
Courtesy of Kingston Technology Company, Inc

Smart digital cameras include all the features of point-and-shoot cameras and also enable you to connect wirelessly via Wi-Fi. Using the wireless capability, you instantly can save captured photos or videos on a networked computer or the cloud, share them on your online social network, upload them to a video sharing site, send them via email, and more. With a smart digital camera, you typically can download apps (just like on a smartphone) from an app store.

Digital cameras store captured images on storage media in the camera or on some type of memory card. Although most cameras enable you to review, edit, print, and share photos directly from the camera, some users prefer to transfer photos from a digital camera or the memory card to a computer's hard drive to perform these tasks.

Photo Quality   Resolution affects the quality of digital camera photos. **Resolution** is the number of horizontal and vertical pixels in a display. A *pixel* (short for picture element) is the smallest element in an electronic image (Figure 3-18). Digital camera resolution typically is stated in *megapixels (MP)*, or millions of pixels. For example, a 16 MP resolution means 16 million pixels. The greater the number of pixels the camera uses to capture a picture, the better the quality of the picture but the larger the file size and the more expensive the camera. Most digital cameras provide a means to adjust the resolution. At a lower resolution, you can capture and store more images in the camera.

The actual photographed resolution is known as the *optical resolution*. Some manufacturers state enhanced resolution, instead of, or in addition to, optical resolution. The *enhanced resolution* usually is higher because it uses a special formula to add pixels between those generated by the optical resolution. Be aware that some manufacturers compute a digital camera's megapixels from the enhanced resolution, instead of optical resolution.

Figure 3-18   A pixel is the smallest element in an electronic image.
© Lingong / Dreamstime.com

Portable and Digital Media Players

A **portable media player** is a mobile device on which you can store, organize, and play or view digital media (Figure 3-19). Smartphones and other mobile devices often can function as a portable media player. Portable media players enable you to listen to music; view photos; watch videos, movies, and television shows; and even record audio and video. Some include a digital camera and also offer a calendar, address book, games, and other apps. Others communicate wirelessly with other devices or computers and enable you to synchronize your digital media with a computer, another mobile device, or cloud storage.

Figure 3-19   Some portable media players have touch screens; others have touch-sensitive pads or buttons that enable you to access your media library.
© iStockphoto / Stephen Krow; © iStockphoto / rzelich; © iStockphoto / AleksVF

BTW

EarPods
Apple uses the term, *EarPods*, to refer to earbuds they designed to match the shape of the human ear.

Portable media players usually require a set of *earbuds*, which are small speakers that rest inside each ear canal. Available in a variety of sizes and colors, some portable media player models have a touch screen. Others have a *touch-sensitive pad*, which is an input device that contains buttons and/or wheels you operate with a thumb or finger. Using the touch-sensitive pad, you can scroll through and play music; view pictures; watch videos or movies; navigate through song, picture, or movie lists; display a menu; adjust volume; customize settings; and perform other actions. Some portable media players have only button controls.

Portable media players are a mobile type of digital media player. A **digital media player** or *streaming media player* is a device, typically used in a home, that streams digital media from a computer or network to a television, projector, or some other entertainment device (Figure 3-20). Some can stream from the Internet, enabling users to access video on websites. Some users opt for a digital media player instead of subscribing to cable or satellite subscription services to watch television programs.

Your collection of stored digital media is called a *media library*. Portable media players and some digital media players house your media library on a storage device in the player and/or on some type of memory card. With most, you transfer the digital media from a computer or the Internet, if the device is Internet capable, to the player's media library. Read How To 2-3 in Module 2 for instructions about how to download digital media from online services.

digital media player

Figure 3-20 A digital media player streams media to a home entertainment device.
Courtesy of Apple, Inc.

Mini Feature 3-3: Mobile Device Buyer's Guide

When purchasing a smartphone, digital camera, or portable or digital media player, you should consider several factors. Read Mini Feature 3-3 for tips to consider when purchasing these mobile devices.

 MINI FEATURE 3-3

Mobile Device Buyer's Guide

Mobile devices such as smartphones, digital cameras, and portable and digital media players are extremely popular. Research the manufacturers and then consider the following guidelines before purchasing a mobile device.

Smartphone Purchase Guidelines

1. Choose a mobile service provider and plan that satisfies your needs and budget. Choose a sufficient voice, text, and data plan that is appropriate.

2. Decide on the size, style, and weight of the smartphone that will work best for you.

3. Determine whether you prefer an on-screen keyboard, keypad, or mini keyboard.

4. Select a smartphone that is compatible with the program you want to use for synchronizing your email messages, contacts, calendar, and other data.

5. Choose a smartphone with sufficient battery life that meets your lifestyle.

6. Make sure your smartphone has enough memory and storage for contacts, email messages, photos, videos, and apps.

7. Consider purchasing accessories such as extra batteries, earbuds, screen protectors, and carrying cases.

© iStockphoto / luxxtek; Courtesy of Nokia; Courtesy of Nokia

Digital Camera Purchase Guidelines

1. Determine the type of digital camera that meets your needs, such as a point-and-shoot camera or SLR camera.

2. Choose a camera with an appropriate resolution.

3. Evaluate memory cards, because different cameras require different memory cards.

4. Consider a camera with built-in photo editing features.

5. Make sure that you can see the screen easily.

6. If the photos you plan to take will require you to zoom, choose a camera with an appropriate optical zoom.

7. Purchase accessories such as extra batteries and battery chargers, extra memory cards, lenses, and carrying cases.

Portable or Digital Media Player Purchase Guidelines

1. Choose a device with sufficient storage capacity for your media library and apps.

2. Consider how the portable or digital media player will connect to the Internet. Some devices connect using a wired and/or wireless connection. Choose a player that is compatible with the type of connection you can provide.

3. Read reviews about sound quality. If you are purchasing a portable device, consider higher-quality earbuds, headphones, or external speakers.

4. Select a player that is compatible with other devices you already own.

5. Consider additional memory cards to increase the storage capacity of your portable or digital media player.

6. Consider the accessories. If your portable or digital media player connects to a television or other display, consider purchasing a keyboard so that you can type easily. If the device is portable, consider additional batteries or a protective case.

✸ **Consider This:** Although most smartphones also can function as digital media players and digital cameras, would you have a separate digital media player and digital camera? Why?

E-Book Readers

An **e-book reader** (short for electronic book reader), or *e-reader*, is a mobile device that is used primarily for reading e-books and other digital publications (Figure 3-21). An *e-book*, or digital book, is an electronic version of a printed book, readable on computers and other mobile devices. Digital publications include books, newspapers, and magazines. Mobile computers and devices that display text also can function as e-book readers.

E-book readers usually are smaller than tablets but larger than smartphones. Most e-book reader models can store thousands of books, have a touch screen, and are Internet capable with built-in wireless technology. You use an on-screen keyboard to navigate, search, make selections, take notes, and highlight. Some have a *text-to-speech feature*, where the device speaks the contents of the printed page. E-book readers are available with an electronic paper black-and-white screen or with a color screen. Most have settings to adjust text size and

Figure 3-21 E-book readers enable you to read e-books and other digital publications such as newspapers and magazines.
© iStockPhoto / Petar Chernaev

for various lighting conditions, such as bright sunlight or dim lighting. Batteries usually have a long life, providing more than 75 hours of use before needing to be recharged.

Similar to how a portable media player stores digital media, e-book readers store digital publications in a library on a storage device in the e-book reader and/or on memory cards. You typically transfer the digital publication from a computer or the Internet, if the device is Internet capable, to the e-book reader. Read How To 2-3 in Module 2 for instructions about how to download digital media from online services.

 CONSIDER THIS

Do you need a separate e-book reader if you have a tablet or other device that can function as an e-book reader?
If you want the flexibility of reading on one device while using a tablet or other device for separate tasks, you will want to purchase a separate e-book reader. Also, e-book readers have a design suited for optimal readability of on-screen text and a longer battery life.

 Internet Research

Which activity trackers are the most widely used?

Search for: popular activity trackers

Wearable Devices

A **wearable device** or *wearable* is a small, mobile computing device designed to be worn by a consumer (Figure 3-22). These devices often communicate with a mobile device or computer using Bluetooth. Three popular types of wearable devices are activity trackers, smartwatches, and smartglasses.

An *activity tracker* is a wearable device that monitors fitness-related activities such as distance walked, heart rate, pulse, calories consumed, and sleep patterns. These devices typically sync, usually wirelessly, with a web or mobile app on your computer or mobile device to extend the capability of the wearable device.

A *smartwatch* is a wearable device that, in addition to keeping time, can communicate wirelessly with a smartphone to make and answer phone calls, read and send messages, access the web, play music, work with apps such as fitness trackers and GPS, and more. Most include a touch screen.

Smartglasses, also called *smart eyewear*, are wearable head-mounted eyeglass-type devices that enable the user to view information or take photos and videos that are projected to a miniature screen in the user's field of vision. For example, the device wearer could run an app while wearing smartglasses that display flight status information when he or she walks into an airport. Users control the device through voice commands or by touching controls on its frame. Some smartglasses also include mobile apps, such as fitness trackers and GPS.

activity tracker communicates with health fitness app on smartphone

smartwatch wirelessly communicates with compatible smartphone

smartglasses, such as Google Glass shown here, respond to voice instruction to access note taking and other apps

Figure 3-22   Three popular wearable devices include activity trackers, smartwatches, and smartglasses.
© iStockPhoto / Petar Chernaev; © iStockPhoto / Chesky_W; © iStockPhoto / scanrail; © iStockPhoto / Wavebreak;
Source: Google Inc

Internet Research

How does augmented reality apply to smartglasses?

Search for: augmented reality

Game Devices

A **game console** is a mobile computing device designed for single-player or multiplayer video games. Gamers often connect the game console to a television or a monitor so that they can view gameplay on the screen. Some models also allow you to listen to music and watch movies or view photos. Typically weighing between 3 and 11 pounds, many game console models include storage for games and other media. Optical disc drives in the game consoles provide access to games and movies on optical disc. Some use memory cards and accept USB flash drives. Game consoles that are Internet capable enable gamers to download games, stream games or movies, and play with others online. Some gamers connect keyboards or webcams so that they more easily can send text messages or conduct video chats with other gamers.

A **handheld game device** is a small mobile device that contains a screen, speakers, controls, and game console all in one unit. Some include a stylus. Some handheld game device models have touch screens and built-in digital cameras. Some are Internet capable for downloading games and apps. Most handheld game devices can communicate wirelessly with other similar devices for multiplayer gaming.

With a game console or computer video game, players direct movements and actions of on-screen objects via a controller, voice, or air gestures. Game controllers include gamepads, joysticks and wheels, dance pads, and a variety of motion-sensing controllers (Figure 3-23). The following list describes each of these types of game controllers. Most communicate via wired or wireless technology.

gamepad   joystick   pedals and wheel

dance pad   motion-sensing game controller   balance board

Figure 3-23   Game players have a variety of ways to direct movements and actions of on-screen objects.
© iStockphoto / peng wu; © aquariagirl1970 / Shutterstock.com; © George Dolgikh / Shutterstock.com; Courtesy of DDR Game; © iStockphoto / Florea Marius Catalin; © Stuartkey / Dreamstime.com

- A *gamepad*, which is held with both hands, controls the movement and actions of players or objects in video games or computer games. On the gamepad, users press buttons with their thumbs or move sticks in various directions to trigger events. Several gamepads can communicate with the game console simultaneously for multiplayer gaming.
- Users running flight and driving simulation software often use a joystick or wheel. A *joystick* is a handheld vertical lever, mounted on a base, that you move in different directions to control the actions of the simulated vehicle or player. The lever usually includes buttons, called triggers, that you press to initiate certain events. A *wheel* is a steering-wheel-type input device that users turn to simulate driving a car, truck, or other vehicle. Most wheels also include foot pedals for acceleration and braking actions.
- A *dance pad* is a flat, electronic device divided into panels that users press with their feet in response to instructions from a music video game. These games test the user's ability to step on the correct panel at the correct time, following a pattern that is synchronized with the rhythm or beat of a song.

Internet Research

Which video games are the most widely used?

Search for: popular video games

- *Motion-sensing game controllers* allow users to guide on-screen elements with air gestures, that is, by moving their body or a handheld input device through the air. Some motion-sensing game controllers are sold with a particular type of game; others are general purpose. Sports games, for example, use motion-sensing game controllers, such as baseball bats and golf clubs. With general-purpose motion-sensing game controllers, you simulate batting, golfing, and other actions with a universal handheld device or no device at all.
- Other controllers include those used for music and fitness games. Controllers that resemble musical instruments, such as guitars, drums, keyboards, and microphones work with music video games that enable game players to create sounds and music by playing the instrument. Fitness games often communicate with a *balance board*, which is shaped like a weight scale and contains sensors that measure a game player's balance and weight. Read Ethics & Issues 3-3 to consider whether games and apps are qualified to provide medical advice.

ETHICS & ISSUES 3-3

Are Fitness Video Games and Apps Qualified to Provide Medical Advice?

Most video games and smartphone apps provide a workout only for your fingers. A host of games and apps, however, attempt to track calories, suggest workout routines, and more. Because you can take your smartphone anywhere, one advantage is that apps can provide tips for eating healthfully at a restaurant, act as a pedometer to track your steps, and send reminders to exercise. Wearable fitness devices can track your steps or use GPS to trace your route when running or biking. Another advantage is you can receive instant feedback and support from fitness apps and games that

allow you to post workouts, calorie counts, and even weight loss to online social networks. Some apps even reward you for working out.

Some critics find fault with these apps, claiming that medical personnel have not evaluated either the game or app developers, or the games and apps themselves. Because they do not take into account the amount of lean muscle mass and body fat, health and weight loss goals can be miscalculated. Experts say that games that simulate sports, such as tennis, burn half the calories you would burn if you participated in the actual sport. Some medical professionals also note that apps do not consider a participant's

medical history when recommending activities. Proponents of fitness-related games and apps say that the games encourage people to be more active and can provide positive feedback, especially the elderly and children who might otherwise not get much physical activity.

Consider This: Should game and app developers provide medical advice? Why or why not? Can fitness-related games provide a quality workout? Can an app give accurate calorie recommendations? Why or why not? As long as the games make people more active, should you ignore a games' shortcomings? Why or why not?

Embedded Computers

An **embedded computer** is a special-purpose computer that functions as a component in a larger product. Embedded computers are everywhere — at home, in your car, and at work. The following list identifies a variety of everyday products that contain embedded computers.

- **Consumer electronics:** Mobile phones, digital phones, digital televisions, cameras, video recorders, DVD players and recorders, answering machines
- **Home automation devices:** Thermostats, sprinkling systems, security systems, vacuum systems, appliances, lights
- **Automobiles:** Antilock brakes, engine control modules, electronic stability control, airbag control unit, cruise control, navigation systems and GPS receivers
- **Process controllers and robotics:** Remote monitoring systems, power monitors, machine controllers, medical devices
- **Computer devices and office machines:** Keyboards, printers, fax and copy machines

Because embedded computers are components in larger products, they usually are small and have limited hardware. These computers perform various functions, depending on the requirements of the product in which they reside. Embedded computers in printers, for example, monitor the amount of paper in the tray, check the ink or toner level, signal if a paper jam has occurred, and so on. Figure 3-24 shows some of the many embedded computers in vehicles. Read Ethics & Issues 3-4 to consider whether in-vehicle technology fosters a false sense of security.

Smartphone apps, such as the OnStar RemoteLink app shown here, remotely start the engine, unlock doors, stream music through the vehicle's sound system, display driving directions, and more.

Adaptive cruise control systems detect if vehicles in front of you are too close and, if necessary, adjust the vehicle's throttle, may apply brakes, and/or sound an alarm.

Cars equipped with wireless communications capabilities, called *telematics*, include features such as navigation systems, remote diagnosis and alerts, and Internet access.

Tire pressure monitoring systems send warning signals if tire pressure is insufficient.

Advanced airbag systems have crash-severity sensors that determine the appropriate level to inflate the airbag, reducing the chance of airbag injury in low-speed accidents.

Electronic stability control automatically applies brakes, and may reduce engine power, when you lose control of steering or traction.

Drive-by-wire systems sense pressure on the gas pedal and communicate electronically to the engine how much and how fast to accelerate.

Figure 3-24   Some of the embedded computers designed to improve your safety, security, and performance in today's vehicles.

© Nir Levy / Shutterstock.com; © Santiago Cornejo / Shutterstock.com; © iStockphoto / narvikk; © iStockphoto / kenneth-cheung; © iStockphoto / Marcin Laska; © iStockPhoto / pagadesign; Source: OnStar, LLC

 ETHICS & ISSUES 3-4

Does In-Vehicle Technology Foster a False Sense of Security?

Embedded computers in vehicles can guide you when backing out of a driveway, warn you if a vehicle or object is in your blind spot, or alert you to unsafe road conditions. Apps can track gas mileage or notify you when your car needs an oil change or other services. Recently, all new cars were required to include electronic stability control, which can assist with steering the car in case of skidding, and backup cameras. Other technologies adjust vehicle speed or headlight usage, and can even activate the brakes.

All of this technology is intended to make driving safer.

Critics of in-vehicle technology claim that it can provide drivers with a false sense of security. If you rely on a sensor for assistance while backing up, parking, or changing lanes, for example, you may miss other obstructions that could cause a crash. Reliance on electronic stability control or other crash-avoidance technologies may cause you to drive faster than conditions allow or to pay less attention to the distance between your vehicle and others.

The effect on new, teen drivers is especially of concern. If teens learn to drive using vehicles equipped with features such as video rearview mirrors, they may be unable to drive older, less-equipped vehicles safely. Many apps and devices help parents protect their teens while driving. Apps can program mobile devices to block incoming calls or text messages while the vehicle is moving. GPS can track a vehicle's location and speed. Sensors can monitor seatbelt usage and number of passengers in the vehicle.

Consider This: Does in-vehicle technology make driving safer? Why or why not? What basic skills should all drivers have, regardless of their vehicle's technology?

 CONSIDER THIS

Can embedded computers use the Internet to communicate with other computers and devices?
Many already do, on a small scale. For example, a Smart TV enables you to browse the web, stream video from online media services, listen to Internet radio, communicate with others on social media sites, play online games, and more — all while watching a television show.

A trend, called the *Internet of Things*, describes an environment where processors are embedded in every product imaginable (things), and those 'things' communicate with one another via the Internet (i.e., alarm clocks, coffeemakers, apps vehicles, refrigerators, phones, washing machines, doorbells, streetlights, thermostats, navigation systems, etc.). For example, when your refrigerator detects the milk is low, it sends your phone a text message that you need milk and adds a 'buy milk' task to your scheduling app. On the drive home, your phone determines the closest grocery store that has the lowest milk price and sends the address of that grocery store to your vehicle's navigation system, which, in turn, gives you directions to the store. In the store, your phone directs you to the dairy aisle, where it receives an electronic coupon from the store for the milk. Because this type of environment provides an efficient means to track or monitor status, inventory, behavior, and more — without human intervention — it sometimes is referred to as machine-to-machine (M2M) communications.

Putting It All Together

Industry experts typically classify computers and mobile devices in six categories: personal computers (desktop), mobile computers and mobile devices, game consoles, servers, supercomputers, and embedded computers. A computer's size, speed, processing power, and price determine the category it best fits. Due to rapidly changing technology, however, the distinction among categories is not always clear-cut. Table 3-3 summarizes the categories of computers discussed on the previous pages.

Table 3-3   Categories of Computers and Mobile Devices

Category	Physical Size	Number of Simultaneously Connected Users	General Price Range
Personal computers (desktop)	Fits on a desk	Usually one (can be more if networked)	Several hundred to several thousand dollars
Mobile computers and mobile devices	Fits on your lap or in your hand	Usually one	Less than a hundred dollars to several thousand dollars
Game consoles	Small box or handheld device	One to several	Several hundred dollars or less
Servers	Small cabinet to room full of equipment	Two to thousands	Several hundred to several million dollars
Supercomputers	Full room of equipment	Hundreds to thousands	Half a million to several billion dollars
Embedded computers	Miniature	Usually one	Embedded in the price of the product

© Cengage Learning

🕐 NOW YOU SHOULD KNOW

Be sure you understand the material presented in the sections titled Cloud Computing, Mobile Devices, Game Devices, Embedded Computers, and Putting It All Together, as it relates to the module objectives.
Now you should know . . .

- When you are using cloud computing (Objective 4)
- What you should consider when purchasing a mobile device (Objective 5)
- What types of controllers you might use with game consoles (Objective 6)
- When you are using an embedded computer (Objective 7)

 BTW

Instead of the term, port, the term, *jack*, sometimes is used to identify audio and video ports (i.e., audio jack or video jack).

Ports and Connections

Computers and mobile devices connect to peripheral devices through ports or by using wireless technologies. A **port** is the point at which a peripheral device (i.e., keyboard, printer, monitor, etc.) attaches to or communicates with a computer or mobile device so that the peripheral device can send data to or receive information from the computer or mobile device. Most computers and mobile devices have ports (Figure 3-25). Some ports have a micro or mini version for mobile devices because of the smaller sizes of these devices.

A **connector** joins a cable to a port. A connector at one end of a cable attaches to a port on the computer or mobile device, and a connector at the other end of the cable attaches to a port on the peripheral device. Table 3-4 shows a variety of ports you may find on a computer or mobile device. USB and Thunderbolt are more general-purpose ports that allow connections to a wide variety of devices; other ports are more specific and connect a single type of device.

Figure 3-25 Most computers and mobile devices have ports so that you can connect the computer or device to peripherals.
Courtesy of Gateway; © Ultraone / Dreamstime.com; Courtesy of Lenovo; © iStockphoto / Nikada; © eduard ionescu / Shutterstock

Table 3-4   Popular Ports and Connectors

Port Type	Connector Photo	Port Photo	Port Type	Connector Photo	Port Photo
DisplayPort (audio/video)			Mini USB		
DVI (digital video interface)			Mini HDMI (audio/video)		
HDMI (audio/video)			Network (Ethernet)		
Headphones			Speaker		
Lightning			Thunderbolt		
Microphone			USB (Type A)		
Micro USB			USB (Type B)		
Mini DisplayPort			VGA		

© Cengage Learning; © Steveheap / Dreamstime.com; © iStockphoto / Hans Martens; © iStockphoto / Ksenia Krylova; © iStockphoto / Lusoimages; © Jorge Salcedo / Shutterstock.com; © Aarrows / Dreamstime.com; © iStockphoto / Lusoimages; © Pcheruvi / Dreamstime.com; © iStockphoto / Potapova Vaeriya; © iStockphoto / Jivko Kazakov; © iStockphoto / TimArbaev; © iStockphoto / Ashok Rodrigues; © iStockphoto / Jon Larson; © Aarrows / Dreamstime.com; © iStockphoto / Denis Sokolov; © Germán Ariel Berra / Shutterstock.com; © Aarrows / Dreamstime.com; © iStockphoto / Li Ding; © iStockphoto / TimArbaev; © Stockphoto / Matthew Brown; © Jorge Salcedo /Shutterstock.com; © Pcheruvi / Dreamstime.com; © Anton Malcev / Photos.com; © iStockphoto / alexander kirch; © iStockphoto / Nick Smith; © Stockphoto / Mohamed Badawi; © Jorge Salcedo /Shutterstock © iStockphoto / Brandon Laufenberg; © getIT / Shutterstock.com; © stavklem / Shutterstock. com; © iStockphoto / Lusoimages; © exan / Shutterstock; © iStockPhoto / NikiLitov; © iStockPhoto / Peter Hermus; © Jarp / Fotolia; Courtesy of Samsung

USB Ports

A **USB port**, short for universal serial bus port, can connect up to 127 different peripheral devices together with a single connector. Devices that connect to a USB port include the following: card reader, digital camera, external hard drive, game console, joystick, modem, mouse, optical disc drive, portable media player, printer, scanner, smartphone, digital camera, speakers, USB flash drive, and webcam. In addition to computers and mobile devices, you find USB ports in vehicles, airplane seats, and other public locations.

Several USB versions have been released, with newer versions (i.e., USB 3.0) transferring data and information faster than earlier ones (i.e., USB 2.0). Newer versions are *backward compatible*, which means they support older USB devices as well as newer ones. Keep in mind, though, that older USB devices do not run any faster in a newer USB port. In addition to transferring data, cables plugged into USB ports also may be able to transfer power to recharge many smartphones and tablets. Newer versions of USB can charge connected mobile devices even when the computer is not in use.

To attach multiple peripheral devices using a single USB port, you can use a USB hub. A *USB hub* is a device that plugs in a USB port on the computer or mobile device and contains multiple USB ports, into which you plug cables from USB devices. Some USB hubs are wireless. That is, a receiver plugs into a USB port on the computer and the USB hub communicates wirelessly with the receiver. Read Secure IT 3-4 for tips when using USB charging stations.

 SECURE IT 3-4

Public USB Charging Stations — Safe or Not?

Although you might be tempted to recharge your smartphone or mobile device at a public charging station, think twice before plugging your USB cable into the charging kiosk's port. The station may be *juice jacking*, which occurs when a hacker steals data from or transfers malware to the device via a USB cable at a charging station. (A hacker is someone who accesses a computer or network illegally.)

This process is possible because the USB cable is used for two purposes: supplying power and syncing data. It can occur within one minute after plugging into the charger.

Anything on the device is susceptible, including photos, contacts, and music, and some malware can create a full backup of your data, leaving you prone to identity theft. Once the phone or mobile device is infected, it can continue to transmit data via Wi-Fi. Security experts claim that the only method of erasing this malware is to restore the device to its factory settings.

Charging stations are common in airports, business centers, and conference rooms. While most are safe, you can reduce the possibility of juice jacking by taking these precautions:

- Use a travel charger, also called a power bank, which can recharge a device several times before needing recharging itself.

- Keep the phone or mobile device locked so that it requires a password to sync data with another device. Turning off the device while charging may not provide sufficient protection against accessing the storage media.

- Use a power-only USB cable that does not allow data transmission.

Consider This: Should warning signs be posted by public charging stations? Would you use a public charging kiosk if your smartphone or mobile device was running low on battery power?

Port Replicators and Docking Stations

Instead of connecting peripheral devices directly to ports on a mobile computer, some mobile users prefer the flexibility of port replicators and docking stations. A *port replicator* is an external device that provides connections to peripheral devices through ports built into the device. The mobile user accesses peripheral devices by connecting the port replicator to a USB port or a special port on the mobile computer. Port replicators sometimes disable ports on the mobile computer to prevent conflicts among the devices on the computer and port replicator.

A docking station is similar to a port replicator, but it has more functionality. A *docking station*, which is an external device that attaches to a mobile computer or device, contains a power connection and provides connections to peripheral devices (Figure 3-26). Docking stations also may include slots for memory cards, optical disc drives, and other devices. With the mobile computer or device in the docking station, users can work with a full-sized keyboard, a mouse, and other desktop peripheral devices from their laptop or tablet.

Wireless Device Connections

Instead of connecting computers and mobile devices to peripheral devices with a cable, some peripheral devices use wireless communications technologies, such as Bluetooth, Wi-Fi, and NFC.

Bluetooth **Bluetooth** technology uses short-range radio signals to transmit data between two Bluetooth-enabled computers or devices. In addition to computers, mobile devices and many peripheral devices, such as a mouse, keyboard, printer, or headset, and many vehicles and consumer electronics are Bluetooth enabled. Bluetooth devices have to be within about 33 feet of each other, but the range can be extended with additional equipment. If you have a computer that is not Bluetooth enabled, you can purchase a Bluetooth wireless port adapter that will convert an existing USB port into a Bluetooth port. Read How To 3-1 for instructions about setting up two Bluetooth devices to communicate with each other.

Figure 3-26 Docking stations often are used with tablets and other mobile computers, providing connections to peripheral devices.
Courtesy of Fujitsu Technology Solutions; © Cengage Learning

✦ HOW TO 3-1

Pair Bluetooth Devices

Before two Bluetooth devices will communicate with each other, they might need to be paired. *Pairing* is the process of initiating contact between two Bluetooth devices and allowing them to communicate with each other. It is important to have the documentation for the Bluetooth devices you are pairing readily available. The following steps will help you pair two Bluetooth devices.

1. Make sure the devices you intend to pair are charged completely or plugged into an external power source.

2. Turn on the devices to pair, ensuring they are within your immediate reach.

3. If necessary, enable Bluetooth on the devices you are pairing.

4. Place one device in *discoverable mode*, which means it is waiting for another Bluetooth device to locate its signal. If you are connecting a smartphone to a Bluetooth headset, for example,

the smartphone would need to be in discoverable mode.

5. Refer to the other device's documentation and follow the necessary steps to locate the discoverable device from the other device you are pairing.

6. After no more than about 30 seconds, the devices should initiate communications.

7. You may be required to enter a passkey (similar to a PIN) on one device for the other device with which you are pairing. For example, if you are pairing a smartphone with a Bluetooth headset, you may be required to enter the Bluetooth headset's passkey on the smartphone. In this case, you would refer to the Bluetooth headset's documentation to obtain the passkey. Common passkeys are 0000 and 1234.

8. After entering the correct passkey, the two devices should be paired successfully.

※ **Consider This:** Why is a passkey required when pairing two Bluetooth devices? Do you need to pair Bluetooth devices before each use?

© Normal Chan / Shutterstock.com

Wi-Fi   Short for wireless fidelity, **Wi-Fi** uses radio signals that conform to 802.11 standards, which were developed by the Institute of Electrical and Electronics Engineers (IEEE).

Computers and devices that have the appropriate Wi-Fi capability can communicate via radio waves with other Wi-Fi computers or devices. Most mobile computers and devices are Wi-Fi enabled, along with routers and other communications devices. For successful Wi-Fi communications in open or outdoor areas free from interference, the Wi-Fi computers or devices should be within 300 feet of each other. In closed areas, the wireless range is about 100 feet. To obtain communications at the maximum distances, you may need to install extra hardware. Read How To 3-2 for instructions about connecting a phone to a Wi-Fi network.

✹ HOW TO 3-2

Connect Your Phone to a Wi-Fi Network to Save Data Charges

Many of today's data plans limit the amount of data you can transfer each month on your mobile service provider's network. Connecting a smartphone to a Wi-Fi network enables you to transfer data without using your phone's data plan and risking costly overages. The following steps describe how to connect your phone to a Wi-Fi network.

1. Make sure you are in a location where a Wi-Fi network is available. Obtain any necessary information you need to connect to the Wi-Fi network.
2. Navigate to the settings on your phone.
3. Locate and enable Wi-Fi in your phone's settings.

4. When your phone displays a list of available wireless networks, choose the network to which you want to connect.
5. If necessary, enter any additional information, such as a password, required to connect to the network.
6. Your phone should indicate when it successfully is connected to the network.
7. When you are finished using the Wi-Fi connection or are not within range of the Wi-Fi network, disable Wi-Fi on your phone to help conserve battery life.

✹ **Consider This:** If you have a data plan allowing unlimited data and you are within range of a Wi-Fi network, is it better to use your mobile service provider's network or the Wi-Fi network? Why?

Google Inc.

NFC   NFC (near field communications) uses close-range radio signals to transmit data between two NFC-enabled devices. Examples of NFC-enabled devices include smartphones, digital cameras, computers, televisions, and terminals. Other objects, such as credit cards and tickets, also use NFC technology. For successful communications, the devices either touch or are within an inch or two of each other.

✹ CONSIDER THIS

What are some uses of NFC devices?
- Pay for goods and services (i.e., smartphone to terminal)
- Share contacts, photos, and other files (i.e., smartphone to smartphone or digital camera to television)
- Download apps (i.e., computer to smartphone)
- Gain access or admittance (i.e., smartphone to terminal)

Protecting Hardware

Users rely on computers and mobile devices to create, store, and manage important information. Thus, you should take measures to protect computers and devices from theft, vandalism, and failure.

Hardware Theft and Vandalism

Companies, schools, and other organizations that house many computers are at risk of hardware theft and vandalism, especially those with smaller computers that easily can fit in a backpack or briefcase. Mobile users are susceptible to hardware theft because the size and weight of their computers and devices make them easy to steal. Thieves may target laptops of company executives so that they can use the stolen computer to access confidential company information illegally.

To help reduce the chances of theft, companies and schools use a variety of security measures. Physical access controls, such as locked doors and windows, usually are adequate to protect the equipment. Many businesses, schools, and some homeowners install alarm systems for additional security. School computer labs and other facilities with a large number of semifrequent users often attach additional physical security devices, such as cables that lock the equipment to a desk, cabinet, or floor. Mobile users sometimes lock their mobile computers temporarily to a stationary object, for example, a table in a hotel room. Small locking devices also exist that require a key to access a hard drive or optical disc drive.

Users also can install a security or device-tracking app on their mobile computers and devices. Some security apps shut down the computer and sound an alarm if the computer moves beyond a specified distance. Others can be configured to photograph the thieves when they use the computer. Device-tracking apps use GPS, Wi-Fi, IP addresses, and other means to determine the location of a lost or stolen computer or device.

Users can configure computers and mobile devices to require identification before allowing access. For example, you can require entry of a user name and password to use the computer or device. Some computers and mobile devices have built-in or attached fingerprint readers (Figure 3-27), which can be used to verify a user's identity before allowing access. A *fingerprint reader* captures curves and indentations of a fingerprint. This type of security does not prevent theft, but it renders the computer or device useless if it is stolen.

Hardware Failure

Hardware can fail for a variety of reasons: aging hardware; random events, such as electrical power problems; and even errors in programs or apps. Not only could hardware failure require you to replace or repair a computer or mobile device, but it also can cause loss of software, data, and information.

One of the more common causes of system failure is an electrical power variation, which can cause loss of data and loss of equipment. If computers and mobile devices are connected to a network, a single power disturbance can damage multiple devices at once. Electrical disturbances that can cause damage include undervoltages and overvoltages.

Figure 3-27 Some mobile computers and devices include fingerprint readers, which can be used to verify a user's identity.

fingerprint reader

- An **undervoltage** occurs when the electrical supply or voltage drops, often defined as more than five percent, below the normal volts. A *brownout* is a prolonged (more than a minute) undervoltage. A *blackout* is a complete power failure. Undervoltages can cause data loss but generally do not cause equipment damage.
- An **overvoltage**, or **power surge**, occurs when the incoming electrical supply or voltage increases, often defined as more than five percent, above the normal volts. A momentary overvoltage, called a *spike*, occurs when the increase in power lasts for less than one millisecond (thousandth of a second). Uncontrollable disturbances such as lightning bolts can cause spikes. Overvoltages can cause immediate and permanent damage to hardware.

To protect against electrical power variations, use a surge protector. A **surge protector**, also called a *surge suppressor*, uses electrical components to provide a stable current flow and minimize the chances of an overvoltage reaching the computer and other electronic equipment (Figure 3-28). Sometimes resembling a power strip, the computer and other devices plug in the surge protector, which plugs in the power source.

Figure 3-28 Circuits inside a surge protector safeguard against electrical power variations.
© iStockPhoto / missisya

The surge protector absorbs small overvoltages — generally without damage to the computer and equipment. To protect the computer and other equipment from large overvoltages, such as those caused by a lightning strike, some surge protectors stop working completely when an overvoltage reaches a certain level. Surge protectors also usually protect the computer from undervoltages. No surge protectors are 100 percent effective. Large power surges can bypass the protector. Repeated small overvoltages can weaken a surge protector permanently. Some experts recommend replacing a surge protector every two to three years.

For additional electrical protection, some users connect an uninterruptible power supply to the computer. An **uninterruptible power supply** (**UPS**) is a device that contains surge protection circuits and one or more batteries that can provide power during a temporary or permanent loss of power (Figure 3-29). A UPS connects your computer and a power source. Read How To 3-3 for purchasing suggestions regarding surge protectors and UPSs.

Figure 3-29   If power fails, a UPS uses batteries to provide electricity for a limited amount of time.
© rendeep kumar r / Shutterstock

 HOW TO 3-3

Evaluate Surge Protectors and UPSs

Electrical power surges are a part of everyday life, and they are especially prevalent during thunderstorms and peak energy consumption periods. These unavoidable occurrences can damage or ruin sensitive electronic equipment. The processor in a computer is particularly sensitive to fluctuations in current. Two devices can help protect electronic components: a surge protector and an uninterruptible power supply (UPS).

Purchase the best surge protector you can afford. Typically, the amount of protection offered by a surge protector is proportional to its cost. That is, the more expensive the surge protector, the more protection it offers. When evaluating surge protectors and UPSs, they should meet or exceed these specifications:

• Sufficient outlets to accommodate each device needing protection

• Individual on/off switch for each device

• Built-in fuse

• UL 1449 rating that ensures quality control and testing

• Joule rating of at least 600

• Indicator light showing the device is functioning properly

• Warranty for damages to any connected equipment

• Low clamping voltage

• High energy-absorption rating

• Low response time, preferably less than ten nanoseconds

• Protection for a modem, communications lines, and cables

 Consider This: What other factors might you consider while evaluating surge protectors? Why?

 CONSIDER THIS

What other measures can organizations implement if their computers must remain operational at all times?

Some companies use duplicate components or duplicate computers to protect against hardware failure. A *fault-tolerant computer* has duplicate components so that it can continue to operate when one of its main components fail. Airline reservation systems, communications networks, ATMs, and other systems that must be operational at all times use duplicate components, duplicate computers, or fault-tolerant computers.

Health Concerns of Using Technology

The widespread use of technology has led to some important user health concerns. You should be proactive and minimize your chance of risk.

Repetitive Strain Injuries

A *repetitive strain injury* (*RSI*) is an injury or disorder of the muscles, nerves, tendons, ligaments, and joints. Technology-related RSIs include tendonitis and carpal tunnel syndrome.

- Tendonitis is inflammation of a tendon due to repeated motion or stress on that tendon.
- Carpal tunnel syndrome (CTS) is inflammation of the nerve that connects the forearm to the palm of the hand.

Repeated or forceful bending of the wrist can cause tendonitis of the wrist or CTS. Symptoms of tendonitis of the wrist include extreme pain that extends from the forearm to the hand, along with tingling in the fingers. Symptoms of CTS include burning pain when the nerve is compressed, along with numbness and tingling in the thumb and first two fingers.

Long-term computer work can lead to tendonitis or CTS. Factors that cause these disorders include prolonged typing, prolonged mouse usage, or continual shifting between the mouse and the keyboard. If untreated, these disorders can lead to permanent physical damage.

 CONSIDER THIS

What can you do to prevent technology-related tendonitis or CTS?
Follow these precautions:

- Take frequent breaks to exercise your hands and arms (Figure 3-30).
- Do not rest your wrists on the edge of a desk. Instead, place a wrist rest between the keyboard and the edge of your desk.
- Place the mouse at least six inches from the edge of the desk. In this position, your wrist is flat on the desk.
- Minimize the number of times you switch between the mouse and the keyboard.
- Keep your forearms and wrists level so that your wrists do not bend.
- Avoid using the heel of your hand as a pivot point while typing or using the mouse.
- Keep your shoulders, arms, hands, and wrists relaxed while you work.
- Maintain good posture.
- Stop working if you experience pain or fatigue.

Hand Exercises
- Spread fingers apart for several seconds while keeping wrists straight.
- Gently push back fingers and then thumb.
- Dangle arms loosely at sides and then shake arms and hands.

Figure 3-30 To reduce the chance of developing tendonitis or carpal tunnel syndrome, take frequent breaks during computer sessions to exercise your hands and arms.
© iStockphoto / Denis Kartavenko; © Oleksiy Mark / Shutterstock.com; © Cengage Learning

Other Physical Risks

With the growing use of earbuds and headphones in computers and mobile devices, some users are experiencing hearing loss. Read How To 3-4 for guidelines for evaluating earbuds and headphones.

Computer vision syndrome (*CVS*) is a technology-related health condition that affects eyesight. You may have CVS if you have sore, tired, burning, itching, or dry eyes; blurred or double vision after prolonged staring at a display device; headache or sore neck; difficulty shifting focus between a display device and documents; difficulty focusing on the screen image; color fringes or after-images when you look away from the display device; and increased sensitivity to light. Eyestrain associated with CVS is not thought to have serious or long-term consequences. Figure 3-31 outlines some techniques you can follow to ease eyestrain.

People who spend their workday using the computer sometimes complain of lower back pain, muscle fatigue, and emotional fatigue. Lower back pain sometimes is caused from poor posture. Always sit properly in the chair while you work. To alleviate back pain, muscle fatigue, and emotional fatigue, take a 15- to 30-minute break every 2 hours — stand up, walk around, stretch, and relax.

Techniques to Ease Eyestrain

- Every 10 to 15 minutes, take an eye break.
  - Look into the distance and focus on an object for 20 to 30 seconds.
  - Roll your eyes in a complete circle.
  - Close your eyes and rest them for at least one minute.
- Blink your eyes every five seconds.
- Place your display about an arm's length away from your eyes with the top of the screen at or below eye level.
- Use large fonts.
- If you wear glasses, ask your doctor about computer glasses.
- Adjust the lighting.

Figure 3-31 Following these tips may help reduce eyestrain while using technology.
© grublee / Shutterstock.com

 HOW TO 3-4

Evaluate Earbuds and Headphones

Earbuds and headphones are used to listen to music and other audio files on computers and mobile devices. Selecting the proper product not only depends on the style you prefer, but also the type of audio you will be playing. Prices for earbuds and headphones can range from only a few dollars to several hundred dollars, so it is important to know what you are purchasing. The following guidelines describe what to look for when evaluating earbuds and headphones.

- Determine which style you prefer. Earbuds rest inside your ear, while headphones rest over your ear. Experiment with both types

and determine which is more comfortable for you.

- Determine the quality you desire. If you listen to music casually and typically do not notice variations in sound quality, a higher-end product might not be necessary. Alternatively, if sound quality is important, you may consider a more expensive set. Note that a higher price does not always indicate better quality; read online product reviews for information about the sound quality of various products.

- Decide whether you would like a noise cancelling feature. *Noise cancelling* helps block external noise while you are

listening to the audio on your device. Noise cancelling headphones sometimes require batteries, and you are able to turn the noise cancelling feature on and off. If you will be listening to audio in locations where you also need to hear what is going on around you, consider purchasing a product without this feature.

Consider This: Based on your preferences and needs, which type of product (earbuds or headphones) is best for you? Locate a product online that meets your specifications. What brand is it? How much does it cost? Where is this product available?

Internet Research

What is a text neck?

Search for: text neck

Another way to help prevent these injuries is to be sure your workplace is designed ergonomically. **Ergonomics** is an applied science devoted to incorporating comfort, efficiency, and safety into the design of items in the workplace. Ergonomic studies have shown that using the correct type and configuration of chair, keyboard, display, and work surface helps users work comfortably and efficiently and helps protect their health (Figure 3-32). You can hire an ergonomic consultant to evaluate your workplace and recommend changes.

viewing angle: 20° to center of screen **viewing distance:** 18 to 28 inches

arms: elbows at about 90° and arms and hands approximately parallel to floor

keyboard height: 23 to 28 inches depending on height of user

adjustable height chair with 4 or 5 legs for stability

feet flat on floor

Figure 3-32 A well designed work area should be flexible to allow adjustments to the height and build of different individuals.
© Science Photo Library / Alamy

Behavioral Health Risks

Some technology users become obsessed with computers, mobile devices, and the Internet. **Technology addiction** occurs when technology use consumes someone's entire social life. Technology addiction is a growing health problem, but it can be treated through therapy and support groups.

People suffering from *technology overload* feel distressed when deprived of technology, even for a short length of time, or feel overwhelmed with the amount of technology they are required to manage. To cope with the feelings of distraction and to control the impact that technology can have on work and relationships, set aside technology-free time.

 CONSIDER THIS

How can you tell if you are addicted to technology?
Symptoms of a user with technology addiction include the following:

- Craves computer time
- Overjoyed when using a computer or mobile device
- Unable to stop using technology
- Irritable when not using technology
- Neglects family and friends
- Problems at work or school

✔ NOW YOU SHOULD KNOW

Be sure you understand the material presented in the sections titled Ports and Connections, Protecting Hardware, and Health Concerns of Using Technology as it relates to the module objectives.
Now you should know…

- How you can connect a peripheral device to a computer or mobile device (Objective 8)
- How you can protect your hardware from theft, vandalism, and failure (Objective 9)
- How you can minimize your risk of health-related injuries and disorders that can result from using technology (Objective 10)

✔ Summary

This module presented characteristics of and purchasing guidelines for laptops, tablets, desktops, smartphones, digital cameras, and portable and digital media players. It also discussed servers, supercomputers, point-of-sale terminals, ATMs, self-service kiosks, e-book readers, wearable devices, game devices, embedded computers, and cloud computing. It presented a variety of ports and connections, ways to protect hardware, and health concerns of using technology use along with preventive measures.

TECHNOLOGY @ WORK

Energy Management

When you walk into your office at the start of a new day, you give little thought to the fact that the lights are on and the temperature is comfortable. For all you know, the air conditioner and lighting were on all night; however, energy management systems are hard at work conserving energy and reducing energy costs. When you return home, you also might take for granted the fact that your dryer automatically stops when it senses that your clothes are dry, or that your dishwasher or washing machine uses only enough water to sufficiently clean its contents. Individuals in the energy management field always are looking for ways to use technology to manage energy use.

Building automation systems are devices that can control various building components, such as complex air conditioning systems and lighting systems. Building automation systems adjust these components to provide a comfortable, safe working environment without wasting energy. For example, in an office building where employees all work weekdays from 8:00 a.m. until 5:00 p.m., the

building automation system might prompt the air conditioner to turn on one or two hours before the first employees arrive. After the employees leave for the day, the air conditioner either may turn off for the evening or maintain a higher temperature to conserve energy. Some systems used in hotel rooms may include motion sensors that turn off the air conditioner if they sense no motion or noise in the room. Cruise ship cabins and hotel rooms with doors to a balcony may automatically shut down the air conditioner if the door is left open. Air conditioning systems often are one of the largest consumers of energy, and money spent toward automating one of these systems often can be recovered in smaller electricity bills. In addition to controlling the air conditioning system, building automation systems also can control and monitor lighting. Many newer buildings include motion and sound sensors in each room and automatically turn off lights when the rooms are unoccupied. Lighting in common areas of these buildings might turn off after hours when the building is unoccupied. Alternatively, if the building

has plenty of natural light coming in, sensors automatically can turn off lights when sufficient sunlight is available, or turn on the lights when the sunlight decreases.

The energy management field has made significant advancements because of computer technologies. Businesses not only are able to reduce their energy costs, but they also are conserving energy at the same time.

☀ **Consider This:** In what other ways do computers and technology play a role in the energy management field?

© Viktor Gladkov / Shutterstock

Study Guide

The Study Guide exercise reinforces material you should know for the module exam.

Instructions: Answer the questions below using the format that helps you remember best or that is required by your instructor. Possible formats may include one or more of these options: write the answers; create a document that contains the answers; record answers as audio or video using a webcam, smartphone, or portable media player; post answers on a blog, wiki, or website; or highlight answers in the book/e-book.

1. List types of computers and mobile devices.

2. Describe how personal computers often are differentiated.

3. Explain how to avoid malware infections.

4. Define the term, motherboard.

5. Describe the roles of the processor and memory.

6. Differentiate among traditional and ultrathin laptops, tablets, phablets, and handheld computers.

7. To interact with a tablet, you may use a touch screen or a(n) _____.

8. List steps to protect yourself from webcam spying.

9. List considerations when purchasing a mobile computer. Explain the importance of built-in ports and slots.

10. A(n) _____ desktop may be less expensive and take up less space.

11. Identify types of desktop users and explain how each user's computer needs may differ.

12. Identify how you can purchase the appropriate desktop computer for your needs.

13. Describe the purpose and functions of a server. Differentiate among rack, blade, and tower servers.

14. Define virtualization as it relates to servers. Define the terms, server farm and mainframe.

15. Define the terms, terminal and thin client. List the advantages of a thin client.

16. Identify situations where POS terminals, ATMs, and self-service kiosks might be used. List ATM safety guidelines.

17. A(n) _____ is used to solve complex, sophisticated mathematical calculations, such as those used in petroleum exploration.

18. List cloud computing resources. Describe how businesses use cloud computing to manage resources.

19. List types of mobile devices. Describe features of a smartphone.

20. Explain the issues surrounding the recycling of e-waste.

21. Identify methods for typing on a smartphone.

22. List options provided by text, picture/video message, and voicemail services.

23. Distinguish between push and pull notifications.

24. _____ occurs when a person's attention is diverted, such as by talking on a mobile phone.

25. Describe the types of digital cameras, how they store captured images, and how to transfer photos to a computer.

26. Explain how resolution affects digital picture quality.

27. Identify the features of portable media and digital media players.

28. List considerations when purchasing different types of mobile devices.

29. List features of e-book readers and wearable devices.

30. Identify types of game controllers.

31. Explain whether fitness video games are an effective form of exercise.

32. List products that contain embedded computers. List the disadvantages of in-vehicle technology.

33. Describe the trend, the Internet of Things.

34. Describe categories of computers and mobile devices, and identify general characteristics of size, user type, and price.

35. Explain how a computer uses ports and connectors.

36. List devices that connect to a USB port. Explain risks of using public USB charging stations.

37. Define the term, backward compatible.

38. Distinguish between a port replicator and a docking station.

39. Describe the following technologies: Bluetooth, Wi-Fi, and NFC.

40. _____ is the process of initiating contact between two Bluetooth devices.

41. List steps to connect your phone to a Wi-Fi network.

42. List methods for securing against hardware theft and vandalism.

43. Define the terms, undervoltage and overvoltage, and explain how each can damage a computer or data.

44. Describe the purposes of surge protectors and UPS devices. Explain the purpose a fault-tolerant computer.

45. Identify causes and types of repetitive strain injuries. List symptoms of CVS.

46. List guidelines for evaluating earbuds and headphones.

47. Describe the role of ergonomics in a workplace.

48. List symptoms of technology addiction. Define the term, technology overload.

49. Describe how technology is used in the energy management industry.

You should be able to define the Primary Terms and be familiar with the Secondary Terms listed below.

Key Terms

Primary Terms (shown in **bold-black** characters in the module)

all-in-one (114)	e-book reader (129)	NFC (138)	tablet (112)
Bluetooth (137)	embedded computer	overvoltage (140)	technology addiction
cloud computing (121)	(132)	port (134)	(144)
computer (108)	ergonomics (144)	portable media player	undervoltage (140)
computer vision	game console (131)	(127)	uninterruptible power
syndrome (143)	handheld game device	power surge (140)	supply (UPS) (140)
connector (135)	(131)	resolution (127)	USB port (136)
desktop (114)	laptop (111)	server (116)	wearable device (130)
digital camera (125)	mobile computer (108)	smartphone (123)	Wi-Fi (138)
digital media player (128)	mobile device (108)	surge protector (140)	

Secondary Terms (shown in *italic* characters in the module)

all-in-one desktop (114)	*handheld computer (112)*	*rack server (116)*	*telematics (133)*
activity tracker (130)	*home server (116)*	*repetitive strain injury (RSI) (142)*	*terminal (117)*
application server (116)	*Internet of Things (133)*	*server farm (117)*	*text-to-speech feature (129)*
ATM (118)	*jack (134)*	*server virtualization (117)*	*thin client (117)*
backup server (116)	*joystick (131)*	*slate tablet (112)*	*touch-sensitive pad (128)*
backward compatible (136)	*juice jacking (136)*	*SLR camera (125)*	*tower (114)*
balance board (132)	*kiosk (119)*	*smart digital camera (125)*	*tower server (116)*
bar code reader (118)	*list server (116)*	*smart eyewear (130)*	*ultrabook (111)*
blackout (140)	*mail server (116)*	*smartglasses (130)*	*USB hub (136)*
blade server (116)	*mainframe (117)*	*smartwatch (130)*	*virtual keyboard (124)*
brownout (140)	*media library (128)*	*SMS (short message service) (124)*	*virtualization (117)*
building automation systems (145)	*megapixel (MP) (127)*	*spike (140)*	*visual voice mail (125)*
charge-coupled device (CCD) (125)	*MMS (multimedia message*	*storage server (116)*	*voice mail (125)*
common short code (CSC) (124)	*service) (124)*	*streaming media player (128)*	*wearable (130)*
convertible tablet (112)	*motherboard (110)*	*stylus (112)*	*web server (116)*
CPU (110)	*motion-sensing game controller (132)*	*supercomputer (120)*	*wheel (131)*
CVS (143)	*network server (116)*	*surge suppressor (140)*	*workstation (114)*
dance pad (131)	*noise cancelling (143)*	*swipe keyboard app (123)*	
database server (116)	*notebook computer (111)*	*system unit (114)*	
discoverable mode (137)	*on-screen keyboard (123)*	*technology overload (144)*	
docking station (136)	*optical resolution (127)*		
domain name server (116)	*pairing (137)*		
DVD kiosk (120)	*peripheral device (108)*		
earbuds (128)	*personal computer (108)*		
EarPods (128)	*phablet (112)*		
e-book (129)	*PIN (118)*		
enhanced resolution (127)	*pixel (127)*		
e-reader (129)	*point-and-shoot camera (125)*		
fault-tolerant computer (141)	*port replicator (136)*		
file server (116)	*portable keyboard (124)*		
fingerprint reader (139)	*POS terminal (118)*		
FTP server (116)	*predictive text (123)*		
game server (116)	*print server (116)*		
gamepad (131)	*processor (110)*		
gaming desktop (114)	*pull notification (124)*		
Google Street View (111)	*push notification (124)*		

phablet (112)

Checkpoint

The Checkpoint exercises test your knowledge of the module concepts. The page number containing the answer appears in parentheses after each exercise. The Consider This exercises challenge your understanding of module concepts.

True/False   Mark T for True and F for False.

_____ 1. Malware authors often focus on social media, with the goal of stealing personal information. (110)

_____ 2. The disadvantages of a virtual server are that it is difficult to manage and takes a long time to create and configure. (117)

_____ 3. A mainframe is a small terminal that looks like a desktop, but has limited capabilities and components. (117)

_____ 4. Thin clients contain powerful hard drives. (117)

_____ 5. Applications requiring complex, sophisticated mathematical calculations use mainframes. (120)

_____ 6. Most computers and electronic devices are analog, which use only two discrete states: on and off. (125)

_____ 7. SLR cameras are much heavier and larger than point-and-shoot cameras. (125)

_____ 8. Because embedded computers are components in larger products, they usually are small and have limited hardware. (132)

_____ 9. Instead of the term, port, the term, connector, sometimes is used to identify audio and video ports. (134)

_____ 10. Newer versions of USB are backward compatible, which means they support only new USB devices, not older ones. (136)

_____ 11. A port replicator is an external device that provides connections to peripheral devices through ports built into the device. (136)

_____ 12. Because the processor in a computer is particularly sensitive to fluctuations in current, you always should use a surge protector. (141)

Multiple Choice   Select the best answer.

1. Which of the following is *not* true of ultrathin laptops? (111)
   a. They weigh less than traditional laptops.
   b. They have a shorter battery life.
   c. Many have fewer ports than traditional laptops.
   d. They do not include an optical disc drive.

2. Some people use the term _____ to refer to the case that contains and protects the motherboard, internal hard drive, memory, and other electronic components of the computer from damage. (114)
   a. system unit
   b. phablet
   c. thin client
   d. USB hub

3. Power users may work with a high-end desktop, sometimes called a(n) _____, that is designed to handle intense calculations and powerful graphics. (114)
   a. laptop
   b. gaming desktop
   c. server farm
   d. workstation

4. Services provided by _____ include storing content and controlling access to hardware, software, and other resources on a network. (116)
   a. jacks
   b. servers
   c. fault-tolerant computers
   d. mainframes

5. A dedicated server that backs up and restores files, folders, and media is referred to as a _____. (116)
   a. web server
   b. file server
   c. storage server
   d. backup server

6. A four- or five-digit number assigned to a specific content or mobile service provider is referred to as a(n) _____. (124)
   a. CSC
   b. MMS
   c. SMS
   d. SLR

7. A(n) __ is a special-purpose computer that functions as a component in a larger product. (132)
   a. server
   b. embedded computer
   c. thin client
   d. ultrabook

8. A(n) _____ can connect up to 127 different peripheral devices together with a single connector. (136)
   a. SLR device
   b. USB port
   c. port replicator
   d. docking station

Checkpoint

Matching   Match the terms with their definitions.

_____ 1. peripheral device (108)

_____ 2. motherboard (110)

_____ 3. CPU (110)

_____ 4. slate tablet (112)

_____ 5. phablet (112)

_____ 6. server virtualization (117)

_____ 7. thin client (117)

_____ 8. kiosk (119)

_____ 9. push notification (124)

_____ 10. fault-tolerant computer (141)

a. term used to refer to a device that combines the features of a smartphone with a tablet

b. computer with duplicate components so that it can continue to operate when one of its main components fail

c. tablet that does not contain a physical keyboard

d. component you connect to a computer or mobile device to expand its capabilities

e. terminal that looks like a desktop but has limited capabilities and components

f. the use of software to enable a physical server to emulate the hardware and computing capabilities of one or more servers

g. electronic component that interprets and carries out the basic instructions that operate a computer

h. freestanding terminal that usually has a touchscreen for user input

i. message that initiates from a sending location without a request from the receiver

j. the main circuit board of a personal computer

✳ Consider This   Answer the following questions in the format specified by your instructor.

1. Answer the critical thinking questions posed at the end of these elements in this module: Ethics & Issues (111, 122, 132, 133), How To (137, 138, 141, 143), Mini Features (113, 115, 128), Secure IT (110, 119, 125, 136), and Technology @ Work (145).

2. How do malware authors use social media to spread infection? (110)

3. What are the two main components of the motherboard? (110)

4. How do ultrathin laptops differ from traditional laptops? (111)

5. What privacy issues have arisen with webcams in mobile devices? (111)

6. What are the two types of tablets? (112)

7. What is a stylus? (112)

8. What is in the system unit? (114)

9. What are the features of a gaming desktop? (114)

10. Who might use a workstation? (114)

11. What additional requirements are associated with a dedicated server? (116)

12. What are the three form factors for servers? (116)

13. What are the advantages of virtual servers? (117)

14. How does a POS terminal serve as input? (118)

15. What are some examples of self-serve kiosks? (119)

16. How does cloud computing allow businesses to more efficiently manage resources? (122)

17. What are three types of cloud computing? (122)

18. What information might you receive from a web to mobile text message? (124)

19. For what purpose is a common short code (CSC) used? (124)

20. How do push notifications differ from pull notifications? (124)

21. How do SLR cameras differ from point-and-shoot cameras? (125)

22. What is the difference between enhanced and optical resolution? (127)

23. What are three popular wearable devices? (130)

24. Why are embedded computers usually small with limited hardware? (132)

25. What are some types of ports you might find on a computer or mobile device? (135)

26. What is the purpose of a docking station? (137)

27. What is necessary before two Bluetooth devices can communicate? (138)

28. Why might you want to connect your phone to a Wi-Fi network? (138)

29. How does a surge protector work? What is the purpose of an uninterruptible power supply? (140)

30. How can you prevent RSIs and CTS? (142)

✳ Problem Solving

The Problem Solving exercises extend your knowledge of module concepts by seeking solutions to practical problems with technology that you may encounter at home, school, or work. The Collaboration exercise should be completed with a team.

Instructions: You often can solve problems with technology in multiple ways. Determine a solution to the problems in these exercises by using one or more resources available to you (such as a computer or mobile device, articles on the web or in print, blogs, podcasts, videos, television, user guides, other individuals, electronics or computer stores, etc.). Describe your solution, along with the resource(s) used, in the format requested by your instructor (brief report, presentation, discussion, blog post, video, or other means).

Personal

1. **Slow Computer Performance** Your computer is running exceptionally slow. Not only does it take the operating system a long time to start, but programs also are not performing as well as they used to perform. How might you resolve this?

2. **Faulty ATM** When using an ATM to deposit a check, the ATM misreads the amount of the check and credits your account the incorrect amount. What can you do to resolve this?

Source: Google

3. **Wearable Device Not Syncing** Your wearable device synchronized with your smartphone this morning when you turned it on, but the two devices no longer are synchronized. What might be wrong, and what are your next steps?

4. **Battery Draining Quickly** Although the battery on your smartphone is fully charged, it drains quickly. In some instances when the phone shows that the battery has 30% remaining, it shuts down immediately. What might be wrong?

5. **Potential Virus Infection** While using your laptop, a message is displayed stating that your computer is infected with a virus and you should tap or click a link to download a program designed to remove the virus. How will you respond?

Professional

6. **Excessive Phone Heat** While using your smartphone, you notice that throughout the day it gets extremely hot, making it difficult to hold up to your ear. What steps can you take to correct this problem?

7. **Server Not Connecting** While traveling on a business trip, your phone suddenly stops synchronizing your email messages, calendar information, and contacts. Upon further investigation, you notice an error message stating that your phone is unable to connect to the server. What are your next steps?

8. **Mobile Device Synchronization** When you plug your smartphone into your computer to synchronize the data, the computer does not recognize that the smartphone is connected. What might be the problem?

9. **Cloud Service Provider** Your company uses a cloud service provider to back up the data on each employee's computer. Your computer recently crashed, and you need to obtain the backup data to restore to your computer; however, you are unable to connect to the cloud service provider's website. What are your next steps?

10. **Connecting to a Projector** Your boss asked you to give a presentation to your company's board of directors. When you enter the boardroom and attempt to connect your laptop to the projector, you realize that the cable to connect your laptop to the projector does not fit in any of the ports on your laptop. What are your next steps?

Collaboration

11. **Technology in Energy Management** Your science instructor is teaching a lesson about how technology has advanced the energy management field. Form a team of three people to prepare a brief report about how technology and energy management are connected. One team member should research how computers play a role in conserving energy. Another team member should research other types of technology present in today's homes and buildings that can conserve energy, and the third team member should research other benefits (such as cost savings) resulting from proper energy management.

The How To: Your Turn exercises present general guidelines for fundamental skills when using a computer or mobile device and then require that you determine how to apply these general guidelines to a specific program or situation.

How To: Your Turn

Instructions: You often can complete tasks using technology in multiple ways. Figure out how to perform the tasks described in these exercises by using one or more resources available to you (such as a computer or mobile device, articles on the web or in print, online or program help, user guides, blogs, podcasts, videos, other individuals, trial and error, etc.). Summarize your 'how to' steps, along with the resource(s) used, in the format requested by your instructor (brief report, presentation, discussion, blog post, video, or other means).

❶ Synchronize a Device

Synchronizing a mobile device with the cloud or a computer provides a backup location for your data should your device fail, or become lost or stolen. While companies such as Google and Apple typically will allow you to download your purchased apps again free of charge, you also should synchronize your data so that it is available in the event a problem with your device arises. The following steps guide you through the process of synchronizing a device.

© iStockPhoto / Krystian Nawrocki

Synchronize with the Cloud

a. Search for an app compatible with your device that allows you to synchronize the data on your device with the cloud. Some device manufacturers, such as Apple, provide a service to synchronize your device with the cloud.

b. If necessary, download and install the app.

c. The first time you run the app, you may need to enter some personal information so that you are able to sign in and access your data in the future.

d. Configure the app to synchronize at your desired interval. If you are synchronizing a smartphone, keep in mind that synchronizing with the cloud will require a data plan. Be sure your data plan supports the amount of data that will be synchronized.

e. Once you have configured the synchronization settings successfully, select the option to manually synchronize your device at this time.

Synchronize with a Computer

a. Install and run the app designed to synchronize your device with your computer. For instance, iTunes is used to synchronize Apple devices with a computer.

b. Connect the device to the computer using the synchronization cable provided.

c. When the synchronization is complete, a message will inform you that it is safe to disconnect the device. Do not disconnect the device before the synchronization is complete, as that may damage the data on the device.

Retrieve Synchronized Data

If you lose your device or the data on your device, you can retrieve the data previously synchronized. To retrieve data synchronized previously, follow the instructions in the program or app used to synchronize your data.

Exercises

1. What type of device are you attempting to synchronize? What programs and apps are available to synchronize your device with the cloud? What programs and apps are available to synchronize your device with a computer?

2. Which program or app did you use to synchronize your device? Why did you choose that program or app instead of the others?

3. How long did it take to synchronize your device? What data on your device did the program or app synchronize?

❷ Find, Download, and Read an E-Book on an E-Book Reader

Most e-book readers enable you to find and download new e-books without having to connect to a computer first. To search for and download an e-book, you need to establish an Internet connection through either Wi-Fi or a mobile data plan. The following steps guide you through the process of finding, downloading, and reading an e-book on an e-book reader.

a. Turn on your e-book reader and establish an Internet connection.

b. Navigate to the store on your e-book reader where you can search for and download e-books.

c. Locate the option to search available e-books and then enter the desired search text. You usually can search by the book's title, author, or genre.

✺ How To: Your Turn

d. Perform the search and then browse the search results for the book you want to download and install.

e. Select the option to download the book. Please note that many books cost money to download. If your payment information was entered previously, you may be charged for downloading this e-book. If you do not want to be charged, locate and download an e-book that is free.

f. When the download is complete, return to your list of installed e-books.

g. Select the e-book you have just downloaded to read the e-book.

Exercises

1. What type of e-book reader do you have? Are you happy with the selection of e-books on your e-book reader?

2. In addition to e-book readers, what other types of devices allow you to read e-books?

3. Do e-books cost more or less than traditional print books? What are the advantages and disadvantages of using e-books?

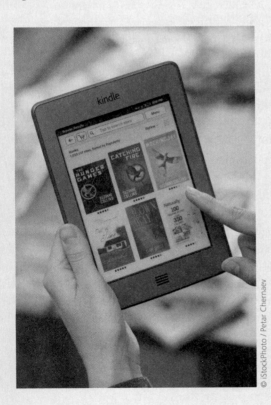

© iStockPhoto / Petar Chernaev

③ Manage Power for Mobile Computers and Devices

Configuring power management settings on mobile computers and devices will help ensure your battery life is maximized. The following steps guide you

through the process of configuring power management features on mobile computers and devices.

a. Display the Control Panel or Settings on your mobile computer or device.

b. Tap or click the option to display power management or battery settings.

c. If necessary, select a power plan setting to view or modify.

d. Make the necessary adjustments to the settings that affect power consumption. For example, configure the display to dim or turn off after 30 seconds of inactivity. This will allow you enough time to read what is on the screen without having to touch the screen or move the mouse.

e. Save all changes.

Exercises

1. What power management settings have you configured on your mobile computer or device?

2. Compare battery life on your device before and after configuring power management settings. Have you noticed an improvement in battery life? If so, how vmuch?

3. What other power management settings are you able to configure on your mobile computer or device?

Google Inc.

How To: Your Turn

4 **Use your Mobile Device Ergonomically**

Individuals are using various mobile devices, such as phones and tablets, more frequently, and using these devices ergonomically can help prevent unnecessary injury. The following guidelines will help you use your mobile device ergonomically:

- Use shortcuts and abbreviations whenever possible to avoid excessive hand movement.
- Make sure your hands, wrists, and arms are at a natural angle, and avoid holding the device in a position that causes discomfort.
- Use hands-free devices and voice recognition features whenever possible to avoid hand movement.
- Do not use the device for extended periods of time without taking frequent breaks.
- Avoid resting the device on your lap during use.
- Sit in an upright position or stand when using the device.
- Consider using a separate keyboard and mouse if you will be interacting with the device extensively.
- Use the device in a setting with natural light.

Exercises

1. Have you been following the above guidelines while using mobile computers and devices? If not, what have you been doing differently?
2. What types of health risks might nonergonomic use of a mobile device pose?
3. What are some additional guidelines you can follow to help minimize health risks while using your mobile device?

© Marcin Balcerzak / Shutterstock

5 **Transfer Media from a Mobile Device to a Computer**

Many individuals take photos and record videos using mobile devices such as digital cameras, smartphones, and tablets. After taking the photos and recording the videos, transferring them to a computer allows you easily to create backup copies, edit the media, and create digital albums. The following steps describe multiple ways to transfer media from a mobile device to a computer.

To transfer photos from a mobile device to a computer using a memory card:

a. Safely remove the memory card from the mobile device.
b. Properly insert the memory card into the appropriate memory card slot on the computer.
c. When the computer detects the memory card, navigate to the location of the media to transfer.
d. Select the files to transfer and then drag them to the destination folder on the computer.
e. Use the operating system's "Eject" or "Safely Remove" feature to remove the memory card from the computer safely and insert it back in the mobile device.

To transfer photos from a mobile device to a computer using a USB cable:

a. Connect the cable to the mobile device and to the computer.
b. When the computer detects the mobile device, navigate to the location on the mobile device containing the media to transfer.
c. Select the files to transfer and then drag them to the destination folder on the computer.
d. Disconnect the USB cable from the computer and from the mobile device.
    Some mobile devices also allow you to transfer media using wireless technologies, such as Bluetooth and Wi-Fi. The steps required to transfer photos wirelessly vary greatly for each device. Thus, read your mobile device's documentation to see if and how you can transfer media to your computer wirelessly. Be aware that transferring photos using your mobile data plan could increase your data charges. Consider using Wi-Fi or Bluetooth to transfer the media.

Exercises

1. Of the above techniques, which way do you find is easiest to transfer media from your mobile device to a computer? Why?
2. What other technologies might you be able to use to transfer media from a mobile device to a computer?
3. Would you rather transfer media from your mobile device to a computer, or transfer it to the cloud? Why?

✳ Internet Research

The Internet Research exercises broaden your understanding of module concepts by requiring that you search for information on the web.

Instructions: Use a search engine or another search tool to locate the information requested or answers to questions presented in the exercises. Describe your findings, along with the search term(s) you used and your web source(s), in the format requested by your instructor (brief report, presentation, discussion, blog post, video, or other means).

❶ Making Use of the Web
Retail and Auctions

E-retailers are changing the ways consumers shop for goods. One market research firm reports that nearly three-fourths of shoppers complete one-half of all their transactions online. As shoppers grow increasingly loyal to e-commerce, retail websites have become more sophisticated, and brick-and-mortar stores have adapted to the online presence. Nearly 90 percent of smartphone owners use their devices to compare prices, locate promotional offers, and determine directions and store hours.

Online auctions offer another convenient method of shopping for and selling practically anything imaginable. Most auction sites organize products in categories and provide photos and descriptions. eBay is one of thousands of Internet auction websites and is the world's largest personal online trading community. In addition, craigslist is a free online equivalent of classified advertisements.

Research This: (a) Visit two retail websites and search for the latest e-book readers. Which features do these websites offer compared with the same offerings in brick-and-mortar stores? What are the advantages and disadvantages of shopping online? What policies do these websites offer for returning items? Which items have you purchased online?

(b) Visit an auction website and search for two objects pertaining to your favorite musical artist, sports team, or celebrity. For example, search for an autographed photo or ticket stubs. Describe these two items. How many people have bid on these items? Who are the sellers? What are the opening and current bids?

Source: eBay

❷ Social Media

Businesses know that using social media is an efficient and effective method of building brand loyalty and promoting the exchange of ideas. The informal communication between consumers and company representatives can help maintain credibility and promote trust. According to a recent study, more than 70 percent of American Internet users visit online social networks, and 65 percent of these people discover particular brands, products, and services by reading material posted on these websites. Twitter, Facebook, and other social media often are used to befriend customers, give a positive feeling about services and goods, engage readers, and market new ideas. Subscribers share their opinions, thoughts, and experiences, either positive or negative, through product and service reviews.

Research This: Visit at least three Twitter, Facebook, or other online social network sites and review the content. How many Twitter followers or Facebook 'likes' does the website have? Identify three organizations, businesses, products, or causes that have a presence on Facebook, Twitter, or other online social networks. How many followers or fans do they have? Which posts are engaging and promote positive attitudes about the company and the products or services offered? How many user-generated reviews and product ratings are shown? How do the online social networks encourage sharing opinions? In which ways do the companies respond to and interact with followers and fans? If negative posts are written, does the company respond professionally and positively?

❸ Search Skills
Search Operators

Search engines provide operators, or special symbols, that will help narrow down search results. Use quotation marks around search text to search for an exact word or phrase. For example, type the following as your search text: "wireless communications technologies" (be sure to include the quotation marks) to search for those three words in that exact order. Search results will display matching pages with the quoted search phrase highlighted or in bold.

Internet Research

To match one or more words in a phrase, you can use an asterisk (*), also called a wildcard operator, as part of your search text. Each asterisk represents one or more words. For example, type the following as your search text: "wireless * technologies" (with the quotation marks) to find search results that match wireless communications technologies, wireless Internet technologies, wireless and related technologies, and others. If you are searching for a phrase or quotation with many words, consider using the asterisk wildcard operator in place of some of the words in the search text. This technique is useful if you have a quotation, and you want to find out who said it or where it may have appeared.

Source: Google

Research This: Create search queries using quotation marks and/or the wildcard operator to answer the following questions and use a search engine to find the answers. (1) Someone once said, "Life is not fair, get used to it." Who was it? (2) What are three websites containing digital camera reviews? (3) How do businesses use near field communications? (4) Find five different words that complete the phrase, handheld ___ devices, by typing appropriate search text into a search engine.

4 Security

Surge protectors and uninterruptible power supplies offer protection from electrical power surges, as you learned in the Protecting Hardware section of this module. While these surges are part of everyday life, they are more likely to occur during thunderstorms and peak energy consumption periods. These unavoidable occurrences can damage or ruin sensitive electronic equipment. The processor in a computer is particularly sensitive to the fluctuations in current. When shopping for a surge protector, purchase the best product you can afford. Typically, the amount of protection offered by a surge protector is proportional to its cost. That is, the more expensive the surge protector, the more protection it offers.

Research This: Visit an electronics store or view websites with a variety of surge protectors from several manufacturers. Read the packaging or specifications to determine many of the features. Compare at least three surge protectors by creating a table using these headings: manufacturer, model, price, Joule rating (a Joule is the unit of energy the device can absorb before it can be damaged; the higher the Joule rating, the better the protection), warranty, energy-absorption rating, response time, and other features. Which surge protector do you recommend? Why?

5 Cloud Services
Data Providers and Mashups (DaaS)

The web has made it possible for many information providers to make business, housing, weather, demographic, and other data available on demand to third parties. Accessing online data on demand is an example of DaaS (data as a service), a service of cloud computing that provides current data over the Internet for download, analysis, or use in new applications.

Mashups are apps that combine data from one or more online data providers. Mapping mashups are popular because users can visualize locations associated with data originating from a variety of online sources, including real estate listings, crime statistics, current Tweets, live traffic conditions, or digital photos.

Research This: (1) Use a search engine to find two different online data markets. Write a report sharing the sources or focus of information each provides, the availability of visualization tools to preview data, and how developers can access or incorporate the data into their own apps and websites. (2) Use a search engine to find a popular mapping mashup based on data from one of the sources listed above, or another topic. Identify the provider of the data and the provider of the maps on which the data is displayed. (3) Use a search engine to find an app or website that will help you create your own map mashup showing locations of your online data: Facebook friends, Flickr or Instagram photos, or Tweets. Take a screenshot of the mashup you made.

Critical Thinking

The Critical Thinking exercises challenge your assessment and decision-making skills by presenting real-world situations associated with module concepts. The Collaboration exercise should be completed with a team.

Instructions: Evaluate the situations below, using personal experiences and one or more resources available to you (such as articles on the web or in print, blogs, podcasts, videos, television, user guides, other individuals, electronics or computer stores, etc.). Perform the tasks requested in each exercise and share your deliverables in the format requested by your instructor (brief report, presentation, discussion, blog post, video, or other means).

1. Technology Purchases

You are the director of information technology at a company that specializes in designing and selling customizable sportswear for local high school and college sports teams. Most of the technology equipment is out of date and must be replaced. You need to evaluate the requirements of individual employees so that you can order replacements.

Do This: Determine the type of computer or mobile device that might be most appropriate for the following employees: a graphic designer who exclusively works in the office, a cashier who is responsible for assisting customers with purchases, and a sales representative who travels to various locations and needs wireless communications capabilities. Consider the varying requirements of each, including mobility, security, and processing capabilities. Discuss various options that might work for each user, and considerations when purchasing each type of device.

2. Game Devices

You manage a youth recreation center and have been given a grant to purchase a game console and accessories, along with fitness games, for use at the center.

Do This: Use the web to research three popular recent game consoles. Choose five characteristics to compare the game consoles, such as Internet capabilities, multiplayer game support, storage capacity, television connection, and game controllers. Research fitness games for each console and what accessories are needed to run the games. Determine the goals of each game, such as skill-building, weight loss, or entertainment. Read user reviews of each game, as well as professional reviews by gaming industry experts. If possible, survey your friends and classmates to learn about their experiences with each game, such as heart rate while playing the games, any fitness goals reached, and their enjoyment of the game.

3. Case Study

Amateur Sports League You are the new manager for a nonprofit amateur soccer league. The league would like to purchase a digital camera to upload pictures of players, games, and fundraising events to its Facebook page and its website.

Do This: You need to prepare information about digital camera options to present to the board of directors. First, research the cost and quality differences between point-and-shoot cameras and SLR cameras. Use the web to find a recent model of both camera types and compare the reviews, as well as the costs, for each. Make a list of additional features, such as video capabilities, editing capabilities, lens, megapixels, GPS, flash, and zoom. Determine how each camera stores the images, the amount of storage available, and how to transfer images to a computer or mobile device. Explore whether software is included with the camera that can be used to edit, store, or organize the images after they are transferred to a computer. Compare your findings with the camera capabilities of a recent model smartphone. Determine what type of camera would be best for the league's needs and the capabilities that are most important.

Courtesy of Samsung

Collaboration

4. National Security Uses for Technology

Technology is an integral part of military operations. Many military research projects use simulators that resemble civilian computer games. Your company has been contacted by the Department of Defense for a research project.

Do This: Form a four-member team, and then form two two-member groups. Assign each group one of the following topics to research: (1) How have mobile computers and cloud computing affected issues of national security? (2) How can the utilization of microchips worn by soldiers, or wearable computers, be integrated into civilian use? Meet with your team and discuss your findings. Determine any advantages or disadvantages, as well as any legal ramifications that may arise.

PROGRAMS AND APPS: Productivity, Graphics, Security, and Other Tools

4

People use a variety of programs and apps on their computers and mobile devices.

"I use my computer and mobile devices to complete homework assignments, pay bills, edit digital photos, post social media updates, and play games. I also use an antivirus program. What other programs and apps could I need?"

While you may be familiar with some of the content in this module, do you know how to ...

- Determine safe websites for downloading software?
- Ensure you are not plagiarizing Internet content?
- Safely use a personal finance app?
- Use project management software?
- Avoid risks when using payment apps?
- Edit and share photos?
- Use voice command personal assistant apps?
- Identify different types of viruses and malware?
- Recognize a virus hoax?
- Protect your smartphone against malware threats?
- Recognize a phishing message?
- Uninstall a program or remove an app?
- Compress and uncompress files and folders?

In this module, you will discover how to perform these tasks along with much more information essential to this course.

© Rashevskyi Viacheslav / Shutterstock

✔ Objectives

After completing this module, you will be able to:

1 Identify the general categories of programs and apps

2 Describe how an operating system interacts with applications and hardware

3 Differentiate among the ways you can acquire programs and apps: retail, custom, web app, mobile app, mobile web app, shareware, freeware, open source, and public-domain

4 Identify the key features of productivity applications: word processing, presentation, spreadsheet, database, note taking, calendar and contact management, project management, accounting, personal finance, legal, tax preparation, document management, support services, and enterprise computing

5 Identify the key features of graphics and media applications: computer-aided design, desktop publishing, paint/image editing, photo editing and photo management, video and audio editing, multimedia and website authoring, media player, and disc burning

6 Identify the uses of personal interest applications: lifestyle, medical, entertainment, convenience, and education

7 Identify the purpose of software used in communications

8 Identify the key features of security tools: personal firewall, antivirus programs, malware removers, and Internet filters

9 Identify the key features of file, disk, and system management tools: file manager, search, image viewer, uninstaller, disk cleanup, disk defragmenter, screen saver, file compression, PC maintenance, and backup and restore

Programs and Apps

Using programs and apps, you can accomplish a variety of tasks on computers and mobile devices (Figure 4-1). Recall from Module 1 that a **program**, or **software**, consists of a series of related instructions, organized for a common purpose, that tells the computer what tasks to perform and how to perform them. An **application**, or **app**, sometimes called *application software*, consists of programs designed to make users more productive and/or assist them with personal tasks.

An *operating system* is a set of programs that coordinates all the activities among computer or mobile device hardware. Other programs, often called *tools* or *utilities*, enable you to perform maintenance-type tasks usually related to managing devices, media, and programs used by computers and mobile devices. The operating system and other tools are collectively known as *system software* because they consist of the programs that control or maintain the operations of the computer and its devices.

Role of the Operating System

Internet Research

Which mobile operating system is the most widely used?

Search for: mobile operating system market share

To use applications, such as a browser or word processing program on a desktop or laptop, your computer must be running an operating system. Similarly, a mobile device must be running an operating system to run a mobile app, such as a navigation or payment app. Desktop operating systems include Mac OS, Windows, Linux, and Chrome OS. Mobile operating systems include Android, iOS, and Windows Phone. The operating system, therefore, serves as the interface between the user, the applications and other programs, and the computer's or mobile device's hardware (Figure 4-2).

Figure 4-1 Users work with a variety of programs and apps, some of which are shown in this figure.

An Example of How an Operating System Interacts with a User, an Application, and Hardware

Step 2
The user instructs the operating system to run an application, such as a word processing application, which appears on the user's screen. The user then instructs the application to print a document.

document to be printed

Step 1
An operating system user interface is displayed on the screen when a user turns on a computer.

Print button

Step 3
The application sends the print instruction to the computer's operating system (software), which is running on the computer.

Step 4
The operating system sends the print instruction to the printer (hardware), which prints the document.

Figure 4-2 This figure shows how the operating system is the interface between the user, the application, and the hardware.
© photoguy_76 / Fotolia; © Cengage Learning; © restyler / Shutterstock.com; © StockLite / Shutterstock; Source: Microsoft

Each time you start a computer or mobile device, the operating system is loaded (copied) from the computer's hard drive or mobile device's storage media into memory. Once the operating system is loaded, it coordinates all the activities of the computer or mobile device. This includes running applications and transferring data among input and output devices and memory. While the computer or mobile device is running, the operating system remains in memory.

Obtaining Software

Software is available in a variety of forms: retail, custom, web app, mobile app, mobile web app, shareware, freeware, open source, and public domain.

- *Retail software* is mass-produced, copyrighted software that meets the needs of a wide variety of users, not just a single user or company. Some retail software, such as an operating system, is preinstalled on new computers and mobile devices. You also can purchase retail software from local stores and on the web. With online purchases, you may be able to download purchased programs immediately instead of waiting for the software to arrive by mail.
- *Custom software* performs functions specific to a business or industry. Sometimes a company cannot locate retail software that meets its unique requirements. In this case, the company may use software developers to create tailor-made custom software. Custom software usually costs more than retail software.
- A *web app* is an application stored on a web server that you access through a browser. Users typically interact with web apps directly by visiting a website, but some web apps also can be accessed locally offline. Many websites provide free access to their apps. Some charge a one-time fee, while others charge recurring monthly or annual subscription fees. You may be able to use part of a web app free and pay for access to a more comprehensive program or pay a fee when a certain action occurs.
- A *mobile app* is an application you download from a mobile device's app store, sometimes called a *marketplace*, or other location on the Internet to a smartphone or other mobile device. Some mobile apps are preinstalled on a new mobile computer or device. Many mobile apps are free; others have a minimal cost — often less than a few dollars.
- A *mobile web app* is a web app that is optimized for display in a browser on a mobile device, regardless of screen size or orientation. Many app developers opt for web delivery because they do not have to create a different version for each mobile device's app store. Many web apps use a responsive design, which means the app displays properly on any computer or device.
- *Shareware* is copyrighted software that is distributed at no cost for a trial period. To use a shareware program beyond that period, you send payment to the software developer or you might be billed automatically unless you cancel within a specified period of time. Some developers trust users to send payment if software use extends beyond the stated trial period. Others render the software useless if no payment is received after the trial period expires. In some cases, a scaled-down version of the software is distributed free, and payment entitles the user to the fully functional product.
- *Freeware* is copyrighted software provided at no cost by an individual or a company that retains all rights to the software. Thus, software developers typically cannot incorporate freeware in applications they intend to sell. The word, free, in freeware indicates the software has no charge.
- *Open source software* is software provided for use, modification, and redistribution. This software has no restrictions from the copyright holder regarding modification of the software's internal instructions and its redistribution. Open source software usually can be downloaded from a web server on the Internet, often at no cost. Promoters of open source software state two main advantages: users who modify the software share their improvements with others, and customers can personalize the software to meet their needs.
- *Public-domain software* has been donated for public use and has no copyright restrictions. Anyone can copy or distribute public-domain software to others at no cost.

Thousands of shareware, freeware, and public-domain programs are available on the Internet for users to download. Examples include communications, graphics, and game programs. Read Secure IT 4-1 for tips about safely downloading shareware, freeware, or public-domain software.

 SECURE IT 4-1

Safe Downloading Websites

Websites tempt potential customers with catchy offers for software promising to speed up the computer or to obtain the latest versions of games and music. The temptation to download shareware, freeware, and public-domain software is high, especially when the cost of such useful or fun programs is free or extremely reasonable. This action could be dangerous, however, because some of these websites are filled with virus-infected software just waiting to be installed on an unsuspecting user's computer or mobile device.

Before downloading any software, consider these factors when locating and evaluating shareware, freeware, or public-domain websites:

- Search for popular shareware, freeware, and public-domain download websites.

The software generally is organized into evaluation categories, such as outstanding and recommended, or grouped into purpose, such as tools and gaming.

- Look for websites with programs for your particular type of computer or mobile device. Some websites exclusively offer Windows- or Apple-based products.

- Obtain the latest versions of shareware, freeware, and public-domain software. Many developers update their programs frequently in an effort to include new features and to thwart viruses. The newest versions, therefore, often are safer and easier to use than previous versions.

- Locate websites with a variety of programs in a specific category. For example, if you need antivirus software, you can search

to find which shareware, freeware, and public-domain software is available.

- Read ratings for and reviews of products. Often, comments from users provide guidance in selecting the most desirable software for your needs.

If you follow these tips, you may find shareware, freeware, and public-domain software to be one of the best software bargains in the marketplace.

 Consider This: Have you ever used or downloaded programs or apps from a shareware, freeware, or public-domain software website? If so, what software did you acquire? If not, would you consider locating shareware, freeware, or public-domain software for your particular needs? Why or why not?

 CONSIDER THIS

What is software as a service?

Software as a service (SaaS) describes a computing environment where an Internet server hosts and deploys applications. Editing projects or photos, sending email messages, and managing finances are common consumer tasks of SaaS applications. For an exercise related to SaaS, see the Internet Research: Cloud Services exercise at the end of this module.

Installing Software

Recall from Module 1 that you typically need to install desktop apps on a computer. Installing is the process of setting up the software to work with a computer, printer, and other hardware. Mobile apps typically install automatically after you download the app from the device's app store. You usually do not need to install web apps before you can use them, but you may need to install plug-ins, such as Java or Flash, so that the web apps work.

 BTW

Syncing Apps
When you install an app on one computer or device, it also will install automatically on any other computers and devices on the same subscription plan.

During installation of software or before the first use, a program or app may ask you to register and/or activate the software. *Software registration* typically is optional and usually involves submitting your name and other personal information to the software manufacturer or developer. Registering the software often entitles you to product support. *Product activation* is a technique that some software manufacturers use to ensure that you do not install the software on more computers than legally licensed. Usually, the software can be run a preset number of times, has limited functionality, or does not function until you activate it via the Internet or by phone. Thus, activation is a required process for programs that request it. Some software allows multiple activations; for example, you can install it and run it on a laptop and a desktop. Registering and/ or activating software also usually entitles you to free program updates for a specified time period, such as a year.

Many desktop and mobile apps use an *automatic update* feature, where the updates can be configured to download and install automatically. With web apps, by contrast, you always access the latest version of the software.

☀ **CONSIDER THIS** ————————————————————————————

What is a license agreement?

A *license agreement,* sometimes called an end-user license agreement (*EULA*), is the right to use a program or app. The license agreement provides specific conditions for use of the software, which a user typically must accept before using the software (Figure 4-3). Unless otherwise specified by a license agreement, you do not have the right to copy, loan, borrow, rent, or in any way distribute programs or apps. Doing so is a violation of copyright law; it also is a federal crime.

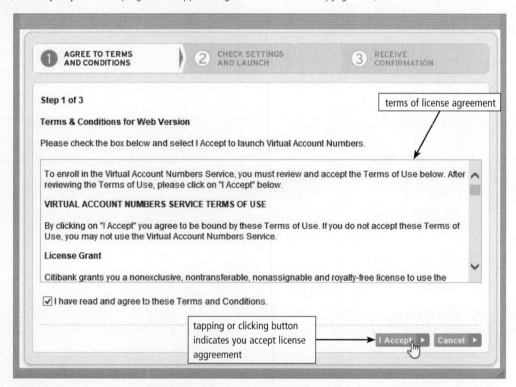

Figure 4-3 A user must accept the terms in a license agreement before using the software.
Source: Citigroup Inc

Categories of Programs and Apps

With programs and apps, you can work on a variety of projects — such as creating letters, memos, reports, and other documents; developing presentations; preparing and filing taxes; drawing and altering images; recording and enhancing audio and video clips; obtaining directions or maps; playing games individually or with others; composing email and other messages; protecting computers and mobile devices from malware; organizing media; locating files; and much more. Table 4-1 categorizes popular categories of programs and apps by their general use.

Table 4-1 Programs and Apps by Category

Category	Types of Programs and Apps	
Productivity (Business and Personal)	• Word Processing • Presentation • Spreadsheet • Database • Note Taking • Calendar and Contact Management • Project Management	• Accounting • Personal Finance • Legal • Tax Preparation • Document Management • Support Services • Enterprise Computing
Graphics and Media	• Computer-Aided Design (CAD) • Desktop Publishing • Paint/Image Editing • Photo Editing and Photo Management • Clip Art/Image Gallery	• Video and Audio Editing • Multimedia and Website Authoring • Media Player • Disc Burning
Personal Interest	• Lifestyle • Medical • Entertainment • Convenience • Education	
Communications	• Blog • Browser • Chat Room • Online Discussion • Email • File Transfer	• Internet Phone • Internet Messaging • Mobile Messaging • Videoconference • Web Feeds
Security	• Personal Firewall • Antivirus • Malware Removers • Internet Filters	
File, Disk, and System Management	• File Manager • Search • Image Viewer • Uninstaller • Disk Cleanup	• Disk Defragmenter • Screen Saver • File Compression • PC Maintenance • Backup and Restore

✳ CONSIDER THIS

Are the categories of programs and apps shown in Table 4-1 mutually exclusive?
Programs and apps listed in one category may be used in other categories. For example, photo editing applications, which appear in the graphics and media category, often also are used for business or personal productivity. Additionally, the programs and apps in the last three categories (communications; security; and file, disk, and system management) often are used in conjunction with or to support programs and apps in the first three categories (productivity, graphics and media, and personal interest). For example, email appears in the communications category but also is a productivity application.

Productivity Applications

Productivity applications can assist you in becoming more effective and efficient while performing daily activities at work, school, and home. Productivity applications include word processing, presentation, spreadsheet, database, note taking, calendar and contact management, project management, accounting, personal finance, legal, tax preparation, document management, and enterprise computing.

A variety of manufacturers offer productivity apps in each of these areas, ranging from desktop to mobile to web apps. Many have a desktop version and a corresponding mobile version adapted for smaller screen sizes and/or touch screens.

Developing Projects

With productivity applications, users often create, edit, format, save, and distribute projects. Projects include documents, presentations, spreadsheets, notes, calendars, contact lists, budgets, and more.

During the process of developing a project, you likely will switch back and forth among the following activities.

1. When you *create* a project, you enter text or numbers, insert images, add contacts, schedule appointments, and perform other tasks using a variety of input methods, such as a keyboard, a mouse, touch, or voice.
2. To *edit* a project means to make changes to its existing content. Common editing tasks include inserting, deleting, cutting, copying, and pasting.
    a. Inserting involves adding text, images, or other content.
    b. Deleting involves removing text, images, or other content.
    c. Cutting is the process of removing content and storing it in a temporary storage location, called a *clipboard*.
    d. Copying is the process of placing content on a clipboard, with the content remaining in the project. Read Ethics & Issues 4-1 for a discussion about unethical copying.
    e. Pasting is the process of transferring content from a clipboard to a specific location in a project.

 ETHICS & ISSUES 4-1

What Can Schools and Employers Do to Prevent Internet Plagiarism?

The Internet has made it easier for students and employees to plagiarize; in contrast, it also provides tools that schools and employers can use to detect illegal copying. Schools often have specific rules about what constitutes plagiarism. Employees, such as journalists, are expected to follow ethical guidelines when copying or citing content.

The Internet offers many ways for students to cheat intentionally, including websites that allow you to purchase a research paper. Students may not realize that copying information without properly citing it also is plagiarism. Students who intentionally plagiarize blame competition. Teachers have several tools to catch plagiarists,

including services that compare papers to others on the Internet and produce a report highlighting content resembling previously published writing.

A journalist might be expected not only to produce multiple articles daily but also to use social media to keep readers engaged. This pressure tempts some journalists to copy content, sometimes without giving credit or linking to the original source. The laws against plagiarism are the same whether copying content from a respected news source, a personal blog, or social media. The pressures of time and expectations of content can create high-profile cases of plagiarism that affect not only the journalist but the news source for which he or she writes.

Some argue that the best way to prevent cheating is to educate. First, teach the values and discuss the consequences of cheating. Next, teach how to cite sources properly and summarize information. Before copying or paraphrasing another person's work, contact him or her to request permission. When in doubt, check with a librarian, editor, or instructor.

Consider This: How should educators and employers deal with plagiarism? Should schools use a paper-comparison service in an attempt to stop cheating? Why or why not? Does linking to the original source excuse a journalist who copies content? Why or why not?

3. When users *format* a project, they change its appearance. Formatting is important because the overall look of a project significantly can affect its capability to communicate information clearly. Examples of formatting tasks are changing the font, font size, and font style (Figure 4-4).

   a. A *font* is a name assigned to a specific design of characters. Cambria and Calibri are examples of fonts.

   b. *Font size* indicates the size of the characters in a particular font. Font size is gauged by a measurement system called points. A single point is about 1/72 of an inch in height.

   c. A *font style* adds emphasis to a font. Bold, italic, underline, and color are examples of font styles.

4. During the process of creating, editing, and formatting a project, the computer or mobile device holds it in memory. To keep the project for future use requires that you save it. When you *save* a project, the computer transfers the project from memory to a local storage medium, such as a USB flash drive or hard drive, or cloud storage, so that you can retrieve it later.

5. You can distribute a project as a hard copy or electronically. A *hard copy* is information that exists on a physical medium, such as paper. To generate a hard copy, you *print* a project. Sending electronic files via email or posting them for others to view, on websites for example, saves paper and printer supplies. Many users opt for electronic distribution because it contributes to green computing.

Figure 4-4 The Cambria and Calibri fonts are shown in two font sizes and a variety of font styles.
© Cengage Learning

✳ **CONSIDER THIS** —————————————————————————————

How often should you save a project, and why do some apps not require you save?
Saving at regular intervals, such as every 5 or 10 minutes, ensures that the majority of your work will not be lost in the event of a power loss or system failure. Many programs have an AutoSave feature that automatically saves open projects at specified time intervals, such as every 10 minutes.

   Some web and mobile apps, such as online productivity apps, save your work instantly as you type. These apps and the document both are stored on the cloud. Thus, the app automatically saves your changes to a cloud server with every keystroke.

✳ **CONSIDER THIS** —————————————————————————————

What is a clip art/image gallery?
Applications often include a **clip art/image gallery**, which is a collection of clip art and photos. Some applications contain links to additional clips available on the web or are available as web apps. You also can purchase clip art/image gallery software that contains thousands of images.

   In addition to clip art and photos, many clip art/image galleries provide fonts, animations, sounds, video clips, and audio clips. You can use the images, fonts, and other items from the clip art/image gallery in all types of projects, including documents, brochures, worksheets, and slide shows.

Word Processing

Word processing software, sometimes called a word processor, is an application that allows users to create and manipulate documents containing mostly text and sometimes graphics (Figure 4-5). Millions of people use word processing software on their computers and mobile devices every day to develop documents such as letters, memos, reports, mailing labels, newsletters, and webpages.

A major advantage of using word processing software is that it enables users to change their written words easily. Word processing software also has many features to make documents look professional and visually appealing. For example, you can change the font, size, and color of characters; apply special effects, such as three-dimensional shadows; use built-in styles to format documents; and organize text in newspaper-style columns.

Most word processing software allows users to incorporate graphics, such as digital photos and clip art, in documents. In Figure 4-5, a user inserted an image of a tractor in the document. With word processing software, you easily can modify the appearance of an image after inserting it in the document.

You can use word processing software to define the size of the paper on which to print and to specify the margins. A feature, called wordwrap, allows users to type words in a paragraph continually without pressing the ENTER key at the end of each line. While you edit a paragraph or change the paragraph margins, the words in the paragraph automatically wrap, or reflow within the paragraph. As you type more lines of text than can be displayed on the screen, the top portion of the document moves upward, or scrolls, off the screen.

Internet Research
What are the guidelines for writing business letters?
Search for: business letter writing

document is displayed in window

image

printed document

Figure 4-5 Word processing software enables users to create professional and visually appealing documents.
Microsoft; © Cengage Learning

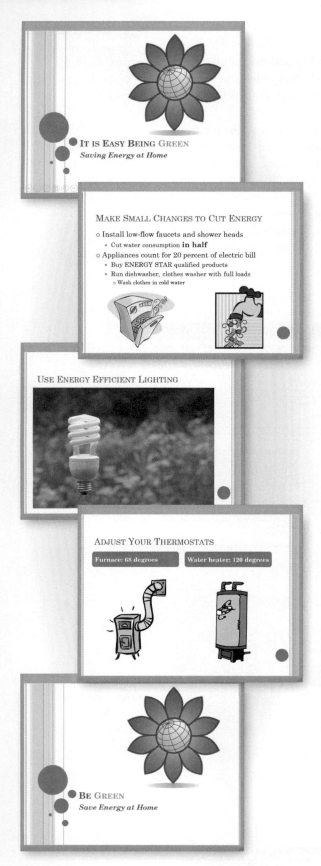

Figure 4-6 This presentation created with presentation software consists of five slides.
Source: Microsoft; © Cengage Learning

Word processing software typically includes tools to assist you with the writing process. For example, a spelling checker reviews the spelling of individual words, sections of a document, or the entire document. A grammar checker detects passive voice, run-on sentences, and grammatical errors. A format checker identifies extraneous spaces, capitalization errors, and more.

Presentation

Presentation software is an application that allows users to create visual aids for presentations to communicate ideas, messages, and other information to a group. The presentations can be viewed as slides, sometimes called a *slide show*, that are displayed on a large monitor or on a projection screen from a computer or mobile device (Figure 4-6).

Presentation software typically provides a variety of predefined presentation formats that define complementary colors for backgrounds, text, and graphical accents on the slides. This software also provides a variety of layouts for each individual slide such as a title slide, a two-column slide, and a slide with clip art, a chart, a table, or a diagram. In addition, you can enhance any text, charts, and graphics on a slide with 3-D effects, animation, and other special effects, such as shading, shadows, and textures.

When building a presentation, users can set the slide timing so that the presentation automatically displays the next slide after a preset delay. Presentation software allows you to apply special effects to the transition between slides. One slide, for example, might fade away as the next slide appears.

Presentation software typically includes a clip gallery that provides images, photos, video clips, and audio clips to enhance presentations. Some audio and video editing applications work with presentation software, providing users with an easy means to record and insert video, music, and audio commentary in a presentation.

You can view or print a finished presentation in a variety of formats, including a hard copy outline of text from each slide and handouts that show completed slides. Presentation software also incorporates features such as checking spelling, formatting, researching, and creating webpages from existing slide shows.

Spreadsheet

Spreadsheet software is an application that allows users to organize data in columns and rows and perform calculations on the data. These columns and rows collectively are called a **worksheet**. Most spreadsheet software has basic features to help users create, edit, and format worksheets. A spreadsheet file also is known as a workbook because it can contain thousands of related individual worksheets. Data is organized vertically in columns and horizontally in rows on each worksheet (Figure 4-7).

Each worksheet usually can have thousands of columns and rows. One or more letters identify each column, and a number identifies each row. Only a small fraction of these columns and rows are visible on the screen at one time. Scrolling through the worksheet displays different parts of it on the screen.

A cell is the intersection of a column and row. The spreadsheet software identifies cells by the column and row in which they are located. For example, the intersection of column B and row 4 is referred to as cell B4. As shown in Figure 4-7, cell B4 contains the number, $1,000.29, which represents the wages for January.

Many of the worksheet cells shown in Figure 4-7 contain a number, called a value, that can be used in a calculation. Other cells, however, contain formulas that generate values. A formula performs calculations on the data in the worksheet and displays the resulting value in a cell, usually the cell containing the formula. When creating a worksheet, you can enter your own formulas. In Figure 4-7, for example, cell B17 could contain the formula =B9+B10+B11+B12+ B13+B14+B15+B16, which would add (sum) the contents of cells B9, B10, B11, B12, B13, B14, B15, and B16. That is, this formula calculates the total expenses for January.

A *function* is a predefined formula that performs common calculations, such as adding the values in a group of cells or generating a value such as the time or date. For example, the function =SUM(B9:B16) instructs the spreadsheet application to add all of the numbers in the range of cells B9 through B16. Spreadsheet applications contain many built-in functions.

One of the more powerful features of spreadsheet software is its capability to recalculate the rest of the worksheet when data in a cell changes. Spreadsheet software's capability of recalculating data also makes it a valuable budgeting, forecasting, and decision-making tool. Another standard feature of spreadsheet software is charting, which depicts the data in graphical form, such as bar charts or pie charts. A visual representation of data through charts often makes it easier for users to see at a glance the relationship among the numbers.

BTW
Formulas
In many spreadsheet apps, a formula begins with an equal sign (=).

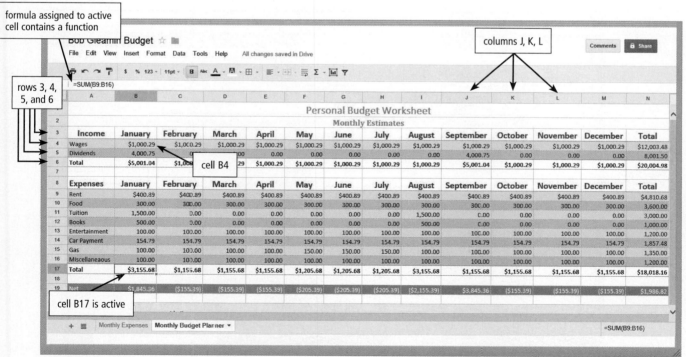

Figure 4-7 With spreadsheet software, you create worksheets that contain data arranged in columns and rows, and you can perform calculations on the data in the worksheets.
Source: Google Inc.

Database

A **database** is a collection of data organized in a manner that allows access, retrieval, and use of that data. In a manual database, you might record data on paper and store it in a filing cabinet. With a database stored electronically, such as the one shown in Figure 4-8, the computer stores the data on a storage medium, such as a hard drive or optical disc, or on cloud storage.

Database software is an application that allows users to create, access, and manage a database. Using database software, you can add, change, and delete data in a database; sort and retrieve data from the database; and create forms and reports using the data in the database.

With most personal computer database programs, a database consists of a collection of tables, organized in rows and columns. Each row, called a record, contains data about a given item in the database, which is often a person, product, object, or event. Each column, called a field, contains a specific category of data within a record. The Publishing database shown in Figure 4-8 consists of two tables: a Customer table and a Book Rep table. The Customer table contains 15 records (rows), each storing data about one customer. The customer data is grouped into 10 fields (columns): CU # (customer number), Customer Name, Street, City, State, Postal Code, Amount Paid, Current Due, Returns, and BR # (book rep number). The Current Due field, for instance, contains the amount of money the customer owes the publisher. The Customer and Book Rep tables relate to each other through a common field, BR # (book rep number).

Users run queries to retrieve data. A query is a request for specific data from the database. For example, a query might request a list of customers whose balance is greater than $20,000. After obtaining the results of a query, database applications can present them on the screen, send them to a printer, or save them in a file.

 CONSIDER THIS

When should you use a database instead of a spreadsheet program?
Although databases and spreadsheets both store data, these programs have different purposes and capabilities. Spreadsheet programs are ideal for calculating results or creating charts from value in the worksheet. You should use a database program, however, if want to collect, reorganize and filter data, and/or create reports from the data.

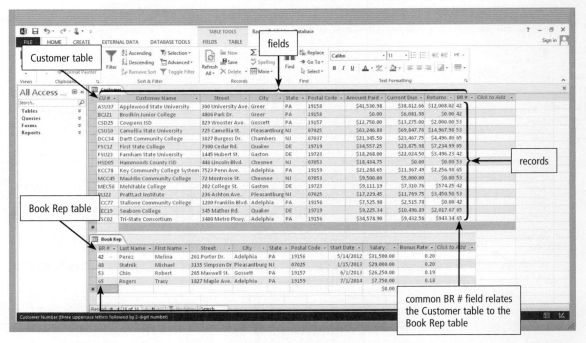

Figure 4-8　This database contains two tables: one for customers and one for book reps. The Customer table has 15 records and 10 fields; the Book Rep table has 4 records and 10 fields.
Source: Microsoft

Note Taking

Note taking software is an application that enables users to enter typed text, handwritten comments, drawings, sketches, photos, and links anywhere on a page and then save the page as part of a notebook (Figure 4-9). Users also can include audio recordings as part of their notes. Some enable users to sync their notes to the cloud so that they can access the notes on any computer or mobile device. Many note taking applications also include a calendar feature.

Users find note taking software convenient during meetings, class lectures and conferences, and in libraries and other settings that previously required pencil and paper for recording thoughts and discussions.

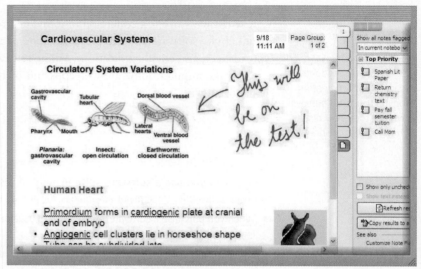

Figure 4-9 With note taking software, mobile users can handwrite notes, draw sketches, insert photos and links, and type text.
Source: Microsoft

Calendar and Contact Management

Calendar and contact management software is an application that helps you organize your calendar, keep track of contacts, and share this information with other users, who can view it on their computers and mobile devices (Figure 4-10). This software provides a way for individuals and workgroups to organize, find, view, and share appointment and contact information easily. Although sometimes available separately, calendar and contact management software often exists as a unit in a single program. Many email applications include calendar and contact management features.

Figure 4-10 Users can share schedules with other users via calendar and contact management applications.
Google Inc.

Calendar and contact management applications enable you to synchronize information. This means that all of your computers and mobile devices, along with your organization's server or cloud storage, have the latest version of any updated information.

Software Suite

A **software suite** is a collection of individual related applications available together as a unit. Productivity software suites typically include, at a minimum, word processing, presentation, spreadsheet, and email applications. While several productivity suites are designed to be installed on a local computer, some are web apps and/or mobile web apps that enabling you to share and collaborate with projects stored on the cloud.

BTW

Forms and Surveys
Some online productivity suites support creating online forms for surveys, which store their results in online spreadsheets.

 CONSIDER THIS

Why would you use a software suite instead of a stand-alone application?
Software suites offer three major advantages: lower cost, ease of use, and integration.

- When you purchase a software suite, the suite usually costs significantly less than purchasing each application individually, or as stand-alone applications.

- Software suites provide ease of use because the applications in the suite normally use a consistent interface and share features, such as clip art and spelling checker.

- Applications in a software suite often are integrated, which makes it easy to share information among them. For example, you can copy a chart created from a worksheet in a spreadsheet program and paste it into a slideshow in the presentation software.

Project Management

Project management software is an application that allows a user to plan, schedule, track, and analyze the events, resources, and costs of a project. Project management software helps users manage project variables, allowing them to complete a project on time and within budget. A marketing manager, for example, might use project management software to schedule the processes required in a product launch (Figure 4-11). Read How To 4-1 to learn how you can manage a project using project management software.

Figure 4-11 With project management software, you can plan and schedule the tasks and processes required in a project.
Courtesy of CS Odessa

HOW TO 4-1

Manage a Project Using Project Management Software

Several project management programs and apps exist that are both free and fee based. Project management programs and apps are designed for projects of specific sizes, so be sure to research the various programs and apps on the market and choose one that best suits your needs. To manage a project using project management software, follow these steps:

1. Make sure you understand the project in its entirety, as well as the steps you must take to bring the project to completion.

2. Determine the date by which the project must be completed.

3. Verify you have the appropriate resources (people and materials) to complete the project. If you do not have the necessary resources, you should obtain them.

4. Determine the order of the steps that must be taken to bring the project to completion. Identify steps that must be taken before other steps, as well as steps that can be completed at the same time as other steps.

5. Verify the feasibility of the plan.

6. During the project, it will be necessary to update the progress and possibly adjust dates. Changes to the project and its dates should be communicated to the entire project team.

✸ **Consider This:** Do you think project management software can help individuals complete a project more quickly? Why or why not?

✸ **CONSIDER THIS**

Does the term, project, have two meanings in the technology field?
Yes. As discussed earlier in this module, a project can be a deliverable you create using application software, such as a document, presentation, spreadsheet, notes, calendar, contact list, budget, and more. A project also describe the collection of tasks and processes required to develop a solution to a problem.

Accounting

Accounting software is an application that helps businesses of all sizes record and report their financial transactions. With accounting software, business users perform accounting activities related to the general ledger, accounts receivable, accounts payable, purchasing, invoicing (Figure 4-12), and payroll functions. Accounting software also enables business users to write and print checks, track checking account activity, and update and reconcile balances on demand.

Most accounting software supports online credit checks, bill payment, direct deposit, and payroll services. Some offer more complex features, such as job costing and estimating, time tracking, multiple company reporting, foreign currency reporting, and forecasting the amount of raw materials needed for products. The cost of accounting software for small businesses ranges from less than one hundred to several thousand dollars. Accounting software for large businesses can cost several hundred thousand dollars.

Figure 4-12 Accounting software helps businesses record and report their financial transactions.
Courtesy of Intuit

Personal Finance

Personal finance software is a simplified accounting application that helps home users and small/home office users balance their checkbooks, pay bills, track personal income and expenses, verify account balances, transfer funds, track investments, and evaluate financial plans (Figure 4-13). Personal finance software helps determine where, and for what purpose, you are spending money so that you can manage your finances.

Most personal finance software includes financial planning features, such as analyzing home and personal loans, preparing income taxes, and managing retirement savings. Other features include managing home inventory and setting up budgets. Most of these applications also offer a variety of online services, such as online banking and online investing. Read Secure IT 4-2 for safety tips when using personal finance apps on your smartphone or other mobile device.

Figure 4-13 Personal finance software assists home users with tracking personal accounts.
Courtesy of Intuit

Legal

Legal software is an application that assists in the preparation of legal documents and provides legal information to individuals, families, and small businesses (Figure 4-14). Legal software provides standard contracts and documents associated with buying, selling, and renting property; estate planning; marriage and divorce; and preparing a will or living trust. By answering a series of questions or completing a form, the legal software tailors the legal document to specific needs. Read Ethics & Issues 4-2 to consider whether an attorney should review documents created with legal software.

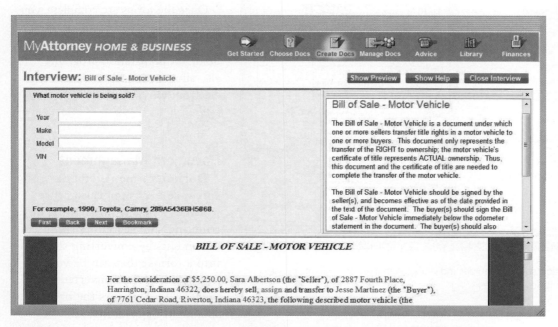

Figure 4-14 Legal software assists individuals, families, and small businesses in the preparation of legal documents.

Source: Avanquest Software

 ETHICS & ISSUES 4-2

Should an Attorney Review Documents Created with Legal Software?

If you want to sublet your apartment or buy or sell a used car, should you seek legal help? Hiring an attorney to create a lease or sale agreement can cost hundreds of dollars. Legal software or website services, on the other hand, typically cost less than $100 and sometimes are free. While it is tempting to opt for the route that will save money, you should evaluate the program to make sure it is up to date, addresses the latest laws and provisions that are specific to your state, and includes a legal dictionary. If you use a program that is out of date or creates an incomplete or invalid legal document, the cost for an attorney to correct the document

could exceed the amount you originally spent on the program.

A lease that you create or sign regarding subletting or renting an apartment should have provisions for payment of any damages, breaking or extending the agreement, and who is responsible for routine maintenance and repair. In some states, the property owner must disclose any mold, lead paint, or water quality issues. Sales agreements, such as for used cars, should include language that protects the buyer from undisclosed damage to the car, as well as clearly specify any further responsibility of the car seller.

Attorneys caution against using legal software unless you intend to have an attorney review the document. Not only can

they validate the accuracy of the document, attorneys claim they can provide for gaps in the software; further, they are versed in laws specific to your state or circumstance. Others argue that any legal document is better than a verbal agreement and can protect both parties.

Consider This: Would you use legal software to create a legal document? Why or why not? Would you sign a legal document created with software without consulting an attorney? Why or why not? How do mistakes made as a result of using legal software differ from mistakes that result from human error?

Tax Preparation

Tax preparation software is an application that can guide individuals, families, or small businesses through the process of filing federal and state taxes (Figure 4-15). These programs forecast tax liability and offer money-saving tax tips, designed to lower your tax bill. After you answer a series of questions and complete basic forms, the software creates and analyzes your tax forms to search for missed potential errors and deduction opportunities.

Once the forms are complete, you can print any necessary paperwork; then, they are ready for filing. Some tax preparation programs also allow you to file your tax forms electronically, a process called *e-filing*.

Figure 4-15 Tax preparation software guides individuals, families, or small businesses through the process of filing federal taxes.
Source: 2nd Story Software

Document Management

Document management software is an application that provides a means for sharing, distributing, and searching through documents by converting them into a format that can be viewed by any user. The converted document, which mirrors the original document's appearance, can be viewed and printed without the software that created the original document. Some document management software allows users to edit content and add comments to the converted document (Figure 4-16).

Many businesses use document management software to share and distribute company brochures, literature, and other documents electronically. Home users distribute flyers, announcements, and graphics electronically. A popular electronic image file format that document management software uses to save converted documents is **PDF** (Portable Document Format), developed by Adobe Systems.

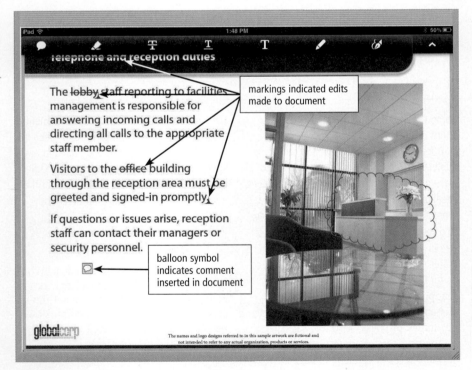

Figure 4-16 Users can edit content and add comments to a converted document.
Source: Adobe Systems Incorporated

To view and print a PDF file, you need Adobe Reader software, which can be downloaded free from Adobe's website.

 CONSIDER THIS

Can you create a PDF file only in document management applications?
No. Many productivity applications, such as word processing and spreadsheet programs, provide a method of saving a project as a PDF. This enables other users to view your document without requiring the application that created the project.

Enterprise Computing

A large organization, commonly referred to as an enterprise, requires special computing solutions because of its size and geographic distribution. A typical enterprise consists of a wide variety of departments, centers, and divisions — collectively known as functional units. Nearly every enterprise has the following functional units: human resources, accounting and finance, engineering or product development, manufacturing, marketing, sales, distribution, customer service, and information technology.

Software used in functional units is not mutually exclusive; however, each functional unit in an enterprise uses specific software, as outlined below.

- Human resources software manages employee information, such as pay rate, benefits, personal information, performance evaluations, training, and vacation time.
- Accounting software manages everyday transactions, such as sales and payments to suppliers. Finance software helps managers budget, forecast, and analyze.
- Engineering or product development software allows engineers to develop plans for new products and test their product designs.
- Manufacturing software assists in the assembly process, as well as in scheduling and managing the inventory of parts and products.
- Marketing software allows marketing personnel to create marketing campaigns, target demographics, and track their effectiveness.
- Sales software enables the salesforce to manage contacts, schedule meetings, log customer interactions, manage product information, and take customer orders.
- Distribution software analyzes and tracks inventory and manages product shipping status.
- Customer service software manages the day-to-day interactions with customers, such as phone calls, email messages, web interactions, and messaging sessions.
- Information technology staff use a variety of programs and apps to maintain and secure the hardware and software in an enterprise.

Mini Feature 4-1: Web and Mobile Apps for Personal and Business Productivity

A variety of applications provide a service intended to make business or personal tasks easier to accomplish. Some applications focus on a single service, while others provide several services in a single application. Read Mini Feature 4-1 to learn about some popular web and mobile apps for personal and business productivity.

✦ MINI FEATURE 4-1

Web and Mobile Apps for Personal and Business Productivity

Whether you are checking appointments, sending or reading email messages, arranging travel, banking or looking up information online, making a purchase, scanning QR (quick response) codes or bar codes, or checking in with friends on online social networks, web and mobile apps can assist your personal and business productivity.

Calendar and Email

Maintaining a calendar and checking email messages are common tasks of calendar and email web and mobile apps. Calendar apps keep track of your appointments and synchronize information entered on a mobile device with your online or desktop calendar software. Email mobile apps integrate with your device's address book to display names from your device's contact list that match a recipient's name as you type it, and with your device's photo gallery for sending photos.

Travel

Purchasing flights, hotels, rental cars, or travel services is a common online task for personal and business travelers. Travel apps display available options and allow you to filter results. Many allow you to share travel plans with your online social networks.

Source: Kayak

Financial

You can access bank accounts or investments using a financial app. Financial mobile apps track expenses as you spend money and notify you when a bill is due. To help secure information, financial mobile apps can disable access if your device is stolen or lost. Some banking mobile apps allow you to upload a photo of a check taken with the device's camera to process the deposit.

Reference

Dictionaries, encyclopedias, books, and directories are available online as reference apps. Many have associated mobile apps that format information for mobile devices, or take advantage of their features. For example, rather than typing a search term in a dictionary web app to look up its definition, a mobile app also might offer voice input. On the mobile version

of an encyclopedia app, you might shake the device to display random topics or redisplay the app's home screen. Some reference mobile apps also can download information directly to your phone for offline access.

Retail

Online marketplaces and payment services support buying and selling items and transferring funds from one party to another. Marketplace apps enable customers to research products, enter or examine product reviews, and make purchases. A retail store mobile app might use a device's GPS to offer special deals closest to the customer's location. You also might use a device's camera to scan a product's bar code and then place the item in a shopping cart. Payment services allow customers to send money or pay for items using mobile devices. Read Secure IT 4-3 for safety tips when using payment apps.

Scanning

Scanning apps use a mobile device's camera to scan a QR code or bar code. A **QR code** is a square-shaped graphic that represents a web address or other information. A QR code reader app scans a QR code, and then displays its corresponding information. A bar code scanner reads a bar code and may provide product information, price, or reviews. Some supermarkets provide shopping apps for customers to scan bar codes of items they purchase. These apps create a customized shopping list, ordering items by their aisle location in the store, to provide a more efficient shopping experience.

© iStockPhoto / franckreporter

Online Social Networks

Many users connect with family, friends, and coworkers using online social network mobile apps. Online social network web apps often integrate instant messaging and video chat communications. Online social network mobile apps allow users to include photos and videos from their device in their updates easily.

✸ **Consider This:** Compare the web and mobile versions of the same app for personal and business productivity. Which features are common to both? Which features in the mobile version are not found in the web version? Which features in the web version are not found in the mobile version? Why do you think the developers made these decisions? Which features would you like to see that are missing from either version of the app?

SECURE IT 4-3

Avoiding Risks Using Payment Apps

Paying for coffee at the local coffee shop or buying tools at the hardware store has become streamlined with the advent of mobile payment apps. More than 15 percent of Starbucks transactions are accomplished using a smartphone app instead of using cash or credit card, and many merchants are accepting this form of payment as mobile wallet apps become more secure. The users enjoy the convenience of maintaining control when they scan their phone at the checkout counter instead of handing a credit card to a clerk. This security factor becomes even more pronounced at restaurants, where unscrupulous employees can take credit cards away from the table and then have full access to the personal information on the cards.

Mobile payment providers state that using their apps is more secure than using plastic credit cards. The apps use a payment system on phones equipped with an *NFC chip*, which stores data that is transmitted to a contactless terminal and verified as a legitimate sale. A smartphone user never enters an account number at the cash register because all financial information is stored on the mobile payment system. If, however, an unauthorized charge is made, the Electronic Fund Transfer Act protects users as long as the claim is made promptly, generally within two days.

If you use your smartphone to make purchases, follow this advice from the security experts:

- Use a password on your phone.
- Select a payment app that requires you to enter a password to start the transaction.
- Choose a payment app that issues a receipt so that you can verify every purchase.

- Be vigilant about checking mobile transactions against monthly statements from the credit card company.

 Consider This: Should additional merchants allow payments using mobile apps? Should merchants be required to pay when customers use payment apps, like they do when customers use credit cards? Why or why not? Where would you like to pay for transactions using your smartphone?

Google Inc.

 NOW YOU SHOULD KNOW

Be sure you understand the material presented in the sections titled Programs and Apps and Productivity Applications as it relates to the module objectives.
Now you should know ...

- What categories of programs and apps you might find on a computer or mobile device (Objective 1)
- Why you need an operating system on computers and mobile devices (Objective 2)
- How you can obtain software (Objective 3)
- Which productivity applications might be suited to your needs (Objective 4)

Graphics and Media Applications

In addition to productivity applications, many people work with software designed specifically for their field of work. Power users, such as engineers, architects, desktop publishers, and graphic artists, often use sophisticated software that allows them to work with graphics and media. Many of these applications incorporate user-friendly interfaces or scaled-down versions, making it possible for the home and small business users also to create projects using these types of programs.

Graphics and media applications include computer-aided design, desktop publishing, paint/image editing, photo editing and photo management, video and audio editing, multimedia and website authoring, media players, and disc burning.

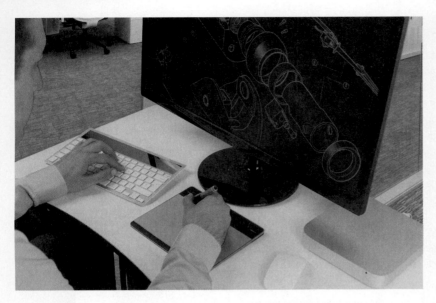

Figure 4-17 Architects use CAD software to design building structures.
© iStockPhoto / GordanD

Computer-Aided Design

Computer-aided design (CAD) software is a type of application that assists professionals and designers in creating engineering, architectural, and scientific designs and models. For example, engineers create design plans for vehicles and security systems. Architects design building structures and floor plans (Figure 4-17). Scientists design drawings of molecular structures.

Three-dimensional CAD programs allow designers to rotate designs of 3-D objects to view them from any angle. Some CAD software even can generate material lists for building designs.

Home and small business users work with less sophisticated design and modeling software. These applications usually contain thousands of predrawn plans that users can customize to meet their needs. For example, *home design/landscaping software* is an application that assists users with the design, remodeling, or improvement of a home, deck, or landscape.

Desktop Publishing

Desktop publishing software (DTP software) is an application that enables designers to create sophisticated publications that contain text, graphics, and many colors. Professional DTP software is ideal for the production of high-quality color projects such as textbooks, corporate newsletters, marketing literature, product catalogs, and annual reports. Designers and graphic artists can print finished publications on a color printer, take them to a professional printer, or post them on the web in a format that can be viewed by those without DTP software.

Figure 4-18 With personal DTP software, such as Microsoft Publisher shown here, home users can create newsletters.
Courtesy of Joy Starks; Source: Microsoft

Home and small business users create newsletters, brochures, flyers, advertisements, postcards, greeting cards, letterhead, business cards, banners, calendars, logos, and webpages using personal DTP software (Figure 4-18). Although many word processing programs include DTP features, home and small business users often prefer to create DTP projects using DTP software because of its enhanced features. These programs typically guide you through the development of a project by asking a series of questions. Then, you can print a finished publication on a color printer or post it on the web.

Many personal DTP programs also include paint/image editing software and photo editing and photo management software (discussed next), enabling users to embellish their publications with images.

Paint/Image Editing

Graphic artists, multimedia professionals, technical illustrators, and desktop publishers use paint software and image editing software to create and modify graphics, such as those used in DTP projects and webpages. **Paint software**, also called *illustration software*, is an application that allows users to draw pictures, shapes, and other graphics with various on-screen tools, such as a pen, brush, eyedropper, and paint bucket. **Image editing software** is an application that provides the capabilities of paint software and also includes the capability to enhance and modify existing photos and images. Modifications can include adjusting or enhancing image colors, adding special effects such as shadows and glows, creating animations, and image stitching (combining multiple images into a larger image).

Paint/image editing software for the home or small business user provides an easy-to-use interface; includes various simplified tools that allow you to draw pictures, shapes, and other images (Figure 4-19); and provides the capability of modifying existing graphics and photos. These products also include many templates to assist you in adding images to projects, such as greeting cards, banners, calendars, signs, labels, business cards, and letterhead.

Figure 4-19   Home users can purchase affordable paint/image editing programs that enable them to draw images.
DrawPlus X5 © Serif (Europe) Ltd, | www.serif.com

Photo Editing and Photo Management

Photo editing software is a type of image editing software that allows users to edit and customize digital photos. With photo editing software, users can retouch photos, crop images, remove red-eye, erase blemishes, restore aged photos, add special effects, enhance image quality, change image shapes, color-correct images, straighten images, remove or rearrange objects in a photo, add layers, and more (Figure 4–20). Many applications also provide a means for creating digital photo albums.

Figure 4-20   With photo editing software, users can edit digital photos, such as by adjusting the appearance of images as shown here.
PhotoPlus X6 © Serif (Europe) Ltd | www.serif.com

When you purchase a digital camera, it usually includes photo editing software. Many digital cameras also include basic photo editing software so that you can edit the image directly on the camera. Read How To 4-2 for instructions about editing and sharing photos. Read Ethics & Issues 4-3 to consider issues related to altering digital photos.

With **photo management software**, you can view, organize, sort, catalog, print, and share digital photos. Some photo editing software includes photo management functionality. Many online photo storage services enable you to create scrapbooks — selecting photos, adding captions, selecting backgrounds, and more.

⚙ HOW TO 4-2

Edit and Share Photos

When you take a photo using a digital camera or smartphone, you sometimes may want to edit the photo to remove unwanted areas, correct imperfections, or change its file size. Many apps allow you to edit photos easily. Several are simple to use and do not require advanced photo editing experience. Before editing a photo, you first should make a backup of the original photo. The table below describes common ways to edit photos using a photo editing app.

After you have edited a photo to your satisfaction, you may want to share the photo with others. Many mobile devices, such as smartphones and tablets, as well as most photo editing apps, have built-in options that allow you to share photos. To share a photo on a mobile device or from within a photo editing app, follow these steps:

1. Open the photo to share.
2. Select the sharing option in the photo editing app or on the mobile device.
3. Choose the method by which to share the photo. Common ways to share

photos include sending the photo as an email attachment, posting the photo to an online social network or photo sharing site, and sending the photo as a picture message to another mobile device.

❋ **Consider This:** Examine your digital camera or other mobile device with a camera feature. Which of the photo editing features discussed here does it have? Did you notice any photo editing features in addition to those listed here?

ACTION	PURPOSE	STEPS
Crop	Removes unwanted areas of a photo	1. Select cropping tool. 2. Adjust photo border to define area(s) of the photo to keep and discard.
Remove *red-eye*	Removes the appearance of red eyes caused by the camera flash	1. Select red-eye removal tool. 2. Tap or click areas of the photo with the red-eye effect *or* drag a border around the affected areas.
Resize	Changes the physical dimensions of the photo	1. Select resizing tool. 2. Drag sizing handles to increase or decrease the photo's dimensions *or* type the desired height and width in the appropriate text boxes.
Compress	Decreases the photo's file size	1. Select option to compress photo. 2. Choose desired level of compression.
Adjust *sharpness*	Increases or decreases crispness of objects in the photo	1. Select option to adjust sharpness. 2. Drag sharpness slider to desired value *or* type the desired sharpness level into appropriate text box.
Adjust *brightness*	Adjusts lightness or darkness in the photo	1. Select option to adjust brightness. 2. Drag brightness slider to desired value *or* type the desired brightness level into appropriate text box.
Adjust *contrast*	Adjusts the difference in appearance between light and dark areas of the photo	1. Select option to adjust contrast. 2. Drag contrast slider to desired value *or* type the desired contrast level into appropriate text box.

⚙ ETHICS & ISSUES 4-3

Is It Ethical to Alter Digital Photos?

Many commercial artists, photojournalists, and creators of magazine covers and billboards use photo editing software to alter digital photos. Artists use photo editing software to enhance digital photos by changing colors, adding or removing objects, and more. When does photo manipulation become unethical?

In several high-profile cases, news sources published intentionally altered photos that misrepresented the facts, in one case publishing photos of an aging world leader edited to remove his hearing aid. One school received criticism when it altered necklines on yearbook photos to be more modest.

Real estate agents on occasion have altered photos of homes for online listings or print brochures. Also making news are celebrity or model photos that artists retouch to change their physical appearance.

The National Press Photographers Association expresses reservations about digital altering and subscribes to the following belief: "As [photo]journalists we believe the guiding principle of our profession is accuracy; therefore, we believe it is wrong to alter the content of a photo in any way ... that deceives the public." Yet, some insist that the extent to which a photo "deceives the public" is in the eye of the beholder. Many differentiate between

technical manipulation to improve photo quality and an intent to deceive. Some governments are attempting to legislate photo manipulation. One country banned a magazine in which a celebrity's appearance appeared visibly altered. Some celebrities refuse to allow airbrushing or other manipulation of photos of them.

Consider This: Is it ethical to alter digital photos? Why or why not? Does the answer depend on the reason for the alteration, the extent of the alteration, or some other factor? Should magazines stop altering pictures of people to change their appearance? Why or why not?

Video and Audio Editing

Video editing software is an application that allows professionals to modify a segment of a video, called a clip. For example, users can reduce the length of a video clip, reorder a series of clips, or add special effects such as words that move across the screen. Video editing software typically includes audio editing capabilities. **Audio editing software** is an application that enables users to modify audio clips, produce studio-quality soundtracks, and add audio to video clips (Figure 4-21). Most television shows and movies are created or enhanced using video and audio editing software.

Many home users work with easy-to-use video and audio editing software, which is much simpler to use than its professional counterpart, for small-scale movie making projects. With these programs, home users can edit home movies, add music or other sounds to the video, and share their movies on the web. Some operating systems include video editing and audio editing applications.

Figure 4-21 With audio editing software, users modify audio clips.

Source: Adobe Systems Incorporated

Multimedia and Website Authoring

Multimedia authoring software allows users to combine text, graphics, audio, video, and animation in an interactive application (Figure 4-22). With this software, users control the placement of text and images and the duration of sounds, video, and animation. Once created, multimedia presentations often take the form of interactive computer-based presentations or web-based presentations designed to facilitate learning, demonstrate product functionality, and elicit direct user participation. Training centers, educational institutions, and online magazine publishers use multimedia authoring software to develop interactive applications. These applications may be distributed on an optical disc, over a local area network, or via the Internet as web apps.

Website authoring software helps users of all skill levels create related webpages that include graphics, video, audio, animation, special effects with interactive content, and blog posts. In addition, many website authoring programs allow users to organize, manage, and maintain websites. Website authoring software often has capabilities of multimedia authoring software.

 CONSIDER THIS

What is computer-based or web-based training?

Computer-based training (*CBT*) is a type of education in which students learn by using and completing exercises with instructional software. *Web-based training* (*WBT*) is a type of CBT that uses Internet technology to deliver the training. CBT and WBT typically consist of self-directed, self-paced instruction about a topic so that the user becomes actively involved in the learning process instead of being a passive recipient of information. Beginning athletes use CBT programs to learn the intricacies of participating in a sport. The military and airlines use CBT simulations to train pilots to fly in various conditions and environments. WBT is popular in business, industry, and schools for teaching new skills or enhancing existing skills of employees, teachers, and students.

Figure 4-22 Multimedia authoring software allows you to create dynamic presentations that include text, graphics, audio, video, and animation.
Courtesy of Matchware Inc.

Media Player

A **media player** is a program that allows you to view images and animations, listen to audio, and watch video files on your computer or mobile device (Figure 4-23). Media players also may enable you to organize media files by genre, artist, or other category; create playlists; convert files to different formats; connect to and purchase media from an online media store or market-place; stream radio stations' broadcasting over the Internet; download podcasts; burn audio CDs; and transfer media to portable media players.

Figure 4-23 A media player.
Source: Rhapsody

Disc Burning

Disc burning software writes text, graphics, audio, and video files on a recordable or rewritable disc. This software enables home users easily to back up contents of their hard drive on an optical disc (CD/DVD) and make duplicates of uncopyrighted music or movies. Disc burning software usually also includes photo editing, audio editing, and video editing capabilities.

Personal Interest Applications

Countless desktop, mobile, and web apps are designed specifically for lifestyle, medical, entertainment, convenience, or education activities. Most of the programs in this category are relatively inexpensive; many are free. Some applications focus on a single service, while others provide several services in a single application.

- Lifestyle applications: Access the latest news or sports scores, check the weather forecast, compose music, research genealogy, find recipes, or locate nearby restaurants, gas stations, or points of interest.
- Medical applications: Research symptoms, establish a fitness or health program, track exercise activity, refill prescriptions, count calories, or monitor sleep patterns.

Internet Research

What is geocaching?

Search for: geocaching basics

- Entertainment applications: Listen to music or the radio, view photos, watch videos or shows, read a book or other publication, organize and track fantasy sports teams, and play games individually or with others.
- Convenience applications: Obtain driving directions or your current location, remotely start your vehicle or unlock/lock the doors, set an alarm or timer, check the time, calculate a tip, use your phone as a flashlight, or use a personal assistant that acts on your voice commands (read How To 4-3 for instructions about using personal assistant apps).
- Education applications: Access how-to guides, learn or fine-tune a particular skill, follow a tutorial, run a simulation, assist children with reading and other elementary skills, or support academics.

HOW TO 4-3

Use Features in Voice Command Personal Assistant and Mobile Search Apps

Many mobile operating systems include a virtual personal assistant that processes voice commands and performs certain tasks. Some mobile search apps also act on spoken commands.. For example, you can issue voice commands to set an alarm, add an appointment to your calendar, send a text message, or run an app. The following table describes ways to use features in voice command personal assistant apps:

Task	Sample Voice Command(s)
Change phone settings	"Turn on Wi-Fi." "Turn off Bluetooth."
Dial a number	"Call Madelyn's Cell." "Call Mom Home." "Dial 407-555-8275."
Obtain information	"When was George Washington born?" "How many ounces are in a pound?" "What is the closest Chinese restaurant?"
Obtain driving instructions	"Navigate to 123 Main Street, Orlando, Florida." "Navigate to The Home Depot." "Navigate to Manchester, New Hampshire."
Perform a search	"What is the gas mileage for a Ford Explorer?" "Search butterfly lifespan."
Run an app	"Run calendar." "Run email."
Schedule a meeting	"Schedule a meeting with Traci at the library at 3:00 p.m. tomorrow."
Send a text message	"Text Samuel meet me at the pool."
Set a reminder	"Remind me to go grocery shopping tomorrow."
Set a timer	"Set timer for five minutes."
Set an alarm	"Set an alarm for 6:00 a.m. tomorrow." "Set an alarm for 6:30 a.m. every weekday."

Consider This: What other voice commands are available on your phone? Do you use voice commands? Why or why not?

Mini Feature 4-2: Web and Mobile Apps for Media and Personal Interest

A variety of applications provide a service intended to make media and personal interest tasks easier to accomplish. Some applications focus on a single service, while others provide several services in a single application. Read Mini Feature 4-2 to learn about some popular web and mobile apps for media and personal interests.

⚙ MINI FEATURE 4-2

Web and Mobile Apps for Media and Personal Interests

Whether sharing, viewing, and purchasing media, such as photos; streaming audio and video; or playing games by yourself or with others, countless web and mobile apps are available to meet your needs. You also can use web and mobile apps to look up news, sports, and weather; obtain maps and directions; help you reach your health and fitness goals; and assist you with academic objectives.

Media Sharing

With media sharing mobile apps, you use the digital camera on your mobile device to take quality photos and/or videos and then instantly can share the photos or videos on online social networks. Using the corresponding media sharing web app, you can categorize, tag, organize, and rank the media posted by you, your friends, and your contacts.

Streaming Audio and Video

Podcasts, video blogs, clips or episodes from a television show, or even entire movies are available through a variety of streaming media web and mobile apps. Some services are available only with membership, and may charge a monthly fee. Others are free, but include ads. Streaming media enables you to view and listen to content without downloading it to your computer or device, saving valuable disc or media storage space.

Gaming

Game web and mobile apps often offer a social component, enabling you to chat within the game environment, find friends who play the same game apps, and post your scores on social media. Word, puzzle, and board games are just some examples of apps you can play by yourself or with friends or others using the same apps.

News, Sports, and Weather

Many apps provide access to the latest news, stories, current events, sports scores, sporting events, and weather forecasts. Some of these mobile apps use GPS technology to provide current or customized information based on the location of your mobile device. You also can configure these apps to deliver text messages and other types of alerts to your device when certain events occur, such as when a football team scores a touchdown or when severe weather is near.

Mapping

Using your mobile device's GPS capability, you can use mapping mobile apps to obtain directions, maps, and recommendations for restaurants or other points of interest based on your current location. Some mapping apps even help you to locate friends based on their GPS signals (if they enable you to do so). Others allow you to share your current location on social media using a check-in feature. Web apps help you decide on a route, print directions or a map, and even find amenities along your route, such as public rest stops or restaurants.

Health and Fitness

Losing weight, training for a race, or following a low-calorie diet are some uses of health and fitness apps. Using a mobile device as a pedometer or GPS receiver can help you count your steps or create a map of a route you run and then update your profile with the data

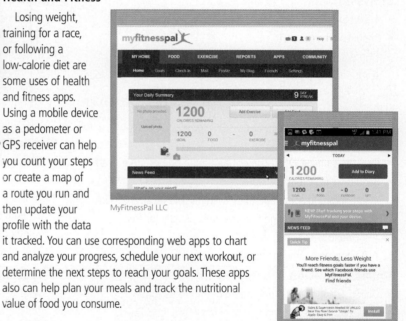

MyFitnessPal LLC

it tracked. You can use corresponding web apps to chart and analyze your progress, schedule your next workout, or determine the next steps to reach your goals. These apps also can help plan your meals and track the nutritional value of food you consume.

Academic

If you need to study terms or topics, flash card apps can provide reinforcement. This book's premium content for example, has an accompanying Flash Cards app designed to improve your retention of module key terms. Schools often subscribe to educational apps that provide students with games, quizzes, and lessons about course topics. Using these apps, teachers can keep track of students' progress and pinpoint areas where they may need extra help. You also can access complete college or high school courses and take advantage of free or fee-based digital content provided by publishers and teachers.

⚙ **Consider This:** Which web and mobile apps have you used for media sharing; streaming audio and video; gaming; news, sports, and weather; mapping; health and fitness; and education? Will you try others after reading this mini feature? Why or why not?

BTW

Mobile Communications Apps

Most of the communications apps in Table 4-2 are available as mobile apps, as well.

Communications Applications

One of the main reasons people use computers is to communicate and share information with others. Earlier modules presented a variety of communications applications, which are summarized in Table 4-2. Read Ethics & Issues 4-4 to consider whether your email provider should be allowed to read or scan your email messages.

Table 4-2 Communications Applications

Blog
- Time-stamped articles, or posts, in diary or journal format, usually listed in reverse chronological order
- Bloggers (author) use blogging software to create/maintain blog
  - Some blog services provide blogging software so users do not have to install it on their own servers

Browsing
- Allows users to access and view webpages on the Internet
- Requires browser
  - Integrated in most operating systems
  - Alternative browsers are available on the web for download, usually for free

Chat
- Real-time, online typed conversation with one or more users
- Requires chat client software
  - Integrated in some operating systems and most browsers
  - Available for download on the web, usually for free
  - Included with some paid ISPs
  - Built into some websites

Online Discussion
- Online areas where users have written discussions
- May require a reader program
- Integrated in some operating systems, email programs, and browsers

Email
- Messages and files sent via a network, such as the Internet
- Requires an email program
  - Integrated in many software suites and operating systems
  - Available free at portals on the web
  - Included with a paid ISP
  - Can be purchased separately

File Transfer
- Method of uploading files to and downloading files from servers on the Internet
- May require an FTP client program
  - Integrated in some operating systems
  - Available for download on the web; many free or open source alternatives are available
  - Many applications (such as web editing software) that require frequent transfer of files to the Internet have built-in FTP capabilities

Internet Phone
- Allows users to speak to other users via an Internet connection
- Requires a microphone, a speaker, a high-speed Internet connection, and VoIP software
  - Some subscription services also require a separate phone and VoIP router
  - With a webcam, some services also support video chat or videoconferences

Internet Messaging
- Real-time exchange of messages, files, images, audio, and/or video with another online user
- Requires messaging software
  - Integrated in some operating systems
  - Available for download on the web, usually for free, or available as a browser plug-in
  - Included with some paid ISPs

Mobile Messaging
- Short text, picture, or video messages sent and received, mainly on mobile devices
- May require messaging plan from mobile service provider
  - Requires messaging software
  - Integrated in most mobile devices
  - Available for download on the web, usually for free

Videoconference
- Meeting between geographically separated people who use a network to transmit video/audio
- Requires videoconferencing software, a microphone, a speaker, and a webcam

Web Feeds
- Keeps track of changes made to blogs by checking feeds
- Requires a feed reader
  - Integrated in some email programs and browsers
  - Available for download on the web, usually for free

ETHICS & ISSUES 4-4

Should Your Email Provider Be Allowed to Read or Scan Your Email?

When using any email program or service, you expect the app to scan incoming and outgoing mail to prevent the spread of malware. One web-based email service recently released a service update that includes automatic scanning of all email messages in order to provide targeted advertisements. Privacy experts point out that the scan includes all email messages sent or received, whether or not both the sender and recipient subscribe to the service.

Ad-supported web services, including email, often collect information in your profile, as well as your search results and other Internet activity. When you agree to use these services, you give consent to this type of monitoring. In this case, the extent of the monitoring exceeds the policies of other web-based services. In a court filing, one email provider stated that users of web-based services have no "reasonable expectation" of privacy with respect to the content of email messages.

A further complication to this instance is that many educational institutions use this service for email, collaboration software, and more. The service admits to collecting data from students, even when the school has opted out of ad displays. Laws are unclear whether collecting student data is legal. Several schools have joined to create a class-action lawsuit against the provider. Many argue that collection of student data, which could include grades received and more, is a violation of the Family Educational Rights and Privacy Act (FERPA). Although FERPA predates cloud-based Internet services, it states that "schools must have written permission from the parent or eligible student in order to release any information from a student's education record."

Consider This: Should an email service provider disclose data collection practices? Why or why not? Is it ethical for an email provider to scan email sent by a nonsubscriber? Why or why not? Is collecting student data a violation of FERPA? Why or why not?

✔ NOW YOU SHOULD KNOW

Be sure you understand the material presented in the sections titled Graphics and Media Applications, Personal Interest Applications, and Communications Applications, as it relates to the module objectives.
Now you should know ...

- When you might use a graphics or media application (Objective 5)
- Which personal interest applications you would find useful (Objective 6)
- When you are interacting with communications applications (Objective 7)

Security Tools

To protect your computers and mobile devices, you can use one or more security tools. Security tools include personal firewalls, antivirus programs, malware removers, and Internet filters. Although some of these tools are included with the operating system, you also can purchase stand-alone programs that offer improvements or added functionality.

Personal Firewall

A **personal firewall** is a security tool that detects and protects a personal computer and its data from unauthorized intrusions (Figure 4-24). Personal firewalls constantly monitor all transmissions to and from a computer or mobile device and may inform a user of attempted intrusions. When connected to the Internet, your computer or mobile device is vulnerable to attacks from

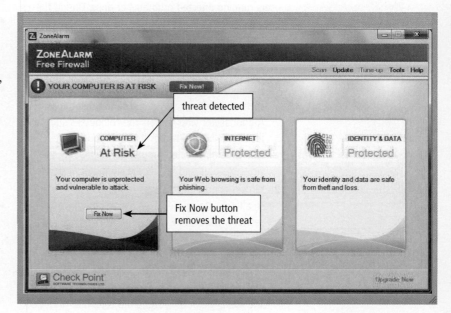

Figure 4-24 This personal firewall detected a threat to the computer and provided a means to remove the threat.
Courtesy of Checkpoint Software Technologies Ltd.

hackers who try to access a computer or network illegally. These attacks may destroy your data, steal information, damage your computer, or carry out some other malicious action.

 CONSIDER THIS

What is a hardware firewall?

A *hardware firewall* is a device intended to stop network intrusions before they attempt to affect your computer or network maliciously. Many routers also can function as a hardware firewall.

Mini Feature 4-3: Viruses and Malware

A computer **virus** is a potentially damaging program that affects a computer or device negatively by altering the way it works. This occurs without the user's knowledge or permission. Once the virus is in a computer or device, it can spread and may damage your files, programs and apps, and operating system. Read Mini Feature 4-3 to learn more about viruses and other malware.

 MINI FEATURE 4-3

Viruses and Malware

Viruses do not generate by chance. The programmer of a virus, known as a virus author, intentionally writes a virus program. Writing a virus program usually requires significant programming skills. The virus author ensures the virus can replicate itself, conceal itself, monitor for certain events, and then deliver its payload. A *payload* is the destructive event or prank the virus delivers. Viruses can infect all types of computers and devices. Most variations of viruses have two phases involved in their execution: infection and delivery.

The first step in the infection phase is activation of the virus. The most common way viruses spread is by users running infected programs or apps. During the infection phase, viruses typically perform one or more of the following actions:

1. First, a virus replicates by attaching itself to program files. A macro virus hides in a macro, which is a standard feature of many productivity applications, such as word processing and spreadsheet apps. A boot sector virus targets the computer's start-up files. A file virus attaches itself to program files. The next time an infected program or app is run, the virus executes and infects the computer or device.

2. Viruses conceal themselves to avoid detection. A stealth virus disguises itself by hiding in fake code sections, which it inserts within working code in a file. A polymorphic virus actually changes its code as it delivers the infection.

3. Finally, viruses watch for a certain condition or event and activate when that condition or event occurs. The event might be starting the computer or device, or reaching a date on the system clock. A logic bomb activates when it detects a specific condition

(say, a name deleted from the employee list). A time bomb is a logic bomb that activates on a particular date or time. If the triggering condition does not exist, the virus simply replicates.

During the delivery phase, the virus unleashes its payload, which might be a harmless prank that displays a meaningless message — or it might be destructive, corrupting or deleting data and files. The most dangerous viruses do not have an obvious payload. Instead, they quietly modify files. One way antivirus software detects computer viruses is by monitoring files for unknown changes.

In addition to viruses, other malware includes worms, trojan horse programs, and rootkits.

- A *worm* resides in active memory and replicates itself over a network to infect computers and devices, using up system resources and possibly shutting down the system.

- A *trojan horse* is a destructive program disguised as a real program, such as a screen saver. When a user runs a seemingly innocent program, a trojan horse hiding inside can capture information, such as user names and passwords, from your computer or enable someone to control your computer remotely. Unlike viruses, trojan horses do not replicate themselves.

- A *rootkit* is a program that easily can hide and allow someone to take full control of your computer from a remote location, often for nefarious purposes. For example, a rootkit can hide in a folder on your computer. The folder appears empty because the rootkit has instructed your computer not to display the contents of the folder. Rootkits can be very dangerous and often require special software to detect and remove.

Studies show that malware can infect an unprotected computer within minutes after connecting to the Internet. Due to the increasing threat of viruses attacking your computer, it is more important than ever to protect your computer from viruses and other malware. Secure IT 1-2 in Module 1 lists steps you can follow to protect your computer from a virus infection.

Consider This: If your computer or mobile device is infected with a virus or malware, how will you know? How will you find instructions for removing a virus?

Signs of Virus Infection

- An unusual message or image is displayed on the computer screen.
- An unusual sound or music plays randomly.
- The available memory is less than what should be available.
- A program or file suddenly is missing.
- An unknown program or file mysteriously appears.
- The size of a file changes without explanation.
- A file becomes corrupted.
- A program or file does not work properly.
- System properties change.
- The computer operates much slower than usual.

© Cengage Learning

Antivirus Programs

To protect a computer from virus attacks, users should install an antivirus program and keep it updated by purchasing revisions or upgrades to the software. An **antivirus program** protects a computer against viruses by identifying and removing any computer viruses found in memory, on storage media, or on incoming files (Figure 4-25). Antivirus programs scan for programs that attempt to modify a computer's start-up files, the operating system, and other programs that normally are read from but not modified. In addition, many antivirus programs automatically scan files downloaded from the web, email attachments, opened files, and all types of removable media inserted in the computer or mobile device.

If an antivirus program identifies an infected file, it attempts to remove the malware. If the antivirus program cannot remove the infection, it often quarantines the infected file. A *quarantine* is a separate area of a hard drive that holds the infected file until the infection can be removed. This step ensures other files will not become infected. Quarantined files remain on your computer or mobile device until you delete them or restore them.

Most antivirus programs also include protection against other malware, such as worms, trojan horses, and spyware. When you purchase a new computer, it may include a trial version of antivirus software. Many email servers also have antivirus programs installed to check incoming and outgoing email messages for viruses and other malware. Read Secure IT 4-4 for tips about recognizing virus hoaxes.

BTW

Antivirus and Malware Detection Programs
You should run only one antivirus program on your computer but can run more than one malware detection program.

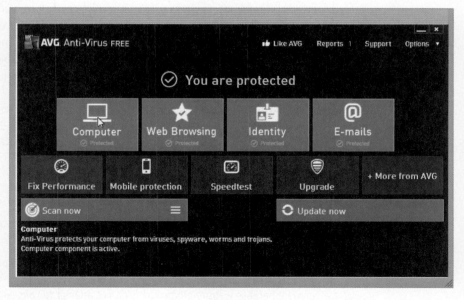

Figure 4-25   An antivirus program scans memory, media, and incoming email messages and attachments for viruses and attempts to remove any viruses it finds.
Courtesy of Checkpoint Software Technologies Ltd.

SECURE IT 4-4

Recognizing Virus Hoaxes

Computer hoaxes spread across the Internet in record time and often are the source of urban legends. These hoaxes take several forms and often disappear for months or years at a time, only to resurface some time later.

Most alarming to some users are the computer virus hoaxes that warn the computer is infected and needs immediate attention. Some warnings state the problem is so severe that the computer or device will explode or that the entire hard drive will be erased in a matter of seconds. The warnings cite prominent companies, such as Microsoft and Intel Security. These messages claim to offer a solution to the problem, generally requesting a fee for a program to download. Snopes.com compiles these hoaxes and describes their sources and histories.

In reality, these fake messages are generated by unscrupulous scammers preying upon gullible people who panic and follow the directions in the message. These users divulge credit card information and then often download files riddled with viruses.

If you receive one of these virus hoaxes, never respond to the message. Instead, delete it. Most importantly, never forward it to an unsuspecting friend or coworker. If you receive the virus hoax from someone you know, send him or her a separate email message with information about the hoax.

 Consider This: Have you ever received a virus hoax? If so, what action did you take?

 CONSIDER THIS

How do antivirus programs detect viruses?

Many antivirus programs identify viruses by looking for virus signatures. A *virus signature,* also called a virus definition, is a known specific pattern of virus code. Computer users should update their antivirus program's signature files regularly. This extremely important activity allows the antivirus program to protect against viruses written since the antivirus program was released and/or its last update. Most antivirus programs contain an automatic update feature or regularly prompts users to download the updated virus signatures, usually at least once a week. The vendor usually provides this service to registered users at no cost for a specified time.

Spyware, Adware, and Other Malware Removers

Spyware is a type of program placed on a computer or mobile device without the user's knowledge that secretly collects information about the user and then communicates the information it collects to some outside source while the user is online. Some vendors or employers use spyware to collect information about program usage or employees. Internet advertising firms often collect information about users' web browsing habits. Spyware can enter your computer when you install a new program, through a graphic on a webpage or in an email message, or through malware.

Adware is a type of program that displays an online advertisement in a banner or pop-up or pop-under window on webpages, email messages, or other Internet services. Sometimes, Internet advertising firms hide spyware in adware.

A **spyware remover** is a type of program that detects and deletes spyware and similar programs. An **adware remover** is a program that detects and deletes adware. Malware removers detect and delete spyware, adware, and other malware. Read Secure IT 4-5 for measures you can take to protect your mobile device from malware.

 CONSIDER THIS

Are cookies spyware?

A *cookie* is a small text file that a web server stores on your computer. Cookie files typically contain data about you, such as your user name, viewing preferences, or shopping cart contents. Cookies are not considered spyware because website programmers do not attempt to conceal the cookies.

SECURE IT 4-5

Malware Risks to Mobile Devices

Practically every smartphone is vulnerable to hacking attacks. Threats to smartphones and mobile devices are growing in record numbers due to the rising popularity of these products and the variety of marketplace sources for downloading apps.

Often the malware is disguised as a popular app and steals personal and sensitive information and phone numbers. It also can allow hackers to control the mobile device from remote locations. Once the hacker takes over the device, all the information on it is available, including passwords and account numbers. One of the fastest growing threats within mobile apps is *toll fraud malware*,

which is a malicious mobile app that uses a variety of fraudulent schemes to charge unsuspecting users for premium messaging services.

Smartphone users can take several precautions to guard against malware threats. They include:

- Read reviews of apps and the companies that create them before downloading the apps to your mobile device.
- Use mobile malware and antivirus protection.
- Turn off location-based apps that track your movements.
- Do not connect to unknown wireless networks.

- Keep the operating system up to date.
- Enable the screen lock feature, and use a strong password to unlock the device.
- Reset the mobile device before selling or trading it in.
- Practice the same safe computing measures you take on your home computer.

Consider This: Which of these guidelines do you follow now when using your smartphone or mobile device? How will you modify your usage after reading these tips?

Internet Filters

Filters are programs that remove or block certain items from being displayed. Four widely used Internet filters are anti-spam programs, web filters, phishing filters, and pop-up and pop-under blockers.

Anti-Spam Programs   **Spam** is an unsolicited email message or posting sent to many recipients or forums at once. Spam is considered Internet junk mail. The content of spam ranges from selling a product or service, to promoting a business opportunity, to advertising offensive material. Spam also may contain links or attachments that contain malware.

An **anti-spam program** is a filtering program that attempts to remove spam before it reaches your inbox or forum. If your email program does not filter spam, many anti-spam programs are available at no cost on the web. ISPs often filter spam as a service for their subscribers.

Web Filters   **Web filtering software** is a program that restricts access to certain material on the web. Some restrict access to specific websites; others filter websites that use certain words or phrases. Many businesses use web filtering software to limit employee's web access. Some schools, libraries, and parents use this software to restrict access to websites that are not educational.

Phishing Filters   **Phishing** is a scam in which a perpetrator sends an official looking email message that attempts to obtain your personal and/or financial information (Figure 4-26). Some phishing messages ask you to reply with your information; others direct you to a phony website or a pop-up or pop-under window that looks like a legitimate website, which then collects your information.

A **phishing filter** is a program that warns or blocks you from potentially fraudulent or suspicious websites. Some browsers include phishing filters.

Internet Research

What are current phishing scams?

Search for: recent phishing scams

Figure 4-26   An example of a phishing email message.
Source: Andrew Levine

Pop-Up and Pop-Under Blockers A *pop-up ad* is an Internet advertisement that suddenly appears in a new window on top of a webpage. Similarly, a *pop-under ad* is an Internet advertisement that is hidden behind the browser window so that it will be viewed when users close their browser windows. A **pop-up blocker** or **pop-under blocker** is a filtering program that stops pop-up or pop-under ads from displaying on webpages. Many browsers include these blockers. You also can download pop-up and pop-under blockers from the web at no cost.

File, Disk, and System Management Tools

To perform maintenance-type tasks related to managing a computer, its devices, or its programs, you can use one or more file, disk, and system management tools. Functions provided by these tools include the following: managing files, searching, viewing images, uninstalling software, cleaning up disks, defragmenting disks, setting up screen savers, compressing files, maintaining a personal computer, and backing up files and disks. Although some of these tools are included with the operating system, you also can purchase stand-alone programs that offer improvements or added functionality.

File Manager
A **file manager** is a tool that performs functions related to file management. Some of the file management functions that a file manager performs are displaying a list of files on a storage medium (Figure 4-27); organizing files in folders; and copying, renaming, deleting, moving, and sorting files. A **folder** is a specific named location on a storage medium that contains related files. Operating systems typically include a file manager.

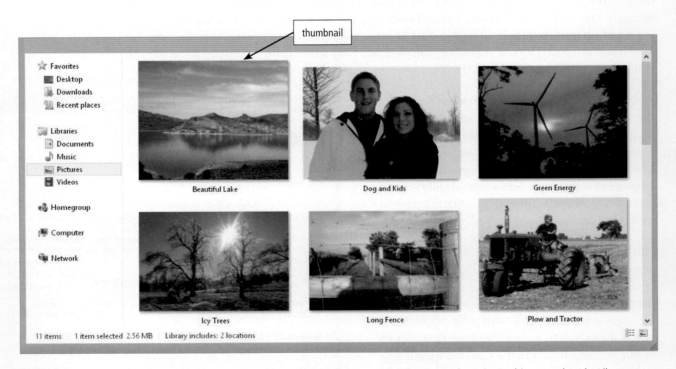

Figure 4-27 With a file manager, you can view files containing documents, photos, and music. In this case, thumbnails of photos are displayed.
Source: Microsoft

Search

A **search tool** is a program, usually included with an operating system, that attempts to locate a file, contact, calendar event, app or any other item stored on your computer or mobile device based on criteria you specify (Figure 4-28). The criteria could be a word(s), date, location, and other similar properties. Search tools can look through documents, photos, music, calendars, contacts, and other items on your computer or mobile device and/or on the Internet, combining search results in a single location.

Search tools typically use an index to assist with locating items quickly. An *index* stores a variety of information about a file, including its name, date created, date modified, author name, and so on. When you enter search criteria, instead of looking through every file and folder on the storage medium, the search tool looks through the index first to find a match. Each entry in the index contains a link to the actual file on the storage media for easy retrieval.

Figure 4-28 This search displays all files on the mobile device that match the search critieria, Map. Notice the search results show map apps, email with a map, and a calendar event.
Source: Apple Inc

Image Viewer

An **image viewer** is a tool that allows users to display, copy, and print the contents of a graphics file, such as a photo (Figure 4-29). With an image viewer, users can see images without having to open them in a paint or image editing program. Many image viewers include some photo editing capabilities. Most operating systems include an image viewer.

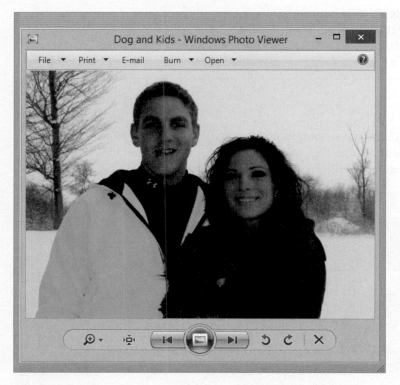

Figure 4-29 An image viewer allows users to see the contents of a photo file.
Source: Microsoft

Uninstaller

An **uninstaller** is a tool that removes a program, as well as any associated entries in the system files. When you install a program, the operating system records the information it uses to run the software in the system files. The uninstaller deletes files and folders from the hard drive, as well as removes program entries from the system files. Read How To 4-4 for instructions about uninstalling programs and removing apps from your computers and mobile devices.

HOW TO 4-4

Uninstall a Program or Remove an App
You may choose to uninstall a program or remove an app from your computer or mobile device for a variety of reasons. For example, you may uninstall a program if you need more space on your hard drive, or if you no longer have a use for that program. Uninstalling unwanted programs and apps will keep your hard drive free from clutter and maximize your computer or mobile device's performance. The following steps describe how to uninstall a program or remove an app.

Windows
1. Open the Control Panel.
2. Tap or click the option to uninstall a program.

3. Tap or click to select the program to uninstall.
4. Tap or click the Uninstall button and then follow the prompts on the screen.

Mac
1. Open the Finder.
2. Tap or click Applications in the left pane.
3. Scroll to display the app you wish to uninstall.
4. Drag the app's icon to the Trash.

iPhone, iPad, or iPod Touch
1. Press and hold the icon for the app you wish to delete until the app icons begin to animate.

2. Tap the X on the icon for the app you wish to delete to remove the app from your device.

Android
1. Display the Settings menu.
2. Tap the command to display a list of installed applications.
3. Tap the application to uninstall.
4. Tap the Uninstall button.
5. Tap the OK button.

 Consider This: In addition to the reasons stated here, what other reasons might you choose to uninstall an app from your computer or mobile device?

 CONSIDER THIS

Can you use a file manager to delete a program?
If an uninstaller exists and you remove software from a computer by deleting the files and folders associated with the program without running the uninstaller, the system file entries might not be updated. This may cause the operating system to display error messages when you start the computer.

Disk Cleanup

A **disk cleanup** tool searches for and removes unnecessary files (Figure 4-30). Unnecessary files may include downloaded program files, temporary Internet files, deleted files, and unused program files. Operating systems usually include a disk cleanup tool.

searching for unnecessary files

Figure 4-30 A disk cleanup tool searches for and removes unnecessary files.
Source: Microsoft

Disk Defragmenter

A **disk defragmenter** is a tool that reorganizes the files and unused space on a computer's hard disk so that the operating system accesses data more quickly and programs run faster. When an operating system stores data on a disk, it places the data in the first available sector (a storage location on a disk in the shape of an arc). The operating system attempts to place data in sectors that are contiguous (next to each other), but this is not always possible. When the contents of a file are scattered across two or more noncontiguous sectors, the file is fragmented.

Fragmentation slows down file access and, thus, the performance of the entire computer. Defragmenting the disk, or reorganizing it so that the files are stored in contiguous sectors, solves this problem (Figure 4-31). Operating systems usually include a disk defragmenter.

BTW

SSDs
Defragmenting is necessary only on hard disks. You do not need to defragment an SSD (solid-state drive).

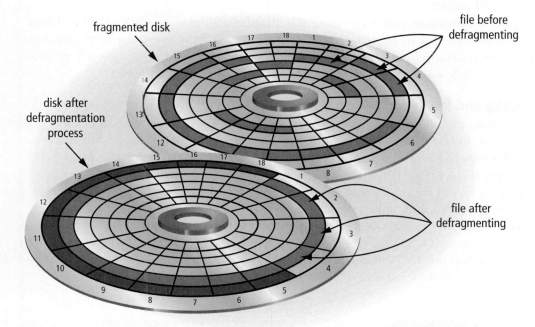

Figure 4-31 A fragmented disk has many files stored in noncontiguous sectors. Defragmenting reorganizes the files so that they are located in contiguous sectors, which speeds access time.
© Cengage Learning

Screen Saver

A **screen saver** is a tool that causes a display device's screen to show a moving image or blank screen if no keyboard or mouse activity occurs for a specified time. When you press a key on the keyboard, tap the screen, or move the mouse, the screen saver disappears and the screen returns to the previous state.

 CONSIDER THIS

What is the purpose of a screen saver?
Screen savers originally were developed to prevent a problem called ghosting, in which images could be etched permanently on a monitor's screen. Although ghosting is not as severe of a problem with today's displays, manufacturers continue to recommend that users install screen savers for this reason. Screen savers also are popular for security, business, and entertainment purposes. To secure a computer, users configure their screen saver to require a password to deactivate.

File Compression

A **file compression tool** shrinks the size of a file(s). A compressed file takes up less storage space than the original file. Compressing files frees up room on the storage media. You may need to compress a file so that it will fit on a smaller storage medium, such as a USB flash drive. Attaching a compressed file to an email message, for example, reduces the time needed for file transmission. Uploading and downloading compressed files to and from the Internet reduces the file transmission time.

Compressed files sometimes are called **zipped files**. When you receive or download a compressed file, you must uncompress it. To **uncompress** (or unzip or expand) a file, you restore it to its original form. Some operating systems include file compression and uncompression capabilities.

PC Maintenance

A **PC maintenance tool** is a program that identifies and fixes operating system problems, detects and repairs drive problems, and includes the capability of improving a computer's performance. Additionally, some personal computer maintenance utilities continuously monitor a computer while you use it to identify and repair problems before they occur.

Backup and Restore

A **backup tool** allows users to copy, or back up, selected files or the contents of an entire storage medium to another storage location, such as another hard drive, optical disc, USB flash drive, or cloud storage (Figure 4-32). During the backup process, the backup tool monitors progress and alerts you if it needs additional media, such as another disc. Many backup programs compress files during the backup process. By compressing the files, the backup program requires less storage space for the backup files than for the original files.

Because they are compressed, you usually cannot use backup files in their backed up form. In the event you need to use a backup file, a **restore tool** reverses the process and returns backed up files to their original form. Backup tools work with a restore tool. You should back up files and disks regularly in the event your originals are lost, damaged, or destroyed.

Figure 4-32 A backup tool allows users to copy files, folders, or the entire contents from one storage medium to another location.
Source: Acronis

NOW YOU SHOULD KNOW ————————————————————————

Be sure you understand the material presented in the sections titled Security Tools and File, Disk, and System Management Tools as it relates to the module objectives.

Now you should know ...

- Why you should use personal firewalls, antivirus programs, malware removers, and Internet filters (Objective 8)
- Which file, disk, and system management tools you would find useful (Objective 9)

Summary

This module presented a variety of programs and apps available for computers and mobile devices. You learned about the role of the operating system and the various ways software is distributed. The module presented the features of a variety of productivity applications, graphics and media applications, and personal interest applications. It reviewed several communications applications and then presented features of a variety of security tools and file, disk, and system management tools.

TECHNOLOGY @ WORK ————————————————————————

Entertainment

Do you wonder how music on the radio sounds so perfectly in tune, how animated motion pictures are created, or how one controls and technology lighting during a concert? Not only does the entertainment industry rely on computers and technology to advertise and sell their services, computers also assist in other aspects, including audio and video composition, lighting control, computerized animation, and computer gaming.

Entertainment websites provide music and movies you can purchase and download to your computer or mobile device; live news broadcasts, performances, and sporting events; games you can play with other online users; and much more.

As early as 1951, computers were used to record and play music. Today, computers play a much larger role in the music industry. For example, if you are listening to a song on the radio and notice that not one note is out of tune, it is possible that a program or app was used to change individual notes without altering the rest of the song.

Many years ago, creating cartoons or animated motion pictures was an extremely time-consuming task because artists were responsible for sketching thousands of drawings by hand. Currently, artists use computers to create these drawings in a fraction of the time, which significantly reduces the time and cost of development. Technology also is used in other areas of movie production to add visual effects.

Technology also is used in the gaming industry. While some game developers create games from scratch, others might use game engines that simplify the development process. For example, LucasArts created the GrimE game engine, which is designed to create adventure games.

During a concert, lighting technicians use computer programs to control lights by turning them off and on, changing their color, or changing their placement at specified intervals. In fact, once a performance begins, the technicians often merely are standing by, monitoring the computer as it performs most of the work. A significant amount of time and

effort, however, is required to program the computer to execute its required tasks during a live show.

The next time you listen to a song, watch a movie, play a game, or attend a concert, think about the role technology plays in contributing to your entertainment.

Consider This: How else might computers and technology be used in the entertainment industry?

© Horizons WWP / Alamy

Study Guide

The Study Guide exercise reinforces material you should know for the module exam.

Instructions: Answer the questions below using the format that helps you remember best or that is required by your instructor. Possible formats may include one or more of these options: write the answers; create a document that contains the answers; record answers as audio or video using a webcam, smartphone, or portable media player; post answers on a blog, wiki, or website; or highlight answers in the book/e-book.

1. List categories of programs and apps. _____ is another word for program.

2. Define these terms: operating system, tools, and system software.

3. List examples of desktop and mobile operating systems.

4. Describe how an operating system interacts with the computer.

5. _____ software performs functions specific to a business or industry.

6. Differentiate among web apps, mobile apps, and mobile web apps.

7. List any restrictions for shareware, freeware, open source, and public-domain software.

8. Explain considerations for safely downloading software and apps.

9. Describe steps to register and activate software.

10. Explain the purpose of a license agreement.

11. List types of productivity applications.

12. Describe the activities that occur during project development.

13. Differentiate among font, font size, and font style.

14. Explain the impact of the Internet on plagiarism.

15. Applications often include a(n) _____ gallery, which is a collection of clip art and photos.

16. Identify functions of the following software: word processing, presentation, spreadsheet, database, note taking, calendar and contact management, software suite, project management, accounting, personal finance, legal, tax preparation, and document management.

17. Identify tools word processing programs provide that can assist you when writing.

18. Define the following terms: worksheet and function.

19. Describe when you should use a database and when to use a spreadsheet.

20. List advantages of using a software suite.

21. Identify ways you can manage a project using project management software.

22. List safety considerations when using personal finance apps.

23. Describe issues that might arise when using legal software.

24. Name the types of software used by various functional units in an enterprise.

25. Identify functions of the following apps: calendar and email, scanning, financial, reference, retail, travel, and online social networks.

26. Identify risks when using payment apps.

27. Identify functions of the following software: computer-aided design, desktop publishing, paint/image editing, photo editing and photo management, video and audio editing, multimedia and website authoring, media player, and disc burning.

28. List ways to edit digital photos. Identify issues surrounding altered digital photos.

29. _____ authoring software allows users to combine text, graphics, audio, video, and animation in an interactive application.

30. Define the terms, CBT and WBT.

31. List types of personal interest applications.

32. Describe ways to use voice command personal assistant apps.

33. Identify functions of the following apps: media sharing; streaming audio and video; game; news, sports, and weather; mapping; health and fitness; and academic.

34. Identify types of communications applications.

35. List issues surrounding an email provider scanning users' emails.

36. Identify functions of the following tools: personal firewalls, hardware firewalls, antivirus programs, malware removers, and Internet filters.

37. Describe ways a virus infects programs or apps.

38. List types of malware. Identify signs of a virus infection.

39. Explain the risks of and how to avoid computer virus hoaxes.

40. A virus _____ is a known specific pattern of virus code. Differentiate between spyware and adware.

41. Identify ways to avoid malware when using a mobile device.

42. List and describe four types of Internet filters.

43. Identify functions of the following tools: file manager, search, image viewer, uninstaller, disk cleanup, disk defragmenter, screen saver, file compression, PC maintenance, and backup and restore.

44. Define the terms, folder and index.

45. List steps to uninstall a program or remove an app.

46. Describe the disk defragmentation process.

47. Compressed files are sometimes called _____ files.

48. List storage media for backups.

49. Describe uses of technology in the entertainment industry.

STUDENT ASSIGNMENTS

You should be able to define the Primary Terms and be familiar with the Secondary Terms listed below.

Key Terms

Primary Terms   (shown in **bold-black** characters in the module)

accounting software (173)

adware remover (192)

anti-spam program (193)

antivirus program (191)

app (158)

application (158)

audio editing software (183)

backup tool (198)

calendar and contact management software (171)

clip art/image gallery (166)

computer-aided design (180)

database (170)

database software (170)

desktop publishing software (180)

disc burning software (185)

disk cleanup (196)

disk defragmenter (197)

document management software (176)

file compression tool (198)

file manager (194)

folder (194)

image editing software (181)

image viewer (195)

legal software (175)

media player (185)

multimedia authoring software (184)

note taking software (171)

paint software (181)

PC maintenance tool (198)

PDF (176)

personal finance software (174)

personal firewall (189)

phishing (193)

phishing filter (193)

photo editing software (181)

photo management software (182)

pop-under blocker (194)

pop-up blocker (194)

presentation software (168)

program (158)

project management software (172)

QR code (178)

restore tool (198)

screen saver (197)

search tool (195)

software (158)

software suite (172)

spam (193)

spreadsheet software (168)

spyware remover (192)

tax preparation software (176)

uncompress (198)

uninstaller (195)

video editing software (183)

virus (190)

web filtering software (193)

website authoring software (184)

word processing software (167)

worksheet (168)

zipped files (198)

Secondary Terms   (shown in *italic* characters in the module)

adware (192)

application software (158)

automatic update (163)

brightness (182)

clipboard (165)

compress (182)

computer-based training (CBT) (184)

contrast (182)

cookie (192)

create (165)

crop (182)

custom software (161)

edit (165)

e-filing (176)

EULA (163)

font (166)

font size (166)

font style (166)

format (166)

freeware (161)

function (169)

hard copy (166)

hardware firewall (190)

home design/landscaping software (180)

illustration software (181)

index (195)

license agreement (163)

marketplace (161)

mobile app (161)

mobile web app (161)

NFC chip (179)

open source software (161)

operating system (158)

payload (190)

pop-under ad (194)

pop-up ad (194)

print (166)

product activation (162)

productivity applications (165)

public-domain software (161)

quarantine (191)

red-eye (182)

resize (182)

retail software (161)

rootkit (190)

save (165)

security suite (189)

shareware (161)

sharpness (182)

slide show (168)

software as a service (SaaS) (162)

software registration (162)

spyware (192)

system software (158)

toll fraud malware (193)

tools (158)

trial version (161)

trojan horse (190)

utilities (158)

virus signature (192)

web app (161)

web-based training (WBT) (184)

worm (190)

database software (170)

Checkpoint

The Checkpoint exercises test your knowledge of the module concepts. The page number containing the answer appears in parentheses after each exercise. The Consider This exercises challenge your understanding of module concepts.

True/False   Mark T for True and F for False.

_____ 1. Application software serves as the interface between the user, the apps, and the computer's or mobile device's hardware. (158)

_____ 2. While a computer or mobile device is running, the operating system remains in memory. (160)

_____ 3. Open source software is mass-produced, copyrighted software that meets the needs of a wide variety of users. (161)

_____ 4. When downloading shareware, freeware, or public-domain software, it is good practice to seek websites with ratings for and reviews of products. (162)

_____ 5. With web apps, you always access the latest version of the software. (163)

_____ 6. With database software, users run functions to retrieve data. (170)

_____ 7. Software suites offer three major advantages: lower cost, ease of use, and integration. (172)

_____ 8. A PDF file can be viewed and printed without the software that created the original document. (176)

_____ 9. The military and airlines use CBT simulations to train pilots to fly in various conditions and environments. (184)

_____ 10. A router also can function as a hardware firewall. (190)

_____ 11. A worm is a destructive program designed as a real program. (190)

_____ 12. Cookies typically are considered a type of spyware. (192)

Multiple Choice   Select the best answer.

1. _____ software performs functions specific to a business or industry. (161)
   a. Retail
   b. Open source
   c. Shareware
   d. Custom

2. A(n) _____ is the right to use a program or app. (163)
   a. license agreement
   b. product activation
   c. software registration
   d. automatic update

3. _____ software is an application that allows users to organize data in columns and rows and perform calculations on the data. (168)
   a. Spreadsheet
   b. Database
   c. Presentation
   d. Document management

4. Mobile payment apps use a payment system on phones equipped with a(n) _____, which stores data that is transmitted to a contactless terminal and verified as a legitimate sale. (179)
   a. QR chip
   b. EULA
   c. NFC chip
   d. trojan horse

5. _____ is a type of application that assists professionals and designers in creating engineering, architectural, and scientific designs and models. (180)
   a. Enterprise software
   b. CAD software
   c. Public-domain software
   d. A software suite

6. The term _____ refers to removing unwanted areas of a photo. (182)
   a. crop
   b. snip
   c. compress
   d. shrink

7. A(n) _____ is a device intended to stop network intrusions before they attempt to affect your computer or network maliciously. (190)
   a. anti-spam program
   b. pop-under blocker
   c. hardware firewall
   d. quarantine drive

8. _____ is a small text file that a web server stores on your computer. (192)
   a. A pop-under blocker
   b. A cookie
   c. Adware
   d. Spyware

Checkpoint

Matching Match the terms with their definitions.

_____ 1. tools (158)

_____ 2. shareware (161)

_____ 3. software as a service (162)

_____ 4. QR code (178)

_____ 5. CBT (184)

_____ 6. personal firewall (189)

_____ 7. payload (190)

_____ 8. worm (190)

_____ 9. quarantine (191)

_____ 10. phishing (193)

a. destructive event or prank a virus was created to deliver

b. copyrighted software that is distributed at no cost for a trial period

c. malware that resides in active memory and replicates itself over a network to infect computers and devices, using up the system resources and possibly shutting down the system

d. program that enables you to perform maintenance-type tasks usually related to managing devices, media, and programs used by computers and mobile devices

e. computing environment where an Internet server hosts and deploys applications

f. security tool that detects and protects a personal computer and its data from unauthorized intrusions

g. type of education in which students learn by using and completing exercises with instructional software

h. scam in which a perpetrator sends an official looking email message that attempts to obtain personal and/or financial information

i. square-shaped graphic that represents a web address or other information

j. separate area of a hard drive that holds an infected file until the infection can be removed

✳ Consider This Answer the following questions in the format specified by your instructor.

1. Answer the critical thinking questions posed at the end of these elements in this module: Ethics & Issues (165, 175, 183, 189), How To (173, 182, 186, 196), Mini Features (178, 187, 190), Secure IT (162, 174, 179, 192, 193), and Technology @ Work (199).

2. What is the role of the operating system? (158)

3. What is system software? (158)

4. What are the advantages of open source software? (161)

5. Why do app developers opt for web delivery? (161)

6. What is the difference between software registration and product activation? (162)

7. What activities does a license agreement restrict? (163)

8. What does it mean to edit a project? (165)

9. What is the clipboard? (165)

10. What is meant by font style? (166)

11. How often should you save a project? (166)

12. How does a spreadsheet organize data? (169)

13. How are cells identified in a spreadsheet? (169)

14. When might you choose to use a database instead of a spreadsheet? (170)

15. What features are included in personal finance software? (174)

16. What steps can you take to safeguard your funds and identity when using personal finance apps? (174)

17. Who might use CAD? (180)

18. Should journalists edit or enhance digital photos? Why or why not? (183)

19. What tasks can you accomplish using mapping apps? (187)

20. How does a personal firewall protect your computer? (189)

21. What happens during the delivery phase of a virus? (190)

22. How do a virus, worm, trojan horse, and rootkit differ? (190)

23. In reference to malware, what is a quarantine? (191)

24. What is a phishing scam? (193)

25. Why is spam potentially dangerous? (193)

26. What are the different types of file, disk, and system management tools? (194)

27. How does a search tool locate a file on your computer or mobile device? (195)

28. What is a fragmented disk? (197)

29. How does fragmentation affect a computer's performance? (197)

30. What tasks does a PC maintenance tool perform? (198)

✷ Problem Solving

The Problem Solving exercises extend your knowledge of module concepts by seeking solutions to practical problems with technology that you may encounter at home, school, work, or with nonprofit organizations. The Collaboration exercise should be completed with a team.

Instructions: You often can solve problems with technology in multiple ways. Determine a solution to the problems in these exercises by using one or more resources available to you (such as a computer or mobile device, articles on the web or in print, blogs, podcasts, videos, television, user guides, other individuals, electronics or computer stores, etc.). Describe your solution, along with the resource(s) used, in the format requested by your instructor (brief report, presentation, discussion, blog post, video, or other means).

Personal

1. **Antivirus Program Not Updating**   You are attempting to update your antivirus program with the latest virus definitions, but you receive an error message. What steps will you take to resolve this issue?

2. **Operating System Does Not Load**   Each time you turn on your computer, the operating system attempts to load for approximately 30 seconds and then the computer restarts. You have tried multiple times to turn your computer off and on, but it keeps restarting when the operating system is trying to load. What are your next steps?

3. **Unwanted Programs**   When you displayed a list of programs installed on your computer so that you could uninstall one, you noticed several installed programs that you do not remember installing. Why might these programs be on your computer?

Source: Microsoft

4. **News Not Updating**   Each morning, you run an app on your smartphone to view the news for the current day. For the past week, however, you notice that the news displayed in the app is out of date. In fact, the app now is displaying news that is nearly one week old. Why might the app not be updating? What are your next steps?

5. **Incompatible App**   You are using your Android tablet to browse for apps in the Google Play store. You found an app you want to download, but you are unable to download it because a message states it is incompatible with your device. Why might the app be incompatible with your device?

Professional

6. **Videoconference Freezes**   While conducting a videoconference with colleagues around the country, the audio sporadically cuts out and the video freezes. You have attempted several times to terminate and then reestablish the connection, but the same problem continues to occur. What might be the problem?

7. **License Agreement**   You are planning to work from home for several days, but you are unsure of whether you are allowed to install a program you use at work on your home computer. What steps will you take to determine whether you are allowed to install the software on your home computer?

8. **Low on Space**   The computer in your office is running low on free space. You have attempted to remove as many files as possible, but the remaining programs and files are necessary to perform your daily job functions. What steps might you take to free enough space on the computer?

9. **Unacceptable File Size**   Your boss has asked you to design a new company logo using a graphics application installed on your computer. When you save the logo and send it to your boss, she responds that the file size is too large and tells you to find a way to decrease the file size. What might you do to make the image file size smaller?

10. **Disc Burning Not Working**   While attempting to back up some files on your computer on an optical disc, the disc burning software on your computer reports a problem and ejects the disc. When you check the contents of the disc, the files you are trying to back up are not there. What might be wrong?

Collaboration

11. **Technology in Entertainment**   The film department at a local high school is considering developing a movie and has asked for your help. The film teacher would like to incorporate technology wherever possible, in hopes that it would decrease the cost of the movie's production. Form a team of three people to determine what technology can be used to assist in the movie's production. One team member should research the type of technology that can be used during the filming process. Another team member should research the types of hardware and software available for editing footage, and the third team member should research the hardware and software requirements for producing and distributing the media.

The How To: Your Turn exercises present general guidelines for fundamental skills when using a computer or mobile device and then require that you determine how to apply these general guidelines to a specific program or situation.

How To: Your Turn

Instructions: You often can complete tasks using technology in multiple ways. Figure out how to perform the tasks described in these exercises by using one or more resources available to you (such as a computer or mobile device, articles on the web or in print, online or program help, user guides, blogs, podcasts, videos, other individuals, trial and error, etc.). Summarize your 'how to' steps, along with the resource(s) used, in the format requested by your instructor (brief report, presentation, discussion, blog post, video, or other means).

1 Obtain Help about Programs and Apps

Multiple ways are provided to obtain help while using the programs and apps on a computer or mobile device. The program or app developer usually includes a Help feature in the program and/or online. In addition, third parties often post resources online that can provide further assistance. The following steps describe how to obtain help about various programs and apps using various methods.

Help System

You typically can access help in a program or app using one of the following methods:

- Tap or click the Help or Information icon in the program or app. The appearance of Help or Information icons may vary, but typically they are identified by a question mark or the letter 'i' formatted in italic.
- Navigate the program or app's menu to locate the Help command.
- If you are using a program or app on a Windows laptop or desktop, press the F1 key on the keyboard to display Help content.

Online Help

Online help usually is available from the program or app developer. The following steps describe how to obtain online help.

a. Navigate to the program or app developer's website.
b. Locate, and then tap or click a Help or Support link.
c. Select the program or app for which you wish to obtain help to display the help information.

Searching for Help

In addition to obtaining help from within a program or app or on the developer's website, you also can search the web for help as described in the following steps.

a. Navigate to a search engine, such as google.com or yahoo.com.
b. Type the program or app name, as well as the type of help for which you are searching, as the search text, and then press the ENTER key or tap or click the Search (or a similar) button.
c. Scroll through the search results and then tap or click the search result to display more information. Be aware that not all help originates from reputable or accurate sources.

Exercises

1. Under what circumstances would you use each of these methods to obtain help with a program or app you are using?
2. Compare and contrast the different methods of obtaining help. Which method do you think is the best? Why?
3. What are some reputable websites that can provide you with help for the operating system installed on your computer? Why do you consider them reputable?

2 Compress/Uncompress Files and Folders

You may want to compress files if your hard drive is running out of available space. While the operating system may be able to compress some files by 50 percent or more, other files' sizes may not decrease significantly when they are compressed. Compressed files typically are stored by default in a file with a .zip file extension. The following steps describe how to compress a file or folder and then uncompress (expand or extract) the compressed file.

a. Press and hold or right-click the file(s) or folders you wish to compress to display a shortcut menu.
b. Tap or click the option to compress the file(s) or folder(s). (You may need to select a Send to or other command to display the compression options.)
c. If necessary, type the desired file name for the compressed file.

Uncompressing (or expanding) compressed files or folders returns them to their original form. The following steps uncompress a compressed file.

a. Double-tap or double-click the compressed file.
b. If necessary, tap or click the option to uncompress (expand or extract) the file.

or

a. Press and hold or right-click the compressed file to display a shortcut menu.
b. Tap or click the option to uncompress (expand or extract) the file.

❋ How To: Your Turn

Exercises

1. In addition to the operating system's built-in functionality to compress files and folders, what other programs and apps exist that can compress files and folders?
2. In addition to trying to free space on your storage device, for what other reasons might you want to compress files and folders?
3. Try compressing various types of files on your hard drive, such as a Word document and an image. Compare the file sizes before and after compression. What did you notice with each type of file?

③ View Current Virus Threats

One important way to protect your computer or mobile device from viruses is to be aware of current threats. Several websites exist that not only provide a list of current virus threats but also describe how best to protect your computer or mobile device from these threats. As new virus threats are introduced, it is important to make sure your antivirus program is updated and running properly. The following steps describe how to view a list of current virus threats.

a. Run a browser and then navigate to a search engine of your choice.
b. Perform a search for websites that display current virus threats.
c. Review the search results and visit at least two websites that display current virus threats.
d. View the list of virus threats on each of these websites.

or

a. Run a browser and then navigate to a search engine of your choice.
b. Perform a search for websites created by companies that make antivirus software. Some companies that make antivirus software include Symantec, McAfee, and Microsoft.
c. Navigate to one of these company's websites and then search for a link to a webpage displaying current virus threats.
d. Tap or click the link to display current virus threats.

Courtesy of Checkpoint Software Technologies Ltd.

Exercises

1. Which websites did you access? Compare these websites and determine which you think provided the most helpful information. Why, in your opinion, does the website you chose provide the best information?
2. Has your computer or mobile device ever been infected with a virus? If so, what steps have you taken to remove the virus?
3. Is your computer or mobile device adequately protected from viruses? What steps do you take to keep your computer safe?

④ Back Up Your Computer

Backing up your computer is an important way to protect your programs, apps, and data from loss. The frequency at which people back up their computers can vary. For instance, if you create and modify a lot of files on your computer, you may choose to back up your computer frequently. If you rarely use your computer or primarily use your computer for answering email messages and browsing the web, you might not back up your computer as often. The following steps guide you through the process of backing up a computer.

a. Decide which backup program you wish to use. Some operating systems have built-in tools you can use to back up a computer, or you can install a third-party program.
b. Run the program you will use to back up the computer.
c. If necessary, connect the storage device, such as an external hard drive, you will use to store the backup. If you plan to store the backup on an optical disc or another hard drive that already is installed, you will not need to connect an additional storage device.
d. Make sure the storage medium has enough available space for the backed up files. If you are storing the backup on optical discs, make sure you have enough optical discs for the backup.
e. Select the type of backup (full, incremental, differential, or selective) you wish to perform.
f. If you are performing a selective backup, choose the files, programs, and apps you wish to include in the backup.
g. Run the backup. The backup process may take up to several hours, depending on the number of files you are including in the backup.
h. If you are storing the backup on optical discs, the backup program may prompt you to insert new, blank optical discs throughout the backup process.

How To: Your Turn

i. When the backup is complete, store the backup in a safe location. In the event you lose data or information on the computer, you will need to retrieve the backup.

Source: Acronis

Exercises

1. How often do you feel you should back up your computer? Justify your answer.
2. Which storage medium do you feel is most appropriate for your backup? Justify your answer.
3. Research at least three programs that you can use to back up your computer. Which programs did you research? Which program or app do you feel is the best? Why?

5 **Share Your Online Calendar**

If you keep track of your meetings, appointments, and other obligations using an online calendar, you might want to share your calendar with others so that they know when you are available. For instance, you might want to share your calendar with fellow employees so that they can verify your availability before scheduling meetings. Your family members may share their calendars with one another so that it is easier to plan family events when everyone is available. The

following steps describe how to share your online calendar.

a. If necessary, run a browser and navigate to an online calendar.
b. Display the calendar's settings.
c. Select the option to display the calendar's sharing settings.
d. Specify with whom you want to share the calendar.
e. Determine your sharing settings for each person. For example, you may select whether a person only can view your calendar or view and edit your calendar. You also can select the level of detail you want to share with others. For example, you can share the times you are free or busy, or you can share the specific details for each appointment.
f. If necessary, repeat the two previous steps for each additional person with whom you wish to share the calendar.
g. Save the settings.
h. Verify the people with whom you shared the calendar are able to access the calendar.

Exercises

1. For what other reasons might you share your calendar?
2. In addition to the steps outlined previously, in what other ways can you share your calendar online?
3. In addition to sharing online calendars, is it possible to share calendars you create in programs such as Microsoft Outlook? If so, how?

Google Inc.

✴ Internet Research

The Internet Research exercises broaden your understanding of module concepts by requiring that you search for information on the web.

Instructions: Use a search engine or another search tool to locate the information requested or answers to questions presented in the exercises. Describe your findings, along with the search term(s) you used and your web source(s), in the format requested by your instructor (brief report, presentation, discussion, blog post, video, or other means).

❶ Making Use of the Web
Website Creation and Management

Retailers and organizations realize the importance of having a website to promote their goods and services. An online presence helps a business connect with an audience and ultimately builds trust and respect. Innovative and dynamic websites deliver information to current and potential customers and clients. Creating these websites requires a methodology of planning, designing, creating, hosting, and maintaining. A business must identify the website's purpose, demographics of the target audience, appropriate content and functionality, page layout, and usability. Once the website is implemented, it must be monitored to determine usage. Logs list the number of visitors, the browsers they used, and usage patterns. In addition, the website should be maintained to update content and features.

Products are available to help build and manage a website. Most offer well-designed templates that can be customized to accommodate specific personal and business needs. They can include calendars, photos, videos, maps, and blogs. Some of these design and management tools, such as those offered on Google Sites, are available at no cost, while others require fees for specific features, such as technical support or exclusive designs.

Research This: Visit Google Sites and two other online content management systems for building websites. Compare these web apps by creating a table using these headings: Name, Number of Templates, Price, Maximum Storage, Customer Support, and Features. The Features column could include the availability of items such as customizable color schemes, e-commerce, drag and drop, website logs and analytics, and mobile editing. Which website builder would you choose if you were creating a website? Why?

❷ Social Media

Gaming via social media has seen explosive growth in recent years, especially among adult males. Exponential gaming growth has spawned companion businesses that facilitate and manage the gaming experience. Some mobile and desktop apps provide gamers a portal for tracking all their online gaming results in a central location that can be shared with friends and others with similar game interests. These apps integrate with the major Internet messaging services, have personalized news feeds, and incorporate a "suggestion" engine for new game discoveries. Many gaming blogs offer game tricks, work-arounds, and hidden features. Beginning gamers can engage their minds during downtime and expand their circle of online friends.

Research This: Visit at least two online social networks for gamers. How many games are shown? Which topics are featured in community discussions and live chats? Are rewards available? If so, what are they? Which online leagues and tournaments are offered? What are some of the latest news articles about specific games and the gaming industry? Have you participated in gaming online social networks? If so, which ones?

Google Inc.

Internet Research

3 **Search Skills**

Narrowing Your Search Results

One strategy for narrowing search results is to specify what you are or are not looking for as part of your search text. Precede words with a plus sign (+) if you want to ensure that they appear in your search results, and precede a word with a minus sign (-) if you want to exclude that word from search results. For example, typing the phrase, windows +microsoft, will search for information about the operating system; typing the phrase, windows –microsoft, also will find information about windows that are made of glass.

Include the keyword, and, between words or phrases in search text if you want search results to include both words or phrases, or the keyword, or, if search results containing either word or phrase are acceptable. Group terms with parentheses to clarify search text. For example, type the phrase, iPhone and "Steve Jobs" (including the quotation marks), to search for articles about the inventor of the iPhone. Type the phrase, (iPhone or iPad) and "Steve Jobs" (including the parentheses and quotation marks), to search for information about iPhone or iPad devices that also mentions Steve Jobs.

Google, Inc.

Research This: Create search text using the techniques described above or in previous Search Skills exercises, and type it in a search engine to answer these questions. (1) What is an open source FTP application that has versions for both Windows and Mac? (2) Other than TurboTax, what are two examples of online tax preparation software? (3) Find reviews comparing Internet Explorer, Edge, Chrome, and Firefox browsers. (4) What are the more popular calendar management and task management apps on Google Play?

4 **Security**

Virus hoaxes are widespread and sometimes cause panic among Internet users. Secure IT 4-4 in this module gives advice on recognizing and avoiding virus hoaxes. Snopes.com provides further insight on the sources and variations of a wide variety of rumors, deceptions, and folklore.

Research This: Visit snopes.com and type the search text phrase, virus hoaxes & realities, in the Search box at the top of the page. Review the list of the more recent real (indicated by a green dot) and false (indicated by a red dot) rumors circulating on the Internet. Which are the three newest actual warnings, and which are the three latest virus hoaxes? What harm is predicted to occur if a user downloads each of these real or false viruses or views a website laden with malware? What is the origin of the website's name, Snopes?

5 **Cloud Services**

Photo Editing (SaaS)

Online photo editing apps provide browser-based capabilities to modify digital images, and often contain many similar features as their desktop counterparts. They are an example of SaaS (software as a service), a service of cloud computing that provides access to software solutions accessed through a browser. In addition to drawing shapes, touching up colors, and adding filters to images, online photo editing apps allow users to access, store, and share their photos on the cloud. Online photo editing apps often include the ability to share photos with friends easily by sending a link, or posting the photo to online social networks.

Research This: (1) Use a search engine to research various online photo editing apps. Compare the features of two of them as you explore their capabilities. Summarize your findings in a table, regarding image formats you can import or save, sharing capabilities, special editing features, and ways to organize photos online. Which features take advantage of the fact that the app is cloud based? (2) If you have access to computers running two different operating systems, such as Windows and Mac, try running the photo editing app in a browser on both computers. What similarities and differences do you notice between the two versions?

Critical Thinking

The Critical Thinking exercises challenge your assessment and decision-making skills by presenting real-world situations associated with module concepts. The Collaboration exercise should be completed with a team.

Instructions: Evaluate the situations below, using personal experiences and one or more resources available to you (such as articles on the web or in print, blogs, podcasts, videos, television, user guides, other individuals, electronics or computer stores, etc.). Perform the tasks requested in each exercise and share your deliverables in the format requested by your instructor (brief report, presentation, discussion, blog post, video, or other means).

1. File, Disk, and System Management Tools

You are the director of information technology at a company that frequently hires student interns. The interns tend to have limited experience with using file, disk, and system management tools. As part of your job, you lead workshops that teach the interns the many tasks and functions they can perform using these tools.

Do This: Choose three categories of tools, such as disk cleanup, PC maintenance, and file compression. Determine whether your computer's operating system includes these tools. Use the web to research popular tools for each category, whether they can be purchased separately or if they are available only as part of an operating system, and the costs for each tool. Choose one program from each category, and read user reviews and articles by industry experts. Describe situations where you would use each type of tool. Share any experiences you have with using the tools.

2. Web and Mobile App Comparison

You recently purchased a new smartphone and want to research mobile apps that also have accompanying web apps.

Do This: Choose three categories of apps, and find an example for each that has both a free web and mobile version. Read user reviews of each app, and search for articles by industry experts. Research any known safety risks for the apps. If you determine the app is safe, have access to the appropriate device, and would like to test the mobile app, you can download it to a smartphone or other mobile device. Try accessing the web app on a computer. Using your experience or research, note the differences in functionality between the web and mobile app. Is one or the other easier to use? Why or why not?

3. Case Study

Amateur Sports League You are the new manager for a nonprofit amateur soccer league. The league needs productivity software in order to keep track of participant and budget information and to prepare flyers. You prepare information about productivity software options to present to the board of directors.

Do This: Use the web to research popular word processing, spreadsheet, and accounting software. Choose three programs from each category. List common features of each, find pricing information, and note any feedback or ratings by users. Which programs would you recommend? Why? Describe the steps involved in developing a project, creating a flyer for the league as an example. Identify possible uses the league may have for the spreadsheet and accounting software. Compile your findings.

Source: © Cengage Learning

Collaboration

4. Educational Program and App Effectiveness

The principal of the local elementary school has recommended that educational apps should play a major role in the learning process, believing that these apps enable students to learn at their own pace. Some enable teachers to track an individual student's progress and understanding.

Do This: Form a three-member team and research the use of educational apps. Each member of your team should choose a different type of app, such as flash cards, testing, or CBT. List the advantages and disadvantages of using that type of app. If possible, download or access a free version of an educational app from each category and spend some time using it. Read user reviews of popular apps, and search for articles by industry experts. Would you recommend using an app for educational purposes? Why or why not? Meet with your team, and discuss and compile your findings.

DIGITAL SECURITY, ETHICS, AND PRIVACY:
Threats, Issues, and Defenses

5

Users should take precautions to protect their digital content.

"I am careful when browsing the web, use antivirus software, and never open email messages from unknown senders. I use a cloud storage provider to back up my computer and mobile devices. What more do I need to know about digital safety and security?"

While you may be familiar with some of the content in this module, do you know how to . . .

- Avoid risks when playing online games?
- Determine if an email message has been spoofed?
- Tell if your computer or device is functioning as a zombie?
- Set up a personal firewall?
- Protect computers and devices from viruses and other malware?
- Protect your passwords?
- Use two-step verification?
- Prevent your data from being lost on the cloud?
- Follow a disaster recovery plan?
- Secure your wireless network?
- Safeguard your hardware and data from a disaster?
- Protect against a phishing scam?
- Protect yourself from social engineering scams?
- Evaluate your electronic profile?

In this module, you will discover how to perform these tasks along with much more information essential to this course.

© iStockPhoto / Vertigo3d

✔ Objectives

After completing this module, you will be able to:

1 Define the term, digital security risks, and briefly describe the types of cybercriminals

2 Describe various types of Internet and network attacks (malware, botnets, denial of service attacks, back doors, and spoofing) and explain ways to safeguard against these attacks, including firewalls

3 Discuss techniques to prevent unauthorized computer access and use, including access controls, user names, passwords, possessed objects, and biometric devices

4 Explain ways that software manufacturers protect against software piracy

5 Discuss how encryption, digital signatures, and digital certificates work

6 Identify safeguards against hardware theft, vandalism, and failure

7 Explain options available for backing up

8 Identify risks and safeguards associated with wireless communications

9 Recognize issues related to information accuracy, intellectual property rights, codes of conduct, and green computing

10 Discuss issues surrounding information privacy, including electronic profiles, cookies, phishing, spyware and adware, social engineering, privacy laws, employee monitoring, and content filtering

Digital Security Risks

Today, people rely on technology to create, store, and manage their critical information. Thus, it is important that computers and mobile devices, along with the data and programs they store, are accessible and available when needed. It also is crucial that users take measures to protect or safeguard their computers, mobile devices, data, and programs from loss, damage, and misuse. For example, organizations must ensure that sensitive data and information, such as credit records, employee and customer data, and purchase information, is secure. Home users must ensure that their credit card numbers are secure when they make online purchases.

A **digital security risk** is any event or action that could cause a loss of or damage to computer or mobile device hardware, software, data, information, or processing capability. The more common digital security risks include Internet and network attacks, unauthorized access and use, hardware theft, software theft, information theft, and system failure (Figure 5-1).

While some breaches to digital security are accidental, many are intentional. Some intruders do not disrupt a computer or device's functionality; they merely access data, information, or programs on the computer or mobile device before signing out. Other intruders indicate some evidence of their presence either by leaving a message or by deliberately altering or damaging data.

Cybercrime

An intentional breach to digital security often involves a deliberate act that is against the law. Any illegal act involving the use of a computer or related devices generally is referred to as a **computer crime**. The term **cybercrime** refers to online or Internet-based illegal acts such as distributing malicious software or committing identity theft. Software used by cybercriminals sometimes is called *crimeware*. Today, combating cybercrime is one of the FBI's top priorities.

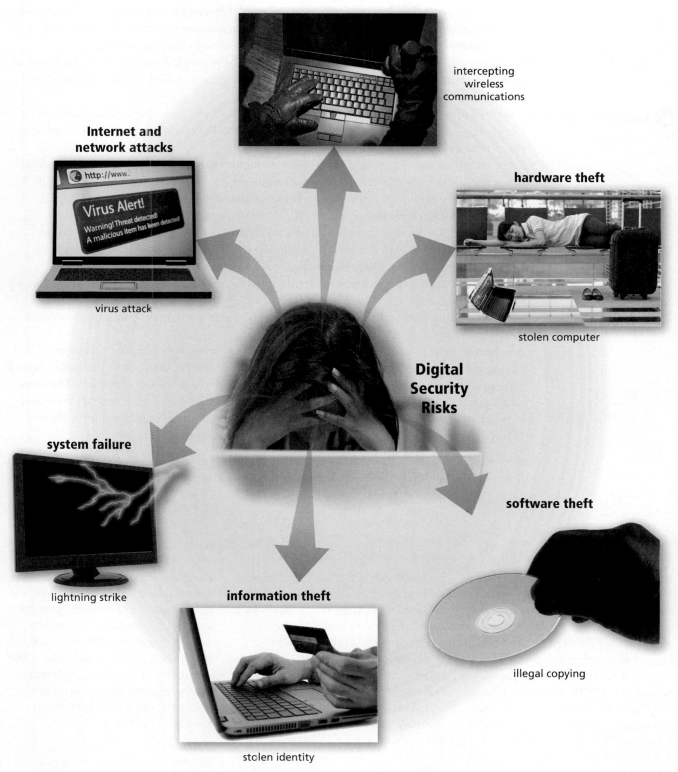

Figure 5-1   Computers and mobile devices, along with the data and programs they store, are exposed to several types of digital security risks.

Perpetrators of cybercrime typically fall into one of these basic categories: hacker, cracker, script kiddie, corporate spy, unethical employee, cyberextortionist, and cyberterrorist.

- The term **hacker**, although originally a complimentary word for a computer enthusiast, now has a derogatory meaning and refers to someone who accesses a computer or network illegally. Some hackers claim the intent of their security breaches is to improve security.
- A **cracker** also is someone who accesses a computer or network illegally but has the intent of destroying data, stealing information, or other malicious action. Both hackers and crackers have advanced computer and network skills.
- A **script kiddie** has the same intent as a cracker but does not have the technical skills and knowledge. Script kiddies often use prewritten hacking and cracking programs to break into computers and networks.
- Some corporate spies have excellent computer and networking skills and are hired to break into a specific computer and steal its proprietary data and information, or to help identify security risks in their own organization. Unscrupulous companies hire corporate spies, a practice known as corporate espionage, to gain a competitive advantage.
- Unethical employees may break into their employers' computers for a variety of reasons. Some simply want to exploit a security weakness. Others seek financial gains from selling confidential information. Disgruntled employees may want revenge.
- A **cyberextortionist** is someone who demands payment to stop an attack on an organization's technology infrastructure. These perpetrators threaten to expose confidential information, exploit a security flaw, or launch an attack that will compromise the organization's network — if they are not paid a sum of money.
- A **cyberterrorist** is someone who uses the Internet or network to destroy or damage computers for political reasons. The cyberterrorist might target the nation's air traffic control system, electricity-generating companies, or a telecommunications infrastructure. The term, *cyberwarfare*, describes an attack whose goal ranges from disabling a government's computer network to crippling a country. Cyberterrorism and cyberwarfare usually require a team of highly skilled individuals, millions of dollars, and several years of planning.

Read Ethics & Issues 5-1 to consider how cybercriminals should be punished. Some organizations hire individuals previously convicted of computer crimes to help identify security risks and implement safeguards because these individuals know how criminals attempt to breach security.

⚡ Internet Research

How do script kiddies use malware?

Search for: script kiddie malware

✺ ETHICS & ISSUES 5-1

How Should Cybercriminals Be Punished?
A hacker received a 10-year jail sentence for selling credit card information from several large corporations, costing one company approximately $200 million. In another case, a hacker accessed the personal online accounts of celebrities, as well as people he knew, and distributed revealing photos and information. He also received 10 years in jail, in part for the emotional distress his actions caused his victims. Do these sentences seem too harsh? Some legal experts point out that the punishment given to some hackers is not in line with crimes of a violent nature.

In addition to the extent of the punishment, other issues surrounding

cybercrime laws include whether an action is defamation or free speech and who should be punished, the hacker or those who were hacked. If a hacker's actions damage the reputation of another via libel or slander, should the hacker be prosecuted under the defamation law or be protected under the First Amendment? A *hacktivist*, which is a type of hacker whose actions are politically or socially motivated, believes his or her actions should be protected under the First Amendment. Should companies whose systems have been breached be punished for their lax security? The Federal Trade Commission (FTC) has fined companies whose security flaws enabled hackers to access their systems.

Legislators have made efforts to define and prevent cybercrime, both with new laws and the expansion of existing laws. Cybercrime laws vary between states and countries, making it difficult to establish what is illegal. Determining who has jurisdiction over a case can create more legal hassles. For example, which area is responsible for determining punishment: where the victim(s) resides or where the criminal lives?

Consider This: Should hacktivism be punishable? Why or why not? Should corporations be liable for damages caused by hackers? Why or why not? Should hackers receive comparable punishment to violent criminals? Why or why not?

Internet and Network Attacks

Information transmitted over networks has a higher degree of security risk than information kept on an organization's premises. In an organization, network administrators usually take measures to protect a network from security risks. On the Internet, where no central administrator is present, the security risk is greater. Internet and network attacks that jeopardize security include malware, botnets, denial of service attacks, back doors, and spoofing.

Malware

Recall that **malware**, short for *malicious software*, consists of programs that act without a user's knowledge and deliberately alter the operations of computers and mobile devices. Table 5-1 summarizes common types of malware, all of which have been discussed in previous modules. Some malware contains characteristics in two or more classes. For example, a single threat could contain elements of a virus, worm, and trojan horse.

Malware can deliver its *payload*, or destructive event or prank, on a computer or mobile device in a variety of ways, such as when a user opens an infected file, runs an infected program, connects an unprotected computer or mobile device to a network, or when a certain condition or event occurs, such as the computer's clock changing to a specific date. A common way that computers and mobile devices become infected with viruses and other malware is through users opening infected email attachments (Figure 5-2). Read Secure IT 5-1 to learn about how malware can affect online gaming.

Internet Research

Does a list of known malware exist?

Search for: malware list

Table 5-1	Common Types of Malware
Type	**Description**
Virus	A potentially damaging program that affects, or infects, a computer or mobile device negatively by altering the way the computer or device works without the user's knowledge or permission.
Worm	A program that copies itself repeatedly, for example in memory or on a network, using up resources and possibly shutting down the computer, device, or network.
Trojan horse	A program that hides within or looks like a legitimate program. Unlike a virus or worm, a trojan horse does not replicate itself to other computers or devices.
Rootkit	A program that hides in a computer or mobile device and allows someone from a remote location to take full control of the computer or device.
Spyware	A program placed on a computer or mobile device without the user's knowledge that secretly collects information about the user and then communicates the information it collects to some outside source while the user is online.
Adware	A program that displays an online advertisement in a banner, pop-up window, or pop-under window on webpages, email messages, or other Internet services.

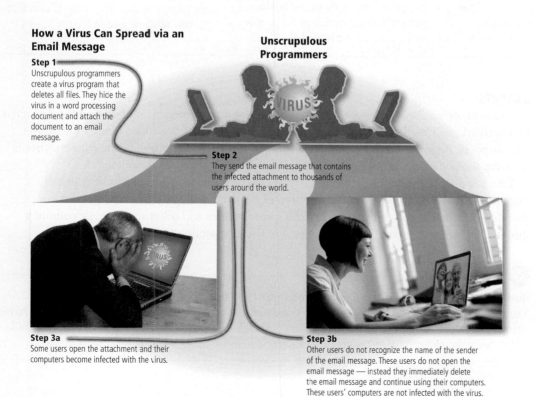

How a Virus Can Spread via an Email Message

Unscrupulous Programmers

Step 1
Unscrupulous programmers create a virus program that deletes all files. They hide the virus in a word processing document and attach the document to an email message.

Step 2
They send the email message that contains the infected attachment to thousands of users around the world.

Step 3a
Some users open the attachment and their computers become infected with the virus.

Step 3b
Other users do not recognize the name of the sender of the email message. These users do not open the email message — instead they immediately delete the email message and continue using their computers. These users' computers are not infected with the virus.

Figure 5-2 This figure shows how a virus can spread via an email message.
© Cengage Learning;
© iStockphoto / Steve Cukrov;
© iStockphoto / Casarsa

CONSIDER THIS

What if you cannot remove malware?
In extreme cases, in order to remove malware from a computer or mobile device, you may need to erase, or reformat, an infected computer's hard drive, or reset a mobile device to its factory settings. For this reason, it is critical you have uninfected (clean) backups of all files. Consider creating recovery media when you purchase a new computer, and be sure to keep all installation media in the event you need to reinstall the computer's operating system and your apps. Seek advice from a technology specialist before performing a format or reformat instruction on your media.

 Internet Research

What are the latest malware threats?

Search for: malware news

 SECURE IT 5-1

Play It Safe to Avoid Online Gaming Risks

Gamers often understand general security issues regarding online behavior, but they may not be aware of a different set of technology and social risks they may encounter as they interact in the online world. Anyone experiencing the joys of playing games online or playing games with others through online services should realize that thieves and hackers lurking behind the scenes may take advantage of security holes and vulnerabilities that can turn a gaming session into a nightmare.

Viruses, worms, and malware can be hidden in downloaded game files, mobile apps, email message attachments, and messaging software. In addition, messages on online social networks may encourage gamers to visit fraudulent websites filled with malware. If the game requires a connection to the Internet, then any computer connected to the game's server is subject to security cyberthreats. Thieves can take control of a remote computer that does not have a high level of security protection and use it to control other computers, or they could break into the computer and install malware to discover personal information.

Malicious users know that the gaming community uses social media intensely, so they also create accounts and attempt to mislead uninformed users into revealing personal information. The thieves may claim to have software updates and free games, when they really are luring users to bogus websites that ask users to set up profiles and accounts.

Gamers should follow these practices to increase their security:

- Before downloading any software or apps, including patches to games, or disclosing any private details, check the developer to be certain the website or the person making the request is legitimate.

- Read the permissions notices to learn what information is being requested or being collected. Avoid games requiring passwords to be saved to an online account on a smartphone.

- Exercise extreme caution if the game requires ActiveX or JavaScript to be enabled or if it must be played in administrator mode.

- Use a firewall and make exceptions to allow only trusted individuals to access your computer or mobile device when playing multiplayer online games.

- Do not share personal information with other gamers whom you meet online.

 Consider This: Have you played online games or downloaded gaming apps and followed the advice listed here? How will you change your gaming behavior now that you are aware of specific security threats?

Botnets

A **botnet**, or *zombie army*, is a group of compromised computers or mobile devices connected to a network, such as the Internet, that are used to attack other networks, usually for nefarious purposes. A compromised computer or device, known as a **zombie**, is one whose owner is unaware the computer or device is being controlled remotely by an outsider.

A *bot* is a program that performs a repetitive task on a network. Cybercriminals install malicious bots on unprotected computers and devices to create a botnet. The perpetrator then uses the botnet to send spam via email, spread viruses and other malware, or commit a distributed denial of service attack (discussed in the next section).

 CONSIDER THIS

How can you tell if your computer or mobile device is functioning as a zombie?
Your computer or mobile device may be a zombie if you notice an unusually high drive activity, a slower than normal Internet connection, or connected devices becoming increasingly unresponsive. The chances of your computer or devices becoming part of a botnet greatly increase if your devices are not protected by an effective firewall.

Denial of Service Attacks

A **denial of service attack (DoS attack)** is an assault whose purpose is to disrupt computer access to an Internet service, such as the web or email. Perpetrators carry out a DoS attack in a variety of ways. For example, they may use an unsuspecting computer to send an influx of confusing data messages or useless traffic to a computer network. The victim computer network slows down considerably and eventually becomes unresponsive or unavailable, blocking legitimate visitors from accessing the network.

A more devastating type of DoS attack is the *distributed DoS attack (DDoS attack)* in which a zombie army is used to attack computers or computer networks. DDoS attacks have been able to stop operations temporarily at numerous websites, including powerhouses such as Yahoo!, eBay, Amazon.com, and CNN.com.

The damage caused by a DoS or DDoS attack usually is extensive. During the outage, retailers lose sales from customers, news websites and search engines lose revenue from advertisers, and time-sensitive information may be delayed. Repeated attacks could tarnish reputations, causing even greater losses.

Internet Research

Are DoS attacks still prevalent?

Search for: news of dos attacks

 CONSIDER THIS ——————————————————————————————

Why would someone execute a Dos or DDoS attack?
Perpetrators have a variety of motives for executing a DoS or DDoS attack. Hactivists, or those who disagree with the beliefs or actions of a particular organization, claim political anger motivates their attacks. Some perpetrators use the attack as a vehicle for extortion. Others simply want the recognition, even though it is negative.

Back Doors

A **back door** is a program or set of instructions in a program that allows users to bypass security controls when accessing a program, computer, or network. Once perpetrators gain access to unsecure computers, they often install a back door or modify an existing program to include a back door, which allows them to continue to access the computer remotely without the user's knowledge. A rootkit can be a back door. Some worms leave back doors, which have been used to spread other worms or to distribute spam from the unsuspecting victim computers.

Programmers often build back doors into programs during system development. These back doors save development time because the programmer can bypass security controls while writing and testing programs. Similarly, a computer repair technician may install a back door while troubleshooting problems on a computer. If a programmer or computer repair technician fails to remove a back door, a perpetrator could use the back door to gain entry to a computer or network.

Spoofing

Spoofing is a technique intruders use to make their network or Internet transmission appear legitimate to a victim computer or network. Two common types of spoofing schemes are IP and email spoofing.

- *IP spoofing* occurs when an intruder computer fools a network into believing its IP address is associated with a trusted source. Perpetrators of IP spoofing trick their victims into interacting with the phony website. For example, the victim may provide confidential information or download files containing viruses, worms, or other malware.
- *Email spoofing* occurs when the sender's address or other components of an email header are altered so that it appears that the email message originated from a different sender. Email spoofing commonly is used in virus hoaxes, spam, and phishing scams (Figure 5-3). Read How To 5-1 to learn about how to determine if an email message has been spoofed.

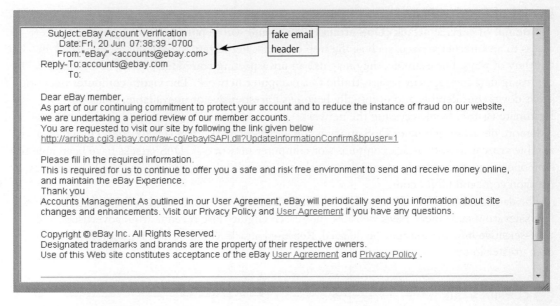

Subject:eBay Account Verification
Date:Fri, 20 Jun 07:38:39 -0700
From:"eBay" <accounts@ebay.com>
Reply-To:accounts@ebay.com
To:

fake email header

Dear eBay member,
As part of our continuing commitment to protect your account and to reduce the instance of fraud on our website, we are undertaking a period review of our member accounts.
You are requested to visit our site by following the link given below
http://arribba.cgi3.ebay.com/aw-cgi/ebayISAPI.dll?UpdateInformationConfirm&bpuser=1

Please fill in the required information.
This is required for us to continue to offer you a safe and risk free environment to send and receive money online, and maintain the eBay Experience.
Thank you
Accounts Management As outlined in our User Agreement, eBay will periodically send you information about site changes and enhancements. Visit our Privacy Policy and User Agreement if you have any questions.

Copyright © eBay Inc. All Rights Reserved.
Designated trademarks and brands are the property of their respective owners.
Use of this Web site constitutes acceptance of the eBay User Agreement and Privacy Policy .

Figure 5-3 With email spoofing, the components of an email header are altered so that it appears the email message originated from a different sender.
Source: Privacy Rights Clearinghouse

 HOW TO 5-1

Determine If an Email Message Has Been Spoofed

Spoofed email messages appear to originate from one source, but in reality originate from another source. Spoofed email messages often are sent by nefarious people attempting to obtain personal information. For example, an email message appearing to be sent from a reputable source, such as your financial institution, may ask you to reply with personal information, such as a password, Social Security number, or account number. If you reply, you will be sending personal information to an unknown third party that could use

the information to steal your identity, make unauthorized purchases, and more. The following steps describe some ways to determine if an email message has been spoofed.

- The email message requests personal information, such as account numbers, passwords, Social Security numbers, and credit card numbers.
- The email message contains spelling and/ or grammatical errors.
- The email message encourages you to tap or click a link that takes you to another website.

- The header in the email message contains a different domain in the MessageID than the domain of the supposed sender.
- The "From" and "Reply-To" email addresses do not match.

If you ever are unsure of whether an email message was spoofed, contact the supposed sender either via phone or a new email message (do not reply to the original email message) to verify the authenticity of the message.

Consider This: Have you ever received a spoofed email message? Did you know it was spoofed? What steps did you take?

Safeguards against Internet and Network Attacks

Methods that protect computers, mobile devices, and networks from attacks include the following:

- Use antivirus software.
- Be suspicious of unsolicited email attachments.
- Scan removable media for malware before using it.
- Implement firewall solutions.
- Back up regularly.

 BTW

Antivirus Programs
In addition to protecting against viruses and other malware, many antivirus programs also include protection from DoS and DDoS attacks.

Secure IT 1-2 in Module 1 provided some measures you can take to protect your computers and mobile devices from malware. Read Secure IT 5-2 for additional tips to protect home users against Internet and network attacks. The next section discusses firewalls in more depth.

SECURE IT 5-2

Protection from Viruses and Other Malware

It is impossible to ensure a virus or malware never will attack a computer, but you can take steps to protect your computer by following these practices:

- **Use virus protection software.** Install a reputable antivirus program and then scan the entire computer to be certain it is free of viruses and other malware. Update the antivirus program and the virus signatures (known specific patterns of viruses) regularly.

- **Use a firewall.** Set up a hardware firewall or install a software firewall that protects your network's resources from outside intrusions.

- **Be suspicious of all unsolicited email and text messages.** Never open an email message unless you are expecting it, *and* it is from a trusted source. When in doubt, ask the sender to confirm the message is legitimate before you open it. Be especially

cautious when deciding whether to tap or click links in email and text messages or to open attachments.

- **Disconnect your computer from the Internet.** If you do not need Internet access, disconnect the computer from the Internet. Some security experts recommend disconnecting from the computer network before opening email attachments.

- **Download software with caution.** Download programs or apps only from websites you trust, especially those with music and video sharing software.

- **Close spyware windows.** If you suspect a pop-up or pop-under window may be spyware, close the window. Never tap or click an Agree or OK button in a suspicious window.

- **Before using any removable media, scan it for malware.** Follow this procedure even for shrink-wrapped software

from major developers. Some commercial software has been infected and distributed to unsuspecting users. Never start a computer with removable media inserted in the computer unless you are certain the media are uninfected.

- **Keep current.** Install the latest updates for your computer software. Stay informed about new virus alerts and virus hoaxes.

- **Back up regularly.** In the event your computer becomes unusable due to a virus attack or other malware, you will be able to restore operations if you have a clean (uninfected) backup.

Consider This: What precautions do you take to prevent viruses and other malware from infecting your computer? What new steps will you take to attempt to protect your computer?

 CONSIDER THIS

How can you determine if your computer or mobile device is vulnerable to an Internet or network attack? You could use an **online security service,** which is a web app that evaluates your computer or mobile device to check for Internet and email vulnerabilities. The online security service then provides recommendations of how to address the vulnerabilities.

Organizations requiring assistance or information about Internet security breaches can contact or visit the website for the *Computer Emergency Response Team Coordination Center,* or *CERT/CC,* which is a federally funded Internet security research and development center.

Firewalls

A **firewall** is hardware and/or software that protects a network's resources from intrusion by users on another network, such as the Internet. All networked and online users should implement a firewall solution.

Organizations use firewalls to protect network resources from outsiders and to restrict employees' access to sensitive data, such as payroll or personnel records. They can implement a firewall solution themselves or outsource their needs to a company specializing in providing firewall protection.

Large organizations often route all their communications through a proxy server, which typically is a component of the firewall. A *proxy server* is a server outside the organization's network that controls which communications pass in and out of the organization's network. That is, a proxy server carefully screens all incoming and outgoing messages. Proxy servers use a variety of screening techniques. Some check the domain name or IP address of the message for legitimacy. Others require that the messages have digital signatures (discussed later in this module).

Home and small/home office users often protect their computers with a personal firewall. As discussed in Module 4, a **personal firewall** is a software firewall that detects and protects a personal computer and its data from unauthorized intrusions. Personal firewalls constantly monitor all transmissions to and from the computer and may inform a user of any attempted intrusions. Both Windows and Mac operating systems include firewall capabilities, including monitoring Internet traffic to and from installed applications. Read How To 5-2 for instructions about setting up a personal firewall.

Some small/home office users purchase a hardware firewall, such as a router or other device that has a built-in firewall, in addition to or instead of a personal firewall. Hardware firewalls stop malicious intrusions before they attempt to affect your computer or network. Figure 5-4 illustrates the purpose of hardware and software firewalls.

Figure 5-4 A firewall is hardware and/or software that protects a home or business's network resources from intrusion by users on another network, such as the Internet.

Courtesy of NETGEAR; © Cengage Learning; Courtesy of CheckPoint Software Technologies; © iStockphoto / Skip Odonnell; Source: Nutrition Blog Network; © iStockphoto / 123render; Source: Microsoft; © Iakov Filimonov / Shutterstock.com; © iStockphoto / Oleksiy Mark; Source: Microsoft; © iStockphoto / Ayaaz Rattansi; Source: Microsoft; © iStockphoto / Oleksiy Mark; Source: Microsoft; © Cengage Learning; Microsoft

HOW TO 5-2

Set Up a Personal Firewall

A personal firewall is a program that helps protect your computer from unauthorized access by blocking certain types of communications. For example, if somebody knows the IP address of your computer and attempts to access it using a browser or other program, the personal firewall can be configured to deny the incoming connection. The following steps describe how to set up a personal firewall.

1. Locate and purchase a personal firewall. You can purchase personal firewalls online and in stores that sell software. Many operating systems include a personal firewall. Computers typically can have only one active personal firewall running at a time. If you purchase a personal firewall, you may need to disable the one that is included with the operating system.

2. If you purchase a personal firewall, follow the instructions to install the program on your computer.

3. Run the personal firewall.

4. If necessary, ensure the personal firewall is enabled.

5. Review the settings for the incoming and outgoing rules. Incoming rules display programs and services that are allowed to access your computer. Outgoing rules display programs and services on your computer that are allowed to communicate with other computers and mobile devices on your network or the Internet.

6. Back up or export your current list of incoming and outgoing rules. If your computer does not function properly after you adjust the rules (in Steps 7 and 8), you will be able to restore the current rules.

7. Adjust your incoming rules to disallow devices, programs, and services you do

not want accessing your computer. Be careful adjusting these settings, as adding or removing rules may hinder a legitimate program's capability to work properly.

8. Adjust your outgoing rules to allow only appropriate programs on your computer to communicate with other computers and mobile devices on your network or the Internet. Examples include a browser, email program, or other communications programs.

9. Save your settings.

10. Test programs on your computer that require Internet access. If any do not function properly, restore the list of rules you backed up or exported in Step 6.

11. Exit the personal firewall.

Consider This: Which programs on your computer should have access to the Internet? Which programs should not?

Unauthorized Access and Use

Unauthorized access is the use of a computer or network without permission. *Unauthorized use* is the use of a computer or its data for unapproved or possibly illegal activities.

Home and business users can be a target of unauthorized access and use. Unauthorized use includes a variety of activities: an employee using an organization's computer to send personal email messages, an employee using the organization's word processing software to track his or her child's soccer league scores, or a perpetrator gaining access to a bank computer and performing an unauthorized transfer.

Safeguards against Unauthorized Access and Use

Organizations take several measures to help prevent unauthorized access and use. At a minimum, they should have a written *acceptable use policy* (*AUP*) that outlines the activities for which the computer and network may and may not be used. An organization's AUP should specify the acceptable use of technology by employees for personal reasons. Some organizations prohibit such use entirely. Others allow personal use on the employee's own time, such as a lunch hour. Whatever the policy, an organization should document and explain it to employees. The AUP also should specify the personal activities, if any, that are allowed on company time. For example, can employees check personal email messages or respond to personal text messages during work hours?

To protect your personal computer from unauthorized intrusions, you should disable file and printer sharing in your operating system (Figure 5-5). This security measure attempts to ensure that others cannot access your files or your printer. You also should be sure to use a firewall. The following sections address other techniques for protecting against unauthorized access and use. The technique(s) used should correspond to the degree of risk that is associated with the unauthorized access.

Figure 5-5 To protect files on your device's hard drive from hackers and other intruders, turn off file and printer sharing on your device.

Source: Microsoft

Access Controls

Many organizations use access controls to minimize the chance that a perpetrator intentionally may access or an employee accidentally may access confidential information on a computer, mobile device, or network. An *access control* is a security measure that defines who can access a computer, device, or network; when they can access it; and what actions they can take while accessing it. In addition, the computer, device, or network should maintain an *audit trail* that records in a file both successful and unsuccessful access attempts. An unsuccessful access attempt could result from a user mistyping his or her password, or it could result from a perpetrator trying thousands of passwords.

Organizations should investigate unsuccessful access attempts immediately to ensure they are not intentional breaches of security. They also should review successful access for irregularities, such as use of the computer after normal working hours or from remote computers. The security program can be configured to alert a security administrator whenever suspicious or irregular activities are suspected. In addition, an organization regularly should review users' access privilege levels to determine whether they still are appropriate.

User Names and Passwords

A **user name** — also called a *user ID* (identification), log on name, or sign in name — is a unique combination of characters, such as letters of the alphabet or numbers, that identifies one specific user. A **password** is a private combination of characters associated with the user name that allows access to certain computer resources.

Most operating systems that enable multiple users to share computers and devices or that access a home or business network require users to enter a user name and a password correctly before they can access the data, information, and programs stored on a computer, mobile device, or network. Many systems that maintain financial, personal, and other confidential information also require a user name and password as part of their sign-in procedure (Figure 5-6).

Some systems assign a user name and/or password to each user. For example, a school may use a combination of letters from a student's first and last names as a user name. For example, Brittany Stearn's user name might be stearns_brit. Some websites use your email address as the user name. Information technology (IT) departments may assign passwords so that they have a record in case the employee leaves or forgets the password.

With other systems, users select their own user names and/or passwords. Many users select a combination of their first and last names for their user

Figure 5-6 Many websites that maintain personal and confidential data, such as Citibank's credit card system, require a user to enter a user name (user ID) and password.

Source: Citigroup Inc

 BTW

Single Sign On
When you enter your user name into a *single sign on* account, such as for Microsoft, Google, Twitter, and Facebook, you automatically are signed in to other accounts and services. Many also recognize your information to provide additional customized content.

names. Many online social networks, media sharing sites, and retail and other websites allow you to choose your own user name. You might select a name that is formed from parts of your real name or nickname and possibly some numbers, if the name you want is taken (such as britstearns04). If you wish to remain more anonymous, choose a user name that combines common words, or reflects your interests (such as guitarboston27).

Once you select a password, change it frequently. Read Secure IT 1-3 in Module 1 for tips about creating strong passwords. Do not disclose your password to anyone or write it on a slip of paper kept near the computer, especially taped to the monitor or under the keyboard. Email and telemarketing scams often ask unsuspecting users to disclose their credit card numbers, so be wary if you did not initiate the inquiry or phone call. Read Secure IT 5-3 for tips about using a password manager.

SECURE IT 5-3

Safely Use a Password Manager

If you use the same password to access your banking, shopping, online social networks, and school accounts, you are not alone. Many people think one password is sufficient protection for all their vital online accounts, but cyberthieves are aware of this flawed thinking and take advantage of this practice. Security experts recommend using different user names and passwords for every account and changing the passwords frequently.

Keeping track of all these accounts can be an overwhelming task. A *password manager*, also called a *password organizer*, is a convenient service that stores all your account information securely. Once you select a service, you download and install the software and create one master password. The first time you view a password-protected website and enter your user name and password, the password manager saves this information. The next time you visit one of these websites or apps, the software supplies the account information automatically. Password managers use two-step verification and advanced encryption techniques (discussed later in this module) to ensure information is stored securely.

Some managers offer the option to generate random passwords, which have a unique combination of jumbled numbers and letters that are difficult for criminals to steal, for each account. Other features include the ability to auto-fill information, such as your name, address, and phone number, on forms and to provide a hint if you have forgotten your master password.

Password manager services can be free to use or may require a small annual fee. Some security experts recommend using a service that charges a fee, stating that these companies may provide more features. Before using any manager, call the company and ask about security measures, the ability to sync with multiple mobile devices, 24-hour customer service via live chat or phone, and limits on the number of passwords that can be saved.

 Consider This: Do you use a password manager? If so, do you feel secure storing all your sign in and password information in this service? If not, how do you keep track of your passwords?

 CONSIDER THIS

Why do some websites allow you to use your email address as a user name?

No two users can have the same email address; that is, your email address is unique to you. This means you can use your email address and password from one website to validate your identity on another website. Facebook, Google, and Twitter, for example, are three popular websites that provide authentication services to other applications. By using your email address from one of these websites to access other websites, you do not have to create or remember separate user names and passwords for the various websites you visit.

In addition to a user name and password, some systems ask users to enter one of several pieces of personal information. Such items can include a grandparent's first name, your favorite food, your first pet's name, or the name of the elementary school you attended. These items should be facts that you easily remember but are not easy for others to discover about you when using a search engine or examining your profiles on online social networks. As with a password, if the user's response does not match information on file, the system denies access.

Passphrase   Instead of passwords, some organizations use passphrases to authenticate users. A *passphrase* is a private combination of words, often containing mixed capitalization and punctuation, associated with a user name that allows access to certain computer resources. Passphrases, which often can be up to 100 characters in length, are more secure than passwords, yet can be easy to remember because they contain words.

PIN   A **PIN** (personal identification number), sometimes called a *passcode*, is a numeric password, either assigned by a company or selected by a user. PINs provide an additional level of security. Select PINs carefully and protect them as you do any other password. For example, do not use the same four digits, sequential digits, or dates others could easily determine, such as birth dates.

BTW
Default Passwords
If a program or device has a default or preset password, such as admin, be sure to change it to prevent unauthorized access.

Why do some websites display distorted characters you must reenter along with your password?

These websites use a CAPTCHA, which stands for Completely Automated Public Turing test to tell Computers and Humans Apart. A *CAPTCHA* is a program developed at Carnegie Mellon University that displays an image containing a series of distorted characters for a user to identify and enter in order to verify that user input is from humans and not computer programs (Figure 5-7).

A CAPTCHA is effective in blocking computer-generated attempts to access a website, because it is difficult to write programs for computers to detect distorted characters, while humans generally can recognize them. For visually impaired users or if words are too difficult to read, the CAPTCHA text can be read aloud; you also have the option of generating a new CAPTCHA.

Figure 5-7 To continue with the ticket order process at the Ticketmaster website, the user must enter the characters in the CAPTCHA, which consists of the letters, themssr neillso, in this case.
Source: Carnegie Mellon University

Possessed Objects

A possessed object is any item that you must possess, or carry with you, in order to gain access to a computer or computer facility. Examples of possessed objects are badges, cards, smart cards, and keys. The card you use in an ATM (automated teller machine), for example, is a possessed object that allows access to your bank account.

Biometric Devices

A **biometric device** authenticates a person's identity by translating a personal characteristic, such as a fingerprint, into a digital code that is compared with a digital code stored in a computer or mobile device verifying a physical or behavioral characteristic. If the digital code in the computer or mobile device does not match the personal characteristic code, the computer or mobile device denies access to the individual.

Biometric devices grant access to programs, computers, or rooms using computer analysis of some biometric identifier. Examples of biometric devices and systems include fingerprint readers, face recognition systems, hand geometry systems, voice verification systems, signature verification systems, iris recognition systems, and retinal scanners.

Fingerprint Reader A **fingerprint reader**, or fingerprint scanner, captures curves and indentations of a fingerprint (Figure 5-8). Organizations use fingerprint readers to secure doors, computers, and software. With the cost of fingerprint readers often less than $100, some home and small business users install fingerprint readers to authenticate users before they can access a personal computer.

Figure 5-8 A fingerprint reader.
© Flynavyjp / Dreamstime.com

The reader also can be set up to perform different functions for different fingers; for example, one finger starts a program and another finger shuts down the computer. External fingerprint readers usually plug into a USB port.

Some laptops, smartphones, and smartwatches have a built fingerprint reader. Using their fingerprint, users can unlock the computer or device, sign in to programs and websites via their fingerprint instead of entering a user name and password, and on some devices, even test their blood pressure and heart rate.

 CONSIDER THIS ⸻⸻⸻⸻⸻⸻⸻⸻⸻

What is a lock screen?

A *lock screen* is a screen that restricts access to a computer or mobile device until a user performs a certain action. Some simply require a user swipe the screen to unlock the screen. Others verify a user's identity by requiring entry of a password, PIN, or passcode; a fingerprint scan; or a gesture swipe (Figure 5-9). Gestures are motions users make on a touch screen with the tip of one or more fingers or their hand. For example, to unlock the screen on a phone, a user could connect the dots on the screen using a pattern previously defined by the user.

Figure 5-9   Some ways users unlock screens include entering a passcode, scanning a fingerprint, and swiping a gesture.
© iStockPhoto / franckreporter; © Alexey Boldin / Shutterstock; © iStockPhoto / Carpe89

Face Recognition System   A *face recognition system* captures a live face image and compares it with a stored image to determine if the person is a legitimate user. Some buildings use face recognition systems to secure access to rooms. Law enforcement, surveillance systems, and airports use face recognition to protect the public. Some mobile devices use face recognition systems to unlock the device. Face recognition programs are becoming more sophisticated and can recognize people with or without glasses, makeup, or jewelry, and with new hairstyles.

Hand Geometry System   A *hand geometry system* measures the shape and size of a person's hand (Figure 5-10). Because hand geometry systems can be expensive, they often are used in larger companies to track workers' time and attendance or as security devices. Colleges use hand geometry systems to verify students' identities. Daycare centers and hospital nurseries use them to identify parents who pick up their children.

Voice Verification System   A *voice verification system* compares a person's live speech with their stored voice pattern. Larger organizations sometimes use voice verification systems as time and attendance devices. Many companies also use this technology for access to sensitive files and networks. Some financial services use voice verification systems to secure phone banking transactions.

Figure 5-10   A hand geometry system verifies identity based on the shape and size of a person's hand.
Courtesy of Ingersoll Rand Security Technologies

Signature Verification System   A *signature verification system* recognizes the shape of your handwritten signature, as well as measures the pressure exerted and the motion used to write the signature. Signature verification systems use a specialized pen and tablet. Signature verification systems often are used to reduce fraud in financial institutions.

 CONSIDER THIS ⸻⸻⸻⸻⸻⸻⸻⸻⸻

Do retailers use a signature verification system for credit card purchases?

No. With a credit card purchase, users sign their name on a signature capture pad using a stylus attached to the device. Software then transmits the signature to a central computer, where it is stored. Thus, the retailers use these systems simply to record your signature.

Iris Recognition System

High security areas use iris recognition systems. The camera in an iris recognition system uses iris recognition technology to read patterns in the iris of the eye (Figure 5-11). These patterns are as unique as a fingerprint. Iris recognition systems are quite expensive and are used by government security organizations, the military, and financial institutions that deal with highly sensitive data. Some organizations use retinal scanners, which work similarly but instead scan patterns of blood vessels in the back of the retina.

Figure 5-11 An iris recognition system.
© iStockPhoto / NKND200; © Robert F. Balazik / Shutterstock.com; © Cengage Learning

✸ CONSIDER THIS

How popular are biometric devices?

Biometric devices are gaining popularity as a security precaution because they are a virtually foolproof method of identification and authentication. For example, some grocery stores, retail stores, and gas stations use *biometric payment*, where the customer's fingerprint is read by a fingerprint reader that is linked to a payment method, such as a checking account or credit card. Users can forget their user names and passwords. Possessed objects can be lost, copied, duplicated, or stolen. Personal characteristics, by contrast, are unique and cannot be forgotten or misplaced.

Biometric devices do have disadvantages. If you cut your finger, a fingerprint reader might reject you as a legitimate user. Hand geometry readers can transmit germs. If you are nervous, a signature might not match the one on file. If you have a sore throat, a voice recognition system might reject you. Many people are uncomfortable with the thought of using an iris scanner.

 BTW

Two-Step Verification
Users should register a landline phone number, alternate email address, or other form of contact beyond a mobile phone number so that they still can access their accounts even if they lose their mobile phone.

 Internet Research

Which websites use two-step verification?

Search for: two-step verification websites

Two-Step Verification

In an attempt to further protect personal data and information from online thieves, many organizations such as financial institutions or universities that store sensitive or confidential items use a two-step verification process. With **two-step verification**, also known as *two-factor verification*, a computer or mobile device uses two separate methods, one after the next, to verify the identity of a user.

ATMs (automated teller machines) usually requires a two-step verification. Users first insert their ATM card into the ATM (Step 1) and then enter a PIN (Step 2) to access their bank account. Most debit cards and some credit cards use PINs. If someone steals these cards, the thief must enter the user's PIN to access the account.

Another use of two-step verification requires a mobile phone and a computer. When users sign in to an account on a computer, they enter a user name and a password (Step 1). Next, they are prompted to enter another authentication code (Step 2), which is sent as a text or voice message or via an app on a smartphone (Figure 5-12). This second code generally is valid for a set time, sometimes only for a few hours. If users do not sign in during this time limit, they must repeat the process and request another verification code. Microsoft and Google commonly use two-step verification when you sign in to their websites. If you sign in from a device you use frequently, you can elect to bypass this step.

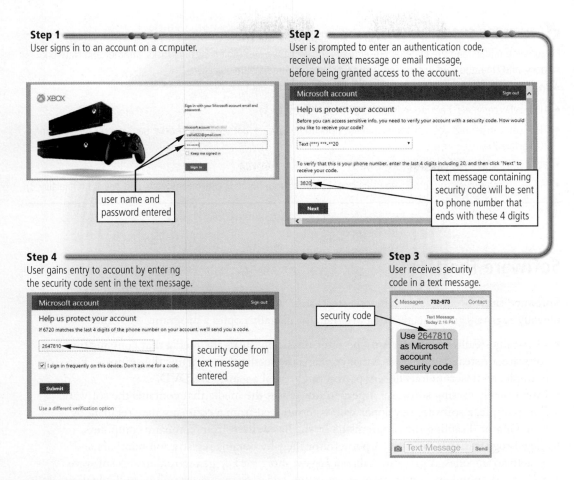

Figure 5-12   This figure shows an example of two-step authentication.
Source: Microsoft

✷ **CONSIDER THIS** ───

Can users circumvent the two-step verification process?
Users may be able to specify a computer as a trusted device during a two-step verification so that future sign-in attempts on that same computer will bypass the two-step verification. Only limited-use computers in safe areas should be identified as a trusted device.

Digital Forensics

Digital forensics, also called *cyberforensics*, is the discovery, collection, and analysis of evidence found on computers and networks. Digital forensics involves the examination of media, programs, data and log files on computers, mobile devices, servers, and networks. Many areas use digital forensics, including law enforcement, criminal prosecutors, military intelligence, insurance agencies, and information security departments in the private sector.

A digital forensics examiner must have knowledge of the law, technical experience with many types of hardware and software products, superior communication skills, familiarity with corporate structures and policies, a willingness to learn and update skills, and a knack for problem solving.

NOW YOU SHOULD KNOW

Be sure you understand the material presented in the sections titled Digital Security Risks, Internet and Network Attacks, and Unauthorized Access and Use, as it relates to the module objectives.
Now you should know ...

- How cybercriminals' backgrounds and intent vary (Objective 1)
- How you can protect your computers and devices from malware, botnets, DoS attacks, back doors, and spoofing (Objective 2)
- Why you should use a firewall (Objective 2)
- How you can prevent unauthorized users from accessing your home or office computers and devices (Objective 3)

Software Theft

Software theft occurs when someone steals software media, intentionally erases programs, illegally registers and/or activates a program, or illegally copies a program.

- Physically stealing software: A perpetrator physically steals the media that contains the software, or steals the hardware that contains the media that contains the software. For example, an unscrupulous library patron might steal a game CD/DVD.
- Intentionally erasing software: A perpetrator erases the media that contains the software. For example, a software developer who is terminated from a company may retaliate by removing or disabling the programs he or she has written from company computers.
- Illegal registration/activation: A perpetrator illegally obtains registration numbers and/or activation codes. A program called a *keygen*, short for key generator, creates software registration numbers and sometimes activation codes. Some unscrupulous individuals create and post keygens so that users can install software without legally purchasing it.
- Illegal copying: A perpetrator copies software from manufacturers. **Software piracy**, often referred to simply as **piracy**, is the unauthorized and illegal duplication of copyrighted software. Piracy is the most common form of software theft.

Safeguards against Software Theft

To protect software media from being stolen, owners should keep original software boxes and media or the online confirmation of purchased software in a secure location, out of sight of prying eyes. All computer users should back up their files and drives regularly, in the event of theft. When some companies terminate a software developer or if the software developer quits, they escort the employee off the premises immediately. These companies believe that allowing terminated employees to remain on the premises gives them time to sabotage files and other network procedures.

Many manufacturers incorporate an activation process into their programs to ensure the software is not installed on more computers than legally licensed. During the **product activation**, which is conducted either online or by phone, users provide the software product's identification number to associate the software with the computer or mobile device on which the software is installed. Usually, the software can be run a preset number of times, has limited functionality, or does not function until you activate it.

To further protect themselves from software piracy, software manufacturers issue users license agreements. As discussed in Module 4, a **license agreement** is the right to use software. That is, you do not own the software. The most common type of license included with software purchased by individual users is a *single-user license agreement*, also called an *end-user license agreement* (*EULA*). The license agreement provides specific conditions for use of the software, which a user must accept before using the software. These terms usually are displayed when you install

 BTW
BSA
To promote understanding of software piracy, a number of major worldwide software companies formed the *Business Software Alliance* (*BSA*). The BSA operates a website and antipiracy hotlines around the world.

 Internet Research
What are the penalties for piracy?
Search for: piracy penalties

the software. Use of the software constitutes acceptance of the terms on the user's part. Figure 5-13 identifies the conditions of a typical single-user license agreement.

To support multiple users' access of software, most manufacturers sell network versions or site licenses of their software, which usually costs less than buying individual stand-alone copies of the software for each computer. A *network license* is a legal agreement that allows multiple users to access the software on the server simultaneously. The network license fee usually is based on the number of users or the number of computers attached to the network. A *site license* is a legal agreement that permits users to install the software on multiple computers — usually at a volume discount.

Typical Conditions of a Single-User License Agreement

You can...

- Install the software on only one computer or device. (Some license agreements allow users to install the software on a specified number of computers and/or mobile devices.)
- Make one copy of the software as a backup.
- Give or sell the software to another individual, but only if the software is removed from the user's computer first.

You cannot...

- Install the software on a network, such as a school computer lab.
- Give copies to friends and colleagues, while continuing to use the software.
- Export the software.
- Rent or lease the software.

Figure 5-13 A user must accept the terms of a license agreement before using the software.
© Cengage Learning

CONSIDER THIS

Can you install software on work computers or work-issued smartphones?
Many organizations and businesses have strict written policies governing the installation and use of software and enforce their rules by checking networked or online computers or mobile devices periodically to ensure that all software is licensed properly. If you are not completely familiar with your school's or employer's policies governing installation of software, check with the information technology department or your school's technology coordinator.

Information Theft

Information theft occurs when someone steals personal or confidential information. Both business and home users can fall victim to information theft. An unethical company executive may steal or buy stolen information to learn about a competitor. A corrupt individual may steal credit card numbers to make fraudulent purchases. Information theft often is linked to other types of cybercrime. For example, an individual first might gain unauthorized access to a computer and then steal credit card numbers stored in a firm's accounting department.

Safeguards against Information Theft

Most organizations will attempt to prevent information theft by implementing the user identification and authentication controls discussed earlier in this module. These controls are best suited for protecting information on computers located on an organization's premises. To further protect information on the Internet and networks, organizations and individuals use a variety of encryption techniques.

Encryption

Encryption is the process of converting data that is readable by humans into encoded characters to prevent unauthorized access. You treat encrypted data just like any other data. That is, you can store it or send it in an email message. To read the data, the recipient must **decrypt**, or decode it. For example, users may specify that an email application encrypt a message before sending it securely. The recipient's email application would need to decrypt the message in order for the recipient to be able to read it.

In the encryption process, the unencrypted, readable data is called *plaintext*. The encrypted (scrambled) data is called *ciphertext*. An *encryption algorithm*, or *cypher*, is a set of steps that can convert readable plaintext into unreadable ciphertext. A simple encryption algorithm might switch the order of characters or replace characters with other characters. Encryption programs typically use more than one encryption algorithm, along with an encryption key. An *encryption key* is a set of characters that the originator of the data uses to encrypt the plaintext and the recipient of the data uses to decrypt the ciphertext.

Two basic types of encryption are private key and public key. With *private key encryption*, also called *symmetric key encryption*, both the originator and the recipient use the same secret key to encrypt and decrypt the data. *Public key encryption*, also called *asymmetric key encryption*, uses two encryption keys: a public key and a private key (Figure 5-14). Public key encryption software generates both the private key and the public key. A message encrypted with a public key can be decrypted only with the corresponding private key, and vice versa. The public key is made known to message originators and recipients. For example, public keys may be posted on a secure webpage or a public-key server, or they may be emailed. The private key, by contrast, should be kept confidential.

Some operating systems and email programs allow you to encrypt the contents of files and messages that are stored on your computer. You also can purchase an encryption program to encrypt files. Many browsers use encryption when sending private information, such as credit card numbers, over the Internet.

Mobile users today often access their company networks through a virtual private network. When a mobile user connects to a main office using a standard Internet connection, a *virtual private network* (*VPN*) provides the mobile user with a secure connection to the company network server, as if the user has a private line. VPNs help ensure that data is safe from being intercepted by unauthorized people by encrypting data as it transmits from a laptop, smartphone, or other mobile device.

An Example of Public Key Encryption

Step 1
The sender creates a document to be sent via email to the receiver.

Step 2
The sender uses the receiver's public key to encrypt a message.

Step 3
The receiver uses his or her private key to decrypt the message.

Step 4
The receiver can read or print the decrypted message.

CONFIDENTIAL
The new plant will be located...

AA311C253
430250C
4CAD078
32EC8EF

CONFIDENTIAL
The new plant will be located...

Figure 5-14 This figure shows an example of public key encryption.
© Cengage Learning

Digital Signatures and Certificates

A **digital signature** is an encrypted code that a person, website, or organization attaches to an electronic message to verify the identity of the message sender. Digital signatures often are used to ensure that an impostor is not participating in an Internet transaction. That is, digital signatures can help to prevent email forgery. A digital signature also can verify that the content of a message has not changed.

A **digital certificate** is a notice that guarantees a user or a website is legitimate. E-commerce applications commonly use digital certificates. Browsers often display a warning message if a website does not have a valid digital certificate.

A website that uses encryption techniques to secure its data is known as a **secure site** (Figure 5-15). Web addresses of secure sites often begin with https instead of http. Secure sites typically use digital certificates along with security protocols.

 CONSIDER THIS ———————————————————————————

Who issues digital certificates?

A *certificate authority* (*CA*) is an organization that issues digital certificates. Each CA is a trusted third party that takes responsibility for verifying the sender's identity before issuing a certificate. Individuals and companies can purchase digital certificates from one of more than 35 online CA providers. The cost varies depending on the desired level of data encryption, with the strongest levels recommended for financial and e-commerce transactions.

Figure 5-15 Web addresses of secure sites, such as the Amazon.com checkout, often begin with https instead of http. Browsers also often display a lock symbol in the window, which you usually can tap or click to see the associated digital certificate.

Source: Amazon.com and Microsoft

Mini Feature 5-1: Cloud Data Privacy

Privacy and security concerns arise when consumers and businesses consider moving their data to an online storage service. Read Mini Feature 5-1 to learn about privacy issues surrounding cloud data storage. Read Ethics & Issues 5-2 to consider who is responsible for data left on the cloud.

MINI FEATURE 5-1

Cloud Data Privacy

Privacy and security concerns arise when consumers and businesses consider moving their data to an online storage service. While the cloud offers a tremendous amount of storage space at a relatively low cost, the security of data and the reliability of cloud companies trigger concerns.

When people register for a cloud computing service, they sign a written contract or tap or click an online OK or Agree button to affirm they read and understand the terms of the agreement. Any data saved on the cloud is entrusted to the third-party provider, which has a legal obligation to protect the data from security breaches. The company also must guard against data loss due to physical disasters, such as power outages, cooling failures, and fire. When data has been compromised, many states require the company to disclose the issue to the data owner promptly.

The Cloud Security Alliance (CSA) warns of hackers who register for the service with a credit card or for a free trial period and then unleash malware in an attempt to gain access to passwords. Because the registration and validation procedure for accessing the cloud is relatively anonymous, authorities can have difficulty locating the abusers.

Another concern arises when transferring data over a network to the cloud. When the data is traveling to or from a computer and the cloud service, it is subject to interception. To minimize risk, security experts emphasize that the web address of the website you are visiting must begin with https, and the data should be encrypted and authenticated.

Law enforcement's access to the data raises another security issue. Email messages stored on a private server belong to the company or individual who owns the computer, so law enforcement officials must obtain a search warrant to read a particular user's messages. In contrast, law enforcement officials can access email messages stored on the cloud by requesting the information from the company that owns the cloud service. The user might not be notified of the search until up to 90 days after the search occurred; moreover, the search may occur without limitations and may include continuous monitoring of an individual's email communications.

International laws and industry regulations protect sensitive and personal data. Germany has some of the strictest cloud data privacy laws, and, in general, the European Union's privacy regulations are more protective that those in the United States. In much of Europe, for example, consumers must agree to have their personal information collected, and they can review the data for accuracy. The education, health care, and financial services industries in the United States have strict data privacy regulations that affect cloud storage. For example, the Family Educational Rights and Privacy Act (FERPA) regulates the confidentiality of students' educational records, so colleges must obtain students' consent to share data with cloud storage providers and other third parties.

Cloud storage companies have increased their privacy and security features in recent years. Many allow consumers and businesses to protect files with passwords or require two-step authentication to access files, to delete data if a mobile device has been stolen or lost, and to delete data that has been stored past an expiration date.

✷ **Consider This:** How much of your personal data is stored on the cloud? Do you have concerns about the security of this data? Have you ever received a notice that any of your online data has been compromised? Should online social networks or email providers give more explicit notice that data is stored on the cloud? Should law enforcement officials be able to access your data without your consent? Why or why not?

⊛ ETHICS & ISSUES 5-2

Who Is Responsible for Data Left on the Cloud?

Businesses often contract with cloud storage providers for data storage. Many businesses also use cloud storage providers to store customer data. This data could include contact information, credit card numbers, and ordering history.

Ownership of cloud data becomes an issue when a cloud storage provider or the business using the cloud services closes. Other issues include what happens if the business fails to pay the cloud storage provider, or when a contract ends. Many feel that it is the responsibility of the business owner to remove and destroy company data before a contract ends. Supporters of this argument believe that cloud storage providers should not be accessing data they host. Others contend that if a business fails to remove and destroy its data before its cloud storage contract ends, cloud storage providers should return the data, or remove the data permanently.

An ongoing debate exists related to who is responsible for cloud data security. Many experts put the responsibility of securing data in the hands of the data owner. Others advocate for a shared security model, in which the cloud storage provider includes security tools, but the company provides additional security as needed.

Ownership and security of data should be included in any contract between a business and cloud storage provider. Contracts also should specify what happens in a variety of scenarios, including if either party stops its operations, or if hackers access the data.

Consider This: If a business stops its operations, who should remove its data from cloud storage? Why? If a customer does not remove its data before a contract ends, should a cloud storage provider return the data, or can it remove or sell the data? Why or why not? Who is responsible for data security? Why?

Hardware Theft, Vandalism, and Failure

Users rely on computers and mobile devices to create, store, and manage important information. As discussed in Module 3, you should take measures to protect computers and devices from theft, vandalism, and failure.

Hardware theft is the act of stealing digital equipment. Hardware vandalism involves defacing or destroying digital equipment. Hardware can fail for a variety of reasons: aging hardware, natural or man-made disasters, or random events such as electrical power problems, and even errors in programs or apps. Figure 5-16 summarizes the techniques you can use to safeguard hardware from theft, vandalism, and failure.

Hardware Theft and Vandalism Safeguards
- Physical access controls (i.e., locked doors and windows)
- Alarm system
- Physical security devices (i.e., cables and locks)
- Device-tracking app

Hardware Failure Safeguards
- Surge protector
- Uninterruptible power supply (UPS)
- Duplicate components or duplicate computers
- Fault-tolerant computer

Figure 5-16 Summary of safeguards against hardware theft, vandalism, and failure.
© Cengage Learning; © iStockphoto / Norebbo

Backing Up — The Ultimate Safeguard

To protect against data loss caused by hardware/software/information theft or system failure, users should back up computer and mobile device files regularly. As previously described, a **backup** is a duplicate of a file, program, or media that can be used if the original is lost, damaged, or destroyed; and to **back up** a file means to make a copy of it. In the case of system failure or the discovery of corrupted files, you **restore** the files by copying the backed up files to their original location on the computer or mobile device.

If you choose to back up locally, be sure to use high-quality media. A good choice for a home user might be optical discs or an external hard drive. Keep your backup media in a fireproof and heat-proof safe or vault, or offsite. *Off-site* means in a location separate from where you typically store or use your computer or mobile device. Keeping backup copies off-site minimizes the chance that a single disaster, such as a fire, would destroy both the original and the backup media. An off-site location can be a safe deposit box at a bank, a briefcase, or cloud storage or cloud backup.

Cloud storage provides storage to customers, usually along with synchronization services but often on smaller amounts of data. By contrast, cloud backup provides only backup and retrieval services, but generally provides continuous data protection (discussed next) to the cloud. More customers are opting for cloud backup because it saves them the cost of maintaining hardware (Figure 5-17).

Backup programs are available from many sources. Most operating systems include a backup program. Backup devices, such as external disk drives, also include backup programs. Numerous stand-alone backup tools exist. Cloud storage providers may offer backup services. Users of a cloud backup service install software on their computers that backs up files to the cloud as they are modified.

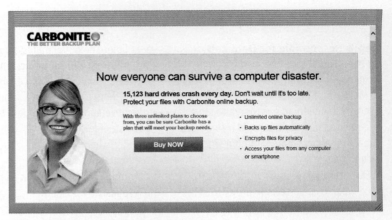

Figure 5-17 Cloud storage, such as Carbonite shown here, is a popular method for off-site backups.
Source: Carbonite, Inc.

Business and home users can perform four types of backup: full, differential, incremental, or selective. A fifth type, continuous data protection, often is used only by large enterprises to back up data to an in-house network storage device purchased and maintained by the enterprise. Cloud backup services, a sixth option, are providing continuous data protection capabilities at a lower cost. Table 5-2 summarizes the purpose, advantages, and disadvantages of each of these backup methods.

Some users implement a three-generation backup policy to preserve three copies of important files. The *grandparent* is the oldest copy of the file. The *parent* is the second oldest copy of the file. The *child* is the most recent copy of the file. When a new backup is performed, the child becomes the parent, the parent becomes the grandparent, and the media on which the grandparent copy was stored may be erased and reused for a future backup.

Table 5-2 Various Backup Methods

Type of Backup	Description	Advantages	Disadvantages
Full backup	Copies all of the files on media in the computer.	Fastest recovery method. All files are saved.	Longest backup time.
Differential backup	Copies only the files that have changed since the last full backup.	Fast backup method. Requires minimal storage space to back up.	Recovery is time-consuming because the last full backup plus the differential backup are needed.
Incremental backup	Copies only the files that have changed since the last full or incremental backup.	Fastest backup method. Requires minimal storage space to back up. Only most recent changes saved.	Recovery is most time-consuming because the last full backup and all incremental backups since the last full backup are needed.
Selective backup	Users choose which folders and files to include in a backup.	Fast backup method. Provides great flexibility.	Difficult to manage individual file backups. Least manageable of all the backup methods.
Continuous data protection (CDP)	All data is backed up whenever a change is made.	The only real-time backup. Very fast recovery of data.	Very expensive and requires a great amount of storage.
Cloud backup	Files are backed up to the cloud as they change.	Cloud backup provider maintains backup hardware. Files may be retrieved from anywhere with an Internet connection on any device.	Requires an Internet connection, otherwise files are marked for backup when the computer goes back online.

Mini Feature 5-2: Disaster Recovery

A **disaster recovery plan** is a written plan that describes the steps an organization would take to restore its computer operations in the event of a disaster. Read Mini Feature 5-2 to learn about steps an organization takes in the event of a disaster.

⚙ MINI FEATURE 5-2

Disaster Recovery

A disaster can be natural or man-made (hackers, viruses, etc.). Each company and each department or division within an organization usually has its own disaster recovery plan. The following scenario illustrates how an organization might implement a disaster recovery plan.

Rosewood Associates is a consulting firm that helps clients use social media for marketing and customer outreach. Last week, a fire broke out in the office suite above Rosewood. The heat and smoke, along with water from the sprinkler system, caused extensive damage. As a result, Rosewood must replace all computers, servers, and storage devices. Also, the company lost all of the data it had not backed up.

Rosewood currently backs up its systems daily to an internal server and weekly to a remote cloud server. Because of damage to the internal server, the company lost several days of data. Rosewood does not have a plan for replacing hardware. Thus, they will lose several additional days of productivity while purchasing, installing, and configuring new hardware.

To minimize the chance of this type of loss in the future, the company hired you as a consultant to help create a disaster recovery plan. You first discuss the types of disasters that can strike, as shown in the table. You then explain that the goal of a disaster recovery plan is to prevent, detect, and correct system threats, and to restore the most critical systems first.

A disaster recovery plan typically contains these four components: emergency plan, backup plan, recovery plan, and test plan.

Emergency Plan: An emergency plan specifies the steps Rosewood will take as soon as a disaster strikes. The emergency plan is organized by type of disaster, such as fire, flood, or earthquake, and includes:

1. Names and phone numbers of people and organizations to notify (company management, fire and police department, clients, etc.)
2. Computer equipment procedures, such as equipment or power shutoff, and file removal; employees should follow these procedures only if it is safe to do so
3. Employee evacuation procedures
4. Return procedures (who can enter the facility and what actions they are to perform)

Backup Plan: The backup plan specifies how Rosewood will use backup files and equipment to resume computer operations, and includes:

1. The location of backup data, supplies, and equipment
2. Who is responsible for gathering backup resources and transporting them to an alternate computer facility
3. The methods by which data will be restored from cloud storage

Considerations for Disaster Recovery

Disaster Type	What to Do First	What Might Occur	What to Include in the Plan
Natural (earthquake, hurricane, tornado, etc.)	Shut off power Evacuate, if necessary Pay attention to advisories Do not use phone lines if lightning occurs	Power outage Phone lines down Structural damage to building Road closings, transportation interruptions Flooding Equipment damage	Generator Satellite phone, list of employee phone numbers Alternate worksite Action to be taken if employees are not able to come to work/leave the office Wet/dry vacuums Make and model numbers and vendor information to get replacements
Man-made (hazardous material spill, terrorist attacks, fire, hackers, malware, etc.)	Notify authorities (fire departments, etc.) of immediate threat Attempt to suppress fire or contain spill, if safe to do so Evacuate, if necessary	Data loss Dangerous conditions for employees Criminal activity, such as data hacking and identity theft Equipment damage	Backup data at protected site Protective equipment and an evacuation plan Contact law enforcement Make and model numbers and vendor information to obtain replacements

© Cengage Learning

4. A schedule indicating the order and approximate time each application should be up and running

Recovery Plan: The recovery plan specifies the actions Rosewood will take to restore full computer operations. As with the emergency plan, the recovery plan differs for each type of disaster. You recommend that Rosewood set up planning committees. Each committee would be responsible for different forms of recovery, such as replacing hardware or software.

Test Plan: The test plan includes simulating various levels of disasters and recording Rosewood's ability to recover. You run a test in which the employees follow the steps in the disaster recovery plan. The test uncovers a few needed recovery actions not specified in the plan, so you modify the plan. A few days later, you run another test without giving the employees any advance notice to test the plan again.

☀ **Consider This:** For what kinds of natural and man-made disasters should a company plan? What roles can cloud storage providers play in helping to recover from a disaster? How involved should employees be in developing and testing disaster recovery plans?

© iStockphoto / Hans Laubel;
© iStockphoto / William Sen;
© Gewoldi / Photos.com

Figure 5-18 Wireless access points or routers around campus allow students to access the school network wirelessly from their classrooms, the library, dorms, and other campus locations.
© Robert Kneschke / Shutterstock.com; © iStockphoto / CEFutcher; © Natalia Siverina / Shutterstock.com; © Downunderphoto / Fotolia; © Natalia Siverina / Shutterstock.com; © Cengage Learning

Wireless Security

Billions of home and business users have laptops, smartphones, and other mobile devices to access the Internet, send email and Internet messages, chat online, or share network connections — all wirelessly. Home users set up wireless home networks. Mobile users access wireless networks in hot spots at airports, hotels, shopping malls, bookstores, restaurants, and coffee shops. Schools have wireless networks so that students can access the school network using their mobile computers and devices as they move from building to building (Figure 5-18).

Although wireless access provides many conveniences to users, it also poses additional security risks. Some perpetrators connect to other's wireless networks to gain free Internet access; others may try to access an organization's confidential data.

To access a wireless network, the individual must be in range of the wireless network. Some intruders intercept and monitor communications as they transmit through the air. Others connect to a network through an unsecured wireless access point (WAP) or combination router/WAP. Read How To 5-3 for instructions about ways to secure a wireless network, in addition to using firewalls.

 HOW TO 5-3

Secure Your Wireless Network
When you set up a wireless network, it is important to secure the network so that only your computers and mobile devices can connect to it. Unsecured wireless networks can be seen and accessed by neighbors and others nearby, which may make it easier for them to connect to and access the data on the computers and mobile devices on your network. The following list provides suggestions for securing your wireless network.

- Immediately upon connecting your wireless access point and/or router, change the password required to access administrative features. If the password remains at its default setting, others may possibly be able to connect to and configure your wireless network settings.

- Change the *SSID* (service set identifier), which is a network name, from the default to something that uniquely identifies your network, especially if you live in close proximity to other wireless networks.

- Do not broadcast the SSID. This will make it more difficult for others to detect your

wireless network. When you want to connect a computer or mobile device to your wireless network, it will be necessary to enter the SSID manually.

- Enable an encryption method such as WPA2 (Wi-Fi Protected Access 2), and specify a password or passphrase that is difficult for others to guess. The most secure passwords and passphrases contain more than eight characters, uppercase and lowercase letters, numbers, and special characters.

- Enable and configure the MAC (Media Access Control) address control feature. A *MAC address* is a unique hardware identifier for your computer or device. The *MAC address control* feature specifies the computers and mobile devices that can connect to your network. If a computer or device is not specified, it will not be able to connect.

- Choose a secure location for your wireless router so

that unauthorized people cannot access it. Someone who has physical access to a wireless router can restore factory defaults and erase your settings.

✸ **Consider This:** In addition to safeguarding the data and information on your computers from others, why else might it be a good idea to secure your wireless network?

Home Wi-Fi LAN WWAN Security Advanced	Verizon EvDO Rev Ae	Dormant	

Wi-Fi

Wi-Fi Profiles		
Current Profile	Secure	
Selected Profile	Secure	
Network Name (SSID)	smith	×
802.11 Mode	802.11g + 802.11b	
WMM (Wi-Fi Multimedia)	Off	
	With older Droids and devices that aren't working, use "Backward compatibility".	
Channel	Auto	
Security	WPA2	
Authentication	Open Access	
Network Key	68c2c067	
	8 ~ 63 ASCII characters. For greater security, use a mixture of digits, upper case, lower case, and other symbols.	

Update Profile   Apply   Revert

Source: Verizon Wireless

CONSIDER THIS

Can you detect if someone is accessing your wireless home network?

If you notice the speed of your wireless connection is slower than normal, it may be a sign that someone else is accessing your network. You also may notice indicator lights on your wireless router flashing rapidly when you are not connected to your wireless network. Most wireless routers have a built-in utility that allows you to view the computers currently connected to your network. If you notice a computer that does not belong to you, consult your wireless router's documentation to determine how to remove it from the network.

Mini Feature 5-3: Mobile Security

As the number of smartphones and mobile devices in use increases, the possibility of security breaches and lost devices increases proportionally. Read Mini Feature 5-3 to learn about ways you can protect sensitive and personal data on your mobile devices.

MINI FEATURE 5-3

Mobile Security

The consequences of losing a smartphone or mobile device are significant given the amount of storage and the variety of personal and business data stored. Symantec, one the world's leading online security companies, projects that only one-half of lost or stolen phones eventually will be returned to their owners. Chances are that the people who find the missing phones likely will have viewed much of the content on the devices in a quest to find the owners and possibly to gain access to private information.

The goal, therefore, for mobile device users is to make their data as secure as possible. Follow these steps to protect sensitive and personal data and to fight mobile cybercrime.

- **Be extra cautious locating and downloading apps.** Any device that connects to the Internet is susceptible to mobile malware. Cyberthieves target apps on widely used phones and tablets. Popular games are likely candidates to house malware, and it often is difficult to distinguish the legitimate apps from the fake apps. Obtain mobile device apps from well-known stores, and before downloading anything, read the descriptions and reviews. Look for

misspellings and awkward sentence structure, which could be clues that the app is fake. If something looks awry, do not download. Scrutinize the number and types of permissions the app is requesting. If the list seems unreasonable in length or in the personal information needed, deny permission and uninstall the app.

- **Use a PIN.** Enable the passcode feature on a mobile device as the first step in stopping prying eyes from viewing contents. This four-to-eight-digit code adds a layer of protection. Only emergency functions can be accessed without entering the correct sequence of numbers. This strong code should not be information easily guessed, such as a birthdate.

- **Turn off GPS tracking.** GPS technology can track the mobile device's location as long as it is transmitting and receiving signals to and from satellites. This feature is helpful to obtain directions from your current location, view local news and weather reports, find a lost device, summon emergency personnel, and locate missing children. Serious privacy concerns can arise, however, when the technology is used in malicious ways, such as to stalk individuals or trace their whereabouts. Unless you want to allow others to follow your locations throughout the day, disable the GPS tracking feature until needed.

- **Use mobile security software.** Protection is necessary to stop viruses and spyware and to safeguard personal and business data. Mobile security apps can allow you to lock your mobile

turn off location services until needed

(*Continued*)

device and SIM card remotely, erase the memory, and activate the GPS function. Other apps prevent cyberthieves from hijacking your phone and taking pictures, making recordings, placing calls to fee-imposed businesses, and sending infected messages to all individuals in your contact list. Look for security software that can back up data to a cloud account, set off a screeching alarm on the lost or stolen mobile device, offer live customer service, and provide theft, spam, virus, and malware protection.

- **Avoid tapping or clicking unsafe links.** Tapping or clicking an unknown link can lead to malicious websites. If you receive a text message from someone you do not know or an invitation to tap or click a link, resist the urge to fulfill the request. Your financial institution never will send you a message requesting you to enter your account user name and

password. Malicious links can inject malware on the mobile device to steal personal information or to create toll fraud, which secretly contacts wireless messaging services that impose steep fees on a monthly bill.

 Consider This: As the number of smartphones and mobile devices in use increases, the possibility of security breaches and lost devices increases proportionally. How can manufacturers and wireless carriers emphasize the importance of mobile security and convince users to take the precautions suggested in this mini feature? What mobile security safeguards have you taken to protect your smartphone or mobile device? What steps will you take after reading this mini feature?

✔ NOW YOU SHOULD KNOW

Be sure you understand the material presented in the sections titled Software Theft; Information Theft; Hardware Theft, Vandalism, and Failure; Backing Up – The Ultimate Safeguard; and Wireless Security as it relates to the module objectives.

Now you should know ...

- What actions you are allowed according to a software license agreement (Objective 4)
- Why you would want to use encryption, digital signatures, or digital certificates (Objective 5)
- How you can protect your hardware from theft, vandalism, and failure (Objective 6)
- Which backup method is most suited to your needs (Objective 7)
- How you can protect your wireless communications (Objective 8)

Ethics and Society

As with any powerful technology, computers and mobile devices can be used for both good and bad intentions. The standards that determine whether an action is good or bad are known as ethics.

Technology ethics are the moral guidelines that govern the use of computers, mobile devices, information systems, and related technologies. Frequently discussed areas of computer ethics are unauthorized use of computers, mobile devices, and networks; software theft (piracy); information accuracy; intellectual property rights; codes of conduct; green computing; and information privacy. The questionnaire in Figure 5-19 raises issues in each of these areas.

Previous sections in this module discussed unauthorized use of computers, mobile devices and networks, and software theft (piracy). The following sections discuss issues related to information accuracy, intellectual property rights, codes of conduct, green computing, and information privacy.

Your Thoughts?

		Ethical	Unethical
1.	An organization requires employees to wear badges that track their whereabouts while at work.	☐	☐
2.	A supervisor reads an employee's email message.	☐	☐
3.	An employee uses his computer at work to send email messages to a friend.	☐	☐
4.	An employee sends an email message to several coworkers and blind copies his supervisor.	☐	☐
5.	An employee forwards an email message to a third party without permission from the sender.	☐	☐
6.	An employee uses her computer at work to complete a homework assignment for school.	☐	☐
7.	The vice president of your Student Government Association (SGA) downloads a photo from the web and uses it in a flyer recruiting SGA members.	☐	☐
8.	A student copies text from the web and uses it in a research paper for his English Composition class.	☐	☐
9.	An employee sends political campaign material to individuals on her employer's mailing list.	☐	☐
10.	As an employee in the registration office, you have access to student grades. You look up grades for your friends, so that they do not have to wait for grades to be posted online.	☐	☐
11.	An employee makes a copy of software and installs it on her home computer. No one uses her home computer while she is at work, and she uses her home computer only to finish projects from work.	☐	☐
12.	An employee who has been laid off installs a computer virus on his employer's computer.	☐	☐
13.	A person designing a webpage finds one on the web similar to his requirements, copies it, modifies it, and publishes it as his own webpage.	☐	☐
14.	A student researches using only the web to write a report.	☐	☐
15.	In a society in which all transactions occur online (a cashless society), the government tracks every transaction you make and automatically deducts taxes from your bank account.	☐	☐
16.	Someone copies a well-known novel to the web and encourages others to read it.	☐	☐
17.	A person accesses an organization's network and reports to the organization any vulnerabilities discovered.	☐	☐
18.	Your friend uses a neighbor's wireless network to connect to the Internet and check email.	☐	☐
19.	A company uses recycled paper to print a 50-page employee benefits manual that is distributed to 425 employees.	☐	☐
20.	An employee is fired based on the content of posts on his or her online social network.	☐	☐

Figure 5-19 Indicate whether you think the situation described is ethical or unethical. Be prepared to discuss your answers.
© Cengage Learning

Information Accuracy

Information accuracy is a concern today because many users access information maintained by other people or companies, such as on the Internet. Do not assume that because the information is on the web that it is correct. As discussed in Module 2, users should evaluate the value of a webpage before relying on its content. Be aware that the organization providing access to the information may not be the creator of the information. Read Secure IT 5-4 to consider the risks associated with inaccurate data.

SECURE IT 5-4

Risks Associated with Inaccurate Data

Mapping and navigation software is invaluable for locating unfamiliar destinations. Problems arise, however, when satellite images are outdated or when the desired address cannot be found on a map. Inaccurate data can result in lost revenues for businesses when potential customers cannot find the storefront. It also has caused accidents when drivers followed turn-by-turn GPS directions and drove the wrong way on one-way streets, made illegal turns, or ended at ponds where a road stopped.

Business owners can report incorrect address data to some mapping services. They can, for example, state that the satellite image needs updating, their address has changed, the directions are incorrect, or the street names are inaccurate. In some cases,

the maps and addresses are updated quickly, often within a day.

Data entry errors also can lead to lost business, lawsuits, and expenses. In an extreme example, a $125 million Mars Climate Orbiter spacecraft was lost in space because Lockheed Martin engineers performed calculations using English units (pounds) to fire the thrusters guiding the spacecraft, but NASA engineers assumed the data was in metric units (Newtons) and sent the spacecraft 60 miles off course. In another unit conversion error, an axle broke on a Space Mountain roller coaster car at Tokyo Disneyland because it was the wrong size; the error occurred when engineers performed calculations to convert the original Space Mountain master plan from English units to metric units.

In the business world, mistakes can occur when software has not been updated or when employees are overworked, distracted, or faced with repetitive tasks. Software should have safeguards to verify valid data has been entered, such as checking that phone numbers have 10 numeric characters. Data cleaning software can eliminate duplicate database records, locate missing data, and correct discrepancies.

Consider This: Have you ever used a mapping app or website and encountered incorrect information? Would you consider notifying mapping companies of errors in their satellite images or directions? What steps can companies take to help employees enter data accurately?

Figure 5-20 This digitally edited photo shows a fruit that looks like an apple on the outside and an orange on the inside.
© Cengage Learning.

Internet Research

What is meant by fair use?

Search for: fair use definition

Internet Research

What is creative commons?

Search for: creative commons

In addition to concerns about the accuracy of computer input, some individuals and organizations raise questions about the ethics of using computers to alter output, primarily graphic output, such as a retouched photo. With graphics equipment and software, users easily can digitize photos and then add, change (Figure 5-20), or remove images.

Intellectual Property Rights

Intellectual property (*IP*) refers to unique and original works, such as ideas, inventions, art, writings, processes, company and product names, and logos. *Intellectual property rights* are the rights to which creators are entitled for their work. Certain issues arise surrounding IP today because many of these works are available digitally and easily can be redistributed or altered without the creator's permission.

A *copyright* gives authors, artists, and other creators of original work exclusive rights to duplicate, publish, and sell their materials. A copyright protects any tangible form of expression.

A common infringement of copyright is piracy, where people illegally copy software, movies, and music. Many areas are not clear-cut with respect to the law, because copyright law gives the public fair use to copyrighted material. The issues surround the phrase, fair use, which allows use for educational and critical purposes. This vague definition is subject to widespread interpretation and raises many questions:

- Should individuals be able to download contents of your website, modify it, and then put it on the web again as their own?
- Should a faculty member have the right to print material from the web and distribute it to all members of the class for teaching purposes only?
- Should someone be able to scan photos or pages from a book, publish them on the web, and allow others to download them?
- Should someone be able to put the lyrics of a song on the web?
- Should students be able to take term papers they have written and post them on the web, making it tempting for other students to download and submit them as their own work?

These issues with copyright law led to the development of *digital rights management* (DRM), a strategy designed to prevent illegal distribution of movies, music, and other digital content.

Codes of Conduct

A **code of conduct** is a written guideline that helps determine whether a specification is ethical/unethical or allowed/not allowed. An IT code of conduct focuses on acceptable use of technology. Employers and schools often specify standards for the ethical use of technology in an IT code of conduct and then distribute these standards to employees and students (Figure 5-21). You also may find codes of conduct online that define acceptable forms of communications for websites where users post commentary or other communications, such as blogs, wikis, online discussions, and so on.

Sample IT Code of Conduct

1. Technology may not be used to harm other people.
2. Employees may not meddle in others' files.
3. Employees may use technology only for purposes in which they have been authorized.
4. Technology may not be used to steal.
5. Technology may not be used to bear false witness.
6. Employees may not copy or use software illegally.
7. Employees may not use others' technology resources without authorization.
8. Employees may not use others' intellectual property as their own.
9. Employees shall consider the social impact of programs and systems they design.
10. Employees always should use technology in a way that demonstrates consideration and respect for fellow humans.

Figure 5-21   Sample IT code of conduct employers may distribute to employees.
© Cengage Learning; © iStockphoto / Oleksiy Mark

Green Computing

People use, and often waste, resources such as electricity and paper while using technology. Recall from Module 1 that **green computing** involves reducing the electricity and environmental waste while using computers, mobile devices, and related technologies. Figure 5-22 summarizes measures users can take to contribute to green computing.

Personal computers, displays, printers, and other devices should comply with guidelines of the ENERGY STAR program. The United States Department of Energy (DOE) and the United States Environmental Protection Agency (EPA) developed the *ENERGY STAR program* to help reduce the amount of electricity used by computers and related devices. This program encourages manufacturers to create energy-efficient devices. For example, many devices switch to sleep or power save mode after a specified number of inactive minutes or hours. Computers and devices that meet the ENERGY STAR guidelines display an ENERGY STAR label (shown in Figure 5-22).

Enterprise data centers and computer facilities consume large amounts of electricity from computer hardware and associated devices and utilities, such as air conditioning, coolers, lighting, etc. Organizations can implement a variety of measures to reduce electrical waste:

- Consolidate servers by using virtualization.
- Purchase high-efficiency equipment.
- Use sleep modes and other power management features for computers and devices.
- Buy computers and devices with low power consumption processors and power supplies.
- When possible, use outside air to cool the data center or computer facility.

Some organizations continually review their *power usage effectiveness* (PUE), which is a ratio that measures how much power enters the computer facility or data center against the amount of power required to run the computers and devices.

Green Computing Tips

1. Conserve Energy
   a. Use computers and devices that comply with the ENERGY STAR program.
   b. Do not leave a computer or device running overnight.
   c. Turn off the monitor, printer, and other devices when not in use.

2. Reduce Environmental Waste
   a. Use paperless methods to communicate.
   b. Recycle paper and buy recycled paper.
   c. Recycle toner and ink cartridges, computers, mobile devices, printers, and other devices.
   d. Telecommute.
   e. Use videoconferencing and VoIP for meetings.

Figure 5-22   A list of suggestions to make computing healthy for the environment.
US Environmental Protection Agency, ENERGY STAR program; © Roman Sotola / Shutterstock.com; © Cengage Learning

Internet Research

Where can I recycle outdated electronics?

Search for: recycle old electronics

CONSIDER THIS —————————————————————————

Should you save out-of-date computers and devices?
Users should not store obsolete computers and devices in their basement, storage room, attic, warehouse, or any other location. Computers, monitors, and other equipment contain toxic materials and potentially dangerous elements including lead, mercury, and flame retardants. In a landfill, these materials release into the environment. Recycling and refurbishing old equipment are much safer alternatives for the environment. Manufacturers can use the millions of pounds of recycled raw materials to make products such as outdoor furniture and automotive parts. Before recycling, refurbishing, or discarding your old computer, be sure to erase, remove, or destroy its hard drive so that the information it stored remains private.

How to Safeguard Personal Information

1. Fill in only necessary information on rebate, warranty, and registration forms.

2. Do not preprint your phone number or Social Security number on personal checks.

3. Have an unlisted or unpublished phone number.

4. If you have Caller ID, find out how to block your number from displaying on the receiver's system.

5. Do not write your phone number on charge or credit receipts.

6. Ask merchants not to write credit card numbers, phone numbers, Social Security numbers, and driver's license numbers on the back of your personal checks.

7. Purchase goods with cash, rather than credit or checks.

8. Avoid shopping club and buyer cards.

9. If merchants ask personal questions, find out why they want to know before releasing the information.

10. Inform merchants that you do not want them to distribute your personal information.

11. Request, in writing, to be removed from mailing lists.

12. Obtain your credit report once a year from each of the three major credit reporting agencies (Equifax, Experian, and TransUnion) and correct any errors.

13. Request a free copy of your medical records once a year from the Medical Information Bureau.

14. Limit the amount of information you provide to websites. Fill in only required information.

15. Install a cookie manager to filter cookies.

16. Clear your history file when you are finished browsing.

17. Set up a free email account. Use this email address for merchant forms.

18. Turn off file and printer sharing on your Internet connection.

19. Install a personal firewall.

20. Sign up for email filtering through your ISP or use an anti-spam program.

21. Do not reply to spam for any reason.

22. Surf the web anonymously or through an anonymous website.

Figure 5-23 Techniques to keep personal data private.
© iStockphoto / Norebbo; © Cengage Learning

Information Privacy

Information privacy refers to the right of individuals and companies to deny or restrict the collection, use, and dissemination of information about them. Organizations often use huge databases to store records, such as employee records, medical records, financial records, and more. Much of the data is personal and confidential and should be accessible only to authorized users. Many individuals and organizations, however, question whether this data really is private. That is, some companies and individuals collect and use this information without your authorization. Websites often collect data about you, so that they can customize advertisements and send you personalized email messages. Some employers monitor your computer usage and email messages.

Figure 5-23 lists measures you can take to make your personal data more private. The following sections address techniques companies and employers use to collect your personal data.

Electronic Profiles

When you fill out a printed form, such as a magazine subscription or contest entry, or an online form to sign up for a service, create a profile on an online social network, or register a product warranty, the merchant that receives the form usually stores the information you provide in a database. Likewise, every time you tap or click an advertisement on the web or perform a search online, your information and preferences enter a database. Some merchants may sell or share the contents of their databases with national marketing firms and Internet advertising firms. By combining this data with information from public records, such as driver's licenses and vehicle registrations, these firms can create an electronic profile of individuals. Electronic profiles may include personal details, such as your age, address, phone number, marital status, number and ages of dependents, interests, and spending habits.

Direct marketing supporters claim that using information in this way lowers overall selling costs, which lowers product prices. Critics contend that the information in an electronic profile reveals more about an individual than anyone has a right to know. They argue that companies should inform people if they plan to provide personal information to others, and people should have the right to deny such use. Many websites allow people to specify whether they want their personal information shared or preferences retained (Figure 5-24).

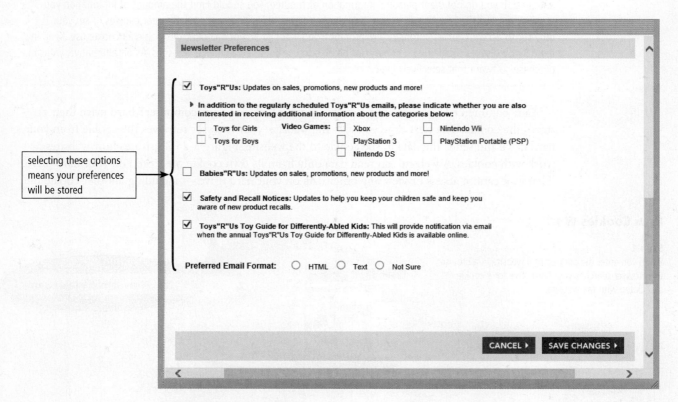

selecting these options means your preferences will be stored

Figure 5-24 Many companies, such as Toys"R"Us shown here, allow users to specify whether they want the company to retain their preferences.
Source: Geoffrey, LLC

Cookies

A **cookie** is a small text file that a web server stores on your computer. Cookie files typically contain data about you, such as your user name, postal code, or viewing preferences. Websites use cookies for a variety of purposes:

- Most websites that allow for personalization use cookies to track user preferences. These cookies may obtain their values when a user fills in an online form requesting personal information. Some websites, for example, store user names in cookies in order to display a personalized greeting that welcomes the user, by name, back to the website. Other websites allow users to customize their viewing experience with preferences, such as local news headlines, the local weather forecast, or stock quotes.
- Some websites use cookies to store user names and/or passwords, so that users do not need to enter this information every time they sign in to the website.
- Online shopping sites generally use a *session cookie* to keep track of items in a user's shopping cart. This way, users can start an order during one web session and finish it on another day in another session. Session cookies usually expire after a certain time, such as a week or a month.

- Some websites use cookies to track how often users visit a site and the webpages they visit while at the website.
- Websites may use cookies to target advertisements. These websites store a user's interests and browsing habits in the cookie.

 CONSIDER THIS

Do websites ever sell information stored in cookies?

Some websites sell or trade information stored in your cookies to advertisers — a practice many believe to be unethical. If you do not want personal information distributed, you should limit the amount of information you provide to a website or adjust how your browser handles cookies. You can regularly clear cookies or set your browser to accept cookies automatically, prompt if you want to accept a cookie, or disable all cookie use. Keep in mind if you disable cookie use, you may not be able to use some e-commerce websites. As an alternative, you can purchase software that selectively blocks cookies.

Many commercial websites send a cookie to your browser; your computer's hard drive then stores the cookie. The next time you visit the website, your browser retrieves the cookie from your hard drive and sends the data in the cookie to the website. Figure 5-25 illustrates how websites work with cookies. A website can read data only from its own cookie file stored on your hard drive. That is, it cannot access or view any other data on your hard drive — including another cookie file.

How Cookies Work

Step 1
When you enter the address of a website in a browser, the browser searches your hard drive for a cookie associated with the website.

cookies

http://www.omahasteaks.com

CUSTOM COMBOS $69⁹⁹

Internet

identification number

cookie information

Step 3
If the website does not receive cookie information, and is expecting it, the website creates an identification number for you in its database and sends that number to your browser. The browser in turn creates a cookie file based on that number and stores the cookie file on your hard drive. The website now can update information in the cookie file whenever you access the website.

Step 2
If the browser finds a cookie, it sends information in the cookie file to the website.

web server for www.omahasteaks.com

Figure 5-25 This figure shows how cookies work.
© Alex Staroseltsev / Shutterstock.com; Source: Omaha Steaks International, Inc; © iStockphoto / Norman Chan; © Cengage Learning

Phishing

Recall from Module 4 that **phishing** is a scam in which a perpetrator sends an official looking email message that attempts to obtain your personal and/or financial information. These messages look legitimate and request that you update credit card numbers, Social Security numbers, bank account numbers, passwords, or other private information. Read How To 5-4 for instructions about protecting yourself from phishing scams.

HOW TO 5-4

Protect against a Phishing Scam

Phishing scams can be perpetrated via email messages, websites, and even on the phone. The following guidelines will help protect you against a phishing scam.

Phone Scams

- If you receive a phone call from someone claiming to be from a company with which you do business, record his or her name and the time of the call. Do not disclose personal or financial information to the caller. If the caller is offering a product or service and is requesting a payment, call the company back at the number you have on file, and ask to be transferred to the person who called you initially.

- Whenever possible, enter your payment information on secure websites instead of reading credit card numbers or bank account information on the phone. You never know whether the caller is recording your payment information to use later for malicious purposes.

Email Scams

- If you receive an email message from someone requesting you to verify online account or financial information, do not reply with this information.

- Never tap or click links in email messages, even if the message appears to be from someone you know. Nor should you copy and paste the link from the email message to a browser. Instead, type the link's web address into a browser's address bar manually, and make sure you type it correctly. If you are visiting your financial institution's website, make sure the web address you enter matches the web address you have on file for them.

- Do not reply to email messages asking you for financial assistance — even if the email message appears to originate from someone you know. If you receive this type of email message from someone you know, call the person to verify the message's authenticity.

Website Scams

- When visiting a website, such as your financial institution's website, that will require you to enter confidential information, be sure to type the web address correctly. Typing it incorrectly may take you to a phishing website where the information you enter can be collected by an unknown party.

- Make sure websites requiring your confidential information use the https://protocol.

- Websites with misspellings, poor grammar, or formatting problems may indicate a phishing website. Do not enter personal or financial information on a website that looks suspicious.

- Enable the *phishing filter* in your browser that can warn or block you from potentially fraudulent or suspicious websites.

Consider This: Have you experienced a phishing scam? If so, how did it attempt to trick you into providing personal or financial information? How did you respond?

Clickjacking is yet another similar scam. With *clickjacking*, an object that can be tapped or clicked — such as a button, image, or link — on a website, pop-up ad, pop-under ad, or in an email message or text message contains a malicious program. When a user taps or clicks the disguised object, a variety of nefarious events may occur. For example, the user may be redirected to a phony website that requests personal information, or a virus may download to the computer or mobile device. Browsers typically include clickjacking protection.

Internet Research
Which phishing scams are prevalent?
Search for: recent phishing scams

Spyware and Adware

Recall from Module 4 that **spyware** is a program placed on a computer or mobile device without the user's knowledge that secretly collects information about the user and then communicates the information it collects to some outside source while the user is online. Some vendors or employers use spyware to collect information about program usage or employees. Internet advertising firms often collect information about users' web browsing habits. Spyware can enter your computer when you install a new program, through malware, or through a graphic on a webpage or in an email message.

Adware is a program that displays an online advertisement in a banner, a pop-up window, or pop-under window on webpages, email messages, or other Internet services. Adware on mobile phones is known as *madware*, for mobile adware. Sometimes, spyware is hidden in adware.

To remove spyware and adware, you can obtain spyware removers, adware removers, or malware removers that can detect and delete spyware and adware. Some operating systems and browsers include spyware and adware removers.

Social Engineering

As related to the use of technology, **social engineering** is defined as gaining unauthorized access to or obtaining confidential information by taking advantage of the trusting human nature of some victims and the naivety of others. Some social engineers trick their victims into revealing confidential information, such as user names and passwords, on the phone, in person, or on the Internet. Techniques they use include pretending to be an administrator or other authoritative figure, feigning an emergency situation, or impersonating an acquaintance. Social engineers also obtain information from users who do not destroy or conceal information properly. These perpetrators sift through company dumpsters, watch or film people dialing phone numbers or using ATMs, and snoop around computers or mobile devices looking for openly displayed confidential information.

To protect yourself from social engineering scams, follow these tips:

- Verify the identity of any person or organization requesting personal or confidential information.
- When relaying personal or confidential information, ensure that only authorized people can hear your conversation.
- When personal or confidential information appears on a computer or mobile device, ensure that only authorized people can see your screen.
- Shred all sensitive or confidential documents.
- After using a public computer, clear the cache in its browser.
- Avoid using public computers to conduct banking or other sensitive transactions.

Privacy Laws

The concern about privacy has led to the enactment of federal and state laws regarding the storage and disclosure of personal data, some of which are shown in Table 5-3. Common points in some of these laws are as follows:

1. Information collected and stored about individuals should be limited to what is necessary to carry out the function of the business or government agency collecting the data.
2. Once collected, provisions should be made to protect the data so that only those employees within the organization who need access to it to perform their job duties have access to it.
3. Personal information should be released outside the organization collecting the data only when the person has agreed to its disclosure.
4. When information is collected about an individual, the individual should know that the data is being collected and have the opportunity to determine the accuracy of the data.

Read Ethics & Issues 5-3 to consider the legal issues surrounding your digital footprint.

Table 5-3 Major U.S. Government Laws Concerning Privacy

Law	Purpose
Children's Internet Protection Act	Protects minors from inappropriate content when accessing the Internet in schools and libraries
Children's Online Privacy Protection Act (COPPA)	Requires websites to protect personal information of children under 13 years of age
Computer Abuse Amendments Act	Outlaws transmission of harmful computer code such as viruses
Digital Millennium Copyright Act (DMCA)	Makes it illegal to circumvent antipiracy schemes in commercial software; outlaws sale of devices that copy software illegally
Electronic Communications Privacy Act (ECPA)	Provides the same right of privacy protection of the postal delivery service and phone companies to various forms of electronic communications, such as voice mail, email, and mobile phones
Financial Modernization Act	Protects consumers from disclosure of their personal financial information and requires institutions to alert customers of information disclosure policies
Freedom of Information Act (FOIA)	Enables public access to most government records
HIPAA (Health Insurance Portability and Accountability Act)	Protects individuals against the wrongful disclosure of their health information
PATRIOT (Provide Appropriate Tools Required to Intercept and Obstruct Terrorism)	Gives law enforcement the right to monitor people's activities, including web and email habits
Privacy Act	Forbids federal agencies from allowing information to be used for a reason other than that for which it was collected

ETHICS & ISSUES 5-3

Do You Have the Right to Be Digitally Forgotten?

Privacy experts, such as The Institute for Responsible Online and Cell-Phone Communication (IROC2), warn that "Your digital activity is public and permanent" and is available permanently to anyone using a search engine. Does it have to be? Do you have a "right to be forgotten" as was ruled by a court in the European Union recently?

In this case, the court ordered a popular search engine to remove links to information that was "inadequate, irrelevant, or no longer relevant." The content in question included many factual articles published by a major news source. Examples included stories about a university student arrested for driving while intoxicated and a referee who lied about a mistake. Free speech advocates criticize the law. They state that a government should not be able to deny access to accurate information. Others argue that a person should be able to request removal of information that is damaging to his or her reputation. Some are concerned that negative incidents may be necessary information for an employer to know about a job seeker, or for those considering a relationship with another person. You can never truly delete your digital footprint because everything you do online has the potential to be forwarded, captured as a screenshot, or archived in databases.

Among the debated issues is whether the rights of a private citizen should differ from those of a public figure. Many argue that different rules apply for celebrities, politicians, and others who choose such professions. Some feel that the responsibility rests on search engines to provide methods that enable individuals to comment on, explain, or select what information is displayed when they are the subject of an Internet search. For example, Google developed the Google Inactive Account Manager, where you can specify what happens to your data after a period of inactivity.

Consider This: Does a government have a right to legislate search engine links? Why or why not? In what, if any, situations should individuals be able to request removal of digital content? Should search engines provide users with tools to control what information about them appears? Why or why not?

Employee Monitoring

Employee monitoring involves the use of computers, mobile devices, or cameras to observe, record, and review an employee's use of a technology, including communications such as email messages, keyboard activity (used to measure productivity), and websites visited. Many programs exist that easily allow employers to monitor employees. Further, it is legal for employers to use these programs.

 CONSIDER THIS

Do employers have the right to read employee email messages?

Actual policies vary widely. Some organizations declare that they will review email messages regularly, and others state that email messages are private. In some states, if a company does not have a formal email policy, it can read email messages without employee notification.

Content Filtering

One of the more controversial issues that surround the Internet is its widespread availability of objectionable material, such as prejudiced literature, violence, and obscene photos. Some believe that such materials should be banned. Others believe that the materials should be filtered, that is, restricted.

Content filtering is the process of restricting access to certain material. Many businesses use content filtering to limit employees' web access. These businesses argue that employees are unproductive when visiting inappropriate or objectionable websites. Some schools, libraries, and parents use content filtering to restrict access to minors. Content filtering opponents argue that banning any materials violates constitutional guarantees of free speech and personal rights. Read Ethics & Issues 5-4 to consider whether content filtering violates first amendment rights.

ETHICS & ISSUES 5-4

Does Content Filtering in a Public Library Violate First Amendment Rights?

Among the resources libraries offer are Internet-enabled computers. The use of content filtering software on library computers controls the type of information a patron can access. Free speech advocates argue that this violates the First Amendment because it restricts library patrons from viewing certain websites and content.

The Children's Internet Protection Act (CIPA) requires that schools and libraries use content filtering software in order to receive certain federal funds. The purpose of CIPA is to restrict access to objectionable material, protect children when communicating online,

prohibit children from sharing personal information, and restrict children's identities or accounts being hacked. Proponents of CIPA claim it is necessary to protect children. CIPA does allow libraries to turn off the filters, if an adult patrons requests it. Some libraries use content filtering software on computers used only by children.

Critics of content filtering software argue that the programs do not always work as intended. They can overfilter content, blocking information or education websites based on a single word. Some websites and services that filtering software may block include online social networks, or software platforms, such as Google Drive, which students may need to access to submit assignments.

Conversely, they can underfilter content, which could result in access to webpages with inappropriate media. Others argue that it gives unequal access to students doing research who rely on library computers to do schoolwork and those who have unfiltered Internet access at home.

Libraries typically have a policy stating acceptable use of the Internet. Libraries' policies also should state whether they use content filtering software, so that the patrons are aware.

Consider This: Is it fair for a government to require that libraries use content filtering software? Why or why not? Do free speech laws cover content on the Internet? Why or why not?

Web filtering software is a program that restricts access to specified websites. Some also filter sites that use specific words (Figure 5-26). Others allow you to filter email messages, chat rooms, and programs. Many Internet security programs include a firewall, antivirus program, and filtering capabilities combined. Browsers also often include content filtering capabilities.

Figure 5-26   Web filtering software restricts access to specified websites.
Courtesy of ContentWatch, Inc.

NOW YOU SHOULD KNOW

Be sure you understand the material presented in the sections titled Ethics and Society and Information Privacy as it relates to the module objectives.

Now you should know ...

- What issues you might encounter with respect to information accuracy, intellectual property, codes of conduct, and green computing (Objective 9)
- How you can make your personal data more private (Objective 10)
- Why your computer might have a cookie (Objective 10)

Summary

This module presented a variety of digital security risks. You learned about cybercrime and cybercriminals. The module discussed risks and safeguards associated with Internet and network attacks, unauthorized access and use, software theft, information theft, and hardware theft, vandalism, and failure. It presented various backup strategies and methods of securing wireless communications. You learned about ethical issues in society and various ways to protect the privacy of personal information.

TECHNOLOGY @ WORK

National and Local Security

Since 2001, the federal government, local governments, businesses, and individuals have been implementing aggressive new security measures because of the increase in terrorist activity. A security threat can exist anywhere, and it is nearly impossible for humans alone to protect the country. As a result, technology now assists governments, law enforcement officials, business owners, and other individuals with monitoring and maintaining security.

Advancements in computer vision enable computers to monitor indoor and outdoor areas that might be subject to a high volume of criminal activity. For example, some cities are installing cameras in problematic areas. A program analyzes the output from the camera and can determine whether two or more people in close proximity to one another might be engaged in a physical confrontation. If the computer detects suspicious behavior, it automatically notifies local law enforcement.

Computers also use facial recognition to identify individuals who do not belong in a particular area. For example, one theme park takes a picture of individuals they escort out of and ban from the park. As visitors walk from their cars to the park, surveillance cameras positioned in strategic locations scan visitors' faces and compare them with the database containing images of those who are banned from the park. If the computer finds a match, it alerts a security officer who then can investigate the situation. Thousands of people visit theme parks each day, and computers make it easier to perform the otherwise impossible task of identifying those who might be trespassing.

The federal government, particularly the Department of Homeland Security, uses a computerized No Fly List to track individuals who are not authorized to travel on commercial flights within the United States. When an individual makes a reservation, a computer compares his or her name to the names on the No Fly List. If the computer finds a match, the individual must prove that he or she is not the person on the list before being allowed to board an aircraft.

Whether you are walking outside, visiting an attraction, or traveling, the chances are good that computers are, in some way, ensuring your safety.

Consider This: In what other ways do computers and technology play a role in national and local security?

Study Guide

The Study Guide exercise reinforces material you should know for the module exam.

Instructions: Answer the questions below using the format that helps you remember best or that is required by your instructor. Possible formats may include one or more of these options: write the answers; create a document that contains the answers; record answers as audio or video using a webcam, smartphone, or portable media player; post answers on a blog, wiki, or website; or highlight answers in the book/e-book.

1. Define the terms, digital security risk, computer crime, cybercrime, and crimeware.

2. Differentiate among hackers, crackers, script kiddies, cyberextortionists, and cyberterrorists. Identify issues with punishing cybercriminals.

3. List common types of malware. A(n) ___ is the destructive event or prank malware delivers.

4. Identify risks and safety measures when gaming.

5. Define these terms: botnet, zombie, and bot.

6. Describe the damages caused by and possible motivations behind DoS and DDoS attacks.

7. A(n) ___ allows users to bypass security controls when accessing a program, computer, or network.

8. Define the term, spoofing. How can you tell if an email is spoofed?

9. List ways to protect against Internet and network attacks.

10. Describe the purpose of an online security service.

11. Define the terms, firewall and proxy server. List steps to set up a personal firewall.

12. Give examples of unauthorized access and use of a computer or network.

13. Identify what an AUP should specify. Why might you disable file and printer sharing?

14. Explain how an organization uses access controls and audit trails.

15. Differentiate among user names, passwords, passphrases, and pass codes.

16. List tips for using a password manager safely.

17. What is a single sign on account? PIN stands for ___.

18. Describe the purpose of a CAPTCHA.

19. Define the terms, possessed objects and biometric devices.

20. What is the purpose of a lock screen?

21. Describe how companies use the following recognition, verification, or payment systems: fingerprint, face, hand, voice, signature, and iris. List disadvantages of biometric devices.

22. Explain the two-step verification process.

23. Define the term, digital forensics. Name areas in which digital forensics are used.

24. Define the terms, software theft, keygen, and software piracy. Identify methods to prevent software theft.

25. Explain the process of product activation.

26. Describe the following license agreement types: single- or end-user, network, and site. List conditions provided in a license agreement.

27. Give examples of information theft. How can you protect yourself from information theft?

28. Describe the functions of an encryption algorithm and an encryption key. Differentiate between private and public key encryption.

29. Unencrypted data is called ___; encrypted data is called ___.

30. Describe the purpose of a VPN.

31. Define these terms: digital signature, digital certificate, and secure site.

32. List concerns and responsibilities regarding cloud data storage and privacy.

33. Describe what occurs during hardware theft or vandalism.

34. Define the terms, backup and restore.

35. List six types of backups. Describe the three-generation backup policy.

36. Identify the components of a disaster recovery plan.

37. Describe security risks associated with wireless access. Identify ways to secure your wireless network.

38. List guidelines to protect your mobile device data.

39. Describe technology ethics, information accuracy, intellectual property rights, copyrights, and codes of conduct.

40. Describe issues surrounding inaccurate data.

41. List measures users can take to contribute to green computing.

42. Explain how companies, websites, and employers might infringe on your right to information privacy.

43. Describe how the following techniques are used to collect personal data: electronic profiles, cookies, phishing, clickjacking, spyware, adware, and madware.

44. How can you protect against phishing scams?

45. Identify methods to protect yourself from social engineering scams.

46. List examples of privacy laws. Should you be able to remove personal information from the Internet? Why or why not?

47. Describe what a company might track when monitoring employees.

48. Define and identify issues surrounding content and web filtering.

49. Describe uses of technology in the national and local security industry.

You should be able to define the Primary Terms and be familiar with the Secondary Terms listed below.

Key Terms

Primary Terms (shown in **bold-black** characters in the module)

adware (244)
back door (217)
back up (233)
backup (233)
biometric device (224)
botnet (216)
code of conduct (241)
computer crime (212)
content filtering (247)
cookie (243)
cracker (214)
cybercrime (212)
cyberextortionist (214)
cyberterrorist (214)

decrypt (229)
denial of service attack
  (DoS attack) (217)
digital certificate (231)
digital forensics (227)
digital security risk (212)
digital signature (231)
disaster recovery plan
  (234)
employee monitoring
  (247)
encryption (229)
fingerprint reader (224)
firewall (219)

green computing (241)
hacker (214)
information privacy (242)
information theft (229)
license agreement (228)
malware (215)
online security service
  (219)
password (222)
personal firewall (220)
phishing (244)
PIN (223)
piracy (228)
product activation (228)

restore (233)
script kiddie (214)
secure site (231)
social engineering (245)
software piracy (228)
software theft (228)
spoofing (217)
spyware (215)
technology ethics (238)
two-step verification (226)
user name (242)
web filtering software
  (248)
zombie (216)

Secondary Terms (shown in *italic* characters in the module)

acceptable use policy (AUP) (231)
access control (222)
adware (215)
asymmetric key encryption (230)
audit trail (222)
biometric payment (226)
bot (216)
Business Software Alliance
  (BSA) (228)
CAPTCHA (224)
CERT/CC (219)
certificate authority (CA) (231)
child (234)
ciphertext (230)
clickjacking (245)
cloud backup (234)
Computer Emergency Response Team
  Coordination Center (219)
continuous data protection
  (CDP) (234)
copyright (240)
crimeware (212)
cyberforensics (227)
cyberwarfare (214)
cypher (230)

differential backup (234)
digital rights management (240)
distributed DoS attack (DDoS
  attack) (217)
email spoofing (217)
encryption algorithm (230)
encryption key (230)
end-user license agreement
  (EULA) (228)
ENERGY STAR program (241)
face recognition system (225)
full backup (234)
grandparent (234)
hacktivist (214)
hand geometry system (225)
incremental backup (234)
intellectual property (IP) (240)
intellectual property rights (240)
IP spoofing (217)
keygen (228)
lock screen (225)
MAC address (236)
MAC address control (236)
madware (245)
malicious software (215)

network license (229)
off-site (233)
parent (234)
passcode (223)
passphrase (223)
password manager (223)
password organizer (223)
payload (215)
phishing filter (244)
plaintext (230)
power usage effectiveness
  (PUE) (241)
private key encryption (230)
proxy server (219)
public key encryption (230)
rootkit (215)
selective backup (234)
session cookie (243)
signature verification
  system (225)
single sign on (222)
single-user license
  agreement (228)
site license (229)
spyware (215)

SSID (236)
symmetric key encryption (230)
trojan horse (215)
two-factor verification (226)
unauthorized access (221)
unauthorized use (221)
user ID (222)
virtual private network
  (VPN) (230)
virus (215)
voice verification system (225)
worm (215)
zombie army (216)

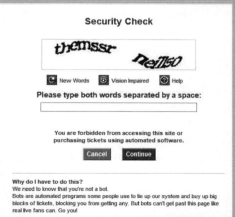

CAPTCHA (224)

Checkpoint

The Checkpoint exercises test your knowledge of the module concepts. The page number containing the answer appears in parentheses after each exercise. The Consider This exercises challenge your understanding of module concepts.

True/False   Mark T for True and F for False.

_____ 1. Any illegal act involving the use of a computer or related devices generally is referred to as a crimeware. (212)

_____ 2. A rootkit displays an online advertisement in a banner or pop-up window on webpages, email, or other Internet services. (215)

_____ 3. Viruses, worms, and other malware can be hidden in downloaded game files and mobile apps. (216)

_____ 4. An audit trail records in a file both successful and unsuccessful access attempts. (222)

_____ 5. It is good practice to change your password frequently. (222)

_____ 6. Intentionally erasing software would be considered software theft. (228)

_____ 7. A typical license agreement allows you to rent or lease the software. (229)

_____ 8. Unencrypted, readable data is called ciphertext. (230)

_____ 9. Private key encryption also is called asymmetric key encryption. (230)

_____ 10. VPNs encrypt data to help ensure that the data is safe from being intercepted by unauthorized people. (230)

_____ 11. When data is traveling to or from a computer to a cloud service, it is subject to interception. (232)

_____ 12. A good practice to secure your wireless network is to immediately broadcast the SSID. (236)

Multiple Choice   Select the best answer.

1. A _____ is someone who demands payment to stop an attack on an organization's technology infrastructure. (214)
   a. cyberterrorist
   b. script kiddie
   c. cracker
   d. cyberextortionist

2. _____ is a program that hides in a computer or mobile device and allows someone from a remote location to take full control of the computer or device. (215)
   a. A rootkit
   b. Spyware
   c. A trojan horse
   d. Adware

3. A _____ is a program or set of instructions in a program that allows users to bypass security controls when accessing a program, computer, or network. (217)
   a. zombie
   b. botnet
   c. back door
   d. session cookie

4. An employee using an organization's computer to send personal email messages might be an example of _____. (221)
   a. cybercrime
   b. hardware vandalism
   c. intellectual property rights violation
   d. unauthorized access and use

5. A _____ is a private combination of words, often up to 100 characters in length and containing mixed capitalization and punctuation, associated with a user name that allows access to certain computer resources. (223)
   a. passphrase
   b. private key
   c. passcode
   d. encryption algorithm

6. A(n) _____ is a set of characters that the originator of the data uses to encrypt the text and the recipient of the data uses to decrypt the text. (230)
   a. cipher
   b. plaintext
   c. public key
   d. encryption key

7. A(n) _____ backup method is the only real-time back up, providing very fast recovery of data. (234)
   a. selective
   b. full
   c. incremental
   d. continuous data protection

8. Online shopping websites generally use a _____ to keep track of items in a user's shopping cart. (243)
   a. phishing filter
   b. session cookie
   c. location sharing algorithm
   d. keygen

Checkpoint

Matching Match the terms with their definitions.

_____ 1. script kiddie (214)

_____ 2. zombie (216)

_____ 3. bot (216)

_____ 4. spoofing (217)

_____ 5. access control (222)

_____ 6. keygen (228)

_____ 7. digital certificate (231)

_____ 8. technology ethics (238)

_____ 9. digital rights management (240)

_____ 10. cookie (243)

a. compromised computer or device whose owner is unaware the computer or device is being controlled remotely by an outsider

b. technique intruders use to make their network or Internet transmission appear legitimate to a victim computer or network

c. program that performs a repetitive task on a network

d. small text file that a web server stores on your computer

e. notice that guarantees a user or website is legitimate

f. strategy designed to prevent illegal distribution of movies, music, and other digital content

g. program that creates software registration numbers and sometimes activation codes

h. hacker who does not have the technical skills and knowledge of a cracker

i. security measure that defines who can access a computer, device, or network; when they can access it; and what actions they can take while accessing it

j. moral guidelines that govern the use of computers, mobile devices, information systems, and related technologies

✳ Consider This   Answer the following questions in the format specified by your instructor.

1. Answer the critical thinking questions posed at the end of these elements in this module: Ethics & Issues (214, 233, 246, 247), How To (218, 221, 236, 244), Mini Features (232, 235, 237), Secure IT (216, 219, 223, 240), and Technology @ Work (249).

2. What are some common digital security risks? (212)

3. How does a hacker differ from a cracker? (214)

4. What is cyberwarfare? (214)

5. What is a hacktivist? (214)

6. How does malware deliver its payload? (215)

7. What is a botnet? (216)

8. What practices should gamers follow to increase their security? (216)

9. What is the purpose of a DoS attack? (217)

10. Why would a programmer or computer repair technician build a back door? (217)

11. How is email spoofing commonly used? (217)

12. What are methods to protect computers, mobile devices, and networks from attacks? (218)

13. Who would an organization requiring assistance or information about Internet security breach contact? (219)

14. What screening techniques do proxy servers use? (219)

15. How does unauthorized access differ from unauthorized use? (221)

16. What is a single sign-on account? (222)

17. What is a password manager? (223)

18. Are passphrases more secure than passwords? Why or why not? (223)

19. How are fingerprint readers used with personal computers and mobile devices? (225)

20. What conditions are found in a typical single-user license agreement? (229)

21. Who issues digital certificates? (231)

22. What is meant by a three-generation backup policy? (234)

23. What should you include in a disaster recovery plan for natural disasters? What should you include for man-made disasters? (235)

24. What steps can you take to secure your wireless network? (236)

25. How can mobile security apps protect your mobile device data? (237)

26. What are some questions that arise surrounding fair use with respect to copyrighted material? (240)

27. What role does the ENERGY STAR program play in green computing? (241)

28. For what purposes do websites use cookies? (243)

29. What is clickjacking? (245)

✳ Problem Solving

The Problem Solving exercises extend your knowledge of module concepts by seeking solutions to practical problems with technology that you may encounter at home, school, work, or with nonprofit organizations. The Collaboration exercise should be completed with a team.

Instructions: You often can solve problems with technology in multiple ways. Determine a solution to the problems in these exercises by using one or more resources available to you (such as a computer or mobile device, articles on the web or in print, blogs, podcasts, videos, television, user guides, other individuals, electronics or computer stores, etc.). Describe your solution, along with the resource(s) used, in the format requested by your instructor (brief report, presentation, discussion, blog post, video, or other means).

Personal

1. **No Browsing History**   While using the browser on your tablet, you realize that it is not keeping a history of websites you have visited. Why might this be happening, and what is the first step you will take to correct this problem?

2. **Phishing Scam**   You just received an email message from someone requesting personal identification information.

Source: Privacy Rights Clearinghouse

Believing the message was legitimate, you provided the requested information to the original sender. You now realize, however, that you might have fallen victim to a phishing scam. What are your next steps?

3. **Suspicious File Attachment**   You receive an email message that appears to be from someone you know. When you try to open the attachment, nothing happens. You attempt to open the attachment two more times without any success. Several minutes later, your computer is running slower and you are having trouble running apps. What might be wrong?

4. **Antivirus Software Outdated**   After starting your computer and signing in to the operating system, a message is displayed stating that your virus definitions are out of date and need to be updated. What are your next steps?

5. **Laptop's Physical Security**   You plan to start taking your laptop to school so that you can record notes in class. You want to make sure, however, that your computer is safe if you ever step away from it for a brief period of time. What steps can you take to ensure the physical security of your laptop?

Professional

6. **Corporate Firewall Interference**   You installed a new browser on your work computer because you no longer wish to use the default browser provided with the operating system. When you run the new browser, an error message appears stating that a user name and password are required to configure the firewall and allow this program to access the Internet. Why has this happened?

7. **Problems with CAPTCHA**   You are signing up for an account on a website and encounter a CAPTCHA. You attempt to type the characters you see on the screen, but an error message appears stating that you have entered the incorrect characters. You try two more times and get the same result. You are typing the characters to the best of your ability but think you still might be misreading at least one of the characters. What are your next steps?

8. **Unclear Acceptable Use Policy**   You read your company's acceptable use policy, but it is not clear about whether you are able to use the computer in your office to visit news websites on your lunch break. How can you determine whether this type of activity is allowed?

9. **Two-Step Verification Problem**   A website you are attempting to access requires two-step verification. In addition to entering your password, you also have to enter a code that it sends to you as a text message. You no longer have the same phone number, so you are unable to receive the text message. What are your next steps?

10. **Issue with Virus Protection**   You receive a notification that the antivirus program on your computer is not enabled. While attempting to enable the antivirus program, an error message is displayed stating that a problem has prevented the antivirus program from being enabled. What are your next steps?

Collaboration

11. **Technology in National and Local Security**   National and local security agencies often use technology to protect citizens. For example, computers are used to maintain a No Fly List, which contains a list of individuals not cleared to board a commercial aircraft. Form a team of three people to create a list of the various ways technology helps to keep the public safe. One team member should research how local agencies, such as police departments, use technology to ensure security. Another team member should research ways national security agencies use technology to protect the public from threats, and the last team member should research ways that private businesses use technology to enhance security. Compile these findings into a report and submit it to your instructor.

The How To: Your Turn exercises present general guidelines for fundamental skills when using a computer or mobile device and then require that you determine how to apply these general guidelines to a specific program or situation.

How To: Your Turn

Instructions: You often can complete tasks using technology in multiple ways. Figure out how to perform the tasks described in these exercises by using one or more resources available to you (such as a computer or mobile device, articles on the web or in print, online or program help, user guides, blogs, podcasts, videos, other individuals, trial and error, etc.). Summarize your 'how to' steps, along with the resource(s) used, in the format requested by your instructor (brief report, presentation, discussion, blog post, video, or other means).

① Evaluating Your Electronic Profile

When you make purchases online, tap or click advertisements, follow links, and complete online forms requesting information about yourself, you are adding to your electronic profile. While an electronic profile may help businesses guide you toward products and services that are of interest to you, some people view them as an invasion of privacy. The following steps guide you through the process of locating online information about yourself and taking steps to remove the information, if possible.

a. Run a browser.

b. Navigate to a search engine of your choice.

c. Perform a search for your full name.

d. In the search results, follow a link that you feel will display a webpage containing information about you. If the link's destination does not contain information about you, navigate back to the search results and follow another link.

e. Evaluate the webpage that contains information about you. If you wish to try removing the information, locate a link that allows you to contact the site owner(s) or automatically request removal of the information.

f. Request that your information be removed from the website. Some websites may not honor your request for removal. If you feel that the information must be removed, you may need to solicit legal advice.

g. If the search results display information from an account you have on an online social network, such as Facebook or LinkedIn, you may need to adjust your privacy settings so that the information is not public. If the privacy settings do not allow you to hide your information, you may need to consider deleting the account.

h. Repeat Steps d – g for the remaining search results. When you no longer see relevant search results for the search engine you used, search for other variations of your name (use your middle initial instead of your middle name, exclude your middle name, or consider

using commonly used nicknames instead of your first name).

i. Use other search engines to search for different variations of your name. Some search engines uncover results that others do not.

j. If you have an account on an online social network, navigate to the website's home page and, without signing in, search for your name. If information appears that you do not want to be public, you may need to adjust your privacy settings or remove your account.

k. Follow up with requests you have made to remove your online information.

Exercises

1. What personal information have you uncovered online? Did you have any idea that the information was there?

2. What additional steps can you take to prevent people and businesses from storing information about you?

3. What steps might you be able to take if you are unsuccessful with your attempts to remove online information that identifies you?

✳ How To: Your Turn

❷ Update Virus Definitions

In addition to installing or activating an antivirus program on your computer or mobile device to keep it safe from viruses, it also is necessary to keep the virus definitions updated so that the antivirus program can search for and detect new viruses on your computer or mobile device. New virus definitions can be released as often as once per day, depending on the number of new viruses that are created. Antivirus programs either can search for and install new virus definitions automatically at specified intervals, or you can update the virus signatures manually. The following steps describe how to update the virus definitions for an antivirus program.

Source: Microsoft

Update Virus Definitions Manually

a. If necessary, establish an Internet connection so that you will be able to update the virus definitions.
b. Run an antivirus program.
c. Tap or click the button to check for updated virus definitions.
d. If new virus definitions are available for the antivirus program, tap or click the link to download the definitions to the computer or mobile device.
e. When the update is complete, tap or click the button to scan the computer or mobile device for viruses.

Configure Automatic Updates for Virus Definitions

a. If necessary, establish an Internet connection so that you will be able to update the virus definitions.
b. Run an antivirus program.
c. Tap or click the option to update virus definitions automatically.
d. Tap or click the option to display the virus definition update schedule.
e. To provide the maximum protection from viruses, configure the antivirus program to update definitions as frequently as possible.
f. After configuring the update schedule, tap or click the button to update virus definitions manually.
g. When the update is complete, tap or click the button to scan the computer or mobile device for viruses.

Exercises

1. What antivirus program, if any, currently is installed on your computer? Is it scheduled to update virus definitions automatically?
2. In addition to downloading and installing virus definitions from within the antivirus program, are other ways available to obtain the latest virus definitions?
3. In addition to keeping the antivirus program's virus definitions current, what other ways can you protect a computer or mobile device from viruses?

❸ Determine Whether a Computer or Mobile Device Is Secured Properly

Several steps are required to secure a computer or mobile device properly. In addition to installing antivirus software and updating the virus definitions regularly, you also should install and configure a firewall, keep the operating system up to date, and be careful not to open suspicious email messages, visit unsecure webpages, or download untrusted files while using the Internet. The following steps guide you through the process of making sure your computer or mobile device is secured properly by verifying antivirus software is installed and running, a firewall is enabled and configured, and the operating system is up to date.

Verify Antivirus Software

a. Use the search tool in the operating system or scan the programs on the computer or mobile device for antivirus software. Some operating systems include antivirus software.
b. If you are unable to locate antivirus software on the computer or mobile device, obtain an antivirus program and install it.
c. Run the antivirus program.
d. Verify the virus definitions in the antivirus program are up to date.

Verify the Firewall

a. Use the search tool in the operating system or scan the programs, apps, and settings on the computer or mobile device to access and configure the firewall.
b. If you are unable to locate a firewall on the computer or mobile device, obtain a firewall program and install it.
c. Run the firewall program.
d. View the firewall settings and verify the firewall is turned on.
e. View the list of programs, apps, and features allowed through the firewall. If you do not recognize or use one or more of the programs, apps, or features, remove them from the list of allowed programs, apps, and features.

Verify Operating System Updates

a. If necessary, establish an Internet connection.

b. Navigate to the area of the operating system where you can access the button, link, or command to search for operating system updates. For example, in Microsoft Windows, you would display the settings for Windows Update.

c. Tap or click the button, link, or command to check for updates.

d. If no updates are available, your operating system is up to date. If the operating system locates additional updates, download and install the updates. **NOTE: If the computer or mobile device you are using does not belong to you, check with its owner before downloading and installing updates for the operating system.**

Source: Microsoft

Exercises

1. Before you began this exercise, was your computer or mobile device secured properly? How did you know your computer or mobile device was secured properly? If it was not, what actions did you need to perform to secure it?

2. Which programs, apps, and features do you think are safe to allow through your firewall? Which programs, apps, and features do you feel are not safe to allow through your firewall?

3. What additional ways can you properly secure your computer?

4 Clear Your Browsing History

A browser keeps track of the webpages that you have visited previously unless you have changed your settings. Although you can clear the browsing history on your computer or mobile device, your Internet service provider still may have logs that show a history of websites you have visited. The following steps guide you through the process of clearing your browsing history.

a. Run the browser.

b. Display the browser's settings.

c. If necessary, navigate to the settings that configure the browser's security settings. These settings often are found in the Security, Safety, or Privacy category.

How To: Your Turn

d. Select the option to delete the browsing history. In addition to deleting the list of websites you have visited, you also may be able to clear passwords the browser has remembered, clear cookies and temporary internet files, clear data you entered in forms, and clear a history of downloads.

e. When the browsing history has been deleted, run the browser again.

f. Follow the above steps for each additional browser you have installed on your computer or mobile device.

Exercises

1. What are some reasons why you might want to delete your browsing history?

2. Can you configure your browser to automatically delete your browsing history? If so, how?

3. What are the advantages of keeping your browsing history? If you do keep your browsing history, how long do you keep it?

5 Configure a Browser's Cookie Settings

As discussed in this module, cookies can be used for a variety of reasons. Websites can install cookies on your computer or mobile device that can store information on your computer or mobile device, or track your browsing habits. You can configure a browser's settings to disallow websites from storing and accessing cookies on your computer or mobile device. The following steps guide you through the process of configuring a browser's cookie settings.

a. Run the browser.

b. Display the browser's settings.

c. Navigate to the settings that configure the browser's cookie settings. These settings often are found in the Security, Safety, or Privacy category.

d. Configure how the browser handles first-party cookies and third-party cookies. Some users choose to reject all cookies. To function properly, however, some websites require that you accept their cookies.

e. Save the changes to the settings.

f. Run the browser again.

Exercises

1. What is the difference between first-party cookies and third-party cookies?

2. Configure the browser to deny all first-party and third-party cookies and then navigate to five websites you visit most frequently. Do the websites display any differently now that you are denying all cookies? Describe your browsing experience while the browser is configured to deny all cookies.

3. What security risks are associated with cookies?

❋ Internet Research

The Internet Research exercises broaden your understanding of module concepts by requiring that you search for information on the web.

Instructions: Use a search engine or another search tool to locate the information requested or answers to questions presented in the exercises. Describe your findings, along with the search term(s) you used and your web source(s), in the format requested by your instructor (brief report, presentation, discussion, blog post, video, or other means).

① Making Use of the Web
News, Weather, and Sports

Apps on tablets, smartphones, and other mobile devices are changing the delivery of the day's major news, weather, and sports stories. In one study, approximately one-half of American adults reported that they get some of their news on a tablet or mobile device. They view video and photos from eyewitnesses and fans, read analyses from investigators and coaches, and comment on stories. Men and college-educated people are the heaviest users of mobile news websites, and they are likely to read in-depth investigations and analyses. Online social networks also are a major source of information for many people.

Research This: (a) Visit two news websites or apps and locate one national event covered in both sources. Compare the coverage of the two stories. What information is provided in addition to the text, such as video, graphics, or links to related articles? Which story offers a better analysis? Which source is easier to navigate and read? Then, using another website or app, locate and read today's top international news story. What did you learn by reading the story? Were you aware of this event prior to reading the online story? Does the coverage include videos and photos to increase your comprehension?

(b) Visit a weather website or app and obtain the five-day forecast for your hometown. Include details about information that supplements the current and forecast conditions, such as a pollen or air quality index, storm tracking, travel advisories, or season summaries.

(c) Visit a sports website or app and read the first story reported. Describe the coverage of this event. Which sources are quoted in the story? Which links are included to other stories? Describe the features provided on this website, such as the ability to chat, customize the page for your favorite teams, or share the content with media sharing sites.

② Social Media

Sharing photos on your social media sites of yesterday's visit to the ballpark might be at the top of today's to-do list, but these images might be just the clues cyberthieves need to access your account. Facebook, in particular, is one website that scammers and advertisers use to gather information regarding your whereabouts and your personal life. Their malicious attacks begin with a visit to your timeline or other record of your activities. Searching for keywords on your page, they send targeted messages appearing to originate from trusted friends. If you open their attachments or tap or click their links, you have given these unscrupulous individuals access to your account. In addition, you may think you have crafted a password no one could guess. With your page open for others to view, however, the thieves scour the contents in hopes of locating starting clues, such as children's names, anniversary dates, and pet breeds, which could be hints to cracking your password.

Research This: In the Help section of an online social network you use, search for information about changing your profile's security and privacy settings. What steps can you take to mitigate the chance of becoming the victim of a hack? For example, can you adjust the connection settings to restrict who can see stories, send friend requests and messages, or search for you by name or contact information? Can you hide certain posts or block people from posting on your page? Can you report posts if they violate the website's terms? What are other potential threats to someone accessing your account?

③ Search Skills
Social Media Search

Search engines provide access to millions of search results by finding webpages, documents, images, or

NATIONAL WEATHER SERVICE

National Forecast Maps

Internet Research ✷

other information that match the search text you provide. Recommendations from people who use social media to share what they have read can be a possible alternative to using a search engine. People who take the time to Tweet pin an article or image on Twitter or Pinterest often do so because they found it useful, and hope others will as well.

To search Twitter, type the search text, search twitter, in a search engine to find the web address for the Twitter Search website, or sign in to Twitter with your credentials. In the Search Twitter text box, type the search text. For example, type the text, best mapping app, to find recommendations of links to articles or websites about mapping apps. You also can search Twitter for hashtags (a keyword preceded by a # symbol) to find Tweets about current events or popular discussion topics.

To search Pinterest, sign in to your Pinterest account and then type the search text into the search box. For example, type the search text, information security, into the search box to view related pins from Pinterest users. Pinterest users often pin links to infographics, images, and websites.

Source: Pinterest

Research This: Use Twitter and Pinterest to search for information about the following topics and then compare your results with those you would find using a search engine such as Bing, Google, or Yahoo!. (1) green computing, (2) computer virus, (3) cybercrime, and (4) malware. How are the results different? What type of information are you more likely to find on Twitter, on Pinterest, and using a search engine?

4 Security

Digital certificates and signatures detect a sender's identity and verify a document's authenticity. In this

module you learned that many e-commerce companies use them in an attempt to prevent digital eavesdroppers from intercepting confidential information. The online certificate authority (CA) vendors generate these certificates using a standard, called X.509, which is coordinated by the International Telecommunication Union and uses algorithms and encryption technology to identify the documents.

Research This: Visit websites of at least two companies that issue digital certificates. Compare products offered, prices, and certificate features. What length of time is needed to issue a certificate? What is a green address bar, and when is one issued? What business or organization validation is required? Then, visit websites of at least two companies that provide digital signatures. Compare signing and sending requirements, types of supported signatures, and available security features. Which documents are required to obtain a digital signature? When would a business need a Class 2 rather than a Class 3 digital signature?

5 Cloud Services

Cloud Security (SecaaS)

Antivirus software offers regular, automatic updates in order to protect a server, computer, or device from viruses, malware, or other attacks. Antivirus software is an example of cloud security, or security as a service (SecaaS), a service of cloud computing that delivers virus definitions and security software to users over the Internet as updates become available, with no intervention from users. Security as a service is a special case of software as a service, but is limited to security software solutions.

Individuals and enterprise users take advantage of antivirus software and security updates. Enterprise cloud users interact with cloud security solutions via a web interface to configure apps that provide protection to email servers, preventing spam before it arrives, keeping data secure, and watching for online threats and viruses. As the use of cloud-based resources continues, the market for security as a service solutions is expected to increase significantly in coming years.

Research This: (1) Use a search engine to find two different providers of security as a service solutions. Research the different solutions they provide, and report your findings. (2) How are enterprise security requirements different from those of individual users?

Critical Thinking

The Critical Thinking exercises challenge your assessment and decision-making skills by presenting real-world situations associated with module concepts. The Collaboration exercise should be completed with a team.

Instructions: Evaluate the situations below, using personal experiences and one or more resources available to you (such as articles on the web or in print, blogs, podcasts, videos, television, user guides, other individuals, electronics or computer stores, etc.). Perform the tasks requested in each exercise and share your deliverables in the format requested by your instructor (brief report, presentation, discussion, blog post, video, or other means).

1. Online Gaming Safety

You and your friend frequently play a popular online role-playing game. Your friend's computer had a virus recently, which was traced back to a malware-infected website. Your friend tells you that she visited the website after following a link while playing the game. What risks are involved when playing online games?

Do This: Use the web to find articles about incidents of malware infections associated with online gaming. Research tips for increasing security when playing online games. Did you find other threats and security tips in addition to the ones mentioned in this module? Have you ever downloaded updates to a game? If so, how did you ensure the updates were safe? Locate a list of games that are known to cause malware infections. Share your findings and any online gaming security problems you have experienced with the class.

2. Ensuring Safety and Security Online

You work in the information technology department for a large enterprise. An increasing number of users are contacting the help desk complaining about slow computer performance. Help desk representatives frequently attribute the decreased performance to malware. Although the help desk has installed security software on each computer, users also must practice safe computing. Your manager asked you to prepare information that teaches employees how to guard against malware and other security threats.

Do This: Include information such as how to determine if a website is safe, how to identify email and other spoofing schemes, guidelines for downloading programs and apps, email attachment safety, and how to avoid phishing scams. Create a list of how organizations use common safeguards to protect other users on the network, such as firewalls, proxy servers, user names and passwords, access controls, and audit trails.

3. Case Study

Amateur Sports League You are the new manager for a nonprofit amateur soccer league. The league's board of directors asked you to develop a disaster recovery plan for its main office. The main office consists of a small storefront with two back rooms: one room is the office, with all of the electronic equipment and paper files; the other is for storage of nonelectronic equipment. The staff members — you, an administrative assistant, and an information technology (IT) specialist — work in the office. The electronic equipment in the office includes two desktops, a laptop, an external hard drive for backups, a wireless router, and two printers. In addition, each staff member has a smartphone.

Do This: Choose either a natural or man-made disaster. Create a disaster recovery plan that outlines emergency strategies, backup procedures, recovery steps, and a test plan. Assign staff members roles for each phase of the disaster recovery plan.

Collaboration

4. **Implementing Biometric Security** You are the chief technology officer of a large company. You have been reading an article about computer security that discussed several examples of security breaches, including thieves breaking into an office and stealing expensive equipment, and a recently terminated employee gaining access to the office after hours and corrupting data. Because of these incidents, your company would like to start using biometric devices to increase its security.

Do This: Form a three-member team and research the use of biometric devices to protect equipment and data. Each member of your team should choose a different type of biometric device, such as fingerprint readers, face recognition systems, and hand geometry systems. Find products for each device type, and research costs and user reviews. Search for articles by industry experts. Would you recommend using the biometric device for security purposes? Why or why not? Meet with your team, discuss and compile your findings, and then share with the class.

Courtesy of Ingersoll Rand Security Technologies

Notes

Notes

Office 2016 and Windows 10: Essential Concepts and Skills

Objectives

You will have mastered the material in this module when you can:

- Use a touch screen
- Perform basic mouse operations
- Start Windows and sign in to an account
- Identify the objects on the Windows 10 desktop
- Identify the apps in and versions of Microsoft Office 2016
- Run an app
- Identify the components of the Microsoft Office ribbon

- Create folders
- Save files
- Change screen resolution
- Perform basic tasks in Microsoft Office apps
- Manage files
- Use Microsoft Office Help and Windows Help

This introductory module covers features and functions common to Office 2016 apps, as well as the basics of Windows 10.

Roadmap

In this module, you will learn how to perform basic tasks in Windows and the Office apps. The following roadmap identifies general activities you will perform as you progress through this module:

1. SIGN IN to an account
2. USE WINDOWS
3. USE Office APPS
4. FILE and Folder MANAGEMENT
5. SWITCH between APPS

6. SAVE and Manage FILES

7. CHANGE SCREEN RESOLUTION

8. EXIT Office APPS

9. USE ADDITIONAL Office APPS

10. USE Office and Windows HELP

At the beginning of the step instructions throughout each module, you will see an abbreviated form of this roadmap. The abbreviated roadmap uses colors to indicate module progress: gray means the module is beyond that activity, blue means the task being shown is covered in that activity, and black means that activity is yet to be covered. For example, the following abbreviated roadmap indicates the module would be showing a task in the USE APPS activity.

1 SIGN IN | 2 USE WINDOWS | 3 USE APPS | 4 FILE MANAGEMENT | 5 SWITCH APPS | 6 SAVE FILES

7 CHANGE SCREEN RESOLUTION | 8 EXIT APPS | 9 USE ADDITIONAL APPS | 10 USE HELP

Use the abbreviated roadmap as a progress guide while you read or step through the instructions in this module.

Introduction to the Windows 10 Operating System

Windows 10 is the newest version of Microsoft Windows, which is a popular and widely used operating system (Figure 1). An **operating system (OS)** is a set of programs that coordinate all the activities among computer or mobile device hardware.

Figure 1

The Windows operating system simplifies the process of working with documents and apps by organizing the manner in which you interact with the computer. Windows is used to run apps. An application, or **app**, consists of programs designed to make users more productive and/or assist them with personal tasks, such as word processing or browsing the web.

Using a Touch Screen and a Mouse

Windows users who have computers or devices with touch screen capability can interact with the screen using gestures. A **gesture** is a motion you make on a touch screen with the tip of one or more fingers or your hand. Touch screens are convenient because they do not require a separate device for input. Table 1 presents common ways to interact with a touch screen.

Table 1 Touch Screen Gestures

Motion	Description	Common Uses	Equivalent Mouse Operation
Tap	Quickly touch and release one finger one time.	Activate a link (built-in connection). Press a button. Run a program or an app.	Click
Double-tap	Quickly touch and release one finger two times.	Run a program or an app. Zoom in (show a smaller area on the screen, so that contents appear larger) at the location of the double-tap.	Double-click
Press and hold	Press and hold one finger to cause an action to occur, or until an action occurs.	Display a shortcut menu (immediate access to allowable actions). Activate a mode enabling you to move an item with one finger to a new location.	Right-click
Drag, or slide	Press and hold one finger on an object and then move the finger to the new location.	Move an item around the screen. Scroll.	Drag
Swipe	Press and hold one finger and then move the finger horizontally or vertically on the screen.	Select an object. Swipe from edge to display a bar such as the Action Center, Apps bar, and Navigation bar (all discussed later).	Drag
Stretch	Move two fingers apart.	Zoom in (show a smaller area on the screen, so that contents appear larger).	None
Pinch	Move two fingers together.	Zoom out (show a larger area on the screen, so that contents appear smaller).	None

If you are using your finger on a touch screen and are having difficulty completing the steps in this module, consider using a stylus. Many people find it easier to be precise with a stylus than with a finger. In addition, with a stylus you see the pointer. If you still are having trouble completing the steps with a stylus, try using a mouse.

Will your screen look different if you are using a touch screen?
The Windows and Microsoft Office interface varies slightly if you are using a touch screen. For this reason, you might notice that your screen looks slightly different from the screens in the module.

Windows users who do not have touch screen capabilities typically work with a mouse that has at least two buttons. For a right-handed user, the left button usually is

CONSIDER THIS

BTW
Pointer
If you are using a touch screen, the pointer may not appear on the screen as you perform touch gestures. The pointer will reappear when you begin using the mouse.

the primary mouse button, and the right mouse button is the secondary mouse button. Left-handed people, however, can reverse the function of these buttons.

Table 2 explains how to perform a variety of mouse operations. Some apps also use keys in combination with the mouse to perform certain actions. For example, when you hold down the CTRL key while rolling the mouse wheel, text on the screen may become larger or smaller based on the direction you roll the wheel. The function of the mouse buttons and the wheel varies depending on the app.

Table 2 Mouse Operations

Operation	Mouse Action	Example*	Equivalent Touch Gesture
Point	Move the mouse until the pointer on the desktop is positioned on the item of choice.	Position the pointer on the screen.	None
Click	Press and release the primary mouse button, which usually is the left mouse button.	Select or deselect items on the screen or run an app or app feature.	Tap
Right-click	Press and release the secondary mouse button, which usually is the right mouse button.	Display a shortcut menu.	Press and hold
Double-click	Quickly press and release the primary mouse button twice without moving the mouse.	Run an app or app feature.	Double-tap
Triple-click	Quickly press and release the primary mouse button three times without moving the mouse.	Select a paragraph.	Triple-tap
Drag	Point to an item, hold down the primary mouse button, move the item to the desired location on the screen, and then release the mouse button.	Move an object from one location to another or draw pictures.	Drag or slide
Right-drag	Point to an item, hold down the right mouse button, move the item to the desired location on the screen, and then release the right mouse button.	Display a shortcut menu after moving an object from one location to another.	Press and hold, then drag
Rotate wheel	Roll the wheel forward or backward.	Scroll vertically (up and down).	Swipe
Free-spin wheel	Whirl the wheel forward or backward so that it spins freely on its own.	Scroll through many pages in seconds.	Swipe
Press wheel	Press the wheel button while moving the mouse.	Scroll continuously.	None
Tilt wheel	Press the wheel toward the right or left.	Scroll horizontally (left and right).	None
Press thumb button	Press the button on the side of the mouse with your thumb.	Move forward or backward through webpages and/or control media, games, etc.	None

*Note: The examples presented in this column are discussed as they are demonstrated in this chapter.

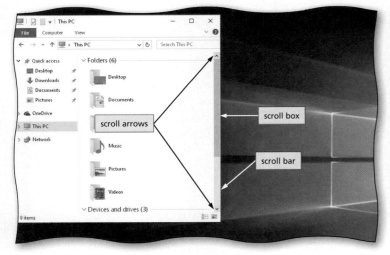

© 2015 Cengage Learning

Scrolling

A **scroll bar** is a horizontal or vertical bar that appears when the contents of an area may not be visible completely on the screen (Figure 2). A scroll bar contains **scroll arrows** and a **scroll box** that enable you to view areas that currently cannot be seen on the screen. Clicking the up and down scroll arrows moves the screen content up or down one line. You also can click above or below the scroll box to move up or down a section, or drag the scroll box up or down to move to a specific location.

Figure 2

Keyboard Shortcuts

In many cases, you can use the keyboard instead of the mouse to accomplish a task. To perform tasks using the keyboard, you press one or more keyboard keys, sometimes identified as a **keyboard shortcut**. Some keyboard shortcuts consist of a single key, such as the F1 key. For example, to obtain help in many apps, you can press the F1 key. Other keyboard shortcuts consist of multiple keys, in which case a plus sign separates the key names, such as CTRL+ESC. This notation means to press and hold down the first key listed, press one or more additional keys, and then release all keys. For example, to display the Start menu, press CTRL+ESC, that is, hold down the CTRL key, press the ESC key, and then release both keys.

Starting Windows

It is not unusual for multiple people to use the same computer in a work, educational, recreational, or home setting. Windows enables each user to establish a **user account**, which identifies to Windows the resources, such as apps and storage locations, a user can access when working with the computer.

Each user account has a user name and may have a password and an icon, as well. A **user name** is a unique combination of letters or numbers that identifies a specific user to Windows. A **password** is a private combination of letters, numbers, and special characters associated with the user name that allows access to a user's account resources. An icon is a small image that represents an object; thus, a **user icon** is a picture associated with a user name.

When you turn on a computer, Windows starts and displays a **lock screen** consisting of the time and date (Figure 3). To unlock the screen, click the lock screen. Depending on your computer's settings, Windows may or may not display a sign-in screen that shows the user names and user icons for users who have accounts on the computer. This **sign-in screen** enables you to sign in to your user account and makes the computer available for use. Clicking the user icon begins the process of signing in, also called logging on, to your user account.

BTW
Minimize Wrist Injury
Computer users frequently switch between the keyboard and the mouse during a word processing session; such switching strains the wrist. To help prevent wrist injury, minimize switching. For instance, if your fingers already are on the keyboard, use keyboard keys to scroll. If your hand already is on the mouse, use the mouse to scroll. If your hand is on the touch screen, use touch gestures to scroll.

lock screen

current date and time

2:57
Wednesday, September 23

Figure 3

At the bottom of the sign-in screen is the 'Connect to Internet' button, 'Ease of access' button, and a Shut down button. Clicking the 'Connect to Internet' button displays a list of each network connection and its status. You also can connect to or disconnect from a network. Clicking the 'Ease of access' button displays the Ease of access menu, which provides tools to optimize a computer to accommodate the needs of the mobility, hearing, and vision impaired users. Clicking the Shut down button displays a menu containing commands related to putting the computer or mobile device in a low-power state, shutting it down, and restarting the computer or mobile device. The commands available on your computer or mobile device may differ.

- The Sleep command saves your work, turns off the computer fans and hard drive, and places the computer in a lower-power state. To wake the computer from sleep mode, press the power button or lift a laptop's cover, and sign in to your account.
- The Shut down command exits running apps, shuts down Windows, and then turns off the computer.
- The Restart command exits running apps, shuts down Windows, and then restarts Windows.

To Sign In to an Account

1 SIGN IN | 2 USE WINDOWS | 3 USE APPS | 4 FILE MANAGEMENT | 5 SWITCH APPS | 6 SAVE FILES
7 CHANGE SCREEN RESOLUTION | 8 EXIT APPS | 9 USE ADDITIONAL APPS | 10 USE HELP

The following steps, which use SCSeries as the user name, sign in to an account based on a typical Windows installation. **Why?** *After starting Windows, you might be required to sign in to an account to access the computer or mobile device's resources.* You may need to ask your instructor how to sign in to your account.

- Click the lock screen (shown in Figure 3) to display a sign-in screen.

- Click the user icon (for SCSeries, in this case) on the sign-in screen, which depending on settings, either will display a second sign-in screen that contains a Password text box (Figure 4) or will display the Windows desktop (Figure 5).

Figure 4

Q&A
Why do I not see a user icon?
Your computer may require you to type a user name instead of clicking an icon.

What is a text box?
A text box is a rectangular box in which you type text.

Why does my screen not show a Password text box?
Your account does not require a password.

- If Windows displays a sign-in screen with a Password text box, type your password in the text box.

2

- Click the Submit button (shown in Figure 4) to sign in to your account and display the Windows desktop (Figure 5).

Q&A

Why does my desktop look different from the one in Figure 5?
The Windows desktop is customizable, and your school or employer may have modified the desktop to meet its needs. Also, your screen resolution, which affects the size of the elements on the screen, may differ from the screen resolution used in this book. Later in this module, you learn how to change screen resolution.

How do I type if my tablet has no keyboard?
You can use your fingers to press keys on a keyboard that appears on the screen, called an on-screen keyboard, or you can purchase a separate physical keyboard that attaches to or wirelessly communicates with the tablet.

Figure 5

The Windows Desktop

The Windows 10 desktop (Figure 5) and the objects on the desktop emulate a work area in an office. Think of the Windows desktop as an electronic version of the top of your desk. You can perform tasks such as placing objects on the desktop, moving the objects around the desktop, and removing items from the desktop.

When you run an app in Windows 10, it appears on the desktop. Some icons also may be displayed on the desktop. For instance, the icon for the **Recycle Bin**, the location of files that have been deleted, appears on the desktop by default. A **file** is a named unit of storage. Files can contain text, images, audio, and video. You can customize your desktop so that icons representing programs and files you use often appear on your desktop.

Introduction to Microsoft Office 2016

Microsoft Office 2016 is the newest version of Microsoft Office, offering features that provide users with better functionality and easier ways to work with the various files they create. This version of Office also is designed to work more optimally on mobile devices and online.

Microsoft Office 2016 Apps

Microsoft Office 2016 includes a wide variety of apps, such as Word, PowerPoint, Excel, Access, Outlook, Publisher, and OneNote:

- **Microsoft Word 2016**, or Word, is a full-featured word processing app that allows you to create professional-looking documents and revise them easily.

- **Microsoft PowerPoint 2016**, or PowerPoint, is a complete presentation app that enables you to produce professional-looking presentations and then deliver them to an audience.

- **Microsoft Excel 2016**, or Excel, is a powerful spreadsheet app that allows you to organize data, complete calculations, make decisions, graph data, develop professional-looking reports, publish organized data to the web, and access real-time data from websites.

- **Microsoft Access 2016**, or Access, is a database management system that enables you to create a database; add, change, and delete data in the database; ask questions concerning the data in the database; and create forms and reports using the data in the database.

- **Microsoft Outlook 2016**, or Outlook, is a communications and scheduling app that allows you to manage email accounts, calendars, contacts, and access to other Internet content.

- **Microsoft Publisher 2016**, or Publisher, is a desktop publishing app that helps you create professional-quality publications and marketing materials that can be shared easily.

- **Microsoft OneNote 2016**, or OneNote, is a note taking app that allows you to store and share information in notebooks with other people.

Microsoft Office 2016 Suites

A **suite** is a collection of individual apps available together as a unit. Microsoft offers a variety of Office suites, including a stand-alone desktop app, Microsoft Office 365, and Microsoft Office Online. **Microsoft Office 365**, or Office 365, provides plans that allow organizations to use Office in a mobile setting while also being able to communicate and share files, depending upon the type of plan selected by the organization. **Microsoft Office Online** includes apps that allow you to edit and share files on the web using the familiar Office interface.

During the Office 365 installation, you select a plan, and depending on your plan, you receive different apps and services. Office Online apps do not require a local installation and can be accessed through OneDrive and your browser. **OneDrive** is a cloud storage service that provides storage and other services, such as Office Online, to computer users.

 How do you sign up for a OneDrive account?

- Use your browser to navigate to onedrive.live.com.

- Create a Microsoft account by clicking the Sign up button and then entering your information to create the account.

- Sign in to OneDrive using your new account or use it in Office to save your files on OneDrive.

CONSIDER THIS

Apps in a suite, such as Microsoft Office, typically use a similar interface and share features. Once you are comfortable working with the elements and the interface and performing tasks in one app, the similarity can help you apply the knowledge and skills you have learned to another app(s) in the suite. For example, the process for saving a file in Word is the same in PowerPoint, Excel, and some of the other Office apps. While briefly showing how to use several Office apps, this module illustrates some of the common functions across the apps and identifies the characteristics unique to these apps.

Running and Using an App

To use an app, you must instruct the operating system to run the app. Windows provides many different ways to run an app, one of which is presented in this section (other ways to run an app are presented throughout this module). After an app is running, you can use it to perform a variety of tasks. The following pages use Word to discuss some elements of the Office interface and to perform tasks that are common to other Office apps.

Word

Word is a full-featured word processing app that allows you to create many types of personal and business documents, including flyers, letters, memos, resumes, reports, fax cover sheets, mailing labels, and newsletters. Word also provides tools that enable you to create webpages and save these webpages directly on a web server. Word has many features designed to simplify the production of documents and add visual appeal. Using Word, you easily can change the shape, size, and color of text. You also can include borders, shading, tables, images, pictures, charts, and web addresses in documents.

To Run an App Using the Start Menu and Create a Blank Document

1 SIGN IN | 2 USE WINDOWS | 3 USE APPS | 4 FILE MANAGEMENT | 5 SWITCH APPS | 6 SAVE FILES
7 CHANGE SCREEN RESOLUTION | 8 EXIT APPS | 9 USE ADDITIONAL APPS | 10 USE HELP

Across the bottom of the Windows 10 desktop is the taskbar. The taskbar contains the **Start button**, which you use to access apps, files, folders, and settings. A **folder** is a named location on a storage medium that usually contains related documents.

Clicking the Start button displays the Start menu. The **Start menu** allows you to access programs, folders, and files on the computer or mobile device and contains commands that allow you to start programs, store and search for documents, customize the computer or mobile device, and sign out of a user account or shut down the computer or mobile device. A **menu** is a list of related items, including folders, programs, and commands. Each **command** on a menu performs a specific action, such as saving a file or obtaining help. *Why? When you install an app, for example, the app's name will be added to the All apps list on the Start menu.*

The following steps, which assume Windows is running, use the Start menu to run an Office app and create a blank document based on a typical installation. You may need to ask your instructor how to run an Office app on your computer. Although the steps illustrate running the Word app, the steps to run any Office app are similar.

1

- Click the Start button on the Windows 10 taskbar to display the Start menu (Figure 6).

Figure 6

2

• Click All apps at the bottom of the left pane of the Start menu to display a list of apps installed on the computer or mobile device. If necessary, scroll to display the app you wish to run (Figure 7).

Figure 7

3

• If the app you wish to run is located in a folder, click or scroll to and then click the folder in the All apps list to display a list of the folder's contents.

• Click, or scroll to and then click, the program name (Microsoft Word 2016, in this case) in the list to run the selected program (Figure 8).

Figure 8

4

- Click the Blank document thumbnail on the Word start screen to create a blank Word document in the Word window (Figure 9).

Q&A

What happens when you run an app?

Some apps provide a means for you to create a blank document, as shown in Figure 8; others immediately display a blank document in an app window, such as the Word window shown in Figure 9. A **window** is a rectangular area that displays data and information. The top of a window has a **title bar**, which is a horizontal space that contains the window's name.

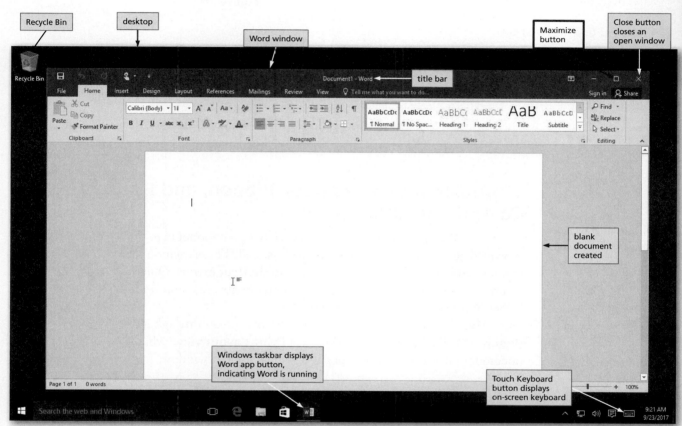

Figure 9

Other Ways

1. Type app name in search box, click app name in results list
2. Double-click file created in app you want to run

---

1 SIGN IN | 2 USE WINDOWS | 3 USE APPS | 4 FILE MANAGEMENT | 5 SWITCH APPS | 6 SAVE FILES
7 CHANGE SCREEN RESOLUTION | 8 EXIT APPS | 9 USE ADDITIONAL APPS | 10 USE HELP

To Maximize a Window

Sometimes content is not visible completely in a window. One method of displaying the entire contents of a window is to **maximize** it, or enlarge the window so that it fills the entire screen. The following step maximizes the Word window; however, any Office app's window can be maximized using this step. *Why? A maximized window provides the most space available for using the app.*

①

- If the app window is not maximized already, click the Maximize button (shown in Figure 9) next to the Close button on the window's title bar (the Word window title bar, in this case) to maximize the window (Figure 10).

Figure 10

Q&A

What happened to the Maximize button?

It changed to a Restore Down button, which you can use to return a window to its size and location before you maximized it.

How do I know whether a window is maximized?

A window is maximized if it fills the entire display area and the Restore Down button is displayed on the title bar.

Other Ways

1. Double-click title bar
2. Drag title bar to top of screen

Word Document Window, Ribbon, and Elements Common to Office Apps

The Word window consists of a variety of components to make your work more efficient and documents more professional. These include the document window, ribbon, Tell Me box, mini toolbar, shortcut menus, Quick Access Toolbar, and Microsoft Account area. Most of these components are common to other Microsoft Office apps; others are unique to Word.

You view a portion of a document on the screen through a **document window** (Figure 11). The default (preset) view is **Print Layout view**, which shows the document on a mock sheet of paper in the document window.

Scroll Bars   You use a scroll bar to display different portions of a document in the document window. At the right edge of the document window is a vertical scroll bar. If a document is too wide to fit in the document window, a horizontal scroll bar also appears at the bottom of the document window. On a scroll bar, the position of the scroll box reflects the location of the portion of the document that is displayed in the document window.

Status Bar   The **status bar**, located at the bottom of the document window above the Windows taskbar, presents information about the document, the progress of current tasks, and the status of certain commands and keys; it also provides controls for viewing the document. As you type text or perform certain tasks, various indicators and buttons may appear on the status bar.

The left side of the status bar in Figure 11 shows the current page followed by the total number of pages in the document, the number of words in the document, and an icon to check spelling and grammar. The right side of the status bar includes buttons and controls you can use to change the view of a document and adjust the size of the displayed document.

Ribbon   The ribbon, located near the top of the window below the title bar, is the control center in Word and other Office apps (Figure 12). The ribbon provides easy, central access to the tasks you perform while creating a document. The ribbon consists

Figure 11

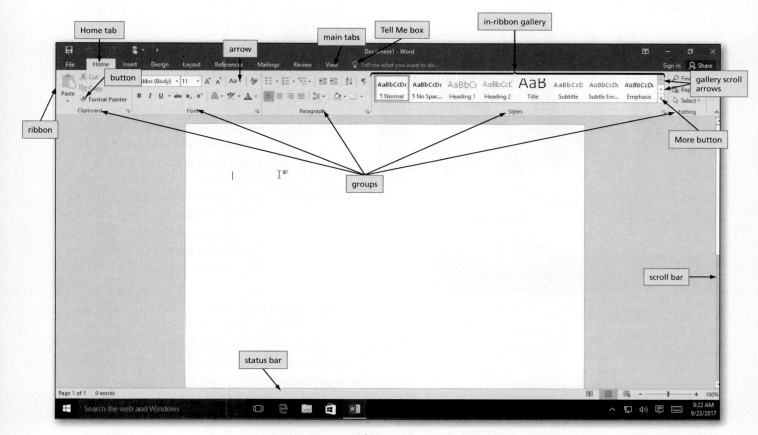

Figure 12

of tabs, groups, and commands. Each **tab** contains a collection of groups, and each **group** contains related commands. When you run an Office app, such as Word, it initially displays several main tabs, also called default or top-level tabs. All Office apps have a Home tab, which contains the more frequently used commands.

Figure 13

In addition to the main tabs, the Office apps display **tool tabs**, also called contextual tabs (Figure 13), when you perform certain tasks or work with objects such as pictures or tables. If you insert a picture in a Word document, for example, the Picture Tools tab and its related subordinate Format tab appear, collectively referred to as the Picture Tools Format tab. When you are finished working with the picture, the Picture Tools Format tab disappears from the ribbon. Word and other Office apps determine when tool tabs should appear and disappear based on tasks you perform. Some tool tabs, such as the Table Tools tab, have more than one related subordinate tab.

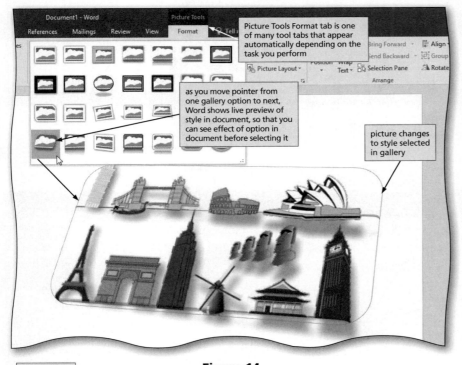

Figure 14

Items on the ribbon include buttons, boxes, and galleries (shown in Figure 12). A **gallery** is a set of choices, often graphical, arranged in a grid or in a list. You can scroll through choices in an in-ribbon gallery by clicking the gallery's scroll arrows. Or, you can click a gallery's More button to view more gallery options on the screen at a time.

Some buttons and boxes have arrows that, when clicked, also display a gallery; others always cause a gallery to be displayed when clicked. Most galleries support **live preview**, which is a feature that allows you to point to a gallery choice and see its effect in the document — without actually selecting the choice (Figure 14). Live preview works only if you are using a mouse; if you are using a touch screen, you will not be able to view live previews.

Some commands on the ribbon display an image to help you remember their function. When you point to a command on the ribbon, all or part of the command glows in a shade of gray, and a ScreenTip appears on the screen. A **ScreenTip** is an on-screen note that provides the name of the command, available keyboard shortcut(s), a description of the command, and sometimes instructions for how to obtain help about the command (Figure 15).

Figure 15

Some groups on the ribbon have a small arrow in the lower-right corner, called a **Dialog Box Launcher**, that when clicked, displays a dialog box or a task pane with additional options for the group (Figure 16). When presented with a dialog box, you make selections and must close the dialog box before returning to the document. A **task pane**, in contrast to a dialog box, is a window that can remain open and visible while you work in the document.

BTW
Touch Mode
The Office and Windows interfaces may vary if you are using touch mode. For this reason, you might notice that the function or appearance of your touch screen differs slightly from this module's presentation.

Figure 16

Tell Me Box The **Tell Me box**, which appears to the right of the tabs on the ribbon, is a type of search box that helps you to perform specific tasks in an Office app (Figure 17). As you type in the Tell Me box, the word-wheeling feature displays search results that are refined as you type. For example, if you want to center text in a document, you can type "center" in the Tell Me box and then select the appropriate command. The Tell Me box also lists the last five commands accessed from the box.

Mini Toolbar The **mini toolbar**, which appears automatically based on tasks you perform, contains commands related to changing the appearance of text in a document (Figure 18). If you do not use the mini toolbar, it disappears from the screen. The buttons, arrows, and boxes on the mini toolbar vary, depending on whether you are using Touch mode versus Mouse mode. If you right-click an item in the document window, Word displays both the mini toolbar and a shortcut menu, which is discussed in a later section in this module.

All commands on the mini toolbar also exist on the ribbon. The purpose of the mini toolbar is to minimize hand or mouse movement.

Figure 17

BTW
Turning Off the Mini Toolbar
If you do not want the mini toolbar to appear, click File on the ribbon to open the Backstage view, click the Options tab in the Backstage view, if necessary, click General (Options dialog box), remove the check mark from the 'Show Mini Toolbar on selection' check box, and then click the OK button.

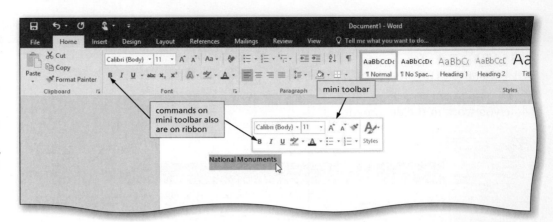

Figure 18

Quick Access Toolbar The **Quick Access Toolbar**, located initially (by default) above the ribbon at the left edge of the title bar, provides convenient, one-click access to frequently used commands (shown in Figure 15). The commands on the Quick Access Toolbar always are available, regardless of the task you are performing. The Touch/Mouse Mode button on the Quick Access Toolbar allows you to switch between Touch mode and Mouse mode. If you primarily are using touch gestures, Touch mode will add more space between commands in menus and on the ribbon so that they are easier to tap. While touch gestures are convenient ways to interact with Office apps, not all features are supported when you are using Touch mode. If you are using a mouse, Mouse mode will not add the extra space between buttons and commands. The Quick Access Toolbar is discussed in more depth later in the module.

KeyTips If you prefer using the keyboard instead of the mouse, you can press the ALT key on the keyboard to display **KeyTips**, or keyboard code icons, for certain commands (Figure 19). To select a command using the keyboard, press the letter or number displayed in the KeyTip, which may cause additional KeyTips related to the selected command to appear. To remove KeyTips from the screen, press the ALT key or the ESC key until all KeyTips disappear, or click anywhere in the app window.

Microsoft Account Area In this area, you can use the Sign in link to sign in to your Microsoft account. Once signed in, you will see your account information, as well as a picture if you have included one in your Microsoft account.

Figure 19

To Display a Different Tab on the Ribbon

1 SIGN IN | 2 USE WINDOWS | 3 USE APPS | 4 FILE MANAGEMENT | 5 SWITCH APPS | 6 SAVE FILES
7 CHANGE SCREEN RESOLUTION | 8 EXIT APPS | 9 USE ADDITIONAL APPS | 10 USE HELP

When you run Word, the ribbon displays nine main tabs: File, Home, Insert, Design, Layout, References, Mailings, Review, and View. The tab currently displayed is called the **active tab**.

The following step displays the Insert tab, that is, makes it the active tab. *Why? When working with an Office app, you may need to switch tabs to access other options for working with a document.*

- Click Insert on the ribbon to display the Insert tab (Figure 20).

Experiment

- Click the other tabs on the ribbon to view their contents. When you are finished, click Insert on the ribbon to redisplay the Insert tab.

Figure 20

Other Ways

1. Press ALT, press letter corresponding to tab to display
2. Press ALT, press LEFT ARROW or RIGHT ARROW until desired tab is displayed

To Collapse and Expand the Ribbon and Use Full Screen Mode

1 SIGN IN | 2 USE WINDOWS | 3 USE APPS | 4 FILE MANAGEMENT | 5 SWITCH APPS | 6 SAVE FILES
7 CHANGE SCREEN RESOLUTION | 8 EXIT APPS | 9 USE ADDITIONAL APPS | 10 USE HELP

To display more of a document or other item in the window of an Office app, some users prefer to collapse the ribbon, which hides the groups on the ribbon and displays only the main tabs, or to use **Full Screen mode**, which hides all the commands and just displays the document. Each time you run an Office app, the ribbon appears the same way it did the last time you used that Office app. The modules in this book, however, begin with the ribbon appearing as it did at the initial installation of the software.

The following steps collapse, expand, and restore the ribbon in an Office app and then switch to Full Screen mode. **Why?** *If you need more space on the screen to work with your document, you may consider collapsing the ribbon or switching to Full Screen mode to gain additional workspace.*

- Click the 'Collapse the Ribbon' button on the ribbon (shown in Figure 20) to collapse the ribbon (Figure 21).

Q&A | What happened to the 'Collapse the Ribbon' button?
The 'Pin the ribbon' button replaces the 'Collapse the Ribbon' button when the ribbon is collapsed. You will see the 'Pin the ribbon' button only when you expand a ribbon by clicking a tab.

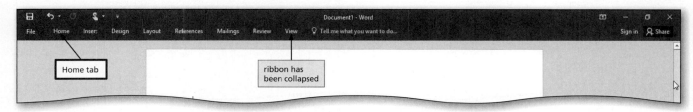

Figure 21

2

- Click Home on the ribbon to expand the Home tab (Figure 22).

Q&A Why would I click the Home tab?
If you want to use a command on a collapsed ribbon, click the main tab to display the groups for that tab. After you select a command on the ribbon and resume working in the document, the groups will be collapsed once again. If you decide not to use a command on the ribbon, you can collapse the groups by clicking the same main tab or clicking in the app window.

Experiment

- Click Home on the ribbon to collapse the groups again. Click Home on the ribbon to expand the Home tab.

Figure 22

3

- Click the 'Pin the ribbon' button on the expanded Home tab to restore the ribbon.
- Click the 'Ribbon Display Options' button to display the Ribbon Display Options menu (Figure 23).

Figure 23

4

- Click Auto-hide Ribbon to hide all the commands from the screen (Figure 24).
- Click the ellipsis to temporarily display the ribbon.
- Click the 'Ribbon Display Options' button to display the Ribbon Display Options menu (shown in Figure 23).
- Click 'Show Tabs and Commands' to exit Full Screen mode.

Figure 24

Other Ways

1. Double-click a main tab on the ribbon
2. Press CTRL+F1

To Use a Shortcut Menu to Relocate the Quick Access Toolbar

1 SIGN IN | 2 USE WINDOWS | 3 USE APPS | 4 FILE MANAGEMENT | 5 SWITCH APPS | 6 SAVE FILES
7 CHANGE SCREEN RESOLUTION | 8 EXIT APPS | 9 USE ADDITIONAL APPS | 10 USE HELP

When you right-click certain areas of the Word and other Office app windows, a shortcut menu will appear. A **shortcut menu** is a list of frequently used commands that relate to an object. **Why?** *You can use shortcut menus to access common commands quickly.* When you right-click the status bar, for example, a shortcut menu appears with commands related to the status bar. When you right-click the Quick Access Toolbar, a shortcut menu appears with commands related to the Quick Access Toolbar. The following steps use a shortcut menu to move the Quick Access Toolbar, which by default is located on the title bar.

1

- Right-click the Quick Access Toolbar to display a shortcut menu that presents a list of commands related to the Quick Access Toolbar (Figure 25).

Figure 25

- Click 'Show Quick Access Toolbar Below the Ribbon' on the shortcut menu to display the Quick Access Toolbar below the ribbon (Figure 26).

Figure 26

- Right-click the Quick Access Toolbar to display a shortcut menu (Figure 27).

④

- Click 'Show Quick Access Toolbar Above the Ribbon' on the shortcut menu to return the Quick Access Toolbar to its original position (shown in Figure 25).

Figure 27

Other Ways

1. Click 'Customize Quick Access Toolbar' button on Quick Access Toolbar, click 'Show Below the Ribbon' or 'Show Above the Ribbon'

To Customize the Quick Access Toolbar

1 SIGN IN | 2 USE WINDOWS | 3 USE APPS | 4 FILE MANAGEMENT | 5 SWITCH APPS | 6 SAVE FILES
7 CHANGE SCREEN RESOLUTION | 8 EXIT APPS | 9 USE ADDITIONAL APPS | 10 USE HELP

The Quick Access Toolbar provides easy access to some of the more frequently used commands in the Office apps. By default, the Quick Access Toolbar contains buttons for the Save, Undo, and Redo commands. If your computer or mobile device has a touch screen, the Quick Access Toolbar also might display the Touch/Mouse Mode button. You can customize the Quick Access Toolbar by changing its location in the window, as shown in the previous steps, and by adding more buttons to reflect commands you would like to access easily. The following steps add the Quick Print button to the Quick Access Toolbar. *Why? Adding the Quick Print button to the Quick Access Toolbar speeds up the process of printing.*

①

- Click the 'Customize Quick Access Toolbar' button to display the Customize Quick Access Toolbar menu (Figure 28).

◄ Which commands are listed on the
Q&A Customize Quick Access Toolbar menu?
It lists commands that commonly are added to the Quick Access Toolbar.

Figure 28

2

- Click Quick Print on the Customize Quick Access Toolbar menu to add the Quick Print button to the Quick Access Toolbar (Figure 29).

Q&A How would I remove a button from the Quick Access Toolbar?
You would right-click the button you wish to remove and then click 'Remove from Quick Access Toolbar' on the shortcut menu or click the 'Customize Quick Access Toolbar' button on the Quick Access Toolbar and then click the button name in the Customize Quick Access Toolbar menu to remove the check mark.

Figure 29

To Enter Text in a Document

1 SIGN IN | 2 USE WINDOWS | 3 USE APPS | 4 FILE MANAGEMENT | 5 SWITCH APPS | 6 SAVE FILES
7 CHANGE SCREEN RESOLUTION | 8 EXIT APPS | 9 USE ADDITIONAL APPS | 10 USE HELP

The first step in creating a document is to enter its text by typing on the keyboard. By default, Word positions text at the left margin as you type. The following steps type this first line of a flyer. *Why? To begin creating a flyer, for example, you type the headline in the document window.*

1

- Type **VISIT NATIONAL MONUMENTS** as the text (Figure 30).

Q&A What is the blinking vertical bar to the right of the text?
The blinking bar is the insertion point, which indicates where text, graphics, and other items will be inserted in the document. As you type, the insertion point moves to the right, and when you reach the end of a line, it moves down to the beginning of the next line.

What if I make an error while typing?

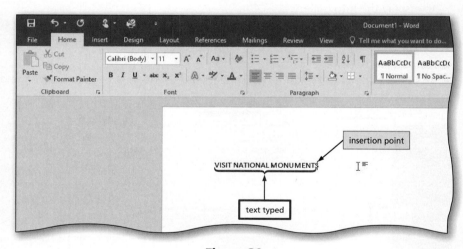

Figure 30

You can press the BACKSPACE key until you have deleted the text in error and then retype the text correctly.

2

- Press the ENTER key to move the insertion point to the beginning of the next line (Figure 31).

Q&A Why did blank space appear between the entered text and the insertion point?
Each time you press the ENTER key, Word creates a new paragraph and inserts blank space between the two paragraphs. Depending on your settings, Office may or may not insert a blank space between the two paragraphs.

Figure 31

Document Properties

You can organize and identify your files by using **document properties**, which are the details about a file, such as the project author, title, and subject. For example, a class name or document topic can describe the file's purpose or content.

CONSIDER THIS

Why would you want to assign document properties to a document?

Document properties are valuable for a variety of reasons:

- Users can save time locating a particular file because they can view a file's document properties without opening the file.

- By creating consistent properties for files having similar content, users can better organize their files.

- Some organizations require users to add document properties so that other employees can view details about these files.

To Change Document Properties

1 SIGN IN | 2 USE WINDOWS | 3 USE APPS | 4 FILE MANAGEMENT | 5 SWITCH APPS | 6 SAVE FILES
7 CHANGE SCREEN RESOLUTION | 8 EXIT APPS | 9 USE ADDITIONAL APPS | 10 USE HELP

You can change the document properties while working with the file in an Office app. When you save the file, the Office app (Word, in this case) will save the document properties with the file. The following steps change document properties. *Why? Adding document properties will help you identify characteristics of the file without opening it.*

①

- Click File on the ribbon to open the Backstage view and then, if necessary, click the Info tab in the Backstage view to display the Info gallery.
- Click to the right of the Comments property in the Properties list, and type `CIS 101 Assignment` in the text box (Figure 32).

Q&A
What is the Backstage view?
The **Backstage view** contains a set of commands that enable you to manage documents and provides data about the documents.

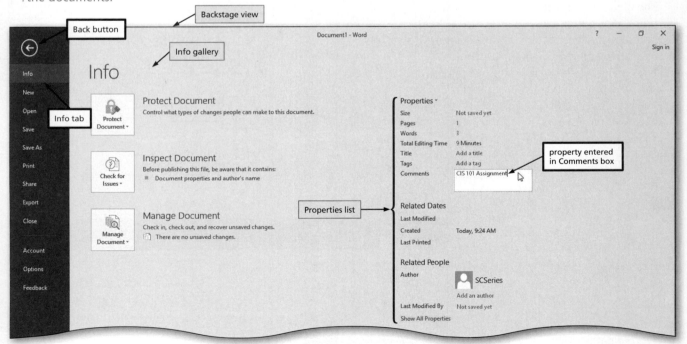

Figure 32

②

- Click the Back button in the upper-left corner of the Backstage view to return to the document window.

Printing, Saving, and Organizing Files

BTW
File Type
Depending on your Windows settings, the file type .docx may be displayed immediately to the right of the file name after you save the file. The file type .docx is a Word 2016 document.

While you are creating a document, the computer or mobile device stores it in memory. When you save a document, the computer or mobile device places it on a storage medium, such as a hard disk, solid state drive (SSD), USB flash drive, or optical disc. The storage medium can be permanent in your computer, may be portable where you remove it from your computer, or may be on a web server you access through a network or the Internet.

A saved document is referred to as a file. A **file name** is the name assigned to a file when it is saved. When saving files, you should organize them so that you easily can find them later. Windows provides tools to help you organize files.

Printing a Document

After creating a document, you may want to print it. Printing a document enables you to distribute it to others in a form that can be read or viewed but typically not edited.

CONSIDER THIS

What is the best method for distributing a document?
The traditional method of distributing a document uses a printer to produce a hard copy. A **hard copy** or **printout** is information that exists on a physical medium, such as paper. Hard copies can be useful for the following reasons:

• Some people prefer proofreading a hard copy of a document rather than viewing it on the screen to check for errors and readability.

• Hard copies can serve as a backup reference if your storage medium is lost or becomes corrupted and you need to recreate the document

Instead of distributing a hard copy of a document, users can distribute the document as an electronic image that mirrors the original document's appearance. The electronic image of the document can be sent as an email attachment, posted on a website, or copied to a portable storage medium, such as a USB flash drive. Two popular electronic image formats, sometimes called fixed formats, are PDF by Adobe Systems and XPS by Microsoft. In Word, you can create electronic image files through the Save As dialog box and the Export, Share, and Print tabs in the Backstage view. Electronic images of documents, such as PDF and XPS, can be useful for the following reasons:

• Users can view electronic images of documents without the software that created the original document (e.g., Word). For example, to view a PDF file you use a program called Adobe Reader, which can be downloaded free from Adobe's website.

• Sending electronic documents saves paper and printer supplies. Society encourages users to contribute to **green computing**, which involves reducing the electricity consumed and environmental waste generated when using computers, mobile devices, and related technologies.

To Print a Document

1 SIGN IN | 2 USE WINDOWS | 3 USE APPS | 4 FILE MANAGEMENT | 5 SWITCH APPS | 6 SAVE FILES
7 CHANGE SCREEN RESOLUTION | 8 EXIT APPS | 9 USE ADDITIONAL APPS | 10 USE HELP

With the document opened, you may want to print it. *Why? Because you want to see how the text will appear on paper, you want to print a hard copy on a printer.* The following steps print a hard copy of the contents of the document.

• Click File on the ribbon to open the Backstage view.
• Click the Print tab in the Backstage view to display the Print gallery (Figure 33).

Q&A How can I print multiple copies of my document?
Increase the number in the Copies box in the Print gallery.

What if I decide not to print the document at this time?
Click the Back button in the upper-left corner of the Backstage view to return to the document window.

②

- Verify that the selected printer will print a hard copy of the document. If necessary, click the Printer Status button to display a list of available printer options and then click the desired printer to change the currently selected printer.

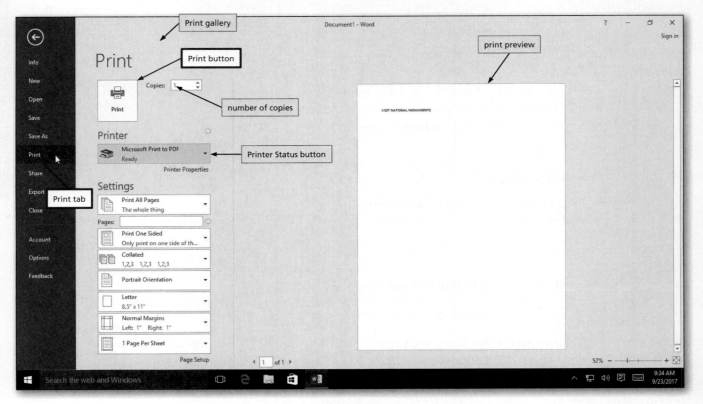

Figure 33

③

- Click the Print button in the Print gallery to print the document on the currently selected printer.
- When the printer stops, retrieve the hard copy (Figure 34).

Q&A

What if I want to print an electronic image of a document instead of a hard copy?

You would click the Printer Status button in the Print gallery and then select the desired electronic image option, such as Microsoft XPS Document Writer, which would create an XPS file.

Figure 34

Other Ways

1. Press CTRL+P

Organizing Files and Folders

A file contains data. This data can range from a research paper to an accounting spreadsheet to an electronic math quiz. You should organize and store files in folders to avoid misplacing a file and to help you find a file quickly.

If you are taking an introductory computer class (CIS 101, for example), you may want to design a series of folders for the different subjects covered in the class. To accomplish this, you can arrange the folders in a hierarchy for the class, as shown in Figure 35.

Figure 35

The hierarchy contains three levels. The first level contains the storage medium, such as a hard drive. The second level contains the class folder (CIS 101, in this case), and the third level contains seven folders, one each for a different Office app that will be covered in the class (Word, PowerPoint, Excel, Access, Outlook, Publisher, and OneNote).

When the hierarchy in Figure 35 is created, the storage medium is said to contain the CIS 101 folder, and the CIS 101 folder is said to contain the separate Office folders (i.e., Word, PowerPoint, Excel, etc.). In addition, this hierarchy easily can be expanded to include folders from other classes taken during additional semesters.

The vertical and horizontal lines in Figure 35 form a pathway that allows you to navigate to a drive or folder on a computer or network. A **path** consists of a drive letter (preceded by a drive name when necessary) and colon, to identify the storage device, and one or more folder names. A hard disk typically has a drive letter of C. Each drive or folder in the hierarchy has a corresponding path.

By default, Windows saves documents in the Documents folder, music in the Music folder, photos in the Pictures folder, videos in the Videos folder, and downloads in the Downloads folder.

The following pages illustrate the steps to organize the folders for this class and save a file in one of those folders:

1. Create the folder identifying your class.
2. Create the Word folder in the folder identifying your class.
3. Create the remaining folders in the folder identifying your class (one each for PowerPoint, Excel, Access, Outlook, Publisher, and OneNote).
4. Save a file in the Word folder.
5. Verify the location of the saved file.

To Create a Folder

When you create a folder, such as the CIS 101 folder shown in Figure 35, you must name the folder. A folder name should describe the folder and its contents. A folder name can contain spaces and any uppercase or lowercase characters, except a backslash (\), slash (/), colon (:), asterisk (*), question mark (?), quotation marks ("), less than symbol (<), greater than symbol (>), or vertical bar (|). Folder names cannot be CON, AUX, COM1, COM2, COM3, COM4, LPT1, LPT2, LPT3, PRN, or NUL. The same rules for naming folders also apply to naming files.

The following steps create a class folder (CIS 101, in this case) in the Documents folder. *Why? When storing files, you should organize the files so that it will be easier to find them later.*

- Click the File Explorer button on the taskbar to run the File Explorer.
- If necessary, double-click This PC in the navigation pane to expand the contents of your computer.
- Click the Documents folder in the navigation pane to display the contents of the Documents folder in the file list (Figure 36).

Figure 36

- Click the New folder button on the Quick Access Toolbar to create a new folder with the name, New folder, selected in a text box (Figure 37).

Q&A

Why is the folder icon displayed differently on my computer or mobile device?
Windows might be configured to display contents differently on your computer or mobile device.

Figure 37

③

- Type **CIS 101** (or your class code) in the text box as the new folder name.
- If requested by your instructor, add your last name to the end of the folder name.
- Press the ENTER key to change the folder name from New folder to a folder name identifying your class (Figure 38).

Q&A What happens when I press the ENTER key?

The class folder (CIS 101, in this case) is displayed in the file list, which contains the folder name, date modified, type, and size.

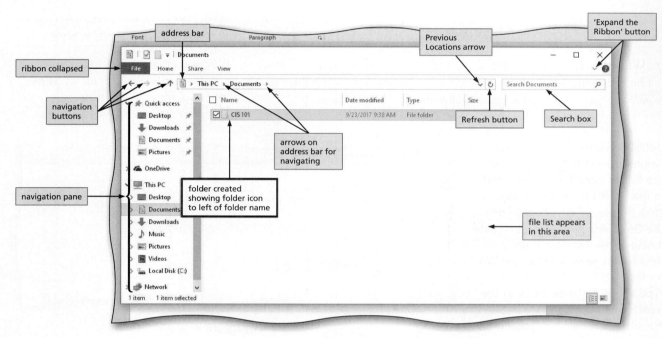

Figure 38

Other Ways

1. Press CTRL+SHIFT+N
2. Click the New folder button (Home tab | New group)

Folder Windows

The File Explorer window (shown in Figure 38) is called a folder window. Recall that a folder is a specific named location on a storage medium that contains related files. Most users rely on **folder windows** for finding, viewing, and managing information on their computers. Folder windows have common design elements, including the following (shown in Figure 38).

- The **address bar** provides quick navigation options. The arrows on the address bar allow you to visit different locations on the computer or mobile device.
- The buttons to the left of the address bar allow you to navigate the contents of the navigation pane and view recent pages.
- The **Previous Locations arrow** displays the locations you have visited.
- The **Refresh button** on the right side of the address bar refreshes the contents of the folder list.
- The **Search box** contains the dimmed words, Search Documents. You can type a term in the search box for a list of files, folders, shortcuts, and elements containing that term within the location you are searching.

- The **ribbon** contains four tabs used to accomplish various tasks on the computer related to organizing and managing the contents of the open window. This ribbon works similarly to the ribbon in the Office apps.
- The **navigation pane** on the left contains the Quick access area, the OneDrive area, the This PC area, and the Network area.
- The **Quick Access area** shows locations you access frequently. By default, this list contains links only to your Desktop, Downloads, Documents, and Pictures.

To Create a Folder within a Folder

1 SIGN IN | 2 USE WINDOWS | 3 USE APPS | 4 FILE MANAGEMENT | 5 SWITCH APPS | 6 SAVE FILES
7 CHANGE SCREEN RESOLUTION | 8 EXIT APPS | 9 USE ADDITIONAL APPS | 10 USE HELP

With the class folder created, you can create folders that will store the files you create using each Office app. The following step creates a Word folder in the CIS 101 folder (or the folder identifying your class). *Why? To be able to organize your files, you should create a folder structure.*

- Double-click the icon or folder name for the CIS 101 folder (or the folder identifying your class) in the file list to open the folder.
- Click the New folder button on the Quick Access Toolbar to create a new folder with the name, New folder, selected in a text box folder.
- Type Word in the text box as the new folder name.
- Press the ENTER key to rename the folder (Figure 39).

Figure 39

Other Ways
1. Press CTRL+SHIFT+N
2. Click the New folder button (Home tab | New group)

To Create the Remaining Folders

The following steps create the remaining folders in the folder identifying your class (in this case, CIS 101).

1 Click the New folder button on the Quick Access Toolbar to create a new folder with the name, New folder, selected in a text box.

2 Type **PowerPoint** in the text box as the new folder name.

3 Press the ENTER key to rename the folder.

4 Repeat Steps 1 through 3 to create each of the remaining folders, using Excel, Access, Outlook, Publisher, and OneNote as the folder names (Figure 40).

Figure 40

To Expand a Folder, Scroll through Folder Contents, and Collapse a Folder

Folder windows display the hierarchy of items and the contents of drives and folders in the file list. You might want to expand a folder in the navigation pane to view its contents, scroll through its contents, and collapse it when you are finished viewing its contents. *Why? When a folder is expanded, you can see all the folders it contains. By contrast, a collapsed folder hides the folders it contains.* The following steps expand, scroll through, and then collapse the folder identifying your class (CIS 101, in this case).

1

- Double-click the Documents folder in the This PC area of the navigation pane, which expands the folder to display its contents and displays a black arrow to the left of the Documents folder icon (Figure 41).

Figure 41

2

- Double-click the CIS 101 folder, which expands the folder to display its contents and displays a black arrow to the left of the folder icon (Figure 42).

Experiment

- Drag the scroll box down or click the down scroll arrow on the vertical scroll bar to display additional folders at the bottom of the navigation pane. Drag the scroll box up or click the scroll bar above the scroll box to move the scroll box to the top of the navigation pane. Drag the scroll box down the scroll bar until the scroll box is halfway down the scroll bar.

Figure 42

3

• Double-click the folder identifying your class (CIS 101, in this case) to collapse the folder (Figure 43).

Q&A Why are some folders indented below others?

A folder contains the indented folders below it.

Figure 43

Other Ways

1. Point to display arrows in navigation pane, click arrow to expand or collapse

2. Select folder to expand or collapse using arrow keys, press RIGHT ARROW to expand; press LEFT ARROW to collapse

To Switch from One App to Another

1 SIGN IN | 2 USE WINDOWS | 3 USE APPS | 4 FILE MANAGEMENT | 5 SWITCH APPS | 6 SAVE FILES
7 CHANGE SCREEN RESOLUTION | 8 EXIT APPS | 9 USE ADDITIONAL APPS | 10 USE HELP

The next step is to save the Word file containing the headline you typed earlier. Word, however, currently is not the active window. You can use the button on the taskbar and live preview to switch to Word and then save the document in the Word document window.

Why? *By clicking the appropriate app button on the taskbar, you can switch to the open app you want to use.* The steps below switch to the Word window; however, the steps are the same for any active Office app currently displayed as a button on the taskbar.

1

• Point to the Word app button on the taskbar to see a live preview of the open document(s) or the window title(s) of the open document(s), depending on your computer's configuration (Figure 44).

Q&A What if I am using a touch screen?

Live preview will not work if you are using a touch screen. If you are using a touch screen and do not have a mouse, proceed to Step 2.

Figure 44

2

- Click the button or the live preview to make the app associated with the app button the active window (Figure 45).

Q&A What if multiple documents are open in an app?
Click the desired live preview to switch to the window you want to use.

Figure 45

Other Ways

1. Press ALT+TAB until app you wish to display is selected

To Save a File in a Folder

1 SIGN IN | 2 USE WINDOWS | 3 USE APPS | 4 FILE MANAGEMENT | 5 SWITCH APPS | 6 SAVE FILES
7 CHANGE SCREEN RESOLUTION | 8 EXIT APPS | 9 USE ADDITIONAL APPS | 10 USE HELP

With the folders for storing your files created, you can save the Word document. *Why? Without saving a file, you may lose all the work you have done and will be unable to reuse or share it with others later.* The following steps save a file in the Word folder contained in your class folder (CIS 101, in this case) using the file name, National Monuments.

1

- Click the Save button (shown in Figure 45) on the Quick Access Toolbar, which depending on settings, will display either the Save As gallery in the Backstage view (Figure 46) or the Save As dialog box (Figure 47).

Q&A What if the Save As gallery is not displayed in the Backstage view?
Click the Save As tab to display the Save As gallery.

How do I close the Backstage view?
Click the Back button in the upper-left corner of the Backstage view to return to the app window.

Figure 46

- If your screen displays the Backstage view, click This PC, if necessary, to display options in the right pane related to saving on your computer or mobile device; if your screen already displays the Save As dialog box, proceed to Step 3.

Q&A What if I wanted to save on OneDrive instead?
You would click OneDrive. Saving on OneDrive is discussed in a later section in this module.

- Click the Browse button in the left pane to display the Save As dialog box (Figure 47).

Q&A Why does a file name already appear in the File name box?
Word automatically suggests a file name the first time you save a document. The file name normally consists of the first few words contained in the document. Because the suggested file name is selected, you do not need to delete it; as soon as you begin typing, the new file name replaces the selected text.

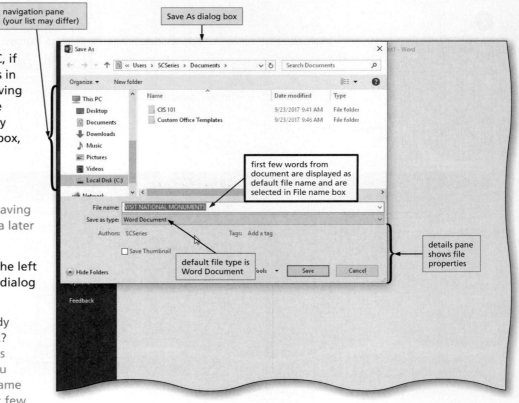

navigation pane (your list may differ)

Save As dialog box

first few words from document are displayed as default file name and are selected in File name box

default file type is Word Document

details pane shows file properties

Figure 47

- Type **National Monuments** in the File name box (Save As dialog box) to change the file name. Do not press the ENTER key after typing the file name because you do not want to close the dialog box at this time (Figure 48).

Q&A What characters can I use in a file name?
The only invalid characters are the backslash (\), slash (/), colon (:), asterisk (*), question mark (?), quotation mark ("), less than symbol (<), greater than symbol (>), and vertical bar (|).

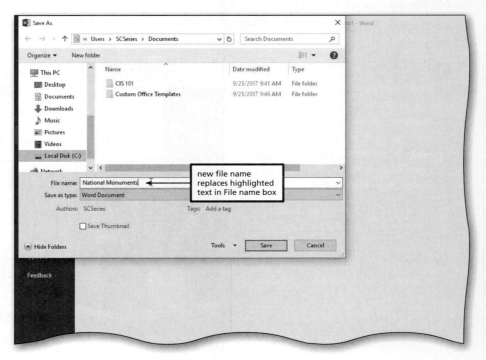

new file name replaces highlighted text in File name box

Figure 48

4

- Navigate to the desired save location (in this case, the Word folder in the CIS 101 folder [or your class folder] in the Documents folder) by performing the tasks in Steps 4a and 4b.

4a

- If the Documents folder is not displayed in the navigation pane, drag the scroll bar in the navigation pane until Documents appears.

- If the Documents folder is not expanded in the navigation pane, double-click Documents to display its folders in the navigation pane.

- If your class folder (CIS 101, in this case) is not expanded, double-click the CIS 101 folder to select the folder and display its contents in the navigation pane (Figure 49).

Figure 49

Q&A What if I do not want to save in a folder?

Although storing files in folders is an effective technique for organizing files, some users prefer not to store files in folders. If you prefer not to save this file in a folder, select the storage device on which you wish to save the file and then proceed to Step 5.

4b

- Click the Word folder in the navigation pane to select it as the new save location and display its contents in the file list (Figure 50).

Figure 50

5

- Click the Save button (Save As dialog box) to save the document in the selected folder in the selected location with the entered file name (Figure 51).

Q&A How do I know that the file is saved?
While an Office app is saving a file, it briefly displays a message on the status bar indicating the amount of the file saved. In addition, the file name appears on the title bar.

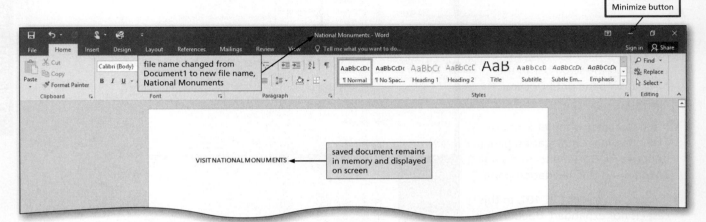

Figure 51

Other Ways

1. Click File on ribbon, click Save As in Backstage view, click This PC, click Browse button, type file name (Save As dialog box), navigate to desired save location, click Save button
2. Press F12, type file name (Save As dialog box), navigate to desired save location, click Save button

CONSIDER THIS

How often should you save a document?
It is important to save a document frequently for the following reasons:

- The document in memory might be lost if the computer is turned off or you lose electrical power while an app is running.
- If you run out of time before completing a project, you may finish it at a future time without starting over.

Navigating in Dialog Boxes

Navigating is the process of finding a location on a storage device. While saving the National Monuments file, for example, Steps 4a and 4b navigated to the Word folder located in the CIS 101 folder in the Documents folder. When performing certain functions in Windows apps, such as saving a file, opening a file, or inserting a picture in an existing document, you most likely will have to navigate to the location where you want to save the file or to the folder containing the file you want to open or insert. Most dialog boxes in Windows apps requiring navigation follow a similar procedure; that is, the way you navigate to a folder in one dialog box, such as the Save As dialog box, is similar to how you might navigate in another dialog box, such as the Open dialog box. If you chose to navigate to a specific location in a dialog box, you would follow the instructions in Steps 4a and 4b.

1 SIGN IN | 2 USE WINDOWS | 3 USE APPS | 4 FILE MANAGEMENT | 5 SWITCH APPS | 6 SAVE FILES
7 CHANGE SCREEN RESOLUTION | 8 EXIT APPS | 9 USE ADDITIONAL APPS | 10 USE HELP

To Minimize and Restore a Window

Before continuing, you can verify that the Word file was saved properly. To do this, you will minimize the Word window and then open the CIS 101 window so that you can verify the file is stored in the CIS 101 folder on the hard drive. A **minimized window** is an open window that is hidden from view but can be displayed quickly by clicking the window's button on the taskbar.

In the following example, Word is used to illustrate minimizing and restoring windows; however, you would follow the same steps regardless of the Office app you are using. *Why? Before closing an app, you should make sure your file saved correctly so that you can find it later.*

The following steps minimize the Word window, verify that the file is saved, and then restore the minimized window.

- Click the Minimize button on the app's title bar (shown in Figure 51) to minimize the window (Figure 52).

Q&A Is the minimized window still available?
The minimized window, Word in this case, remains available but no longer is the active window. It is minimized as a button on the taskbar.

- If the File Explorer window is not open on the screen, click the File Explorer button on the taskbar to make the File Explorer window the active window.

Figure 52

- Double-click the Word folder in the file list to select the folder and display its contents (Figure 53).

Q&A Why does the File Explorer button on the taskbar change?
A selected app button indicates that the app is active on the screen. When the button is not selected, the app is running but not active.

- After viewing the contents of the selected folder, click the Word button on the taskbar to restore the minimized window (as shown in Figure 51).

Figure 53

Other Ways

1. Right-click title bar, click Minimize on shortcut menu, click taskbar button in taskbar button area
2. Press WINDOWS+M, press WINDOWS+SHIFT+M
3. Click Word app button on taskbar to minimize window. Click Word app button again to restore window.

To Save a File on OneDrive

1 SIGN IN | 2 USE WINDOWS | 3 USE APPS | 4 FILE MANAGEMENT | 5 SWITCH APPS | 6 SAVE FILES
7 CHANGE SCREEN RESOLUTION | 8 EXIT APPS | 9 USE ADDITIONAL APPS | 10 USE HELP

One of the features of Office is the capability to save files on OneDrive so that you can use the files on multiple computers or mobile devices without having to use an external storage device, such as a USB flash drive. Storing files on OneDrive also enables you to share files more efficiently with others, such as when using Office Online and Office 365.

In the following example, Word is used to save a file on OneDrive. *Why? Storing files on OneDrive provides more portability options than are available from storing files in the Documents folder.*

You can save files directly on OneDrive from within an Office app. The following steps save the current Word file on OneDrive. These steps require you have a Microsoft account and an Internet connection.

- Click File on the ribbon to open the Backstage view.

Q&A What is the purpose of the File tab?
The File tab opens the Backstage view for each Office app.

- Click the Save As tab in the Backstage view to display the Save As gallery.
- Click OneDrive to display OneDrive saving options or a Sign In button, if you are not signed in already to your Microsoft account (Figure 54).

Figure 54

- If your screen displays a Sign In button (shown in Figure 54), click it to display the Sign in dialog box (Figure 55).

Q&A What if the Sign In button does not appear?
If you already are signed into your Microsoft account, the Sign In button will not be displayed. In this case, proceed to Step 3.

- Follow the instructions on the screen to sign in to your Microsoft account.

Figure 55

3

- If necessary, click OneDrive in the left pane.
- In the Backstage view, click the Documents folder in the right pane to display the Save As dialog box (Figure 56).

4

- Click the Save button (Save As dialog box) to save the file on OneDrive.

Figure 56

To Sign Out of a Microsoft Account

If you are using a public computer or otherwise wish to sign out of your Microsoft account, you should sign out of the account from the Accounts gallery in the Backstage view. Signing out of the account is the safest way to make sure that nobody else can access online files or settings stored in your Microsoft account. *Why? For security reasons, you should sign out of your Microsoft account when you are finished using a public or shared computer. Staying signed in to your Microsoft account might enable others to access your files.*

The following steps sign out of a Microsoft account from Word. You would use the same steps in any Office app. If you do not wish to sign out of your Microsoft account, read these steps without performing them.

1 Click File on the ribbon to open the Backstage view.

2 Click the Account tab to display the Account gallery (Figure 57).

3 Click the Sign out link, which displays the Remove Account dialog box. If a Can't remove Windows accounts dialog box appears instead of the Remove Account dialog box, click the OK button and skip the remaining steps.

Q&A Why does a Can't remove Windows accounts dialog box appear?
If you signed in to Windows using your Microsoft account, then you also must sign out from Windows, rather than signing out from within Word. When you are finished using Windows, be sure to sign out at that time.

4 Click the Yes button (Remove Account dialog box) to sign out of your Microsoft account on this computer.

Q&A Should I sign out of Windows after removing my Microsoft account?
When you are finished using the computer, you should sign out of Windows for maximum security.

5 Click the Back button in the upper-left corner of the Backstage view to return to the document.

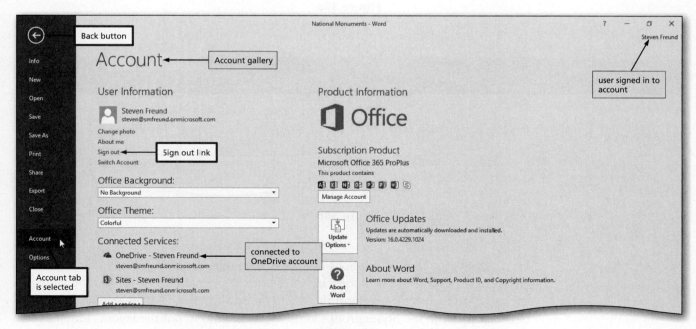

Figure 57

Screen Resolution

Screen resolution indicates the number of pixels (dots) that the computer uses to display the letters, numbers, graphics, and background you see on the screen. When you increase the screen resolution, Windows displays more information on the screen, but the information decreases in size. The reverse also is true: as you decrease the screen resolution, Windows displays less information on the screen, but the information increases in size.

Screen resolution usually is stated as the product of two numbers, such as 1366 × 768 (pronounced "thirteen sixty-six by seven sixty-eight"). A 1366 × 768 screen resolution results in a display of 1366 distinct pixels on each of 768 lines, or about 1,050,624 pixels. Changing the screen resolution affects how the ribbon appears in Office apps and some Windows dialog boxes. Figure 58 shows the Word ribbon at screen resolutions of 1366 × 768 and 1024 × 768. All of the same commands are available regardless of screen resolution. The app (Word, in this case), however, makes changes to the groups and the buttons within the groups to accommodate the various screen resolutions. The result is that certain commands may need to be accessed differently depending on the resolution chosen. A command that is visible on the ribbon and available by clicking a button at one resolution may not be visible and may need to be accessed using its Dialog Box Launcher at a different resolution.

Figure 58a

Figure 58b

Comparing the two ribbons in Figure 58, notice the changes in content and layout of the groups and galleries. In some cases, the content of a group is the same in each resolution, but the layout of the group differs. For example, the same gallery and buttons appear in the Styles groups in the two resolutions, but the layouts differ. In other cases, the content and layout are the same across the resolution, but the level of detail differs with the resolution.

To Change the Screen Resolution

If you are using a computer to step through the modules in this book and you want your screen to match the figures, you may need to change your screen's resolution. *Why? The figures in this book use a screen resolution of 1366 × 768.* The following steps change the screen resolution to 1366 × 768. Your computer already may be set to 1366 × 768. Keep in mind that many computer labs prevent users from changing the screen resolution; in that case, read the following steps for illustration purposes.

1

- Click the Show desktop button, which is located at the far-right edge of the taskbar, to display the Windows desktop.

- Right-click an empty area on the Windows desktop to display a shortcut menu that contains a list of commands related to the desktop (Figure 59).

Q&A Why does my shortcut menu display different commands?
Depending on your computer's hardware and configuration, different commands might appear on the shortcut menu.

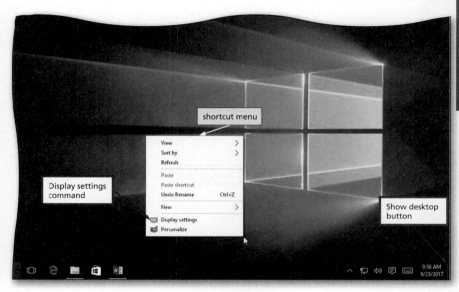

Figure 59

2

- Click Display settings on the shortcut menu to open the Settings app window. If necessary, scroll to display the 'Advanced display settings' link (Figure 60).

Figure 60

3

- Click 'Advanced display settings' in the Settings window to display the advanced display settings.
- If necessary, scroll to display the Resolution box (Figure 61).

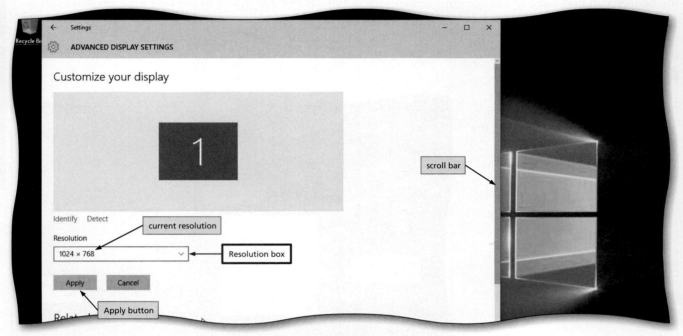

Figure 61

4

- Click the Resolution box to display a list of available screen resolutions (Figure 62).
- If necessary, scroll to and then click 1366 × 768 to select the screen resolution.

Q&A

What if my computer does not support the 1366 × 768 resolution? Some computers do not support the 1366 × 768 resolution. In this case, select a resolution that is close to the 1366 × 768 resolution.

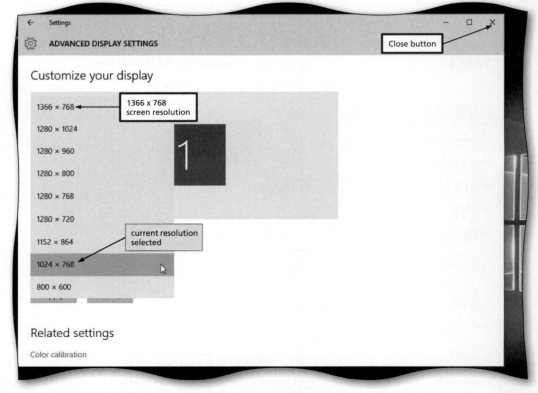

Figure 62

5

- Click the Apply button (Advanced Display Settings window) (shown in Figure 61) to change the screen resolution and display a confirmation message (Figure 63).
- Click the Keep changes button to accept the new screen resolution.
- Click the Close button (shown in Figure 62) to close the Settings app window.

Figure 63

Other Ways

1. Click Start button, click Settings, click System, click Display, click 'Advanced display settings,' select desired resolution in Resolution box, click Apply button, click Keep changes button

2. Type **screen resolution** in search box, click 'Change the screen resolution,' select desired resolution in Resolution box, click Apply, click Keep changes

To Exit an Office App with One Document Open

1 SIGN IN | 2 USE WINDOWS | 3 USE APPS | 4 FILE MANAGEMENT | 5 SWITCH APPS | 6 SAVE FILES
7 CHANGE SCREEN RESOLUTION | 8 EXIT APPS | 9 USE ADDITIONAL APPS | 10 USE HELP

When you exit an Office app, such as Word, if you have made changes to a file since the last time the file was saved, the Office app displays a dialog box asking if you want to save the changes you made to the file before it closes the app window. *Why? The dialog box contains three buttons with these resulting actions: the Save button saves the changes and then exits the Office app, the Don't Save button exits the Office app without saving changes, and the Cancel button closes the dialog box and redisplays the file without saving the changes.*

If no changes have been made to an open document since the last time the file was saved, the Office app will close the window without displaying a dialog box.

The following steps exit an Office app. In the following example, Word is used to illustrate exiting an Office app; however, you would follow the same steps regardless of the Office app you were using.

1

- If necessary, click the Word app button on the taskbar to display the Word window on the desktop (Figure 64).

Figure 64

- Click the Close button to close the document and exit Word. If a Microsoft Word dialog box appears, click the Save button to save any changes made to the document since the last save.

Q&A What if I have more than one document open in an Office app?
You could click the Close button for each open document. When you click the last open document's Close button, you also exit the Office app. As an alternative that is more efficient, you could right-click the app button on the taskbar and then click 'Close all windows' on the shortcut menu, or press ALT+F4 to close all open documents and exit the Office app.

Other Ways

1. Right-click the Office app button on Windows taskbar, click Close window on shortcut menu
2. Press ALT+F4

To Copy a Folder to OneDrive

1 SIGN IN | 2 USE WINDOWS | 3 USE APPS | **4 FILE MANAGEMENT** | 5 SWITCH APPS | 6 SAVE FILES
7 CHANGE SCREEN RESOLUTION | 8 EXIT APPS | **9 USE ADDITIONAL APPS** | **10 USE HELP**

To back up your files or easily make them available on another computer or mobile device, you can copy them to OneDrive. The following steps copy your CIS 101 folder to OneDrive. If you do not have access to a OneDrive account, read the following steps without performing them. *Why? It often is good practice to have a backup of your files so that they are available in case something happens to your original copies.*

- Click the File Explorer button on the taskbar to make the folder window the active window.
- Click Documents in the This PC area of the navigation pane to display the CIS 101 folder in the file list.

Q&A What if my CIS 101 folder is stored in a different location?
Use the navigation pane to navigate to the location of your CIS 101 folder. The CIS 101 folder should be displayed in the file list once you have located it.

- Click the CIS 101 folder in the file list to select it (Figure 65).

Figure 65

- Click Home on the ribbon to display the Home tab.
- Click the Copy to button (Home tab | Organize group) to display the Copy to menu (Figure 66).

Figure 66

❸

- Click Choose location on the Copy to menu to display the Copy Items dialog box.
- Click OneDrive (Copy Items dialog box) to select it (Figure 67).

Figure 67

❹

- Click the Copy button (Copy Items dialog box) to copy the selected folder to OneDrive.
- Click OneDrive in the navigation pane to verify the CIS 101 folder displays in the file list (Figure 68).

Q&A
Why does a Microsoft OneDrive dialog box display when I click OneDrive in the navigation pane?
If you are not currently signed in to Windows using a Microsoft account, you will manually need to sign in to a Microsoft account to save files to OneDrive. Follow the instructions on the screen to sign in to your Microsoft account.

Figure 68

Other Ways

1. In File Explorer, select folder to copy, click Copy button (Home tab | Clipboard group), display contents of OneDrive in file list, click Paste button (Home tab | Clipboard group)

2. In File Explorer, select folder to copy, press CTRL+C, display contents of OneDrive in file list, press CTRL+V

3. Drag folder to copy to OneDrive in navigation pane

To Unlink a OneDrive Account

If you are using a public computer and are not signed in to Windows with a Microsoft account, you should unlink your OneDrive account so that other users cannot access it. *Why? If you do not unlink your OneDrive account, other people using the same user account on the computer will be able to view, remove, and add to files stored in your OneDrive account.*

The following steps unlink your OneDrive account. If you do not wish to sign out of your Microsoft account, read these steps without performing them.

①

• Click the 'Show hidden icons' button on the Windows taskbar to show a menu of hidden icons (Figure 69).

Figure 69

②

• Right click the OneDrive icon (shown in Figure 69) to display a shortcut menu (Figure 70).

Figure 70

❸

- Click Settings on the shortcut menu to display the Microsoft OneDrive dialog box (Figure 71).

Figure 71

❹

- If necessary, click the Settings tab.
- Click the Unlink OneDrive button (Microsoft OneDrive dialog box) to unlink the OneDrive account (Figure 72).
- When the Microsoft OneDrive dialog box appears with a Welcome to OneDrive message, click the Close button.
- Minimize the File Explorer window.

Figure 72

Break Point: If you wish to take a break, this is a good place to do so. To resume at a later time, continue to follow the steps from this location forward.

Additional Microsoft Office Apps

The previous section used Word to illustrate common features of Office and some basic elements unique to Word. The following sections present elements unique to PowerPoint, Excel, and Access, as well as illustrate additional common features of Office.

In the following pages, you will learn how to do the following:

1. Run an Office app (PowerPoint) using the search box.
2. Create two small documents in the same Office app (PowerPoint).
3. Close one of the documents.
4. Reopen the document just closed.
5. Create a document in a different Office app (Excel).
6. Save the document with a new file name.
7. Create a file in a different Office app (Access).
8. Close the file and then open the file.

PowerPoint

PowerPoint is a full-featured presentation app that allows you to produce compelling presentations to deliver and share with an audience (Figure 73). A PowerPoint **presentation** also is called a **slide show**. PowerPoint contains many features to design, develop, and organize slides, including formatting text, adding and editing video and audio clips, creating tables and charts, applying artistic effects to pictures, animating graphics, and collaborating with friends and colleagues. You then can turn your presentation into a video, broadcast your slide show on the web, or create a photo album.

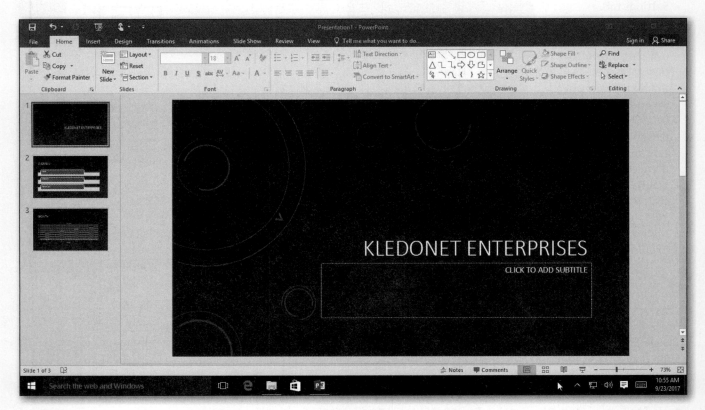

Figure 73

To Run an App Using the Search Box

The following steps, which assume Windows is running, use the search box to run the PowerPoint app based on a typical installation; however, you would follow similar steps to run any Office app. *Why? Some people prefer to use the search box to locate and run an app, as opposed to searching through a list of all apps on the Start menu.* You may need to ask your instructor how to run apps for your computer.

- Type **PowerPoint 2016** as the search text in the search box and watch the search results appear in the search results (Figure 74).

Q&A

Do I need to type the complete app name or use correct capitalization?

No, you need to type just enough characters of the app name for it to appear in the search results. For example, you may be able to type PowerPoint or powerpoint, instead of PowerPoint 2016.

2

- Click the app name, PowerPoint 2016 in this case, in the search results to run PowerPoint (Figure 75).

Figure 74

Figure 75

3
- Click the Blank Presentation thumbnail to create a blank presentation and display it in the PowerPoint window.
- If the app window is not maximized, click the Maximize button on its title bar to maximize the window (Figure 76).

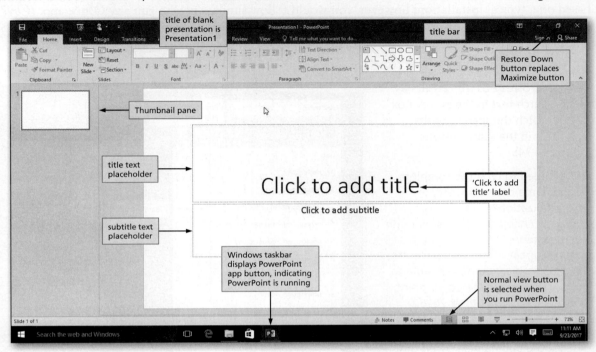

Figure 76

The PowerPoint Window and Ribbon

The PowerPoint window consists of a variety of components to make your work more efficient and documents more professional: the window, ribbon, mini toolbar, shortcut menus, Quick Access Toolbar, and Microsoft Account area. Many of these components are common to other Office apps and have been discussed earlier in this module. Other components, discussed in the following paragraphs and later in subsequent modules, are unique to PowerPoint.

The basic unit of a PowerPoint presentation is a **slide**. A slide may contain text and objects, such as graphics, tables, charts, and drawings. **Layouts** are used to position this content on the slide. When you create a new presentation, the default **Title Slide** layout appears (shown in Figure 76). The purpose of this layout is to introduce the presentation to the audience. PowerPoint includes several other built-in standard layouts.

The default slide layouts are set up in **landscape orientation**, where the slide width is greater than its height. In landscape orientation, the slide size is preset to 13.3 inches wide and 7.5 inches high when printed on a standard sheet of paper measuring 11 inches wide and 8.5 inches high.

Placeholders   **Placeholders** are boxes with dashed or solid borders that are displayed when you create a new slide. All layouts except the Blank slide layout contain placeholders. Depending on the particular slide layout selected, title and subtitle placeholders are displayed for the slide title and subtitle; a content placeholder is displayed for text or a table, chart, picture, graphic, or movie. The title slide in Figure 76 has two text placeholders for the main heading, or title, and the subtitle.

Ribbon   The ribbon in PowerPoint is similar to the one in Word and the other Microsoft Office apps. When you run PowerPoint, the ribbon displays nine main tabs: File, Home, Insert, Design, Transitions, Animations, Slide Show, Review, and View.

To Enter Content in a Title Slide

With the exception of a blank slide, PowerPoint assumes every new slide has a title. Many of PowerPoint's layouts have both a title text placeholder and at least one content placeholder. To make creating a presentation easier, any text you type after a new slide appears becomes title text in the title text placeholder. As you begin typing text in the title text placeholder, the title text also is displayed in the Slide 1 thumbnail in the Thumbnail pane. The title for this presentation is Mara's Marbles. The following step enters a presentation title on the title slide. *Why? In general, every presentation should have a title to describe what the presentation will be covering.*

1
- Click the 'Click to add title' label located inside the title text placeholder (shown in Figure 76) to select the placeholder.
- Type **Mara's Marbles** in the title text placeholder. Do not press the ENTER key because you do not want to create a new line of text (Figure 77).

Figure 77

To Save a File in a Folder

The following steps save the presentation in the PowerPoint folder in the class folder (CIS 101, in this case) in the Documents folder using the file name, Mara's Marbles.

1 Click the Save button on the Quick Access Toolbar (shown in Figure 77), which depending on settings will display either the Save As gallery in the Backstage view or the Save As dialog box.

2 If your screen displays the Backstage view, click This PC, if necessary, to display options in the right pane related to saving on your computer; if your screen already displays the Save As dialog box, proceed to Step 4.

3 Click the Browse button in the left pane to display the Save As dialog box.

4 If necessary, type **Mara's Marbles** in the File name box (Save As dialog box) to change the file name. Do not press the ENTER key after typing the file name because you do not want to close the dialog box at this time.

5 Navigate to the desired save location (in this case, the PowerPoint folder in the CIS 101 folder [or your class folder] in the Documents folder). For specific instructions, perform the tasks in Steps 5a through 5e.

5a If the Documents folder is not displayed in the navigation pane, slide to scroll or drag the scroll bar in the navigation pane until Documents appears.

5b If the Documents folder is not expanded in the navigation pane, double-click Documents to display its folders in the navigation pane.

5c If the Documents folder is not expanded in the navigation pane, double-click Documents to display its folders in the navigation pane.

5d If your class folder (CIS 101, in this case) is not expanded, double-click the CIS 101 folder to select the folder and display its contents in the navigation pane.

5e Click the PowerPoint folder in the navigation pane to select it as the new save location and display its contents in the file list.

6 Click the Save button (Save As dialog box) to save the presentation in the selected folder in the selected location with the entered file name.

To Create a New Office Document from the Backstage View

1 SIGN IN | 2 USE WINDOWS | 3 USE APPS | 4 FILE MANAGEMENT | 5 SWITCH APPS | 6 SAVE FILES
7 CHANGE SCREEN RESOLUTION | 8 EXIT APPS | 9 USE ADDITIONAL APPS | **10 USE HELP**

As discussed earlier, the Backstage view contains a set of commands that enable you to manage documents and data about the documents. *Why? From the Backstage view in PowerPoint, for example, you can create, open, print, and save presentations. You also can share documents, manage versions, set permissions, and modify document properties. In other Office 2016 apps, the Backstage view may contain features specific to those apps.* The following steps create a file, a blank presentation in this case, from the Backstage view.

1
• Click File on the ribbon to open the Backstage view (Figure 78).

Q&A
What is the purpose of the Info tab in the Backstage view?
The Info tab, which is selected by default when you click File on the ribbon, allows you to protect your document, inspect your document, and manage versions of your document as well as view all the file properties, such as when the file was created.

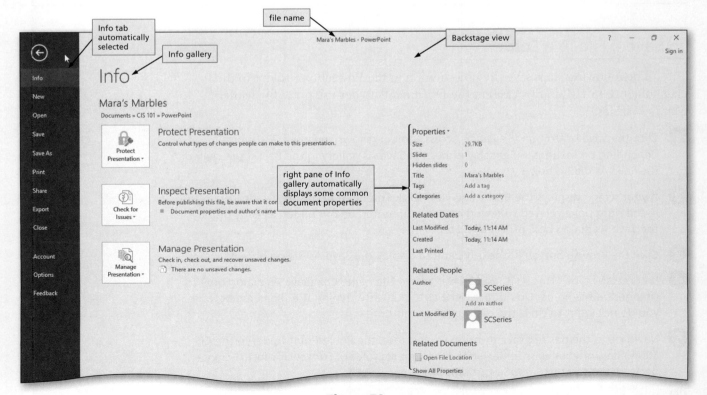

Figure 78

2

- Click the New tab in the Backstage view to display the New gallery (Figure 79).

Q&A Can I create documents through the Backstage view in other Office apps? Yes. If the Office app has a New tab in the Backstage view, the New gallery displays various options for creating a new file.

Figure 79

3

- Click the Blank Presentation thumbnail in the New gallery to create a new presentation.

Other Ways

1. Press CTRL + N

To Enter Content in a Title Slide of a Second PowerPoint Presentation

The presentation title for this presentation is Visiting National Monuments. The following steps enter a presentation title on the title slide.

1 Click the title text placeholder to select it.

2 Type `Visiting National Monuments` in the title text placeholder. Do not press the ENTER key.

To Save a File in a Folder

The following steps save the second presentation in the PowerPoint folder in the class folder (CIS 101, in this case) in the Documents folder using the file name, Visiting National Monuments.

1 Click the Save button on the Quick Access Toolbar, which depending on settings will display either the Save As gallery in the Backstage view or the Save As dialog box.

2 If your screen displays the Backstage view, click This PC, if necessary, to display options in the right pane related to saving on your computer; if your screen already displays the Save As dialog box, proceed to Step 4.

3 Click the Browse button in the left pane to display the Save As dialog box.

④ If necessary, type `Visiting National Monuments` in the File name box (Save As dialog box) to change the file name. Do not press the ENTER key after typing the file name because you do not want to close the dialog box at this time.

⑤ If necessary, navigate to the desired save location (in this case, the PowerPoint folder in the CIS 101 folder [or your class folder] in the Documents folder). For specific instructions, perform the tasks in Steps 5a through 5e in the previous section titled To Save a File in a Folder.

⑥ Click the Save button (Save As dialog box) to save the presentation in the selected folder on the selected drive with the entered file name.

To Close an Office File Using the Backstage View

1 SIGN IN | 2 USE WINDOWS | 3 USE APPS | 4 FILE MANAGEMENT | 5 SWITCH APPS | 6 SAVE FILES
7 CHANGE SCREEN RESOLUTION | 8 EXIT APPS | 9 USE ADDITIONAL APPS | 10 USE HELP

Sometimes, you may want to close an Office file, such as a PowerPoint presentation, entirely and start over with a new file. You also may want to close a file when you are done working with it. *Why? You should close a file when you are done working with it so that you do not make inadvertent changes to it.* The following steps close the current active Office file, that is, the Visiting National Monuments presentation, without exiting the active app (PowerPoint, in this case).

①

- Click File on the ribbon to open the Backstage view (Figure 80).

②

- Click Close in the Backstage view to close the open file (Visiting National Monuments, in this case) without exiting the active app.

Q&A What if the Office app displays a dialog box about saving?
Click the Save button if you want to save the changes, click the Don't Save button if you want to ignore the changes since the last time you saved, and click the Cancel button if you do not want to close the document.

Can I use the Backstage view to close an open file in other Office apps, such as Word and Excel?
Yes.

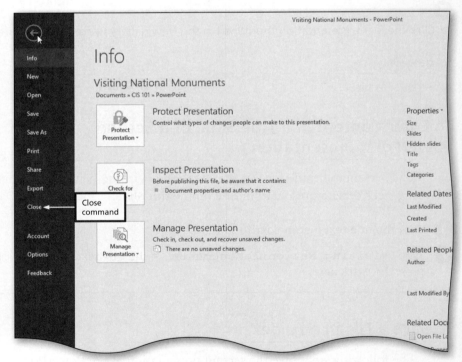

Figure 80

Other Ways

1. Press CTRL+F4

To Open a Recent Office File Using the Backstage View

1 SIGN IN | 2 USE WINDOWS | 3 USE APPS | 4 FILE MANAGEMENT | 5 SWITCH APPS | 6 SAVE FILES
7 CHANGE SCREEN RESOLUTION | 8 EXIT APPS | 9 USE ADDITIONAL APPS | 10 USE HELP

You sometimes need to open a file that you recently modified. *Why? You may have more changes to make, such as adding more content or correcting errors.* The Backstage view allows you to access recent files easily. The following steps reopen the Visiting National Monuments file just closed.

①

• Click File on the ribbon to open the Backstage view.
• Click the Open tab in the Backstage view to display the Open gallery (Figure 81).

②

• Click the desired file name in the Recent list, Visiting National Monuments in this case, to open the file.

Q&A Can I use the Backstage view to open a recent file in other Office apps, such as Word and Excel?
Yes, as long as the file name appears in the list of recent files.

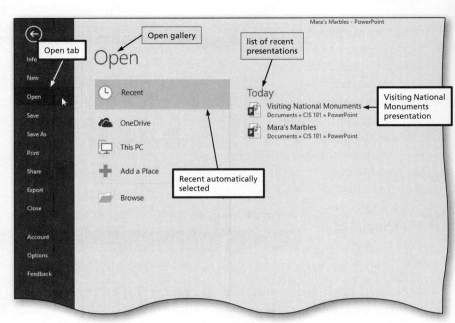

Figure 81

Other Ways

1. Click File on ribbon, click Open in Backstage view, click This PC, click Browse button, navigate to file (Open dialog box), click Open button

To Exit an Office App

You are finished using PowerPoint. Thus, you should exit this Office app. The following steps exit PowerPoint.

① If you have one Office document open, click the Close button on the right side of the title bar to close the document and exit the Office app; or if you have multiple Office documents open, right-click the app button on the taskbar and then click 'Close all windows' on the shortcut menu, or press ALT+F4 to close all open documents and exit the Office app.

Q&A If I am using a touch screen, could I press and hold the Close button until all windows close and the app exits?
Yes.

② If a dialog box appears, click the Save button to save any changes made to the document since the last save.

Excel

Excel is a powerful spreadsheet app that allows users to organize data, complete calculations, make decisions, graph data, develop professional-looking reports (Figure 82), publish organized data to the web, and access real-time data from websites. The four major parts of Excel are:

• **Workbooks and Worksheets:** A **workbook** is like a notebook. Inside the workbook are sheets, each of which is called a **worksheet**. Thus, a workbook is a collection of worksheets. Worksheets allow users to enter, calculate, manipulate, and analyze data, such as numbers and text. The terms worksheet and spreadsheet are interchangeable.

• **Charts:** Excel can draw a variety of charts, such as column charts and pie charts.

• **Tables:** Tables organize and store data within worksheets. For example, once a user enters data into a worksheet, an Excel table can sort the data, search for specific data, and select data that satisfies defined criteria.

Figure 82

• **Web Support:** Web support allows users to save Excel worksheets or parts of a worksheet in a format that a user can view in a browser, so that a user can view and manipulate the worksheet using a browser. Excel web support also provides access to real-time data, such as stock quotes, using web queries.

To Create a New Blank Office Document from File Explorer

1 SIGN IN | 2 USE WINDOWS | 3 USE APPS | 4 FILE MANAGEMENT | 5 SWITCH APPS | 6 SAVE FILES
7 CHANGE SCREEN RESOLUTION | 8 EXIT APPS | 9 USE ADDITIONAL APPS | 10 USE HELP

File Explorer provides a means to create a blank Office document without running an Office app. The following steps use File Explorer to create a blank Excel document. *Why? Sometimes you might need to create a blank document and then return to it later for editing.*

1

• If necessary, click the File Explorer button on the taskbar to make the folder window the active window.

• If necessary, double-click the Documents folder in the navigation pane to expand the Documents folder.

• If necessary, double-click your class folder (CIS 101, in this case) in the navigation pane to expand the folder.

• Click the Excel folder in the navigation pane to display its contents in the file list.

• With the Excel folder selected, right-click an open area in the file list to display a shortcut menu.

• Point to New on the shortcut menu to display the New submenu (Figure 83).

Figure 83

- Click 'Microsoft Excel Worksheet' on the New submenu to display an icon and text box for a new file in the current folder window with the file name, New Microsoft Excel Worksheet, selected (Figure 84).

Figure 84

3

- Type **Silver Sky Hardware** in the text box and then press the ENTER key to assign a new file name to the new file in the current folder (Figure 85).

Figure 85

To Run an App from File Explorer and Open a File

1 SIGN IN | 2 USE WINDOWS | 3 USE APPS | 4 FILE MANAGEMENT | 5 SWITCH APPS | 6 SAVE FILES
7 CHANGE SCREEN RESOLUTION | 8 EXIT APPS | 9 USE ADDITIONAL APPS | 10 USE HELP

Previously, you learned how to run an Office app using the Start menu and the search box. The following steps, which assume Windows is running, use File Explorer to run the Excel app based on a typical installation. *Why? Another way to run an Office app is to open an existing file from File Explorer, which causes the app in which the file was created to run and then open the selected file.* You may need to ask your instructor how to run Office apps for your computer.

1

- If necessary, display the file to open in the folder window in File Explorer (shown in Figure 85).
- Right-click the file icon or file name (Silver Sky Hardware, in this case) to display a shortcut menu (Figure 86).

Figure 86

2

- Click Open on the shortcut menu to open the selected file in the app used to create the file, Excel in this case (Figure 87).
- If the window is not maximized, click the Maximize button on the title bar to maximize the window.

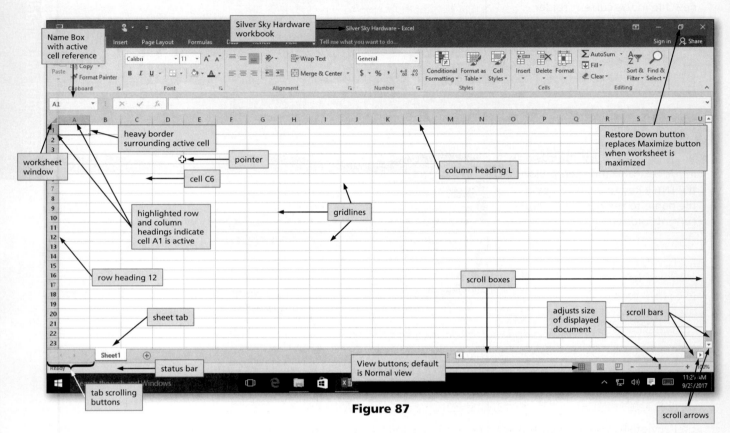

Figure 87

Instead of using File Explorer, can I run Excel using the same method shown previously for Word and PowerPoint?
Yes, you can use any method of running an Office app to run Excel.

BTW
The Worksheet Size and Window
The 16,384 columns and 1,048,576 rows in Excel make for a huge worksheet that — if you could imagine — takes up the entire side of a building to display in its entirety. Your computer screen, by comparison, is a small window that allows you to view only a minute area of the worksheet at one time. While you cannot see the entire worksheet, you can move the window over the worksheet to view any part of it.

Unique Features of Excel

The Excel window consists of a variety of components to make your work more efficient and worksheets more professional. These include the worksheet window, ribbon, Tell Me box, mini toolbar and shortcut menus, Quick Access Toolbar, and Microsoft Account area. Some of these components are common to other Office apps; others are unique to Excel.

Excel opens a new workbook with one worksheet. If necessary, you can add additional worksheets.

Each worksheet has a sheet name that appears on a **sheet tab** at the bottom of the workbook. For example, Sheet1 is the name of the active worksheet displayed in the Silver Sky Hardware workbook. You can add more sheets to the workbook by clicking the New sheet button.

The Worksheet The worksheet is organized into a rectangular grid containing vertical columns and horizontal rows. A column letter above the grid, also called the **column heading**, identifies each column. A row number on the left side of the grid, also called the **row heading**, identifies each row.

The intersection of each column and row is a cell. A **cell** is the basic unit of a worksheet into which you enter data. Each worksheet in a workbook has 16,384 columns and 1,048,576 rows for a total of 17,179,869,184 cells. Only a small fraction of the active worksheet appears on the screen at one time.

A cell is referred to by its unique address, or **cell reference**, which is the coordinates of the intersection of a column and a row. To identify a cell, specify the column letter first, followed by the row number. For example, cell reference C6 refers to the cell located at the intersection of column C and row 6 (Figure 87).

One cell on the worksheet, designated the **active cell**, is the one into which you can enter data. The active cell in Figure 87 is A1. The active cell is identified in three ways. First, a heavy border surrounds the cell; second, the active cell reference shows immediately above column A in the Name box; and third, the column heading A and row heading 1 are highlighted so that it is easy to see which cell is active (Figure 87).

The horizontal and vertical lines on the worksheet itself are called **gridlines**. Gridlines make it easier to see and identify each cell in the worksheet. If desired, you can turn the gridlines off so that they do not show on the worksheet. While learning Excel, gridlines help you to understand the structure of the worksheet.

The pointer in Figure 87 has the shape of a block plus sign. The pointer appears as a block plus sign whenever it is located in a cell on the worksheet. Another common shape of the pointer is the block arrow. The pointer turns into the block arrow when you move it outside the worksheet or when you drag cell contents between rows or columns.

Ribbon   When you run Excel, the ribbon displays eight main tabs: File, Home, Insert, Page Layout, Formulas, Data, Review, and View. The Formulas and Data tabs are specific to Excel. The Formulas tab allows you to work with Excel formulas, and the Data tab allows you to work with data processing features such as importing and sorting data.

Formula Bar   As you type, Excel displays the entry in the **formula bar**, which appears below the ribbon (Figure 88). You can make the formula bar larger by dragging the sizing handle at the bottom of the formula bar or clicking the expand button to the right of the formula bar. Excel also displays the active cell reference in the **Name box** on the left side of the formula bar.

BTW
Customizing the Ribbon
In addition to customizing the Quick Access Toolbar, you can add items to and remove items from the ribbon. To customize the ribbon, click File on the ribbon to open the Backstage view, click the Options tab in the Backstage view, and then click Customize Ribbon in the left pane of the Options dialog box. More information about customizing the ribbon is presented in a later module.

Figure 88

To Enter a Worksheet Title

1 SIGN IN | 2 USE WINDOWS | 3 USE APPS | 4 FILE MANAGEMENT | 5 SWITCH APPS | 6 SAVE FILES
7 CHANGE SCREEN RESOLUTION | 8 EXIT APPS | 9 USE ADDITIONAL APPS | 10 USE HELP

To enter data into a cell, you first must select it. The easiest way to select a cell (make it active) is to use the mouse to move the block plus sign pointer to the cell and then click. An alternative method is to use the arrow keys that are located just to the right of the typewriter keys on the keyboard. An arrow key selects the cell adjacent to the active cell in the direction of the arrow on the key.

In Excel, any set of characters containing a letter, hyphen (as in a telephone number), or space is considered text. **Text** is used to place titles, such as worksheet titles, column titles, and row titles, on the worksheet. The following steps enter the worksheet title in cell A1. *Why? A title informs others as to the contents of the worksheet, such as information regarding a company.*

1

- If it is not already the active cell, click cell A1 to make it the active cell.
- Type **Silver Sky Hardware** in cell A1 (Figure 89).

Figure 89

2

- Click the Enter button to complete the entry and enter the worksheet title in cell A1 (Figure 90).

Q&A

Why do some commands on the ribbon appear dimmed?
Excel dims the commands that are unavailable for use at the current time.

Figure 90

Other Ways

1. To complete entry, click any cell other than active cell
2. To complete entry, press ENTER, HOME, PAGE UP, PAGE DOWN, END, UP ARROW, DOWN ARROW, LEFT ARROW, or RIGHT ARROW

To Save an Existing Office File with the Same File Name

1 SIGN IN | 2 USE WINDOWS | 3 USE APPS | 4 FILE MANAGEMENT | 5 SWITCH APPS | 6 SAVE FILES
7 CHANGE SCREEN RESOLUTION | 8 EXIT APPS | 9 USE ADDITIONAL APPS | 10 USE HELP

Saving frequently cannot be overemphasized. *Why? You have made modifications to the file (spreadsheet) since you created it. Thus, you should save again. Similarly, you should continue saving files frequently so that you do not lose the changes you have made since the time you last saved the file.* You can use the same file name, such as Silver Sky Hardware, to save the changes made to the document. The following step saves a file again with the same file name.

1

- Click the Save button on the Quick Access Toolbar to overwrite the previously saved file (Silver Sky Hardware, in this case) in the Excel folder (Figure 91).

Figure 91

Other Ways

1. Press CTRL+S
2. Press SHIFT+F12

To Save a File with a New File Name

You might want to save a file with a different file name or to a different location. For example, you might start a homework assignment with a data file and then save it with a final file name for submission to your instructor, saving it to a location designated by your instructor. The following steps save a file with a different file name.

1 Click the File tab to open the Backstage view.

2 Click the Save As tab to display the Save As gallery.

3 If necessary, click This PC to display options in the right pane related to saving on your computer.

4 Click the Browse button in the left pane to display the Save As dialog box.

5 Type `Silver Sky Hardware Sales Summary` in the File name box (Save As dialog box) to change the file name. Do not press the ENTER key after typing the file name because you do not want to close the dialog box at this time.

6 If necessary, navigate to the desired save location (in this case, the Excel folder in the CIS 101 folder [or your class folder] in the Documents folder). For specific instructions, perform the tasks in Steps 5a through 5e in the previous section titled To Save a File in a Folder, replacing the PowerPoint folder with the Excel folder.

7 Click the Save button (Save As dialog box) to save the worksheet in the selected folder on the selected drive with the entered file name.

To Exit an Office App

You are finished using Excel. The following steps exit Excel.

1 If you have one Office document open, click the Close button on the right side of the title bar to close the document and exit the Office app; or if you have multiple Office documents open, right-click the app button on the taskbar and then click 'Close all windows' on the shortcut menu, or press ALT + F4 to close all open documents and exit the Office app.

2 If a dialog box appears, click the Save button to save any changes made to the file since the last save.

Access

The term **database** describes a collection of data organized in a manner that allows access, retrieval, and use of that data. **Access** is a database management system. A **database management system** is software that allows you to use a computer to create a database; add, change, and delete data in the database; create queries that allow you to ask questions concerning the data in the database; and create forms and reports using the data in the database.

To Run an App

The following steps, which assume Windows is running, run the Access app based on a typical installation. You may need to ask your instructor how to run apps for your computer.

1 Type `Access 2016` as the search text in the search box and watch the search results appear in the search results.

2 Click the app name, Access 2016 in this case, in the search results to run Access.

3 If the window is not maximized, click the Maximize button on its title bar to maximize the window (Figure 92).

Q&A Do I have to run Access using these steps?

No. You can use any previously discussed method of running an Office app to run Access.

Figure 92

Unique Elements in Access

You work on objects such as tables, forms, and reports in the **Access work area**. Figure 93 shows a work area with multiple objects open. **Object tabs** for the open objects appear at the top of the work area. You select an open object by clicking its tab. In the figure, the Customer List table is the selected object. To the left of the work area is the Navigation Pane, which contains a list of all the objects in the database. You use this pane to open an object. You also can customize the way objects are displayed in the Navigation Pane.

Because the Navigation Pane can take up space in the window, you may not have as much open space for working as you would with Word or Excel. You can use the 'Shutter Bar Open/Close Button' to minimize the Navigation Pane when you are not using it, which allows more space to work with tables, forms, reports, and other database elements.

Figure 93

Ribbon When you run Access, the ribbon displays five main tabs: File, Home, Create, External Data, and Database Tools. Access has unique groupings such as Sort & Filter and Records that are designed specifically for working with databases. Many of the formatting options are reserved for the tool tabs that appear when you are working with forms and reports.

To Create an Access Database

1 SIGN IN | 2 USE WINDOWS | 3 USE APPS | 4 FILE MANAGEMENT | 5 SWITCH APPS | 6 SAVE FILES
7 CHANGE SCREEN RESOLUTION | 8 EXIT APPS | 9 USE ADDITIONAL APPS | 10 USE HELP

Unlike the other Office apps, Access saves a database when you first create it. When working in Access, you will add data to an Access database. As you add data to a database, Access automatically saves your changes rather than waiting until you manually save the database or exit Access. Recall that in Word and Excel, you entered the data first and then saved it.

Because Access automatically saves the database as you add and change data, you do not always have to click the Save button on the Quick Access Toolbar. Instead, the Save button in Access is used for saving the objects (including tables, queries, forms, reports, and other database objects) a database contains. You can use either the 'Blank desktop database' option or a template to create a new database. If you already know the organization of your database, you would use the 'Blank desktop database' option. If not, you can use a template. Templates can guide you by suggesting some commonly used database organizations.

The following steps use the 'Blank desktop database' option to create a database named Rimitoein Electronics in the Access folder in the class folder (CIS 101, in this case) in the Documents folder. *Why? You have decided to use Microsoft Access to maintain large amounts of data.*

①

- Click the 'Blank desktop database' thumbnail (shown in Figure 92) to select the database type.
- Type **Rimitoein Electronics** in the File Name text box (Blank desktop database dialog box) to enter the new file name. Do not press the ENTER key after typing the file name because you do not want to create the database at this time (Figure 94).

Figure 94

②

- Click the 'Browse for a location to put your database' button to display the File New Database dialog box.
- Navigate to the location for the database, that is, the Documents folder, then to the folder identifying your class (CIS 101, in this case), and then to the Access folder (Figure 95). For specific instructions, perform the tasks in Steps 5a through 5e in the previous section titled To Save a File in a Folder, replacing the PowerPoint folder with the Access folder.

 Why does the 'Save as type' box say Microsoft Access 2007-2016 Databases?

Microsoft Access database formats change with some new versions of Microsoft Access. The most recent format is the Microsoft Access 2007-2016 Databases format, which was released with Access 2007.

Figure 95

- Click the OK button (File New Database dialog box) to select the Access folder as the location for the database and close the dialog box (Figure 96).

- Click the Create button (Blank desktop database dialog box) to create the database on the selected drive in the selected folder with the file name, Rimitoein Electronics (Figure 97).

◄ Q&A How do I know that the Rimitoein Electronics database is created?

The file name of the database appears on the title bar.

Figure 96

Figure 97

To Close an Office File

Assume you need to close the Access database and return to it later. The following step closes an Office file.

1 Click File on the ribbon to open the Backstage view and then click Close in the Backstage view to close the open file (Rimitoein Electronics, in this case) without exiting the active app.

◄ Q&A Why is Access still on the screen?

When you close a database, the app remains running.

To Open an Existing Office File

Assume you wish to continue working on an existing file, that is, a file you previously saved. Earlier in this module, you learned how to open a recently used file through the Backstage view. The following step opens a database, specifically the Rimitoein Electronics database, that recently was saved. *Why? Because the file has been created already, you just need to reopen it.*

- Click File on the ribbon to open the Backstage view and then click Open in the Backstage view to display the Open gallery in the Backstage view.
- Click This PC to display recent folders accessed on your computer.
- Click the Browse button to display the Open dialog box.
- If necessary, navigate to the location of the file to open.
- Click the file to open, Rimitoein Electronics in this case, to select the file (Figure 98).
- Click the Open button (Open dialog box) to open the file. If necessary, click the Enable Content button.

Q&A | Why did the Security Warning appear?

The Security Warning appears when you open an Office file that might contain harmful content. The files you create in this module are not harmful, but you should be cautious when opening files from other people.

Figure 98

Other Ways

1. Press CTRL+O   2. Navigate to file in File Explorer window, double-click file name

To Exit an Office App

You are finished using Access. The following step exits Access.

1 Click the Close button on the right side of the title bar to close the file and exit the Office app.

Other Office Apps

In addition to the Office apps discussed thus far, three other apps are useful when collaborating and communicating with others: Outlook, Publisher, and OneNote.

Outlook

Outlook is a powerful communications and scheduling app that helps you communicate with others, keep track of contacts, and organize your calendar. Apps such as Outlook provide a way for individuals and workgroups to organize, find, view, and share information easily. Outlook allows you to send and receive email messages and provides a means to organize contacts. Users can track email messages, meetings, and notes related to a particular contact. Outlook's Calendar, People, Tasks, and Notes components aid in this organization. Contact information readily is available from the Outlook Calendar, Mail, People, and Task components by accessing the Search Contacts feature.

Email is the transmission of messages and files over a computer network. Email has become an important means of exchanging information and files between business associates, classmates and instructors, friends, and family. Businesses find that using email to send documents electronically saves both time and money. Parents with students away at college or relatives who live across the country find that communicating by email is an inexpensive and easy way to stay in touch with their family members. Exchanging email messages is a widely used service of the Internet.

The Outlook Window   Figure 99 shows an Outlook window, which is divided into three panes: the Navigation pane, the message pane to the left of center, and the Reading pane to the right of center.

Figure 99

When an email message is open in Outlook, it is displayed in a Message window (Figure 100). When you open a message, the Message tab on the ribbon appears, which contains the more frequently used commands.

Figure 100

Publisher

Publisher is a powerful desktop publishing (DTP) app that assists you in designing and producing professional-quality documents that combine text, graphics, illustrations, and photos. DTP software provides additional tools beyond those typically found in word processing apps, including design templates, graphic manipulation tools, color schemes or libraries, advanced layout and printing tools, and web components. For large jobs, businesses use DTP software to design publications that are camera ready, which means the files are suitable for outside commercial printing. In addition, DTP software can be used to create webpages and interactive web forms.

Publisher is used by people who regularly produce high-quality color publications, such as newsletters, brochures, flyers, logos, signs, catalogs, cards, and business forms. Publisher has many features designed to simplify production and make publications visually appealing. Using Publisher, you easily can change the shape, size, and color of text and graphics. You can include many kinds of graphical objects, including mastheads, borders, tables, images, pictures, charts, and web objects in publications, as well as integrate spreadsheets and databases.

The Publisher Window   Publisher initially displays a list of publication types. **Publication types** are typical publications used by desktop publishers. The more popular types are displayed in the center of the window.

Once you select a publication type, a dialog box is displayed to allow you to create the publication (Figure 101). Some templates are installed with Publisher, and others are available online. In Figure 101, the Business newsletter publication dialog box is displayed.

BTW
Running Publisher
When you first run Publisher, the New templates gallery usually is displayed in the Backstage view. If it is not displayed, click File on the ribbon, click the Options tab in the Backstage view, click General (Publisher Options dialog box), and then click 'Show the New template gallery when starting Publisher' to select the check box in the right pane.

Figure 101

When you select the desired template, Publisher creates the publication and sets it up for you to edit. Figure 102 shows the Business newsletter publication that Publisher creates when default options are selected.

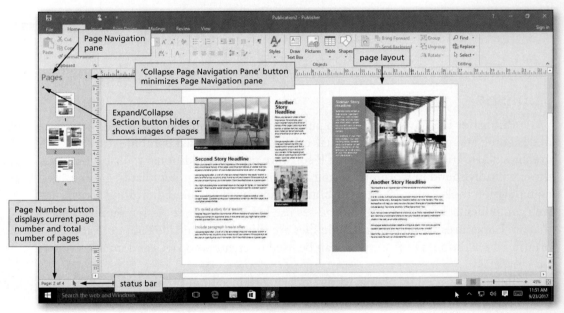

Figure 102

OneNote

OneNote is a note taking app that assists you in entering, saving, organizing, searching, and using notes. It enables you to create pages, which are organized in sections, just as in a physical notebook. In OneNote, you can type notes anywhere on a page and then easily move the notes around on the page. You can create lists and outlines, use handwriting to enter notes, and create drawings. If you use a tablet to add handwritten notes to a document, OneNote can convert the handwriting to text. It also can perform searches on the handwritten entries. Pictures and data from other apps easily are incorporated in your notes.

In addition to typing and handwriting, you can take audio notes. For example, you could record conversations during a meeting or lecture. As you record, you can take additional notes. When you play back the audio notes, you can synchronize the additional notes you took; that is, OneNote will show you during playback the exact points at which you added the notes. A variety of note flags, which are symbols that call your attention to notes on a page, enable you to flag notes as being important. You then can use the Note Flags summary to view the flagged notes, which can be sorted in a variety of ways.

OneNote includes tools to assist you with organizing a notebook and navigating its contents. It also includes a search feature, making it easy to find the specific notes in which you are interested. For short notes that you always want to have available readily, you can use Side Notes, which are used much like the sticky notes that you might use in a physical notebook.

OneNote Window   All activity in OneNote takes place in the **notebook** (Figure 103). Like a physical notebook, the OneNote notebook consists of notes that are placed on **pages**. The pages are grouped into **sections**, which can be further grouped into **folders**. (No folders are shown in the notebook in the figure.) You can use the Search box to search for specific text in your notes.

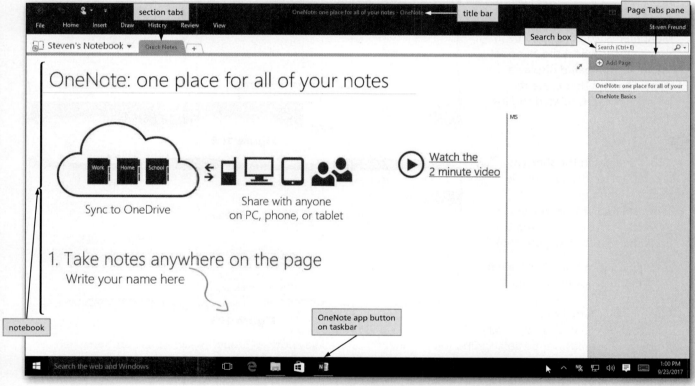

Figure 103

You can add pages to the notebook using the Add Page button in the Page Tabs pane. If page tabs are displayed, you can switch to a page by clicking its tab. Figure 103 shows the Quick Notes page being displayed for the notebook.

Break Point: If you wish to take a break, this is a good place to do so. To resume at a later time, continue to follow the steps from this location forward.

Renaming, Moving, and Deleting Files

Earlier in this module, you learned how to organize files in folders, which is part of a process known as **file management**. The following sections cover additional file management topics including renaming, moving, and deleting files.

OFF 68   Office 2016 and Windows 10 Module   Essential Concepts and Skills

1 SIGN IN | 2 USE WINDOWS | 3 USE APPS | **4 FILE MANAGEMENT** | 5 SWITCH APPS | 6 SAVE FILES
7 CHANGE SCREEN RESOLUTION | 8 EXIT APPS | 9 USE ADDITIONAL APPS | **10 USE HELP**

To Rename a File

In some circumstances, you may want to change the name of, or rename, a file or a folder. *Why? You may want to distinguish a file in one folder or drive from a copy of a similar file, or you may decide to rename a file to better identify its contents.* The following steps change the name of the National Monuments file in the Word folder to National Monuments Flyer.

- If necessary, click the File Explorer button on the taskbar to make the folder window the active window.
- Navigate to the location of the file to be renamed (in this case, the Word folder in the CIS 101 [or your class folder] folder in the Documents folder) to display the file(s) it contains in the file list.
- Right-click the National Monuments icon or file name in the file list to select the National Monuments file and display a shortcut menu that presents a list of commands related to files (Figure 104).

Figure 104

- Click Rename on the shortcut menu to place the current file name in a text box.
- Type **National Monuments Flyer** in the text box and then press the ENTER key (Figure 105).

Q&A

Are any risks involved in renaming files that are located on a hard drive?
If you inadvertently rename a file that is associated with certain apps, the apps may not be able to find the file and, therefore, may not run properly. Always use caution when renaming files.

Can I rename a file when it is open?
No, a file must be closed to change the file name.

Figure 105

Other Ways

1. Select file, press F2, type new file name, press ENTER   2. Select file, click Rename (Home tab | Organize group), type new file name, press ENTER

To Move a File

Why? At some time, you may want to move a file from one folder, called the source folder, to another, called the destination folder. When you move a file, it no longer appears in the original folder. If the destination and the source folders are on the same media, you can move a file by dragging it. If the folders are on different media, then you will need to right-drag the file, and then click Move here on the shortcut menu. The following step moves the Silver Sky Hardware Sales Summary file from the Excel folder to the OneNote folder.

- In File Explorer, navigate to the location of the file to be moved (in this case, the Excel folder in the CIS 101 folder [or your class folder] in the Documents folder).
- Click the Excel folder in the navigation pane to display the files it contains in the right pane (Figure 106).
- Drag the Silver Sky Hardware Sales Summary file in the right pane to the OneNote folder in the navigation pane.

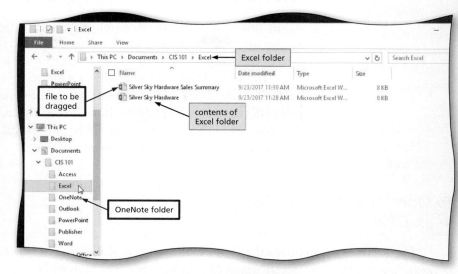

Figure 106

Other Ways

1. Right-click file to move, click Cut on shortcut menu, right-click destination folder, click Paste on shortcut menu

2. Select file to move, press CTRL+X, select destination folder, press CTRL+V

To Delete a File

1 SIGN IN | 2 USE WINDOWS | 3 USE APPS | **4 FILE MANAGEMENT** | 5 SWITCH APPS | 6 SAVE FILES
7 CHANGE SCREEN RESOLUTION | 8 EXIT APPS | 9 USE ADDITIONAL APPS | **10 USE HELP**

A final task you may want to perform is to delete a file. Exercise extreme caution when deleting a file or files. When you delete a file from a hard drive, the deleted file is stored in the Recycle Bin where you can recover it until you empty the Recycle Bin. If you delete a file from removable media, such as a USB flash drive, the file is deleted permanently. The next steps delete the Visiting National Monuments file from the PowerPoint folder. *Why? When a file no longer is needed, you can delete it to conserve space on your storage location.*

- In File Explorer, navigate to the location of the file to be deleted (in this case, the PowerPoint folder in the CIS 101 folder [or your class folder] in the Documents folder).
- Click the Visiting National Monuments icon or file name in the right pane to select the file.
- Right-click the selected file to display a shortcut menu (Figure 107).

- Click Delete on the shortcut menu to delete the file.
- If a dialog box appears, click the Yes button to delete the file.

Q&A Can I use this same technique to delete a folder?

Yes. Right-click the folder and then click Delete on the shortcut menu. When you delete a folder, all of the files and folders contained in the folder you are deleting, together with any files and folders on lower hierarchical levels, are deleted as well. For example, if you delete the CIS 101 folder, you will delete all folders and files inside the CIS 101 folder.

Figure 107

Other Ways

1. Select file, press DELETE

Microsoft Office and Windows Help

At any time while you are using one of the Office apps, you can use Office Help to display information about all topics associated with the app. To illustrate the use of Office Help, this section uses Word. Help in other Office apps operates in a similar fashion.

In Office, Help is presented in a window that has browser-style navigation buttons. Each Office app has its own Help home page, which is the starting Help page that is displayed in the Help window. If your computer is connected to the Internet, the contents of the Help page reflect both the local help files installed on the computer and material from Microsoft's website.

To Open the Help Window in an Office App

1 SIGN IN | 2 USE WINDOWS | 3 USE APPS | 4 FILE MANAGEMENT | 5 SWITCH APPS | 6 SAVE FILES
7 CHANGE SCREEN RESOLUTION | 8 EXIT APPS | 9 USE ADDITIONAL APPS | **10 USE HELP**

The following step opens the Word Help window. ***Why?*** *You might not understand how certain commands or operations work in Word, so you can obtain the necessary information using help.*

- Run an Office app, in this case Word.
- Click the Blank document thumbnail to display a blank document.
- Press F1 to open the app's Help window (Figure 108).

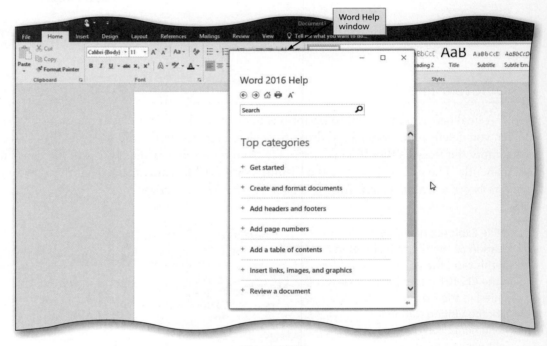

Figure 108

Moving and Resizing Windows

At times, it is useful, or even necessary, to have more than one window open and visible on the screen at the same time. You can resize and move these open windows so that you can view different areas of and elements in the window. In the case of the Help window, for example, it could be covering document text in the Word window that you need to see.

To Move a Window by Dragging

1 SIGN IN | **2 USE WINDOWS** | 3 USE APPS | 4 FILE MANAGEMENT | 5 SWITCH APPS | 6 SAVE FILES
7 CHANGE SCREEN RESOLUTION | 8 EXIT APPS | 9 USE ADDITIONAL APPS | 10 USE HELP

You can move any open window that is not maximized to another location on the desktop by dragging the title bar of the window. ***Why?*** *You might want to have a better view of what is behind the window or just want to move the window so that you can see it better.* The following step drags the Word Help window to the upper-left corner of the desktop.

1

- Drag the window title bar (the Word Help window title bar, in this case) so that the window moves to the upper-left corner of the desktop, as shown in Figure 109.

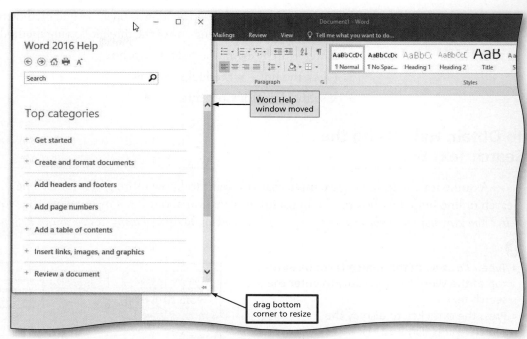

Figure 109

To Resize a Window by Dragging

1 SIGN IN | 2 USE WINDOWS | 3 USE APPS | 4 FILE MANAGEMENT | 5 SWITCH APPS | 6 SAVE FILES
7 CHANGE SCREEN RESOLUTION | 8 EXIT APPS | 9 USE ADDITIONAL APPS | 10 USE HELP

A method used to change the size of the window is to drag the window borders. The following step changes the size of the Word Help window by dragging its borders. *Why? Sometimes, information is not visible completely in a window, and you want to increase the size of the window.*

1

- If you are using a mouse, point to the lower-right corner of the window (the Word Help window, in this case) until the pointer changes to a two-headed arrow.
- Drag the bottom border downward to display more of the active window (Figure 110).

Q&A
Can I drag other borders on the window to enlarge or shrink the window?
Yes, you can drag the left, right, and top borders and any window corner to resize a window.

Q&A
Will Windows remember the new size of the window after I close it?
Yes. When you reopen the window, Windows will display it at the same size it was when you closed it.

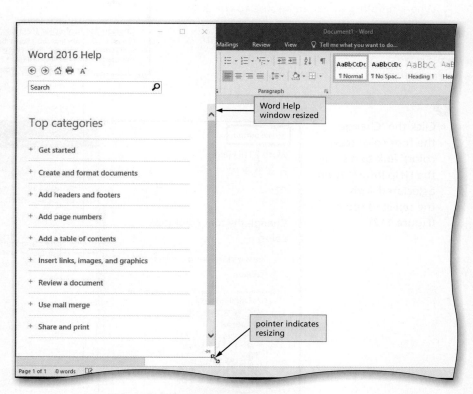

Figure 110

Using Office Help

Once an Office app's Help window is open, several methods exist for navigating Help. You can search for help by using any of the three following methods from the Help window:

1. Enter search text in the Search text box.
2. Click the links in the Help window.
3. Use the Table of Contents.

To Obtain Help Using the Search Text Box

1 SIGN IN | 2 USE WINDOWS | 3 USE APPS | 4 FILE MANAGEMENT | 5 SWITCH APPS | 6 SAVE FILES
7 CHANGE SCREEN RESOLUTION | 8 EXIT APPS | 9 USE ADDITIONAL APPS | **10 USE HELP**

Assume for the following example that you want to know more about fonts. The following steps use the 'Search online help' text box to obtain useful information about fonts by entering the word, fonts, as search text. *Why? You may not know the exact help topic you are looking to find, so using keywords can help narrow your search.*

- Type **fonts** in the Search text box at the top of the Word Help window to enter the search text.
- Press the ENTER key to display the search results (Figure 111).

Q&A Why do my search results differ?
If you do not have an Internet connection, your results will reflect only the content of the Help files on your computer. When searching for help online, results also can change as material is added, deleted, and updated on the online Help webpages maintained by Microsoft.

Q&A Why were my search results not very helpful?
When initiating a search, be sure to check the spelling of the search text; also, keep your search specific to return the most accurate results.

Figure 111

- Click the 'Change the font color (text color)' link to display the Help information associated with the selected topic (Figure 112).

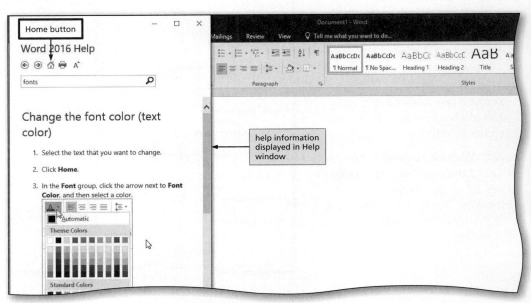

Figure 112

❸

- Click the Home button in the Help window to clear the search results and redisplay the Help home page (Figure 113).
- Click the Close button in the Word 2016 Help window to close the window.

Figure 113

Obtaining Help while Working in an Office App

Help in the Office apps provides you with the ability to obtain help directly, without opening the Help window and initiating a search. For example, you may be unsure about how a particular command works, or you may be presented with a dialog box that you are not sure how to use.

Figure 114 shows one option for obtaining help while working in an Office app. If you want to learn more about a command, point to its button and wait for the ScreenTip to appear. If the Help icon and 'Tell me more' link appear in the ScreenTip, click the 'Tell me more' link or press the F1 key while pointing to the button to open the Help window associated with that command.

Figure 115 shows a dialog box that contains a Help button. Clicking the Help button or pressing the F1 key while the dialog box is displayed opens a Help window. The Help window contains help about that dialog box, if available. If no help file is available for that particular dialog box, then the main Help window opens.

As mentioned previously, the Tell Me box is available in most Office apps and can perform a variety of functions. One of these functions is to provide easy access to commands by typing a description of the command.

Figure 114

Figure 115

To Obtain Help Using the Tell Me Box

If you are having trouble finding a command in an Office app, you can use the Tell Me box to search for the function you are trying to perform. As you type, the Tell Me box will suggest commands that match the search text you are entering. *Why? You can use the Tell Me box to quickly access commands you otherwise may be unable to find on the ribbon.* The following step finds information about margins.

- Type **margins** in the Tell Me box and watch the search results appear.
- Point to Adjust Margins to display a submenu displaying the various margin settings (Figure 116).
- Click an empty area of the document window to close the search results.

- Exit Microsoft Word.

Figure 116

Using the Windows Search Box

One of the more powerful Windows features is the Windows search box. The search box is a central location from where you can type search text and quickly access related Windows commands or web search results. In addition, **Cortana** is a new search tool in Windows that you can access using the search box. It can act as a personal assistant by performing functions such as providing ideas; searching for apps, files, and folders; and setting reminders. In addition to typing search text in the search box, you also can use your computer or mobile device's microphone to give verbal commands.

To Use the Windows Search Box

The following step uses the Windows search box to search for a Windows command. *Why? Using the search box to locate apps, settings, folders, and files can be faster than navigating windows and dialog boxes to search for the desired content.*

- Type **notification** in the search box to display the search results. The search results include related Windows settings, Windows Store apps, and web search results (Figure 117).
- Click an empty area of the desktop to close the search results.

Figure 117

Summary

In this module, you learned how to use the Windows interface, several touch screen and mouse operations, file and folder management, some basic features of some Microsoft Office apps (including Word, PowerPoint, Excel, and Access), and discovered the common elements that exist among these different Office apps. You also were introduced to additional Office apps, including Outlook, Publisher, and OneNote. Topics covered included signing in, using Windows, using apps, file management, switching between apps, saving files, changing screen resolution, exiting apps, using additional apps, and using help.

What guidelines should you follow to plan your projects?

The process of communicating specific information is a learned, rational skill. Computers and software, especially Microsoft Office 2016, can help you develop ideas and present detailed information to a particular audience and minimize much of the laborious work of drafting and revising projects. No matter what method you use to plan a project, it is beneficial to follow some specific guidelines from the onset to arrive at a final product that is informative, relevant, and effective. Use some aspects of these guidelines every time you undertake a project, and others as needed in specific instances.

1. Determine the project's purpose.

    a) Clearly define why you are undertaking this assignment.

    b) Begin to draft ideas of how best to communicate information by handwriting ideas on paper; composing directly on a laptop, tablet, or mobile device; or developing a strategy that fits your particular thinking and writing style.

2. Analyze your audience.

    a) Learn about the people who will read, analyze, or view your work.

    b) Determine their interests and needs so that you can present the information they need to know and omit the information they already possess.

    c) Form a mental picture of these people or find photos of people who fit this profile so that you can develop a project with the audience in mind.

3. Gather possible content.

    a) Locate existing information that may reside in spreadsheets, databases, or other files.

    b) Conduct a web search to find relevant websites.

    c) Read pamphlets, magazine and newspaper articles, and books to gain insights of how others have approached your topic.

    d) Conduct personal interviews to obtain perspectives not available by any other means.

    e) Consider video and audio clips as potential sources for material that might complement or support the factual data you uncover.

4. Determine what content to present to your audience.

    a) Write three or four major ideas you want an audience member to remember after reading or viewing your project.

    b) Envision your project's endpoint, the key fact you wish to emphasize, so that all project elements lead to this final element.

    c) Determine relevant time factors, such as the length of time to develop the project, how long readers will spend reviewing your project, or the amount of time allocated for your speaking engagement.

    d) Decide whether a graph, photo, or artistic element can express or enhance a particular concept.

    e) Be mindful of the order in which you plan to present the content, and place the most important material at the top or bottom of the page, because readers and audience members generally remember the first and last pieces of information they see and hear.

How should you submit solutions to questions in the assignments identified with a symbol?

Every assignment in this book contains one or more questions with a symbol. These questions require you to think beyond the assigned file. Present your solutions to the question in the format required by your instructor. Possible formats may include one or more of these options: write the answer; create a document that contains the answer; present your answer to the class; discuss your answer in a group; record the answer as audio or video using a webcam, smartphone, or portable media player; or post answers on a blog, wiki, or website.

Apply Your Knowledge

Reinforce the skills and apply the concepts you learned in this module.

Creating a Folder and a Document

Instructions: You will create a PowerPoint Assignments folder and then create a PowerPoint presentation and save it in the folder.

Perform the following tasks:

1. Open the File Explorer window and then double-click to open the Documents folder.
2. Click the New folder button on the Quick Access Toolbar to display a new folder icon and text box for the folder name.
3. Type **PowerPoint Assignments** in the text box to name the folder. Press the ENTER key to create the folder in the Documents folder.
4. Run PowerPoint and create a new blank presentation.
5. Enter **Technology Update** in the title text placeholder (Figure 118).
6. Click the Save button on the Quick Access Toolbar. Navigate to the PowerPoint folder in the Documents folder and then save the document using the file name, Apply 1 Presentation.
7. If your Quick Access Toolbar does not show the Quick Print button, add the Quick Print button to the Quick Access Toolbar. Print the presentation using the Quick Print button on the Quick Access Toolbar. When you are finished printing, remove the Quick Print button from the Quick Access Toolbar.
8. Submit the printout to your instructor.
9. Exit PowerPoint.
10. ✳ What other commands might you find useful to include on the Quick Access Toolbar?

Figure 118

Extend Your Knowledge

Extend the skills you learned in this module and experiment with new skills. You will use Help to complete the assignment.

Using Help

Instructions: Use Office Help to perform the following tasks.

Perform the following tasks:

1. Run Word.
2. Click the Microsoft Word Help button to open the Word Help window (Figure 119).
3. Search Word Help to answer the following questions.

    a. What are the steps to create a hanging indent?

    b. What is mail merge?
4. With the Word app still running, run PowerPoint.
5. Click the Microsoft PowerPoint Help button on the title bar to open the PowerPoint Help window.
6. Search PowerPoint Help to answer the following questions.

    a. How can you create a Venn diagram?

    b. How do you add slide numbers to each slide?
7. Exit PowerPoint.
8. Run Excel.
9. Click the Microsoft Excel Help button to open the Excel Help window.
10. Search Excel Help to answer the following questions.

    a. What different types of charts are available in Excel?

    b. What is Flash Fill?
11. Exit Excel.
12. Run Access.
13. Click the Microsoft Access Help button to open the Access Help window.
14. Search Access Help to answer the following questions.

    a. What is a query?

    b. What are data types?
15. Exit Access.
16. Type the answers from your searches in a new blank Word document. Save the document with a new file name and then submit it in the format specified by your instructor.
17. Exit Word.
18. ✸ What search text did you use to perform the searches above? Did it take multiple attempts to search and locate the exact information for which you were searching?

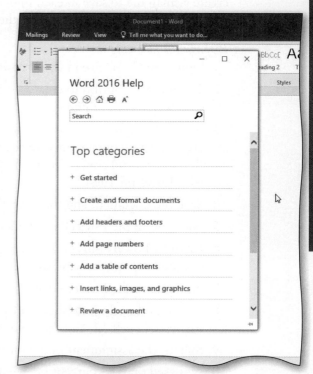

Figure 119

Expand Your World
Creating Office Online Documents

Create a solution that uses cloud or web technologies by learning and investigating on your own from general guidance.

Instructions: Create the folders shown in Figure 120. Then, using the respective Office Online app, create a small file to save in each folder (i.e., create a Word document to save in the Word folder, a PowerPoint presentation to save in the PowerPoint folder, and so on).

Perform the following tasks:

1. Sign in to OneDrive in your browser.

2. Use the New button to create the folder structure shown in Figure 120.

3. In the Word folder, use the New button to create a Word document with the file name, Reminders, and containing the text, Lunch with Lucas on Tuesday.

Figure 120

4. Save the document and then exit the app.

5. Navigate to the PowerPoint folder.

6. Create a PowerPoint presentation called Widget Sales with one slide containing the title text, Online Presentation, and then exit the app.

7. Navigate to the Excel folder.

8. Create an Excel spreadsheet called Widget Sales Analysis containing the text, Sales Cost Analysis, in cell A1, and then exit the app.

9. Submit the assignment in the format specified by your instructor.

10. ✸ Based on your current knowledge of OneDrive, do you think you will use it? What about the Office Online apps?

In the Labs

Design, create, modify, and/or use files following the guidelines, concepts, and skills presented in this module. Labs 1 and 2, which increase in difficulty, require you to create solutions based on what you learned in the module; Lab 3 requires you to apply your creative thinking and problem-solving skills to design and implement a solution.

Lab 1: Creating Folders for a Bookstore

Problem: Your friend works for a local bookstore. He would like to organize his files in relation to the types of books available in the store. He has seven main categories: fiction, biography, children, humor, social science, nonfiction, and medical. You are to create a folder structure similar to Figure 121.

Perform the following tasks:

1. Click the File Explorer button on the taskbar and display the contents of the Documents folder.

2. In the Documents folder, create the main folder and name it Book Categories.

3. Navigate to the Book Categories folder.

Figure 121

4. Within the Book Categories folder, create a folder for each of the following: Fiction, Biography, Children, Humor, Social Science, Nonfiction, and Medical.

5. Within the Fiction folder, create two additional folders, one for Science Fiction and the second for Western.

6. Submit the assignment in the format specified by your instructor.

7. ❋ Think about how you use your computer for various tasks (consider personal, professional, and academic reasons). What folders do you think will be required on your computer to store the files you save?

Lab 2: **Creating Office Documents and Saving Them in Appropriate Folders**

Problem: You are taking a class that requires you to create a Word, PowerPoint, Excel, and Access file. You will save these files to folders named for four different Office apps (Figure 122).

Perform the following tasks:

1. Create the folders shown in Figure 122.

2. Create a Word document containing the text, Week 1 Notes.

3. In the Backstage view, click Save As and then click This PC.

4. Click the Browse button to display the Save As dialog box.

© 2015 Cengage Learning

Figure 122

5. Click Documents to open the Documents folder.

6. Navigate to the Word folder and then save the file in the Word folder.

7. Create a PowerPoint presentation with one slide containing the title text, In-Class Presentation, and then save it in the PowerPoint folder.

8. Create an Excel spreadsheet containing the text, Financial Spreadsheet, in cell A1 and then save it in the Excel folder.

9. Save an Access database named, My Movie Database, in the Access folder.

10. Submit the assignment in the format specified by your instructor.

11. ✷ Based on your current knowledge of Word, PowerPoint, Excel, and Access, which app do you think you will use most frequently? Why?

Lab 3: **Consider This: Your Turn**

Performing Research about Malware

Problem: You have just installed a new computer with the Windows operating system. Because you want to be sure that it is protected from the threat of malware, you decide to research malware, malware protection, and removing malware.

Part 1: Research the following three topics: malware, malware protection, and removing malware. Use the concepts and techniques presented in this module to use the search box to find information regarding these topics. Create a Word document that contains steps to properly safeguard a computer from malware, ways to prevent malware, as well as the different ways to remove malware or a virus should your computer become infected. Submit your assignment in the format specified by your instructor.

Part 2: You made several decisions while searching for this assignment. What decisions did you make? What was the rationale behind these decisions? How did you locate the required information about malware?

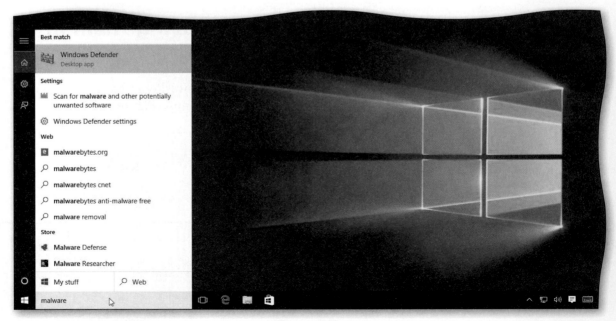

Figure 123

1 Creating, Formatting, and Editing a Word Document with a Picture

Objectives

You will have mastered the material in this module when you can:

- Enter text in a Word document
- Check spelling as you type
- Format paragraphs
- Format text
- Undo and redo commands or actions
- Change theme colors

- Insert digital pictures in a Word document
- Resize pictures
- Format pictures
- Add a page border
- Adjust spacing
- Correct errors and revise a document

Introduction

To advertise a sale, promote a business, publicize an event, or convey a message to the community, you may want to create a flyer and hand it out in person or post it in a public location. Libraries, schools, community organizations, grocery stores, coffee shops, and other places often provide bulletin boards or windows for flyers. You also see flyers posted on webpages, on social media, or in email messages.

Flyers announce personal items for sale or rent (car, boat, apartment); events, such as garage or block sales; services being offered (animal care, housecleaning, lessons, tours); membership, sponsorship, or donation requests (club, community organization, charity); and other messages, such as a lost or found pet.

Project — Flyer with a Picture

Individuals and businesses create flyers to gain public attention. Flyers, which usually are a single page in length, are an inexpensive means of reaching the community. Many flyers, however, go unnoticed because they are designed poorly.

The project in this module follows general guidelines and uses Word to create the flyer shown in Figure 1–1. This colorful, eye-catching flyer announces surfing lessons. The picture of the surfer riding a wave, taken with a digital camera, entices passersby or viewers to stop and look at the flyer. The headline on the flyer is large and colorful to draw attention into the text. The body copy below the picture briefly describes what is included in the lessons, along with a bulleted list that concisely highlights important information. The signature line of the flyer calls attention to the contact phone number. The word, expert, and the signature line are in a different color so that they stand apart from the rest of the text on the flyer. Finally, the graphical page border nicely frames and complements the contents of the flyer.

Figure 1–1

In this module, you will learn how to create the flyer shown in Figure 1–1. The following roadmap identifies general activities you will perform as you progress through this module:

1. ENTER TEXT in a new document.
2. FORMAT the TEXT in the flyer.
3. INSERT a PICTURE, called Surfer, in the flyer.
4. FORMAT the PICTURE in the flyer.
5. ENHANCE the PAGE with a border and spacing.
6. CORRECT errors AND REVISE text in the flyer.

To Run Word and Specify Settings

If you are using a computer to step through the project in this module and you want your screens to match the figures in this book, you should change your screen's resolution to 1366 × 768. For information about how to change a computer's resolution, refer to the Office and Windows module at the beginning of this book.

1 Run Word and create a blank document in the Word window.

2 If the Word window is not maximized, click the Maximize button on its title bar to maximize the window.

3 If the Print Layout button on the status bar is not selected (shown in Figure 1–2), click it so that your screen is in Print Layout view.

Q&A | What is Print Layout view?
The default (preset) view in Word is **Print Layout view**, which shows the document on a mock sheet of paper in the document window.

4 If Normal (Home tab | Styles group) is not selected in the Styles gallery (shown in Figure 1–2), click it so that your document uses the Normal style.

Q&A | What is the Normal style?
When you create a document, Word formats the text using a particular style. The default style in Word is called the **Normal style**, which is discussed later in this book.

What if rulers appear on my screen?
Click View on the ribbon to display the View tab and then remove the check mark from the View Ruler check box (View tab | Show group).

Entering Text

The first step in creating a document is to enter its text. With the projects in this book, you enter text by typing on the keyboard. By default, Word positions text you type at the left margin. In a later section of this module, you will learn how to format, or change the appearance of, the entered text.

For an introduction to Office and instructions about how to perform basic tasks in Office apps, read the Office and Windows module at the beginning of this book, where you can learn how to run an application, use the ribbon, save a file, open a file, print a file, exit an application, use Help, and much more.

For an introduction to Windows and instructions about how to perform basic Windows tasks, read the Office and Windows module at the beginning of this book, where you can learn how to resize windows, change screen resolution, create folders, move and rename files, use Windows Help, and much more.

BTW
The Word Window
The modules in this book begin with the Word window appearing as it did at the initial installation of the software. Your Word window may look different depending on your screen resolution and other Word settings.

To Type Text

To begin creating the flyer in this module, type the headline in the document window. *Why? The headline is the first line of text in the Surf Flyer.* The following steps type the first line of text in the document.

● Type **Surf's Up!** as the headline (Figure 1–2).

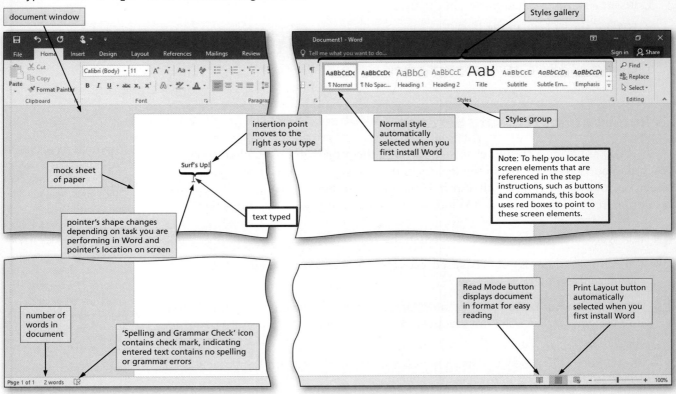

Figure 1–2

Q&A | What if I make an error while typing?
You can press the BACKSPACE key until you have deleted the text in error and then retype the text correctly.

What is the purpose of the 'Spelling and Grammar Check' icon on the status bar?
The **'Spelling and Grammar Check' icon** displays either a check mark to indicate the entered text contains no spelling or grammar errors, or an X to indicate that it found potential errors. Word flags potential errors in the document with a red, green, or blue wavy underline. Later in this module, you will learn how to fix flagged errors.

● Press the ENTER key to move the insertion point to the beginning of the next line (Figure 1–3).

Q&A | Why did blank space appear between the headline and the insertion point?
Each time you press the ENTER key, Word creates a new paragraph and inserts blank space between the two paragraphs. Later in this module, you will learn how to increase and decrease the spacing between paragraphs.

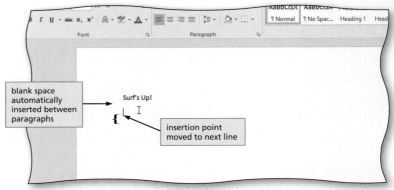

Figure 1–3

How do you use the touch keyboard with a touch screen?

To display the on-screen touch keyboard, tap the Touch Keyboard button on the Windows taskbar as shown in the Office and Windows module at the beginning of this book. When finished using the touch keyboard, tap the X button on the touch keyboard to close the keyboard.

To Display Formatting Marks

You may find it helpful to display formatting marks while working in a document. *Why? Formatting marks indicate where in a document you pressed the* ENTER *key,* SPACEBAR, *and other nonprinting characters.* A **formatting mark** is a character that Word displays on the screen but is not visible on a printed document. For example, the paragraph mark (¶) is a formatting mark that indicates where you pressed the ENTER key. A raised dot (·) shows where you pressed the SPACEBAR. Formatting marks are discussed as they appear on the screen.

Depending on settings made during previous Word sessions, your Word screen already may display formatting marks (Figure 1–4). The following step displays formatting marks, if they do not show already on the screen.

- If the Home tab is not the active tab, click Home on the ribbon to display the Home tab.
- If it is not selected already, click the 'Show/Hide ¶' button (Home tab | Paragraph group) to display formatting marks on the screen (Figure 1–4).

Q&A What if I do not want formatting marks to show on the screen?

You can hide them by clicking the 'Show/Hide ¶' button (Home tab | Paragraph group) again. It is recommended that you display formatting marks so that you visually can identify when you press the ENTER key, SPACEBAR, and other keys associated with nonprinting characters. Most of the document windows presented in this book, therefore, show formatting marks.

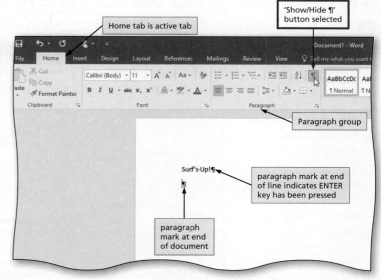

Figure 1–4

Other Ways

1. Press CTRL+SHIFT+*

To Insert a Blank Line

In the flyer, the digital picture of the surfer appears between the headline and body copy. You will not insert this picture, however, until after you enter and format all text. *Why? Although you can format text and insert pictures in any order, for illustration purposes, this module formats all text first before inserting the picture. Thus, you leave a blank line in the document as a placeholder for the picture.*

To enter a blank line in a document, press the ENTER key without typing any text on the line. The following step inserts one blank line below the headline.

- Press the ENTER key
  to insert a blank line
  in the document
  (Figure 1–5).

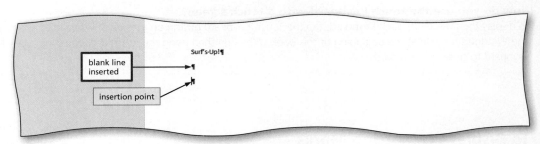

Figure 1–5

To Zoom Page Width

1 ENTER TEXT | 2 FORMAT TEXT | 3 INSERT PICTURE
4 FORMAT PICTURE | 5 ENHANCE PAGE | 6 CORRECT & REVISE

The next step in creating this flyer is to enlarge the contents that appear on the screen. *Why? You would like the text on the screen to be larger so that it is easier to read.* The document currently displays at 100% (shown in Figure 1–6). With Word, you can zoom page width, which zooms (enlarges or shrinks) the mock sheet of paper on the screen so that it is the width of the Word window. The following steps zoom page width.

- Click View on the
  ribbon to display
  the View tab
  (Figure 1–6).

Q&A Why did the groups
on the ribbon
change?
When you switch
from one tab to
another on the
ribbon, the groups
on the ribbon
change to show
commands related to
the selected tab.

Figure 1–6

- Click the Page Width
  button (View tab |
  Zoom group) to
  display the page the
  same width as the
  document window
  (Figure 1–7).

Q&A If I change the zoom,
will the document
print differently?
Changing the zoom
has no effect on the
printed document.

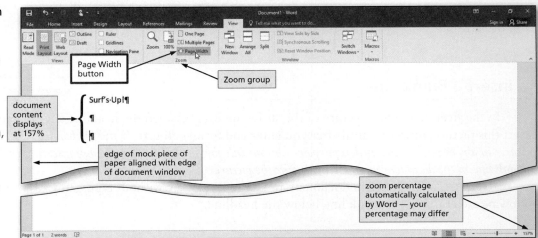

Figure 1–7

What are the other predefined zoom options?
Through the View tab | Zoom group or the Zoom dialog box (Zoom button in Zoom group), you can zoom to one page (an entire single page appears in the document window), many pages (multiple pages appear at once in the document window), page width, text width, and a variety of set percentages. Whereas page width zoom places the edges of the page at the edges of the document window, text width zoom places the document contents at the edges of the document window.

Other Ways

1. Click Zoom button (View tab | Zoom group), click Page width (Zoom dialog box), click OK button

Wordwrap

Wordwrap allows you to type words in a paragraph continually without pressing the ENTER key at the end of each line. As you type, if a word extends beyond the right margin, Word also automatically positions that word on the next line along with the insertion point.

Word creates a new paragraph each time you press the ENTER key. Thus, as you type text in the document window, do not press the ENTER key when the insertion point reaches the right margin. Instead, press the ENTER key only in these circumstances:

1. To insert a blank line(s) in a document (as shown in previous steps)
2. To begin a new paragraph
3. To terminate a short line of text and advance to the next line
4. To respond to questions or prompts in Word dialog boxes, task panes, and other on-screen objects

BTW
Zooming
If text is too small for you to read on the screen, you can zoom the document by dragging the Zoom slider on the status bar or by clicking the Zoom Out or Zoom In buttons on the status bar. Changing the zoom has no effect on the printed document.

1 ENTER TEXT | 2 FORMAT TEXT | 3 INSERT PICTURE
4 FORMAT PICTURE | 5 ENHANCE PAGE | 6 CORRECT & REVISE

To Wordwrap Text as You Type

The next step in creating the flyer is to type the body copy. *Why? In many flyers, the body copy text appears below the headline.* The following steps illustrate how the body copy text wordwraps as you enter it in the document, which means you will not have to press the ENTER key at the end of the line.

1

- Type the first sentence of the body copy: `Learn to surf or improve your form and skills on the waves through expert instruction from our award-winning surf school.`

 Why does my document wrap on different words?
The printer connected to a computer is one factor that can control where wordwrap occurs for each line in a document. Thus, it is possible that the same document could wordwrap differently if printed on different printers.

2

- Press the ENTER key to position the insertion point on the next line in the document (Figure 1–8).

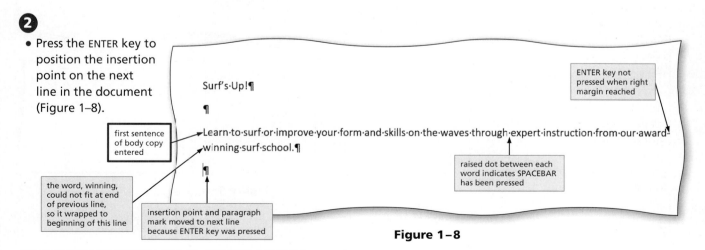

Figure 1–8

Spelling and Grammar Check

As you type text in a document, Word checks your typing for possible spelling and grammar errors. If all of the words you have typed are in Word's dictionary and your grammar is correct, as mentioned earlier, the Spelling and Grammar Check icon on the status bar displays a check mark. Otherwise, the icon shows an X. In this case, Word flags the potential error(s) in the document window with a red, green, or blue wavy underline.

- A red wavy underline means the flagged text is not in Word's dictionary (because it is a proper name or misspelled).

- A green wavy underline indicates the text may be incorrect grammatically.

- A blue wavy underline indicates the text may contain a contextual spelling error, such as the misuse of homophones (words that are pronounced the same but that have different spellings or meanings, such as one and won).

Although you can check the entire document for spelling and grammar errors at once, you also can check flagged errors as they appear on the screen.

A flagged word is not necessarily misspelled. For example, many names, abbreviations, and specialized terms are not in Word's main dictionary. In these cases, you can instruct Word to ignore the flagged word. As you type, Word also detects duplicate words while checking for spelling errors. For example, if your document contains the phrase, to the the store, Word places a red wavy underline below the second occurrence of the word, the.

To Check Spelling and Grammar as You Type

1 ENTER TEXT | 2 FORMAT TEXT | 3 INSERT PICTURE
4 FORMAT PICTURE | 5 ENHANCE PAGE | 6 CORRECT & REVISE

In the following steps, the word, group, has been misspelled intentionally as goup. **Why?** These steps illustrate Word's check spelling as you type feature. If you are completing this project on a computer, your flyer may contain different or no misspelled words, depending on the accuracy of your typing.

- Type **Private or goup** and then press the SPACEBAR, so that a red wavy line appears below the misspelled word (Figure 1–9).

Q&A | What if Word does not flag my spelling and grammar errors with wavy underlines?
To verify that the check spelling and grammar as you type features are enabled, click File on the ribbon to open the Backstage view and then click the Options tab in the Backstage view. When the Word Options dialog box is displayed, click Proofing in the left pane and then ensure the 'Check spelling as you type' and 'Mark grammar errors as you type' check boxes contain check marks. Also ensure the 'Hide spelling errors in this document only' and 'Hide grammar errors in this document only' check boxes do not contain check marks. Click the OK button to close the Word Options dialog box.

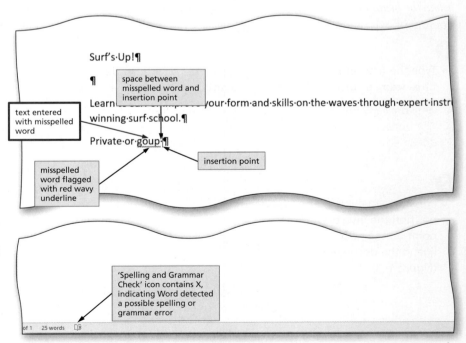

Figure 1–9

2

- Right-click the flagged word (goup, in this case) to display a shortcut menu that presents a list of suggested spelling corrections for the flagged word (Figure 1–10).

Q&A What if, when I right-click the misspelled word, my desired correction is not in the list on the shortcut menu?
You can click outside the shortcut menu to close the shortcut menu and then retype the correct word.

What if a flagged word actually is, for example, a proper name and spelled correctly?
Right-click it and then click Ignore All on the shortcut menu to instruct Word not to flag future occurrences of the same word in this document.

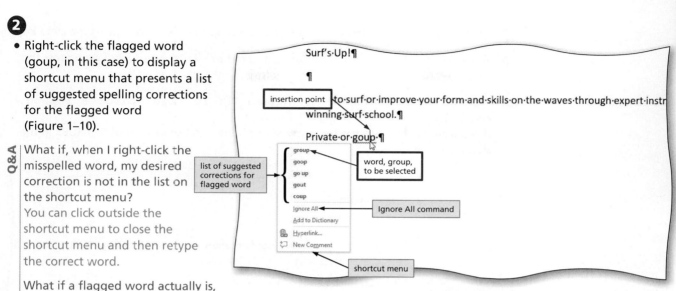

Figure 1–10

3

- Click group on the shortcut menu to replace the misspelled word in the document with a correctly spelled word (Figure 1–11).

Figure 1–11

Other Ways

1. Click 'Spelling and Grammar Check' icon on status bar, click desired word in Spelling pane, click Change button, click OK button

To Enter More Text

In the flyer, the text yet to be entered includes the remainder of the body copy, which will be formatted as a bulleted list, and the signature line. The following steps enter the remainder of text in the flyer.

1 Press the END key to move the insertion point to the end of the current line.

2 Type **lessons** and then press the ENTER key.

③ Type `Photo and video packages available` and then press the ENTER key.

④ Type `Reef shoes and surfboard rental included` and then press the ENTER key.

⑤ Type the signature line in the flyer (Figure 1–12): `To sign up for a lesson, call 555-SURF!`
If requested by your instructor, enter your phone number instead of 555-SURF in the signature line.

Figure 1–12

BTW

Organizing Files and Folders
You should organize and store files in folders so that you easily can find the files later. For example, if you are taking an introductory technology class called CIS 101, a good practice would be to save all Word files in a Word folder in a CIS 101 folder. For a discussion of folders and detailed examples of creating folders, refer to the Office and Windows module at the beginning of this book.

⑥ Save the flyer on your hard drive, OneDrive, or other storage location using Surf Flyer as the file name.

Q&A Why should I save the flyer at this time?
You have performed many tasks while creating this flyer and do not want to risk losing work completed thus far. For information about how to save, refer to the Office and Windows module at the beginning of this book.

CONSIDER THIS

How should you organize text in a flyer?
The text in a flyer typically is organized into three areas: headline, body copy, and signature line.

- The **headline** is the first line of text on the flyer. It conveys the product or service being offered (such as a car for sale, lessons, or sightseeing tours) or the benefit that will be gained (such as a convenience, better performance, greater security, higher earnings, or more comfort), or it can contain a message (such as a lost or found pet).

- The **body copy** consists of text between the headline and the signature line. This text highlights the key points of the message in as few words as possible. It should be easy to read and follow. While emphasizing the positive, the body copy must be realistic, truthful, and believable.

- The **signature line**, which is the last line of text on the flyer, contains contact information or identifies a call to action.

Navigating a Document

You view only a portion of a document on the screen through the document window. At some point when you type text or insert graphics, Word probably will **scroll** the top or bottom portion of the document off the screen. Although you cannot see the text and graphics once they scroll off the screen, they remain in the document.

You can use touch gestures, the keyboard, or a mouse to scroll to a different location in a document and/or move the insertion point around a document. If you are using a touch screen, simply use your finger to slide the document up or down to display a different location in the document and then tap to move the insertion point to a new location. When you use the keyboard, the insertion point automatically moves when you press the desired keys. For example, the previous steps used the END key to move the insertion point to the end of the current line. Table 1–1 outlines various techniques to navigate a document using the keyboard.

Table 1–1 Moving the Insertion Point with the Keyboard			
Insertion Point Direction	**Key(s) to Press**	**Insertion Point Direction**	**Key(s) to Press**
Left one character	LEFT ARROW	Up one paragraph	CTRL+UP ARROW
Right one character	RIGHT ARROW	Down one paragraph	CTRL+DOWN ARROW
Left one word	CTRL+LEFT ARROW	Up one screen	PAGE UP
Right one word	CTRL+RIGHT ARROW	Down one screen	PAGE DOWN
Up one line	UP ARROW	To top of document window	ALT+CTRL+PAGE UP
Down one line	DOWN ARROW	To bottom of document window	ALT+CTRL+PAGE DOWN
To end of line	END	To beginning of document	CTRL+HOME
To beginning of line	HOME	To end of document	CTRL+END

© 2015 Cengage Learning

With the mouse, you can use the scroll arrows or the scroll box on the scroll bar to display a different portion of the document in the document window and then click the mouse to move the insertion point to that location. Table 1–2 explains various techniques for using the scroll bar to scroll vertically with the mouse.

Table 1–2 Using the Scroll Bar to Scroll Vertically with the Mouse			
Scroll Direction	**Mouse Action**	**Scroll Direction**	**Mouse Action**
Up	Drag the scroll box upward.	Down one screen	Click anywhere below the scroll box on the vertical scroll bar.
Down	Drag the scroll box downward.	Up one line	Click the scroll arrow at the top of the vertical scroll bar.
Up one screen	Click anywhere above the scroll box on the vertical scroll bar.	Down one line	Click the scroll arrow at the bottom of the vertical scroll bar.

© 2015 Cengage Learning

Formatting Paragraphs and Characters

With the text for the flyer entered, the next step is to **format**, or change the appearance of, its text. A paragraph encompasses the text from the first character in the paragraph up to and including its paragraph mark (¶). **Paragraph formatting** is the process of changing the appearance of a paragraph. For example, you can center or add bullets to a paragraph. Characters include letters, numbers, punctuation marks, and symbols. **Character formatting** is the process of changing the way characters appear on the screen and in print. You use character formatting to emphasize certain words and improve readability of a document. For example, you can color, italicize, or underline characters. Often, you apply both paragraph and character formatting to the same text. For example, you may center a paragraph (paragraph formatting) and underline some of the characters in the same paragraph (character formatting).

Although you can format paragraphs and characters before you type, many Word users enter text first and then format the existing text. Figure 1–13a shows the flyer in this module before formatting its paragraphs and characters. Figure 1–13b shows the flyer after formatting. As you can see from the two figures, a document that is formatted is easier to read and looks more professional. The following sections discuss how to format the flyer so that it looks like Figure 1–13b.

BTW

Minimize Wrist Injury
Computer users frequently switch among the keyboard, the mouse, and touch gestures during a word processing session; such switching strains the wrist. To help prevent wrist injury, minimize switching. For instance, if your hand already is on the mouse, use the mouse to scroll. If your fingers already are on the keyboard, use keyboard keys to scroll. If your fingertips already are on the screen, use your finger to slide the document to a new location.

Figure 1–13a Unformatted Flyer

Figure 1–13b Formatted Flyer

Figure 1–13

Font, Font Sizes, and Themes

Characters that appear on the screen are a specific shape and size. The **font**, or typeface, defines the appearance and shape of the letters, numbers, and special characters. In Word, the default font usually is Calibri (shown in Figure 1–14). You can leave characters in the default font or change them to a different font. **Font size** specifies the size of the characters and is determined by a measurement system called points. A single **point** is about 1/72 of one inch in height. The default font size in Word typically is 11 (Figure 1–14). Thus, a character with a font size of 11 is about 11/72 or a little less than 1/6 of one inch in height. You can increase or decrease the font size of characters in a document.

A document **theme** is a set of unified formats for fonts, colors, and graphics. Word includes a variety of document themes to assist you with coordinating these visual elements in a document. The default theme fonts are Calibri Light for headings and Calibri for body text. By changing the document theme, you quickly can give your document a new look. You also can define your own document themes.

How do I know which formats to use in a flyer?
In a flyer, consider the following formatting suggestions.

- **Increase the font size of characters.** Flyers usually are posted on a bulletin board or in a window. Thus, the font size should be as large as possible so that passersby easily can read the flyer. To give the headline more impact, its font size should be larger than the font size of the text in the body copy. If possible, make the font size of the signature line larger than the body copy but smaller than the headline.

- **Change the font of characters.** Use fonts that are easy to read. Try to use only two different fonts in a flyer; for example, use one for the headline and the other for all other text. Too many fonts can make the flyer visually confusing.

- **Change the paragraph alignment.** The default alignment for paragraphs in a document is **left-aligned**, that is, flush at the left margin of the document with uneven right edges. Consider changing the alignment of some of the paragraphs to add interest and variety to the flyer.

- **Highlight key paragraphs with bullets.** A bulleted paragraph is a paragraph that begins with a dot or other symbol. Use bulleted paragraphs to highlight important points in a flyer.

- **Emphasize important words.** To call attention to certain words or lines, you can underline them, italicize them, or bold them. Use these formats sparingly, however, because overuse will minimize their effect and make the flyer look too busy.

- **Use color.** Use colors that complement each other and convey the meaning of the flyer. Vary colors in terms of hue and brightness. Headline colors, for example, can be bold and bright. Signature lines should stand out more than body copy but less than headlines. Keep in mind that too many colors can detract from the flyer and make it difficult to read.

To Center a Paragraph

The headline in the flyer currently is left-aligned (shown in Figure 1–14). *Why? Word, by default, left-aligns text, unless you specifically change the alignment.* You want the headline to be **centered**, that is, positioned horizontally between the left and right margins on the page. Recall that Word considers a single short line of text, such as the one-word headline, a paragraph. Thus, you will center the paragraph containing the headline. The following steps center a paragraph.

1

- Click Home on the ribbon to display the Home tab.
- Click somewhere in the paragraph to be centered (in this case, the headline) to position the insertion point in the paragraph to be centered (Figure 1–14).

Figure 1–14

2

- Click the Center button (Home tab | Paragraph group) to center the paragraph containing the insertion point (Figure 1–15).

Q&A

What if I want to return the paragraph to left-aligned?
You would click the Center button again or click the Align Left button (Home tab | Paragraph group).

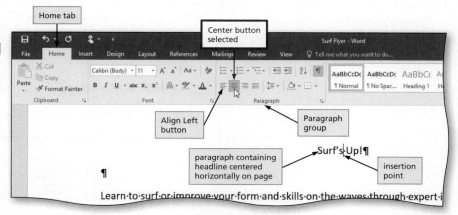

Figure 1–15

Other Ways

1. Right-click paragraph (or if using touch, tap 'Show Context Menu' button on mini toolbar), click Paragraph on shortcut menu, click Indents and Spacing tab (Paragraph dialog box), click Alignment arrow, click Centered, click OK button

2. Click Paragraph Settings Dialog Box Launcher (Home tab or Layout tab | Paragraph group), click Indents and Spacing tab (Paragraph dialog box), click Alignment arrow, click Centered, click OK button

3. Press CTRL+E

To Center Another Paragraph

In the flyer, the signature line is to be centered to match the paragraph alignment of the headline. The following steps center the signature line.

1 Click somewhere in the paragraph to be centered (in this case, the signature line) to position the insertion point in the paragraph to be formatted.

2 Click the Center button (Home tab | Paragraph group) to center the paragraph containing the insertion point (shown in Figure 1–16).

BTW

File Type
Depending on your Windows settings, the file type .docx may be displayed on the title bar immediately to the right of the file name after you save the file. The file type .docx identifies a Word 2016 document.

BTW
The Ribbon and Screen Resolution
Word may change how the groups and buttons within the groups appear on the ribbon, depending on the computer or mobile device's screen resolution. Thus, your ribbon may look different from the ones in this book if you are using a screen resolution other than 1366 × 768.

Formatting Single versus Multiple Paragraphs and Characters

As shown in the previous sections, to format a single paragraph, simply position the insertion point in the paragraph to make it the current paragraph and then format the paragraph. Similarly, to format a single word, position the insertion point in the word to make it the current word, and then format the word.

To format multiple paragraphs or words, however, you first must select the paragraphs or words you want to format and then format the selection.

1 ENTER TEXT | 2 FORMAT TEXT | **3 INSERT PICTURE**
4 FORMAT PICTURE | 5 ENHANCE PAGE | 6 CORRECT & REVISE

To Select a Line

The default font size of 11 point is too small for a headline in a flyer. To increase the font size of the characters in the headline, you first must select the line of text containing the headline. ***Why?*** *If you increase the font size of text without selecting any text, Word will increase the font size only of the word containing the insertion point.* The following step selects a line.

- Move the pointer to the left of the line to be selected (in this case, the headline) until the pointer changes to a right-pointing block arrow (Figure 1–16).

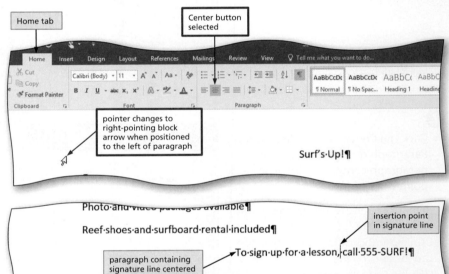

Figure 1–16

2

- While the pointer is a right-pointing block arrow, click the mouse button to select the entire line to the right of the pointer (Figure 1–17).

Q&A

What if I am using a touch screen?
You would double-tap to the left of the line to be selected to select the line.

Why is the selected text shaded gray?
If your screen normally displays dark letters on a light background, which is the default setting in Word, then selected text is displayed with a light shading color, such as gray, on the dark letters. Note that the selection that appears on the text does not print.

Figure 1–17

Other Ways

1. Drag pointer through line   2. With insertion point at beginning of desired line, press CRTL+SHIFT+DOWN ARROW

To Change the Font Size of Selected Text

The next step is to increase the font size of the characters in the selected headline. *Why? You would like the headline to be as large as possible and still fit on a single line, which in this case is 72 point.* The following steps increase the font size of the headline from 11 to 72 point.

1

- With the text selected, click the Font Size arrow (Home tab | Font group) to display the Font Size gallery (Figure 1–18).

Q&A

What is the Font Size arrow?
The Font Size arrow is the arrow to the right of the Font Size box, which is the text box that displays the current font size.

Why are the font sizes in my Font Size gallery different from those in Figure 1–18?
Font sizes may vary depending on the current font and your printer driver.

What happened to the mini toolbar?
The mini toolbar disappears if you do not use it. These steps use the Font Size arrow on the Home tab instead of the Font Size arrow on the mini toolbar.

Figure 1–18

2

- Point to 72 in the Font Size gallery to display a live preview of the selected text at the selected point size (Figure 1–19).

Q&A

What is live preview?
Recall from the Office and Windows module at the beginning of this book that live preview is a feature that allows you to point to a gallery choice and see its effect in the document — without actually selecting the choice.

Can I use live preview on a touch screen?
Live preview is not available on a touch screen.

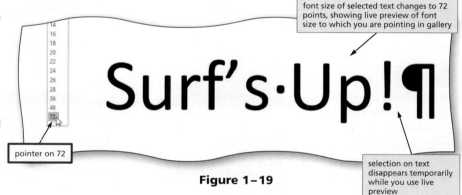

Figure 1–19

Experiment

- Point to various font sizes in the Font Size gallery and watch the font size of the selected text change in the document window.

3

- Click 72 in the Font Size gallery to increase the font size of the selected text.

Other Ways

1. Click Font Size arrow on mini toolbar, click desired font size in Font Size gallery	2. Right-click selected text (or, if using touch, tap 'Show Context Menu' button on mini toolbar), click Font on shortcut menu, click Font tab (Font dialog box), select desired font size in Size list, click OK button	3. Click Font Dialog Box Launcher, (Home tab | Font group) click Font tab (Font dialog box), select desired font size in Size list, click OK button	4. Press CTRL+D, click Font tab (Font dialog box), select desired font size in Size list, click OK button

To Change the Font of Selected Text

The default theme font for headings is Calibri Light and for all other text, called body text in Word, is Calibri. Many other fonts are available, however, so that you can add variety to documents.

The following steps change the font of the headline from Calibri to Rockwell Extra Bold. **Why?** *To draw more attention to the headline, you change its font so that it differs from the font of other text in the flyer.*

1

• With the text selected, click the Font arrow (Home tab | Font group) to display the Font gallery (Figure 1–20).

Q&A

Will the fonts in my Font gallery be the same as those in Figure 1–20?
Your list of available fonts may differ, depending on the type of printer you are using and other settings.

What if the text no longer is selected?
Follow the steps described earlier to select a line.

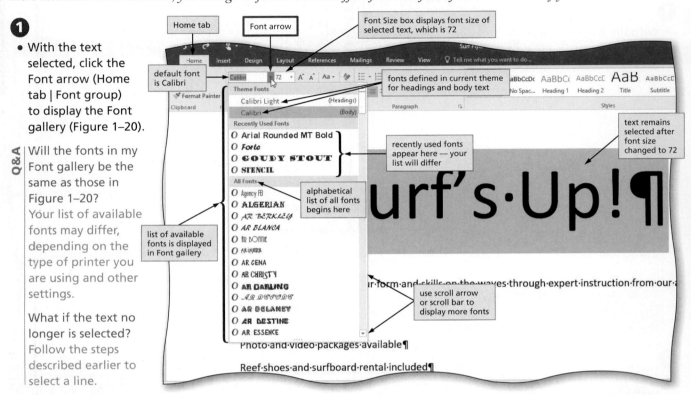

Figure 1–20

2

• If necessary, scroll through the Font gallery to display Rockwell Extra Bold (or a similar font).

• Point to 'Rockwell Extra Bold' (or a similar font) to display a live preview of the selected text in the selected font (Figure 1–21).

Experiment

• Point to various fonts in the Font gallery and watch the font of the selected text change in the document window.

Figure 1–21

❸

- Click 'Rockwell Extra Bold' (or a similar font) in the Font gallery to change the font of the selected text.

Q&A If the font I want to use appears in the Recently Used Fonts list in the Font gallery, could I click it there instead?
Yes.

Other Ways

1. Click Font arrow on mini toolbar, click desired font in Font gallery

2. Right-click selected text (or, if using touch, tap 'Show Context Menu' button on mini toolbar), click Font on shortcut menu, click Font tab (Font dialog box), select desired font in Font list, click OK button

3. Click Font Dialog Box Launcher (Home tab | Font group), click Font tab (Font dialog box), select desired font in Font list, click OK button

4. Press CTRL+D, click Font tab (Font dialog box), select desired font in Font list, click OK button

To Change the Case of Selected Text

1 ENTER TEXT | 2 FORMAT TEXT | **3 INSERT PICTURE**
4 FORMAT PICTURE | 5 ENHANCE PAGE | 6 CORRECT & REVISE

The headline currently shows the first letter in each word capitalized, which sometimes is referred to as initial cap. The following steps change the headline to uppercase. *Why? To draw more attention to the headline, you would like the entire line of text to be capitalized, or in uppercase letters.*

❶

- With the text selected, click the Change Case button (Home tab | Font group) to display the Change Case gallery (Figure 1–22).

Figure 1–22

❷

- Click UPPERCASE in the Change Case gallery to change the case of the selected text (Figure 1–23).

Q&A What if a ruler appears on the screen or the pointer shape changes?
If you are using a mouse, depending on the position of your pointer and locations you click on the screen, a ruler may appear automatically or the pointer's shape may change. Simply move the mouse and the ruler should disappear and/or the pointer shape will change.

Figure 1–23

Other Ways

1. Right-click selected text (or, if using touch, tap 'Show Context Menu' button on mini toolbar), click Font on shortcut menu, click Font tab (Font dialog box), select All caps in Effects area, click OK button

2. Click Font Dialog Box Launcher (Home tab | Font group), click Font tab (Font dialog box), select All caps in Effects area, click OK button

3. Press SHIFT+F3 repeatedly until text is desired case

To Apply a Text Effect to Selected Text

Word provides many text effects to add interest and variety to text. The following steps apply a text effect to the headline. *Why? You would like the text in the headline to be even more noticeable.*

1

- With the text selected, click the 'Text Effects and Typography' button (Home tab | Font group) to display the Text Effects and Typography gallery (Figure 1–24).

Figure 1–24

2

- Point to 'Fill - White, Outline - Accent 2, Hard Shadow - Accent 2' (fourth text effect in third row) to display a live preview of the selected text with the selected text effect (Figure 1–25).

Figure 1–25

 Experiment

- Point to various text effects in the Text Effects and Typography gallery and watch the text effects of the selected text change in the document window.

3

- Click 'Fill - White, Outline - Accent 2, Hard Shadow - Accent 2' to change the text effect of the selected text.

4

- Click anywhere in the document window to remove the selection from the selected text.

Other Ways

1. Right-click selected text (or, if using touch, tap 'Show Context Menu' button on mini toolbar), click Font on shortcut menu, click Font tab (Font dialog box), click Text Effects button, expand Text Fill or Text Outline section and then select the desired text effect(s) (Format Text Effects dialog box), click OK button, click OK button

2. Click Font Dialog Box Launcher (Home tab | Font group), click Font tab (Font dialog box), click Text Effects button, expand Text Fill or Text Outline section and then select desired text effect (Format Text Effects dialog box), click OK button, click OK button

To Shade a Paragraph

When you **shade** text, Word colors the rectangular area behind any text or graphics. If the text to shade is a paragraph, Word shades the area from the left margin to the right margin of the current paragraph. To shade a paragraph, place the insertion point in the paragraph. To shade any other text, you must first select the text to be shaded.

This flyer uses a shading color for the headline. *Why? To make the headline of the flyer more eye-catching, you shade it.* The following steps shade a paragraph.

1

- Click somewhere in the paragraph to be shaded (in this case, the headline) to position the insertion point in the paragraph to be formatted.

- Click the Shading arrow (Home tab | Paragraph group) to display the Shading gallery (Figure 1–26).

Figure 1–26

Q&A What if I click the Shading button by mistake?
Click the Shading arrow and proceed with Step 2. Note that if you are using a touch screen, you may not have a separate Shading button.

Why does my Shading gallery display different colors?
Your color scheme setting may display colors in a different order or may be different from Office, which is the default color scheme. To change the color scheme, click Design on the ribbon, click the Theme Colors button (Design tab | Document Formatting group), and then click Office in the Theme Colors gallery.

🔍 Experiment

- Point to various colors in the Shading gallery and watch the shading color of the current paragraph change.

2

- Click 'Orange, Accent 2, Darker 25%' (sixth color in fifth row) to shade the current paragraph (Figure 1–27).

Q&A What if I apply a dark shading color to dark text?
When the font color of text is Automatic, the color usually is black. If you select a dark shading color,

Figure 1–27

Word automatically may change the text color to white so that the shaded text is easier to read.

Other Ways

1. Click Borders arrow (Home tab | Paragraph group), click Borders and Shading, click Shading tab (Borders and Shading dialog box), click Fill arrow, select desired color, click OK button

To Select Multiple Lines

The next formatting step for the flyer is to increase the font size of the characters between the headline and the signature line. ***Why?*** *You want this text to be easier to read from a distance.*

To change the font size of the characters in multiple lines, you first must select all the lines to be formatted. The following steps select multiple lines.

- Scroll, if necessary, so that all text below the headline is displayed on the screen.

- Move the pointer to the left of the first paragraph to be selected until the pointer changes to a right-pointing block arrow (Figure 1–28).

Figure 1–28

Q&A What if I am using a touch screen?
You would tap to position the insertion point in the text to select.

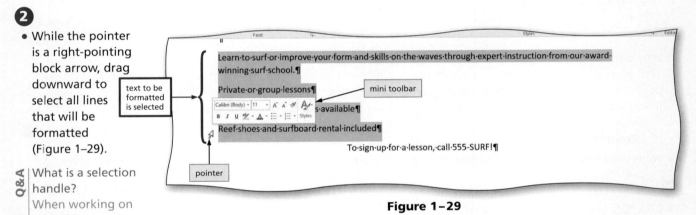

- While the pointer is a right-pointing block arrow, drag downward to select all lines that will be formatted (Figure 1–29).

Figure 1–29

Q&A What is a selection handle?
When working on a touch screen, a **selection handle** (small circle) appears below the insertion point. Using a fingertip, you drag a selection handle to select text.

Other Ways

1. With insertion point at beginning of desired line, press SHIFT+DOWN ARROW repeatedly until all lines are selected

BTW
Formatting Marks
With some fonts, the formatting marks will not be displayed properly on the screen. For example, the raised dot that signifies a blank space between words may be displayed behind a character instead of in the blank space, causing the characters to look incorrect.

To Change the Font Size of Selected Text

The characters between the headline and the signature line in the flyer currently are 11 point. To make them easier to read from a distance, this flyer uses a 24-point font size for these characters. The following steps change the font size of the selected text.

1 With the text selected, click the Font Size arrow (Home tab | Font group) to display the Font Size gallery.

2 Click 24 in the Font Size gallery to increase the font size of the selected text.

3 Click anywhere in the document window to remove the selection from the text.

4 If necessary, scroll so that you can see all the resized text on the screen (Figure 1–30).

Figure 1–30

To Bullet a List of Paragraphs

1 ENTER TEXT | 2 FORMAT TEXT | 3 INSERT PICTURE
4 FORMAT PICTURE | 5 ENHANCE PAGE | 6 CORRECT & REVISE

A **bulleted list** is a series of paragraphs, each beginning with a bullet character. The next step is to format the three paragraphs about the lessons that are above the signature line in the flyer as a bulleted list.

To format a list of paragraphs with bullets, you first must select all the lines in the paragraphs. *Why? If you do not select all paragraphs, Word will place a bullet only in the paragraph containing the insertion point.* The following steps bullet a list of paragraphs.

1

- Move the pointer to the left of the first paragraph to be selected until the pointer changes to a right-pointing block arrow.

- Drag downward until all paragraphs that will be formatted with a bullet character are selected (Figure 1–31).

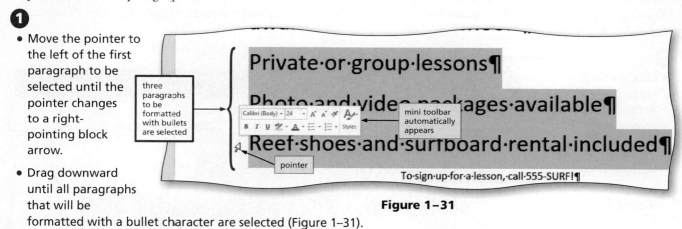

Figure 1–31

Q&A What if I am using a touch screen?

Tap to position the insertion point in the text to select and then drag the selection handle(s) as necessary to select the text that will be formatted.

2

- Click the Bullets button (Home tab | Paragraph group) to place a bullet character at the beginning of each selected paragraph (Figure 1–32).

Q&A

Why does my screen display a Bullets gallery?
If you are using a touch screen, you may not have a separate Bullets button and Bullets arrow. In this case, select the desired bullet style in the Bullets gallery.

What if I accidentally click the Bullets arrow?
Press the ESCAPE key to remove the Bullets gallery from the screen and then repeat Step 2.

How do I remove bullets from a list or paragraph?
Select the list or paragraph and then click the Bullets button again, or click the Bullets arrow and then click None in the Bullet Library.

Figure 1–32

Other Ways

1. Right-click selected paragraphs, click Bullets button on mini toolbar

To Undo and Redo an Action

1 ENTER TEXT | 2 FORMAT TEXT | 3 INSERT PICTURE
4 FORMAT PICTURE | 5 ENHANCE PAGE | 6 CORRECT & REVISE

Word provides a means of canceling your recent command(s) or action(s). For example, if you format text incorrectly, you can undo the format and try it again. When you point to the Undo button, Word displays the action you can undo as part of a ScreenTip.

If, after you undo an action, you decide you did not want to perform the undo, you can redo the undone action. Word does not allow you to undo or redo some actions, such as saving or printing a document. The following steps undo the bullet format just applied and then redo the bullet format. *Why? These steps illustrate the undo and redo actions.*

1

- Click the Undo button on the Quick Access Toolbar to reverse your most recent action (in this case, remove the bullets from the paragraphs) (Figure 1–33).

Figure 1–33

2

- Click the Redo button on the Quick Access Toolbar to reverse your most recent undo (in this case, place a bullet character on the paragraphs again) (shown in Figure 1–32).

Other Ways

1. Press CTRL+Z to undo; press CTRL+Y to redo

To Italicize Text

1 ENTER TEXT | 2 FORMAT TEXT | 3 INSERT PICTURE
4 FORMAT PICTURE | 5 ENHANCE PAGE | 6 CORRECT & REVISE

Italic text has a slanted appearance. The next step is to italicize the word, expert, in the flyer to further emphasize it. As with a single paragraph, if you want to format a single word, you do not need to select it. *Why?* *To format a single word, you simply position the insertion point somewhere in the word and apply the desired format.* The following step italicizes a word.

1

- Click somewhere in the word to be italicized (expert, in this case) to position the insertion point in the word to be formatted.

- Click the Italic button (Home tab | Font group) to italicize the word containing the insertion point (Figure 1–34).

Q&A How would I remove an italic format?
You would click the Italic button a second time, or you immediately could click the Undo button on the Quick Access Toolbar or press CTRL+Z.

Figure 1–34

How can I tell what formatting has been applied to text?
The selected buttons and boxes on the Home tab show formatting characteristics of the location of the insertion point. With the insertion point in the word, expert, the Home tab shows these formats: 24-point Calibri italic font.

Why did the appearance of the Redo button change?
It changed to a Repeat button. When it is a Repeat button, you can click it to repeat your last action. For example, you can select different text and then click the Repeat button to apply (repeat) the italic format to the selected text.

Other Ways

1. Click Italic button on mini toolbar

2. Right-click selected text (or, if using touch, tap 'Show Context Menu' button on mini toolbar), click Font on shortcut menu, click Font tab (Font dialog box), click Italic in Font style list, click OK button

3. Click Font Dialog Box Launcher (Home tab | Font group), click Font tab (Font dialog box), click Italic in Font style list, click OK button

4. Press CTRL+I

To Color Text

The following steps change the color of the word, expert. *Why? To emphasize the word even more, you change its color.*

- With the insertion point in the word to format, click the Font Color arrow (Home tab | Font group) to display the Font Color gallery (Figure 1–35).

Q&A What if I click the Font Color button by mistake?
Click the Font Color arrow and then proceed with Step 2. Note that you may not have a separate Font Color button if you are using a touch screen.

Figure 1–35

Experiment

- If you are using a mouse, point to various colors in the Font Color gallery and watch the color of the current word change.

- Click 'Orange, Accent 2, Darker 25%' (sixth color in fifth row) to change the color of the text (Figure 1–36).

Q&A How would I change the text color back to black?
You would position the insertion point in the word or select the text, click the Font Color arrow (Home tab | Font group) again, and then click Automatic in the Font Color gallery.

Learn·to·su text color changed improve·your·form·and·skills·on·
the·waves·through·*expert*·instruction·from·our·
award-winning·surf·school.¶

  •··Private·or·group·lessons¶

  •··Photo·and·video·packages·available¶

Figure 1–36

Other Ways

1. Click Font Color arrow on mini toolbar, click desired color	2. Right-click selected text (or, if using touch, tap 'Show Context Menu' button on mini toolbar), click Font on shortcut menu, click Font tab (Font dialog box), click Font color arrow, click desired color, click OK button	3. Click Font Dialog Box Launcher (Home tab | Font group), click Font tab (Font dialog box), click Font color arrow, click desired color, click OK button

To Use the Mini Toolbar to Format Text

Recall from the Office and Windows module at the beginning of this book that the mini toolbar automatically appears based on certain tasks you perform. *Why? Word places commonly used buttons and boxes on the mini toolbar for your convenience. If you do not use the mini toolbar, it disappears from the screen.* All commands on the mini toolbar also exist on the ribbon.

The following steps use the mini toolbar to change the color and font size of text in the signature line of the flyer.

1

- Move the pointer to the left of the line to be selected until the pointer changes to a right-pointing block arrow and then click to select the line and display the mini toolbar (Figure 1–37).

Q&A What if I am using a touch screen?
Double-tap to the left of the line to be selected to select the line and then tap the selection to display the mini toolbar. If you are using a touch screen, the buttons and boxes on the mini toolbar differ. For example, it contains a 'Show Context Menu' button at the far-right edge, which you tap to display a shortcut menu.

2

- Click the Font Size arrow on the mini toolbar to display the Font Size gallery.
- Point to 28 in the Font Size gallery to display a live preview of the selected font size (Figure 1–38).

3

- Click 28 in the Font Size gallery to increase the font size of the selected text.

Figure 1–37

Figure 1–38

4

- With the text still selected and the mini toolbar still displayed, click the Font Color arrow on the mini toolbar to display the Font Color gallery.
- Point to 'Orange, Accent 2, Darker 25%' (sixth color in the fifth row) to display a live preview of the selected font color (Figure 1–39).

Figure 1–39

5

- Click 'Orange, Accent 2, Darker 25%' to change the color of the selected text.
- Click anywhere in the document window to remove the selection from the text.

To Select a Group of Words

1 ENTER TEXT | 2 FORMAT TEXT | 3 INSERT PICTURE
4 FORMAT PICTURE | 5 ENHANCE PAGE | 6 CORRECT & REVISE

To emphasize the contact phone number (555-SURF), this text is underlined in the flyer. Because the phone number is separated with a hyphen, Word considers it a group of words. To format a group of words, you first must select them. ***Why?*** *If you underline text without selecting any text first, Word will underline only the word containing the insertion point.* The following steps select a group of words.

1

- Position the pointer immediately to the left of the first character of the text to be selected, in this case, the 5 in 555 (Figure 1–40).

Q&A Why did the shape of the pointer change?
The pointer's shape is an I-beam when positioned in unselected text in the document window.

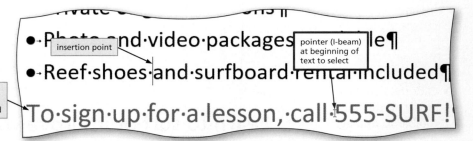

Figure 1–40

2

- Drag the pointer through the last character of the text to be selected, in this case, the F in the phone number (Figure 1–41).

Q&A Why did the pointer shape change again?
When the pointer is positioned in selected text, its shape is a left-pointing block arrow.

Figure 1–41

Other Ways

1. With insertion point at beginning of first word in group, press CTRL+SHIFT+RIGHT ARROW repeatedly until all words are selected

To Underline Text

Underlined text prints with an underscore (_) below each character. In the flyer, the contact phone number, 555-SURF, in the signature line is underlined. *Why? Underlines are used to emphasize or draw attention to specific text.* The following step formats selected text with an underline.

1

- With the text selected, click the Underline button (Home tab | Font group) to underline the selected text (Figure 1–42).

Q&A What if my screen displays an Underline gallery? If you are using a touch screen, you may not have a separate Underline button and Underline arrow. In this case, select the desired underline style in the Underline gallery.

Figure 1–42

If a button exists on the mini toolbar, can I click that instead of using the ribbon? Yes.

How would I remove an underline?
You would click the Underline button a second time, or you immediately could click the Undo button on the Quick Access Toolbar.

Other Ways			
1. Click Underline button on mini toolbar	2. Right-click text (or, if using touch, tap 'Show Context Menu' button on mini toolbar), click Font on shortcut menu, click Font tab (Font dialog box), click Underline style box arrow, click desired underline style, click OK button	3. Click Font Dialog Box Launcher (Home tab | Font group), click Font tab (Font dialog box), click Underline style arrow, click desired underline style, click OK button	4. Press CTRL+U

To Bold Text

Bold characters appear somewhat thicker and darker than those that are not bold. The following steps format the text, award-winning, in bold characters. *Why? To further emphasize this text, it is bold in the flyer.* Recall that if you want to format a single word, you simply position the insertion point in the word and then format the word. To format text that consists of more than one word, as you have learned previously, you select the text first.

1

- Select the text to be formatted (the text, award-winning, in this case); that is, position the pointer immediately to the left of the first character of the text to be selected and then drag the pointer through the last character of the text to be selected.

Q&A What if I am using a touch screen?
Tap to position the insertion point in the text you want to select and then drag the selection handle(s) to select the text to be formatted.

②

- With the text selected, click the Bold button (Home tab | Font group) to bold the selected text (Figure 1–43).

How would I remove a bold format?

You would click the Bold button a second time, or you immediately could click the Undo button on the Quick Access Toolbar.

③

- Click anywhere in the document window to remove the selection from the screen.

Figure 1–43

Other Ways

1. Click Bold button on mini toolbar	2. Right-click selected text (or, if using touch, tap 'Show Context Menu' button on mini toolbar), click Font on shortcut menu, click Font tab (Font dialog box), click Bold in Font style list, click OK button	3. Click Font Dialog Box Launcher (Home tab | Font group), click Font tab (Font dialog box), click Bold in Font style list, click OK button	4. Press CTRL+B

1 ENTER TEXT | 2 FORMAT TEXT | 3 INSERT PICTURE
4 FORMAT PICTURE | 5 ENHANCE PAGE | 6 CORRECT & REVISE

To Zoom One Page

Earlier in this module, you changed the zoom to page width so that the text on the screen was larger and easier to read. In the next set of steps, you want to see the entire page (as a mock sheet of paper) on the screen at once. *Why? You want be able to see the effect of adjusting colors in the document as a whole.* The next step displays a single page in its entirety in the document window as large as possible.

①

- Click View on the ribbon to display the View tab.
- Click the One Page button (View tab | Zoom group) to display the entire page in the document window as large as possible (Figure 1–44).

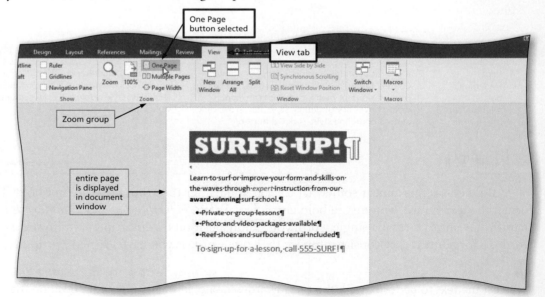

Figure 1–44

Other Ways

1. Click Zoom button (View tab | Zoom group), click Whole page (Zoom dialog box), click OK button

What colors should I choose when creating documents?

When choosing color, associate the meaning of the color with your message:

- Red expresses danger, power, or energy and often is associated with sports or physical exertion.

- Brown represents simplicity, honesty, and dependability.

- Orange denotes success, victory, creativity, and enthusiasm.

- Yellow suggests sunshine, happiness, hope, liveliness, and intelligence.

- Green symbolizes growth, healthiness, harmony, and healing and often is associated with safety or money.

- Blue indicates integrity, trust, importance, confidence, and stability.

- Purple represents wealth, power, comfort, extravagance, magic, mystery, and spirituality.

- White stands for purity, goodness, cleanliness, precision, and perfection.

- Black suggests authority, strength, elegance, power, and prestige.

- Gray conveys neutrality and, thus, often is found in backgrounds and other effects.

To Change Theme Colors

1 ENTER TEXT | 2 FORMAT TEXT | 3 INSERT PICTURE
4 FORMAT PICTURE | 5 ENHANCE PAGE | 6 CORRECT & REVISE

A **color scheme** in Word is a document theme that identifies complementary colors for text, background, accents, and links in a document. With more than 20 predefined color schemes, Word provides a simple way to coordinate colors in a document.

The default color scheme is called Office. In the flyer, you will change the color scheme. *Why? You want the colors in the flyer to represent integrity, trust, confidence, stability, healthiness, harmony, blooming, and safety, which are conveyed by shades of blues and greens. In Word, the Blue color scheme uses these colors.* The following steps change theme colors.

1

- Click Design on the ribbon to display the Design tab.

- Click the Theme Colors button (Design tab | Document Formatting group) to display the Theme Colors gallery.

- Point to Blue in the Theme Colors gallery to display a live preview of the selected theme color (Figure 1–45).

 Experiment

- Point to various color schemes in the Theme Colors gallery and watch the colors change in the document.

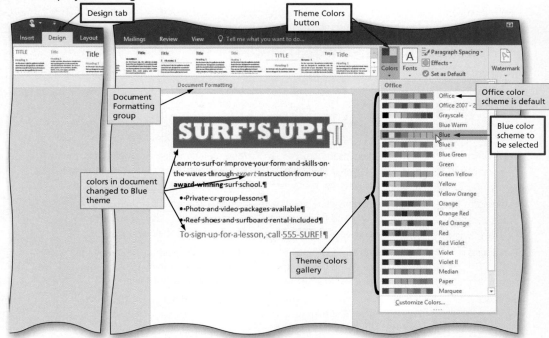

Figure 1–45

2

- Click Blue in the Theme Colors gallery to change the document theme colors.

 What if I want to return to the original color scheme?

You would click the Theme Colors button again and then click Office in the Theme Colors gallery.

To Zoom Page Width

Because the document contents are small when displayed on one page, the next steps zoom page width again.

BTW
Selecting Nonadjacent Items
In Word, you can use keyboard keys to select nonadjacent items, that is, items not next to each other. This is helpful when you are applying the same formatting to multiple items. To select nonadjacent items (text or graphics), select the first item, such as a word or paragraph, as usual; then, press and hold down the CTRL key. While holding down the CTRL key, select additional items.

1 Click View on the ribbon to display the View tab.

2 Click the Page Width button (View tab | Zoom group) to display the page the same width as the document window (shown earlier in the module in Figure 1–7).

3 Save the flyer again on the same storage location with the same file name.

Q&A Why should I save the flyer again?
You have made several modifications to the flyer since you last saved it; thus, you should save it again.

Selecting Text

In many of the previous steps, you have selected text. Table 1–3 summarizes the techniques used to select various items.

Table 1–3 Techniques for Selecting Text			
Item to Select	Touch	Mouse	Keyboard (where applicable)
Block of text	Tap to position insertion point in text to select and then drag selection handle(s) to select text.	Click at beginning of selection, scroll to end of selection, position pointer at end of selection, hold down SHIFT key, and then click; or drag through the text.	
Character(s)	Tap to position insertion point in text to select and then drag selection handle(s) to select text.	Drag through character(s).	SHIFT+RIGHT ARROW or SHIFT+LEFT ARROW
Document		Move pointer to left of text until pointer changes to right-pointing block arrow and then triple-click.	CTRL+A
Graphic	Tap the graphic.	Click the graphic.	
Line	Double-tap to left of line to be selected.	Move pointer to left of line until pointer changes to right-pointing block arrow and then click.	HOME, then SHIFT+END or END, then SHIFT+HOME
Lines	Tap to position insertion point in text to select and then drag selection handle(s) to select text.	Move pointer to left of first line until pointer changes to right-pointing block arrow and then drag up or down.	HOME, then SHIFT+DOWN ARROW or END, then SHIFT+UP ARROW
Paragraph	Tap to position insertion point in text to select and then drag selection handle(s) to select text.	Triple-click paragraph; or move pointer to left of paragraph until pointer changes to right-pointing block arrow and then double-click.	CTRL+SHIFT+DOWN ARROW or CTRL+SHIFT+UP ARROW
Paragraphs	Tap to position insertion point in text to select and then drag selection handle(s) to select text.	Move pointer to left of paragraph until pointer changes to right-pointing block arrow, double-click, and then drag up or down.	CTRL+SHIFT+DOWN ARROW or CTRL+SHIFT+UP ARROW repeatedly
Sentence	Tap to position insertion point in text to select and then drag selection handle(s) to select text.	Press and hold down CTRL key and then click sentence.	
Word	Double-tap word.	Double-click word.	CTRL+SHIFT+RIGHT ARROW or CTRL+SHIFT+LEFT ARROW
Words	Tap to position insertion point in text to select and then drag selection handle(s) to select text.	Drag through words.	CTRL+SHIFT+RIGHT ARROW or CTRL+SHIFT+LEFT ARROW repeatedly

Break Point: If you wish to take a break, this is a good place to do so. You can exit Word now. To resume at a later time, run Word, open the file called Surf Flyer, and continue following the steps from this location forward. For a detailed example of exiting Word, running Word, and opening a file, refer to the Office and Windows module at the beginning of the book.

Inserting and Formatting a Picture in a Word Document

With the text formatted in the flyer, the next step is to insert a digital picture in the flyer and format the picture. Flyers usually contain a graphical image(s), such as a picture, to attract the attention of passersby. In the following sections, you will perform these tasks:

1. Insert a digital picture into the flyer.
2. Reduce the size of the picture.
3. Change the look of the picture.

CONSIDER THIS

How do I locate a graphic file to use in a document?
To use a graphic in a Word document, the image must be stored digitally in a file. Files containing graphics are available from a variety of sources:

• The web has images available, some of which are free, while others require a fee.

• You can take a picture with a digital camera or smartphone and **download** it, which is the process of copying the digital picture from the camera or phone to your computer.

• With a scanner, you can convert a printed picture, drawing, or diagram to a digital file.

If you receive a picture from a source other than yourself, do not use the file until you are certain it does not contain a virus. A **virus** is a computer program that can damage files and programs on your computer. Use an antivirus program to verify that any files you use are virus free.

To Center Another Paragraph

In the flyer, the digital picture of a surfer should be centered on the blank line below the headline. The blank paragraph below the headline currently is left-aligned. The following steps center this paragraph.

1 Click Home on the ribbon to display the Home tab.

2 Click somewhere in the paragraph to be centered (in this case, the blank line below the headline) to position the insertion point in the paragraph to be formatted.

3 Click the Center button (Home tab | Paragraph group) to center the paragraph containing the insertion point (shown in Figure 1–46).

To Insert a Picture

1 ENTER TEXT | 2 FORMAT TEXT | **3 INSERT PICTURE**
4 FORMAT PICTURE | 5 ENHANCE PAGE | 6 CORRECT & REVISE

The next step in creating the flyer is to insert a digital picture of a surfer in the flyer on the blank line below the headline. The picture, which was taken with a digital camera, is available on the Data Files. Please contact your instructor for information about accessing Data Files.

The following steps insert a picture, which, in this example, is located in the Module 01 folder in the Data Files folder. ***Why?*** *It is good practice to organize and store files in folders so that you easily can find the files at a later date.*

1

- If necessary, position the insertion point at the location where you want to insert the picture (in this case, on the centered blank paragraph below the headline).

- Click Insert on the ribbon to display the Insert tab (Figure 1–46).

Figure 1–46

2

- Click the From File button (Insert tab | Illustrations group) (shown in Figure 1–46) to display the Insert Picture dialog box (shown in Figure 1–47).

3

- Navigate to the desired picture location (in this case, the Module 01 folder in the Data Files folder). For a detailed example of this procedure, refer to Steps 4a and 4b in the To Save a File in a Folder section in the Office and Windows module at the beginning of this book.

Figure 1–47

- Click Surfing to select the file (Figure 1–47).

4

- Click the Insert button (Insert Picture dialog box) to insert the picture at the location of the insertion point in the document (Figure 1–48).

Q&A What are the symbols around the picture?

A selected graphic appears surrounded by a **selection rectangle**, which has small squares and circles, called **sizing handles**, at each corner and middle location.

What is the purpose of the Layout Options button?

When you click the Layout Options button, Word provides options for changing how the graphic is positioned with text in the document.

Figure 1–48

How do you know where to position a graphic on a flyer?

The content, size, shape, position, and format of a graphic should capture the interest of passersby, enticing them to stop and read the flyer. Often, the graphic is the center of attention and visually the largest element on a flyer. If you use colors in the graphical image, be sure they are part of the document's color scheme.

CONSIDER THIS

1 ENTER TEXT | 2 FORMAT TEXT | **3 INSERT PICTURE**
4 FORMAT PICTURE | 5 ENHANCE PAGE | 6 CORRECT & REVISE

To Zoom the Document

In the steps in the following sections, you will work with the picture just inserted. The next task is to adjust the zoom percentage. *Why? Currently, you can see only a small amount of text with the picture. Seeing more of the document at once helps you determine the appropriate size for the picture.* The following step zooms the document.

1

 Experiment

- Repeatedly click the Zoom Out and Zoom In buttons on the status bar and watch the size of the document change in the document window.

What if I am using a touch screen?
Repeatedly pinch (move two fingers together on the screen) and stretch (move two fingers apart on the screen) and watch the size of the document change in the document window.

• Click the Zoom Out or Zoom In button as many times as necessary until the Zoom button on the status bar displays 40% on its face (Figure 1–49).

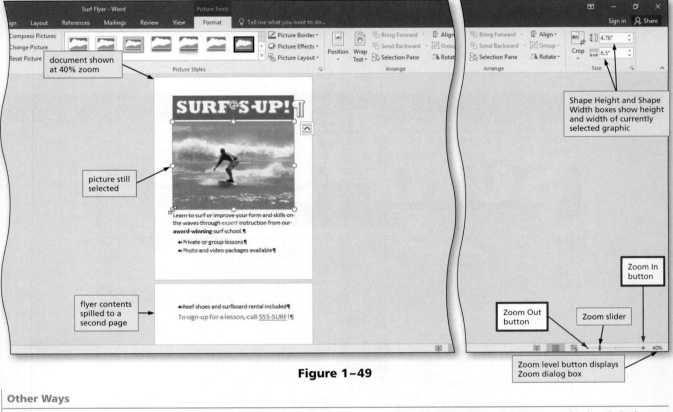

Figure 1–49

Other Ways

1. Drag Zoom slider on status bar
2. Click Zoom level button on status bar, select desired zoom percent or type (Zoom dialog box), click OK button
3. Click Zoom button (View tab | Zoom group), select desired zoom percent or type (Zoom dialog box), click OK button

To Resize a Graphic

Resizing includes both increasing and reducing the size of a graphic. The next step is to resize the picture so that it is smaller in the flyer. **Why?** *You want the graphic and all the text on the flyer to fit on a single sheet of paper.* The following steps resize a selected graphic.

1

• Be sure the graphic still is selected.

 What if my graphic (picture) is not selected?
To select a graphic, click it.

• Point to the lower-left corner sizing handle on the picture so that the pointer shape changes to a two-headed arrow (Figure 1–50).

Figure 1–50

- Drag the sizing handle diagonally inward until the lower-left corner of the picture is positioned approximately as shown in Figure 1–51. Do not release the mouse button at this point.

Q&A What if I am using a touch screen?
Drag a corner of the graphic, without lifting your finger, until the graphic is the desired size.

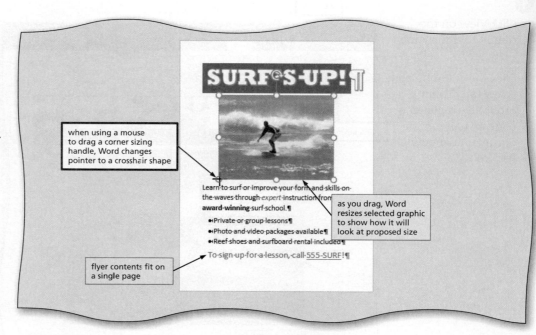

when using a mouse to drag a corner sizing handle, Word changes pointer to a crosshair shape

as you drag, Word resizes selected graphic to show how it will look at proposed size

flyer contents fit on a single page

Figure 1–51

- Release the mouse button to resize the graphic, which, in this case, should have a height of about 3.7″ and a width of about 5.06″.

Q&A How can I see the height and width measurements?
Look in the Size group on the Picture Tools Format tab to see the height and width measurements of the currently selected graphic (shown in Figure 1–49).

What if the graphic is the wrong size?
Repeat Steps 1, 2, and 3, or enter the desired height and width values in the Shape Height and Shape Width boxes (Picture Tools Format tab | Size group).

What if I want to return a graphic to its original size and start again?
With the graphic selected, click the Size Dialog Box Launcher (Picture Tools Format tab | Size group), click the Size tab (Layout dialog box), click the Reset button, and then click the OK button.

Other Ways
1. Enter height and width of graphic in Shape Height and Shape Width boxes (Picture Tools Format tab | Size group) 2. Click Advanced Layout: Size Dialog Box Launcher (Picture Tools Format tab | Size group), click Size tab (Layout dialog box), enter desired height and width values in boxes, click OK button

1 ENTER TEXT | 2 FORMAT TEXT | 3 INSERT PICTURE

To Zoom 100%

4 FORMAT PICTURE | 5 ENHANCE PAGE | 6 CORRECT & REVISE

In the next series of steps, you will format the picture. Earlier in this module, you changed the zoom to 40% so that you could see more of the page while resizing the graphic. The following step zooms the screen to 100%. *Why? You want the contents of the image to be enlarged a bit, while still seeing some of the text in the document.*

1

- Click View on the ribbon to display the View tab.

- Click the 100% button (View tab | Zoom group) to display the page at 100% in the document window (Figure 1–52).

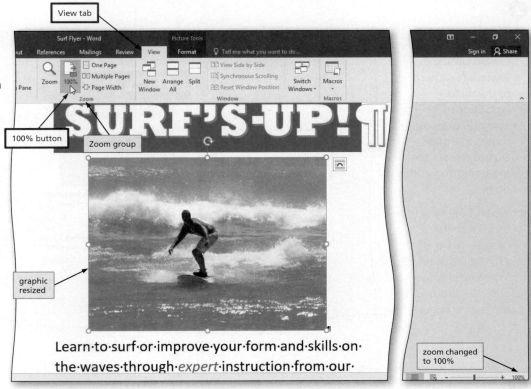

Figure 1–52

Other Ways

1. Click Zoom button (View tab | Zoom group), click 100% (Zoom dialog box), click OK button

---

1 ENTER TEXT | 2 FORMAT TEXT | 3 INSERT PICTURE
4 FORMAT PICTURE | 5 ENHANCE PAGE | 6 CORRECT & REVISE

To Apply a Picture Style

A **style** is a named group of formatting characteristics. Word provides more than 25 picture styles. *Why? Picture styles enable you easily to change a picture's look to a more visually appealing style, including a variety of shapes, angles, borders, and reflections.* The flyer in this module uses a style that applies an oval shape to the picture. The following steps apply a picture style to a picture.

1

- Ensure the graphic still is selected and then click Picture Tools Format on the ribbon to display the Picture Tools Format tab (Figure 1–53).

Q&A

What if my graphic (picture) is not selected?
To select a graphic, click it.

What is the white circle attached to top of the selected graphic?
It is called a rotate handle. When you drag a graphic's **rotate handle,** the graphic moves in either a clockwise or counterclockwise direction.

Figure 1–53

②

- Click the More button in the Picture Styles gallery (Picture Tools Format tab | Picture Styles group) (shown in Figure 1–53) to expand the gallery.

- Point to 'Soft Edge Oval' in the Picture Styles gallery to display a live preview of that style applied to the picture in the document (Figure 1–54).

 Experiment

- Point to various picture styles in the Picture Styles gallery and watch the style of the picture change in the document window.

③

- Click 'Soft Edge Oval' in the Picture Styles gallery (sixth style in third row) to apply the style to the selected picture.

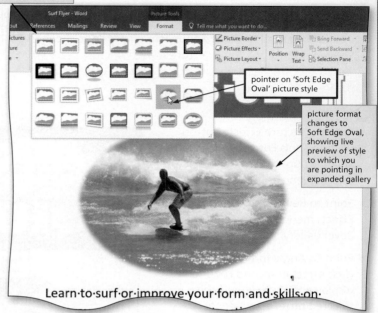

Figure 1–54

Other Ways

1. Right-click picture, click 'Picture Styles' on mini toolbar, select desired style

To Apply Picture Effects

1 ENTER TEXT | 2 FORMAT TEXT | 3 INSERT PICTURE
4 FORMAT PICTURE | 5 ENHANCE PAGE | 6 CORRECT & REVISE

Word provides a variety of picture effects, such as shadows, reflections, glow, soft edges, bevel, and 3-D rotation. The difference between the effects and the styles is that each effect has several options, providing you with more control over the exact look of the image.

In this flyer, the picture has a slight lime green glow effect and beveled edges. The following steps apply picture effects to the selected picture. **Why?** *Picture effects enable you to further customize a picture.*

①

- With the picture still selected, click the Picture Effects button (Picture Tools Format tab | Picture Styles group) to display the Picture Effects menu.

- Point to Glow on the Picture Effects menu to display the Glow gallery.

- Point to 'Lime, 5 pt glow, Accent color 6' in the Glow Variations area (rightmost glow in first row) to display a live preview of the selected glow effect applied to the picture in the document window (Figure 1–55).

 Experiment

- If you are using a mouse, point to various glow effects in the Glow gallery and watch the picture change in the document window.

Figure 1–55

2

- Click 'Lime, 5 pt glow, Accent color 6' in the Glow gallery to apply the selected picture effect.

Q&A

What if I wanted to discard formatting applied to a picture?
You would click the Reset Picture button (Picture Tools Format tab | Adjust group). To reset formatting and size, you would click the Reset Picture arrow (Picture Tools Format tab | Adjust group) and then click 'Reset Picture & Size' on the Reset Picture menu.

3

- Click the Picture Effects button (Picture Tools Format tab | Picture Styles group) to display the Picture Effects menu again.

- Point to Bevel on the Picture Effects menu to display the Bevel gallery.

- Point to Angle in the Bevel area (first effect in second row) to display a live preview of the selected bevel effect applied to the picture in the document window (Figure 1–56).

 Experiment

- If you are using a mouse, point to various bevel effects in the Bevel gallery and watch the picture change in the document window.

Figure 1–56

4

- Click Angle in the Bevel gallery to apply the selected picture effect.

Other Ways

1. Right-click picture (or, if using touch, tap 'Show Context Menu' button on mini toolbar), click Format Object or Format Picture on shortcut menu, click Effects button (Format Picture task pane), select desired options, click Close button

2. Click Format Shape Dialog Box Launcher (Picture Tools Format tab | Picture Styles group), click Effects button (Format Picture task pane), select desired options, click Close button

BTW

Touch Screen Differences
The Office and Windows interfaces may vary if you are using a touch screen. For this reason, you might notice that the function or appearance of your touch screen differs slightly from this module's presentation.

Enhancing the Page

With the text and graphics entered and formatted, the next step is to look at the page as a whole and determine if it looks finished in its current state. As you review the page, answer these questions:

- Does it need a page border to frame its contents, or would a page border make it look too busy?

- Is the spacing between paragraphs and graphics on the page adequate? Do any sections of text or graphics look as if they are positioned too closely to the items above or below them?

- Does the flyer have too much space at the top or bottom? Should the contents be centered vertically?

You determine that a graphical, color-coordinated border would enhance the flyer. You also notice that the flyer would look better proportioned if it had a little more space above and below the picture. You also want to ensure that the contents are centered vertically. The following sections make these enhancements to the flyer.

To Add a Page Border

In Word, you can add a border around the perimeter of an entire page. The flyer in this module has a lime border. *Why? This border color complements the color of the flyer contents.* The following steps add a page border.

1

- Click Design on the ribbon to display the Design tab.

- Click the 'Borders and Shading' button (Design tab | Page Background group) to display the Borders and Shading dialog box (Figure 1–57).

Figure 1–57

2

- Scroll to, if necessary, and then click the sixth border style in the Style list (Borders and Shading dialog box) to select the style.

- Click the Color arrow to display a Color palette (Figure 1–58).

Figure 1–58

- Click 'Lime, Accent 6, Lighter 40%' (rightmost color in fourth row) in the Color palette to select the color for the page border.
- Click the Width arrow to display the Width list and then click 4 ½ pt to select the thickness of the page border (Figure 1–59).

- Click the OK button to add the border to the page (shown in Figure 1–60).

Q&A What if I wanted to remove the border?
You would click None in the Setting list in the Borders and Shading dialog box.

Figure 1–59

To Zoom One Page

The next steps zoom one page so that you can see the entire page on the screen at once.

1 Click View on the ribbon to display the View tab.

2 Click the One Page button (View tab | Zoom group) to display the entire page in the document window as large as possible.

To Change Spacing before and after Paragraphs

1 ENTER TEXT | 2 FORMAT TEXT | 3 INSERT PICTURE
4 FORMAT PICTURE | 5 ENHANCE PAGE | 6 CORRECT & REVISE

The default spacing above (before) a paragraph in Word is 0 points and below (after) is 8 points. In the flyer, you want to increase the spacing below the paragraph containing the headline and above the signature line. *Why? The flyer spacing will look more balanced with spacing increased above and below these paragraphs.* The following steps change the spacing above and below a paragraph.

- Position the insertion point in the paragraph to be adjusted, in this case, the paragraph containing the headline.

Q&A What happened to the Picture Tools Format tab?
When you click outside of a graphic or press a key to scroll through a document, Word deselects the graphic and removes the Picture Tools Format tab from the screen. That is, this tab appears only when a graphic is selected.

- Click Layout on the ribbon to display the Layout tab.
- Click the Spacing After up arrow (Layout tab | Paragraph group) so that 12 pt is displayed in the Spacing After box to increase the space below the current paragraph (Figure 1–60).

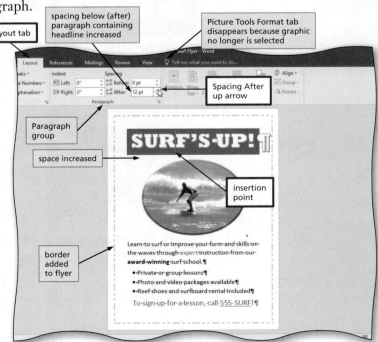

Figure 1–60

2

- Position the insertion point in the paragraph to be adjusted, in this case, the paragraph containing the signature line.

- Click the Spacing Before up arrow (Layout tab | Paragraph group) as many times as necessary so that 12 pt is displayed in the Spacing Before box to increase the space above the current paragraph (Figure 1–61).

- If the text flows to two pages, reduce the spacing above and below paragraphs as necessary.

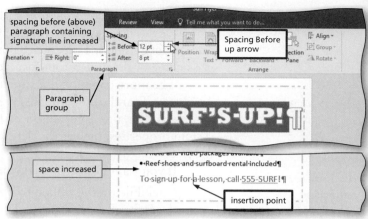

Figure 1–61

Other Ways

1. Right-click paragraph (or, if using touch, tap 'Show Context Menu' button on mini toolbar), click Paragraph on shortcut menu, click Indents and Spacing tab (Paragraph dialog box), enter spacing before and after values, click OK button

2. Click Paragraph Settings Dialog Box Launcher (Home tab or Layout tab | Paragraph group), click Indents and Spacing tab (Paragraph dialog box), enter spacing before and after values, click OK button

To Center Page Contents Vertically

1 ENTER TEXT | 2 FORMAT TEXT | 3 INSERT PICTURE
4 FORMAT PICTURE | 5 ENHANCE PAGE | 6 CORRECT & REVISE

In Word, you can center the page contents vertically. *Why? This places the same amount of space at the top and bottom of the page.* The following steps center page contents vertically.

1

- If necessary, click Layout on the ribbon to display the Layout tab.

- Click the Page Setup Dialog Box Launcher (Layout tab | Page Setup group) to display the Page Setup dialog box.

- Click the Layout tab (Page Setup dialog box) to display the Layout sheet (Figure 1–62).

Figure 1–62

2

- Click the Vertical alignment arrow (Page Setup dialog box) to display the list of alignment options and then click Center in the list (Figure 1–63).

3

- Click the OK button to center the page contents vertically on the screen (shown in Figure 1–1 at the beginning of this module).

Q&A

What if I wanted to change the alignment back?

You would select the Top vertical alignment from the Vertical alignment list in the Layout sheet (Page Setup dialog box).

Figure 1–63

TO CHANGE DOCUMENT PROPERTIES

Word helps you organize and identify your files by using **document properties**, which, as discussed in the Office and Windows module at the beginning of this book, are the details about a file, such as the project author, title, and subject. For example, a class name or document topic can describe the file's purpose or content.

The more common document properties are standard and automatically updated properties. **Standard properties** are associated with all Microsoft Office files and include author, title, and subject. **Automatically updated properties** include file system properties, such as the date you create or change a file, and statistics, such as the file size.

If you wanted to change document properties, you would follow these steps.

1. Click File on the ribbon to open the Backstage view and then, if necessary, click the Info tab in the Backstage view to display the Info gallery.

2. If the property you wish to change is displayed in the Properties list in the right pane of the Info gallery, try to click to the right of the property. If a text box appears to the right of the property, type the text for the property in the text box and then click the Back button in the upper-left corner of the Backstage view to return to the Word window. Skip the remaining steps.

3. If the property you wish to change is not displayed in the Properties list in the right pane of the Info gallery or you cannot change it in the Info gallery, click the Properties button in the right pane to display the Properties menu and then click Advanced Properties on the Properties menu to display the Properties dialog box. If necessary, click the Summary tab (Properties dialog box) to display the Summary sheet, fill in the appropriate text boxes, and then click the OK button.

Q&A | Why are some of the document properties in the dialog box already filled in?
The person who installed Office 2016 on your computer or network may have set or customized the properties.

To Save the Document and Exit Word

Although you still need to make some edits to this document, you want to exit Word and resume working on the project at a later time. Thus, the following steps save the document and exit Word. For a detailed example of the procedure summarized below, refer to the Office and Windows module at the beginning of this book.

1 Save the flyer again on the same storage location with the same file name.

2 Close the open document and exit Word.

Break Point: If you wish to take a break, this is a good place to do so. To resume at a later time, continue following the steps from this location forward.

Correcting Errors and Revising a Document

After creating a document, you may need to change it. For example, the document may contain an error, or new circumstances may require you to add text to the document.

Types of Changes Made to Documents

The types of changes made to documents normally fall into one of the three following categories: additions, deletions, or modifications.

Additions Additional words, sentences, or paragraphs may be required in a document. Additions occur when you omit text from a document and want to insert it later. For example, you may want to add your email address to the flyer.

Deletions Sometimes, text in a document is incorrect or no longer is needed. For example, you may discover that the lessons no longer include reef shoes. In this case, you would delete the words, reef shoes, from the flyer.

Modifications If an error is made in a document or changes take place that affect the document, you might have to revise a word(s) in the text. For example, the phone number may change.

To Run Word, Open a Document, and Specify Settings

Once you have created and saved a document, you may need to retrieve it from storage. For example, you might want to revise the document or distribute it. Earlier in this module you saved the flyer using the file name, Surf Flyer. The following steps run Word, open this document, and specify settings. For a detailed example of the procedures summarized below for running Word or opening a document, refer to the Office and Windows module.

1 Run Word.

2 Open the document named Surf Flyer from the Recent list or use the Open dialog box to navigate to the location of the file and then open it in the Word window.

3 If the Word window is not maximized, click the Maximize button on its title bar to maximize the window.

4 Click View on the ribbon to display the View tab and then click the 100% button (View tab | Zoom group) to display the page at 100% in the document window.

To Insert Text in an Existing Document

1 ENTER TEXT | 2 FORMAT TEXT | 3 INSERT PICTURE
4 FORMAT PICTURE | 5 ENHANCE PAGE | **6 CORRECT & REVISE**

Word inserts text to the left of the insertion point. The text to the right of the insertion point moves to the right and downward to fit the new text. The following steps insert the word, today, to the left of the word, or, in the flyer. **Why?** *These steps illustrate the process of inserting text.*

1

• Scroll through the document and then click to the left of the location of text to be inserted (in this case, the o in or) to position the insertion point where text should be inserted (Figure 1–64).

Figure 1–64

- Type **today** and then press the SPACEBAR to insert the word to the left of the insertion point (Figure 1–65).

Q&A
Why did the text move to the right as I typed?
In Word, the default typing mode is **insert mode**, which means as you type a character, Word moves all the characters to the right of the typed character one position to the right.

Figure 1–65

To Delete Text

1 ENTER TEXT | 2 FORMAT TEXT | 3 INSERT PICTURE
4 FORMAT PICTURE | 5 ENHANCE PAGE | **6 CORRECT & REVISE**

It is not unusual to type incorrect characters or words in a document. As discussed earlier in this module, you can click the Undo button on the Quick Access Toolbar to undo a command or action immediately — this includes typing. Word also provides other methods of correcting typing errors.

To delete an incorrect character in a document, simply click next to the incorrect character and then press the BACKSPACE key to erase to the left of the insertion point, or press the DELETE key to erase to the right of the insertion point.

To delete a word or phrase, you first must select the word or phrase. The following steps select the word, today, which was just added in the previous steps, and then delete the selection. *Why? These steps illustrate the process of selecting a word and then deleting selected text.*

- Double-click the word to be selected (in this case, today) to select the word (Figure 1–66).

- Press the DELETE key to delete the selected text.

Q&A
What if I am using a touch screen?
Tap the selected text to display the mini toolbar and then tap the Cut button on the mini toolbar to delete the selected text.

Figure 1–66

Other Ways

1. Right-click selected item, click Cut on shortcut menu
2. Select item, press BACKSPACE to delete to left of insertion point or press DELETE to delete to right of insertion point
3. Select item, press CTRL+X

To Move Text

1 ENTER TEXT | 2 FORMAT TEXT | 3 INSERT PICTURE
4 FORMAT PICTURE | 5 ENHANCE PAGE | **6 CORRECT & REVISE**

An efficient way to move text a short distance is drag-and-drop editing. With **drag-and-drop editing**, you select the item to be moved, drag the selected item to the new location, and then drop, or insert, it in the new location. Another technique for moving text is the cut-and-paste technique, which is discussed in the next module.

The following steps use drag-and-drop editing to move text. *Why? While proofreading the flyer, you realize that the body copy would read better if the last two bulleted paragraphs were reversed.*

- Position the pointer in the paragraph to be moved (in this case, the last bulleted item) and then triple-click to select the paragraph.

- With the pointer in the selected text, press and hold down the mouse button, which displays a small dotted box with the pointer (Figure 1–67).

Figure 1–67

- Drag the insertion point to the location where the selected text is to be moved, as shown in Figure 1–68.

Figure 1–68

- Release the mouse button to move the selected text to the location of the dotted insertion point (Figure 1–69).

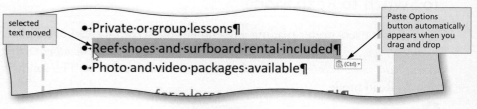

Figure 1–69

Q&A What if I accidentally drag text to the wrong location?
Click the Undo button on the Quick Access Toolbar and try again.

Can I use drag-and-drop editing to move any selected item?
Yes, you can select words, sentences, phrases, and graphics and then use drag-and-drop editing to move them.

What is the purpose of the Paste Options button?
If you click the Paste Options button, a menu appears that allows you to change the format of the item that was moved. The next module discusses the Paste Options menu.

- Click anywhere in the document window to remove the selection from the bulleted item.

Q&A What if I am using a touch screen?
If you have a stylus, you can follow Steps 1 through 3 using the stylus. If you are using your finger, you will need to use the cut-and-paste technique: tap to position the insertion point in the text to be moved and then drag the selection handles as necessary to select the text that you want to move; tap the selection to display the mini toolbar and then tap the Cut button on the mini toolbar to remove the text; tap to position the insertion point at the location where you want to move the text; display the Home tab and then tap the Paste button on the Home tab to place the text at the location of the insertion point. The next module discusses this procedure in more depth.

Other Ways

1. Click Cut button (Home tab | Clipboard group), click where text or object is to be pasted, click Paste button (Home tab | Clipboard group)

2. Right-click selected text, click Cut on mini toolbar or shortcut menu, right-click where text or object is to be pasted, click Paste on mini toolbar or 'Keep Source Formatting' on shortcut menu

3. Press CTRL+X, position insertion point where text or object is to be pasted, press CTRL+V

To Save and Print the Document

It is a good practice to save a document before printing it, in the event you experience difficulties printing. The following steps save and print the document. For a detailed example of the procedure summarized next for saving and printing a document, refer to the Office and Windows module at the beginning of this book.

BTW
Conserving Ink and Toner
If you want to conserve ink or toner, you can instruct Word to print draft quality documents by clicking File on the ribbon to open the Backstage view, clicking the Options tab in the Backstage view to display the Word Options dialog box, clicking Advanced in the left pane (Word Options dialog box), scrolling to the Print area in the right pane, placing a check mark in the 'Use draft quality' check box, and then clicking the OK button. Then, use the Backstage view to print the document as usual.

1 Save the flyer again on the same storage location with the same file name.

2 If requested by your instructor, print the flyer.

Q&A
What if one or more of my borders do not print?
Click the Page Borders button (Design tab | Page Background group), click the Options button (Borders and Shading dialog box), click the Measure from arrow and click Text, change the four text boxes to 15 pt, and then click the OK button in each dialog box. Try printing the document again. If the borders still do not print, adjust the boxes in the dialog box to a number smaller than 15 point.

To Switch to Read Mode

Some users prefer reading a document on-screen instead of on paper. *Why? If you are not composing a document, you can switch to* **Read mode***, which hides the ribbon and other writing tools so that more content fits on the screen. Read mode is intended to make it easier to read a document.* The following step switches from Print Layout view to Read mode.

1

- Click the Read Mode button on the status bar to switch to Read mode (Figure 1–70).

 Experiment

- Click the arrows to advance forward and then move backward through the document.

Q&A
Besides reading, what can I do in Read mode?
You can zoom, copy text, highlight text, search, add comments, and more.

Figure 1–70

Other Ways

1. Click Read Mode button (View tab | Views group)

BTW
Distributing a Document
Instead of printing and distributing a hard copy of a document, you can distribute the document electronically. Options include sending the document via email; posting it on cloud storage (such as OneDrive) and sharing the file with others; posting it on social media, a blog, or other website; and sharing a link associated with an online location of the document. You also can create and share a PDF or XPS image of the document, so that users can view the file in Acrobat Reader or XPS Viewer instead of in Word.

To Switch to Print Layout View

The next steps switch back to Print Layout view. *Why? If you want to show the document on a mock sheet of paper in the document window, along with the ribbon and other writing tools, you should switch to Print Layout view.* The following step switches to Print Layout view.

1

- Click the Print Layout button on the status bar to switch to Print Layout view (Figure 1–71).

- Because the project now is complete, you can exit Word.

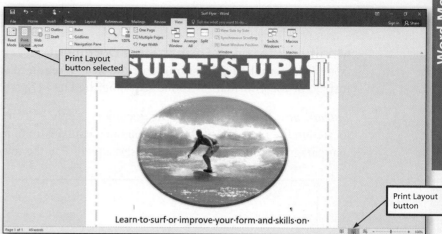

Figure 1–71

Other Ways

1. Click Print Layout button (View tab | Views group)   2. Click View on the ribbon, click Edit Document

Summary

In this module, you have learned how to enter text in a document, correct spelling errors as you type, format paragraphs and characters, insert and format a picture, add a page border, adjust paragraph and page spacing, and correct errors and revise a document.

What decisions will you need to make when creating your next flyer?

Use these guidelines as you complete the assignments in this module and create your own flyers outside of this class.

1. Choose the text for the headline, body copy, and signature line — using as few words as possible to make a point.

2. Format various elements of the text.

   a) Select appropriate font sizes for text in the headline, body copy, and signature line.

   b) Select appropriate fonts for text in the headline, body copy, and signature line.

   c) Adjust paragraph alignment, as appropriate.

   d) Highlight key paragraphs with bullets.

   e) Emphasize important words.

   f) Use color to convey meaning and add appeal.

3. Find an eye-catching graphic(s) that conveys the overall message and meaning of the flyer.

4. Establish where to position and how to format the graphical image(s) so that the image grabs the attention of passersby and draws them into reading the flyer.

5. Determine whether the flyer needs enhancements, such as a graphical, color-coordinated border, or spacing adjustments to improve readability or overall appearance.

6. Correct errors and revise the document as necessary.

   a) Post the flyer on a wall and make sure all text and images are legible from a distance.

   b) Ask someone else to read the flyer and give you suggestions for improvements.

7. Determine the best method for distributing the document, such as printing, sending via email, or posting on the web or social media.

Apply Your Knowledge

Reinforce the skills and apply the concepts you learned in this module.

Modifying Text and Formatting a Document

Note: To complete this assignment, you will be required to use the Data Files. Please contact your instructor for information about accessing the Data Files.

Instructions: Run Word. Open the document, Apply 1–1 Graduation Flyer Unformatted, which is located in the Data Files. The flyer you open contains an unformatted flyer. You are to modify text, format paragraphs and characters, and insert a picture in the flyer to create the flyer shown in Figure 1–72.

Figure 1–72

Perform the following tasks:
1. Correct each spelling (red wavy underline) and grammar (green and blue wavy underlines) error by right-clicking the flagged text and then clicking the appropriate correction on the shortcut menu.

2. Delete the word, degree, in the sentence below the headline.

3. Insert the word, need, between the words, or directions (so that it reads: Questions or need directions?), in the second to last line of the flyer.

4. Change the word, on, to the word, by, in the last line so that the text reads: Please RSVP by May 18.

5. If requested by your instructor, change the phone number in the flyer to your phone number.

6. Center the headline and the last two paragraphs of the flyer.

7. Select the third, fourth, and fifth paragraphs of text in the flyer and add bullets to the selected paragraphs.

8. Change the theme colors to the Blue II color scheme.

9. Change the font and font size of the headline to 48-point Arial Rounded MT Bold, or a similar font. Change the case of the word, Celebrate, in the headline to uppercase letters. Apply the text effect called Fill - Dark Green, Accent 1, Outline - Background 1, Hard Shadow - Accent 1 to the entire headline. Change the font color of the headline text to Dark Green, Accent 5, Darker 25%.

10. Change the font size of the sentence below the headline, the bulleted list, and the last line of flyer to 26 point.

11. Use the mini toolbar to change the font size of the sentence below the bulleted list to 18 point.

12. Switch the last two bulleted paragraphs. That is, select the '125 Park Court in Condor' bullet and move it so that it is the second bulleted paragraph.

13. Select the words, open house, in the paragraph below the headline and italicize these words. Undo this change and then redo the change.

14. Select the text, Saturday, May 27, in the first bulleted paragraph and bold this text. Change the font color of this same text to Dark Red.

15. Underline the word, and, in the third bulleted paragraph.

16. Bold the text, Please RSVP by May 18., in the last line of the flyer. Shade this same text Dark Green, Accent 5, Darker 50%. If the font color does not automatically change to a lighter color, change its color to White, Background 1.

17. Change the zoom so that the entire page is visible in the document window.

18. Insert the picture of the graduate centered on the blank line below the headline. The picture is called Graduation and is available on the Data Files. Resize the picture so that it is approximately 2.9" × 2.89". Apply the Simple Frame, Black picture style to the inserted picture.

19. Change the spacing before the first bulleted paragraph to 12 points and the spacing after the last bulleted paragraph to 24 points.

20. The entire flyer should fit on a single page. If it flows to two pages, resize the picture or decrease spacing before and after paragraphs until the entire flyer text fits on a single page.

21. Change the zoom to text width, then page width, then 100% and notice the differences.

22. If requested by your instructor, enter the text, Graduation Open House, as the keywords in the document properties. Change the other document properties, as specified by your instructor.

23. Click File on the ribbon and then click Save As. Save the document using the file name, Apply 1–1 Graduation Flyer Formatted.

24. Print the document. Switch to Read Mode and browse pages through the document. Switch to Print Layout view.

25. Submit the revised document, shown in Figure 1–72, in the format specified by your instructor.

26. Exit Word.

27. ✷ If this flyer were announcing a victory parade instead of a graduation, which color scheme would you apply and why?

Extend Your Knowledge

Extend the skills you learned in this module and experiment with new skills. You may need to use Help to complete the assignment.

Modifying Text and Picture Formats and Adding Page Borders

Note: To complete this assignment, you will be required to use the Data Files. Please contact your instructor for information about accessing the Data Files.

Figure 1–73

Instructions: Run Word. Open the document, Extend 1–1 Painting Lessons Flyer Draft, from the Data Files. You will enhance the look of the flyer shown in Figure 1–73. *Hint:* Remember, if you make a mistake while formatting the picture, you can reset it by using the Reset Picture button or Reset Picture arrow (Picture Tools Format tab | Adjust group).

Perform the following tasks:

1. Use Help to learn about the following: remove bullets, grow font, shrink font, art page borders, decorative underline(s), picture bullets, picture border shading, picture border color, shadow picture effects, and color saturation and tone.

2. Remove the bullet from the last paragraph of the flyer.

3. Select the text, Painting Lessons, and use the 'Increase Font Size' button (Home tab | Font group) to increase its font size.

4. Add an art page border to the flyer. If the border is not in color, add color to it if the border supports color.

5. Change the solid underline below the word, all, to a decorative underline. Change the color of the underline.

6. Change the style of the bullets to picture bullet(s). Adjust the hanging indent, if necessary, to align the text in the bulleted list.

7. Change the color of the picture border. Add a shadow picture effect to the picture.

8. Change the color saturation and color tone of the picture.

9. If requested by your instructor, change the name of the art studio (Bakersfield) to your last name.

10. Save the revised document with the file name, Extend 1–1 Painting Lessons Flyer Final, and then submit it in the format specified by your instructor.

11. ✷ In this assignment, you changed the bullets to picture bullets. Which bullet character did you select and why?

Expand Your World

Create a solution that uses cloud or web technologies by learning and investigating on your own from general guidance.

Using Word Online to Create a Flyer with a Picture

Note: To complete this assignment, you will be required to use the Data Files. Please contact your instructor for information about accessing the Data Files.

Instructions: You will use Word Online to prepare a flyer. The text for the unformatted flyer is shown in Figure 1–74. You will enter the text in Word Online and then use its tools to enhance the look of the flyer.

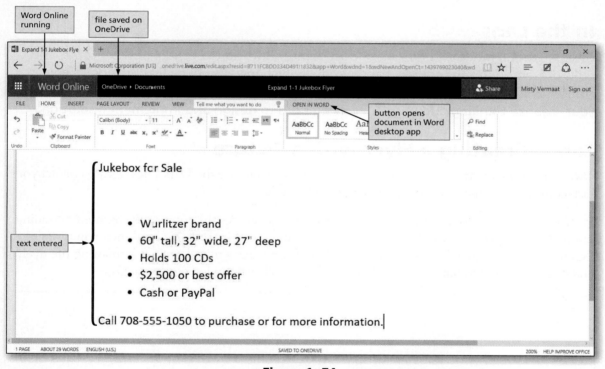

Figure 1–74

Perform the following tasks:

1. Run a browser. Search for the text, Word Online, using a search engine. Visit several websites to learn about Word Online. Navigate to the Office Online website. You will need to sign in to your OneDrive account.

2. Create a new blank Word document using Word Online. Name the document Expand 1–1 Jukebox Flyer.

3. Notice the differences between Word Online and the Word desktop app you used to create the project in this module.

4. Enter the text in the flyer, shown in Figure 1–74, checking spelling as you type.

5. Insert the picture called Jukebox, which is located in the Data Files.

Continued >

STUDENT ASSIGNMENTS

6. Use the features available in Word Online, along with the concepts and techniques presented in this module, to format this flyer. Be sure to change the font and font size of text, center a paragraph(s), italicize text, color text, underline text, and apply a picture style. Resize the picture. Adjust spacing above and below paragraphs as necessary. The flyer should fit on a single page.

7. If requested by your instructor, replace the phone number in the flyer with your phone number.

8. Save the document again. Click the button to open the document in the Word desktop app. If necessary, sign in to your Microsoft account when prompted. Notice how the document appears in the Word desktop app.

9. Using either Word Online or the Word desktop app, submit the document in the format requested by your instructor. Exit Word Online. If necessary, sign out of your OneDrive account and your Microsoft account in Word.

10. ✷ What is Word Online? Which features that are covered in this module are not available in Word Online? Do you prefer using Word Online or the Word desktop app? Why?

In the Labs

Design, create, modify, and/or use a document following the guidelines, concepts, and skills presented in this module. Labs 1 and 2, which increase in difficulty, require you to create solutions based on what you learned in the module; Lab 3 requires you to apply your creative thinking and problem-solving skills to design and implement a solution.

Lab 1: **Creating a Flyer with a Picture**

Note: To complete this assignment, you will be required to use the Data Files. Please contact your instructor for information about accessing the Data Files.

Problem: Your boss asked you to prepare a flyer that advertises the company's commodity trading seminars. First, you prepare the unformatted flyer shown in Figure 1–75a, and then you format it so that it looks like Figure 1–75b. *Hint:* Remember, if you make a mistake while formatting the flyer, you can use the Undo button on the Quick Access Toolbar to undo your last action.

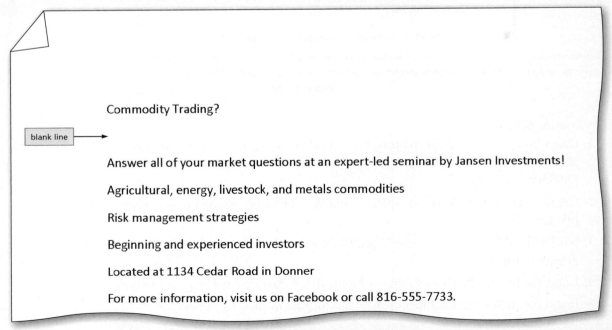

Commodity Trading?

blank line →

Answer all of your market questions at an expert-led seminar by Jansen Investments!

Agricultural, energy, livestock, and metals commodities

Risk management strategies

Beginning and experienced investors

Located at 1134 Cedar Road in Donner

For more information, visit us on Facebook or call 816-555-7733.

Figure 1–75a Unformatted Text

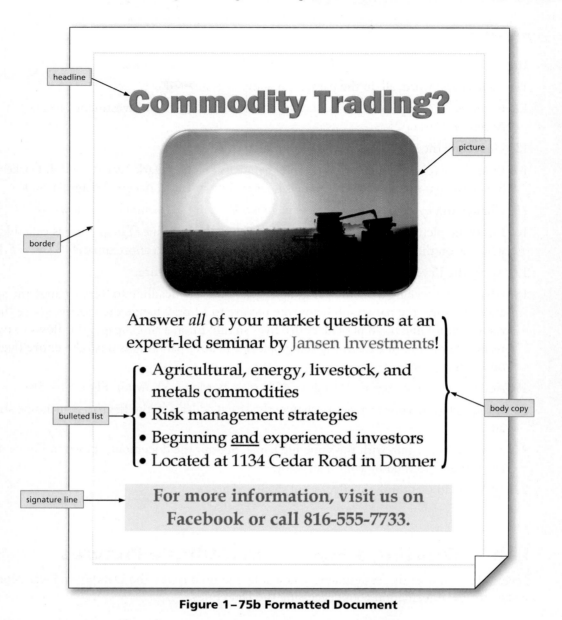

Figure 1–75b Formatted Document

Perform the following tasks:

1. Run Word. Display formatting marks on the screen.

2. Type the flyer text, unformatted, as shown in Figure 1–75a, inserting a blank line between the headline and the body copy. If Word flags any misspelled words as you type, check their spelling and correct them.

3. Save the document using the file name, Lab 1–1 Commodity Trading Flyer.

4. Center the headline and the signature line.

5. Change the theme colors to Green.

6. Change the font size of the headline to 48 point and the font to Franklin Gothic Heavy or a similar font. Apply the text effect called Fill - Dark Teal, Accent 4, Soft Bevel.

7. Change the font size of body copy between the headline and the signature line to 24 point.

8. Change the font size of the signature line to 26 point.

9. Change the font of the body copy and signature line to Book Antiqua.

Continued >

In the Labs *continued*

10. Bullet the four lines (paragraphs) of text above the signature line.

11. Italicize the word, all, in the paragraph above the bulleted list.

12. In the same paragraph, change the color of the words, Jansen Investments, to Dark Teal, Accent 4, Darker 25%.

13. Underline the word, and, in the third bulleted paragraph.

14. Bold the text in the signature line and change its color to Dark Teal, Accent 4, Darker 25%. Shade the paragraph containing the signature line in Lime, Accent 2, Lighter 80%.

15. Change the zoom so that the entire page is visible in the document window.

16. Insert the picture centered on a blank line below the headline. The picture is called Harvest, which is on the Data Files. Reduce the size of the picture to approximately 3.29" × 5.11".

17. Apply the Bevel Rectangle picture style to the inserted picture.

18. Change the spacing after the paragraph containing the headline to 0 pt. Change the spacing above (before) the paragraph below the picture to 12 pt. Change the spacing above (before) the signature line to 18 pt. The entire flyer should fit on a single page. If it flows to two pages, resize the picture or decrease spacing before and after paragraphs until the entire flyer text fits on a single page.

19. Add a ½-pt Lime, Accent 3, Lighter 40% page border, as shown in Figure 1–75b.

20. If requested by your instructor, change the street address in the flyer to your home street address.

21. Save the flyer again with the same file name. Submit the document, shown in Figure 1–75b, in the format specified by your instructor.

22. ✸ Why do you think this flyer used shades of green?

Lab 2: **Creating a Flyer with Multiple Pictures**

Note: To complete this assignment, you will be required to use the Data Files. Please contact your instructor for information about accessing the Data Files.

Problem: Your boss at Gingham Travel has asked you to prepare a flyer that promotes its business. You prepare the flyer shown in Figure 1–76. *Hint*: Remember, if you make a mistake while formatting the flyer, you can use the Undo button on the Quick Access Toolbar to undo your last action.

Perform the following tasks:

1. Run Word. Type the flyer text, unformatted. If Word flags any misspelled words as you type, check their spelling and correct them.

2. Save the document using the file name, Lab 1–2 Spring Break Flyer.

3. Change the theme colors to the Aspect color scheme.

4. Add bullets to the four paragraphs shown in the figure. Center all paragraphs, except the paragraphs containing the bulleted list.

5. Change the font size of both lines in the headline to 48 point. Change the font of the first line in the headline to Ravie, or a similar font, and the second line in the headline to Arial Rounded MT Bold, or a similar font. Apply this text effect to the first line in the headline: Fill - Dark Purple, Accent 1, Outline - Background 1, Hard Shadow - Accent 1. Shade the second line of the headline to the Dark Green, Accent 4 color, and change the font color to White, Background 1.

Figure 1–76

6. Change the font of all text below the headline to Arial Rounded MT Bold. Change the font size of the company name to 28 point, the company address to 24 point, and the bulleted list and signature line to 22 point.

7. Change the color of the company name and address to Dark Green, Accent 4, Darker 25%. Underline the company name.

8. Italicize the word, and, in the first bulleted paragraph.

9. Bold the word, Discounted, in the second bulleted paragraph. Change the color of this same word to Dark Purple, Accent 5.

10. Shade the signature line to the Dark Green, Accent 4 color, and change the font color to White, Background 1.

11. Change the zoom so that the entire page is visible in the document window.

12. Insert two pictures on the same blank line below the headline. The pictures are called Spring Break - Florida and Spring Break - New York, which are both in the Data Files.

Continued >

In the Labs *continued*

13. Resize the top picture so that it is approximately 2.4" × 3". Apply the Simple Frame, White picture style to both pictures. Apply the Perspective Right 3-D Rotation picture effect to the picture on the left and the Perspective Left 3-D Rotation to the picture on the right. Resize the pictures, if necessary, so that they fit on the same line. Add space as necessary between the two pictures.

14. Change the spacing before and after the paragraph containing the company name to 0 pt, the spacing after the company address to 12 pt, and the spacing before the signature line to 12 pt. The entire flyer should fit on a single page. If it flows to two pages, resize the pictures or decrease spacing before and after paragraphs until the entire flyer text fits on a single page.

15. Add the 6-point page border shown in Figure 1–76, using the color Dark Purple, Accent 5.

16. Center the page contents vertically.

17. If requested by your instructor, change the company name to your last name.

18. Save the flyer again with the same file name. Submit the document, shown in Figure 1–76, in the format specified by your instructor.

19. ✴ Why do you think this flyer used shades of purple and green?

Lab 3: **Consider This: Your Turn**

Design and Create an Antique Store Flyer

Note: To complete this assignment, you will be required to use the Data Files. Please contact your instructor for information about accessing the Data Files.

Problem: Your boss at Antiques Galore has asked you to prepare a flyer that promotes its business.

Perform the following tasks:

Part 1: The flyer should contain two digital pictures appropriately resized; the Data Files contains two pictures called Vintage Phone and Vintage Scale, or you can use your own digital pictures if they are appropriate for the topic of the flyer. The flyer should contain the headline, Antiques Galore, and this signature line: Questions? Call 312-555-2000 or find us on Facebook. The body copy consists of the following text, in any order: We sell all types of vintage items and also buy items individually or as an entire estate. Bring your items in for a free appraisal!; 1,200 square foot shop; Collectibles, costume jewelry, furniture, paintings, pottery, toys, and more!; Affordable items with new inventory daily; Located at 229 Center Street in Snow Hill; Open from 9:00 a.m. to 8:00 p.m. daily.

Use the concepts and techniques presented in this module to create and format this flyer. Be sure to check spelling and grammar. Submit your assignment and answers to the Part 2 critical thinking questions in the format specified by your instructor.

Part 2: ✴ You made several decisions while creating the flyer in this assignment: where to place text, how to format the text (i.e., font, font size, paragraph alignment, bulleted paragraphs, underlines, italics, bold, color, etc.), which graphics to use, where to position the graphics, how to format the graphics, and which page enhancements to add (i.e., borders and spacing). What was the rationale behind each of these decisions? When you proofread the document, what further revisions did you make and why? How would you recommend distributing this flyer?

2 Creating a Research Paper with References and Sources

Objectives

You will have mastered the material in this module when you can:

- Describe the MLA documentation style for research papers
- Modify a style
- Change line and paragraph spacing in a document
- Use a header to number pages of a document
- Apply formatting using keyboard shortcuts
- Modify paragraph indentation

- Insert and edit citations and their sources
- Add a footnote to a document
- Insert a manual page break
- Create a bibliographical list of sources
- Cut, copy, and paste text
- Find text and replace text
- Find a synonym
- Check spelling and grammar at once
- Look up information

Introduction

In both academic and business environments, you will be asked to write reports. Business reports range from proposals to cost justifications to five-year plans to research findings. Academic reports focus mostly on research findings.

A **research paper** is a document you can use to communicate the results of research findings. To write a research paper, you learn about a particular topic from a variety of sources (research), organize your ideas from the research results, and then present relevant facts and/or opinions that support the topic. Your final research paper combines properly credited outside information along with personal insights. Thus, no two research papers — even if they are about the same topic — will or should be the same.

Project — Research Paper

When preparing a research paper, you should follow a standard documentation style that defines the rules for creating the paper and crediting sources. A variety of documentation styles exists, depending on the nature of the research paper. Each style

BTW

APA Appendix

If you are required to create a research paper that uses APA style instead of MLA style, you can visit www.cengagebrain.com for the steps required to create this module's research paper. Alternately, you can utilize any number of APA guidelines available in print or online, or ask your instructor.

requires the same basic information; the differences in styles relate to requirements for presenting the information. For example, one documentation style uses the term, bibliography, for the list of sources, whereas another uses the term, references, and yet a third prefers the term, works cited. Two popular documentation styles for research papers are the **Modern Language Association of America (MLA)** and **American Psychological Association (APA)** styles. This module uses the MLA documentation style because it is used in a wide range of disciplines.

The project in this module follows research paper guidelines and uses Word to create the short research paper shown in Figure 2–1. This paper, which discusses using headphones and earbuds safely, follows the MLA documentation style. Each page contains a page number. The first two pages present the name and course information (student name, instructor name, course name, and paper due date), paper title, an introduction with a thesis statement, details that support the thesis, and a conclusion. This section of the paper also includes references to research sources and a footnote. The third page contains a detailed, alphabetical list of the sources referenced in the research paper. All pages include a header at the upper-right edge of the page.

In this module, you will learn how to create the research paper shown in Figure 2–1. The following roadmap identifies general activities you will perform as you progress through this module:

1. CHANGE the DOCUMENT SETTINGS.
2. CREATE the HEADER for each page of the research paper.
3. TYPE the RESEARCH PAPER text WITH CITATIONS.
4. CREATE an ALPHABETICAL WORKS CITED page.
5. PROOFREAD AND REVISE the RESEARCH PAPER.

MLA Documentation Style

The research paper in this project follows the guidelines presented by the MLA. To follow the MLA documentation style, use a 12-point Times New Roman or similar font. Double-space text on all pages of the paper using one-inch top, bottom, left, and right margins. Indent the first word of each paragraph one-half inch from the left margin. At the right margin of each page, place a page number one-half inch from the top margin. On each page, precede the page number with your last name.

The MLA documentation style does not require a title page. Instead, place your name and course information in a block at the left margin beginning one inch from the top of the page. Center the title one double-spaced line below your name and course information.

BTW

APA Documentation Style

In the APA style, a separate title page is required instead of placing name and course information on the paper's first page. Double-space all pages of the paper with one-inch top, bottom, left, and right margins. Indent the first word of each paragraph one-half inch from the left margin. In the upper-right margin of each page, including the title page, place a running head that consists of the page number preceded by a brief summary of the paper title.

In the text of the paper, place author references in parentheses with the page number(s) of the referenced information. The MLA documentation style uses in-text **parenthetical references** instead of noting each source at the bottom of the page or at the end of the paper. In the MLA documentation style, notes are used only for optional content or bibliographic notes.

If used, content notes elaborate on points discussed in the paper, and bibliographic notes direct the reader to evaluations of statements in a source or provide a means for identifying multiple sources. Use a superscript (raised number) both to signal that a note exists and to sequence the notes (shown in Figure 2–1). Position notes at the bottom of the page as footnotes or at the end of the paper as endnotes. Indent the first line of each note one-half inch from the left margin. Place one space following the superscripted number before beginning the note text. Double-space the note text (shown in Figure 2–1).

Figure 2–1

The MLA documentation style uses the term, works cited, to refer to the bibliographic list of sources at the end of the paper. The **works cited** page alphabetically lists sources that are referenced directly in the paper. Place the list of sources on a separate numbered page. Center the title, Works Cited, one inch from the top margin. Double-space all lines. Begin the first line of each source at the left margin, indenting subsequent lines of the same source one-half inch from the left margin. List each source by the author's last name or, if the author's name is not available, by the title of the source.

Changing Document Settings

The MLA documentation style defines some global formats that apply to the entire research paper. Some of these formats are the default in Word. For example, the default left, right, top, and bottom margin settings in Word are one inch, which meets the MLA documentation style. You will modify, however, the font, font size, and line and paragraph spacing.

To Run Word and Specify Settings

If you are using a computer to step through the project in this module and you want your screens to match the figures in this book, you should change your screen's resolution to 1366 × 768. For information about how to change a computer's resolution, refer to the Office and Windows module at the beginning of this book.

1 Run Word and create a blank document in the Word window.

2 If the Word window is not maximized, click the Maximize button on its title bar to maximize the window.

3 If the Print Layout button on the status bar is not selected (shown in Figure 2–2), click it so that your screen is in Print Layout view.

4 If Normal (Home tab | Styles group) is not selected in the Styles gallery (shown in Figure 2–2), click it so that your document uses the Normal style.

5 Display the View tab. To display the page the same width as the document window, if necessary, click the Page Width button (View tab | Zoom group).

6 Display the Home tab. If the 'Show/Hide ¶' button (Home tab | Paragraph group) is not selected already, click it to display formatting marks on the screen.

Styles

When you create a document, Word formats the text using a particular style. A **style** is a named group of formatting characteristics, including font and font size. The default style in Word is called the **Normal style**, which most likely uses an 11-point Calibri font. If you do not specify a style for text you type, Word applies the Normal style to the text. In addition to the Normal style, Word has many other built-in, or predefined, styles that you can use to format text. Styles make it easy to apply many formats at once to text. You can modify existing styles and create your own styles. Styles are discussed as they are used in this book.

For an introduction to Office and instructions about how to perform basic tasks in Office apps, read the Office and Windows module at the beginning of this book, where you can learn how to run an application, use the ribbon, save a file, open a file, print a file, exit an application, use Help, and much more.

For an introduction to Windows and instructions about how to perform basic Windows tasks, read the Office and Windows module at the beginning of this book, where you can learn how to resize windows, change screen resolution, create folders, move and rename files, use Windows Help, and much more.

BTW
Style Formats
To see the formats assigned to a particular style in a document, click the Styles Dialog Box Launcher (Home tab | Styles group) and then click the Style Inspector button in the Styles task pane. Position the insertion point in the style in the document and then point to the Paragraph formatting or Text level formatting areas in the Style Inspector task pane to display a ScreenTip describing formats assigned to the location of the insertion point. You also can click the Reveal Formatting button in the Style Inspector task pane or press SHIFT+F1 to display the Reveal Formatting task pane.

To Modify a Style

The MLA documentation style requires that all text in the research paper use a 12-point Times New Roman or similar font. If you change the font and font size using buttons on the ribbon, you will need to make the change many times during the course of creating the paper. **Why?** *Word formats various areas of a document based on the Normal style, which uses an 11-point Calibri font. For example, body text, headers, and bibliographies all display text based on the Normal style.*

Thus, instead of changing the font and font size for various document elements, a more efficient technique is to change the Normal style for this document to use a 12-point Times New Roman font. **Why?** *By changing the Normal style, you ensure that all text in the document will use the format required by the MLA.* The following steps change the Normal style.

- Right-click Normal in the Styles gallery (Home tab | Styles group) to display a shortcut menu related to styles (Figure 2–2).

Figure 2–2

- Click Modify on the shortcut menu to display the Modify Style dialog box (Figure 2–3).

Figure 2–3

3

- Click the Font arrow (Modify Style dialog box) to display the Font list. Scroll to and then click Times New Roman in the list to change the font for the style being modified.
- Click the Font Size arrow (Modify Style dialog box) and then click 12 in the Font Size list to change the font size for the style being modified.
- Ensure that the 'Only in this document' option button is selected (Figure 2–4).

Figure 2–4

Q&A Will all future documents use the new font and font size?

No, because the 'Only in this document' option button is selected. If you wanted all future documents to use a new setting, you would select the 'New documents based on this template' option button.

4

- Click the OK button (Modify Style dialog box) to update the Normal style to the specified settings.

Other Ways

1. Click Styles Dialog Box Launcher, click arrow next to style name, click Modify on menu, change settings (Modify Style dialog box), click OK button

2. Press ALT+CTRL+SHIFT+S, click arrow next to style name, click Modify on menu, change settings (Modify Style dialog box), click OK button

---

BTW

Line Spacing
If the top of a set of characters or a graphical image is chopped off, then line spacing may be set to Exactly. To remedy the problem, change line spacing to 1.0, 1.15, 1.5, 2.0, 2.5, 3.0, or At least (in the Paragraph dialog box), all of which accommodate the largest font or image.

Adjusting Line and Paragraph Spacing

Line spacing is the amount of vertical space between lines of text in a paragraph. **Paragraph spacing** is the amount of space above and below a paragraph. By default, the Normal style places 8 points of blank space after each paragraph and inserts a vertical space equal to 1.08 lines between each line of text. It also automatically adjusts line height to accommodate various font sizes and graphics.

The MLA documentation style requires that you double-space the entire research paper. That is, specifying a document use **double-space** means that the amount of vertical space between each line of text and above and below paragraphs should be equal to one blank line. The next sets of steps adjust line spacing and paragraph spacing according to the MLA documentation style.

To Change Line Spacing

1 CHANGE DOCUMENT SETTINGS | 2 CREATE HEADER | 3 TYPE RESEARCH PAPER WITH CITATIONS
4 CREATE ALPHABETICAL WORKS CITED | 5 PROOFREAD & REVISE RESEARCH PAPER

The following steps change the line spacing to 2.0 to double-space lines in a paragraph. *Why? The lines of the research paper should be double-spaced, according to the MLA documentation style.*

1

- Click the 'Line and Paragraph Spacing' button (Home tab | Paragraph group) to display the Line and Paragraph Spacing gallery (Figure 2–5).

Q&A
What do the numbers in the Line and Paragraph Spacing gallery represent?
The options 1.0, 2.0, and 3.0 set line spacing to single, double, and triple, respectively. Similarly, the 1.15, 1.5, and 2.5 options set line spacing to 1.15, 1.5, and 2.5 lines. All of these options adjust line spacing automatically to accommodate the largest font or graphic on a line.

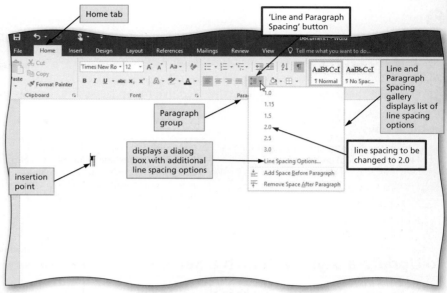

Figure 2–5

2

- Click 2.0 in the Line and Paragraph Spacing gallery to change the line spacing at the location of the insertion point.

Q&A
Can I change the line spacing of existing text?
Yes. Select the text first and then change the line spacing as described in these steps.

Other Ways

1. Right-click paragraph (or, if using touch, tap 'Show Context Menu' on mini toolbar), click Paragraph on shortcut menu, or click Indents and Spacing tab (Paragraph dialog box), click Line spacing arrow, select desired spacing, click OK button

2. Click Paragraph Settings Dialog Box Launcher (Home tab or Layout tab | Paragraph group), click Indents and Spacing tab (Paragraph dialog box), click Line spacing arrow, select desired spacing, click OK button

3. Press CTRL+2 for double-spacing

To Remove Space after a Paragraph

1 CHANGE DOCUMENT SETTINGS | 2 CREATE HEADER | 3 TYPE RESEARCH PAPER WITH CITATIONS
4 CREATE ALPHABETICAL WORKS CITED | 5 PROOFREAD & REVISE RESEARCH PAPER

The following steps remove space after a paragraph. *Why? The research paper should not have additional blank space after each paragraph, according to the MLA documentation style.*

1

- Click the 'Line and Paragraph Spacing' button (Home tab | Paragraph group) to display the Line and Paragraph Spacing gallery (Figure 2–6).

Q&A
Why does a check mark appear to the left of 2.0 in the gallery?
The check mark indicates the currently selected line spacing.

Figure 2–6

- Click 'Remove Space After Paragraph' in the Line and Paragraph Spacing gallery so that no blank space appears after paragraphs.

Q&A
◄ Can I remove space after existing paragraphs?
Yes. Select the paragraphs first and then remove the space as described in these steps.

Other Ways

1. Adjust Spacing After arrows (Layout tab | Paragraph group) until 0 pt is displayed	2. Right-click paragraph (or, if using touch, tap 'Show Context Menu' on mini toolbar), click Paragraph on shortcut menu, click Indents and Spacing tab (Paragraph dialog box), adjust After arrows until 0 pt is displayed, click OK button	3. Click Paragraph Settings Dialog Box Launcher (Home tab or Layout tab | Paragraph group), click Indents and Spacing tab (Paragraph dialog box), adjust After arrows until 0 pt is displayed, click OK button

To Update a Style to Match a Selection

1 CHANGE DOCUMENT SETTINGS | 2 CREATE HEADER | 3 TYPE RESEARCH PAPER WITH CITATIONS
4 CREATE ALPHABETICAL WORKS CITED | 5 PROOFREAD & REVISE RESEARCH PAPER

To ensure that all paragraphs in the paper will be double-spaced and do not have space after the paragraphs, you want the Normal style to include the line and paragraph spacing changes made in the previous two sets of steps. The following steps update the Normal style. *Why? You can update a style to reflect the settings of the location of the insertion point or selected text. Because no text has been typed in the research paper yet, you do not need to select text prior to updating the Normal style.*

- Right-click Normal in the Styles gallery (Home tab | Styles group) to display a shortcut menu (Figure 2–7).

- Click 'Update Normal to Match Selection' on the shortcut menu to update the selected (or current) style to reflect the settings at the location of the insertion point.

Figure 2–7

Other Ways

1. Click Styles Dialog Box Launcher, click arrow next to style name, click 'Update Normal to Match Selection'	2. Press ALT+CTRL+SHIFT+S, click arrow next to style name in Styles pane, click 'Update Normal to Match Selection'

Creating a Header

BTW

The Ribbon and Screen Resolution
Word may change how the groups and buttons within the groups appear on the ribbon, depending on the computer or mobile device's screen resolution. Thus, your ribbon may look different from the ones in this book if you are using a screen resolution other than 1366 x 768.

A **header** is text and/or graphics that print at the top of each page in a document. Similarly, a **footer** is text and/or graphics that print at the bottom of every page. In Word, headers print in the top margin one-half inch from the top of every page, and footers print in the bottom margin one-half inch from the bottom of each page, which meets the MLA documentation style. In addition to text and graphics, headers and footers can include document information, such as the page number, current date, current time, and author's name.

In this research paper, you are to precede the page number with your last name placed one-half inch from the upper-right edge of each page. The procedures in the following sections enter your name and the page number in the header, as specified by the MLA documentation style.

To Switch to the Header

The following steps switch from editing the document text to editing the header. *Why? To enter text in the header, you instruct Word to edit the header.*

1
- Click Insert on the ribbon to display the Insert tab.
- Click the 'Add a Header' button (Insert tab | Header & Footer group) to display the Add a Header gallery (Figure 2–8)

🔎 **Experiment**
- Click the down scroll arrow in the Add a Header gallery to see the available built-in headers.

Q&A Can I use a built-in header for this research paper?
None of the built-in headers adheres to the MLA documentation style; thus, you should enter your own header content instead of using a built-in header for this research paper.

How would I remove a header from a document?
You would click Remove Header in the Add a Header gallery. Similarly, to remove a footer, you would click Remove Footer in the Add a Footer gallery.

Figure 2–8

2
- Click Edit Header in the Add a Header gallery to switch from the document text to the header, which allows you to edit the contents of the header (Figure 2–9).

Q&A How do I remove the Header & Footer Tools Design tab from the ribbon?
When you are finished editing the header, you will close it, which removes the Header & Footer Tools Design tab.

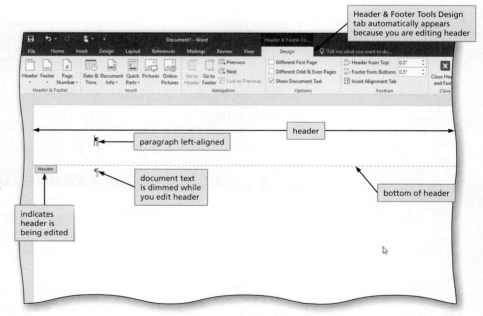

Figure 2–9

Other Ways

1. Double-click dimmed header   2. Right-click header in document, click Edit Header button that appears

To Right-Align a Paragraph

The paragraph in the header currently is left-aligned (shown in Figure 2–9). The following steps right-align this paragraph. *Why? Your last name and the page number should print **right-aligned**; that is, they should print at the right margin, according to the MLA documentation style.*

- Click Home on the ribbon to display the Home tab.

- Click the Align Right button (Home tab | Paragraph group) to right-align the current paragraph (Figure 2–10).

Q&A

What if I wanted to return the paragraph to left-aligned?
You would click the Align Right button again, or click the Align Left button (Home tab | Paragraph group).

Figure 2–10

Other Ways

1. Right-click paragraph (or, if using touch, tap 'Show Context Menu' button on mini toolbar), click Paragraph on shortcut menu, click Indents and Spacing tab (Paragraph dialog box), click Alignment arrow, click Right, click OK button

2. Click Paragraph Settings Dialog Box Launcher (Home tab or Layout tab | Paragraph group), click Indents and Spacing tab (Paragraph dialog box), click Alignment arrow, click Right, click OK button

3. Press CTRL+R

BTW

Footers
If you wanted to create a footer, you would click the 'Add a Footer' button (Insert tab | Header & Footer group) and then select the desired built-in footer or click Edit Footer in the Add a Footer gallery to create a customized footer; or, you could double-click the dimmed footer.

To Enter Text

The following step enters the last name right-aligned in the header area.

 Type **Carter** and then press the SPACEBAR to enter the last name in the header.

If requested by your instructor, enter your last name instead of Carter in the header.

To Insert a Page Number

The following steps insert a page number at the location of the insertion point. *Why? The MLA documentation style requires a page number following the last name in the header.*

1

- Click Header & Footer Tools Design on the ribbon to display the Header & Footer Tools Design tab.
- Click the 'Add Page Numbers' button (Header & Footer Tools Design tab | Header & Footer group) to display the Add Page Numbers menu.

Q&A Why does the button name in the step differ from the name on the face of the button in the figure?
The text that appears on the face of the button may vary, depending on screen resolution. The name that appears in the ScreenTip (when you point to the button), however, never changes. For this reason, this book uses the name that appears in the ScreenTip to identify buttons, boxes, and other on-screen elements.

- Point to Current Position on the Add Page Numbers menu to display the Current Position gallery (Figure 2–11).

Experiment

- Click the down scroll arrow in the Current Position gallery to see the available page number formats.

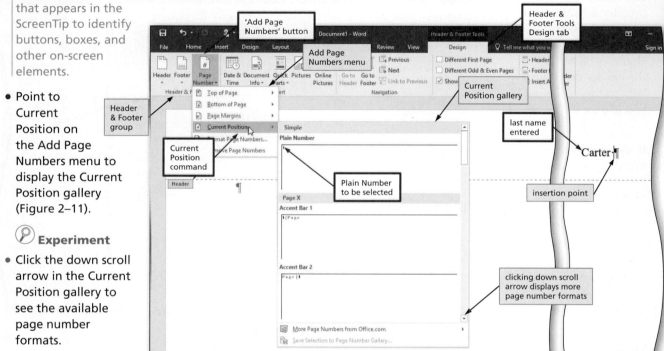

Figure 2–11

2

- If necessary, scroll to the top of the Current Position gallery.
- Click Plain Number in the Current Position gallery to insert an unformatted page number at the location of the insertion point (Figure 2–12).

Figure 2–12

Other Ways

1. Click 'Add Page Numbers' button (Insert tab | Header & Footer group)

2. Click 'Explore Quick Parts' button (Insert tab | Text group or Header & Footer Tools Design tab | Insert group), click Field on Explore Quick Parts menu, select Page in Field names list (Field dialog box), select desired format in Format list, click OK button

To Close the Header

The next task is to switch back to the document text. *Why? You are finished entering text in the header.* The following step closes the header.

1

- Click the 'Close Header and Footer' button (Header & Footer Tools Design tab | Close group) (shown in Figure 2–12) to close the header and switch back to the document text (Figure 2–13).

Q&A

How do I make changes to existing header text?
Switch to the header using the steps described previously in the section titled To Switch to the Header, edit the header as you would edit text in the document window, and then switch back to the document text.

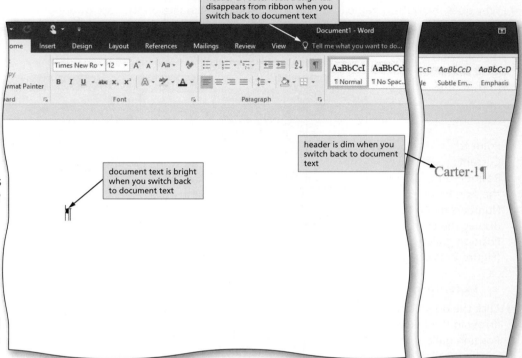

Header & Footer Tools Design tab disappears from ribbon when you switch back to document text

document text is bright when you switch back to document text

header is dim when you switch back to document text

Carter·1¶

Figure 2–13

Other Ways

1. Double-click dimmed document text

Typing the Research Paper Text

The text of the research paper in this module encompasses the first two pages of the paper. You will type the text of the research paper and then modify it later in the module, so that it matches Figure 2–1 shown at the beginning of this module.

CONSIDER THIS

What should you consider when writing the first draft of a research paper?
As you write the first draft of a research paper, be sure it includes the proper components, uses credible sources, and does not contain any plagiarized material.

- **Include an introduction, body, and conclusion.** The first paragraph of the paper introduces the topic and captures the reader's attention. The body, which follows the introduction, consists of several paragraphs that support the topic. The conclusion summarizes the main points in the body and restates the topic.

- **Evaluate sources for authority, currency, and accuracy.** Be especially wary of information obtained on the web. Any person, company, or organization can publish a webpage on the Internet. When considering the source, consider the following:

  - Authority: Does a reputable institution or group support the source? Is the information presented without bias? Are the author's credentials listed and verifiable?

  - Currency: Is the information up to date? Are dates of sources listed? What is the last date revised or updated?

  - Accuracy: Is the information free of errors? Is it verifiable? Are the sources clearly identified?

- **Acknowledge all sources of information; do not plagiarize.** Sources of research include books, magazines, newspapers, and the Internet. As you record facts and ideas, list details about the source: title, author, place of publication, publisher, date of publication, etc. When taking notes, be careful not to **plagiarize**. That is, do not use someone else's work and claim it to be your own. If you copy information directly, place it in quotation marks and identify its source. Not only is plagiarism unethical, but it is considered an academic crime that can have severe punishments, such as failing a course or being expelled from school.

When you summarize, paraphrase (rewrite information in your own words), present facts, give statistics, quote exact words, or show a map, chart, or other graphic, you must acknowledge the source. Information that commonly is known or accessible to the audience constitutes common knowledge and does not need to be acknowledged. If, however, you question whether certain information is common knowledge, you should document it — just to be safe.

To Enter Name and Course Information

As discussed earlier in this module, the MLA documentation style does not require a separate title page for research papers. Instead, place your name and course information in a block at the top of the page, below the header, at the left margin. The following steps enter the name and course information in the research paper.

BTW
Date Formats
The MLA style prefers the day-month-year (10 October 2017) or month-day-year (October 10, 2017) format.

1 Type `Oswald Carter` as the student name and then press the ENTER key.

2 Type `Ms. Ruiz` as the instructor name and then press the ENTER key.

3 Type `English 104` as the course name and then press the ENTER key.

4 Type `October 10, 2017` as the paper's due date and then press the ENTER key (Figure 2–14).

If requested by your instructor, enter your name and course information instead of the information shown above.

Q&A Why did the word, October, appear on the screen as I began typing the month name?
Word has an AutoComplete feature, where it predicts some words or phrases as you are typing and displays its prediction in a ScreenTip. If the AutoComplete prediction is correct, you can press the ENTER key (or, if using touch, tap the ScreenTip) to instruct Word to finish your typing with the word or phrase that appears in the ScreenTip.

student name entered on line 1 → Oswald·Carter¶

instructor name entered on line 2 → Ms.·Ruiz¶

one blank line is displayed each time you press ENTER key because text is double-spaced

course name entered on line 3 → English·104¶

paper due date entered on line 4 → October·10,·2017¶

¶

insertion point

Figure 2–14

To Click and Type

The next task is to enter the title of the research paper centered between the page margins. In Module 1, you used the Center button (Home tab | Paragraph group) to center text and graphics. As an alternative, if you are using a mouse, you can use Word's Click and Type feature to format and enter text, graphics, and other items. *Why? With **Click and Type**, you can double-click a blank area of the document window and Word automatically formats the item you type or insert according to the location where you double-clicked.* The following steps use Click and Type to center and then type the title of the research paper.

1

Figure 2–15

 Experiment

- Move the pointer around the document below the entered name and course information and observe the various icons that appear with the I-beam.

- Position the pointer in the center of the document at the approximate location for the research paper title until a center icon appears below the I-beam (Figure 2–15).

Q&A
What are the other icons that appear in the Click and Type pointer?
A left-align icon appears to the right of the I-beam when the Click and Type pointer is in certain locations on the left side of the document window. A right-align icon appears to the left of the I-beam when the Click and Type pointer is in certain locations on the right side of the document window.

What if I am using a touch screen?
Tap the Center button (Home tab | Paragraph group) and then proceed to Step 3 because the Click and Type feature does not work with a touch screen.

2

- Double-click to center the paragraph mark and insertion point between the left and right margins.

3

- Type `Safely Using Headphones and Earbuds` as the paper title and then press the ENTER key to position the insertion point on the next line (Figure 2–16).

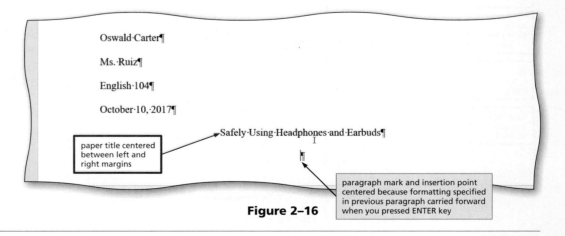

Figure 2–16

Keyboard Shortcuts

Word has many **keyboard shortcuts**, sometimes called shortcut keys or keyboard key combinations, for your convenience while typing. Table 2–1 lists the common keyboard shortcuts for formatting characters. Table 2–2 lists common keyboard shortcuts for formatting paragraphs.

Table 2–1 Keyboard Shortcuts for Formatting Characters

Character Formatting Task	Keyboard Shortcut	Character Formatting Task	Keyboard Shortcut
All capital letters	CTRL+SHIFT+A	Italic	CTRL+I
Bold	CTRL+B	Remove character formatting (plain text)	CTRL+SPACEBAR
Case of letters	SHIFT+F3	Small uppercase letters	CTRL+SHIFT+K
Decrease font size	CTRL+SHIFT+<	Subscript	CTRL+EQUAL SIGN
Decrease font size 1 point	CTRL+[	Superscript	CTRL+SHIFT+PLUS SIGN
Double-underline	CTRL+SHIFT+D	Underline	CTRL+U
Increase font size	CTRL+SHIFT+>	Underline words, not spaces	CTRL+SHIFT+W
Increase font size 1 point	CTRL+]		

© 2015 Cengage Learning

Table 2–2 Keyboard Shortcuts for Formatting Paragraphs

Paragraph Formatting	Keyboard Shortcut	Paragraph Formatting	Keyboard Shortcut
1.5 line spacing	CTRL+5	Justify paragraph	CTRL+J
Add/remove one line above paragraph	CTRL+0 (ZERO)	Left-align paragraph	CTRL+L
Center paragraph	CTRL+E	Remove hanging indent	CTRL+SHIFT+T
Decrease paragraph indent	CTRL+SHIFT+M	Remove paragraph formatting	CTRL+Q
Double-space lines	CTRL+2	Right-align paragraph	CTRL+R
Hanging indent	CTRL+T	Single-space lines	CTRL+1
Increase paragraph indent	CTRL+M		

© 2015 Cengage Learning

To Format Text Using a Keyboard Shortcut

The paragraphs below the paper title should be left-aligned, instead of centered. Thus, the next step is to left-align the paragraph below the paper title. When your fingers already are on the keyboard, you may prefer using keyboard shortcuts to format text as you type it.

The following step left-aligns a paragraph using the keyboard shortcut CTRL+L. (Recall from Module 1 that a notation such as CTRL+L means to press the letter L on the keyboard while holding down the CTRL key.)

1 Press CTRL+L to left-align the current paragraph, that is, the paragraph containing the insertion point (shown in Figure 2–17).

Q&A Why would I use a keyboard shortcut instead of the ribbon to format text?
Switching between the mouse and the keyboard takes time. If your hands are already on the keyboard, use a keyboard shortcut. If your hand is on the mouse, use the ribbon.

2 Save the research paper on your hard drive, OneDrive, or other storage location using the file name, Headphones and Earbuds Paper.

Q&A Why should I save the research paper at this time?
You have performed many tasks while creating this flyer and do not want to risk losing work completed thus far.

BTW
Keyboard Shortcuts
To print a complete list of keyboard shortcuts in Word, press F1 to display the Word Help window, type **keyboard shortcuts** in the Search box in the Word Help window, press the ENTER key, click the Keyboard shortcuts for Microsoft Word link, click the Print button in the Help window, and then click the Print button in the Print dialog box.

To Display the Rulers

According to the MLA documentation style, the first line of each paragraph in the research paper is to be indented one-half inch from the left margin. Although you can use a dialog box to indent paragraphs, Word provides a quicker way through the **horizontal ruler**. This ruler is displayed at the top edge of the document window just below the ribbon. Word also provides a **vertical ruler** that is displayed along the left edge of the Word window. The following step displays the rulers. *Why? You want to use the horizontal ruler to indent paragraphs.*

- If necessary, scroll the document so that the research paper title is at the top of the document window.
- Click View on the ribbon to display the View tab.
- If the rulers are not displayed, click the View Ruler check box (View tab | Show group) to place a check mark in the check box and display the horizontal and vertical rulers on the screen (Figure 2–17).

Q&A | What tasks can I accomplish using the rulers?
You can use the rulers to indent paragraphs, set tab stops, change page margins, and adjust column widths.

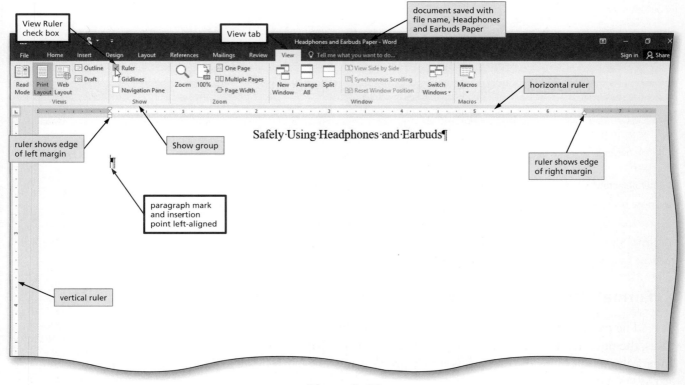

Figure 2–17

To First-Line Indent Paragraphs

If you are using a mouse, you can use the horizontal ruler, usually simply called the **ruler**, to indent just the first line of a paragraph, which is called a **first-line indent**. The left margin on the ruler contains two triangles above a square. The **'First Line Indent' marker** is the top triangle at the 0" mark on the ruler (shown in Figure 2–18). The bottom triangle is discussed later in this module. The small square at the 0" mark is the Left Indent marker. The **Left Indent marker** allows you to change the entire left margin, whereas the 'First Line Indent' marker indents only the first line of the paragraph.

The following steps first-line indent paragraphs in the research paper. *Why? The first line of each paragraph in the research paper is to be indented one-half inch from the left margin, according to the MLA documentation style.*

1

- With the insertion point on the paragraph mark below the research paper title, point to the 'First Line Indent' marker on the ruler (Figure 2–18).

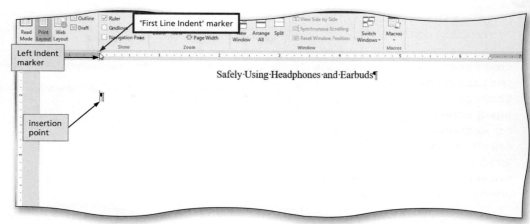

Figure 2–18

2

- Drag the 'First Line Indent' marker to the .5" mark on the ruler to display a vertical dotted line in the document window, which indicates the proposed indent location of the first line of the paragraph (Figure 2–19).

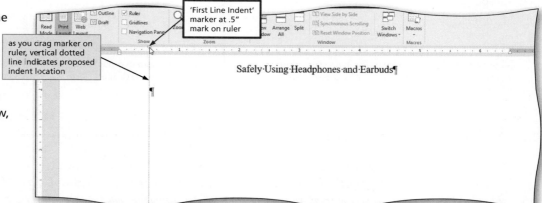

Figure 2–19

3

- Release the mouse button to place the 'First Line Indent' marker at the .5" mark on the ruler, or one-half inch from the left margin (Figure 2–20).

 What if I am using a touch screen?
If you are using a touch screen, you cannot drag the 'First Line Indent' marker and must follow these steps instead: tap the Paragraph Settings Dialog Box Launcher (Home tab or Layout tab | Paragraph group) to display the Paragraph dialog box, tap the Indents and Spacing tab (Paragraph dialog box), tap the Special arrow, tap First line, and then tap the OK button.

Figure 2–20

- Type `People often listen to sound from their computers or portable devices through headphones or earbuds.` and notice that Word automatically indents the first line of the paragraph by one-half inch (Figure 2–21).

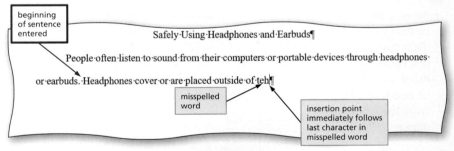

Figure 2–21

Q&A Will I have to set a first-line indent for each paragraph in the paper?

No. Each time you press the ENTER key, paragraph formatting in the previous paragraph carries forward to the next paragraph. Thus, once you set the first-line indent, its format carries forward automatically to each subsequent paragraph you type.

Other Ways

1. Right-click paragraph (or, if using touch, tap 'Show Context Menu' button on mini toolbar), click Paragraph on shortcut menu, click Indents and Spacing tab (Paragraph dialog box), click Special arrow, click First line, click OK button

2. Click Paragraph Settings Dialog Box Launcher (Home tab or Layout tab | Paragraph group), click Indents and Spacing tab (Paragraph dialog box), click Special arrow, click First line, click OK button

---

To AutoCorrect as You Type

1 CHANGE DOCUMENT SETTINGS | 2 CREATE HEADER | 3 TYPE RESEARCH PAPER WITH CITATIONS
4 CREATE ALPHABETICAL WORKS CITED | 5 PROOFREAD & REVISE RESEARCH PAPER

Word has predefined many commonly misspelled words, which it automatically corrects for you. ***Why?*** *As you type, you may make typing, spelling, capitalization, or grammar errors. Word's **AutoCorrect** feature automatically corrects these kinds of errors as you type them in the document. For example, if you type the characters, ahve, Word automatically changes it to the correct spelling, have, when you press the* SPACEBAR *or a punctuation mark key, such as a period or comma.*

The following steps intentionally misspell the word, the, as teh to illustrate the AutoCorrect feature.

- Press the SPACEBAR.
- Type the beginning of the next sentence, misspelling the word, the, as follows: `Headphones cover or are placed outside of teh` (Figure 2–22).

Figure 2–22

- Press the SPACEBAR and watch Word automatically correct the misspelled word.
- Type the rest of the sentence (Figure 2–23): `ear, whereas earbuds rest inside the ear canal.`

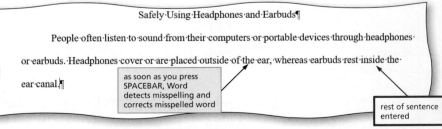

Figure 2–23

To Use the AutoCorrect Options Button

The following steps illustrate the AutoCorrect Options button and menu. ***Why?*** *If you are using a mouse, when you position the pointer on text that Word automatically corrected, a small blue box appears below the text. If you point to the small blue box, Word displays the AutoCorrect Options button. When you click the **AutoCorrect Options button**, Word displays a menu that allows you to undo a correction or change how Word handles future automatic corrections of this type.*

- Position the pointer in the text automatically corrected by Word (the word, the, in this case) to display a small blue box below the automatically corrected word (Figure 2–24).

Figure 2–24

- Point to the small blue box to display the AutoCorrect Options button.
- Click the AutoCorrect Options button to display the AutoCorrect Options menu (Figure 2–25).
- Press the ESC key to remove the AutoCorrect Options menu from the screen.

Q&A Do I need to remove the AutoCorrect Options button from the screen?
No. When you move the pointer, the AutoCorrect Options button will disappear from the screen. If, for some reason, you wanted to remove the AutoCorrect Options button from the screen, you could press the ESC key a second time.

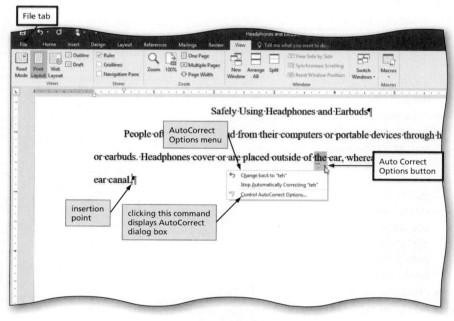

Figure 2–25

To Create an AutoCorrect Entry

The next steps create an AutoCorrect entry. ***Why?*** *In addition to the predefined list of AutoCorrect spelling, capitalization, and grammar errors, you can create your own AutoCorrect entries to add to the list. For example, if you tend to mistype the word computer as comptuer, you should create an AutoCorrect entry for it.*

❶

- Click File on the ribbon (shown in Figure 2–25) to open the Backstage view (Figure 2–26).

Figure 2–26

❷

- Click the Options tab in the Backstage view to display the Word Options dialog box.
- Click Proofing in the left pane (Word Options dialog box) to display proofing options in the right pane.
- Click the AutoCorrect Options button in the right pane to display the AutoCorrect dialog box.
- When Word displays the AutoCorrect dialog box, type **comptuer** in the Replace text box.
- Press the TAB key and then type **computer** in the With text box (Figure 2–27).

Figure 2–27

Q&A How would I delete an existing AutoCorrect entry?
You would select the entry to be deleted in the list of defined entries in the AutoCorrect dialog box and then click the Delete button (AutoCorrect dialog box).

❸

- Click the Add button (AutoCorrect dialog box) to add the entry alphabetically to the list of words to correct automatically as you type. (If your dialog box displays a Replace button instead, click it and then click the Yes button in the Microsoft Word dialog box to replace the previously defined entry.)
- Click the OK button (AutoCorrect dialog box) to close the dialog box.
- Click the OK button (Word Options dialog box) to close the dialog box.

The AutoCorrect Dialog Box

In addition to creating AutoCorrect entries for words you commonly misspell or mistype, you can create entries for abbreviations, codes, and so on. For example, you could create an AutoCorrect entry for asap, indicating that Word should replace this text with the phrase, as soon as possible.

If, for some reason, you do not want Word to correct automatically as you type, you can turn off the Replace text as you type feature by clicking the Options tab in the Backstage view, clicking Proofing in the left pane (Word Options dialog box), clicking the AutoCorrect Options button in the right pane (shown in Figure 2–27), removing the check mark from the 'Replace text as you type' check box, and then clicking the OK button in each open dialog box.

The AutoCorrect sheet in the AutoCorrect dialog box (Figure 2–27) contains other check boxes that correct capitalization errors if the check boxes are selected:

- If you type two capital letters in a row, such as TH, Word makes the second letter lowercase, Th.
- If you begin a sentence with a lowercase letter, Word capitalizes the first letter of the sentence.
- If you type the name of a day in lowercase letters, such as tuesday, Word capitalizes the first letter in the name of the day, Tuesday.
- If you leave the CAPS LOCK key on and begin a new sentence, such as after, Word corrects the typing, After, and turns off the CAPS LOCK key.

If you do not want Word to perform any of these corrections automatically, simply remove the check mark from the appropriate check box in the AutoCorrect dialog box.

Sometimes, you do not want Word to AutoCorrect a particular word or phrase. For example, you may use the code, WD., in your documents. Because Word automatically capitalizes the first letter of a sentence, the character you enter following the period will be capitalized (in the previous sentence, it would capitalize the letter i in the word, in). To allow the code, WD., to be entered into a document and still leave the AutoCorrect feature turned on, you would set an exception. To set an exception to an AutoCorrect rule, click the Options tab in the Backstage view, click Proofing in the left pane (Word Options dialog box), click the AutoCorrect Options button in the right pane, click the Exceptions button (Figure 2–27), click the appropriate tab in the AutoCorrect Exceptions dialog box, type the exception entry in the text box, click the Add button, click the Close button (AutoCorrect Exceptions dialog box), and then click the OK button in each of the remaining dialog boxes.

To Enter More Text

The next task is to continue typing text in the research paper up to the location of the in-text parenthetical reference. The following steps enter this text.

1 With the insertion point positioned at the end of the first paragraph in the paper, as shown in Figure 2–25, press the SPACEBAR and then type these three sentences, intentionally misspelling the word sound as sould: `With these listening devices, only the individual wearing the device hears the sould. Using headphones or earbuds improperly can lead to permanent hearing loss. Items that may protect hearing include quality of these devices and volume levels.`

Q&A | Why is the word, sound, misspelled?
Later in this module, you will use Word's check spelling and grammar at once feature to check the entire document for errors.

BTW
Automatic Corrections
If you do not want to keep a change made automatically by Word and you immediately notice the automatic correction, you can undo the change by clicking the Undo button on the Quick Access Toolbar or pressing CTRL+Z. You also can undo a correction through the AutoCorrect Options button (Word Options dialog box) (shown in Figure 2–27).

BTW
Spacing after Punctuation
Because word processing documents use variable character fonts, it often is difficult to determine in a printed document how many times someone has pressed the SPACEBAR between sentences. Thus, the rule is to press the SPACEBAR only once after periods, colons, and other punctuation marks.

2 Press the ENTER key to start a new paragraph.

3 Type **The features of certain headphones and earbuds can help to prevent hearing loss. Higher-quality headphones and earbuds tend to produce a clearer sound, enabling wearers to listen at a lower volume** and then press the SPACEBAR (Figure 2–28).

Figure 2–28

Citations

Both the MLA and APA guidelines suggest the use of in-text parenthetical references (placed at the end of a sentence), instead of footnoting each source of material in a paper. These parenthetical references, called citations in Word, guide the reader to the end of the paper for complete information about the source.

Word provides tools to assist you with inserting citations in a paper and later generating a list of sources from the citations. With a documentation style selected, Word automatically formats the citations and list of sources according to that style. The process for adding citations in Word is as follows:

1. Modify the documentation style, if necessary.
2. Insert a citation placeholder.
3. Enter the source information for the citation.

You can combine Steps 2 and 3, where you insert the citation placeholder and enter the source information at once. Or, you can insert the citation placeholder as you write and then enter the source information for the citation at a later time. While creating the research paper in this module, you will use both methods.

To Change the Bibliography Style

1 CHANGE DOCUMENT SETTINGS | 2 CREATE HEADER | 3 TYPE RESEARCH PAPER WITH CITATIONS
4 CREATE ALPHABETICAL WORKS CITED | 5 PROOFREAD & REVISE RESEARCH PAPER

The first step in inserting a citation is to be sure the citations and sources will be formatted using the correct documentation style, called the bibliography style in Word. **_Why?_** _You want to ensure that Word is using the MLA documentation style for this paper._ The following steps change the specified documentation style.

- Click References on the ribbon to display the References tab.
- Click the Bibliography Style arrow (References tab | Citations & Bibliography group) to display the Bibliography Style gallery, which lists predefined documentation styles (Figure 2–29).

- Click 'MLA Seventh Edition' in the Bibliography Style gallery to change the documentation style to MLA.

Q&A What if I am using a different edition of a documentation style shown in the Bibliography Style gallery?

Select the closest one and then, if necessary, perform necessary edits before submitting the paper.

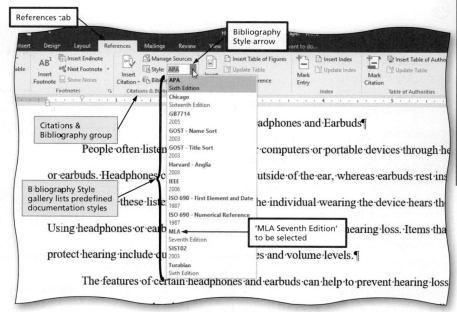

Figure 2–29

What details are required for sources?

During your research, be sure to record essential publication information about each of your sources. Following is a sample list of types of required information for the MLA documentation style.

- Book: full name of author(s), complete title of book, edition (if available), volume (if available), publication city, publisher name, publication year, and publication medium

- Magazine: full name of author(s), complete title of article, magazine title, issue number (if available), date of magazine, page numbers of article, publication medium, and date viewed (if medium is a website)

- Website: full name of author(s), title of website, website publisher or sponsor (if none, write N.p.), publication date (if none, write n.d.), publication medium, and date viewed

CONSIDER THIS

To Insert a Citation and Create Its Source

1 CHANGE DOCUMENT SETTINGS | 2 CREATE HEADER | **3 TYPE RESEARCH PAPER WITH CITATIONS**
4 CREATE ALPHABETICAL WORKS CITED | 5 PROOFREAD & REVISE RESEARCH PAPER

With the documentation style selected, the next task is to insert a citation at the location of the insertion point and enter the source information for the citation. You can accomplish these steps at once by instructing Word to add a new source. The following steps add a new source for a magazine (periodical) article on the web. *Why? The material preceding the insertion point was summarized from an online magazine article.*

- With the insertion point at the location for the citation (as shown in Figure 2–28), click the Insert Citation button (References tab | Citations & Bibliography group) to display the Insert Citation menu (Figure 2–30).

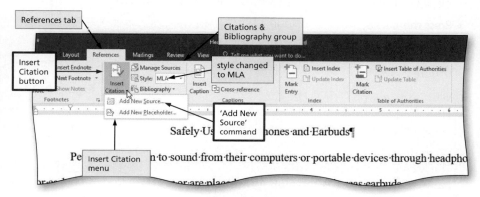

Figure 2–30

2

- Click 'Add New Source' on the Insert Citation menu to display the Create Source dialog box (Figure 2–31).

Q&A What are the Bibliography Fields in the Create Source dialog box?
A **field** is a placeholder for data whose contents can change. You enter data in some fields; Word supplies data for others. In this case, you enter the contents of the fields for a particular source, for example, the author name in the Author field.

Figure 2–31

Experiment

- Click the 'Type of Source' arrow and then click one of the source types in the list, so that you can see how the list of fields changes to reflect the type of source you selected.

3

- If necessary, click the 'Type of Source' arrow (Create Source dialog box) and then click 'Article in a Periodical', so that the list shows fields required for a magazine (periodical).

- Click the Author text box. Type `Tu, Mingzhu Lin` as the author.

- Click the Title text box. Type `Headphones and Earbuds` as the article title.

- Press the TAB key and then type `Technology and Trends Today` as the periodical title.

- Press the TAB key and then type `2017` as the year.

- Press the TAB key and then type `Aug.` as the month.

- Press the TAB key twice and then type `n. pag.` as the number of pages.

- Press the TAB key and then type `Web` as the medium (Figure 2–32).

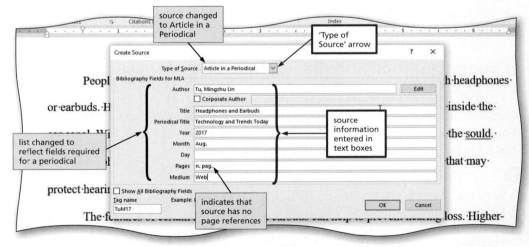

Figure 2–32

Q&A Why is the month abbreviated?
The MLA documentation style abbreviates all months, except May, June, and July, when they appear in a source.

What does the n. pag. entry mean in the Pages text box?
The MLA documentation style uses the abbreviation n. pag. for no pagination, which indicates the source has no page references. This is common for web sources.

4

- Place a check mark in the 'Show All Bibliography Fields' check box so that Word displays all fields available for the selected source, including the date viewed (accessed) fields.

- If necessary, scroll to the bottom of the Bibliography Fields list to display the date viewed (accessed) fields.

- Click the Year Accessed text box. Type 2017 as the year.

- Press the TAB key and then type Oct. as the month accessed.

- Press the TAB key and then type 3 as the day accessed (Figure 2–33).

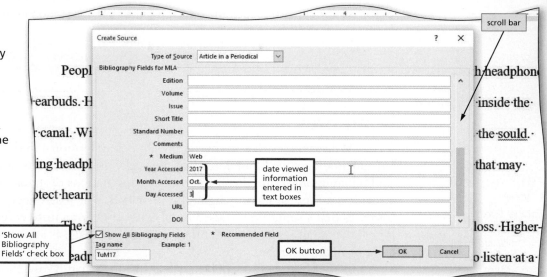

Figure 2–33

Q&A What if some of the text boxes disappear as I enter the fields?
With the 'Show All Bibliography Fields' check box selected, the dialog box may not be able to display all fields at the same time. In this case, some may scroll up off the screen.

5

- Click the OK button to close the dialog box, create the source, and insert the citation in the document at the location of the insertion point.
- Press the END key to move the insertion point to the end of the line, if necessary, which also deselects the citation.
- Press the PERIOD key to end the sentence (Figure 2–34).

Figure 2–34

To Enter More Text

The next task is to continue typing text in the research paper up to the location of the footnote. The following steps enter this text.

1 Press the SPACEBAR.

2 Type the next sentences (Figure 2–35):
Properly designed headphones

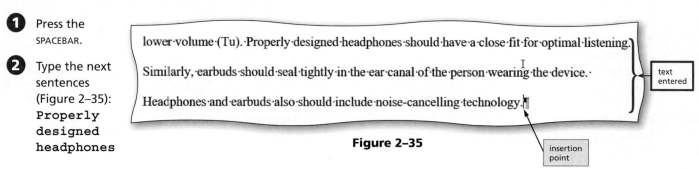

Figure 2–35

```
should have a close fit for optimal listening. Similarly,
earbuds should seal tightly in the ear canal of the person
wearing the device. Headphones and earbuds also should
include noise-cancelling technology.
```

③ Save the research paper again on the same storage location with the same file name.

Q&A Why should I save the research paper again?
You have made several modifications to the research paper since you last saved it; thus, you should save it again.

Footnotes

As discussed earlier in this module, notes are optional in the MLA documentation style. If used, content notes elaborate on points discussed in the paper, and bibliographic notes direct the reader to evaluations of statements in a source or provide a means for identifying multiple sources. The MLA documentation style specifies that a superscript (raised number) be used for a **note reference mark** to signal that a note exists either at the bottom of the page as a **footnote** or at the end of the document as an **endnote**.

In Word, **note text** can be any length and format. Word automatically numbers notes sequentially by placing a note reference mark both in the body of the document and to the left of the note text. If you insert, rearrange, or remove notes, Word renumbers any subsequent note reference marks according to their new sequence in the document.

To Insert a Footnote Reference Mark

1 CHANGE DOCUMENT SETTINGS | 2 CREATE HEADER | **3 TYPE RESEARCH PAPER WITH CITATIONS**
4 CREATE ALPHABETICAL WORKS CITED | 5 PROOFREAD & REVISE RESEARCH PAPER

The following step inserts a footnote reference mark in the document at the location of the insertion point and at the location where the footnote text will be typed. **Why?** *You will insert a content note elaborating on noise-cancelling technology, which you want to position as a footnote.*

①

• With the insertion point positioned as shown in Figure 2–35, click the Insert Footnote button (References tab | Footnotes group) to display a note reference mark (a superscripted 1) in two places: (1) in the document window at the location of the insertion point and (2) at the bottom of the page where the footnote will be positioned, just below a separator line (Figure 2–36).

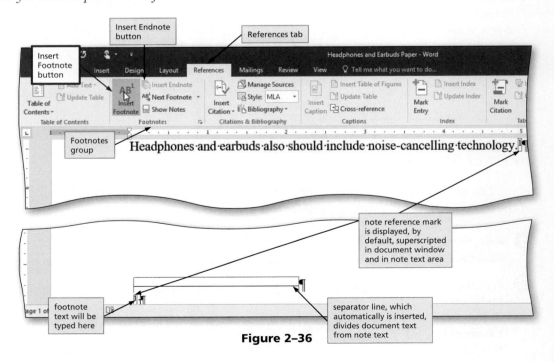

Figure 2–36

Q&A

What if I wanted notes to be positioned as endnotes instead of as footnotes?

You would click the Insert Endnote button (References tab | Footnotes group), which places the separator line and the endnote text at the end of the document, instead of the bottom of the page containing the reference.

Other Ways

1. Press ALT+CTRL+F

To Enter Footnote Text

The following step types the footnote text to the right of the note reference mark below the separator line.

1 Type the footnote text up to the citation (shown in Figure 2–37): `Gupta and Padro state that effective noise-cancelling technology reduces the interference of sounds from the surrounding environment, reducing the volume level required by headphones and earbuds` and then press the SPACEBAR.

To Insert a Citation Placeholder

1 CHANGE DOCUMENT SETTINGS | 2 CREATE HEADER | **3 TYPE RESEARCH PAPER WITH CITATIONS**
4 CREATE ALPHABETICAL WORKS CITED | **5 PROOFREAD & REVISE RESEARCH PAPER**

Earlier in this module, you inserted a citation and its source at once. In Word, you also can insert a citation without entering the source information. ***Why?*** *Sometimes, you may not have the source information readily available and would prefer to enter it at a later time.*

The following steps insert a citation placeholder in the footnote, so that you can enter the source information later.

1

- With the insertion point positioned as shown in Figure 2–37, click the Insert Citation button (References tab | Citations & Bibliography group) to display the Insert Citation menu (Figure 2–37).

Figure 2–37

- Click 'Add New Placeholder' on the Insert Citation menu to display the Placeholder Name dialog box.
- Type **Gupta** as the tag name for the source (Figure 2–38).

Q&A
What is a tag name?
A tag name is an identifier that links a citation to a source. Word automatically creates a tag name when you enter a source. When you create a citation placeholder, enter a meaningful tag name, which will appear in the citation placeholder until you edit the source.

Figure 2–38

- Click the OK button (Placeholder Name dialog box) to close the dialog box and insert the entered tag name in the citation placeholder in the document (shown in Figure 2–39).
- Press the PERIOD key to end the sentence.

Q&A
What if the citation is in the wrong location?
Click the citation to select it and then drag the citation tab (on the upper-left corner of the selected citation) to any location in the document.

Footnote Text Style

When you insert a footnote, Word formats it using the Footnote Text style, which does not adhere to the MLA documentation style. For example, notice in Figure 2–37 that the footnote text is single-spaced, left-aligned, and a smaller font size than the text in the research paper. According to the MLA documentation style, notes should be formatted like all other paragraphs in the paper.

You could change the paragraph formatting of the footnote text to first-line indent and double-spacing and then change the font size from 10 to 12 point. If you use this technique, however, you will need to change the format of the footnote text for each footnote you enter into the document.

A more efficient technique is to modify the format of the Footnote Text style so that every footnote you enter in the document will use the formats defined in this style.

1 CHANGE DOCUMENT SETTINGS | 2 CREATE HEADER | 3 TYPE RESEARCH PAPER WITH CITATIONS
4 CREATE ALPHABETICAL WORKS CITED | 5 PROOFREAD & REVISE RESEARCH PAPER

To Modify a Style Using a Shortcut Menu

The Footnote Text style specifies left-aligned single-spaced paragraphs with a 10-point font size for text. The following steps modify the Footnote Text style. *Why? To meet MLA documentation style, the footnotes should be double-spaced with a first-line indent and a 12-point font size for text.*

1

- Right-click the note text in the footnote to display a shortcut menu related to footnotes (Figure 2–39).

shortcut menu

Style command

insertion point

footnote paragraphs should be formatted the same as other paragraphs in research paper

¹Gupta and Padro state that effective noise-cancelling technology reduces the interference of sounds from the surrounding environment, reducing the volume level required by headphones and earbuds (Gupta).¶

citation placeholder inserted

Figure 2–39

2

- Click Style on the shortcut menu to display the Style dialog box. If necessary, click the Category arrow, click All styles in the Category list, and then click Footnote Text in the Styles list to select the style to modify.

- Click the Modify button (Style dialog box) to display the Modify Style dialog box.

- Click the Font Size arrow (Modify Style dialog box) to display the Font Size list and then click 12 in the Font Size list to change the font size.

- Click the Double Space button to change the line spacing.

- Click the Format button to display the Format menu (Figure 2–40).

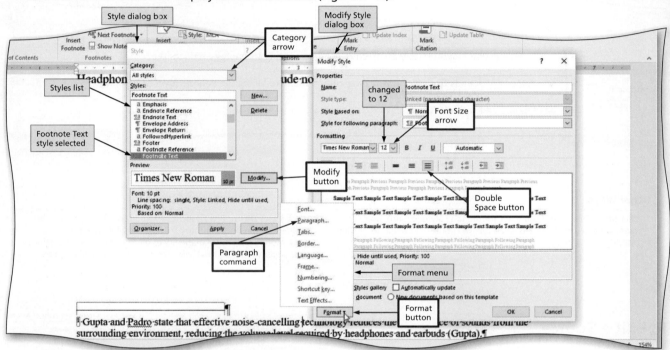

Figure 2–40

3

- Click Paragraph on the Format menu (Modify Style dialog box) to display the Paragraph dialog box.

- Click the Special arrow in the Indentation area (Paragraph dialog box) and then click First line (Figure 2–41).

Figure 2–41

4

- Click the OK button (Paragraph dialog box) to close the dialog box.
- Click the OK button (Modify Style dialog box) to close the dialog box.
- Click the Apply button (Style dialog box) to apply the style changes to the footnote text (Figure 2–42).

 Will all footnotes use this modified style?

Yes. Any future footnotes entered in the document will use a 12-point font with the paragraphs first-line indented and double-spaced.

Figure 2–42

Other Ways

1. Click Styles Dialog Box Launcher (Home tab | Styles group), point to style name in list, click style name arrow, click Modify, change settings (Modify Style dialog box), click OK button

2. Click Styles Dialog Box Launcher (Home tab | Styles group), click Manage Styles button in task pane, select style name in list, click Modify button (Manage Styles dialog box), change settings (Modify Style dialog box), click OK button in each dialog box

---

To Edit a Source

1 CHANGE DOCUMENT SETTINGS | 2 CREATE HEADER | 3 TYPE RESEARCH PAPER WITH CITATIONS
4 CREATE ALPHABETICAL WORKS CITED | 5 PROOFREAD & REVISE RESEARCH PAPER

When you typed the footnote text for this research paper, you inserted a citation placeholder for the source. The following steps edit a source. **Why?** *Assume you now have the source information and are ready to enter it.*

1

- Click somewhere in the citation placeholder to be edited, in this case (Gupta), to select the citation placeholder.

- Click the Citation Options arrow to display the Citation Options menu (Figure 2–43).

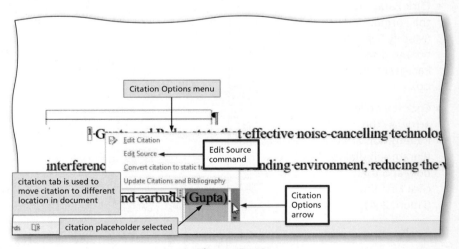

Figure 2–43

What is the purpose of the tab to the left of the selected citation?

If, for some reason, you wanted to move a citation to a different location in the document, you would select the citation and then drag the citation tab to the desired location.

2

- Click Edit Source on the Citation Options menu to display the Edit Source dialog box.
- If necessary, click the 'Type of Source' arrow (Edit Source dialog box) and then click Book, so that the list shows fields required for a book.
- Because this source has two authors, click the Edit button to display the Edit Name dialog box, which assists you with entering multiple author names.
- Type **Gupta** as the first author's last name; press the TAB key and then type **Elena** as the first name; press the TAB key and then type **Maia** as the middle name (Figure 2–44).

Q&A What if I already know how to punctuate the author entry properly?
You can enter the name directly in the Author box.

Figure 2–44

3

- Click the Add button (Edit Name dialog box) to add the first author name to the Names list.
- Type **Padro** as the second author's last name; press the TAB key and then type **Adelbert** as the first name; press the TAB key and then type **Luis** as the middle name.
- Click the Add button (Edit Name dialog box) to add the second author name to the Names list (Figure 2–45).

Figure 2–45

- Click the OK button (Edit Name dialog box) to add the author names that appear in the Names list to the Author box in the Edit Source dialog box.

- Click the Title text box (Edit Source dialog box). Type **Hearing Protection Methods** as the book title.

- Press the TAB key and then type **2017** as the year.

- Press the TAB key and then type **Orlando** as the city.

- Press the TAB key and then type **Palm Press** as the publisher.

- Press the TAB key and then type **Print** as the medium (Figure 2–46).

Figure 2–46

- Click the OK button to close the dialog box, create the source, and update the citation to display both author last names (shown in Figure 2–47).

Other Ways

1. Click Manage Sources button (References tab | Citations & Bibliography group), click placeholder source in Current List, click Edit button (Source Manager dialog box)

To Edit a Citation

1 CHANGE DOCUMENT SETTINGS | 2 CREATE HEADER | 3 TYPE RESEARCH PAPER WITH CITATIONS
4 CREATE ALPHABETICAL WORKS CITED | 5 PROOFREAD & REVISE RESEARCH PAPER

In the MLA documentation style, if a source has page numbers, you should include them in the citation. Thus, Word provides a means to enter the page numbers to be displayed in the citation. Also, if you reference the author's name in the text, you should not list it again in the parenthetical citation. Instead, just list the page number(s) in the citation. To do this, you instruct Word to suppress author and title. *Why? If you suppress the author, Word automatically displays the title, so you need to suppress both the author and title if you want just the page number(s) to be displayed.* The following steps edit the citation, suppressing the author and title but displaying the page numbers.

❶

- If necessary, click somewhere in the citation to be edited, in this case somewhere in (Gupta and Padro), which selects the citation and displays the Citation Options arrow.

- Click the Citation Options arrow to display the Citation Options menu (Figure 2–47).

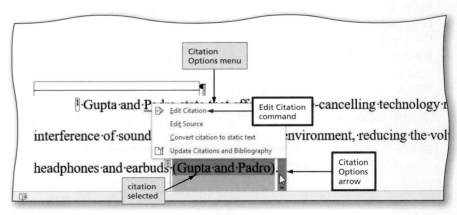

Figure 2–47

2

- Click Edit Citation on the Citation Options menu to display the Edit Citation dialog box.

- Type 75-78 in the Pages text box (Edit Citation dialog box).

- Click the Author check box to place a check mark in it.

- Click the Title check box to place a check mark in it (Figure 2–48).

Figure 2–48

3

- Click the OK button to close the dialog box, remove the author names from the citation in the footnote, suppress the title from showing, and add page numbers to the citation.

- Press the END key to move the insertion point to the end of the line, which also deselects the citation (Figure 2–49).

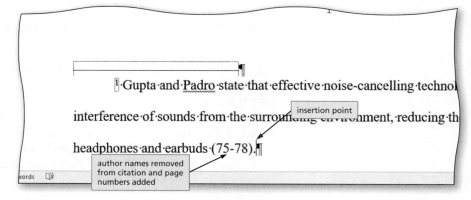

Figure 2–49

Working with Footnotes and Endnotes

You edit footnote text just as you edit any other text in the document. To delete or move a note reference mark, however, the insertion point must be in the document text (not in the footnote text).

To delete a note, select the note reference mark in the document text (not in the footnote text) by dragging through the note reference mark and then click the Cut button (Home tab | Clipboard group). Or, click immediately to the right of the note reference mark in the document text and then press the BACKSPACE key twice, or click immediately to the left of the note reference mark in the document text and then press the DELETE key twice.

To move a note to a different location in a document, select the note reference mark in the document text (not in the footnote text), click the Cut button (Home tab | Clipboard group), click the location where you want to move the note, and then click the Paste button (Home tab | Clipboard group). When you move or delete notes, Word automatically renumbers any remaining notes in the correct sequence.

If you are using a mouse and position the pointer on the note reference mark in the document text, the note text is displayed above the note reference mark as a ScreenTip. To remove the ScreenTip, move the pointer.

If, for some reason, you wanted to change the format of note reference marks in footnotes or endnotes (i.e., from 1, 2, 3 to A, B, C), you would click the Footnote & Endnote Dialog Box Launcher (References tab | Footnotes group) to display the Footnote and Endnote dialog box, click the Number format arrow (Footnote and Endnote dialog box), click the desired number format in the list, and then click the Apply button.

BTW

Footnote and Endnote Location
You can change the location of footnotes from the bottom of the page to the end of the text by clicking the Footnote & Endnote Dialog Box Launcher (References tab | Footnotes group), clicking the Footnotes arrow (Footnote and Endnote dialog box), and then clicking Below text. Similarly, clicking the Endnotes arrow (Footnote and Endnote dialog box) enables you to change the location of endnotes from the end of the document to the end of a section.

If, for some reason, you wanted to change a footnote number, you would click the Footnote & Endnote Dialog Box Launcher (References tab | Footnotes group) to display the Footnote and Endnote dialog box, enter the desired number in the Start at box, and then click the Apply button (Footnote and Endnote dialog box).

If, for some reason, you wanted to convert footnotes to endnotes, you would click the Footnote & Endnote Dialog Box Launcher (References tab | Footnotes group) to display the Footnote and Endnote dialog box, click the Convert button (Footnote and Endnote dialog box), select the 'Convert all footnotes to endnotes' option button (Convert Notes dialog box), click the OK button (Convert Notes dialog box), and then click the Close button (Footnote and Endnote dialog box).

To Enter More Text

The next task is to continue typing text in the body of the research paper. The following steps enter this text.

1 Position the insertion point after the note reference mark in the document and then press the ENTER key.

2 Type the first three sentences in the third paragraph of the research paper (shown in Figure 2–50): `The volume level of the sound that transmits from headphones or earbuds into the ear of a person wearing this type of device has been linked to hearing loss. The volume should be set low enough that other people nearby cannot hear the sound being transmitted. The quieter the sounds, the less possibility of hearing damage.`

1 CHANGE DOCUMENT SETTINGS | 2 CREATE HEADER | **3 TYPE RESEARCH PAPER WITH CITATIONS**
4 CREATE ALPHABETICAL WORKS CITED | 5 PROOFREAD & REVISE RESEARCH PAPER

To Count Words

Often when you write papers, you are required to compose the papers with a minimum number of words. The minimum requirement for the research paper in this module is 275 words. You can look on the status bar and see the total number of words thus far in a document. For example, Figure 2–50 shows the research paper has 231 words, but you are not sure if that count includes the words in your footnote. The following steps display the Word Count dialog box. ***Why?*** *You want to verify that the footnote text is included in the count.*

1
- Click the Word Count indicator on the status bar to display the Word Count dialog box.

- If necessary, place a check mark in the 'Include textboxes, footnotes and endnotes' check box (Word Count dialog box) (Figure 2–50).

Figure 2–50

Why do the statistics in my Word Count dialog box differ from those in Figure 2–50?
Depending on the accuracy of your typing, your statistics may differ.

2
- Click the Close button (Word Count dialog box) to close the dialog box.

Q&A Can I display statistics for just a section of the document?
Yes. Select the section and then click the Word Count indicator on the status bar to display statistics about the selected text.

Other Ways

1. Click Word Count button (Review tab | Proofing group)   2. Press CTRL+SHIFT+G

Automatic Page Breaks

As you type documents that exceed one page, Word automatically inserts page breaks, called **automatic page breaks** or **soft page breaks**, when it determines the text has filled one page according to paper size, margin settings, line spacing, and other settings. If you add text, delete text, or modify text on a page, Word recalculates the location of automatic page breaks and adjusts them accordingly.

Word performs page recalculation between the keystrokes, that is, in between the pauses in your typing. Thus, Word refers to the automatic page break task as **background repagination**. An automatic page break will occur in the next set of steps.

To Enter More Text and Insert a Citation Placeholder

The next task is to type the remainder of the third paragraph in the body of the research paper. The following steps enter this text and a citation placeholder at the end of the paragraph.

1 With the insertion point positioned at the end of the third sentence in the third paragraph, as shown in Figure 2–50, press the SPACEBAR.

2 Type the rest of the third paragraph: **Further, listening at a higher volume for extended periods of time could be unsafe. One expert suggests people should listen at only 30 percent maximum** and then press the SPACEBAR.

Q&A Why does the text move from the second page to the first page as I am typing?
Word, by default, will not allow the first line of a paragraph to be by itself at the bottom of a page (an **orphan**) or the last line of a paragraph to be by itself at the top of a page (a **widow**). As you type, Word adjusts the placement of the paragraph to avoid orphans and widows.

3 Click the Insert Citation button (References tab | Citations & Bibliography group) to display the Insert Citation menu. Click 'Add New Placeholder' on the Insert Citation menu to display the Placeholder Name dialog box.

4 Type **Chamberlain** as the tag name for the source.

5 Click the OK button (Placeholder Name dialog box) to close the dialog box and insert the tag name in the citation placeholder (shown in Figure 2–51).

6 Press the PERIOD key to end the sentence.

BTW
Page Break Locations
As you type, your page break may occur at different locations depending on Word settings and the type of printer connected to the computer.

To Hide and Show White Space

With the page break and header, it is difficult to see the entire third paragraph at once on the screen. With the screen in Print Layout view, you can hide white space, which is the space that is displayed at the top and bottom of pages (including headers and footers) and also the space between pages. The following steps hide white space, if your screen displays it, and then shows white space. *Why? You want to see as much of the third paragraph as possible at once, which spans the bottom of the first page and the top of the second page.*

1

• Position the pointer in the document window in the space between pages so that the pointer changes to a 'Hide White Space' button (Figure 2–51).

Q&A What if I am using a touch screen?
Proceed to step 2.

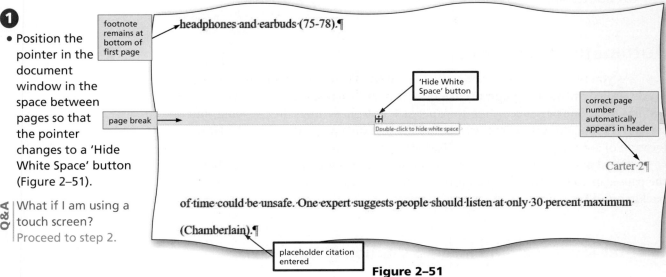

Figure 2–51

2

• Double-click while the pointer is a 'Hide White Space' button to hide white space.

Q&A What if I am using a touch screen?
Double-tap in the space between pages.

Does hiding white space have any effect on the printed document?
No.

3

• Position the pointer in the document window on the page break between pages so that the pointer changes to a 'Show White Space' button (Figure 2–52).

Figure 2–52

4

- Double-click while the pointer is a 'Show White Space' button to show white space.

Q&A What if I am using a touch screen?
Double-tap the page break.

Other Ways

1. Click File on ribbon, click Options tab in Backstage view, click Display in left pane (Word Options dialog box), remove or select check mark from 'Show white space between pages in Print Layout view' check box, click OK button

To Edit a Source

When you typed the third paragraph of the research paper, you inserted a citation placeholder, Chamberlain, for the source. You now have the source information, which is for a website, and are ready to enter it. The following steps edit the source for the Chamberlain citation placeholder.

1 Click somewhere in the citation placeholder to be edited, in this case (Chamberlain), to select the citation placeholder.

2 Click the Citation Options arrow to display the Citation Options menu.

3 Click Edit Source on the Citation Options menu to display the Edit Source dialog box.

4 If necessary, click the 'Type of Source' arrow (Edit Source dialog box); scroll to and then click Web site, so that the list shows fields required for a Web site.

5 Place a check mark in the 'Show All Bibliography Fields' check box to display more fields related to Web sites.

6 Click the Author text box. Type `Chamberlain, Megan Lynn` as the author.

7 Click the 'Name of Web Page' text box. Type `Understanding How Volume Levels Affect Hearing` as the webpage name.

8 Click the Production Company text box. Type `Course Technology` as the production company.

9 Click the Year Accessed text box. Type `2017` as the year accessed (Figure 2–53).

Figure 2–53

10 Press the TAB key and then type `Sept.` as the month accessed.

11 Press the TAB key and then type `16` as the day accessed.

12 Press the TAB key as many times as necessary to move the insertion point to the Medium text box and then type `Web` as the Medium.

Q&A Do I need to enter a web address (URL)?
The latest MLA documentation style update does not require the web address in the source.

13 Click the OK button to close the dialog box and create the source.

BTW
Organizing Files and Folders
You should organize and store files in folders so that you easily can find the files later. For example, if you are taking an introductory technology class called CIS 101, a good practice would be to save all Word files in a Word folder in a CIS 101 folder. For a discussion of folders and detailed examples of creating folders, refer to the Office and Windows module at the beginning of this book.

To Enter More Text

The next task is to type the last paragraph of text in the research paper. The following steps enter this text.

1 Press the END key to position the insertion point at the end of the third paragraph and then press the ENTER key.

2 Type the last paragraph of the research paper (Figure 2–54): `More and more people are using headphones and earbuds with their computers and portable devices. Using high-quality listening devices and lowering the volume can help to lessen potential hearing loss from the use of headphones and earbuds.`

3 Save the research paper again on the same storage location with the same file name.

Figure 2–54

Break Point: If you wish to take a break, this is a good place to do so. You can exit Word now. To resume at a later time, run Word, open the file called Headphones and Earbuds Paper, and continue following the steps from this location forward. For a detailed example of exiting Word, running Word, and opening a file, refer to the Office and Windows module at the beginning of the book.

Creating an Alphabetical Works Cited Page

According to the MLA documentation style, the **works cited page** is a list of sources that are referenced directly in a research paper. You place the list on a separate numbered page with the title, Works Cited, centered one inch from the top margin. The works are to be alphabetized by the author's last name or, if the work has no author, by the work's title. The first line of each entry begins at the left margin. Indent subsequent lines of the same entry one-half inch from the left margin.

What is a bibliography?

A **bibliography** is an alphabetical list of sources referenced in a paper. Whereas the text of the research paper contains brief references to the source (the citations), the bibliography lists all publication information about the source. Documentation styles differ significantly in their guidelines for preparing a bibliography. Each style identifies formats for various sources, including books, magazines, pamphlets, newspapers, websites, television programs, paintings, maps, advertisements, letters, memos, and much more. You can find information about various styles and their guidelines in printed style guides and on the web.

CONSIDER THIS

To Page Break Manually

1 CHANGE DOCUMENT SETTINGS | 2 CREATE HEADER | 3 TYPE RESEARCH PAPER WITH CITATIONS
4 CREATE ALPHABETICAL WORKS CITED | 5 PROOFREAD & REVISE RESEARCH PAPER

The next step is to insert a manual page break following the body of the research paper. ***Why?*** *According to the MLA documentation style, the works cited are to be displayed on a separate numbered page.*

A **manual page break**, or **hard page break**, is one that you force into the document at a specific location. Word never moves or adjusts manual page breaks. Word, however, does adjust any automatic page breaks that follow a manual page break. Word inserts manual page breaks immediately above or to the left of the location of the insertion point. The following step inserts a manual page break after the text of the research paper.

1

- Verify that the insertion point is positioned at the end of the text of the research paper, as shown in Figure 2–54.

- Click Insert on the ribbon to display the Insert tab.

- Click the 'Insert a Page Break' button (Insert tab | Pages group) to insert a manual page break immediately to the left of the insertion point and position the insertion point immediately below the manual page break (Figure 2–55).

Figure 2–55

Other Ways

1. Press CTRL+ENTER

To Apply a Style

The works cited title is to be centered between the margins of the paper. If you simply issue the Center command, the title will not be centered properly. ***Why?*** *It will be to the right of the center point because earlier you set the first-line indent for paragraphs to one-half inch.*

To properly center the title of the works cited page, you could drag the 'First Line Indent' marker back to the left margin before centering the paragraph, or you could apply the Normal style to the location of the insertion point. Recall that you modified the Normal style for this document to 12-point Times New Roman with double-spaced, left-aligned paragraphs that have no space after the paragraphs.

To apply a style to a paragraph, first position the insertion point in the paragraph and then apply the style. The following step applies the modified Normal style to the location of the insertion point.

- Click Home on the ribbon to display the Home tab.

- With the insertion point on the paragraph mark at the top of page 3 (as shown in Figure 2–55) even if Normal is selected, click Normal in the Styles gallery (Home tab | Styles group) to apply the Normal style to the paragraph containing the insertion point (Figure 2–56).

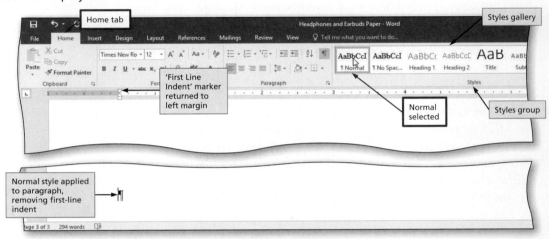

Figure 2–56

Other Ways

1. Click Styles Dialog Box Launcher (Home tab | Styles group), select desired style in Styles task pane

2. Press CTRL+SHIFT+S, click Style Name arrow in Apply Styles task pane, select desired style in list

To Center Text

The next task is to enter the title, Works Cited, centered between the margins of the paper. The following steps use a keyboard shortcut to format the title.

1 Press CTRL+E to center the paragraph mark.

2 Type `Works Cited` as the title.

3 Press the ENTER key.

4 Press CTRL+L to left-align the paragraph mark (shown in Figure 2–57).

To Create a Bibliographical List

While typing the research paper, you created several citations and their sources. The next task is to use Word to format the list of sources and alphabetize them in a **bibliographical list**. ***Why?*** *Word can create a bibliographical list with each element of the source placed in its correct position with proper punctuation, according to the specified style, saving you time looking up style guidelines. For example, in this research paper, the book source will list, in* *this order, the author name(s), book title, publisher city, publishing company name, and publication year with the correct punctuation between each element according to the MLA documentation style.* The following steps create an MLA-styled bibliographical list from the sources previously entered.

1

- Click References on the ribbon to display the References tab.

- With the insertion point positioned as shown in Figure 2–57, click the Bibliography button (References tab | Citations & Bibliography group) to display the Bibliography gallery (Figure 2–57).

Q&A Will I select the Works Cited option from the Bibliography gallery? No. The title it inserts is not formatted according to the MLA documentation style. Thus, you will use the Insert Bibliography command instead.

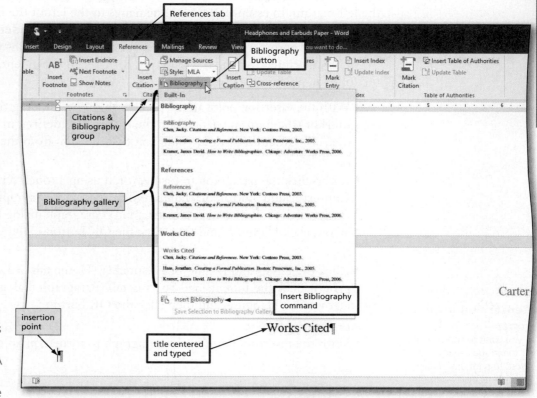

Figure 2–57

2

- Click Insert Bibliography in the Bibliography gallery to insert a list of sources at the location of the insertion point.

- If necessary, scroll to display the entire list of sources in the document window (Figure 2–58).

Q&A What is the n.d. in the first work? The MLA documentation style uses the abbreviation n.d. for no date (for example, no date appears on the webpage).

Carter·3¶

Works·Cited¶

Chamberlain,·Megan·Lynn.·*Understanding·How·Volume·Levels·Affect·Hearing.*·n.d.·Course·
        Technology.·Web.·16·Sept.·2017.¶

Gupta,·Elena·Maia·and·Adelbert·Luis·Padro.·*Hearing·Protection·Methods.*·Orlando:·Palm·Press,·
        2017.·Print.¶

Tu,·Mingzhu·Lin.·"Headphones·and·Earbuds."·*Technology·and·Trends·Today*·Aug.·2017:·n.·pag.·
        Web.·3·Oct.·2017.¶

Figure 2–58

- Save the research paper again on the same storage location with the same file name.

To Format Paragraphs with a Hanging Indent

Notice in Figure 2–58 that the first line of each source entry begins at the left margin, and subsequent lines in the same paragraph are indented one-half inch from the left margin. In essence, the first line hangs to the left of the rest of the paragraph; thus, this type of paragraph formatting is called a **hanging indent**. The Bibliography style in Word automatically formats the works cited paragraphs with a hanging indent.

If you wanted to format paragraphs with a hanging indent, you would use one of the following techniques.

- With the insertion point in the paragraph to format, drag the **Hanging Indent marker** (the bottom triangle) on the ruler to the desired mark on the ruler (i.e., .5") to set the hanging indent at that location from the left margin.

or

- Right-click the paragraph to format (or, if using a touch screen, tap the 'Show Context Menu' button on the mini toolbar), click Paragraph on the shortcut menu, click the Indents and Spacing tab (Paragraph dialog box), click the Special arrow, click Hanging, and then click the OK button.

or

- Click the Paragraph Dialog Box Launcher (Home tab or Layout tab | Paragraph group), click the Indents and Spacing tab (Paragraph dialog box), click the Special arrow, click Hanging, and then click the OK button.

or

- With the insertion point in the paragraph to format, press CTRL+T.

Proofreading and Revising the Research Paper

As discussed in Module 1, once you complete a document, you might find it necessary to make changes to it. Before submitting a paper to be graded, you should proofread it. While **proofreading**, ensure all the source information is correct and look for grammatical, typographical, and spelling errors. Also ensure that transitions between sentences flow smoothly and the sentences themselves make sense.

To assist you with the proofreading effort, Word provides several tools. You can go to a page, copy text, find text, replace text, insert a synonym, check spelling and grammar, and look up information. The following pages discuss these tools.

BTW

Conserving Ink and Toner

If you want to conserve ink or toner, you can instruct Word to print draft quality documents by clicking File on the ribbon to open the Backstage view, clicking the Options tab in the Backstage view to display the Word Options dialog box, clicking Advanced in the left pane (Word Options dialog box), scrolling to the Print area in the right pane, placing a check mark in the 'Use draft quality' check box, and then clicking the OK button. Then, use the Backstage view to print the document as usual.

CONSIDER THIS

What should you consider when proofreading and revising a paper?

As you proofread the paper, look for ways to improve it. Check all grammar, spelling, and punctuation. Be sure the text is logical and transitions are smooth. Where necessary, add text, delete text, reword text, and move text to different locations. Ask yourself these questions:

- Does the title suggest the topic?
- Is the thesis clear?
- Is the purpose of the paper clear?
- Does the paper have an introduction, body, and conclusion?
- Does each paragraph in the body relate to the thesis?
- Is the conclusion effective?
- Are sources acknowledged correctly?

To Modify a Source

While proofreading the paper, you notice an error in the magazine title; specifically, the word, and, should be removed. If you modify the contents of any source, the list of sources automatically updates. *Why? Word automatically updates the contents of fields, and the bibliography is a field.* The following steps delete a word from the title of the magazine article.

- Click the Manage Sources button (References tab | Citations & Bibliography group) to display the Source Manager dialog box.
- Click the source you wish to edit in the Current List, in this case the article by Tu, to select the source.
- Click the Edit button (Source Manager dialog box) to display the Edit Source dialog box.
- In the Periodical Title text box, delete the word, and, from the title (Figure 2–59).

Figure 2–59

- Click the OK button (Edit Source dialog box) to close the dialog box.
- If a Microsoft Word dialog box appears, click its Yes button to update all occurrences of the source.
- Click the Close button (Source Manager dialog box) to update the list of sources and close the dialog box.

To Update a Field

Depending on settings, the bibliography field may not automatically reflect the edited magazine title. Thus, the following steps update the bibliography field. *Why? Because the bibliography is a field, you may need to instruct Word to update its contents.*

1

- Right-click anywhere in the bibliography text to display a shortcut menu related to fields (Figure 2–60).

Q&A What if I am using a touch screen?
Press and hold anywhere in the bibliography text and then tap the 'Show Context Menu' button on the mini toolbar.

Figure 2–60

Why are all the words in the bibliography shaded gray?
By default, Word shades selected fields gray.

What if the bibliography field is not shaded gray?
Click File on the ribbon to open the Backstage view, click the Options tab in the Backstage view, click Advanced in the left pane (Word Options dialog box), scroll to the 'Show document content' area, click the Field shading arrow, click When selected, and then click the OK button.

2

- Click Update Field on the shortcut menu to update the selected field (Figure 2–61).

Q&A Can I update all fields in a document at once?
Yes. Select the entire document and then follow these steps.

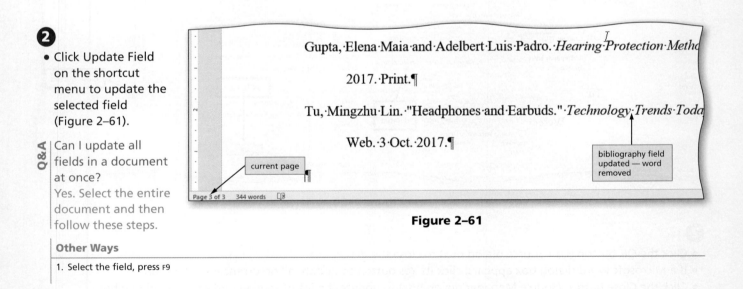

Figure 2–61

Other Ways

1. Select the field, press F9

TO CONVERT A FIELD TO REGULAR TEXT

If, for some reason, you wanted to convert a field, such as the bibliography field, to regular text, you would perform the following steps. Keep in mind, though, once you convert the field to regular text, it no longer is a field that can be updated.

1. Click somewhere in the field to select it, in this case, somewhere in the bibliography.

2. Press CTRL+SHIFT+F9 to convert the selected field to regular text.

To Go to a Page

The next task in revising the paper is to modify text on the second page of the document. *Why? You want to copy text from one location to another on the second page.* You could scroll to the desired location in the document, or you can use the Navigation Pane to browse through pages in a document. The following steps display the top of the second page in the document window and position the insertion point at the beginning of that page.

1

- Click View on the ribbon to display the View tab.

- Place a check mark in the 'Open the Navigation Pane' check box (View tab | Show group) to open the Navigation Pane on the left side of the Word window.

- If necessary, click the Pages tab in the Navigation Pane to display thumbnails of the pages in the document.

- Scroll to, if necessary, and then click the thumbnail of the second page to display the top of the selected page in the top of the document window (Figure 2–62).

Q&A What is the Navigation Pane?
The Navigation Pane is a window that enables you to browse through headings in a document, browse through pages in a document, or search for text in a document.

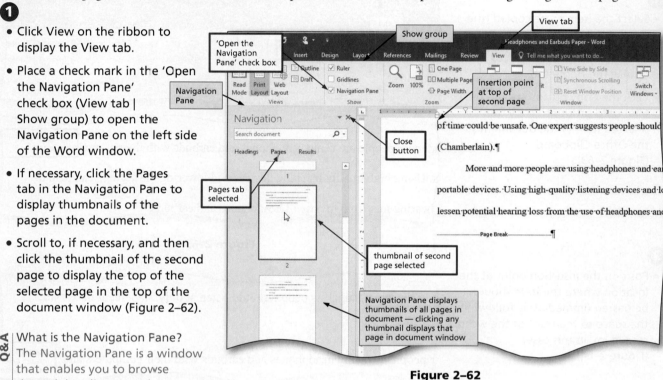

Figure 2–62

2

- Click the Close button in the Navigation Pane to close the pane.

Other Ways
1. Click Find arrow (Home tab | Editing group), click Go To on Find menu, click Go To tab (Find and Replace dialog box), enter page number, click Go To button   2. Click Page Number indicator on status bar, click Pages tab in Navigation Pane, click thumbnail of desired page (Navigation Pane)   3. Press CTRL+G, enter page number (Find and Replace dialog box), click Go To button

Copying, Cutting, and Pasting

While proofreading the research paper, you decide it would read better if the word, volume, in the second sentence of the last paragraph also appeared after the word, maximum, in the last sentence of the previous paragraph. You could type the word at the desired location, but you decide to use the Office Clipboard. The **Office Clipboard** is a temporary storage area that holds up to 24 items (text or graphics) copied from any Office program. The Office Clipboard works with the copy, cut, and paste commands:

- **Copying** is the process of placing items on the Office Clipboard, leaving the item in the document.

- **Cutting** removes the item from the document before placing it on the Office Clipboard.

- **Pasting** is the process of copying an item from the Office Clipboard into the document at the location of the insertion point.

To Copy and Paste

In the research paper, you copy a word from one location to another. *Why? The sentence reads better with the word, volume, inserted after the word, maximum.* The following steps copy and paste a word.

1

- Select the item to be copied (the word, volume, in this case).
- Click Home on the ribbon to display the Home tab.
- Click the Copy button (Home tab | Clipboard group) to copy the selected item in the document to the Office Clipboard (Figure 2–63).

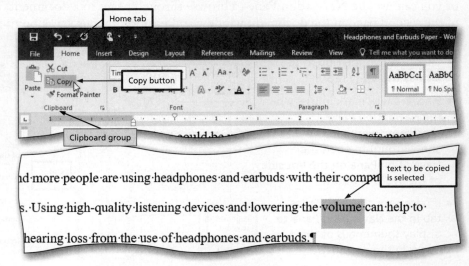

Figure 2–63

2

- Position the insertion point at the location where the item should be pasted (immediately following the space to the right of the word, maximum, in this case) (Figure 2–64).

Figure 2–64

3

- Click the Paste button (Home tab | Clipboard group) to paste the copied item in the document at the location of the insertion point (Figure 2–65).

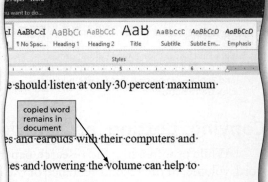

Q&A What if I click the Paste arrow by mistake?
Click the Paste arrow again to remove the Paste menu and repeat Step 3.

Figure 2–65

Other Ways

1. Click Copy on shortcut menu (or, if using touch, tap Copy on mini toolbar), right-click where item is to be pasted, click 'Keep Source Formatting' in Paste Options area on shortcut menu (or, if using touch, tap Paste on mini toolbar)

2. Select item, press CTRL+C, position insertion point at paste location, press CTRL+V

To Display the Paste Options Menu

When you paste an item or move an item using drag-and-drop editing, which was discussed in the previous module, Word automatically displays a Paste Options button near the pasted or moved text (shown in Figure 2–65). *Why? The Paste Options button allows you to change the format of a pasted item. For example, you can instruct Word to format the pasted item the same way as where it was copied (the source) or format it the same way as where it is being pasted (the destination).* The following steps display the Paste Options menu.

1

- Click the Paste Options button to display the Paste Options menu (Figure 2–66).

Q&A What are the functions of the buttons on the Paste Options menu?

In general, the left button indicates the pasted item should look the same as it did in its original location (the source). The second button formats the pasted text to match the rest of the item where it was pasted (the destination). The third button removes all formatting from the pasted item. The 'Set Default Paste' command displays the Word Options dialog box. Keep in mind that the buttons shown on a Paste Options menu will vary, depending on the item being pasted.

Figure 2–66

2

- Click anywhere to remove the Paste Options menu from the window.

Other Ways
1. CTRL or ESC (to remove the Paste Options menu)

To Find Text

While proofreading the paper, you would like to locate all occurrences of the word, portable. *Why? You are contemplating changing occurrences of this word to the word, mobile.* The following steps find all occurrences of specific text in a document.

1

- Click the Find button (Home tab | Editing group) to display the Navigation Pane.

Q&A What if I am using a touch screen?

Tap the Find button (Home tab | Editing group) and then tap Find on the menu.

- If necessary, click the Results tab in the Navigation Pane, which displays a Search box where you can type text for which you want to search (Figure 2–67).

Figure 2–67

- Type **portable** in the Navigation Pane Search box to display all occurrences of the typed text, called the search text, in the Navigation Pane and to highlight the occurrences of the search text in the document window (Figure 2–68).

Figure 2–68

Experiment

- Click both occurrences in the Navigation Pane and watch Word display the associated text in the document window.

Experiment

- Type various search text in the Navigation Pane Search box, and watch Word both list matches in the Navigation Pane and highlight matches in the document window.

- Click the Close button in the Navigation Pane to close the pane.

Other Ways

1. Click Find arrow (Home tab | Editing group), click Find on Find menu, enter search text in Navigation Pane
2. Click Page Number indicator on status bar, enter search text in Navigation Pane
3. Press CTRL+F, enter search text in Navigation Pane

To Replace Text

1 CHANGE DOCUMENT SETTINGS | 2 CREATE HEADER | 3 TYPE RESEARCH PAPER WITH CITATIONS
4 CREATE ALPHABETICAL WORKS CITED | 5 PROOFREAD & REVISE RESEARCH PAPER

You decide to change all occurrences of the word, portable, to the word, mobile. *Why? The term, mobile devices, is more commonly used than portable devices.* Word's find and replace feature locates each occurrence of a word or phrase and then replaces it with text you specify. The following steps find and replace text.

- Click the Replace button (Home tab | Editing group) to display the Replace sheet in the Find and Replace dialog box.
- If necessary, type **portable** in the Find what box (Find and Replace dialog box).
- Type **mobile** in the Replace with box (Figure 2–69).

Figure 2–69

- Click the Replace All button to instruct Word to replace all occurrences of the Find what text with the Replace with text (Figure 2–70). If Word displays a dialog box asking if you want to continue searching from the beginning of the document, click the Yes button.

portable changed to mobile

dialog box indicates 2 replacements were made

OK button

Replace All button

Find Next button

after clicking OK button (Microsoft Word dialog box), Cancel button changes to Close button

Figure 2–70

Q&A Does Word search the entire document?

If the insertion point is at the beginning of the document, Word searches the entire document; otherwise, Word may search from the location of the insertion point to the end of the document and then display a dialog box asking if you want to continue searching from the beginning. You also can search a section of text by selecting the text before clicking the Replace or Replace All button.

- Click the OK button (Microsoft Word dialog box) to close the dialog box.
- Click the Close button (Find and Replace dialog box) to close the dialog box.

Other Ways

1. Press CTRL+H

Find and Replace Dialog Box

The Replace All button (Find and Replace dialog box) replaces all occurrences of the Find what text with the Replace with text. In some cases, you may want to replace only certain occurrences of a word or phrase, not all of them. To instruct Word to confirm each change, click the Find Next button (Find and Replace dialog box) (shown in Figure 2–70), instead of the Replace All button. When Word locates an occurrence of the text, it pauses and waits for you to click either the Replace button or the Find Next button. Clicking the Replace button changes the text; clicking the Find Next button instructs Word to disregard the replacement and look for the next occurrence of the Find what text.

If you accidentally replace the wrong text, you can undo a replacement by clicking the Undo button on the Quick Access Toolbar. If you used the Replace All button, Word undoes all replacements. If you used the Replace button, Word undoes only the most recent replacement.

BTW

Finding Formatting
To search for formatting or a special character, click the More button in the Find and Replace dialog box (shown in Figure 2–69). To find formatting, use the Format button in the Find dialog box. To find a special character, use the Special button.

To Find and Insert a Synonym

1 CHANGE DOCUMENT SETTINGS | 2 CREATE HEADER | 3 TYPE RESEARCH PAPER WITH CITATIONS
4 CREATE ALPHABETICAL WORKS CITED | 5 PROOFREAD & REVISE RESEARCH PAPER

In this project, you would like a synonym for the word, lessen, in the last paragraph of the research paper. *Why? When writing, you may discover that you used the same word in multiple locations or that a word you used was not quite appropriate, which is the case here.* In these instances, you will want to look up a **synonym**, or a word similar in meaning, to the duplicate or inappropriate word. A **thesaurus** is a book of synonyms. Word provides synonyms and a thesaurus for your convenience. The following steps find a suitable synonym.

1

- Right-click the word for which you want to find a synonym (in this case, lessen) to display a shortcut menu.
- Point to Synonyms on the shortcut menu to display a list of synonyms for the word you right-clicked (Figure 2–71).

Q&A

◄ What if I am using a touch screen?
Press and hold the word for which you want a synonym, tap the 'Show Context Menu' button on the mini toolbar, and then tap Synonyms on the shortcut menu.

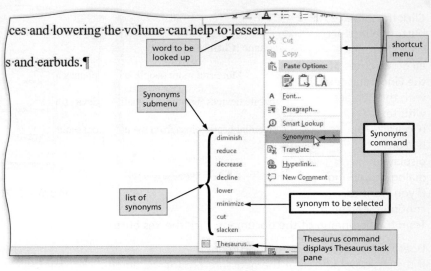

Figure 2–71

2

- Click the synonym you want (in this case, minimize) on the Synonyms submenu to replace the selected word in the document with the selected synonym (Figure 2–72).

Q&A

◄ What if the synonyms list on the shortcut menu does not display a suitable word?
You can display the thesaurus in the Thesaurus task pane by clicking Thesaurus on the Synonyms submenu. The Thesaurus task pane displays a complete thesaurus, in which you can look up synonyms for various meanings of a word. You also can look up an antonym, or word with an opposite meaning.

More·and·more·people·are·using·headphones·and·earbuds·with·the
mobile·devices.·Using·high-quality·listening·devices·and·lowering·the·vol
minimize·potential·hearing·loss·from·the·use·of·headphones·and·earbuds.¶

word, lessen,
changed to minimize

Figure 2–72

Other Ways

1. Click Thesaurus button (Review tab | Proofing group)
2. Press SHIFT+F7

To Check Spelling and Grammar at Once

1 CHANGE DOCUMENT SETTINGS | 2 CREATE HEADER | 3 TYPE RESEARCH PAPER WITH CITATIONS
4 CREATE ALPHABETICAL WORKS CITED | 5 PROOFREAD & REVISE RESEARCH PAPER

As discussed in Module 1, Word checks spelling and grammar as you type and places a wavy underline below possible spelling or grammar errors. Module 1 illustrated how to check these flagged words immediately. The next steps check spelling and grammar at once. **Why?** *Some users prefer to wait and check their entire document for spelling and grammar errors at once.*

Note: In the following steps, the word, sound, has been misspelled intentionally as sould to illustrate the use of Word's check spelling and grammar at once feature. If you are completing this project on a computer or mobile device, your research paper may contain different misspelled words, depending on the accuracy of your typing.

1

- Press CTRL+HOME because you want the spelling and grammar check to begin from the top of the document.
- Click Review on the ribbon to display the Review tab.

- Click the 'Spelling & Grammar' button (Review tab | Proofing group) to begin the spelling and grammar check at the location of the insertion point, which, in this case, is at the beginning of the document.

- Click the desired word in the list of suggestions in the Spelling task pane (sound, in this case) (Figure 2–73).

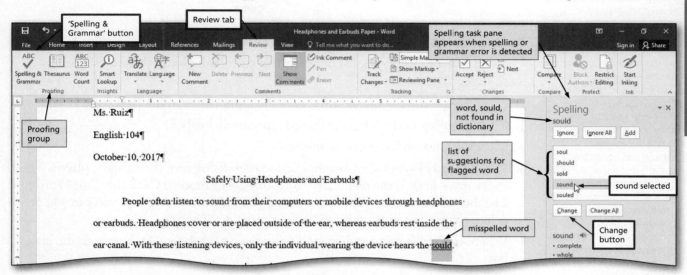

Figure 2–73

2

- With the word, sound, selected in the list of suggestions, click the Change button (Spelling task pane) to change the flagged word to the selected suggestion and then continue the spelling and grammar check until the next error is identified or the end of the document is reached (Figure 2–74).

3

- Because the flagged word is a proper noun and spelled correctly, click the Ignore All button (Spelling task pane) to ignore this and future occurrences of the flagged proper noun and then continue the spelling and grammar check until the next error is identified or the end of the document is reached.

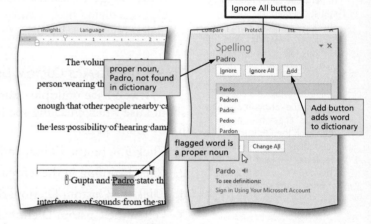

Figure 2–74

4

- When the spelling and grammar check is finished and Word displays a dialog box, click its OK button.

Q&A Can I check spelling of just a section of a document?
Yes, select the text before starting the spelling and grammar check.

Other Ways

1. Click 'Spelling and Grammar Check' icon on status bar
2. Press F7

The Main and Custom Dictionaries

As shown in the previous steps, Word may flag a proper noun as an error because the proper noun is not in its main dictionary. You may want to add some proper nouns that you use repeatedly, such as a company name or employee names, to Word's dictionary. To prevent Word from flagging proper nouns as errors, you can add the proper nouns to the custom dictionary. To add a correctly spelled word to the custom dictionary, click the Add button (Spelling task pane) or right-click the flagged word

BTW
Readability Statistics
You can instruct Word to display readability statistics when it has finished a spelling and grammar check on a document. Three readability statistics presented are the percent of passive sentences, the Flesch Reading Ease score, and the Flesch-Kincaid Grade Level score. The Flesch Reading Ease score uses a 100-point scale to rate the ease with which a reader can understand the text in a document. A higher score means the document is easier to understand. The Flesch-Kincaid Grade Level score rates the text in a document on a U.S. school grade level. For example, a score of 10.0 indicates a student in the tenth grade can understand the material. To show readability statistics when the spelling check is complete, open the Backstage view, click the Options tab in the Backstage view, click Proofing in the left pane (Word Options dialog box), place a check mark in the 'Show readability statistics' check box, and then click the OK button. Readability statistics will be displayed the next time you check spelling and grammar at once in the document.

(or, if using touch, press and hold and then tap 'Show Context Menu' button on the mini toolbar) and then click 'Add to Dictionary' on the shortcut menu. Once you have added a word to the custom dictionary, Word no longer will flag it as an error.

To View or Modify Entries in a Custom Dictionary

To view or modify the list of words in a custom dictionary, you would follow these steps.

1. Click File on the ribbon and then click the Options tab in the Backstage view.
2. Click Proofing in the left pane (Word Options dialog box).
3. Click the Custom Dictionaries button.
4. When Word displays the Custom Dictionaries dialog box, if necessary, place a check mark next to the dictionary name to view or modify. Click the 'Edit Word List' button (Custom Dictionaries dialog box). (In this dialog box, you can add or delete entries to and from the selected custom dictionary.)
5. When finished viewing and/or modifying the list, click the OK button in the dialog box.
6. Click the OK button (Custom Dictionaries dialog box).
7. If the 'Suggest from main dictionary only' check box is selected in the Word Options dialog box, remove the check mark. Click the OK button (Word Options dialog box).

To Set the Default Custom Dictionary

If you have multiple custom dictionaries, you can specify which one Word should use when checking spelling. To set the default custom dictionary, you would follow these steps.

1. Click File on the ribbon and then click the Options tab in the Backstage view.
2. Click Proofing in the left pane (Word Options dialog box).
3. Click the Custom Dictionaries button.
4. When the Custom Dictionaries dialog box is displayed, place a check mark next to the desired dictionary name. Click the Change Default button (Custom Dictionaries dialog box).
5. Click the OK button (Custom Dictionaries dialog box).
6. If the 'Suggest from main dictionary only' check box is selected in the Word Options dialog box, remove the check mark. Click the OK button (Word Options dialog box).

To Look Up Information

1 CHANGE DOCUMENT SETTINGS | 2 CREATE HEADER | 3 TYPE RESEARCH PAPER WITH CITATIONS
4 CREATE ALPHABETICAL WORKS CITED | 5 PROOFREAD & REVISE RESEARCH PAPER

If you are connected to the Internet, you can use the Insights task pane to search through various forms of reference information, including images, on the web and/or look up a definition of a word. The following steps use the Insights task pane to look up a definition of a word. *Why? Assume you want to see some images and know more about the word, headphones.*

1

- Position the insertion point in the word you want to look up (in this case, headphones).
- Click the Smart Lookup button (Review tab | Insights group) to open the Insights task pane (Figure 2–75).

Q&A Why does my Insights task pane look different? Depending on your settings, your Insights task pane may appear different from the figure shown here.

Figure 2–75

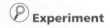 **Experiment**

- With the Explore tab selected in the Insights task pane, scroll through the information and images that appear in the Insights task pane. Click the Define tab in the Insights task pane to see a definition of the current word. Click the Explore tab to redisplay information from the web and images of the current word. Click one of the More links in the Insights task pane to view additional information. Click the Back button at the top of the Insights task pane to return to the previous display.

Q&A Can I copy information from the Insights task pane into my document?
Yes, you can use the Copy and Paste commands. When using Word to insert material from the Insights task pane or any other online reference, however, be careful not to plagiarize.

2

- Click the Close button in the Insights task pane.

Q&A Is the Research task pane from previous Word editions still available?
Yes. While holding down the ALT key, you can click the word you want to look up (such as headphones) to open the Research task pane and display a dictionary entry for the ALT+clicked word.

To Zoom Multiple Pages

1 CHANGE DOCUMENT SETTINGS | 2 CREATE HEADER | 3 TYPE RESEARCH PAPER WITH CITATIONS
4 CREATE ALPHABETICAL WORKS CITED | 5 PROOFREAD & REVISE RESEARCH PAPER

The next steps display multiple pages in the document window at once. *Why? You want to be able to see all pages in the research paper on the screen at the same time. You also hide formatting marks and the rulers so that the display is easier to view.*

1

- Click Home on the ribbon to display the Home tab.
- If the 'Show/Hide ¶' button (Home tab | Paragraph group) is selected, click it to hide formatting marks.
- Click View on the ribbon to display the View tab.

- If the rulers are displayed, click the View Ruler check box (View tab | Show group) to remove the check mark from the check box and remove the horizontal and vertical rulers from the screen.

- Click the Multiple Pages button (View tab | Zoom group) to display all three pages at once in the document window (Figure 2–76).

Q&A
Why do the pages appear differently on my screen?
Depending on settings, Word may display all the pages as shown in Figure 2–76 or may show the pages differently.

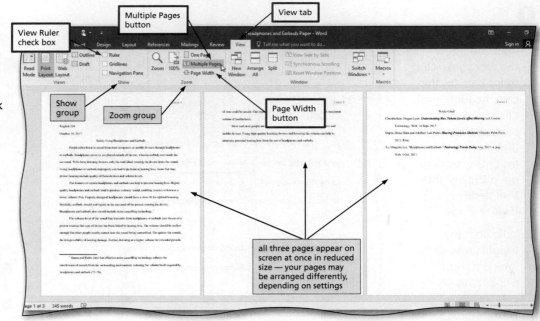

Figure 2–76

2
- When finished, click the Page Width button (View tab | Zoom group) to return to the page width zoom.

To Change Read Mode Color

1 CHANGE DOCUMENT SETTINGS | 2 CREATE HEADER | 3 TYPE RESEARCH PAPER WITH CITATIONS
4 CREATE ALPHABETICAL WORKS CITED | 5 PROOFREAD & REVISE RESEARCH PAPER

You would like to read the entire research paper using Read mode but would like to change the background color of the Read mode screen. **Why?** *You prefer a different background color for reading on the screen.* The following steps change the color of the screen in Read mode.

1
- Click the Read Mode button on the status bar to switch to Read mode.
- Click the View tab to display the View menu.
- Point to Page Color on the View menu to display the Page Color submenu (Figure 2–77).

Figure 2–77

- Click Inverse on the Page Color submenu to change the color of the Read mode screen to inverse (Figure 2–78).

- When finished, click the Print Layout button (shown in Figure 2–77) on the status bar to return to Print Layout view.

Figure 2–78

To Save and Print the Document and Exit Word

The following steps save and print the document and then exit Word. For a detailed example of the procedure summarized below, refer to the Office and Windows module at the beginning of this book.

1 Save the research paper again on the same storage location with the same file name.

2 If requested by your instructor, print the research paper.

3 Exit Word.

Summary

In this module, you have learned how to modify styles, adjust line and paragraph spacing, use headers to number pages, insert and edit citations and their sources, add footnotes, create a bibliographical list of sources, update a field, go to a page, copy and paste text, find and replace text, check spelling and grammar, and look up information.

What decisions will you need to make when creating your next research paper?

Use these guidelines as you complete the assignments in this module and create your own research papers outside of this class.

1. Select a topic.

    a) Spend time brainstorming ideas for a topic.

    b) Choose a topic you find interesting.

    c) For shorter papers, narrow the scope of the topic; for longer papers, broaden the scope.

    d) Identify a tentative thesis statement, which is a sentence describing the paper's subject matter.

2. Research the topic and take notes, being careful not to plagiarize.

3. Organize your notes into related concepts, identifying all main ideas and supporting details in an outline.

4. Write the first draft from the outline, referencing all sources of information and following the guidelines identified in the required documentation style.

5. Create the list of sources, using the formats specified in the required documentation style.

6. Proofread and revise the paper.

CONSIDER THIS: PLAN AHEAD

Apply Your Knowledge

Reinforce the skills and apply the concepts you learned in this module.

Revising Text and Paragraphs in a Document

Note: To complete this assignment, you will be required to use the Data Files. Please contact your instructor for information about accessing the Data Files.

Instructions: Run Word. Open the document, Apply 2-1 3-D Printers Paragraph Draft, which is located in the Data Files. The document you open contains a paragraph of text. You are to revise the document as follows: move a word, move another word and change the format of the moved word, change paragraph indentation, change line spacing, find all occurrences of a word, replace all occurrences of a word with another word, locate a synonym, and edit the header. The modified paragraph is shown in Figure 2–79.

Figure 2–79

Perform the following tasks:

1. Copy the text, printers, from the second sentence and paste it in the third sentence after the underlined word, liquid.

2. Select the underlined word, liquid, in the third sentence. Use drag-and-drop editing to move the selected word, liquid, so that it is before the word, polymer, in the last sentence. (If you are using a touch screen, use the cut and paste commands to move the word.) Click the Paste Options button that displays to the right of the moved word, liquid. Remove the underline format from the moved word by clicking 'Keep Text Only' on the Paste Options menu.

3. Display the ruler, if necessary. Use the ruler to indent the first line of the paragraph one-half inch. (If you are using a touch screen, use the Paragraph dialog box.)

4. Change the line spacing of the paragraph to double.

5. Use the Navigation Pane to find all occurrences of the word, printer. How many are there?

6. Use the Find and Replace dialog box to replace all occurrences of the word, 3D, with the word, 3-D. How many replacements were made?

7. Use the Navigation Pane to find the word, finished. Use Word's thesaurus to change the word, finished, to the word, complete. What other words are in the list of synonyms?

8. Switch to the header so that you can edit it. In the first line of the header, change the word, Draft, to the word, Modified, so that it reads: 3-D Printers Paragraph Modified.

9. In the second line of the header, insert a page number (a plain number with no formatting) one space after the word, Page.

10. Change the alignment of both lines of text in the header from left-aligned to right-aligned. Switch back to the document text.

11. If requested by your instructor, enter your first and last name on a separate line below the page number in the header.

12. Click File on the ribbon and then click Save As. Save the document using the file name, Apply 2-1 3-D Printers Paragraph Modified.

13. Submit the modified document, shown in Figure 2–79, in the format specified by your instructor.

14. Use the Insights task pane to look up the word prosthetics. Click the Explore tab in the Insights task pane. Which web articles appeared? What images appeared? Click the Define tab in the Insights task pane. Which dictionary was used?

15. ✸ Answer the questions posed in #5, #6, #7, and #14. How would you find and replace a special character, such as a paragraph mark?

Extend Your Knowledge

Extend the skills you learned in this module and experiment with new skills. You may need to use Help to complete the assignment.

Working with References and Proofing Tools

Note: To complete this assignment, you will be required to use the Data Files. Please contact your instructor for information about accessing the Data Files.

Instructions: Run Word. Open the document, Extend 2-1 Databases Paper Draft, from the Data Files. You will add another footnote to the paper, convert the footnotes to endnotes, modify the Endnote Text style, change the format of the note reference marks, use Word's readability statistics, translate the document to another language (Figure 2–80), and convert the document from MLA to APA documentation style.

Perform the following tasks:

1. Use Help to learn more about footers, footnotes and endnotes, readability statistics, bibliography styles, AutoCorrect, and Word's translation features.

2. Delete the footer from the document.

3. Insert a second footnote at an appropriate place in the research paper. Use the following footnote text: A data warehouse is a huge database that stores and manages the data required to analyze past and current transactions.

4. Change the location of the footnotes from bottom of page to below text. How did the placement of the footnotes change?

5. Convert the footnotes to endnotes. Where are the endnotes positioned?

6. Modify the Endnote Text style to 12-point Times New Roman font, double-spaced text with a hanging-line indent.

7. Change the format of the note reference marks to capital letters (A, B, etc.).

Continued >

Extend Your Knowledge *continued*

8. Add an AutoCorrect entry that replaces the word, buziness, with the word, business. Type the following sentence as the first sentence in the last paragraph of the paper, misspelling the word, business, as buziness to test the AutoCorrect entry: **Organizations often use a database to manage buziness or other functions.** Delete the AutoCorrect entry that replaces buziness with the word, business.

9. Display the Word Count dialog box. How many words, characters without spaces, characters with spaces, paragraphs, and lines are in the document? Be sure to include footnote and endnote text in the statistics.

10. Check spelling of the document, displaying readability statistics. What are the Flesch-Kincaid Grade Level and the Flesch Reading Ease score? Modify the paper to increase the reading ease score. How did you modify the paper? What are the new statistics?

11. If requested by your instructor, change the student name at the top of the paper to your name, including the last name in the header.

12. Save the revised document with the file name, Extend 2-1 Databases Paper Modified, and then submit it in the format specified by your instructor.

13. If you have an Internet connection, translate the research paper into a language of your choice using the Translate button (Review tab | Language group), as shown in Figure 2–80. Submit the translated document in the format specified by your instructor. Use the Mini Translator to hear how to pronounce three words in your paper.

14. Select the entire document and then change the documentation style from MLA to APA. Save the APA version of the document with a new file name. Compare the APA version to the MLA version. If you have a hard copy of each and your instructor requests it, circle the differences between the two documents.

15. ✸ Answer the questions posed in #4, #5, #9, and #10. Where did you insert the second footnote and why?

Figure 2–80

Expand Your World

Create a solution that uses cloud or web technologies by learning and investigating on your own from general guidance.

Using an Online Bibliography Tool to Create a List of Sources

Instructions: Assume you are using a computer or mobile device that does not have Word but has Internet access. To make use of time between classes, you use an online bibliography tool to create a list of sources that you can copy and paste into the Works Cited pages of a research paper that is due tomorrow.

Perform the following tasks:

1. Run a browser. Search for the text, online bibliography tool, using a search engine. Visit several of the online bibliography tools and determine which you would like to use to create a list of sources. Navigate to the desired online bibliography tool.

2. Use the online bibliography tool to enter list of sources shown below (Figure 2–81):

   Alverez, Juan and Tracy Marie Wilson. *Radon in the Home*. Chicago: Martin Publishing, 2017. Print.

   Buchalski, Leonard Adam. *Radon and Your Health*. Los Angeles: Coastal Works, 2017. Print.

   Johnson, Shantair Jada. "Radon Facts." *Environment Danger* Aug. 2017. Web. 31 Aug. 2017.

   Slobovnik, Vincent Alexander. *The Radon Guide*. Aug. 2017. Course Technology. Web. 18 Sept. 2017.

   Wakefield, Ginger Lynn and Bethany Olivia Ames. "Radon Removal Systems." *Living Well Today* Aug. 2017. Web. 3 Oct. 2017.

   Zhao, Shen Li. *Radon Testing Procedures*. Sept. 2017. Course Technology. Web. 8 Sept. 2017.

3. If requested by your instructor, replace the name in one of the sources above with your name.

4. Search for another source that discusses radon issues in the home. Add that source.

5. Copy and paste the list of sources into a Word document.

6. Save the document with the file name, Expand 2-1 Radon Issues Sources. Submit the document in the format specified by your instructor.

7. ✴ Which online bibliography tools did you evaluate? Which one did you select to use and why? Do you prefer using the online bibliography tool or Word to create sources? Why? What differences, if any, did you notice between the list of sources created with the online bibliography tool and the lists created when you use Word?

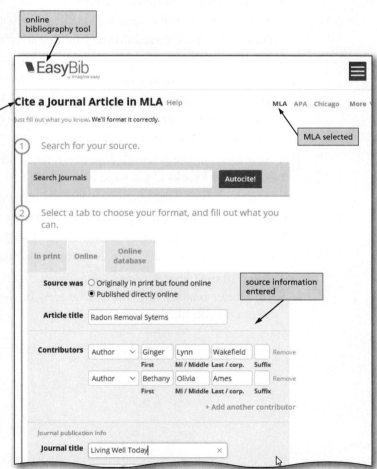

Figure 2–81

In the Labs

Design, create, modify, and/or use a document following the guidelines, concepts, and skills presented in this module. Labs 1 and 2, which increase in difficulty, require you to create solutions based on what you learned in the module; Lab 3 requires you to apply your creative thinking and problem-solving skills to design and implement a solution.

Lab 1: **Preparing a Short Research Paper**

Problem: You are a college student currently enrolled in an introductory English class. Your assignment is to prepare a short research paper (300–350 words) in any area of interest to you. The requirements are that the paper be presented according to the MLA documentation style and have three references. At least one of the three references must be from the web. You prepare the paper shown in Figure 2–82, which discusses wearable devices.

Perform the following tasks:

1. Run Word. If necessary, display formatting marks on the screen.
2. Modify the Normal style to the 12-point Times New Roman font.
3. Adjust line spacing to double.
4. Remove space below (after) paragraphs.
5. Update the Normal style to reflect the adjusted line and paragraph spacing.
6. Create a header to number pages.
7. Type the name and course information at the left margin. If requested by your instructor, use your name and course information instead of the information shown in Figure 2–82a. Center and type the title.
8. Set a first-line indent to one-half inch for paragraphs in the body of the research paper.
9. Type the research paper as shown in Figures 2–82a and 2–82b. Change the bibliography style to MLA. As you insert citations, enter their source information (shown in Figure 2–82c). Edit the citations so that they are displayed according to Figures 2–82a and 2–82b.
10. At the end of the research paper text, press the ENTER key and then insert a manual page break so that the Works Cited page begins on a new page. Enter and format the works cited title (Figure 2–82c). Use Word to insert the bibliographical list (bibliography).
11. Check the spelling and grammar of the paper at once.
12. Save the document using the file name, Lab 2–1 Wearable Devices Paper. Submit the document, shown in Figure 2–82, in the format specified by your instructor.
13. ✳ Read the paper in Print Layout view. Switch to Read mode and scroll through the pages. Do you prefer reading in Print Layout view or Read mode? Why? In Read mode, which of the page colors do you like best and why?

Hakimi 1

Farrah Iman Hakimi

Mr. Danshov

English 103

November 15, 2017

Wearable Devices

A wearable device or wearable is a small, mobile computing device designed to be worn by a consumer. These devices often communicate with a mobile device or computer using Bluetooth. Three popular types of wearable devices are activity trackers, smartwatches, and smart glasses.

An activity tracker is a wearable device that monitors fitness-related activities such as distance walked, heart rate, pulse, calories consumed, and sleep patterns. These devices typically sync, usually wirelessly, with a web or mobile app on your computer or mobile device to extend the capability of the wearable device (Pappas 32-41).

A smartwatch is a wearable device that, in addition to keeping time, can communicate wirelessly with a smartphone to make and answer phone calls, read and send messages, access the web, play music, work with apps such as fitness trackers and GPS, and more. Most include a touch screen (Carter and Schmidt).

Smart glasses, also called smart eyewear, are wearable head-mounted eyeglass-type devices that enable the user to view information or take photos and videos that are projected to a miniature screen in the user's field of vision. For example, the device wearer could run an app while wearing smart glasses that display flight status information when he or she walks into an airport. Users control the device through voice commands or by touching controls on its frame. Some smart glasses also include mobile apps, such as fitness trackers and GPS (Yazzie).

Figure 2–82a

Continued >

In the Labs *continued*

Hakimi 2

Activity trackers, smartwatches, and smart eyewear are available from a variety of

manufacturers. Before making a purchase, consumers should research costs and features of all

options to determine the device that best suits their requirements.

Figure 2–82b

Hakimi 3

Works Cited

Carter, Calvin J. and Karl Hans Schmidt. "Smartwatch Review." *Technology Trends* Aug. 2017:

n. pag. Web. 12 October 2017.

Pappas, Anastasia Maria. *Activity Trackers and Other Wearable Devices*. Dallas: Western Star

Publishing, 2017. Print.

Yazzie, Nina Tamaya. *Evaluating Today's Smart Glasses*. 25 Aug. 2017. Course Technology.

Web. 25 Sept. 2017.

Figure 2–82c

Lab 2: **Preparing a Research Report with a Footnote**

Problem: You are a college student enrolled in an introductory technology class. Your assignment is to prepare a short research paper (350–400 words) in any area of interest to you. The requirements are that the paper be presented according to the MLA documentation style, contain at least one note positioned as a footnote, and have three references. At least one of the three references must be from the web. You prepare a paper about two-step verification (Figure 2–83).

Perform the following tasks:
1. Run Word. Modify the Normal style to the 12-point Times New Roman font. Adjust line spacing to double and remove space below (after) paragraphs. Update the Normal style to include the adjusted line and paragraph spacing. Create a header to number pages. Type the name and course information at the left margin. If requested by your instructor, use your name and course information instead of the information shown in Figure 2–83a. Center and type the title. Set a first-line indent for paragraphs in the body of the research paper.

2. Type the research paper as shown in Figures 2–83a and 2–83b. Insert the footnote as shown in Figure 2–83a. Change the Footnote Text style to the format specified in the MLA documentation

Wagner 1

Bryan Wagner

Dr Rosenberg

Technology 104

October 27, 2017

Two-Step Verification

In an attempt to protect personal data and information from online thieves, many
organizations, such as financial institutions or universities, that store sensitive or confidential
items use a two-step verification process. With two-step verification, a computer or mobile
device uses two separate methods, one after the next, to verify the identity of a user.

ATMs (automated teller machines) usually require a two-step verification. Users first
insert their ATM card into the ATM (Step 1) and then enter a PIN, or personal identification
number, (Step 2) to access their bank account. If someone steals these cards, the thief must enter
the user's PIN to access the account (Tanaka).

Another use of two-step verification requires a mobile phone and a computer or mobile
device.[1] When users sign in to an account on a computer or mobile device, they enter a user
name and password (Step 1). Next, they are prompted to enter another authentication code (Step
2), which is sent as a text or voice message or via an app on a smartphone. This second code
generally is valid for a set time, sometimes only for a few minutes or hours. If users do not sign
in during this time limit, they must repeat the process and request another verification code

---

[1] According to Moore and O'Sullivan, users should register an alternate mobile phone
number, landline phone number, email address, or other form of contact beyond a mobile phone
number so that they still can access their accounts even if they lose their mobile phone (54).

Figure 2–83a

Wagner 2

(Marcy). Microsoft and Google commonly use two-step verification when users sign in to these
websites (Moore and O'Sullivan).

Some organizations use two separate methods to verify the identity of users. These two-
step verification procedures are designed to protect users' sensitive and confidential items from
online thieves.

Figure 2–83b

Continued >

STUDENT ASSIGNMENTS

In the Labs *continued*

style. Change the bibliography style to MLA. As you insert citations, use the following source information, entering it according to the MLA style:

a. Type of Source: Article in a Periodical
   Author: Hana Kei Tanaka
   Article Title: Safeguards against Unauthorized Access and Use
   Periodical Title: Technology Today
   Year: 2017
   Month: Sept.
   Pages: no pages used
   Medium: Web
   Year Accessed: 2017
   Month Accessed: Oct.
   Day Accessed: 3

b. Type of Source: Web site
   Author: Fredrick Lee Marcy
   Name of webpage: Two-Step Verification
   Year/Month/Date: none given
   Production Company: Course Technology
   Medium: Web
   Year Accessed: 2017
   Month Accessed: Sept.
   Day Accessed: 18

c. Type of Source: Book
   Author: Aaron Bradley Moore and Brianna Clare O'Sullivan
   Title: Authentication Techniques
   Year: 2017
   City: Detroit
   Publisher: Great Lakes Press
   Medium: Print

3. At the end of the research paper text, press the ENTER key once and insert a manual page break so that the Works Cited page begins on a new page. Enter and format the works cited title. Use Word to insert the bibliographical list.

4. Check the spelling and grammar of the paper.

5. Save the document using the file name, Lab 2–2 Two-Step Verification Paper. Submit the document, shown in Figure 2–83, in the format specified by your instructor.

6. ✳ This paper uses web sources. What factors should you consider when selecting web sources?

Lab 3: **Consider This: Your Turn**

Create a Research Paper about Wireless Communications
Note: To complete this assignment, you will be required to use the Data Files. Please contact your instructor for information about accessing the Data Files.

Problem: As a student in an introductory computer class, your instructor has assigned a brief research paper that discusses wireless communications.

Perform the following tasks:
Part 1: The source for the text in your research paper is in a file called Lab 2–3 Consider This Your Turn Wireless Communications Notes, which is located in the Data Files. If your instructor requests, use the Insights task pane to obtain information from another source and include that information as a note positioned as a footnote in the paper, along with entering its corresponding source information as appropriate. Add an AutoCorrect entry to correct a word you commonly mistype. If necessary, set the default dictionary. Add one of the source last names to the dictionary.

Using the concepts and techniques presented in this module, organize the notes in the text in the file on the Data Files, rewording as necessary, and then create and format this research paper according to the MLA documentation style. Be sure to check spelling and grammar of the finished paper. Submit your assignment and answers to the critical thinking questions in the format specified by your instructor.

Part 2: ✳ You made several decisions while creating the research paper in this assignment: how to organize the notes, where to place citations, how to format sources, and which source on the web to use for the footnote text (if requested by your instructor). What was the rationale behind each of these decisions? When you proofread the document, what further revisions did you make and why?

3 Creating a Business Letter with a Letterhead and Table

Objectives

You will have mastered the material in this module when you can:

- Change margins
- Insert and format a shape
- Change text wrapping
- Insert an online picture and format it
- Insert a symbol
- Add a border to a paragraph
- Clear formatting
- Convert a hyperlink to regular text

- Apply a style
- Set and use tab stops
- Insert the current date
- Create, modify, and insert a building block
- Insert a Word table, enter data in the table, and format the table
- Address and print an envelope

Introduction

In a business environment, people use documents to communicate with others. Business documents can include letters, memos, newsletters, proposals, and resumes. An effective business document clearly and concisely conveys its message and has a professional, organized appearance. You can use your own creative skills to design and compose business documents. Using Word, for example, you can develop the content and decide on the location of each item in a business document.

Project — Business Letter with a Letterhead and Table

At some time, you more than likely will prepare a business letter. Contents of business letters include requests, inquiries, confirmations, acknowledgements, recommendations, notifications, responses, thank you letters, invitations, offers, referrals, complaints, and more.

The project in this module follows generally accepted guidelines for writing letters and uses Word to create the business letter shown in Figure 3–1. This business

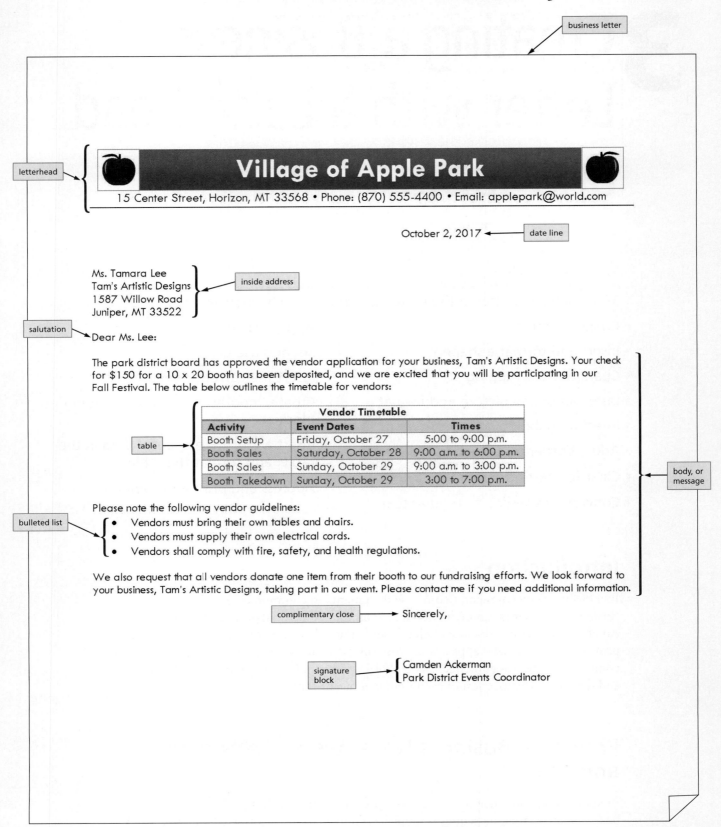

Figure 3–1

letter is a letter from the park district events coordinator at the Village of Apple Park that confirms a vendor application to participate in its community event. The letter includes a custom letterhead, as well as all essential business letter components: date line, inside address, salutation, body, complimentary close, and signature block. To easily present the vendor timetable during the event, the letter shows this information in a table. The vendor guidelines appear in a bulleted list.

In this module, you will learn how to create the letter shown in Figure 3–1. The following roadmap identifies general activities you will perform as you progress through this module:

1. CREATE AND FORMAT a LETTERHEAD WITH GRAPHICS.

2. SPECIFY the LETTER FORMATS according to business letter guidelines.

3. INSERT a TABLE in the letter.

4. FORMAT the TABLE in the letter.

5. INSERT a BULLETED LIST in the letter.

6. ADDRESS an ENVELOPE for the letter.

To Run Word and Change Word Settings

If you are using a computer to step through the project in this module and you want your screens to match the figures in this book, you should change your screen's resolution to 1366 × 768. For information about how to change a computer's resolution, refer to the Office and Windows module at the beginning of this book.

The following steps run Word, display formatting marks, and change the zoom to page width.

1 Run Word and create a blank document in the Word window. If necessary, maximize the Word window.

2 If the Print Layout button on the status bar is not selected (shown in Figure 3–2), click it so that your screen is in Print Layout view.

3 If the 'Show/Hide ¶' button (Home tab | Paragraph group) is not selected already, click it to display formatting marks on the screen.

4 To display the page the same width as the document window, if necessary, click the Page Width button (View tab | Zoom group).

For an introduction to Windows and instructions about how to perform basic Windows tasks, read the Office and Windows module at the beginning of this book, where you can learn how to resize windows, change screen resolution, create folders, move and rename files, use Windows Help, and much more.

For an introduction to Office and instructions about how to perform basic tasks in Office apps, read the Office and Windows module at the beginning of this book, where you can learn how to run an application, use the ribbon, save a file, open a file, print a file, exit an application, use Help, and much more.

To Change Margin Settings

1 CREATE & FORMAT LETTERHEAD WITH GRAPHICS | 2 SPECIFY LETTER FORMATS
3 INSERT TABLE | 4 FORMAT TABLE | 5 INSERT BULLETED LIST | 6 ADDRESS ENVELOPE

Word is preset to use standard 8.5-by-11-inch paper, with 1-inch top, bottom, left, and right margins. The business letter in this module uses .75-inch left and right margins and 1-inch top and bottom margins. *Why? You would like more text to fit from left to right on the page.*

When you change the default (preset) margin settings, the new margin settings affect every page in the document. If you wanted the margins to affect just a portion of the document, you would divide the document into sections (discussed in a later module), which enables you to specify different margin settings for each section. The following steps change margin settings.

1

- Display the Layout tab.

- Click the Adjust Margins button (Layout tab | Page Setup group) to display the Adjust Margins gallery (Figure 3–2).

2

- Click Moderate in the Adjust Margins gallery to change the margins to the specified settings.

Q&A

What if the margin settings I want are not in the Adjust Margins gallery?

You can click Custom Margins in the Adjust Margins gallery and then enter your desired margin values in the top, bottom, left, and right boxes in the Page Setup dialog box.

Figure 3–2

Other Ways

1. Position pointer on margin boundary on ruler; when pointer changes to two-headed arrow, drag margin boundary on ruler

Creating a Letterhead

The cost of preprinted letterhead can be high. An alternative is to create your own letterhead and save it in a file. When you want to create a letter at a later time, you can start by using the letterhead file. The following sections create a letterhead and then save it in a file for future use.

What is a letterhead?

A **letterhead** is the section of a letter that identifies an organization or individual. Often, the letterhead appears at the top of a letter. Although you can design and print a letterhead yourself, many businesses pay an outside firm to design and print their letterhead, usually on higher-quality paper. They then use the professionally preprinted paper for external business communications.

If you do not have preprinted letterhead paper, you can design a creative letterhead. It is important the letterhead appropriately represent the essence of the organization or individual (i.e., formal, technical, creative, etc.). That is, it should use text, graphics, formats, and colors that reflect the organization or individual. The letterhead should leave ample room for the contents of the letter.

When designing a letterhead, consider its contents, placement, and appearance.

- **Contents of letterhead.** A letterhead should contain these elements:
  - Complete legal name of the individual, group, or company
  - Complete mailing address: street address including building, room, suite number, or post office box, along with city, state, and postal code
  - Phone number(s) and fax number, if applicable
  - Email address

– Website address, if applicable

– Many letterheads also include a logo or other image; if an image is used, it should express the organization or individual's personality or goals

• **Placement of elements in the letterhead.** Many letterheads center their elements across the top of the page. Others align some or all of the elements with the left or right margins. Sometimes, the elements are split between the top and bottom of the page. For example, a name and logo may be at the top of the page with the address at the bottom of the page.

• **Appearance of letterhead elements.** Use fonts that are easy to read. Give the organization or individual name impact by making its font size larger than the rest of the text in the letterhead. For additional emphasis, consider formatting the name in bold, italic, or a different color. Choose colors that complement each other and convey the goals of the organization or individual.

When finished designing the letterhead, determine if a divider line would help to visually separate the letterhead from the remainder of the letter.

The letterhead for the letter in this module consists of the organization's name, appropriate graphics, postal address, phone number, and email address. The name and graphics are enclosed in a rectangular shape (shown in Figure 3–1), and the contact information is below the shape. You will follow these general steps to create the letterhead in this module:

1. Insert and format a shape.
2. Enter and format the organization name in the shape.
3. Insert, format, and position the images in the shape.
4. Enter the contact information below the shape.
5. Add a border below the contact information.

BTW

The Ribbon and Screen Resolution
Word may change how the groups and buttons within the groups appear on the ribbon, depending on the computer or mobile device's screen resolution. Thus, your ribbon may look different from the ones in this book if you are using a screen resolution other than 1366 x 768.

1 CREATE & FORMAT LETTERHEAD WITH GRAPHICS | 2 SPECIFY LETTER FORMATS
3 INSERT TABLE | 4 FORMAT TABLE | 5 INSERT BULLETED LIST | 6 ADDRESS ENVELOPE

To Insert a Shape

Word has a variety of predefined shapes, which are a type of drawing object, that you can insert in documents. A **drawing object** is a graphic that you create using Word. Examples of shape drawing objects include rectangles, circles, triangles, arrows, flowcharting symbols, stars, banners, and callouts. The following steps insert a rectangle shape in the letterhead. *Why? The organization's name is placed in a rectangle for emphasis and visual appeal.*

• Display the Insert tab.

• Click the 'Draw a Shape' button (Insert tab | Illustrations group) to display the Draw a Shape gallery (Figure 3–3).

Figure 3–3

- Click the Rectangle shape in the Rectangles area in the Draw a Shape gallery, which removes the gallery.

Q&A What if I am using a touch screen?
The shape is inserted in the document window. Skip Steps 3 and 4, and proceed to Step 5.

- Position the pointer (a crosshair) in the approximate location for the upper-left corner of the desired shape (Figure 3–4).

Q&A What is the purpose of the crosshair pointer?
You drag the crosshair pointer from the upper-left corner to the lower-right corner to form the desired location and size of the shape.

Figure 3–4

- Drag the mouse to the right and downward to form the boundaries of the shape, as shown in Figure 3–5. Do not release the mouse button.

Figure 3–5

- Release the mouse button so that Word draws the shape according to your drawing in the document window.

5

- Verify your shape is the same approximate height and width as the one in this project by reviewing, and if necessary changing, the values in the Shape Height box and Shape Width boxes (Drawing Tools Format tab | Size group) to 0.53" and 5.7" by typing each value in the respective box and then pressing the ENTER key (Figure 3–6).

Q&A What is the purpose of the rotate handle?
When you drag an object's **rotate handle**, which is the white circle on the top of the object, Word rotates the object in the direction you drag the mouse.

What if I wanted to delete a shape and start over?
With the shape selected, you would press the DELETE key.

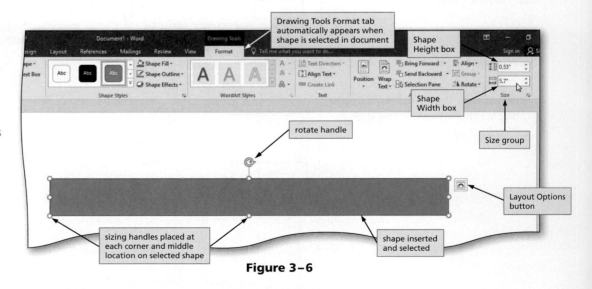

Figure 3–6

Floating versus Inline Objects

When you insert an object in a document, Word inserts it as either an inline object or a floating object. An **inline object** is an object that is part of a paragraph. With inline objects, you change the location of the object by setting paragraph options, such as centered, right-aligned, and so on. For example, when you inserted the picture of the surfer in Module 1, Word inserted it as an inline object. A **floating object**, by contrast, is an object that can be positioned at a specific location in a document or in a layer over or behind text in a document. The shape you just inserted is a floating object. You have more flexibility with floating objects because you can position a floating object anywhere on the page.

In addition to changing an object from inline to floating and vice versa, Word provides several floating options, which (along with inline) are called text wrapping options because they affect how text wraps with or around the object. Table 3–1 presents the various text wrapping options.

Table 3–1 Text Wrapping Options

Text Wrapping Option	Object Type	How It Works
In Line with Text	Inline	Object positioned according to paragraph formatting; for example, if paragraph is centered, object will be centered with any text in the paragraph.
Square	Floating	Text wraps around object, with text forming a box around the object.
Tight	Floating	Text wraps around object, with text forming to shape of the object.
Through	Floating	Object appears at beginning, middle, or end of text. Moving object changes location of text.
Top and Bottom	Floating	Object appears above or below text. Moving object changes location of text.
Behind Text	Floating	Object appears behind text.
In Front of Text	Floating	Object appears in front of text and may cover the text.

To Change an Object's Position

1 CREATE & FORMAT LETTERHEAD WITH GRAPHICS | 2 SPECIFY LETTER FORMATS
3 INSERT TABLE | 4 FORMAT TABLE | 5 INSERT BULLETED LIST | 6 ADDRESS ENVELOPE

You can specify an object's vertical position on a page (top, middle, bottom) and its horizontal position (left, center, right). The following steps change the position of an object, specifically, the rectangle shape. *Why? You want the shape to be centered at the top of the page in the letterhead.*

1

• With the shape still selected, click the Position Object button (Drawing Tools Format tab | Arrange group) to display the Position Object gallery (Figure 3–7).

Q&A What if the shape is not still selected? Click the shape to select it.

Figure 3–7

ⓟ Experiment

- Point to various options in the Position Object gallery and watch the shape move to the selected position option.

❷

- Click 'Position in Top Center with Square Text Wrapping' in the Position Object gallery so that the object does not cover the document and is centered at the top of the document.

Other Ways

1. Click Layout Options button attached to graphic (shown in Figure 3–8), click See more link in Layout Options gallery, click Horizontal Alignment arrow and select alignment (Layout dialog box), click Vertical Alignment arrow and select alignment, click OK button

2. Click Advanced Layout: Size Dialog Box Launcher (Drawing Tools Format tab | Size group), click Position tab (Layout dialog box), click Horizontal Alignment arrow and select alignment, click Vertical Alignment arrow and select alignment, click OK button

To Change an Object's Text Wrapping

1 CREATE & FORMAT LETTERHEAD WITH GRAPHICS | 2 SPECIFY LETTER FORMATS
3 INSERT TABLE | 4 FORMAT TABLE | 5 INSERT BULLETED LIST | 6 ADDRESS ENVELOPE

When you insert a shape in a Word document, the default text wrapping is In Front of Text, which means the object will cover any text behind it. The previous steps, which changed the shape's position, changed the text wrapping to Square. In the letterhead, you want the shape's text wrapping to be Top and Bottom. **Why?** *You want the letterhead above the contents of the letter when you type it, instead of covering the contents of the letter.* The following steps change an object's text wrapping.

❶

- With the shape still selected, click the Layout Options button attached to the graphic to display the Layout Options gallery (Figure 3–8).

❷

- Click 'Top and Bottom' in the Layout Options gallery so that the object does not cover the document text (shown in Figure 3–9).

Q&A

How can I tell that the text wrapping has changed?
Because the letter has no text, you need to look at the paragraph mark, which now is positioned below the shape instead of to its left.

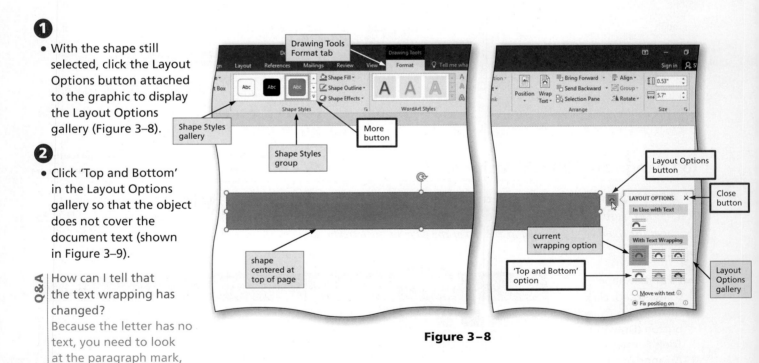

Figure 3–8

- Click the Close button in the Layout Options gallery to close the gallery.

Other Ways

1. Right-click object (or, if using touch, tap 'Show Context Menu' button on mini toolbar), point to Wrap Text on shortcut menu, click desired wrapping option

2. Click Wrap Text button (Drawing Tools Format tab | Arrange group), select desired wrapping option

To Apply a Shape Style

Why apply a shape style? Word provides a Shape Styles gallery so that you easily can change the appearance of the shape. The following steps apply a shape style to the rectangle shape.

- With the shape still selected, click the More button (shown in Figure 3–8) in the Shape Styles gallery (Drawing Tools Format tab | Shape Styles group) to expand the gallery.

Q&A What if the shape no longer is selected?
Click the shape to select it.

- Point to 'Moderate Effect - Gray-50%, Accent 3' (fourth effect in fifth row) in the Shape Styles gallery to display a live preview of that style applied to the shape in the document (Figure 3–9).

Experiment

- Point to various styles in the Shape Styles gallery and watch the style of the shape change in the document.

Figure 3–9

- Click 'Moderate Effect - Gray-50%, Accent 3' in the Shape Styles gallery to apply the selected style to the shape.

Other Ways
1. Right-click shape, click 'Shape Quick Styles' button on mini toolbar, select desired style	2. Click Format Shape Dialog Box Launcher (Drawing Tools Format tab | Shape Styles group), click 'Fill & Line' button (Format Shape task pane), expand Fill section, select desired colors, click Close button

To Add Text to a Shape

The following steps add text (the organization name) to a shape. *Why? In the letterhead for this module, the name is in the shape. Similarly, an individual could put his or her name in a shape on a letterhead in order to create personalized letterhead.*

- Right-click the shape to display a mini toolbar and/or shortcut menu (Figure 3–10).

Figure 3–10

2

- Click Add Text on the shortcut menu to place an insertion point in the shape.

What if I am using a touch screen?
Tap the Edit Text button on the mini toolbar.

Why do the buttons on my mini toolbar differ?
If you are using a mouse in Mouse mode, the buttons on your mini toolbar will differ from those that appear when you use a touch screen in Touch mode.

- If the insertion point and paragraph mark are not centered in the shape, click the Center button (Home tab | Paragraph group) to center them.

- Type **Village of Apple Park** as the name in the shape (Figure 3–11).

  If requested by your instructor, enter your name instead of the name shown in Figure 3–11.

Figure 3–11

To Use the 'Increase Font Size' Button

1 CREATE & FORMAT LETTERHEAD WITH GRAPHICS | 2 SPECIFY LETTER FORMATS
3 INSERT TABLE | 4 FORMAT TABLE | 5 INSERT BULLETED LIST | 6 ADDRESS ENVELOPE

In previous modules, you used the Font Size arrow (Home tab | Font group) to change the font size of text. Word also provides an 'Increase Font Size' button (Home tab | Font group), which increases the font size of selected text each time you click the button. The following steps use the 'Increase Font Size' button to increase the font size of the name in the shape to 26 point. **Why?** *You want the name to be as large as possible in the shape.*

1

- Drag through the text to be formatted (in this case, the name in the shape).

2

- If necessary, display the Home tab.

- Repeatedly click the 'Increase Font Size' button (Home tab | Font group) until the Font Size box displays 26 to increase the font size of the selected text (Figure 3–12).

What if I click the 'Increase Font Size' button (Home tab | Font group) too many times, causing the font size to be too big?
Click the 'Decrease Font Size' button (Home tab | Font group) until the desired font size is displayed.

Figure 3–12

Experiment

- Repeatedly click the 'Increase Font Size' and 'Decrease Font Size' buttons (Home tab | Font group) and watch the font size of the selected text change in the document window. When you are finished experimenting with these two buttons, set the font size to 26.

Other Ways

1. Press CTRL+SHIFT+>

To Bold Selected Text

To make the name stand out even more, bold it. The following steps bold the selected text.

1 With the text selected, click the Bold button (Home tab | Font group) to bold the selected text (shown in Figure 3–13).

2 Click anywhere in the text in the shape to remove the selection and place the insertion point in the shape.

To Change the Document Theme

1 CREATE & FORMAT LETTERHEAD WITH GRAPHICS | 2 SPECIFY LETTER FORMATS
3 INSERT TABLE | 4 FORMAT TABLE | 5 INSERT BULLETED LIST | 6 ADDRESS ENVELOPE

A **document theme** is a coordinated combination of colors, fonts, and effects. The current default document theme is Office, which uses Calibri and Calibri Light as its font and shades of grays and blues primarily. The following steps change the document theme to Circuit for the letter in this module. *Why? You want to use shades of reds and oranges in the letterhead because those colors are associated with energy, success, creativity, and enthusiasm.*

1

• Display the Design tab.

• Click the Themes button (Design tab | Document Formatting group) to display the Themes gallery.

• Point to Circuit in the Themes gallery to display a live preview of that theme applied to the document (Figure 3–13).

Experiment

• Point to various themes in the Themes gallery and watch the color scheme and font set change in the document window.

Figure 3–13

2

• Click Circuit in the Themes gallery to change the document theme.

To Insert an Online Picture

1 CREATE & FORMAT LETTERHEAD WITH GRAPHICS | 2 SPECIFY LETTER FORMATS
3 INSERT TABLE | 4 FORMAT TABLE | 5 INSERT BULLETED LIST | 6 ADDRESS ENVELOPE

Files containing graphics are available from a variety of sources. In the Module 1 flyer, you inserted a digital picture taken with a camera. In this project, you insert a picture from the web. Microsoft Office applications can access a collection of royalty-free photos and animations.

The letterhead in this project contains a picture of an apple (shown in Figure 3–1). **Why?** *Because the name of the organization is Village of Apple Park, an apple is an appropriate image for this letterhead.* The following steps insert an online picture in the document.

1

- If necessary, click the paragraph mark below the shape to position the insertion point where you want to insert the picture.

- Display the Insert tab.

- Click the Online Pictures button (Insert tab | Illustrations group) to display the Insert Pictures dialog box.

- Type **apple** in the Search box (Insert Pictures dialog box) to specify the search text, which indicates the type of image you want to locate (Figure 3–14).

Figure 3–14

2

- Click the Search button to display a list of online pictures that matches the entered search text.

- Scroll through the list of pictures to locate the one shown in Figure 3–15, or a similar image.

Q&A

Why is my list of pictures different from Figure 3–15? The online images are continually updated.

What is Creative Commons? **Creative Commons** is a nonprofit organization that provides several standard licensing options that owners of creative works may specify when granting permission for others to use their digital content, such as the online pictures that appear in the Bing Image Search. Be sure to follow an image's guidelines when using it in a document.

Figure 3–15

What if I cannot locate the image in Figure 3–15, and I would like to use that exact image?
The image is located in the Data Files. You can click the Cancel button and then click the From File button (Insert tab | Illustrations group), navigate to the file called apple-02.wmf in the Data Files, and then click the Insert button (Insert Picture dialog box).

❸

- If necessary, click the 'Show all web results' button to display more images that match the search text.
- Click the desired picture to select it.
- Click the Insert button to insert the selected image in the document at the location of the insertion point. If necessary, scroll to display the image (picture) in the document window (Figure 3–16).

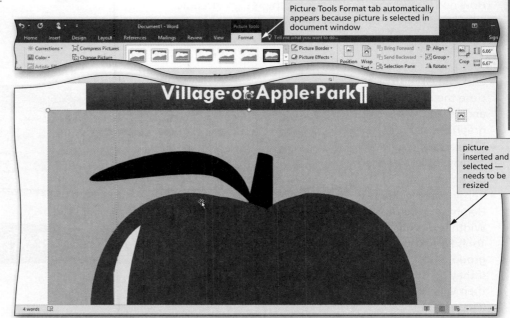

Figure 3–16

To Resize a Graphic to a Percent of the Original Size

1 CREATE & FORMAT LETTERHEAD WITH GRAPHICS | 2 SPECIFY LETTER FORMATS
3 INSERT TABLE | 4 FORMAT TABLE | 5 INSERT BULLETED LIST | 6 ADDRESS ENVELOPE

Instead of dragging a sizing handle to change the graphic's size, as you learned in Module 1, you can specify that the graphic be resized to a percent of its original size. In this module, the graphic is resized to 8 percent of its original size. **Why?** *The original size of the picture is too large for the letterhead.* The following steps resize a graphic to a percent of the original.

❶

- With the graphic still selected, click the Advanced Layout: Size Dialog Box Launcher (Picture Tools Format tab | Size group) to display the Size sheet in the Layout dialog box.

 What if the graphic is not selected or the Picture Tools Format tab is not on the ribbon?
Click the graphic to select it or double-click the graphic to make the Picture Tools Format tab the active tab.

❷

- In the Scale area (Layout dialog box), double-click the current value in the Height box to select it.
- Type 8 in the Height box and then press the TAB key to display the same percent value in the Width box (Figure 3–17).

Figure 3–17

Q&A

Why did Word automatically fill in the value in the Width box?
When the 'Lock aspect ratio' check box (Layout dialog box) is selected, Word automatically maintains the size proportions of the graphic.

How do I know to use 8 percent for the resized graphic?
The larger graphic consumed too much room on the page. Try various percentages to determine the size that works best in the letterhead design.

3

- Click the OK button to close the dialog box and resize the selected graphic.
- If necessary, scroll to display the top of the document
- Verify that the Shape Height and Shape Width boxes (Picture Tools Format tab | Size group) display 0.53". If they do not, change their values to 0.53" (Figure 3–18).

Figure 3–18

Other Ways

1. Click Layout Options button attached to graphic, click See more link in the Layout Options gallery, click Size tab (Layout dialog box), enter height and width values, click OK button

2. Right-click graphic, click 'Size and Position' on shortcut menu, enter height and width values (Layout dialog box), click OK button

To Change the Color of a Graphic

1 CREATE & FORMAT LETTERHEAD WITH GRAPHICS | 2 SPECIFY LETTER FORMATS
3 INSERT TABLE | 4 FORMAT TABLE | 5 INSERT BULLETED LIST | 6 ADDRESS ENVELOPE

In Word, you can change the color of a graphic. The apple image (graphic) currently is a bright red color. The following steps change the color of the graphic. *Why? Because the image in this project will be placed beside the rectangle shape, you prefer to use lighter colors.*

1

- With the graphic still selected (shown in Figure 3–18), click the Color button (Picture Tools Format tab | Adjust group) to display the Color gallery.
- Point to Washout in the Color gallery (fourth color in first row) to display a live preview of that color applied to the selected graphic in the document (Figure 3–19).

Figure 3–19

Experiment

- Point to various colors in the Color gallery and watch the color of the graphic change in the document.

②

- Click Washout in the Color gallery to change the color of the selected graphic.

Q&A How would I change a graphic back to its original colors?
With the graphic selected, you would click No Recolor, which is the upper-left color in the Color gallery.

Other Ways

1. Click Format Shape Dialog Box Launcher (Picture Tools Format tab | Picture Styles group), click Picture button (Format Picture task pane), expand Picture Color section, select desired options

2. Right-click graphic (or, if using touch, tap 'Show Context Menu' button on mini toolbar), click Format Picture on shortcut menu (or, if using touch, tap Format Object), click Picture button (Format Picture task pane), expand Picture Color section, select desired options

---

To Set a Transparent Color in a Graphic

1 CREATE & FORMAT LETTERHEAD WITH GRAPHICS | 2 SPECIFY LETTER FORMATS
3 INSERT TABLE | 4 FORMAT TABLE | 5 INSERT BULLETED LIST | 6 ADDRESS ENVELOPE

In Word, you can make one color in a graphic transparent; that is, you remove the color. You would make a color transparent if you wanted to remove part of a graphic or see text or colors behind a graphic. The following steps set the light green background around the apple in a transparent color. *Why? You prefer the light green color to be transparent.*

❶

- With the graphic still selected, click the Color button (Picture Tools Format tab | Adjust group) to display the Color gallery (Figure 3–20).

Figure 3–20

❷

- Click 'Set Transparent Color' in the Color gallery to display a pen pointer in the document window.

Q&A What if I am using a touch screen?
You may need to use a stylus or mouse to perform these steps.

- Position the pen pointer in the graphic where you want to make the color transparent (Figure 3–21).

Q&A Can I make multiple colors in a graphic transparent?
No, you can make only one color transparent.

Figure 3–21

- Click the location in the graphic where you want the color to be transparent (Figure 3–22).

Q&A What if I make the wrong color transparent? Click the Undo button on the Quick Access Toolbar, or press CTRL+Z, and then repeat these steps.

graphic selected

light shade of green around apple made transparent, showing white here because page color behind graphic is white

Figure 3–22

To Adjust the Brightness and Contrast of a Graphic

1 CREATE & FORMAT LETTERHEAD WITH GRAPHICS | 2 SPECIFY LETTER FORMATS
3 INSERT TABLE | 4 FORMAT TABLE | 5 INSERT BULLETED LIST | 6 ADDRESS ENVELOPE

In Word, you can adjust the brightness, or lightness, of a graphic and also the **contrast**, or the difference between the lightest and darkest areas of the graphic. The following steps decrease the brightness and contrast of the apple graphic, each by 20%. **Why?** *You want to darken the graphic slightly to increase its emphasis on the page and, at the same time, decrease the difference between the light and dark areas of the graphic.*

- If necessary, display the Picture Tools Format tab.

- With the graphic still selected (shown in Figure 3–22), click the Corrections button (Picture Tools Format tab | Adjust group) to display the Corrections gallery.

- Point to 'Brightness: -20% Contrast: -20%' (second image in second row) in the Corrections gallery to display a live preview of that correction applied to the graphic in the document (Figure 3–23).

 Experiment

- Point to various corrections in the Corrections gallery and watch the brightness and contrast of the graphic change in the document.

Corrections button

Picture Tools Format tab

Adjust group

Corrections gallery

pointer on 'Brightness: -20% Contrast: -20%'

graphic changes to Brightness: -20% Contrast: -20%, showing live preview of correction to which you are pointing in gallery

Figure 3–23

- Click 'Brightness: -20% Contrast: -20%' in the Corrections gallery to change the brightness and contrast of the selected graphic.

Other Ways

1. Click Format Shape Dialog Box Launcher (Picture Tools Format tab | Picture Styles group), click Picture button (Format Picture task pane), expand Picture Corrections section, select desired options

2. Right-click graphic (or, if using touch, tap 'Show Context Menu' button on mini toolbar), click Format Picture on shortcut menu (or, if using touch, tap Format Object on shortcut menu), click Picture button (Format Picture task pane), expand Picture Corrections section, select desired options

To Change the Border Color on a Graphic

The apple graphic currently has no border (outline). The following steps change the border color on the graphic. *Why? You would like the graphic to have a lime border so that it is in the same color family as the leaf on the apple.*

1

- Click the Picture Border arrow (Picture Tools Format tab | Picture Styles group) to display the Picture Border gallery.
- Point to 'Lime, Accent 1, Darker 25%' (fifth theme color in fifth row) in the Picture Border gallery to display a live preview of that border color around the picture (Figure 3–24).

Figure 3–24

 What if I click the Picture Border button by mistake?

Click the Picture Border arrow and proceed with Step 2.

🔍 Experiment

- Point to various colors in the Picture Border gallery and watch the border color on the graphic change in the document window.

2

- Click 'Lime, Accent 1, Darker 25%' in the Picture Border gallery to change the picture border color.

How would I remove a border from a graphic?

With the graphic selected, you would click No Outline in the Picture Border gallery.

Can I remove all formatting applied to a graphic and start over?

Yes. With the graphic selected, you would click the Reset Picture button (Picture Tools Format tab | Adjust group).

To Change an Object's Text Wrapping

The apple graphic is to be positioned to the left of the shape. By default, when you insert a picture, it is formatted as an inline graphic. Inline graphics cannot be moved to a precise location on a page. Recall that inline graphics are part of a paragraph and, thus, can be positioned according to paragraph formatting, such as centered or left-aligned. To move the graphic to the left of the shape, you format it as a floating object with In Front of Text wrapping. The following steps change a graphic's text wrapping.

1 If necessary, click the graphic to select it.

2 Click the Layout Options button attached to the graphic to display the Layout Options gallery.

3 Click 'In Front of Text' in the Layout Options gallery so that you can position the object on top of any item in the document, in this case, on top of the rectangular shape.

4 Click the Close button to close the gallery.

To Move a Graphic

1 CREATE & FORMAT LETTERHEAD WITH GRAPHICS | 2 SPECIFY LETTER FORMATS
3 INSERT TABLE | 4 FORMAT TABLE | 5 INSERT BULLETED LIST | 6 ADDRESS ENVELOPE

The following steps move a graphic. *Why? In this letterhead, the first apple graphic is positioned to the left of the shape.*

- Position the pointer in the graphic so that the pointer has a four-headed arrow attached to it (Figure 3–25).

when pointer has four-headed arrow attached to it, you can drag floating graphic to any location in document

Figure 3–25

- Drag the graphic to the left of the shape, as shown in Figure 3–26.

Q&A What if I moved the graphic to the wrong location?
Repeat these steps. You can drag a floating graphic to any location in a document.

Why do green lines appear on my screen as I drag a graphic?
You have alignment guides set, which help you line up graphics. To set alignment guides, click the Align Objects button (Picture Tools Format tab | Arrange group) and then click 'Use Alignment Guides'.

graphic moved to left of the shape

Figure 3–26

To Copy a Graphic

In this project, the same apple graphic is to be placed to the right of the shape. Instead of performing the same steps to insert and format a second identical apple graphic, you can copy the graphic to the Office Clipboard, paste the graphic from the Office Clipboard, and then move the graphic to the desired location.

You use the same steps to copy a graphic as you used in Module 2 to copy text. The following steps copy a graphic.

1 If necessary, click the graphic to select it.

2 Display the Home tab.

3 Click the Copy button, shown in Figure 3–27 (Home tab | Clipboard group), to copy the selected item to the Office Clipboard.

To Use Paste Options

1 CREATE & FORMAT LETTERHEAD WITH GRAPHICS | 2 SPECIFY LETTER FORMATS
3 INSERT TABLE | 4 FORMAT TABLE | 5 INSERT BULLETED LIST | 6 ADDRESS ENVELOPE

The following steps paste a graphic using the Paste Options gallery. *Why? Recall from Module 2 that you can specify the format of a pasted item using Paste Options.*

1

• Click the Paste arrow (Home tab | Clipboard group) to display the Paste gallery.

Q&A What if I accidentally click the Paste button?
Click the Paste Options button below the graphic pasted in the document to display a Paste Options gallery.

• Point to the 'Keep Source Formatting' button in the Paste gallery to display a live preview of that paste option (Figure 3–27).

Experiment

• Point to the two buttons in the Paste gallery and watch the appearance of the pasted graphic change.

Figure 3–27

Q&A What do the buttons in the Paste gallery mean?
The 'Keep Source Formatting' button indicates the pasted graphic should have the same formats as it did in its original location. The Picture button removes some formatting from the graphic.

Why are these paste buttons different from the ones in Module 2?
The buttons that appear in the Paste gallery differ depending on the item you are pasting. Use live preview to see how the pasted object will look in the document.

2

• Click the 'Keep Source Formatting' button in the Paste gallery to paste the object using the same formatting as the original.

To Move a Graphic

The next step is to move the second apple graphic so that it is positioned to the right of the rectangle shape. The following steps move a graphic.

1 If you are using a mouse, position the pointer in the graphic so that the pointer has a four-headed arrow attached to it.

2 Drag the graphic to the location shown in Figure 3–28.

To Flip a Graphic

The following steps flip a graphic horizontally. ***Why?*** *In this letterhead, you want the leaves on the apple graphics to point toward the edge of the paper.*

1

- If necessary, display the Picture Tools Format tab.

- With the graphic still selected, click the Rotate Objects button (Picture Tools Format tab | Arrange group) to display the Rotate Objects gallery (Figure 3–28).

🔍 **Experiment**

- Point to the various rotate options in the Rotate Options gallery and watch the picture rotate in the document window.

Figure 3–28

2

- Click Flip Horizontal in the Rotate Options gallery, so that Word flips the graphic to display its mirror image (shown in Figure 3–29).

Q&A | Can I flip a graphic vertically?
Yes, you would click Flip Vertical in the Rotate Options gallery. You also can rotate a graphic clockwise or counterclockwise by clicking 'Rotate Right 90°' and 'Rotate Left 90°', respectively, in the Rotate Options gallery.

- Save the letterhead on your hard drive, OneDrive, or other storage location using the file name, Apple Park Letterhead.

Q&A | Why should I save the letterhead at this time?
You have performed many tasks while creating this letterhead and do not want to risk losing work completed thus far.

To Format and Enter Text

The contact information for the letterhead in this project is located on the line below the shape containing the name. The following steps format and then enter the mailing address in the letterhead.

1 Position the insertion point on the line below the shape containing the name.

2 If necessary, display the Home tab. Click the Center button (Home tab | Paragraph group) to center the paragraph.

3 Click the 'Increase Font Size' button (Home tab | Font group) to increase the font size to 12 point.

4 Type **15 Center Street, Horizon, MT 33568** and then press the SPACEBAR (shown in Figure 3–29).

To Insert a Symbol from the Symbol Dialog Box

Word provides a method of inserting dots and other symbols, such as letters in the Greek alphabet and mathematical characters, that are not on the keyboard. The following steps insert a dot symbol, sometimes called a bullet symbol, in the letterhead. *Why? You want a visual separator between the mailing address and phone number in the letterhead and also between the phone number and email address.*

- If necessary, position the insertion point as shown in Figure 3–29.
- Display the Insert tab.
- Click the 'Insert a Symbol' button (Insert tab | Symbols group) to display the Insert a Symbol gallery (Figure 3–29).

Q&A | What if the symbol I want to insert already appears in the Insert a Symbol gallery?
You can click any symbol shown in the Insert a Symbol gallery to insert it in the document.

Figure 3–29

- Click More Symbols in the Insert a Symbol gallery to display the Symbol dialog box.
- If the font in the Font box is not (normal text), click the Font arrow (Symbol dialog box) and then scroll to and click (normal text) to select this font.
- If the subset in the Subset box is not General Punctuation, click the Subset arrow and then scroll and click General Punctuation to select this subset.
- In the list of symbols, if necessary, scroll to the dot symbol shown in Figure 3–30 and then click the symbol to select it.
- Click the Insert button (Symbol dialog box) to place the selected symbol in the document to the left of the insertion point (Figure 3–30).

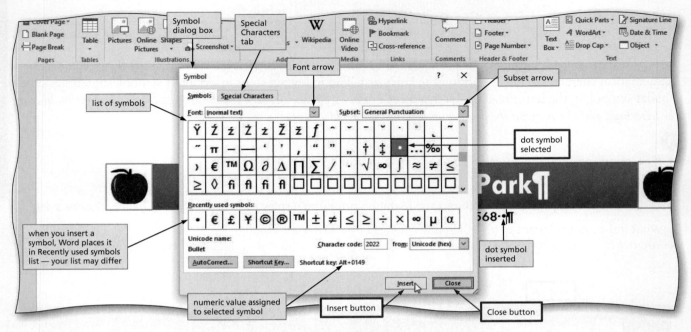

Figure 3–30

Q&A

Why is the Symbol dialog box still open?

The Symbol dialog box remains open, allowing you to insert additional symbols.

- Click the Close button (Symbol dialog box) to close the dialog box.

To Insert a Symbol from the Insert a Symbol Gallery

1 CREATE & FORMAT LETTERHEAD WITH GRAPHICS | 2 SPECIFY LETTER FORMATS

3 INSERT TABLE | 4 FORMAT TABLE | 5 INSERT BULLETED LIST | 6 ADDRESS ENVELOPE

In the letterhead, another dot symbol separates the phone number from the email address. The following steps use the Insert a Symbol gallery to insert a dot symbol between the phone number and email address. *Why? Once you insert a symbol using the Symbol dialog box, Word adds that symbol to the Insert a Symbol gallery so that it is more readily available.*

1

- Press the SPACEBAR, type **Phone: (870) 555-4400** and then press the SPACEBAR.

2

- Click the 'Insert a Symbol' button (Insert tab | Symbols group) to display the Insert a Symbol gallery (Figure 3–31).

Figure 3–31

Q&A Why is the dot symbol now in the Insert a Symbol gallery?
When you insert a symbol from the Symbol dialog box, Word automatically adds the symbol to the Insert a Symbol gallery.

❸

• Click the dot symbol in the Insert a Symbol gallery to insert the symbol at the location of the insertion point (shown in Figure 3–32).

To Enter Text

The following steps enter the email address in the letterhead.

❶ Press the SPACEBAR.

❷ Type `Email: applepark@world.com` to finish the text in the letterhead (Figure 3–32).

BTW

Inserting Special Characters
In addition to symbols, you can insert a variety of special characters, including dashes, hyphens, spaces, apostrophes, and quotation marks. Click the Special Characters tab in the Symbol dialog box (shown in Figure 3–30), click the desired character in the Character list, click the Insert button, and then click the Close button (Symbol dialog box).

Figure 3–32

To Bottom Border a Paragraph

1 CREATE & FORMAT LETTERHEAD WITH GRAPHICS | 2 SPECIFY LETTER FORMATS
3 INSERT TABLE | 4 FORMAT TABLE | 5 INSERT BULLETED LIST | 6 ADDRESS ENVELOPE

In Word, you can draw a solid line, called a **border**, at any edge of a paragraph. That is, borders may be added above or below a paragraph, to the left or right of a paragraph, or in any combination of these sides.

The letterhead in this project has a border that extends from the left margin to the right margin immediately below the mailing address, phone, and email address information. ***Why?*** *The horizontal line separates the letterhead from the rest of the letter.* The following steps add a bottom border to a paragraph.

❶

• Display the Home tab.

• With the insertion point in the paragraph to border, click the Borders arrow (Home tab | Paragraph group) to display the Borders gallery (Figure 3–33).

Figure 3–33

● Click Bottom Border in the Borders gallery to place a border below the paragraph containing the insertion point (Figure 3–34).

Figure 3–34

Q&A If the face of the Borders button displays the border icon I want to use, can I click the Borders button instead of using the Borders arrow?
Yes.

How would I remove an existing border from a paragraph?
If, for some reason, you wanted to remove a border from a paragraph, you would position the insertion point in the paragraph, click the Borders arrow (Home tab | Paragraph group), and then click No Border in the Borders gallery.

Other Ways

1. Click 'Borders and Shading' button (Design tab | Page Background group), click Borders tab (Borders and Shading dialog box), select desired border options, click OK button

To Clear Formatting

1 CREATE & FORMAT LETTERHEAD WITH GRAPHICS | 2 SPECIFY LETTER FORMATS
3 INSERT TABLE | 4 FORMAT TABLE | 5 INSERT BULLETED LIST | 6 ADDRESS ENVELOPE

The next step is to position the insertion point below the letterhead, so that you can type the contents of the letter. When you press the ENTER key at the end of a paragraph containing a border, Word moves the border forward to the next paragraph. The paragraph also retains all current settings, such as the center format. Instead, you want the paragraph and characters on the new line to use the Normal style: black font with no border.

Word uses the term, **clear formatting**, to refer to returning the formats to the Normal style. The following steps clear formatting at the location of the insertion point. *Why? You do not want to retain the current formatting in the new paragraph.*

● With the insertion point between the email address and paragraph mark at the end of the contact information line (as shown in Figure 3–34), press the ENTER key to move the insertion point and paragraph to the next line (Figure 3–35).

Figure 3–35

2

- Click the 'Clear All Formatting' button (Home tab | Font group) to apply the Normal style to the location of the insertion point (Figure 3–36).

Figure 3–36

Other Ways		
1. Click More button in Styles gallery (Home tab | Styles group), click Clear Formatting	2. Click Styles Dialog Box Launcher (Home tab | Styles group), click Clear All in Styles task pane	3. Select text, press CTRL+SPACEBAR, press CTRL+Q

AutoFormat As You Type

As you type text in a document, Word automatically formats some of it for you. For example, when you press the ENTER key or SPACEBAR after typing an email address or web address, Word automatically formats the address as a hyperlink, that is, in a different color and underlined. In Figure 3–35, for example, Word formatted the email address as a hyperlink because you pressed the ENTER key at the end of the line. Table 3–2 outlines commonly used AutoFormat As You Type options and their results.

Table 3–2 Commonly Used AutoFormat As You Type Options		
Typed Text	**AutoFormat As You Type Feature**	**Example**
Quotation marks or apostrophes	Changes straight quotation marks or apostrophes to curly ones	"the" becomes "the"
Text, a space, one hyphen, one or no spaces, text, space	Changes the hyphen to an en dash	ages 20-45 becomes ages 20–45
Text, two hyphens, text, space	Changes the two hyphens to an em dash	Two types--yellow and red becomes Two types—yellow and red
Web or email address followed by SPACEBAR or ENTER key	Formats web or email address as a hyperlink	www.cengagebrain.com becomes www.cengagebrain.com
Number followed by a period, hyphen, right parenthesis, or greater than sign and then a space or tab followed by text	Creates a numbered list	1. Word 2. PowerPoint becomes 1. Word 2. PowerPoint
Asterisk, hyphen, or greater than sign and then a space or tab followed by text	Creates a bulleted list	* Home tab * Insert tab becomes • Home tab • Insert tab
Fraction and then a space or hyphen	Condenses the fraction entry so that it consumes one space instead of three	1/2 becomes ½
Ordinal and then a space or hyphen	Makes part of the ordinal a superscript	3rd becomes 3rd

To Convert a Hyperlink to Regular Text

The email address in the letterhead should be formatted as regular text; that is, it should not be a different color or underlined. ***Why?*** *Hyperlinks are useful only in online documents, and this letter will be printed instead of distributed electronically.* The following steps remove a hyperlink format.

- Right-click the hyperlink (in this case, the email address) to display a shortcut menu (or, if using a touch screen, press and hold the hyperlink and then tap the 'Show Context Menu' button on the mini toolbar) (Figure 3–37).

Figure 3–37

2

- Click Remove Hyperlink on the shortcut menu to remove the hyperlink format from the text.
- Position the insertion point on the paragraph mark below the border because you are finished with the letterhead (Figure 3–38).

Q&A

Could I have used the AutoCorrect Options button instead of the Remove Hyperlink command?
Yes. Alternatively, you could have pointed to the small blue box at the beginning of the hyperlink, clicked the AutoCorrect Options button, and then clicked Undo Hyperlink on the AutoCorrect Options menu.

Figure 3–38

- Save the letterhead again on the same storage location with the same file name.

Other Ways

1. With insertion point in hyperlink, click 'Add a Hyperlink' button (Insert tab | Links group), click Remove Link button

Break Point: If you wish to take a break, this is a good place to do so. You can exit Word now. To resume at a later time, run Word, open the file called Apple Park Letterhead, and continue following the steps from this location forward.

Creating a Business Letter

With the letterhead for the business letter complete, the next task is to create the remainder of the content in the letter. The following sections use Word to create a business letter that contains a table and a bulleted list.

What should you consider when writing a business letter?

A finished business letter should look like a symmetrically framed picture with evenly spaced margins, all balanced below an attractive letterhead. The letter should be well written, properly formatted, logically organized, and use visuals where appropriate. The content of a letter should contain proper grammar, correct spelling, logically constructed sentences, flowing paragraphs, and sound ideas.

Be sure to include all essential elements, use proper spacing and formats, and determine which letter style to use.

- **Include all essential letter elements.** All business letters contain the same basic elements, including the date line, inside address, message, and signature block (shown in Figure 3–1 at the beginning of this module). If a business letter does not use a letterhead, then the top of the letter should include return address information in a heading.

- **Use proper spacing and formats for the contents of the letter below the letterhead.** Use a font that is easy to read, in a size between 8 and 12 point. Add emphasis with bold, italic, and bullets where appropriate, and use tables to present numeric information. Paragraphs should be single-spaced, with double-spacing between paragraphs.

- **Determine which letter style to use.** You can follow many different styles when creating business letters. A letter style specifies guidelines for the alignment and spacing of elements in the business letter.

If possible, keep the length of a business letter to one page. Be sure to proofread the finished letter carefully.

To Save a Document with a New File Name

The current open file has the name Apple Park Letterhead, which is the name of the organization letterhead. Because you want the letterhead file to remain intact so that you can reuse it, you save the document with a new file name. The following step saves a document with a new file name. For a detailed example of the procedure summarized below, refer to the Office and Windows module at the beginning of this book.

 Save the letter on your hard drive, OneDrive, or other storage location using a new file name, Lee Vendor Letter.

BTW

Organizing Files and Folders

You should organize and store files in folders so that you easily can find the files later. For example, if you are taking an introductory technology class called CIS 101, a good practice would be to save all Word files in a Word folder in a CIS 101 folder. For a discussion of folders and detailed examples of creating folders, refer to the Office and Windows module at the beginning of this book.

To Apply a Style

1 CREATE & FORMAT LETTERHEAD WITH GRAPHICS | 2 SPECIFY LETTER FORMATS
3 INSERT TABLE | 4 FORMAT TABLE | 5 INSERT BULLETED LIST | 6 ADDRESS ENVELOPE

Recall that the Normal style in Word places 8 points of blank space after each paragraph and inserts a vertical space equal to 1.08 lines between each line of text. You will need to modify the spacing used for the paragraphs in the business letter. *Why? Business letters should use single spacing for paragraphs and double spacing between paragraphs.*

Word has many built-in, or predefined, styles that you can use to format text. The No Spacing style, for example, defines line spacing as single and does not insert any additional blank space between lines when you press the ENTER key. To apply a style to a paragraph, you first position the insertion point in the paragraph. The following step applies the No Spacing style to a paragraph.

1

- With the insertion point positioned in the paragraph to be formatted, click No Spacing in the Styles gallery (Home tab | Styles group) to apply the selected style to the current paragraph (Figure 3–39).

Will this style be used in the rest of the document?

Yes. The paragraph formatting, which includes the style, will carry forward to subsequent paragraphs each time you press the ENTER key.

Figure 3–39

Other Ways

1. Click Styles Dialog Box Launcher (Home tab | Styles group), click desired style in Styles task pane

2. Press CTRL+SHIFT+S, click Style Name arrow in Apply Styles task pane, click desired style in list

What elements should a business letter contain?

Be sure to include all essential business letter elements, properly spaced, in your letter:

- The **date line**, which consists of the month, day, and year, is positioned two to six lines below the letterhead.

- The **inside address**, placed three to eight lines below the date line, usually contains the addressee's courtesy title plus full name, job title, business affiliation, and full geographical address.

- The **salutation**, if present, begins two lines below the last line of the inside address. If you do not know the recipient's name, avoid using the salutation "To whom it may concern" — it is impersonal. Instead, use the recipient's title in the salutation, e.g., Dear Personnel Director. In a business letter, use a colon (:) at the end of the salutation; in a personal letter, use a comma.

- The body of the letter, the **message**, begins two lines below the salutation. Within the message, paragraphs are single-spaced with one blank line between paragraphs.

- Two lines below the last line of the message, the **complimentary close** is displayed. Capitalize only the first word in a complimentary close.

- Type the **signature block** at least four blank lines below the complimentary close, allowing room for the author to sign his or her name.

What are the common styles of business letters?

Three common business letter styles are the block, the modified block, and the modified semi-block. Each style specifies different alignments and indentations.

- In the block letter style, all components of the letter begin flush with the left margin.

- In the modified block letter style, the date, complimentary close, and signature block are positioned approximately one-half inch to the right of center or at the right margin. All other components of the letter begin flush with the left margin.

- In the modified semi-block letter style, the date, complimentary close, and signature block are centered, positioned approximately one-half inch to the right of center or at the right margin. The first line of each paragraph in the body of the letter is indented one-half to one inch from the left margin. All other components of the letter begin flush with the left margin.

The business letter in this project follows the modified block style.

Using Tab Stops to Align Text

A **tab stop** is a location on the horizontal ruler that tells Word where to position the insertion point when you press the TAB key on the keyboard. Word, by default, places a tab stop at every one-half inch mark on the ruler. You also can set your own custom tab stops. Tab settings are a paragraph format. Thus, each time you press the ENTER key, any custom tab stops are carried forward to the next paragraph.

To move the insertion point from one tab stop to another, press the TAB key on the keyboard. When you press the TAB key, a **tab character** formatting mark appears in the empty space between the tab stops.

When you set a custom tab stop, you specify how the text will align at a tab stop. The tab marker on the ruler reflects the alignment of the characters at the location of the tab stop. Table 3–3 shows types of tab stop alignments in Word and their corresponding tab markers.

Table 3–3 Types of Tab Stop Alignments			
Tab Stop Alignment	**Tab Marker**	**Result of Pressing TAB Key**	**Example**
Left Tab	⌞	Left-aligns text at the location of the tab stop	toolbar ruler
Center Tab	⊥	Centers text at the location of the tab stop	toolbar ruler
Right Tab	⌟	Right-aligns text at the location of the tab stop	toolbar ruler
Decimal Tab	⊥	Aligns text on decimal point at the location of the tab stop	45.72 223.75
Bar Tab	ı	Aligns text at a bar character at the location of the tab stop	toolbar ruler

To Display the Ruler

One way to set custom tab stops is by using the horizontal ruler. Thus, the following steps display the ruler in the document window.

1 If the rulers are not showing, display the View tab.

2 Click the View Ruler check box (View tab | Show group) to place a check mark in the check box and display the horizontal and vertical rulers on the screen (shown in Figure 3–40).

To Set Custom Tab Stops

1 CREATE & FORMAT LETTERHEAD WITH GRAPHICS | 2 SPECIFY LETTER FORMATS
3 INSERT TABLE | 4 FORMAT TABLE | 5 INSERT BULLETED LIST | 6 ADDRESS ENVELOPE

The first required element of the business letter is the date line, which in this letter is positioned two lines below the letterhead. The date line contains the month, day, and year, and begins four inches from the left margin. *Why? Business letter guidelines specify to begin the date line approximately one-half inch to the right of center. Thus, you should set a custom tab stop at the 4" mark on the ruler.* The following steps set a left-aligned tab stop.

①

- With the insertion point on the paragraph mark below the border (shown in Figure 3–39), press the ENTER key so that a blank line appears above the insertion point.

- If necessary, click the tab selector at the left edge of the horizontal ruler until it displays the type of tab you wish to use, which is the Left Tab icon in this case.

- Position the pointer on the 4" mark on the ruler, which is the location of the desired custom tab stop (Figure 3–40).

Q&A What is the purpose of the tab selector? Before using the ruler to set a tab stop, ensure the correct tab stop icon appears in the tab selector. Each time you click the tab selector, its icon changes. The Left Tab icon is the default. For a list of the types of tab stops, see Table 3–3.

Figure 3–40

②

- Click the 4" mark on the ruler to place a tab marker at that location (Figure 3–41).

Q&A What if I click the wrong location on the ruler? You can move a custom tab stop by dragging the tab marker to the desired location on the ruler. Or, you can remove an existing custom tab stop by pointing to the tab marker on the ruler and then dragging the tab marker down and out of the ruler.

Figure 3–41

What if I am using a touch screen? Display the Home tab, tap the Paragraph Settings Dialog Box Launcher (Home tab | Paragraph group), tap the Tabs button (Paragraph dialog box), type 4 in the Tab stop position box (Tabs dialog box), tap the Set button, and then tap the OK button to set a custom tab stop and place a corresponding tab marker on the ruler.

Other Ways

1. Click Paragraph Dialog Box Launcher (Home tab or Layout tab | Paragraph group), click Tabs button (Paragraph dialog box), type tab stop position (Tabs dialog box), click Set button, click OK button

To Insert the Current Date in a Document

The next step is to enter the current date at the 4" tab stop in the document. *Why? The date in this letter will be positioned according to the guidelines for a modified block style letter.* In Word, you can insert a computer's system date in a document. The following steps insert the current date in the letter.

1

- Press the TAB key to position the insertion point at the location of the tab stop in the current paragraph.
- Display the Insert tab.
- Click the 'Insert Date and Time' button (Insert tab | Text group) to display the Date and Time dialog box.
- Select the desired format (Date and Time dialog box), in this case October 2, 2017.
- If the Update automatically check box is selected, click the check box to remove the check mark (Figure 3–42).

Q&A Why should the Update automatically check box not be selected?

In this project, the date at the top of the letter always should show today's date (for example, October 2, 2017). If, however, you wanted the date always to change to reflect the current computer date (for example, showing the date you open or print the letter), then you would place a check mark in this check box.

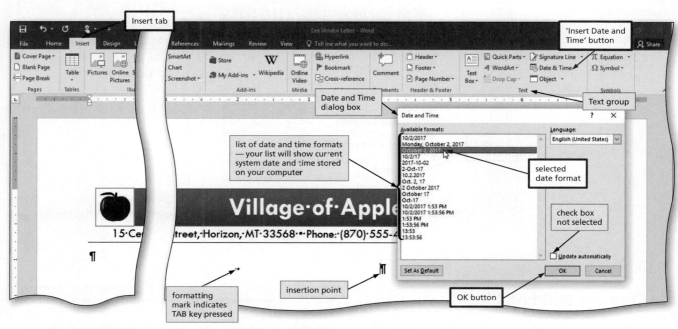

Figure 3–42

2

- Click the OK button to insert the current date at the location of the insertion point (Figure 3–43).

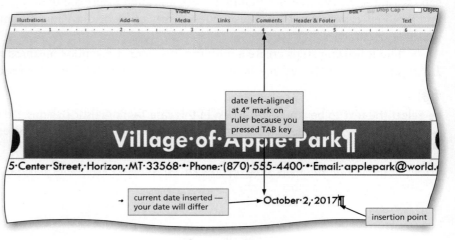

Figure 3–43

BTW
Tabs Dialog Box
You can use the Tabs dialog box to set, change the alignment of, and remove custom tab stops. To display the Tabs dialog box, click the Paragraph Settings Dialog Box Launcher (Home tab or Layout tab | Paragraph group) and then click the Tabs button (Paragraph dialog box). To set a custom tab stop, enter the desired tab position (Tabs dialog box) and then click the Set button. To change the alignment of a custom tab stop, click the tab stop position to be changed, click the new alignment, and then click the Set button. To remove an existing tab stop, click the tab stop position to be removed and then click the Clear button. To remove all tab stops, click the Clear All button in the Tabs dialog box.

To Enter the Inside Address and Salutation

The next step in composing the business letter is to type the inside address and salutation. The following steps enter this text.

1 With the insertion point at the end of the date (shown in Figure 3–43), press the ENTER key three times.

2 Type **Ms. Tamara Lee** and then press the ENTER key.

3 Type **Tam's Artistic Designs** and then press the ENTER key.

4 Type **1587 Willow Road** and then press the ENTER key.

5 Type **Juniper, MT 33522** and then press the ENTER key twice.

6 Type **Dear Ms. Lee:** to complete the inside address and salutation entries. Scroll up, if necessary (Figure 3–44).

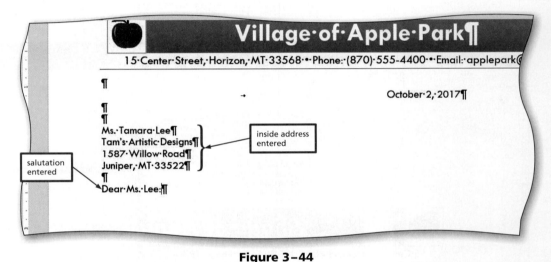

Figure 3–44

To Create a Building Block

1 CREATE & FORMAT LETTERHEAD WITH GRAPHICS | 2 SPECIFY LETTER FORMATS
3 INSERT TABLE | 4 FORMAT TABLE | 5 INSERT BULLETED LIST | 6 ADDRESS ENVELOPE

If you use the same text or graphic frequently, you can store the text or graphic as a **building block** and then insert the stored building block entry in the open document, as well as in future documents. That is, you can create the entry once as a building block and then insert the building block when you need it. In this way, you avoid entering text or graphics inconsistently or incorrectly in different locations throughout the same or multiple documents.

The following steps create a building block for the vendor business name, Tam's Artistic Designs. *Why? Later, you will insert the building block in the document instead of typing the vendor business name again.*

1
• Select the text to be a building block, in this case Tam's Artistic Designs. Do not select the paragraph mark at the end of the text because you do not want the paragraph to be part of the building block.

 Why is the paragraph mark not part of the building block?
Select the paragraph mark only if you want to store paragraph formatting, such as indentation and line spacing, as part of the building block.

- Click the 'Explore Quick Parts' button (Insert tab | Text group) to display the Explore Quick Parts gallery (Figure 3–45).

Figure 3–45

- Click 'Save Selection to Quick Part Gallery' in the Explore Quick Parts gallery to display the Create New Building Block dialog box.

- Type **tad** in the Name text box (Create New Building Block dialog box) to replace the proposed building block name (Tam's Artistic, in this case) with a shorter building block name (Figure 3–46).

- Click the OK button to store the building block entry and close the dialog box.
- If Word displays another dialog box, click the Yes button to save changes to the building blocks.

Figure 3–46

Q&A | Will this building block be available in future documents?
When you exit Word, a dialog box may appear asking if you want to save changes to the building blocks. Click the Save button if you want to use the new building block in future documents.

To Modify a Building Block

1 CREATE & FORMAT LETTERHEAD WITH GRAPHICS | 2 SPECIFY LETTER FORMATS
3 INSERT TABLE | 4 FORMAT TABLE | 5 INSERT BULLETED LIST | 6 ADDRESS ENVELOPE

When you save a building block in the Explore Quick Parts gallery, the building block is displayed at the top of the Explore Quick Parts gallery. When you point to the building block in the Explore Quick Parts gallery, a ScreenTip displays the building block name. If you want to display more information when the user points to the building block, you can include a description in the ScreenTip.

The following steps modify a building block to include a description and change its category to AutoText. **Why?** *Because you want to reuse this text, you place it in the AutoText gallery, which also is accessible through the Explore Quick Parts gallery.*

1

- Click the 'Explore Quick Parts' button (Insert tab | Text group) to display the Explore Quick Parts gallery.

- Right-click the Tam's Artistic Design building block to display a shortcut menu (Figure 3–47).

Figure 3–47

2

- Click Edit Properties on the shortcut menu to display the Modify Building Block dialog box, filled in with information related to the selected building block.

- Click the Gallery arrow (Modify Building Block dialog box) and then click AutoText to change the gallery in which the building block will be placed.

- Type **Event Vendor** in the Description text box (Figure 3–48).

3

- Click the OK button to store the building block entry and close the dialog box.

- Click the Yes button when asked if you want to redefine the building block entry.

Figure 3–48

To Insert a Building Block

1 CREATE & FORMAT LETTERHEAD WITH GRAPHICS | 2 SPECIFY LETTER FORMATS
3 INSERT TABLE | 4 FORMAT TABLE | 5 INSERT BULLETED LIST | 6 ADDRESS ENVELOPE

The vendor business name, Tam's Artistic Designs, appears in the first sentence in the body of the letter. You will type the building block name, tad, and then instruct Word to replace this building block name with the stored building block entry, Tam's Artistic Designs. The following steps insert a building block. **Why?** *Instead of typing the name, you will insert the stored building block.*

1

- Click to the right of the colon in the salutation and then press the ENTER key twice to position the insertion point one blank line below the salutation.

- Type the beginning of the first sentence as follows, entering the building block name as shown: **The park district board has approved the vendor application for your business, tad** (Figure 3–49).

Figure 3–49

❷

- Press the F3 key to instruct Word to replace the building block name (tad) with the stored building block entry (Tam's Artistic Designs).

- Press the PERIOD key (Figure 3–50).

Figure 3–50

Other Ways

1. Click 'Explore Quick Parts' button (Insert tab | Text group), if necessary point to AutoText, select desired building block

2. Click 'Explore Quick Parts' button (Insert tab | Text group), click Building Blocks Organizer, select desired building block, click Insert button

Building Blocks versus AutoCorrect

In Module 2, you learned how to use the AutoCorrect feature, which enables you to insert and create AutoCorrect entries, similarly to how you created and inserted building blocks in this module. The difference between an AutoCorrect entry and a building block entry is that the AutoCorrect feature makes corrections for you automatically as soon as you press the SPACEBAR or type a punctuation mark, whereas you must instruct Word to insert a building block. That is, you enter the building block name and then press the F3 key, or click the Explore Quick Parts button and select the building block from one of the galleries or the Building Blocks Organizer.

To Insert a Nonbreaking Space

1 CREATE & FORMAT LETTERHEAD WITH GRAPHICS | 2 SPECIFY LETTER FORMATS
3 INSERT TABLE | 4 FORMAT TABLE | 5 INSERT BULLETED LIST | 6 ADDRESS ENVELOPE

Some compound words, such as proper nouns, dates, units of time and measure, abbreviations, and geographic destinations, should not be divided at the end of a line. These words either should fit as a unit at the end of a line or be wrapped together to the next line.

Word provides two special characters to assist with this task: the nonbreaking space and the nonbreaking hyphen. A **nonbreaking space** is a special space character that prevents two words from splitting if the first word falls at the end of a line. Similarly, a **nonbreaking hyphen** is a special type of hyphen that prevents two words separated by a hyphen from splitting at the end of a line.

The following steps insert a nonbreaking space between the two words, Fall Festival. **Why?** *You want these two words to appear on the same physical line.*

- With the insertion point at the end of the first sentence in the body of the letter (as shown in Figure 3–50), press the SPACEBAR.

- Type `Your check for $150 for a 10 x 20 booth has been deposited, and we are excited that you will be participating in our Fall` and then press CTRL+SHIFT+SPACEBAR to insert a nonbreaking space after the entered word (Figure 3–51).

Figure 3–51

- Type `Festival` and then press PERIOD key (Figure 3–52).

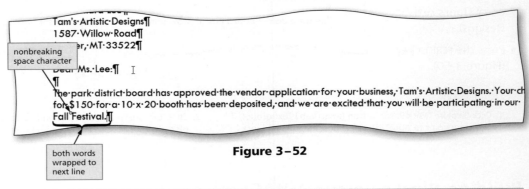

Figure 3–52

Other Ways

1. Click 'Insert a Symbol' button (Insert tab | Symbols group), click More Symbols, click Special Characters tab (Symbol dialog box), click Nonbreaking Space in Character list, click Insert button, click Close button

---

BTW
Nonbreaking Hyphen
If you wanted to insert a nonbreaking hyphen, you would press CTRL+SHIFT+HYPHEN.

To Enter Text

The next step in creating the letter is to enter the rest of the text in the first paragraph. The following steps enter this text.

1 Press the SPACEBAR.

2 Type this sentence: `The table below outlines the timetable for vendors:`

3 Press the ENTER key twice to place a blank line between paragraphs (shown in Figure 3–53).

Q&A Why does my document wrap on different words?
Differences in wordwrap may relate to the printer connected to your computer. Thus, it is possible that the same document could wordwrap differently if associated with a different printer.

4 Save the letterhead again on the same storage location with the same file name.

Break Point: If you wish to take a break, this is a good place to do so. You can exit Word now. To resume at a later time, run Word, open the file called Lee Vendor Letter, and continue following the steps from this location forward.

Tables

The next step in composing the business letter is to place a table listing the vendor timetable (shown in Figure 3–1). A Word **table** is a collection of rows and columns. The intersection of a row and a column is called a **cell**, and cells are filled with data.

The first step in creating a table is to insert an empty table in the document. When inserting a table, you must specify the total number of rows and columns required, which is called the **dimension** of the table. The table in this project has three columns. You often do not know the total number of rows in a table. Thus, many Word users create one row initially and then add more rows as needed. In Word, the first number in a dimension is the number of columns, and the second is the number of rows. For example, in Word, a 3×1 (pronounced "three by one") table consists of three columns and one row.

To Insert an Empty Table

1 CREATE & FORMAT LETTERHEAD WITH GRAPHICS | 2 SPECIFY LETTER FORMATS

3 INSERT TABLE | 4 FORMAT TABLE | 5 INSERT BULLETED LIST | 6 ADDRESS ENVELOPE

The next step is to insert an empty table in the letter. The following steps insert a table with three columns and one row at the location of the insertion point. *Why? The first column will identify the activity, the second will identify the event dates, and the third will identify the activity times. You will start with one row and add them as needed.*

❶

- Scroll the document so that you will be able to see the table in the document window.

- Display the Insert tab.

- With the insertion point positioned as shown in Figure 3–53, click the 'Add a Table' button (Insert tab | Tables group) to display the Add a Table gallery (Figure 3–53).

Experiment

- Point to various cells on the grid to see a preview of various table dimensions in the document window.

Figure 3–53

❷

- Position the pointer on the cell in the first row and third column of the grid to preview the desired table dimension in the document (Figure 3–54).

Figure 3–54

- Click the cell in the first row and third column of the grid to insert an empty table with one row and three columns in the document.
- If necessary, scroll the document so that the table is visible (Figure 3–55).

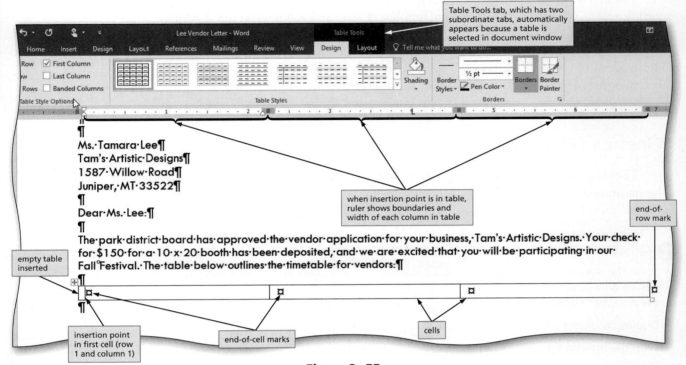

Figure 3–55

What are the small circles in the table cells?

Each table cell has an **end-of-cell mark**, which is a formatting mark that assists you with selecting and formatting cells. Similarly, each row has an **end-of-row mark**, which you can use to add columns to the right of a table. Recall that formatting marks do not print on a hard copy. The end-of-cell marks currently are left-aligned, that is, positioned at the left edge of each cell.

Other Ways

1. Click 'Add a Table' button (Insert tab | Tables group), click Insert Table in Add a Table gallery, enter number of columns and rows (Insert Table dialog box), click OK button

---

To Enter Data in a Table

The next step is to enter data in the cells of the empty table. The data you enter in a cell wordwraps just as text wordwraps between the margins of a document. To place data in a cell, you click the cell and then type.

To advance rightward from one cell to the next, press the TAB key. When you are at the rightmost cell in a row, press the TAB key to move to the first cell in the next row; do not press the ENTER key. *Why? The ENTER key is used to begin a new paragraph within a cell.* One way to add new rows to a table is to press the TAB key when the insertion point is positioned in the bottom-right corner cell of the table. The following step enters data in the first row of the table and then inserts a blank second row.

- With the insertion point in the left cell of the table, type **Activity** and then press the TAB key to advance the insertion point to the next cell.

- Type **Event Dates** and then press the TAB key to advance the insertion point to the next cell.
- Type **Times** and then press the TAB key to add a second row at the end of the table and position the insertion point in the first column of the new row (Figure 3–56).

Figure 3–56

Q&A How do I edit cell contents if I make a mistake?
Click in the cell and then correct the entry.

To Enter More Data in a Table

The following steps enter the remaining data in the table.

1 Type **Booth Setup** and then press the TAB key to advance the insertion point to the next cell. Type **Friday, October 27** and then press the TAB key to advance the insertion point to the next cell. Type **5:00 to 9:00 p.m.** and then press the TAB key to add a row at the end of the table and position the insertion point in the first column of the new row.

2 In the third row, type **Booth Sales** in the first column, **Saturday, October 28** in the second column, and **9:00 a.m. to 6:00 p.m.** in the third column. Press the TAB key to position the insertion point in the first column of a new row.

3 In the fourth row, type **Booth Sales** in the first column, **Sunday, October 29** in the second column, and **9:00 a.m. to 3:00 p.m.** in the third column. Press the TAB key.

4 In the fifth row, type **Booth Takedown** in the first column, **Sunday, October 29** in the second column, and **3:00 to 7:00 p.m.** in the third column (Figure 3–57).

BTW

Tables
For simple tables, such as the one just created, Word users often select the table dimension in the Add a Table gallery to create the table. For a more complex table, such as one with a varying number of columns per row, Word has a Draw Table feature that allows users to draw a table in the document using a pencil pointer. To use this feature, click the 'Add a Table' button (Insert tab | Tables group) and then click Draw Table on the Add a Table menu.

Figure 3–57

To Apply a Table Style

Word provides a gallery of more than 90 table styles, which include a variety of colors and shading. *Why? Table styles allow you to change the basic table format to a more visually appealing style.* The following steps apply a table style to the table in the letter.

- If the First Column check box in the Table Style Options group (Table Tools Design tab) contains a check mark, click the check box to remove the check mark because you do not want the first column in the table formatted differently from the rest of the table. Be sure the remaining check marks match those in the Table Style Options group (Table Tools Design tab) as shown in Figure 3–58.

Q&A

What if the Table Tools Design tab no longer is the active tab?
Click in the table and then display the Table Tools Design tab.

What do the options in the Table Style Options group mean?
When you apply table styles, if you want the top row of the table (header row), a row containing totals (total row), first column, or last column to be formatted differently, select those check boxes. If you want the rows or columns to alternate with colors, select Banded Rows or Banded Columns, respectively.

- With the insertion point in the table, click the More button in the Table Styles gallery (Table Tools Design tab | Table Styles group), shown in Figure 3–57, to expand the gallery.

- Scroll and then point to 'Grid Table 6 Colorful - Accent 3' in the Table Styles gallery to display a live preview of that style applied to the table in the document (Figure 3–58).

Figure 3–58

Experiment

- Point to various styles in the Table Styles gallery and watch the format of the table change in the document window.

3

- Click 'Grid Table 6 Colorful - Accent 3' in the Table Styles gallery to apply the selected style to the table. Scroll up, if necessary (Figure 3–59).

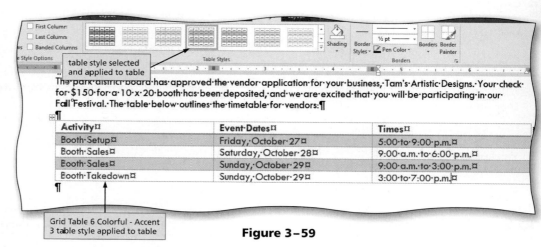

Figure 3–59

Experiment

- Select and remove check marks from various check boxes in the Table Style Options group and watch the format of the table change in the document window. When finished experimenting, be sure the check marks match those shown in Figure 3–58.

To Resize Table Columns to Fit Table Contents

1 CREATE & FORMAT LETTERHEAD WITH GRAPHICS | 2 SPECIFY LETTER FORMATS
3 INSERT TABLE | 4 FORMAT TABLE | 5 INSERT BULLETED LIST | 6 ADDRESS ENVELOPE

The table in this project currently extends from the left margin to the right margin of the document. The following steps instruct Word to fit the width of the columns to the contents of the table automatically. *Why? You want each column to be only as wide as the longest entry in the table. That is, the first column must be wide enough to accommodate the words, Booth Takedown, and the second column should be only as wide as the words, Saturday, October 28, and so on.*

1

- With the insertion point in the table, display the Table Tools Layout tab.

- Click the AutoFit button (Table Tools Layout tab | Cell Size group) to display the AutoFit menu (Figure 3–60).

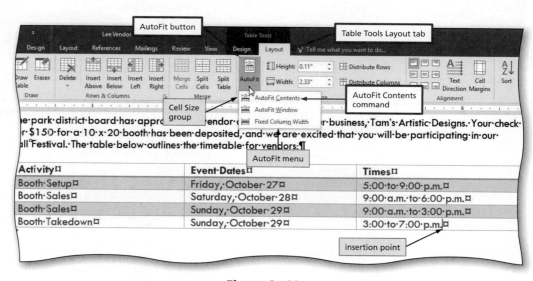

Figure 3–60

2

- Click AutoFit Contents on the AutoFit menu, so that Word automatically adjusts the widths of the columns based on the text in the table (Figure 3–61).

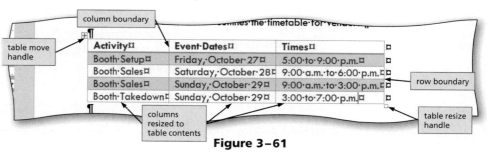

Figure 3–61

Q&A | Can I resize columns manually?
Yes, you can drag a **column boundary**, the border to the right of a column, until the column is the desired width. Similarly, you can resize a row by dragging the **row boundary**, the border at the bottom of a row, until the row is the desired height. You also can resize the entire table by dragging the **table resize handle**, which is a small square that appears when you point to a corner of the table.

What causes the table move handle and table resize handle to appear and disappear from the table?
They appear whenever you position the pointer in the table.

Other Ways

1. Double-click column boundary

To Select a Column

1 CREATE & FORMAT LETTERHEAD WITH GRAPHICS | 2 SPECIFY LETTER FORMATS
3 INSERT TABLE | 4 FORMAT TABLE | 5 INSERT BULLETED LIST | 6 ADDRESS ENVELOPE

The next task is to change the alignment of the data in cells in the third column of the table. To do this, you first must select the column. *Why? If you want to format the contents of a single cell, simply position the insertion point in the cell. To format a series of cells, you first must select them.* The following step selects a column.

• Position the pointer at the boundary above the column to be selected, the third column in this case, so that the pointer changes to a downward pointing arrow and then click to select the column (Figure 3–62).

Q&A | What if I am using a touch screen?
Position the insertion point in the third column, tap the Select Table button (Table Tools Layout tab | Table group), and then tap Select Column on the Select Table menu.

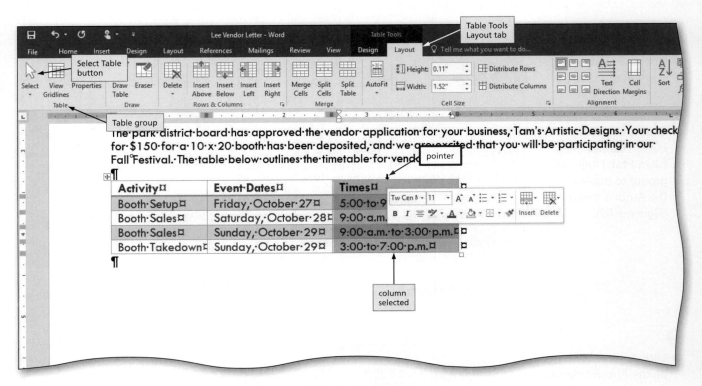

Figure 3–62

Other Ways

1. Click Select Table button (Table Tools Layout tab | Table group), click Select Column in Select Table gallery

Selecting Table Contents

When working with tables, you may need to select the contents of cells, rows, columns, or the entire table. Table 3–4 identifies ways to select various items in a table.

Table 3–4 Selecting Items in a Table	
Item to Select	**Action**
Cell	Point to left edge of cell and then click when the pointer changes to a small solid upward angled pointing arrow. Or Position insertion point in cell, click Select Table button (Table Tools Layout tab | Table group), and then click Select Cell on the Select Table menu.
Column	Point to border at top of column and then click when the pointer changes to a small solid downward-pointing arrow. Or Position insertion point in column, click Select Table button (Table Tools Layout tab | Table group), and then click Select Column on the Select Table menu.
Row	Point to the left of the row and then click when pointer changes to a right-pointing block arrow. Or Position insertion point in row, click Select Table button (Table Tools Layout tab | Table group), and then click Select Row on the Select Table menu.
Multiple cells, rows, or columns adjacent to one another	Drag through cells, rows, or columns.
Multiple cells, rows, or columns not adjacent to one another	Select first cell, row, or column (as described above) and then hold down CTRL key while selecting next cell, row, or column.
Next cell	Press TAB key.
Previous cell	Press SHIFT+TAB
Table	Point somewhere in table and then click table move handle that appears in upper-left corner of table (shown in Figure 3-63). Or Position insertion point in table, click Select Table button (Table Tools Layout tab | Table group), and then click Select Table on the Select Table menu.

BTW

Word Help
At any time while using Word, you can find answers to questions and display information about various topics through Word Help. Used properly, this form of assistance can increase your productivity and reduce your frustrations by minimizing the time you spend learning how to use Word. For instructions about Word Help and exercises that will help you gain confidence in using it, read the Office and Windows module at the beginning of this book.

To Align Data in Cells

1 CREATE & FORMAT LETTERHEAD WITH GRAPHICS | 2 SPECIFY LETTER FORMATS
3 INSERT TABLE | 4 FORMAT TABLE | 5 INSERT BULLETED LIST | 6 ADDRESS ENVELOPE

The next step is to change the alignment of the data in cells in the third column of the table. In addition to aligning text horizontally in a cell (left, center, or right), you can align it vertically within a cell (top, center, bottom). When the height of the cell is close to the same height as the text, however, differences in vertical alignment are not readily apparent, which is the case for this table. The following step centers data in cells. *Why? The column containing the times would look better if its contents are centered.*

- With the cells (column) selected, as shown in Figure 3–62, click the desired alignment, in this case the 'Align Top Center' button (Table Tools Layout tab | Alignment group) to center the contents of the selected cells (Figure 3–63).

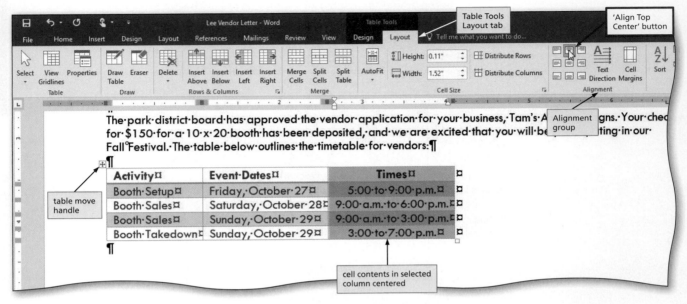

Figure 3–63

To Center a Table

1 CREATE & FORMAT LETTERHEAD WITH GRAPHICS | 2 SPECIFY LETTER FORMATS
3 INSERT TABLE | 4 FORMAT TABLE | 5 INSERT BULLETED LIST | 6 ADDRESS ENVELOPE

When you first create a table, it is left-aligned; that is, it is flush with the left margin. In this letter, the entire table should be centered between the margins of the page. To center a table, you first select the entire table. The following steps select and center a table using the mini toolbar. *Why? Recall that you can use buttons and boxes on the mini toolbar instead of those on the ribbon.*

- Position the pointer in the table so that the table move handle appears (shown in Figure 3–63).

Q&A What if the table move handle does not appear?
You also can select a table by clicking the Select Table button (Table Tools Layout tab | Table group) and then clicking Select Table on the menu.

2

- Click the table move handle to select the entire table (Figure 3–64).

Figure 3–64

Q&A | What if I am using a touch screen?
Tap the Select Table button (Table Tools Layout tab | Table group) and then tap Select Table on the Select Table menu to select the table.

3

- Click the Center button on the mini toolbar to center the selected table between the left and right page margins (Figure 3–65).

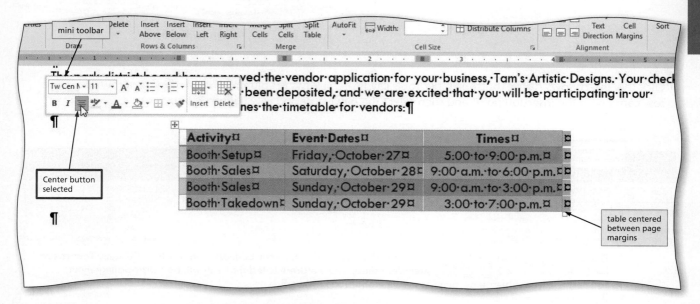

Figure 3–65

Q&A | Could I have clicked the Center button on the Home tab?
Yes. If the command you want to use is not on the currently displayed tab on the ribbon and it is available on the mini toolbar, use the mini toolbar instead of switching to a different tab. This technique minimizes mouse movement.

What if I am using a touch screen?
Display the Home tab and then tap the Center button (Home tab | Paragraph group) to center the table.

To Insert a Row in a Table

1 CREATE & FORMAT LETTERHEAD WITH GRAPHICS | 2 SPECIFY LETTER FORMATS
3 INSERT TABLE | 4 FORMAT TABLE | 5 INSERT BULLETED LIST | 6 ADDRESS ENVELOPE

The next step is to insert a row at the top of the table. *Why?* *You want to place a title on the table.* As discussed earlier, you can insert a row at the end of a table by positioning the insertion point in the bottom-right corner cell and then pressing the TAB key. You cannot use the TAB key to insert a row at the beginning or middle of a table. Instead, you use the 'Insert Rows Above' or 'Insert Rows Below' command (Table Tools Layout tab | Rows & Columns group) or the Insert Control (shown in Figure 3–70). The following steps insert a row at the top of a table.

- Position the insertion point somewhere in the first row of the table because you want to insert a row above this row (Figure 3–66).

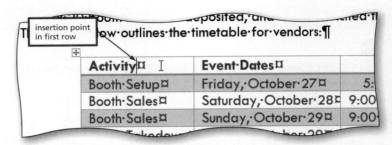

Figure 3–66

2
- Click the 'Insert Rows Above' button (Table Tools Layout tab | Rows & Columns group) to insert a row above the row containing the insertion point and then select the newly inserted row (Figure 3–67).

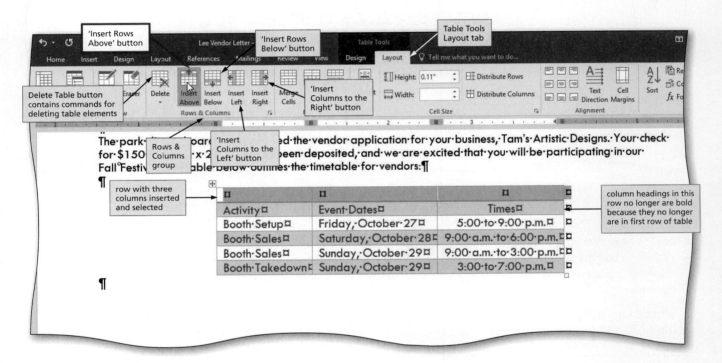

Figure 3–67

Q&A

Do I have to insert rows above the row containing the insertion point?
No. You can insert below the row containing the insertion point by clicking the 'Insert Rows Below' button (Table Tools Layout tab | Rows & Columns group).

Why did the colors in the second row change?
The table style specifies to format the header row differently, which is the first row.

Other Ways

1. Point to the left of the table and click the desired Insert Control

2. Right-click row, point to Insert on shortcut menu (or, if using touch, tap Insert Table button on mini toolbar), click desired option on Insert submenu

To Insert a Column in a Table

BTW
Resizing Table Columns and Rows
To change the width of a column or height of a row to an exact measurement, hold down the ALT key while dragging markers on the ruler. Or, enter values in the 'Table Column Width' or 'Table Row Height' boxes (Table Tools Layout tab | Cell Size group).

If you wanted to insert a column in a table, instead of inserting rows, you would perform the following steps.

1. Point above the table and then click the desired Insert Control.

or

1. Position the insertion point in the column to the left or right of where you want to insert the column.
2. Click the 'Insert Columns to the Left' button (Table Tools Layout tab | Rows & Columns group) to insert a column to the left of the current column, or click the 'Insert Columns to the Right' button (Table Tools Layout tab | Rows & Columns group) to insert a column to the right of the current column.

or

1. Right-click the table, point to Insert on the shortcut menu (or, if using touch, tap Insert Table button on the mini toolbar), and then click 'Insert Columns to the Left' or 'Insert Columns to the Right' on the Insert submenu (or, if using touch, tap Insert Left or Insert Right).

To Merge Cells

1 CREATE & FORMAT LETTERHEAD WITH GRAPHICS | 2 SPECIFY LETTER FORMATS
3 INSERT TABLE | 4 FORMAT TABLE | 5 INSERT BULLETED LIST | 6 ADDRESS ENVELOPE

The row just inserted has one cell for each column, in this case, three cells (shown in Figure 3–67). The top row of the table, however, is to be a single cell that spans all rows. *Why? The top row contains the table title, which should be centered above the columns of the table.* Thus, the following steps merge the three cells into a single cell.

• With the cells to merge selected (as shown in Figure 3–67), click the Merge Cells button (Table Tools Layout tab | Merge group) to merge the selected cells into a single cell (Figure 3–68).

Figure 3–68

- Position the insertion point in the first row and then type **Vendor Timetable** as the table title (Figure 3–69).

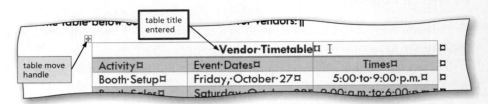

Figure 3–69

BTW

Moving Tables

If you wanted to move a table to a new location, you would point to the upper-left corner of the table until the table move handle appears (shown in Figure 3–69), point to the table move handle, and then drag it to move the entire table to a new location.

To Split Table Cells

Instead of merging multiple cells into a single cell, sometimes you want to split a single cell into multiple cells. If you wanted to split cells, you would perform the following steps.

1. Position the insertion point in the cell to split.
2. Click the Split Cells button (Table Tools Layout tab | Merge group) (or, if using touch, tap 'Show Context Menu' button on mini toolbar), or right-click the cell and then click Split Cells on the shortcut menu, to display the Split Cells dialog box.
3. Enter the number of columns and rows into which you want the cell split (Split Cells dialog box).
4. Click the OK button.

BTW

Tab Character in Tables

In a table, the TAB key advances the insertion point from one cell to the next. To insert a tab character in a cell, you must press CTRL+TAB.

To Split a Table

Instead of splitting table cells into multiple cells, sometimes you want to split a single table into multiple cells. If you wanted to split a table, you would perform the following steps.

1. Position the insertion point in the cell where you want the table to be split.
2. Click the Split Table button (Table Tools Layout tab | Merge group) to split the table into two tables at the location of the insertion point.

To Change the Font of Text in a Table Row

When you added a row to the top of the table for the title, Word moved the bold format from the column headings (which originally were in the first row of the table) to the title row (which now is the first row). Because you would like the columns headings bold also, the following steps select a table row and bold its contents.

1 Select the row containing the column headings (Figure 3–70).

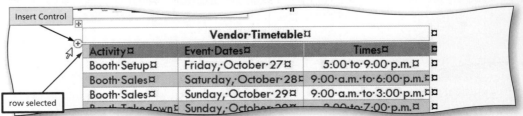

Figure 3–70

② With the text selected, click the Bold button (Home tab | Font group) to bold the selected text.

Q&A What is the symbol that appeared to the left of the table?
When you select a row or column in a table, Word displays an Insert Control. You can click the **Insert Control** to add a row or column to the table at that location.

Deleting Table Data

If you want to delete row(s) or delete column(s) from a table, position the insertion point in the row(s) or column(s) to delete, click the Delete Table button (Table Tools Layout tab | Rows & Columns group), and then click Delete Rows or Delete Columns on the Delete Table menu. Or, select the row or column to delete, right-click the selection, and then click Delete Rows or Delete Columns on the mini toolbar or shortcut menu.

To delete the contents of a cell, select the cell contents and then press the DELETE or BACKSPACE key. You also can drag and drop or cut and paste the contents of cells. To delete an entire table, select the table, click the Delete Table button (Table Tools Layout tab | Rows & Columns group), and then click Delete Table on the Delete Table menu. To delete the contents of a table and leave an empty table, you would select the table and then press the DELETE key.

To Add More Text

The table now is complete. The next step is to enter text below the table. The following steps enter text.

① Position the insertion point on the paragraph mark below the table and then press the ENTER key.

② Type **Please note the following vendor guidelines:** and then press the ENTER key (shown in Figure 3–71).

BTW
AutoFormat Options
Before you can use them, AutoFormat options must be enabled. To check if an AutoFormat option is enabled, click File on the ribbon to open the Backstage view, click the Options tab in the Backstage view, click Proofing in the left pane (Word Options dialog box), click the AutoCorrect Options button, click the AutoFormat As You Type tab, select the appropriate check boxes, and then click the OK button in each open dialog box.

To Bullet a List as You Type

1 CREATE & FORMAT LETTERHEAD WITH GRAPHICS | 2 SPECIFY LETTER FORMATS
3 INSERT TABLE | 4 FORMAT TABLE | **5 INSERT BULLETED LIST** | **6 ADDRESS ENVELOPE**

In Module 1, you learned how to apply bullets to existing paragraphs. If you know before you type that a list should be bulleted, you can use Word's AutoFormat As You Type feature to bullet the paragraphs as you type them (see Table 3–2 shown earlier in this module). *Why? The AutoFormat As You Type feature saves you time because it applies formats automatically.* The following steps add bullets to a list as you type.

①
• Press the ASTERISK key (*) as the first character on the line (Figure 3–71).

②
• Press the SPACEBAR to convert the asterisk to a bullet character.

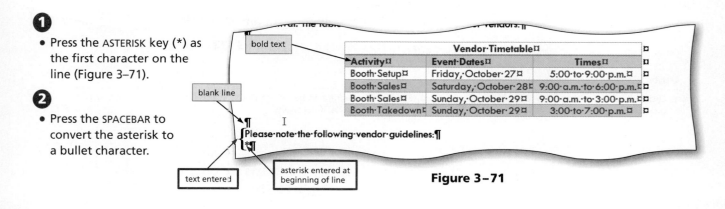

Figure 3–71

What if I did not want the asterisk converted to a bullet character?
You could undo the AutoFormat by clicking the Undo button; pressing CTRL+Z; clicking the AutoCorrect Options button that appears to the left of the bullet character as soon as you press the SPACEBAR and then clicking Undo Automatic Bullets on the AutoCorrect Options menu; or clicking the Bullets button (Home tab | Paragraph group).

3

- Type **Vendors must bring their own tables and chairs.** as the first bulleted item.

- Press the ENTER key to place another bullet character at the beginning of the next line (Figure 3–72).

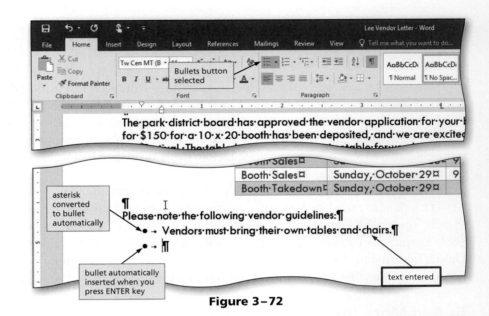

Figure 3–72

4

- Type **Vendors must supply their own electrical cords.** and then press the ENTER key.

- Type **Vendors shall comply with fire, safety, and health regulations.** and then press the ENTER key.

- Press the ENTER key to turn off automatic bullets as you type (Figure 3–73).

Why did automatic bullets stop?
When you press the ENTER key without entering any text after the automatic bullet character, Word turns off the automatic bullets feature.

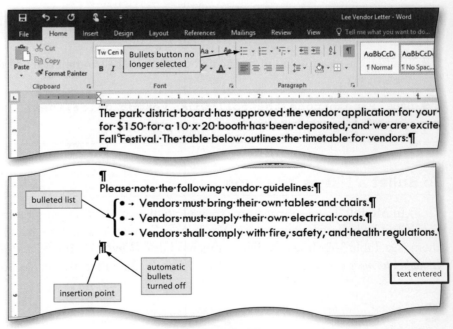

Figure 3–73

Other Ways

1. Click Bullets arrow (Home tab | Paragraph group), click desired bullet style

2. Right-click paragraph to be bulleted, click Bullets button on mini toolbar, click desired bullet style, if necessary

To Enter More Text and then Save and Print the Letter

The following steps enter the remainder of text in the letter.

1 With the insertion point positioned on the paragraph below the bulleted list, press the ENTER key and then type the paragraph shown in Figure 3–74, making certain you use the building block name, tad, to insert the organization name.

2 Press the ENTER key twice. Press the TAB key to position the insertion point at the tab stop set at the 4" mark on the ruler. Type **Sincerely,** and then press the ENTER key four times.

3 Press the TAB key to position the insertion point at the tab stop set at the 4" mark on the ruler. Type **Camden Ackerman** and then press the ENTER key.

If requested by your instructor, enter your name instead of the name stated above.

4 Press the TAB key to position the insertion point at the tab stop set at the 4" mark on the ruler. Type **Park District Events Coordinator** to finish the letter. Scroll up, if necessary (Figure 3–74).

5 Save the letter again on the same storage location with the same file name.

6 If requested by your instructor, print the letter.

BTW

Conserving Ink and Toner

If you want to conserve ink or toner, you can instruct Word to print draft quality documents by clicking File on the ribbon to open the Backstage view, clicking the Options tab in the Backstage view to display the Word Options dialog box, clicking Advanced in the left pane (Word Options dialog box), scrolling to the Print area in the right pane, placing a check mark in the 'Use draft quality' check box, and then clicking the OK button. Then, use the Backstage view to print the document as usual.

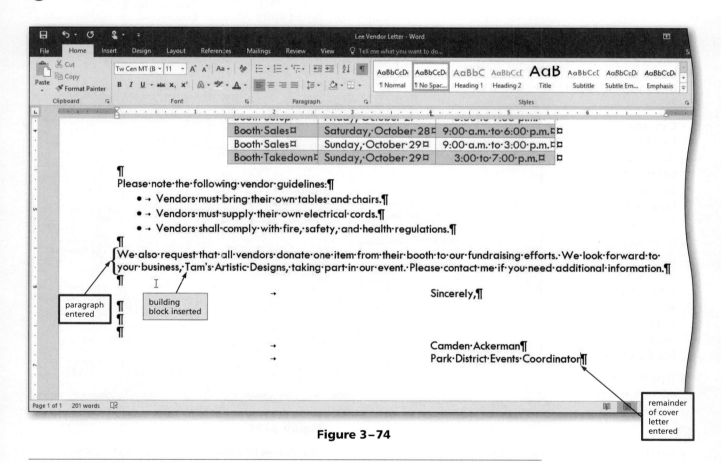

Figure 3–74

Addressing and Printing Envelopes and Mailing Labels

With Word, you can print mailing address information on an envelope or on a mailing label. Computer-printed addresses look more professional than handwritten ones.

To Address and Print an Envelope

1 CREATE & FORMAT LETTERHEAD WITH GRAPHICS | 2 SPECIFY LETTER FORMATS
3 INSERT TABLE | 4 FORMAT TABLE | 5 INSERT BULLETED LIST | 6 ADDRESS ENVELOPE

The following steps address and print an envelope. If you are in a lab environment, check with your instructor before performing these steps. ***Why?*** *Some printers may not accommodate printing envelopes; others may stop printing until an envelope is inserted.*

- Scroll through the letter to display the inside address in the document window.
- Drag through the inside address to select it (Figure 3–75).

Figure 3–75

- Display the Mailings tab.

- Click the Create Envelopes button (Mailings tab | Create group) to display the Envelopes and Labels dialog box.

- If necessary, click the Envelopes tab (Envelopes and Labels dialog box), which automatically displays the selected delivery address in the dialog box.

- Type the return address as shown in Figure 3–76.

Figure 3–76

- Insert an envelope in your printer, as shown in the Feed area of the dialog box (your Feed area may be different depending on your printer).

- If your printer can print envelopes, click the Print button (Envelopes and Labels dialog box) to print the envelope; otherwise, click the Cancel button to close the dialog box.

- Because the project now is complete, you can exit Word.

Envelopes and Labels

Instead of printing the envelope immediately, you can add it to the document by clicking the 'Add to Document' button (Envelopes and Labels dialog box) (shown in Figure 3–76). To specify a different envelope or label type (identified by a number on the box of envelopes or labels), click the Options button (Envelopes and Labels dialog box) (shown in Figure 3–76).

Instead of printing an envelope, you can print a mailing label. To do this, click the Labels button (Mailings tab | Create group) (shown in Figure 3–76) and then type the delivery address in the Delivery address box. To print the same address on all labels on the page, select the 'Full page of the same label' option button in the Print area. Click the Print button (Envelopes and Labels dialog box) to print the label(s).

Summary

In this module, you have learned how to use Word to change margins, insert and format a shape, change text wrapping, insert and format a picture, move and copy graphics, insert symbols, add a border, clear formatting, convert a hyperlink to regular text, set and use tab stops, insert the current date, create and insert building blocks, insert and format tables, and address and print envelopes and mailing labels.

What decisions will you need to make when creating your next business letter?

Use these guidelines as you complete the assignments in this module and create your own business letters outside of this class.

1. Create a letterhead.
   a) Ensure that the letterhead contains a complete legal name, mailing address, phone number, and if applicable, fax number, email address, web address, logo, or other image.
   b) Place elements in the letterhead in a visually appealing location.
   c) Format the letterhead with appropriate fonts, font sizes, font styles, and color.
2. Compose an effective business letter.
   a) Include a date line, inside address, message, and signature block.
   b) Use proper spacing and formats for letter contents.
   c) Follow the alignment and spacing guidelines based on the letter style used (i.e., block, modified block, or modified semi-block).
   d) Ensure the message is well written, properly formatted, and logically organized.

CONSIDER THIS: PLAN AHEAD

BTW
Distributing a Document
Instead of printing and distributing a hard copy of a document, you can distribute the document electronically. Options include sending the document via email; posting it on cloud storage (such as OneDrive) and sharing the file with others; posting it on social media, a blog, or other website; and sharing a link associated with an online location of the document. You also can create and share a PDF or XPS image of the document, so that users can view the file in Acrobat Reader or XPS Viewer instead of in Word.

BTW
Saving a Template
As an alternative to saving the letterhead as a Word document, you could save it as a template. To do so, click File on the ribbon to open the Backstage view, click the Export tab to display the Export gallery, click 'Change File Type', click Template in the right pane, click the Save As button, enter the template file name (Save As dialog box), if necessary select the Templates folder, and then click the Save button in the dialog box. To use the template, tap or click File on the ribbon to open the Backstage view, click the New tab to display the New gallery, click the PERSONAL tab in the New gallery, and then click the template icon or file name.

Apply Your Knowledge

Reinforce the skills and apply the concepts you learned in this module.

Working with Tabs and a Table

Note: To complete this assignment, you will be required to use the Data Files. Please contact your instructor for information about accessing the Data Files.

Instructions: Run Word. Open the document called Apply 3–1 Fall Semester Schedule Draft located on the Data Files. The document is a Word table that you are to edit and format. The revised table is shown in Figure 3–77.

Fall Semester Schedule

Class/Activity	Monday	Tuesday	Wednesday	Thursday	Friday	Saturday
ENG 101	9:30-11:00 a.m.		9:30-11:00 a.m.			
COM 110		12:30-2:00 p.m.		12:30-2:00 p.m.		
MAT 120	1:00-2:00 p.m.		1:00-2:00 p.m.		1:00-2:00 p.m.	
CHM 102	3:30-5:00 p.m.		3:30-5:00 p.m.		3:00-5:00 p.m.	
MUS 152		9:30-11:00 a.m.		9:30-11:00 a.m.		
Yoga	6:00-7:00 p.m.			3:00-4:00 p.m.		8:00-9:00 a.m.
Work		4:00-8:00 p.m.			8:00-11:00 a.m.	1:00-4:00 p.m.

Figure 3–77

Perform the following tasks:

1. Change the document theme to Organic.

2. In the line containing the table title, Fall Semester Schedule, remove the tab stop at the 1" mark on the ruler.

3. Set a centered tab at the 3" mark on the ruler. Move the centered tab stop to the 3.5" mark on the ruler.

4. Bold the characters in the title. Use the 'Increase Font Size' button to increase their font size to 14. Change their color to Red, Accent 4, Darker 25%.

5. In the table, delete the row containing the HIS 107 class.

6. In the table, delete the Sunday column.

7. Insert a column between the Monday and Wednesday columns. Fill in the column as follows:

Column Title – Tuesday

COM 110 – 12:30-2:00 p.m.

MUS 152 – 9:30-11:00 a.m.

If the column heading, Tuesday, is not bold, apply the bold format to the text in this cell.

8. Insert a new row at the bottom of the table. In the first cell of the new row, enter the word, Work, in the cell. If this cell's contents are bold, remove the bold format. Fill in the cells in the remainder of the row as follows:

Tuesday – 4:00-8:00 p.m.

Friday – 8:00-11:00 a.m.

Saturday – 1:00-4:00 p.m.

9. In the Table Style Options group (Table Tools Design tab), ensure that these check boxes have check marks: Header Row, Banded Rows, and First Column. The Total Row, Last Column, and Banded Columns check boxes should not have check marks.

10. Apply the Grid Table 5 Dark - Accent 4 style to the table.

11. Select the entire table. Click the 'Decrease Font Size' button once to decrease the font size of all characters in the table to 10 point.

12. Make all columns as wide as their contents (AutoFit Contents). Note that you may need to perform this step a couple of times to achieve the desired results.

13. Align center left all cells in the first column.

14. Align center the column headings containing the weekday names.

15. Align center right all cells containing times.

16. Center the table between the left and right margins of the page.

17. If requested by your instructor, enter your name on the line below the table.

18. Save the document using the file name, Apply 3–1 Fall Semester Schedule Modified, and submit the document (shown in Figure 3–77) in the format specified by your instructor.

19. ✳ If you wanted to add a row to the middle of the table, how would you add the row?

Extend Your Knowledge

Extend the skills you learned in this module and experiment with new skills. You may need to use Help to complete the assignment.

Working with Formulas, Graphics, Sorting, Picture Bullets, and Mailing Labels

Note: To complete this assignment, you will be required to use the Data Files. Please contact your instructor for information about accessing the Data Files.

Instructions: Run Word. Open the document called Extend 3–1 Donation Letter Draft located on the Data Files. You will use the Format Picture task pane, group objects, enter formulas in the table, change the table style, sort paragraphs, use picture bullets, move tabs, and print mailing labels.

Perform the following tasks:
1. Use Help to learn about grouping objects, entering formulas, sorting, picture bullets, and printing mailing labels.

Continued >

Extend Your Knowledge *continued*

2. Select the graphic of the globe in the hand, click the Format Shape Dialog Box Launcher (Picture Tools Format tab | Picture Styles group) to display the Format Picture task pane, and then click the Picture button in the task pane (Figure 3–78). Experiment with all the buttons in the task pane and modify the look of the graphic to your preferences.

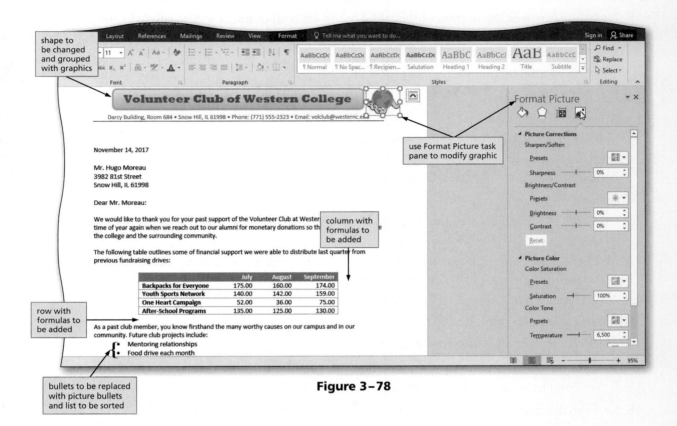

Figure 3–78

3. Select the shape around the Volunteer Club of Western College title and then use the Edit Shape button (Drawing Tools Format tab | Insert Shapes group) to change the shape to your preference. Position the globe in the hand graphic in the desired location to the right of the shape.

4. Copy and paste the modified globe in the hand graphic, flip it horizontally, and then position it on the opposite site of the shape. Group the two globe in hand graphics with the shape at the top of the letterhead. Change the text wrapping of the grouped shape to Top and Bottom.

5. Add a row to the bottom of the table. Insert the word, Total, in the first column of the new row. In the cell to contain the total for September, use the Formula dialog box to insert a formula that adds the cells in the column so that the total amount is displayed; in the dialog box, select a number format so that the total displays with dollar signs. *Hint:* Click the Formula button (Table Tools Format tab | Data group). Repeat this process for the August and July totals. Which formula did you use? Which number format?

6. Add a column to the right of the table. Insert the word, Total, as the column heading for the new column. Use the Formula dialog box to insert a formula that adds the cells each row so that the total amount is displayed. Use the same number format as you used in the previous step. Which formula did you use? What is the grand total for the quarter?

7. Position the insertion point in the table and one at a time, select and deselect each check box in the Table Style Options group. What are the functions of each check box: Header Row, Total Row, Banded Rows, First Column, Last Column, and Banded Columns? Select the check boxes you prefer for the table.

8. Sort the paragraphs in the bulleted list.

9. Change the bullets in the bulleted list to picture bullets.

10. Set a tab stop for the date line at the 4" mark on the ruler. Move the tab stops in the complimentary close and signature block from the 3.5" mark to the 4" mark on the ruler.

11. If requested by your instructor, change the name in the signature block to your name.

12. Save the revised document using the file name, Extend 3–1 Donation Letter Modified, and then submit it in the format specified by your instructor.

13. If requested by your instructor, print a single mailing label for the letter and then a full page of mailing labels, each containing the address shown in Figure 3–78.

14. ✳ Answer the questions posed in #5, #6, and #7. Why would you group objects? Which picture bullet did you use and why?

Expand Your World

Create a solution that uses cloud or web technologies by learning and investigating on your own from general guidance.

Using Google Docs to Upload and Edit Files

Notes:
- To complete this assignment, you will be required to use the Data Files. Please contact your instructor for information about accessing the Data Files.

- To complete this assignment, you will use a Google account, which you can create at no cost. If you do not have a Google account and do not want to create one, read this assignment without performing the instructions.

Instructions: You have created a letter in Word at your office and want to proofread and edit it at home. The problem is that you do not have Word at home. You do, however, have an Internet connection at home. Because you have a Google account, you upload your Word document to Google Drive so that you can view and edit it later from a computer that does not have Word installed.

Perform the following tasks:
1. In Word, open the document, Expand 3–1 Inquiry Letter in Word, from the Data Files. Look through the letter so that you are familiar with its contents and formats. If desired, print the letter so that you easily can compare it to the Google Docs converted file. Close the document.

2. Run a browser. Search for the text, google docs, using a search engine. Visit several websites to learn about Google Docs and Google Drive. Navigate to the Google website. Read about how to create files in Google Docs and upload files to Google Drive. If you do not have a Google account and you want to create one, follow the instructions to create an account. If you do not have a Google account and you do not want to create one, read the remaining instructions without performing them. If you have a Google account, sign in to your account.

3. If necessary, display Google Drive. Upload the file, Expand 3–1 Inquiry Letter in Word, to Google Drive.

Continued >

Expand Your World *continued*

4. Rename the file on Google Drive to Expand 3–1 Inquiry Letter in Google. Open the file in Google Docs (Figure 3–79). What differences do you see between the Word document and the Google Docs converted document?

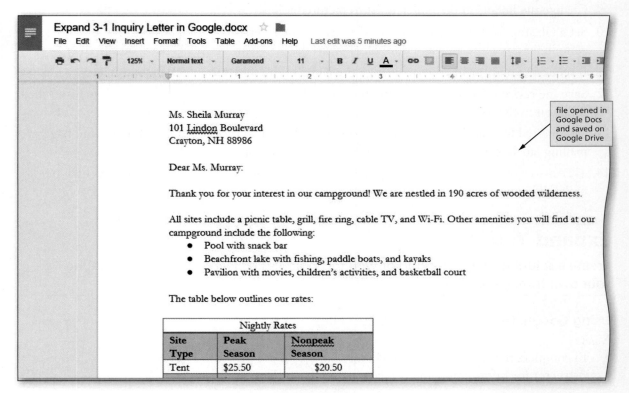

Figure 3–79

5. Fix the document in Google Docs so that it looks appealing, based on the concepts and techniques learned in this module. Add another item to the bulleted list: Fully-stocked camp store with attached laundry facilities. Add a row to the table: Pavilion, $20.00, $40.00. Insert a horizontal line below the line containing the mailing address.

6. If requested by your instructor, change the name in the signature block to your name.

7. Download the revised document to your local storage media, changing its format to Microsoft Word. Submit the document in the format requested by your instructor.

8. ✳ What is Google Drive? What is Google Docs? Answer the question posed in #4. Do you prefer using Google Docs or Word? Why?

In the Labs

Design, create, modify, and/or use a document following the guidelines, concepts, and skills presented in this module. Labs 1 and 2, which increase in difficulty, require you to create solutions based on what you learned in the module; Lab 3 requires you to apply your creative thinking and problem-solving skills to design and implement a solution.

Lab 1: **Creating a Letter with a Letterhead**

Problem: As a junior at your school, you are seeking a summer internship. One letter you prepare is shown in Figure 3–80.

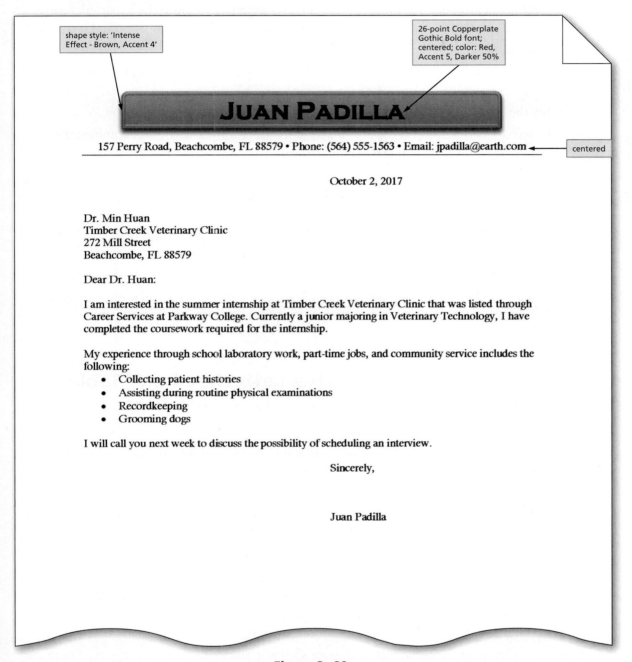

Figure 3–80

Perform the following tasks:

1. Run Word. Create a new blank document. Change the theme to Slate.

2. Create the letterhead shown at the top of Figure 3–80, following these guidelines:

   a. Insert the Rounded Same Side Corner Rectangle shape at an approximate height of 0.53" and width of 5.4". Change position of the shape to 'Position in Top Center with Square Text

Continued >

In the Labs *continued*

Wrapping'. Change the text wrapping for the shape to Top and Bottom. Add the student name, Juan Padilla, to the shape. Format the shape and its text as indicated in the figure.

b. Insert the dot symbols as shown in the contact information. Remove the hyperlink format from the email address. If necessary, clear formatting after entering the bottom border.

c. Save the letterhead with the file name, Lab 3–1 Padilla Letterhead.

3. Create the letter shown in Figure 3–80 using the modified block letter style, following these guidelines:

a. Apply the No Spacing Quick Style to the document text (below the letterhead).

b. Set a left-aligned tab stop at the 3.5" mark on the ruler for the date line, complimentary close, and signature block. Insert the current date.

c. Bullet the list as you type it.

d. If requested by your instructor, change the name in the shape and the signature block to your name.

e. Check the spelling of the letter. Save the letter with Lab 3–1 Internship Letter as the file name and then submit it in the format specified by your instructor.

4. If your instructor permits, address and print an envelope or a mailing label for the letter.

5. ✸ The letter in this assignment uses the modified block letter style. If you wanted to use the modified semi-block letter style, what changes would you make to this letter?

Lab 2: **Creating a Letter with a Letterhead and Table**

Note: To complete this assignment, you may be required to use the Data Files. Please contact your instructor for information about accessing the Data Files.

Problem: As the community education class coordinator, you are responsible for sending class registration confirmation letters. You prepare the letter shown in Figure 3–81.

Perform the following tasks:

1. Run Word. Create a new blank document. Change the theme to Berlin. Change the margins to 1" top and bottom and .75" left and right (Moderate).

2. Create the letterhead shown at the top of Figure 3–81, following these guidelines:

a. Insert the Horizontal Scroll shape at an approximate height of 0.74" and width of 6.32". Change the position of the shape to 'Position in Top Center with Square Text Wrapping'. Change the text wrapping for the shape to Top and Bottom. Add the name to the shape. Format the shape and its text as indicated in the figure.

b. Insert a picture of a rose, similar to the one shown in the figure (the exact figure, if required, is located in the Data Files). Resize the picture, change its text wrapping to In Front of Text, and move it to the left on the shape. Change its color tone to Temperature: 4700K. Copy the picture and move the copy of the image to the right on the shape, as shown in the figure. Flip the copied image horizontally.

c. Insert the small open diamond symbols as shown in the contact information. Remove the hyperlink format from the email address. If necessary, clear formatting after entering the bottom border.

d. Save the letterhead with the file name, Lab 3–2 Rosewood Letterhead.

3. Create the letter shown in Figure 3–81, following these guidelines:

a. Apply the No Spacing Quick Style to the document text (below the letterhead).

b. Set a left-aligned tab stop at the 4" mark on the ruler for the date line, complimentary close, and signature block. Insert the current date.

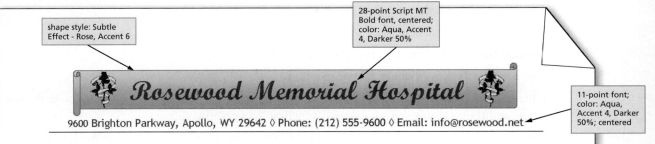

28-point Script MT Bold font, centered; color: Aqua, Accent 4, Darker 50%

shape style: Subtle Effect - Rose, Accent 6

11-point font; color: Aqua, Accent 4, Darker 50%; centered

Rosewood Memorial Hospital

9600 Brighton Parkway, Apollo, WY 29642 ◊ Phone: (212) 555-9600 ◊ Email: info@rosewood.net

October 16, 2017

Ms. Natalia Zajak
88 Sycamore Street
Apollo, WY 29642

Dear Ms. Zajak:

Thank you for your interest in our community education classes. We look forward to seeing you! The table below confirms the classes in which you are registered during November:

table style: Grid Table 5 Dark - Accent 4; table style options: Header Row and Banded Rows

bold text

November Class Registration Confirmation			
Class	**Date**	**Time**	**Location**
Diabetes Risk Assessment	November 6	5:00 to 6:00 p.m.	Suite 101
First Aid and CPR	November 11	9:00 a.m. to 3:00 p.m.	Suite 220
Healthy Cooking	November 14	4:00 to 5:00 p.m.	Suite 203
Basics of Meditation	November 17	11:00 a.m. to 12:30 p.m.	Suite 124

Please note the following:
- Arrive 10 minutes early for all classes.
- No outside food or drink allowed in classrooms.
- Kindly give 48-hour cancellation notice.

If you have any questions, please contact me via email at jgreen@rosewood.net or phone at 212-555-9612.

Sincerely,

Jerome Green
Community Education Class Coordinator

Figure 3–81

Continued >

In the Labs *continued*

c. If requested by your instructor, change the name in the inside address and salutation to your name.

d. Insert and center the table. Format the table as specified in the figure. Make all columns as wide as their contents (AutoFit Contents). Left-align the Class, Date, and Location columns. Center the Time column.

e. Bullet the list as you type it.

f. Convert the email address to regular text.

g. Use nonbreaking hyphens in the phone number.

h. Check the spelling of the letter. Save the letter with Lab 3–2 Confirmation Letter as the file name and then submit it in the format specified by your instructor.

4. If your instructor permits, address and print an envelope or a mailing label for the letter.

5. ✷ What is the purpose of the nonbreaking hyphens in this letter? Why do you think the picture in this letter used a text wrapping of In Front of Text? If the table used banded columns instead of banded rows, how would its appearance change?

Lab 3: **Consider This: Your Turn**

Create a Letter to a Potential Employer

Note: To complete this assignment, you may be required to use the Data Files. Please contact your instructor for information about accessing the Data Files.

Problem: As an intern in the career development office at your school, your boss has asked you to prepare a sample letter to a potential employer. Students seeking employment will use this letter as a reference document when creating their own letters.

Perform the following tasks:

Part 1:   Using your name, mailing address, phone number, and email address, create a letterhead for the letter. Once the letterhead is designed, write the letter to this potential employer: Ms. Latisha Adams, Personnel Director, Cedar Plank Hotels, 85 College Grove Lane, P.O. Box 582, Gartner, TX 74812.

The draft wording for the letter is as follows:

First paragraph:
I am responding to your advertisement in the Texas Post for the Assistant Manager position. I have the credentials you are seeking and believe I can be a valuable asset to Cedar Plank Hotels.

Second paragraph:
In May, I will be earning my bachelor's degree in Hospitality Management from Greenville College. My relevant coursework includes the following:

Below the second paragraph, insert the following table:

Restaurant management	18 hours
Nutrition	15 hours
Tourism management	12 hours
Hotel management	12 hours

Third paragraph:

In addition to my college coursework, I have the following experience:

Below the third paragraph, insert the following items as a bulleted list:

Assistant to school cafeteria director; Volunteer in Hope Mission kitchen; Developed website and Facebook page for local cafe.

Last paragraph:

I look forward to hearing from you to schedule an interview and to discuss my career opportunities at Cedar Plank Hotels.

The letter should contain a letterhead that uses a shape and picture(s); a table with an appropriate table title, column headings, and table style applied (unformatted table shown above); and a bulleted list (to present the experience). Insert nonbreaking spaces in the company name. Create a building block for the company name, edit the building block so that it has a ScreenTip, and insert the building block whenever you have to enter the company name.

Use the concepts and techniques presented in this module to create and format a letter according to a letter style, creating appropriate paragraph breaks and rewording the draft as necessary. The unformatted paragraphs in the letter are in a file called Lab 3–1 Letter Paragraphs, which is located on the Data Files. If you prefer, you can copy and paste this text into your letter instead of typing the paragraphs yourself. Use your name in the signature line in the letter. Be sure to check the spelling and grammar of the finished letter. Submit your assignment in the format specified by your instructor.

Part 2: ✺ You made several decisions while creating the letter in this assignment: where to position elements in the letterhead, how to format elements in the letterhead, which graphics to use in the letterhead, which theme to use in the letter, which font size to use for the letter text, which table style to use, and which letter style to use. What was the rationale behind each of these decisions?

1 Creating and Editing a Presentation with Pictures

Objectives

You will have mastered the material in this module when you can:

- Select and change a document theme and variant
- Create a title slide and a text slide with a multilevel bulleted list
- Add new slides and change slide layouts
- Insert pictures into slides with and without content placeholders
- Move and resize pictures

- Change font size and color
- Bold and italicize text
- Duplicate a slide
- Arrange slides
- Select slide transitions
- View a presentation in Slide Show view

Introduction

A PowerPoint **presentation**, also called a **slide show**, can help you deliver a dynamic, professional-looking message to an audience. PowerPoint allows you to produce slides to use in an academic, business, or other environment. The collection of slides in a presentation is called a **deck**, resembling a deck of cards that are stacked on top of each other. A common use of slide decks is to enhance an oral presentation. A speaker might desire to convey information, such as urging students to volunteer at a fund-raising event, explaining changes in employee compensation packages, or describing a new laboratory procedure. The PowerPoint slides should reinforce the speaker's message and help the audience retain the information presented. Custom slides can fit your specific needs and contain diagrams, charts, tables, pictures, shapes, video, sound, and animation effects to make your presentation more effective. An accompanying handout gives audience members reference notes and review material for your presentation.

Project — Presentation with a Bulleted List and Pictures

In this module's project, you will follow proper design guidelines and learn to use PowerPoint to create, save, and view the slides shown in Figures 1–1a through 1–1e. The objective is to produce a presentation, titled Tall Oaks, to promote three programs at the nature center. This slide show has a variety of pictures and visual elements to add interest and give facts about the events. Some of the text has formatting and color enhancements. Transitions help one slide flow gracefully into the next during a slide show.

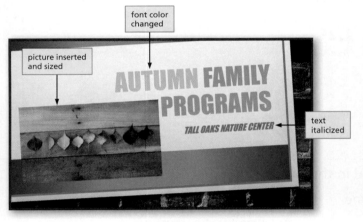

(a) Slide 1 (Title Slide with Picture)

(b) Slide 2 (Multilevel Bulleted List with Picture)

(c) Slide 3 (Comparison Layout and Pictures)

(d) Slide 4 (Title and Illustration)

(e) Slide 5 (Closing Slide)

Figure 1–1

In this module, you will learn how to perform basic tasks using PowerPoint. The following roadmap identifies general activities you will perform as you progress through this module:

1. INSERT the four PRESENTATION SLIDES, using various layouts.
2. ENTER the TEXT for the slides.
3. FORMAT the TEXT on each slide.
4. INSERT GRAPHICAL ELEMENTS, including pictures.
5. SIZE AND POSITION the graphical elements.
6. ENHANCE the SLIDE SHOW by adding a closing slide and transition.
7. DISPLAY the SLIDES.

For an introduction to Office and instructions about how to perform basic tasks in Office apps, read the Office and Windows module at the beginning of this book, where you can learn how to run an application, use the ribbon, save a file, open a file, print a file, exit an application, use Help, and much more.

Choosing a Document Theme and Variant

You easily can give the slides in a presentation a professional and integrated appearance by using a theme. A document **theme** is a specific design with coordinating colors, fonts, and special effects such as shadows and reflections. Several themes are available when you run PowerPoint, each with a specific name. Using one of the formatted themes makes creating a professional-looking presentation easier and quicker than using the Blank Presentation template, where you would need to make all design decisions.

Each theme has a set of four alternate designs, called **variants**. Each variant has the same overall composition, but the colors, fonts, and design elements differ. Once you select a theme, you then can select a variation that best fits your overall design needs. If you later decide that another theme or variant would better fit the presentation's general theme, you can change these elements while you are developing slides.

For an introduction to Windows and instructions about how to perform basic Windows tasks, read the Office and Windows module at the beginning of this book, where you can learn how to resize windows, change screen resolution, create folders, move and rename files, use Windows Help, and much more.

To Choose a Document Theme and Variant

1 INSERT PRESENTATION SLIDES | 2 ENTER TEXT | 3 FORMAT TEXT | 4 INSERT GRAPHICAL ELEMENTS
5 SIZE & POSITION | 6 ENHANCE SLIDE SHOW | 7 DISPLAY SLIDES

When you begin creating a new PowerPoint presentation, you need to select a theme. You either can start with no design elements by using the Blank Presentation, or you can select one of the available professionally designed themes. The following steps apply the Berlin theme and then change the variant. *Why? The title slide will have text and a picture, so you want to select a theme, like Berlin, with an uncluttered background. The presentation discusses three events occurring at the nature center, and green is the color commonly associated with nature's forests and grasslands. The default Berlin theme is predominantly orange and black, but one of its variants is green and is an appropriate choice to relate to the nature concept.*

BTW
The PowerPoint Window
The modules in this book begin with the PowerPoint window appearing as it did at the initial installation of the software. Your PowerPoint window may look different depending on your screen resolution and other PowerPoint settings.

1

- Run PowerPoint and point to the Berlin theme on the Recent screen (Figure 1–2).

Q&A I do not see the Berlin theme. What should I do?
Your list of available templates may differ from those shown in the figure. You may need to scroll down to locate the Berlin theme or enter "Berlin" in the Search box.

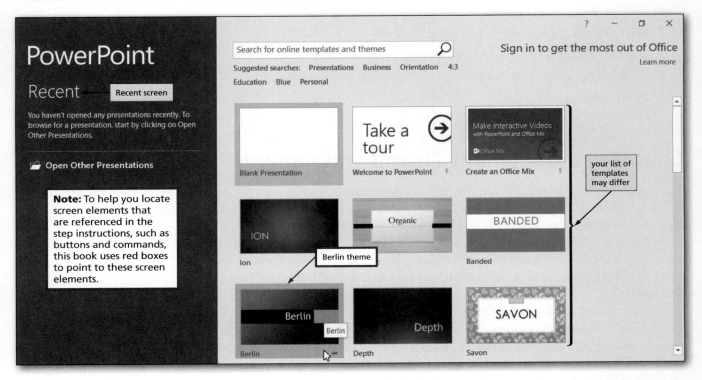

Figure 1–2

2

- Click the Berlin theme to display a theme preview dialog box with a thumbnail view of the theme and its variants (Figure 1–3).

Q&A Can I see previews of other themes?
Yes. Click the right or left arrows on the sides of the theme preview dialog box.

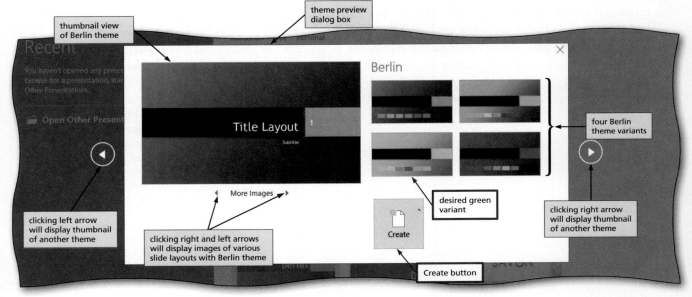

Figure 1–3

3

- Click the lower-left (green) variant to view a preview of that style applied to the thumbnail.

Q&A Can I see previews of the Berlin theme and green variant applied to layouts other than the title slide?
Yes. Click the right or left arrows beside the words, More Images, below the thumbnail. Three other layouts will be displayed: Title and Content, Two Content, and Photo.

- Click the Create button to apply the Berlin theme and green variant to the presentation and to display Slide 1 (Figure 1–4).

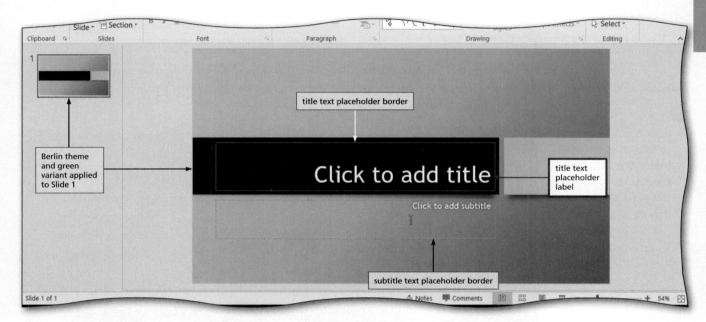

Figure 1–4

Creating a Title Slide

When you open a new presentation, the default **Title Slide** layout appears. The purpose of this layout is to introduce the presentation to the audience. PowerPoint includes other standard layouts for each of the themes. The slide layouts are set up in **landscape orientation**, where the slide width is greater than its height. In landscape orientation, the slide size is preset to 10 inches wide and 7.5 inches high when printed on a standard sheet of paper measuring 11 inches wide and 8.5 inches high.

Placeholders are boxes with dotted or hatch-marked borders that are displayed when you create a new slide. Most layouts have both a title text placeholder and at least one content placeholder. Depending on the particular slide layout selected, title and subtitle placeholders are displayed for the slide title and subtitle; a content text placeholder is displayed for text, art, or a table, chart, picture, graphic, or movie. The title slide has two text placeholders where you can type the main heading, or title, of a new slide and the subtitle.

With the exception of the Blank slide layout, PowerPoint assumes every new slide has a title. To make creating a presentation easier, any text you type after a new slide appears becomes title text in the title text placeholder. The following steps create the title slide for this presentation.

BTW
PowerPoint Screen Resolution
If you are using a computer or mobile device to step through the project in this module and you want your screens to match the figures in this book, you should change your screen's resolution to 1366 x 768. For information about how to change a computer's resolution, refer to the Office and Windows module at the beginning of this book.

CONSIDER THIS

How do I choose the words for the slide?

All presentations should follow the 7 × 7 rule, which states that each slide should have a maximum of seven lines, and each line should have a maximum of seven words. PowerPoint designers must choose their words carefully and, in turn, help viewers read the slides easily.

Avoid line wraps. Your audience's eyes want to stop at the end of a line. Thus, you must plan your words carefully or adjust the font size so that each point displays on only one line.

To Enter the Presentation Title

1 INSERT PRESENTATION SLIDES | 2 ENTER TEXT | 3 FORMAT TEXT | 4 INSERT GRAPHICAL ELEMENTS

5 SIZE & POSITION | 6 ENHANCE SLIDE SHOW | 7 DISPLAY SLIDES

The presentation title for Project 1 is Autumn Family Programs. *Why? The presentation discusses three programs that will be held during the fall months.* The following steps create the slide show's title.

 1

• Click the label, 'Click to add title', located inside the title text placeholder to select the placeholder (Figure 1–5).

Figure 1–5

 2

• Type **Autumn Family Programs** in the title text placeholder. Do not press the ENTER key (Figure 1–6).

Figure 1–6

Correcting a Mistake When Typing

If you type the wrong letter, press the BACKSPACE key to erase all the characters back to and including the one that is incorrect. If you mistakenly press the ENTER key after typing the title and the insertion point is on the new line, simply press the BACKSPACE key to return the insertion point to the right of the last letter in the word, Programs.

By default, PowerPoint allows you to reverse up to the last 20 changes by clicking the Undo button on the Quick Access Toolbar. The ScreenTip that appears when you point to the Undo button changes to indicate the type of change just made. For example, if you type text in the title text placeholder and then point to the Undo button, the ScreenTip that appears is Undo Typing. For clarity, when referencing the Undo button in this project, the name displaying in the ScreenTip is used. You can reapply a change that you reversed with the Undo button by clicking the Redo button on the Quick Access Toolbar. Clicking the Redo button reverses the last undo action. The ScreenTip name reflects the type of reversal last performed.

BTW
Touch Screen Differences
The Office and Windows interfaces may vary if you are using a touch screen. For this reason, you might notice that the function or appearance of your touch screen differs slightly from this module's presentation.

Paragraphs

Text in the subtitle text placeholder supports the title text. It can appear on one or more lines in the placeholder. To create more than one subtitle line, you press the ENTER key after typing some words. PowerPoint creates a new line, which is the second paragraph in the placeholder. A **paragraph** is a segment of text with the same format that begins when you press the ENTER key and ends when you press the ENTER key again. This new paragraph is the same level as the previous paragraph. A **level** is a position within a structure, such as an outline, that indicates the magnitude of importance. PowerPoint allows for five paragraph levels.

How do you use the touch keyboard with a touch screen?

To display the on-screen keyboard, tap the Touch Keyboard button on the Windows taskbar. When finished using the touch keyboard, tap the X button on the touch keyboard to close the keyboard.

CONSIDER THIS

To Enter the Presentation Subtitle Paragraph

1 INSERT PRESENTATION SLIDES | 2 ENTER TEXT | 3 FORMAT TEXT | 4 INSERT GRAPHICAL ELEMENTS
5 SIZE & POSITION | 6 ENHANCE SLIDE SHOW | 7 DISPLAY SLIDES

The first subtitle paragraph is related to the title. *Why? The subtitle gives an additional detail, the nature center's name.* The following steps enter the presentation subtitle.

- Click the label, 'Click to add subtitle', located inside the subtitle text placeholder to select the placeholder (Figure 1–7).

Figure 1–7

- Type **Tall Oaks Nature Center** but do not press the ENTER key (Figure 1–8).

subtitle text entered in placeholder

Figure 1–8

To Zoom a Slide

You can **zoom** the view of the slide on the screen so that the text or other content is enlarged or shrunk. When you zoom in, you get a close-up view of your slide; when you zoom out, you see more of the slide at a reduced size. You will be modifying the text and other slide components as you create the presentation, so you can enlarge the slide on the screen. *Why? Zooming the slide can help you see slide elements more clearly so that you can position them precisely where desired.* The following step changes the zoom to 70 percent.

Experiment

- Repeatedly click the Zoom In and Zoom Out buttons on the status bar and watch the size of the slide change in the Slide pane.

- Click the Zoom In or Zoom Out button as many times as necessary until the Zoom button on the status bar displays 70% on its face (Figure 1–9).

Q&A If I change the zoom percentage, will the slide display differently when I run the presentation?
No. Changing the zoom helps you develop the slide content and does not affect the slide show.

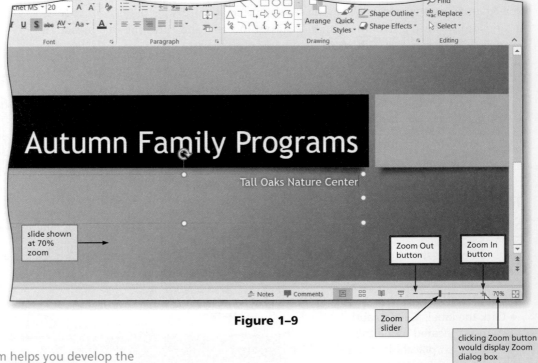

slide shown at 70% zoom

Zoom Out button

Zoom In button

Zoom slider

clicking Zoom button would display Zoom dialog box

Figure 1–9

Other Ways

1. Drag Zoom slider on status bar

2. Click Zoom level button on status bar, select desired zoom percent or type (Zoom dialog box), click OK button

3. Click Zoom button (View tab | Zoom group), select desired zoom percent or type (Zoom dialog box), click OK button

4. For touch screens: Pinch two fingers together in Slide pane (zoom out) or stretch two fingers apart (zoom in)

Formatting Characters in a Presentation

Recall that each document theme determines the color scheme, font set, and layout of a presentation. You can use a specific document theme and then change the characters' formats any time before, during, or after you type the text.

Fonts and Font Styles

Characters that appear on the screen are a specific shape and size. Examples of how you can modify the appearance, or **format**, of these typed characters on the screen and in print include changing the font, style, size, and color. The **font**, or typeface, defines the appearance and shape of the letters, numbers, punctuation marks, and symbols. **Style** indicates how the characters are formatted. PowerPoint's text font styles include regular, italic, bold, and bold italic. **Size** specifies the height of the characters and is gauged by a measurement system that uses points. A **point** is 1/72 of an inch in height. Thus, a character with a font size of 36 is 36/72 (or 1/2) of an inch in height. **Color** defines the hue of the characters.

This presentation uses the Berlin document theme, which has particular font styles and font sizes. The Berlin document theme default title text font is named Trebuchet MS. It has no special effects, and its size is 54 point. The Berlin default subtitle text font also is Trebuchet MS with a font size of 20 point.

To Select a Paragraph

1 INSERT PRESENTATION SLIDES | 2 ENTER TEXT | 3 FORMAT TEXT | 4 INSERT GRAPHICAL ELEMENTS
5 SIZE & POSITION | 6 ENHANCE SLIDE SHOW | 7 DISPLAY SLIDES

You can use many techniques to format characters. When you want to apply the same formats to multiple words or paragraphs, it is helpful to select these words. **Why?** *It is efficient to select the desired text and then make the desired changes to all the characters simultaneously.* The first formatting change you will make will apply to the title slide subtitle. The following step selects this paragraph.

- Triple-click the paragraph, Tall Oaks Nature Center, in the subtitle text placeholder to select the paragraph (Figure 1–10).

Figure 1–10

Other Ways
1. Position pointer to left of first paragraph and drag to end of line

To Italicize Text

Different font styles often are used on slides. *Why? These style changes make the words more appealing to the reader and emphasize particular text.* **Italic** text has a slanted appearance. Used sparingly, it draws the readers' eyes to these characters. The following step adds emphasis to the line of the subtitle text by changing regular text to italic text.

• With the subtitle text still selected, click the Italic button on the mini toolbar to italicize that text on the slide (Figure 1–11).

Q&A If I change my mind and decide not to italicize the text, how can I remove this style?
Immediately click the Undo button on the Quick Access Toolbar, click the Italic button a second time, or press CTRL+Z.

Figure 1–11

Other Ways

1. Right-click selected text, click Italic button in mini toolbar near shortcut menu
2. Select text, click Italic button (Home tab | Font group)
3. Click Font dialog box launcher (Home tab | Font group), click Font tab (Font dialog box), click Italic in Font style list, click OK button
4. Select text, press CTRL+I

To Increase Font Size

Why? To add emphasis, you increase the font size for the subtitle text. The 'Increase Font Size' button on the mini toolbar increases the font size in preset increments. The following step uses this button to increase the font size.

• With the text, Tall Oaks Nature Center, selected, click the 'Increase Font Size' button on the mini toolbar four times to increase the font size of the selected text from 20 to 36 point (Figure 1–12).

Figure 1–12

Other Ways

1. Click Font Size arrow on mini toolbar, click desired font size in Font Size gallery
2. Click 'Increase Font Size' button (Home tab | Font group)
3. Click Font Size arrow (Home tab | Font group), click desired font size in Font size gallery
4. Press CTRL+SHIFT+>

To Select a Word

PowerPoint designers use many techniques to emphasize words and characters on a slide. To accentuate the word, Autumn, on your slide, you want to increase the font size and change the font color to orange for this word in the title text. To make these changes, you should begin by selecting the word, Autumn. *Why? You could perform these actions separately, but it is more efficient to select the word and then change the font attributes.* The following step selects a word.

- Position the pointer somewhere in the word to be selected (in this case, in the word, Autumn).
- Double-click the word to select it (Figure 1–13).

Figure 1–13

Other Ways

1. Position pointer before first character, press CTRL+SHIFT+RIGHT ARROW   2. Position pointer before first character, drag right to select word

---

To Change the Text Color

PowerPoint allows you to use one or more text colors in a presentation. You decide to change the color of the word you selected, Autumn. *Why? The color, orange, is associated with that season, and you want to add more emphasis, subtly, to this word in your title slide text.* The following steps add emphasis to this word by changing the font color from white to orange.

- With the word, Autumn, selected, click the Font Color arrow on the mini toolbar to display the Font Color gallery, which includes Theme Colors and Standard Colors (Figure 1–14).

Q&A If the mini toolbar disappears from the screen, how can I display it once again?
Right-click the text, and the mini toolbar should appear.

🔍 **Experiment**

- Point to various colors in the gallery and watch the word's font color change.

Figure 1–14

2

- Click Orange in the Standard Colors row on the mini toolbar (third color from left) to change the font color to Orange (Figure 1–15).

Why did I select the color Orange?
Orange is one of the 10 standard colors associated with every document theme, and it is a universal color representing the fall colors. The new color will emphasize the fact that the presentation focuses on programs suited for this time of year.

What is the difference between the colors shown in the Theme Colors area and the Standard Colors?
The 10 colors in the top row of the Theme Colors area are two text, two background, and six accent colors in the Berlin theme; the five colors in each column under the top row display different transparencies. The Standard Colors are available in every document theme.

Figure 1–15

3

- Click outside the selected area to deselect the word.

4

- Save the presentation on your hard disk, OneDrive, or other storage location using Tall Oaks as the file name.

Why should I save the presentation at this time?
You have performed many tasks while creating this presentation and do not want to risk losing work completed thus far.

Other Ways
1. Right-click selected text, click Font on shortcut menu, click Font Color button, click desired color
2. Click Font Color arrow (Home tab | Font group), click desired color

Adding a New Slide to a Presentation

With the text for the title slide for the presentation created, the next step is to add the first text slide immediately after the title slide. Usually, when you create a presentation, you add slides with text, pictures, graphics, or charts. Some placeholders allow you to double-click the placeholder and then access other objects, such as videos, charts, diagrams, and organization charts. You can change the layout for a slide at any time during the creation of a presentation.

To Add a New Text Slide with a Bulleted List

1 INSERT PRESENTATION SLIDES | 2 ENTER TEXT | 3 FORMAT TEXT | **4 INSERT GRAPHICAL ELEMENTS**
5 SIZE & POSITION | 6 ENHANCE SLIDE SHOW | 7 DISPLAY SLIDES

When you add a new slide, PowerPoint uses the Title and Content slide layout. This layout provides a title placeholder and a content area for text, art, charts, and other graphics. A vertical scroll bar appears in the Slide pane when you add the second slide. *Why? The scroll bar allows you to move from slide to slide easily.* A small image of this slide also appears in the Slides tab. The following step adds a new slide with the Title and Content slide layout.

1

- Click the New Slide button (Home tab | Slides group) to insert a new slide with the Title and Content layout (Figure 1–16).

Q&A

Why does the bullet character display a white dot?
The Berlin document theme determines the bullet characters. Each paragraph level has an associated bullet character.

I clicked the New Slide arrow instead of the New Slide button. What should I do?
Click the Title and Content slide thumbnail in the Berlin layout gallery.

How do I know which slide number I am viewing?
The left edge of the status bar shows the current slide number followed by the total number of slides in the document. In addition, the slide number is displayed to the left of the slide thumbnail.

What are those six icons grouped in the middle of the Slide pane?
You can click one of the icons to insert a specific type of content: table, chart, SmartArt graphic, pictures, online pictures, or video.

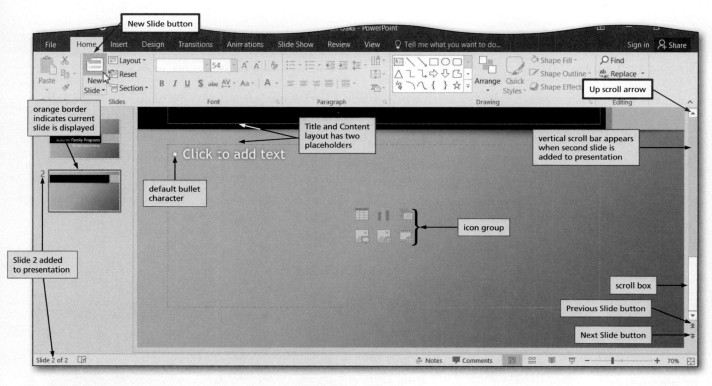

Figure 1–16

Other Ways

1. Click New Slide button (Insert tab | Slides group)   2. Press CTRL+M

Creating a Text Slide with a Multilevel Bulleted List

The information in the Slide 2 text placeholder is presented in a bulleted list with three levels. A **bulleted list** is a list of paragraphs, each of which may be preceded by a bullet character, such as a dot, arrow, or checkmark. Most themes display a bullet character at the start of a paragraph by default. A slide that consists of more than one

BTW
The Ribbon and Screen Resolution
PowerPoint may change how the groups and buttons within the groups appear on the ribbon, depending on the computer or mobile device's screen resolution. Thus, your ribbon may look different from the ones in this book if you are using a screen resolution other than 1366 x 768.

BTW
File Type
Depending on your Windows settings, the file type .pptx may be displayed on the title bar immediately to the right of the file name after you save the file. The file type .pptx identifies a PowerPoint document.

level of bulleted text is called a **multilevel bulleted list slide**. In a multilevel bulleted list, a lower-level paragraph is a subset of a higher-level paragraph. It usually contains information that supports the topic in the paragraph immediately above it.

As you can see in Figure 1–1b, two of the Slide 2 paragraphs appear at the same level, called the first level: Enjoy a hike on natural surface trails, and 9 a.m. every Saturday. Beginning with the second level, each paragraph indents to the right of the preceding level and is pushed down to a lower level. For example, if you increase the indent of a first-level paragraph, it becomes a second-level paragraph. The second and fourth paragraphs on Slide 2 are second-level paragraphs. The last paragraph, Extra supplies will be available, is a third-level paragraph.

Creating a text slide with a multilevel bulleted list requires several steps. Initially, you enter a slide title in the title text placeholder. Next, you select the content text placeholder. Then, you type the text for the multilevel bulleted list, increasing and decreasing the indents as needed. The next several sections add a slide with a multilevel bulleted list.

To Enter a Slide Title

PowerPoint assumes every new slide has a title. *Why? The audience members read the title and then can begin to focus their attention on the information being presented on that slide.* The title for Slide 2 is Morning Bird Walks. The following step enters this title.

- If necessary, click the Up scroll arrow several times until the entire title text placeholder is visible.

- Click the label 'Click to add title', to select it and then type `Morning Bird Walks` in the title text placeholder. Do not press the ENTER key (Figure 1–17).

Figure 1–17

To Select a Text Placeholder

1 INSERT PRESENTATION SLIDES | **2 ENTER TEXT** | 3 FORMAT TEXT | **4 INSERT GRAPHICAL ELEMENTS**
5 SIZE & POSITION | **6 ENHANCE SLIDE SHOW** | **7 DISPLAY SLIDES**

Why? *Before you can type text into a content placeholder, you first must select it.* The following step selects the text placeholder on Slide 2.

- Click the label, 'Click to add text', to select the content placeholder (Figure 1–18).

Q&A Why does my pointer have a different shape?
If you move the pointer away from the bullet, it will change shape.

Figure 1–18

Other Ways

1. Press CTRL+ENTER

To Type a Multilevel Bulleted List

1 INSERT PRESENTATION SLIDES | **2 ENTER TEXT** | 3 FORMAT TEXT | **4 INSERT GRAPHICAL ELEMENTS**
5 SIZE & POSITION | **6 ENHANCE SLIDE SHOW** | **7 DISPLAY SLIDES**

The content placeholder provides an area for the text characters. When you click inside a placeholder, you then can type or paste text. As discussed previously, a bulleted list is a list of paragraphs, each of which is preceded by a bullet. A paragraph is a segment of text ended by pressing the ENTER key. The theme determines the bullets for each level. *Why?* *The bullet variations are determined by the specific paragraph levels, and they generally vary in size, shape, and color.*

The content text placeholder is selected, so the next step is to type the multilevel bulleted list that consists of six paragraphs, as shown in Figure 1–1b. Creating a lower-level paragraph is called **demoting** text; creating a higher-level paragraph is called **promoting** text. The following steps create a multilevel bulleted list consisting of three levels.

- Type **Enjoy a hike on natural surface trails** and then press the ENTER key (Figure 1–19).

Figure 1–19

- Click the 'Increase
  List Level' button
  (Home tab |
  Paragraph group)
  to indent the
  second paragraph
  below the first and
  create a second-
  level paragraph
  (Figure 1–20).

Q&A Why does the bullet
for this paragraph
have a different
size?
A different bullet
is assigned to each
paragraph level.

Figure 1–20

- Type
  **Approximately
  1.5 miles** and
  then press the ENTER
  key (Figure 1–21).

Figure 1–21

- Click the 'Decrease
  List Level' button
  (Home tab |
  Paragraph group)
  so that the second-
  level paragraph
  becomes a first-
  level paragraph
  (Figure 1–22).

Q&A Can I delete bullets
on a slide?
Yes. If you do
not want bullets
to display in
a particular
paragraph, click the
Bullets button (Home
tab | Paragraph group) or right-click the paragraph
and then click the Bullets button on the shortcut menu.

Figure 1–22

Other Ways

1. Press TAB to promote paragraph; press SHIFT+TAB to demote paragraph

To Type the Remaining Text for Slide 2

The following steps complete the text for Slide 2.

1 Type `9 a.m. every Saturday` and then press the ENTER key.

2 Click the 'Increase List Level' button (Home tab | Paragraph group) to demote the paragraph to the second level.

3 Type `Bring binoculars and a field guide` and then press the ENTER key to add a new paragraph at the same level as the previous paragraph.

4 Click the 'Increase List Level' button (Home tab | Paragraph group) to demote the paragraph to the third level.

5 Type `Extra supplies will be available` but do not press the ENTER key (Figure 1–23).

Q&A I pressed the ENTER key in error, and now a new bullet appears after the last entry on this slide. How can I remove this extra bullet?
Press the BACKSPACE key twice.

Figure 1–23

BTW
Automatic Spelling Correction
As you type, PowerPoint automatically corrects some misspelled words. For example, if you type availalbe, PowerPoint automatically corrects the misspelling and displays the word, available, when you press the SPACEBAR or type a punctuation mark. To see a complete list of automatically corrected words, click File on the ribbon to open the Backstage view, click the Options tab in the Backstage view, click Proofing in the left pane (PowerPoint Options dialog box), click the AutoCorrect Options button, and then scroll through the list near the bottom of the dialog box.

To Select a Group of Words

1 INSERT PRESENTATION SLIDES | 2 ENTER TEXT | 3 FORMAT TEXT | 4 INSERT GRAPHICAL ELEMENTS
5 SIZE & POSITION | 6 ENHANCE SLIDE SHOW | 7 DISPLAY SLIDES

PowerPoint designers use many techniques to emphasize words and characters on a slide. To highlight the day of the week when the walks are held, you want to bold and increase the font size of the words, every Saturday, in the body text. The following steps select two words. *Why? You could perform these actions separately, but it is more efficient to select the words and then change the font attributes.*

1

- Position the pointer immediately to the left of the first character of the text to be selected (in this case, the e in the word, every) (Figure 1–24).

Figure 1–24

- Drag the pointer through the last character of the text to be selected (in this case, the y in the word, Saturday) (Figure 1–25).

Figure 1–25

Other Ways

1. Press CTRL+SHIFT+RIGHT ARROW repeatedly until desired words are selected

---

1 INSERT PRESENTATION SLIDES | 2 ENTER TEXT | 3 FORMAT TEXT | 4 INSERT GRAPHICAL ELEMENTS
5 SIZE & POSITION | 6 ENHANCE SLIDE SHOW | 7 DISPLAY SLIDES

To Bold Text

Why? *Bold characters display somewhat thicker and darker than those that display in a regular font style.* Clicking the Bold button on the mini toolbar is an efficient method of bolding text. To add more emphasis to the fact that the body needs nature for cooling purposes, you want to bold the words, every Saturday. The following step bolds this text.

- With the words, every Saturday, selected, click the Bold button on the mini toolbar to bold the two words (Figure 1–26).

Figure 1–26

Other Ways

1. Right-click selected text, click Font on shortcut menu, click Font tab (Font dialog box), click Bold in Font style list, click OK button

2. Select text, click Bold button (Home tab | Font group)

3. Click Font dialog box launcher (Home tab | Font group), click Font tab (Font dialog box), click Bold in Font style list, click OK button

4. Select text, press CTRL+B

To Increase Font Size

The following steps increase the font size from 24 to 28 point. *Why?* *To add emphasis, you increase the font size for the words, every Saturday.*

1 With the words, every Saturday, still selected, click the 'Increase Font Size' button on the mini toolbar once (Figure 1–27).

2 Click outside the selected area to deselect the two words.

Figure 1–27

Adding New Slides, Changing Slide Layouts, and Changing the Theme

Slide 3 in Figure 1–1c contains two pictures: a grasshopper and a dragonfly. Slide 4 in Figure 1–1d contains an illustration of a firefly and does not contain a bulleted list. When you add a new slide, PowerPoint applies the Title and Content layout. This layout and the Title Slide layout for Slide 1 are the default styles. A **layout** specifies the arrangement of placeholders on a slide. These placeholders are arranged in various configurations and can contain text, such as the slide title or a bulleted list, or they can contain content, such as SmartArt graphics, pictures, charts, tables, and shapes. The placement of the text, in relationship to content, depends on the slide layout. You can specify a particular slide layout when you add a new slide to a presentation or after you have created the slide.

Using the **layout gallery**, you can choose a slide layout. The nine layouts in this gallery have a variety of placeholders to define text and content positioning and formatting. Three layouts are for text: Title Slide, Section Header, and Title Only. Five are for text and content: Title and Content, Two Content, Comparison, Content with Caption, and Picture with Caption. The Blank layout has no placeholders. If none of these standard layouts meets your design needs, you can create a **custom layout**. A custom layout specifies the number, size, and location of placeholders, background content, and optional slide and placeholder-level properties.

When you change the layout of a slide, PowerPoint retains the text and objects and repositions them into the appropriate placeholders. Using slide layouts eliminates the need to resize objects and the font size because PowerPoint automatically sizes the objects and text to fit the placeholders. At any time when creating the slide content, you can change the theme and variant to give the presentation a different look and feel.

BTW

Customizing a Slide Layout
PowerPoint provides a wide variety of slide layouts for each theme, but you can customize the layouts to make your deck unique. Display the View tab, click Slide Master (View tab | Master Views group), select the thumbnail below the slide master in the left pane that you would like to customize, and then make the desired modifications.

To Add a New Slide and Enter a Slide Title and Headings

1 INSERT PRESENTATION SLIDES | 2 ENTER TEXT | 3 FORMAT TEXT | 4 INSERT GRAPHICAL ELEMENTS
5 SIZE & POSITION | 6 ENHANCE SLIDE SHOW | 7 DISPLAY SLIDES

The text on Slide 3 in Figure 1–1c consists of a title and two headings. The appropriate layout for this slide is named Comparison. *Why? The Comparison layout has two headings and two text placeholders adjacent to each other, so an audience member easily can compare and contrast the items shown side by side.* The following steps add Slide 3 to the presentation with the Comparison layout and then enter the title and heading text for this slide.

1

• Click the New Slide arrow in the Slides group to display the Berlin layout gallery (Figure 1–28).

Figure 1–28

2

• Click Comparison to add Slide 3 and apply that layout (Figure 1–29).

Figure 1–29

- Type `Afternoon Insect Identification` in the title text placeholder.

- Click the left heading placeholder with the label, 'Click to add text', to select this placeholder (Figure 1–30).

Figure 1–30

- Type `Grasshoppers` and then press the ENTER key.

- Type `(also known as locusts)` but do not press the ENTER key.

- Select the right heading placeholder and then type `Dragonflies` and press the ENTER key.

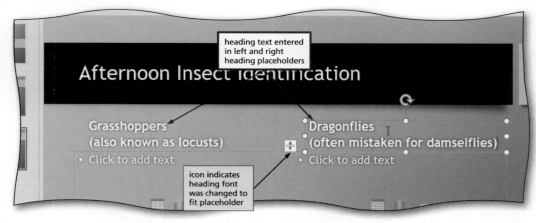

Figure 1–31

- Type `(often mistaken for damselflies)` but do not press the ENTER key (Figure 1–31).

Q&A | What is the white box with the arrow between the placeholders?
The text is too large to fit in the placeholder using the default font and paragraph attributes, so PowerPoint adjusts the text so it displays properly. That icon informs you that the font was altered.

To Add a Slide with the Title Only Layout

1 INSERT PRESENTATION SLIDES | 2 ENTER TEXT | 3 FORMAT TEXT | **4 INSERT GRAPHICAL ELEMENTS**
5 SIZE & POSITION | **6 ENHANCE SLIDE SHOW** | **7 DISPLAY SLIDES**

The following steps add Slide 4 to the presentation with the Title Only slide layout style. *Why? The only text on the slide is the title, and the majority of the slide content is the illustration.*

1

- If necessary, click Home on the ribbon to display the Home tab.

- Click the New Slide arrow (Home tab | Slides group) to display the Berlin layout gallery (Figure 1–32).

Figure 1–32

2

- Click Title Only to add a new slide and apply that layout to Slide 4 (Figure 1–33).

Figure 1–33

To Enter a Slide Title

The only text on Slide 4 is the title. The following step enters the title text for this slide.

1 Type **Twilight Firefly Hikes** as the title text but do not press the ENTER key (Figure 1–34).

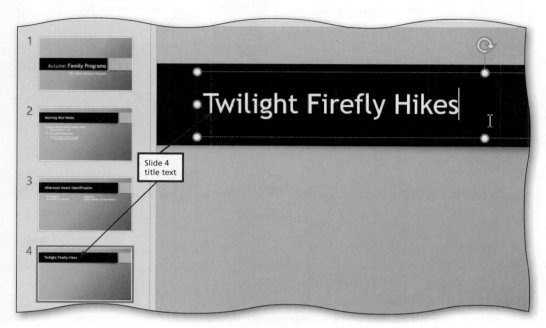

Figure 1–34

To Change the Theme

1 INSERT PRESENTATION SLIDES | 2 ENTER TEXT | 3 FORMAT TEXT | 4 INSERT GRAPHICAL ELEMENTS
5 SIZE & POSITION | 6 ENHANCE SLIDE SHOW | 7 DISPLAY SLIDES

A theme provides consistency in design and color throughout the entire presentation by setting the color scheme, font set, and layout of a presentation. This collection of formatting choices includes a set of colors (the Theme Colors group), a set of heading and content text fonts (the Theme Fonts group), and a set of lines and fill effects (the Theme Effects group). These groups allow you to choose and change the appearance of all the slides or individual slides in your presentation. *Why? At any time while creating the slide deck, you may decide to switch the theme so that the slides have a totally different appearance.* The following steps change the theme for this presentation from Berlin to Main Event.

1

- Click Design on the ribbon to display the Design tab (Figure 1–35).

Figure 1–35

2

- Click the More button (Design tab | Themes group) to expand the gallery, which shows more theme gallery options. If necessary, scroll down to the bottom of the gallery to view the Main Event thumbnail (Figure 1–36).

🔍 **Experiment**

- Point to various document themes in the Themes gallery and watch the colors and fonts change on the title slide.

Figure 1–36

Q&A Are the themes displayed in a specific order?
No. Your themes might be in a different order than shown here.

How can I determine the theme names?
If you point to a theme, a ScreenTip with the theme's name appears on the screen.

3

- Click the Main Event theme to apply this theme to all four slides (Figure 1–37).

Q&A If I decide at some future time that this design does not fit the theme of my presentation, can I apply a different design?
Yes. You can repeat these steps at any time while creating your presentation.

Figure 1–37

PowerPoint Module 1

To Change the Variant

When you began creating this presentation, you selected the Berlin theme and then chose a green variant. You can change the color variation at any time for any theme. **Why?** *The new Main Event theme has a default red color, but you want to emphasize the green color associated with nature, just like you initially did when you chose the green variant for the Berlin theme.* The following steps change the variant from red to green.

- Point to the green variant (Design tab | Variants group) to see a preview of the green variant on Slide 4 (Figure 1–38).

Experiment

- Point to the orange, green, and blue variants and watch the colors change on the slide.

Figure 1–38

- Click the green variant to apply this color to all four slides (Figure 1–39).

Q&A If I decide at some future time that this color variation does not fit the theme of my presentation, can I apply a different variant?
Yes. You can repeat these steps at any time.

Figure 1–39

- Save the presentation again on the same storage location with the same file name.

Q&A Why should I save the presentation again?
You have made several modifications to the presentation since you last saved it. Thus, you should save it again.

Break Point: If you wish to take a break, this is a good place to do so. You can exit PowerPoint now. To resume at a later time, run PowerPoint, open the file called Tall Oaks, and continue following the steps from this location forward. For a detailed example of exiting PowerPoint, running PowerPoint, and opening a file, refer to the Office and Windows module at the beginning of the book.

PowerPoint Views

The PowerPoint window display varies depending on the view. A **view** is the mode in which the presentation appears on the screen. You will use some views when you are developing slides and others when you are delivering your presentation. When creating a presentation, you most likely will use Normal, Slide Sorter, Notes Pane, and Outline views. When presenting your slides to an audience, you most likely will use Slide Sorter, Presenter, and Reading views.

The default view is **Normal view**, which is composed of three areas that allow you to work on various aspects of a presentation simultaneously. The large area in the middle, called the **Slide pane**, displays the slide you currently are developing and allows you to enter text, tables, charts, graphics, pictures, video, and other elements. As you create the slides, miniature views of the individual slides, called thumbnails, are displayed in the **Slides tab** on the left of the screen. You can rearrange the thumbnails in this pane. The **Notes pane**, by default, is hidden at the bottom of the window. If you want to type notes to yourself or remarks to share with your audience, you can click the Notes button in the status bar to open the Notes pane. After you have created at least two slides, a **scroll bar** containing **scroll arrows** and **scroll boxes** will appear on the right edge of the window.

To Move to Another Slide in Normal View

1 INSERT PRESENTATION SLIDES | 2 ENTER TEXT | 3 FORMAT TEXT | 4 INSERT GRAPHICAL ELEMENTS
5 SIZE & POSITION | 6 ENHANCE SLIDE SHOW | 7 DISPLAY SLIDES

Why? *When creating or editing a presentation in Normal view (the view you are currently using), you often want to display a slide other than the current one.* Before continuing with developing this project, you want to display the title slide. You can click the desired slide in the Slides tab or drag the scroll box on the vertical scroll bar; if you are using a touch screen, you can tap the desired slide in the Slides tab. When you drag the scroll box, the **slide indicator** shows the number and title of the slide you are about to display. Releasing shows the slide. The following steps move from Slide 4 to Slide 1 using the scroll box in the Slide pane.

- Position the pointer on the scroll box.
- Press and hold down the mouse button so that Slide: 4 of 4 Twilight Firefly Hikes appears in the slide indicator (Figure 1–40).

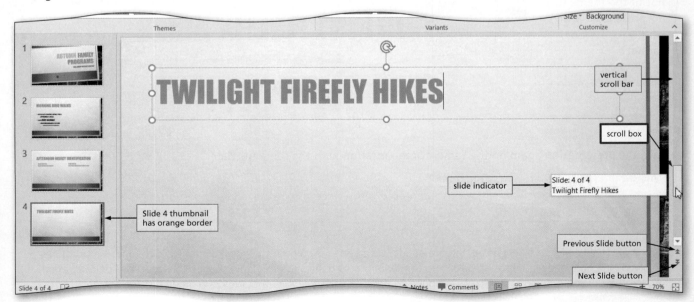

Figure 1–40

2

• Drag the scroll box up the vertical scroll bar until Slide: 1 of 4 Autumn Family Programs appears in the slide indicator (Figure 1–41).

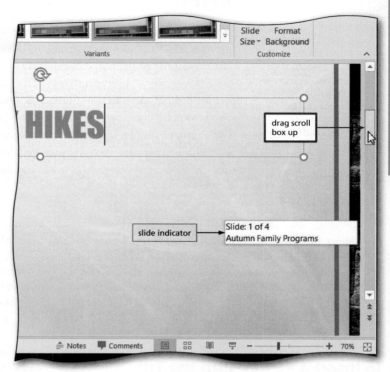

Figure 1–41

3

• Release so that Slide 1 appears in the Slide pane and the Slide 1 thumbnail has an orange border in the Slides tab (Figure 1–42).

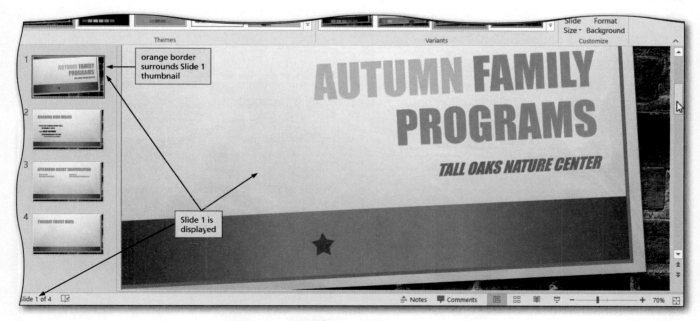

Figure 1–42

Other Ways

1. Click Next Slide button or Previous Slide button to move forward or back one slide

2. Click slide in Slides tab

3. Press PAGE DOWN or PAGE UP to move forward or back one slide

Inserting Pictures into Slides

Adding pictures can help increase the visual and audio appeal of many slides. These images may include photographs, illustrations, and other artwork. If you have a Microsoft account, you can add pictures from websites, including Flickr and OneDrive.

You can add pictures to your presentation in two ways. One way is by selecting one of the slide layouts that includes a content placeholder with a Pictures button. A second method is by clicking the Pictures button in the Images area on the Insert tab. Clicking the Pictures button opens the Insert Picture dialog box. The **Insert Picture dialog box** allows you to search for picture files that are stored on your computer or a storage device. Contact your instructor if you need the pictures used in the following steps.

CONSIDER THIS

How can you design a title slide that holds your audience's attention?
Develop a slide that reflects the content of your presentation but does so in a thought-provoking way. A title, at the very least, should prepare your audience for the material they are about to see and hear. Look for ways to focus attention on your theme and the method in which you plan to present this theme. A unique photograph or graphic can help generate interest. You may decide to introduce your topic with a startling fact, a rhetorical question, or a quotation. The device you choose depends upon your audience, the occasion, and the presentation's purpose.

To Insert a Picture into the Title Slide

1 INSERT PRESENTATION SLIDES | 2 ENTER TEXT | 3 FORMAT TEXT | 4 INSERT GRAPHICAL ELEMENTS
5 SIZE & POSITION | 6 ENHANCE SLIDE SHOW | 7 DISPLAY SLIDES

Slide 1 uses the Title Slide layout, which has two placeholders for text but none for graphical content. You desire to place a graphic on Slide 1. *Why? It is likely that your viewers will see an image on this slide before they read any text, so you want to include a picture to create interest in the presentation and introduce your audience to the topic.* For this presentation, you will insert a photograph of several leaves that have changed colors. Later in this module, you will resize and position the picture in an appropriate location. The following steps add a picture to Slide 1.

- Click Insert on the ribbon to display the Insert tab.
- Click the Pictures button (Insert tab | Images group) to display the Insert Picture dialog box.

Q&A What should I do if no pictures are displayed when I click the Pictures button?
You may need to click the Online Pictures button instead of the Pictures button.

- Navigate to the Data Files and the Module 01 folder. Click the Autumn Leaves picture to select that file (Figure 1–43).

Q&A Why do I see only a list of file names and not thumbnails of the pictures in my folder?
Your view is different from the view shown in Figure 1–43.

Figure 1–43

❸

- Click the Insert button (Insert Picture dialog box) to insert the picture into Slide 1 (Figure 1–44).

Q&A Can I double-click the picture or file name instead of selecting it and clicking the Insert button?
Yes. Either method inserts the picture.

Why is this picture displayed in this location on the slide?
The slide layout does not have a content placeholder, so PowerPoint inserts the file in an area of the slide. You will move and resize the picture later in this module.

Figure 1–44

To Insert a Picture into a Slide without a Content Placeholder

The next step is to add an owl picture to Slide 2. This slide has a bulleted list in the text placeholder, so the icon group does not display in the center of the placeholder. Later in this module, you will resize the inserted picture. The following steps add one picture to Slide 2.

❶ Click the Slide 2 thumbnail in the Slides tab to display Slide 2.

❷ Click Insert on the ribbon to display the Insert tab and then click the Pictures button (Insert tab | Images group) to display the Insert Picture dialog box.

❸ If necessary, scroll down the list of files, click Owl to select the file, and then click the Insert button to insert the picture into Slide 2 (Figure 1–45).

Q&A Why is my picture a different size from the one shown in Figure1-1b?
The clip was inserted into the slide and not into a content placeholder. You will resize the picture later in this module.

BTW

Wrapping Text around a Photo
PowerPoint does not allow you to wrap text around a picture or other graphics, such as tables, shapes, and charts. This feature, however, is available in Word.

Figure 1–45

To Insert a Picture
into a Content Placeholder

Slide 3 uses the Comparison layout, which has a content placeholder below each of the two headings. You desire to insert pictures into both content placeholders. ***Why?*** *You want to display two insects that participants likely will identify during the program at the nature center.* The following steps insert a picture of a grasshopper into the left content placeholder and a dragonfly into the right content placeholder on Slide 3.

1

- Click the Slide 3 thumbnail in the Slides tab to display Slide 3 (Figure 1–46).

Figure 1–46

2

- Click the Pictures icon in the left content placeholder to select that placeholder and to open the Insert Picture dialog box.

- If necessary, scroll down the list of files, click Grasshopper to select the file, and then double-click to insert the picture into the left content placeholder (Figure 1–47).

Figure 1–47

Skitter Photo/StockSnap.io

Q&A Do I need to select the file name before double-clicking to insert the picture?

No. You just can double-click the file name.

❸

- Click the Pictures icon in the right content placeholder to select that placeholder and to open the Insert Picture dialog box.

- If necessary, scroll down the list to display the Dragonfly file name and then insert this picture into the right content placeholder (Figure 1–48).

Figure 1–48

To Insert a Picture into a Slide without a Content Placeholder

Next, you will add a picture to Slide 4. This picture is an illustration, not an actual photograph, of a firefly. You will not insert this file into a content placeholder, so it will display in the center of the slide. Later in this module, you will resize this picture. You locate and insert illustrations in the same manner you used to insert photos. The following steps add an illustration picture to Slide 4.

❶ Click the Slide 4 thumbnail in the Slides tab.

❷ Display the Insert tab, click the Pictures button, and then insert the Firefly file into Slide 4 (Figure 1–49).

Figure 1–49

Break Point: If you wish to take a break, this is a good place to do so. You can save your presentation and then exit PowerPoint now. To resume at a later time, run PowerPoint, open the file called Tall Oaks, and continue following the steps from this location forward.

Resizing Photos and Illustrations

Sometimes it is necessary to change the size of pictures and illustrations. **Resizing** includes enlarging or reducing the size of a graphic. You can resize these images using a variety of techniques. One method involves changing the size of a picture by specifying exact dimensions in a dialog box. Another method involves sliding or dragging one of the graphic's sizing handles to the desired location. A selected graphic appears surrounded by a **selection rectangle**, which has small circles, called **sizing handles** or move handles, at each corner and middle location.

To Proportionally Resize Pictures

1 INSERT PRESENTATION SLIDES | 2 ENTER TEXT | 3 FORMAT TEXT | 4 INSERT GRAPHICAL ELEMENTS

5 SIZE & POSITION | 6 ENHANCE SLIDE SHOW | 7 DISPLAY SLIDES

Why? On Slides 1, 2, and 4, the picture and illustration sizes are too large to display aesthetically on the slides. At times it is important to maintain the proportions of a picture, such as when a person is featured prominently. To change the size of a picture and keep the width and height in proportion to each other, drag the corner sizing handles to view how the image will look on the slide. Using these corner handles maintains the graphic's original proportions. If, however, the proportions do not need to be maintained precisely, as with the owl picture on Slide 2, drag the side sizing handles to alter the proportions so that the graphic's height and width become larger or smaller. The following steps proportionally decrease the size of the Slide 1 picture using a corner sizing handle.

- Click the Slide 1 thumbnail in the Slides tab to display Slide 1.

- Click the leaves picture to select it and display the selection rectangle.

- Point to the lower-right corner sizing handle on the picture so that the pointer changes to a two-headed arrow (Figure 1–50).

Q&A I am using a touch screen and do not see a two-headed arrow when I press and hold the lower-right sizing handle. Why?

Touch screens may not display pointers; you can just press and slide sizing handles to resize.

Figure 1–50

● Drag the sizing handle diagonally toward the upper-left corner of the slide until the lower-right sizing handle or the crosshair is positioned approximately as shown in Figure 1–51.

Q&A What if the picture is not the same size as the one shown in Figure 1–51?
Repeat Steps 1 and 2.

Can I drag any corner sizing handle diagonally inward toward the opposite corner to resize the picture?
Yes.

● Release to resize the picture.

Figure 1–51

To Nonproportionally Resize the Photograph on Slide 2

Why? *The height of the owl picture in Slide 2 extends from the top to the bottom of the slide. The width, however, will cover some of the text when the picture is positioned on the right side of the slide.* The width of this picture can be decreased slightly without negatively distorting the original image. You can decrease the width of a picture by sliding or dragging one of the sizing handles on the sides of the image. The following steps resize the width of the nature bottle picture using a sizing handle along the side of the image.

● Display Slide 2 and then click the owl picture to select it and display the selection rectangle.

● Click the Zoom Out button as many times as necessary until the Zoom level is 50%.

● Point to the middle sizing handle on the bottom edge of the picture so that the pointer changes to a two-headed arrow (Figure 1–52).

Figure 1–52

- Drag the sizing handle upward until the sizing handle or crosshair is positioned on the top of the green bar, as shown in Figure 1–53.

Q&A What if the picture is not the same size as the one shown in Figure 1–53?
Repeat Steps 1 and 2.

Figure 1–53

- Release to resize the picture.
- Click outside the picture to deselect it (Figure 1–54).

Q&A What if I want to return the picture to its original size and start again?
With the picture selected, click the Reset Picture arrow (Picture Tools Format tab | Adjust group) and then click Reset Picture & Size in the Reset Picture gallery.

What happened to the Picture Tools Format tab?
When you click outside the picture, PowerPoint deselects the object and removes the Picture Tools Format tab from the screen.

Figure 1–54

To Resize the Illustration on Slide 4

The firefly picture illustration on Slide 4 can be reduced slightly to fit entirely on the slide. You resize an illustration in the same manner that you resize a photograph. You want to maintain the proportions of the character and nature in this illustration, so you will drag one of the corner sizing handles. The following steps resize this illustration using a corner sizing handle.

1 Display Slide 4 and then click the firefly illustration to select it.

2 Drag any corner sizing handle on the illustration diagonally inward until the illustration is positioned and resized approximately as shown in Figure 1–55.

illustration
resized on
Slide 4

Figure 1–55

To Move Pictures

Why? *After you insert a photo or an illustration on a slide, you might want to reposition it. The leaves picture on Slide 1 could be moved to the lower-left side of the slide, the owl on Slide 2 could be moved to the right side of the slide, and the illustration on Slide 4 could be positioned in the center of the slide.* PowerPoint displays **Smart Guides** automatically when a picture, shape, or other object is moved and is close to lining up with another slide element. These layout guides, which display as dashed lines, help you align slide elements vertically and horizontally. They display when aligning to the left, right, top, bottom, and middle of placeholders and other objects on a slide. For example, a Smart Guide will display to help you align the right or left edge of a picture in relation to a text placeholder or to another picture. The following steps center the illustration on Slide 4 and move the pictures on Slides 2 and 1.

1

- If necessary, click the firefly illustration on Slide 4 to select it.

- With the four-headed arrow displaying, drag the illustration downward and toward the left until the horizontal Smart Guide is displayed under the title text placeholder and the vertical Smart Guide is displayed through the center of the slide, as shown in Figure 1–56, and then release.

- If necessary, select the illustration and then use the ARROW keys to position it precisely as shown in Figure 1–56.

Q&A The firefly still is not located exactly where I want it to display. What can I do to align the image?
Press the CTRL key while you press the ARROW keys. This key combination moves the illustration in smaller increments than when you press only an ARROW key.

TWILIGHT FIREFLY HIKES

horizontal
Smart Guide

vertical Smart
Guide

pointer changes
to four-headed
arrow

Figure 1–56

- Display Slide 2 and then click the owl picture to select it.
- Drag the picture downward and to the right until the horizontal Smart Guide is displayed above the title text placeholder and the right edge is aligned with the vertical gray bar on the right side of the slide (Figure 1–57).

Figure 1–57

- Display Slide 1 and then click the leaves picture to select it.
- Drag the picture downward until the horizontal Smart Guide is displayed under the title text placeholder and the vertical Smart Guide is displayed near the left side of the slide, as shown in Figure 1–58, and then release.

Can I move the picture in small increments?
Yes. To move or nudge the picture in very small increments, hold down the CTRL key with the picture selected while pressing the ARROW keys. You cannot perform this action using a touch screen.

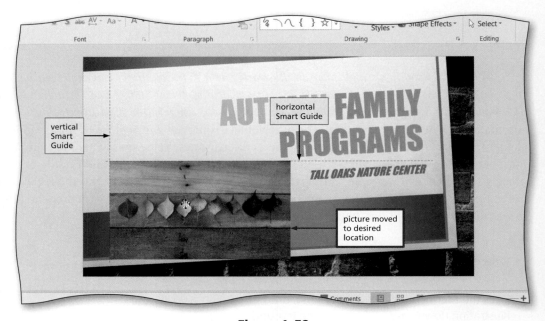

Figure 1–58

To Rotate a Picture

1 INSERT PRESENTATION SLIDES | 2 ENTER TEXT | 3 FORMAT TEXT | 4 INSERT GRAPHICAL ELEMENTS
5 SIZE & POSITION | 6 ENHANCE SLIDE SHOW | 7 DISPLAY SLIDES

Why? *The Main Event Title Slide layout is angled, so the picture would complement the design by being angled, too.* Dragging the **rotation handle** above a selected object allows you to rotate an object in any direction. The following steps rotate the leaves picture.

1

- With the leaves picture selected, position the mouse pointer over the rotation handle so that it changes to a Free Rotate pointer (Figure 1–59).

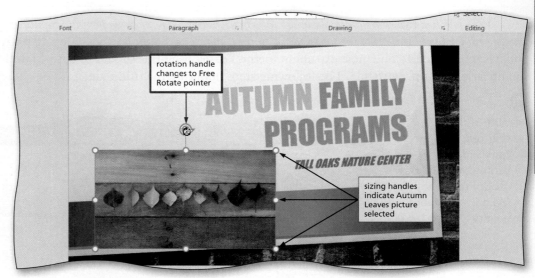

Figure 1–59

2

- Drag the rotation handle counterclockwise and then move the picture so that it is displayed as shown in Figure 1–60.

Figure 1–60

Ending a Slide Show with a Closing Slide

All the text for the slides in the Tall Oaks slide show has been entered. This presentation thus far consists of a title slide, one text slide with a multilevel bulleted list, a third slide with a Comparison layout, and a fourth slide for an illustration. A closing slide that resembles the title slide is the final slide to create.

What factors should you consider when developing a closing slide for the presentation?
After the last slide appears during a slide show, the default PowerPoint setting is to end the presentation with a **black slide**. This black slide appears only when the slide show is running and concludes the slide show, so your audience never sees the PowerPoint window. It is a good idea, however, to end your presentation with a final closing slide to display at the end of the presentation. This slide ends the presentation gracefully and should be an exact copy, or a very similar copy, of your title slide. The audience will recognize that the presentation is drawing to a close when this slide appears. It can remain on the screen when the audience asks questions, approaches the speaker for further information, or exits the room.

CONSIDER THIS

To Duplicate a Slide

Why? *When two slides contain similar information and have the same format, duplicating one slide and then making minor modifications to the new slide saves time and increases consistency.* Slide 5 will have the same layout and design as Slide 1. The most expedient method of creating this slide is to copy Slide 1 and then make minor modifications to the new slide. The following steps duplicate the title slide.

- With Slide 1 selected, click the New Slide arrow (Home tab | Slides group) to display the Main Event layout gallery (Figure 1–61).

Figure 1–61

- Click 'Duplicate Selected Slides' in the Main Event layout gallery to create a new Slide 2, which is a duplicate of Slide 1 (Figure 1–62).

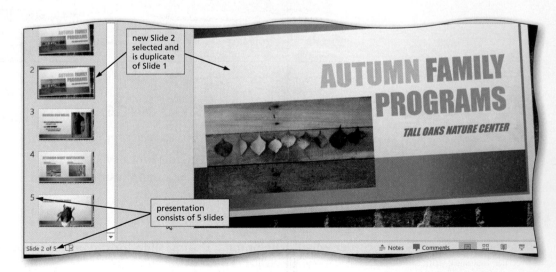

Figure 1–62

To Arrange a Slide

The new Slide 2 was inserted directly below Slide 1 because Slide 1 was the selected slide. This duplicate slide needs to display at the end of the presentation directly after the final title and content slide. ***Why?*** *It is a closing slide that reinforces the concept presented in Slide 1 and indicates to your audiences that your presentation is ending.*

Changing slide order is an easy process and is best performed in the Slides tab. When you click the thumbnail and begin to drag it to a new location, the remaining thumbnails realign to show the new sequence. When you release, the slide drops into the desired location. Hence, this process of sliding or dragging and then dropping the thumbnail in a new location is called **drag and drop**. You can use the drag-and-drop method to move any selected item, including text and graphics. The following step moves the new Slide 2 to the end of the presentation so that it becomes a closing slide.

- With Slide 2 selected, drag the Slide 2 slide thumbnail below the last slide in the Slides tab so that it becomes the new Slide 5 (Figure 1–63).

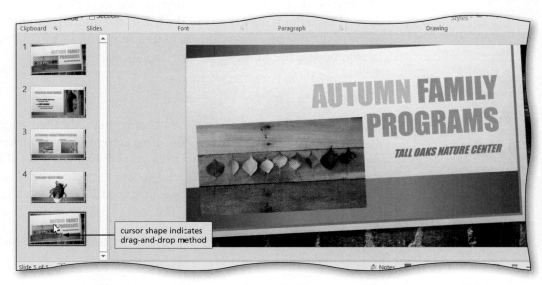

Figure 1–63

Other Ways	
1. Click Slide Sorter button on status bar, drag thumbnail to new location	2. Click Slide Sorter button (View tab | Presentation Views group), click slide thumbnail, drag thumbnail to new location

Break Point: If you wish to take a break, this is a good place to do so. Be sure to save the Tall Oaks file again and then you can exit PowerPoint. To resume at a later time, run PowerPoint, open the file called Tall Oaks, and continue following the steps from this location forward.

Making Changes to Slide Text Content

After creating slides in a presentation, you may find that you want to make changes to the text. Changes may be required because a slide contains an error, the scope of the presentation shifts, or the style is inconsistent. This section explains the types of changes that commonly occur when creating a presentation.

You generally make three types of changes to text in a presentation: additions, replacements, and deletions.

- Additions are necessary when you omit text from a slide and need to add it later. You may need to insert text in the form of a sentence, word, or single character. For example, you may want to add the presenter's middle name on the title slide.
- Replacements are needed when you want to revise the text in a presentation. For example, you may want to substitute the word, *their*, for the word, *there*.

• Deletions are required when text on a slide is incorrect or no longer is relevant to the presentation. For example, a slide may look cluttered. Therefore, you may want to remove one of the bulleted paragraphs to add more space.

Editing text in PowerPoint basically is the same as editing text in a word processing program. The following sections illustrate the most common changes made to text in a presentation.

BTW

Selecting Nonadjacent Text
In PowerPoint, you can use keyboard keys to select letters, numbers, or special characters not next to each other. This is especially helpful when you are applying the same formatting to multiple words. To select nonadjacent text, select the first item, such as a word or paragraph, as usual; then, press and hold down the CTRL key. While holding down the CTRL key, select additional items.

Replacing Text in an Existing Slide

When you need to correct a word or phrase, you can replace the text by selecting the text to be replaced and then typing the new text. As soon as you press any key on the keyboard, the selected text is deleted and the new text is displayed.

PowerPoint inserts text to the left of the insertion point. The text to the right of the insertion point moves to the right (and shifts downward if necessary) to accommodate the added text.

Deleting Text

You can delete text using one of many methods. One is to use the BACKSPACE key to remove text just typed. The second is to position the insertion point to the left of the text you want to delete and then press the DELETE key. The third method is to drag through the text you want to delete and then click the Cut button on the mini toolbar, press DELETE or BACKSPACE key, or press CTRL+X. Use the third method when deleting large sections of text.

To Delete Text in a Placeholder

1 INSERT PRESENTATION SLIDES | 2 ENTER TEXT | **3 FORMAT TEXT** | 4 INSERT GRAPHICAL ELEMENTS
5 SIZE & POSITION | 6 ENHANCE SLIDE SHOW | **7 DISPLAY SLIDES**

Why? *To keep the ending slide clean and simple, you want to edit a few words in the slide title and subtitle text.* The following steps change Autumn to Register For and then change Tall Oaks Nature Center to Call 555-8928 today! in the placeholders.

• With Slide 5 selected, position the pointer immediately to the left of the first character of the text to be selected in the title text placeholder (in this case, the A in the word, Autumn).

• Drag the pointer through the last character of the text to be selected (in this case, the n in the word, Autumn) (Figure 1–64).

Q&A Can I drag from left to right or right to left?
Yes. Either direction will select the letters.

Could I also have selected the word, Autumn, by double-clicking it?
Yes. Either method works to select a word.

Figure 1–64

2

- Press the DELETE key to delete the selected text.

- Type **Register for** as the first words in the title text placeholder (Figure 1–65).

Q&A Could I have typed these words while the word, Autumn, was selected without cutting the text first?
Yes. Either method works to replace words. You will use this alternate method in the next step.

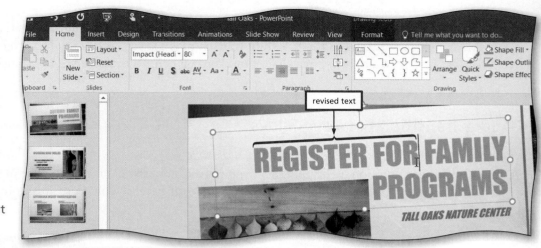

Figure 1–65

Why does the text display with all capital letters despite the fact that I am typing uppercase and lowercase letters?
The Main Event theme uses the All Caps effect for the title and subtitle text. This effect converts lowercase letters to uppercase letters.

3

- Position the pointer anywhere in the subtitle text placeholder other than on the picture and then triple-click to select all the text, Tall Oaks Nature Center (Figure 1–66).

Figure 1–66

4

- Type **Call 816-555-8928 today!** as the new subtitle text (Figure 1-67).

- If requested by your instructor, change the last four digits of the phone number in the subtitle text placeholder, 8928, to the last four digits of your phone number.

Figure 1–67

Other Ways

1. Right-click selected text, click Cut on shortcut menu   2. Select text, press DELETE or BACKSPACE key   3. Select text, press CTRL+X

Adding a Transition

PowerPoint includes a wide variety of visual and sound effects that can be applied to text or content. A **slide transition** is a special effect used to progress from one slide to the next in a slide show. You can control the speed of the transition effect and add a sound.

To Add a Transition between Slides

1 INSERT PRESENTATION SLIDES | 2 ENTER TEXT | 3 FORMAT TEXT | 4 INSERT GRAPHICAL ELEMENTS
5 SIZE & POSITION | 6 ENHANCE SLIDE SHOW | 7 DISPLAY SLIDES

Why? *Transitions add interest when you advance the slides in a presentation and make a slide show presentation look professional.* In this presentation, you apply the Wind transition in the Exciting category to all slides and change the transition speed from 2 seconds to 3 seconds. The following steps apply this transition to the presentation.

- Click the Transitions tab on the ribbon and then point to the More button (Transitions tab | Transition to This Slide group) in the Transition to This Slide gallery (Figure 1–68).

Q&A
Is a transition applied now?
No. None, the first slide icon in the Transition to This Slide group, is selected, which indicates no transition has been applied.

Figure 1–68

- Click the More button to expand the Transitions gallery.
- Point to the Wind transition in the Exciting category in the Transitions gallery (Figure 1–69).

Figure 1–69

3

- Click Wind in the Exciting category in the Transitions gallery to view a preview of this transition and to apply this transition to the closing slide.

Q&A

Why does a star appear next to Slide 5 in the Slides tab?
The star indicates that a transition animation effect is applied to that slide.

- Click the Duration up arrow (Transitions tab | Timing group) four times to change the transition speed from 02.00 seconds to 03.00 seconds (Figure 1–70).

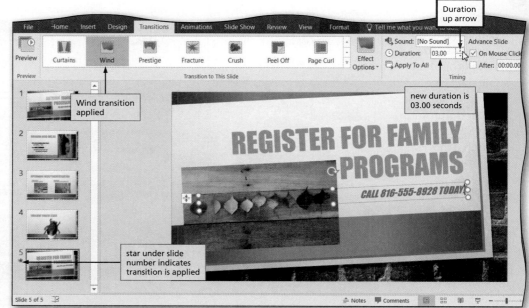

Figure 1–70

Q&A

Why did the time change from the default 02.00 to 03.00?
Each transition has a default duration time. The default Wind transition time is 02.00 seconds.

4

- Click the Preview Transitions button (Transitions tab | Preview area) to view the transition and the new transition time (Figure 1–71).

Q&A

Can I adjust the duration time I just set?
Yes. Click the Duration up or down arrows or type a speed in the Duration box and preview the transition until you find the time that best fits your presentation.

Figure 1–71

5

- Click the 'Apply To All' button (Transitions tab | Timing group) to apply the Wind transition and the increased transition time to Slides 1 through 4 in the presentation (Figure 1–72).

Q&A What if I want to apply a different transition and duration to each slide in the presentation? Repeat Steps 2 and 3 for each slide individually.

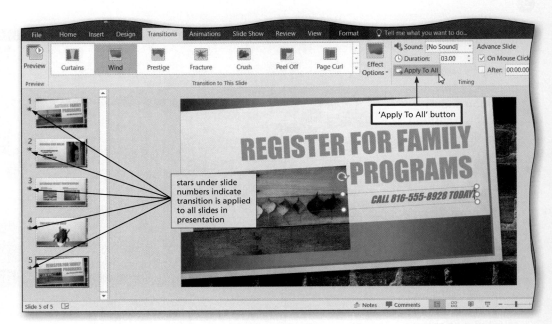

Figure 1–72

Document Properties

PowerPoint helps you organize and identify your files by using **document properties**, which are the details about a file such as the project author, title, and subject. For example, a class name or presentation topic can describe the file's purpose or content.

CONSIDER THIS

Why would you want to assign document properties to a presentation?

Document properties are valuable for a variety of reasons:

- Users can save time locating a particular file because they can view a file's document properties without opening the presentation.

- By creating consistent properties for files having similar content, users can better organize their presentations.

- Some organizations require PowerPoint users to add document properties so that other employees can view details about these files.

The more common document properties are standard and automatically updated properties. **Standard properties** are associated with all Microsoft Office files and include author, title, and subject. **Automatically updated properties** include file system properties, such as the date you create or change a file, and statistics, such as the file size.

BTW

Printing Document Properties

PowerPoint 2016 does not allow you to print document properties. This feature, however, is available in other Office 2016 apps, including Word and Excel.

To Change Document Properties

To change document properties, you would follow these steps.

1. Click File on the ribbon to open the Backstage view and then, if necessary, click the Info tab in the Backstage view to display the Info gallery.

2. If the property you wish to change is displayed in the Properties list in the right pane of the Info gallery, try to click that property. If a text box with that property is displayed, type the text for the property in the box, and then click the Back button in the upper-left corner of the Backstage view to return to the PowerPoint window. Skip the remaining steps.

3. If the property you wish to change is not displayed in the Properties list in the right pane of the Info gallery or you cannot change it in the Info gallery, click the Properties button in the right pane to display the Properties menu, and then click Advanced Properties on the Properties menu to display the Summary tab in the Properties dialog box.

Q&A Why are some of the document properties in my Document Information Panel already filled in?
The person who installed Office 2016 on your computer or network may have set or customized the properties.

4. Type the desired text in the appropriate property boxes.

5. Click the OK button (Properties dialog box) to close the dialog box

6. Click the Back button in the upper-left corner of the Backstage view to return to the PowerPoint presentation window.

Viewing the Presentation in Slide Show View

The 'Start From Beginning' button, located in the Quick Access Toolbar, allows you to show a presentation using a computer. As the name implies, the first slide to be displayed always will be Slide 1. You also can run a presentation starting with the slide currently displaying when you click the Slide Show button on the status bar. In either case, PowerPoint displays the slides on the full screen without any of the PowerPoint window objects, such as the ribbon. The full-screen slide hides the toolbars, menus, and other PowerPoint window elements.

BTW
PowerPoint Help
At any time while using PowerPoint, you can find answers to questions and display information about various topics through PowerPoint Help. Used properly, this form of assistance can increase your productivity and reduce your frustrations by minimizing the time you spend learning how to use PowerPoint. For instructions about PowerPoint Help and exercises that will help you gain confidence in using it, read the Office and Windows module at the beginning of this book.

To Start Slide Show View

1 INSERT PRESENTATION SLIDES | 2 ENTER TEXT | 3 FORMAT TEXT | 4 INSERT GRAPHICAL ELEMENTS
5 SIZE & POSITION | 6 ENHANCE SLIDE SHOW | **7 DISPLAY SLIDES**

Why? *You run a presentation for your audience so they can see the slides in their entirety and view any transitions or other effects added to the slides.* When making a presentation, you use **Slide Show view**. You can start Slide Show view from Normal view or Slide Sorter view. Slide Show view begins when you click the 'Start From Beginning' button or the Slide Show button. The following steps start Slide Show view starting with Slide 1.

1

• Point to the 'Start From Beginning' button (Figure 1–73).

Q&A What would have displayed if I had clicked the Slide Show button instead of the 'Start From Beginning' button?
When you click the Slide Show button to start the presentation, PowerPoint begins the show with the currently displayed slide, which in this case is Slide 5. Only Slide 5 would display during the slide show.

Figure 1–73

②

- Click the 'Start From Beginning' button to display the transition and the title slide (Figure 1–74).

Q&A

Where is the PowerPoint window? When you run a slide show, the PowerPoint window is hidden. It will reappear once you end your slide show.

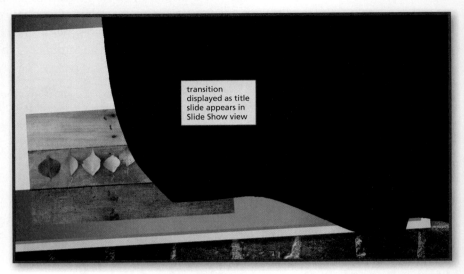

Figure 1–74

Other Ways		
1. Display Slide 1, click Slide Show button on status bar	2. Click 'Start From Beginning' button (Slide Show tab | Start Slide Show group)	3. Press F5

To Move Manually through Slides in a Slide Show

1 INSERT PRESENTATION SLIDES | 2 ENTER TEXT | 3 FORMAT TEXT | 4 INSERT GRAPHICAL ELEMENTS

5 SIZE & POSITION | 6 ENHANCE SLIDE SHOW | **7 DISPLAY SLIDES**

After you begin Slide Show view, you can move forward or backward through the slides. PowerPoint allows you to advance through the slides manually or automatically. During a slide show, each slide in the presentation shows on the screen, one slide at a time. Each time you click, the next slide appears. The following steps move manually through the slides. *Why? You can control the length of time each slide is displayed and change the preset order if you need to review a slide already shown or jump ahead to another slide designed to display later in the presentation.*

①

- Click each slide until Slide 5 (Register for Family Programs) is displayed (Figure 1–75).

Heather Wilson Smith/ StockSnap.io

Figure 1–75

- Click Slide 5 so that the black slide appears with a message announcing the end of the slide show (Figure 1–76).

I see a small toolbar in the lower-left corner of my slide. What is this toolbar?

You may see the Slide Show toolbar when you begin running a slide show and then click a slide or move the pointer. The buttons on this toolbar allow you to navigate to the next slide or the previous slide, to mark up the current slide, or to change the current display. If you do not see the toolbar, hover the mouse near the lower-left corner of the screen.

Figure 1–76

- Click the black slide to return to Normal view in the PowerPoint window.

Other Ways

1. Press PAGE DOWN to advance one slide at a time, or press PAGE UP to go back one slide at a time

2. Press RIGHT ARROW or DOWN ARROW to advance one slide at a time, or press LEFT ARROW or UP ARROW to go back one slide at a time

3. If Slide Show toolbar is displayed, click Next Slide or Previous Slide button on toolbar

To Save and Print the Presentation

It is a good practice to save a presentation before printing it, in the event you experience difficulties printing. For a detailed example of the procedure summarized below for saving and printing a presentation, refer to the Office and Windows module at the beginning of this book.

1 Save the presentation again on the same storage location with the same file name.

2 Print the presentation.

Do I have to wait until my presentation is complete to print it?

No, you can print a presentation at any time while you are creating it.

3 Because the project now is complete, you can exit PowerPoint.

BTW
Conserving Ink and Toner
If you want to conserve ink or toner, you can instruct PowerPoint to print draft quality documents by clicking File on the ribbon to open the Backstage view, clicking the Options tab in the Backstage view to display the PowerPoint Options dialog box, clicking Advanced in the left pane (PowerPoint Options dialog box), scrolling to the Print area in the right pane, not placing a check mark in the High quality check box, and then clicking the OK button. Then, use the Backstage view to print the document as usual.

BTW
Distributing a Document
Instead of printing and distributing a hard copy of a document, you can distribute the document electronically. Options include sending the document via email; posting it on cloud storage (such as OneDrive) and sharing the file with others; posting it on social media, a blog, or other website; and sharing a link associated with an online location of the document. You also can create and share a PDF or XPS image of the document, so that users can view the file in Acrobat Reader or XPS Viewer instead of in PowerPoint.

Summary

In this module, you learned how to use PowerPoint to create and enhance a presentation. Topics covered included applying and changing a document theme and variant, creating a title slide and text slides with a bulleted list, inserting pictures and then resizing and moving them on a slide, formatting and editing text, adding a slide transition, and viewing the presentation in Slide Show view.

CONSIDER THIS: PLAN AHEAD

What decisions will you need to make when creating your next presentation?
Use these guidelines as you complete the assignments in this module and create your own slide show decks outside of this class.

1. Determine the content you want to include on your slides.

2. Determine which theme and variant are appropriate.

3. Identify the slide layouts that best communicate your message.

4. Format various text elements to emphasize important points.

    a) Select appropriate font sizes.

    b) Emphasize important words with bold or italic type and color.

5. Locate graphical elements, such as pictures, that reinforce your message.

    a) Size and position them aesthetically on slides.

6. Determine a storage location for the presentation.

7. Determine the best method for distributing the presentation.

Apply Your Knowledge

Reinforce the skills and apply the concepts you learned in this module.

Modifying Character Formats and Paragraph Levels and Moving an Illustration

Note: To complete this assignment, you will be required to use the Data Files. Please contact your instructor for information about accessing the Data Files.

Instructions: Run PowerPoint. Open the presentation called Apply 1-1 Email Fraud, which is located in the Data Files.

The two slides in the presentation discuss phishing, which is a scam in which a perpetrator attempts to obtain an individual's personal and/or financial information. The document you open is an unformatted presentation. You are to modify the document theme, indent the paragraphs, resize and move the image, and format the text so the slides look like Figure 1–77.

Perform the following tasks:

1. Change the document theme to Droplet. Select the blue (third) variant.

2. On the title slide, use your name in place of Student Name and bold and italicize your name.

3. If requested by your instructor, change your first name to your grandmother's first name on the title slide.

4. Increase the title text font size to 60 point and then bold this text. Resize and position the illustration using the Smart Guides to align the image with the bottom of the subtitle placeholder and the right edge of the placeholders, as shown in Figure 1–77a.

5. On Slide 2, increase the indent of the second, third, and fourth paragraphs to second-level paragraphs. Then combine paragraphs six and seven (Work related and Personal) to read, **Work and personal messages can contain threats**, as shown in Figure 1–77b. Increase the indent of this paragraph to second level.

(a) Slide 1 (Title Slide with a Picture)

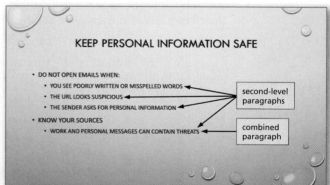

(b) Slide 2 (Multilevel Bulleted List)

Figure 1–77

6. Apply the Ripple transition in the Exciting category to both slides. Change the duration to 3.00 seconds. Click the 'Start From Beginning' button to start the show from the first slide. Then click to display each slide and again to end the presentation.

Continued >

Apply Your Knowledge *continued*

7. Save the presentation using the file name, Apply 1-1 Phishing.

8. Submit the revised document in the format specified by your instructor.

9. ✳ In Step 5 you combined two paragraphs and added text. How did this action improve the slide content?

Extend Your Knowledge

Extend the skills you learned in this module and experiment with new skills. You may need to use Help to complete the assignment.

Changing Slide Theme, Layout, and Text

Note: To complete this assignment, you will be required to use the Data Files. Please contact your instructor for information about accessing the Data Files.

Instructions: Run PowerPoint. Open the presentation called Extend 1-1 Waterfalls, which is located in the Data Files. Slide 1 is shown in Figure 1-78. You are aware that geologists have classified many types of waterfalls, including cascade and cataract, and the three slides in this file are part of a presentation you are developing for your geology class on this topic. Choose a theme, format the slides, and create a closing slide.

Perform the following tasks:

1. Change the document theme to Slice and the variant to green.

2. On Slide 1, format the text using techniques you learned in this module, such as changing the font size and color and bolding and italicizing words.

3. Replace the text, Student Name, with your name. In addition, delete the bullet preceding your name because, in most cases, a bullet is displayed as the first character in a list consisting of several paragraphs, not just one line of text. To delete the bullet, position the insertion point in the paragraph and then click the Bullets button (Home tab | Paragraph group).

4. Resize the picture and move it to an appropriate area on the slide.

5. On Slide 2, add bullets to the three paragraphs. To add bullets, select the paragraphs and then click the Bullets button (Home tab | Paragraph group). Insert the picture called Cascade, which is located in the Data Files, resize it, and then move it to an appropriate area on the slide.

6. On Slide 3, add bullets to the two paragraphs. Insert the picture called Cataract, which is located in the Data Files, resize it, and then move it to an appropriate area on the slide.

7. Create a closing slide using the title slide as a guide. Change the subtitle text to Natural Wonders and then underline this text. Insert the two waterfall pictures, Cascade and Cataract, and then size and move all three pictures to appropriate places on the slide.

change theme and variant

resize and move picture

delete bullet

substitute your name

format title text

WATERFALL CLASSIFICATIONS WORLDWIDE

Student Name

Jan Erik Waider/StockSnap.io

Figure 1–78

8. Apply the Drape transition in the Exciting category to all slides and then change the duration for Slide 1 to 3.50 seconds. Click the 'Start From Beginning' button to start the show from the first slide. Then click to display each slide and again to end the presentation.

9. Save the presentation using the file name, Extend 1-1 Natural Wonders.

10. Submit the revised document in the format specified by your instructor.

11. If requested by your instructor, replace your last name on Slide 1 with the name of your hometown.

12. ✷ How did you determine the appropriate size and location of the three pictures on the closing slide?

Expand Your World

Create a solution that uses cloud and web technologies by learning and investigating on your own from general guidance.

Modifying and Exporting a Presentation

Note: To complete this assignment, you will be required to use the Data Files. Please contact your instructor for information about accessing the Data Files.

Instructions: Run PowerPoint. Open the presentation called Expand 1-1 Youth Group, which is located in the Data Files. The local youth group in your community is sponsoring a talent show, and you are part of a committee to publicize the event. You want to share the one slide you developed with some of the participants, so you have decided to store the file on OneDrive. You are going to modify the slide you have created, shown in Figure 1–79, and save it to OneDrive.

Perform the following tasks:

1. Insert the pictures called Musician and Singers, which are located in the Data Files. Size and then move them to the areas indicated in Figure 1–79. Use the guides to help you position the pictures.

2. If requested to do so by your instructor, change the words, Phoenix, AZ, to the town and state where you were born.

3. Save the presentation using the file name, Expand 1-1 Talent Show.

4. Export the file to your OneDrive account.

5. Submit the assignment in the format specified by your instructor.

6. ✷ When would you save one of your files for school or your job to OneDrive? Do you think using OneDrive enhances collaboration efforts? Why?

Figure 1–79

In the Labs

Design, create, modify, and/or use a presentation following the guidelines, concepts, and skills presented in this module. Labs 1 and 2, which increase in difficulty, require you to create solutions based on what you learned in the module; Lab 3 requires you to apply your creative thinking and problem-solving skills to design and implement a solution.

Lab 1: **Creating a Presentation with Pictures**

Note: To complete this assignment, you will be required to use the Data Files. Please contact your instructor for information about accessing the Data Files.

Problem: Your friend, Bobby, has expanded her Bake Shoppe and wants to publicize new offerings. She has asked you to help her create a presentation that showcases pastries and breads. You prepare the PowerPoint presentation shown in Figure 1–80.

Perform the following tasks:

1. Run PowerPoint. Create a new presentation using the Retrospect document theme. Do not change the variant.
2. Using Figure 1–80a, create the title slide. Type the title text and subtitle text shown in the figure. Decrease the font size of the title text to 60 point and bold this text. Change the font color to Orange, Accent 1 (in Theme Colors row).

(a) Slide 1 (Title Slide)

(b) Slide 2

(c) Slide 3

(d) Slide 4 (Closing Slide)

Figure 1–80

3. On Slide 1, insert the illustration called Bakery, which is located in the Data Files. Move the illustration up to the top of the slide and then use the Smart Guides to align its left and right edges with the sides of the text placeholders. Use the lower-center sizing handle to resize this illustration so that it fits above the title text.

4. Replace the words, Anytown, USA, with your hometown city and state.

5. Create Slide 2 using the Title Only layout. Type the title text, Fresh Daily, bold this text, and then change the font color to Orange, Accent 1 (in Theme Colors row). Insert the picture called Doughnut, which is located in the Data Files, resize it as shown in Figure 1–80b, and then move it to the left side of the slide. Insert the picture called Muffin, which is located in the Data Files, and then resize and move it to the right side of the slide, as shown in the figure.

6. Using Figure 1–80c as a guide, create Slide 3 using the Picture with Caption layout. Insert the picture called Bread, which is located in the Data Files. Type the title text, Artisan Breads, increase the font size to 48 point, and then bold this text. Type `All natural ingredients` as the subtitle text, press the Tab key four times, and then type `No preservatives` in the placeholder. Increase this subtitle text size to 28 point.

7. Create a closing slide by duplicating Slide 1. Change the subtitle text using Figure 1–80d as a guide.

8. Apply the Clock transition in the Exciting category to all slides. Change the duration to 2.00 seconds.

9. Click the 'Start From Beginning' button to start the show from the first slide. Then click to display each slide and again to end the presentation.

10. Save the presentation using the file name, Lab 1-1 Bake. Submit the document in the format specified by your instructor.

11. ✳ What is the significance of changing the font color on Slides 1 and 2 but not Slide 3?

Lab 2: Creating a Presentation with Bulleted Lists and Pictures

Note: To complete this assignment, you will be required to use the Data Files. Please contact your instructor for information about accessing the Data Files.

Problem: The history museum in your town is a popular destination for residents, tourists, and researchers. Among the more popular exhibits are the dinosaurs, mummies, and antiques. You want to highlight these three attractions, so you create the presentation shown in Figure 1–81.

Perform the following tasks:

1. Run PowerPoint. Create a new presentation using the Quotable document theme.

2. Using Figure 1–81, create the title slide. Use your name in place of Student Name.

3. If requested by your instructor, substitute the name of your hometown in place of your last name.

4. On Slide 1 (Figure 1–81a), italicize the text, History Museum. Increase the font size of the subtitle text, Popular Exhibits, to 32 point and the font size of your name to 24 point. Change the font color of the title text to Dark Blue (in Standard Colors row).

5. Create the three slides shown in Figures 1-81b, 1-81c, and 1-81d. Use the Comparison layout for Slide 2, the Section Header layout for Slide 3, and the Two Content layout for Slide 4. Change the color of the title text on these three text slides to Dark Blue. Increase the font size of the subtitle text on Slides 2 and 3 to 24 point.

Continued >

In the Labs *continued*

(a) Slide 1 (Title Slide)

(b) Slide 2

(c) Slide 3

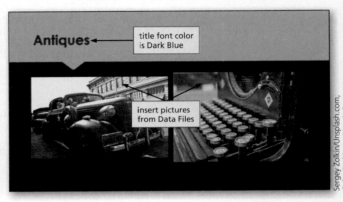

(d) Slide 4

Figure 1–81

6. Add the pictures shown in Figures 1-81a through 1-81d using the guides on Slides 1 and 3 to help align them. The pictures to be inserted are called Museum Icon, Girls in Museum, T-rex Skeleton, T-rex 3D, Pharaoh, Car, and Typewriter, and they are located in the Data Files. Zoom the slides and then resize the pictures when necessary.

7. Apply the Gallery transition in the Exciting category to all slides. Change the duration to 2.25 seconds.

8. Click the 'Start From Beginning' button to start the show from the first slide. Then click to display each slide and again to end the presentation.

9. Save the presentation using the file name, Lab 1-2 History Museum.

10. Submit the revised document in the format specified by your instructor.

11. ✴ How does changing the title text font color to Dark Blue complement the theme color?

Lab 3: **Consider This: Your Turn**

Design and Create a Presentation about the Building Construction Technology Program

Note: To complete this assignment, you will be required to use the Data Files. Please contact your instructor for information about accessing the Data Files.

Part 1: Your school is expanding the courses offered in the Building Construction Technology Program, and the department chair has asked you to help promote the program. He informs you that students obtain hands-on experience using the latest methods of construction, and they receive instruction in the classroom and in the lab. The capstone courses are held in the field, where students build an actual energy-efficient home from the ground up. The skills learned and experience gained prepare students for careers in carpentry, masonry, plumbing, electrical, project supervision, cost estimating, and drafting. Use the concepts and techniques presented in this module to prepare a presentation with a minimum of four slides that showcase the Building Construction Technology program. Select a suitable theme, and include a title slide, bulleted list, closing slide, and transition. The presentation should contain pictures and illustrations resized appropriately. Several pictures are available in the Data Files: Backhoe, Concrete, Hammer, Hard Hat, Measuring Tape, Nail, and Tool Belt. Review and revise your presentation as needed. Submit your assignment in the format specified by your instructor.

Part 2: ✺ You made several decisions while creating the presentation in this assignment: what theme to use, where to place text, how to format the text (font, font size, paragraph alignment, bulleted paragraphs, italics, bold, color). You decided which images to use and where to position them. You also chose a transition. What was the rationale behind each of these decisions? When you reviewed the slides, what further revisions did you make and why? Where would you recommend showing this slide show?

2 | Enhancing a Presentation with Pictures, Shapes, and WordArt

Objectives

You will have mastered the material in this module when you can:

- Search for and download an online theme
- Insert and format pictures
- Insert and size a shape
- Apply effects to a shape
- Add text to a shape

- Change the text font
- Insert a picture to create a background
- Insert and format WordArt
- Format slide backgrounds
- Find and replace text and check spelling
- Add and print speaker notes

Introduction

In our visually oriented culture, audience members enjoy viewing effective graphics. Whether reading a document or viewing a PowerPoint presentation, people increasingly want to see photographs, artwork, graphics, and a variety of typefaces. Researchers have known for decades that documents with visual elements are more effective than those that consist of only text because the illustrations motivate audiences to study the material. People remember at least one-third more information when the document they are seeing or reading contains visual elements. These graphics help clarify and emphasize details, so they appeal to audience members with differing backgrounds, reading levels, attention spans, and motivations.

Project — Presentation with Pictures, Shapes, and WordArt

The project in this module focuses on publicizing a basketball camp held each summer for children living in the park district. Professionals teach boys and girls a variety of offensive and defensive skills during this fun and educational event. The presentation shown in Figure 2–1 follows graphical guidelines and has a variety of illustrations and visual elements that are colorful and appealing to child athletes and their parents. For example, the pictures have particular shapes and effects. The enhanced type has a style that blends well with the formatted background and illustrations. Pictures and type are formatted using picture styles and WordArt, which give the presentation a professional look. You plan to present the material during winter and spring sports tournaments, so you want to add notes explaining concepts you will be discussing during these events.

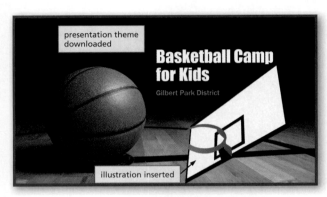

(a) Slide 1 (Title Slide)

(b) Slide 2 (Formatted Picture)

(c) Slide 3 (Shapes Inserted and Formatted)

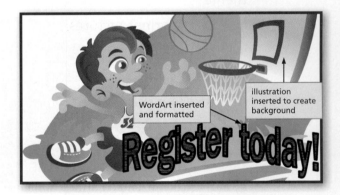

(d) Slide 4 (Picture Background)

Figure 2–1

For an introduction to Windows and instructions about how to perform basic Windows tasks, read the Office and Windows module at the beginning of this book, where you can learn how to resize windows, change screen resolution, create folders, move and rename files, use Windows Help, and much more.

In this module, you will learn how to create the slides shown in Figure 2–1. The following roadmap identifies general activities you will perform as you progress through this module:

1. DOWNLOAD a theme and SELECT SLIDES for the presentation.
2. INSERT and FORMAT PICTURES for the slides.
3. INSERT and FORMAT SHAPES on one slide.
4. FORMAT SLIDE BACKGROUNDS with a gradient, texture, and picture fill.
5. INSERT and FORMAT WORDART by changing the shape, fill, and outline.
6. REVIEW, REVISE, and PRINT SLIDES by finding a synonym, checking spelling, and adding speaker notes.

Downloading a Theme and Editing Slides

In Module 1, you selected a theme and then typed the content for the title and text slides. In this module, you will type the slide content for the title and text slides, select a background, insert and format pictures and shapes, and then insert and format WordArt. To begin creating the four slides in this presentation, you will download a theme, delete unneeded slides in this downloaded presentation, and then enter text in three of the four slides.

To Search for and Download an Online Theme

1 DOWNLOAD & SELECT SLIDES | 2 INSERT & FORMAT PICTURES | 3 INSERT & FORMAT SHAPES
4 FORMAT SLIDE BACKGROUNDS | 5 INSERT & FORMAT WORDART | 6 REVIEW, REVISE, & PRINT SLIDES

PowerPoint displays many themes that are varied and appealing and give you an excellent start at designing a presentation. At times, however, you may have a specific topic and design concept and could use some assistance in starting to develop the presentation. Microsoft offers hundreds of predesigned themes and templates that could provide you with an excellent starting point. ***Why?*** *You can search for one of these ready-made presentations, or you can browse one of the predefined categories, such as business and education. The themes and templates can save you time and help you develop content.* The following steps search for a theme with a basketball concept.

- Run PowerPoint and then type **basketball** in the 'Search for online templates and themes' box (Figure 2–2).

Q&A Why are my theme thumbnails displaying in a different order?
The order changes as you choose themes for presentations. In addition, Microsoft occasionally adds and modifies the themes, so the order may change.

Can I choose one of the keywords listed below the 'Search for online templates and themes' box?
Yes. Click one of the terms in the Suggested searches list to display a variety of templates and themes relating to those topics.

Figure 2–2

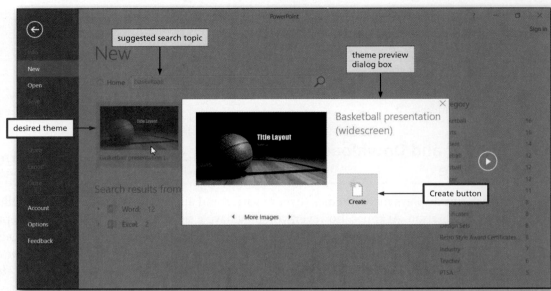

- Click the Start searching button (the magnifying glass) or press the ENTER key to search for and display all themes with the keyword, basketball.
- Click the 'Basketball presentation (widescreen)' theme to display a theme preview dialog box with a thumbnail view of the theme (Figure 2–3).

Figure 2–3

Q&A Can I see previews of the slides in this theme?
Yes. Click the right or left arrows beside the words, More Images, below the thumbnail. On some devices, a preview of all slides starts automatically after you tap the theme.

- Click the Create button to download the theme and open a presentation with that theme in PowerPoint.

To Delete a Slide

1 DOWNLOAD & SELECT SLIDES | 2 INSERT & FORMAT PICTURES | 3 INSERT & FORMAT SHAPES
4 FORMAT SLIDE BACKGROUNDS | 5 INSERT & FORMAT WORDART | 6 REVIEW, REVISE, & PRINT SLIDES

The downloaded theme has nine slides with a variety of layouts. You will use four different layouts in your Basketball Camp presentation, so you can delete the slides you downloaded that you will not need. *Why? Deleting the extra slides now helps reduce clutter and helps you focus on the layouts you will use.* The following steps delete the extra slides.

- Click the Slide 3 thumbnail in the Slides tab to select this slide.
- Press and hold the SHIFT key, scroll down, and then click the thumbnail for Slide 7 to select slides 3 through 7 (Figure 2–4).

Q&A Do I need to select consecutive slides?
No. You can select an individual slide to delete. You also can select nonconsecutive slides by pressing and holding the CTRL key down and then clicking the thumbnails of the slides you want to delete.

Why did I press and hold down the SHIFT key instead of the CTRL key?
Holding down the SHIFT key selects consecutive slides between the first and last selected slides, whereas holding the CTRL key selects only the slides you click.

Figure 2–4

• Right-click any selected slide to display the shortcut menu (Figure 2–5).

Figure 2–5

• Click Delete Slide to delete the selected slides from the presentation (Figure 2–6).

Figure 2–6

Other Ways	
1. Select slide(s), press DELETE	2. Select slide(s), press BACKSPACE

To Create a Title Slide

Recall from Module 1 that the title slide introduces the presentation to the audience. In addition to introducing the presentation, this project uses the title slide to capture the audience's attention by using title text and an illustration. *Why? The presentation focuses on basketball, so the picture of a ball and court on the title slide can be supplemented with a backboard illustration that you will insert later on this slide.* The following steps create the slide show's title slide.

 Display Slide 1, select the text in the title text placeholder, and then type **Basketball Camp for Kids** as the title text.

◁ | Why do I have to select the text in the placeholder before typing?
Q&A | This downloaded template includes text in some of the placeholders that must be replaced with your own text.

For an introduction to Office and instructions about how to perform basic tasks in Office apps, read the Office and Windows module at the beginning of this book, where you can learn how to run an application, use the ribbon, save a file, open a file, print a file, exit an application, use Help, and much more.

BTW
PowerPoint Screen Resolution
If you are using a computer or mobile device to step through the project in this module and you want your screens to match the figures in this book, you should change your screen's resolution to 1366 x 768. For information about how to change a computer's resolution, refer to the Office and Windows module at the beginning of this book.

2 Click the subtitle text placeholder, select the text in that placeholder, and then type **Gilbert Park District** as the subtitle text (Figure 2–7).

- If requested by your instructor, type the name of the city or county in which you were born instead of the word, Gilbert.

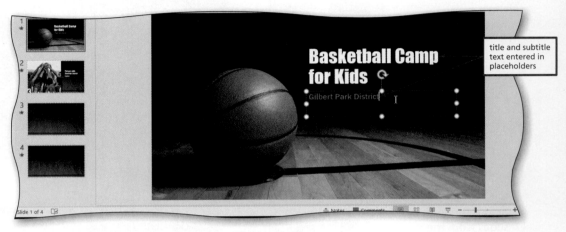

Figure 2–7

BTW

Touch Screen Differences
The Office and Windows interfaces may vary if you are using a touch screen. For this reason, you might notice that the function or appearance of your touch screen differs slightly from this module's presentation.

To Create the First Text Slide

The first text slide you create in Module 2 emphasizes two benefits of attending the weekly camp: receiving professional instruction and developing friendships. The following steps create the Slide 2 text slide using the Picture with Caption layout.

1 Display Slide 2, select the text in the title text placeholder, and then type **Learn from pros and make acquaintances** in the placeholder.

2 Select the text in the caption placeholder and then type **Classes meet weekday mornings throughout the summer** in this placeholder (Figure 2–8).

BTW

The Ribbon and Screen Resolution
PowerPoint may change how the groups and buttons within the groups appear on the ribbon, depending on the computer or mobile device's screen resolution. Thus, your ribbon may look different from the ones in this book if you are using a screen resolution other than 1366 × 768.

Figure 2–8

To Create the Second Text Slide

The second text slide you create shows three skills that will be taught: ball handling, offensive moves, and defensive strategies. The following steps add a title to Slide 3, which uses the Title Only layout, and save the presentation.

1 Display Slide 3 and then type `You will lern…` in the title text placeholder. The word, lern, is misspelled intentionally; the red wavy line indicates the misspelling (Figure 2-9).

2 Save the presentation using `Basketball Camp` as the file name.

Figure 2–9

Inserting and Formatting Pictures in a Presentation

With the text entered in three of the four slides, the next step is to insert pictures into Slides 1 and 2 and then format the pictures. These graphical images draw the viewers' eyes to the slides and help them retain the information presented.

In the following pages, you will perform these tasks:

1. Insert an illustration into Slide 1.
2. Resize the illustration.
3. Change the Slide 2 photo.
4. Change the photo's brightness and contrast.
5. Change the photo's style and effect.
6. Add and modify the photo's border.

BTW

Organizing Files and Folders
You should organize and store files in folders so that you easily can find the files later. For example, if you are taking an introductory technology class called CIS 101, a good practice would be to save all PowerPoint files in a PowerPoint folder in a CIS 101 folder. For a discussion of folders and detailed examples of creating folders, refer to the Office and Windows module at the beginning of this book.

To Insert a Picture into a Slide without a Content Placeholder

1 DOWNLOAD & SELECT SLIDES | 2 INSERT & FORMAT PICTURES | 3 INSERT & FORMAT SHAPES
4 FORMAT SLIDE BACKGROUNDS | 5 INSERT & FORMAT WORDART | 6 REVIEW, REVISE, & PRINT SLIDES

In Module 1, you inserted photos and an illustration into slides without a content placeholder. *Why? Some slide layouts do not have a content placeholder, so you must insert and move the pictures to appropriate locations on the slide.* The illustration for Slide 1 is available in the Data Files. Contact your instructor if you need the pictures used in the following steps. The instructions in this module show the required files in the Module 02 folder in the Data Files folder. The following steps insert an illustration into the title slide.

1

- Display Slide 1 and then click Insert on the ribbon to display the Insert tab.
- Click the Pictures button (Insert tab | Images group) to display the Insert Picture dialog box.

2

- If necessary, navigate to the PowerPoint Module 02 folder and then click Backboard to select the file name (Figure 2–10).

 What if Backboard is not displayed in the navigation pane?
Drag the navigation pane scroll bar (Insert Picture dialog box) until Backboard appears. If this file is not in the list, see your instructor.

Why do I see just file names and not thumbnails of the pictures in my folder?
Your view is different from the view shown in Figure 2–10.

Figure 2–10

3

- Click the Insert button (Insert Picture dialog box) to insert the illustration into Slide 1.
- Drag the upper-left sizing handle diagonally toward the lower-right corner of the slide until the crosshair is positioned approximately as shown in Figure 2–11.

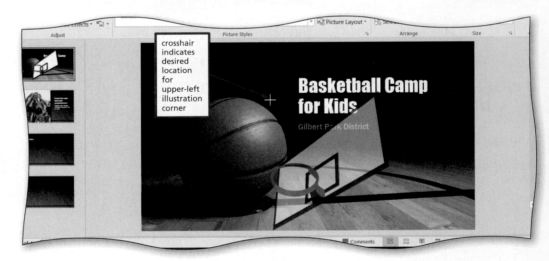

Figure 2–11

4

- Release to resize the illustration.
- Drag the illustration to the right until the vertical Smart Guide is displayed near the right side of the slide, as shown in Figure 2–12, and then release.

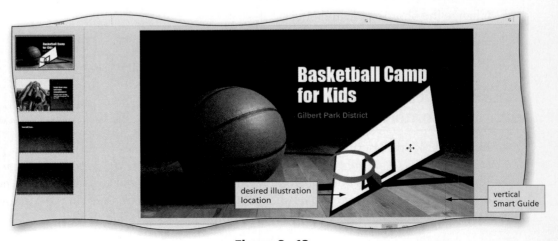

Figure 2–12

To Change a Picture

Why? *The downloaded theme included the photo of several team members on Slide 2. You need to change the photo because those players are wearing green uniforms, which are not the clothes your camp participants will wear.* The next task in the presentation is to change the default picture on Slide 2 to one of the pictures in the Data Files. The following steps change the Slide 2 photo to the Teamwork photo, which, in this example, is located in the Module 02 folder in the Data Files folder.

 1

- Display Slide 2 and then right-click the picture to display the shortcut menu (Figure 2–13).

Q&A Why are the Style and Crop buttons displayed near the shortcut menu on my screen?
These two buttons display either above or below the shortcut menu depending upon where you right-click on the screen.

Figure 2–13

 2

- Click Change Picture to display the Insert Pictures dialog box (Figure 2–14).

Figure 2–14

3

- Click the Browse button in the 'From a file' area to display the Insert Picture dialog box.
- If necessary, navigate to the PowerPoint Module 02 folder, scroll down, and then click Teamwork to select the file (Figure 2–15).

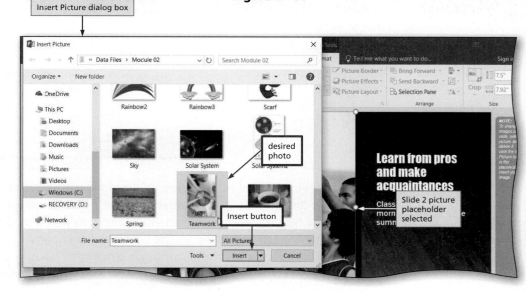

Figure 2–15

4

- Click the Insert button (Insert Picture dialog box) to insert the photo into the Slide 2 picture placeholder.
- Click the gray text box on the right side of the slide to select this object (Figure 2–16).

Q&A Why should I select and then delete this gray text box?
When you delete the box, the slide will expand to the right to fill that space and you will be able to view a larger slide image.

Figure 2–16

5

- Press the DELETE key to delete this text box.

Q&A Could I have followed the directions in the gray box on the right to change the image?
Yes, either method works. You also could have selected the gray box and then clicked the Cut button (Home tab | Clipboard group) button to delete the text box.

Other Ways

1. Click Change Picture button (Picture Tools Format tab | Adjust group)

To Correct a Picture

1 DOWNLOAD & SELECT SLIDES | 2 INSERT & FORMAT PICTURES | 3 INSERT & FORMAT SHAPES
4 FORMAT SLIDE BACKGROUNDS | 5 INSERT & FORMAT WORDART | 6 REVIEW, REVISE, & PRINT SLIDES

A photo's color intensity can be modified by changing the brightness and contrast. **Brightness** determines the overall lightness or darkness of the entire image, whereas **contrast** is the difference between the darkest and lightest areas of the image. The brightness and contrast are changed in predefined percentage increments. The following step decreases the brightness and increases the contrast. *Why? Altering the photo's brightness will coordinate with the dark colors on the basketball court while increasing the contrast will sharpen the image. It is important for the audience to recognize the basketball and the players' overlapping hands but not focus on each aspect of this photo.*

1

- Select the Teamwork photo on Slide 2 and then click Format on the ribbon to display the Picture Tools Format tab.

- Click the Corrections button (Picture Tools Format tab | Adjust group) to display the Corrections gallery.

- Scroll down to display the last row of images in the Corrections gallery and then point to Brightness: –20% Contrast: +40% (second picture in last Brightness/Contrast row) to display a live preview of these corrections on the picture (Figure 2–17).

Figure 2–17

Q&A   Can I use live preview on a touch screen?
Live preview is not available on a touch screen.

Why is a gray border surrounding the pictures in the center of the Sharpen/Soften and Brightness/Contrast areas of the gallery?
The image on Slide 2 currently has normal sharpness, brightness, and contrast (0%), which is represented by these center images in the gallery.

Experiment

- Point to various pictures in the Brightness/Contrast area and watch the brightness and contrast change on the picture in Slide 2.

- Click Brightness: –20% Contrast: +40% to apply this correction to the Teamwork photo.

Q&A   How can I remove all effects from the picture?
Click the Reset Picture button (Picture Tools Format tab | Adjust group).

Other Ways

1. Click Picture Corrections Options (Corrections gallery), move Brightness or Contrast sliders or enter number in box next to slider (Format Picture pane)

To Apply a Picture Style

1 DOWNLOAD & SELECT SLIDES | 2 INSERT & FORMAT PICTURES | 3 INSERT & FORMAT SHAPES
4 FORMAT SLIDE BACKGROUNDS | 5 INSERT & FORMAT WORDART | 6 REVIEW, REVISE, & PRINT SLIDES

A **style** is a named group of formatting characteristics. The picture on Slide 2 emphasizes the concept of teamwork in this sport, and you can increase its visual appeal by applying a style. *Why? PowerPoint provides more than 25 picture styles that enable you easily to change a picture's look to a more visually appealing style, including a variety of shapes, angles, borders, and reflections.* You want to use a style that applies a shadow to the Teamwork photo. The following steps apply a picture style to the Slide 2 photo.

- With the Slide 2 picture selected and the Picture Tools Format tab displaying, click the More button in the Picture Styles gallery (Picture Tools Format tab | Picture Styles group) (shown in Figure 2–17) to expand the gallery.
- Point to Bevel Rectangle in the Picture Styles gallery (last style in third row) to display a live preview of that style applied to the picture in the document (Figure 2–18).

Figure 2–18

 Experiment

- Point to various picture styles in the Picture Styles gallery and watch the style of the picture change in the document window.

2

- Click Bevel Rectangle in the Picture Styles gallery to apply the style to the selected picture.

To Add a Picture Border

1 DOWNLOAD & SELECT SLIDES | **2 INSERT & FORMAT PICTURES** | **3 INSERT & FORMAT SHAPES**
4 FORMAT SLIDE BACKGROUNDS | 5 INSERT & FORMAT WORDART | 6 REVIEW, REVISE, & PRINT SLIDES

The next step is to add a border to the Slide 2 picture. *Why? Some picture styles do not have a border; others, such as the Bevel Rectangle style you applied to this picture, do have this edging. This border is small, and you want a larger edge around the photo to draw attention to the graphic.* The following steps add a border to the Teamwork picture.

- With the Slide 2 picture still selected, click the Picture Border arrow (Picture Tools Format tab | Picture Styles group) to display the Picture Border gallery.

Q&A | What if the Picture Tools Format tab no longer is displayed on my ribbon?
Click the picture to display the Picture Tools Format tab.

2

- Point to Weight on the Picture Border gallery to display the Weight gallery.

- Point to 6 pt to display a live preview of this line weight on the picture (Figure 2–19).

Q&A Can I make the line width more than 6 pt?
Yes. Click More Lines, Click Solid line in the Line section of the Format Picture pane, and then increase the amount in the Width box.

Figure 2–19

 Experiment

- Point to various line weights in the Weight gallery and watch the line thickness change.

3

- Click 6 pt to add this line weight to the picture.

To Change a Picture Border Color

1 DOWNLOAD & SELECT SLIDES | 2 INSERT & FORMAT PICTURES | 3 INSERT & FORMAT SHAPES
4 FORMAT SLIDE BACKGROUNDS | 5 INSERT & FORMAT WORDART | 6 REVIEW, REVISE, & PRINT SLIDES

The default color for the border you added to the Slide 2 picture is white, but you will change the border color to black. *Why? The black color coordinates with other elements on the slide, especially the lines on the basketball and the court.* The following steps change the Slide 2 picture border color.

1

- With the Slide 2 photo still selected, click the Picture Border arrow (Picture Tools Format tab | Picture Styles group) to display the Picture Border gallery again.

2

- Point to Black, Background 1 (first color in first row) in the Picture Border gallery to display a live preview of that border color on the picture (Figure 2–20).

Figure 2–20

Experiment

- Point to various colors in the Picture Border gallery and watch the border on the picture change in the slide.

- Click Black, Background 1 in the Picture Border gallery to change the picture border color.

To Apply Picture Effects

1 DOWNLOAD & SELECT SLIDES | 2 INSERT & FORMAT PICTURES | 3 INSERT & FORMAT SHAPES
4 FORMAT SLIDE BACKGROUNDS | 5 INSERT & FORMAT WORDART | 6 REVIEW, REVISE, & PRINT SLIDES

Why? Picture effects allow you to further customize a picture. PowerPoint provides a variety of picture effects, including shadows, reflections, glow, soft edges, bevel, and 3-D rotation. The difference between the effects and the styles is that each effect has several options, providing you with more control over the exact look of the image.

In this presentation, the photo on Slide 2 has a brown glow effect and a bevel applied to its edges. The following steps apply picture effects to the selected picture.

1

- With the Slide 2 picture still selected, click the Picture Effects button (Picture Tools Format tab | Picture Styles group) to display the Picture Effects menu.

Q&A What if the Picture Tools Format tab no longer is displayed on my ribbon?
Click the picture to display the Picture Tools Format tab.

- Point to Glow on the Picture Effects menu to display the Glow gallery.

- Point to Brown, 18 pt glow, Accent color 3 in the Glow Variations area (third glow in last row) to display a live preview of the selected glow effect applied to the picture in the document window (Figure 2–21).

Figure 2–21

 Experiment

- Point to various glow effects in the Glow gallery and watch the picture change in the document window.

- Click Brown, 18 pt glow, Accent color 3 in the Glow gallery to apply the selected picture effect.

- Click the Picture Effects button (Picture Tools Format tab | Picture Styles group) to display the Picture Effects menu again.
- Point to Bevel on the Picture Effects menu to display the Bevel gallery.
- Point to Angle (first bevel in second Bevel row) to display a live preview of the selected bevel effect applied to the Slide 2 picture (Figure 2–22).

Figure 2–22

 Experiment

- Point to various bevel effects in the Bevel gallery and watch the picture change in the slide.

4

- Click Angle in the Bevel gallery to apply the selected picture effect.

Other Ways

1. Right-click picture, click Format Picture on shortcut menu, select desired options (Format Picture pane), click Close button

2. Click Format Shape pane launcher (Picture Tools Format tab | Picture Styles group), select desired options (Format Picture pane), click Close button

Break Point: If you wish to take a break, this is a good place to do so. Be sure to save the Basketball Camp file again and then you can exit PowerPoint. To resume at a later time, run PowerPoint, open the file called Basketball Camp, and continue following the steps from this location forward.

Inserting and Formatting a Shape

One method of getting the audience's attention and reinforcing the major concepts being presented is to have graphical elements on the slide. PowerPoint provides a wide variety of predefined shapes that can add visual interest to a slide. Shape elements include lines, basic geometrical shapes, arrows, equation shapes, flowchart symbols, stars, banners, and callouts. After adding a shape to a slide, you can change its default characteristics by adding text, bullets, numbers, and styles. You also can combine multiple shapes to create a more complex graphic.

The predefined shapes are found in the Shapes gallery. This collection is found on the Home tab | Drawing group and the Insert tab | Illustrations group. Once you have inserted and selected a shape, the Drawing Tools Format tab is displayed, and the Shapes gallery also is displayed in the Insert Shapes group.

BTW

Inserting Special Characters
Along with adding shapes to a slide, you can insert characters not found on your keyboard, such as the section sign (§), the copyright sign (©), and Greek capital letters (e.g., Δ, Ω, and ß). To insert these characters, click the Insert tab and then click the Symbol button (Insert tab | Symbols group). When the Symbol dialog box is displayed, you can use the same font you currently are using in your presentation, or you can select another font. The Webdings, Wingdings, Wingdings 2, and Wingdings 3 fonts have a variety of symbols.

Slide 3 in this presentation is enhanced in a variety of ways. First, an oval, an arrow, and a pentagon shape are inserted on the slide and formatted. Then, text is added to the oval and pentagon and formatted. The pentagon is copied, and the text is modified in this new shape. Finally, the arrow shape is duplicated twice and moved into position.

To Add a Shape

1 DOWNLOAD & SELECT SLIDES | 2 INSERT & FORMAT PICTURES | 3 INSERT & FORMAT SHAPES

4 FORMAT SLIDE BACKGROUNDS | 5 INSERT & FORMAT WORDART | 6 REVIEW, REVISE, & PRINT SLIDES

Many of the shapes included in the Shapes gallery can direct the viewer to important aspects of the presentation. The following steps add an oval shape, which displays as a circle, to Slide 3. *Why? A circle shape complements the basketball photo on Slide 1 and helps reinforce the presentation's basketball theme.*

- Display Slide 3 and then, if necessary, click the Home tab (Figure 2–23).

Figure 2–23

- Click the Shapes More button (Home tab | Drawing group) shown in Figure 2–23 to display the Shapes gallery (Figure 2–24).

Q&A I do not see a Shapes More button and the three rows of the shapes shown in Figure 2–24. Instead, I have a Shapes button. Why?
Monitor dimensions and resolution affect how buttons display on the ribbon. Click the Shapes button to display the entire Shapes gallery.

Figure 2–24

3

- Click the Oval shape in the Basic Shapes area of the Shapes gallery.

Q&A
Why did my pointer change shape?
The pointer changed to a plus shape to indicate the Oval shape has been added to the Clipboard.

- Position the pointer (a crosshair) near the center of the slide, as shown in Figure 2–25.

Figure 2–25

4

- Click Slide 3 to insert the Oval shape.

Other Ways

1. Click Shapes button (Insert tab | Illustrations group)

To Resize a Shape

1 DOWNLOAD & SELECT SLIDES | 2 INSERT & FORMAT PICTURES | 3 INSERT & FORMAT SHAPES
4 FORMAT SLIDE BACKGROUNDS | 5 INSERT & FORMAT WORDART | 6 REVIEW, REVISE, & PRINT SLIDES

The next step is to resize the Oval shape. *Why? The oval should be enlarged so that it is a focal point in the middle area of the slide.* The following steps resize the selected shape.

1

- Press and hold down the SHIFT key and then drag the upper-left corner sizing handle until the shape is resized approximately as shown in Figure 2–26 and the top is aligned with a horizontal Smart Guide.

Q&A
Why did I need to press the SHIFT key while enlarging the shape?
Holding down the SHIFT key while dragging keeps the proportions of the original shape.

What if my shape is not selected?
To select a shape, click it.

If I am using a touch screen, how can I maintain the shape's original proportion?
If you drag one of the corner sizing handles, the object should stay in proportion.

Figure 2–26

2

- Release to resize the shape.
- Drag the shape until the vertical Smart Guide is displayed in the middle of the oval and the horizontal Smart Guide is displayed at the top of the oval, as shown in Figure 2–27, and then release.

Q&A What if I want to move the shape to a precise location on the slide?
With the shape selected, press the ARROW keys or the CTRL+ARROW keys to move the shape to the desired location.

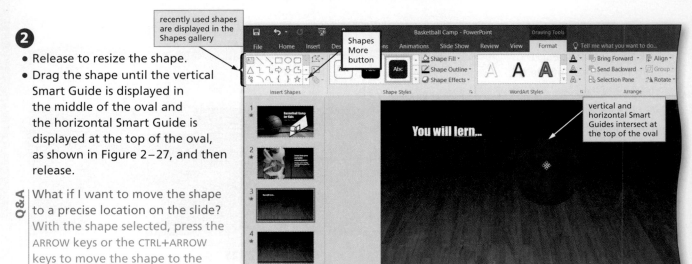

Figure 2–27

Other Ways

1. Enter shape height and width in Height and Width boxes (Drawing Tools Format tab | Size group)
2. Click Size and Position pane launcher (Drawing Tools Format tab | Size group), click Size tab, enter desired height and width values in boxes, click Close button

---

To Add Other Shapes

1 DOWNLOAD & SELECT SLIDES | 2 INSERT & FORMAT PICTURES | **3 INSERT & FORMAT SHAPES**
4 FORMAT SLIDE BACKGROUNDS | 5 INSERT & FORMAT WORDART | 6 REVIEW, REVISE, & PRINT SLIDES

Ovals, squares, arrows, stars, and equation shapes are among the items included in the Shapes gallery. These shapes can be combined to show relationships among the elements, and they can help illustrate the basic concepts presented in your slide show. *Why? Arrows are especially useful in showing the relationship among slide elements and guiding the viewer's eyes to move from one shape to the next.* More than two dozen arrow shapes are displayed in the Block Arrows section of the Shapes gallery. The following steps add one of these arrows and the pentagon shapes to Slide 3.

1

- Click the Shapes More button (Drawing Tools Format tab | Insert Shapes group) shown in Figure 2–27 to display the Shapes gallery (Figure 2–28).

Q&A When I inserted the Oval shape, I selected it on the Home tab. Is the same Shapes gallery also displayed on the Drawing Tools Format tab?
Yes. The Shapes gallery is displayed on this tab once an object is inserted and selected on the slide.

Figure 2–28

2

- Click the Curved Left Arrow shape in the Block Arrows area of the Shapes gallery.
- Position the pointer to the right of the oval shape in Slide 3 and then click to insert the Curved Left Arrow shape.

3

- Press and hold down the SHIFT key and then drag a corner sizing handle until the arrow shape is approximately the size shown in Figure 2–29.

Q&A If I am using a touch screen, how can I maintain the Oval shape's original proportion?
The object should stay in proportion when you drag one of the corner sizing handles.

- If necessary, drag the Curved Left Arrow shape to the right side of the oval, as shown in Figure 2–29, and then release.

Figure 2–29

4

- Display the Shapes gallery and then click the Regular Pentagon shape in the Basic Shapes area of the gallery (shown in Figure 2–28).
- Position the pointer toward the lower-left side of the Curved Left Arrow shape and then click to insert the Regular Pentagon shape.

5

- Press and hold down the SHIFT key and then drag a corner sizing handle to resize the pentagon shape so that it is the size shown in Figure 2–30.
- Drag the pentagon shape so that its tip is placed at the intersection of the horizontal Smart Guide above the pentagon and the vertical Smart Guide in the middle of the shape, as shown in Figure 2–30, and then release.

Figure 2–30

To Apply a Shape Style

1 DOWNLOAD & SELECT SLIDES | 2 INSERT & FORMAT PICTURES | 3 INSERT & FORMAT SHAPES
4 FORMAT SLIDE BACKGROUNDS | 5 INSERT & FORMAT WORDART | 6 REVIEW, REVISE, & PRINT SLIDES

Formatting text in a shape follows the same techniques as formatting text in a placeholder. You can change font, font color and size, and alignment. You later will add information about a skill to the Oval shape, but first you want to apply a shape style. *Why? The style will give depth and dimension to the object.* The Quick Styles gallery has a variety of styles that change depending upon the theme applied to the presentation. The following steps apply a style to the oval.

1

• Display the Home tab, click the oval to select it, and then click the Quick Styles button (Home tab | Drawing group) (Figure 2–31).

Figure 2–31

2

• Point to Light 1 Outline, Colored Fill – Black, Dark 1 in the Quick Styles gallery (first shape in third Theme Styles row) to display a live preview of that style applied to the oval in the slide (Figure 2–32).

Figure 2–32

Experiment

- Point to various styles in the Quick Styles gallery and watch the style of the shape change.

3

- Click Light 1 Outline, Colored Fill – Black, Dark 1 in the Quick Styles gallery to apply the selected style to the oval.

Other Ways
1. Click Shape Styles More button (Drawing Tools Format tab | Shape Styles group), select style
2. Right-click shape, click Style button on mini toolbar, select desired style

To Apply Another Style

You later will add text to the oval and pentagon about particular skills taught at the camp, but now you want to format the arrow and pentagon shapes. *Why? You can apply shape styles to the arrow and pentagon that will coordinate with the oval's style. A light style color in the arrow shape will help join darker style colors of the oval and rectangle. This formatting will add interest and emphasize the relationship between basketball playing skills.* The following steps apply styles to the arrow and pentagon shapes.

1 Click the arrow shape to select it.

2 Click the Quick Styles button (Home tab | Drawing group) to display the Quick Styles gallery and then apply the Colored Outline – Black, Dark 1 style (first style in first Theme Styles row) to the arrow shape.

3 Click the pentagon shape to select it and then click the Quick Styles button.

4 Click Subtle Effect – Black, Dark 1 (first style in fourth Theme Styles row) to apply that style to the pentagon shape (Figure 2–33).

BTW

Deleting a Shape
If you want to delete a shape you have added to a slide, click that shape to select it and then press the delete key. If you want to DELETE multiple shapes, press the CTRL key while clicking the undesired shapes and then press the DELETE key.

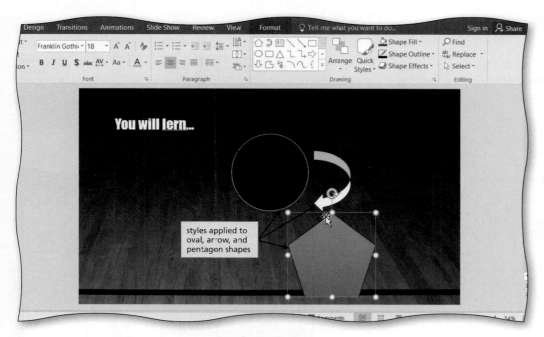

Figure 2–33

To Add Text to a Shape

The three shapes on Slide 3 help call attention to the key aspects of your presentation. *Why? Your goal is to emphasize key skills the campers will learn.* The next step is to add this information to Slide 3. The following steps add text to the oval and pentagon shapes.

- With the pentagon selected, type **Offensive moves** to add the text in the shape.

- Click the oval to select it and then type **Ball handling skills** to add the text in the shape (Figure 2–34).

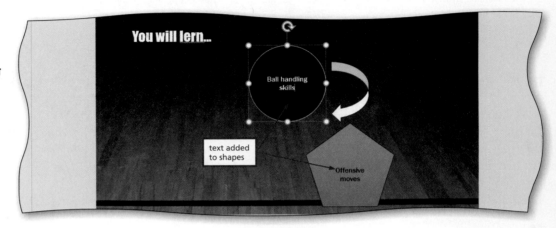

Figure 2–34

To Change the Font

The default theme font is Franklin Gothic Medium. To draw more attention to text in the shapes and to help differentiate these slide elements from the title text, you want to change the font to Century Schoolbook. *Why? Century Schoolbook is a serif typeface, meaning the ends of some of the letter are adorned with small decorations, called serifs. These adornments slow down the viewer's reading speed, which might help them retain the information they saw.* To change the font, you must select the letters you want to format. In Module 1, you selected a paragraph and then formatted the characters, and you follow the same procedure to change the font. The following steps change the text font in the shape.

- With the oval selected, triple-click the text to select all the characters and display the mini toolbar (Figure 2–35).

Figure 2–35

- Click the Font arrow to display the Font gallery (Figure 2–36).

Q&A Will the fonts in my Font gallery be the same as those shown in Figure 2–36?
Your list of available fonts may differ, depending on what fonts you have installed and the type of printer you are using.

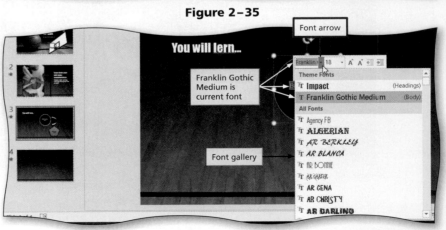

Figure 2–36

❸

- Drag or scroll through the Font gallery and then point to Century Schoolbook (or a similar font) to display a live preview of the title text in the Century Schoolbook font (Figure 2–37).

🔍 **Experiment**

- Point to various fonts in the Font gallery and watch the subtitle text font change in the slide.

- Click Century Schoolbook (or a similar font) to change the font of the selected text to Century Schoolbook.

Figure 2–37

Other Ways

1. Click Font arrow (Home tab | Font group), click desired font in Font gallery
2. Right-click selected text, click Font on shortcut menu (Font dialog box), click Font tab, select desired font in Font list, click OK button
3. Click Font dialog box launcher (Home tab | Font group), click Font tab (Font dialog box), select desired font in Font list, click OK button
4. Press CTRL+SHIFT+F, click Font tab (Font dialog box), select desired font in the Font list, click OK button
5. Right-click selected text, click Font arrow on mini toolbar, select desired font

To Format the Text

To increase readability, you can format the oval text by increasing the font size, bolding the characters, and changing the font color to orange. The following steps format the oval text.

❶ With the oval text selected, click the Increase Font Size button (Home tab | Font group) two times to increase the font size to 24 pt.

❷ Click the Bold button (Home tab | Font group) to bold the text.

❸ Click the Font Color arrow and change the color to Orange (third color in Standard Colors row) (Figure 2–38).

Q&A | What should I do if one or more letters of the word, handling, wrap to the third line in the shape?
Press and hold down the SHIFT key and then drag a corner sizing handle outward slightly to resize the oval shape.

Could I also add a shadow behind the text to add depth and help the letters display prominently?
Yes. Select the text and then click the Text Shadow button (Home tab | Font group).

Figure 2–38

Other Ways

1. Right-click selected text, click desired text format button on mini toolbar

BTW
Shadowing Text
Adding a shadow to text
gives depth and helps the
letters display prominently
by adding a shadow behind
them. To add a shadow,
select the text and then click
the Text Shadow button
(Home tab | Font group).

Format Painter

To save time and avoid formatting errors, you can use the Format Painter to apply custom formatting to other places in your presentation quickly and easily. You can use this feature in three ways:

- To copy only character attributes, such as font and font effects, select text that has these qualities.

- To copy both character attributes and paragraph attributes, such as alignment and indentation, select the entire paragraph.

- To apply the same formatting to multiple words, phrases, or paragraphs, double-click the Format Painter button and then select each item you want to format. You then can press the ESC key or click the Format Painter button to turn off this feature.

To Format Text Using the Format Painter

1 DOWNLOAD & SELECT SLIDES | 2 INSERT & FORMAT PICTURES | 3 INSERT & FORMAT SHAPES
4 FORMAT SLIDE BACKGROUNDS | 5 INSERT & FORMAT WORDART | 6 REVIEW, REVISE, & PRINT SLIDES

Why? *To save time and duplicated effort, you quickly can use the Format Painter to copy formatting attributes from the oval shape text and apply them to pentagon shape text.* The following steps use the Format Painter to copy formatting features.

- With the oval text still selected, double-click the Format Painter button (Home tab | Clipboard group).
- Move the pointer off the ribbon (Figure 2–39).

Q&A Why does the Format Painter button on my screen display only a paint brush and not the words, Format Painter?
Monitor dimensions and resolution affect how buttons display on the ribbon.

Why did my pointer change shape?
The pointer changed shape by adding a paintbrush to indicate that the Format Painter function is active.

Figure 2–39

2

- Triple-click the pentagon text to apply the format to all characters (Figure 2–40).
- Click the Format Painter button or press the ESC key to turn off the Format Painter feature.

Q&A What should I do if one or more letters of the word, Offensive, wrap to a second line in the shape?
Press and hold down the SHIFT key and then drag a corner sizing handle outward slightly to resize the pentagon shape.

Figure 2–40

Other Ways

1. Select text, double-click Format Painter button on mini toolbar

To Copy and Paste a Shape

1 DOWNLOAD & SELECT SLIDES | 2 INSERT & FORMAT PICTURES | 3 INSERT & FORMAT SHAPES
4 FORMAT SLIDE BACKGROUNDS | 5 INSERT & FORMAT WORDART | 6 REVIEW, REVISE, & PRINT SLIDES

Good basketball players have both offensive and defensive skills. You already have created the shape stating the campers will work on refining their offensive talents. You now need to create a second shape with information about defensive instruction that will be provided at the camp. The following steps copy the pentagon shape and then change the text. *Why? You could repeat all the steps you performed to create the first pentagon, but it is much more efficient to duplicate the shape and then edit the text.*

1

- With the pentagon shape selected, click the Copy button (Home tab | Clipboard group) (Figure 2–41).

Figure 2–41

2

- Click the Paste button (Home tab | Clipboard group) to insert a duplicate Regular Pentagon shape on Slide 3.
- Drag the new pentagon shape to the left of the original pentagon shape, as shown in Figure 2–42.
- In the left pentagon shape, select the text, Offensive moves, and then type `Defensive mindset` as the replacement text (Figure 2–42).

Q&A What should I do if one or more letters of the word, Defensive, wrap to a second line in the shape?
Press and hold down the SHIFT key and then drag a corner sizing handle outward slightly to resize the pentagon shape.

Figure 2–42

3

- Select the arrow shape and then click the Copy button (Home tab | Clipboard group) (Figure 2–43).

Figure 2–43

4

- Click the Paste button (Home tab | Clipboard group) two times to insert two duplicate arrow shapes on Slide 3.
- Drag one of the duplicate arrow shapes between the two pentagon shapes and then drag the other duplicate arrow shape between the left pentagon shape and the oval shape (Figure 2–44).

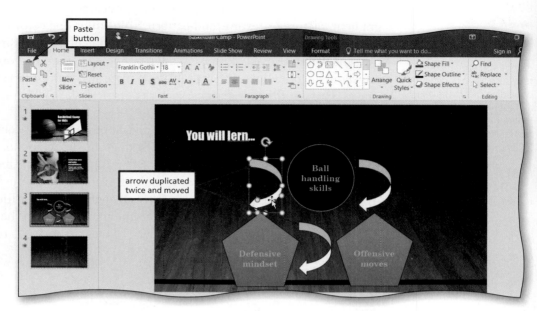

Figure 2–44

5

- With the left arrow selected, drag its rotation handle clockwise or counterclockwise so that it is displayed as shown in Figure 2–45. Repeat this procedure for the other two arrows, and then adjust the shapes' locations on Slide 3 so that the arrows touch their adjacent shapes (Figure 2–45).

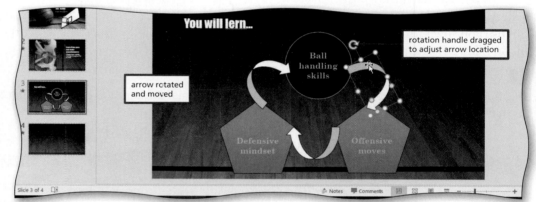

Figure 2–45

- If the end of an arrow is underneath an oval or a pentagon shape, select the arrow, click the Drawing Tools Format tab, and then click the Bring Forward button (Drawing Tools Format tab | Arrange group) to bring the arrow on top of the shape.

Other Ways

1. Right-click selected shape, click Copy on shortcut menu, right-click blank area, click Paste on shortcut menu
2. Select shape, press CTRL+C, press CTRL+V

Break Point: If you wish to take a break, this is a good place to do so. Be sure to save the Basketball Camp file again and then you can exit PowerPoint. To resume at a later time, run PowerPoint, open the file called Basketball Camp, and continue following the steps from this location forward.

Formatting Slide Backgrounds

A slide's background is an integral part of a presentation because it can generate audience interest. Every slide can have the same background, or different backgrounds can be used in a presentation. This background is considered **fill**, which is the content

BTW
**Undo Text
Formatting Changes**
To remove a formatting
change you have made to
text, such as an underline
or bolding, select the text
and then click the button
that originally applied the
format. For example, to undo
bolding, select the text and
then click the Bold button.
If you apply a format and
then immediately decide to
remove this effect, click the
Undo button on the Quick
Access Toolbar.

that makes up the interior of a shape, line, or character. Four fills are available: solid, gradient, picture or texture, and pattern. **Solid fill** is one color used throughout the entire slide. **Gradient fill** is one color shade gradually progressing to another shade of the same color or one color progressing to another color. **Picture or texture fill** uses a specific file or an image that simulates a material, such as cork, granite, marble, or canvas. **Pattern fill** adds designs, such as dots or dashes, which repeat in rows across the slide.

Once you add a fill, you can adjust its appearance. For example, you can adjust its **transparency**, which allows you to see through the background, so that any text on the slide is visible. You also can select a color that is part of the theme or a custom color. You can use an **offset**, another background feature, to move the background away from the slide borders in varying distances by percentage. A **tiling option** repeats the background image many times vertically and horizontally on the slide; the smaller the tiling percentage, the greater the number of times the image is repeated.

To Insert a Texture Fill

1 DOWNLOAD & SELECT SLIDES | 2 INSERT & FORMAT PICTURES | 3 INSERT & FORMAT SHAPES
4 FORMAT SLIDE BACKGROUNDS | 5 INSERT & FORMAT WORDART | 6 REVIEW, REVISE, & PRINT SLIDES

Why? Various texture fills are available to give your background a unique look. The 24 pictures in the Texture gallery give the appearance of a physical object, such as water drops, sand, tissue paper, and a paper bag. You also can use your own texture pictures for custom backgrounds. The following steps insert the Brown marble texture fill on Slide 2 in the presentation.

- Display Slide 2. Click the Design tab and then click the Format Background button (Design tab | Customize group) to display the Format Background pane (Figure 2–46).

Figure 2–46

2

- With the Fill section displaying (Format Background pane), if necessary, click 'Picture or texture fill' and then click the Texture button to display the Texture gallery (Figure 2–47).

Figure 2–47

3

- Click the Brown marble texture (first texture in third row) to insert this texture fill as the background on Slide 2 (Figure 2–48).

Q&A

Is a live preview available to see the various textures on this slide?
No. Live preview is not an option with the background textures and fills.

Could I insert this background on all four slides simultaneously?
Yes. You would click the 'Apply to All' button to insert the Brown marble background on all slides.

Figure 2–48

Other Ways

1. Right-click background, click Format Background on shortcut menu, select desired options (Format Background pane)

To Format the Background Texture Fill Transparency

Why? *The Brown marble texture on Slide 2 is dark, and its pattern may detract from the photo and text.* One method of reducing this darkness is to change the transparency. The **Transparency slider** indicates the amount of opaqueness. The default setting is 0, which is fully opaque. The opposite extreme is 100%, which is fully transparent. To change the transparency, you can move the Transparency slider or enter a number in the box next to the slider. The following step adjusts the texture transparency to 15%.

- Click the Transparency slider (Format Background pane) and drag it to the right until 15% is displayed in the Transparency box (Figure 2–49).

Q&A Can I move the slider in small increments so that I can get a precise percentage easily?
Yes. Click the up or down arrows in the Transparency box to move the slider in 1% increments.

Figure 2–49

To Insert a Gradient Fill

Although you selected Brown marble texture fill on Slide 2 and changed the transparency, you decide that another type of background may be more suitable for Slide 3. *Why?* *The Brown marble texture does not offer sufficient contrast with the oval symbol and may detract from the messages presented in the three symbols.* For each theme, PowerPoint provides 30 preset **gradient fills** with five designs for each of the six major theme colors. Each fill has one dark color shade that gradually lightens to either another shade of the same color or another color. The following steps replace the background on Slide 3 to a preset gradient fill.

- Display Slide 3. With the Fill section displaying (Format Background pane), click Gradient fill in the Format Background pane (shown in Figure 2–49) and then click the Preset gradients button to display the Preset gradients gallery (Figure 2–50).

Q&A Are the backgrounds displayed in a specific order?
Yes. The first row has light colors at the top of the background; the middle rows have darker fills at the bottom; the bottom row has overall dark fills on all edges.

Is a live preview available to see the various gradients on this slide?
No. Live preview is not an option with the background textures and fills.

Figure 2–50

2

- Click Bottom Spotlight – Accent 3 (third fill in fourth row) to apply that style to Slide 3 (Figure 2–51).

Q&A
If I decide later that this background gradient does not fit the theme of my presentation, can I apply a different background?
Yes. You can repeat these steps at any time while creating your presentation.

Figure 2–51

Other Ways

1. Click Design tab on ribbon, click Format Background button (Customize group), select desired options (Format Background pane)
2. Right-click background, click Format Background on shortcut menu, select desired options (Format Background pane)

To Insert a Picture to Create a Background

Why? *For variety and interest, you want to use an illustration as the Slide 4 background.* This picture is stored in the Data Files folder. PowerPoint will stretch the height and width of this picture to fill the slide area. The following steps insert the illustration, Basketball Boy, on Slide 4 only.

1

- Display Slide 4. With the Fill section displaying (Format Background pane), if necessary, click 'Picture or texture fill' and then click the File button (Format Background pane) to display the Insert Picture dialog box. If necessary, navigate to the Module 02 folder in the Data Files folder or the location where your data files are located.

Figure 2–52

- Click Basketball Boy to select the file name (Figure 2–52).

- Click the Insert button (Insert Picture dialog box) to insert the Basketball Boy illustration as the Slide 4 background (Figure 2–53).

Q&A What if I do not want to use this picture?
Click the Undo button on the Quick Access Toolbar or click the Reset Background button at the bottom of the Format Background pane.

Figure 2–53

To Format the Background Picture Fill Transparency

1 DOWNLOAD & SELECT SLIDES | 2 INSERT & FORMAT PICTURES | 3 INSERT & FORMAT SHAPES
4 FORMAT SLIDE BACKGROUNDS | 5 INSERT & FORMAT WORDART | 6 REVIEW, REVISE, & PRINT SLIDES

Why? *The Basketball Boy illustration on Slide 4 has vibrant colors that will conflict with the WordArt you will add later in this project.* You can adjust the transparency of picture in the same manner that you change the transparency of a slide texture. The following steps adjust the transparency of the background picture to 30% and then close the Format Background pane.

- Click the Transparency slider and drag it to the right until 30% is displayed in the Transparency box (Figure 2–54).

2

- Click the Close button (Format Background pane) to close the pane and return to Slide 4.

Figure 2–54

Inserting and Formatting WordArt

One method of adding appealing visual elements to a presentation is by using **WordArt** styles. This feature is found in other Microsoft Office applications, including Word and Excel. This gallery of decorative effects allows you to type new text or convert existing text to WordArt. You then can add elements such as fills, outlines, and effects.

WordArt **fill** in the interior of a letter can consist of a solid color, texture, picture, or gradient. The WordArt **outline** is the exterior border surrounding each letter or symbol. PowerPoint allows you to change the outline color, weight, and style. You also can add an **effect**, which helps add emphasis or depth to the characters. Some effects are shadows, reflections, glows, bevels, and 3-D rotations.

To Insert WordArt

1 DOWNLOAD & SELECT SLIDES | 2 INSERT & FORMAT PICTURES | 3 INSERT & FORMAT SHAPES
4 FORMAT SLIDE BACKGROUNDS | 5 INSERT & FORMAT WORDART | 6 REVIEW, REVISE, & PRINT SLIDES

The basketball camp is a very popular event among boys and girls in the community, and the sessions fill every year. Parents need to register their student early to reserve a place. You want to emphasize this concept, and the last slide in the presentation is an excellent location to urge your audience to take action. *Why? Audience members remember the first and last things they see and hear.* You quickly can add a visual element to the slide by selecting a WordArt style from the WordArt Styles gallery and then applying it to some text. The following steps insert WordArt.

1
- Display the Insert tab and then click the WordArt button (Insert tab | Text group) to display the WordArt gallery (Figure 2–55).

Figure 2–55

2
- Click 'Fill – Red, Accent 2, Outline – Accent 2' (third style in first row) to insert the WordArt object (Figure 2–56).

Figure 2–56

3
- Type `Register today!` in the object as the WordArt text (Figure 2–57).

Q&A Why did the Drawing Tools Format tab appear automatically in the ribbon?
It appears when you select text to which you could add a WordArt style or other effect.

Figure 2–57

To Change the WordArt Shape

Why? *The WordArt text is useful to emphasize the need to register children early for camp. You further can emphasize this text by changing its shape.* PowerPoint provides a variety of graphical shapes that add interest to WordArt text. The following steps change the WordArt shape to Chevron Up.

1

• With the WordArt object still selected, click the Text Effects button (Drawing Tools Format tab | WordArt Styles group) to display the Text Effects menu (Figure 2–58).

Figure 2–58

2

• Point to Transform in the Text Effects menu to display the WordArt Transform gallery (Figure 2–59).

Figure 2–59

3

• Point to the Chevron Up effect in the Warp area (first effect in second row in Warp area) to display a live preview of that text effect applied to the WordArt object (Figure 2–60).

Figure 2–60

Experiment

- Point to various effects in the Transform gallery and watch the format of the text and borders change.

Q&A How can I see the preview of a Transform effect if the gallery overlays the WordArt letters?
Move the WordArt box to the left or right side of the slide and then repeat Steps 1 and 2.

4

- Click the Chevron Up shape to apply this text effect to the WordArt object.

Q&A Can I change the shape I applied to the WordArt?
Yes. Position the insertion point in the box and then repeat Steps 1 and 2.

5

- Drag the lower-right sizing handle diagonally toward the lower-right corner of the slide until the crosshair is positioned approximately as shown in Figure 2–61.

crosshair indicates lower-right WordArt location

Figure 2–61

6

- Release to resize the WordArt object.
- Drag the WordArt object toward the right side of the slide until it is positioned approximately as shown in Figure 2–62.

WordArt object moved to desired location

Figure 2–62

To Apply a WordArt Text Fill

1 DOWNLOAD & SELECT SLIDES | 2 INSERT & FORMAT PICTURES | 3 INSERT & FORMAT SHAPES
4 FORMAT SLIDE BACKGROUNDS | 5 INSERT & FORMAT WORDART | 6 REVIEW, REVISE, & PRINT SLIDES

Various texture fills are available to give your WordArt characters a unique look. You used a texture fill to add interest to the Slide 3 background. The following steps add the Medium wood texture as a fill for the WordArt characters. *Why? The brown fill coordinates well with the red WordArt outline and is similar to the color of the basketball court in the Slide 1 and Slide 2 backgrounds.*

❶

- With the WordArt object selected, click the Text Fill arrow (Drawing Tools Format tab | WordArt Styles group) to display the Text Fill gallery.
- Point to Texture in the Text Fill gallery to display the Texture gallery.

❷

- If necessary, scroll down and then point to the Medium wood texture (last texture in last row) to display a live preview of that texture applied to the WordArt object (Figure 2–63).

Figure 2–63

🔍 Experiment

- Point to various styles in the Texture gallery and watch the fill change.

❸

- Click the Medium wood texture to apply this texture as the fill for the WordArt object.

Q&A | Can I apply this texture simultaneously to text that appears in more than one place on my slide?
Yes. You can select one area of text, press and then hold the CTRL key while you select the other text, and then apply the texture.

To Change the Weight of the WordArt Outline

1 DOWNLOAD & SELECT SLIDES | 2 INSERT & FORMAT PICTURES | 3 INSERT & FORMAT SHAPES
4 FORMAT SLIDE BACKGROUNDS | 5 INSERT & FORMAT WORDART | 6 REVIEW, REVISE, & PRINT SLIDES

The letters in the WordArt style applied have an outline around the edges. You can increase the width of the outlines. **Why?** *The thicker line will emphasize this characteristic and add another visual element.* As with fonts, lines also are measured in points, and PowerPoint gives you the option to change the line **weight**, or thickness, starting with ¼ point (pt) and increasing in ¼-point increments. Other outline options include modifying the color and the line style, such as changing to dots or dashes or a combination of dots and dashes. The following steps change the WordArt outline weight to 6 pt.

1

- With the WordArt object still selected, click the Text Outline arrow (Drawing Tools Format tab | WordArt Styles group) to display the Text Outline gallery.
- Point to Weight in the gallery to display the Weight list.
- Point to 6 pt to display a live preview of this line weight on the WordArt text outline (Figure 2–64).

Figure 2–64

Q&A Can I make the line width more than 6 pt?

Yes. Click More Lines and increase the amount in the Width box.

Experiment

- Point to various line weights in the Weight list and watch the line thickness change.

2

- Click 6 pt to apply this line weight to the WordArt text outline.

Q&A Must my text have an outline?

No. To delete the outline, click No Outline in the Text Outline gallery.

To Change the Color of the WordArt Outline

1 DOWNLOAD & SELECT SLIDES | 2 INSERT & FORMAT PICTURES | 3 INSERT & FORMAT SHAPES

4 FORMAT SLIDE BACKGROUNDS | 5 INSERT & FORMAT WORDART | 6 REVIEW, REVISE, & PRINT SLIDES

Why? The WordArt outline color and the boy's shorts are similar, so you can add contrast by changing one of these slide elements. The following steps change the WordArt outline color.

1

- With the WordArt object still selected, display the Text Outline gallery.
- Point to Black, Background 1 (first color in Theme Colors row) to display a live preview of this outline color (Figure 2–65).

Figure 2–65

Experiment

- Point to various colors in the gallery and watch the outline colors change.

2

- Click Black, Background 1 to apply this color to the WordArt outline.

- Click outside of the WordArt box to deselect this slide element (Figure 2–66).

WordArt object formatted

Figure 2–66

Reviewing and Revising Individual Slides

The text, pictures, and shapes for all slides in the Basketball Camp presentation have been entered. Once you complete a slide show, you might decide to change elements. PowerPoint provides several tools to assist you with making changes. They include finding and replacing text, inserting a synonym, checking spelling, and printing speaker notes. The following pages discuss these tools.

Replace Dialog Box

BTW
Finding and Replacing Text
When finding and replacing text, you do not need to display the slide that contains the word for which you are searching. You can perform this action when any slide is displayed. To see the results of the search and replace action, however, you need to display the slide where the change occurred.

At times, you might want to change all occurrences of a word or phrase to another word or phrase. For example, an instructor may have one slide show to accompany a lecture for several introductory classes, and he wants to update slides with the particular class name and section that appear on several slides. He manually could change the characters, but PowerPoint includes an efficient method of replacing one word with another. The Find and Replace feature automatically locates specific text and then replaces it with desired text.

In some cases, you may want to replace only certain occurrences of a word or phrase, not all of them. To instruct PowerPoint to confirm each change, click the Find Next button in the Replace dialog box instead of the Replace All button. When PowerPoint locates an occurrence of the text, it pauses and waits for you to click either the Replace button or the Find Next button. Clicking the Replace button changes the text; clicking the Find Next button instructs PowerPoint to disregard that particular instance and look for the next occurrence of the Find what text.

To Find and Insert a Synonym

1 DOWNLOAD & SELECT SLIDES | 2 INSERT & FORMAT PICTURES | 3 INSERT & FORMAT SHAPES
4 FORMAT SLIDE BACKGROUNDS | 5 INSERT & FORMAT WORDART | 6 REVIEW, REVISE, & PRINT SLIDES

Why? *When reviewing your slide show, you may decide that a particular word does not express the exact usage you intended or that you used the same word on multiple slides.* In these cases, you could find a **synonym**, or word similar in meaning, to replace the inappropriate or duplicate word. PowerPoint provides a **thesaurus**, which is a list of synonyms and antonyms, to help you find a replacement word.

In this project, you want to find a synonym to replace the word, acquaintances, on Slide 2. The following steps locate an appropriate synonym and replace the word.

1

- Display Slide 2 and then place the insertion point in the word, acquaintances.

- Right-click to display a shortcut menu related to the word, acquaintances. Then, point to Synonyms on the shortcut menu to display a list of synonyms for this word (Figure 2–67).

Q&A How do I locate a synonym for multiple words?
You need to select all the words and then right-click to display the shortcut menu.

If I am using a touch screen, how do I find a synonym?
Tap the Thesaurus button (Review tab | Proofing group) to display the Thesaurus pane for the selected word. Then, in the pane, tap the arrow next to the word to display a shortcut menu.

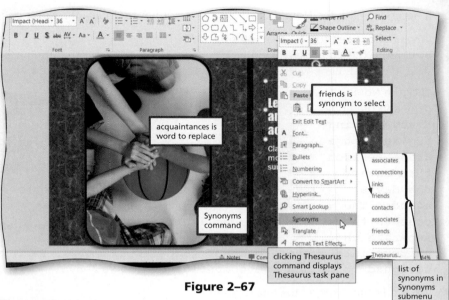

Figure 2–67

2

- Click the synonym you want (friends) on the Synonyms submenu to replace the word, acquaintances, in the presentation with the word, friends (Figure 2–68).

Q&A What if a suitable word does not display in the Synonyms submenu?
You can display the Thesaurus pane by clicking Thesaurus on the Synonyms submenu. A complete thesaurus with synonyms displays in the pane along with an antonym, which is a word with an opposite meaning.

Figure 2–68

Other Ways

1. Click Thesaurus (Review tab | Proofing group)

2. Press SHIFT+F7

To Add Notes

1 DOWNLOAD & SELECT SLIDES | 2 INSERT & FORMAT PICTURES | 3 INSERT & FORMAT SHAPES
4 FORMAT SLIDE BACKGROUNDS | 5 INSERT & FORMAT WORDART | 6 REVIEW, REVISE, & PRINT SLIDES

Why? *As you create slides, you may find material you want to state verbally and do not want to include on the slide. After adding these comments, you can print a set of speaker notes that will print below a small image of the slide.* You can type and format comments in the **Notes pane** as you work in Normal view and then print this information as **notes pages**. The Notes pane is hidden until you click the Notes button on the status bar to open the pane. If you want to close the Notes pane, click the Notes button again. Charts, tables, and pictures added to the Notes pane also print on these pages. The following steps add text to the Notes pane on Slides 2, 3, and 4.

Note: In the following step, the word, skills, has been misspelled intentionally as skils to illustrate the use of PowerPoint's spell check feature. Your slides may contain different misspelled words, depending upon the accuracy of your typing.

❶

• If necessary, click the Notes button on the status bar to display the Notes pane for Slide 2.

Q&A | Why might I need to click the Notes button?
By default, the Notes pane is closed when you begin a new presentation. Once you display the Notes pane for any slide, the Notes pane will remain open unless you click the Notes button to close it.

• Click the Notes pane and then type `Every morning begins with a group session that covers the day's agenda. The coaches then separate the`

Figure 2–69

`campers into groups to cover fundamental skils. Each morning ends with a contest designed to be fun and competitive.` (Figure 2–69).

Q&A | What if I cannot see all the lines I typed?
You can drag the splitter bar up to enlarge the Notes pane. Clicking the Notes pane scroll arrows or swiping up or down on the Notes pane allows you to view the entire text.

❷

• Display Slide 3, click the Notes pane, and then type `Campers will gain confidence while learning sportsmanship and strategies.` (Figure 2–70).

Figure 2–70

❸

• Display Slide 4 and then type `Space is limited. Every camper will receive a t-shirt, snacks, and water. Parents are encouraged to attend the awards ceremony at the end of the camp session.` in the Notes pane (Figure 2–71).

Figure 2–71

1 DOWNLOAD & SELECT SLIDES | 2 INSERT & FORMAT PICTURES | 3 INSERT & FORMAT SHAPES
4 FORMAT SLIDE BACKGROUNDS | 5 INSERT & FORMAT WORDART | 6 REVIEW, REVISE, & PRINT SLIDES

To Find and Replace Text

While reviewing your slides, you realize that the camp will be held in the afternoon, not in the morning. To change this word throughout a presentation, you could view each slide, look for the word, morning, delete the word, and then type the replacement word, afternoon. A more efficient and effective method of performing this action is to use PowerPoint's Find and Replace feature. *Why? This method locates each occurrence of a word or phrase automatically and then replaces it with specified text.* The word, morning, displays three times in the slides and notes. The following steps use Find and Replace to replace all occurrences of the word, morning, with the word, afternoon.

❶

- If necessary, display the Home tab and then click the Replace button (Home tab | Editing group) to display the Replace dialog box.

- Type **morning** in the Find what box (Replace dialog box).

- Click the Replace with box and then type **afternoon** in the box (Figure 2–72).

Figure 2–72

❷

- Click the Replace All button (Replace dialog box) to instruct PowerPoint to replace all occurrences of the Find what word, morning, with the Replace with word, afternoon (Figure 2–73).

Q&A If I accidentally replaced the wrong text, can I undo this replacement?

Yes. Press CTRL+Z or click the Undo button on the Quick Access Toolbar to undo all replacements. If you had clicked the Replace button instead of the Replace All button, PowerPoint would undo only the most recent replacement.

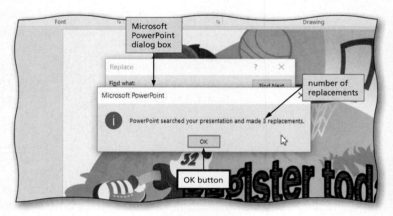

Figure 2–73

❸

- Click the OK button (Microsoft PowerPoint dialog box).

- Click the Close button (Replace dialog box).

Other Ways

1. Press CTRL+H

Checking Spelling

After you create a presentation, you should check it visually for spelling errors and style consistency. In addition, you can use PowerPoint's Spelling tool to identify possible misspellings on the slides and in the notes. You should proofread your presentation carefully by pointing to each word and saying it aloud as you point to it. Be mindful of commonly misused words such as its and it's, through and though, and to and too.

PowerPoint checks the entire presentation for spelling mistakes using a standard dictionary contained in the Microsoft Office group. This dictionary is shared with the other Microsoft Office applications such as Word and Excel. A custom dictionary is available if you want to add special words such as proper names, cities, and acronyms.

BTW

Formatting Notes Pane Text

You can format text in the Notes pane in the same manner you format text on a slide. To add emphasis, for example, you can italicize key words or change the font color and size.

When checking a presentation for spelling errors, PowerPoint opens the standard dictionary and the custom dictionary file, if one exists. When a word appears in the Spelling pane, you can perform one of several actions, as described in Table 2–1.

The standard dictionary contains commonly used English words. It does not, however, contain many proper names, abbreviations, technical terms, poetic contractions, or antiquated terms. PowerPoint treats words not found in the dictionaries as misspellings.

Table 2–1 Spelling Pane Buttons and Actions

Button Name/Action	When to Use	Action
Ignore	Word is spelled correctly but not found in dictionaries	PowerPoint continues checking rest of the presentation but will flag that word again if it appears later in document.
Ignore All	Word is spelled correctly but not found in dictionaries	PowerPoint ignores all occurrences of the word and continues checking rest of presentation.
Add	Add word to custom dictionary	PowerPoint opens custom dictionary, adds word, and continues checking rest of presentation.
Change	Word is misspelled	Click proper spelling of the word in Suggestions list. PowerPoint corrects word, continues checking rest of presentation, but will flag that word again if it appears later in document.
Change All	Word is misspelled	Click proper spelling of word in Suggestions list. PowerPoint changes all occurrences of misspelled word and continues checking rest of presentation.
Listen to the pronunciation	To hear the pronunciation of a word	Click the audio speaker icon next to the properly spelled word near the bottom of the Spelling pane.
View synonyms	See some synonyms for the correctly spelled word	View the bullet list of synonyms below the correctly spelled word near the bottom of the Spelling pane.
Close	Stop spelling checker	PowerPoint closes spelling checker and returns to PowerPoint window.

To Check Spelling

1 DOWNLOAD & SELECT SLIDES | 2 INSERT & FORMAT PICTURES | 3 INSERT & FORMAT SHAPES
4 FORMAT SLIDE BACKGROUNDS | 5 INSERT & FORMAT WORDART | 6 REVIEW, REVISE, & PRINT SLIDES

Why? *Although PowerPoint's spelling checker is a valuable tool, it is not infallible. You should not rely on the spelling checker to catch all your mistakes.* The following steps check the spelling on all slides in the Basketball Camp presentation.

1

• Click Review on the ribbon to display the Review tab.

• Click the Spelling button (Review Tab | Proofing group) to start the spelling checker and display the Spelling pane (Figure 2–74).

Figure 2–74

2

- With the word, skils, selected in the list and in the Notes pane, click the Change button (Spelling pane) to replace the misspelled flagged word, skils, with the selected correctly spelled word, skills, and then continue the spelling check (Figure 2–75).

Figure 2–75

Q&A Could I have clicked the Change All button instead of the Change button?
Yes. When you click the Change All button, you change the current and future occurrences of the misspelled word. The misspelled word, skils, appears only once in the presentation, so clicking the Change or the Change All button in this instance produces identical results.

Occasionally a correctly spelled word is flagged as a possible misspelled word. Why?
Your custom dictionary does not contain the word, so it is seen as spelled incorrectly. You can add this word to a custom dictionary to prevent the spelling checker from flagging it as a mistake.

3

- Replace the misspelled word, lern, with the word, learn.
- Continue checking all flagged words in the presentation. When the Microsoft PowerPoint dialog box appears, click the OK button (Microsoft PowerPoint dialog box) to close the spelling checker and return to the slide where a possible misspelled word appeared.

Other Ways

1. Click Spell Check icon on status bar	2. Right-click flagged word, click correct word	3. Press F7

To Insert a Slide Number

PowerPoint can insert the slide number on your slides automatically to indicate where the slide is positioned within the presentation. The number location on the slide is determined by the presentation theme. You have the option to not display this slide number on the title slide. To insert a slide number on all slides except the title slide, you would follow these steps.

1. Display the Insert tab and then click the Slide Number button (Insert tab | Text group) to display the Header and Footer dialog box.

2. Click the Slide number check box (Header and Footer dialog box) to place a check mark in it.

Q&A Can I prevent the slide number from being displayed on the title slide?
Yes. Click the 'Don't show on title slide' check box (Header and Footer dialog box) to place a check mark in it.

3. Click the 'Apply to All' button (Header and Footer dialog box) to close the dialog box and insert the slide number.

Q&A How does clicking the 'Apply to All' button differ from clicking the Apply button?
The Apply button inserts the slide number only on the currently displayed slide, whereas the 'Apply to All' button inserts the slide number on every slide.

BTW

PowerPoint Help
At any time while using PowerPoint, you can find answers to questions and display information about various topics through PowerPoint Help. Used properly, this form of assistance can increase your productivity and reduce your frustrations by minimizing the time you spend learning how to use PowerPoint. For instructions about PowerPoint Help and exercises that will help you gain confidence in using it, read the Office and Windows module at the beginning of this book.

To Add a Transition between Slides

A final enhancement you will make in this presentation is to change the transition from Fade to Wipe for all slides and increase the transition duration. The following steps apply this transition to the presentation.

1 Click Transitions on the ribbon and then click the Wipe transition (Transitions tab | Transition to This Slide group) to apply this transition.

2 Click the Duration up arrow in the Timing group four times to change the transition speed from 01.00 to 02.00.

3 Click the Preview Transitions button (Transitions tab | Preview area) to view the new transition and time.

4 Click the 'Apply To All' button (Transitions tab | Timing group) to apply this transition and speed to all four slides in the presentation (Figure 2–76).

Q&A Can I apply a particular transition or duration to one slide and then change the transition or timing for a different slide in the presentation?

Yes. Select a slide and then select a transition and duration. Do not click the 'Apply To All' button. Repeat this process to apply the transition and duration to individual slides.

Figure 2–76

How can I use handouts to organize my speech?

As you develop a lengthy presentation with many visuals, handouts can help you organize your material. Print handouts with the maximum number of slides per page. Use scissors to cut each thumbnail and then place these miniature slide images adjacent to each other on a flat surface. Any type on the thumbnails will be too small to read, so the images will need to work with only the support of the verbal message you provide. You can rearrange these thumbnails as you organize your speech. When you return to your computer, you can rearrange the slides on your screen to match the order of your thumbnail printouts. Begin speaking the actual words you want to incorporate in the body of the talk. This process of glancing at the thumbnails and hearing yourself say the key ideas of the speech is one of the best methods of organizing and preparing for the actual presentation. Ultimately, when you deliver your speech in front of an audience, the images on the slides or on your note cards should be sufficient to remind you of the accompanying verbal message.

To Print Speaker Notes

Why? *Comments added to slides in the Notes pane give the speaker information that supplements the text on the slide.* They will print with a small image of the slide at the top and the comments below the slide. The following steps print the speaker notes.

1

• Display Slide 1, click File on the ribbon to open the Backstage view, and then click the Print tab in the Backstage view to display Slide 1 in the Print gallery.

• Click 'Full Page Slides' in the Settings area to display the Print gallery (Figure 2–77).

Q&A Why does the preview of my slide appear in black and white?

Your printer determines how the preview appears. If your printer is not capable of printing color images, the preview will not appear in color.

Figure 2–77

2

• Click Notes Pages in the Print Layout area to select this option and then click the Next Page button three times to display a preview of Slide 4 (Figure 2–78).

Q&A Can I preview Slides 1, 2, or 3 now?

Yes. Click the Previous Page button to preview the other slides.

Figure 2–78

- Verify that the printer listed on the Printer Status button will print a hard copy of the presentation. If necessary, click the Printer Status button to display a list of available printer options and then click the desired printer to change the currently selected printer.

- Click the Print button in the Print gallery to print the notes pages on the currently selected printer.

- When the printer stops, retrieve the hard copy.

Q&A | I am not using a color printer, so why do the background images display in the figures but not in my printout?
Graphics are displayed depending upon the settings in the Print gallery. For example, the background will print if Color is specified whereas it will not with a Grayscale or Pure Black and White setting.

Other Ways

1. Press CTRL+P, select desired options

To Save and Print the Presentation

It is a good practice to save a presentation before printing it, in the event you experience difficulties printing. For a detailed example of the procedure summarized below for saving and printing a presentation, refer to the Office and Windows module at the beginning of this book.

1 Save the presentation again on the same storage location with the same file name.

2 Print the presentation.

Q&A | Do I have to wait until my presentation is complete to print it?
No, you can follow these steps to print a presentation at any time while you are creating it.

3 Because the project now is complete, you can exit PowerPoint.

BTW
Conserving Ink and Toner
If you want to conserve ink or toner, you can instruct PowerPoint to print draft quality documents by clicking File on the ribbon to open the Backstage view, clicking the Options tab in the Backstage view to display the PowerPoint Options dialog box, clicking Advanced in the left pane (PowerPoint Options dialog box), scrolling to the Print area in the right pane, not placing a check mark in the High quality check box, and then clicking the OK button. Then, use the Backstage view to print the document as usual.

BTW
Distributing a Document
Instead of printing and distributing a hard copy of a document, you can distribute the document electronically. Options include sending the document via email; posting it on cloud storage (such as OneDrive) and sharing the file with others; posting it on social media, a blog, or other website; and sharing a link associated with an online location of the document. You also can create and share a PDF or XPS image of the document, so that users can view the file in Acrobat Reader or XPS Viewer instead of in PowerPoint.

BTW
Printing Document Properties
PowerPoint 2016 does not allow you to print document properties. This feature, however, is available in other Office 2016 apps, including Word and Excel.

Summary

In this module, you have learned how to insert and format pictures, add and format shapes, insert and format WordArt, add and format slide backgrounds, find and replace text, check spelling, add notes, and print speaker notes.

What decisions will you need to make when creating your next presentation?

Use these guidelines as you complete the assignments in this module and create your own slide show decks outside of this class.

1. Determine if an online theme can help you design and develop the presentation efficiently and effectively.

2. Identify personal pictures that would create interest and promote the message being presented.

3. Consider modifying pictures.

    a) Add corrections.

    b) Add styles.

    c) Add effects.

    d) Add and format borders.

4. Locate shapes that supplement the verbal and written message.

    a) Size and position them aesthetically on slides.

    b) Add styles.

5. Develop WordArt that emphasizes major presentation messages.

    a) Modify the shape.

    b) Change the weight and color to coordinate with slide elements.

6. Format individual slide backgrounds.

    a) Add and modify fills.

    b) Insert a picture background.

7. Change fonts to emphasize particular slide components.

8. Search for synonyms that help express your thoughts.

9. Create speaker notes.

10. Check spelling.

Apply Your Knowledge

Reinforce the skills and apply the concepts you learned in this module.

Changing the Background and Adding Photos and WordArt

Note: To complete this assignment, you will be required to use the Data Files. Please contact your instructor for information about accessing the Data Files.

Instructions: Run PowerPoint. Open the presentation called Apply 2–1 Bees, which is located in the Data Files. The four slides in the presentation discuss bee stings. The document you open is an unformatted presentation. You are to add pictures, apply picture styles, add WordArt, change slide layouts, and apply a transition so the slides look like Figure 2–79.

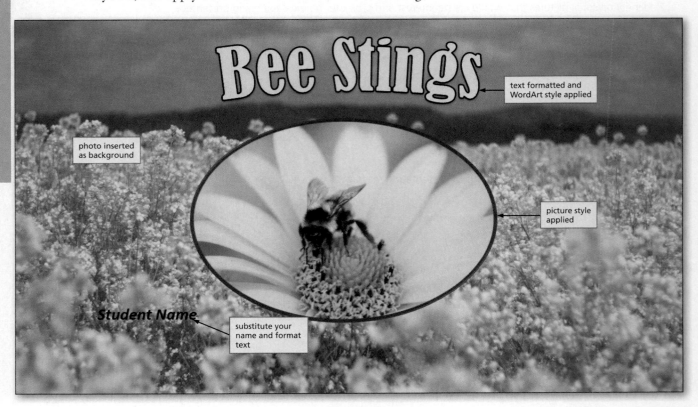

(a) Slide 1

Figure 2–79

Perform the following tasks:

1. On the title slide, use your name in place of Student Name and then bold and italicize this text (Figure 2–79a).

2. If requested to do so by your instructor, change your first name to your mother's first name on the title slide.

3. Increase the title text font size to 96 point and change the font to Bernard MT Condensed. Apply the WordArt style, Fill – White, Outline – Accent 1, Shadow (in first row). Change text fill color to Yellow (in Standard Colors row). Change text outline to Black, Text 1 (in first Theme Colors row) and then change the outline weight to 2¼ pt. Apply the Transform text effect, Arch Up (in Follow Path row) to this text.

4. Apply the Beveled Oval, Black picture style to the picture on Slide 1 and then move the picture to the center of the slide as shown in Figure 2–79a. Use the vertical Smart Guide to align the picture in this location.

5. Create a background on Slide 1 by inserting the photo, Spring, which is located in the Data Files.

6. On Slide 2, change the layout to Title and Content. Increase the title text font to 54 point, change the font color to Green (in Standard Colors row), and then bold this text. Increase the list font size to 32 point, as shown in Figure 2–79b.

7. Create a background on Slides 2 and 3 by inserting the Light Gradient – Accent 4 gradient fill (in first Preset gradients row).

8. On Slide 2, insert the picture, Bee2, move it to the right side of the slide, and then apply the Soft Edge Rectangle picture style to the picture.

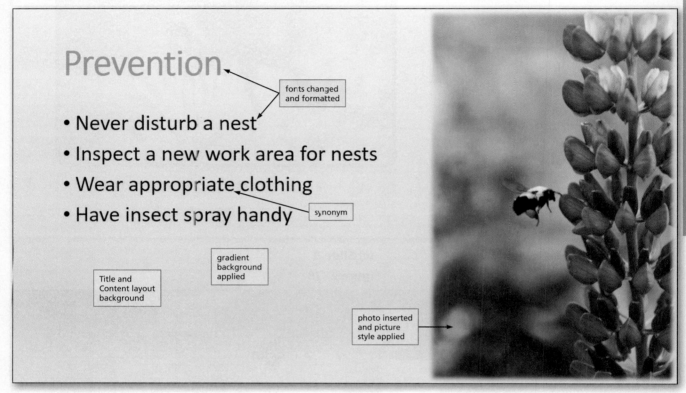

(b) Slide 2

Figure 2–79

9. On Slide 2, type **Wear long pants and a long-sleeved shirt when hiking or working outside.** in the Notes pane.

10. Replace the word, proper, with the synonym, appropriate.

11. On Slide 3 (Figure 2–79c), increase the title text font to 54 point, change the font color to Green (in Standard Colors row), and then bold this text. Increase the list font size to 24 point. Insert the photo, Bee3, and then apply the Reflected Bevel, Black picture style and change the picture brightness to Brightness: +20% Contrast: 0% (Normal) (in Brightness/Contrast area).

12. Type **Apply ice to control swelling.** in the Notes pane.

13. Create a new Slide 4 with the blank layout. Create a background on Slide 4 by inserting the photo, Hiking. Insert the illustration, Bee4. Resize this illustration and move it to the woman's right arm, as shown in Figure 2–79d.

14. On Slide 4, insert the Oval Callout shape (in first row in Callouts area) and then move it to the right side of the woman's head. Apply the Subtle Effect – Gold, Accent 4 (in fourth row) shape style to the callout. Size the shape as shown in the figure. Type **I am glad I have insect repellent in my backpack** in the shape. Bold and italicize this text and then change the font size to 20 point, as shown in Figure 2–79d.

15. Apply the Wind transition in the Exciting category to all slides. Change the duration to 2.50 seconds.

Continued >

Apply Your Knowledge *continued*

(c) Slide 3

Figure 2–79

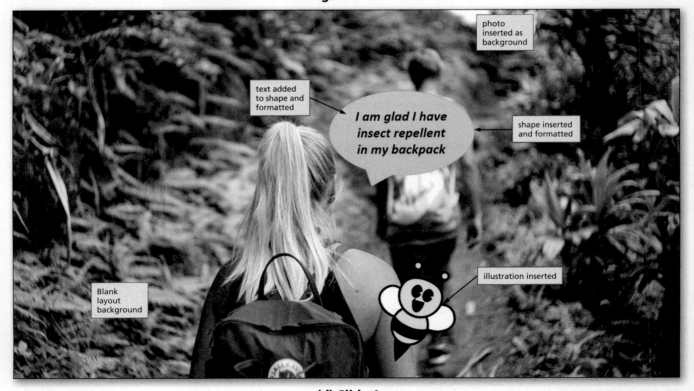

(d) Slide 4

Figure 2–79

16. Save the presentation using the file name, Apply 2–1 Bee Stings.

17. Submit the revised document in the format specified by your instructor.

18. ✦ In Step 4 you applied the Beveled Oval, Black picture style to the photo on Slide 1. How did this style enhance the photo and the slide?

Extend Your Knowledge

Extend the skills you learned in this module and experiment with new skills. You may need to use Help to complete the assignment.

Changing Slide Backgrounds, Inserting Shapes and WordArt, and Finding and Replacing Text

Note: To complete this assignment, you will be required to use the Data Files. Please contact your instructor for information about accessing the Data Files.

Instructions: Run PowerPoint. Open the presentation, Extend 2–1 Monarch, which is located in the Data Files. You will create backgrounds including inserting a photo to create a background, apply a WordArt Style and effect, add shapes, and find and replace text to create the presentation.

Perform the following tasks:

1. Change the document theme to Basis and choose the orange variant (third variant).

2. Find and replace the words, stay alive, with the word, survive, on all slides.

3. On all slides, create a background by inserting the photo, Sky. Change the transparency to 25%.

4. On the title slide (Figure 2–80a), apply the WordArt style, Fill - Black, Text 1, Outline – Background 1, Hard Shadow – Accent 1 (second style in third row), to the title text, and then increase the font size to 72 point. Apply the WordArt Glow text effect, Red, 18 pt glow, Accent color 3 (in Glow Variations area), and then italicize this text. Also, align the text in the middle of the text box by clicking the Align Text button (Home tab | Paragraph group) and then selecting Middle in the Align Text gallery. You may need to use Help for assistance in aligning this text.

(a) Slide 1

Figure 2–80

Continued >

Extend Your Knowledge *continued*

5. If requested to do so by your instructor, add your current or previous pet's name as the Slide 1 subtitle text in place of Student Name.

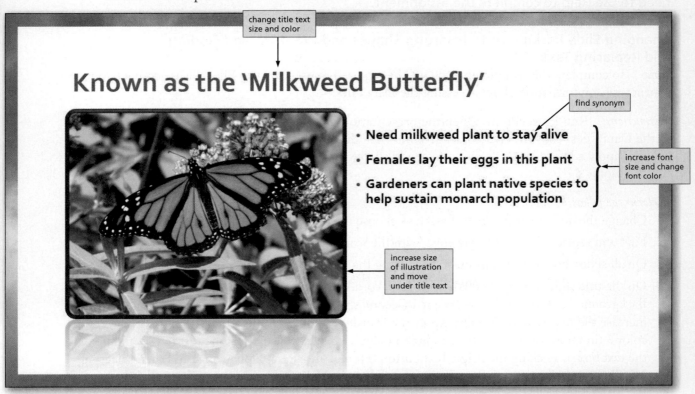

(b) Slide 2

Figure 2–80

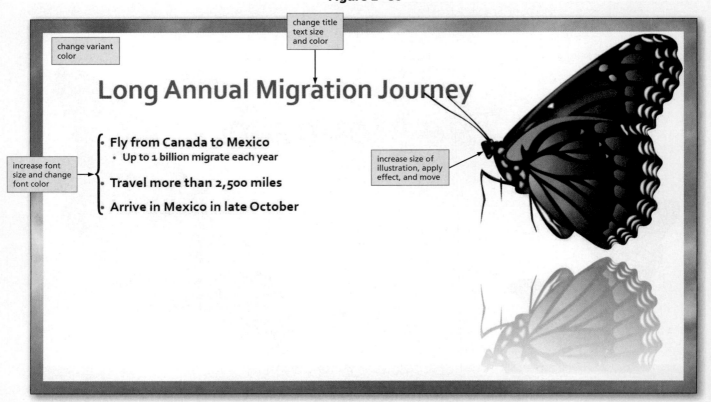

(c) Slide 3

Figure 2–80

(d) Slide 4

Figure 2–80

6. On Slide 1, move the butterfly illustration in the upper-left corner to the lower-left corner of the slide. Change the butterfly illustration in the upper-right corner of the slide to the illustration, Monarch2. Increase the size of this illustration to approximately 6.26" × 5.44" and move it to the lower-right side of the slide as shown in Figure 2–80a. *Hint*: Use the Size group on the Picture Tools Format tab to enter these measurements for the illustration.

7. On Slides 2 and 3, increase the font size of the first-level paragraphs to 20 point and the one second-level paragraph on Slide 3 to 16 point. Also, change the color of this text to Black, Text 1 (in first Theme Colors row) and then bold this text.

8. On Slide 2 (Figure 2–80b), increase the size of the illustration to approximately 4.14" × 5.53", apply the Reflected Bevel, Black picture style, and then move it under the title text.

9. On Slide 3 (Figure 2–80c), increase the size of the illustration to approximately 4.35" × 5.2", apply the Half Reflection, 8 pt offset reflection picture effect (Reflection Variations area), and then move this illustration to the upper-right corner of the slide.

10. On Slides 2, 3, and 4, decrease the size of the title text to 40 point and then bold this text.

11. On Slide 4 (Figure 2–80d), insert the Right Arrow shape (in Block Arrows area) and position it on the globe illustration near the Canada–United States border. Size the shape as shown in the figure. Type **Canada to Mexico** in the shape. Bold this text and then change the font size to 24 point. Apply the Light 1 Outline, Colored Fill – Orange, Accent 4 shape style (in third Theme Styles row) to the shape.

12. On Slide 4, insert a Curved Arrow Connector shape by displaying the Shapes gallery, clicking this shape (in Lines area), and then positioning the pointer over central Canada in the globe illustration. Then, click and drag the pointer to central Mexico. Size this arrow so it is approximately 0.84" × 1.91". Hint: You can size a shape in the same manner as you size a picture or illustration.

Continued >

Extend Your Knowledge *continued*

13. With the Curved Arrow Connector selected, click the Shape Outline button (Drawing Tools Format tab | Shape Styles group) to display the Shape Outline gallery and then click the Red, Accent 1 style (in first Theme Styles row) to apply this style to this arrow shape. Change the shape outline weight to 6 pt.

14. Apply an appropriate transition to all slides.

15. Save the presentation using the file name, Extend 2–1 Monarch Migration.

16. Submit the revised document in the format specified by your instructor.

17. ✳ In this assignment, you changed the transparency of the inserted background picture on all the slides to 25%. How did this transparency change enhance your slides?

Expand Your World

Create a solution that uses cloud and web technologies by learning and investigating on your own from general guidance.

Modifying a Presentation Using PowerPoint Online

Note: To complete this assignment, you will be required to use the Data Files. Please contact your instructor for information about accessing the Data Files.

Instructions: The park district director in your community is planning a basketball camp for next summer. He has asked you to help him promote this event, and he wants to focus on the skills boys and girls will learn and develop. You inform him that you have created a Basketball Camp presentation for your computer class, and he would like you to customize the content of these slides slightly to promote the summer camp.

Perform the following tasks:
1. Run a browser. Search for the text, PowerPoint Online, using a search engine. Visit several websites to learn about PowerPoint Online. Navigate to the Office Online website. You will need to sign in to your Microsoft account. Run PowerPoint Online.

2. Locate the Basketball Camp presentation in the Recent list and then click the file name to open the file. Click the Edit Presentation button and then click 'Edit in PowerPoint Online' and display the ribbon. Modify the presentation you created for the Basketball Camp presentation by adding the name and address of the nearest park district headquarters on the title slide. In addition, add the date that is the first Saturday in June next year and a starting time of 1 p.m.

3. If requested by your instructor, add the name of one of your high school teachers as the park district director's name on the title slide.

4. Save the presentation using the file name, Expand 2–1 Basketball Camp.

5. Submit the assignment in the format specified by your instructor.

6. ✳ Other than the content the director asked you to include on the title slide, how does the presentation you created using PowerPoint Online differ from the presentation you created in the Module 2 project? Which tabs are not available in PowerPoint Online? View the Home, Design, and Transitions tabs. Do you think the formatting functions, themes, and transitions are adequate to develop effective presentations? Why or why not?

In the Labs

Design, create, modify, and/or use a presentation following the guidelines, concepts, and skills presented in this module. Labs 1 and 2, which increase in difficulty, require you to create solutions based on what you learned in the module; Lab 3 requires you to apply your creative thinking and problem-solving skills to design and implement a solution.

Lab 1: Creating a Presentation, Inserting Photos, Applying Picture Styles, and Inserting Shapes

Note: To complete this assignment, you will be required to use the Data Files. Please contact your instructor for information about accessing the Data Files.

Problem: Your astronomy class is studying the dwarf planet, Pluto, and the New Horizon probe that has been taking photographs of this planet. Prepare the PowerPoint presentation shown in Figure 2–81.

Perform the following tasks:

1. Run PowerPoint. Create a new presentation using the Celestial theme.

2. On Slide 1, insert the photo, Pluto1, as shown in Figure 2–81a. Apply the Metal Oval picture style to the picture, decrease the size of the picture slightly, and then move it to the left side of the slide as shown in the figure.

3. Type **Pluto Up Close** as the Slide 1 title text. Press the ENTER key after the words, PLUTO and UP, so the text is displayed on three lines. Change the font to Britannic Bold and increase the font size to 88 point. Apply the WordArt style Gradient Fill – Gray (first style in

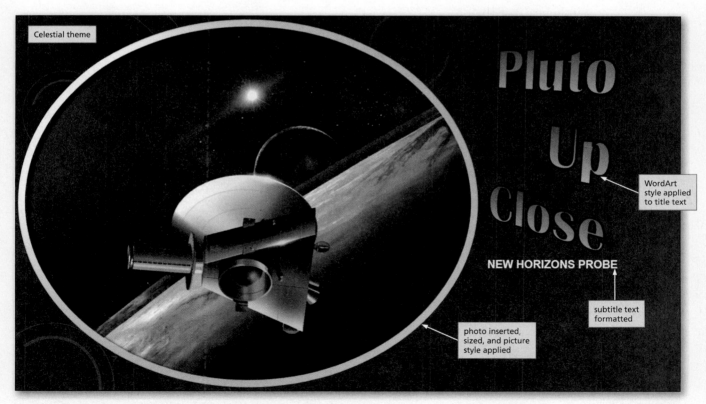

(a) Slide 1

Figure 2–81

Continued >

In the Labs *continued*

second row). Change the text outline color to Black, Background 1 (in Theme Colors row) and the text outline weight to 3 pt. Also, apply the Perspective Heroic Extreme Left 3-D Rotation (in Perspective area) to this text. Type **New Horizons Probe** as the subtitle text. Change the font to Arial, decrease the font size to 16 point, and then bold this text.

4. Insert four new slides. Create Slides 2 and 5 with the Two Content layout, Slide 3 with the Panoramic Picture with Caption layout, and Slide 4 with the Title Only layout.

5. Using Figures 2–81b through 2–81e as a guide, type the title and content text. On Slide 2, change the title font to Arial, increase the font size to 44 point, and then change the font color to Red (in Standard Colors row). Use the Format Painter to apply these formatting changes to the title text on Slides 4 and 5.

6. On Slide 3, change the font size of the two paragraphs to 24 point and then bold this text.

7. On Slide 5, change the bulleted list font size to 28 point and then bold this text.

8. Using Figures 2–81b through 2–81e as a guide, insert all illustrations on Slides 2 through 5. The pictures and illustration to be inserted, which are available in the Data Files, are called Pluto2 (for Slide 2), Solar System (for Slide 3), Pluto3 (for Slide 4), and Solar System2 (for Slide 5).

9. Size the pictures and then use the Smart Guides to position these images. You may want to zoom the slides to help you align these graphic elements.

10. On Slide 2, apply the Bevel Perspective picture style to the picture, change the picture border color to Red, and then change the border weight to 3 pt, as shown in Figure 2–81b.

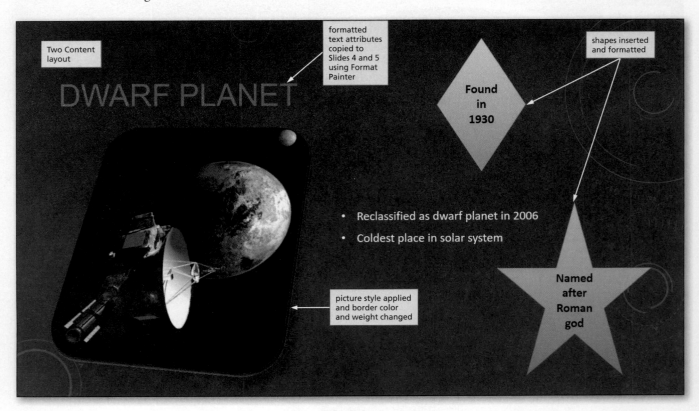

(b) Slide 2

Figure 2–81

11. On Slide 2, insert the Diamond shape located in the Basic Shapes area to the right of the title text. Apply the Subtle Effect – Olive Green, Accent 4 shape style (in Theme Styles area) to the shape, type `Found in 1930` in the shape, and then bold this text. Insert the 5-Point Star shape located in the Stars and Banners area in the lower-right corner of the slide. Apply the Subtle Effect – Blue, Accent 2 shape style (in Theme Styles area) to the shape, type `Named after Roman god` in the shape, and then bold this text. Adjust the size and position of these two shapes, as shown in the figure.

12. On Slide 3, insert the Sun shape located in the Basic Shapes area on the lower-right corner of the slide. Apply the Intense Effect – Gold, Accent 5 shape style (in Theme Styles area) to the shape. Size the shape as shown in the figure. Type the text, `Pluto takes 248 earth years to orbit the sun` in the shape and then bold this text, as shown in Figure 2–81c.

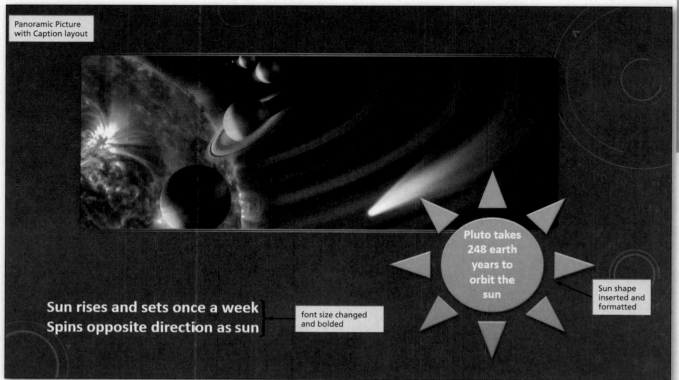

(c) Slide 3

Figure 2–81

13. On Slide 4, insert the Oval shape. Select this shape, hold down the SHIFT key, and then draw a circle .75" × .75", as shown in Figure 2–81d. *Hint:* Use the Size group in the Drawing Tools Format tab to enter the exact measurement of the shape. Change the shape fill gradient to Linear Down (in first Light Variations area). Then copy and paste this shape four times. Move the five shapes around the Pluto illustration, as shown in the figure.

14. On Slide 5, apply the Simple Frame, White picture style to the illustration. Insert the Left Arrow shape located in the Block Arrows area to the right of the illustration. Change the shape fill to Red. Size the shape as shown in the figure. Type `Pluto` in the shape and then bold this text, as shown in Figure 2–81e.

15. On Slide 2, type `Pluto was discovered on February 18, 1930, by Clyde Tombaugh of the Lowell Observatory.` in the Notes pane.

16. On Slide 3, type `It takes five hours for the sun's rays to reach Pluto. It takes only eight minutes for the sun's rays to reach Earth.` in the Notes pane.

Continued >

In the Labs *continued*

(d) Slide 4

Figure 2–81

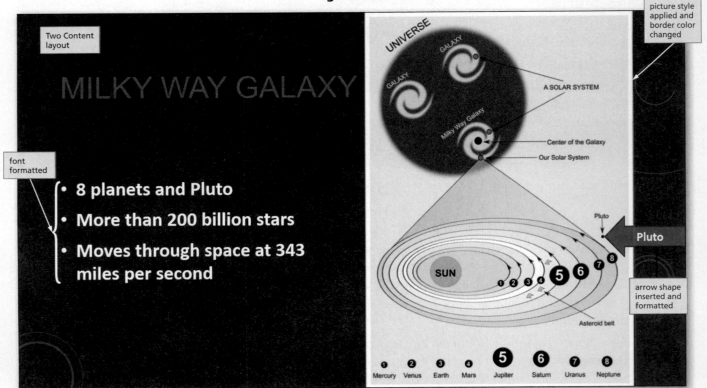

(e) Slide 5

Figure 2–81

17. If requested by your instructor, type the name of the city or county in which you were born into the title placeholder on Slide 3.

18. Apply the Vortex transition in the Exciting category to all slides. Change the duration to 3.0 seconds.

19. Check the spelling and correct any errors. Save the presentation using the file name, Lab 2–1 Pluto Up Close.

20. Print the notes pages.

21. Submit the document in the format specified by your instructor.

22. ✺ In Step 2, you applied the Metal Oval picture style to the picture. How did this improve the design of the slide? Why did you put a 3 pt red border on the picture on Slide 2?

Lab 2: Creating a Presentation Using an Online Theme Template, Shapes, and WordArt

Note: To complete this assignment, you will be required to use the Data Files. Please contact your instructor for information about accessing the Data Files.

Problem: Your local library has hired a singer for the summer reading program. Her weekly show is centered around music and art, and one of her songs is about the colors of the rainbow. In addition to her backdrop of rainbow colors, you decide to develop a presentation to teach the children more about rainbows. You create the presentation shown in Figure 2–82.

Perform the following tasks:

1. Run PowerPoint and then search for an online template by typing   **nature**   in the 'Search for online templates and themes' box. Choose the template called Nature presentation, illustrated landscape design (widescreen).

2. Delete Slides 12 and 13, delete Slides 6 through 10, and then delete Slides 3 and 4. Duplicate Slide 2 and then move Slide 4 to the end of the presentation.

3. Type the title and text content for all slides, as shown in Figures 2–82a through 2–82e.

(a) Slide 1

Figure 2–82

Continued >

In the Labs *continued*

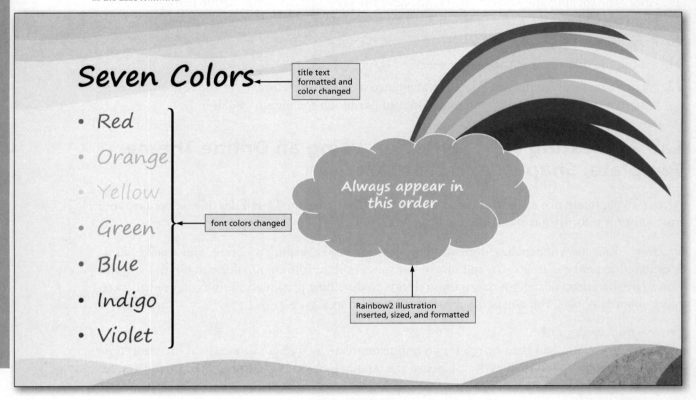

(b) Slide 2

Figure 2–82

(c) Slide 3

Figure 2–82

4. Insert the illustrations shown in Figures 2–82b through 2–82d from the Data Files. The illustrations are called Rainbow1 (for Slide 1), Rainbow2 (for Slide 2), Rainbow3 (for Slide 3), and People (for Slide 4). Size the illustrations using Figure 2–82 as a guide.

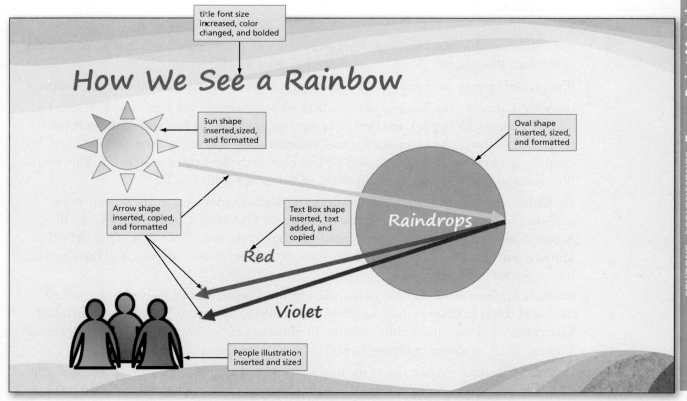

(d) Slide 4

Figure 2–82

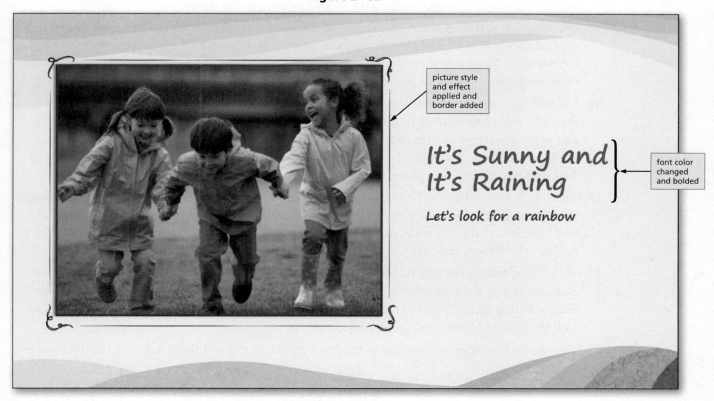

(e) Slide 5

Figure 2–82

5. On the title slide, select the title text and then apply the WordArt style Fill – White, Outline –
Accent 1, Shadow (fourth style in first row). Increase the font size to 72 point. Change the text
fill to Red (in Standard Colors row), the text outline color to Purple (in Standard Colors row),

Continued >

In the Labs *continued*

and the text outline weight to 3 pt. Also, apply the Arch Up transform effect (Follow Path area), to this text. Position this WordArt, as shown in Figure 2–82a.

6. If requested by your instructor, add the name of your hometown in the subtitle placeholder.

7. On Slide 2, increase the font size of the title to 40 point, change the font color to Black, Text 2 (in first Theme Colors row), and then bold this text. Increase the font size of the bulleted list to 28 point. Change the font color for each bulleted paragraph to the color that is named. For example, the first bulleted paragraph is Red, so change the font color to Red. Use Blue for the Blue text and Dark Blue for the Indigo text, as shown in Figure 2–82b.

8. On Slide 2, insert the Cloud shape, located in the Basic Shapes area, at the bottom of the rainbow illustration. Change the shape style to Light 1, Outline, Colored Fill – Light Blue, Accent 2 (in third Theme Styles row). Size the shape as shown in the figure. Type **Always appear in this order** in the shape, increase the font size to 20 point, and then bold this text, as shown in Figure 2–82b.

9. On Slide 3, increase the font size of the title text to 40 point, change the font color to Red, and then bold this text. Change the font color of the bulleted list text to Dark Blue (in Standard Colors row). For the illustration, apply the Brightness: +20% Contrast: +40% (in Brightness/ Contrast area), as shown in Figure 2–82c.

10. On Slide 4, increase the font size of the title text to 40 point, change the font color to Red, and then bold this text, as shown in Figure 2–82d. Insert the Sun shape, located in the Basic Shapes area, in the upper left area of the slide below the title text. Change the shape fill color to Yellow (in Standard Colors row) and then apply the From Top Left Corner gradient (in Dark Variations area) to the shape. Size and position the shape as shown in the figure.

11. On Slide 4, insert the Oval shape located in the Basic Shapes area, resize the shape so that it is approximately 3" × 3", and then change the Shape Fill color to Light Blue, Accent 2 (in Theme Colors row). Move this shape to the area shown in the figure. Type **Raindrops** in the shape, increase the font size to 24 point, and then bold this text.

12. On Slide 4, insert the Arrow shape, located in the Lines area, from the edge of the sun shape to the right side of the blue shape, as shown in Figure 2–82d. Change the weight to 6 pt. Copy and paste this arrow two times and use the sizing handles to position the arrows, as shown in the figure. Change the upper Arrow shape outline color to Yellow, the middle Arrow shape to Red, and the lower Arrow shape to Purple.

13. On Slide 4, insert the Text Box shape, located in the Basic Shapes area, type **Red** in the shape, change the font color to Red, increase the font size to 24 point, and then bold this text. Copy and paste this shape one time, change the text to **Violet,** and then change the font color to Purple. Move these two text box shapes to the areas shown in the figure.

14. On Slide 5, change the title text font color to Red and then bold this text, as shown in Figure 2–82e. Change the font color of the text to Purple and then bold this text. Apply the Simple Frame, White picture style to the picture. Add a 3 pt Purple border and then apply the Offset Left shadow (in Outer area) picture effect.

15. Change the transition to Origami in the Exciting category to all slides. Change the duration to 2.5 seconds.

16. Check spelling and correct all errors. Save the presentation using the file name, Lab 2–2 About Rainbows.

17. Submit the revised document in the format specified by your instructor.

18. ✹ You searched for an online rainbow theme. Do you think any of the other themes would have worked well for your presentation? Does choosing specific slide layouts while beginning the exercise help save time creating the presentation?

Lab 3: **Consider This: Your Turn**

Design and Create a Presentation about Learning to Knit and Crochet

Note: To complete this assignment, you will be required to use the Data Files. Please contact your instructor for information about accessing the Data Files.

Part 1: More than 50 million people knit or crochet to create fun and useful items, to relax, or to exchange ideas with fellow hobbyists at a regional guild or group. The local craft store in your community is offering a series of classes on knitting and crocheting techniques, and the manager has asked you to help promote the event. The introductory course includes instruction on selecting yarn, hooks, and needles; reading patterns; and making basic stitches. The intermediate and advanced courses include knitting in the round; making sleeves, button holes, and cables; and bead and filet crocheting. Classes are scheduled for four weeks on consecutive Saturdays beginning the first week of every month. All students will learn new skills and complete a fashionable project, which could include creating afghans, hats, and scarves for community residents in need. Use the concepts and techniques presented in this module to prepare a presentation to promote the classes. Select a suitable theme, and include a title slide, bulleted lists, shapes, and WordArt. The presentation should contain photos and illustrations appropriately resized. Six photos and illustrations are available in the Data Files: Green Yarn, Mitten, Two Mittens, Penguin, Quilt, and Scarf. Apply picture styles and effects. Add a title slide and closing slide to complete your presentation. Format the title slide with a shape. Format the background with at least one picture and apply a background texture to at least one slide. Review and revise your presentation as needed. Submit your assignment in the format specified by your instructor.

Part 2: ✹ You made several decisions while creating the presentation in this assignment: where to place text, how to format the text (such as font, font size, and where to use WordArt), which graphical image(s) to use, what styles and effects to apply, where to position the graphical images, how to format the graphical images, and which shapes to use to add interest to the presentation. What was the rationale behind each of these decisions? When you reviewed the document, what further revisions did you make and why? Where would you recommend showing this slide show?

3 Reusing a Presentation and Adding Media and Animation

Objectives

You will have mastered the material in this module when you can:

- Color a photo
- Add an artistic effect to a photo
- Align paragraph text
- Change views
- Ungroup, change the color of, and regroup an illustration
- Copy a slide element from one slide to another
- Insert and edit a video clip

- Insert an audio clip
- Control audio and video clips
- Insert entrance, emphasis, and exit effects
- Control animation timing
- Change theme colors
- Change a theme and variant on one slide
- Print handouts

BTW
Media in Presentations
Well-produced video and audio clips add value to a presentation when they help explain a concept that cannot be captured in a photo or illustration. Before you insert these files on a slide, however, consider whether they really add any value to your overall slide show. Audiences quickly tire of extraneous movement and sounds on slides, and they will find such media clips annoying. The audience's attention should focus primarily on the presenter; extraneous or inappropriate media files may divert their attention and, in turn, decrease the quality of the presentation.

Introduction

At times, you will need to revise a PowerPoint presentation. Changes may include inserting and adding effects to photos, altering the colors of photos and illustrations, and updating visual elements displayed on a slide. Applying a different theme, changing fonts, and substituting graphical elements can give a slide show an entirely new look. Adding media, including sounds, video, and music, can enhance a presentation and help audience members retain the information being presented. Adding animation can reinforce important points and enliven a presentation.

Project — Presentation with Video, Audio, Animation, and Photos with Effects

The project in this module follows graphical guidelines and uses PowerPoint to create the presentation shown in Figure 3–1. The slides in this revised presentation, which discusses the Spokes Bike Club, have a variety of audio and visual elements. For example, the photos in the slides' backgrounds have artistic effects applied that soften the images and help the audience focus on other elements on the slides. The bicycle wheel photo has colors that blend well with the background. The bullet list is animated with entrance, emphasis, and exit effects. The video has been edited to play only one portion and has effects to add audience interest. Bicycle riding sounds integrate with the visual elements.

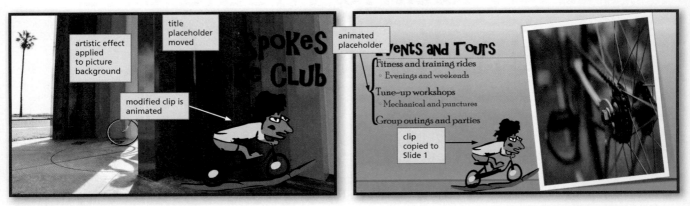

(a) Slide 1 (Title Slide with Picture Background, Modified Clip, and Animated Clip)

(b) Slide 2 (Bulleted List)

(c) Slide 3 (Picture Background and Video Clip)

(d) Slide 4 (Video Playing Full Screen)

Figure 3–1

For an introduction to Windows and instructions about how to perform basic Windows tasks, read the Office and Windows module at the beginning of this book, where you can learn how to resize windows, change screen resolution, create folders, move and rename files, use Windows Help, and much more.

Overall, the slides have myriad media elements and effects that are exciting for your audience to watch and hear.

In this module, you will learn how to create the slides shown in Figure 3–1. The following roadmap identifies general activities you will perform as you progress through this module:

1. INSERT and ADD EFFECTS to photos, including changing colors and styles.

2. MODIFY PLACEHOLDERS on the slides by moving and changing sizes.

3. MODIFY and COPY an ILLUSTRATION to customize its appearance.

4. ADD MEDIA files to slides.

5. ANIMATE SLIDE CONTENT with entrance, emphasis, and exit effects.

6. CUSTOMIZE SLIDE ELEMENTS by changing a theme and variant on one slide and changing the theme colors.

Inserting Photos and Adding Effects

The Spokes Bike Club presentation consists of three slides that have some text, a clip art image, a formatted background, and a transition applied to all slides. You will insert a photo into one slide and then modify it and another photo by adding artistic effects and recoloring. You also will copy the clip art from Slide 2 to Slide 1 and modify the objects in this clip. In Module 2, you inserted photos, made corrections, and added styles and effects; the new effects you apply in this module will add to your repertoire of photo enhancements that increase interest in your presentation.

In the following pages, you will perform these tasks:

1. Insert the first photo into Slide 1.

2. Recolor the Slide 1 photo.

3. Add an artistic effect to the Slide 3 photo.

4. Send the Slide 1 photo back behind all other slide objects.

To Insert and Resize a Photo into a Slide without Content Placeholders

The first step is to insert a photo into Slide 1. This photo is available in the Data Files. Please contact your instructor for information about accessing the required file. The following steps insert a photo into Slide 1.

1 Run PowerPoint and then open the presentation, Spokes, from the Data Files.

2 Save the presentation using the file name, Spokes Bike Club.

3 With Slide 1 displaying, click Insert on the ribbon to display the Insert tab and then click the Pictures button (Insert tab | Images group) to display the Insert Picture dialog box.

4 If necessary, navigate to the photo location (in this case, the Module 03 folder in the Data Files folder).

5 Click Hidden Bike to select the file.

6 Click the Insert button (Insert Picture dialog box) to insert the photo into Slide 1.

7 Drag the sizing handles to resize the photo so that it covers the entire slide. You can click the Height and Width arrows (Picture Tools Format tab | Size group) to adjust the picture size so that it is approximately 7.5" x 13.33" (Figure 3–2).

BTW

PowerPoint Screen Resolution
If you are using a computer or mobile device to step through the project in this module and you want your screens to match the figures in this book, you should change your screen's resolution to 1366 x 768. For information about how to change a computer's resolution, refer to the Office and Windows module at the beginning of this book.

BTW

Organizing Files and Folders
You should organize and store files in folders so that you easily can find the files later. For example, if you are taking an introductory technology class called CIS 101, a good practice would be to save all PowerPoint files in a PowerPoint folder in a CIS 101 folder. For a discussion of folders and detailed examples of creating folders, refer to the Office and Windows module at the beginning of this book.

For an introduction to Office and instructions about how to perform basic tasks in Office apps, read the Office and Windows module at the beginning of this book, where you can learn how to run an application, use the ribbon, save a file, open a file, print a file, exit an application, use Help, and much more.

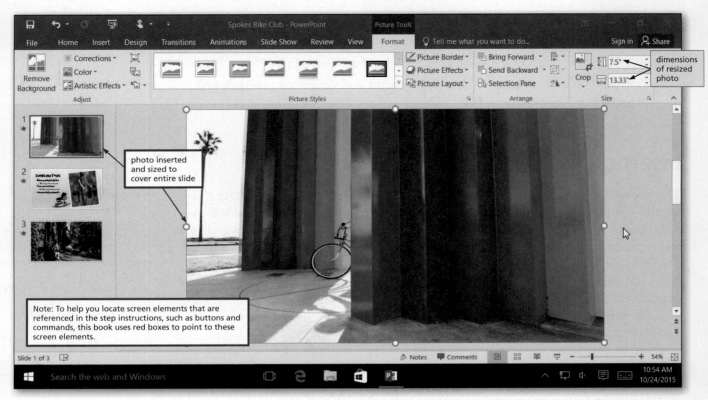

Figure 3–2

Adjusting Photo Colors

PowerPoint allows you to adjust colors to match or add contrast to slide elements by coloring photos. The Color gallery has a wide variety of preset formatting combinations. The thumbnails in the gallery display the more common color saturation, color tone, and recolor adjustments. **Color saturation** changes the intensity of colors. High saturation produces vivid colors; low saturation produces gray tones. **Color tone** affects the coolness, called blue, or the warmness, called orange, of photos. When a digital camera does not measure the tone correctly, a **color cast** occurs, and, as a result, one color dominates the photo. **Recolor** effects convert the photo into a wide variety of hues. The more common are **grayscale**, which changes the color photo into black, white, and shades of gray, and **sepia**, which changes the photo colors into brown, gold, and yellow, reminiscent of a faded photo. You also can fine-tune the color adjustments by clicking the Picture Color Options and More Variations commands in the Color gallery.

To Color a Photo

1 INSERT & ADD EFFECTS | 2 MODIFY PLACEHOLDERS | 3 MODIFY & COPY ILLUSTRATIONS
4 ADD MEDIA | 5 ANIMATE SLIDE CONTENT | 6 CUSTOMIZE SLIDE ELEMENTS

The Office theme and text on Slides 1 and 2 are simple and fulfill the need to communicate the presentation's bicycling message. The photos on Slides 1 and 3 help set the tone of riding on an open road and enjoying the freedom that biking brings. You may want to add an effect to photos. *Why? An effect adds variety to the presentation and helps enhance ordinary photos.* The following steps recolor the Slide 1 photo to intensify the bright colors.

1

- With Slide 1 displaying and the Hidden Bike photo selected, click the Color button (Picture Tools Format tab | Adjust group) to display the Color gallery (Figure 3–3).

Q&A Why does the Adjust group look different on my screen?
Your monitor is set to a different resolution. See the Office 2016 and Windows 10 module for an explanation of screen resolution and the appearance of the ribbon.

Why are gray borders surrounding the thumbnails in the Color Saturation, Color Tone, and Recolor areas in the gallery?
The gray borders show the color saturation, tone, and recolor settings currently in effect for the image on Slide 1.

Figure 3–3

2

- Point to Saturation: 400% (last thumbnail in Color Saturation row) to display a live preview of this adjustment on the photo.

 Experiment

- Point to various thumbnails in the Color Saturation area and watch the saturation change on the photo in Slide 1.

- Click Saturation: 400% to apply this saturation to the Hidden Bike photo (Figure 3–4).

Q&A Could I have applied this recoloring to the photo if it had been a background instead of a file inserted into the slide?
No. Artistic effects and recoloring cannot be applied to backgrounds.

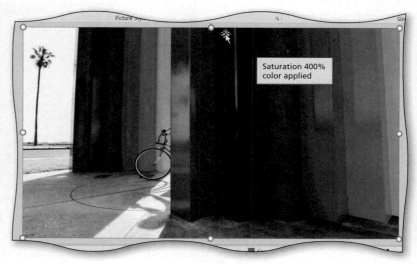

Figure 3–4

Other Ways

1. Click Format Picture on shortcut menu, click Picture icon, click Picture Color, use Saturation slider (Format Picture pane)

To Add an Artistic Effect to a Photo

1 INSERT & ADD EFFECTS | 2 MODIFY PLACEHOLDERS | 3 MODIFY & COPY ILLUSTRATIONS
4 ADD MEDIA | 5 ANIMATE SLIDE CONTENT | 6 CUSTOMIZE SLIDE ELEMENTS

Artists use a variety of techniques to create effects in their paintings. They can vary the amount of paint on their brushstroke, use fine bristles to add details, mix colors to increase or decrease intensity, and smooth their paints together to blend the colors. You, likewise, can add similar effects to your photos using PowerPoint's built-in artistic effects. *Why? The completed Slide 3 will have both a photo and a video, so applying an artistic effect to the photo will provide a contrast between the two images.* The following steps add an artistic effect to the Slide 3 photo.

1

- Display Slide 3 and select the photo.
- Click the Artistic Effects button (Picture Tools Format tab | Adjust group) to display the Artistic Effects gallery (Figure 3–5).

Figure 3–5

2

- Point to Cement (first thumbnail in fourth row) to display a live preview of this effect on the photo.

Experiment

- Point to various artistic effects and watch the hues change on the photo in Slide 3.
- Click Cement to apply this artistic effect to the photo (Figure 3–6).

Figure 3–6

Q&A

Can I adjust a photo by recoloring and applying an artistic effect?

Yes. You can apply both a color and an effect. You may prefer at times to mix these adjustments to create a unique image.

Other Ways

1. Click Format Picture on shortcut menu, click Effects icon, click Artistic Effects

To Change the Stacking Order

1 INSERT & ADD EFFECTS | 2 MODIFY PLACEHOLDERS | 3 MODIFY & COPY ILLUSTRATIONS
4 ADD MEDIA | 5 ANIMATE SLIDE CONTENT | 6 CUSTOMIZE SLIDE ELEMENTS

The objects on a slide stack on top of each other, much like individual cards in a deck. To change the order of these objects, you use the Bring Forward and Send Backward commands. **Bring Forward** moves an object toward the top of the stack, and **Send Backward** moves an object underneath another object. When you click the Bring Forward arrow, PowerPoint displays a menu with an additional command, **Bring to Front**, which moves a selected object to the top of the stack. Likewise, when you click the Send Backward arrow, the **Send to Back** command moves the selected object underneath all objects on the slide. The following steps arrange the Slide 1 photo. *Why? On this slide, the photo is on top of the placeholders, so you no longer can see the text. If you send the photo to the bottom of the stack on the slide, the letters will become visible.*

- Display Slide 1 and then select the Hidden Bike photo.
- Click the Picture Tools Format tab and then click the Send Backward arrow (Picture Tools Format tab | Arrange group) to display the Send Backward menu (Figure 3–7).

Q&A How can I see objects that are not on the top of the stack?
Press TAB or SHIFT + TAB to display each slide object.

Figure 3–7

- Click 'Send to Back' to move the photo underneath all slide objects (Figure 3–8).

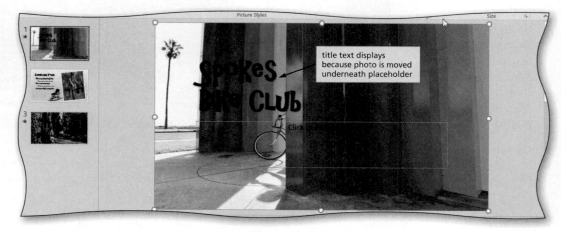

Figure 3–8

Other Ways

1. Click Send Backward arrow (Picture Tools Format tab | Arrange group), press K
2. Right-click photo, point to 'Send to Back' on shortcut menu, click 'Send to Back'

Modifying Placeholders

You have become familiar with inserting text and graphical content in the three types of placeholders: title, subtitle, and content. These placeholders can be moved, resized, and deleted to meet desired design requirements. In addition, placeholders can be added to a slide when needed. After you have modified the placeholder locations, you can view thumbnails of all your slides simultaneously by changing views.

In the following pages, you will perform these tasks:

1. Resize the Slide 1 title text placeholder.
2. Align the Slide 1 title text.
3. Move the Slide 1 title text placeholder.
4. Delete the Slide 1 subtitle text placeholder.
5. Change views.

BTW
The Ribbon and Screen Resolution
PowerPoint may change how the groups and buttons within the groups appear on the ribbon, depending on the computer or mobile device's screen resolution. Thus, your ribbon may look different from the ones in this book if you are using a screen resolution other than 1366 x 768.

To Resize a Placeholder

When the Slide 1 title placeholder is selected, the AutoFit button displays on the left side of the placeholder because the two lines of text exceed the placeholder's borders. PowerPoint attempts to reduce the font size when the text does not fit, and you can click this button to resize the existing text in the placeholder so the spillover text will fit within the borders. The following step increases the Slide 1 title text placeholder size. *Why?* *The two lines of text exceed the placeholder's borders, so you can resize the placeholder and fit the letters within the rectangle.*

- With Slide 1 displaying, click somewhere in the title text paragraphs to position the insertion point in the placeholder. Click the border of the title text placeholder to select it and then point to the top-middle sizing handle.
- Drag the top title text placeholder border upward to enlarge the placeholder (Figure 3–9).

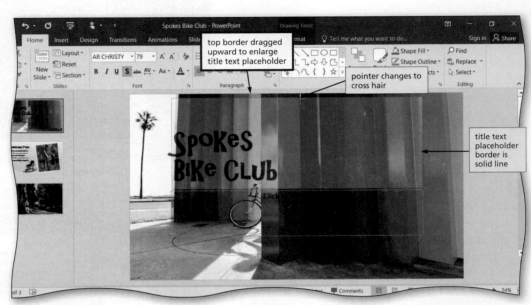

Figure 3–9

Q&A Can I drag other sizing handles to enlarge or shrink the placeholder?

Yes, you also can drag the left, right, top, and corner sizing handles to resize a placeholder. When you drag a corner sizing handle, the box keeps the same proportion and simply enlarges or shrinks the overall shape.

To Align Paragraph Text

The presentation theme determines the formatting characteristics of fonts and colors. It also establishes paragraph formatting, including the alignment of text. Some themes **center** the text paragraphs between the left and right placeholder borders, while others **left-align** the paragraph so that the first character of a text line is near the left border or **right-align** the paragraph so that the last character of a text line is near the right border. The paragraph also can be **justified** so that the text is aligned to both the left and right borders. When PowerPoint justifies text, it adds extras spaces between the words to fill the entire line.

The words, Spokes Bike Club, are left-aligned in the Slide 1 title text placeholder. Later, you will add an illustration on the right side of the slide below this text, so you desire to right-align the paragraph. *Why?* *Both the text and the picture will be located on the right side of the slide, so the alignments complement each other.* The following steps change the alignment of the Slide 1 title text placeholder.

• With the Home tab displayed, click somewhere in the title text paragraph of Slide 1 to position the insertion point in the text to be formatted (Figure 3–10).

Figure 3–10

• Click the Align Right button (Home tab | Paragraph group) to move the text to the right side of the title text placeholder (Figure 3–11).

Q&A What if I want to return the paragraph to left-alignment? Click the Align Left button (Home tab | Paragraph group).

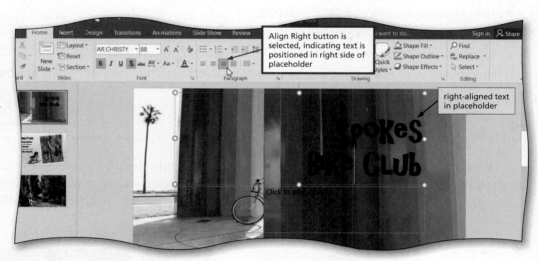

Figure 3–11

Other Ways

1. Right-click paragraph, click Align Right button on mini toolbar

2. Right-click paragraph, click Paragraph on shortcut menu, click Alignment arrow (Paragraph dialog box), click Right, click OK button

3. Click Paragraph dialog box launcher (Home tab | Paragraph group), click Alignment arrow (Paragraph dialog box), click Right, click OK button

4. Press CTRL+R

To Move a Placeholder

1 INSERT & ADD EFFECTS | 2 MODIFY PLACEHOLDERS | 3 MODIFY & COPY ILLUSTRATIONS
4 ADD MEDIA | 5 ANIMATE SLIDE CONTENT | 6 CUSTOMIZE SLIDE ELEMENTS

Why? If you desire to have a placeholder appear in a different area of the slide, you can move it to a new location. The theme layouts determine where the text and content placeholders display on the slide. The Slide 1 title text placeholder currently displays in the middle third of the slide, but the text in this placeholder would be more aesthetically pleasing if it were moved to the upper-right corner of the slide. The following step moves the Slide 1 title text placeholder.

- Click the border of the Slide 1 title text placeholder to select it.
- With the title text placeholder border displaying as a solid line or fine dots, point to an area of the left border between the middle and lower sizing handles so that the pointer changes to a four-headed arrow.

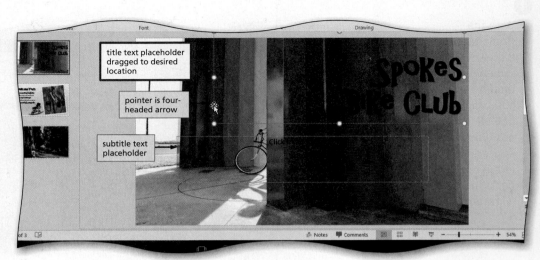

Figure 3–12

Q&A

Can I click any part of the border to select it?
Yes. You can click any of the four border lines.

How do I know if the placeholder is selected?
The selection handles are displayed.

- Drag the placeholder upward and to the right, as shown in Figure 3–12.
- If requested by your instructor, replace with word, Spokes, with the name of the city in which you were born.

To Delete a Placeholder

1 INSERT & ADD EFFECTS | 2 MODIFY PLACEHOLDERS | 3 MODIFY & COPY ILLUSTRATIONS
4 ADD MEDIA | 5 ANIMATE SLIDE CONTENT | 6 CUSTOMIZE SLIDE ELEMENTS

When you run a slide show, empty placeholders do not display. You may desire to delete unused placeholders from a slide. *Why? So they are not a distraction when you are designing slide content.* The subtitle text placeholder on Slide 1 is not required for this presentation, so you can remove it. The following steps remove the Slide 1 subtitle text placeholder.

- Click a border of the subtitle text placeholder so that it displays as a solid or finely dotted line (Figure 3–13).

2

- Press the DELETE key to remove the subtitle text placeholder.

Figure 3–13

Q&A

Can I also click the Cut button to delete the placeholder?
Yes. Generally, however, the Cut button is used when you desire to remove a selected slide element, place it on the Clipboard, and then paste it in another area. The DELETE key is used when you do not want to reuse that particular slide element.

Other Ways

1. Select placeholder, press BACKSPACE

2. Right-click placeholder border, click Cut on shortcut menu

TO ADD A TEXT BOX

You occasionally may need to insert a small amount of text in an area of a slide where no content placeholder is located. A text box allows you to emphasize or set off text that you consider important for your audience to read. To add a text box to a slide, you would perform the following steps.

1. Click the Text Box button (Insert tab | Text group), click the slide, and then drag the object to the desired location on the slide.
2. Click inside the text box to add or paste text.
3. If necessary, change the look and style of the text box characters by using formatting features (Home tab | Font group).

Changing Views

You have been using **Normal view** to create and edit your slides. Once you completed your slides in projects for previous modules, you reviewed the final products by displaying each slide in **Slide Show view**, which occupies the full computer screen. You were able to view how the transitions, graphics, and effects will display in an actual presentation before an audience.

PowerPoint has other views to help review a presentation for content, organization, and overall appearance. **Slide Sorter view** allows you to look at several slides at one time. **Reading view** is similar to Slide Show view because each slide displays individually, but the slides do not fill the entire screen. Using this view, you easily can progress through the slides forward or backward with simple controls at the bottom of the window. Switching between Slide Sorter, Reading, and Normal views helps you review your presentation, assess whether the slides have an attractive design and adequate content, and make sure they are organized for the most impact. After reviewing the slides, you can change the view to Normal so that you may continue working on the presentation.

To Change Views

1 INSERT & ADD EFFECTS | 2 MODIFY PLACEHOLDERS | 3 MODIFY & COPY ILLUSTRATIONS
4 ADD MEDIA | 5 ANIMATE SLIDE CONTENT | 6 CUSTOMIZE SLIDE ELEMENTS

Why? *You have made several modifications to the slides, so you should check for balance and consistency.* The following steps change the view from Normal view to Slide Sorter view, then Reading view, and back to Normal view.

1

- Click the Slide Sorter view button on the right side of the status bar to display the presentation in Slide Sorter view (Figure 3–14).

 Why is Slide 1 selected?
It is the current slide in the Slides tab.

Figure 3–14

- Click the Reading View button on the right side of the status bar to display Slide 1 of the presentation in Reading view (Figure 3–15).

Figure 3–15

- Click the Next button two times to advance through the presentation.
- Click the Previous button two times to display Slide 2 and then Slide 1.
- Click the Menu button to display commonly used commands (Figure 3–16).

- Click End Show to return to Slide Sorter view, which is the view you were using before Reading view.
- Click the Normal view button to display the presentation in Normal view.

Figure 3–16

Modifying and Copying an Illustration

Slides 1 and 2 (shown in Figures 3–1a and 3–1b) contain an illustration of a biker that was inserted and then modified. You may want to modify an illustration for various reasons. Many times, you cannot find an illustration that precisely represents your topic. For example, you want a picture of a red flower with red petals, but the only available picture has yellow petals.

Occasionally, you may want to remove or change a portion of an illustration or you might want to combine two or more illustrations. For example, you can use one illustration for the background and another photo as the foreground. Other times, you may want to combine an illustration with another type of object. In this presentation, the biker has a brown shirt, and you want to change the color to yellow. In addition, the bike hubs are black, and you want to change them to yellow. The illustration has a blue background, which is not required to display on the slide. You will ungroup the illustration, change the color of the shirt and hubs, and remove the blue background.

Modifying the clip on Slide 2 and then copying it to Slide 1 requires several steps. In the following pages, you will perform these tasks:

1. Zoom Slide 2 to examine the illustration.

2. Ungroup the illustration.

3. Change objects' color.

4. Delete objects.

5. Regroup the illustration.

6. Copy the illustration from Slide 2 to Slide 1.

To Zoom a Slide

You will be modifying small areas of the illustration, so it will help you select the relevant pieces if the graphic is enlarged. The following step changes the zoom to 90 percent.

1 Display Slide 2 and then drag the Zoom slider or click the Zoom level button or the Zoom In button to change the zoom level to 90%. If necessary, click the Down scroll arrow several times so that the entire graphic is visible (Figure 3–17).

Figure 3–17

To Ungroup an Illustration

1 INSERT & ADD EFFECTS | 2 MODIFY PLACEHOLDERS | **3 MODIFY & COPY ILLUSTRATIONS**
4 ADD MEDIA | 5 ANIMATE SLIDE CONTENT | 6 CUSTOMIZE SLIDE ELEMENTS

The next step is to ungroup the biker illustration, also called a clip, on Slide 2. When you **ungroup** an illustration, PowerPoint breaks it into its component objects. A clip may be composed of a few individual objects or several complex groups of objects. These groups can be ungrouped repeatedly until they decompose into individual objects. *Why? Because an illustration is a collection of complex groups of objects, you may need to ungroup a complex object into less complex objects before being able to modify a specific object.* When you ungroup a clip and click the Yes button in the Microsoft PowerPoint dialog box, PowerPoint converts the clip to a PowerPoint object. The following steps ungroup an illustration.

1

- Click the biker clip to select it and then click Format on the ribbon to display the Picture Tools Format tab.
- Click the Group Objects button (Picture Tools Format tab | Arrange group) to display the Group Objects menu (Figure 3–18).

Q&A
Why does the Group Objects button look different on my screen?
Your monitor is set to a different resolution. See the Office 2016 and Windows 10 module for an explanation of screen resolution and the appearance of the ribbon.

Figure 3–18

- Click Ungroup on the Group Objects menu to display the Microsoft PowerPoint dialog box (Figure 3–19).

Figure 3–19

- Click the Yes button (Microsoft PowerPoint dialog box) to convert the clip to a Microsoft Office drawing.

Q&A What happens if I click the No button?
The clip will remain displayed on the slide as an illustration and will not ungroup.

- Click Format on the ribbon to display the Drawing Tools Format tab. Click the Group Objects button (Drawing Tools Format tab | Arrange group) and then click Ungroup again to display the objects that form the biker clip (Figure 3–20).

Q&A Why does the ribbon change from the Picture Tools Drawing tab to the Drawing Tools Format tab and show different options this time?
The illustration has become a drawing object, so tools related to drawing now display.

Why do all those circles display in the clip?
The circles are sizing handles for each of the clip's objects, which resemble pieces of a jigsaw puzzle.

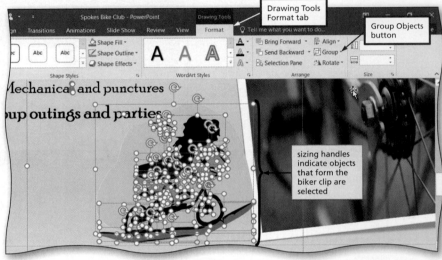

Figure 3–20

Other Ways

1. Right-click clip, point to Group on shortcut menu, click Ungroup   2. Press CTRL+SHIFT+G

To Change the Color of a Clip Object

1 INSERT & ADD EFFECTS | 2 MODIFY PLACEHOLDERS | 3 MODIFY & COPY ILLUSTRATIONS
4 ADD MEDIA | 5 ANIMATE SLIDE CONTENT | 6 CUSTOMIZE SLIDE ELEMENTS

Now that the biker illustration is ungrouped, you can change the color of the objects. You must exercise care when selecting the correct object to modify. **Why?** *A clip might be composed of hundreds of objects.* The following steps change the color of the biker's shirt from brown to yellow.

- Click an area of the slide that is not part of the clip to deselect all the clip pieces.
- Click the biker's shirt to display sizing handles around the brown colored area (Figure 3–21).

Q&A What if I selected a different area by mistake?
Click outside the clip and retry.

Figure 3–21

- Click the Shape Fill arrow (Drawing Tools Format tab | Shape Styles group) to display the Shape Fill gallery.
- Point to Yellow (fourth color in Standard Colors row) to display a live preview of the shirt color (Figure 3–22).

🔎 **Experiment**

- Point to various colors and watch the biker's shirt color change.

Figure 3–22

- Click the color Yellow to change the biker's shirt color (Figure 3–23).

Q&A Why is the bar under the Shape Fill button now yellow?
The button displays the last fill color selected.

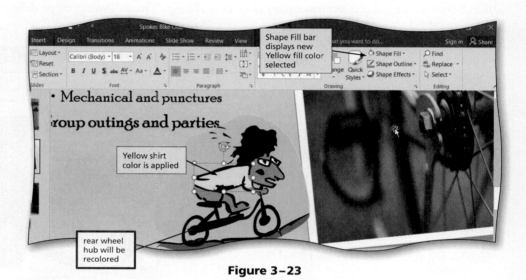

Figure 3–23

4

- Click the rear wheel hub to select it.
- Click the Shape Fill button (Drawing Tools Format tab | Shape Styles group) to change the wheel hub color to Yellow (Figure 3–24).

Q&A Why did I not need to click the Shape Fill arrow to select this color?
PowerPoint uses the last fill color selected. This color displays in the bar under the bucket icon on the button.

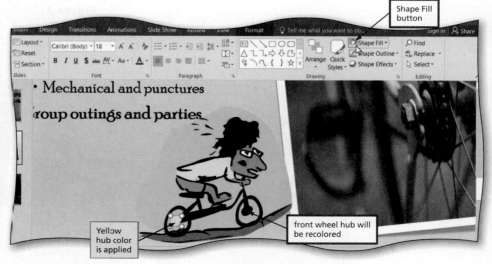

Figure 3–24

5

• Change the front wheel hub color to Yellow (Figure 3–25).

Q&A

Can I select multiple objects so I can color them simultaneously?
Yes. While pressing the SHIFT key, click the desired elements to select them.

Figure 3–25

Other Ways

1. Click Shape Fill arrow (Home tab | Drawing group)
2. Right-click object, click Fill button below shortcut menu
3. Right-click object, click Format Shape on shortcut menu, click 'Fill & Line' icon

To Delete a Clip Object

1 INSERT & ADD EFFECTS | 2 MODIFY PLACEHOLDERS | 3 MODIFY & COPY ILLUSTRATIONS
4 ADD MEDIA | 5 ANIMATE SLIDE CONTENT | 6 CUSTOMIZE SLIDE ELEMENTS

With the biker's shirt and hub colors changed, you want to delete the blue background object. *Why? This object clutters the slide and is not a necessary element of the clip.* The following steps delete this object.

1

• Click the background in any area where the blue color displays to select this object (Figure 3–26).

Q&A

Can I select multiple objects so I can delete them simultaneously?
Yes. While pressing the SHIFT key, click the unwanted elements to select them.

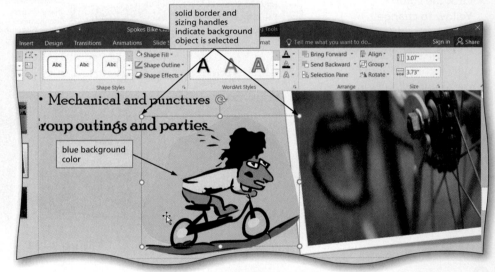

Figure 3–26

2

• Press the DELETE key to delete this object (Figure 3–27).

Figure 3–27

3

- Click one black sweat droplet, press the SHIFT key, and then click the other five sweat droplets to select all six objects (Figure 3–28).

Q&A What can I do if I am having difficulty selecting just these six objects?
Try increasing the zoom, or select a few objects at a time and then delete them.

- Press the DELETE key to delete these objects.

Figure 3–28

To Regroup Objects

1 INSERT & ADD EFFECTS | 2 MODIFY PLACEHOLDERS | 3 MODIFY & COPY ILLUSTRATIONS
4 ADD MEDIA | 5 ANIMATE SLIDE CONTENT | 6 CUSTOMIZE SLIDE ELEMENTS

When you ungrouped the biker clip, you eliminated the embedding data or linking information that tied all the individual pieces together. If you attempt to move or size this clip now, you might encounter difficulties because it consists of multiple objects and is no longer one unified piece. Dragging or sizing affects only a selected object, not the entire collection of objects, so you must use caution when objects are not completely regrouped. You can **regroup** all of the ungrouped objects so they are reassembled into a single unit. The individual pieces of the biker clip now will be regrouped. *Why? When they are regrouped, they cannot be accidentally moved or manipulated.* The following steps regroup these objects into one object.

1

- Position the selection pointer (the left-pointing arrow) in the lower-left corner of the biker illustration and then drag diagonally to the upper-right corner of the illustration so that the entire illustration is covered with a gray box (Figure 3–29).

Q&A Must I drag diagonally from left to right?
No. You can drag in any direction as long as the gray box covers all the clip.

Figure 3–29

- Release the mouse to display all the selected pieces of the illustration.
- Click the Drawing Tools Format tab, and then click the Group Objects button (Drawing Tools Format tab | Arrange group) to display the Group Objects menu (Figure 3–30).

- Click Regroup to recombine all the clip objects.

Figure 3–30

- Use the Zoom slider to change the zoom level to 60%.

Other Ways

1. Right-click selected clip, point to Group on shortcut menu, click Regroup

To Copy a Clip from One Slide to Another

1 INSERT & ADD EFFECTS | 2 MODIFY PLACEHOLDERS | 3 MODIFY & COPY ILLUSTRATIONS
4 ADD MEDIA | 5 ANIMATE SLIDE CONTENT | 6 CUSTOMIZE SLIDE ELEMENTS

The biker clip on Slide 2 also can display in its modified form on the title slide. You first must copy it using the Office Clipboard and then paste it in the desired location. The **Office Clipboard** is a temporary storage location that can hold a maximum of 24 text or graphics items copied from any Office program. *Why? You have made modifications to the illustration that you would like to duplicate on the title slide.* The same procedure of copying and pasting objects works for copying and pasting text from one placeholder to another. The following steps copy this slide element from Slide 2 to Slide 1.

- With the biker illustration on Slide 2 selected, display the Home tab and then click the Copy button (Home tab | Clipboard group) (Figure 3–31).

- Display Slide 1 and then click the Paste button (Home tab | Clipboard group), shown in Figure 3–31, to insert the biker illustration into the title slide.

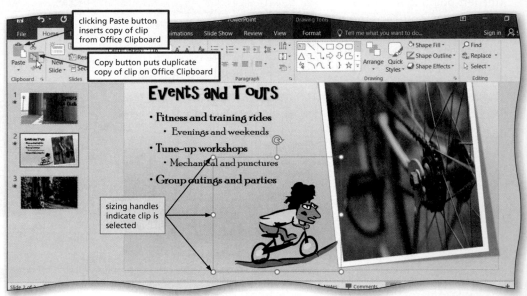

Figure 3–31

Q&A Is the clip deleted from the Office Clipboard when I paste it into the slide?
No.

- Increase the biker illustration size by dragging one of the corner sizing handles outward until the biker is the size shown in Figure 3–32 (approximately 5.24" x 6.55" as indicated on the Drawing Tools Format tab). Drag the biker to the location shown in this figure.

Figure 3–32

Break Point: If you wish to take a break, this is a good place to do so. Be sure to save the Spokes Bike Club file again and then you can quit PowerPoint. To resume at a later time, start PowerPoint, open the file called Spokes Bike Club, and continue following the steps from this location forward.

Adding Media to Slides

Media files can enrich a presentation if they are used correctly. Video files can be produced with a camera and editing software, and sound files can come from the Internet, files stored on your computer, or an audio track on a CD. To hear the sounds, you need a sound card and speakers or headphones on your system.

Once an audio or video clip is inserted into a slide, you can specify options that affect how the file is displayed and played. For example, you can have the video play automatically when the slide is displayed, or you can click the video frame when you are ready to start the playback. You also can have the video fill the entire slide, which is referred to as **full screen**. If you decide to play the slide show automatically and have it display full screen, you can drag the video frame to the gray area off the slide so that it does not display briefly before going to full screen. You can select the 'Loop until Stopped' option to have the video repeat until you click the next slide, or you can choose to not have the video frame display on the slide until you click the slide.

If your video clip has recorded sounds, the volume controls give you the option to set how loudly this audio will play. They also allow you to mute the sound so that your audience will hear no background noise or music.

In the following pages, you will perform these tasks:

1. Insert a video file into Slide 3.
2. Trim the video file to shorten the play time.
3. Add video options that determine the clip's appearance and playback.
4. Insert an audio file into Slide 1.
5. Add audio options that determine the clip's appearance and playback.
6. Resize the Slide 3 video clip.
7. Add a video style to the Slide 3 clip.
8. Add a border to the Slide 3 clip and then change the border weight and color.

BTW
Using Codecs
Video and audio content developers use a codec (**co**mpressor/**dec**ompressor) to reduce the file size of digital media. The reduced file size helps transfer files across the Internet quickly and smoothly and helps save space on storage media. Your computer can play any compressed file if the specific codec used to compress the file is available on your computer. If the codec is not installed or is not recognized, your computer attempts to download this file from the Internet. Many codec files are available to download from the Internet at no cost.

To Insert a Video File

Slide 3 has another photo of a biker, and you have a video clip of a person riding a bike through a wooded area. You want to use a majority of the clip and eliminate a few seconds from the beginning and end. PowerPoint allows you to insert this clip into your slide and then trim the file. *Why? You want to play just a portion of the video when you preview the clip or run the slide show.* This clip is available in the Data Files. The following steps insert this video clip into Slide 3.

1

- Display Slide 3 and then display the Insert tab. Click the Insert Video button (Insert tab | Media group) to display the Insert Video menu (Figure 3–33).

Figure 3–33

2

- Click 'Video on My PC' on the Insert Video menu to display the Insert Video dialog box.
- If the list of files for Module 03 is not displayed in the Insert Video dialog box, navigate to the location where the files are located.
- Click Mountain Bike Video to select the file (Figure 3–34).

Figure 3–34

3

- Click the Insert button (Insert Video dialog box) to insert the video clip into Slide 3 (Figure 3–35).

Q&A Can I adjust the color of a video clip? Yes. You can correct the brightness and contrast, and you also can recolor a video clip using the same methods you learned in this module to color a photo.

Figure 3–35

To Trim a Video File

1 INSERT & ADD EFFECTS | 2 MODIFY PLACEHOLDERS | 3 MODIFY & COPY ILLUSTRATIONS
4 ADD MEDIA | 5 ANIMATE SLIDE CONTENT | 6 CUSTOMIZE SLIDE ELEMENTS

Why? *The Mountain Bike Video file has a running time of slightly more than 32 seconds. Much of the video is the same view of the bike path through the woods, so you decide to delete a few seconds from the beginning and the end to shorten the duration.* PowerPoint's **Trim Video** feature allows you to trim the beginning and end of your clip by designating your desired Start Time and End Time. These precise time measurements are accurate to one-thousandth of a second. The start point is indicated by a green marker, and the end point is indicated by a red marker. The following steps trim the Mountain Bike Video clip.

1

- With the video clip selected on Slide 3, click the Play/Pause button in the video controls underneath the video to play the entire video.

Q&A Can I play the video by clicking the Play button in the Preview group?
Yes. This Play button plays the entire clip. You may prefer to click the Play/Pause button displayed in the video controls to stop the video and examine one of the frames.

Figure 3–36

- Click Playback on the ribbon to display the Video Tools Playback tab.
- Click the Trim Video button (Video Tools Playback tab | Editing group) to display the Trim Video dialog box (Figure 3–36).

2

- Point to the start point, which is indicated by the green marker on the right side, so that the pointer changes to a two-headed arrow.
- Slide or drag the green marker to the right until the Start Time is approximately 00:05.991 (Figure 3–37).

Figure 3–37

- Point to the end point, which is indicated by the red marker on the right side, so that the pointer changes to a two-headed arrow.
- Slide or drag the red marker to the left until the End Time is 00:29.100 (Figure 3–38).

Q&A Can I specify the start or end times without dragging the markers?

Yes. You can enter the time in the Start Time or End Time boxes, or you can click the Start Time or End Time box arrows. You also can click the Next Frame and Previous Frame buttons (Trim Video dialog box).

Figure 3–38

- Click the Play/Pause button (Trim Video dialog box) to review the shortened video clip.
- Click the OK button (Trim Video dialog box) to set the Start Time and End Time and to close the Trim Video dialog box.

Other Ways

1. Right-click clip, click Trim on shortcut menu

To Add Video Options

1 INSERT & ADD EFFECTS | 2 MODIFY PLACEHOLDERS | 3 MODIFY & COPY ILLUSTRATIONS
4 ADD MEDIA | 5 ANIMATE SLIDE CONTENT | 6 CUSTOMIZE SLIDE ELEMENTS

Once the video clip is inserted into Slide 3, you can specify that the video plays automatically when the slide is displayed. **Why?** *When you are giving your presentation, you do not want to click the mouse to start the video.* You also can adjust the volume of the sound recorded on the file. The following steps add the option of playing the video full screen automatically and also decrease the volume of the clip.

- With the Video Tools Playback tab displaying, click the Start arrow (Video Tools Playback tab | Video Options group) to display the Start menu (Figure 3–39).

Q&A What does the On Click option do?

The video clip would begin playing when a presenter clicks the frame during the slide show.

Figure 3–39

- Click Automatically in the Start menu to run the video clip automatically when the slide is displayed.

- Click the 'Play Full Screen' check box (Video Tools Playback tab | Video Options group) to place a check mark in it.
- Click the Volume button (Video Tools Playback tab | Video Options group) to display the Volume menu (Figure 3–40).

4

- Click Medium on the Volume menu to set the audio volume.

Figure 3–40

To Insert an Audio File

1 INSERT & ADD EFFECTS | 2 MODIFY PLACEHOLDERS | 3 MODIFY & COPY ILLUSTRATIONS
4 ADD MEDIA | 5 ANIMATE SLIDE CONTENT | 6 CUSTOMIZE SLIDE ELEMENTS

If you have a digital audio recorder or an app on your smartphone or mobile device, you can record sounds to insert into your presentation. The following steps insert an audio clip into Slide 1. *Why? An audio clip of pedaling sounds adds interest to the start of your presentation when Slide 1 is displayed.*

- Display Slide 1 and then click Insert on the ribbon to display the Insert tab.
- Click the Insert Audio button (Insert tab | Media group) to display the Insert Audio menu (Figure 3–41).

Figure 3–41

- Click 'Audio on My PC' on the Insert Audio menu to open the Insert Audio dialog box.
- If the list of files for Module 03 is not displayed in the Insert Audio dialog box, navigate to the location where the files are located.
- Click Pedaling Sounds to select the file (Figure 3–42).

Figure 3–42

- Click the Insert button (Insert Audio dialog box) to insert the audio clip into Slide 1 (Figure 3–43).

Q&A

Why does a sound icon display on the slide?
The icon indicates an audio file is inserted.

Do the audio control buttons have the same functions as the video control buttons that displayed when I inserted the Mountain Bike Video clip?
Yes. The controls include playing and pausing the sound, moving back or forward 0.25 seconds, audio progress, elapsed time, and muting or unmuting the sound.

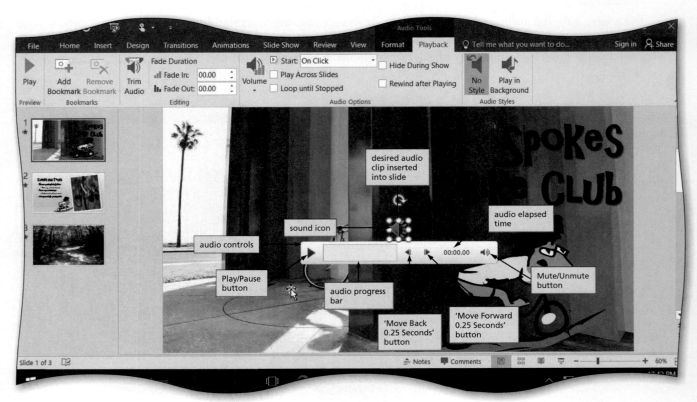

Figure 3–43

4

- Drag the sound icon to the lower-left corner of the slide (Figure 3–44).

Must I move the icon on the slide?

No. Although your audience will not see the icon when you run the slide show, it is easier for you to see the audio controls in this area of this slide.

Figure 3–44

To Add Audio Options

1 INSERT & ADD EFFECTS | 2 MODIFY PLACEHOLDERS | 3 MODIFY & COPY ILLUSTRATIONS
4 ADD MEDIA | 5 ANIMATE SLIDE CONTENT | 6 CUSTOMIZE SLIDE ELEMENTS

Once an audio clip is inserted into a slide, you can specify options that control playback and appearance. As with the video options you applied to the Mountain Bike Video clip, the audio clip can play either automatically or when clicked, it can repeat the clip while a particular slide is displayed, and you can drag the sound icon off the slide and set the volume. The following steps add the options of starting automatically, playing until the slide no longer is displayed, and hiding the sound icon on the slide. *Why? You do not want to click the screen to start the sound, so you do not need to see the icon. In addition, you want the pedaling sound to repeat while the slide is displayed to coordinate with the bicycle picture prominently shown and to keep the audience's attention focused on the topic of riding a bike.*

1

- If necessary, click Playback on the ribbon to display the Audio Tools Playback tab. Click the Start arrow (Audio Tools Playback tab | Audio Options group) to display the Start menu (Figure 3–45).

2

- Click Automatically in the Start menu.

Does the On Click option function the same way for an audio clip as On Click does for a video clip?

Yes. If you were to select On Click, the sound would begin playing only after the presenter clicks Slide 1 during a presentation.

Figure 3–45

• Click the 'Loop until Stopped' check box (Audio Tools Playback tab | Audio Options group) to place a check mark in it.

Q&A What is the difference between the 'Loop until Stopped' option and the 'Play Across Slides' option?
The audio clip in the 'Loop until Stopped' option repeats for as long as one slide is displayed. In contrast, the 'Play Across Slides' option would play the clip only once, but it would continue to play while other slides in the presentation are displayed. Once the end of the clip is reached, the sound would end and not repeat.

• Click the 'Hide During Show' check box (Audio Tools Playback tab | Audio Options group) to place a check mark in it (Figure 3–46).

Q&A Why would I want the icon to display during the show?
If you had selected the On Click option, you would need to find this icon on the slide and click it to start playing the clip.

Can I adjust the sound's volume?
Yes. You can adjust the volume or mute the sound by clicking the Volume button (Audio Tools Playback tab | Audio Options group) or by clicking the Mute/Unmute button on the Media Controls bar and using the volume slider.

Figure 3–46

BTW
Ideal Decibels for Creativity
When you need to be creative, move to an environment filled with moderate background noise, such as a coffee shop. Researchers at the University of British Columbia state that a noise level of approximately 70 decibels, which is the sound of a quiet conversation or highway noise from afar, fosters original ideas. Anything louder than this ambient noise level decreases the thought process.

TO TRIM AN AUDIO FILE

PowerPoint's **Trim Audio** feature allows you to set the beginning and end of a clip. You select the desired sound to play by designating a Start Time and End Time, which are accurate to one-thousandth of a second. As with the video file markers, the Start Time is indicated by a green marker and the End Time is indicated by a red marker. To trim an audio file, you would perform the following steps.

1. Select the sound icon on the slide and then click the Trim Audio button (Audio Tools Playback tab | Editing group).

2. Drag the green marker to the right until the desired Start Time is displayed.

3. Drag the red marker to the left until the desired End Time is displayed.

4. Click the Play/Pause button (Trim Audio dialog box) to review the shortened audio clip.

5. Click the OK button to set the Start Time and End Time and to close the Trim Audio dialog box.

To Resize a Video

The default Mountain Bike Video frame size can be changed. You resize a video clip in the same manner that you resize photos and illustrations. The following steps will decrease the Mountain Bike Video frame using a sizing handle. ***Why?*** *You want to fit the video near the center of the slide.*

- Display Slide 3 and select the video frame. Click Format on the ribbon to display the Video Tools Format tab (Figure 3–47).

Figure 3–47

❷

- With the video selected, drag any corner sizing handle diagonally inward until the frame is resized to approximately 5.5" x 9.78".
- Drag the clip to the location shown in Figure 3–48.

Figure 3–48

To Add a Video Style

The video styles are similar to the photo styles you applied in Module 2 and include various shapes, angles, borders, and reflections. The following steps apply a video style to the Mountain Bike Video clip on Slide 3. ***Why?*** *The Mountain Bike Video clip on Slide 3 displays full screen when it is playing, but you decide to increase the visual appeal of the clip when it is not playing by applying a video style.*

- With the video selected and the Video Tools Format tab displaying, click the More button in the Video Styles gallery (Video Tools Format tab | Video Styles group) (shown in Figure 3–48) to expand the gallery.
- Point to Reflected Perspective Right in the Intense area of the Video Styles gallery (sixth style in first row) to display a live preview of that style applied to the video frame on the slide (Figure 3–49).

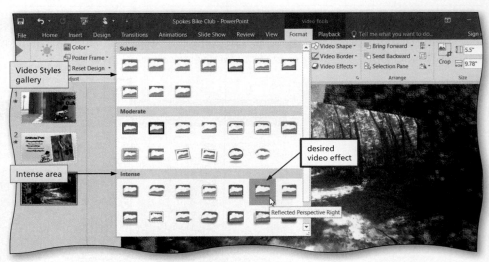

Figure 3–49

Experiment

- Point to various photo styles in the Video Styles gallery and watch the style of the video frame change in the document window.

- Click Reflected Perspective Right in the Video Styles gallery to apply the style to the selected video and then move the video to the location displayed in Figure 3–50.

Q&A

Can I preview the movie clip?

Yes. Point to the clip and then click the Play button on the ribbon (Preview group) or the Play/Pause button on the video controls below the video.

Figure 3–50

To Add a Video Border

You have added borders to photos, and this design element can be added to video frames. The following steps apply a border to the Mountain Bike Video clip. **Why?** *A border adds visual interest and distinguishes the video frame from the photo background.*

- With the video clip selected, click the Video Border button (Video Tools Format tab | Video Styles group) and then point to Weight on the Video Border gallery to display the Weight gallery.

- Point to 2¼ pt to display a live preview of this line weight on the video frame (Figure 3–51).

🔍 **Experiment**

- Point to various line weights in the Weight gallery and watch the line thickness change.

- Click 2¼ pt to add this line weight to the video.

Figure 3–51

To Change a Video Border Color

1 INSERT & ADD EFFECTS | 2 MODIFY PLACEHOLDERS | 3 MODIFY & COPY ILLUSTRATIONS
4 ADD MEDIA | 5 ANIMATE SLIDE CONTENT | 6 CUSTOMIZE SLIDE ELEMENTS

Once you have added a border to a video, you can modify the default color. The following steps change the video border color to yellow. *Why? Yellow is used as an accent color in many components of the Spokes Bike Club slides.*

- With the video clip selected, click the Video Border button (Video Tools Format tab | Video Styles group) and then point to Yellow (fourth color in Standard Colors row) to display a live preview of this border color on the video frame (Figure 3–52).

🔍 **Experiment**

- Point to various colors in the gallery and watch the line colors change.

- Click Yellow to change the video border color.

Figure 3–52

Other Ways

1. Click Format Video on shortcut menu, click Fill & Line icon, click Color button

Break Point: If you wish to take a break, this is a good place to do so. Be sure to save the Spokes Bike Club file again and then you can quit PowerPoint. To resume at a later time, start PowerPoint, open the file called Spokes Bike Club, and continue following the steps from this location forward.

Animating Slide Content

Animation includes special visual and sound effects applied to text or other content. You already are familiar with one form of animation: transitions between slides. To add visual interest and clarity to a presentation, you can animate various parts of an individual slide, including pictures, shapes, text, and other slide elements. For example, each paragraph on the slide can spin as it is displayed. Individual letters and shapes also can spin or move in various motions. PowerPoint has a variety of built-in animations that will fade, wipe, or fly-in text and graphics.

Custom Animations

BTW
Animation Effect Icon Colors
Animation effects allow you to control how objects enter, move on, and exit slides. Using a traffic signal analogy may help you remember the sequence of events. Green icons indicate when the animation effect starts on the slide. Yellow icons represent the object's motion; use them with caution so they do not distract from the message you are conveying to your audience. Red icons indicate when the object stops appearing on a slide.

You can create your own **custom animations** to meet your unique needs. Custom animation effects are grouped in categories: entrance, exit, emphasis, and motion paths. **Entrance effects**, as the name implies, determine how slide elements first appear on a slide. **Exit effects** work in the opposite manner as entrance effects: They determine how slide elements disappear. **Emphasis effects** modify text and objects displayed on the screen. For example, letters may darken or increase in font size. The entrance, exit, and emphasis animations are grouped into categories: Basic, Subtle, Moderate, and Exciting. You can set the animation speed to Very Fast, Fast, Medium, Slow, or Very Slow.

The Slide 2 illustration shows a person riding a bike. When the slide is displayed, the audience will see this biker enter from the lower-left corner, move across the slide, stop beside the bicycle picture, rock slightly, and then continue across the slide toward the right corner.

In the following pages, you will perform these tasks:

1. Apply an entrance effect to the biker illustration and then change the direction.
2. Apply emphasis and exit effects.
3. Change the exit effect direction.
4. Preview the animation sequence.
5. Modify the entrance, emphasis, and exit effects' timing.
6. Animate text paragraphs.

To Animate an Illustration Using an Entrance Effect

1 INSERT & ADD EFFECTS | 2 MODIFY PLACEHOLDERS | 3 MODIFY & COPY ILLUSTRATIONS
4 ADD MEDIA | 5 ANIMATE SLIDE CONTENT | 6 CUSTOMIZE SLIDE ELEMENTS

The biker you modified will not appear on Slide 2 when you display the slide. Instead, it will enter the slide from the lower-left corner. *Why? The biker is facing right, so he will appear to be pedaling forward.* It will then continue across the slide until it reaches the lower-right side of the photo. Entrance effects are colored green in the Animation gallery. The following step applies an entrance effect to the biker illustration in Slide 2.

①

- Display Slide 2, select the biker clip, and then click Animations on the ribbon to display the Animations tab.
- Click the Fly In animation in the Animation gallery (Animations tab | Animation group) to display a live preview of this animation and to apply this entrance animation to the biker illustration (Figure 3–53).

Q&A Are more entrance animations available?
Yes. Click the More button in the Animation gallery to see additional animations. You can select one of the 13 entrance animations that are displayed, or you can click the 'More Entrance Effects' command to expand the selection. You can click any animation to see a preview of the effect.

Q&A

Why does the number 1 appear in a box on the left side of the clip? The 1 is a sequence number and indicates Fly In is the first animation that will appear on the slide when you click the slide.

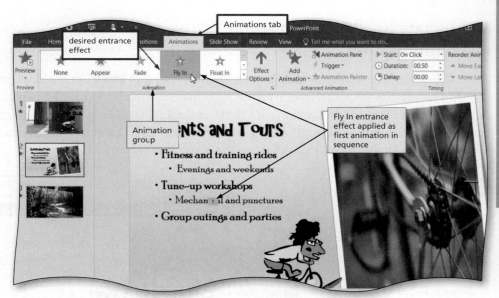

Figure 3–53

To Change Animation Direction

1 INSERT & ADD EFFECTS | 2 MODIFY PLACEHOLDERS | 3 MODIFY & COPY ILLUSTRATIONS
4 ADD MEDIA | 5 ANIMATE SLIDE CONTENT | 6 CUSTOMIZE SLIDE ELEMENTS

Why? *By default, the illustration appears on the slide by entering from the bottom edge, and you want it to enter from the left.* You can modify this direction and specify that it enters from another side or from a corner. The following steps change the biker entrance animation to enter from the left.

1

- Click the Effect Options button (Animations tab | Animation group) to display the Direction gallery (Figure 3–54).

Q&A

Why does a pink box appear around the From Bottom arrow? From Bottom is the default entrance direction applied to the animation.

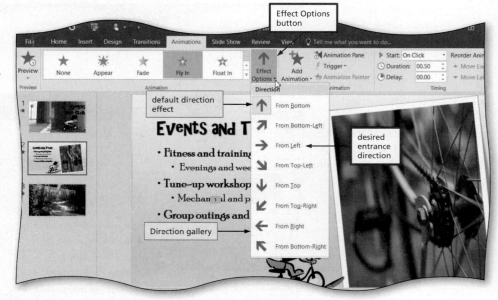

Figure 3–54

2

- Click the From Left arrow to see a preview of this animation and apply this direction to the entrance animation.

Q&A

Can I change this entrance effect? Yes. Repeat Step 1 to select another direction.

To Animate an Illustration Using an Emphasis Effect

Why? The biker will enter the slide from the left corner and stop beside the bicycle photo. You then want it to rock slightly. PowerPoint provides several effects that you can apply to a picture once it appears on a slide. These movements are categorized as emphasis effects, and they are colored yellow in the Animation gallery. You already have applied an entrance effect to the biker, so you want to add another animation to this illustration. The following steps apply an emphasis effect to the biker after the entrance effect.

1

- Select the biker illustration and then click the Add Animation button (Animations tab | Advanced Animation group) to display the Animation gallery (Figure 3–55).

 Are more emphasis effects available in addition to those shown in the Animation gallery?
Yes. To see additional emphasis effects, click 'More Emphasis Effects' in the lower portion of the Animation gallery. The effects are arranged in the Basic, Subtle, Moderate, and Exciting categories.

Figure 3–55

2

- Click Teeter (third effect in the first Emphasis row) to see a preview of this animation and to apply this emphasis effect to the biker illustration (Figure 3–56).

 Do I need to use both an entrance and an emphasis effect, or can I use only an emphasis effect?
You can use one or the other effect, or both effects.

Why does the number 2 appear in a box below the number 1 on the left side of the illustration?
The 2 in the numbered tag indicates a second animation is applied in the animation sequence.

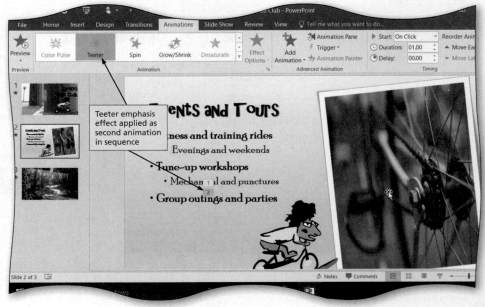

Figure 3–56

To Animate an Illustration Using an Exit Effect

The animated biker will enter the slide from the lower-left corner, stop beside the bicycle photo, and then teeter. It then will continue across the slide and exit in the lower-right corner. To continue this animation sequence, you first need to apply an exit effect. As with the entrance and emphasis effects, PowerPoint provides a wide variety of effects that you can apply to remove an illustration from a slide. These exit effects are colored red in the Animation gallery. You already have applied the Fly In entrance effect, so you will apply the Fly Out exit effect. *Why? It would give continuity to the animation sequence.* The following steps add this exit effect to the biker illustration after the emphasis effect.

1

- Select the biker illustration and then click the Add Animation button (Animations tab | Advanced Animation group) again to display the Animation gallery.
- Scroll down to display all the exit effects in the gallery (Figure 3–57).

Q&A Are more exit effects available in addition to those shown in the Animation gallery?
Yes. To see additional exit effects, click 'More Exit Effects' in the lower portion of the Animation gallery. The effects are arranged in the Basic, Subtle, Moderate, and Exciting categories.

Figure 3–57

2

- Click Fly Out to see a preview of this animation and to add this exit effect to the sequence of biker illustration animations (Figure 3–58).

Q&A How can I tell that this exit effect has been applied?
The Fly Out effect is displayed in the Animation gallery (Animations tab | Animation group), and the number 3 is displayed to the left of the biker illustration.

How can I delete an animation effect?
Click the number associated with the animation you wish to delete and then press the DELETE key.

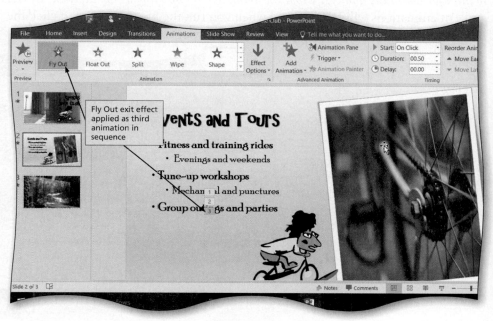

Figure 3–58

To Change Exit Animation Direction

The default direction for a picture to exit a slide is To Bottom. In this presentation, you want the biker to exit in the lower-right corner. *Why? To give the impression it is continuing down a bike path across the slide.* The following steps change the exit animation direction from To Bottom to To Right.

1 Click the Effect Options button (Animations tab | Animation group) to display the Direction gallery (Figure 3–59).

2 Click the To Right arrow to apply this direction to the exit animation effect.

Figure 3–59

1 INSERT & ADD EFFECTS | 2 MODIFY PLACEHOLDERS | 3 MODIFY & COPY ILLUSTRATIONS
4 ADD MEDIA | 5 ANIMATE SLIDE CONTENT | 6 CUSTOMIZE SLIDE ELEMENTS

To Preview an Animation Sequence

Why? Although you have not completed developing the presentation, you should view the animation you have added to check for continuity and verify that the animation is displaying as you expected. By default, the entrance, emphasis, and exit animations will be displayed when you run the presentation and click the slide. The following step runs the presentation and displays the three animations.

1

- Click the Preview button (Animations tab | Preview group) to view all the Slide 2 animations (Figure 3–60).

Q&A Why does a red square appear in the middle of the circle on the Preview button when I click that button?
The red square indicates the animation sequence is in progress. Ordinarily, a green arrow is displayed in the circle.

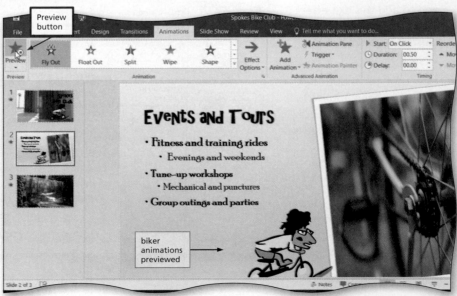

Figure 3–60

To Modify Entrance Animation Timing

The three animation effects are displayed quickly. To create a dramatic effect, you can change the timing. The default setting is to start each animation with a click, but you can change this setting so that the entrance effect is delayed until a specified number of seconds has passed. The following steps modify the start, delay, and duration settings for the entrance animation. *Why? You want the slide title text to display and then, a few seconds later, the biker to start to move across the slide slowly.*

- Click the tag numbered 1 on the left side of the biker illustration and then click the Start arrow (Animations tab | Timing group) to display the Start menu (Figure 3–61).

- Click After Previous to change the start option.

Q&A Why did the numbered tags change from 1, 2, 3 to 0, 1, 2?
The first animation now occurs automatically without a click. The first and second clicks now will apply the emphasis and exit animations.

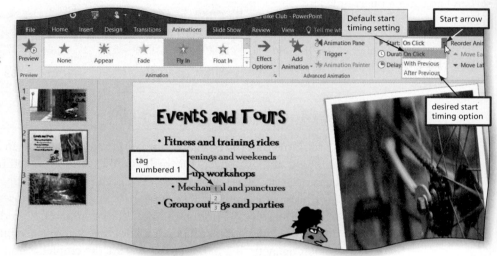

Figure 3–61

What is the difference between the With Previous and After Previous settings?
The With Previous setting starts the effect simultaneously with any prior animation; the After Previous setting starts the animation after a prior animation has ended. If the prior animation is fast or a short duration, it may be difficult for a viewer to discern the difference between these two settings.

- Click the Duration up arrow (Animations tab | Timing group) several times to increase the time from 00.50 second to 02.00 seconds (Figure 3–62).
- Click the Preview button to view the animations.

Q&A What is the difference between the duration time and the delay time?
The duration time is the length of time in which the animation occurs; the delay time is the length of time that passes before the animation begins.

Can I type the speed in the Duration box instead of clicking the arrow to adjust the speed?
Yes. Typing the numbers allows you to set a precise timing.

Figure 3–62

4

- Click the Delay up arrow (Animations tab | Timing group) several times to increase the delay time from 00.00 seconds to 03.00 seconds (Figure 3–63).
- Click the Preview button to view the animations.

Q&A

Can I adjust the delay time I just set?
Yes. Click the Delay up or down arrows and run the slide show to display Slide 2 until you find the time that best fits your presentation.

Figure 3–63

To Modify Emphasis and Exit Timings

Now that the entrance animation settings have been modified, you can change the emphasis and exit effects for the biker illustration. The emphasis effect can occur once the entrance effect has concluded, and then the exit effect can commence. The biker will start moving slowly, but he will increase his speed after he pauses briefly. You, consequently, will shorten the duration of the exit effect compared with the duration of the entrance effect. The animation sequence should flow without stopping, so you will not change the default delay timing of 00.00 seconds for the emphasis and exit effects. The following steps modify the start and duration settings for the emphasis and exit animations.

1 Click the tag numbered 1, which represents the emphasis effect, on the left side of the biker illustration.

2 Click the Start arrow (Animations tab | Timing group) to display the Start menu and then click After Previous to change the start option.

3 Click the Duration up arrow (Animations tab | Timing group) several times to increase the time to 02.00 seconds.

4 Click the tag numbered 1, which now represents the exit effect, click the Start arrow, and then click After Previous.

5 Click the Duration up arrow twice to increase the time to 01.00 seconds.

6 Preview the Slide 2 animation (Figure 3–64).

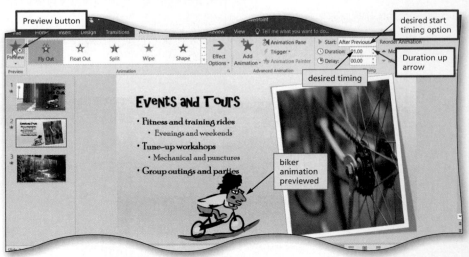

Figure 3–64

To Animate Content Placeholder Paragraphs

The biker illustration on Slide 2 has one entrance, one emphasis, and one exit animation. You decide to add similar animations to the five bulleted paragraphs in the Slide 2 content placeholder. *Why? For a special effect, you can add several emphasis animations to one slide element.* The following steps add one entrance and two emphasis animations to the bulleted list paragraphs.

- Double-click the Slide 2 content placeholder border so that it displays as a solid line (Figure 3–65).

Figure 3–65

- Click the More button (shown in Figure 3–65) in the Animation group (Animations tab | Animation group) to expand the Animation gallery (Figure 3–66).

Figure 3–66

- Click the Fade entrance effect in the Animation gallery (second effect in first row) to add and preview this animation.
- Change the Start option to With Previous.
- Change the Duration time to 02.00 seconds (Figure 3–67).

Q&A Do I need to change the delay time?
No. The paragraphs can start appearing on the slide when the biker exit effect is beginning.

Figure 3–67

- Click the Add Animation button (Animations tab | Advanced Animation group), scroll down to display the entire Emphasis area, and then click the Font Color emphasis animation effect (last effect in third row).
- Change the Start option to After Previous (Figure 3–68).
- Preview the Slide 2 animation.

Figure 3–68

5

- Click the Add Animation button, scroll down to display the entire Emphasis area again, and then click the Underline emphasis animation effect (first effect in the fourth row).

Q&A Why do the animation effects display differently in the Animation gallery on my screen?
The width of the Animation gallery and the order of the animations may vary, especially if you are using a tablet.

- Change the Start option to With Previous (Figure 3–69).

Q&A Why is a second set of animation numbered tags starting with 0 displaying on the left side of the content placeholder?
They represent the three animations associated with the paragraphs in that placeholder.

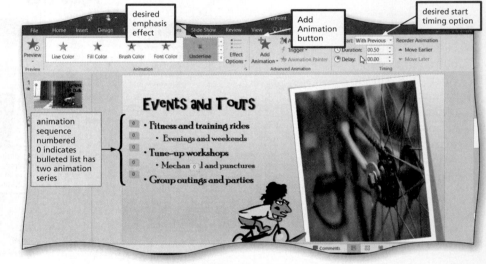

Figure 3–69

BTW
PowerPoint Help
At any time while using PowerPoint, you can find answers to questions and display information about various topics through PowerPoint Help. Used properly, this form of assistance can increase your productivity and reduce your frustrations by minimizing the time you spend learning how to use PowerPoint. For instructions about PowerPoint Help and exercises that will help you gain confidence in using it, read the Office and Windows module at the beginning of this book.

Customizing Slide Elements

PowerPoint's varied themes and layouts help give presentations a unified and aesthetically pleasing look. You may, however, desire to modify the default settings to give your slides a unique quality. One of the easier methods of developing a custom show is to change a theme for one or more slides, not an entire presentation. Similarly, you can change the variant for one or more slides to give a coordinating look to the slides in your deck. One other method of altering your slides slightly is to change the default colors associated with a particular theme.

The animated elements on Slide 2 help emphasize the events and tours that members of the Spokes Bike Club can experience. Changing the theme colors for that slide to yellow coordinates with the yellow slide elements.

To Change the Theme and Variant on One Slide

The Office theme applied to the presentation is appropriate for this topic. The font and placeholder locations are simple and add variety without calling attention to the design elements. The following steps change the theme and variant for Slide 2. *Why? To call attention to the material in the bulleted list on Slide 2, you can apply an equally effective theme that has a design element on the bottom that resembles a bike path. You then can modify this new theme by changing the variant on one slide.*

1

- With Slide 2 displaying, display the Design tab and then click the More button (Design tab | Themes group) to expand the Theme gallery.
- Point to the Retrospect theme to see a preview of that theme on Slide 2 (Figure 3–70).

Experiment

- Point to various document themes in the Themes gallery and watch the colors and fonts change on Slide 2.

Figure 3–70

2

- Right-click the Retrospect theme to display a shortcut menu (Figure 3–71).

Figure 3–71

3

- Click 'Apply to Selected Slides' to apply the Retrospect theme to Slide 2.
- Right-click the green variant (second variant in row) to display a shortcut menu (Figure 3–72).

Figure 3–72

- Click 'Apply to Selected Slides' to apply the green variant to Slide 2 (Figure 3–73).

Figure 3–73

To Change the Theme Colors

1 INSERT & ADD EFFECTS | 2 MODIFY PLACEHOLDERS | 3 MODIFY & COPY ILLUSTRATIONS
4 ADD MEDIA | 5 ANIMATE SLIDE CONTENT | 6 CUSTOMIZE SLIDE ELEMENTS

Every theme has 10 standard colors: two for text, two for backgrounds, and six for accents. The following steps change the theme colors for the Spokes Bike Club slides. *Why? You can change the look of your presentation and add variety by applying the colors from one theme to another theme.*

- Click the More button (shown in Figure 3–73) in the Variants group to expand the gallery.
- Point to Colors in the menu to display the Colors gallery (Figure 3–74).

Experiment

- Point to various color rows in the gallery and watch the colors change on Slide 2.

Figure 3–74

- Click Green in the gallery to change the Slide 2 theme colors (Figure 3–75).

BTW

Printing Document Properties
PowerPoint 2016 does not allow you to print document properties. This feature, however, is available in other Office 2016 apps, including Word and Excel.

Figure 3–75

To Run a Slide Show with Media

All changes are complete, so you now can view the Spokes Bike Club presentation. The following steps start Slide Show view.

1 Click the 'Start From Beginning' button on the Show tab to display the title slide and listen to the bicycle engine sound. Allow the audio clip to repeat several times.

2 Press the SPACEBAR to display Slide 2. Watch the biker and bulleted list animations.

3 Press the SPACEBAR to display Slide 3. Watch the video clip.

4 Press the SPACEBAR to end the slide show and then press the SPACEBAR again to exit the slide show.

To Preview and Print a Handout

1 INSERT & ADD EFFECTS | 2 MODIFY PLACEHOLDERS | 3 MODIFY & COPY ILLUSTRATIONS
4 ADD MEDIA | 5 ANIMATE SLIDE CONTENT | 6 CUSTOMIZE SLIDE ELEMENTS

Printing handouts is useful for reviewing a presentation. You can analyze several slides displayed simultaneously on one page. Additionally, many businesses distribute handouts of the slide show before or after a presentation so attendees can refer to a copy. Each page of the handout can contain reduced images of one, two, three, four, six, or nine slides. The three-slides-per-page handout includes lines beside each slide so that your audience can write notes conveniently. The following steps preview and print a presentation handout with two slides per page. *Why? Two of the slides are predominantly pictures, so your audience does not need full pages of those images. The five bulleted paragraphs on Slide 2 can be read easily on one-half of a sheet of paper.*

1

- Click File on the ribbon to open the Backstage view and then click the Print tab.
- Click the Previous Page button to display Slide 1 in the Print gallery.
- Click 'Full Page Slides' in the Settings area to display the Full Page Slides gallery (Figure 3–76).

Q&A Why does the preview of my slide appear in black and white?
Your printer determines how the preview appears. If your printer is not capable of printing color images, the preview will appear in black and white.

Figure 3–76

BTW

Conserving Ink and Toner
If you want to conserve ink or toner, you can instruct PowerPoint to print draft quality documents by clicking File on the ribbon to open the Backstage view, clicking the Options tab in the Backstage view to display the PowerPoint Options dialog box, clicking Advanced in the left pane (PowerPoint Options dialog box), scrolling to the Print area in the right pane, not placing a check mark in the High quality check box, and then clicking the OK button. Then, use the Backstage view to print the document as usual.

- Click 2 Slides in the Handouts area to select this option and display a preview of the handout (Figure 3–77).

 The current date displays in the upper-right corner of the handout, and the page number displays in the lower-right corner of the footer. Can I change their location or add other information to the header and footer?

Yes. Click the 'Edit Header & Footer' link at the bottom of the Print gallery, click the Notes and Handouts tab (Header and Footer dialog box), and then decide what content to include on the handout page.

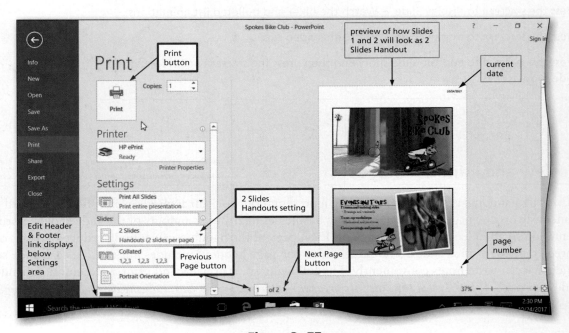

Figure 3–77

- Click the Next Page and Previous Page buttons to display previews of the two pages in the handout.
- Click the Print button in the Print gallery to print the handout.
- When the printer stops, retrieve the printed handout.
- Save the presentation again in the same storage location with the same file name.
- Because the project now is complete, you can exit PowerPoint.

Summary

In this module, you have learned how to adjust photo colors and effects, modify placeholders, modify and copy illustrations, add and format media, animate slide content, customize slides, and print a handout.

BTW
Distributing a Document
Instead of printing and distributing a hard copy of a document, you can distribute the document electronically. Options include sending the document via email; posting it on cloud storage (such as OneDrive) and sharing the file with others; posting it on social media, a blog, or other website; and sharing a link associated with an online location of the document. You also can create and share a PDF or XPS image of the document, so that users can view the file in Acrobat Reader or XPS Viewer instead of in PowerPoint.

What decisions will you need to make when creating your next presentation?

Use these guidelines as you complete the assignments in this module and create your own slide show decks outside of this class.

1. Determine if adjusting photo colors and effects can increase visual appeal.

   a) Change color saturation.

   b) Change tones.

   c) Recolor the image.

2. Vary paragraph alignment.

   a) Themes dictate whether paragraph text is aligned left, center, or right in a placeholder, but you can modify these design decisions when necessary. Moving placeholders and changing paragraph alignment can help create a unique slide.

   b) Different effects are achieved when text alignment shifts in a presentation.

3. Use multimedia selectively.

   a) Locate video, music, and sound files that are appropriate for your audience and that you have permission to use.

   b) Use media files only when necessary, however, because they draw the audience's attention away from the presenter and toward the slides.

   c) Using too many multimedia files can be overwhelming.

4. Use animation sparingly.

   a) PowerPoint audience members usually take notice the first time an animation is displayed on the screen, so be certain the animation will help focus on the precise points being presented during a particular time of the presentation.

   b) Avoid using animation for the sake of using animation. Use animation only when necessary to add emphasis.

   c) Animation overuse annoys and desensitizes audience members.

   d) Carefully decide how text or a slide element enters and exits a slide and how it is displayed once it is present on the slide.

5. Use handouts to organize your speech and to distribute to audiences.

   a) Determine if a handout with two slides per page will help unify your message when you distribute copies to an audience.

Apply Your Knowledge

Reinforce the skills and apply the concepts you learned in this module.

Resizing a Photo by Entering Exact Measurements, Formatting a Video Border, Trimming a Video File, Resizing and Moving a Placeholder, and Animating a Photo and Title

Note: To complete this assignment, you will be required to use the Data Files. Please contact your instructor for information about accessing the Data Files.

Instructions: Run PowerPoint. Open the presentation called Apply 3-1 Cats, which is located in the Data Files. The four slides in the presentation, shown in Figure 3–78, discuss the factors you should consider when adopting a cat. The local pet store is holding a special event for cat adoptions. The document you open is composed of slides containing pictures and a video. You will apply artistic effects or modify some of these graphic elements. You also will move placeholders. In addition, you will animate photos and a title using an entrance effect.

Continued >

Apply Your Knowledge *continued*

(a) Slide 1

Figure 3–78a

Perform the following tasks:

1. On Slide 1 (Figure 3–78a), move the title text placeholder to the upper area of the slide, the subtitle text placeholder to the lower area of the slide, and the green-eyed cat picture to the bottom left corner of the slide, as shown in the figure. Color the green-eyed cat picture by selecting Saturation: 200% from the Color Saturation area, and apply the Paint Brush artistic effect to the picture, as shown in figure. Decrease the picture size to 3.35"×3.88" and apply the Metal Oval picture style to the picture. Apply the Float In animation entrance effect, change the duration to 2.50, and then change the Start timing setting to With Previous.

2. On Slide 1, change the title font to Eras Bold ITC, increase the font size to 72 point, and then change the font color to Dark Blue, Background 2 (in Theme Colors row). Change the size of the title text placeholder to 3.73"×3.75" and then move it to the left area of the slide using the Smart Guides to line it up with the left edge of the picture, as shown in the figure. Apply the Fly In animation and then change the direction to From Right to the title text font and change the duration to 2.00. Change the Start timing setting to After Previous.

3. On Slide 1, change the subtitle font to Arial, increase the font size to 36 point, change the font color to Dark Blue (in Standard Colors row), and then bold and italicize this text.

4. On Slide 2 (Figure 3–78b), change the title text font to Arial, increase the font size to 44 point, bold this text, and then change the font color to Light Green (in Standard Colors row). Align this text left. Use the Format Painter to format the title text font on Slides 3 and 4 with the same features as the title text font on Slide 2.

5. Increase the size of the bulleted list font on Slide 2 to 24 point and then bold this text. Apply the Grow & Turn entrance effect to the bulleted list and then change the duration to 1.75. Change the Start timing setting to After Previous.

6. On Slide 2, increase the size of the right cat picture to approximately 4.12"×4.29" and then apply the Bevel Rectangle picture style to the cat picture. Decrease the size of the kitten picture in the center of the slide to approximately 4.24"×4.98" and then apply the Soft Edge Oval picture style to the kitten picture. Move the cat and kitten pictures to the locations shown in the figure.

7. On Slide 3 (Figure 3–78c), increase the size of the video to 5"×8.88". Apply the Rotated, Gradient video style in the Moderate area to the video, change the border weight to 6 pt, and

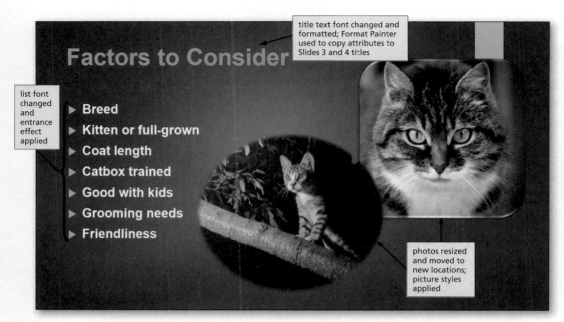

title text font changed and formatted; Format Painter used to copy attributes to Slides 3 and 4 titles

list font changed and entrance effect applied

photos resized and moved to new locations; picture styles applied

(b) Slide 2

Figure 3–78b

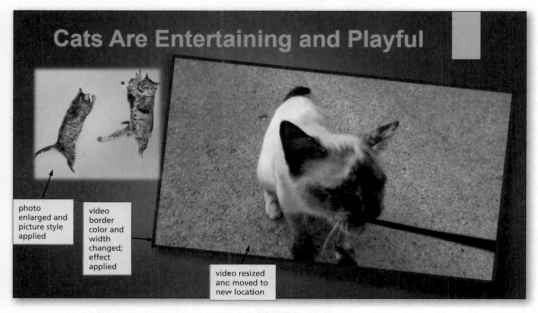

photo enlarged and picture style applied

video border color and width changed; effect applied

video resized and moved to new location

(c) Slide 3

Figure 3–78c

then change the border color to Dark Blue (in Standard Colors row). Move the video to the location shown in the figure. Trim the video so that the Start Time is 00:15.073. Start this video automatically.

8. Increase the size of the picture to approximately 3.1"×3.51" on Slide 3. Apply the Soft Edge Rectangle picture style to the picture.

9. On Slide 4 (Figure 3–78d), reset the picture to its original color and style by clicking the Reset Picture button (Picture Tools Format tab | Adjust group). Increase the size of the picture to approximately 5.75"×10.21", apply the Beveled Oval, Black picture style, and then move the picture to the location shown in the figure.

Continued >

Apply Your Knowledge *continued*

photo enlarged, picture style applied, color changed, and moved to new location

(d) Slide 4

Figure 3–78d

10. If requested by your instructor, add your mother's first name as a second line under the subtitle on Slide 1.

11. Apply the Clock transition in the Exciting category to all the slides. Change the duration to 3.00 seconds.

12. View the presentation and then save the file using the file name, Apply 3–1 Adopt a Cat.

13. Submit the revised document in the format specified by your instructor.

14. ✸ In Step 2, you changed the size of the title text placeholder and then moved it to the upper left area of the slide. How did this style improve the slide? On Slide 3, you trimmed the start time of the video. Why?

Extend Your Knowledge

Extend the skills you learned in this module and experiment with new skills. You may need to use Help to complete the assignment.

Changing Theme Colors, Coloring a Picture, Inserting and Trimming a Video File, Adding a Text Box, and Animating an Illustration

Note: To complete this assignment, you will be required to use the Data Files. Please contact your instructor for information about accessing the Data Files.

Instructions: Run PowerPoint. Open the presentation called Extend 3-1 Swimming, which is located in the Data Files. You will change theme colors, insert a video file, trim a video file, and insert a text box to create the presentation shown in Figure 3–79.

Perform the following tasks:

1. Change the theme variant to Black on Slide 1 only. Change the theme color to Blue II on Slide 3 only.

2. On Slide 1 (Figure 3–79a), change the title text font to Britannic Bold, increase the font size to 48 point, change the font color to Yellow (in Standard Colors row), and then center the text.

(a) Slide 1

Figure 3–79a

Change the font case to UPPERCASE. (*Hint*: The Change Case button is located in the Font group (Home tab | Font group).) Move the title text placeholder to the top of the slide, as shown in the figure. Delete the subtitle text placeholder.

3. Increase the size of the picture on Slide 1 to approximately 6.19" × 11", apply the Moderate Frame, White picture style, and then move the picture to the center of the slide, using the vertical Smart Guide to help you align this picture. Recolor the picture using the Blue, Accent color 3 Dark color (in Recolor area). Adjust the title text placeholder so that the text is below the picture border.

4. On Slide 1, apply the Grow/Shrink Emphasis effect to the Teardrop shape and then change the duration to 3.00. Change the Start timing setting to After Previous.

5. On Slide 2 (Figure 3–79b), change the title text font to Franklin Gothic Heavy, increase the font size to 40 point, change the font color to Dark Blue (in Standard Colors row), and then center the text. Use the Format Painter to apply these attributes to the title text font on Slide 4.

6. Apply the Bevel Perspective picture style to the picture. Increase the size of the picture to approximately 5.01" × 7.63" and then position it on the right side of the slide.

7. On Slide 2, apply the Zoom Entrance effect to the bulleted list, change the duration to 2:00, and then change the Start timing setting to After Previous.

8. On Slide 3 (Figure 3–79c), insert the video file called Swim, which is located in the Data Files. Increase the size of the video to approximately 6.41" × 8.74" and move the video to the location shown in the figure. Apply the Simple Frame, White video style and then change the Video Border color to Yellow (in Standard Colors row). Trim the video so that the End Time is 00:14.151. Start this video automatically.

9. Insert a text box on the left side of Slide 3 and type `Video highlights from one of our swim meets` in the text box, change the font to Arial, change font size to 24 point, and then bold and italicize this text. Adjust the size of the text box so that it measures approximately 2.52" × 2.01", and then use the horizontal Smart Guide to center the text box between the left end of the slide and the left edge of the video file.

Continued >

Extend Your Knowledge *continued*

(b) Slide 2

Figure 3–79b

(c) Slide 3

Figure 3–79c

10. On Slide 4 (Figure 3–79d), increase the size of the swimmer picture to approximately 3.88" × 6.29" and apply the Beveled Oval, Black picture style to the picture. Change the border color to Light Green (in Standard Colors row) and then change the border weight to 6 pt. Position this picture on the left side of the slide under the title using the Smart Guides to align the picture with the left, right, and bottom edges of the placeholder.

11. On Slide 4, apply the Float Out exit effect to the flippers illustration and then change the duration to 5.00. Change the Start timing setting to After Previous.

12. If requested by your instructor, insert a text box on Slide 3 under the text box and add the time of day you were born.

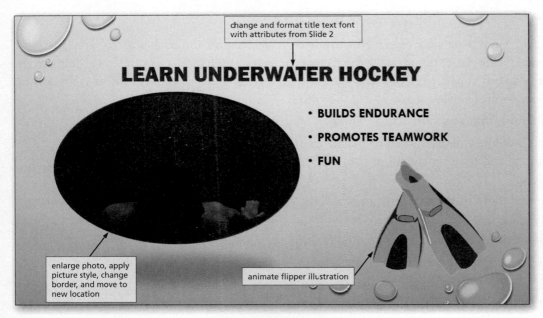

(d) Slide 4

Figure 3–79d

13. Apply an appropriate transition to all slides.

14. View the presentation and then save the file using the file name, Extend 3-1 Galaxy Aquatic Center.

15. Submit the revised document in the format specified by your instructor.

16. ✷ In this assignment, you inserted a video file and trimmed it. How did this enhance the presentation?

Expand Your World

Create a solution that uses cloud or web technologies by learning and investigating on your own from general guidance.

Inserting Video Files from the Web

Instructions: The Spokes Bike Club presentation you created in the module has a video you inserted from the Data Files. The bicyclist in this video mounted a camera on his helmet and recorded his ride through the forest. Using a helmet can help reduce head and brain injury risk and increase rider visibility to motorists and other cyclists. Many organizations promoting bicycling safety have created videos describing how to select and fit a bicycle helmet, and these videos are posted to online websites. PowerPoint allows you to insert online videos easily in a manner similar to how you inserted the Mountain Bike Video clip. You are going to search for and then insert one of these online videos into the Spokes Bike Club presentation.

Perform the following tasks:

1. In PowerPoint, open the Spokes Bike Club file, insert a new Slide 4 with the Title and Content layout, and then type `Helmet Safety Tips` as the title text. Use the Format Painter to copy the title text font formatting from Slide 2 to the new Slide 4 title. Center this title text.

2. Format the Slide 4 background with a gradient or texture fill.

3. Click the Insert Video icon in the content placeholder to display the Insert Video dialog box. Click the YouTube button in the dialog box and then type `bicycling helmet safety` as the search text in the Search YouTube search box.

Continued >

Expand Your World *continued*

4. When the search results are displayed, browse the video frames and click one that appears to fit the theme of this presentation. View the title of the video and its source in the lower-left corner of the dialog box. Then, click the View Larger (magnifying glass) icon in the lower-right corner of the video frame to view a preview of the video.

5. Click the Insert button to insert the video on Slide 4.

6. Add a style to the video and then resize the frame. Start this file automatically during the presentation and have it play full screen, if possible. If necessary, trim the video to the length you desire.

7. If requested to do so by your instructor, add the city where you were born to the Slide 4 title text.

8. View the presentation and then save the file using the file name, Expand 3-1 Spokes.

9. Submit the assignment in the format specified by your instructor.

10. ✺ What criteria did you use to select a particular YouTube video? What decisions did you make to choose a background and video style?

In the Labs

Design, create, modify, and/or use a presentation following the guidelines, concepts, and skills presented in this module. Labs 1 and 2, which increase in difficulty, require you to create solutions based on what you learned in the module; Lab 3 requires you to apply your creative thinking and problem-solving skills to design and implement a solution.

Lab 1: Changing the Stacking Order, Inserting an Audio File, and Animating a Photo, Illustration, and Title

Note: To complete this assignment, you will be required to use the Data Files. Please contact your instructor for information about accessing the Data Files.

Problem: Your local library is featuring information about national parks. Your travel club is planning to visit Yellowstone National Park next year, and you decide to gather some general information to present to the club. You create the slides shown in Figure 3–80.

Perform the following tasks:

1. Run PowerPoint. Open the presentation called Lab 3-1 Yellowstone, which is located in the Data Files. On Slide 1, increase the size of the waterfall picture to 7.5" × 11.54" and then move the picture to the left side of the slide, as shown in Figure 3–80a.

2. On Slide 1, select the title text placeholder. Display the Animation gallery, click 'More Entrance Effects,' and then apply the Expand entrance effect (in Subtle area) to the title text. Change the Start timing option to With Previous and the duration to 03.00 seconds. Bring the title text Forward so that the eagle's wings do not block the title.

3. On Slide 1, decrease the size of the eagle illustration to approximately 4.43" × 5.3" and then move it to the position shown in the figure. Apply the Fly In entrance effect with the From Bottom-Right direction to the illustration and then change the start timing option to After Previous and the duration to 02.50 seconds. Add the Fly Out exit animation with the To Left direction to the eagle illustration and then change the Start timing option to After Previous and the duration to 3.00 seconds.

(a) Slide 1

Figure 3–80a

4. On Slide 2 (Figure 3–80b), change the size of the video so that it measures approximately 5.93" × 8.9". Change the video style to the Canvas, White style (in Intense area) and then change the border weight to 6 pt. Have the video start Automatically. Trim the video by changing the Start Time to 00:28.008 and changing the End Time to 00:50.55. Move the video to the location shown in the figure.

5. On Slide 3 (Figure 3–80c), increase the size of the picture to approximately 6.26" × 8.23" and then apply the Moderate Frame, Black picture style to the picture. Move the picture to the location shown in the figure. Start the audio file Automatically and hide this file during the show. Trim the audio file so that the Start Time is at 01:00 and the End Time is at 02:00.

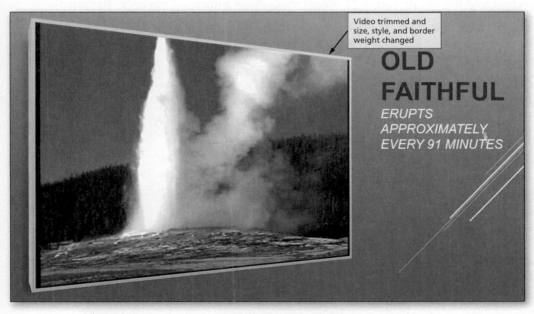

(b) Slide 2

Figure 3–80b

Continued >

In the Labs *continued*

(c) Slide 3

Figure 3–80c

6. On Slide 4 (Figure 3–80d), apply the Moderate Frame, Black picture style to the bear picture. Apply the Metal Oval picture style to the wolf picture. Move the two pictures to the locations shown, and bring the wolf picture forward, as shown in the figure.

7. Apply the Fade entrance effect to the two pictures. Change the Start timing option to After Previous and the duration to 02.50.

8. Insert the audio file called Wolves, which is located in the Data Files. Change the volume to Medium, start Automatically, and hide the audio file during the show.

9. On Slide 5 (Figure 3–80e) apply the Metal Oval picture style to the four fish pictures. Apply the Bounce entrance effect to the upper left picture and then change the Start timing option to After Previous and the duration to 5.25. Apply these same animation effects to the remaining three pictures in a clockwise order.

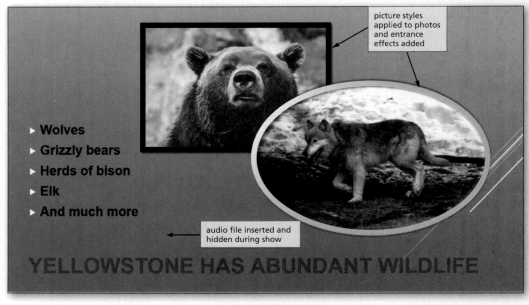

(d) Slide 4

Figure 3–80d

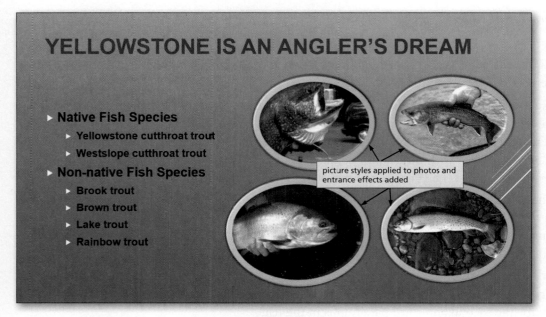

(e) Slide 5

Figure 3–80e

10. Apply the Wind transition in the Exciting category to all the slides. Change the duration to 2.50 seconds.

11. If requested by your instructor, insert a text box on Slide 2 and add the name of the street where you lived as a child.

12. View the presentation and then save the file using the file name, Lab 3–1 Visiting Yellowstone.

13. Submit the document in the format specified by your instructor.

14. ✹ On Slide 1, why did you bring the title text to the front of the eagle illustration? Why did you choose the Bounce entrance effect with a 05.25 duration on the four fish pictures on Slide 5?

Lab 2: Adding Audio Options, Ungrouping a Clip, Changing the Color of a Clip Object, Deleting a Clip Object, and Regrouping Objects

Note: To complete this assignment, you will be required to use the Data Files. Please contact your instructor for information about accessing the Data Files.

Problem: You work at a nature center and are asked to do a PowerPoint presentation on how to attract hummingbirds to your yard. You create the presentation shown in Figure 3–81.

Perform the following tasks:
1. Run PowerPoint. Open the presentation called Lab 3-2 Hummingbirds, which is located in the Data Files. On Slide 1 (Figure 3–81a), change the volume of the audio file to High and then select Start Automatically, 'Play Across Slides', 'Loop until Stopped', 'Rewind after Playing', and 'Hide During Show'.

2. Copy the hummingbird illustration from Slide 2 (Figure 3–81b) to Slide 1 and then delete it from Slide 2. Decrease the size of this illustration so that it measures approximately

Continued >

In the Labs *continued*

1.71" × 1.87" and then move it to the location shown in Figure 3–81a. Apply the Fly In 'From Top–Right' entrance effect to the illustration, change the Start timing setting to After Previous, and then change the duration to 02.50.

3. Increase the title text font on Slide 1 to 72 point, bold the text, and then change the color of the title text font to Red (in Standard Colors). Decrease the size of the title text placeholder to approximately 1.65" × 7.62" and then position the title on top of the red rectangle. Apply the Fly In entrance effect with the From Top direction to the title, change the Start timing option to After Previous, and then change the duration to 02.50.

4. On Slide 1, change the shape fill color of the red rectangle to Lime, Accent 1 (in first Theme Colors row). Decrease the size of the rectangle shape to approximately 1.7" × 6.96", as shown in the figure. Increase the font size of the three paragraphs in the rectangle shape to 28 point and then bold this text.

5. On Slide 1, apply the Appear entrance effect to the first paragraph in the list and then change the start timing option to After Previous and the duration to 02.50. Apply the same animation settings for the second and third paragraphs in the list.

6. On Slide 2 (Figure 3–81b), move the video to the right side of the slide, increase the size to approximately 5.84" × 8.2", apply the Beveled Oval, Black video style (in Moderate area) to the video, change the video border color to Red (in Standard Colors), and then change the border weight to 3 pt. Trim the video so that the End Time is 00:17.88. Change the volume to High and then start the video automatically.

7. On Slide 2 (Figure 3–81b), apply the Float In entrance effect to the title text and then change the direction to Float Down. Change the start timing option to With Previous and the duration to 03.00.

8. On Slide 3 (Figure 3–81c), apply the Shape entrance effect to the title text and then change the Start timing option to With Previous and the duration to 3.00.

9. On Slide 3, select the hummingbird and flowers illustration and zoom in to view the three pink flowers. Ungroup this illustration. Select the three pink flowers and change their fill color to Red (in Standard Colors). Delete the three green leaves in the middle of the dark green stem.

(a) Slide 1

Figure 3–81a

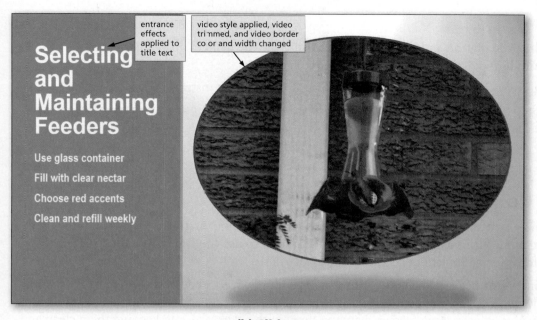

(b) Slide 2

Figure 3–81b

(c) Slide 3

Figure 3–81c

Regroup the illustration, increase the size to approximately 3.14" × 4.85", and then zoom out and move it to the area shown in the figure.

10. On Slide 3, apply the Reflected Bevel, White picture style to the flower picture. Resize the picture to approximately 3.1" × 4.17" and then move it to the right side of the slide, as shown in the figure. Apply the Zoom entrance effect to this picture. Change the Start timing option to On Click and the duration to 2.00.

11. If requested by your instructor, insert a text box at the lower-right corner of Slide 2 and type the color of your eyes in the text box.

12. Change the transition to None for all slides.

Continued >

In the Labs *continued*

13. View the presentation and then save the file using the file name, Lab 3–2 Attracting Hummingbirds.

14. Submit the revised document in the format specified by your instructor.

15. ✳ In Step 9, you changed the color of the three flowers from pink to red. Why? Why did you change the volume of the audio file to High?

Lab 3: **Consider This: Your Turn**

Design and Create a Presentation about Winter Bird Feeding

Note: To complete this assignment, you will be required to use the Data Files. Please contact your instructor for information about accessing the Data Files.

Part 1: Winter storms in cold climates can affect wild birds. Ice and deep snow reduce the natural food supply, and birds, consequently, have a difficult time surviving and thriving. People can help the birds by buying or making feeders, hanging them in the backyard, and keeping them clean and full. Nutritious winter seed foods include mixes of black oil sunflowers, hulled peanuts, and white millet. Suet and peanut butter are high-energy foods that help the birds stay warm. Providing water also helps the birds from becoming dehydrated. Place the feeders at least 10 feet from shrubs and compact the snow beneath them. Use the concepts and techniques presented in this module to create a presentation with this information to show at your local garden center. Select a suitable theme, change the theme colors, and then include a title slide, photos, and illustration. The Data Files contain a video called Birds in Winter and photos and illustrations called Bird Feeder, Red Jay, and Birds in Tree. Trim the video file and add a style. The illustration can be ungrouped, and you can change the color of it and the photos to add some visual interest to the presentation. Add animation to the slide content using effects and timing. Review and revise your presentation as needed and then save the file using the file name, Lab 3-3 Winter Bird Feeding. Submit your assignment in the format specified by your instructor.

Part 2: ✳ You made several decisions while creating the presentation in this assignment: selecting a theme and changing the theme colors, coloring and adding effects to the illustration and photos, trimming the video and adding a style, and adding animation. What was the rationale behind each of these decisions? When you reviewed the document, what further revisions did you make and why? Where would you recommend showing this slide show?

1 Creating a Worksheet and a Chart

Objectives

You will have mastered the material in this module when you can:

- Describe the Excel worksheet
- Enter text and numbers
- Use the Sum button to sum a range of cells
- Enter a simple function
- Copy the contents of a cell to a range of cells using the fill handle
- Apply cell styles
- Format cells in a worksheet

- Create a 3-D pie chart
- Change a worksheet name and sheet tab color
- Change document properties
- Preview and print a worksheet
- Use the AutoCalculate area to display statistics
- Correct errors on a worksheet

Introduction

Almost every organization collects vast amounts of data. Often, data is consolidated into a summary so that people in the organization better understand the meaning of the data. An Excel worksheet allows data to be summarized and charted easily. A **chart** conveys a visual representation of data. In this module, you will create a worksheet that includes a chart. The data in the worksheet and chart comprise a personal budget that contains monthly estimates for each income and expense category.

Project — Personal Budget Worksheet and Chart

The project in this module follows proper design guidelines and uses Excel to create the worksheet and chart shown in Figure 1–1a and Figure 1–1b. The worksheet contains budget data for Linda Fox. She has compiled a list of her expenses and sources of income and wants to use this information to create an easy-to-read worksheet to see how much she will be ahead or behind each month. In addition, she would like a 3-D pie chart to show her estimated expenses by category for each of the 12 months.

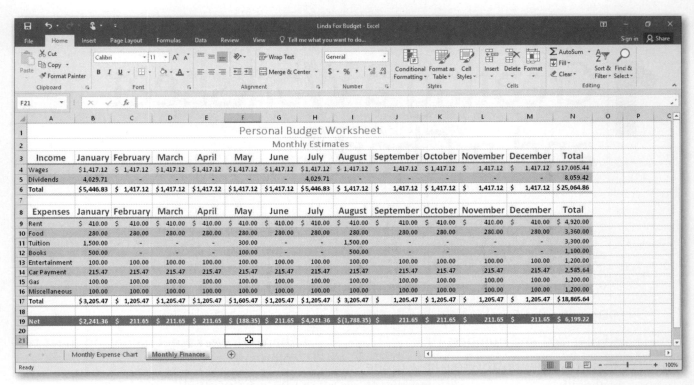

Figure 1–1(a) Personal Budget Worksheet

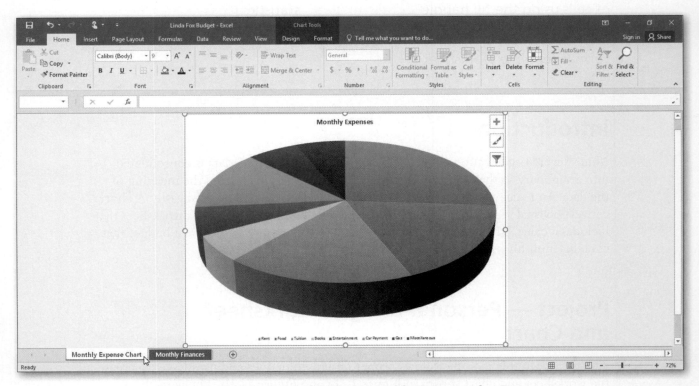

Figure 1–1(b) Pie Chart Showing Monthly Expenses by Category

The first step in creating an effective worksheet is to make sure you understand what is required. The person or persons requesting the worksheet may supply their requirements in a requirements document, or you can create one. A requirements document includes a needs statement, a source of data, a summary of calculations, and any other special requirements for the worksheet, such as charting and web support. Figure 1–2 shows the requirements document for the new workbook to be created in this module.

Worksheet Title	Personal Budget Worksheet
Word	A yearly projection of Linda Fox's personal budget
Source of data	Data supplied by Linda Fox includes monthly estimates for income and expenses
Calculations	The following calculations must be made: 1. For each month, a total for income and expenses 2. For each budget item, a total for the item 3. For the year, total all income and expenses 4. Net = ncome – expenses

Figure 1–2

In this module, you will learn how to perform basic workbook tasks using Excel. The following roadmap identifies general activities you will perform as you progress through this module:

1. ENTER TEXT in a blank worksheet.

2. CALCULATE SUMS AND USE FORMULAS in the worksheet.

3. FORMAT TEXT in the worksheet.

4. INSERT a pie CHART into the worksheet.

5. Assign a NAME to the sheet TAB.

6. PREVIEW AND PRINT the WORKSHEET.

For an introduction to Windows and instructions about how to perform basic Windows tasks, read the Office and Windows module at the beginning of this book, where you can learn how to resize windows, change screen resolution, create folders, move and rename files, use Windows Help, and much more.

CONSIDER THIS

Why is it important to plan a worksheet?
The key to developing a useful worksheet is careful planning. Careful planning can reduce your effort significantly and result in a worksheet that is accurate, easy to read, flexible, and useful. When analyzing a problem and designing a worksheet solution, what steps should you follow?

• Define the problem, including need, source of data, calculations, charting, and web or special requirements.

• Design the worksheet.

• Enter the data and formulas.

• Test the worksheet.

After carefully reviewing the requirements document (Figure 1–2) and making the necessary decisions, the next step is to design a solution or draw a sketch of the worksheet based on the requirements, including titles, column and row headings, the location of data values, and the 3-D pie chart, as shown in Figure 1–3. The dollar signs and commas that you see in the sketch of the worksheet indicate formatted numeric values.

sketch of worksheet and chart →

Personal Budget Worksheet

Income	January	December	Total
Wages	$99,999.99	$99,999.99	$99,999.99
Dividend			
Total	$99,999.99	$99,999.99	$99,999.99
Expenses	January	December	Total
Rent	$99,999.99	$99,999.99	$99,999.99
Food			
Tuition			
Books			
Entertainment			
Car payment			
Gas			
Miscellaneous			
Total	$99,999.99	$99,999.99	$99,999.99
Net	$99,999.99	$99,999.99	$99,999.99

Monthly Expenses

Legend of Expenses

Figure 1–3

With a good understanding of the requirements document, an understanding of the necessary decisions, and a sketch of the worksheet, the next step is to use Excel to create the worksheet and chart.

Selecting a Cell

To enter data into a cell, you first must select it. The easiest way to **select** a cell (make it active) is to use the mouse to move the block plus sign pointer to the cell and then click.

An alternative method is to use the arrow keys that are located just to the right of the alphanumeric keys on a standard keyboard. An arrow key selects the cell adjacent to the active cell in the direction of the arrow on the key.

You know a cell is selected, or active, when a heavy border surrounds the cell and the active cell reference appears in the Name box on the left side of the formula bar. Excel also changes the color of the active cell's column and row headings to a darker shade.

Entering Text

In Excel, any set of characters containing a letter, hyphen (as in a telephone number), or space is considered **text**. Text is used for titles, such as column and row titles, on the worksheet.

Worksheet titles and subtitles should be as brief and meaningful as possible. A worksheet title could include the name of the organization, department, or a

For an introduction to Office and instructions about how to perform basic tasks in Office apps, read the Office and Windows module at the beginning of this book, where you can learn how to run an application, use the ribbon, save a file, open a file, print a file, exit an application, use Help, and much more.

BTW
Touch Screen Differences
The Office and Windows interfaces may vary if you are using a touch screen. For this reason, you might notice that the function or appearance of your touch screen differs slightly from this module's presentation.

description of the content of the worksheet. A worksheet subtitle, if included, could include a more detailed description of the content of the worksheet. Examples of worksheet titles are January 2018 Payroll and Year 2018 Projected Budget, and examples of subtitles are Finance Department and Monthly Projections, respectively.

As shown in Figure 1–4, data in a worksheet is identified by row and column titles so that the meaning of each entry is clear. Rows typically contain information such as categories of data. Columns typically describe how data is grouped in the worksheet, such as by month or by department.

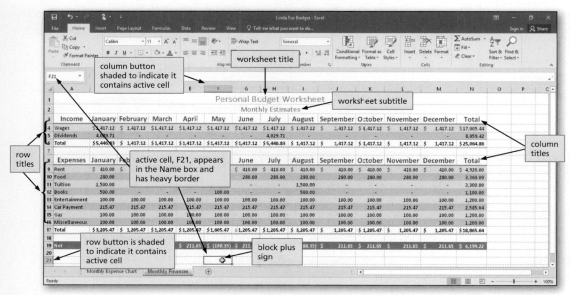

Figure 1–4

BTW

Excel Screen Resolution
If you are using a computer to step through the project in this module and you want your screens to match the figures in this book, you should change your screen's resolution to 1366 x 768. For information about how to change a computer's resolution, refer to the Office and Windows module at the beginning of this book.

To Enter the Worksheet Titles

1 ENTER TEXT | 2 CALCULATE SUMS & USE FORMULAS | 3 FORMAT TEXT
4 INSERT CHART | 5 NAME TAB | 6 PREVIEW & PRINT WORKSHEET

As shown in Figure 1–4, the worksheet title, Personal Budget Worksheet, identifies the purpose of the worksheet. The worksheet subtitle, Monthly Estimates, identifies the type of data contained in the worksheet. *Why? A title and subtitle help the reader to understand clearly what the worksheet contains.* The following steps enter the worksheet titles in cells A1 and A2. Later in this module, the worksheet titles will be formatted so that they appear as shown in Figure 1–4.

1

- Run Excel and create a blank workbook in the Excel window.

- If necessary, click cell A1 to make cell A1 the active cell (Figure 1–5).

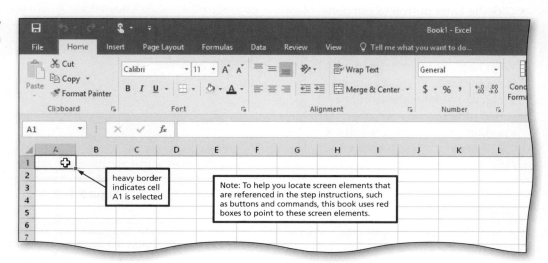

Figure 1–5

2

- Type **Personal Budget Worksheet** in cell A1 (Figure 1–6).

 Q&A Why did the appearance of the formula bar change?

Excel displays the title in the formula bar and in cell A1. When you begin typing a cell entry, Excel enables two additional boxes in the formula bar: the Cancel button and the Enter button. Clicking the Enter button completes an entry. Clicking the Cancel button cancels an entry.

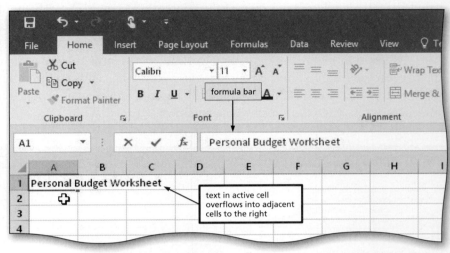

Figure 1–6

3

- Click the Enter button to complete the entry and enter the worksheet title (Figure 1–7).

 Q&A Why does the entered text appear in three cells?

When the text is longer than the width of a cell, Excel displays the overflow characters in adjacent cells to the right as long as those adjacent cells contain no data. If the adjacent cells contain data, Excel hides the overflow characters. The overflow characters are visible in the formula bar whenever that cell is active.

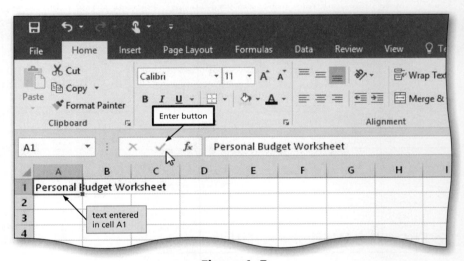

Figure 1–7

4

- Click cell A2 to select it.

- Type **Monthly Estimates** as the cell entry.

- Click the Enter button to complete the entry and enter the worksheet subtitle (Figure 1–8).

Q&A What happens when I click the Enter button?

When you complete an entry by clicking the Enter button, the insertion point disappears and the cell in which the text is entered remains the active cell.

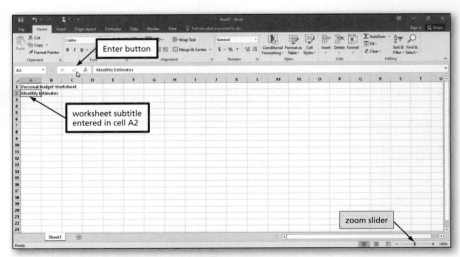

Figure 1–8

Other Ways

1. To complete entry, click any cell other than active cell

2. To complete entry, press ENTER

3. To complete entry, press HOME, PAGE UP, PAGE DOWN, END, UP ARROW, DOWN ARROW, LEFT ARROW, or RIGHT ARROW

Why is it difficult to read the text on my screen?

If you are having trouble reading the cell values in your spreadsheet, you can zoom in to make the cells larger. When you zoom in, fewer columns and rows display on your screen, and you might have to scroll more often. To zoom in, drag the zoom slider on the right of the status bar, or click the plus button on the zoom slider, until you reach your desired zoom level. In addition to the zoom slider, you also can zoom by clicking the Zoom button (View tab | Zoom group), selecting a desired zoom percentage (Zoom dialog box), and then clicking the OK button (Zoom dialog box).

AutoCorrect

The **AutoCorrect** feature of Excel works behind the scenes, correcting common mistakes when you complete a text entry in a cell. AutoCorrect makes three types of corrections for you:

1. Corrects two initial uppercase letters by changing the second letter to lowercase.
2. Capitalizes the first letter in the names of days.
3. Replaces commonly misspelled words with their correct spelling. For example, it will change the misspelled word *recieve* to *receive* when you complete the entry. AutoCorrect will correct the spelling of hundreds of commonly misspelled words automatically.

To Enter Column Titles

1 ENTER TEXT | 2 CALCULATE SUMS & USE FORMULAS | 3 FORMAT TEXT
4 INSERT CHART | 5 NAME TAB | 6 PREVIEW & PRINT WORKSHEET

The worksheet is divided into two parts, income and expense, as shown in Figure 1–4. Grouping income and expense data by month is a common method for organizing budget data. The column titles shown in row 3 identify the income section of the worksheet and indicate that the income values will be grouped by month. Likewise, row 8 is clearly identified as the expense section and similarly indicates that the expense values will be estimated on a per month basis. The following steps enter the column titles in row 3. ***Why?*** *Data entered in columns should be identified using column titles to identify what the column contains.*

- Click cell A3 to make it the active cell.

- Type **Income** to begin entry of a column title in the active cell (Figure 1–9).

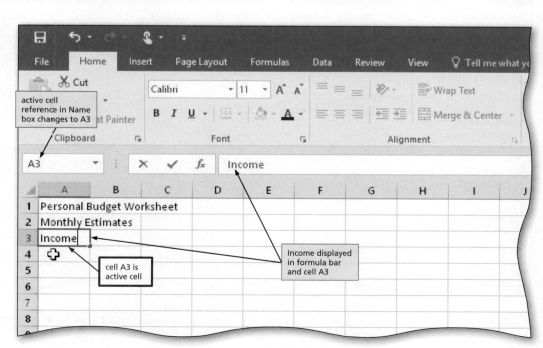

Figure 1–9

2

- Press the RIGHT ARROW key to enter the column title and make the cell to the right the active cell (Figure 1–10).

Q&A
Why is the RIGHT ARROW key used to complete the entry in the cell?

Pressing an arrow key to complete an entry makes the adjacent cell in the direction of the arrow (up, down, left, or right) the next active cell. However, if your next entry is in a nonadjacent cell, you can complete your current entry by clicking the next cell in which you plan to enter data. You also can press the ENTER key and then click the appropriate cell for the next entry.

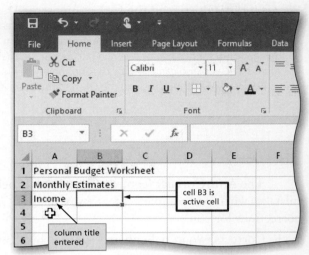

Figure 1–10

3

- Repeat Steps 1 and 2 to enter the remaining column titles; that is, enter **January** in cell B3, **February** in cell C3, **March** in cell D3, **April** in cell E3, **May** in cell F3, **June** in cell G3, **July** in cell H3, **August** in cell I3, **September** in cell J3, **October** in cell K3, **November** in cell L3, **December** in cell M3, and **Total** in cell N3 (complete the last entry in cell N3 by clicking the Enter button in the formula bar).

- Click cell A8 to select it.

- Repeat Steps 1 and 2 to enter the remaining column titles; that is, enter **Expenses** in cell A8, **January** in cell B8, **February** in cell C8, **March** in cell D8, **April** in cell E8, **May** in cell F8, **June** in cell G8, **July** in cell H8, **August** in cell I8, **September** in cell J8, **October** in cell K8, **November** in cell L8, **December** in cell M8, and **Total** in cell N8 (complete the last entry in cell N8 by clicking the Enter button in the formula bar) (Figure 1–11).

Figure 1–11

To Enter Row Titles

The next step in developing the worksheet for this project is to enter the row titles in column A. For the Personal Budget Worksheet data, the row titles contain a list of income types and expense types. Each income or expense item should be placed in its own row. *Why? Entering one item per row allows for maximum flexibility, in case more income or expense items are added in the future.* The following steps enter the row titles in the worksheet.

1

- Click cell A4 to select it.

- Type **Wages** and then click cell A5 or press the DOWN ARROW key to enter a row title (Figure 1–12).

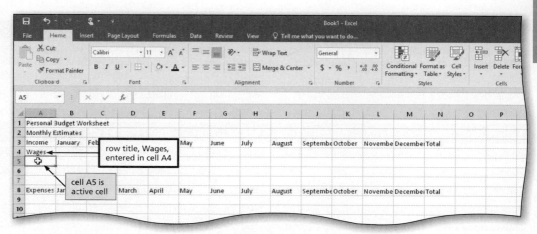

Figure 1–12

2

- Repeat Step 1 to enter the remaining row titles in column A; that is, enter **Dividends** in cell A5, **Total** in cell A6, **Rent** in cell A9, **Food** in cell A10, **Tuition** in cell A11, **Books** in cell A12, **Entertainment** in cell A13, **Car Payment** in cell A14, **Gas** in cell A15, **Miscellaneous** in cell A16, **Total** in cell A17, and **Net** in cell A19 (Figure 1–13).

Q&A Why is the text left-aligned in the cells?
Excel automatically left-aligns the text in the cell. Excel treats any combination of numbers, spaces, and nonnumeric characters as text. For example, Excel would recognize the following entries as text: 401AX21, 921–231, 619 321, 883XTY. How to change the text alignment in a cell is discussed later in this module.

Figure 1–13

Entering Numbers

In Excel, you enter a **number** into a cell to represent an amount or value. A number can contain only the following characters:

0 1 2 3 4 5 6 7 8 9 + − ( ) , / . $ % E e

If a cell entry contains any other keyboard character (including spaces), Excel interprets the entry as text and treats it accordingly. The use of special characters is explained when they are used in this book.

To Enter Numbers

The Personal Budget Worksheet numbers used in Module 1 are summarized in Table 1–1. These numbers, which represent yearly income and expense amounts, are entered in rows 4–5 and 9–16. *Why?* *One of the most powerful features of Excel is the ability to perform calculations on numeric data. Before you can perform calculations, you first must enter the data.* The following steps enter the numbers in Table 1–1 one row at a time.

Table 1–1 Personal Budget Worksheet

Income	January	February	March	April	May	June	July	August	September	October	November	December
Wages	1417.12	1417.12	1417.12	1417.12	1417.12	1417.12	1417.12	1417.12	1417.12	1417.12	1417.12	1417.12
Dividends	4029.71	0	0	0	0	0	4029.71	0	0	0	0	0

Expenses	January	February	March	April	May	June	July	August	September	October	November	December
Rent	410	410	410	410	410	410	410	410	410	410	410	410
Food	280	280	280	280	280	280	280	280	280	280	280	280
Tuition	1500	0	0	0	300	0	0	1500	0	0	0	0
Books	500	0	0	0	100	0	0	500	0	0	0	0
Entertainment	100	100	100	100	100	100	100	100	100	100	100	100
Car Payment	215.47	215.47	215.47	215.47	215.47	215.47	215.47	215.47	215.47	215.47	215.47	215.47
Gas	100	100	100	100	100	100	100	100	100	100	100	100
Miscellaneous	100	100	100	100	100	100	100	100	100	100	100	100

1

- Click cell B4 to select it.

- Type **1417.12** and then press the RIGHT ARROW key to enter the data in the selected cell and make the cell to the right (cell C4) the active cell (Figure 1–14).

Q&A Do I need to enter dollar signs, commas, or trailing zeros for the amounts?
You are not required to type dollar signs, commas, or trailing zeros. When you enter a dollar value that has cents, however, you must add the decimal point and the numbers representing the cents. Later in this module, you will learn how to format numbers with dollar signs, commas, and trailing zeros to improve their appearance and readability.

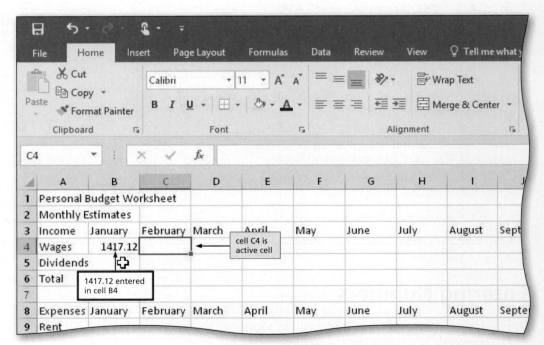

Figure 1–14

2

- Enter   **1417.12**   in cells C4, D4, E4, F4, G4, H4, I4, J4, K4, L4, and M4 to complete the first row of numbers in the worksheet (Figure 1–15).

Q&A | Why are the numbers right-aligned?
When you enter numeric data in a cell, Excel recognizes the values as numbers and automatically right-aligns the values in order to vertically align decimal and integer values.

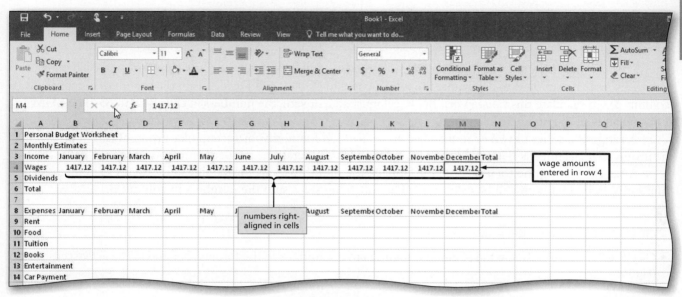

Figure 1–15

3

- Click cell B5 to select it and complete the entry in the previously selected cell.

- Enter the remaining numbers provided in Table 1–1 for each of the nine remaining budget items in row 5 and rows 9–16 (Figure 1–16).

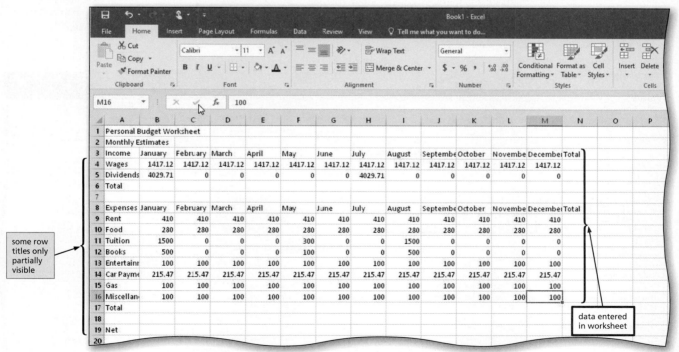

Figure 1–16

Calculating a Sum

The next step in creating the worksheet is to perform any necessary calculations, such as calculating the column and row totals. In Excel, you easily can perform calculations using a **function**, or a predefined formula. When you use functions, Excel performs the calculations for you, which helps to prevent errors and allows you to work more efficiently.

To Sum a Column of Numbers

1 ENTER TEXT | 2 CALCULATE SUMS & USE FORMULAS | 3 FORMAT TEXT
4 INSERT CHART | 5 NAME TAB | 6 PREVIEW & PRINT WORKSHEET

As stated in the requirements document in Figure 1–2, totals are required for each month and each budget item. The first calculation is to determine the total income for Wages and Dividends in the month of January (column B). To calculate this value in cell B6, Excel must add, or sum, the numbers in cells B4 and B5. The **SUM function** adds all the numbers in a range of cells. ***Why?*** *Excel's SUM function is an efficient means to accomplish this task.*

A **range** is a series of two or more adjacent cells in a column, row or rectangular group of cells. For example, the group of adjacent cells B4 and B5 is a range. Many Excel operations are performed on a range of cells.

After calculating the total income for January, the monthly totals for income and expenses and the yearly total for each budget item will be calculated. The following steps sum the numbers in column B.

- Click cell B6 to make it the active cell.
- Click the Sum button (Home tab | Editing group) to enter a formula in the formula bar and in the active cell (Figure 1–17).

Q&A

What if my screen displays the Sum menu?
If you are using a touch screen, you may not have a separate Sum button and Sum arrow. In this case, select the desired option (Sum) on the Sum menu.

How does Excel know which cells to sum?
Excel automatically selects what it considers to be your choice of the range to sum. When proposing the range, Excel first looks for a range of cells with numbers above the active cell and then to the left. If Excel proposes the wrong range, you can correct it by dragging through the correct range before pressing the ENTER key. You also can enter the correct range by typing the beginning cell reference, a colon (:), and the ending cell reference.

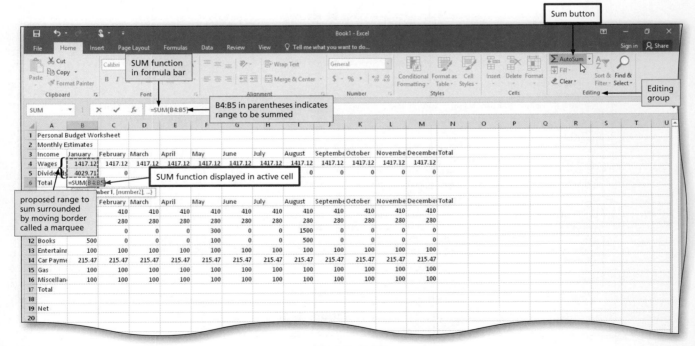

Figure 1–17

2

- Click the Enter button in the formula bar to enter the sum in the active cell.

Q&A What is the purpose of the arrow next to the Sum button on the ribbon?

The Sum arrow (shown in Figure 1–17) displays a list of functions that allow you to easily determine the average of a range of numbers, the number of items in a selected range, or the maximum or minimum value of a range.

3

- Repeat Steps 1 and 2 to enter the SUM function in cell B17 (Figure 1–18).

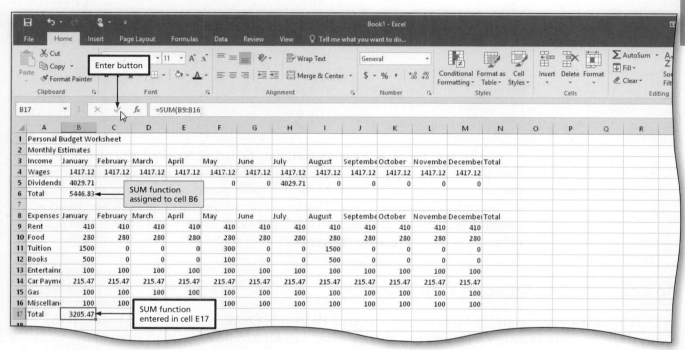

Figure 1–18

Other Ways

1. Click Insert Function button in formula bar, select SUM in Select a function list, click OK button (Insert Function dialog box), click OK button

   (Function Arguments dialog box)

2. Click Sum arrow (Home tab | Editing group), click More Functions in list, scroll to and

   then click SUM (Insert Function dialog box), click OK button, select range (Function Arguments dialog box), click OK button

3. Type **=s** in cell, select SUM in list, select range, click Enter button

4. Press ALT+EQUAL SIGN (=) twice

Using the Fill Handle to Copy a Cell to Adjacent Cells

You want to calculate the totals for income during each month in cells C6:M6. Table 1–2 illustrates the similarities between the function and range used in cell B6 and the function and ranges required to sum the totals in cells C6, D6, E6, F6, G6, H6, I6, J6, K6, L6, and M6.

To calculate each total for each range across the worksheet, you could follow the same steps shown previously in Figure 1–17 and Figure 1–18. A more efficient method, however, would be to copy the SUM function from cell B6 to the range C6:M6. The cell being copied is called the **source area** or **copy area**. The range of cells receiving the copy is called the **destination area** or **paste area**.

Table 1–2 Sum Function Entries in Row 6

Cell	SUM Function Entries	Result
B6	=SUM(B4:B5)	Sums cells B4 and B5
C6	=SUM(C4:C5)	Sums cells C4 and C5
D6	=SUM(D4:D5)	Sums cells D4 and D5
E6	=SUM(E4:E5)	Sums cells E4 and E5
F6	=SUM(F4:F5)	Sums cells F4 and F5
G6	=SUM(G4:G5)	Sums cells G4 and G5
H6	=SUM(H4:H5)	Sums cells H4 and H5
I6	=SUM(I4:I5)	Sums cells I4 and I5
J6	=SUM(J4:J5)	Sums cells J4 and J5
K6	=SUM(K4:K5)	Sums cells K4 and K5
L6	=SUM(L4:L5)	Sums cells L4 and L5
M6	=SUM(M4:M5)	Sums cells M4 and M5

Although the SUM function entries in Table 1–2 are similar to each other, they are not exact copies. The range in each SUM function entry uses cell references that are one column to the right of the previous column. When you copy formulas that include cell references, Excel automatically adjusts them for each new position, resulting in the SUM function entries illustrated in Table 1–2. Each adjusted cell reference is called a **relative reference**.

1 ENTER TEXT | 2 CALCULATE SUMS & USE FORMULAS | 3 FORMAT TEXT
4 INSERT CHART | 5 NAME TAB | 6 PREVIEW & PRINT WORKSHEET

To Copy a Cell to Adjacent Cells in a Row

The easiest way to copy the SUM formula from cell B6 to cells C6:M6 is to use the fill handle. *Why? Using the fill handle copies content to adjacent cells more efficiently.* The **fill handle** is the small green square located in the lower-right corner of the heavy border around the active cell. The following steps use the fill handle to copy cell B6 to the adjacent cells C6:M6.

1

- With cell B6 active, point to the fill handle to activate it. Your pointer changes to a crosshair (Figure 1–19).

Q&A
Why is my fill handle not a green square?
If you are using a touch screen, the fill handle appears as a black and white rectangle with a blue down arrow in it.

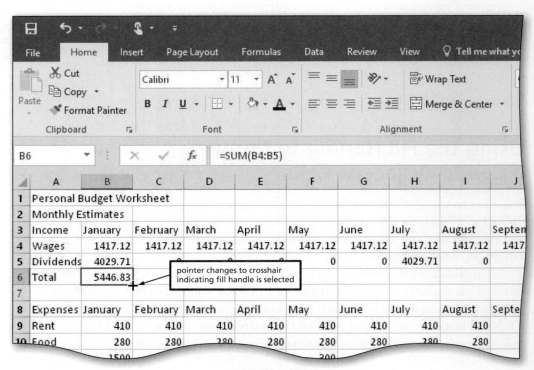

Figure 1–19

2

- Drag the fill handle
to select the
destination area,
range C6:M6, which
will draw a heavy
green border around
the source area
and the destination
area (Figure 1–20).
Do not release the
mouse button.

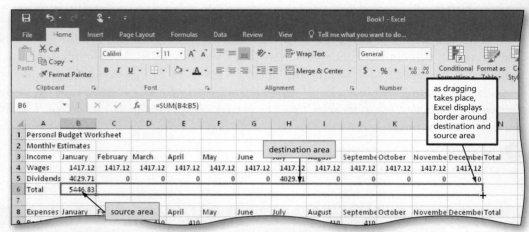

Figure 1–20

3

- Release the mouse
button to copy the
SUM function from
the active cell to the
destination area and
calculate the sums
(Figure 1–21).

Q&A What is the purpose
of the 'Auto Fill
Options' button?
The 'Auto Fill
Options' button
allows you to choose
whether you want to
copy the values from
the source area to
the destination area
with the existing
formatting, without
the formatting, or
with the formatting
but without the
functions.

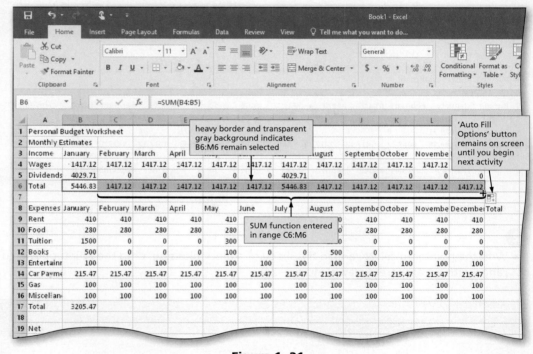

Figure 1–21

4

- Repeat Steps 1–3
to copy the SUM
function from
cell B17 to the
range C17:M17
(Figure 1–22).

Expenses	January	Febru...				June	July	Augu...			...be	December	Total
9 Rent	410	410	410	410	410	410	410	410	410	410	410	410	
10 Food	280	280	280	280	280	280	280	280	280	280	280	280	
11 Tuition	1500	0	0	0	300	0	0	1500	0	0	0	0	
12 Books	500	0	0	0	100	0	0	500	0	0	0	0	
13 Entertainr	100	100	100	100	100	100	100	100	100	100	100	100	
14 Car Payme	215.47	215.47	215.47	215.47	215.47	215.47	215.47	215.47	215.47	215.47	215.47	215.47	
15 Gas	100	100	100	100	100	100	100	100	100	100	100	100	
16 Misce lan	100	100	100	100	100	100	100	100	100	100	100	100	
17 Total	3205.47	1205.47	1205.47	1205.47	1605.47	1205.47	1205.47	3205.47	1205.47	1205.47	1205.47	1205.47	
18													
19 Net													
20													

SUM function in range C17:M17

Figure 1–22

Other Ways

1. Select source area, click Copy button (Home tab | Clipboard group),
select destination area, click Paste button (Home tab | Clipboard group)

2. Right-click source area, click Copy on shortcut menu, select and right-
click destination area, click Paste on shortcut menu

To Calculate Multiple Totals at the Same Time

The next step in building the worksheet is to determine the total income, total expenses, and total for each budget item in column N. To calculate these totals, you use the SUM function similar to how you used it to total the income and expenses for each month in rows 6 and 17.

In this example, however, Excel will determine totals for all of the rows at the same time. ***Why?*** *By determining multiple totals at the same time, the number of steps to add totals is reduced.* The following steps sum multiple totals at once.

1
- Click cell N4 to make it the active cell (Figure 1–23).

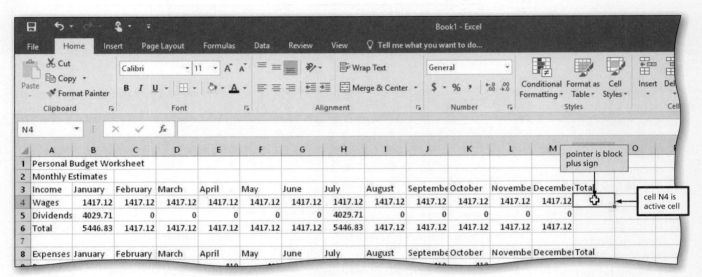

Figure 1–23

2
- With the pointer in cell N4 and in the shape of a block plus sign, drag the pointer down to cell N6 to highlight the range with a transparent view (Figure 1–24).

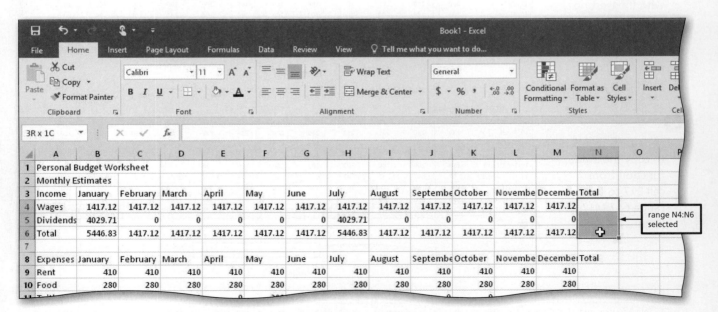

Figure 1–24

❸

- Click the Sum button (Home tab | Editing group) to calculate the sums of the corresponding rows (Figure 1–25).

Q&A How does Excel create unique totals for each row?

If each cell in a selected range is adjacent to a row of numbers, Excel assigns the SUM function to each cell when you click the Sum button.

Figure 1–25

❹

- Repeat Steps 1–3 to select cells N9 to N17 and calculate the sums of the corresponding rows (Figure 1–26).

Figure 1–26

To Enter a Formula Using the Keyboard

The net for each month, which will appear in row 19, is equal to the income total in row 6 minus the expense total in row 17. The formula needed in the worksheet is noted in the requirements document as follows:

Net (row 19) = Income (row 6) – Expenses (row 17)

The following steps enter the net formula in cell B19 using the keyboard. **Why?** *Sometimes a predefined function does not fit your needs; therefore, you enter a formula of your own.*

1

- Select cell B19 to deselect the selected range.

- Type **=b6-b17** in the cell. The formula is displayed in the formula bar and the current cell, and colored borders are drawn around the cells referenced in the formula (Figure 1–27).

Q&A

What occurs on the worksheet as I enter the formula?

The equal sign (=) preceding b6–b17 in the formula alerts Excel that you are entering a formula or function and not text. Because the most common error when entering a formula is to reference the wrong cell, Excel highlights the cell references in the formula in color, and uses same colors to highlight the borders of the cells to help you ensure that your cell references are correct. The minus sign (–) following b6 in the formula is the arithmetic operator that directs Excel to perform the subtraction operation.

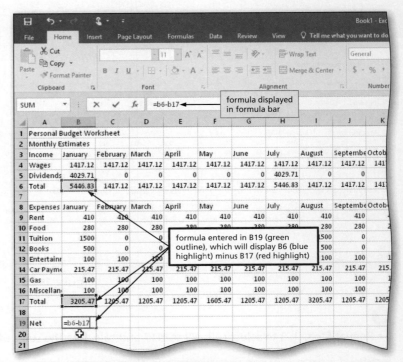

Figure 1–27

2

- Click cell C19 to complete the arithmetic operation, display the result in the worksheet, and select the cell to the right (Figure 1–28).

8	Expenses	January	February	March	April	May	June	July	August	Septembe	October	Novembe	Dec
9	Rent	410	410	410	410	410	410	410	410	410	410	410	
10	Food	280	280	280	280	280	280	280	280	280	280	280	
11	Tuition	1500	0	0	0	300	0	0	1500	0	0	0	
12	Books	500	0	0	0	100	0	0	500	0	0	0	
13	Entertainr	100	100	100	100	100	100	100	100	100	100	100	
14	Car Payme	215.47	215.47	215.47	215.47	215.47	215.47	215.47	215.47	215.47	215.47	215.47	
15	Gas	100	100	100	100	100	100	100	100	100	100	100	
16	Miscellan	100	100	100	100	100	100	100	100	100	100	100	
17	Total	3205.47	1205.47	1205.47	1205.47	1605.47	1205.47	1205.47	3205.47	1205.47	1205.47	1205.47	12
18													
19	Net	2241.36											
20													
21													
22													
23													

cell C19 selected

sum displayed

Figure 1–28

To Copy a Cell to Adjacent Cells in a Row

The easiest way to copy the SUM formula from cell B19 to cells C19, D19, E19, F19, G19, H19, I19, J19, K19, L19, M19, and N19 is to use the fill handle. The following steps use the fill handle to copy the formula in cell B19 to the adjacent cells C19:N19.

1 Select cell B19.

2 Drag the fill handle to select the destination area, range C19:N19, which draws a shaded border around the source area and the destination area. Release the mouse button to copy the simple formula function from the active cell to the destination area and calculate the results.

3 Save the worksheet on your hard drive, OneDrive, or other storage location using Linda Fox Budget as the file name.

Q&A | Why should I save the workbook at this time?
You have performed many tasks while creating this workbook and do not want to risk losing work completed thus far.

Break Point: If you wish to take a break, this is a good place to do so. You can exit Excel. To resume at a later time, run Excel, open the file called Linda Fox Budget, and continue following the steps from this location forward.

Formatting the Worksheet

The text, numeric entries, and functions for the worksheet now are complete. The next step is to format the worksheet. You **format** a worksheet to emphasize certain entries and make the worksheet easier to read and understand.

Figure 1–29a shows the worksheet before formatting. Figure 1–29b shows the worksheet after formatting. As you can see from the two figures, a worksheet that is formatted not only is easier to read but also looks more professional.

To change the unformatted worksheet in Figure 1–29a so that it looks like the formatted worksheet in Figure 1–29b, the following tasks must be completed:

What steps should I consider when formatting a worksheet?
The key to formatting a worksheet is to consider the ways you can enhance the worksheet so that it appears professional. When formatting a worksheet, consider the following steps:

• Identify in what ways you want to emphasize various elements of the worksheet.

• Increase the font size of cells.

• Change the font color of cells.

• Center the worksheet titles, subtitles, and column headings.

• Modify column widths to best fit text in cells.

• Change the font style of cells.

CONSIDER THIS

(a) Unformatted Worksheet

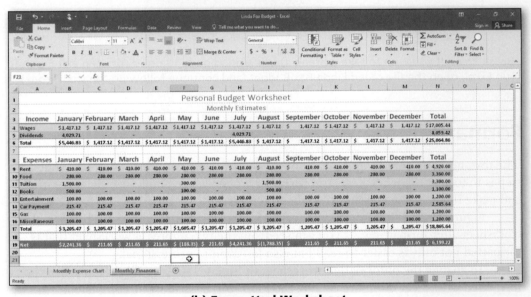

(b) Formatted Worksheet

Figure 1–29

1. Change the font, change the font style, increase the font size, and change the font color of the worksheet titles in cells A1 and A2.

2. Center the worksheet titles in cells A1 and A2 across columns A through N.

3. Format the body of the worksheet. The body of the worksheet, range A3:N19, includes the column titles, row titles, and numbers. Formatting the body of the worksheet changes the numbers to use a dollars-and-cents format, with dollar signs in rows 4 and 9 and in the total rows (row 6 and 17); changes the styles of some rows; adds underlining that emphasizes portions of the worksheet; and modifies the column widths to fit the text in the columns and make the text and numbers readable.

Although the formatting procedures are explained in the order described above, you could make these format changes in any order. Modifying the column widths, however, usually is done last because other formatting changes may affect the size of data in the cells in the column.

Font Style, Size, and Color

The characters that Excel displays on the screen are a specific font, style, size, and color. The **font**, or font face, defines the appearance and shape of the letters, numbers, and special characters. Examples of fonts include Calibri, Cambria, Times New Roman, Arial, and Courier. **Font style** indicates how the characters are emphasized. Common font styles include regular, bold, underline, and italic. The **font size** specifies the size of the characters. Font size is gauged by a measurement system called points. A single point is 1/72 of one inch in height. Thus, a character with a **point size** of 10 is 10/72 of one inch in height. Finally, Excel has a wide variety of **font colors** from which to choose to define the color of the characters.

When Excel first runs, the default font for the entire workbook is Calibri, with a font size, font style, and font color of 11-point regular black. You can change the font characteristics in a single cell, a range of cells, the entire worksheet, or the entire workbook.

1 ENTER TEXT | 2 CALCULATE SUMS & USE FORMULAS | 3 FORMAT TEXT
4 INSERT CHART | 5 NAME TAB | 6 PREVIEW & PRINT WORKSHEET

To Change a Cell Style

You can change several characteristics of a cell, such as the font, font size, and font color, all at once by assigning a predefined cell style to a cell. A **cell style** is a predefined font, font size, and font color that you can apply to a cell. **Why?** *Using the predefined styles provides a consistent appearance to common portions of your worksheets, such as worksheet titles, worksheet subtitles, column headings, and total rows.* The following steps assign the Title cell style to the worksheet title in cell A1.

- Click cell A1 to make cell A1 the active cell.
- Click the Cell Styles button (Home tab | Styles group) to display the Cell Styles gallery (Figure 1–30).

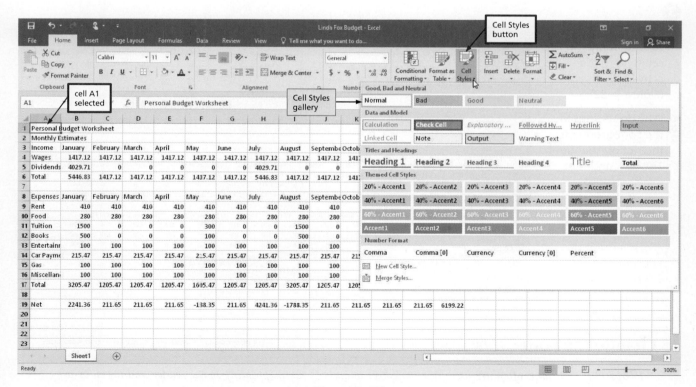

Figure 1–30

2

- Point to the Title cell style in the Titles and Headings area of the Cell Styles gallery to see a live preview of the cell style in the active cell (Figure 1–31).

Q&A Can I use live preview on a touch screen?
Live preview is not available on a touch screen.

Experiment

- Point to other cell styles in the Cell Styles gallery to see a live preview of those cell styles in cell A1.

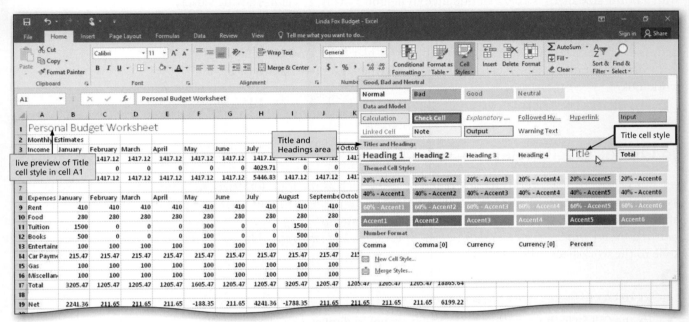

Figure 1–31

3

- Click the Title cell style to apply the cell style to the active cell (Figure 1–32).

Q&A Why do settings in the Font group on the ribbon change?
The font and font size change to reflect the font changes applied to the active cell, cell A1, as a result of applying the Title cell style.

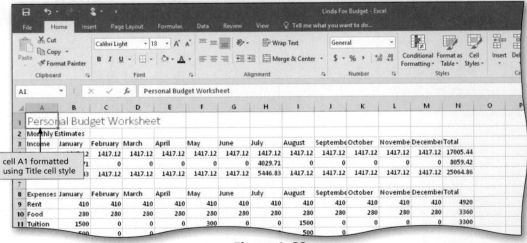

Figure 1–32

1 ENTER TEXT | 2 CALCULATE SUMS & USE FORMULAS | 3 FORMAT TEXT
4 INSERT CHART | 5 NAME TAB | 6 PREVIEW & PRINT WORKSHEET

To Change the Font

Why? *Different fonts often are used in a worksheet to make it more appealing to the reader and to relate or distinguish data in the worksheet.* The following steps change the worksheet subtitle's font to Calibri Light.

1

- Click cell A2 to make it the active cell.

- Click the Font arrow (Home tab | Font group) to display the Font gallery. If necessary, scroll to Calibri Light.

- Point to Calibri Light in the Font gallery to see a live preview of the selected font in the active cell (Figure 1–33).

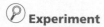 **Experiment**

- Point to several other fonts in the Font gallery to see a live preview of the other fonts in the selected cell.

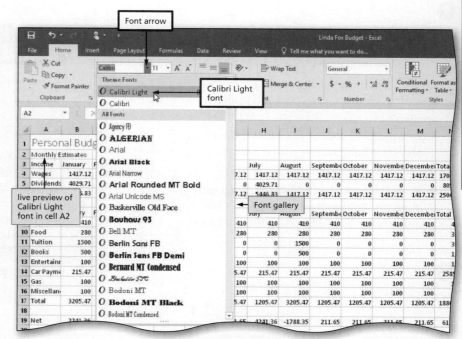

Figure 1–33

2

- Click Calibri Light in the Font gallery to change the font of the worksheet subtitle to Calibri Light (Figure 1–34).

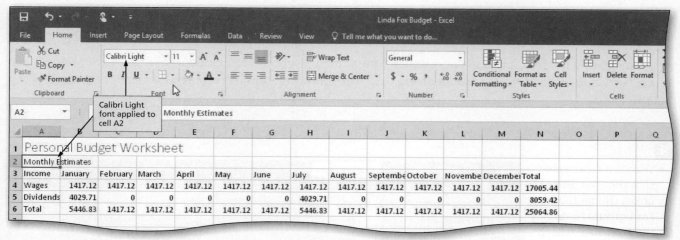

Figure 1–34

Other Ways

1. Click Font Settings Dialog Box Launcher, click Font tab (Format Cells dialog box), click desired font in Font list, click OK button

2. Right-click cell to display mini toolbar, click Font box arrow on mini toolbar, click desired font in Font gallery

3. Right-click selected cell, click Format Cells on shortcut menu, click Font tab (Format Cells dialog box), click desired font, click OK button

1 ENTER TEXT | 2 CALCULATE SUMS & USE FORMULAS | 3 FORMAT TEXT
4 INSERT CHART | 5 NAME TAB | 6 PREVIEW & PRINT WORKSHEET

To Apply Bold Style to a Cell

Bold, or boldface, text has a darker appearance than normal text. ***Why?*** *You apply bold style to a cell to emphasize it or make it stand out from the rest of the worksheet.* The following steps apply bold style to the worksheet title and subtitle.

- Click cell A1 to make it active and then click the Bold button (Home tab | Font group) to change the font style of the active cell to bold (Figure 1–35).

Q&A

What if a cell already has the bold style applied?
If the active cell contains bold text, then Excel displays the Bold button with a darker gray background.

How do I remove the bold style from a cell?
Clicking the Bold button (Home tab | Font group) a second time removes the bold style.

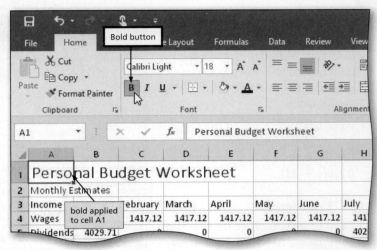

Figure 1–35

2

- Repeat Step 1 to bold cell A2.

Other Ways

1. Click Font Settings Dialog Box Launcher, click Font tab (Format Cells dialog box), click Bold in Font style list, click OK button
2. Right-click selected cell, click Bold button on mini toolbar
3. Right-click selected cell, click Format Cells on shortcut menu, click Font tab (Format Cells dialog box), click Bold, click OK button
4. Press CTRL+B

To Increase the Font Size of a Cell Entry

1 ENTER TEXT | 2 CALCULATE SUMS & USE FORMULAS | 3 FORMAT TEXT
4 INSERT CHART | 5 NAME TAB | 6 PREVIEW & PRINT WORKSHEET

Increasing the font size is the next step in formatting the worksheet subtitle. *Why? You increase the font size of a cell so that the entry stands out and is easier to read.* The following steps increase the font size of the worksheet subtitle in cell A2.

1

- With cell A2 selected, click the Font Size arrow (Home tab | Font group) to display the Font Size gallery.

- Point to 14 in the Font Size gallery to see a live preview of the active cell with the selected font size (Figure 1–36).

Experiment

- If you are using a mouse, point to several other font sizes in the Font Size list to see a live preview of those font sizes in the selected cell.

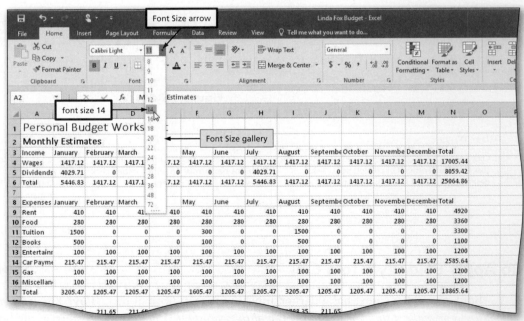

Figure 1–36

1

- Click 14 in the Font Size gallery to change the font size in the active cell (Figure 1–37).

Q&A

Can I choose a font size that is not in the Font Size gallery?
Yes. An alternative to selecting a font size in the Font Size gallery is to click the Font Size box (Home tab | Font group), type the font size you want, and then press the ENTER key.

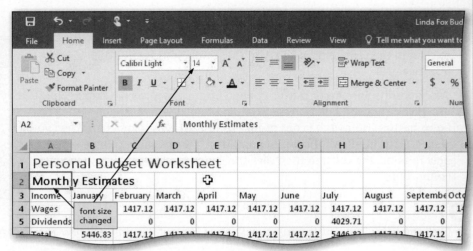

Figure 1–37

Other Ways

1. Click 'Increase Font Size' button (Home tab | Font group) or 'Decrease Font Size' button (Home tab | Font group)

2. Click Font Settings Dialog box Launcher, click Font tab (Format Cells dialog box), click desired size in Size list, click OK button

3. Right-click cell to display mini toolbar, click Font Size arrow on mini toolbar, click desired font size in Font Size gallery

4. Right-click selected cell, click Format Cells on shortcut menu, click Font tab (Format Cells dialog box), select font size in Size box, click OK button

---

1 ENTER TEXT | **2** CALCULATE SUMS & USE FORMULAS | **3** FORMAT TEXT
4 INSERT CHART | **5** NAME TAB | **6** PREVIEW & PRINT WORKSHEET

To Change the Font Color of a Cell Entry

The next step is to change the color of the font in cells A1 and A2 to orange. ***Why?*** *Changing the font color of cell entries can help the text stand out more. You also can change the font colors to match the company or product's brand colors.* The following steps change the font color of a cell entry.

1

- Click cell A1 and then click the Font Color arrow (Home tab | Font group) to display the Font Color gallery.

- Point to 'Orange, Accent 2' (column 6, row 1) in the Theme Colors area of the Font Color gallery to see a live preview of the font color in the active cell (Figure 1–38).

Experiment

- Point to several other colors in the Font Color gallery to see a live preview of other font colors in the active cell.

Q&A

How many colors are in the Font Color gallery?
You can choose from approximately 70 different font colors in the Font Color gallery. Your Font Color gallery may have more or fewer colors, depending on the color settings of your operating system. The Theme Colors area contains colors that are included in the current workbook's theme.

Figure 1–38

- Click 'Orange, Accent 2' (column 6, row 1) in the Font Color gallery to change the font color of the worksheet title in the active cell (Figure 1–39).

Q&A Why does the Font Color button change after I select the new font color?
When you choose a color on the Font Color gallery, Excel changes the Font Color button (Home tab | Font group) to your chosen color. Then when you want to change the font color of another cell to the same color, you need only to select the cell and then click the Font Color button (Home tab | Font group).

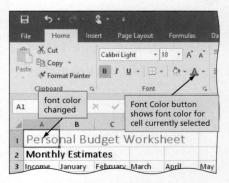

Figure 1–39

3

- Click the Font Color button to apply Orange, Accent 2 (column 6, row 1) to cell A2.

Other Ways

1. Click Font Settings Dialog Box Launcher, click Font tab (Format Cells dialog box), click desired color in Color list, click OK button

2. Right-click the cell to display mini toolbar, click Font Color arrow on mini toolbar, click desired font color in Font Color gallery

3. Right-click selected cell, click Format Cells on shortcut menu, click Font tab (Format Cells dialog box), select color in Font Color gallery, click OK button

---

To Center Cell Entries across Columns by Merging Cells

1 ENTER TEXT | 2 CALCULATE SUMS & USE FORMULAS | 3 FORMAT TEXT
4 INSERT CHART | 5 NAME TAB | 6 PREVIEW & PRINT WORKSHEET

The final step in formatting the worksheet title and subtitle is to center them across columns A through N. **Why?** *Centering a title across the columns used in the body of the worksheet improves the worksheet's appearance.* To do this, the 14 cells in the range A1:N1 are combined, or merged, into a single cell that is the width of the columns in the body of the worksheet. The 14 cells in the range A2:N2 are merged in a similar manner. **Merging cell**s involves creating a single cell by combining two or more selected cells. The following steps center the worksheet title and subtitle across columns by merging cells.

1

- Select cell A1 and then drag to cell N1 to highlight the range to be merged and centered (Figure 1–40).

Q&A What if a cell in the range B1:N1 contains data?
For the 'Merge & Center' button (Home tab | Alignment group) to work properly, all the cells except the leftmost cell in the selected range must be empty.

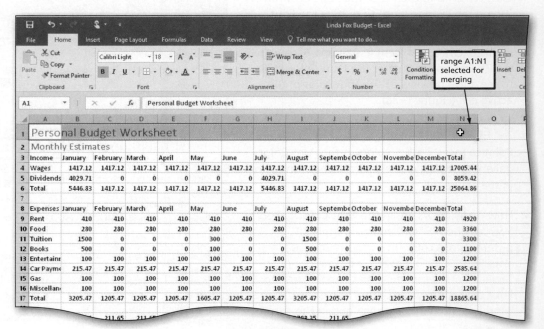

Figure 1–40

2

- Click the 'Merge & Center' button (Home tab | Alignment group) to merge cells A1 through N1 and center the contents of the leftmost cell across the selected columns (Figure 1–41).

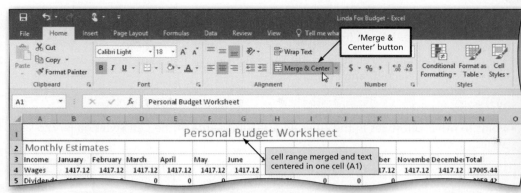

Figure 1–41

Q&A What if my screen displays a Merge & Center menu?

Select the desired option on the Merge & Center menu if you do not have a separate 'Merge & Center' button and 'Merge & Center' arrow.

What happened to cells B1 through N1?

After the merge, cells B1 through N1 no longer exist. The new cell A1 now extends across columns A through N.

3

- Repeat Steps 1 and 2 to merge and center the worksheet subtitle across cells A2 through N2 (Figure 1–42).

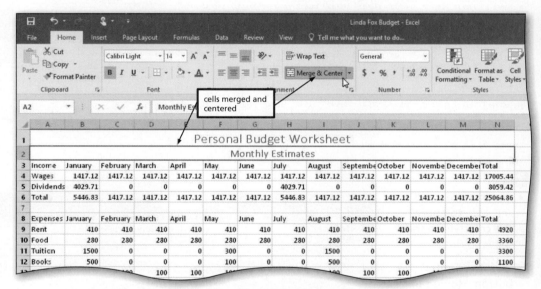

Figure 1–42

Q&A Are cells B1 through N1 and B2 through N2 lost forever?

No. The opposite of merging cells is **splitting** a merged cell. After you have merged multiple cells into one cell, you can unmerge, or split, the cell to display the original range of cells. You split a merged cell by selecting it and clicking the 'Merge & Center' button. For example, if you click the 'Merge & Center' button a second time in Step 2, it will split the merged cell A1 into cells A1, B1, C1, D1, E1, F1, G1, H1, I1, J1, K1, L1, M1, and N1, and move the title to it's original location in cell A1.

Other Ways

1. Right-click selection, click 'Merge & Center' button on mini toolbar
2. Right-click selected cell, click Format Cells on shortcut menu, click Alignment tab (Format Cells dialog box), select 'Center Across Selection' in Horizontal list, click OK button

1 ENTER TEXT | **2** CALCULATE SUMS & USE FORMULAS | **3 FORMAT TEXT**
4 INSERT CHART | **5 NAME TAB** | **6 PREVIEW & PRINT WORKSHEET**

To Format Rows Using Cell Styles

The next step to format the worksheet is to format the rows. **Why?** *Row titles and the total row should be formatted so that the column titles and total row can be distinguished from the data in the body of the worksheet. Data rows can be formatted to make them easier to read as well.* The following steps format the column titles and total row using cell styles in the default worksheet theme.

- Click cell A3 and then drag to cell N3 to select the range.

- Click the Cell Styles button (Home tab | Styles group) to display the Cell Styles gallery.

- Point to the Heading 1 cell style in the Titles and Headings area of the Cell Styles gallery to see a live preview of the cell style in the selected range (Figure 1–43).

Experiment

- Point to other cell styles in the Titles and Headings area of the Cell Styles gallery to see a live preview of other styles.

Figure 1–43

- Click the Heading 1 cell style to apply the cell style to the selected range.

- Click the Center button (Home tab | Alignment group) to center the column headings in the selected range.

- Select the range A8 to N8 (Figure 1–44).

Figure 1–44

- Apply the Heading 1 cell style format and then center the headings (Figure 1–45).

Figure 1–45

- Format the range A6:N6 and A17:N17 with the Total cell style format.

- Format the range A19:N19 with the Accent2 cell style format.

- Format the range A4:N4, A9:N9, A11:N11, A13:N13, A15:N15 with the 20% - Accent2 cell style format.

- Format the range A5:N5, A10:N10, A12:N12, A14:N14, A16:N16 with the 40% - Accent2 cell style format. Deselect the selected ranges

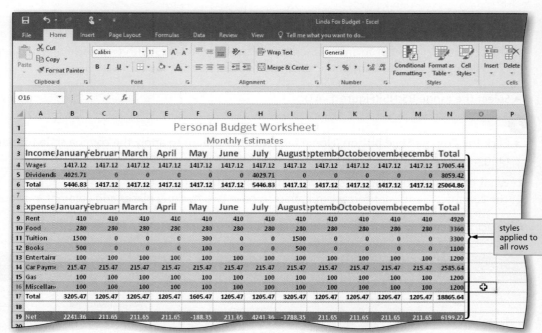

Figure 1–46

1 ENTER TEXT | 2 CALCULATE SUMS & USE FORMULAS | 3 FORMAT TEXT
4 INSERT CHART | 5 NAME TAB | 6 PREVIEW & PRINT WORKSHEET

To Format Numbers in the Worksheet

The requirements document requested that numbers in the first row and last row of each section should be formatted to use a dollar-and-cents format, while other numbers receive a comma format. *Why? Using a dollar-and-cents format for selected cells makes it clear to users of the worksheet that the numbers represent dollar values without cluttering the entire worksheet with dollar signs, and applying the comma format makes larger numbers easier to read.* Excel allows you to apply various number formats, many of which are discussed in later modules. The following steps use buttons on the ribbon to format the numbers in the worksheet.

- Select the range
B4:N4.

- Click the 'Accounting
Number Format'
button (Home tab |
Number group) to
apply the accounting
number format
to the cells in the
selected range.

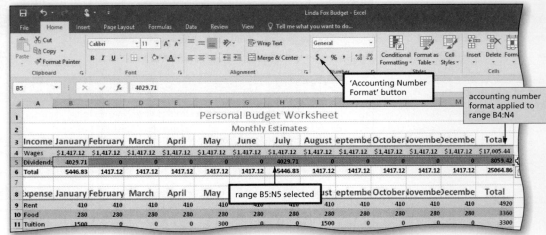

Figure 1–47

Q&A What if my
screen displays an
Accounting Number
Format menu?
If you are using a touch
screen, you may not
have a separate 'Accounting Number Format' button and 'Accounting Number Format' arrow. In this case, select
the desired option on the Accounting Number Format menu.

What effect does the accounting number format have on the selected cells?
The accounting number format causes numbers to be displayed with two decimal places and to align vertically.
Cell widths are adjusted automatically to accommodate the new formatting.

- Select the range B5:N5 (Figure 1–47).

2

- Click the Comma Style button (Home tab | Number group) to apply the comma style format to the selected
range.

Q&A What effect does the comma style format have on the selected cells?
The comma style format formats numbers to have two decimal places and commas as thousands separators.

- Select the range B6:N6 to make it the active range (Figure 1–48).

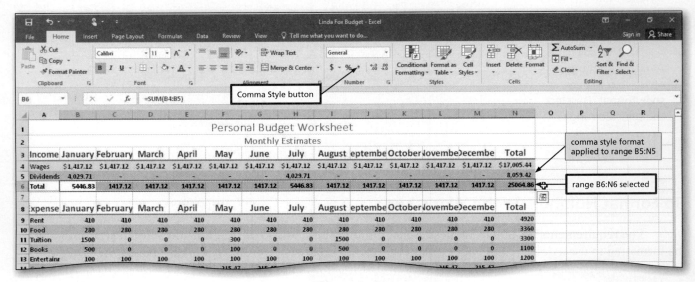

Figure 1–48

3

- Click the 'Accounting Number Format' button (Home tab | Number group) to apply the accounting number format
to the cells in the selected range.

4

- Format the ranges B9:N9, B17:N17, and B19:N19 with the accounting number format.

- Format the range B10:N16 with the comma style format. Click cell A1 to deselect the selected ranges (Figure 1–49).

Q&A How do I select the range B10:N16?

Select this range the same way as you select a range of cells in a column or row; that is, click the first cell in the range (B10, in this case) and drag to the last cell in the range (N16, in this case).

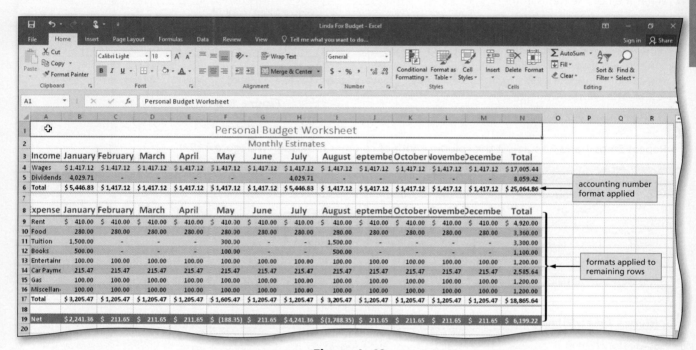

Figure 1–49

Other Ways

1. Click 'Accounting Number Format' or Comma Style button on mini toolbar

2. Right-click selected cell, click Format Cells on shortcut menu, click Number tab (Format Cells dialog box), select Accounting in Category list or select Number and click 'Use 1000 Separator', click OK button

To Adjust the Column Width

1 ENTER TEXT | 2 CALCULATE SUMS & USE FORMULAS | 3 FORMAT TEXT
4 INSERT CHART | 5 NAME TAB | 6 PREVIEW & PRINT WORKSHEET

The last step in formatting the worksheet is to adjust the width of the columns so that each title is visible. **Why?** *To make a worksheet easy to read, the column widths should be adjusted appropriately.* Excel offers other methods for adjusting cell widths and row heights, which are discussed later in this book. The following steps adjust the width of columns A through N so that the contents of the columns are visible.

1

- Point to the boundary on the right side of the column A heading above row 1 to change the pointer to a split double arrow (Figure 1–50).

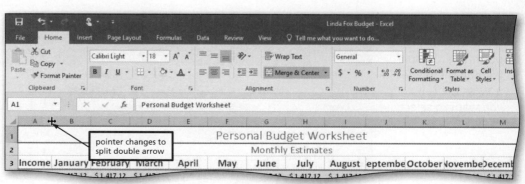

Figure 1–50

2

- Double-click the boundary to adjust the width of the column to accommodate the width of the longest item in the column (Figure 1–51).

Q&A

What if all of the items in the column are already visible?

If all of the items are shorter in length than the width of the column and you double-click the column boundary, Excel will reduce the width of the column.

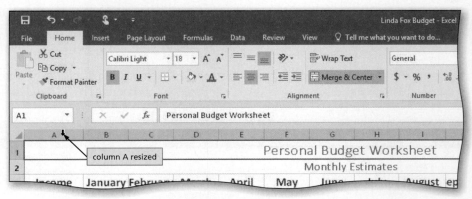

Figure 1–51

3

- Repeat Steps 1 and 2 to adjust the column width of columns B through N (Figure 1–52).

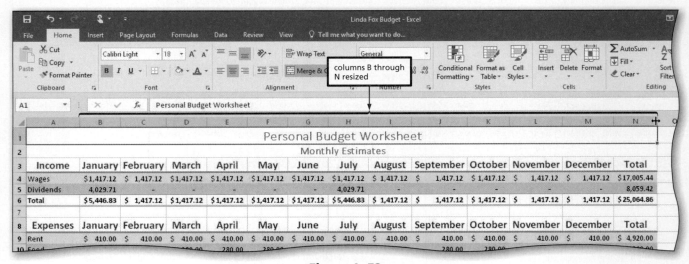

Figure 1–52

To Use the Name Box to Select a Cell

1 ENTER TEXT | 2 CALCULATE SUMS & USE FORMULAS | 3 FORMAT TEXT
4 INSERT CHART | 5 NAME TAB | 6 PREVIEW & PRINT WORKSHEET

The next step is to chart the monthly expenses. To create the chart, you need to identify the range of the data you want to feature on the chart and then select it. In this case you want to start with cell A3. Rather than clicking cell A3 to select it, you will select the cell by using the Name box, which is located to the left of the formula bar. **Why?** *You might want to use the Name box to select a cell if you are working with a large worksheet and it is faster to type the cell name rather than scrolling to and clicking it.* The following steps select cell A3 using the Name box.

1

- Click the Name box in the formula bar and then type **a3** as the cell you want to select (Figure 1–53).

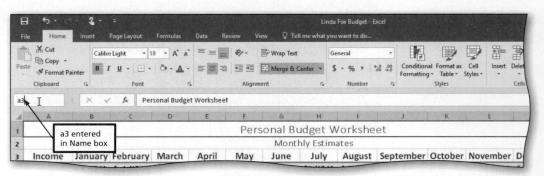

Figure 1–53

2

- Press the ENTER key to change the active cell in the Name box and make cell A3 the active cell (Figure 1–54).

cell A3 is active cell

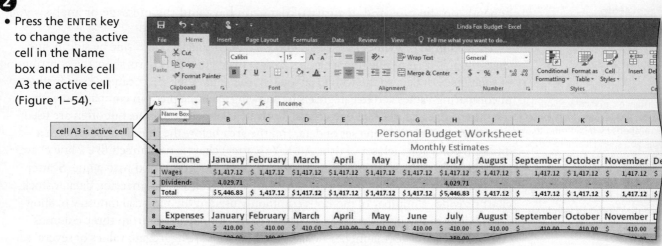

Figure 1–54

Other Ways to Select Cells

As you will see in later modules, in addition to using the Name box to select any cell in a worksheet, you also can use it to assign names to a cell or range of cells. Excel supports several additional ways to select a cell, as summarized in Table 1–3.

Table 1–3 Selecting Cells in Excel	
Key, Box, or Command	**Function**
ALT+PAGE DOWN	Selects the cell one worksheet window to the right and moves the worksheet window accordingly.
ALT+PAGE UP	Selects the cell one worksheet window to the left and moves the worksheet window accordingly.
ARROW	Selects the adjacent cell in the direction of the arrow on the key.
CTRL+ARROW	Selects the border cell of the worksheet in combination with the arrow keys and moves the worksheet window accordingly. For example, to select the rightmost cell in the row that contains the active cell, press CTRL+RIGHT ARROW. You also can press the END key, release it, and then press the appropriate arrow key to accomplish the same task.
CTRL+HOME	Selects cell A1 or the cell one column and one row below and to the right of frozen titles and moves the worksheet window accordingly.
Find command on Find & Select menu (Home tab | Editing group) or SHIFT+F5	Finds and selects a cell that contains specific contents that you enter in the Find and Replace dialog box. If necessary, Excel moves the worksheet window to display the cell. You also can press CTRL+F to display the Find and Replace dialog box.
Go To command on Find & Select menu (Home tab | Editing group) or F5	Selects the cell that corresponds to the cell reference you enter in the Go To dialog box and moves the worksheet window accordingly. You also can press CTRL+G to display the Go To dialog box.
HOME	Selects the cell at the beginning of the row that contains the active cell and moves the worksheet window accordingly.
Name box	Selects the cell in the workbook that corresponds to the cell reference you enter in the Name box.
PAGE DOWN	Selects the cell down one worksheet window from the active cell and moves the worksheet window accordingly.
PAGE UP	Selects the cell up one worksheet window from the active cell and moves the worksheet window accordingly.

© 2014 Cengage Learning

Break Point: If you wish to take a break, this is a good place to do so. Be sure to save the Linda Fox Budget file again and then you can exit Excel. To resume at a later time, run Excel, open the file called Linda Fox Budget, and continue following the steps from this location forward.

Adding a Pie Chart to the Worksheet

Excel includes 15 chart types from which you can choose, including column, line, pie, bar, area, X Y (scatter), stock, surface, radar, treemap, sunburst,

BTW
Excel Help
At any time while using
Excel, you can find answers
to questions and display
information about various
topics through Excel Help.
Used properly, this form of
assistance can increase your
productivity and reduce your
frustrations by minimizing the
time you spend learning how
to use Excel. For instructions
about Excel Help and
exercises that will help you
gain confidence in using it,
read the Office and Windows
module at the beginning of
this book.

histogram, box & whisker, waterfall, and combo. The type of chart you choose depends on the type and quantity of data you have and the message or analysis you want to convey.

A column or cylinder chart is a good way to compare values side by side. A line chart often is used to illustrate changes in data over time. Pie charts show the contribution of each piece of data to the whole, or total, of the data. A pie chart can go even further in comparing values across categories by showing each pie piece in comparison with the others. Area charts, like line charts, illustrate changes over time, but often are used to compare more than one set of data, and the area below the lines is filled in with a different color for each set of data. An X Y (scatter) chart is used much like a line chart, but each piece of data is represented by a dot and is not connected with a line. Scatter charts are typically used for viewing scientific, statistical, and engineering data. A stock chart provides a number of methods commonly used in the financial industry to show fluctuations in stock market data. A surface chart compares data from three columns and/or rows in a 3-D manner. A radar chart can compare aggregate values of several sets of data in a manner that resembles a radar screen, with each set of data represented by a different color. A combo chart allows you to combine multiple types of charts.

Excel 2016 includes five new charts. Treemap and sunburst charts are hierarchy charts, used to compare parts to a whole. A treemap chart uses nested rectangles to show data in a hierarchy. A sunburst chart stacks multiple pie charts on one another to illustrate related data. New statistical charts include histogram and box & whisker charts. A histogram chart shows the distribution of data. A box & whisker chart, or box plot, is used to display variation within a set of data. The new waterfall chart is used to visualize increases and decreases within a set of data and is grouped with stock charts.

As outlined in the requirements document in Figure 1–2, the budget worksheet should include a pie chart to graphically represent the yearly expense totals for each item in Linda Fox's budget. The pie chart shown in Figure 1–55 is on its own sheet in the workbook. The pie chart resides on a separate sheet, called a **chart sheet**, which contains only the chart.

Figure 1–55

In this worksheet, the ranges you want to chart are the nonadjacent ranges A9:A16 (expense titles) and N9:N16 (yearly expense totals). The expense titles in the range A9:A16 will identify the slices of the pie chart; these entries are called category names. The range N9:N16 contains the data that determines the size of the slices in the pie; these entries are called the **data series**. Because eight budget items are being charted, the 3-D pie chart contains eight slices.

To Add a 3-D Pie Chart

1 ENTER TEXT | 2 CALCULATE SUMS & USE FORMULAS | 3 FORMAT TEXT
4 INSERT CHART | 5 NAME TAB | 6 PREVIEW & PRINT WORKSHEET

Why? *When you want to see how each part relates to the whole, you use a pie chart.* The following steps draw the 3-D pie chart.

- Select the range A9:A16 to identify the range of the category names for the 3-D pie chart.

- While holding down the CTRL key, select the nonadjacent range N9:N16.

- Click Insert on the ribbon to display the Insert tab.

- Click the 'Insert Pie or Doughnut Chart' button (Insert tab | Charts group) to display the Insert Pie or Doughnut Chart gallery (Figure 1–56).

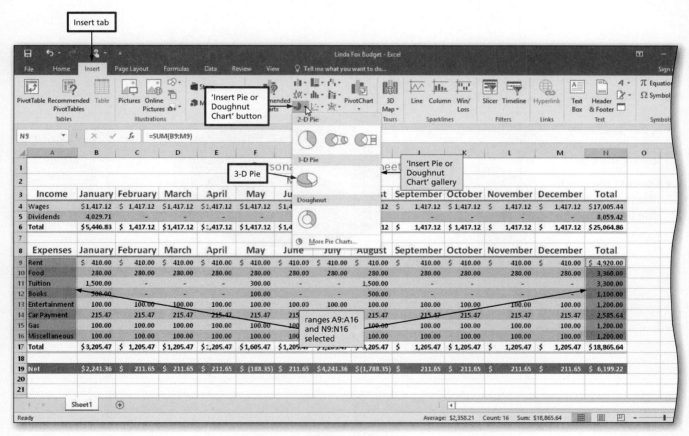

Figure 1–56

②

- Click 3-D Pie in the Insert Pie or Doughnut Chart gallery to insert the chart in the worksheet (Figure 1–57).

Q&A Why have new tabs appeared on the ribbon?

The new tabs provide additional options and functionality when you are working with certain objects, such as charts, and only display when you are working with those objects.

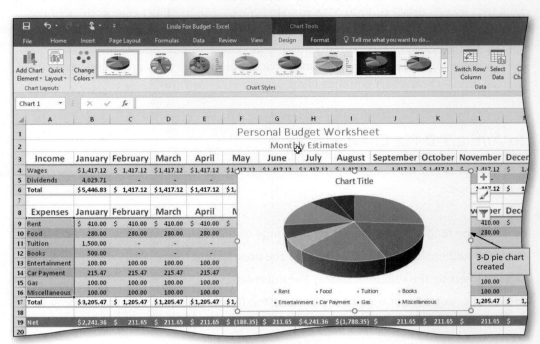

Figure 1–57

③

- Click and drag to select all the text in the chart title.

- Type **Monthly Expenses** to specify the title.

- Deselect the chart title to view the new title (Figure 1–58).

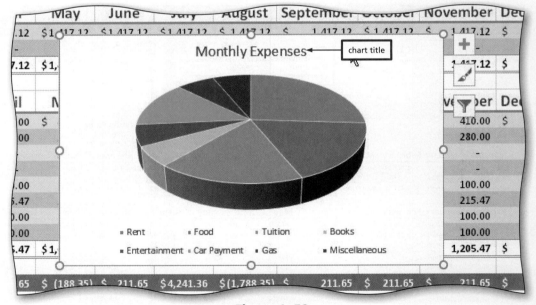

Figure 1–58

1 ENTER TEXT | 2 CALCULATE SUMS & USE FORMULAS | 3 FORMAT TEXT
4 INSERT CHART | 5 NAME TAB | 6 PREVIEW & PRINT WORKSHEET

To Apply a Style to a Chart

Why? *If you want to enhance the appearance of a chart, you can apply a chart style.* The following steps apply Style 5 to the 3-D pie chart.

①

- Click the Chart Styles button to display the Chart Styles gallery.

- Scroll in the Chart Style gallery to display the Style 5 chart style (Figure 1–59).

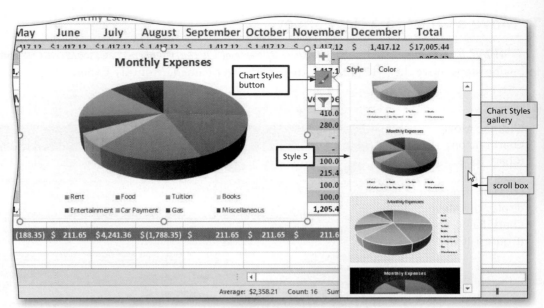

Figure 1–59

②

- Click Style 5 in the Chart Styles gallery to change the chart style to Style 5 (Figure 1–60).

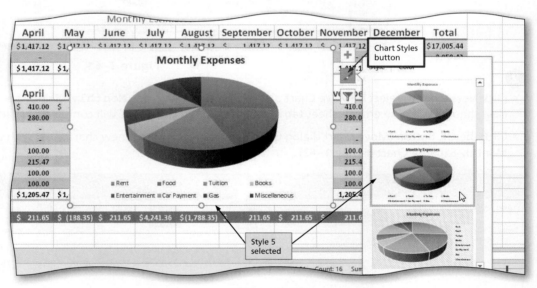

Figure 1–60

③

- Click the Chart Styles button to close the Chart Styles gallery.

Changing the Sheet Tab Names

The sheet tabs at the bottom of the window allow you to navigate between any worksheet in the workbook. You click the sheet tab of the worksheet you want to view in the Excel window. By default, the worksheets are named Sheet1, Sheet2, and so on. The worksheet names become increasingly important as you move toward more sophisticated workbooks, especially workbooks in which you reference cells between worksheets.

BTW

Exploding a Pie Chart

If you want to draw attention to a particular slice in a pie chart, you can offset the slice so that it stands out from the rest. A pie chart with one or more slices offset is referred to as an exploded pie chart. To offset a slice, click the slice two times to select it (do not double-click) and then drag the slice outward.

EX 38   Excel Module 1   Creating a Worksheet and a Chart

1 ENTER TEXT | 2 CALCULATE SUMS & USE FORMULAS | 3 FORMAT TEXT
4 INSERT CHART | 5 NAME TAB | 6 PREVIEW & PRINT WORKSHEET

To Move a Chart to a New Sheet

Why? *By moving a chart to its own sheet, the size of the chart will increase, which can improve readability.* The following steps move the 3-D pie chart to a chart sheet named, Monthly Expenses.

1

- Click the Move Chart button (Chart Tools Design tab | Location group) to display the Move Chart dialog box (Figure 1–61).

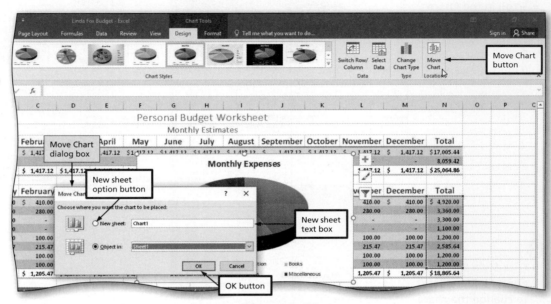

Figure 1–61

2

- Click New sheet to select it (Move Chart dialog box) and then type **Monthly Expense Chart** in the New sheet text box to enter a sheet tab name for the worksheet that will contain the chart.

- Click the OK button (Move Chart dialog box) to move the chart to a new chart sheet with the sheet tab name, Monthly Expense Chart (Figure 1–62).

Figure 1–62

To Change the Sheet Tab Name

You decide to change the name of the Sheet1 tab to Monthly Finances. ***Why?*** *Use simple, meaningful names for each sheet tab. Sheet tab names often match the worksheet title. If a worksheet includes multiple titles in multiple sections of the worksheet, use a sheet tab name that encompasses the meaning of all of the sections.* The following steps rename the sheet tab.

❶

- Double-click the sheet tab labeled Sheet1 in the lower-left corner of the window.

- Type **Monthly Finances** as the sheet tab name and then press the ENTER key to assign the new name to the sheet tab (Figure 1–63).

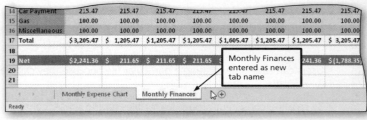

Q&A What is the maximum length for a sheet tab name?

Sheet tab names can be up to 31 characters (including spaces) in length. Longer worksheet names, however, mean that fewer sheet tabs will display on your screen. If you have multiple worksheets with long sheet tab names, you may have to scroll through sheet tabs.

Figure 1–63

❷

- Right-click the sheet tab labeled, Monthly Finances, in the lower-left corner of the window to display a shortcut menu.

- Point to Tab Color on the shortcut menu to display the Tab Color gallery (Figure 1–64).

Figure 1–64

❸

- Click a color that matches your shirt in the Theme Colors area to change the color of the tab (Figure 1–65).

- If necessary, click Home on the ribbon to display the Home tab.

- Save the workbook again on the same storage location with the same file name.

Q&A Why should I save the workbook again?

You have made several modifications to the workbook since you last saved it. Thus, you should save it again.

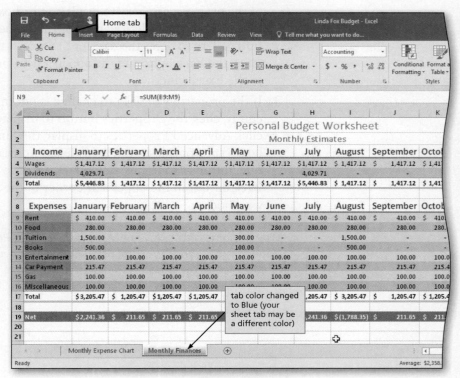

Figure 1–65

Document Properties

Excel helps you organize and identify your files by using **document properties**, which are the details about a file such as the project author, title, and subject. For example, you could use the class name or topic to describe the workbook's purpose or content in the document properties.

Why would you want to assign document properties to a workbook?
Document properties are valuable for a variety of reasons:

• Users can save time locating a particular file because they can view a file's document properties without opening the workbook.

• By creating consistent properties for files having similar content, users can better organize their workbooks.

• Some organizations require Excel users to add document properties so that other employees can view details about these files.

Common document properties include standard properties and those that are automatically updated. **Standard properties** are associated with all Microsoft Office files and include author, title, and subject. **Automatically updated properties** include file system properties, such as the date you create or change a file, and statistics, such as the file size.

TO CHANGE DOCUMENT PROPERTIES

To change document properties, you would follow these steps.

1. Click File on the ribbon to open the Backstage view and then, if necessary, click the Info tab in the Backstage view to display the Info gallery. The Properties list is found in the right pane of the Info gallery.

2. If the property you wish to change is in the Properties list, click to the right of the property category to display a text box. (Note that not all properties are editable.) Type the desired text for the property and then click anywhere in the Info gallery to enter the data, or press TAB to navigate to the next property. Click the Back button in the upper-left corner of the Backstage view to return to the Excel window.

3. If the property you wish to change is not in the Properties list or you cannot edit it, click the Properties button to display the Properties menu, and then click Advanced Properties to display the Summary tab in the Properties dialog box. Type your desired text in the appropriate property text boxes. Click the OK button (Properties dialog box) to close the dialog box and then click the Back button in the upper-left corner of the Backstage view to return to the workbook.

Q&A Why do some of the document properties in my Properties dialog box contain data?
Depending on where you are using Office 2016, your school, university, or place of employment may have customized the properties.

Printing a Worksheet

After creating a worksheet, you may want to print it. Printing a worksheet enables you to distribute the worksheet to others in a form that can be read or viewed but not edited. It is a good practice to save a workbook before printing a worksheet, in the event you experience difficulties printing.

CONSIDER THIS

What is the best method for distributing a workbook?

The traditional method of distributing a workbook uses a printer to produce a hard copy. A **hard copy** or **printout** is information that exists on paper. Hard copies can be useful for the following reasons:

- Some people prefer proofreading a hard copy of a workbook rather than viewing it on the screen to check for errors and readability.

- Hard copies can serve as a backup reference if your storage medium is lost or becomes corrupted and you need to recreate the workbook.

Instead of distributing a hard copy of a workbook, users can distribute the workbook as an electronic image that mirrors the original workbook's appearance. An electronic image of a workbook is not an editable file; it simply displays a picture of the workbook. The electronic image of the workbook can be sent as an email attachment, posted on a website, or copied to a portable storage medium such as a USB flash drive. Two popular electronic image formats, sometimes called fixed formats, are PDF by Adobe Systems and XPS by Microsoft. In Excel, you can create electronic image files through the Save As dialog box and the Export, Share, and Print tabs in the Backstage view. Electronic images of workbooks, such as PDF and XPS, can be useful for the following reasons:

- Users can view electronic images of workbooks without the software that created the original workbook (e.g., Excel). Specifically, to view a PDF file, you use a program called Adobe Reader, which can be downloaded free from Adobe's website. Similarly, to view an XPS file, you use a program called XPS Viewer, which is included in the latest version of Windows.

- Sending electronic workbooks saves paper and printer supplies. Society encourages users to contribute to **green computing**, which involves reducing the electricity consumed and environmental waste generated when using computers, mobile devices, and related technologies.

To Preview and Print a Worksheet in Landscape Orientation

1 ENTER TEXT | 2 CALCULATE SUMS & USE FORMULAS | 3 FORMAT TEXT
4 INSERT CHART | 5 NAME TAB | **6 PREVIEW & PRINT WORKSHEET**

Pages printed in **portrait orientation** have the short (8½") edge at the top of the printout; the printed page is taller than it is wide. **Landscape orientation** prints the long (11") edge at the top of the paper; the printed page is wider than it is tall. With the completed workbook saved, you may want to print it. *Why? Because the worksheet is included in a report delivered in person, you will print a hard copy on a printer.* The following steps print a hard copy of the contents of the worksheet.

- Click File on the ribbon to open the Backstage view.

- Click the Print tab in the Backstage view to display the Print gallery (Figure 1–66).

Q&A How can I print multiple copies of my worksheet?
Increase the number in the Copies box in the Print gallery.

What if I decide not to print the worksheet at this time?
Click the Back button in the upper-left corner of the Backstage view to return to the workbook window.

Figure 1–66

2

- Verify that the printer listed on the Printer Status button will print a hard copy of the workbook. If necessary, click the Printer Status button to display a list of available printer options and then click the desired printer to change the currently selected printer.

3

- Click the Portrait Orientation button in the Settings area and then select Landscape Orientation to change the orientation of the page to landscape.

- Click the No Scaling button and then select 'Fit Sheet on One Page' to print the entire worksheet on one page (Figure 1–67).

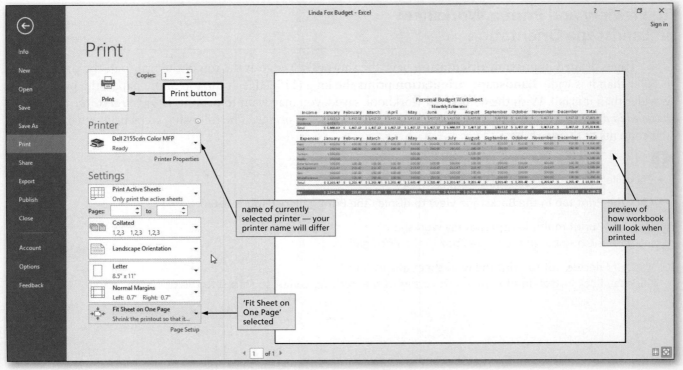

Figure 1–67

4

- Click the Print button in the Print gallery to print the worksheet in landscape orientation on the currently selected printer.

- When the printer stops, retrieve the hard copy (Figure 1–68).

Q&A Do I have to wait until my worksheet is complete to print it?
No, you can print a document at any time while you are creating it.

Personal Budget Worksheet
Monthly Estimates

Income	January	February	March	April	May	June	July	August	September	October	November	December	Total
Wages	$ 1,417.12	$ 1,417.12	$ 1,417.12	$ 1,417.12	$ 1,417.12	$ 1,417.12	$ 1,417.12	$ 1,417.12	$ 1,417.12	$ 1,417.12	$ 1,417.12	$ 1,417.12	$ 17,005.44
Dividends	4,029.71	-	-	-	-	-	4,029.71	-	-	-	-	-	8,059.42
Total	$ 5,446.83	$ 1,417.12	$ 1,417.12	$ 1,417.12	$ 1,417.12	$ 1,417.12	$ 5,446.83	$ 1,417.12	$ 1,417.12	$ 1,417.12	$ 1,417.12	$ 1,417.12	$ 25,064.86

Expenses	January	February	March	April	May	June	July	August	September	October	November	December	Total
Rent	$ 410.00	$ 410.00	$ 410.00	$ 410.00	$ 410.00	$ 410.00	$ 410.00	$ 410.00	$ 410.00	$ 410.00	$ 410.00	$ 410.00	$ 4,920.00
Food	280.00	280.00	280.00	230.00	280.00	280.00	280.00	280.00	280.00	280.00	280.00	280.00	3,360.00
Tuition	1,500.00	-	-	-	300.00	-	-	1,500.00	-	-	-	-	3,300.00
Books	500.00	-	-	-	100.00	-	-	500.00	-	-	-	-	1,100.00
Entertainment	100.00	100.00	100.00	100.00	100.00	100.00	100.00	100.00	100.00	100.00	100.00	100.00	1,200.00
Car Payment	215.47	215.47	215.47	215.47	215.47	215.47	215.47	215.47	215.47	215.47	215.47	215.47	2,585.64
Gas	100.00	100.00	100.00	100.00	100.00	100.00	100.00	100.00	100.00	100.00	100.00	100.00	1,200.00
Miscellaneous	100.00	100.00	100.00	100.00	100.00	100.00	100.00	100.00	100.00	100.00	100.00	100.00	1,200.00
Total	$ 3,205.47	$ 1,205.47	$ 1,205.47	$ 1,205.47	$ 1,605.47	$ 1,205.47	$ 1,205.47	$ 3,205.47	$ 1,205.47	$ 1,205.47	$ 1,205.47	$ 1,205.47	$ 18,865.64

| Net | $ 2,241.36 | $ 211.65 | $ 211.65 | $ 211.65 | $ (188.35) | $ 211.65 | $ 4,241.36 | $ (1,788.35) | $ 211.65 | $ 211.65 | $ 211.65 | $ 211.65 | $ 6,199.22 |

Figure 1–68

Other Ways

1. Press CTRL+P to open Print Gallery, press ENTER

Autocalculate

You easily can obtain a total, an average, or other information about the numbers in a range by using the **AutoCalculate area** on the status bar. First, select the range of cells containing the numbers you want to check. Next, right-click the AutoCalculate area to display the Customize Status Bar shortcut menu (Figure 1–69). The check marks indicate that the calculations are displayed in the status bar; more than one may be selected. The functions of the AutoCalculate commands on the Customize Status Bar shortcut menu are described in Table 1–4.

Table 1–4 Commonly Used Status Bar Commands

Command	Function
Average	AutoCalculate area displays the average of the numbers in the selected range
Count	AutoCalculate area displays the number of non-empty cells in the selected range
Numerical Count	AutoCalculate area displays the number of cells containing numbers in the selected range
Minimum	AutoCalculate area displays the lowest value in the selected range
Maximum	AutoCalculate area displays the highest value in the selected range
Sum	AutoCalculate area displays the sum of the numbers in the selected range

BTW

Distributing a Workbook
Instead of printing and distributing a hard copy of a workbook, you can distribute the workbook electronically. Options include sending the workbook via email; posting it on cloud storage (such as OneDrive) and sharing the file with others; posting it on social media, a blog, or other website; and sharing a link associated with an online location of the workbook. You also can create and share a PDF or XPS image of the workbook, so that users can view the file in Acrobat Reader or XPS Viewer instead of in Excel.

To Use the AutoCalculate Area to Determine a Maximum

The following steps determine the largest monthly total in the budget. *Why? Sometimes, you want a quick analysis, which can be especially helpful when your worksheet contains a lot of data.*

- Select the range B19:M19. Right-click the status bar to display the Customize Status Bar shortcut menu (Figure 1–69).

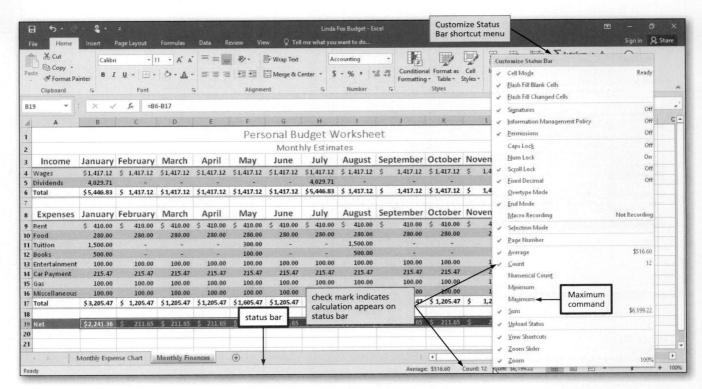

Figure 1–69

2

- Click Maximum on the shortcut menu to display the Maximum value in the range B19:M19 in the AutoCalculate area of the status bar.

- Click anywhere on the worksheet to close the shortcut menu (Figure 1–70).

Figure 1–70

• Right-click the AutoCalculate area and then click Maximum on the shortcut menu to deselect it. The Maximum value will no longer appear on the status bar.

• Close the shortcut menu.

• Save the workbook using the same file name in the same storage location.

• If desired, sign out of your Microsoft account.

• Exit Excel.

Correcting Errors

You can correct data entry errors on a worksheet using one of several methods. The method you choose will depend on the extent of the error and whether you notice it while entering the data or after you have entered the incorrect data into the cell.

Correcting Errors while Entering Data into a Cell

If you notice an error while you are entering data into a cell, press the BACKSPACE key to erase the incorrect character(s) and then enter the correct character(s). If the error is a major one, click the Cancel box in the formula bar or press the ESC key to erase the entire entry and then reenter the data.

Correcting Errors after Entering Data into a Cell

If you find an error in the worksheet after entering the data, you can correct the error in one of two ways:

1. If the entry is short, select the cell, retype the entry correctly, and then click the Enter button or press the ENTER key. The new entry will replace the old entry.

2. If the entry in the cell is long and the errors are minor, using Edit mode may be a better choice than retyping the cell entry. In **Edit mode**, Excel displays the active cell entry in the formula bar and a flashing insertion point in the active cell, and you can edit the contents directly in the cell — a procedure called **in-cell editing.**

   a. Double-click the cell containing the error to switch Excel to Edit mode (Figure 1–71).

   b. Make corrections using the following in-cell editing methods.

      (1) To insert new characters between two characters, place the insertion point between the two characters and begin typing. Excel inserts the new characters to the left of the insertion point.

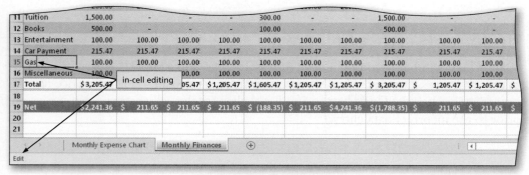

Figure 1–71

(2) To delete a character in the cell, move the insertion point to the left of the character you want to delete and then press the DELETE key, or place the insertion point to the right of the character you want to delete and then press the BACKSPACE key. You also can drag to select the character or adjacent characters you want to delete and then press the DELETE key or CTRL+X, or click the Cut button (Home tab | Clipboard group).

(3) When you are finished editing an entry, click the Enter button or press the ENTER key.

There are two ways for entering data in Edit mode: Insert mode and Overtype mode. In the default **Insert mode**, as you type a character, Excel inserts the character and moves all characters to the right of the typed character one position to the right. You can change to Overtype mode by pressing the INSERT key. In **Overtype mode**, Excel replaces, or overtypes, the character to the right of the insertion point. The INSERT key toggles the keyboard between Insert mode and Overtype mode.

While in Edit mode, you may have reason to move the insertion point to various points in the cell, select portions of the data in the cell, or switch from inserting characters to overtyping characters. Table 1–5 summarizes the more common tasks performed during in-cell editing.

Table 1–5 Summary of In-Cell Editing Tasks

	Task	Mouse Operation	Keyboard
1.	Move the insertion point to the beginning of data in a cell.	Point to the left of the first character and click.	Press HOME
2.	Move the insertion point to the end of data in a cell.	Point to the right of the last character and click.	Press END
3.	Move the insertion point anywhere in a cell.	Point to the appropriate position and click the character.	Press RIGHT ARROW or LEFT ARROW
4.	Highlight one or more adjacent characters.	Drag through adjacent characters.	Press SHIFT+RIGHT ARROW or SHIFT+LEFT ARROW
5.	Select all data in a cell.	Double-click the cell with the insertion point in the cell if the data in the cell contains no spaces.	
6.	Delete selected characters.	Click the Cut button (Home tab | Clipboard group).	Press DELETE
7.	Delete characters to the left of the insertion point.		Press BACKSPACE
8.	Delete characters to the right of the insertion point.		Press DELETE
9.	Toggle between Insert and Overtype modes.		Press INSERT

Undoing the Last Cell Entry

The Undo button on the Quick Access Toolbar (Figure 1–72) allows you to erase recent cell entries. Thus, if you enter incorrect data in a cell and notice it immediately, click the Undo button and Excel changes the cell entry to what it was prior to the incorrect data entry.

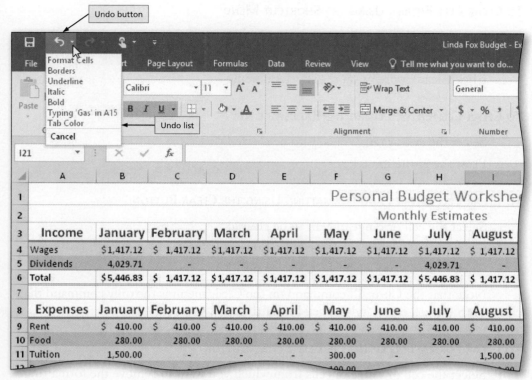

Figure 1–72

Excel remembers the last 100 actions you have completed. Thus, you can undo up to 100 previous actions by clicking the Undo arrow to display the Undo list and then clicking the action to be undone (Figure 1–72). You can drag through several actions in the Undo list to undo all of them at once. If no actions are available for Excel to undo, then the dimmed appearance of the Undo button indicates that it is unavailable.

The Redo button, next to the Undo button on the Quick Access Toolbar, allows you to repeat previous actions; that is, if you accidentally undo an action, you can use the Redo button to perform the action again.

Clearing a Cell or Range of Cells

If you enter data into the wrong cell or range of cells, you can erase, or clear, the data using one of the first four methods listed below. The fifth method clears the formatting from the selected cells. To clear a cell or range of cells, you would perform the following steps:

TO CLEAR CELL ENTRIES USING THE FILL HANDLE

1. Select the cell or range of cells and then point to the fill handle so that the pointer changes to a crosshair.
2. Drag the fill handle back into the selected cell or range until a shadow covers the cell or cells you want to erase.

TO CLEAR CELL ENTRIES USING THE SHORTCUT MENU

1. Select the cell or range of cells to be cleared.
2. Right-click the selection.
3. Click Clear Contents on the shortcut menu.

TO CLEAR CELL ENTRIES USING THE BACKSPACE KEY

1. Select the cell or range of cells to be cleared.
2. Press the BACKSPACE key.

TO CLEAR CELL ENTRIES AND FORMATTING USING THE CLEAR BUTTON

1. Select the cell or range of cells to be cleared.
2. Click the Clear button (Home tab | Editing group).
3. Click Clear Contents on the Clear menu.

Note that the Clear All command on the Clear menu is the only command that clears both the cell entry and the cell formatting.

TO CLEAR FORMATTING USING THE CELL STYLES BUTTON

1. Select the cell or range of cells from which you want to remove the formatting.
2. Click the Cell Styles button (Home tab | Styles group) and then click Normal in the Cell Styles gallery.

As you are clearing cell entries, always remember that you should *never press the SPACEBAR to clear a cell*. Pressing the SPACEBAR enters a blank character. A blank character is interpreted by Excel as text and is different from an empty cell, even though the cell may appear empty.

Clearing the Entire Worksheet

If the required worksheet edits are extremely extensive or if the requirements drastically change, you may want to clear the entire worksheet and start over. To clear the worksheet or delete an embedded chart, you would use the following steps.

TO CLEAR THE ENTIRE WORKSHEET

1. Click the Select All button on the worksheet. The Select All button is located above the row 1 identifier and to the left of the column A heading.
2. Click the Clear button (Home tab | Editing group) and then click Clear All on the menu to delete both the entries and formats.

The Select All button selects the entire worksheet. Instead of clicking the Select All button, you can press CTRL+A. To clear an unsaved workbook, click the Close Window button on the workbook's title bar or click the Close button in the Backstage view. Click the No button if the Microsoft Excel dialog box asks if you want to save changes. To start a new, blank workbook, click the New button in the Backstage view.

Summary

In this module you have learned how to create a personal budget worksheet and chart. Topics covered included selecting a cell, entering text, entering numbers, calculating a sum, using the fill handle, formatting a worksheet, adding a pie chart, changing sheet tab names, printing a worksheet, AutoCalculate, and correcting errors.

CONSIDER THIS: PLAN AHEAD

What decisions will you need to make when creating workbooks and charts in the future?

1. Determine the workbook structure.

    a) Determine the data you will need for your workbook.

    b) Sketch a layout of your data and your chart.

2. Create the worksheet.

    a) Enter titles, subtitles, and headings.

    b) Enter data, functions, and formulas.

3. Format the worksheet.

    a) Format the titles, subtitles, and headings using styles.

    b) Format the totals.

    c) Format the numbers.

    d) Format the text.

    e) Adjust column widths.

4. Create the chart.

    a) Determine the type of chart to use.

    b) Determine the chart title and data.

    c) Format the chart.

Apply Your Knowledge

Reinforce the skills and apply the concepts you learned in this module.

Changing the Values in a Worksheet

Note: To complete this assignment, you will be required to use the Data Files. Please contact your instructor for information about accessing the required files.

Instructions: Run Excel. Open the workbook Apply 1–1 Lima Wholesale (Figure 1–73a). The workbook you open contains sales data for Lima Wholesale. You are to apply formatting to the worksheet and move the chart to a new sheet tab.

Table 1–6 New Worksheet Data	
Cell	**Change Cell Contents To**
A2	Monthly Departmental Sales
B5	15242.36
C7	114538.23
D5	25747.85
E6	39851.44
F7	29663.77
G6	19885.41

Perform the following tasks:

1. Make the changes to the worksheet described in Table 1–6 so that the worksheet appears as shown in Figure 1–73b. As you edit the values in the cells containing numeric data, watch the totals in row 8, the totals in column H, and the chart change.

2. Change the worksheet title in cell A1 to the Title cell style and then merge and center it across columns A through H.

3. Use buttons in the Font group on the Home tab on the ribbon to change the worksheet subtitle in cell A2 to 16-point font and then center it across columns A through H. Change the font color of cell A2 to Dark Blue, Text 2, Darker 25%.

4. Apply the worksheet name, Monthly Sales, and the Dark Blue, Text 2, Darker 25% color to the sheet tab.

5. Move the chart to a new sheet called Sales Analysis Chart (Figure 1–73c). Change the chart title to SALES TOTALS.

6. If requested by your instructor, replace Lima in cell A1 with your last name.

7. Save the workbook using the file name, Apply 1–1 Lima Wholesale Sales Analysis.

8. Submit the revised workbook as specified by your instructor and exit Excel.

9. ✳ Besides the styles used in the worksheet, what other changes could you make to enhance the worksheet?

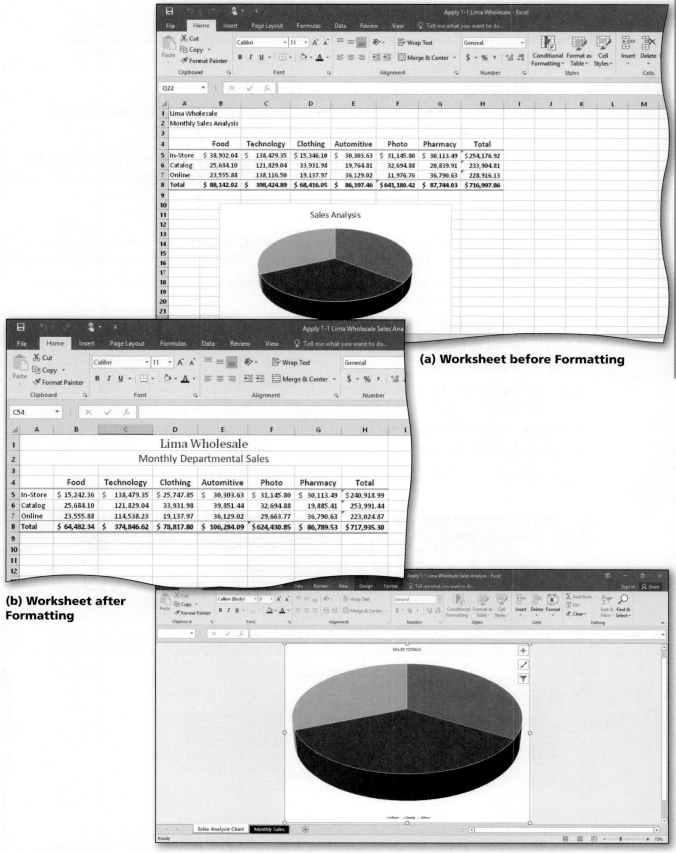

(a) Worksheet before Formatting

(b) Worksheet after Formatting

(c) 3-D Pie Chart on Separate Sheet

Figure 1–73

Extend Your Knowledge

Extend the skills you learned in this module and experiment with new skills. You may need to use Help to complete the assignment.

Creating Styles and Formatting a Worksheet

Note: To complete this assignment, you will be required to use the Data Files. Please contact your instructor for information about accessing the required files.

Instructions: Run Excel. Open the workbook Extend 1–1 Dasminne Grocery (Figure 1–74). The workbook you open contains sales data for Dasminne Grocery. You are to create styles and format a worksheet using them.

Perform the following tasks:

1. Select cell A4. Use the New Cell Style command in the Cell Styles gallery to create a style that uses the Blue, Accent 1, Darker 50% font color (row 6, column 5). Name the style, MyHeadings.

2. Select cell A5. Use the New Cell style dialog box to create a style that uses the Blue, Accent 1, Darker 25% (row 5, column 5) font color. Name the style, MyRows.

3. Select cell ranges B4:G4 and A5:A8. Apply the MyHeadings style to the cell ranges.

4. Select the cell range B5:G7. Apply the MyRows style to the cell range.

5. Apply a worksheet name to the sheet tab and apply a color of your choice to the sheet tab.

6. If requested by your instructor, change the font color for the text in cells A1 and A2 to the color of your eyes, if available.

7. Save the workbook using the file name, Extend 1–1 Dasminne Grocery Third Quarter.

8. Submit the revised workbook as specified by your instructor and exit Excel.

9. ✷ What other styles would you create to improve the worksheet's appearance?

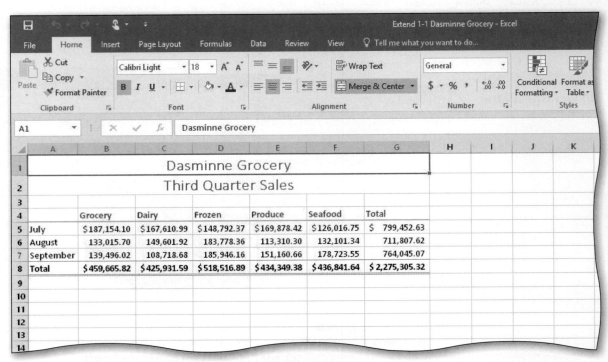

Figure 1–74

Expand Your World

Create a solution that uses cloud or web technologies by learning and investigating on your own from general guidance.

College Loan Calculator

Instructions: You are tasked with determining how long it will take you to pay back your college loans. You decide to download and use one of Excel's templates to create your worksheet.

Perform the following tasks:

1. Click the New tab in the Backstage view and then search for and click the College loan calculator template to download it.

2. Enter data for your estimated salary after graduation, the date you will begin paying back loans, as well as fictitious (but realistic) information for four loans, including loan number, lender, loan amount, annual interest rate, beginning date, and length (in years).

3. Save the file as Expand 1-1: College Loans. Print the worksheet.

4. Submit the assignment as specified by your instructor.

5. ✳ Which template would you use if you wanted to plan and keep track of a budget for a wedding?

In the Labs

Design, create, modify, and/or use a workbook following the guidelines, concepts, and skills presented in this module. Labs 1 and 2, which increase in difficulty, require you to create solutions based on what you learned in the module; Lab 3 requires you to apply your creative thinking and problem-solving skills to design and implement a solution.

Lab 1: First Quarter Revenue Analysis Worksheet

Problem: You work as a spreadsheet specialist for Katie's Kicks, which has four regional shops in the state of Florida. Your manager has asked you to develop a first quarter revenue analysis similar to the one shown in Figure 1–75.

Perform the following tasks:

1. Run Excel and create a new blank workbook. Enter the worksheet title, Katie's Kicks, in cell A1 and the worksheet subtitle, First Quarter Revenue Analysis, in cell A2. Beginning in row 4, enter the region data shown in Table 1–7.

Table 1–7 Katie's Kicks				
	North	South	East	West
Sneakers	72714.58	77627.29	76607.31	49008.32
Shoes	45052.23	69165.66	76243.41	84844.01
Sandals	77630.94	78684.24	56601.25	72716.68
Accessories	65423.73	77690.69	58383.67	54433.07
Miscellaneous	55666.92	78618.97	47317.09	68594.40

2. Create totals for each region, product, and company grand total.

3. Format the worksheet title with the Title cell style. Center the title across columns A through F.

Continued >

In the Labs *continued*

4. Format the worksheet subtitle to 16-point Calibri Light, and change the font color to Blue-Gray, Text 2. Center the subtitle across columns A through F.

5. Use Cell Styles to format the range A4:F4 with the Heading 3 cell style, the range B4:F4 with the Accent1 cell style, and the range A10:F10 with the Total cell style.

6. Center the column titles in row 4. Apply the accounting number format to the ranges B5:F5 and B10:F10. Apply the comma style format to the range B6:F9. Adjust any column widths to the widest text entry in each column.

7. Select the ranges B4:E4 and B10:E10 and then insert a 3-D pie chart. Apply the Style 3 chart style to the chart. Move the chart to a new worksheet named Revenue Analysis Chart. Change the chart title to First Quarter Revenue Analysis.

8. Rename the Sheet1 tab, First Quarter, and apply the Green color to the sheet tab.

9. If requested by your instructor, change the font color of the text in cells A1 and A2 to the color of the shirt you currently are wearing.

10. Save the workbook using the file name, Lab 1-1 Katie's Kicks.

11. Preview and print the worksheet in landscape orientation.

12. ✸ If you wanted to chart the item totals instead of the regions, which ranges would you use to create the chart?

13. Submit the assignment as specified by your instructor.

(a) Worksheet

(b) Pie Chart

Figure 1–75

Lab 2: **Sales Analysis Worksheet**

Problem: As the chief accountant for Davis Mobile Concepts, a leading car audio dealer serving four states, you have been asked by the vice president to create a worksheet to analyze the yearly sales for each state (Figure 1–76). The packages and corresponding sales by state for the year are shown in Table 1–8.

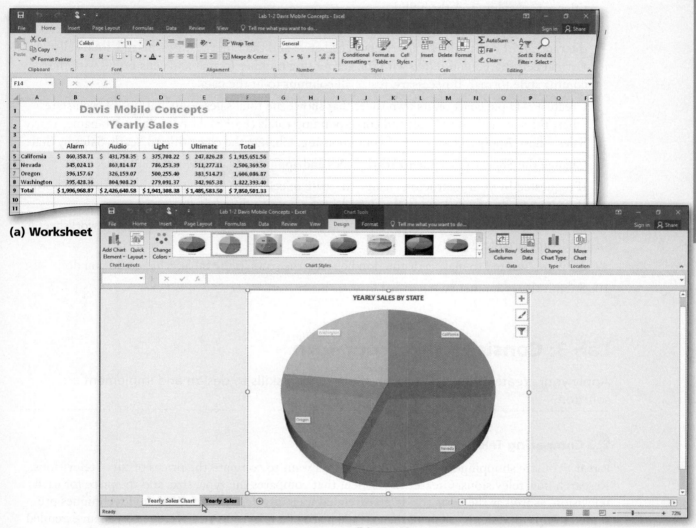

(a) Worksheet

(b) Pie Chart

Figure 1–76

Perform the following tasks:

1. Create the worksheet shown in Figure 1–76a using the data in Table 1–8.

Table 1–8 Davis Mobile Concepts				
	Alarm	**Audio**	**Light**	**Ultimate**
California	860358.71	431758.35	375708.22	247826.28
Nevada	345024.13	863814.87	786253.39	511277.11
Oregon	396157.67	326159.07	500255.40	383514.73
Washington	395428.36	804908.29	279091.37	342965.38

Continued >

In the Labs *continued*

2. Use the SUM function to determine total revenue for each of the four packages, the totals for each state, and the company total. Add column and row headings for the totals row and totals column, as appropriate.

3. Format the worksheet title and subtitle with the Title cell style and center them across columns A through F. Use the Font group on the ribbon to format the worksheet title and subtitle as 18-point Arial Black. Format the title and subtitle with Green, Accent 6 font color. Center the titles across columns A through F.

4. Format the range B4:F4 with the Heading 2 cell style and center the text in the cells. Format the range A5:F8 with the 20% - Accent6 cell style and the range A9:F9 with the Total cell style. Format cells B5:F5 and B9:F9 with the accounting number format and cells B6:F8 with the comma style format. If necessary, resize all columns to fit the data.

5. Create a 3-D pie chart on its own sheet that shows the total sales contributions of each state. Chart the state names (A5:A8) and corresponding totals (F5:F8). Use the sheet tab name, Yearly Sales Chart. Apply a chart style of your choosing. Change the chart title to Yearly Sales by State.

6. Change the Sheet1 tab name to Yearly Sales and apply the Orange color to the sheet tab.

7. If requested by your instructor, change the state in cell A8 to the state in which you were born. If your state already is listed in the spreadsheet, choose a different state.

8. Save the workbook using the file name, Lab 1-2 Davis Mobile Concepts. Print the worksheet in landscape orientation.

9. If you wanted to make a distinction between the rows in the table, what could you do?

10. Submit the assignment as specified by your instructor.

Lab 3: **Consider This: Your Turn**

Apply your creative thinking and problem-solving skills to design and implement a solution.

Comparing Televisions

Part 1:   You are shopping for a new television and want to compare the prices of three televisions. Research new televisions. Create a worksheet that compares the type, size, and the price for each television, as well as the costs to add an extended warranty. Use the concepts and techniques presented in this module to calculate the average price of a television and average cost of an extended warranty and to format the worksheet. Submit your assignment in the format specified by your instructor.

Part 2:   Based upon the data you found, how could you chart the information to show the comparisons? Which chart would be the best to use? Include a chart to compare the different television costs.

2 | Formulas, Functions, and Formatting

Objectives

You will have mastered the material in this module when you can:

- Use Flash Fill
- Enter formulas using the keyboard
- Enter formulas using Point mode
- Apply the MAX, MIN, and AVERAGE functions
- Verify a formula using Range Finder
- Apply a theme to a workbook
- Apply a date format to a cell or range

- Add conditional formatting to cells
- Change column width and row height
- Check the spelling on a worksheet
- Change margins and headers in Page Layout view
- Preview and print versions and sections of a worksheet

Introduction

In Module 1, you learned how to enter data, sum values, format a worksheet to make it easier to read, and draw a chart. This module continues to illustrate these topics and presents some new ones.

The new topics covered in this module include using formulas and functions to create a worksheet. Recall from Module 1 that a function is a prewritten formula that is built into Excel. Other new topics include using option buttons, verifying formulas, applying a theme to a worksheet, adding borders, formatting numbers and text, using conditional formatting, changing the widths of columns and heights of rows, checking spelling, generating alternative worksheet displays and printouts, and adding page headers and footers to a worksheet. One alternative worksheet display and printout shows the formulas in the worksheet instead of the values. When you display the formulas in the worksheet, you see exactly what text, data, formulas, and functions you have entered into it.

Project — Worksheet with Formulas and Functions

The project in this module follows proper design guidelines and uses Excel to create the worksheet shown in Figure 2–1. Every two weeks, the owners of Olivia's Art Supply create a salary report by hand, where they keep track of employee payroll data. Before paying employees, the owners must summarize the hours worked, pay rate, and tax information for each employee to ensure that the business properly compensates its employees. This report also includes the following information for each employee: name, email address, number of dependents, hours worked, hourly pay rate, tax information, net pay, and hire date. As the complexity of creating the salary report increases, the owners want to use Excel to make the process easier.

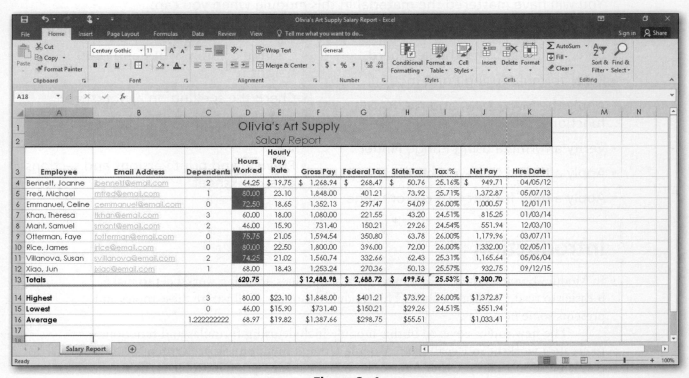

Figure 2–1

Recall that the first step in creating an effective worksheet is to make sure you understand what is required. The people who request the worksheet usually provide the requirements. The requirements document for the Olivia's Art Supply Salary Report worksheet includes the following needs: source of data, summary of calculations, and other facts about its development (Figure 2–2).

Worksheet Title	Olivia's Art Supply Salary Report
Needs	An easy-to-read worksheet that summarizes the company's salary report (Figure 2–3). For each employee, the worksheet is to include the employee's name, email address, number of dependents, hours worked, hourly pay rate, gross pay, federal tax, state tax, total tax percent, net pay, and hire date. The worksheet also should include the total pay for all employees, as well as the highest value, lowest value, and average for each category of data.
Source of Data	Supplied data includes employee names, number of dependents, hours worked, hourly pay rate, and hire dates.
Calculations	The following calculations must be made for each of the employees: 1. Gross Pay = Hours Worked * Hourly Pay Rate 2. Federal Tax = 0.22 * (Gross Pay * Number of Dependents * 24.32) 3. State Tax = 0.04 * Gross Pay 4. Tax % = (Federal Tax + State Tax) / Gross Pay 5. Net Pay = Gross Pay * (Federal Tax + State Tax) 6. Compute the totals for hours worked, gross pay, federal tax, state tax, and net pay 7. Compute the total tax percent 8. Use the MAX and MIN functions to determine the highest and lowest values for number of dependents, hours worked, hourly pay rate, gross pay, federal tax, state tax, total tax percent, and net pay 9. Use the AVERAGE function to determine the average for hours worked, number of dependents, hourly pay rate, gross pay, federal tax, state tax, and net pay

Figure 2–2

In addition, using a sketch of the worksheet can help you visualize its design. The sketch for the Olivia's Art Supply Salary Report worksheet includes a title, a subtitle, column and row headings, and the location of data values (Figure 2–3). It also uses specific characters to define the desired formatting for the worksheet, as follows:

1. The row of Xs below the leftmost column heading defines the cell entries as text, such as employee names.

Figure 2–3

For an introduction to Windows and instructions about how to perform basic Windows tasks, read the Office and Windows module at the beginning of this book, where you can learn how to resize windows, change screen resolution, create folders, move and rename files, use Windows Help, and much more.

For an introduction to Office and instructions about how to perform basic tasks in Office apps, read the Office and Windows module at the beginning of this book, where you can learn how to run an application, use the ribbon, save a file, open a file, print a file, exit an application, use Help, and much more.

2. The rows of Zs and 9s with slashes, dollar signs, decimal points, commas, and percent signs in the remaining columns define the cell entries as numbers. The Zs indicate that the selected format should instruct Excel to suppress leading 0s. The 9s indicate that the selected format should instruct Excel to display any digits, including 0s.

3. The decimal point means that a decimal point should appear in the cell entry and indicates the number of decimal places to use.

4. The slashes in the last column identify the cell entry as a date.

5. The dollar signs that are adjacent to the Zs below the totals row signify a floating dollar sign, or one that appears next to the first significant digit.

6. The commas indicate that the selected format should instruct Excel to display a comma separator only if the number has sufficient digits (values in the thousandths) to the left of the decimal point.

7. The percent sign (%) in the Tax % column indicates a percent sign should appear after the number.

In this module, you will learn how to use functions and create formulas. The following roadmap identifies general activities you will perform as you progress through this module:

1. ENTER FORMULAS in the worksheet.
2. ENTER FUNCTIONS in the worksheet.
3. VERIFY FORMULAS in the worksheet.
4. FORMAT the WORKSHEET.
5. CHECK SPELLING.
6. PRINT the WORKSHEET.

What is the function of an Excel worksheet?

The function, or purpose, of a worksheet is to provide a user with direct ways to accomplish tasks. In designing a worksheet, functional considerations should supersede visual aesthetics. Consider the following when designing your worksheet:

• Avoid the temptation to use flashy or confusing visual elements within the worksheet.

• Understand the requirements document.

• Choose the proper functions and formulas.

• Build the worksheet.

BTW
Touch Screen Differences
The Office and Windows interfaces may vary if you are using a touch screen. For this reason, you might notice that the function or appearance of your touch screen differs slightly from this module's presentation.

Entering the Titles and Numbers into the Worksheet

The first step in creating the worksheet is to enter the titles and numbers into the worksheet. The following sets of steps enter the worksheet title and subtitle and then the salary report data shown in Table 2–1.

To Enter the Worksheet Title and Subtitle

With a good comprehension of the requirements document, an understanding of the necessary decisions, and a sketch of the worksheet, the next step is to use Excel to create the worksheet. The following steps enter the worksheet title and subtitle into cells A1 and A2.

1 Run Excel and create a blank workbook in the Excel window.

2 If necessary, select cell A1. Type `Olivia's Art Supply` in the selected cell and then press the DOWN ARROW key to enter the worksheet title.

3 Type `Salary Report` in cell A2 and then press the DOWN ARROW key to enter the worksheet subtitle.

To Enter the Column Titles

The column titles in row 3 begin in cell A3 and extend through cell K3. The employee names and the row titles begin in cell A4 and continue down to cell A16. The employee data is entered into rows 4 through 12 of the worksheet. The remainder of this section explains the steps required to enter the column titles, payroll data, and row titles, as shown in Figure 2–4, and then to save the workbook. The following steps enter the column titles.

1 With cell A3 selected, type `Employee` and then press the RIGHT ARROW key to enter the column heading.

2 Type `Email Address` in cell B3 and then press the RIGHT ARROW key.

3 In cell C3, type `Dependents` and then press the RIGHT ARROW key.

4 In cell D3, type `Hours` and then press the ALT+ENTER keys to enter the first line of the column heading. Type `Worked` and then press the RIGHT ARROW key to enter the column heading.

Q&A   Why do I use the ALT+ENTER keys?
You press ALT+ENTER in order to start a new line in a cell. The final line can be completed by clicking the Enter button, pressing the ENTER key, or pressing one of the arrow keys. When you see ALT+ENTER in a step, press the ENTER key while holding down the ALT key and then release both keys.

5 Type `Hourly` in cell E3, press the ALT+ENTER keys, type `Pay Rate,` and then press the RIGHT ARROW key.

6 Type `Gross Pay` in cell F3 and then press the RIGHT ARROW key.

7 Type `Federal Tax` in cell G3 and then press the RIGHT ARROW key.

8 Type `State Tax` in cell H3 and then press the RIGHT ARROW key.

9 Type `Tax %` in cell I3 and then press the RIGHT ARROW key.

10 Type `Net Pay` in cell J3 and then press the RIGHT ARROW key.

11 Type `Hire Date` in cell K3 and then press the RIGHT ARROW key.

BTW

Screen Resolution
If you are using a computer or mobile device to step through the project in this module and you want your screens to match the figures in this book, you should change your screen's resolution to 1366 x 768. For information about how to change a computer's resolution, refer to the Office and Windows module at the beginning of this book.

BTW

Wrapping Text
If you have a long text entry, such as a paragraph, you can instruct Excel to wrap the text in a cell. This method is easier than your pressing ALT+ENTER to end each line of text within the paragraph. To wrap text, right-click in the cell, click Format Cells on a shortcut menu, click the Alignment tab, and then click Wrap text. Excel will increase the height of the cell automatically so that the additional lines will fit. If you want to control where each line ends in the cell, rather than letting Excel wrap the text based on the cell width, you must end each line with ALT+ENTER.

To Enter the Salary Data

The salary data in Table 2-1 includes a hire date for each employee. Excel considers a date to be a number and, therefore, it displays the date right-aligned in the cell. The following steps enter the data for each employee, except their email addresses, which will be entered later in this module.

BTW
Two-Digit Years
When you enter a two-digit year value (xx) that is less than 30, Excel changes that value to 20xx; when you enter a value that is 30 or greater (zz), Excel changes the value to 19zz. Use four-digit years, if necessary, to ensure that Excel interprets year values the way you intend.

1 Select cell A4. Type **Bennett, Joanne** and then press the RIGHT ARROW key two times to enter the employee name and make cell C4 the active cell.

2 Type **2** in cell C4 and then press the RIGHT ARROW key.

3 Type **64.25** in cell D4 and then press the RIGHT ARROW key.

4 Type **19.75** in cell E4.

5 Click cell K4 and then type **4/5/12**.

6 Enter the payroll data in Table 2–1 for the eight remaining employees in rows 5 through 12.

Q&A In Step 5, why did the date change from 4/5/12 to 4/5/2012?
When Excel recognizes a date in mm/dd/yy format, it formats the date as mm/dd/yyyy. Most professionals prefer to view dates in mm/dd/yyyy format as opposed to mm/dd/yy format to avoid confusion regarding the intended year. For example, a date displayed as 3/3/50 could imply a date of 3/3/1950 or 3/3/2050.

Table 2–1 Olivia's Art Supply Salary Report Data					
Employee	Email Address	Dependents	Hours Worked	Hourly Pay Rate	Hire Date
Bennett, Joanne		2	64.25	19.75	4/5/12
Fred, Michael		1	80.00	23.10	5/7/13
Emmanuel, Celine		0	72.50	18.65	12/1/11
Khan, Theresa		3	60.00	18.00	1/3/14
Mant, Samuel		2	46.00	15.90	12/3/10
Otterman, Faye		0	75.75	21.05	3/7/11
Rice, James		0	80.00	22.50	2/5/11
Villanova, Susan		2	74.25	21.02	5/6/04
Xiao, Jun		1	68.00	18.43	9/12/15

BTW
The Ribbon and Screen Resolution
Excel may change how the groups and buttons within the groups appear on the ribbon, depending on the computer or mobile device's screen resolution. Thus, your ribbon may look different from the ones in this book if you are using a screen resolution other than 1366 x 768.

Flash Fill

When you are entering data in a spreadsheet, occasionally Excel will recognize a pattern in the data you are entering. **Flash Fill** is an Excel feature that looks for patterns in the data and automatically fills or formats data in remaining cells. For example if column A contains a list of 10 phone numbers without parentheses around the area code or dashes after the prefix, Flash Fill can help create formatted phone numbers with relative ease. To use Flash Fill, simply start entering formatted phone numbers in cells next to the unformatted numbers. After entering a few formatted phone numbers, Flash Fill will suggest similarly formatted phone numbers for the remaining cells in the column. If you do not want to wait for Excel to offer suggestions, type one or two examples and then click the Flash Fill button (Data tab | Data Tools group). Flash fill will autocomplete the remaining cells. If Flash Fill makes a mistake, simply click the Undo button, enter a few more examples, and try again. In addition to formatting data, Flash Fill can perform tasks such as concatenating data from multiple cells and separating data from one cell into multiple cells.

To Use Flash Fill

1 ENTER FORMULAS | 2 ENTER FUNCTIONS | 3 VERIFY FORMULAS
4 FORMAT WORKSHEET | 5 CHECK SPELLING | 6 PRINT WORKSHEET

In the Olivia's Art Supply Salary Report worksheet, you can use Flash Fill to generate email addresses using first and last names from another column in the worksheet. *Why? The Flash Fill feature is a convenient way to avoid entering a lot of data manually.* The following steps use Flash Fill to generate employee email addresses using the names entered in column A.

- Click cell B4 to select it.

- Type **jbennett@ email.com** and then press the DOWN ARROW key to select cell B5.

- Type **mfred@ email.com** and then click the Enter button to enter Michael Fred's email address in cell B5 (Figure 2–4).

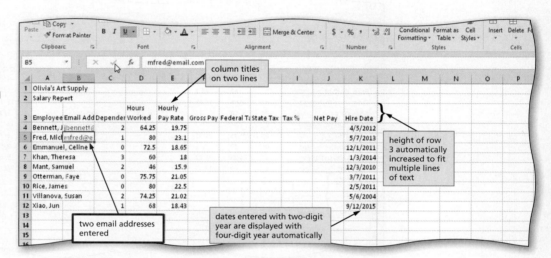

Figure 2–4

- Click Data on the ribbon to select the Data tab.

- Click Flash Fill (Data tab | Data Tools group) to enter similarly formatted email addresses in the range B6:B12.

- Remove the entries from cells B1 and B2 (Figure 2–5).

Q&A

Why was I unable to click the Flash Fill button after entering the first email address?

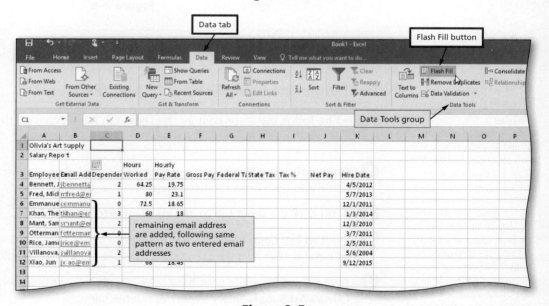

Figure 2–5

One entry might not have been enough for Excel to recognize a pattern. For instance, Flash Fill might have used the letter *j* before each last name in the email address, instead of using the first initial and last name.

What would have happened if I kept typing examples without clicking the Flash Fill button?

As soon as Excel recognized a pattern, it would have displayed suggestions for the remaining cells. Pressing the ENTER key when the suggestions appear will populate the remaining cells.

To Enter the Row Titles

The following steps add row titles for the rows that will contain the totals, highest, lowest, and average amounts.

1 Select cell A13. Type **Totals** and then press the DOWN ARROW key to enter a row header.

2 Type **Highest** in cell A14 and then press the DOWN ARROW key.

3 Type **Lowest** in cell A15 and then press the DOWN ARROW key.

4 Type **Average** in cell A16 and then press the DOWN ARROW key (Figure 2–6).

Figure 2–6

To Change the Sheet Tab Name and Color

The following steps change the sheet tab name, change the tab color, and save the workbook in the Excel folder (for your assignments).

1 Double-click the Sheet1 tab and then enter **Salary Report** as the sheet tab name and then press the ENTER key.

2 Right-click the sheet tab to display the shortcut menu.

3 Point to Tab Color on the shortcut menu to display the Tab Color gallery. Click Green (column 6, row 7) in the Standard Colors area to apply the color to the sheet tab.

4 Save the workbook in your hard drive, OneDrive, or other storage location using Olivia's Art Supply Salary Report as the file name.

Q&A Why should I save the workbook at this time?
You have performed many tasks while creating this workbook and do not want to risk losing work completed thus far.

Entering Formulas

One of the reasons Excel is such a valuable tool is that you can assign a formula to a cell, and Excel will calculate the result. A **formula** consists of cell references, numbers, and arithmetic operators that instruct Excel to perform a calculation. Consider, for example, what would happen if you had to multiply 64.25 by 19.75 and then manually enter the product for Gross Pay, 1,268.94, in cell F4. Every time the values in cells D4 or E4 changed, you would have to recalculate the product and enter the new value in cell F4. By contrast, if you enter a formula in cell F4 to multiply the values in cells D4 and E4, Excel recalculates the product whenever new values are entered into those cells and displays the result in cell F4.

A formula in a cell that contains a reference back to itself is called a **circular reference**. Excel warns you when you create circular references. In almost all cases, circular references are the result of an incorrect formula. A circular reference can be direct or indirect. For example, placing the formula =A1 in cell A1 results in a direct circular reference. A **direct circular reference** occurs when a formula refers to the same cell in which it is entered. An **indirect circular reference** occurs when a formula in a cell refers to another cell or cells that include a formula that refers back to the original cell.

BTW

Entering Numbers in a Range
An efficient way to enter data into a range of cells is to select a range and then enter the first number in the upper-left cell of the range. Excel responds by accepting the value and moving the active cell selection down one cell. When you enter the last value in the first column, Excel moves the active cell selection to the top of the next column.

To Enter a Formula Using the Keyboard

1 ENTER FORMULAS | 2 ENTER FUNCTIONS | 3 VERIFY FORMULAS
4 FORMAT WORKSHEET | 5 CHECK SPELLING | 6 PRINT WORKSHEET

The formulas needed in the worksheet are noted in the requirements document as follows:

1. Gross Pay (column F) = Hours Worked × Hourly Pay Rate
2. Federal Tax (column G) = 0.22 × (Gross Pay − Dependents × 24.32)
3. State Tax (column H) = 0.04 × Gross Pay
4. Tax % (column I) = (Federal Tax + State Tax) / Gross Pay
5. Net Pay (column J) = Gross Pay − (Federal Tax + State Tax)

The gross pay for each employee, which appears in column F, is equal to hours worked in column D times hourly pay rate in column E. Thus, the gross pay for Joanne Bennett in cell F4 is obtained by multiplying 64.25 (cell D4) by 19.75 (cell E4) or = D4 × E4. The following steps enter the initial gross pay formula in cell F4 using the keyboard. *Why? In order for Excel to perform the calculations, you must first enter the formulas.*

1

- With cell F4 selected, type **=d4*e4** in the cell to display the formula in the formula bar and the current cell and to display colored borders around the cells referenced in the formula (Figure 2–7).

Q&A What happens when I enter the formula?
The **equal sign** (=) preceding d4*e4 alerts Excel that you are entering a formula or function — not text. Because the most common error when entering a formula is to reference the wrong cell, Excel colors the cells referenced in the formula. The colored cells help you determine whether the cell references are correct. The asterisk (*) following d4 is the arithmetic operator for multiplication.

Is there a function, similar to the SUM function, that calculates the product of two or more numbers?
Yes. The **PRODUCT function** calculates the product of two or more numbers. For example, the function, =PRODUCT(D4,E4) will calculate the product of cells D4 and E4.

Figure 2–7

2

- Press the RIGHT ARROW key to complete the arithmetic operation indicated by the formula, display the result in the worksheet, and select the cell to the right (Figure 2–8). The number of decimal places on your screen may be different than shown in Figure 2–8, but these values will be adjusted later in this module.

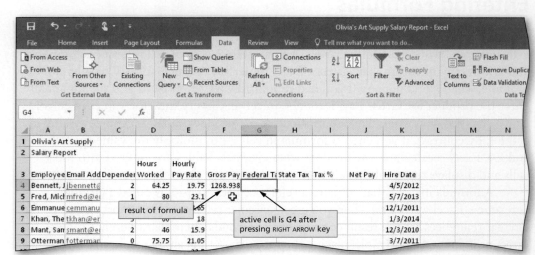

Figure 2–8

BTW
Automatic Recalculation
Every time you enter a value into a cell in the worksheet, Excel automatically recalculates all formulas. You can change to manual recalculation by clicking the Calculation Options button (Formulas tab | Calculation group) and then clicking Manual. In manual calculation mode, pressing the F9 key instructs Excel to recalculate all formulas.

Arithmetic Operations

Excel provides powerful functions and capabilities that allow you to perform arithmetic operations easily and efficiently. Table 2–2 describes multiplication and other valid Excel arithmetic operators.

Table 2–2 Arithmetic Operations Listed in Order of Operations			
Arithmetic Operator	**Meaning**	**Example of Usage**	**Result**
–	Negation	–78	Negative 78
%	Percentage	=23%	Multiplies 23 by 0.01
^	Exponentiation	=3 ^ 4	Raises 3 to the fourth power
*	Multiplication	=61.5 * C5	Multiplies the contents of cell C5 by 61.5
/	Division	=H3 / H11	Divides the contents of cell H3 by the contents of cell H11
+	Addition	=11 + 9	Adds 11 and 9
–	Subtraction	=22 – F15	Subtracts the contents of cell F15 from 22

Order of Operations

BTW
Troubling Formulas
If Excel does not accept a formula, remove the equal sign from the left side and complete the entry as text. Later, after you have entered additional data in the cells reliant on the formula or determined the error, reinsert the equal sign to change the text back to a formula and edit the formula as needed.

When more than one arithmetic operator is involved in a formula, Excel follows the same basic order of operations that you use in algebra. The **order of operations** is the collection of rules that define which mathematical operations take precedence over the others in expressions with multiple operations. Moving from left to right in a formula, the order of operations is as follows: first negation (–), then all percentages (%), then all exponentiations (^), then all multiplications (*) and divisions (/), and, finally, all additions (+) and subtractions (–).

As in algebra, you can use parentheses to override the order of operations. For example, if Excel follows the order of operations, 8 * 3 + 2 equals 26. If you use parentheses, however, to change the formula to 8 * (3 + 2), the result is 40, because the parentheses instruct Excel to add 3 and 2 before multiplying by 8. Table 2–3 illustrates several examples of valid Excel formulas and explains the order of operations.

Table 2–3 Examples of Excel Formulas

Formula	Result
=G15	Assigns the value in cell G15 to the active cell.
=2^4 + 7	Assigns the sum of 16 + 7 (or 23) to the active cell.
=100 + D2 or =D2 +100 or =(100 + D2)	Assigns 100 plus the contents of cell D2 to the active cell.
=25% * 40	Assigns the product of 0.25 times 40 (or 10) to the active cell.
– (K15 * X45)	Assigns the negative value of the product of the values contained in cells K15 and X45 to the active cell. *Tip:* You do not need to type an equal sign before an expression that begins with a minus sign, which indicates a negation.
=(U8 – B8) * 6	Assigns the difference between the values contained in cells U8 and B8 times 6 to the active cell.
=J7 / A5 + G9 * M6 – Z2 ^ L7	Completes the following operations, from left to right: exponentiation (Z2 ^ L7), then division (J7 / A5), then multiplication (G9 * M6), then addition (J7 / A5) + (G9 * M6), and finally subtraction (J7 / A5 + G9 * M6) – (Z2 ^ L7). If cells A5 = 6, G9 = 2, J7 = 6, L7 = 4, M6 = 5, and Z2 = 2, then Excel assigns the active cell the value –5; that is, 6 / 6 + 2 * 5 – 2 ^ 4 = –5.

BTW

Parentheses
Remember that you can use parentheses to override the order of operations. You cannot use brackets or braces in place of parentheses in arithmetic operations.

1 ENTER FORMULAS | 2 ENTER FUNCTIONS | 3 VERIFY FORMULAS
4 FORMAT WORKSHEET | 5 CHECK SPELLING | 6 PRINT WORKSHEET

To Enter Formulas Using Point Mode

The sketch of the worksheet in Figure 2–3 calls for the federal tax, state tax, tax percentage, and net pay for each employee to appear in columns G, H, I, and J, respectively. All four of these values are calculated using formulas in row 4:

Federal Tax (cell G4) = 0.22 × (Gross Pay − Dependents × 24.32) or = 0.22 * (F4 − C4 * 24.32)
State Tax (cell H4) = 0.04 × Gross Pay or = 0.04 * F4
Tax % (cell I4) = (Federal Tax + State Tax) / Gross Pay or = (G4 + H4) / F4
Net Pay (cell J4) = Gross Pay − (Federal Tax + State Tax) or = F4 − (G4 + H4)

An alternative to entering the formulas in cells G4, H4, I4, and J4 using the keyboard is to enter the formulas using the pointer and Point mode. **Point mode** allows you to select cells for use in a formula by using the pointer. The following steps enter formulas using Point mode. **Why?** *Using Point mode makes it easier to create formulas without worrying about typographical errors when entering cell references.*

1

• With cell G4 selected, type =0.22*(to begin the formula and then click cell F4 to add a cell reference in the formula (Figure 2–9).

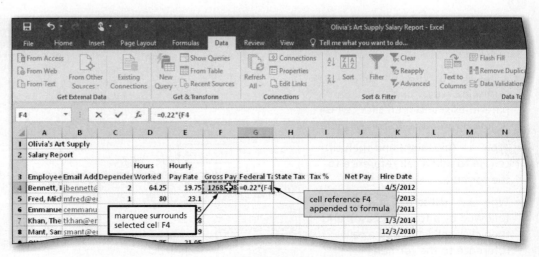

Figure 2–9

2

- Type **–** (minus sign) and then click cell C4 to add a subtraction operator and a reference to another cell to the formula.

- Type ***24.32)** to complete the formula (Figure 2–10).

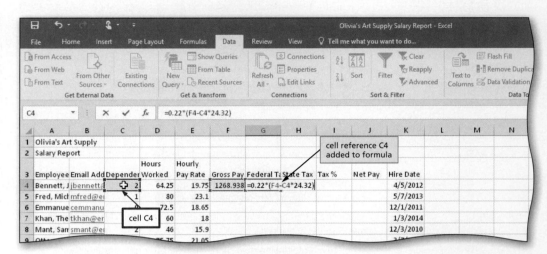

Figure 2–10

3

- Click the Enter button in the formula bar and then select cell H4 to prepare to enter the next formula.

- Type **=0.04*** and then click cell F4 to add a cell reference to the formula (Figure 2–11).

Q&A

Why should I use Point mode to enter formulas?

Using Point mode to enter formulas often is faster and more accurate than using the keyboard, but only when the cell you want to select does not require you to scroll. In many instances, as in these steps, you may want to use

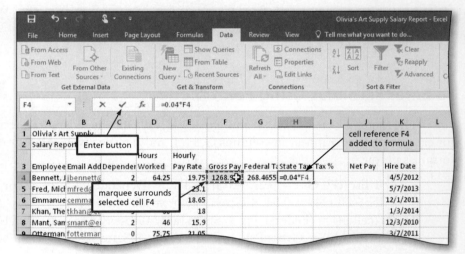

Figure 2–11

both the keyboard and pointer when entering a formula in a cell. You can use the keyboard to begin the formula, for example, and then use the pointer to select a range of cells.

4

- Click the Enter button in the formula bar to enter the formula in cell H4.

- Select cell I4. Type **= (** (equal sign followed by an open parenthesis) and then click cell G4 to add a reference to the formula.

- Type **+** (plus sign) and then click cell H4 to add a cell reference to the formula.

- Type **) /** (close parenthesis followed by a forward slash), and then click cell F4 to add a cell reference to the formula.

- Click the Enter button in the formula bar to enter the formula in cell I4 (Figure 2–12).

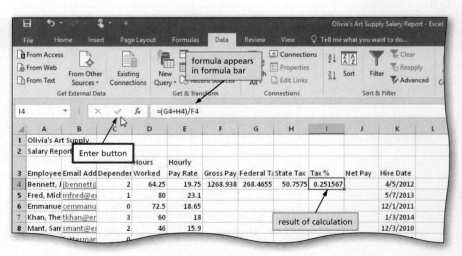

Figure 2–12

5
- Click cell J4, type = (equal sign) and then click cell F4.

- Type – ((minus sign followed by an open parenthesis) and then click cell G4.

- Type + (plus sign), click cell H4, and then type)   (close parenthesis) to complete the formula (Figure 2–13).

- Click the Enter button.

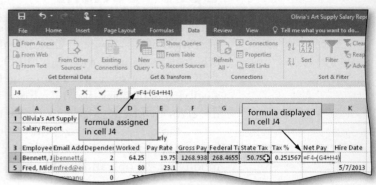

Figure 2–13

To Copy Formulas Using the Fill Handle

The five formulas for Joanne Bennett in cells F4, G4, H4, I4, and J4 now are complete. The next step is to copy them to the range F5:J12. When copying formulas in Excel, the source area is the cell, or range, from which data or formulas are being copied. When a range is used as a source, it sometimes is called the **source range**. The destination area is the cell, or range, to which data or formulas are being copied. When a range is used as a destination, it sometimes is called the **destination range**. Recall from Module 1 that the fill handle is a small square in the lower-right corner of the active cell or active range. The following steps copy the formulas using the fill handle.

1 Select the source range, F4:J4 in this case, activate the fill handle, drag the fill handle down through cell J12, and then continue to hold the mouse button to select the destination range.

2 Release the mouse button to copy the formulas to the destination range (Figure 2–14).

Q&A | How does Excel adjust the cell references in the formulas in the destination area?
Recall that when you copy a formula, Excel adjusts the cell references so that the new formulas contain new cell references corresponding to the new locations and perform calculations using the appropriate values. Thus, if you copy downward, Excel adjusts the row portion of cell references relative to the source cell. If you copy across, then Excel adjusts the column portion of cell references relative to the source cell. Cell references that adjust relative to the location of the source cell are called **relative cell references**.

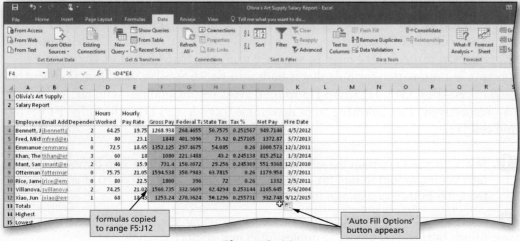

Figure 2–14

Option Buttons

Excel displays option buttons in a worksheet to indicate that you can complete an operation using automatic features such as AutoCorrect, Auto Fill, error checking, and others. For example, the 'Auto Fill Options' button shown in Figure 2–14 appears after a fill operation, such as dragging the fill handle. When an error occurs in a formula in a cell, Excel displays the Trace Error button next to the cell and identifies the cell with the error by placing a green triangle in the upper left of the cell.

Table 2–4 summarizes the option buttons available in Excel. When one of these buttons appears on your worksheet, click its arrow to produce the list of options for modifying the operation or to obtain additional information.

Table 2–4 Option Buttons in Excel

Name	Menu Function
Auto Fill Options	Provides options for how to fill cells following a fill operation, such as dragging the fill handle
AutoCorrect Options	Undoes an automatic correction, stops future automatic corrections of this type, or causes Excel to display the AutoCorrect Options dialog box
Insert Options	Lists formatting options following an insertion of cells, rows, or columns
Paste Options	Specifies how moved or pasted items should appear (for example, with original formatting, without formatting, or with different formatting)
Trace Error	Lists error-checking options following the assignment of an invalid formula to a cell

CONSIDER THIS

Why is the Paste Options button important?
The Paste Options button provides powerful functionality. When performing copy and paste operations, the button allows you great freedom in specifying what it is you want to paste. You can choose from the following options:

- Paste an exact copy of what you copied, including the cell contents and formatting.
- Copy only formulas.
- Copy only formatting.
- Copy only values.
- Copy a combination of these options.
- Copy a picture of what you copied.

BTW
Selecting a Range
You can select a range using the keyboard. Press the F8 key and then use the arrow keys to select the desired range. After you are finished, make sure to press the F8 key to turn off the selection process or you will continue to select ranges.

To Determine Totals Using the Sum Button

The next step is to determine the totals in row 13 for the hours worked in column D, gross pay in column F, federal tax in column G, state tax in column H, and net pay in column J. To determine the total hours worked in column D, the values in the range D4 through D12 must be summed using the SUM function. Recall that a function is a prewritten formula that is built into Excel. Similar SUM functions can be used in cells F13, G13, H13, and J13 to total gross pay, federal tax, state tax, and net pay, respectively. The following steps determine totals in cell D13, the range F13:H13, and cell J13.

1 Select the cell to contain the sum, cell D13 in this case. Click the Sum button (Home tab | Editing group) to sum the contents of the range D4:D12 in cell D13 and then click the Enter button to display a total in the selected cell.

2 Select the range to contain the sums, range F13:H13 in this case. Click the Sum button (Home tab | Editing group) to display totals in the selected range.

❸ Select the cell to contain the sum, cell J13 in this case. Click the Sum button (Home tab | Editing group) to sum the contents of the range J4:J12 in cell J13 and then click the Enter button to display a total in the selected cell (Figure 2–15).

Q&A Why did I have to click the Enter button?

When calculating a sum for a single column, you click the Enter button. If you are calculating the sum for multiple ranges, you click the Sum button.

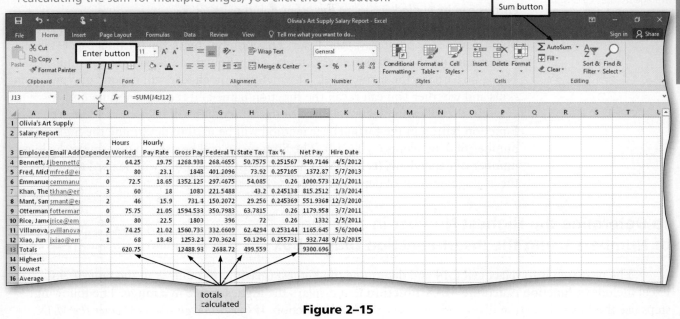

Figure 2–15

To Determine the Total Tax Percentage

With the totals in row 13 determined, the next step is to copy the tax percentage formula in cell I12 to cell I13. The following step copies the tax percentage formula.

❶ Select the cell to be copied, I12 in this case, and then drag the fill handle down through cell I13 to copy the formula (Figure 2–16).

Q&A Why was the SUM function not used for tax percentage in I13?

The total tax percentage is calculated using the totals of the Gross Pay, Federal Tax and State Tax columns, not by summing the tax percentage column.

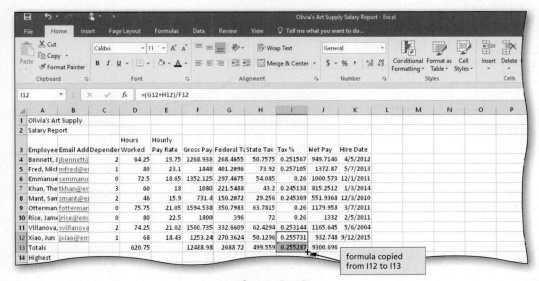

Figure 2–16

Using the AVERAGE, MAX, and MIN Functions

The next step in creating the Olivia's Art Supply Salary Report worksheet is to compute the highest value, lowest value, and average value for the number of dependents listed in the range C4:C12 using the MAX, MIN, and AVERAGE functions in the range C14:C16. Once the values are determined for column C, the entries can be copied across to the other columns.

With Excel, you can enter functions using one of five methods: (1) keyboard, touch gesture, or pointer; (2) the Insert Function button in the formula bar; (3) the Sum menu; (4) the Sum button (Formulas tab | Function Library group); and (5) the Name box area in the formula bar. The method you choose will depend on your typing skills and whether you can recall the function name and required arguments.

In the following sections, three of these methods will be used. The Insert Function button in the formula bar method will be used to determine the highest number of dependents (cell C14). The Sum menu will be used to determine the lowest number of dependents (cell C15). The keyboard and pointer will be used to determine the average number of dependents (cell C16).

To Determine the Highest Number in a Range of Numbers Using the Insert Function Dialog Box

1 ENTER FORMULAS | 2 ENTER FUNCTIONS | 3 VERIFY FORMULAS
4 FORMAT WORKSHEET | 5 CHECK SPELLING | 6 PRINT WORKSHEET

The next step is to select cell C14 and determine the highest (maximum) number in the range C4:C12. Excel includes a function called the **MAX function** that displays the highest value in a range. The following steps use the Insert Function dialog box to enter the MAX function. *Why? Although you could enter the MAX function using the keyboard and Point mode as described previously, an alternative method to entering the function is to use the Insert Function button in the formula bar to open the Insert Function dialog box. The Insert Function dialog box is helpful if you do not remember the name of a function or need to search for a particular function by what it does.*

1

- Select the cell to contain the maximum number, cell C14 in this case.

- Click the Insert Function button in the formula bar to display the Insert Function dialog box.

- Click MAX in the Select a function list (Insert Function dialog box; Figure 2–17). You may need to scroll.

Figure 2–17

 What if the MAX function is not in the Select a function list?
Click the 'Or select a category' arrow to display the list of function categories, select All, and then scroll down and select the MAX function in the Select a function list.

How can I learn about other functions?
Excel has more than 400 functions that perform nearly every type of calculation you can imagine. These functions are categorized in the Insert Function dialog box shown in Figure 2–17. To view the categories, click the 'Or select a category' arrow. Click the name of a function in the Select a function list to display a description of the function.

2

- Click the OK button (Insert Function dialog box) to display the Function Arguments dialog box.

- Replace the text in the Number1 box with the text, **c4:c12** (Function Arguments dialog box) to enter the first argument of the function (Figure 2–18).

Q&A What are the numbers that appear to the right of the Number1 box in the Function Arguments dialog box?
The numbers shown to the right of the Number1 box are the values in the selected range (or if the range is large, the first few numbers only). Excel also displays the value the MAX function will return to cell C14 in the Function Arguments dialog box, shown in Figure 2–18.

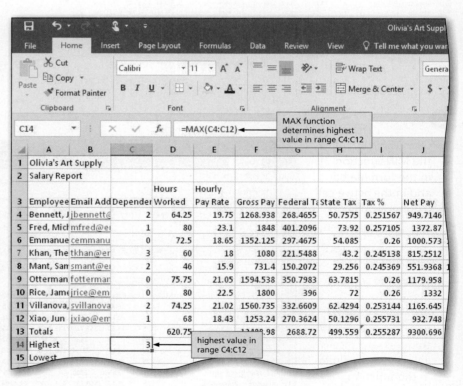

Figure 2–18

3

- Click the OK button (Function Arguments dialog box) to display the highest value in the chosen range in cell C14 (Figure 2–19).

Q&A Why should I not just enter the highest value that I see in the range C4:C12 in cell C14?
In this example, rather than entering the MAX function, you could examine the range C4:C12, determine that the highest number of dependents is 3, and manually enter the number 3 as a constant in cell C14. Excel would display the number similar to how it appears in Figure 2–19. However, because C14 would then contain a constant, Excel would continue to display 3 in cell C14 even if the values in the range change. If you use the MAX function, Excel will recalculate the highest value in the range each time a new value is entered.

Figure 2–19

Other Ways

1. Click Sum arrow (Home tab | Editing group), click Max

2. Click Sum arrow (Formulas tab | Function Library group), click Max

3. Type **=MAX (** in cell, specify range, type **)**

To Determine the Lowest Number in a Range of Numbers Using the Sum Menu

The next step is to enter the **MIN function** in cell C15 to determine the lowest (minimum) number in the range C4:C12. Although you can enter the MIN function using the method used to enter the MAX function, the following steps illustrate an alternative method using the Sum button (Home tab | Editing group). *Why? Using the Sum menu allows you quick access to five commonly used functions, without having to memorize their names or required arguments.*

• Select cell C15 and then click the Sum arrow (Home tab | Editing group) to display the Sum menu (Figure 2–20).

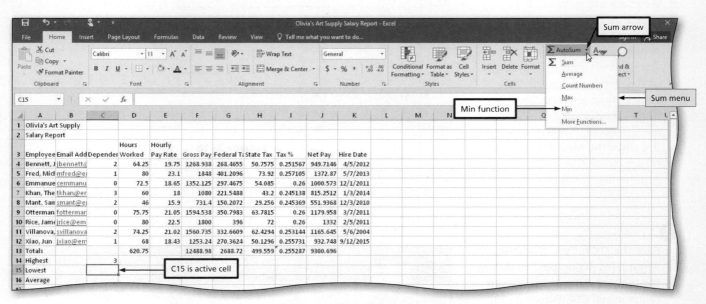

Figure 2–20

2

• Click Min to display the MIN function in the formula bar and in the active cell (Figure 2–21).

Q&A
Why does Excel select the incorrect range?
The range selected by Excel is not always the right one. Excel attempts to guess which cells you want to include in the function by looking for ranges containing numeric data that are adjacent to the selected cell.

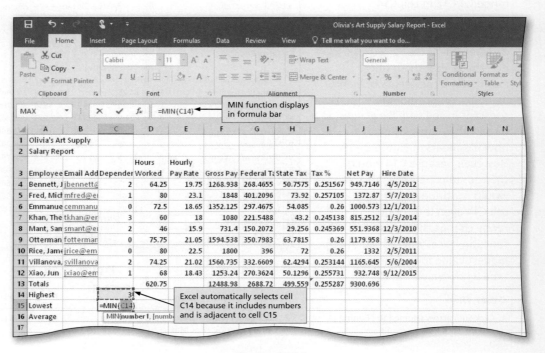

Figure 2–21

3

• Click cell C4 and then drag through cell C12 to update the function with the new range (Figure 2–22).

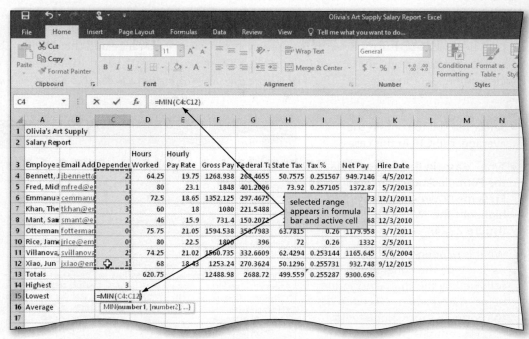

Figure 2–22

4

• Click the Enter button to determine the lowest value in the range C4:C12 and display the result in cell C15 (Figure 2–23).

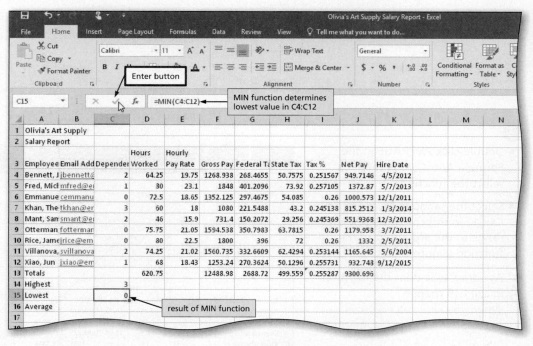

Figure 2–23

Other Ways

1. Click Insert Function button in formula bar, select Statistical category if necessary, click MIN, specify arguments

2. Click Sum arrow (Formulas tab | Function Library group), click Min

3. Type **=MIN(** in cell, fill in arguments, type **)**

To Determine the Average of a Range of Numbers Using the Keyboard

The **AVERAGE function** sums the numbers in a specified range and then divides the sum by the number of cells with numeric values in the range. The following steps use the AVERAGE function to determine the average of the numbers in the range C4:C12. *Why? The AVERAGE function calculates the average of a range of numbers.*

- Select the cell to contain the average, cell C16 in this case.

- Type `=av` in the cell to display the Formula AutoComplete list. Press the DOWN ARROW key to highlight the AVERAGE function (Figure 2–24).

What is happening as I type?
As you type the equal sign followed by the characters in the name of a function, Excel displays the Formula AutoComplete list. This list contains those functions whose names match the letters you have typed.

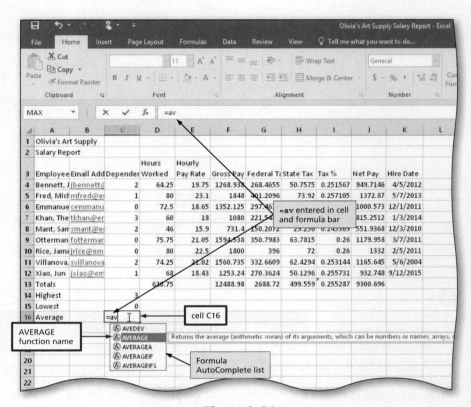

Figure 2–24

- Double-click AVERAGE in the Formula AutoComplete list to select the function.

- Select the range to be averaged, C4:C12 in this case, to insert the range as the argument to the function (Figure 2–25).

As I drag, why does the function in cell C16 change?
When you click cell C4, Excel surrounds cell C4 with a marquee and appends C4 to the left parenthesis in the formula bar. When you begin dragging, Excel appends to the argument a colon (:) and the cell reference of the cell where the pointer is located.

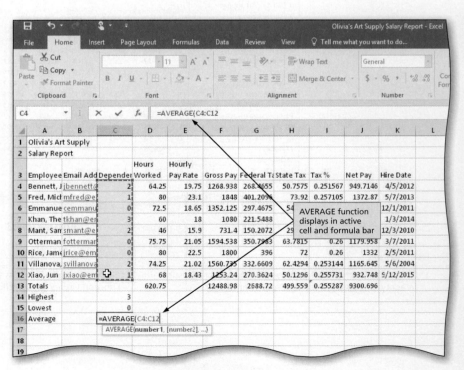

Figure 2–25

3

- Click the Enter button to compute the average of the numbers in the selected range and display the result in the selected cell (Figure 2–26).

Q&A

Can I use the arrow keys to complete the entry instead?

No. While in Point mode, the arrow keys change the selected cell reference in the range you are selecting instead of completing the entry.

What is the purpose of the parentheses in the function?

Most Excel functions require that the argument (in this case, the range C4:C12) be included within parentheses following the function name. In this case, Excel appended the right parenthesis to complete the AVERAGE function when you clicked the Enter button.

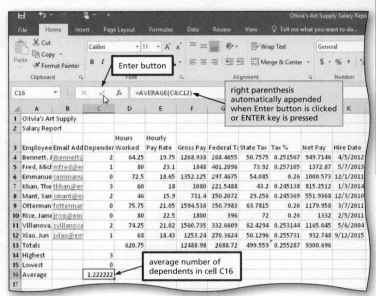

Figure 2–26

To Copy a Range of Cells across Columns to an Adjacent Range Using the Fill Handle

The next step is to copy the AVERAGE, MAX, and MIN functions in the range C14:C16 to the adjacent range D14:J16. The following steps use the fill handle to copy the functions.

1 Select the source range from which to copy the functions, in this case C14:C16.

2 Drag the fill handle in the lower-right corner of the selected range through cell J16 to copy the three functions to the selected range.

3 Select cell I16 and then press the DELETE key to delete the average of the Tax % (Figure 2–27).

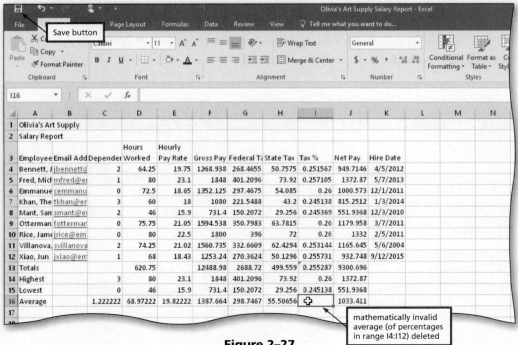

Figure 2–27

4 Save the workbook again on the same storage location with the same file name.

Q&A

Why delete the formula in cell I16?

You deleted the average in cell I16 because averaging this type of percentage is mathematically invalid.

How can I be sure that the function arguments are correct for the cells in range D14:J16?
Remember that Excel adjusts the cell references in the copied functions so that each function refers to the range of numbers above it in the same column. Review the functions in rows 14 through 16 by clicking on individual cells and examining the function as it appears in the formula bar. You should see that the functions in each column reference the appropriate ranges.

Other Ways

1. Select source area, click Copy button (Home tab | Clipboard group), select destination area, click Paste button (Home tab | Clipboard group)

2. Right-click source area, click Copy on shortcut menu; right-click destination area, click Paste icon on shortcut menu

3. Select source area and then point to border of range; while holding down CTRL, drag source area to destination area

4. Select source area, press CTRL+C, select destination area, press CTRL+V

Break Point: If you wish to take a break, this is a good place to do so. You can exit Excel now. To resume at a later time, run Excel, open the file called Olivia's Art Supply Salary Report, and continue following the steps from this location forward.

Verifying Formulas Using Range Finder

One of the more common mistakes made with Excel is to include an incorrect cell reference in a formula. An easy way to verify that a formula references the cells you want it to reference is to use Range Finder. **Range Finder** checks which cells are referenced in the formula assigned to the active cell.

To use Range Finder to verify that a formula contains the intended cell references, double-click the cell with the formula you want to check. Excel responds by highlighting the cells referenced in the formula so that you can verify that the cell references are correct.

To Verify a Formula Using Range Finder

1 ENTER FORMULAS | 2 ENTER FUNCTIONS | 3 VERIFY FORMULAS
4 FORMAT WORKSHEET | 5 CHECK SPELLING | 6 PRINT WORKSHEET

Why? Range Finder allows you to correct mistakes by making immediate changes to the cells referenced in a formula. The following steps use Range Finder to check the formula in cell I4.

1

- Double-click cell I4 to activate Range Finder (Figure 2–28).

2

- Press the ESC key to quit Range Finder and then click anywhere in the worksheet, such as cell A18, to deselect the current cell.

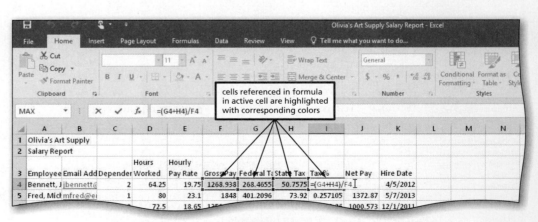

Figure 2–28

Formatting the Worksheet

Although the worksheet contains the appropriate data, formulas, and functions, the text and numbers need to be formatted to improve their appearance and readability.

In Module 1, cell styles were used to format much of the worksheet. This section describes how to change the unformatted worksheet in Figure 2–29a to the formatted worksheet in Figure 2–29b using a theme and other commands on the ribbon. A **theme** formats a worksheet by applying a collection of fonts, font styles, colors, and effects to give it a consistent appearance.

(a) Unformatted Worksheet

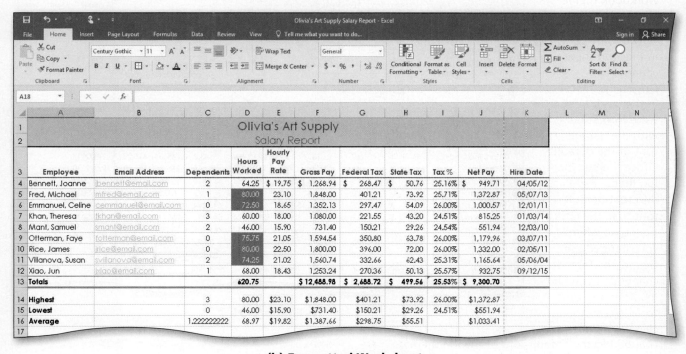

(b) Formatted Worksheet

Figure 2–29

To Change the Workbook Theme

Why? *A company or department may choose a specific theme as their standard theme so that all of their documents have a similar appearance. Similarly, you may want to have a theme that sets your work apart from the work of others. Other Office programs, such as Word and PowerPoint, include the same themes so that all of your Microsoft Office documents can share a common look.* The following steps change the workbook theme to the Ion theme.

①

• Click Page Layout to display the Page Layout tab.

• Click the Themes button (Page Layout tab | Themes group) to display the Themes gallery (Figure 2–30).

🔍 **Experiment**

• Point to several themes in the Themes gallery to preview the themes.

Figure 2–30

②

• Click Ion in the Themes gallery to change the workbook theme (Figure 2–31).

Q&A

Why did the cells in the worksheet change?
Originally, the cells in the worksheet were formatted with the default font of the default Office theme. The Ion theme has a different default font than the Office theme, so when you changed the theme, the font changed. If you had modified the font for any cells, those cells would not have changed to the default font of the Ion theme.

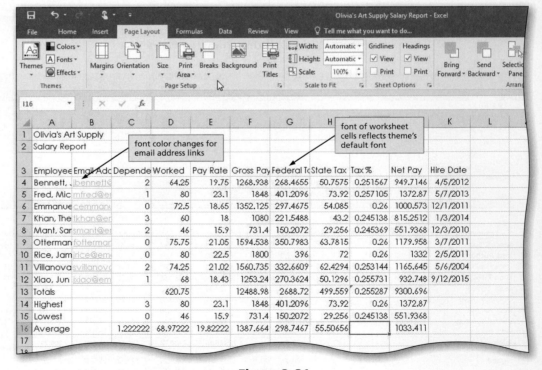

Figure 2–31

To Format the Worksheet Titles

The following steps merge and center the worksheet titles, apply the Title cells style to the worksheet titles, and decrease the font of the worksheet subtitle.

1 Display the Home tab.

2 Select the range to be merged, A1:K1 in this case, and then click the 'Merge & Center' button (Home tab | Alignment group) to merge and center the text in the selected range.

3 Select the range A2:K2 and then click the 'Merge & Center' button (Home tab | Alignment group) to merge and center the text.

4 Select the range to contain the Title cell style, in this case A1:A2, click the Cell Styles button (Home tab | Styles group) to display the Cell Styles gallery, and then click the Title cell style in the Cell Styles gallery to apply the Title cell style to the selected range.

5 Select cell A2 and then click the 'Decrease Font Size' button (Home tab | Font group) to decrease the font size of the selected cell to the next lower font size (Figure 2–32).

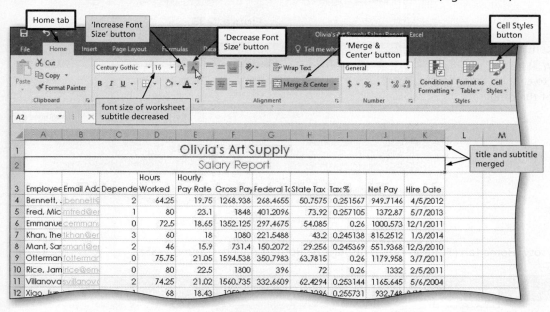

Figure 2–32

Q&A What happens when I click the 'Decrease Font Size' button?

When you click the 'Decrease Font Size' button, Excel assigns the next smaller font size in the Font Size gallery to the selected range. The 'Increase Font Size' button works in a similar manner, assigning the next larger font size in the Font Size gallery to the selected range.

Which colors work best when formatting your worksheet?

Knowing how people perceive colors can help you focus attention on parts of your worksheet. Warmer colors (red and orange) tend to reach toward the reader. Cooler colors (blue, green, and violet) tend to pull away from the reader.

CONSIDER THIS

To Change the Background Color and Apply a Box Border to the Worksheet Title and Subtitle

Why? *A background color and border can draw attention to the title of a worksheet.* The final formats assigned to the worksheet title and subtitle are the blue-gray background color and thick outside border. The following steps complete the formatting of the worksheet titles.

1

• Select the range A1:A2 and then click the Fill Color arrow (Home tab | Font group) to display the Fill Color gallery (Figure 2–33).

🔍 **Experiment**

• Point to a variety of colors in the Fill Color gallery to preview the selected colors in the range A1:A2.

Figure 2–33

2

• Click Blue-Gray, Accent 5, Lighter 60% (column 9, row 3) in the Theme Colors area to change the background color of the range of cells (Figure 2–34).

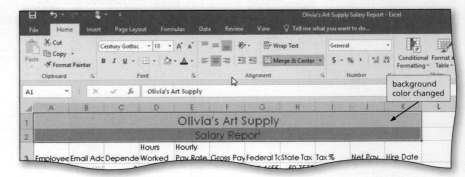

Figure 2–34

3

• Click the Borders arrow (Home tab | Font group) to display the Borders gallery (Figure 2–35).

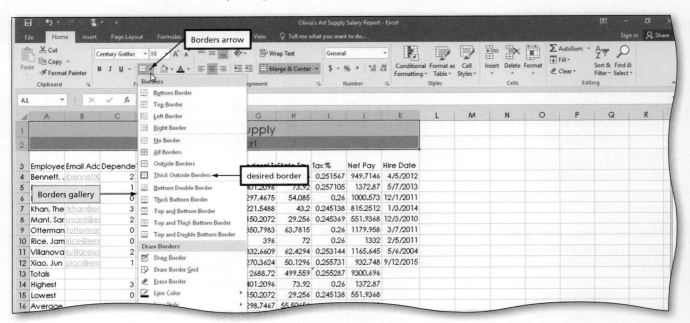

Figure 2–35

4

- Click 'Thick Outside Borders' in the Borders gallery to create a thick outside border around the selected range.

- Click anywhere in the worksheet, such as cell A18, to deselect the current range (Figure 2–36).

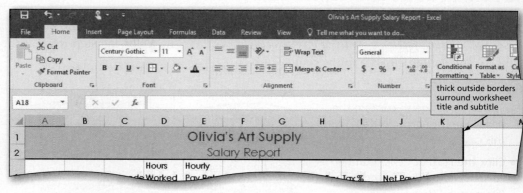

Figure 2–36

Other Ways

1. Click Font Settings Dialog Box Launcher (Home tab | Font group), click Fill tab (Format Cells dialog box), click desired fill, click OK button

2. Right-click range, click Format Cells on shortcut menu, click Fill tab (Format Cells dialog box), click desired fill, click OK button

3. Press CTRL+1, click Fill tab (Format Cells dialog box), click desired fill, click OK button

To Apply a Cell Style to the Column Headings and Format the Total Rows

As shown in Figure 2–29b, the column titles (row 3) should have the Heading 3 cell style and the totals row (row 13) should have the Total cell style. The headings in the range A14:A16 should be bold. The following steps assign these styles and formats to row 3, row 13, and the range A14:A16.

1 Select the range to be formatted, cells A3:K3 in this case.

2 Use the Cell Styles gallery to apply the Heading 3 cell style to the range A3:K3.

3 Click the Center button (Home tab | Alignment group) to center the column headings.

4 Apply the Total cell style to the range A13:K13.

5 Bold the range A14:A16 (Figure 2–37).

BTW

Color Selection
Bright colors jump out of a dark background and are easiest to see. White or yellow text on a dark blue, green, purple, or black background is ideal for highlighting.

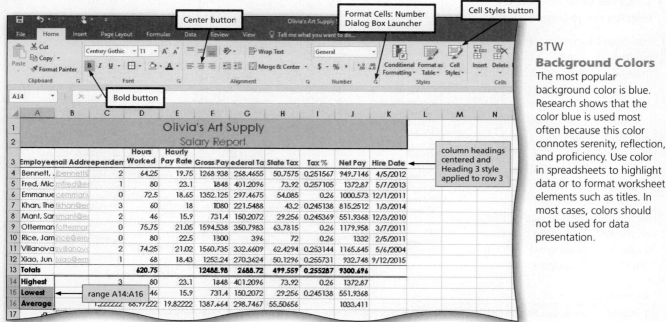

Figure 2–37

BTW

Background Colors
The most popular background color is blue. Research shows that the color blue is used most often because this color connotes serenity, reflection, and proficiency. Use color in spreadsheets to highlight data or to format worksheet elements such as titles. In most cases, colors should not be used for data presentation.

To Format Dates and Center Data in Cells

Why? *You may want to change the format of the dates to better suit your needs. In addition, numbers that are not used in calculations often are centered instead of right-aligned.* The following steps format the dates in the range K4:K12 and center the data in the range C4:C16.

- Select the range to contain the new date format, cells K4:K12 in this case.

- Click the Format Cells: Number Format Dialog Box Launcher (Home tab | Number group) (shown in Figure 2–37) to display the Format Cells dialog box.

- If necessary, click the Number tab (Format Cells dialog box), click Date in the Category list, and then click 03/14/12 in the Type list to choose the format for the selected range (Figure 2–38).

- Click the OK button (Format Cells dialog box) to format the dates in the current column using the selected date format style.

Figure 2–38

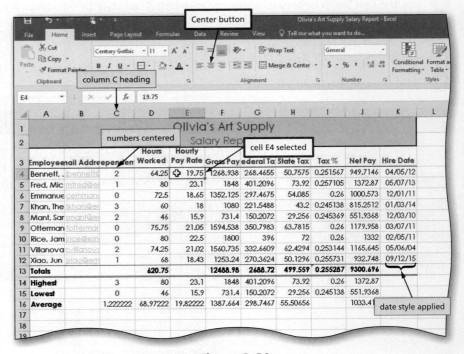

Figure 2–39

- Select the range C4:C16 and then click the Center button (Home tab | Alignment group) to center the data in the selected range.

- Select cell E4 to deselect the selected range (Figure 2–39).

Q&A

How can I format an entire column at once?

Instead of selecting the range C4:C16 in Step 3, you could have clicked the column C heading immediately above cell C1, and then clicked the Center button (Home tab | Alignment group). In this case, all cells in column C down to the last cell in the worksheet would have been formatted to use center alignment. This same procedure could have been used to format the dates in column K.

Other Ways

1. Right-click range, click Format Cells on shortcut menu, click Number tab (Format Cells dialog box), click desired number format, click OK button

2. Press CTRL+1, click Number tab (Format Cells dialog box), click desired number format, click OK button

To Apply an Accounting Number Format and Comma Style Format Using the Ribbon

As shown in Figure 2–29b, the worksheet is formatted to resemble an accounting report. In columns E through H and J, the numbers in the first row (row 4), the totals row (row 13), and the rows below the totals (rows 14 through 16) have dollar signs, while the remaining numbers (rows 5 through 12) in columns E through H and column J do not. The following steps assign formats using the 'Accounting Number Format' button and the Comma Style button. **Why?** *This gives the worksheet a more professional look.*

1 Select the range to contain the accounting number format, cells E4:H4 in this case.

2 While holding down the CTRL key, select cell J4, the range F13:H13, and cell J13 to select the nonadjacent ranges and cells.

3 Click the 'Accounting Number Format' button (Home tab | Number group) to apply the accounting number format with fixed dollar signs to the selected nonadjacent ranges.

Q&A What is the effect of applying the accounting number format?

The 'Accounting Number Format' button assigns a fixed dollar sign to the numbers in the ranges and rounds the figure to the nearest 100th. A fixed dollar sign is one that appears to the far left of the cell, with multiple spaces between it and the first digit in the cell.

4 Select the ranges to contain the comma style format, cells E5:H12 and J5:J12 in this case.

5 Click the Comma Style button (Home tab | Number group) to assign the comma style format to the selected ranges.

6 Select the range D4:D16 and then click the Comma Style button (Home tab | Number group) to assign the comma style format to the selected range (Figure 2–40).

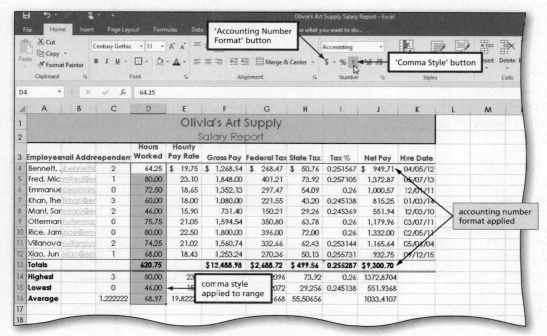

Figure 2–40

To Apply a Currency Style Format with a Floating Dollar Sign Using the Format Cells Dialog Box

1 ENTER FORMULAS | 2 ENTER FUNCTIONS | 3 VERIFY FORMULAS
4 FORMAT WORKSHEET | 5 CHECK SPELLING | 6 PRINT WORKSHEET

Why? *The Currency format places dollar signs immediately to the left of the number (known as floating dollar signs, as they change position depending on the number of digits in the cell) and displays a zero for cells that have a value of zero.* The following steps use the Format Cells dialog box to apply the currency style format with a floating dollar sign to the numbers in the ranges E14:H16 and J14:J16.

- Select the ranges (E14:H16 and J14:J16) and then click the Number Format Dialog Box Launcher (Home tab | Number group) to display the Format Cells dialog box.

- If necessary, click the Number tab to display the Number sheet (Format Cells dialog box).

- Click Currency in the Category list to select the necessary number format category and then click the third style ($1,234.10) in the Negative numbers list to select the desired currency format for negative numbers (Figure 2–41).

Figure 2–41

Q&A How do I decide which number format to use?
Excel offers many ways to format numbers. Once you select a number category, you can select the number of decimal places, whether to include a dollar sign (or a symbol of another currency), and how negative numbers should appear. Selecting the appropriate negative numbers format is important, because some formats add a space to the right of the number in order to align numbers in the worksheet on the decimal points and some do not.

- Click the OK button (Format Cells dialog box) to assign the currency style format with a floating dollar sign to the selected ranges (Figure 2–42).

Q&A What is the difference between using the accounting number style and currency style?
When using the currency style, recall that a floating dollar sign always appears immediately to the left of the first digit. With the accounting number style, the fixed dollar sign always appears on the left side of the cell.

						$268.47	$ 50.7			
5	Fred, Mic	mfred@er	1	80.00	23.10	1,848.00	401.21	73.92	0.257105	1,372.87	05/07/13
6	Emmanue	cemman	0	72.50	18.65	1,352.13	297.47	54.09	0.26	1,000.57	12/01/11
7	Khan, The	tkhan@er	3	60.00	18.00	1,080.00	221.55	43.20	0.245138	815.25	01/03/14
8	Mant, Sar	smant@er	2	46.00	15.90	731.40	150.21	29.26	0.245369	551.94	12/03/10
9	Otterman	fotterman	0	75.75	21.05	1,594.54	350.80	63.78	0.26	1,179.96	03/07/11
10	Rice, Jam	rice@em	0	80.00	22.50	1,800.00	396.00	72.00	0.26	1,332.00	02/05/11
11	Villanova	svillanova	2	74.25	21.02	1,560.74	332.66	62.43	0.253144	1,165.64	05/06/04
12	Xiao, Jun	jxiao@em	1	68.00	18.43	1,253.24	270.36	50.13	0.255731	932.75	09/12/15
13	**Totals**			**620.75**		**$12,488.98**	**$2,688.72**	**$ 499.56**	**0.255287**	**$9,300.70**	
14	**Highest**		3	80.00	$23.10	$1,848.00	$401.21	$73.92	0.26	$1,372.87	
15	**Lowest**		0	46.00	$15.90	$731.40	$150.21	$29.26	0.245138	$551.94	
16	**Average**		1.222222	68.97	$19.82	$1,387.66	$298.75	$55.51		$1,033.41	
17											
18											
19											

Salary Report ⊕

Ready   Average: $532.86

currency style applied to selected ranges

Figure 2–42

Other Ways

1. Press CTRL+1, click Number tab (Format Cells dialog box), click Currency in Category list, select format, click OK button

2. Press CTRL+SHIFT+DOLLAR SIGN ($)

To Apply a Percent Style Format and Use the Increase Decimal Button

The next step is to format the tax percentage in column I. *Why? Currently, Excel displays the numbers as decimal fractions when they should appear as percentages.* The following steps format the range I4:I15 to the percent style format with two decimal places.

1

• Select the range to format, cells I4:I15 in this case.

• Click the Percent Style button (Home tab | Number group) to display the numbers in the selected range as a rounded whole percent.

Q&A

What is the result of clicking the Percent Style button?

The Percent Style button instructs Excel to display a value as a percentage, which is determined by multiplying the cell entry by 100, rounding the result to the nearest percentage, and adding a percent sign. For example, when cell I4 is formatted using the Percent Style buttons, Excel displays the actual value 0.251567 as 25%.

2

• Click the Increase Decimal button (Home tab | Number group) two times to display the numbers in the selected range with two decimal places (Figure 2–43).

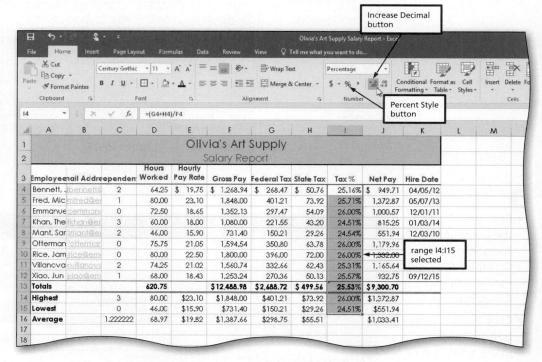

Figure 2–43

Other Ways

1. Right-click selected range, click Format Cells on shortcut menu, click Number tab (Format Cells dialog box), click Percentage in Category list, select format, click OK button
2. Press CTRL+1, click Number tab (Format Cells dialog box), click Percentage in Category list, select format, click OK button
3. Press CTRL+SHIFT+PERCENT SIGN (%)

Conditional Formatting

Conditional formatting offers you the ability to automatically change how a cell appears — the font, font color, background fill, and other options — based on the value in the cell. Excel offers a variety of commonly used conditional formatting rules, along with the ability to create your own custom rules and formatting. The next step is to emphasize the values greater than 72 in column D by formatting them to appear with a blue background and white font color (Figure 2–44).

BTW

Conditional Formatting

You can assign any format to a cell, a range of cells, a worksheet, or an entire workbook conditionally. If the value of the cell changes and no longer meets the specified condition, Excel suppresses the conditional formatting.

To Apply Conditional Formatting

The following steps assign conditional formatting to the range D4:D12. *Why? After formatting, any cell with a value greater than 72 in column D will appear with a blue background and a white font.*

1

- Select the range D4:D12.

- Click the Conditional Formatting button (Home tab | Styles group) to display the Conditional Formatting menu (Figure 2–44).

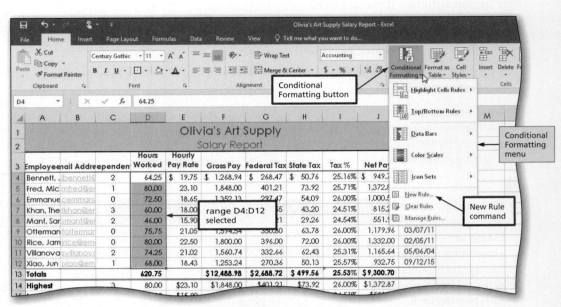

Figure 2–44

2

- Click New Rule on the Conditional Formatting menu to display the New Formatting Rule dialog box.

- Click 'Format only cells that contain' in the Select a Rule Type area (New Formatting Rule dialog box) to change the Edit the Rule Description area.

- In the Edit the Rule Description area, click the arrow in the relational operator box (second box) to display a list of relational operators, and then select greater than to select the desired operator.

- Select the rightmost box, and then type   72   to enter the value of the rule description (Figure 2–45).

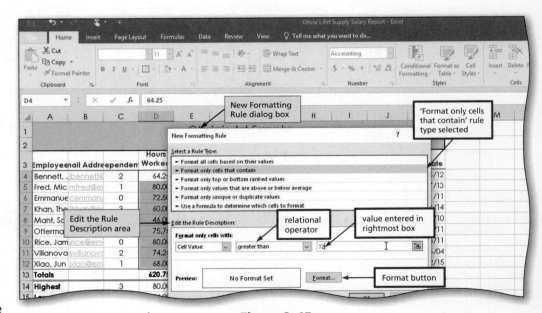

Figure 2–45

Q&A

What do the changes in the Edit the Rule Description area indicate?

The Edit the Rule Description area allows you to view and edit the rules for the conditional format. In this case, the rule indicates that Excel should format only those cells with cell values greater than 72.

❸

- Click the Format button (New Formatting Rule dialog box) to display the Format Cells dialog box.
- If necessary, click the Font tab (Format Cells dialog box) to display the Font sheet. Click the Color arrow to display the Color gallery and then click White, Background 1 (column 1, row 1) in the Color gallery to select the font color (Figure 2–46).

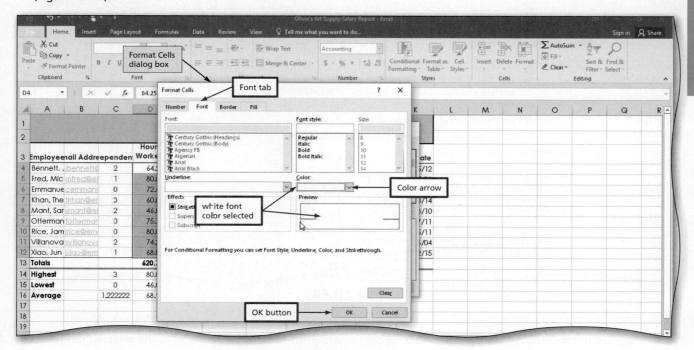

Figure 2–46

❹

- Click the Fill tab (Format Cells dialog box) to display the Fill sheet and then click the blue color in column 9, row 1 to select the background color (Figure 2–47).

Figure 2–47

- Click the OK button (Format Cells dialog box) to close the Format Cells dialog box and display the New Formatting Rule dialog box with the desired font and background colors displayed in the Preview area (Figure 2–48).

Figure 2–48

- Click the OK button (New Formatting Rule dialog box) to assign the conditional format to the selected range.

- Click anywhere in the worksheet, such as cell A18, to deselect the current range (Figure 2–49).

Q&A What should I do if I make a mistake setting up a rule?
If after you have applied the conditional formatting you realize you made a mistake when creating a rule, select the cell(s) with the rule you want to edit, click the Conditional Formatting button (Home tab | Styles group), select the rule you want to edit, and then click either the Edit Rule button (to edit the selected rule) or the Delete Rule button (to delete the selected rule).

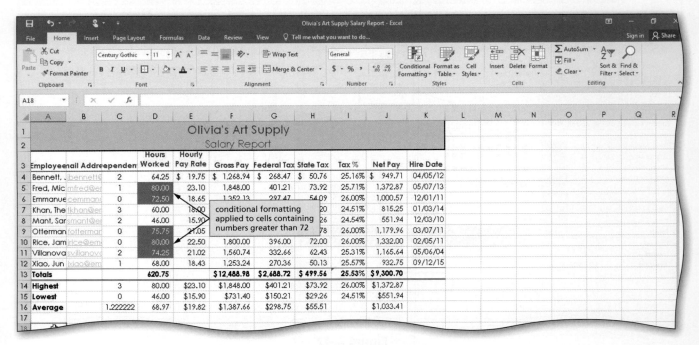

Figure 2–49

Conditional Formatting Operators

As shown in the New Formatting Rule dialog box, when the selected rule type is "Format only the cells that contain," the second text box in the Edit the Rule Description area allows you to select a relational operator, such as greater than, to use in the condition. The eight different relational operators from which you can choose for conditional formatting are summarized in Table 2–5.

Table 2–5 Summary of Conditional Formatting Relational Operators

Relational Operator	Formatting will be applied if...
between	cell value is between two numbers
not between	cell value is not between two numbers
equal to	cell value is equal to a number
not equal to	cell value is not equal to a number
greater than	cell value is greater than a number
less than	cell value is less than a number
greater than or equal to	cell value is greater than or equal to a number
less than or equal to	cell value is less than or equal to a number

Changing Column Width and Row Height

You can change the width of the columns or height of the rows at any time to make the worksheet easier to read or to ensure that an entry fits properly in a cell. By default, all of the columns in a blank worksheet have a width of 8.43 characters, or 64 pixels. This value may change depending on the theme applied to the workbook. For example, when the Ion theme was applied to the workbook in this module, the default width of the columns changed to 8.38 characters. A **character** is defined as a letter, number, symbol, or punctuation mark. An average of 8.43 characters in 11-point Calibri font (the default font used by Excel) will fit in a cell.

The default row height in a blank worksheet is 15 points (or 20 pixels), which easily fits the 11-point default font. Recall from Module 1 that a point is equal to 1/72 of an inch. Thus, 15 points is equal to about 1/5 of an inch.

Another measure of the height and width of cells is pixels. A **pixel**, which is short for picture element, is a dot on the screen that contains a color. The size of the dot is based on your screen's resolution. At the resolution of 1366 × 768 used in this book, 1366 pixels appear across the screen and 768 pixels appear down the screen for a total of 1,049,088 pixels. It is these 1,049,088 pixels that form the font and other items you see on the screen.

1 ENTER FORMULAS | 2 ENTER FUNCTIONS | 3 VERIFY FORMULAS
4 FORMAT WORKSHEET | 5 CHECK SPELLING | 6 PRINT WORKSHEET

To Change Column Width

When changing the column width, you can set the width manually or you can instruct Excel to size the column to best fit. **Best fit** means that the width of the column will be increased or decreased so that the widest entry will fit in the column. *Why? Sometimes, you may prefer more or less white space in a column than best fit provides. To change the white space, Excel allows you to change column widths manually.*

When the format you assign to a cell causes the entry to exceed the width of a column, Excel changes the column width to best fit. If you do not assign a format to a cell or cells in a column, the column width will remain 8.43 characters. Recall from Module 1 that to set a column width to best fit, double-click the right boundary of the column heading above row 1. The following steps change the column widths.

1

- Drag through column headings A, B, and C above row 1 to select the columns.

- Point to the boundary on the right side of column heading C to cause the pointer to become a split double arrow (Figure 2–50).

Q&A

What if I want to make a large change to the column width?
If you want to increase or decrease column width significantly, you can right-click a column heading and then use the Column Width command on the shortcut menu to change the column's width. To use this command, however, you must select one or more entire columns.

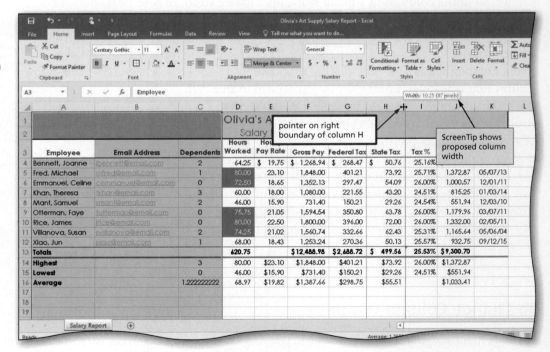

Figure 2–50

2

- Double-click the right boundary of column heading C to change the width of the selected columns to best fit.

- Point to the right boundary of the column H heading above row 1.

- When the pointer changes to a split double arrow, drag until the ScreenTip indicates Width: 10.25 (87 pixels). Do not release the mouse button (Figure 2–51).

Q&A

What happens if I change the column width to zero (0)?
If you decrease the

Figure 2–51

column width to 0, the column is hidden. Hiding cells is a technique you can use to hide data that might not be relevant to a particular report. To instruct Excel to display a hidden column, position the mouse pointer to the right of the column heading boundary where the hidden column is located and then drag to the right.

3

- Release the mouse button to change the column width.

- Click the column D heading above row 1 to select the column.

- While holding down the CTRL key, click the column E heading and then the column I heading above row 1 so that nonadjacent columns are selected.

- Point to the boundary on the right side of the column I heading above row 1.

- Drag until the ScreenTip indicates Width: 7.50 (65 pixels). Do not release the mouse button (Figure 2–52).

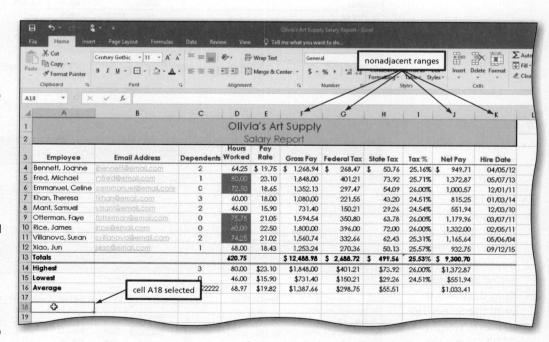

Figure 2–52

4

- Release the mouse button to change the column widths.

- Click the column F heading and drag to select the column G heading.

- While holding down the CTRL key, click the column J heading and drag to select the column K heading above row 1 so that nonadjacent columns are selected.

- Drag the right boundary of column G until the ScreenTip indicates Width: 11.00 (93 pixels).
Release the mouse button to change the column widths.

- Click anywhere in the worksheet, such as cell A18, to deselect the columns (Figure 2–53).

Figure 2–53

Other Ways
1. Click column heading or drag through multiple column headings, right-click selected column, click Column Width on shortcut menu, enter desired column width, click OK button

To Change Row Height

Why? *You also can increase or decrease the height of a row manually to improve the appearance of the worksheet.* When you increase the font size of a cell entry, such as the title in cell A1, Excel increases the row height to best fit so that it can display the characters properly. Recall that Excel did this earlier when multiple lines were entered in a cell in row 3, and when the cell style of the worksheet title and subtitle was changed. The following steps improve the appearance of the worksheet by increasing the height of row 3 to 48.00 points and increasing the height of row 14 to 27.00 points.

- Point to the boundary below row heading 3 until the pointer becomes a split double arrow.

- Drag down until the ScreenTip indicates Height: 48.00 (64 pixels). Do not release the mouse button (Figure 2–54).

Figure 2–54

- Release the mouse button to change the row height.

- Point to the boundary below row heading 14 until the pointer becomes a split double arrow and then drag downward until the ScreenTip indicates Height: 27.00 (36 pixels). Do not release the mouse button (Figure 2–55).

Figure 2–55

❸

- Release the mouse button to change the row height.

- Click anywhere in the worksheet, such as cell A18, to deselect the current cell (Figure 2–56).

Q&A Can I hide a row?

Yes. As with column widths, when you decrease the row height to 0, the row is hidden. To instruct Excel to display a hidden row, position the pointer just below the row heading boundary where the row is hidden and then drag downward. To set a row height to best fit, double-click the bottom boundary of the row heading. You also can hide and unhide rows by right-clicking the row or column heading and selecting the option to hide or unhide the cells.

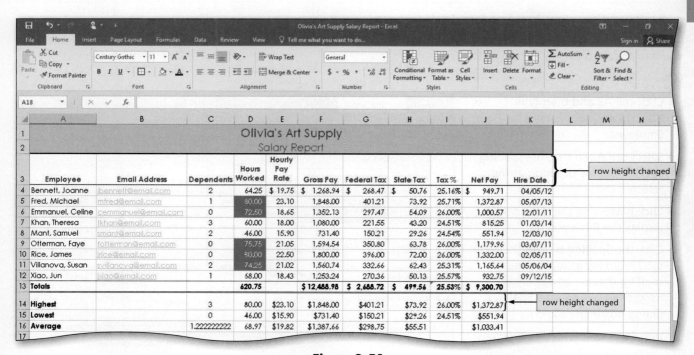

Figure 2–56

Other Ways

1. Right-click row heading or drag through multiple row headings, right-click selected heading, click Row Height on shortcut menu, enter desired row height, click OK button

Break Point: If you wish to take a break, this is a good place to do so. Be sure to save the Olivia's Art Supply Salary Report file again and then you can exit Excel. To resume at a later time, run Excel, open the file called Olivia's Art Supply Salary Report, and continue following the steps from this location forward.

Checking Spelling

Excel includes a **spelling checker** you can use to check a worksheet for spelling errors. The spelling checker looks for spelling errors by comparing words on the worksheet against words contained in its standard dictionary. If you often use specialized terms that are not in the standard dictionary, you may want to add them to a custom dictionary using the Spelling dialog box. When the spelling checker finds a word that is not in either dictionary, it displays the word in the Spelling dialog box. You then can correct it if it is misspelled.

BTW
Spell Checking
While Excel's spell checker is a valuable tool, it is not infallible. You should proofread your workbook carefully by pointing to each word and saying it aloud as you point to it. Be mindful of misused words such as its and it's, through and though, and to and too. Nothing undermines a good impression more than a professional looking report with misspelled words.

Does the spelling checker catch all spelling mistakes?

While Excel's spelling checker is a valuable tool, it is not infallible. You should proofread your workbook carefully by pointing to each word and saying it aloud as you point to it. Be mindful of misused words such as its and it's, through and though, your and you're, and to and too. Nothing undermines a good impression more than a professional report with misspelled words.

To Check Spelling on the Worksheet

1 ENTER FORMULAS | 2 ENTER FUNCTIONS | 3 VERIFY FORMULAS
4 FORMAT WORKSHEET | 5 CHECK SPELLING | 6 PRINT WORKSHEET

Why? *Everything in a worksheet should be checked to make sure there are no spelling errors.* To illustrate how Excel responds to a misspelled word, the following steps purposely misspell the word, Employee, in cell A3 as the word, Empolyee, as shown in Figure 2–57.

1

- Click cell A3 and then type **Empolyee** to misspell the word, Employee.

- Select cell A2 so that the spelling checker begins checking at the selected cell.

- Click Review on the ribbon to display the Review tab.

- Click the Spelling button (Review tab | Proofing group) to use the spelling checker to display the misspelled word in the Spelling dialog box (Figure 2–57).

Q&A What happens when the spelling checker finds a misspelled word?
When the spelling checker identifies that a cell contains a word not in its standard or custom dictionary, it selects that cell as the active cell and displays the Spelling dialog box. The Spelling dialog box displays the word that was not found in the dictionary and offers a list of suggested corrections (Figure 2–58).

Figure 2–57

2

- Verify that the word highlighted in the Suggestion area is correct.

- Click the Change button (Spelling dialog box) to change the misspelled word to the correct word (Figure 2–58).

- Click the Close button to close the Spelling dialog box.

- If a Microsoft Excel dialog box is displayed, click the OK button.

Figure 2–58

- Click anywhere in the worksheet, such as cell A18, to deselect the current cell.

- Display the Home tab.

- Save the workbook again on the same storage location with the same file name.

Q&A What other actions can I take in the Spelling dialog box?

If one of the words in the Suggestions list is correct, select it and then click the Change button. If none of the suggested words are correct, type the correct word in the 'Not in Dictionary' text box and then click the Change button. To change the word throughout the worksheet, click the Change All button instead of the Change button. To skip correcting the word, click the Ignore Once button. To have Excel ignore the word for the remainder of the worksheet, click the Ignore All button.

Other Ways

1. Press F7

Additional Spelling Checker Considerations

Consider these additional guidelines when using the spelling checker:
- To check the spelling of the text in a single cell, double-click the cell to make the formula bar active and then click the Spelling button (Review tab | Proofing group).

- If you select a single cell so that the formula bar is not active and then start the spelling checker, Excel checks the remainder of the worksheet, including notes and embedded charts.

- If you select a cell other than cell A1 before you start the spelling checker, Excel will display a dialog box when the spelling checker reaches the end of the worksheet, asking if you want to continue checking at the beginning.

- If you select a range of cells before starting the spelling checker, Excel checks the spelling of the words only in the selected range.

- To check the spelling of all the sheets in a workbook, right-click any sheet tab, click 'Select All Sheets' on the sheet tab shortcut menu, and then start the spelling checker.

- To add words to the dictionary, such as your last name, click the 'Add to Dictionary' button in the Spelling dialog box (shown in Figure 2–58) when Excel flags the word as not being in the dictionary.

- Click the AutoCorrect button (shown in Figure 2–58) to add the misspelled word and the correct version of the word to the AutoCorrect list. For example, suppose that you misspell the word, do, as the word, dox. When the spelling checker displays the Spelling dialog box with the correct word, do, in the Suggestions list, click the AutoCorrect button. Then, anytime in the future that you type the word, dox, Excel will change it to the word, do.

Printing the Worksheet

Excel allows for a great deal of customization in how a worksheet appears when printed. For example, the margins on the page can be adjusted. A header or footer can be added to each printed page as well. A **header** is text and graphics that print at the

BTW
Error Checking
Always take the time to check the formulas of a worksheet before submitting it to your supervisor. You can check formulas by clicking the Error Checking button (Formulas tab | Formula Auditing group). You also should test the formulas by employing data that tests the limits of formulas. Experienced spreadsheet specialists spend as much time testing a workbook as they do creating it, and they do so before placing the workbook into production.

BTW
Distributing a Workbook
Instead of printing and distributing a hard copy of a workbook, you can distribute the workbook electronically. Options include sending the workbook via email; posting it on cloud storage (such as OneDrive) and sharing the file with others; posting it on social media, a blog, or other website; and sharing a link associated with an online location of the workbook. You also can create and share a PDF or XPS image of the workbook, so that users can view the file in Acrobat Reader or XPS Viewer instead of in Excel.

top of each page. Similarly, a **footer** is text and graphics that print at the bottom of each page. Excel also has the capability to alter the worksheet in Page Layout view. Page Layout view allows you to create or modify a worksheet while viewing how it will look in printed format. The default view that you have worked in up until this point in the book is called Normal view.

To Change the Worksheet's Margins, Header, and Orientation in Page Layout View

1 ENTER FORMULAS | 2 ENTER FUNCTIONS | 3 VERIFY FORMULAS
4 FORMAT WORKSHEET | 5 CHECK SPELLING | **6 PRINT WORKSHEET**

The following steps change to Page Layout view, narrow the margins of the worksheet, change the header of the worksheet, and set the orientation of the worksheet to landscape. *Why? You may want the printed worksheet to fit on one page. You can do that by reducing the page margins and changing the page orientation to fit wider printouts across a sheet of paper. You can use the header to identify the content on each page.* **Margins** are those portions of a printed page outside the main body of the printed document and always are blank when printed. The current worksheet is too wide for a single page and requires landscape orientation to fit on one page in a readable manner.

• Click the Page Layout button on the status bar to view the worksheet in Page Layout view (Figure 2–59).

◄| What are the features of Page Layout view?
Q&A | Page Layout view shows the worksheet divided into pages. A gray background separates each page. The white areas surrounding each page indicate the print margins. The top of each page includes a Header area, and the bottom of each page includes a Footer area. Page Layout view also includes rulers at the top and left margin of the page that assists you in placing objects on the page, such as charts and pictures.

Figure 2–59

2

- Display the Page Layout tab.

- Click the Adjust Margins button (Page Layout tab | Page Setup group) to display the Margins gallery (Figure 2–60).

Figure 2–60

3

- Click Narrow in the Margins gallery to change the worksheet margins to the Narrow margin style.

- Click the center of the Header area above the worksheet title.

- Type **Jayne Smith** and then press the ENTER key. Type **Chief Financial Officer** to complete the worksheet header (Figure 2–61).

- If requested by your instructor, type your name instead of Jayne Smith.

- Select cell A6 to deselect the header.

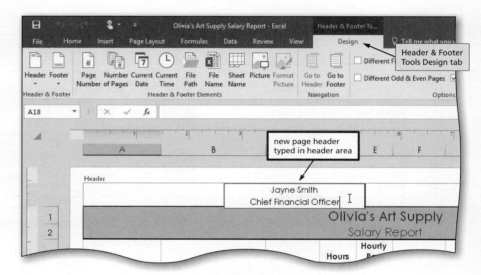

Figure 2–61

Q&A | What else can I place in a header?
You can add additional text, page number information, date and time information, the file path of the workbook, the file name of the workbook, the sheet name of the workbook, and pictures to a header.

4

- Display the Page Layout tab.

- Click the 'Change Page Orientation' button (Page Layout tab | Page Setup group) to display the Change Page Orientation gallery (Figure 2–62).

Figure 2–62

- Click Landscape in the Change Page Orientation gallery to change the worksheet's orientation to landscape (Figure 2–63).

Do I need to change the orientation every time I want to print the worksheet?

No. Once you change the orientation and save the workbook, Excel will save the orientation setting for that workbook until you change it. When you open a new workbook, Excel sets the orientation to portrait.

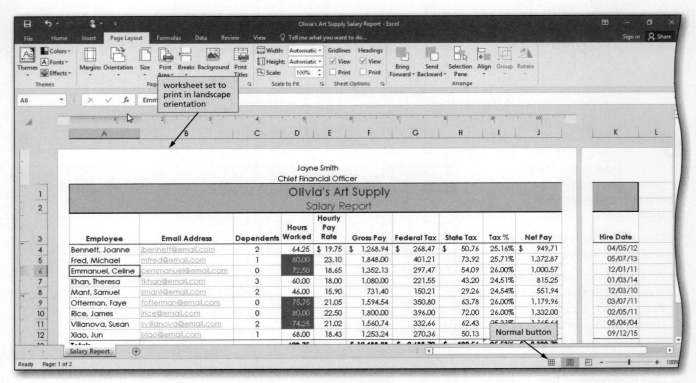

Figure 2–63

Other Ways

1. Click Page Setup Dialog Box Launcher (Page Layout tab | Page Setup group), click Page tab (Page Setup dialog box), click Portrait or Landscape, click OK button

---

To Print a Worksheet

Excel provides multiple options for printing a worksheet. In the following sections, you first print the worksheet and then print a section of the worksheet. The following steps print the worksheet.

1 Click File on the ribbon to open the Backstage view.

2 Click the Print tab in the Backstage view to display the Print gallery.

3 If necessary, click the Printer Status button in the Print gallery to display a list of available Printer options and then click the desired printer to change the currently selected printer.

4 Click the No Scaling button and then select 'Fit Sheet on One Page' to select it.

5 Click the Print button in the Print gallery to print the worksheet in landscape orientation on the currently selected printer.

When the printer stops, retrieve the hard copy (Figure 2–64).

Jayne Smith
Chief Financial Officer

Olivia's Art Supply
Salary Report

Employee	Email Address	Dependents	Hours Worked	Hourly Pay Rate	Gross Pay	Federal Tax	State Tax	Tax %	Net Pay	Hire Date
Bennett, Joanne	jbennett@email.com	2	64.25	$ 19.75	$ 1,268.94	$ 268.47	$ 50.76	25.16%	$ 949.71	04/05/12
Fred, Michael	mfred@email.com	1	80.00	23.10	1,848.00	401.21	73.92	25.71%	1,372.87	05/07/13
Emmanuel. Celine	cemmanuel@email.com	0	72.50	18.65	1,352.13	297.47	54.09	26.00%	1,000.57	12/01/11
Khan, Theresa	tkhan@email.com	3	60.00	18.00	1,080.00	221.55	43.20	24.51%	815.25	01/03/14
Mant, Samuel	smant@email.com	2	46.00	15.90	731.40	150.21	29.26	24.54%	551.94	12/03/10
Otterman, Faye	fotterman@email.com	0	75.75	21.05	1,594.54	350.80	63.78	26.00%	1,179.96	03/07/11
Rice, James	jrice@email.com	0	80.00	22.50	1,800.00	396.00	72.00	26.00%	1,332.00	02/05/11
Villanova, Susan	svillanova@email.com	2	74.25	21.02	1,560.74	332.66	62.43	25.31%	1,165.64	05/06/04
Xiao, Jun	jxiao@email.com	1	68.00	18.43	1,253.24	270.36	50.13	25.57%	932.75	09/12/15
Totals			**620.75**		**$ 12,488.98**	**$ 2,688.72**	**$ 499.56**	**25.53%**	**$ 9,300.70**	
Highest		3	80.00	$23.10	$1,848.00	$401.21	$73.92	26.00%	$1,372.87	
Lowest		0	46.00	$15.90	$731.40	$150.21	$29.26	24.51%	$551.94	
Average		1.222222222	68.97	$19.82	$1,387.66	$298.75	$55.51		$1,033.41	

Figure 2–64

To Print a Section of the Worksheet

1 ENTER FORMULAS | 2 ENTER FUNCTIONS | 3 VERIFY FORMULAS
4 FORMAT WORKSHEET | 5 CHECK SPELLING | 6 PRINT WORKSHEET

You can print portions of the worksheet by selecting the range of cells to print and then clicking the Selection option button in the Print what area in the Print dialog box. **Why?** *To save paper, you only want to print the portion of the worksheet you need, instead of printing the entire worksheet.* The following steps print the range A3:F16.

- Select the range to print, cells A3:F16 in this case.
- Click File on the ribbon to open the Backstage view.
- Click the Print tab to display the Print gallery.
- Click 'Print Active Sheets' in the Settings area (Print tab | Print gallery) to display a list of options that determine what Excel should print (Figure 2–65).

Figure 2–65

2

- Click Print Selection to instruct Excel to print only the selected range.

- Click the Print button in the Print gallery to print the selected range of the worksheet on the currently selected printer (Figure 2–66).

- Click the Normal button on the status bar to return to Normal view.

- Click anywhere in the worksheet, such as cell A18, to deselect the range A3:F16.

Q&A **What can I print?**
Excel includes three options for selecting what to print (Figure 2–65). As shown in the previous steps, the Print Selection option instructs Excel to print the selected range. The 'Print Active Sheets' option instructs Excel to print the active worksheet (the worksheet currently on the screen) or selected worksheets. Finally, the 'Print Entire Workbook' option instructs Excel to print all of the worksheets in the workbook.

Jayne Smith
Chief Financial Officer

Employee	Email Address	Dependents	Hours Worked	Hourly Pay Rate	Gross Pay
Bennett, Joanne	jbennett@email.com	2	64.25	$ 19.75	$ 1,268.94
Fred, Michael	mfred@email.com	1	80.00	23.10	1,848.00
Emmanuel, Celine	cemmanuel@email.com	0	72.50	18.65	1,352.13
Khan, Theresa	tkhan@email.com	3	60.00	18.00	1,080.00
Mant, Samuel	smant@email.com	2	46.00	15.90	731.40
Otterman, Faye	fotterman@email.com	0	75.75	21.05	1,594.54
Rice, James	jrice@email.com	0	80.00	22.50	1,800.00
Villanova, Susan	svillanova@email.com	2	74.25	21.02	1,560.74
Xiao, Jun	jxiao@email.com	1	68.00	18.43	1,253.24
Totals			**620.75**		**$ 12,488.98**
Highest		3	80.00	$23.10	$1,848.00
Lowest		0	46.00	$15.90	$731.40
Average		1.222222222	68.97	$19.82	$1,387.66

Figure 2–66

Other Ways

1. Select range, click Print Area button (Page Layout tab | Page Setup group), click 'Set Print Area', click File tab to open Backstage view, click Print tab, click Print button

Displaying and Printing the Formulas Version of the Worksheet

BTW

Values versus Formulas
When completing class assignments, do not enter numbers in cells that require formulas. Most instructors will check both the values version and formulas version of your worksheets. The formulas version verifies that you entered formulas, rather than numbers, in formula-based cells.

Thus far, you have been working with the values version of the worksheet, which shows the results of the formulas you have entered, rather than the actual formulas. Excel also can display and print the formulas version of the worksheet, which shows the actual formulas you have entered, rather than the resulting values.

The formulas version is useful for debugging a worksheet. **Debugging** is the process of finding and correcting errors in the worksheet. Viewing and printing the formulas version instead of the values version makes it easier to see any mistakes in the formulas.

When you change from the values version to the formulas version, Excel increases the width of the columns so that the formulas do not overflow into adjacent cells, which makes the formulas version of the worksheet significantly wider than the values version. To fit the wide printout on one page, you can use landscape orientation, which already has been selected for the workbook, and the Fit to option in the Page tab in the Page Setup dialog box.

To Display the Formulas in the Worksheet and Fit the Printout on One Page

The following steps change the view of the worksheet from the values version to the formulas version of the worksheet and then print the formulas version on one page. *Why? Printing the formulas in the worksheet can help you verify that your formulas are correct and that the worksheet displays the correct calculations.*

1

• Press CTRL+ACCENT MARK (`) to display the worksheet with formulas.

• Click the right horizontal scroll arrow until column K appears (Figure 2–67).

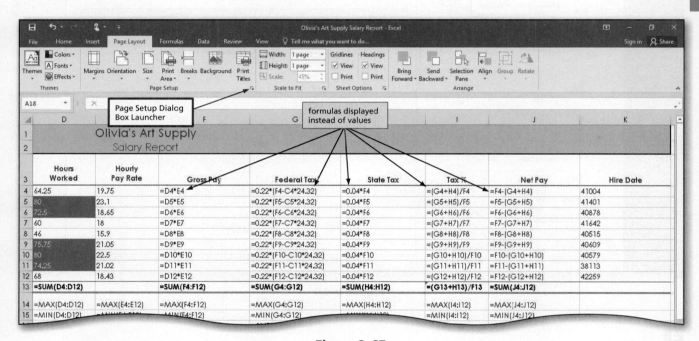

Figure 2–67

2

• Click the Page Setup Dialog Box Launcher (Page Layout tab | Page Setup group) to display the Page Setup dialog box (Figure 2–68).

• If necessary, click Landscape in the Orientation area in the Page tab to select it.

• If necessary, click the Fit to option button in the Scaling area to select it.

Figure 2–68

3

- Click the Print button (Page Setup dialog box) to open the Print tab in the Backstage view. In the Backstage view, select the Print Active Sheets option in the Settings area of the Print gallery (Figure 2–69).

- Click the Print button to print the worksheet.

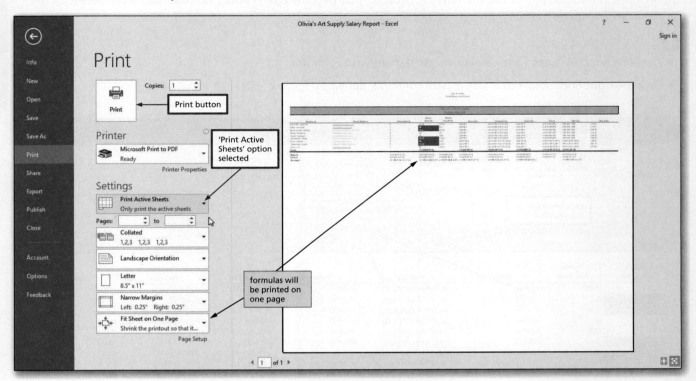

Figure 2–69

4

- After viewing and printing the formulas version, press CTRL+ACCENT MARK (`) to instruct Excel to display the values version.

- Click the left horizontal scroll arrow until column A appears.

To Change the Print Scaling Option Back to 100%

Depending on your printer, you may have to change the Print Scaling option back to 100% after using the Fit to option. Doing so will cause the worksheet to print at the default print scaling of 100%. The following steps reset the Print Scaling option so that future worksheets print at 100%, instead of being resized to print on one page.

1 If necessary, display the Page Layout tab and then click the Page Setup Dialog Box Launcher (Page Layout tab | Page Setup group) to display the Page Setup dialog box.

2 Click the Adjust to option button in the Scaling area to select the Adjust to setting.

3 If necessary, type 100 in the Adjust to box to adjust the print scaling to 100%.

4 Click the OK button (Page Setup dialog box) to set the print scaling to normal.

5 Display the Home tab.

6 Save the workbook again on the same storage location with the same file name.

7 If desired, sign out of your Microsoft account.

8 Exit Excel.

Q&A | What is the purpose of the Adjust to box in the Page Setup dialog box?
The Adjust to box allows you to specify the percentage of reduction or enlargement in the printout of a worksheet. The default percentage is 100%. When you click the Fit to option button, this percentage changes to the percentage required to fit the printout on one page.

Summary

In this module you have learned how to enter formulas, calculate an average, find the highest and lowest numbers in a range, verify formulas using Range Finder, add borders, align text, format numbers, change column widths and row heights, and add conditional formatting to a range of numbers. In addition, you learned how to use the spelling checker to identify misspelled words in a worksheet, print a section of a worksheet, and display and print the formulas version of the worksheet using the Fit to option.

What decisions will you need to make when creating workbooks in the future?

1. Determine the workbook structure.

    a) Determine the formulas and functions you will need for your workbook.

    b) Sketch a layout of your data and functions.

2. Create the worksheet.

    a) Enter the titles, subtitles, and headings.

    b) Enter the data, desired functions, and formulas.

3. Format the worksheet.

    a) Determine the theme for the worksheet.

    b) Format the titles, subtitles, and headings using styles.

    c) Format the totals, minimums, maximums, and averages.

    d) Format the numbers and text.

    e) Resize columns and rows.

CONSIDER THIS: PLAN AHEAD

Apply Your Knowledge

Reinforce the skills and apply the concepts you learned in this module.

Cost Analysis Worksheet

Note: To complete this assignment, you will be required to use the Data Files. Please contact your instructor for information about accessing the required files.

Instructions: Run Excel. Open the workbook Apply 2-1 Proximity Bus. You will enter and copy formulas and functions and apply formatting to the worksheet in order to analyze the costs associated with a bus company's fleet of vehicles, as shown in Figure 2–70.

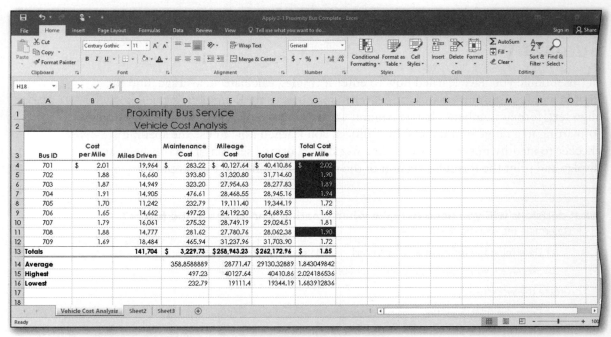

Figure 2–70

Perform the following tasks:

1. Use the following formulas in cells E4, F4, and G4:
   Mileage Cost (cell E4) = Cost per Mile * Miles Driven or = B4 * C4
   Total Cost (cell F4) = Maintenance Cost + Mileage Cost or = D4 + E4
   Total Cost per Mile (cell G4) = Total Cost / Miles Driven or = F4 / C4
   Use the fill handle to copy the three formulas in the range E4:G4 to the range E5:G12.

2. Determine totals for the miles driven, maintenance cost, mileage cost, and total cost in row 13. Copy the formula in cell G12 to G13 to assign the formula in cell G12 to G13 in the total line. If necessary, reapply the Total cell style to cell G13.

3. In the range D14:D16, determine the average value, highest value, and lowest value, respectively, for the values in the range D4:D12. Use the fill handle to copy the three functions to the range E14:G16.

4. Format the worksheet as follows:
   a. Change the workbook theme to Vapor Trail by using the Themes button (Page Layout tab | Themes group)
   b. Cell A1 — change to Title cell style
   c. Cell A2 — change to a font size of 16
   d. Cells A1:A2 — Red, Accent 1, Lighter 60% fill color and a thick outside borders
   e. Cells B4, D4:G4, and D13:G13 — accounting number format with two decimal places and fixed dollar signs by using the 'Accounting Number Format' button (Home tab | Number group)

    f. Cells B5:B12, and D5:G12 — comma style format with two decimal places by using the Comma Style button (Home tab | Number group)

    g. Cells C4:C13 — comma style format with no decimal places.

    h. Cells G4:G12 — apply conditional formatting so that cells with a value greater than 1.85 appear with a red background color and white font

5. If necessary increase the size of any columns that do not properly display data.

6. Switch to Page Layout view. Enter your name, course, laboratory assignment number, and any other information, as specified by your instructor, in the Header area.

7. Preview and print the worksheet in landscape orientation. Save the workbook using the file name, Apply 2-1 Proximity Bus Complete.

8. Use Range Finder to verify the formula in cell G13.

9. Print the range A3:D16. Press CTRL+ACCENT MARK (`) to change the display from the values version of the worksheet to the formulas version. Print the formulas version in landscape orientation on one page by using the Fit to option in the Page tab in the Page Setup dialog box. Press CTRL+ACCENT MARK (`) to change the display of the worksheet back to the values version. Close the workbook without saving it.

10. ✳ Besides adding a header to your document, can you think of anything else that could be added when printing the worksheet?

11. Submit the workbook as specified by your instructor.

Extend Your Knowledge

Extend the skills you learned in this module and experiment with new skills. You may need to use Help to complete the assignment.

Creating a Customer Tracking Worksheet for Jonee's Animal Supply

Note: To complete this assignment, you will be required to use the Data Files. Please contact your instructor for information about accessing the required files.

Instructions: Run Excel. Open the workbook Extend 2–1 Jonee's Animal Supply. You are to apply Flash Fill and four types of conditional formatting to cells in a worksheet (Figure 2–71).

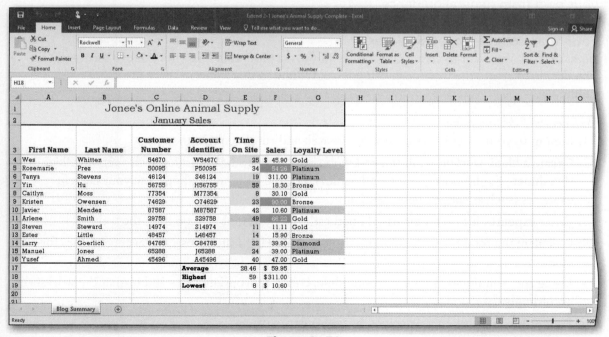

Figure 2–71

Continued >

Extend Your Knowledge *continued*

Perform the following tasks:

1. Add the account identifiers to the cells in the range D4:D16. The account identifier is determined by taking the first initial of the customer's last name followed by the entire customer number. For example, the account identifier for Wes Whitten is W54670. Continue entering two or three account identifiers, then use Flash Fill to complete the remaining cells. If necessary, add the thick bottom border back to cell D16.

2. Select the range E4:E16. Click the Conditional Formatting button (Home tab | Styles group) and then click New Rule on the Conditional Formatting menu. Select 'Format only top or bottom ranked values' in the Select a Rule Type area (New Formatting Rule dialog box).

3. If requested by your instructor, enter any value between 10 and 30 in the text box, (otherwise enter 20) in the Edit the Rule Description (New Formatting Rule dialog box) area, and then click the '% of the selected range' check box to select it.

4. Click the Format button, and choose a light purple background in the Fill sheet to assign this conditional format. Click the OK button in each dialog box and view the worksheet.

5. With range E4:E16 selected, apply a conditional format to the range that uses a yellow background color to highlight cells with scores that are below average. *Hint:* Explore some of the preset conditional rules to assist with formatting this range of cells.

6. With range F4:F16 selected, apply a conditional format to the range that uses a white font and green background to highlight cells that contain a value between 50 and 150.

7. With range G4:G16 selected, apply a conditional format to the range that uses a light gray background color to highlight cells that contain Platinum or Diamond. (*Hint:* You need to apply two separate formats, one for Platinum and one for Diamond.)

8. ✳ When might you want to look for values above the average in a worksheet?

9. Save the workbook using the file name, Extend 2–1 Jonee's Animal Supply Complete. Submit the revised workbook as specified by your instructor.

Expand Your World

Create a solution that uses cloud or web technologies by learning and investigating on your own from general guidance.

Four-Year College Cost Calculator

Instructions: You want to create an estimate of the cost for attending your college for four years. You decide to create the worksheet using Excel Online so that you can share it with your friends online.

Perform the following tasks:

1. Sign in to your Microsoft account on the web and run Excel Online.

2. Create a blank workbook. In the first worksheet, use row headings for each year of college (Freshman, Sophomore, Junior, and Senior). For the column headings, use your current expenses (such as car payment, rent, utilities, tuition, and food).

3. Enter expenses for each year based upon estimates you find by searching the web.

4. Calculate the total for each column. Also determine highest, lowest, and average values for each column.

5. Using the techniques taught in this module, create appropriate titles and format the worksheet accordingly.

6. Submit the assignment as specified by your instructor.

In the Labs

Design, create, modify, and/or use a workbook following the guidelines, concepts, and skills presented in this module. Labs 1 and 2, which increase in difficulty, require you to create solutions based on what you learned in the module; Lab 3 requires you to apply your creative thinking and problem-solving skills to design and implement a solution.

Lab 1: Insurance Premium Worksheet

Problem: You are a part-time assistant in the accounting department at Aylin Insurance, an Orlando-based insurance company. You have been asked to use Excel to generate a report that summarizes the existing balances on annual premiums, similar to the one shown in Figure 2–72. Include the three columns of customer data in Table 2-6 in the report, plus two additional columns to compute a monthly fee and a current balance for each customer. Assume no negative unpaid monthly balances.

Perform the following tasks:

1. Enter and format the worksheet title **Aylin Insurance** and worksheet subtitle **Premium Analysis** in cells A1 and A2. Change the theme of the worksheet to the Berlin theme. Apply the Title cell style to cells A1 and A2. Change the font size in cell A1 to 26 points, and change the font size in cell A2 to 18 points. Merge and center the worksheet title and subtitle across columns A through E. Draw a thick outside border around the range A1:A2.

2. Change the width of column A to 20.00 points. Change the widths of columns B through E to 14.00 points. Change the heights of row 3 to 36.00 points and row 14 to 25.50 points.

Table 2–6 Aylin Insurance Premium Data

Customer	Previous Balance	Payments
Albasco, Robin	1600.72	72.15
Deon, Jade	1518.62	382.3
Goodman, Brad	679.29	80.69
Hill, Raine	1060.42	107.6
Klonde, Albert	1178.83	125.63
Lang, Rose	1280.2	79.85
Moore, Jeffrey	1253.88	389.79
Piper, Taylor	477.11	278.52
Sothens, Mary	821.31	153.14

© 2015 Cengage Learning

Figure 2–72

Continued >

In the Labs *continued*

3. Enter the column titles in row 3 and row titles in the range A13:A16, as shown in Figure 2–72. Center the column titles in the range A3:E3. Apply the Heading 4 cell style to the range A3:E3. Apply the Total cell style to the range A13:E13. Bold the titles in the range A13:A16. Change the font size in the range A3:E16 to 12 points.

4. Enter the data in Table 2-6 in the range A4:C12.

5. Use the following formulas to determine the installment fee in column D and the current balance in column E for the first customer. Copy the two formulas down through the remaining customers.

   a. Installment Fee (cell D4) = 1% * Previous Balance

   b. Current Balance (E4) = Previous Balance – Payments + Installment Fee

6. Determine the totals in row 13.

7. Determine the average, minimum, and maximum values in cells B14:B16 for the range B4:B12, and then copy the range B14:B16 to C14:E16.

8. Format the numbers as follows: (a) assign the currency style with a floating dollar sign to the cells containing numeric data in the ranges B4:E4 and B13:E16, and (b) assign a number style with two decimal places and a thousand's separator (currency with no dollar sign) to the range B5:E12.

9. Use conditional formatting to change the formatting to white font on an orange background in any cell in the range D4:D12 that contains a value greater than 10.

10. Change the worksheet name from Sheet1 to Loan Balance and the sheet tab color to the Orange standard color.

11. Change the worksheet header with your name, course number, and other information as specified by your instructor.

12. Use the spelling checker to check the spelling in the worksheet. Preview and then print the worksheet in landscape orientation. Save the workbook using the file name, Lab 2-1 Aylin Insurance Premium Analysis.

13. ✳ When you created the formula for the installment fee, you used 1%. What would you have to do if the rate changed today to 2% to update the formulas?

Lab 2: **Sales Summary Worksheet**

Problem: You have been asked to build a worksheet for International Moving Company that analyzes the financing needs for the company's first year in business. The company plans to begin operations in January with an initial investment of $750,000.00. The expected revenue and costs for the company's first year are shown in Table 2–7. The desired worksheet is shown in Figure 2–73. The initial investment is shown as the starting balance for January (cell B4). The amount of financing required by the company is shown as the lowest ending balance (cell F18).

Table 2–7 International Moving Company Financing Needs Data		
Month	**Incomes**	**Expenses**
January	1209081	1262911
February	1163811	1381881
March	1300660	1250143
April	1229207	1209498
May	1248369	1355232
June	1196118	1260888
July	1162970	1242599
August	1195824	1368955
September	1305669	1235604
October	1224741	1383254
November	1159644	1411768
December	1210000	1540000

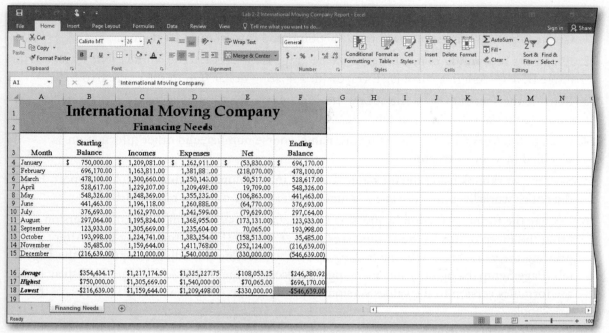

Figure 2–73

Perform the following tasks:

1. Apply the Slate theme to a new workbook.

2. Increase the width of column A to 12.00 and the width of columns B through F to 14.50.

3. Enter the worksheet title **International Moving Company** in cell A1 and the worksheet subtitle **Financing Needs** in cell A2. Enter the column titles in row 3, as shown in Figure 2–73. In row 3, use ALT–ENTER to start a new line in a cell.

4. Enter the financing needs data described in Table 2-7 in columns A, C, and D in rows 4 through 15. Enter the initial starting balance (cell B4) of 750000.00. Enter the row titles in the range A16:A18, as shown in Figure 2–73.

5. For the months of February through December, the starting balance is equal to the previous month's ending balance. Obtain the starting balance for February by setting the starting balance of February to the ending balance of January. Use a cell reference rather than typing in the data. Copy the formula for February to the remaining months.

6. Obtain the net amounts in column E by subtracting the expenses in column D from the incomes in column C. Enter the formula in cell E4 and copy it to the range E5:E15. Obtain the ending balance amounts in column F by adding the starting balance in column B to the net in column E. Enter the formula in cell F4 and copy it to the range F5:F15.

7. In the range B16:B18, use the AVERAGE, MAX, and MIN functions to determine the average value, highest value, and lowest value in the range B4:B15. Copy the range B16:B18 to the range C16:F18.

8. One at a time, merge and center the worksheet title and subtitle across columns A through F. Select cells A1 and A2 and change the background color to Tan, Accent 2 from the theme colors (column 6, row 1). Apply the Title cell style to cells A1 and A2. Change the worksheet title in cell A1 to 26-point. Bold both the title and subtitle. Draw a thick outside border around the range A1:A2.

9. Center the titles in row 3, columns A through F. Apply the Heading 2 cell style to the range A3:F3. Italicize and bold the row titles in the range A16:A18.

10. Draw a thick outside border around the range A16:F18. Change the background color for cell F18 to the same colors applied to the worksheet title in Step 8.

Continued >

In the Labs *continued*

11. Change the row heights of row 3 to 42.00 points and row 16 to 33.00 points.

12. Assign the accounting number format to the range B4:F4. Assign the comma style format to the range B5:F15. Assign a currency format with a floating dollar sign to the range B16:F18.

13. Rename the sheet tab as **Financing Needs**. Apply the Orange color from the standard colors (column 3) to the sheet tab.

14. Change the worksheet header with your name, course number, and other information as specified by your instructor.

15. Save the workbook using the file name, Lab 2-2 International Moving Company Report. Print the entire worksheet in landscape orientation. Next, print only the range A3:B15.

16. Display the formulas version by pressing CTRL+ACCENT MARK (`). Print the formulas version using the Fit to option in the Scaling area in the Page tab (Page Setup dialog box). After printing the worksheet, reset the Scaling option by selecting the Adjust to option in the Page tab (Page Setup dialog box) and changing the percent value to 100%. Change the display from the formulas version to the values version by pressing CTRL+ACCENT MARK (`). Do not save the workbook.

17. Submit the revised workbook as requested by your instructor.

18. ✸ In reviewing the worksheet you created, how do you think the company could obtain a positive result without increasing income or decreasing expenses?

Lab 3: Consider This: Your Turn

Apply your creative thinking and problem-solving skills to design and implement a solution.

Internet Service Summary

Instructions Part 1:   You and your friends have decided to subscribe to a new Internet service provider. You would like to maximize services while keeping costs low. Research and find three Internet service providers in your area. If you cannot find three service providers in your area, you can research three service providers in another area of your choosing. For each company, find the best service package as well as the basic service package. Using the cost figures you find, calculate the cost per month for each service for a year. Include totals, minimum, maximum, and average values. Use the concepts and techniques presented in this module to create and format the worksheet.

Instructions Part 2:   Which companies did you choose for your report? Which services offered the best deals that you would be willing to use?

3 Working with Large Worksheets, Charting, and What-If Analysis

Objectives

You will have mastered the material in this module when you can:

- Rotate text in a cell
- Create a series of month names
- Copy, paste, insert, and delete cells
- Format numbers using format symbols
- Enter and format the system date
- Use absolute and mixed cell references in a formula
- Use the IF function to perform a logical test
- Create and format sparkline charts
- Change sparkline chart types and styles
- Use the Format Painter button to format cells

- Create a clustered column chart on a separate chart sheet
- Use chart filters to display a subset of data in a chart
- Change the chart type and style
- Reorder sheet tabs
- Change the worksheet view
- Freeze and unfreeze rows and columns
- Answer what-if questions
- Goal seek to answer what-if questions
- Use the Smart Lookup Insight
- Understand accessibility features

Introduction

This module introduces you to techniques that will enhance your ability to create worksheets and draw charts. This module also covers other methods for entering values in cells, such as allowing Excel to automatically enter and format values based on a perceived pattern in the existing values. In addition, you will learn how to use absolute cell references and how to use the IF function to assign a value to a cell based on a logical test.

When you set up a worksheet, you should use cell references in formulas whenever possible, rather than constant values. The use of a cell reference allows you to change a value in multiple formulas by changing the value in a single cell. The cell references in a formula are called assumptions. **Assumptions** are values in cells that you can change to determine new values for formulas. This module emphasizes the use of assumptions and shows how to use assumptions to answer what-if questions, such as what happens to the six-month operating income if you decrease the Equipment

BTW
Excel Screen Resolution
If you are using a computer or mobile device to step through the project in this module and you want your screens to match the figures in this book, you should change your screen's resolution to 1366 x 768. For information about how to change a computer's resolution, refer to the Office and Windows module at the beginning of this book.

Repair and Maintenance expenses assumption by 1%. Being able to analyze the effect of changing values in a worksheet is an important skill in making business decisions.

Worksheets are normally much larger than those you created in the previous modules, often extending beyond the size of the Excel window. When you cannot view the entire worksheet on the screen at once, working with a large worksheet can be frustrating. This module introduces several Excel commands that allow you to control what is displayed on the screen so that you can focus on critical parts of a large worksheet. One command allows you to freeze rows and columns so that they remain visible, even when you scroll. Another command splits the worksheet into separate panes so that you can view different parts of a worksheet on the screen at once. Another changes the magnification to allow you to see more content, albeit at a smaller size. This is useful for reviewing the general layout of content on the worksheet.

From your work in Module 1, you know how easily you can create charts in Excel. This module covers additional charting techniques that allow you to convey meaning visually, such as by using sparkline charts or clustered column charts. This module also introduces the Accessibility checker.

Project — Financial Projection Worksheet with What-If Analysis and Chart

The project in this module uses Excel to create the worksheet and clustered column chart shown in Figures 3-1a and 3-1b. Kaitlyn's Ice Cream Shoppe operates kiosks at colleges and universities and serves both hard and soft serve ice cream. Each December and June, the chief executive officer projects monthly sales revenues, costs of goods sold, gross margin, expenses, and operating income for the upcoming six-month period, based on figures from the previous six months. The CEO requires an easy-to-read worksheet that shows financial projections for the upcoming six months to use for procuring partial financing and for determining staffing needs. The worksheet should allow for quick analysis, if projections for certain numbers change, such as the percentage of expenses

(a) Worksheet

Figure 3–1

(b) Clustered Column Chart

Figure 3–1 (Continued)

allocated to commission or the cost of the kiosk rentals. In addition, you need to create a column chart that shows the breakdown of expenses for each month in the period.

The requirements document for the Kaitlyn's Ice Cream Shoppe Six-Month Financial Projection worksheet is shown in Figure 3–2. It includes the needs, source of data, summary of calculations, and chart requirements.

Worksheet Title	Kaitlyn's Ice Cream Shoppe Six-Month Financial Projection
Needs	• A woksheet that shows Kaitlyn's Ice Cream Shoppe projected monthly sales revenue, cost of goods sold, gross margin, expenses, and operating income for a six-month period. • A clustered column chart that shows the expected contribution of each expense category to total expenses.
Source of Data	Data supplied by the business owner includes projections of the monthly sales and expenses based on prior year figures (see Table 3–1). Remaining numbers in the worksheet are based on formulas.
Calculations	The following calculations are needed for each month: • Cost of Goods Sold = Revenue * (1 − Margin) • Gross Margin = Revenue − Cost of Goods Sold • Bonus expense = Predetermined bonus amount if Revenue exceeds the Revenue for Bonus, otherwise Bonus = 0 • Commission expense = Commission percentage × Revenue • Site Rental expense = Kiosk Rental Percentage × Revenue • Marketing expense = Marketing percentage × Revenue • Equipment Repair and Maintenance expense = Equipment Repair and Maintenance percentage × Revenue • Total expenses = sum of all expenses • Operating Income = Gross Margin − Total expenses
Chart Requirements	• Show sparkline charts for revenue and each of the items noted in the calculations area above. • Show a clustered column chart that shows the contributions of each month's expense categories to the total monthly expense figure.

Figure 3–2

Using a sketch of the worksheet can help you visualize its design. The sketch of the worksheet consists of titles, column and row headings, location of data values, calculations, and a rough idea of the desired formatting (Figure 3–3a). The sketch of the clustered column chart shows the expected expenses for each of the six months (Figure 3–3b). The assumptions about income and expenses will be entered at the bottom of the worksheet (Figure 3–3a). The projected monthly sales revenue will be entered in row 4 of the worksheet. The projected monthly sales revenue and the assumptions shown in Table 3–1 will be used to calculate the remaining numbers in the worksheet.

(a) Worksheet

(b) Clustered Column Chart

Figure 3–3

Table 3–1 Kaitlyn's Ice Cream Shoppe Six-Month Financial Projections Data and What-If Assumptions	
Projected Monthly Total Sales Revenues	
January	55,000.00
February	62,500.00
March	67,000.00
April	90,250.00
May	77,500.00
June	74,750.00
What-If Assumptions	
Margin	78.75%
Bonus	$3,500.00
Sales Revenue for Bonus	65,000.00
Commission	25.00%
Site Rental	10.00%
Marketing	5.00%
Equipment Repair and Maintenance	3.50%

With a solid understanding of the requirements document, an understanding of the necessary decisions, and a sketch of the worksheet, the next step is to use Excel to create the worksheet.

In this module, you will learn how to create and use the workbook shown in Figure 3–1. The following roadmap identifies general activities you will perform as you progress through this module:

1. ENTER the HEADINGS and DATA in the worksheet.
2. ENTER FORMULAS and FUNCTIONS in the worksheet.
3. CREATE SPARKLINE CHARTS in a range of cells.
4. FORMAT the WORKSHEET.
5. CREATE a COLUMN CHART on a separate chart sheet.
6. CHANGE VIEWS of the worksheet.
7. ASK WHAT-IF QUESTIONS.

BTW
Excel Help
At any time while using Excel, you can find answers to questions and display information about various topics through Excel Help. Used properly, this form of assistance can increase your productivity and reduce your frustrations by minimizing the time you spend learning how to use Excel. For instructions about Excel Help and exercises that will help you gain confidence in using it, read the Office and Windows module at the beginning of this book.

To Enter the Worksheet Titles and Apply a Theme

The worksheet contains two titles in cells A1 and A2. In the previous modules, titles were centered across the worksheet. With large worksheets that extend beyond the size of a window, it is best to leave titles left-aligned, as shown in the sketch of the worksheet in Figure 3–3a, so that the worksheet will print the title on the first page if the worksheet requires multiple pages. This allows the user to easily find the worksheet title when necessary. The following steps enter the worksheet titles and change the workbook theme to Savon.

1 Run Excel and create a blank workbook in the Excel window.

2 Select cell A1 and then type `Kaitlyn's Ice Cream Shoppe` as the worksheet title.

3 Select cell A2, type `Six-Month Financial Projection` as the worksheet subtitle, and then press the ENTER key to enter the worksheet subtitle.

4 Apply the Savon theme to the workbook.

BTW
The Ribbon and Screen Resolution
Excel may change how the groups and buttons within the groups appear on the ribbon, depending on the computer or mobile device's screen resolution. Thus, your ribbon may look different from the ones in this book if you are using a screen resolution other than 1366 x 768.

BTW
Rotating Text in a Cell
In Excel, you use the Alignment sheet in the Format Cells dialog box (shown in Figure 3–5) to position data in a cell by centering, left-aligning, or right-aligning; indenting; aligning at the top, bottom, or center; and rotating. If you enter 90 in the Degrees box in the Orientation area, the text will appear vertically and read from bottom to top in the cell.

Rotating Text and Using the Fill Handle to Create a Series

The data on the worksheet, including month names and the What-If Assumptions section, now can be added to the worksheet.

What should you take into account when planning a worksheet layout?
Using Excel, you can change text and number formatting in many ways, which affects the visual impact of the worksheet. Rotated text often provides a strong visual appeal. Rotated text also allows you to fit more text into a smaller column width. When laying out a worksheet, keep in mind the content you want to emphasize and the length of the cell titles relative to the numbers.

CONSIDER THIS

To Rotate Text in a Cell

The design of the worksheet calls specifically for data for the six months of the selling season. Because there always will be only six months of data in the worksheet, place the months across the top of the worksheet as column headings rather than as row headings. Place the income and expense categories in rows, as they are more numerous than the number of months. This layout allows you to easily navigate the worksheet. Ideally, a proper layout will create a worksheet that is longer than it is wide.

When you first enter text, its angle is zero degrees (0°), and it reads from left to right in a cell. Excel allows you to rotate text in a cell counterclockwise by entering a number between 1° and 90°. **Why?** *Rotating text is one method of making column headings visually distinct.* The following steps enter the month name, January, in cell B3 and format cell B3 by rotating the text.

- If necessary, click the Home tab and then select cell B3 because this cell will include the first month name in the series of month names.

- Type **January** as the cell entry and then click the Enter button.

- Click the Alignment Settings Dialog Box Launcher (Home tab | Alignment group) to display the Format Cells dialog box (Figure 3–4).

Figure 3–4

2

- Click the 60° point in the Orientation area (Format Cells dialog box) to move the indicator in the Orientation area to the 60° point and display a new orientation in the Degrees box (Figure 3–5).

Figure 3–5

- Click the OK button (Format Cells dialog box) to rotate the text in the active cell and increase the height of the current row to best fit the rotated text (Figure 3–6).

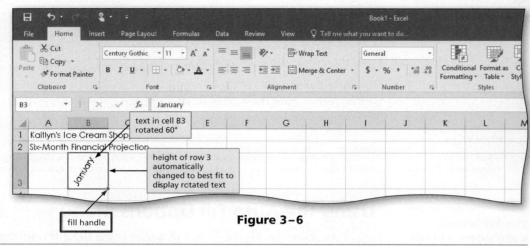

Figure 3–6

Other Ways

1. Right-click selected cell, click Format Cells on shortcut menu, click Alignment tab (Format Cells dialog box), click 60° point, click OK button

To Use the Fill Handle to Create a Series of Month Names

| 1 ENTER HEADINGS & DATA | 2 ENTER FORMULAS & FUNCTIONS | 3 CREATE SPARKLINE CHARTS |
| 4 FORMAT WORKSHEET | 5 CREATE COLUMN CHART | 6 CHANGE VIEWS | 7 ASK WHAT-IF QUESTIONS |

Why? *Once the first month in the series has been entered and formatted, you can complete the data series using the fill handle rather than typing and formatting all the entries.* The following steps use the fill handle and the entry in cell B3 to create a series of month names in cells C3:G3.

- Drag the fill handle on the lower-right corner of cell B3 to the right to select the range to fill, C3:G3 in this case. Do not release the mouse button (Figure 3–7).

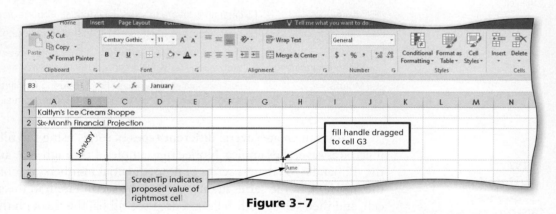

Figure 3–7

2

- Release the mouse button to create a month name series in the selected range and copy the format of the selected cell to the selected range.

- Click the 'Auto Fill Options' button below the lower-right corner of the fill area to display the Auto Fill Options menu (Figure 3–8).

Q&A What if I do not want to copy the format of cell B3 during the auto fill operation?

In addition to creating a series of values, dragging the fill handle instructs Excel to copy the format of cell B3 to the range C3:G3. With some fill operations, you may not want to copy the formats of the source cell or range to the destination cell or range. If this is the case, click the 'Auto Fill Options' button after the range fills and then select the desired option on the Auto Fill Options menu (Figure 3–8).

Figure 3–8

- Click the 'Auto Fill Options' button to hide the Auto Fill Options menu.

- Select cell H3, type **Total**, and then press the RIGHT ARROW key to enter a column heading.

- Type **Chart** in cell I3 and then press the RIGHT ARROW key.

Q&A Why is the word, Total, formatted with a 60° rotation?
Excel tries to save you time by recognizing the format in adjacent cell G3 and applying it to cell H3. Such behavior also occurs when typing the column heading in cell I3.

Other Ways

1. Type text in cell, apply formatting, right-drag fill handle in direction to fill, click Fill Months on shortcut menu

2. Type text in cell, apply formatting, select range, click Fill button (Home tab | Editing group), click Series, click AutoFill (Series dialog box), click OK button

Using the Auto Fill Options Menu

BTW
The Fill Handle
If you drag the fill handle up or to the left, Excel will decrement the series rather than increment the series. To copy a word, such as January or Monday, which Excel might interpret as the start of a series, hold down the CTRL key while you drag the fill handle to a destination area. If you drag the fill handle back into the middle of a cell, Excel erases the contents of the cell.

As shown in Figure 3–8, Fill Series is the default option that Excel uses to fill an area, which means it fills the destination area with a series, using the same formatting as the source area. If you choose another option on the Auto Fill Options menu, Excel changes the contents of the destination range. Following the use of the fill handle, the 'Auto Fill Options' button remains active until you begin the next Excel operation. Table 3–2 summarizes the options on the Auto Fill Options menu.

Table 3–2 Options Available on the Auto Fill Options Menu

Auto Fill Option	Description
Copy Cells	Fill destination area with contents using format of source area. Do not create a series.
Fill Series	Fill destination area with series using format of source area. This option is the default.
Fill Formatting Only	Fill destination area using format of source area. No content is copied unless fill is series.
Fill Without Formatting	Fill destination area with contents, without applying the formatting of source area.
Fill Months	Fill destination area with series of months using format of source area. Same as Fill Series and shows as an option only if source area contains the name of a month.

You can create several different types of series using the fill handle. Table 3–3 illustrates several examples. Notice in examples 4 through 7, 9, and 11 that, if you use the fill handle to create a series of nonsequential numbers or months, you must enter the first item in the series in one cell and the second item in the series in an adjacent cell, and then select both cells and drag the fill handle through the destination area.

BTW
Custom Fill Sequences
You can create your own custom fill sequences for use with the fill handle. For example, if you often type the same list of products or names in Excel, you can create a custom fill sequence. You then can type the first product or name and then use the fill handle automatically to fill in the remaining products or names. To create a custom fill sequence, display the Excel Options dialog box by clicking Options in the Backstage view. Click the Advanced tab (Excel Options dialog box) and then click the 'Edit Custom Lists' button in the General section (Excel Options dialog box).

Table 3–3 Examples of Series Using the Fill Handle

Example	Contents of Cell(s) Copied Using the Fill Handle	Next Three Values of Extended Series
1	4:00	5:00, 6:00, 7:00
2	Qtr2	Qtr3, Qtr4, Qtr1
3	Quarter 1	Quarter 2, Quarter 3, Quarter 4
4	22-Jul, 22-Sep	22-Nov, 22-Jan, 22-Mar
5	2017, 2018	2019, 2020, 2021
6	1, 2	3, 4, 5
7	625, 575	525, 475, 425
8	Mon	Tue, Wed, Thu
9	Sunday, Tuesday	Thursday, Saturday, Monday
10	4th Section	5th Section, 6th Section, 7th Section
11	2205, 2208	2211, 2214, 2217

To Increase Column Widths

Why? In Module 2, you increased column widths after the values were entered into the worksheet. Sometimes, you may want to increase the column widths before you enter values and, if necessary, adjust them later. The following steps increase the column widths.

- Move the pointer to the boundary between column heading A and column heading B so that the pointer changes to a split double arrow in preparation of adjusting the column widths.

- Drag the pointer to the right until the ScreenTip displays the desired column width, Width: 38.00 (309 pixels) in this case. Do not release the mouse button (Figure 3–9).

Figure 3–9

- Release the mouse button to change the width of the column.

- Click column heading B to select the column and then drag through column heading G to select the range in which to change the widths.

- Move the pointer to the boundary between column headings B and C in preparation of resizing column B and then drag the pointer to the right until the ScreenTip displays the desired width, Width: 14.50 (121 pixels) in this case. Do not lift your finger or release the mouse button (Figure 3–10).

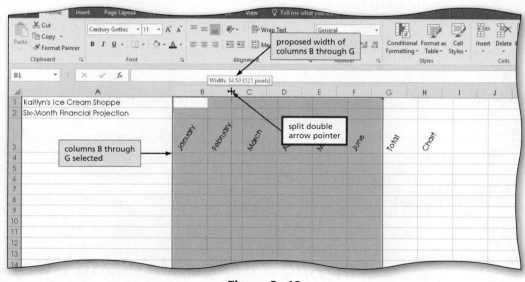

Figure 3–10

- Release the mouse button to change the width of the selected columns.

- If necessary, scroll the worksheet so that column H is visible and then use the technique described in Step 1 to increase the width of column H to 18.00 (149 pixels).

To Enter and Indent Row Titles

Excel allows you to indent text in cells. The following steps enter the row titles in column A and indent several of the row titles to create a visual hierarchy. *Why? You can create a hierarchy by indenting some of the row titles, like in an outline or table of contents.*

- If necessary, scroll the worksheet so that column A and row 4 are visible and then enter **Revenue** in cell A4, **Cost of Goods Sold** in cell A5, **Gross Margin** in cell A6, **Expenses** in cell A8, **Bonus** in cell A9, **Commission** in cell A10, **Site Rental** in cell A11, **Marketing** in cell A12, **Equipment Repair and Maintenance** in cell A13, **Total Expenses** in cell A14, and **Operating Income** in cell A16.

- Select cell A5 and then click the Increase Indent button (Home tab | Alignment group) to increase the indentation of the text in the selected cell.

- Select the range A9:A13 and then click the Increase Indent button (Home tab | Alignment group) to increase the indentation of the text in the selected range (Figure 3–11).

Figure 3–11

- Select cell A18 to finish entering the row titles and deselect the current cell.

Q&A

What happens when I click the Increase Indent button?

The Increase Indent button (Home tab | Alignment group) indents the contents of a cell two spaces to the right each time you click it. The Decrease Indent button decreases the indent by two spaces each time you click it.

Other Ways

1. Right-click range, click Format Cells on shortcut menu, click Alignment tab (Format Cells dialog box), click Left (Indent) in Horizontal list, type number of spaces to indent in Indent box, click OK button (Format Cells dialog box)

Copying a Range of Cells to a Nonadjacent Destination Area

The What-If Assumptions section should be placed in an area of the worksheet that is accessible yet does not impair the view of the main section of the worksheet. As shown in Figure 3–3a, the What-If Assumptions will be placed below the calculations in the worksheet. This will allow the reader to see the main section of the worksheet when first opening the workbook. Additionally, the row titles in the Expenses area are the same as the row titles in the What-If Assumptions table, with the exception of the two additional entries in cells A19 (Margin) and A21 (Sales Revenue for Bonus). Hence, the row titles in the What-If Assumptions table can be created by copying the range A9:A13 to the range A19:A23 and then inserting two rows for the additional entries in cells A19 and A21. You cannot use the fill handle to copy the range because the source area (range A9:A13) is not adjacent to the destination area (range A19:A23).

A more versatile method of copying a source area is to use the Copy button and Paste button (Home tab | Clipboard group). You can use these two buttons to copy a source area to an adjacent or nonadjacent destination area.

BTW

Fitting Entries in a Cell

An alternative to increasing column widths or row heights is to shrink the characters in a cell to fit the current width of the column. To shrink to fit, click Format Cells Alignment Dialog Box Button Launcher (Home tab | Alignment group) and then place a check mark in the 'Shrink to fit' check box in the Text control area (Format Cells dialog box).

To Copy a Range of Cells to a Nonadjacent Destination Area

1 ENTER HEADINGS & DATA | 2 ENTER FORMULAS & FUNCTIONS | 3 CREATE SPARKLINE CHARTS
4 FORMAT WORKSHEET | 5 CREATE COLUMN CHART | 6 CHANGE VIEWS | 7 ASK WHAT-IF QUESTIONS

The Copy button copies the contents and format of the source area to the **Office Clipboard**, a temporary storage area in the computer's memory that allows you to collect text and graphics from any Office document and then paste them into almost any other type of document. The Paste button pastes a copy of the contents of the Office Clipboard in the destination area. *Why? Copying the range of cells rather than reentering the content assures consistency within the worksheet.* The following steps enter the What-If Assumptions row heading and then use the Copy and Paste buttons to copy the range A9:A13 to the nonadjacent range A19:A23.

1

- With cell A18 selected, type **What-If Assumptions** as the new row title and then click the Enter button.

- Select the range A9:A13 and then click the Copy button (Home tab | Clipboard group) to copy the values and formats of the selected range, A9:A13 in this case, to the Office Clipboard.

- Select cell A19, the top cell in the destination area (Figure 3–12).

Q&A Why do I not select the entire destination area?
You are not required to select the entire destination area (A19:A23) because Excel only needs to know the upper-left cell of the destination area. In the case of a single column range, such as A19:A23, the top cell of the destination area (cell A19) also is the upper-left cell of the destination area.

Figure 3–12

2

- Click the Paste button (Home tab | Clipboard group) to copy the values and formats of the last item placed on the Office Clipboard, range A9:A13, to the destination area, A19:A23. If necessary, scroll down to see the complete destination area (Figure 3–13).

Q&A

What if there was data in the destination area before I clicked the Paste button?

Any data contained in the destination area prior to the copy and paste is lost. When you complete a copy, the values and formats in the destination area are replaced with the values and formats of the source area. If you accidentally delete valuable data, click the Undo button on the Quick Access Toolbar or press CTRL+Z.

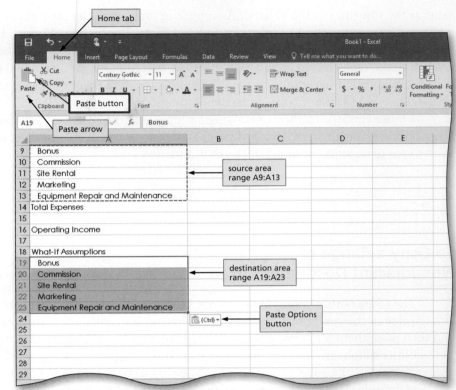

Figure 3–13

3

- Press the ESC key to remove the marquee from the source area and disable the Paste button (Home tab | Clipboard group).

Other Ways

1. Right-click source area, click Copy on shortcut menu, right-click destination area, click Paste icon on shortcut menu
2. Select source area and point to border of range; while holding down CTRL key, drag source area to destination area
3. Select source area, press CTRL+C, select destination area, press CTRL+V

BTW

Copying and Pasting from Other Programs

If you need data in Excel that is stored in another program, copying and pasting likely will help you. You might need to experiment before you are successful, because Excel might attempt to copy formatting or other information that you did not intend to paste from the other program. Trying various Paste Option buttons will solve most of such problems.

BTW

Move It or Copy It

Contrary to popular belief, move and copy operations are not the same. When you move a cell, the data in the original location is cleared and the format of the cell is reset to the default. When you copy a cell, the data and format of the copy area remains intact. In short, you should copy cells to duplicate entries and move cells to rearrange entries.

Using the Paste Options Menu

After you click the Paste button, Excel displays the Paste Options button, as shown in Figure 3–13. If you click the Paste Options arrow and select an option in the Paste Options gallery, Excel modifies the most recent paste operation based on your selection. Table 3–4 summarizes the options available in the Paste Options gallery. When the Paste Options button is visible, you can use keyboard shortcuts to access the paste commands available in the Paste Options gallery. Additionally, you can use combinations of the options in the Paste Options gallery to customize your paste operation. That is, after clicking one of the icons in the Paste Options gallery, you can display the gallery again to further adjust your paste operation. The Paste button (Home tab | Clipboard group) includes an arrow that, when clicked, displays the same options as the Paste Options button.

An alternative to clicking the Paste button is to press the ENTER key. The ENTER key completes the paste operation, removes the marquee from the source area, and disables the Paste button so that you cannot paste the copied source area to other destination areas. The ENTER key was not used in the previous set of steps so that the capabilities of the Paste Options button could be discussed. The Paste Options button does not appear on the screen when you use the ENTER key to complete the paste operation.

Using Drag and Drop to Move or Copy Cells

You also can use the mouse to move or copy cells. First, you select the source area and point to the border of the cell or range. You know you are pointing to the

	Table 3–4 Paste Gallery Commands	
Paste Option Icon	**Paste Option**	**Description**
	Paste	Copy contents and format of source area. This option is the default.
	Formulas	Copy formulas from the source area, but not the contents and format.
	Formulas & Number Formatting	Copy formulas and format for numbers and formulas of source area, but not the contents.
	Keep Source Formatting	Copy contents, format, and styles of source area.
	No Borders	Copy contents and format of source area, but not any borders.
	Keep Source Column Widths	Copy contents and format of source area. Change destination column widths to source column widths.
	Transpose	Copy the contents and format of the source area, but transpose, or swap, the rows and columns.
	Values	Copy contents of source area but not the formatting for formulas.
	Values & Number Formatting	Copy contents and format of source area for numbers or formulas, but use format of destination area for text.
	Values & Source Formatting	Copy contents and formatting of source area but not the formula.
	Formatting	Copy format of source area but not the contents.
	Paste Link	Copy contents and format and link cells so that a change to the cells in source area updates the corresponding cells in destination area.
	Picture	Copy an image of the source area as a picture.
	Linked Picture	Copy an image of the source area as a picture so that a change to the cells in source area updates the picture in destination area.

border of the cell or range when the pointer changes to a four-headed arrow. To move the selected cell or cells, drag the selection to the destination area. To copy a selection, hold down the CTRL key while dragging the selection to the destination area. You know Excel is in Copy mode when a small plus sign appears next to the pointer. Be sure to release the mouse button before you release the CTRL key. Using the mouse to move or copy cells is called **drag and drop**.

Using Cut and Paste to Move Cells

Another way to move cells is to select them, click the Cut button (Home tab | Clipboard group) (Figure 3–12) to remove the cells from the worksheet and copy them to the Office Clipboard, select the destination area, and then click the Paste button (Home tab | Clipboard group) or press the ENTER key. You also can use the Cut command on the shortcut menu, instead of the Cut button on the ribbon.

Inserting and Deleting Cells in a Worksheet

At any time while the worksheet is on the screen, you can insert cells to enter new data or delete cells to remove unwanted data. You can insert or delete individual cells; a range of cells, rows, or columns; or entire worksheets.

BTW
Cutting
When you cut a cell or range of cells using the Cut command on a shortcut menu or Cut button (Home tab | Clipboard group), Excel copies the cells to the Office Clipboard; it does not remove the cells from the source area until you paste the cells in the destination area by either clicking the Paste button (Home tab | Clipboard group) or pressing the ENTER key. When you complete the paste, Excel clears the cell's or range of cell's entries and their formats from the source area.

To Insert a Row

Why? *According to the sketch of the worksheet in Figure 3–3a, two rows must be inserted in the What-If Assumptions table, one above Bonus for the Margin assumption and another between Bonus and Commission for the Sales Revenue for Bonus assumption.* The following steps insert the new rows into the worksheet.

- Right-click row heading 20, the row below where you want to insert a row, to display the shortcut menu and the mini toolbar (Figure 3–14).

Figure 3–14

- Click Insert on the shortcut menu to insert a new row in the worksheet by shifting the selected row and all rows below it down one row.

- Select cell A20 in the new row and then type **Sales Revenue for Bonus** to enter a new row title (Figure 3–15).

Q&A
What is the resulting format of the new row?
The cells in the new row inherit the formats of the cells in the row above them. You can change this behavior by clicking the Insert Options button that appears below the inserted row. Following the insertion of a row, the Insert Options button allows you to select from the following options: (1) 'Format Same As Above', (2) 'Format Same As Below', and (3) Clear Formatting. The 'Format Same as Above' option is the default. The Insert Options button remains active until you begin the next Excel operation. Excel does not display the Insert Options button if the initial row does not contain any formatted data.

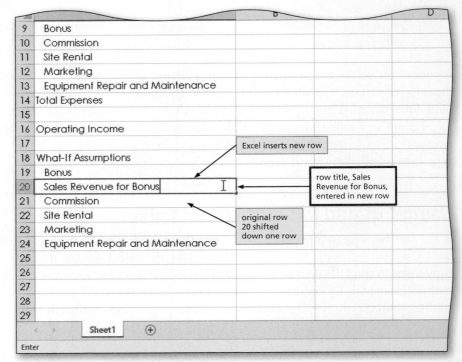

Figure 3–15

❸

- Right-click row heading 19, the row below where you want to insert a row, to display the shortcut menu and the mini toolbar.

- Click Insert on the shortcut menu to insert a new row in the worksheet.

- Click the Insert Options button below row 19 (Figure 3–16).

- Click 'Format Same As Below' on the menu.

- Select cell A19 in the new row and then type **Margin** to enter a new row title.

 What would happen if cells in the shifted rows were included in formulas?

If the rows that shift down included cell references in formulas located in the worksheet, Excel would automatically adjust the cell references in the formulas to their new locations. Thus, in Step 2, if a formula in the worksheet referenced a cell in row 19 before the insert, then Excel would adjust the cell reference in the formula to row 20 after the insert.

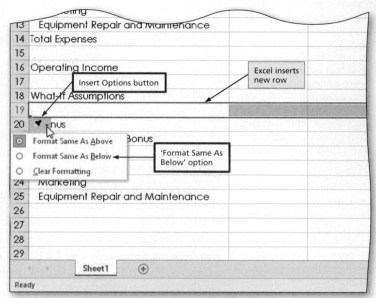

Figure 3–16

❹

- Save the workbook on your hard drive, OneDrive, or other storage location using **Kaitlyn's Ice Cream Shoppe Financial Projection** as the file name.

Other Ways

1. Click Insert Cells arrow (Home tab | Cells group), click 'Insert Sheet Rows'
2. Press CTRL+SHIFT+PLUS SIGN, click Entire row (Insert dialog box), click OK button

---

Inserting Columns

You insert columns into a worksheet in the same way you insert rows. To insert columns, select one or more columns immediately to the right of where you want Excel to insert the new column or columns. Select the number of columns you want to insert, click the Insert arrow (Home tab | Cells group), and then click 'Insert Sheet Columns' in the Insert list; or right-click the selected column(s) and then click Insert on the shortcut menu. The Insert command on the shortcut menu requires that you select an entire column (or columns) to insert a column (or columns). Following the insertion of a column, Excel displays the Insert Options button, which allows you to modify the insertion in a fashion similar to that discussed earlier when inserting rows.

Inserting Single Cells or a Range of Cells

You can use the Insert command on the shortcut menu or the Insert Cells command on the Insert menu — produced by clicking the Insert button (Home tab | Cells group) — to insert a single cell or a range of cells. You should be aware that if you shift a single cell or a range of cells, however, it no longer lines up with its associated cells. To ensure that the values in the worksheet do not get out of order,

BTW

Inserting Multiple Rows
If you want to insert multiple rows, you have two choices. You can insert a single row by using the Insert command on the shortcut menu and then repeatedly press the F4 key to continue inserting rows. Alternatively, you can select a number of existing rows equal to the number of rows that you want to insert. For instance, if you want to insert five rows, select five existing rows in the worksheet, right-click the selected rows, and then click Insert on the shortcut menu.

BTW

Dragging Ranges
You can move and insert a selected cell or range between existing cells by holding down the SHIFT key while you drag the selection to the gridline where you want to insert the selected cell or range. You also can copy and insert by holding down the CTRL+SHIFT keys while you drag the selection to the desired gridline.

spreadsheet experts recommend that you insert only entire rows or entire columns. When you insert a single cell or a range of cells, Excel displays the Insert Options button so that you can change the format of the inserted cell, using options similar to those for inserting rows and columns.

Deleting Columns and Rows

The Delete button (Home tab | Cells group) or the Delete command on the shortcut menu removes cells (including the data and format) from the worksheet. Deleting cells is not the same as clearing cells. The Clear Contents command, described in Module 1, clears the data from the cells, but the cells remain in the worksheet. The Delete command removes the cells from the worksheet and shifts the remaining rows up (when you delete rows) or shifts the remaining columns to the left (when you delete columns). If formulas located in other cells reference cells in the deleted row or column, Excel does not adjust these cell references. Excel displays the error message **#REF!** in those cells to indicate a cell reference error. For example, if cell A7 contains the formula =A4+A5 and you delete row 5, Excel assigns the formula =A4+#REF! to cell A6 (originally cell A7) and displays the error message, #REF!, in cell A6. Excel also displays an Error Options button when you select the cell containing the error message, #REF!, which allows you to select options to determine the nature of the problem.

1 ENTER HEADINGS & DATA | 2 ENTER FORMULAS & FUNCTIONS | 3 CREATE SPARKLINE CHARTS
To Enter Numbers with Format Symbols
4 FORMAT WORKSHEET | 5 CREATE COLUMN CHART | 6 CHANGE VIEWS | 7 ASK WHAT-IF QUESTIONS

The next step in creating the Financial Projection worksheet is to enter the what-if assumptions values in the range B19:B25. The numbers in the table can be entered and then formatted using techniques from Modules 1 and 2, or each number can be entered with **format symbols**, which assign a format to numbers as they are entered. When a number is entered with a format symbol, Excel displays it with the assigned format. Valid format symbols include the dollar sign ($), comma (,), and percent sign (%).

If you enter a whole number, it appears without any decimal places. If you enter a number with one or more decimal places and a format symbol, Excel displays the number with two decimal places. Table 3–5 illustrates several examples of numbers entered with format symbols. The number in parentheses in column 4 indicates the number of decimal places.

Table 3–5 Numbers Entered with Format Symbols			
Format Symbol	**Typed in Formula Bar**	**Displays in Cell**	**Comparable Format**
,	374,149	374,149	Comma(0)
	5,833.6	5,833.60	Comma(2)
$	$58917	$58,917	Currency(0)
	$842.51	$842.51	Currency(2)
	$63,574.9	$63,574.90	Currency(2)
%	85%	85%	Percent(0)
	12.80%	12.80%	Percent(2)
	68.2242%	68.2242%	Percent(4)

Why? In some cases, using a format symbol is the most efficient method for entering and formatting data. The following step enters the numbers in the What-If Assumptions table with format symbols.

1

- Enter the following values, using format symbols to apply number formatting: `78.75%` in cell B19, `3,500.00` in cell B20, `65,000.00` in cell B21, `25.00%` in cell B22, `10.00%` in cell B23, `5.00%` in cell B24, and `3.50%` in cell B25 (Figure 3–17).

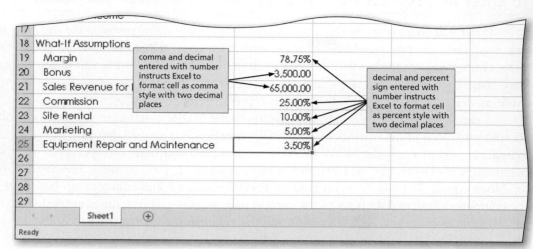

Figure 3–17

Other Ways

1. Right-click range, click Format Cells on shortcut menu, click Number tab (Format Cells dialog box), click category in Category list, select desired format, click OK button

2. Press CTRL+1, click Number tab (Format Cells dialog box), click category in Category list, select desired format, click OK button

---

To Enter the Projected Monthly Sales

The following steps enter the projected revenue, listed previously in Table 3–1, in row 4 and compute the projected six-month revenue in cell H4.

1 If necessary, display the Home tab.

2 Enter `55,000.00` in cell B4, `62,500.00` in cell C4, `67,000.00` in cell D4, `90,250.00` in cell E4, `77,500.00` in cell F4, and `74,750.00` in cell G4.

3 Select cell H4 and then click the Sum button (Home tab | Editing group) twice to create a sum in the selected cell (Figure 3–18).

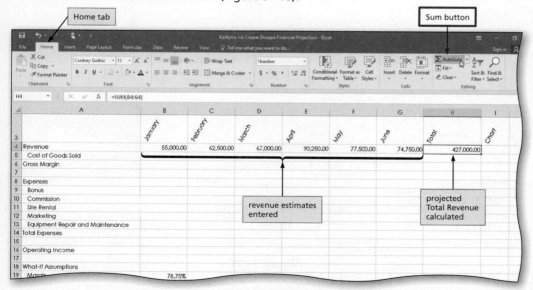

Figure 3–18

To Enter and Format the System Date

Why? *The sketch of the worksheet in Figure 3–3a includes a date stamp on the right side of the heading section. A date stamp shows the date a workbook, report, or other document was created or the time period it represents.* In business, a report often is meaningless without a date stamp. For example, if a printout of the worksheet in this module were distributed to the company's analysts, the date stamp would show when the six-month projections were made, as well as what time period the report represents.

A simple way to create a date stamp is to use the NOW function to enter the system date tracked by your computer in a cell in the worksheet. The **NOW function** is one of 24 date and time functions available in Excel. When assigned to a cell, the NOW function returns a number that corresponds to the system date and time beginning with December 31, 1899. For example, January 1, 1900 equals 1, January 2, 1900 equals 2, and so on. Noon equals .5. Thus, noon on January 1, 1900 equals 1.5 and 6:00 p.m. on January 1, 1900 equals 1.75. If the computer's system date is set to the current date, then the date stamp is equivalent to the current date. The following steps enter the NOW function and then change the format from mm/dd/yyyy hh:mm to mm/dd/yyyy.

❶

- Select cell H1 and then click the Insert Function button in the formula bar to display the Insert Function dialog box.

- Click the 'Or select a category' arrow (Insert Function dialog box) and then select 'Date & Time' to populate the 'Select a function' list with data and time functions.

- Scroll down in the 'Select a function' list and then click NOW to select the required function (Figure 3–19).

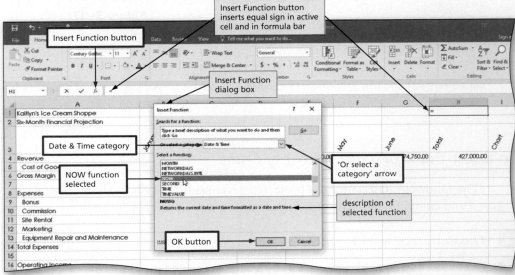

Figure 3–19

❷

- Click the OK button (Insert Function dialog box) to close the Insert Function dialog box and display the Function Arguments dialog box (Figure 3–20).

Q&A
What is meant by 'Formula result = Volatile' in the Function Arguments dialog box?
The NOW function is an example of a volatile function. A **volatile function** is one where the number that the function returns is not constant but changes each time the worksheet is opened. As a result, any formula using the NOW function will have a variable result.

Figure 3–20

- Click the OK button (Function Arguments dialog box) to display the system date and time in the selected cell, using the default date and time format, which is mm/dd/yyyy hh:mm.

Q&A What does the mm/dd/yyyy hh:mm format represent?
The mm/dd/yyyy hh:mm format can be explained as follows: the first mm is the month, dd is the day of the month, yyyy is the year, hh is the hour of the day, and the second mm is the minutes past the hour. Excel applies this date and time format to the result of the NOW function.

- Right-click cell H1 to display a shortcut menu and mini toolbar.

- Click Format Cells on the shortcut menu to display the Format Cells dialog box.

- If necessary, click the Number tab (Format Cells dialog box) to display the Number sheet.

- Click Date in the Category list (Format Cells dialog box) to display the date format options in the Type list. Scroll down in the Type list and then click 3/14/2012 to display a sample of the data in the Sample area in the dialog box (Figure 3–21).

Q&A Why do the dates in the Type box show March 14, 2012 instead of the current date?
March 14, 2012 is just used as a sample date in this version of Office.

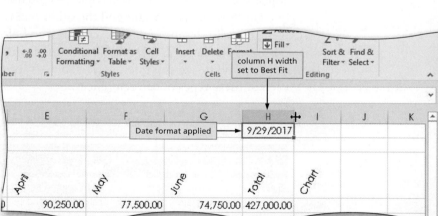

Figure 3–21

4

- Click the OK button (Format Cells dialog box) to display the system date (the result of the NOW function) in the format mm/dd/yyyy.

- Double-click the border between columns H and I to change the width of the column to best fit (Figure 3–22).

🔍 **Experiment**

- If instructed by your professor, select cell H2 and enter the place of your birth.

- Save the workbook again on the same storage location with the same file name.

Q&A Why should I save the workbook again?
You have made several modifications to the workbook since you last saved it. Thus, you should save it again.

Figure 3–22

Other Ways

1. Click 'Date & Time' button (Formulas tab | Function Library group), click NOW
2. Press CTRL+SEMICOLON (this enters the date as a static value, meaning the date will not change when the workbook is opened at a later date)
3. Press CTRL+SHIFT+# to format date as day-month-year

When would you not want to use the system date?
Using the system date results in the date value being updated whenever the worksheet is opened. Think carefully about whether or not this is the result you want. If you want the date to reflect the current date, using the system date is appropriate. If you want to record when the worksheet was created, using a hard-coded date makes more sense. If both pieces of information may be important, consider two date entries in the worksheet: a fixed entry identifying the date the worksheet was created and the volatile system date.

Break Point: If you wish to take a break, this is a good place to do so. You can exit Excel now. To resume at a later time, run Excel, open the file called Kaitlyn's Ice Cream Shoppe Financial Projection, and continue following the steps from this location forward.

BTW
Absolute Referencing
Absolute referencing is one of the more difficult worksheet concepts to understand. One point to keep in mind is that the paste operation is the only operation affected by an absolute cell reference. An absolute cell reference instructs the paste operation to use the same cell reference as it copies a formula from one cell to another.

Absolute Versus Relative Addressing

The next sections describe the formulas and functions needed to complete the calculations in the worksheet.

As you learned in Modules 1 and 2, Excel modifies cell references when copying formulas. However, sometimes while copying formulas you do not want Excel to change a cell reference. To keep a cell reference constant when copying a formula or function (that is, the cell references do not change relative to where you are copying the formula), Excel uses a technique called **absolute cell referencing**. To specify an absolute cell reference in a formula, enter a dollar sign ($) before any column letters or row numbers you want to keep constant in formulas you plan to copy. For example, B4 is an absolute cell reference, whereas B4 is a relative cell reference. Both reference the same cell. The difference becomes apparent when they are copied to a destination area. A formula using the absolute cell reference B4 instructs Excel to keep the cell reference B4 constant (absolute) in the formula as it is copied to the destination area. A formula using the **relative cell reference** B4 instructs Excel to adjust the cell reference as it is copied to the destination area. A cell reference where one factor remains constant and the other one varies is called a **mixed cell reference**. A mixed cell reference includes a dollar sign before the column or the row, not before both. When planning formulas, be aware of when you might need to use absolute, relative, and mixed cell references. Table 3–6 provides some additional examples of each of these types of cell references.

Table 3–6 Examples of Absolute, Relative, and Mixed Cell References		
Cell Reference	**Type of Reference**	**Meaning**
B4	Absolute cell reference	Both column and row references remain the same when you copy this cell, because the cell references are absolute.
B4	Relative cell reference	Both column and row references are relative. When copied to another cell, both the column and row in the cell reference are adjusted to reflect the new location.
B$4	Mixed reference	This cell reference is mixed. The column reference changes when you copy this cell to another column because it is relative. The row reference does not change because it is absolute.
$B4	Mixed reference	This cell reference is mixed. The column reference does not change because it is absolute. The row reference changes when you copy this cell reference to another row because it is relative.

Figure 3–23 illustrates how the type of cell reference used affects the results of copying a formula to a new place in a worksheet. In Figure 3–23a, cells D6:D9 contain formulas. Each formula multiplies the content of cell A2 by 2; the difference between formulas lies in how cell A2 is referenced. Cells C6:C9 identify the type of reference: absolute, relative, or mixed.

Figure 3–23b shows the values that result from copying the formulas in cells D6:D9 to ranges E6:E9, F7:F10, and G11:G14. Figure 3–23c shows the formulas that result from copying the formulas. While all formulas initially multiplied the content of cell A2 by 2, the values and formulas in the destination ranges illustrate how Excel adjusts cell references according to how you reference those cells in original formulas.

(a)

(b)

(c)

Figure 3–23

In the worksheet, you need to enter formulas that calculate the following values for January: cost of goods sold (cell B5), gross margin (cell B6), expenses (range B9:B13), total expenses (cell B14), and operating income (cell B16). The formulas are based on the projected monthly revenue in cell B4 and the assumptions in the range B19:B25.

The calculations for each column (month) are the same, except for the reference to the projected monthly revenue in row 4, which varies according to the month (B4 for January, C4 for February, and so on). Thus, the formulas for January can be entered in column B and then copied to columns C through G. Table 3–7 shows the formulas for determining the January cost of goods sold, gross margin, expenses, total expenses, and operating income in column B.

Table 3–7 Formulas for Determining Cost of Goods Sold, Gross Margin, Expenses, Total Expenses, and Operating Income for January			
Cell	**Row Title**	**Calculation**	**Formula**
B5	Cost of Goods Sold	Revenue times (1 minus Margin %)	=B4 * (1 – B19)
B6	Gross Margin	Revenue minus Cost of Goods Sold	=B4 – B5
B9	Bonus	Bonus equals value in B20 or 0	=IF(B4 >= B21, B20, 0)
B10	Commission	Revenue times Commission %	=B4 * B22
B11	Site Rental	Revenue times Site Rental %	=B4 * B23
B12	Marketing	Revenue times Marketing %	=B4 * B24
B13	Equipment Repair and Maintenance	Revenue times Equipment Repair and Maintenance %	=B4 * B25
B14	Total Expenses	Sum of April Expenses	=SUM(B9:B13)
B16	Operating Income	Gross Margin minus Total Expenses	=B6 – B14

To Enter a Formula Containing Absolute Cell References

1 ENTER HEADINGS & DATA | 2 ENTER FORMULAS & FUNCTIONS | 3 CREATE SPARKLINE CHARTS
4 FORMAT WORKSHEET | 5 CREATE COLUMN CHART | 6 CHANGE VIEWS | 7 ASK WHAT-IF QUESTIONS

Why? *As the formulas are entered in column B for January, as shown in Table 3–7, and then copied to columns C through G (February through June) in the worksheet, Excel will adjust the cell references for each column.* After the copy, the February Commission expense in cell C10 would be =C4 * C22. While the cell reference C4 (February Revenue) is correct, the cell reference C22 references an empty cell. The formula for cell C10 should read =C4 * B22, rather than =C4 * C22, because B22 references the Commission % value in the What-If Assumptions table. In this instance, you must use an absolute cell reference to keep the cell reference in the formula the same, or constant, when it is copied. To enter an absolute cell reference, you can type the dollar sign ($) as part of the cell reference or enter it by pressing the F4 key with the insertion point in or to the right of the cell reference to change it to absolute. The following steps enter the cost of goods sold formula =B4 * (1 – B19) in cell B5 using Point mode.

1

- Click cell B5 to select the cell in which to enter the first formula.

- Type = (equal sign), select cell B4, type * (1−B19 to continue entering the formula, and then press the F4 key to change the cell reference from a relative cell reference to an absolute cell reference. Type) (closing parenthesis) to complete the formula (Figure 3–24).

Q&A

◀ Is an absolute reference required in this formula?

No, a mixed cell reference also could have been used. The formula in cell B5 will be copied across columns, rather than down rows. So, the formula entered in cell B5 in Step 1 could have been entered as =B4*(1−$B19) using a mixed cell reference, rather than =B4*(1−B19), because when you copy a formula across columns, the row does not change. The key is to ensure that column B remains constant as you copy the formula across columns. To change the absolute cell reference to a mixed cell reference, continue to press the F4 key until you achieve the desired cell reference.

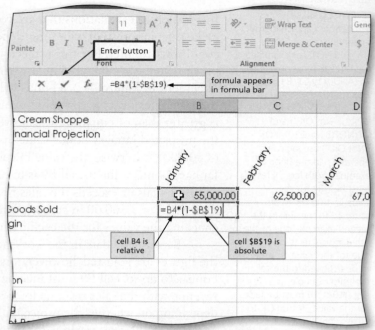

Figure 3–24

2

- Click the Enter button in the formula bar to display the result, 11687.5, instead of the formula in cell B5 (Figure 3–25).

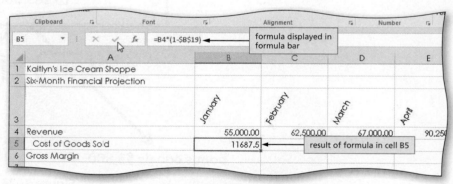

Figure 3–25

3

- Click cell B6 to select the cell in which to enter the next formula, type = (equal sign), click cell B4, type − (minus sign), and then click cell B5 to add a reference to the cell to the formula.

- Click the Enter button in the formula bar to display the result in the selected cell, in this case gross margin for January, 43,312.50, in cell B6 (Figure 3–26).

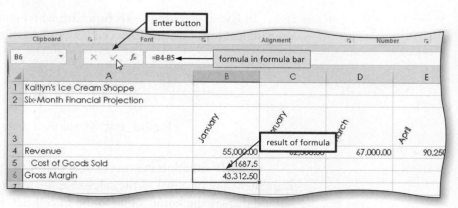

Figure 3–26

Making Decisions — The IF Function

In addition to calculations that are constant across all categories, you may need to make calculations that will differ depending on whether a particular condition or set of conditions are met. For this project, you need to vary compensation according to how much revenue is generated in any particular month. According to the requirements document in Figure 3–2, a bonus will be paid in any month where revenue is greater than the sales revenue for bonus value. If the projected January revenue in cell B4 is greater than or equal to the sales revenue for bonus in cell B21 (65,000.00), then the projected January bonus value in cell B9 is equal to the bonus value in cell B20 (3,500.00); otherwise, the value in cell B9 is equal to 0. One way to assign the projected January bonus value in cell B9 is to manually check to see if the projected revenue in cell B4 equals or exceeds the sales revenue for the bonus amount in cell B21 and, if so, then to enter 3,500.00 in cell B9. You can use this manual process for all six months by checking the values for the each month.

Because the data in the worksheet changes each time a report is prepared or the figures are adjusted, however, it is preferable to have Excel calculate the monthly bonus. To do so, cell B9 must include a formula or function that compares the projected revenue with the sales revenue for bonus value, and displays 3,500.00 or 0.00 (zero), depending on whether the projected January revenue in cell B4 is greater than, equal to, or less than the sales revenue for bonus value in cell B21. This decision-making process is a **logical test**. It can be represented in diagram form, as shown in Figure 3–27.

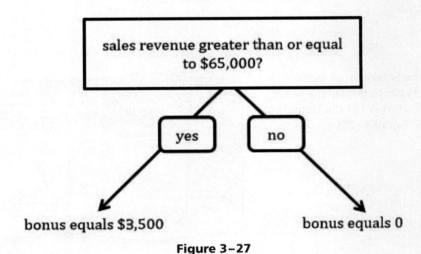

Figure 3–27

In Excel, you use the **IF function** when you want to assign a value to a cell based on a logical test. For example, cell B9 can be assigned the following IF function:

$$\text{=IF(B4>=\$B\$21, \$B\$20, 0)}$$

logical_test   value_if_true   value_if_false

This IF function instructs Excel that if the projected January revenue in cell B4 is greater than or equal to the sales revenue for bonus value in cell B21, then Excel should display the bonus value found in cell B20 in cell B9. If the projected January revenue in cell B4 is not greater than or equal to the sales revenue for bonus value in cell B21, then Excel should display a 0 (zero) in cell B9.

The general form of the IF function is:

$$=IF(logical\_test, value\_if\_true, value\_if\_false)$$

The argument, logical_test, is made up of two expressions and a comparison operator. Each expression can be a cell reference, a number, text, a function, or a formula. In this example, the logical test compares the projected revenue with the sales revenue for bonus, using the comparison operator greater than or equal to. Valid comparison operators, their meanings, and examples of their use in IF functions are shown in Table 3–8. The argument, value_if_true, is the value you want Excel to display in the cell when the logical test is true. The argument, value_if_false, is the value you want Excel to display in the cell when the logical test is false.

Table 3–8 Comparison Operators

Comparison Operator	Meaning	Example
=	Equal to	=IF(A1=A2, "True", "False")
<	Less than	=IF(A1<A2, "True", "False")
>	Greater than	=IF(A1>A2, "True", "False")
>=	Greater than or equal to	=IF(A1>=A2, "True", "False")
<=	Less than or equal to	=IF(A1<=A2, "True", "False")
<>	Not equal to	=IF(A1<>A2, "True", "False")

To Enter an IF Function

1 ENTER HEADINGS & DATA | 2 ENTER FORMULAS & FUNCTIONS | 3 CREATE SPARKLINE CHARTS
4 FORMAT WORKSHEET | 5 CREATE COLUMN CHART | 6 CHANGE VIEWS | 7 ASK WHAT-IF QUESTIONS

Why? *Use an IF function to determine the value for a cell based on a logical test.* The following steps assign the IF function =IF(B4>=B21,B20,0) to cell B9. This IF function determines whether or not the worksheet assigns a bonus for January.

- Click cell B9 to select the cell for the next formula.

- Click the Insert Function button in the formula bar to display the Insert Function dialog box.

- Click the 'Or select a category' arrow (Insert Function dialog box) and then select Logical in the list to populate the 'Select a function' list with logic functions.

- Click IF in the 'Select a function' list to select the required function (Figure 3–28).

Figure 3–28

- Click the OK button (Insert Function dialog box) to display the Function Arguments dialog box.

- Type **b4>=b21** in the Logical_test box to enter a logical test for the IF function.

- Type **b20** in the Value_if_true box to enter the result of the IF function if the logical test is true.

- Type **0** (zero) in the Value_if_false box to enter the result of the IF function if the logical test is false (Figure 3–29).

Figure 3–29

- Click the OK button (Function Arguments dialog box) to insert the IF function in the selected cell (Figure 3–30).

Q&A

Why does cell B9 contain the value 0 (zero)?

The value that Excel displays in cell B9 depends on the values assigned to cells B4, B20, and B21. For example, if the value for January revenue in cell B4 is increased to 65,000.00 or higher, then the IF function in cell B9 will display 3,500.00. If you change the sales revenue for bonus in cell B21 from 65,000.00 to another number and the value in cell B4 is greater than or equal to the value in cell B21, it also will change the results in cell B9.

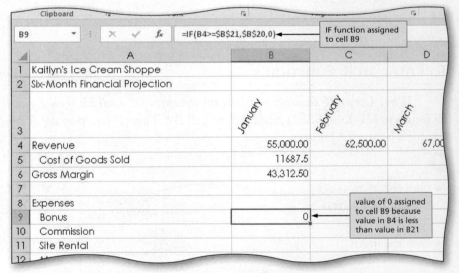

Figure 3–30

Other Ways

1. Click Logical button (Formulas tab | Function Library group), click IF

To Enter the Remaining Formulas for January

The January commission expense in cell B10 is equal to the revenue in cell B4 times the commission assumption in cell B22 (25.00%). The January site rental expense in cell B11 is equal to the projected January revenue in cell B4 times the site rental assumption in cell B23 (10.00%). Similar formulas determine the remaining January expenses in cells B12 and B13.

The total expenses value in cell B14 is equal to the sum of the expenses in the range B9:B13. The operating income in cell B16 is equal to the gross margin in cell B6 minus the total expenses in cell B14. Because the formulas are short, they are typed in the following steps, rather than entered using Point mode.

① Select cell B10. Type **=b4*b22** and then press the DOWN ARROW key to enter the formula in the selected cell. Type **=b4*b23** and then press the DOWN ARROW key to enter the formula in cell B11. Type **=b4*b24,** press the DOWN ARROW key, type **=b4*b25,** and then press the DOWN ARROW key again.

② With cell B14 selected, click the Sum button (Home tab | Editing group) twice to insert a SUM function in the selected cell. Select cell B16 to prepare to enter the next formula. Type **=b6−b14** and then press the ENTER key to enter the formula in the selected cell.

③ Press CTRL+ACCENT MARK (`) to display the formulas version of the worksheet (Figure 3–31).

④ When you are finished viewing the formulas version, press CTRL+ACCENT MARK (`) again to return to the values version of the worksheet.

Q&A | Why should I view the formulas version of the worksheet?
Viewing the formulas version (Figure 3–31) of the worksheet allows you to check the formulas you entered in the range B5:B16. Recall that formulas were entered in lowercase. You can see that Excel converts all the formulas from lowercase to uppercase.

BTW
Replacing a Formula with a Constant
Using the following steps, you can replace a formula with its result so that the cell value remains constant: (1) click the cell with the formula; (2) press the F2 key or click in the formula bar; (3) press the F9 key to display the value in the formula bar; and (4) press the ENTER key.

BTW
Error Messages
When Excel cannot calculate a formula, it displays an error message in a cell. These error messages always begin with a number sign (#). The more commonly occurring error messages are as follows: #DIV/0! (tries to divide by zero); #NAME? (uses a name Excel does not recognize); #N/A (refers to a value not available); #NULL! (specifies an invalid intersection of two areas); #NUM! (uses a number incorrectly); #REF (refers to a cell that is not valid); #VALUE! (uses an incorrect argument or operand); and ##### (refers to cells not wide enough to display entire entry).

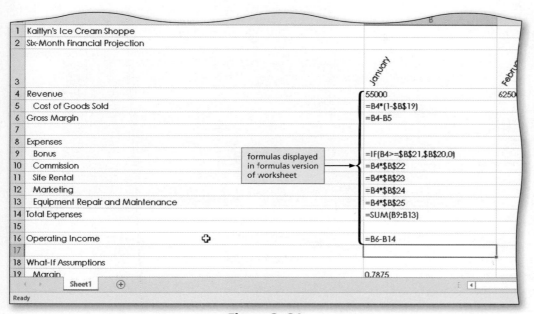

Figure 3–31

To Copy Formulas with Absolute Cell References Using the Fill Handle

1 ENTER HEADINGS & DATA | 2 ENTER FORMULAS & FUNCTIONS | 3 CREATE SPARKLINE CHARTS
4 FORMAT WORKSHEET | 5 CREATE COLUMN CHART | 6 CHANGE VIEWS | 7 ASK WHAT-IF QUESTIONS

Why? Using the fill handle ensures a quick, accurate copy of the formulas. The following steps use the fill handle to copy the January formulas in column B to the other five months in columns C through G.

- Select the range B5:B16 and then point to the fill handle in the lower-right corner of the selected cell, B16 in this case, to display the crosshair pointer (Figure 3–32).

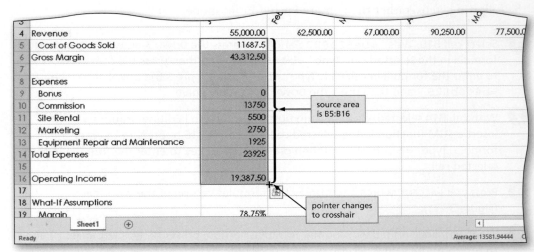

3						
4	Revenue	55,000.00	62,500.00	67,000.00	90,250.00	77,500.0
5	Cost of Goods Sold	11687.5				
6	Gross Margin	43,312.50				
7						
8	Expenses					
9	Bonus	0				
10	Commission	13750		source area is B5:B16		
11	Site Rental	5500				
12	Marketing	2750				
13	Equipment Repair and Maintenance	1925				
14	Total Expenses	23925				
15						
16	Operating Income	19,387.50				
17					pointer changes to crosshair	
18	What-If Assumptions					
19	Margin	78.75%				

Ready   Average: 13581.94444

Figure 3–32

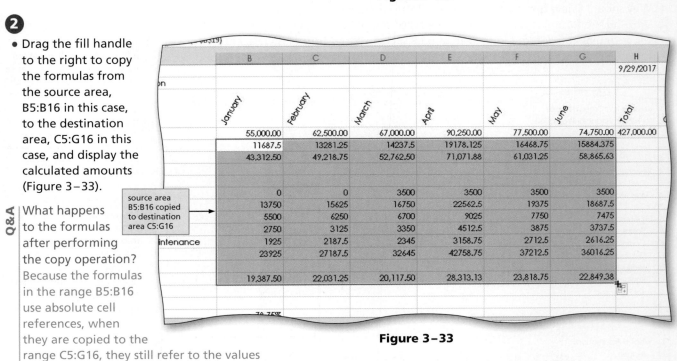

- Drag the fill handle to the right to copy the formulas from the source area, B5:B16 in this case, to the destination area, C5:G16 in this case, and display the calculated amounts (Figure 3–33).

Q&A What happens to the formulas after performing the copy operation? Because the formulas in the range B5:B16 use absolute cell references, when they are copied to the range C5:G16, they still refer to the values in the What-If Assumptions table.

	B	C	D	E	F	G	H
							9/29/2017
	January	February	March	April	May	June	Total
	55,000.00	62,500.00	67,000.00	90,250.00	77,500.00	74,750.00	427,000.00
	11687.5	13281.25	14237.5	19178.125	16468.75	15884.375	
	43,312.50	49,218.75	52,762.50	71,071.88	61,031.25	58,865.63	
	0	0	3500	3500	3500	3500	
	13750	15625	16750	22562.5	19375	18687.5	
	5500	6250	6700	9025	7750	7475	
	2750	3125	3350	4512.5	3875	3737.5	
	1925	2187.5	2345	3158.75	2712.5	2616.25	
	23925	27187.5	32645	42758.75	37212.5	36016.25	
	19,387.50	22,031.25	20,117.50	28,313.13	23,818.75	22,849.38	

source area B5:B16 copied to destination area C5:G16

Figure 3–33

To Determine Row Totals in Nonadjacent Cells

The following steps determine the row totals in column H. To determine the row totals using the Sum button, select only the cells in column H containing numbers in adjacent cells to the left. If, for example, you select the range H5:H16, Excel will display 0s as the sum of empty rows in cells H7, H8, and H15.

1. Select the range H5:H6. While holding down the CTRL key, select the range H9:H14 and cell H16, as shown in Figure 3–34.

2. Click the Sum button (Home tab | Editing group) to display the row totals in the selected ranges (Figure 3–34).

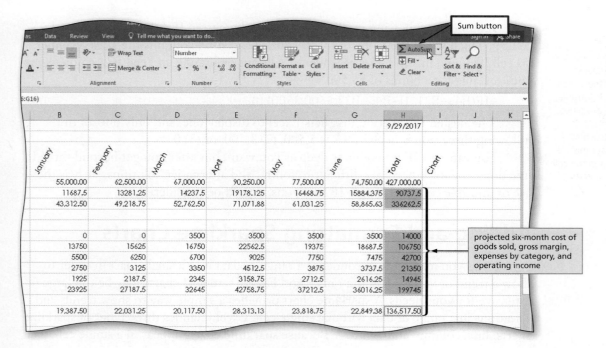

Figure 3–34

3 Save the workbook again on the same storage location with the same file name.

Nested Forms of the IF Function

A **nested IF function** is one in which the action to be taken for the true or false case includes yet another IF function. The second IF function is considered to be nested, or layered, within the first. You can use a nested IF function to add another condition to the decision-making process. Study the nested IF function below, which would add another level of bonus to the compensation at Kaitlyn's Ice Cream Shoppe. In this case, Kaitlyn's Ice Cream Shoppe assigns a bonus for sales of $65,000 and above. For months where sales make that level, additional bonus money is available for sales of $80,000 and above. In this case, three outcomes are possible, two of which involve paying a bonus. Figure 3–35 depicts a decision tree for this logical test.

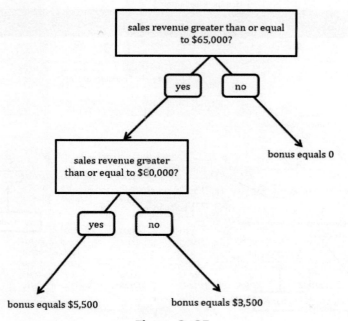

Figure 3–35

BTW

Using IFERROR
Similar to the IF function, the IFERROR function checks a formula for correctness. For example, =IFERROR(formula, "Error Message") examines the formula argument. If an error appears (such as #N/A), Excel displays the Error Message text in the cell instead of the Excel #N/A error.

Assume the following in this example: (1) the nested IF function is assigned to cell B9, which will display one of three values; (2) cell B4 contains the sales revenue; (3) cell B21 contains the sales revenue for a bonus of $3,500; and cell B22 contains the sales revenue for a bonus of $5,500.

=IF(B4>=B21, IF(B4>=B22,5500,3500),0)

The nested IF function instructs Excel to display one, and only one, of the following three values in cell B9: (1) 5,500, (2) 3,500, or (3) 0.

You can nest IF functions as deep as you want, but after you get beyond three IF functions, the logic becomes difficult to follow, and alternative solutions, such as the use of multiple cells and simple IF functions, should be considered.

Adding and Formatting Sparkline Charts

Sometimes you may want to condense a range of data into a small chart in order to show a trend or variation in the range, and Excel's standard charts may be too large or extensive for your needs. A sparkline chart provides a simple way to show trends and variations in a range of data within a single cell. Excel includes three types of sparkline charts: line, column, and win/loss. Because sparkline charts appear in a single cell, you can use them to convey succinct, eye-catching summaries of the data they represent.

To Add a Sparkline Chart to the Worksheet

1 ENTER HEADINGS & DATA | 2 ENTER FORMULAS & FUNCTIONS | 3 CREATE SPARKLINE CHARTS
4 FORMAT WORKSHEET | 5 CREATE COLUMN CHART | 6 CHANGE VIEWS | 7 ASK WHAT-IF QUESTIONS

Each row of monthly data, including those containing formulas, provides useful information that can be summarized by a line sparkline chart. **Why?** *A line sparkline chart is a good choice because it shows trends over the six-month period for each row of data.* The following steps add a line sparkline chart to cell I4 and then use the fill handle to create line sparkline charts in the range I5:I16 to represent the monthly data shown in rows 4 through 16.

- If necessary, scroll the worksheet so that both columns B and I and row 3 are visible on the screen.

- Select cell I4 to prepare to insert a sparkline chart in the cell.

- Display the Insert tab and then click the Line Sparkline button (Insert tab | Sparklines group) to display the Create Sparklines dialog box (Figure 3–36).

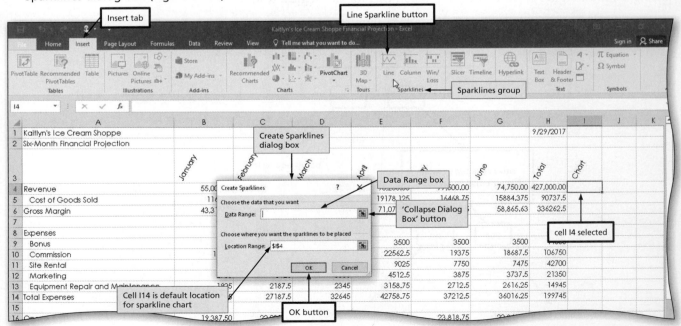

Figure 3–36

2

- Drag through the range B4:G4 to select the range. Do not release the mouse button (Figure 3–37).

Q&A What happened to the Create Sparklines dialog box?

When a dialog box includes a 'Collapse Dialog Box' button (Figure 3–36), selecting cells or a range collapses the dialog box so that only the current text box is visible. This allows you to select your desired range without the dialog box getting in the way. Once the selection is made, the dialog box expands back to its original size. You also can click the 'Collapse Dialog Box' button to make your selection and then click the 'Expand Dialog Box' button (Figure 3–37) to expand the dialog box.

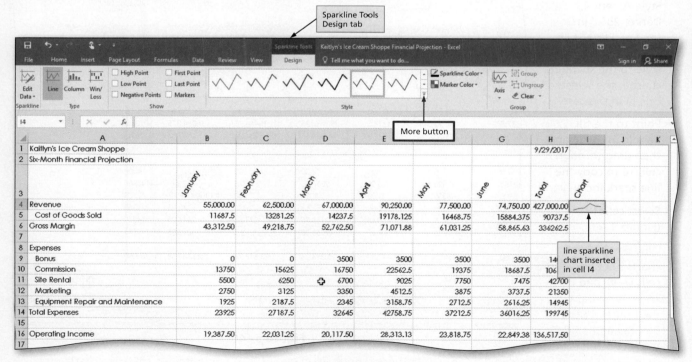

Figure 3–37

3

- Release the mouse button to insert the selected range, B4:G4 in this case, in the Data Range box.

- Click the OK button shown in Figure 3–36 (Create Sparklines dialog box) to insert a line sparkline chart in the selected cell and display the Sparkline Tools Design tab (Figure 3–38).

Figure 3–38

To Change the Sparkline Style and Copy the Sparkline Chart

Why? *The default style option may not provide the visual impact you seek. Changing the sparkline style allows you to alter how the sparkline chart appears.* The following steps change the sparkline chart style.

1

• Click the More button (Sparkline Tools Design tab | Style group) to display the Sparkline Style gallery (Figure 3–39).

Figure 3–39

2

• Click 'Sparkline Style Accent 4, Darker 25%' in the Sparkline Style gallery to apply the style to the sparkline chart in the selected cell, I4 in this case.

• Point to the fill handle in cell I4 and then drag through cell I16 to copy the line sparkline chart.

• Select cell I18 (Figure 3–40).

Q&A
Why do sparkline charts not appear in cells I7, I8, and I15? There is no data in the ranges B7:G7, B8:G8, and B15:G15, so Excel cannot draw

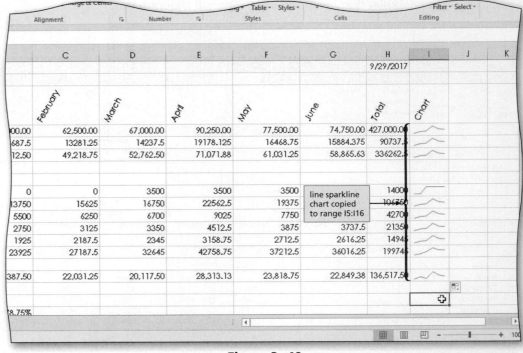

Figure 3–40

sparkline charts. If you added data to cells in those ranges, Excel would then generate line sparkline charts for those rows, because the drag operation defined sparkline charts for cells I7, I8, and I15.

To Change the Sparkline Type

In addition to changing the sparkline chart style, you also can change the sparkline chart type. *Why? You may decide that a different chart type will better illustrate the characteristics of your data.* As shown in Figure 3–40, most of the sparkline charts look similar. Changing the sparkline chart type allows you to decide if a different chart type will better present your data to the reader. The following steps change the line sparkline charts to column sparkline charts.

①

- Select the range I4:I16 to select the sparkline charts.

- Click the Sparkline Tools Design tab to make it the active tab.

- Click the 'Convert to Column Sparkline' button (Sparkline Tools Design tab | Type group) to change the sparkline charts in the selected range to the column type (Figure 3–41).

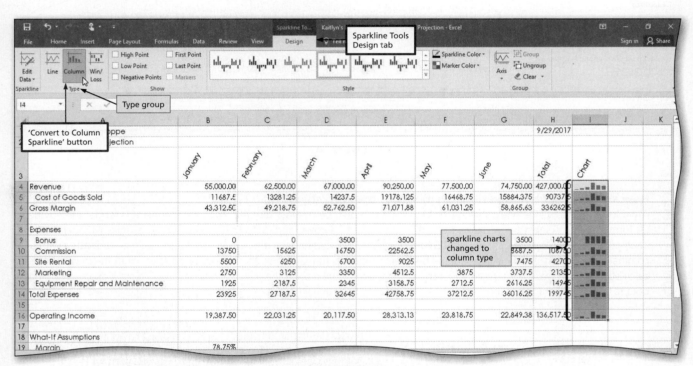

Figure 3–41

②

- Select cell I18.

- Save the workbook again on the same storage location with the same file name.

Formatting the Worksheet

The worksheet created thus far shows the financial projections for the six-month period, from January to June. Its appearance is uninteresting, however, even though some minimal formatting (formatting assumptions numbers, changing the column widths, formatting the date, and formatting the sparkline chart) was performed earlier. This section completes the formatting of the worksheet by making the numbers easier to read and emphasizing the titles, assumptions, categories, and totals, as shown in Figure 3–42.

BTW

Customizing Sparkline Charts
You can customize sparkline charts in a number of ways on the Sparkline Tools Design tab. In the Show group (Sparkline Tools Design tab), you can specify values to show as markers on the chart, such as the highest value, lowest value, any negative numbers, the first point, and the last point. You can change the color of the sparkline and markers in the Style group (Sparkline Tools Design tab).

Figure 3–42

CONSIDER THIS

How should you format various elements of the worksheet?

A worksheet, such as the one presented in this module, should be formatted in the following manner: (1) format the numbers; (2) format the worksheet title, column titles, row titles, and total rows; and (3) format the assumptions table. Numbers in heading rows and total rows should be formatted with a currency symbol. Other dollar amounts should be formatted with a comma style. The assumptions table should be diminished in its formatting so that it does not distract from the main data and calculations in the worksheet. Assigning a smaller font size to the data in the assumptions table would set it apart from other data formatted with a larger font size.

To Assign Formats to Nonadjacent Ranges

1 ENTER HEADINGS & DATA | 2 ENTER FORMULAS & FUNCTIONS | 3 CREATE SPARKLINE CHARTS

4 FORMAT WORKSHEET | 5 CREATE COLUMN CHART | 6 CHANGE VIEWS | 7 ASK WHAT-IF QUESTIONS

The following steps assign formats to the numbers in rows 4 through 16. **Why?** *These formats increase the readability of the data.*

①

- Select the range B4:H4 as the first range to format.

- While holding down the CTRL key, select the nonadjacent ranges B6:H6, B9:H9, B14:H14, and B16:H16, and then release the CTRL key to select nonadjacent ranges.

- Click the Number Format Dialog Box Launcher (Home tab | Number group) to display the Format Cells dialog box.

- Click Currency in the Category list (Format Cells dialog box), if necessary select 2 in the Decimal places box and then select $ in the Symbol list to ensure a dollar sign shows in the cells to be formatted, and select the black font color ($1,234.10) in the Negative numbers list to specify the desired currency style for the selected ranges (Figure 3–43).

Q&A | Why was this particular style chosen for the negative numbers?

In accounting, negative numbers often are shown with parentheses surrounding the value rather than with a negative sign preceding the value. Although the data being used in this module contains no negative numbers, you still must select a negative number format. It is important to be consistent when selecting negative number formats if you are applying different formats in a column; otherwise, the decimal points may not line up.

Why is the Format Cells dialog box used to create the format for the ranges in this step?

The requirements for this worksheet call for a floating dollar sign. You can use the Format Cells dialog box to assign a currency style with a floating dollar sign, instead of using the 'Accounting Number Format' button (Home tab | Number group), which assigns a fixed dollar sign.

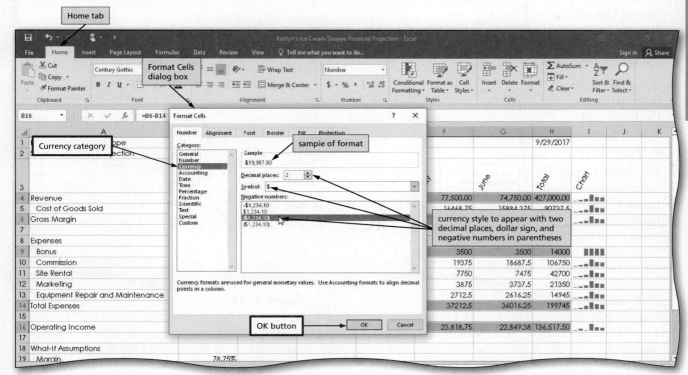

Figure 3–43

2

- Click the OK button (Format Cells dialog box) to close the Format Cells dialog box and apply the desired format to the selected ranges.

- Select the range B5:H5 as the next range to format.

- While holding down the CTRL key, select the range B10:H13, and then release the CTRL key to select nonadjacent ranges.

- Click the Number Format Dialog Box Launcher (Home tab | Number group) to display the Format Cells dialog box.

- Click Currency in the Category list (Format Cells dialog box), if necessary select 2 in the Decimal places box, select None in the Symbol list so that a dollar sign does not show in the cells to be formatted, and select the black font color (1,234.10) in the Negative numbers list (Figure 3–44).

Figure 3–44

3

- Click the OK button (Format Cells dialog box) to close the Format Cells dialog box and apply the desired format to the selected ranges.

- Select an empty cell and display the formatted numbers, as shown in Figure 3–45.

Q&A

Why is the Format Cells dialog box used to create the style for the ranges in Steps 2 and 3?

The Format Cells dialog box is used to assign the comma style instead of the

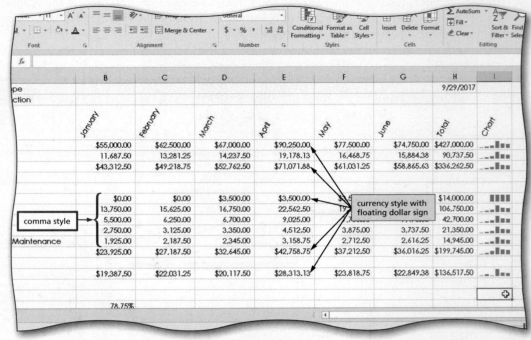

Figure 3–45

Comma Style button (Home tab | Number group), because the Comma Style button assigns a format that displays a dash (–) when a cell has a value of 0. The specifications for this worksheet call for displaying a value of 0 as 0.00 (see cell B9 in Figure 3–45) rather than as a dash. To create a comma style using the Format Cells dialog box, you use a currency style with no dollar sign.

Other Ways

1. Right-click range, click Format Cells on shortcut menu, click Number tab (Format Cells dialog box), click category in Category list, select format, click OK button (Format Cells dialog box)

2. Press CTRL+1, click Number tab (Format Cells dialog box), click category in Category list, select format, click OK button (Format Cells dialog box)

BTW

Toggle Commands
Many of the commands on the ribbon, in galleries, and as shortcut keys function as toggles. For example, if you click Freeze Panes in the Freeze Panes gallery, the command changes to Unfreeze Panes the next time you view the gallery. These types of commands work like on-off switches, or toggles.

To Format the Worksheet Titles

The following steps emphasize the worksheet titles in cells A1 and A2 by changing the font and font size. The steps also format all of the row headers in column A with a bold font style.

1 Press CTRL+HOME to select cell A1 and then click the column A heading to select the column.

2 Click the Bold button (Home tab | Font group) to bold all of the data in the selected column.

3 Increase the font size in cell A1 to 28 point.

4 Increase the font size in cell A2 to 16 point.

5 Select the range A1:I2 and change the fill color to Green, Accent 4 to add a background color to the selected range.

6 With A1:I2 selected, change the font color to White, Background 1.

7 Click an empty cell to deselect the range (Figure 3–46).

Figure 3–46

Other Ways

1. Right-click range, click Format Cells on shortcut menu, click Fill tab (Format Cells dialog box) to color background (or click Font tab to color font), click OK button

2. Press CTRL+1, click Fill tab (Format Cells dialog box) to color background (or click Font tab to color font), click OK button

To Assign Cell Styles to Nonadjacent Rows and Colors to a Cell

The following steps improve the appearance of the worksheet by formatting the headings in row 3 and the totals in rows 6, 14, and 16. Cell A4 also is formatted with a background color and font color.

1 Select the range A3:I3 and apply the Heading 2 cell style.

2 Select the range A6:H6 and while holding down the CTRL key, select the ranges A14:H14 and A16:H16.

3 Apply the Total cell style to the selected nonadjacent ranges.

4 Select cell A4 and click the Fill Color button (Home tab | Font group) to apply the last fill color used (Green, Accent 4) to the cell contents.

5 Click the Font Color button (Home tab | Font group) to apply the last font color used (White, Background 1) to the cell contents (Figure 3–47).

BTW

The Fill and Font Color Buttons
You may have noticed that the color bar at the bottom of the Fill Color and Font Color buttons (Home tab | Font group) (Figure 3–46) changes to the most recently selected color. To apply this same color to a cell background or text, select a cell and then click the Fill Color button to use the color as a background or click the Font Color button to use the color as a font color.

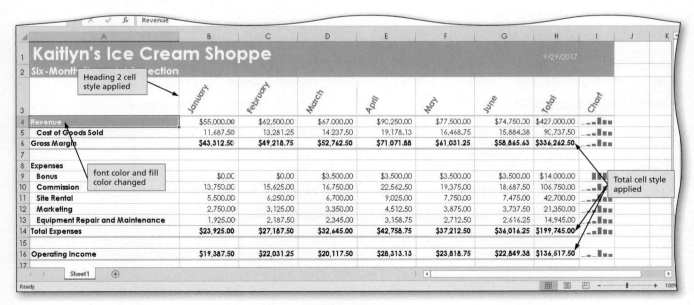

Figure 3–47

To Copy a Cell's Format Using the Format Painter Button

Why? *Using the format painter, you can format a cell quickly by copying a cell's format to another cell or a range of cells.* The following steps use the format painter to copy the format of cell A4 to cells A6 and the range A16:H16.

1

- If necessary, click cell A4 to select a source cell for the format to paint.

- Double-click the Format Painter button (Home tab | Clipboard group) and then move the pointer onto the worksheet to cause the pointer to change to a block plus sign with a paintbrush (Figure 3–48).

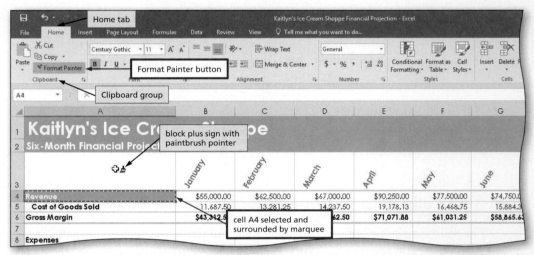

Figure 3–48

2

- Click cell A6 to assign the format of the source cell, A4 in this case, to the destination cell, A6 in this case.

- With the pointer still a block plus sign with a paintbrush, drag through the range A16:H16 to assign the format of the source cell, A4 in this case, to the destination range, A16:H16 in this case.

- Click the Format Painter button or press the ESC key to turn off the format painter.

- Apply the currency style to the range B16:H16 to cause the cells in the range to appear with a floating dollar sign and two decimal places (Figure 3–49).

Q&A Why does the currency style need to be reapplied to the range B16:H16?

Sometimes, the use of the format painter results in unintended outcomes. In this case, changing the background fill color and font color for the range B16:H16 resulted in the loss of the currency style because the format being copied did not include the currency style. Reapplying the currency style to the range results in the proper number style, fill color, and font color.

	Janu	Feb	M	Apr	May	Ju	To	Ch
3								
4 Revenue	$55,000.00	$62,500.00	$67,000.00	$90,250.00	$77,500.00	$74,750.00	$427,000.00	
5 Cost of Goods Sold	11,687.50	13,281.25	14,237.50	19,178.13	16,468.75	15,884.38	90,737.50	
6 Gross Margin	$43,312.50	$49,218.75	$52,762.50	$71,071.88	$61,031.25	$58,865.63	$336,262.50	
7								
8 Expenses								
9 Bonus	$0.00	$0.00	$3,500.00	$3,500.00	$3,500.00	$3,500.00	$14,000.00	
10 Commission			16,750.00	22,562.50	19,375.00	18,687.50	106,750.00	
11 Site Rental			6,700.00	9,025.00	7,750.00	7,475.00	42,700.00	
12 Marketing			3,350.00	4,512.50	3,875.00	3,737.50	21,350.00	
13 Equipment Repair and Maintenance	1,925.00	2,187.50	2,345.00	3,158.75	2,712.50	2,616.25	14,945.00	
14 Total Expenses	$23,925.00	$27,187.50	$32,645.00	$42,758.75	$37,212.50	$36,016.25	$199,745.00	
15								
16 Operating Income	$19,387.50	$22,031.25	$20,117.50	$28,313.13	$23,818.75	$22,849.38	$136,517.50	
17								

format of cell A4 applied to cells A6 and A16:H16 and currency style reapplied to B16:H16

Sheet1

Ready   Average: $39,005.00   Count: 7   Sum: $273,035.00   100%

Figure 3–49

Other Ways

1. Click Copy button (Home tab | Clipboard group), select cell, click Paste arrow (Home tab | Clipboard group), click Formatting button in Paste gallery

2. Right-click cell, click Copy on shortcut menu, right-click cell, click Formatting icon on shortcut menu

To Format the What-If Assumptions Table

The following steps format the What-If Assumptions table, the final step in improving the appearance of the worksheet.

1 Select cell A18.

2 Change the font size to 8 pt.

3 Italicize and underline the text in cell A18.

4 Select the range A19:B25, and change the font size to 8 pt.

5 Select the range A18:B25 and then click the Fill Color button (Home tab | Font group) to apply the most recently used background color to the selected range.

6 Click the Font Color button (Home tab | Font group) to apply the most recently used font color to the selected range.

7 Deselect the range A18:B25 and display the What-If Assumptions table, as shown in Figure 3–50.

8 Save the workbook on the same storage location with the same file name.

Q&A

◄ What happens when I click the Italic and Underline buttons?
When you assign the italic font style to a cell, Excel slants the characters slightly to the right, as shown in cell A18 in Figure 3–50. The underline format underlines only the characters in the cell, rather than the entire cell, as is the case when you assign a cell a bottom border.

BTW

Painting a Format to Nonadjacent Ranges
Double-click the Format Painter button (Home tab | Clipboard group) and then drag through the nonadjacent ranges to paint the formats to the ranges. Click the Format Painter button again to deactivate it.

BTW

Selecting Nonadjacent Ranges
One of the more difficult tasks to learn is selecting nonadjacent ranges. To complete this task, do not hold down the CTRL key when you select the first range because Excel will consider the current active cell to be the first selection, and you may not want the current active cell in the selection. Once the first range is selected, hold down the CTRL key and drag through the nonadjacent ranges. If a desired range is not visible in the window, use the scroll arrows to view the range. You need not hold down the CTRL key while you scroll.

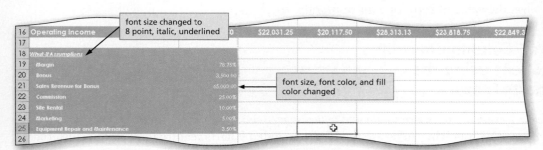

Figure 3–50

Break Point: If you wish to take a break, this is a good place to do so. You can exit Excel now. To resume at a later time, run Excel, open the file called Kaitlyn's Ice Cream Shoppe Financial Projection, and continue following the steps from this location forward.

Adding a Clustered Column Chart to the Workbook

The next step in the module is to create a clustered column chart on a separate sheet in the workbook, as shown in Figure 3–51. Use a clustered column chart to compare values side by side, broken down by category. Each column shows the value for a particular category, by month in this case.

The clustered column chart in Figure 3–51 shows the projected expense amounts, by category, for each of the six months. The clustered column chart allows the user to see how the various expense categories compare with each other each month, and across months.

Recall that charts can either be embedded in a worksheet or placed on a separate chart sheet. The clustered column chart will reside on its own sheet, because if placed on the worksheet, it would not be visible when the worksheet first opens and could be missed.

BTW
Charts
When you change a value on which a chart is dependent, Excel immediately redraws the chart based on the new value. With bar charts, you can drag the bar in the chart in one direction or another to change the corresponding value in the worksheet.

BTW
Chart Items
When you rest the pointer over a chart item, such as a legend, bar, or axis, Excel displays a chart tip containing the name of the item.

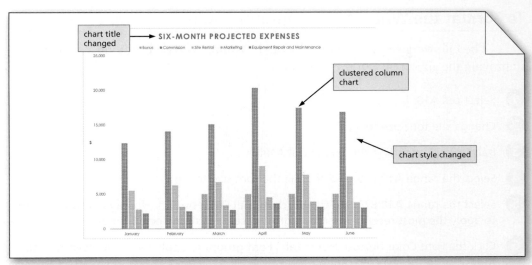

Figure 3–51

In this worksheet, the ranges to chart are the nonadjacent ranges B3:G3 (month names) and A9:G13 (monthly projected expenses, by category). The month names in the range B3:G3 will identify the major groups for the chart; these entries are called **category names**. The range A9:G13 contains the data that determines the individual columns in each month cluster, along with the names that identify each column; these entries are called the **data series**. Because six months of five expense categories are being charted, the chart will contain six clusters of five columns each, unless a category has the value of zero for a given month.

To Draw a Clustered Column Chart on a Separate Chart Sheet Using the Recommended Charts Feature

1 ENTER HEADINGS & DATA | 2 ENTER FORMULAS & FUNCTIONS | 3 CREATE SPARKLINE CHARTS
4 FORMAT WORKSHEET | 5 CREATE COLUMN CHART | 6 CHANGE VIEWS | 7 ASK WHAT-IF QUESTIONS

Why? *This Excel feature evaluates the selected data and makes suggestions regarding which chart types will provide the most suitable representation.* The following steps use the Recommended Charts feature to draw the clustered column chart on a separate chart sheet.

1

- Select the range A3:G3 to identify the range of the categories.

- Hold down the CTRL key and select the data range A9:G13.

- Display the Insert tab.

- Click the Recommended Charts button (Insert tab | Charts group) to display the Insert Chart dialog box with the Recommended Charts tab active (Figure 3–52).

Experiment

- Click the various recommended chart types, reading the description for each of its best use and examining the chart preview.

Figure 3–52

2

- Click the first Clustered Column recommended chart to select it and then click the OK button (Insert Chart dialog box).

- When Excel draws the chart, click the Move Chart button (Chart Tools Design tab | Location group) to display the Move Chart dialog box.

- Click New sheet (Move Chart dialog box) and then type **Expense Chart** in the New sheet text box to enter a sheet tab name for the chart sheet (Figure 3–53).

Figure 3–53

3

- Click the OK button (Move Chart dialog box) to move the chart to a new chart sheet with a new sheet tab name, Expense Chart (Figure 3–54).

Q&A

Why do January and February have only four columns charted?

Both January and February have a value of $0 for the Bonus category. Values of zero are not charted in a column chart, so these two months have one fewer column than the other months.

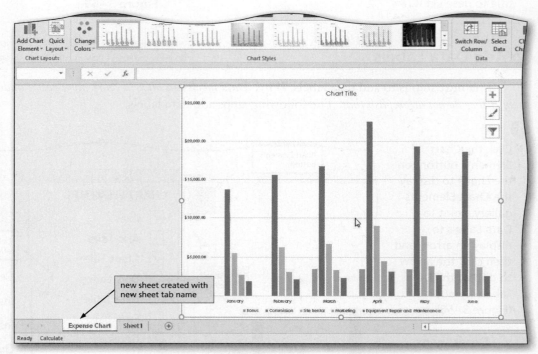

Figure 3–54

Other Ways

1. Select range to chart, PRESS F11

To Insert a Chart Title

The next step is to insert a chart title. ***Why?*** *A chart title identifies the chart content for the viewer.* Before you can format a chart item, such as the chart title, you must select it. The following step inserts a chart title.

- Click anywhere in the chart title placeholder to select it.

- Select the text in the chart title placeholder and then type **Six-Month Projected Expenses** to add a new chart title.

- Select the text in the new title and then display the Home tab.

- Click the Underline button (Home tab | Font group) to assign an underline format to the chart title (Figure 3–55).

- Click anywhere outside of the chart title to deselect it.

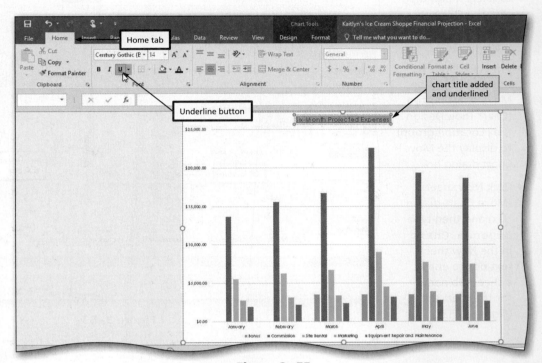

Figure 3–55

To Add Data Labels

The next step is to add data labels. ***Why?*** *Data labels can make a chart more easily understood. You can remove them if they do not accomplish that.* The following steps add data labels.

- Click the Chart Elements button (on the chart) to display the Chart Elements gallery. Point to Data Labels to display an arrow and then click the arrow to display the Data Labels fly-out menu (Figure 3–56).

Experiment

- If you are using a mouse, point to each option on the Data Labels fly-out menu to see a live preview of the data labels.

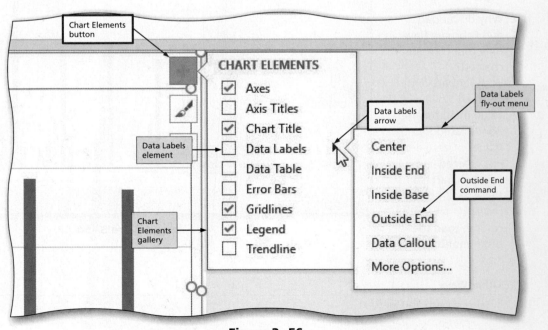

Figure 3–56

2

- Click Outside End on the Data Labels fly-out menu so that data labels are displayed outside the chart at the end of each column.

- Click the Chart Elements button to close the gallery (Figure 3–57).

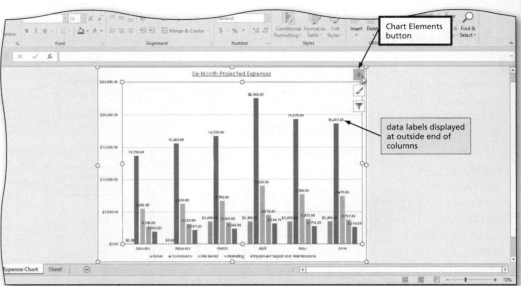

Figure 3–57

To Apply Chart Filters

1 ENTER HEADINGS & DATA | 2 ENTER FORMULAS & FUNCTIONS | 3 CREATE SPARKLINE CHARTS
4 FORMAT WORKSHEET | 5 CREATE COLUMN CHART | 6 CHANGE VIEWS | 7 ASK WHAT-IF QUESTIONS

Why? *With some data, you may find that certain data series or categories make it difficult to examine differences and patterns between other series or categories. Excel allows you to easily filter data series and categories to allow more in-depth examinations of subsets of data.* In this case, filters can be used to temporarily remove the compensation categories Bonus and Commission from the chart, to allow a comparison across the non-compensation expenses. The following steps apply filters to the clustered column chart.

1

- Click the Chart Filters button (on the chart) to display the Chart Filters gallery.

- In the Series section, click the Bonus and Commission check boxes to remove their check marks and then click the Apply button to filter these series from the chart (Figure 3–58).

Q&A What happens when I remove the check marks from Bonus and Commission?
When you remove the check marks from Bonus and Commission, Excel filters the Bonus and Commission series out and redraws the chart without them.

Figure 3–58

2

- Click the Chart Filters button to close the gallery.

To Add an Axis Title to the Chart

Why? Often the unit of measurement or categories for the charted data is not obvious. You can add an axis title, or titles for both axes, for clarity or completeness. The following steps add an axis title for the vertical axis.

- If necessary, click anywhere in the chart area outside the chart to select the chart.

- Click the Chart Elements button to display the Chart Elements gallery. Point to Axis Titles to display an arrow and then click the arrow to display the Axis Titles fly-out menu.

 Experiment

- Point to each option on the fly-out menu to see a live preview of the axes' titles.

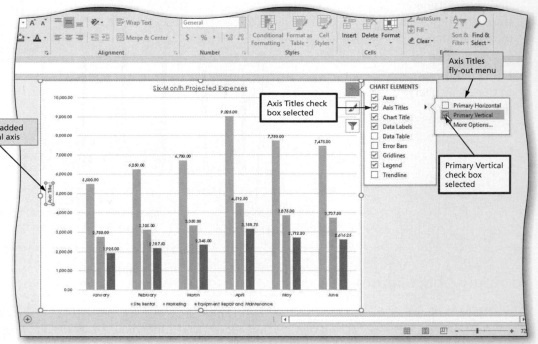

Figure 3–59

- Click Primary Vertical on the Axis Titles fly-out menu to add an axis title to the vertical axis (Figure 3–59).

- Click the Chart Elements button to remove the Chart Elements gallery from the window.

- Select the placeholder text in the vertical axis title and replace it with $ (a dollar sign).

- Right-click the axis title to display a shortcut menu (Figure 3–60).

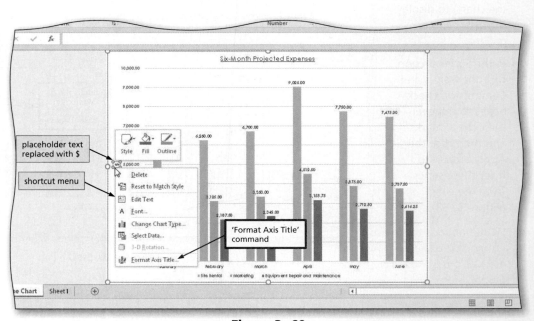

Figure 3–60

3

- Click 'Format Axis Title' on the shortcut menu to open the Format Axis Title task pane.

- If necessary, click the Title Options tab, click the 'Size & Properties' button, and then, if necessary, click the Alignment arrow to expand the Alignment section.

- Click the Text direction arrow to display the Text direction list (Figure 3–61).

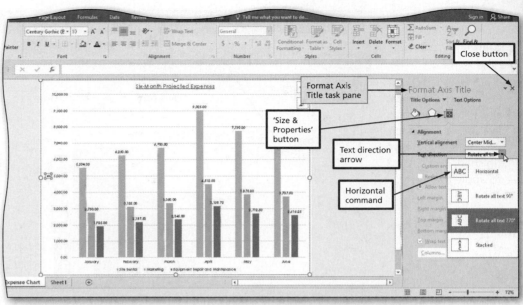

Figure 3–61

- Click Horizontal in the Text direction list to change the orientation of the vertical axis title.

- Click the Close button (shown in Figure 3–61) on the task pane to close the Format Axis Title task pane.

To Change the Chart Style

1 ENTER HEADINGS & DATA | 2 ENTER FORMULAS & FUNCTIONS | 3 CREATE SPARKLINE CHARTS
4 FORMAT WORKSHEET | 5 CREATE COLUMN CHART | 6 CHANGE VIEWS | 7 ASK WHAT-IF QUESTIONS

Why? *You decide that a chart with a different look would better convey meaning to viewers.* The following steps change the chart style.

1

- Click the More button (Chart Tools Design tab | Chart Styles group) (shown in Figure 3–61) to display the Chart Styles gallery (Figure 3–62).

Figure 3–62

2

- Click Style 3 to apply a new style to the chart (Figure 3–63).

Experiment

- Point to the various chart styles to see a live preview of each one. When you have finished, click Style 3 to apply that style.

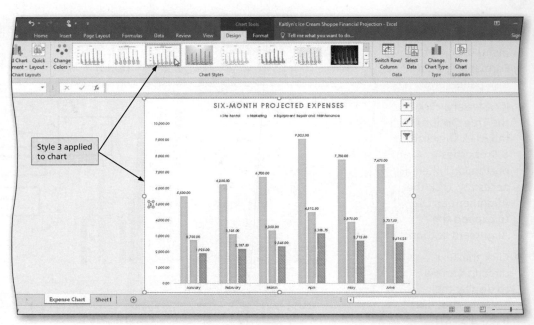

Figure 3–63

To Modify the Chart Axis Number Format

1 ENTER HEADINGS & DATA | 2 ENTER FORMULAS & FUNCTIONS | 3 CREATE SPARKLINE CHARTS
4 FORMAT WORKSHEET | 5 CREATE COLUMN CHART | 6 CHANGE VIEWS | 7 ASK WHAT-IF QUESTIONS

Why? *The two decimal places in the vertical chart axis numbers are not necessary and make the axis appear cluttered.* The following steps format the numbers in the chart axis to contain no decimal places.

1

- Right-click any value on the vertical axis to display the shortcut menu (Figure 3–64).

Figure 3–64

2

- Click Format Axis on the shortcut menu to open the Format Axis task pane.

- If necessary, click the Axis Options tab in the Format Axis task pane and then scroll until Number is visible. Click the Number arrow to expand the Number section and then scroll to review options related to formatting numbers.

- Change the number in the Decimal places text box to 0 (Figure 3–65).

3

- Close the Format Axis task pane.

Figure 3–65

To Remove Filters and Data Labels

You decide that the data labels on the bars are distracting and add no value to the chart. You decide to remove the data labels and filters so that all expense data is once again visible. The following steps remove the data labels and the filters.

1 Click the Chart Elements button to display the Chart Elements gallery.

2 Click the Data Labels check box to remove the check mark for the data labels.

3 Click the Chart Elements button again to close the gallery.

4 Click the Chart Filters button to display the Chart Filters fly-out menu.

5 In the Series section, click Bonus and then Commission, click the Apply button to add the compensation data back into the chart, and then click the Chart Filters button again to close the menu (Figure 3–66).

BTW
Chart Templates
Once you create and format a chart to your liking, consider saving the chart as a template so that you can use it to format additional charts. Save your chart as a chart template by accessing the chart shortcut menu and then selecting 'Save as Template' from that shortcut menu. The chart template will appear in the Templates folder for Charts. When you want to use the template, click the Templates folder in the All Charts sheet (Insert Chart dialog box) and then select your template.

Figure 3–66

Organizing the Workbook

Once the content of the workbook is complete, you can address the organization of the workbook. If the workbook has multiple worksheets, place the worksheet on top that you want the reader to see first. Default sheet names in Excel are not descriptive. Renaming the sheets with descriptive names helps the reader find information that he or she is looking for. Modifying the sheet tabs through the use of color further distinguishes multiple sheets from each other.

To Rename and Color Sheet Tabs

The following steps rename the sheets and color the sheet tabs.

1 Change the color of the Expense Chart sheet tab to Green, Accent 4 (column 8, row 1).

2 Double-click the sheet tab labeled Sheet1 at the bottom of the screen.

3 Type `Six-Month Financial Projection` as the new sheet tab name and then press the ENTER key.

4 Change the sheet tab color of the Six-Month Financial Projection sheet to Blue, Accent 2 (column 6, row 1) and then select an empty cell (Figure 3–67).

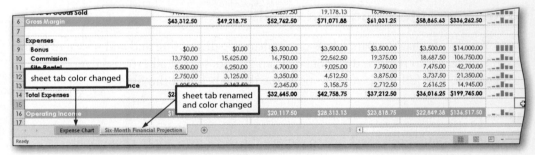

Figure 3–67

To Reorder the Sheet Tabs

1 ENTER HEADINGS & DATA | 2 ENTER FORMULAS & FUNCTIONS | 3 CREATE SPARKLINE CHARTS
4 FORMAT WORKSHEET | 5 CREATE COLUMN CHART | 6 CHANGE VIEWS | 7 ASK WHAT-IF QUESTIONS

Why? *You want the most important worksheets to appear first in a workbook, so you need to change the order of sheets.* The following step reorders the sheets so that the worksheet precedes the chart sheet in the workbook.

1

- Drag the Six-Month Financial Projection tab to the left so that it precedes the Expense Chart sheet tab to rearrange the sequence of the sheets (Figure 3–68).

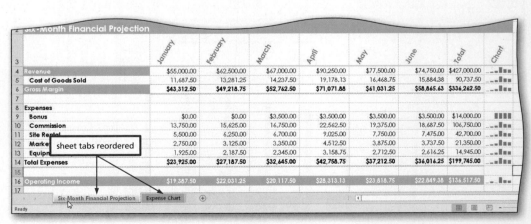

Figure 3–68

Other Ways

1. To move sheet, right-click sheet tab, click Move or Copy on shortcut menu, click OK button

To Check Spelling in Multiple Sheets

BTW
Checking Spelling
Unless you first select a range of cells or an object before starting the spelling checker, Excel checks the entire selected worksheet, including all cell values, cell comments, embedded charts, text boxes, buttons, and headers and footers.

By default, the spelling checker reviews spelling only in the selected sheets. It will check all the cells in the selected sheets, unless you select a range of two or more cells. Before checking the spelling, the following steps select both worksheets in the workbook so that both are checked for any spelling errors.

1 With the Six-Month Financial Projection sheet active, press CTRL+HOME to select cell A1. Hold down the CTRL key and then click the Expense Chart tab to select both sheets.

2 Display the Review tab and then click the Spelling button (Review tab | Proofing group) to check spelling in the selected sheets.

3 Correct any errors and then click the OK button (Spelling dialog box or Microsoft Excel dialog box) when the spelling checker is finished.

To Preview and Print the Worksheet

BTW
Distributing a Workbook
Instead of printing and distributing a hard copy of a workbook, you can distribute the workbook electronically. Options include sending the workbook via email; posting it on cloud storage (such as OneDrive) and sharing the file with others; posting it on social media, a blog, or other website; and sharing a link associated with an online location of the workbook. You also can create and share a PDF or XPS image of the workbook, so that users can view the file in Acrobat Reader or XPS Viewer instead of in Excel.

After checking the spelling, the next step is to preview and print the worksheets. As with spelling, Excel previews and prints only the selected sheets. In addition, because the worksheet is too wide to print in portrait orientation, the orientation must be changed to landscape. The following steps adjust the orientation and scale, preview the worksheets, and then print the worksheets.

1 If both sheets are not selected, hold down the CTRL key and then click the tab of the inactive sheet.

2 Click File on the ribbon to open the Backstage view.

3 Click the Print tab in the Backstage view to display the Print gallery.

4 Click the Portrait Orientation button in the Settings area and then select Landscape Orientation to select the desired orientation.

5 Click the No Scaling button in the Settings area and then select 'Fit Sheet on One Page' to cause the worksheets to print on one page.

6 Verify that the selected printer will print a hard copy of the document. If necessary, click the printer button to display a list of available printer options and then click the desired printer to change the currently selected printer.

7 Click the Print button in the Print gallery to print the worksheet in landscape orientation on the currently selected printer.

8 When the printer stops, retrieve the printed worksheets (shown in Figure 3–69a and Figure 3–69b).

9 Right-click the Six-Month Financial Projection tab, and then click Ungroup Sheets on the shortcut menu to deselect the Expense Chart tab.

10 Save the workbook again on the same storage location with the same file name.

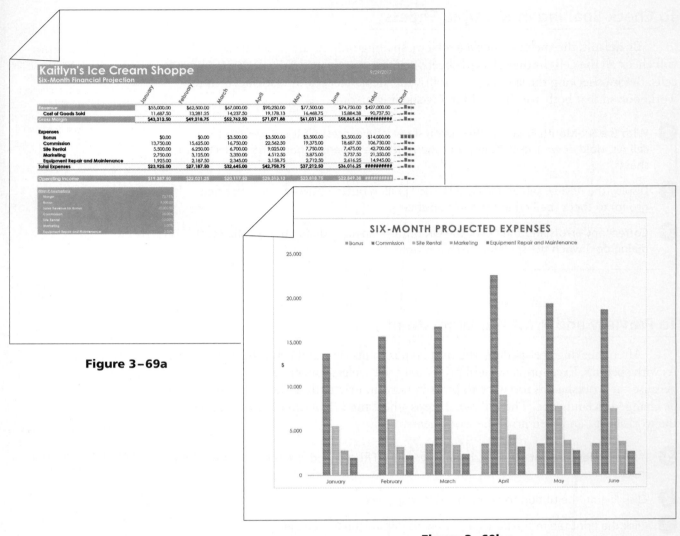

Figure 3–69a

Figure 3–69b

Changing the View of the Worksheet

With Excel, you easily can change the view of the worksheet. For example, you can magnify or shrink the worksheet on the screen. You also can view different parts of the worksheet at the same time by using panes.

To Shrink and Magnify the View of a Worksheet or Chart

1 ENTER HEADINGS & DATA | 2 ENTER FORMULAS & FUNCTIONS | 3 CREATE SPARKLINE CHARTS

4 FORMAT WORKSHEET | 5 CREATE COLUMN CHART | 6 CHANGE VIEWS | 7 ASK WHAT-IF QUESTIONS

You can magnify (zoom in) or shrink (zoom out) the appearance of a worksheet or chart by using the Zoom button (View tab | Zoom group). *Why? When you magnify a worksheet, Excel enlarges the view of the characters on the screen, but shows fewer columns and rows. Alternatively, when you shrink a worksheet, Excel is able to display more columns and rows.* Magnifying or shrinking a worksheet affects only the view; it does not change the window size or the size of the printout of the worksheet or chart. The following steps shrink and magnify the view of the worksheet.

1

- If cell A1 is not active, press CTRL+HOME.

- Display the View tab and then click the Zoom button (View tab | Zoom group) to display a list of magnifications in the Zoom dialog box (Figure 3–70).

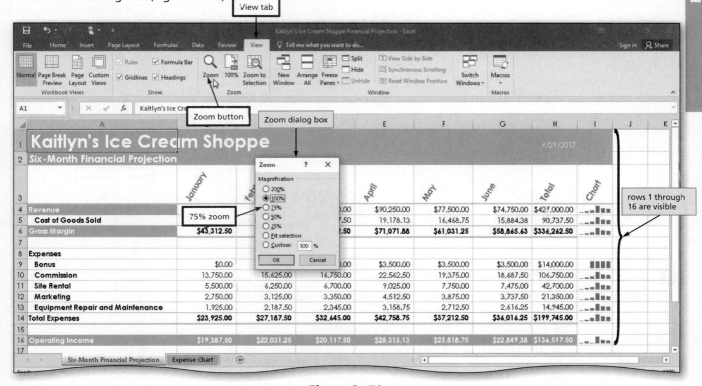

Figure 3–70

2

- Click 75% and then click the OK button (Zoom dialog box) to shrink the display of the worksheet (Figure 3–71). The number of columns and rows appearing on your screen may differ from Figure 3–71.

Figure 3–71

- Click the Zoom Out button on the status bar until the worksheet is displayed at 70% and all worksheet content is visible (Figure 3–72). The number of columns and rows appearing on your screen may differ from Figure 3–72.

Figure 3–72

- Click the 100% button (View tab | Zoom group) to display the worksheet at 100%.

Other Ways

1. Drag zoom slider to increase or decrease zoom level

To Split a Window into Panes

1 ENTER HEADINGS & DATA | 2 ENTER FORMULAS & FUNCTIONS | 3 CREATE SPARKLINE CHARTS
4 FORMAT WORKSHEET | 5 CREATE COLUMN CHART | 6 CHANGE VIEWS | 7 ASK WHAT-IF QUESTIONS

When working with a large worksheet, you can split the window into two or four panes to view different parts of the worksheet at the same time. *Why? Splitting the Excel window into four panes at cell E8 allows you to view all four corners of the worksheet simultaneously.* The following steps split the Excel window into four panes.

- Select cell E8, the intersection of the four proposed panes, as the cell at which to split the window.

- If necessary, display the View tab (Figure 3–73).

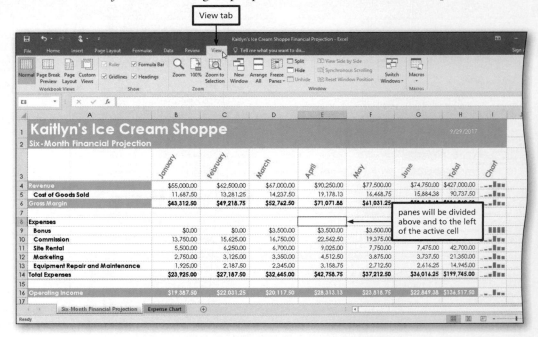

Figure 3–73

2

• Click the Split button (View tab | Window group) to divide the window into four panes.

• Use the scroll arrows to show the four corners of the worksheet at the same time (Figure 3–74).

Q&A What is shown in the four panes?

The four panes in Figure 3–74 show the following: (1) range A1:D7 in the upper-left pane; (2) range E1:J7 in the upper-right pane; (3) range A17:D25 in the lower-left pane; and (4) range E17:J25 in the lower-right pane. The vertical split bar is the vertical bar running up and down the middle of the window. The horizontal split bar is the horizontal bar running across the middle of the window. If you use the scroll bars below the window, you will see that the panes split by the horizontal split bar scroll together horizontally. The panes split by the vertical split bar scroll together vertically when using the scroll bars to the right of the window. To resize the panes, drag either split bar to the desired location.

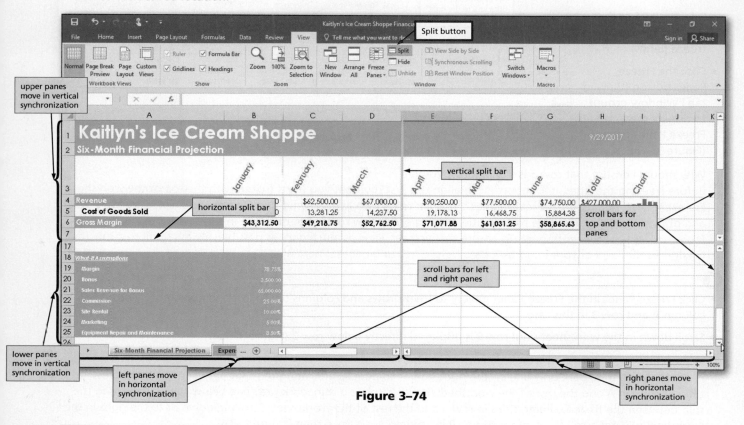

Figure 3–74

To Remove the Panes from the Window

The following step removes the panes from the window.

1 Click the Split button (View tab | Window group) to remove the four panes from the window.

Other Ways

1. Double-click intersection of horizontal and vertical split bars

To Freeze Worksheet Columns and Rows

1 ENTER HEADINGS & DATA | 2 ENTER FORMULAS & FUNCTIONS | 3 CREATE SPARKLINE CHARTS
4 FORMAT WORKSHEET | 5 CREATE COLUMN CHART | 6 CHANGE VIEWS | 7 ASK WHAT-IF QUESTIONS

Why? *Freezing worksheet columns and rows is a useful technique for viewing large worksheets that extend beyond the window.* Normally, when you scroll down or to the right, the column content in the top rows and the row content in the leftmost columns no longer appear on the screen. When the content of these rows and/ or columns helps to identify or define other content still visible on the worksheet, it can make it difficult to remember what the numbers in the visible cells represent. To alleviate this problem, Excel allows you to freeze columns and rows, so that their content, typically column or row titles, remains on the screen, no matter how far down or to the right you scroll. You also may wish to keep numbers visible that you need to see when making changes to content in another part of the worksheet, such as the revenue, cost of goods sold, and gross margin information in rows 4 through 6. The following steps use the Freeze Panes button (View tab | Window group) to freeze the worksheet title and column titles in row 3, and the row titles in column A.

- Scroll the worksheet until Excel displays row 3 as the first row and column A as the first column on the screen.

- Select cell B4 as the cell on which to freeze panes.

- Click the Freeze Panes button (View tab | Window group) to display the Freeze Panes gallery (Figure 3–75).

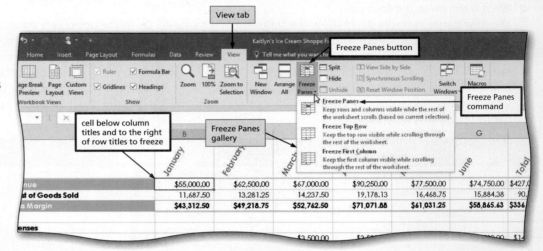

Figure 3–75

Q&A

Why should I ensure that row 3 is the first row visible?

Before freezing the titles, it is important to align the first row that you want frozen with the top of the worksheet. For example, if you used the Freeze Panes button in cell B4 while displaying row 1, then Excel would freeze and display the worksheet title and subtitle, leaving only a few rows of data visible in the Six-Month Financial Projection area of the worksheet. To ensure that you can view as much data as possible, always scroll to a row that maximizes the view of your important data before freezing panes.

- Click Freeze Panes in the Freeze Panes gallery to freeze rows and columns to the left and above the selected cell, column A and row 3 in this case.

- Scroll down in the worksheet until row 9 is displayed directly below row 3 (Figure 3–76).

Q&A

What happens after I click the Freeze Panes command?

Excel displays a thin, dark gray line on the right side of column A, indicating the split between the frozen row titles in column A and the rest of the worksheet. It also displays a thin, dark gray line below row 3, indicating the split between the frozen column titles in row 3 and the rest of the worksheet. Scrolling down or to the right in the worksheet will not scroll the content of row 3 or column A off the screen (Figure 3–76).

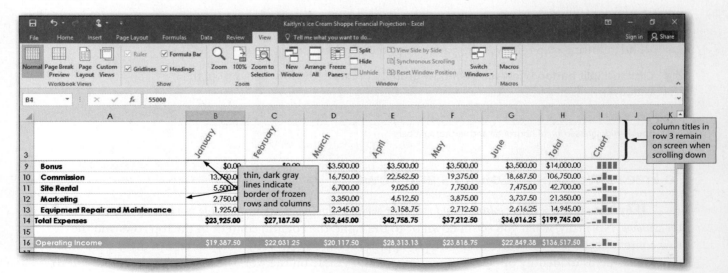

Figure 3–76

To Unfreeze the Worksheet Columns and Rows

Why? *Keep columns and rows frozen only as long as you need to view the worksheet in that configuration.* The following steps unfreeze the titles in column A and row 3 to allow you to work with the worksheet without frozen rows and columns, or to freeze the worksheet at a different location.

1 Press CTRL+HOME to select cell B4 and view the upper-left corner of the screen.

2 Click the Freeze Panes button (View tab | Window group) to display the Freeze Panes gallery.

3 Click Unfreeze Panes in the Freeze Panes gallery to unfreeze the frozen columns and rows.

4 Display the Home tab.

5 Save the workbook again on the same storage location with the same file name.

Q&A | Why does pressing CTRL+HOME select cell B4?
When the titles are frozen and you press CTRL+HOME, Excel selects the upper-leftmost cell of the unfrozen section of the worksheet. For example, in Step 1 of the previous steps, Excel selected cell B4. When the titles are unfrozen, pressing CTRL+HOME selects cell A1.

BTW
Freezing Titles
If you want to freeze only column headings, select the appropriate cell in column A before you click the Freeze Panes button (View tab | Window group). If you want to freeze only row titles, select the appropriate cell in row 1 before you click the Freeze Panes button. To freeze both column headings and row titles, select the cell that is the intersection of the column and row titles before you click the Freeze Panes button.

What-If Analysis

The automatic recalculation feature of Excel is a powerful tool that can be used to analyze worksheet data. Using Excel to scrutinize the impact of changing values in cells that are referenced by formulas in other cells is called **what-if analysis** or sensitivity analysis. When new data is entered, Excel not only recalculates all formulas in a worksheet but also redraws any associated charts.

In the workbook created in this module, many of the formulas are dependent on the assumptions in the range B19:B25. Thus, if you change any of the assumption values, Excel recalculates all formulas. Excel redraws the clustered column chart as well, because it is based on these numbers.

To Analyze Data in a Worksheet by Changing Values

1 ENTER HEADINGS & DATA | 2 ENTER FORMULAS & FUNCTIONS | 3 CREATE SPARKLINE CHARTS
4 FORMAT WORKSHEET | 5 CREATE COLUMN CHART | 6 CHANGE VIEWS | 7 ASK WHAT-IF QUESTIONS

Why? *The effect of changing one or more values in the What-If Assumptions table — essentially posing what-if questions — allows you to review the results of different scenarios.* In this case, you are going to examine what would happen to the six-month operating income (cell H16) if the following changes were made in the What-If Assumptions table: Bonus $3,500.00 to $5,000.00; Commission 25.00% to 22.50%; Equipment Repair and Maintenance 3.50% to 4.00%. To answer a question like this, you need to change only the second, fourth, and seventh values in the What-If Assumptions table. The following step splits the screen, which allows you to view income and expense figures simultaneously, and then changes values in the worksheet to answer a what-if question. When a new value is entered, Excel recalculates the formulas in the worksheet and redraws the clustered column chart to reflect the new data.

- Scroll the worksheet so that row 4 is the first row visible on the worksheet.

- Click in cell A7 to select the row above which to split the window.

- Click the Split button (View tab | Window group) to split the window after row 6.

- Use the scroll arrows in the lower-right pane to scroll the window content until row 9 is the first row visible in the lower part of the screen, as shown in Figure 3–77.

- Enter **5,000** in cell B20, **22.50%** in cell B22, and **4.00%** in cell B25 (Figure 3–77), which causes the six-month operating income in cell H16 to increase from $136,517.50 to $139,057.50.

- Save the workbook again on the same storage location with the same file name.

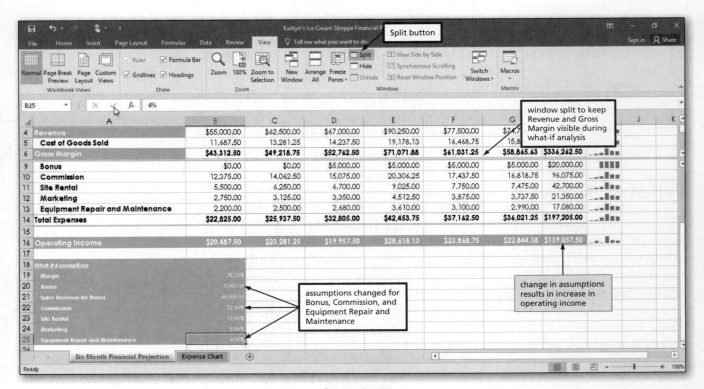

Figure 3–77

To Goal Seek

Why? If you know the result you want a formula to produce, you can use goal seeking to determine the value of a cell on which the formula depends. The previous step, which made changes to the What-If Assumptions table, resulted in an operating income that approaches but does not reach $145,000.00. The following steps use the Goal Seek command (Data tab | Forecast group) to determine what Site Rental percentage (cell B23), in conjunction with the earlier changes in assumptions, will yield a six-month operating income of $145,000 in cell H16, rather than the $139,057.50 calculated in the previous set of steps.

1

- If necessary, use the scroll arrows in the lower pane to ensure that you can view all of the What-If Assumptions table and the Operating Income figures.

- Select cell H16, the cell that contains the six-month operating income.

- Display the Data tab and then click the 'What-If Analysis' button (Data tab | Forecast group) to display the What-If Analysis menu (Figure 3–78).

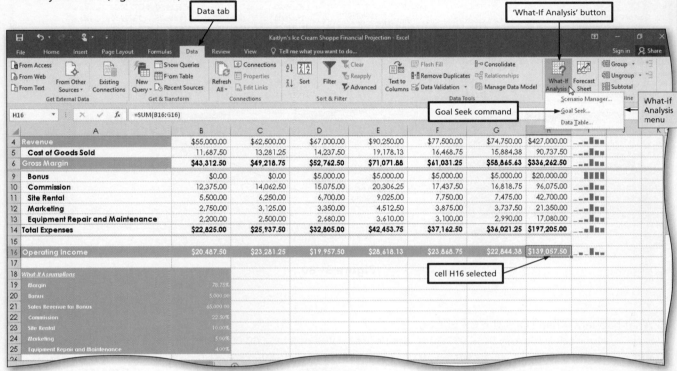

Figure 3–78

2

- Click Goal Seek to display the Goal Seek dialog box with the Set cell box set to the selected cell, H16 in this case.

- Click the To value text box, type **145,000** and then click the 'By changing cell' box to select the 'By changing cell' box.

- Click cell B23 on the worksheet to assign the current cell, B23 in this case, to the 'By changing cell' box (Figure 3–79).

Figure 3–79

- Click the OK button (Goal Seek dialog box) to goal seek for the sought-after value in the To value text box, $145,000.00 in cell H16 in this case (Figure 3–80).

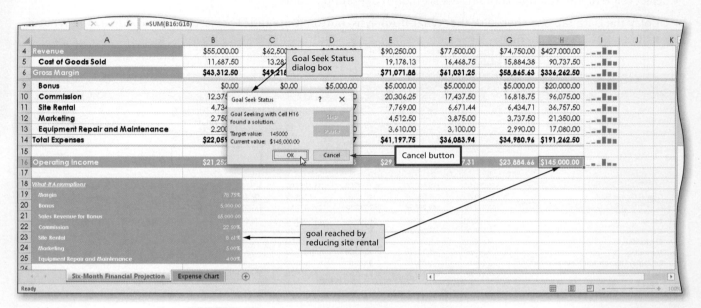

Figure 3–80

What happens when I click the OK button?

Excel changes cell H16 from $139,057.50 to the desired value of $145,000.00. More importantly, Excel changes the Site Rental assumption in cell B23 from 10.00% to 8.61% (Figure 3–80). Excel also displays the Goal Seek Status dialog box. If you click the OK button, Excel keeps the new values in the worksheet. If you click the Cancel button, Excel redisplays the original values.

- Click the Cancel button in the Goal Seek Status dialog box to redisplay the original values in the worksheet.

- Click the Split button (View tab | Window group) to remove the two panes from the window.

Goal Seeking

Goal seeking assumes you can change the value of only one cell referenced directly or indirectly to reach a specific goal for a value in another cell. In this example, to change the six-month operating income in cell H16 to $145,000.00, the Site Rental percentage in cell B23 must decrease by 1.39% from 10.00% to 8.61%.

You can see from this goal seeking example that the cell to change (cell B23) does not have to be referenced directly in the formula or function. For example, the six-month operating income in cell H16 is calculated by the function =SUM(B16:G16). Cell B23 is not referenced in this function. Instead, cell B23 is referenced in the formulas in row 11, on which the monthly operating incomes in row 16 are based. By tracing the formulas and functions, Excel can obtain the desired six-month operating income by varying the value for the Site Rental assumption.

Insights

The Insights feature in Excel uses the Bing search engine and other Internet resources to help you locate more information about the content in your workbooks. One common use of this feature is to look up the definition of a word. When looking up a definition, Excel uses contextual data so that it can return the most relevant information.

To Use the Smart Lookup Insight

1 ENTER HEADINGS & DATA | 2 ENTER FORMULAS & FUNCTIONS | 3 CREATE SPARKLINE CHARTS
4 FORMAT WORKSHEET | 5 CREATE COLUMN CHART | 6 CHANGE VIEWS | 7 ASK WHAT-IF QUESTIONS

Smart Lookup uses Bing and other Internet resources to find useful information about text in your spreadsheet and then displays that information in the Insights task pane. *Why? If you need additional information about some terminology in a workbook you are creating or viewing, Smart Lookup can provide that information.* The following steps use Smart Lookup to look up information about the text in cell A6.

- Select cell A6.
- Display the Review tab and then click Smart Lookup (Review tab | Insights group) to display the Insights task pane containing information about the text in the selected cell (Figure 3–81).

Q&A
Why did I see a 'We value your privacy' message?
This message appears the first time you use the Smart Lookup insight. If you agree to the terms, click the Got it button to continue.

Figure 3–81

- Click the Close button on the Insights task pane to close the task pane.
- If desired, sign out of your Microsoft account.
- Exit Excel.

Accessibility Features

Excel provides a utility that can be used to check a workbook for potential issues related to **accessibility**. Accessibility refers to the practice of removing barriers that may prevent individuals with disabilities from interacting with your data or the app. To use the Check Accessibility command, click File on the ribbon to open the Backstage view, click the Info tab, click the 'Check for Issues' button, and then click Check Accessibility. Excel will check your workbook for content that could prove difficult for people with disabilities to read, either alone or with adaptive tools. The resulting report (Figure 3–82 shows an example) will identify issues and offer suggestions for addressing the reported issues.

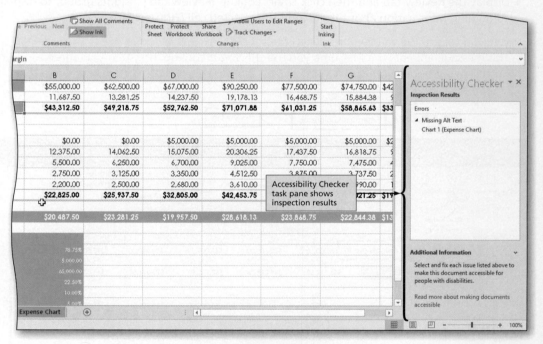

Figure 3–82

Summary

In this module, you learned how to use Excel to create a six-month financial projection workbook. Topics covered included rotating text in a cell, creating a series of month names, entering and formatting the system date, using absolute and mixed cell references, using the IF function, creating and changing sparkline charts, using the format painter, creating a clustered column chart, using chart filters, reordering sheet tabs, changing the worksheet view, freezing and unfreezing rows and columns, answering what-if questions, goal seeking, using Smart Lookup, and understanding accessibility features.

What decisions will you need to make when creating your next worksheet to evaluate and analyze data using what-if analysis?

Use these guidelines as you complete the assignments in this module and create your own worksheets for evaluating and analyzing data outside of this class.

1. Determine the workbook structure.

   a) Determine the data you will need for your worksheet.

   b) Determine the layout of your data on the worksheet.

   c) Determine the layout of the assumptions table on the worksheet.

   d) Determine the location and features of any charts.

2. Create the worksheet.

   a) Enter titles, subtitles, and headings.

   b) Enter data, functions, and formulas.

3. Format the worksheet.

   a) Format the titles, subtitles, and headings.

   b) Format the numbers as necessary.

   c) Format the text.

4. Create and use charts.

   a) Select data to chart.

   b) Select a chart type for selected data.

   c) Format the chart elements.

   d) Filter charts if necessary to view subsets of data.

5. Perform what-if analyses.

   a) Adjust values in the assumptions table to review scenarios of interest.

   b) Use Goal Seek to determine how to adjust a variable value to reach a particular goal or outcome.

Apply Your Knowledge

Reinforce the skills and apply the concepts you learned in this module.

Understanding Logical Tests and Absolute Cell Referencing

Note: To complete this assignment, you will be required to use the Data Files. Please contact your instructor for information about accessing the required files.

Instructions Part 1: For each of the following logical tests, indicate whether an IF function in Excel would return a value of True or False; given the following cell values: C2 = 88; H12 = 15; L3 = 24; M14 = 150; and G4 = 5.

1. C2 > H12   Returned value: _____

2. L3 = G4   Returned value: _____

3. M14 + 15 * H12 / 10 <= L3   Returned value: _____

4. M14 – G4 < H12 / C2   Returned value: _____

5. (C2 + H12) * 2 >= L3 – (C2 / 4) * 2   Returned value: _____

6. L3 + 300 > H12 * G4 + 10   Returned value: _____

7. G4 * M14 >= 2 * (H12 + 25)   Returned value: _____

8. H12 = 10 * (C2 / 8)   Returned value: _____

Instructions Part 2: Write cell L23 as a relative reference, absolute reference, mixed reference with the column varying, and mixed reference with the row varying.

_____   _____   _____   _____

Instructions Part 3: Run Excel. Open the workbook Apply 3-1 Absolute Cell References. You will re-create the numerical grid pictured in Figure 3–83.

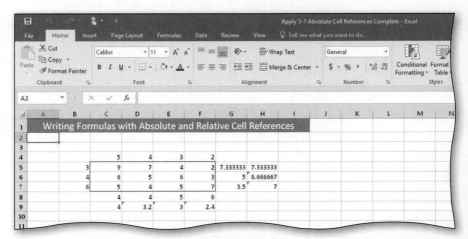

Figure 3–83

Perform the following tasks:

1. Enter a formula in cell C8 that divides the sum of cells C5 through C7 by cell C4. Write the formula so that when you copy it to cells D8:F8, Excel adjusts all the cell references according to the destination cells. Verify your formula by checking it against the values found in cells C8, D8, E8, and F8 in Figure 3–83.

2. Enter a formula in cell G5 that divides the sum of cells C5 through F5 by cell B5. Write the formula so that when you copy the formula to cells G6 and G7, Excel adjusts all the cell references according to the destination cells. Verify your formula by checking it against the values found in cells G5, G6, and G7 in Figure 3–83.

3. Enter a formula in cell C9 that divides the sum of cells C5 through C7 by cell C4. Write the formula using an absolute cell reference so that when you copy the formula to cells D9:F9, cell C4 remains absolute. Verify your formula by checking it against the values found in cells C9, D9, E9, and F9 in Figure 3–83.

4. Enter a formula in cell H5 that divides the sum of cells C5:F5 by cell B5. Write the formula using an absolute cell reference so that when you copy the formula to cells H6 and H7, cell B5 remains absolute. Verify your formula by checking it with the values found in cells H5, H6, and H7 in Figure 3–83.

5. Apply the worksheet name, Cell References, to the sheet tab and apply the Orange, Accent 2 Theme color to the sheet tab.

6. If requested by your instructor, add a dash followed by your name to the worksheet title in cell A1.

7. Save the workbook using the file name, Apply 3-1 Absolute Cell References Complete. Submit the revised workbook as specified by your instructor.

8. ✹ How would you rewrite the formula in cell H5 using relative and mixed cell references only, to come up with the same result as showing in Figure 3–83, and to produce the results currently showing in cells G6 and G7 in cells H6 and H7 when the formula in cell H5 is copied to those cells?

Extend Your Knowledge

Extend the skills you learned in this module and experiment with new skills. You may need to use Help to complete the assignment.

The Fill Handle and Nested IF Functions

Note: To complete this assignment, you will be required to use the Data Files. Please contact your instructor for information about accessing the required files.

Perform the following tasks:

Instructions Part 1: Run Excel. Open the workbook Extend 3-1 Fill and IF. If necessary, make Fill the active sheet.

1. Use the fill handle on one column at a time to propagate the 12 series through row 14, as shown in Figure 3–84. (*Hint:* Search in Help to learn more about the fill handle and Auto Fill.) In cells O2:O13, indicate the actions used with the fill handle to propagate the series. For instance, in cell O2, enter **Drag**. For instances where you need to select something other than the cell in row 2 prior to using the fill handle, enter the selection and then the drag action, **A2:A3 Drag** for example.

2. Select cell D20. While holding down the CTRL key, one at a time drag the fill handle three cells to the right, to the left, up, and down to generate four series of numbers beginning with zero and incremented by one.

3. Select cell H20. Point to the cell border so that the pointer changes to a plus sign with four arrows. Drag the pointer down to cell H22 to move the contents of cell H20 to cell H22.

4. If necessary, select cell H22. Point to the cell border so that the pointer changes to a plus sign with four arrows. While holding down the CTRL key, drag the pointer to cell K22 to copy the contents of cell H22 to cell K22.

Continued >

Extend Your Knowledge *continued*

Figure 3–84

5. Select cell K20. Drag the fill handle in to the center of cell K20 until that the cell is shaded and the cell contents are deleted.

6. Select cell range H2:I14, and insert a 3-D column chart on a new sheet.

7. Change the chart title to Annual Breakdown.

8. Add a data table with no legend keys to the chart.

9. Apply the chart sheet name, Column Chart, to the sheet and move the sheet to follow the Fill sheet.

10. Save the workbook using the file name, Extend 3-1 Fill and IF Complete.

Instructions Part 2: Switch to the IF sheet in the Extend 3-1 Fill and IF Complete workbook.

1. Write an IF function in cell C2 that assigns a grade of 'Pass' if the score in cell B2 is 50 or above, and a grade of 'Fail' if the score in cell B2 is below 50. Copy this function to cells C3:C18.

2. Write a nested IF function in cell D2 that assigns a grade of A for scores between 80 and 100, a grade of B for scores between 65 and 79, a grade of C for scores between 50 and 64, and a grade of F for scores below 50. (*Hint*: Search in Help for nested IF when constructing your function.) Copy this function to cells D3:D18.

3. If requested by your instructor, change the student number in cell A3 on the IF sheet to your student number.

4. Save the workbook and submit the revised workbook as specified by your instructor.

5. ✹ Students who do not take a test receive a score of NS. How would you include a score of NS as a grade in each of Steps 1 and 2?

Expand Your World

Create a solution that uses cloud or web technologies by learning and investigating on your own from general guidance.

Analyzing and Graphing Development Indicators

Note: To complete this assignment, you will be required to use the Data Files. Please contact your instructor for information about accessing the required files.

Instructions: You are working as part of a group creating a report on historical education trends in the developing nation of Mali, comparing three related development indicators concerning school enrollment over time. Your task is to format the worksheet containing the historical data, chart the historical education indicators, and make the chart available to your group using OneDrive. Run Excel and then open the workbook, Expand 3-1 Education Indicators.

Perform the following tasks:

1. Save the workbook using the file name, Expand 3-1 Education Indicators Charted.

2. Format the worksheet using techniques you have learned to present the data in a visually appealing form.

3. Create charts that present the data for each of the three indicators. Think about what interested you in these indicators in the first place, and decide which chart types will best present the data. (*Hint:* If you are not sure which types to use, consider selecting the data and using the Recommended Chart button to narrow down and preview suitable choices.) Format the charts to best present the data in a clear, attractive format.

4. Give each worksheet a descriptive name and color the tabs using theme colors. Reorder the sheets so that the data table appears first, followed by the charts.

5. If requested by your instructor, export the file to OneDrive.

6. Submit the revised workbook as specified by your instructor.

7. ☀ Justify your choice of chart types in Step 3. Explain why you selected these types over other suitable choices.

In the Labs

Design, create, modify and/or use a workbook following the guidelines, concepts, and skills presented in this module. Labs 1 and 2, which increase in difficulty, require you to create solutions based on what you learned in the module; Lab 3 requires you to apply your creative thinking and problem-solving skills to design and implement a solution.

Lab 1: Eight-Year Financial Projection

Problem: Your supervisor in the finance department at August Online Technology has asked you to create a worksheet for the flagship product that will project the annual gross margin, total expenses, operating income, income taxes, and net income for the next eight years based on the assumptions in Table 3–9. The desired worksheet is shown in Figure 3–85.

Table 3–9 August Online Technology Financial Projection Assumptions	
Units Sold in Prior Year	235,411
Unit Cost	$150.00
Annual Sales Growth	3.25%
Annual Price Increase	3.00%
Margin	29.90%

Continued >

In the Labs *continued*

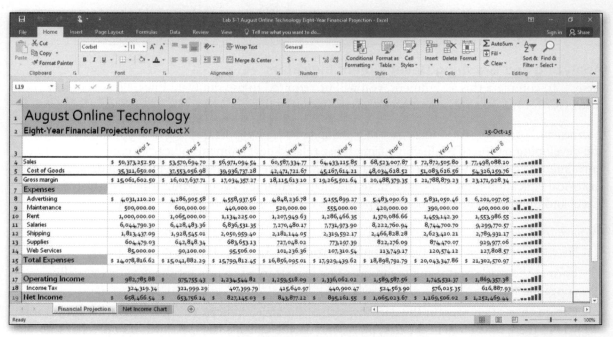

Figure 3–85

Perform the following tasks:

Instructions Part 1: Run Excel, open a blank workbook, and then create the worksheet.

1. Apply the Parallax theme to the worksheet.

2. Enter the worksheet title **August Online Technology** in cell A1 and the subtitle **Eight-Year Financial Projection for Product X** in cell A2. Format the worksheet title in cell A1 to 26-point and the worksheet subtitle in cell A2 to 16-point. Enter the system date in cell I2 using the NOW function. Format the date to the 14-Mar-12 style.

3. Change the following column widths: A = 24.00 characters; B through I = 14.00 characters. Change the heights of rows 7, 15, 17, 19, and 22 to 18.00 points.

4. Enter the eight column titles Year 1 through Year 8 in the range B3:I3 by entering Year 1 in cell B3 and then dragging cell B3's fill handle through the range C3:I3. Format cell B3 as follows:

   a. Increase the font size to 12.
   b. Center and italicize it.
   c. Angle its contents 45 degrees.

5. Use the Format Painter button to copy the format assigned to cell B3 to the range C3:I3.

6. Enter the row titles, as shown in Figure 3-85, in the range A4:A19. Change the font size in cells A7, A15, A17, and A19 to 14-point. Add thick bottom borders to the ranges A3:I3 and A5:I5. Use the Increase Indent button (Home tab | Alignment group) to increase the indent of the row titles in cell A5, the range A8:A14, and cell A18.

7. If requested by your instructor, change the entry in row 14 by inserting your surname prior to the text, Web Services.

8. Enter the table title **Assumptions** in cell A22. Enter the assumptions in Table 3–9 in the range A23:B27. Use format symbols when entering the numbers. Change the font size of the table title in cell A22 to 14-point and underline it.

9. Select the range B4:I19 and then click the Number Format Dialog Box Launcher (Home tab | Number group) to display the Format Cells dialog box. Use the Number category (Format Cells dialog box) to assign the appropriate style that displays numbers with two decimal places and negative numbers in black font and enclosed in parentheses to the range B4:I19.

10. Complete the following entries:

   a. Year 1 Sales (cell B4) = Units Sold in Prior Year * (Unit Cost / (1 – Margin))
   b. Year 2 Sales (cell C4) = Year 1 Sales * (1 + Annual Sales Growth) * (1 + Annual Price Increase). Copy cell C4 to the range D4:I4.
   c. Year 1 Cost of Goods (cell B5) = Year 1 Sales * (1 – Margin). Copy cell B5 to the range C5:I5.
   d. Gross Margin (cell B6) = Year 1 Sales – Year 1 Cost of Goods. Copy cell B6 to the range C6:I6.
   e. Year 1 Advertising (cell B8) = 1250 + 8% * Year 1 Sales. Copy cell B8 to the range C8:I8.
   f. Maintenance (row 9): Year 1 = 500,000; Year 2 = 600,000; Year 3 = 440,000; Year 4 = 520,000; Year 5 = 555,000; Year 6 = 420,000; Year 7 = 390,000; Year 8 = 400,000.
   g. Year 1 Rent (cell B10) = 1,000,000
   h. Year 2 Rent (cell C10) = Year 1 Rent + (6.5% * Year 1 Rent). Copy cell C10 to the range D10:I10.
   i. Year 1 Salaries (cell B11) = 12% * Year 1 Sales. Copy cell B11 to the range C11:I11.
   j. Year 1 Shipping (cell B12) = 3.6% * Year 1 Sales. Copy cell B12 to the range C12:I12.
   k. Year 1 Supplies (cell B13) = 1.2% * Year 1 Sales. Copy cell B13 to the range C13:I13.
   l. Year 1 Web Services (cell B14) = 85,000
   m. Year 2 Web Services (cell C14) = Year 1 Web Services + (6% * Year 1 Web Services). Copy cell C14 to the range D14:I14.
   n. Year 1 Total Expenses (cell B15) = SUM(B8:B14). Copy cell B15 to the range C15:I15.
   o. Year 1 Operating Income (cell B17) = Year 1 Gross Margin – Year 1 Total Expenses. Copy cell B17 to the range C17:I17.
   p. Year 1 Income Tax (cell B18): If Year 1 Operating Income is less than 0, then Year 1 Income Tax equals 0; otherwise Year 1 Income Tax equals 33% * Year 1 Operating Income. Copy cell B18 to the range C18:I18.
   q. Year 1 Net Income (cell B19) = Year 1 Operating Income – Year 1 Income Tax. Copy cell B19 to the range C19:I19.
   r. In cell J4, insert a column sparkline chart (Insert tab | Sparklines group) for cell range B4:I4.
   s. Insert column sparkline charts in cells J5, J6, J8:J15, and J17:J19 using ranges B5:I5, B6:I6, B8:I8 – B15:I15, and B17:I17 – B19:I19 respectively.

11. Apply the Currency number format with a dollar sign, two decimal places, and negative numbers in black with parentheses to the following ranges: B4:I4, B6:I6, B8:I8, B15:I15, B17:I17, and B19:I19. Apply the comma style format to the following ranges: B5:I5 and B9:I14. Apply the Number format with two decimal places and the 1000 separator to the range B18:I18.

12. Change the background colors, as shown in Figure 3–85. Use Blue, Accent 1, Lighter 40% for the background colors.

13. Save the workbook using the file name, Lab 3-1 August Online Technology Eight-Year Financial Projection.

14. Preview the worksheet. Use the Orientation button (Page Layout tab | Page Setup group) to fit the printout on one page in landscape orientation. Preview the formulas version (CTRL+`) of the worksheet in landscape orientation using the Fit to option. Press CTRL+` to instruct Excel to display the values version of the worksheet. Save the workbook again.

Continued >

In the Labs *continued*

Instructions Part 2: Create a chart to present the data, shown in Figure 3–86. If necessary, run Excel and open the workbook Lab 3-1 August Online Technology Eight-Year Financial Projection.

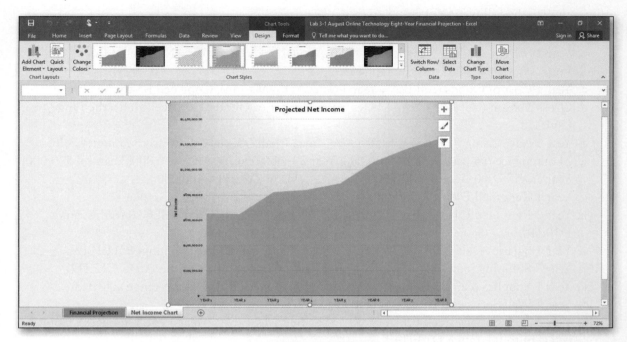

Figure 3–86

1. Use the nonadjacent ranges B3:I3 and B19:I19 to create a Stacked Area chart (*Hint:* use the Recommended Charts button). When the chart appears, click the Move Chart button to move the chart to a new sheet.

2. Change the chart title to **Projected Net Income.**

3. Use the Chart Elements button to add a vertical axis title. Edit the axis title text to read **Net Income.** Bold the axis title.

4. Change the Chart Style to Style 4 in the Chart Styles Gallery (Chart Tools Design tab | Chart Styles group). Use the 'Chart Quick Colors' button (Chart Tools Design tab | Chart Styles group) to change the color scheme to Monochromatic, Color 5.

5. Rename the sheet tabs Financial Projection and Net Income Chart. Rearrange the sheets so that the worksheet is leftmost and change the tab colors to those of your choosing.

6. Click the Financial Projection tab to return to the worksheet. Save the workbook using the same file name (Lab 3-1 August Online Technology Eight-Year Financial Projection) as defined in Part 1.

Instructions Part 3: Use Goal Seek to analyze three different sales scenarios. If necessary, open the workbook Lab 3-1 August Online Technology Eight-Year Financial Projection.

1. Divide the window into two panes between rows 6 and 7. Use the scroll bars to show both the top and bottom of the worksheet. Using the numbers in columns 2 and 3 of Table 3–10, analyze the effect of changing the annual sales growth (cell B25) and annual price increase (cell B26) on the net incomes in row 19. Record the answers for each case and submit the results in a form as requested by your instructor.

Table 3–10 August Online Technology Alternative Projections		
Case	Annual Sales Growth	Annual Price Increase
1	4.25%	2.00%
2	2.25%	3.00%
3	1.25%	4.00%

2. Close the workbook without saving it and then reopen it. Use the 'What-If Analysis' button (Data tab | Forecast group) to goal seek. Determine a margin that would result in a Year 8 net income of $1,500,000. Save the workbook with your needed changes as Lab 3-1 August Online Technology Eight-Year Financial Projection GS. Submit the workbook with the new values or the results of the goal seek as requested by your instructor.

3. ✳ How would you use what-if analysis tools to determine what Annual Sales Growth you would need to achieve in order to keep prices steady over the eight-year projection period?

Lab 2: **Updating a Weekly Payroll Worksheet**

Note: To complete this assignment, you will be required to use the Data Files. Please contact your instructor for information about accessing the required files.

Problem: PHM Reliable Catering is a company that provides catering services to both small and large businesses. You have been asked to update the weekly payroll report to reflect changes in personnel, to update certain mandatory deductions, and to add overtime computations. The final worksheet is shown in Figure 3–87. Run Excel. Open the workbook, Lab 3-2 PHM Reliable Catering Weekly Payroll Report.

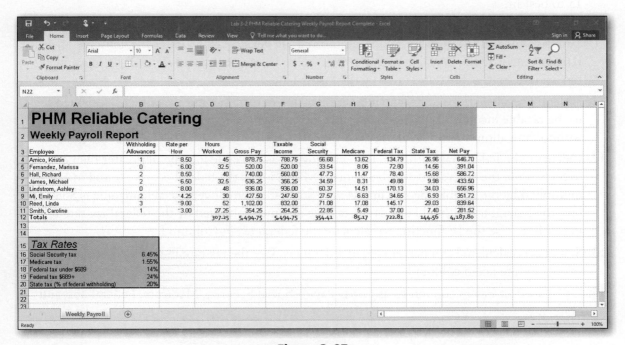

Figure 3–87

Continued >

Perform the following tasks:

1. Save the workbook using the file name, Lab 3-2 PHM Reliable Catering Weekly Payroll Report Complete.

2. Apply the Depth theme to the worksheet.

3. Delete rows 12 through 14 to remove the statistics below the Totals row.

4. Delete column B. Set column A width to 31.00 and columns B through K to 11.00. Select row 3 and set text to wrap in this row using the Wrap Text button (Home tab | Alignment group), and then set the row height to best fit.

5. Delete the record for the employee Evans, Timothy. Add two blank lines directly above the row for Mi, Emily, and add the information for the two new employees listed in Table 3–11.

Table 3–11 PHM Reliable Catering New Employee Data			
Employee	**Withholding Allowances**	**Rate Per Hour**	**Hours Worked**
James, Michael	2	16.50	32.5
Lindstrom, Ashley	0	18.00	48

6. If requested by your instructor, replace one of the employee's names with your name.

7. If necessary, use the fill handle in cell E6 to copy the gross pay formula to the rows of the two new employees.

8. Add the Tax Rates information shown in Figure 3–87 in cells A15:B20 to your worksheet.

9. Change the font size in cell A1 to 28-point. Change the font size in cell A2 to 18-point. Change the font in cell A15 to 18-point italic and underlined. Change the row height for rows 1, 2, and 15 to best fit.

10. Insert three columns to the right of the Gross Pay column. Add the column titles `Taxable Income`, `Social Security`, and `Medicare` in cells F3:H3. Center the contents of cells B3:K3. Calculate the Social Security and Medicare taxes in columns G and H by multiplying the tax rates in the Tax Rates table by the Gross Pay.

11. Federal tax calculations must take into account two tiers of income tax, which are applied to the taxable income. Calculate the taxable income, which is the Gross Pay — (number of withholding allowances × $90).

12. Calculate the federal tax withheld. If an employee has a taxable income of greater than or equal to $689, then the federal tax withheld equals $110.85 plus the federal tax rate found in cell B19 multiplied by the taxable income in excess of $689. If an employees taxable income is $689 or less, the federal tax withheld equals the taxable income multiplied by the federal tax rate found in cell B18. Use the IF function to calculate the federal tax in Column I.

13. State tax is calculated as a percentage of federal tax. Use the tax rate in the Tax Rates table to calculate state tax in column J.

14. Calculate Net Pay in column K, as Gross Pay — Social Security, Medicare, Federal Tax, and State Tax.

15. Use the background color Gold, Accent 5, Darker 25% for the ranges A1:K2 and A15:B20.

16. Center the range B4:B11. Apply the currency style with two decimal places, no dollar signs, and negative numbers in black and parentheses to the range C4:C11 and E4:K12.

17. Apply a Thick Bottom Border to the range A3:K3. Apply the Total cell style to the range A12:K12. Apply a Thick Outside Border to the range A15:B20.

18. Change the sheet tab name to Weekly Payroll and the tab color to match the color used as background color in cell A1.

19. Preview the worksheet. Fit the printout of the worksheet on one page in landscape orientation. Save the workbook again.

20. Submit the workbook as specified by your instructor.

Lab 3: **Consider This: Your Turn**

Apply your creative thinking and problem-solving skills to design and implement a solution.

Transportation Costs

Instructions Part 1: You are thinking about buying a new vehicle, and you want to make sure that you buy one that offers the highest fuel savings. You decide to research hybrid cars as well as gas-only cars. Your friends are also interested in your results. Together, you decide to research the fuel costs associated with various types of vehicles. Research the gas mileage for six vehicles: three should run only on gas, and the others should be hybrid vehicles, combining gas and battery power. After you find the gas mileage for each vehicle, you will use formulas to calculate the fuel cost for one month, one year, and three years. Assume that in a typical month, you will drive 500 miles. Develop a worksheet following the general layout in Table 3–12 that shows the fuel cost analysis. Use the formulas listed in Table 3–13 and the concepts and techniques presented in this module to create the worksheet. You will need to find the average price of gas for your market. Add a chart showing the cost comparisons as an embedded chart.

Table 3–12 Fuel Cost Analysis				
Vehicle	**Miles Per Gallon**	**Fuel Cost 1 Month**	**Fuel Cost 1 Year**	**Fuel Cost 3 Years**
Gas 1		Formula A	Formula B	Formula C
Gas 2		—	—	—
Gas 3		—	—	—
Hybrid 1		—	—	—
Hybrid 2		—	—	—
Hybrid 3		—	—	—
Assumptions				
Distance per Month	500			
Price of Gas				

Table 3–13 Fuel Cost Analysis Formulas
Formula A = (Distance per Month / Miles per Gallon)*Price of Gas
Formula B = ((Distance per Month / Miles per Gallon)*Price of Gas)*12
Formula C = ((Distance Per Month / Miles per Gallon)*Price of Gas)*36

Instructions Part 2: ☀ You made several decisions while creating the workbook for this assignment. Why did you select the chart type used to compare fuel costs? What other costs might you want to consider when making your purchase decision?

PrattLast Associates : Database- C:\Users\Owner\Documents\CIS

Microsoft Access 2016

File   Home   Create   External Data   Database Tools   ♀ Tell me what you want to do...

1 Databases and Database Objects: An Introduction

Objectives

You will have mastered the material in this module when you can:

- Describe the features of the Access window
- Create a database
- Create tables in Datasheet and Design views
- Add records to a table
- Close a database
- Open a database
- Print the contents of a table

- Import data
- Create and use a query
- Create and use a form
- Create and print custom reports
- Modify a report in Layout view
- Perform special database operations
- Design a database to satisfy a collection of requirements

Introduction

The term **database** describes a collection of data organized in a manner that allows access, retrieval, and use of that data. Microsoft Access 2016, usually referred to as simply Access, is a database management system. A **database management system** is software that allows you to use a computer to create a database; add, change, and delete data in the database; ask and answer questions concerning the data; and create forms and reports using the data.

Project — Database Creation

PrattLast Associates is a human resources outsourcing company that provides HR services, such as payroll, hiring, training, and employee benefits management to small and medium-size businesses in the Midwest. Organizations might outsource only one function, such as payroll, or might outsource several functions. While there are many different ways to charge customers, PrattLast charges a set amount per employee per month. The amount varies based on number and type of functions outsourced.

Microsoft Access 2016

File   Home   Create   External Data   Database Tools   ♀ Tell me what you want to do...

PrattLast Associates : Database- C:\Users\Owner\Documents\CIS

Account managers serve their respective client companies by providing HR solutions and understanding the businesses for which they are responsible. The PrattLast account managers can earn bonuses if their client companies elect to outsource additional HR functions. For example, if the business currently outsources only payroll but is convinced by the account manager to add hiring to the outsourced functions, the account manager receives a bonus.

To ensure that operations run smoothly, PrattLast organizes data on its accounts and account managers in a database managed by Access. In this way, PrattLast keeps its data current and accurate and can analyze it for trends; PrattLast can also create a variety of useful reports.

In a **relational database** such as those maintained by Access, a database consists of a collection of tables, each of which contains information on a specific subject. Figure 1–1 shows the database for PrattLast Associates. It consists of two tables: the Account table (Figure 1–1a) contains information about PrattLast accounts, and the Account Manager table (Figure 1–1b) contains information about the account managers to whom these accounts are assigned.

Figure 1–1a Account Table

Figure 1–1b Account Manager Table

The rows in the tables are called **records**. A record contains information about a given person, product, or event. A row in the Account table, for example, contains information about a specific account, such as the account's name, address information, and other data.

The columns in the tables are called fields. A **field** contains a specific piece of information within a record. In the Account table, for example, the fourth field, City, contains the name of the city where the account is located.

The first field in the Account table is AC #, which is an abbreviation for Account Number. PrattLast Associates assigns each account a number; the PrattLast account numbers consist of two uppercase letters followed by a three-digit number.

The account numbers are unique; that is, no two accounts have the same number. Such a field is a **unique identifier**. A unique identifier, as its name suggests, is a way of uniquely identifying each record in the database. A given account number will appear only in a single record in the table. Only one record exists, for example, in which the account number is JM323. A unique identifier is also called a **primary key**. Thus, the Account Number field is the primary key for the Account table. This means the Account Number field can be used to uniquely identify a record in the table. No two records can have the same value in the Account Number field.

The next seven fields in the Account table are Account Name, Street, City, State, Postal Code, Amount Paid, and Current Due. The Amount Paid column contains the amount that the account has paid PrattLast Associates year to date (YTD) prior to the current period. The Current Due column contains the amount due to PrattLast for the current period. For example, account JM323 is JSP Manufacturing Inc. The address is 1200 Franklin Blvd., in Wells, Indiana. The postal code is 46007. The amount paid is $19,739.70 and the current due amount is $2,095.00.

PrattLast assigns a single account manager to work with each account. The last column in the Account table, AM # (an abbreviation for Account Manager Number) gives the number of the account's account manager. The account manager number for JSP Manufacturing is 31.

The first field in the Account Manager table is also AM #, for Account Manager Number. The account manager numbers are unique, so the Account Manager Number field is the primary key of the Account Manager table.

The other fields in the Account Manager table are Last Name, First Name, Street, City, State, Postal Code, Start Date, Salary, and Bonus Rate. The Start Date field gives the date the account manager began working for PrattLast. The Salary field gives the salary paid to the account manager thus far this year. The Bonus Rate gives the potential bonus percentage based on personal performance. The bonus rate applies when the account manager either brings in new business or recommends productivity improvements. For example, account manager 31 is Haydee Rivera. Her address is 325 Twiddy St., in Avondale, Illinois. Her postal code is 60311. Haydee started working for PrattLast on June 3, 2013. So far this year, she has been paid $48,750.00 in salary. Her bonus rate is 0.15 (15%).

The account manager number appears in both the Account table and the Account Manager table, and relates accounts and account managers. Account manager 42, Peter Lu, was recently promoted to account manager and has not yet been assigned any accounts. His account manager number, therefore, does not appear on any row in the Account table.

BTW

Naming Fields
Access 2016 has a number of reserved words, words that have a special meaning to Access. You cannot use these reserved words as field names. For example, Name is a reserved word and could not be used in the Account table to describe an account's name. For a complete list of reserved words in Access 2016, consult Access Help.

How would you find the name of the account manager for Midwest Library Consortium?

In the Account table, you see that the account manager number for account Midwest Library Consortium is 31. To find the name of this account manager, look for the row in the Account Manager table that contains 31 in the AM # column. After you have found it, you know that the account manager for Midwest Library Consortium is Haydee Rivera.

CONSIDER THIS

How would you find all the accounts assigned to Haydee Rivera?
First, look in the Account Manager table to find that her number is 31. You would then look through the Account table for all the accounts that contain 31 in the AM # column. Haydee's accounts are AC001 (Avondale Community Bank), JM323 (JSP Manufacturing Inc.), KC156 (Key Community College System), MI345 (Midwest Library Consortium), and TW001 (Tri-County Waste Disposal).

For an introduction to Windows and instructions about how to perform basic Windows tasks, read the Office and Windows module at the beginning of this book, where you can learn how to resize windows, change screen resolution, create folders, move and rename files, use Windows Help, and much more.

In this module, you will learn how to create and use the database shown in Figure 1–1. The following roadmap identifies general activities you will perform as you progress through this module:

1. **CREATE** the **FIRST TABLE**, Account Manager, using Datasheet view.
2. **ADD RECORDS** to the Account Manager table.
3. **PRINT** the **CONTENTS** of the Account Manager table.
4. **IMPORT RECORDS** into the second table, Account.
5. **MODIFY** the **SECOND TABLE** using Design view.
6. **CREATE** a **QUERY** for the Account table.
7. **CREATE** a **FORM** for the Account table.
8. **CREATE** a **REPORT** for the Account table.

Creating a Database

For an introduction to Office and instructions about how to perform basic tasks in Office apps, read the Office and Windows module at the beginning of this book, where you can learn how to run an application, use the ribbon, save a file, open a file, print a file, exit an application, use Help, and much more.

In Access, all the tables, reports, forms, and queries that you create are stored in a single file called a database. A database is a structure that can store information about multiple types of objects, the properties of those objects, and the relationships among the objects. The first step is to create the database that will hold your tables, reports, forms, and queries. You can use either the Blank desktop database option or a template to create a new database. If you already know the tables and fields you want in your database, you would use the Blank desktop database option. If not, you can use a template. Templates can guide you by suggesting some commonly used databases.

To Create a Database

Because you already know the tables and fields you want in the PrattLast Associates database, you would use the Blank desktop database option rather than using a template. The following steps create the database.

1 Run Access.

2 Using the steps in the "To Create an Access Database" section in the Office and Windows module, create the database on your hard disk, OneDrive, or other storage location using PrattLast Associates as the file name (Figure 1–2).

Q&A

The title bar for my Navigation Pane contains All Tables rather than All Access Objects, as in the figure. Is that a problem?

It is not a problem. The title bar indicates how the Navigation Pane is organized. You can carry out the steps in the text with either organization. To make your screens match the ones in the text, click the Navigation Pane arrow and then click Object Type.

I do not have the Search bar that appears in the figure. Is that a problem?

It is not a problem. If your Navigation Pane does not display a Search bar and you want your screens to match the ones in the text, right-click the Navigation Pane title bar arrow to display a shortcut menu, and then click Search Bar.

Figure 1–2

To Create a Database Using a Template

Ideally, you will design your own database, create a blank database, and then create the tables you have determined that your database should contain. If you are not sure what database design you will need, you could use a template. Templates can guide you by suggesting some commonly used databases. To create a database using a template, you would use the following steps.

1 If you have another database open, close it without exiting Access by clicking File on the ribbon to open the Backstage view and then clicking Close.

2 If you do not see a template that you want, you can search Microsoft Office online for additional templates.

3 Click the template you want to use. Be sure you have selected one that indicates it is for a desktop database.

4 Enter a file name and select a location for the database.

5 Click the Create button to create the database.

The Access Window

The Access window consists of a variety of components to make your work more efficient. These include the Navigation Pane, Access work area, ribbon, shortcut menus, and Quick Access Toolbar. Some of these components are common to other Microsoft Office apps; others are unique to Access.

BTW

Available Templates
The templates gallery includes both desktop and web-based templates. If you are creating an Access database for your own use, select a desktop template. Web-based templates allow you to create databases that you can publish to a SharePoint server.

BTW

Organizing Files and Folders
You should organize and store files in folders so that you easily can find the files later. For example, if you are taking an introductory computer class called CIS 101, a good practice would be to save all Access files in an Access folder in a CIS 101 folder. For a discussion of folders and detailed examples of creating folders, refer to the Office and Windows module at the beginning of this book.

Navigation Pane and Access Work Area

You work on objects such as tables, forms, and reports in the **Access work area**. In the work area in Figure 1–2, a single table, Table1, is open in the work area. **Object tabs** for the open objects appear at the top of the work area. If you have multiple objects open at the same time, you can select one of the open objects by clicking its tab. To the left of the work area is the Navigation Pane. The **Navigation Pane** contains a list of all the objects in the database. You use this pane to open an object. You can also customize the way objects are displayed in the Navigation Pane.

The **status bar**, located at the bottom of the Access window, presents information about the database object, the progress of current tasks, and the status of certain commands and keys; it also provides controls for viewing the object. As you type text or perform certain commands, various indicators might appear on the status bar. The left edge of the status bar in Figure 1–2 shows that the table object is open in **Datasheet view**. In Datasheet view, the table is represented as a collection of rows and columns called a **datasheet**. Toward the right edge are View buttons, which you can use to change the view that currently appears.

Determining Tables and Fields

Once you have created the database, you need to create the tables and fields that your database will contain. Before doing so, however, you need to make some decisions regarding the tables and fields.

Naming Tables and Fields

In creating your database, you must name tables, fields, and other objects. Before beginning the design process, you must understand the rules Access applies to table and field names. These rules are:

1. Names can be up to 64 characters in length.
2. Names can contain letters, digits, and spaces, as well as most of the punctuation symbols.
3. Names cannot contain periods (.), exclamation points (!), accent graves (`), or square brackets ([ ]).
4. Each field in a table must have a unique name.

The approach to naming tables and fields used in this text is to begin the names with an uppercase letter and to use lowercase for the other letters. In multiple-word names, each word begins with an uppercase letter, and there is a space between words (for example, Account Number).

Determining the Primary Key

For each table, you need to determine the primary key, the unique identifier. In many cases, you will have obvious choices, such as Account Number or Account Manager Number. If you do not have an obvious choice, you can use the primary key that Access creates automatically. It is a field called ID. It is an **autonumber field**, which means that Access will assign the value 1 to the first record, 2 to the second record, and so on.

Determining Data Types for the Fields

For each field in your database, you must determine the field's **data type**, that is, the type of data that can be stored in the field. Four of the most commonly used data types in Access are:

1. **Short Text** — The field can contain any characters. A maximum number of 255 characters is allowed in a field whose data type is Short Text.

2. **Number** — The field can contain only numbers. The numbers can be either positive or negative. Fields assigned this type can be used in arithmetic operations. You usually assign fields that contain numbers but will not be used for arithmetic operations (such as postal codes) a data type of Short Text.

3. **Currency** — The field can contain only monetary data. The values will appear with currency symbols, such as dollar signs, commas, and decimal points, and with two digits following the decimal point. Like numeric fields, you can use currency fields in arithmetic operations. Access assigns a size to currency fields automatically.

4. **Date & Time** — The field can contain dates and/or times.

Table 1–1 shows the other data types that are available in Access.

Table 1-1 Additional Data Types	
Data Type	**Description**
Long Text	Field can store a variable amount of text or combinations of text and numbers where the total number of characters may exceed 255.
AutoNumber	Field can store a unique sequential number that Access assigns to a record. Access will increment the number by 1 as each new record is added.
Yes/No	Field can store only one of two values. The choices are Yes/No, True/False, or On/Off.
OLE Object	Field can store an OLE object, which is an object linked to or embedded in the table.
Hyperlink	Field can store text that can be used as a hyperlink address.
Attachment	Field can contain an attached file. Images, spreadsheets, documents, charts, and other elements can be attached to this field in a record in the database. You can view and edit the attached file.
Calculated	Field specified as a calculation based on other fields. The value is not actually stored.

In the Account table, because the Account Number, Account Name, Street, City, and State can all contain letters, their data types should be Short Text. The data type for Postal Code is Short Text instead of Number because you typically do not use postal codes in arithmetic operations; you do not add postal codes or find an average postal code, for example. The Amount Paid and Current Due fields contain monetary data, so their data types should be Currency. The Account Manager Number field contains numbers, but you will not use these numbers in arithmetic operations, so its data type should be Short Text.

Similarly, in the Account Manager table, the data type for the Account Manager Number, Last Name, First Name, Street, City, State, and Postal Code fields should all be Short Text. The Start Date field should have a data type of Date & Time. The Salary field contains monetary amounts, so its data type should be Currency. The Bonus Rate field contains numbers that are not dollar amounts, so its data type should be Number.

For fields whose data type is Short Text, you can change the field size, that is, the maximum number of characters that can be entered in the field. If you set the field size for the State field to 2, for example, Access will not allow the user to enter more than two characters in the field. On the other hand, fields whose data type is Number often require you to change the field size, which is the storage space assigned to the field by Access. Table 1–2 shows the possible field sizes for Number fields.

Table 1-2 Field Sizes for Number Fields	
Field Size	**Description**
Byte	Integer value in the range of 0 to 255
Integer	Integer value in the range of -32,768 to 32,767
Long Integer	Integer value in the range of -2,147,483,648 to 2,147,483,647
Single	Numeric values with decimal places to seven significant digits—requires 4 bytes of storage
Double	Numeric values with decimal places to more accuracy than Single—requires 8 bytes of storage
Replication ID	Special identifier required for replication
Decimal	Numeric values with decimal places to more accuracy than Single or Double—requires 12 bytes of storage.

CONSIDER THIS

What is the appropriate size for the Bonus Rate field?
If the size were Byte, Integer, or Long Integer, only integers could be stored. If you try to store a value that has decimal places, such as 0.18, in fields of these sizes, the portion to the right of the decimal point would be removed, giving a result of 0. To address this problem, the bonus rate should have a size of Single, Double, or Decimal. With such small numbers involved, Single, which requires the least storage of the three, is the appropriate choice.

BTW
Naming Files
The following characters cannot be used in a file name: question mark (?), quotation mark ("), slash (/), backslash (\ ), colon (:), asterisk (*), vertical bar (|), greater than symbol (>), and less than symbol (<).

Creating a Table

To create a table in Access, you must define its structure. That is, you must define all the fields that make up the table and their characteristics. You must also indicate the primary key.

In Access, you can use two different views to create a table: Datasheet view and Design view. In **Datasheet view**, the data in the table is presented in rows and columns, similar to a spreadsheet. Although the main reason to use Datasheet view is to add or update records in a table, you can also use it to create a table or to later modify its structure. The other view, **Design view**, is only used to create a table or to modify the structure of a table.

As you might expect, Design view has more functionality for creating a table than Datasheet view. That is, there are certain actions that can only be performed in Design view. One such action is assigning Single as the field size for the Bonus Rate field. In this module, you will create the first table, the Account Manager table, in Datasheet view. Once you have created the table in Datasheet view, you will use Design view to change the field size.

Whichever view you choose to use, before creating the table, you need to know the names and data types of the fields that will make up the table. You can also decide to enter a description for a particular field to explain important details about the field. When you select this field, this description will appear on the status bar. You might also choose to assign a **caption** to a particular field. If you assign a caption, Access will display the value you assign, rather than the field name, in datasheets and in forms. If you do not assign a caption, Access will display the field name.

When would you want to use a caption?

You would use a caption whenever you want something other than the field name displayed. One common example is when the field name is relatively long and the data in the field is relatively short. In the Account Manager table, the name of the first field is Account Manager Number, but the field contains data that is only two characters long. You will change the caption for this field to AM #, which is much shorter than Account Manager Number yet still describes the field. Doing so will enable you to greatly reduce the width of the column.

The results of these decisions for the fields in the Account Manager table are shown in Table 1–3. The table also shows the data types and field sizes of the fields as well as any special properties that need to be changed. The Account Manager Number field has a caption of AM #, enabling the width of the Account Manager Number column to be reduced in the datasheet.

Table 1-3 Structure of Account Manager Table			
Field Name	**Data Type**	**Field Size**	**Description**
Account Manager Number	Short Text	2	Primary Key **Description:** Unique identifier of account manager **Caption:** AM #
Last Name	Short Text	15	
First Name	Short Text	15	
Street	Short Text	20	
City	Short Text	20	
State	Short Text	2	
Postal Code	Short Text	5	
Start Date	Date/Time	(This appears as Date & Time on the menu of available data types)	
Salary	Currency		
Bonus Rate	Number	Single	Format: Fixed Decimal Places: 2

How do you determine the field size?

You need to determine the maximum number of characters that can be entered in the field. In some cases, it is obvious. Field sizes of 2 for the State field and 5 for the Postal Code field are certainly the appropriate choices. In other cases, you need to determine how many characters you want to allow. In the list shown in Table 1–3, PrattLast decided allowing 15 characters was sufficient for last names. This field size can be changed later if it proves to be insufficient.

What is the purpose of the Format and Decimal Places properties?

The format guarantees that bonus rates will be displayed with a fixed number of decimal places. Setting the decimal places property to 2 guarantees that the rates will be displayed with precisely two decimal places. Thus, a bonus rate of 0.2 will be displayed as 0.20.

To Modify the Primary Key

When you first create your database, Access automatically creates a table for you. You can immediately begin defining the fields. If, for any reason, you do not have this table or inadvertently delete it, you can create the table by clicking Create on the ribbon and then clicking the Table button (Create tab | Tables group). In either case, you are ready to define the fields.

The following steps change the name, data type, and other properties of the first field to match the Account Manager Number field in Table 1–3, which is the primary key. **Why?** *Access has already created the first field as the primary key field, which it has named ID. Account Manager Number is a more appropriate choice.*

1

• Right-click the column heading for the ID field to display a shortcut menu (Figure 1–3).

Why does my shortcut menu look different?
You displayed a shortcut menu for the column instead of the column heading. Be sure you right-click the column heading.

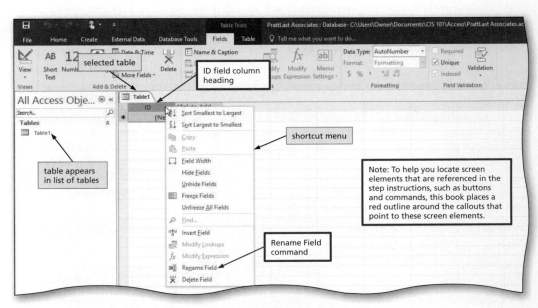

Figure 1–3

2

• Click Rename Field on the shortcut menu to highlight the current name.

• Type `Account Manager Number` to assign a name to the new field.

• Click the white space immediately below the field name to complete the addition of the field (Figure 1–4).

Figure 1–4

Why does the full name of the field not appear?
The default column size is not large enough for Account Manager Number to be displayed in its entirety. You will address this issue in later steps.

3

• Because the data type needs to be changed from AutoNumber to Short Text, click the Data Type arrow (Table Tools Fields tab | Formatting group) to display a menu of available data types (Figure 1–5).

Figure 1–5

- Click Short Text to select the data type for the field (Figure 1–6).

Figure 1–6

- Click the Field Size text box (Table Tools Fields tab | Properties group) to select the current field size, use either the DELETE or BACKSPACE keys to erase the current field size, if necessary, and then type 2 as the new field size.

- Click the Name & Caption button (Table Tools Fields tab | Properties group) to display the Enter Field Properties dialog box.

- Click the Caption text box (Enter Field Properties dialog box), and then type AM # as the caption.

- Click the Description text box, and then type **Unique identifier of account manager** as the description (Figure 1–7).

Figure 1–7

- Click the OK button (Enter Field Properties dialog box) to change the caption and description (Figure 1–8).

Figure 1–8

To Define the Remaining Fields in a Table

1 CREATE FIRST TABLE | 2 ADD RECORDS | 3 PRINT CONTENTS | 4 IMPORT RECORDS
5 MODIFY SECOND TABLE | 6 CREATE QUERY | 7 CREATE FORM | 8 CREATE REPORT

To define an additional field, you click the 'Click to Add' column heading, select the data type, and then type the field name. This is different from the process you used to modify the ID field. The following steps define the remaining fields shown in Table 1–3. These steps do not change the field size of the Bonus Rate field, however. **Why?** *You can only change the field size of a Number field in Design view. Later, you will use Design view to change this field size and change the format and number of decimal places.*

- Click the 'Click to Add' column heading to display a menu of available data types (Figure 1–9).

Figure 1–9

- Click Short Text in the menu of available data types to select the Short Text data type.

- Type `Last Name` to enter a field name.

- Click the blank space below the field name to complete the change of the name. Click the blank space a second time to select the field (Figure 1–10).

Figure 1–10

Q&A

After entering the field name, I realized that I selected the wrong data type. How can I correct it?
Click the Data Type arrow, and then select the correct type.

I inadvertently clicked the blank space before entering the field name. How can I correct the name?
Right-click the field name, click Rename Field on the shortcut menu, and then type the new name.

3

- Change the field size to 15 just as you changed the field size of the Account Manager Number field.

- Using the same technique, add the remaining fields in the Account Manager

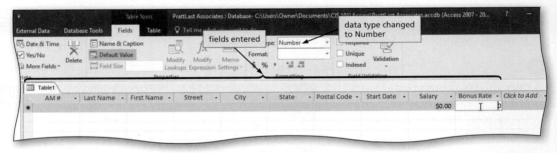

Figure 1–11

table. For the First Name, Street, City, State, and Postal Code fields, use the Short Text data type, but change the field sizes to match Table 1–3. For the Start Date field, change the data type to Date/Time. For the Salary field, change the data type to Currency. For the Bonus Rate field, change the data type to Number (Figure 1–11).

Q&A

I have an extra row between the row containing the field names and the row that begins with the asterisk. What happened? Is this a problem? If so, how do I fix it?
You inadvertently added a record to the table by pressing a key. Even pressing the SPACEBAR would add a record. You now have an unwanted record. To fix it, press the ESC key or click the Undo button to undo the action. You may need to do this more than once.

When I try to move on to specify another field, I get an error message indicating that the primary key cannot contain a null value. How do I correct this?
First, click the OK button to remove the error message. Next, press the ESC key or click the Undo button to undo the action. You may need to do this more than once.

BTW
Touch Screen
Differences
The Office and Windows interfaces may vary if you are using a touch screen. For this reason, you might notice that the function or appearance of your touch screen differs slightly from this module's presentation.

Making Changes to the Structure

When creating a table, check the entries carefully to ensure they are correct. If you discover a mistake while still typing the entry, you can correct the error by repeatedly pressing the BACKSPACE key until the incorrect characters are removed. Then, type the correct characters. If you do not discover a mistake until later, you can use the following techniques to make the necessary changes to the structure:

- To undo your most recent change, click the Undo button on the Quick Access Toolbar. If there is nothing that Access can undo, this button will be dim, and clicking it will have no effect.

- To delete a field, right-click the column heading for the field (the position containing the field name), and then click Delete Field on the shortcut menu.

- To change the name of a field, right-click the column heading for the field, click Rename Field on the shortcut menu, and then type the desired field name.

- To insert a field as the last field, click the 'Click to Add' column heading, click the appropriate data type on the menu of available data types, type the desired field name, and, if necessary, change the field size.

- To insert a field between existing fields, right-click the column heading for the field that will follow the new field, and then click Insert Field on the shortcut menu. Right-click the column heading for the field, click Rename Field on the shortcut menu, and then type the desired field name.

- To move a field, click the column heading for the field to be moved to select the field, and then drag the field to the desired position.

As an alternative to these steps, you might want to start over. To do so, click the Close button for the table, and then click the No button in the Microsoft Access dialog box. Click Create on the ribbon, and then click the Table button to create a table. You then can repeat the process you used earlier to define the fields in the table.

To Save a Table

1 CREATE FIRST TABLE | 2 ADD RECORDS | 3 PRINT CONTENTS | 4 IMPORT RECORDS
5 MODIFY SECOND TABLE | 6 CREATE QUERY | 7 CREATE FORM | 8 CREATE REPORT

The Account Manager table structure is complete. The final step is to save the table within the database. As part of the process, you will give the table a name. The following steps save the table, giving it the name Account Manager. **Why?** *PrattLast has decided that Account Manager is an appropriate name for the table.*

- Click the **Save** button on the Quick Access Toolbar to display the Save As dialog box (Figure 1–12).

Figure 1–12

- Type **Account Manager** to change the name assigned to the table.

- Click the OK button (Save As dialog box) to save the table (Figure 1–13).

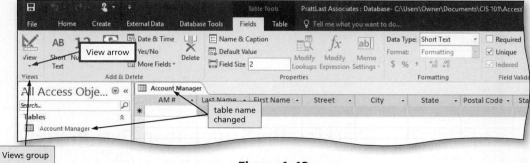

Figure 1–13

Other Ways

1. Click File on the ribbon, click Save in the Backstage view
2. Right-click tab for table, click Save on shortcut menu

3. Press CTRL+S

To View the Table in Design View

Even when creating a table in Datasheet view, Design view can be helpful. *Why? You easily can view the fields, data types, and properties to ensure you have entered them correctly. It is also easier to determine the primary key in Design view.* The following steps display the structure of the Account Manager table in Design view so that you can verify the design is correct.

1

Figure 1–14

- Click the View arrow (Table Tools Fields tab | Views group) to display the View menu (Figure 1–14).

Q&A Could I just click the View button rather than the arrow?
Yes. Clicking the button is equivalent to clicking the command represented by the icon currently appearing on the button. Because the icon on the button in Figure 1–14 is for Design view, clicking the button would display the table in Design view. If you are uncertain, you can always click the arrow and select from the menu.

2

- Click Design View on the View menu to view the table in Design view (Figure 1–15).

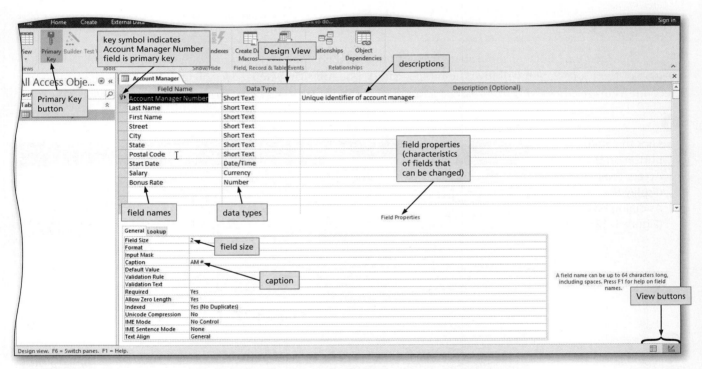

Figure 1–15

Other Ways

1. Click Design View button on status bar

Checking the Structure in Design View

You should use Design view to carefully check the entries you have made. In Figure 1–15, for example, you can see that the Account Manager Number field is the primary key of the Account Manager table by the key symbol in front of the field name. If your table does not have a key symbol, you can click the Primary Key button (Table Tools Design tab | Tools group) to designate a field as the primary key. You can also check that the data type, description, field size, and caption are all correct.

For the other fields, you can see the field name, data type, and description without taking any special action. To see the field size and/or caption for a field, click the field's **row selector**, the small box to the left of the field. Clicking the row selector for the Last Name field, for example, displays the properties for that field. You then can check to see that the field size is correct. In addition, if the field has a caption, you can check to see if that is correct. If you find any mistakes, you can make the necessary corrections on this screen. When you have finished, click the Save button to save your changes.

To Change a Field Size in Design View

1 CREATE FIRST TABLE | 2 ADD RECORDS | 3 PRINT CONTENTS | 4 IMPORT RECORDS
5 MODIFY SECOND TABLE | 6 CREATE QUERY | 7 CREATE FORM | 8 CREATE REPORT

Most field size changes can be made in either Datasheet view or Design view. However, changing the field size for Number fields, such as the Bonus Rate field, can only be done in Design view. Because the values in the Bonus Rate field have decimal places, only Single, Double, or Decimal are possible choices for the field size. The difference between these choices concerns the amount of accuracy, that is, the number of decimal places to which the number is accurate. Double is more accurate than Single, for example, but requires more storage space. Because the rates are only two decimal places, Single is an acceptable choice.

The following steps change the field size of the Bonus Rate field to Single, the format to Fixed, and the number of decimal places to 2. *Why change the format and number of decimal places? Changing the format and number ensures that each value will appear with precisely two decimal places.*

- If necessary, click the vertical scroll bar to display the Bonus Rate field. Click the row selector for the Bonus Rate field to select the field (Figure 1–16).

Figure 1–16

- Click the Field Size box to display the Field Size arrow.

- Click the Field Size arrow to display the Field Size menu (Figure 1–17).

Figure 1–17

Q&A
What would happen if I left the field size set to Long Integer?
If the field size is Long Integer, Integer, or Byte, no decimal places can be stored. For example, a value of .10 would be stored as 0. If you enter rates and the values all appear as 0, chances are you did not change the field size property.

- Click Single to select single precision as the field size.

- Click the Format box to display the Format arrow (Figure 1-18).

Figure 1–18

- Click the Format arrow to display the Format menu.

- Click Fixed to select fixed as the format.

- Click the Decimal Places box to display the Decimal Places arrow.

- Click the Decimal Places arrow to enter the number of decimal places.

- Click 2 to assign the number of decimal places.

- Click the Save button to save your changes (Figure 1–19).

Q&A

Why did the 'Property Update Options' button appear?

You changed the number of decimal places. The 'Property Update Options' button offers a quick way of making the same change everywhere Bonus Rate appears. So far, you have not added any data or created any forms or reports that use the Bonus Rate field, so no such changes are necessary.

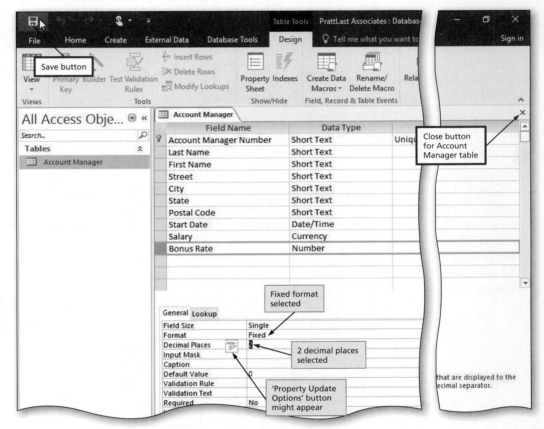

Figure 1–19

To Close the Table

Once you are sure that your entries are correct and you have saved your changes, you can close the table. The following step closes the table.

1. Click the Close button for the Account Manager table to close the table.

Other Ways

1. Right-click tab for table, click Close on shortcut menu

To Add Records to a Table

1 CREATE FIRST TABLE | 2 ADD RECORDS | 3 PRINT CONTENTS | 4 IMPORT RECORDS
5 MODIFY SECOND TABLE | 6 CREATE QUERY | 7 CREATE FORM | 8 CREATE REPORT

Creating a table by building the structure and saving the table is the first step in the two-step process of using a table in a database. The second step is to add records to the table. To add records to a table, the table must be open. When making changes to tables, you work in Datasheet view.

You often add records in phases. *Why? You might not have enough time to add all the records in one session, or you might not have all the records currently available.* The following steps open the Account Manager table in Datasheet view and then add the first two records in the Account Manager table (Figure 1–20).

AM #	Last Name	First Name	Street	City	State	Postal Code	Start Date	Salary	Bonus Rate
42	Lu	Peter	5624 Murray Ave.	Davidson	IN	46007	8/3/2015	$36,750.00	0.09
31	Rivera	Haydee	325 Twiddy St.	Avondale	IL	60311	6/3/2013	$48,750.00	0.15

Figure 1–20

1

- Right-click the Account Manager table in the Navigation Pane to display the shortcut menu (Figure 1–21).

Figure 1–21

2

- Click Open on the shortcut menu to open the table in Datasheet view.

- Click the 'Shutter Bar Open/Close Button' to close the Navigation Pane (Figure 1–22).

Figure 1–22

● Click the first row in the AM # field if necessary to display an insertion point, and type **42** to enter the first account manager number (Figure 1–23).

Figure 1–23

● Press the TAB key to move to the next field.

● Enter the last name, first name, street, city, state, and postal code by typing the following entries, pressing the TAB key after each one: **Lu** as the last name, **Peter** as the first name, **5624 Murray Ave.** as the street, **Davidson** as the city, **IN** as the state, and **46007** as the postal code.

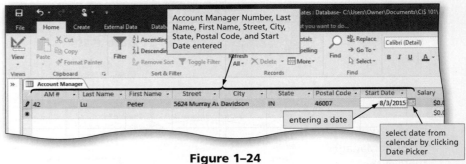

Figure 1–24

● If requested by your instructor, enter your address instead of **5624 Murray Ave.** as the street. If your address is longer than 20 characters, enter the first 20 characters.

● Type **8/3/2015** in the Start Date field (Figure 1–24).

⑤

● Press the TAB key and then type **36750** in the Salary field.

Q&A Do I need to type a dollar sign?
You do not need to type dollar signs or commas. In addition, because the digits to the right of the decimal point are both zeros, you do not need to type either the decimal point or the zeros.

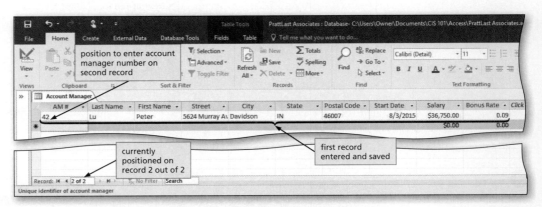

Figure 1–25

● Press the TAB key to complete the entry for the Salary field.

● Type **0.09** in the Bonus Rate field, and then press the TAB key to complete the entry of the first record (Figure 1–25).

Q&A Do I need to type the leading zero for the Bonus Rate?
Typing the leading zero is not necessary. You could type .09 if you prefer. In addition, you would not have to type any final zeros. For example, if you needed to enter 0.20, you could simply type .2 as your entry.

How and when do I save the record?
As soon as you have entered or modified a record and moved to another record, Access saves the original record. This is different from other applications. The rows entered in an Excel worksheet, for example, are not saved until the entire worksheet is saved.

- Use the techniques shown in Steps 3 through 5 to enter the data for the second record (Figure 1–26).

Q&A   Does it matter that I entered account manager 31 after I entered account manager 42? Should the account manager numbers be in order?

The order in which you enter the records is not important. When you close and later reopen the table, the records will be in account manager number order, because the Account Manager Number field is the primary key.

Experiment

- Click the Salary field on either of the records. Be sure the Table Tools Fields tab is selected. Click the Format arrow, and then click each of the formats in the Format box menu to see the effect on the values in the Salary field. When finished, click Currency in the Format box menu.

Q&A   I made a mistake in entering the data. When should I fix it?

It is a good idea to fix it now, although you can fix it later as well. In any case, the following section gives you the techniques you can use to make any necessary corrections. If you want to fix it now, read that section and make your corrections before proceeding to the next step.

Figure 1–26

- Click the Close button for the Account Manager table, shown in Figure 1–26, to close the table (Figure 1–27).

- Exit Access.

Q&A   Is it necessary for me to exit Access at this point?

No. The step is here for two reasons.

First, you will often not be able to add all the records you need to add in one sitting. In such a case, you will add some records, and then exit Access. When you are ready to resume adding the records, you will run Access, open the table, and then continue the addition process. Second, there is a break point coming up in the module. If you want to take advantage of that break, you need to first exit Access.

Figure 1–27

Making Changes to the Data

As you enter data, check your entries carefully to ensure they are correct. If you make a mistake and discover it before you press the TAB key, correct it by pressing the BACKSPACE key until the incorrect characters are removed, and then type the correct characters. If you do not discover a mistake until later, you can use the following techniques to make the necessary corrections to the data:

- To undo your most recent change, click the Undo button on the Quick Access Toolbar. If there is nothing that Access can undo, this button will be dimmed, and clicking it will have no effect.

- To add a record, click the 'New (blank) record' button, click the position for the Account Manager Number field on the first open record, and then add the record. Do not worry about it being in the correct position in the table. Access will reposition the record based on the primary key, in this case, the Account Manager Number.

- To delete a record, click the record selector, shown in Figure 1–22, for the record that you want to delete. Then press the DELETE key to delete the record, and click the Yes button when Access asks you to verify that you want to delete the record.

- To change the contents of one or more fields in a record, the record must be on the screen. If it is not, use any appropriate technique, such as the UP ARROW and DOWN ARROW keys or the vertical scroll bar, to move to the record. If the field you want to correct is not visible on the screen, use the horizontal scroll bar along the bottom of the screen to shift all the fields until the one you want appears. If the value in the field is currently highlighted, you can simply type the new value. If you would rather edit the existing value, you must have an insertion point in the field. You can place the insertion point by clicking in the field or by pressing the F2 key. You then can use the arrow keys, the DELETE key, and the BACKSPACE key for making the correction. You can also use the INSERT key to switch between Insert and Overtype mode. When you have made the change, press the TAB key to move to the next field.

If you cannot determine how to correct the data, you may find that you are "stuck" on the record, in which case Access neither allows you to move to another record nor allows you to close the table until you have made the correction. If you encounter this situation, simply press the ESC key. Pressing the ESC key will remove from the screen the record you are trying to add. You then can move to any other record, close the table, or take any other action you desire.

BTW
AutoCorrect Feature
The AutoCorrect feature of Access corrects common data entry errors. AutoCorrect corrects two capital letters by changing the second letter to lowercase and capitalizes the first letter in the names of days. It also corrects more than 400 commonly misspelled words.

BTW
Other AutoCorrect Options
Using the Office AutoCorrect feature, you can create entries that will replace abbreviations with spelled-out names and phrases automatically. To specify AutoCorrect rules, click File on the ribbon to open the Backstage view, click Options, and then click Proofing in the Access Options dialog box.

Break Point: If you wish to take a break, this is a good place to do so. You can exit Access now. To resume at a later time, run Access, open the database called PrattLast Associates, and continue following the steps from this location forward.

To Add Records to a Table that Contains Data

1 CREATE FIRST TABLE | 2 ADD RECORDS | 3 PRINT CONTENTS | 4 IMPORT RECORDS
5 MODIFY SECOND TABLE | 6 CREATE QUERY | 7 CREATE FORM | 8 CREATE REPORT

You can add records to a table that already contains data using a process almost identical to that used to add records to an empty table. The only difference is that you place the insertion point after the last record before you enter the additional data. To position the insertion point after the last record, you can use the **Navigation buttons**, which are buttons used to move within a table, found near the lower-left corner of the screen when a table is open. *Why not just click the Account Manager Number (AM #) on the first open record? You could click the first open record, but it is a good habit to use the 'New (blank) record' button. Once a table contains more records than will fit on the screen, it is easier to click the 'New (blank) record' button.* The purpose of each Navigation button is described in Table 1–4.

Table 1–4 Navigation Buttons in Datasheet View	
Button	**Purpose**
First record	Moves to the first record in the table
Previous record	Moves to the previous record
Next record	Moves to the next record
Last record	Moves to the last record in the table
New (blank) record	Moves to the end of the table to a position for entering a new record

BTW
Enabling Content
If the database is one that you created, or if it comes from a trusted source, you can enable the content. You should disable the content of a database if you suspect that your database might contain harmful content or damaging macros.

The following steps add the remaining records (Figure 1–28) to the Account Manager table.

AM #	Last Name	First Name	Street	City	State	Postal Code	Start Date	Salary	Bonus Rate
58	Murowski	Karen	168 Truesdale Dr.	Carlton	IL	60313	11/9/2016	$24,000.00	0.08
35	Simson	Mark	1467 Hartwell St.	Walker	IN	46004	5/19/2014	$40,500.00	0.12

Figure 1–28

1

- Run Access, unless it is already running.
- Open the PrattLast Associates database from your hard disk, OneDrive, or other storage location (Figure 1-29).
- If a Security Warning appears, click the Enable Content button.

Figure 1–29

2

- If the Navigation Pane is closed, click the 'Shutter Bar Open/Close Button', shown in Figure 1–27, to open the Navigation Pane (Figure 1–30).

Figure 1–30

3

- Right-click the Account Manager table in the Navigation Pane to display a shortcut menu.

- Click Open on the shortcut menu to open the table in Datasheet view.

Q&A Why do the records appear in a different order than the order in which I entered them?
When you open the table, they are sorted in the order of the primary key. In this case, that means they will appear in Account Manager Number order.

- Close the Navigation Pane by clicking the 'Shutter Bar Open/ Close Button' (Figure 1–31).

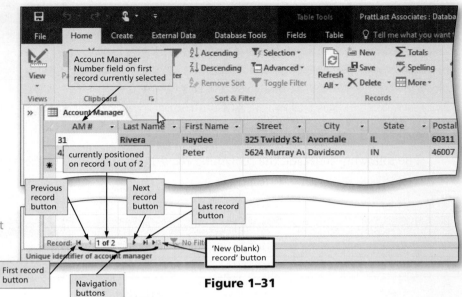

Figure 1–31

4

- Click the 'New (blank) record' button to move to a position to enter a new record (Figure 1–32).

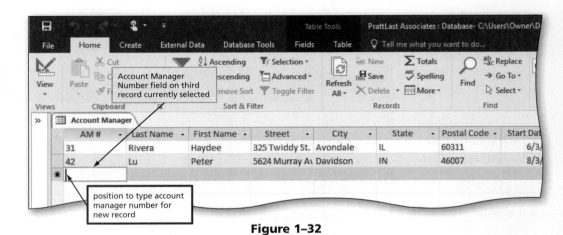

Figure 1–32

5

- Add the records shown in Figure 1–28 using the same techniques you used to add the first two records (Figure 1–33).

6

- Close the table.

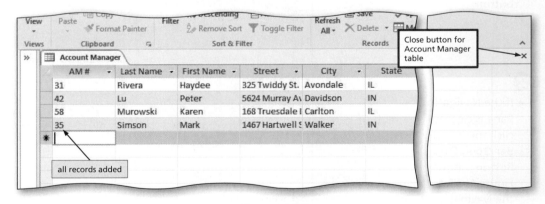

Figure 1–33

Other Ways

1. Click New button (Home tab | Records group)   2. Press CTRL+PLUS SIGN (+)

To Resize Columns in a Datasheet

Access assigns default column sizes, which do not always provide space to display all the data in the field. In some cases, the data might appear but the entire field name will not. You can correct this problem by resizing the column (changing its size) in the datasheet. In some instances, you may want to reduce the size of a column. *Why? Some fields, such as the State field, are short enough that they do not require all the space on the screen that is allotted to them.* Changing a column width changes the layout, or design, of a table. The following steps resize the columns in the Account Manager table and save the changes to the layout.

- Open the Navigation Pane if it is not already open.

- Open the Account Manager table and then close the Navigation Pane.

- Point to the right boundary of the field selector for the Account Manager Number (AM #) field (Figure 1–34) so that the pointer becomes a two-headed arrow.

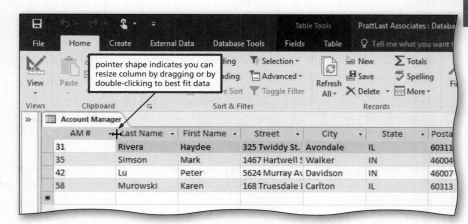

Figure 1–34

Q&A I am using touch and I cannot see the pointer. Is this a problem?
It is not a problem. Remember that if you are using your finger on a touch screen, you will not see the pointer.

②

- Double-click the right boundary of the field selector to resize the field so that it best fits the data.

- Use the same technique to resize all the other fields to best fit the data.

- Save the changes to the layout by clicking the Save button on the Quick Access Toolbar (Figure 1–35).

Figure 1–35

③

- Click the table's Close button (shown in Figure 1–33) to close the table.

Q&A What if I closed the table without saving the layout changes?
You would be asked if you want to save the changes.

Other Ways
1. Right-click field name, click Field Width

What is the best method for distributing database objects?
The traditional method of distributing database objects such as tables, reports, and forms uses a printer to produce a hard copy. A hard copy or printout is information that exists on a physical medium such as paper. Hard copies can be useful for the following reasons:

- Some people prefer proofreading a hard copy of a document rather than viewing it on the screen to check for errors and readability.

- Hard copies can serve as a backup reference if your storage medium is lost or becomes corrupted and you need to recreate the document. Instead of distributing a hard copy, users can distribute the document as an electronic image that mirrors the original document's appearance. The electronic image of the document can be emailed, posted on a website, or copied to a portable storage medium such as a USB flash drive. Two popular electronic image formats, sometimes called fixed formats, are PDF by Adobe Systems and XPS by Microsoft.

In Access, you can create electronic image files through the External Data tab on the ribbon. Electronic images of documents, such as PDF and XPS, can be useful for the following reasons:

- Users can view electronic images of documents without the software that created the original document (e.g., Access). Specifically, to view a PDF file, you use a program called Adobe Reader, which can be downloaded free from Adobe's website. Similarly, to view an XPS file, you use a program called XPS Viewer, which is included in the latest versions of Windows and Edge.

- Sending electronic documents saves paper and printer supplies. Society encourages users to contribute to **green computing**, which involves reducing the electricity consumed and environmental waste generated when using computers, mobile devices, and related technologies.

BTW
Changing Printers
To change the default printer that appears in the Print dialog box, click File on the ribbon, click the Print tab in the Backstage view, click Print in the Print gallery, then click the Name arrow and select the desired printer.

Previewing and Printing the Contents of a Table

When working with a database, you will often need to print a copy of the table contents. Figure 1–36 shows a printed copy of the contents of the Account Manager table. (Yours might look slightly different, depending on your printer.) Because the Account Manager table is substantially wider than the screen, it will also be wider than the normal printed page in portrait orientation. **Portrait orientation** means the printout is across the width of the page. **Landscape orientation** means the printout is across the height of the page. To print the wide database table, you might prefer to use landscape orientation. A convenient way to change to landscape orientation is to preview what the printed copy will look like by using Print Preview. This allows you to determine whether landscape orientation is necessary and, if it is, to change the orientation easily to landscape. In addition, you can also use Print Preview to determine whether any adjustments are necessary to the page margins.

	Account Manager								9/12/2017

AM #	Last Name	First Name	Street	City	State	Postal Code	Start Date	Salary	Bonus Rate
31	Rivera	Haydee	325 Twiddy St.	Avondale	IL	60311	6/3/2013	$48,750.00	0.15
35	Simson	Mark	1467 Hartwell St.	Walker	IN	46004	5/19/2014	$40,500.00	0.12
42	Lu	Peter	5624 Murray Ave.	Davidson	IN	46007	8/3/2015	$36,750.00	0.09
58	Murowski	Karen	168 Truesdale Dr.	Carlton	IL	60313	11/9/2016	$24,000.00	0.08

Figure 1–36

To Preview and Print the Contents of a Table

The following steps use Print Preview to preview and then print the contents of the Account Manager table. *Why? By previewing the contents of the table in Print Preview, you can make any necessary adjustments to the orientation or to the margins before printing the contents.*

1

- If the Navigation Pane is closed, open the Navigation Pane by clicking the 'Shutter Bar Open/ Close Button'.

- Be sure the Account Manager table is selected.

Q&A Why do I have to be sure the Account Manager table is selected? It is the only object in the database.
When the database contains only one object, you do not have to worry about selecting the object. Ensuring that the correct object is selected is a good habit to form, however, to make sure that the object you print is the one you want.

- Click File on the ribbon to open the Backstage view.

- Click the Print tab in the Backstage view to display the Print gallery (Figure 1–37).

Figure 1–37

2

- Click the Print Preview button in the Print gallery to display a preview of what the table will look like when printed (Figure 1–38).

Q&A I cannot read the table. Can I magnify a portion of the table?
Yes. Point the pointer, whose shape will change to a magnifying glass, at the portion of the table that you want to magnify, and then click. You can return to the original view of the table by clicking a second time.

Figure 1–38

- Click the pointer in the position shown in Figure 1–38 to magnify the upper-right section of the table (Figure 1–39).

Q&A My table was already magnified in a different area. How can I see the area shown in the figure? One way is to use the scroll bars to move to the desired portion of the table. You can also click the pointer anywhere in the table to produce a screen like the one shown in Figure 1–38, and then click in the location shown in the figure.

When I magnify the upper-right section, my table moves to the right of the screen and there is a lot of white space. Is that a problem?
No, use the horizontal scroll bar to move the table to the left and reduce the size of the white space.

Figure 1–39

- Click the Landscape button (Print Preview tab | Page Layout group) to change to landscape orientation.

- Click the Margins button arrow (Print Preview tab | Page Size group) and then click Normal, if necessary, to display all the fields (Figure 1–40).

5

- Click the Print button (Print Preview tab | Print group) to display the Print dialog box.

- Click the OK button (Print dialog box) to print the table.

- When the printer stops, retrieve the hard copy of the Account Manager table.

- Click the 'Close Print Preview' button (Print Preview tab | Close Preview group) to close the Print Preview window.

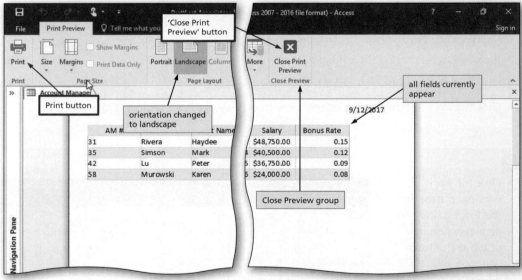

Figure 1–40

Q&A Do I have to select Print Preview before printing the table?
No. If you want to print without previewing, you would select either Print or Quick Print rather than Print Preview.

Other Ways

1. Press CTRL+P, click OK button in Print dialog box

Importing or Linking Data From Other Applications to Access

If your data for a table is stored in an Excel worksheet, you can **import** the data, which means to make a copy of the data as a table in the Access database. In this case, any changes to the data made in Access would not be reflected in the Excel worksheet.

Figure 1–41, which contains the Account data, is an example of the type of worksheet that can be imported. In this type of worksheet, the data is stored as a **list**, that is, a collection of rows and columns in which all the entries in a column represent the same type of data. In this type of list, the first row contains **column headings**, that is, descriptions of the contents of the column, rather than data. In the worksheet in Figure 1–41, for example, the entry in the first column of the first row is Account Number. This indicates that all the other values in this column are account numbers. The fact that the entry in the second column of the first row is Account Name indicates that all the other values in the second column are account names.

BTW

Linking Versus Importing
When you link to the data in the worksheet, the data appears as a table in the Access database but it is maintained in its original form in Excel. Any changes to the Excel data are reflected when the linked table is viewed in Access. In this arrangement, Access would typically be used as a vehicle for querying and presenting the data, with actual updates being made in Excel.

BTW

Importing Data in Other Formats
You can import data into a table from Excel workbooks, Access databases, XML files, ODBC databases such as SQL Server, text files, HTML documents, Outlook folders, and SharePoint lists.

Figure 1–41

Does it matter how the data in the Excel workbook is formatted? If so, how can you be sure the Excel data is formatted in such a way that you can import it?
The format of data in an Excel workbook is important when you want to import it into Access. To ensure the data is in an appropriate format:

1. Make sure the data is in the form of a list; a collection of rows and columns in which all the entries in a column represent the same type of data.

2. Make sure there are no blank rows within the list. If there are, remove them prior to importing or linking.

3. Make sure there are no blank columns within the list. If there are, remove them prior to importing or linking.

4. Determine whether the first row contains column headings that will make appropriate field names in the resulting table. If not, you should consider adding such a row. In general, the process is simpler if the first row in the worksheet contains appropriate column headings.

CONSIDER THIS

The Import process will create a table. In this table, the column headings in the first row of the worksheet become the field names. The rows of the worksheet, other than the first row, become the records in the table. In the process, each field will be assigned the data type that seems the most reasonable, given the data currently in the worksheet. When the Import process is finished, you can use Datasheet view or Design view to modify these data types or to make any other changes to the structure you feel are necessary.

To Import an Excel Worksheet

1 CREATE FIRST TABLE | 2 ADD RECORDS | 3 PRINT CONTENTS | 4 IMPORT RECORDS
5 MODIFY SECOND TABLE | 6 CREATE QUERY | 7 CREATE FORM | 8 CREATE REPORT

You import a worksheet by using the Import Spreadsheet Wizard. In the process, you will indicate that the first row in the worksheet contains the column headings. *Why? You are indicating that Access is to use those column headings as the field names in the Access table.* In addition, you will indicate the primary key for the table. As part of the process, you could, if appropriate, choose not to include all the fields from the worksheet in the resulting table.

The following steps import the Account worksheet.

- Click External Data on the ribbon to display the External Data tab (Figure 1–42).

Figure 1–42

- Click the Excel button (External Data tab | Import & Link group) to display the Get External Data - Excel Spreadsheet dialog box.

- Click the Browse button in the Get External Data - Excel Spreadsheet dialog box.

- Navigate to the location containing the workbook (for example, the Access folder in the CIS 101 folder). For a detailed example of this procedure, refer to the Office and Windows module at the beginning of this book.

- Click the Account workbook, and then click the Open button to select the workbook (Figure 1–43).

Figure 1–43

• With the option button to import the source data to a new table selected, click the OK button to display the Import Spreadsheet Wizard dialog box (Figure 1–44).

Q&A What happens if I select the option button to append records to an existing table?
Instead of the records being placed in a new table, they will be added to an existing table that you specify, provided the value in the primary key field does not duplicate that of an existing record.

Figure 1–44

• Be sure the 'First Row Contains Column Headings' check box is selected. If it is not, click the 'First Row Contains Column Headings' check box to select it.

• Click the Next button (Figure 1–45).

Q&A When would I use the Field Options on the Import Spreadsheet Wizard?
You would use these options if you wanted to change properties for one or more fields. You can change the name, the data type, and whether the field is indexed. You can also indicate that some fields should not be imported.

Figure 1–45

• Because the Field Options need not be specified, click the Next button (Figure 1–46).

Figure 1–46

6

- Click the 'Choose my own primary key' option button (Figure 1–47).

Q&A How do I decide which option button to select?
If one of the fields is an appropriate primary key, choose your own primary key from the list of fields. If you are sure you do not want a primary key, choose 'No primary key'. Otherwise, let Access add the primary key.

Figure 1–47

7

- Because the Account Number field, which is the correct field, is already selected as the primary key, click the Next button.

- Use the DELETE or BACKSPACE keys as necessary to erase the current entry, and then type **Account** in the Import to Table text box.

- Click the Finish button to import the data (Figure 1–48).

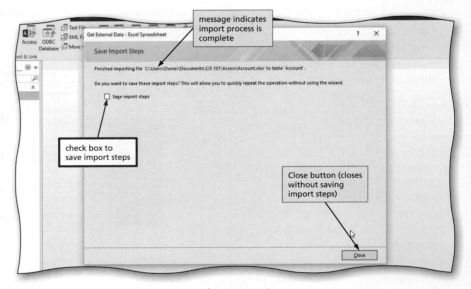

Figure 1–48

8

- Click the 'Save import steps' check box to display the Save import steps options.

- If necessary, type **Import-Account** in the Save as text box.

- Type **Import data from Account workbook into Account table** in the Description text box (Figure 1–49).

Q&A When would I create an Outlook task?
If the import operation is one you will repeat on a regular basis, you can create and schedule the import process just as you can schedule any other Outlook task.

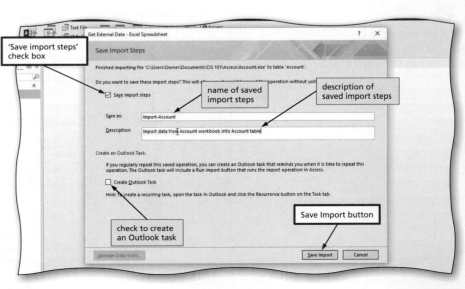

Figure 1–49

9

- Click the Save Import button to save the import steps (Figure 1–50).

Q&A I saved the table as Account Data. How can I change the name? Right-click the table name in the Navigation Pane. Click Rename on the shortcut menu and change the table name to Account.

Figure 1–50

Modifying the Table

The import process has created the Account table. The table has the correct fields and records. There are some details the process cannot handle, however. These include field sizes, descriptions, and captions. You will use Design view to make the necessary changes. The information you need is shown in Table 1–5.

BTW
Creating a Table in Design View
To create a table in Design view, display the Create tab, and then click the Table Design button (Create tab | Tables group). You will then see the same screen as in Figure 1–51, except that there will be no entries. Make all the necessary entries for the fields in your table, save the table, and assign the table a name.

Table 1–5 Structure of Account Table			
Field Name	**Data Type**	**Field Size**	**Notes**
Account Number	Short Text	5	Primary Key **Description:** Account Number (two uppercase letters followed by 3-digit number) **Caption:** AC #
Account Name	Short Text	30	
Street	Short Text	20	
City	Short Text	20	
State	Short Text	2	
Postal Code	Short Text	5	
Amount Paid	Currency		
Current Due	Currency		
Account Manager Number	Short Text	2	**Description:** Account Manager Number (number of account manager for account) **Caption:** AM #

To Modify a Table in Design View

1 CREATE FIRST TABLE | 2 ADD RECORDS | 3 PRINT CONTENTS | 4 IMPORT RECORDS
5 MODIFY SECOND TABLE | 6 CREATE QUERY | 7 CREATE FORM | 8 CREATE REPORT

You will usually need to modify the design of a table created during the import process. *Why? Some properties of a table are not specified during the import process, such as descriptions, captions, and field sizes. You might also need to change a data type.* The following steps make the necessary modifications to the design of the Account table.

1

- Open the Navigation Pane, if necessary.

- Right-click the Account table in the Navigation Pane to display the shortcut menu, and then click Design View on the shortcut menu to open the table in Design view (Figure 1–51).

Figure 1–51

2

- Click the Description (Optional) box for the Account Number field, and then type **Account Number (two uppercase letters followed by a 3-digit number)** as the description.

- With the Account Number field selected, click the Field Size box, erase the current field size, and type **5** as the new field size.

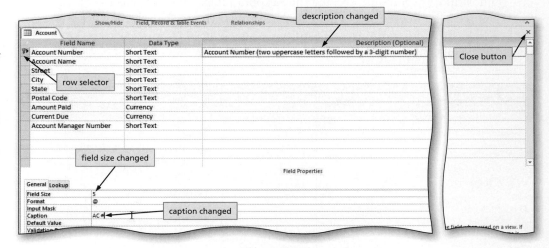

Figure 1–52

- Click the Caption box, and type **AC #** as the caption (Figure 1–52).

Q&A What does the @ symbol represent in the Format box?

The @ symbol is a default format added by Access when the table was imported from Excel.

3

- Make the other changes shown in Table 1–5. To select a field to be changed, click the field's row selector. For most fields, you only need to change the field size. For the Account Manager Number field, you also need to change the description and caption.

- Click the Save button on the Quick Access Toolbar to save your changes.

- Because you know the data will satisfy the new field sizes, click the Yes button when given a message about the possibility of data loss.

Other Ways

1. Press F6 to move between upper and lower panes in Table Design window

Correcting Errors in the Structure

Whenever you create or modify a table in Design view, you should check the entries carefully to ensure they are correct. If you make a mistake and discover it before you press the TAB key, you can correct the error by repeatedly pressing the BACKSPACE key until the incorrect characters are removed. Then, type the correct characters. If you do not discover a mistake until later, you can click the entry, type the correct value, and then press the ENTER key. You can use the following techniques to make changes to the structure:

- If you accidentally add an extra field to the structure, select the field by clicking the row selector (the leftmost column on the row that contains the field to be deleted). Once you have selected the field, press the DELETE key. This will remove the field from the structure.

- If you forget to include a field, select the field that will follow the one you want to add by clicking the row selector, and then press the INSERT key. The remaining fields move down one row, making room for the missing field. Make the entries for the new field in the usual manner.

- If you made the wrong field a primary key field, click the correct primary key entry for the field and then click the Primary Key button (Table Tools Design tab | Tools group).

- To move a field, click the row selector for the field to be moved to select the field, and then drag the field to the desired position.

As an alternative to these steps, you might want to start over. To do so, click the Close button for the window containing the table, and then click the No button in the Microsoft Access dialog box. You then can repeat the process you used earlier to define the fields in the table.

To Close the Table

Now that you have completed and saved the Account table, you can close it. The following step closes the table.

1 Click the Close button for the Account table (see Figure 1–52) to close the table.

To Resize Columns in a Datasheet

You can resize the columns in the datasheet for the Account table just as you resized the columns in the datasheet for the Account Manager table. The following steps resize the columns in the Account table to best fit the data.

1 Open the Account table in Datasheet view.

2 Double-click the right boundary of the field selectors of each of the fields to resize the columns so that they best fit the data.

3 Save the changes to the layout by clicking the Save button on the Quick Access Toolbar.

4 Close the table.

Break Point: If you wish to take a break, this is a good place to do so. You can exit Access now. To resume at a later time, run Access, open the database called PrattLast Associates, and continue following the steps from this location forward.

Additional Database Objects

A database contains many types of objects. Tables are the objects you use to store and manipulate data. Access supports other important types of objects as well; each object has a specific purpose that helps maximize the benefits of a database. Through queries (questions), Access makes it possible to ask complex questions concerning the data in the database and then receive instant answers. Access also allows the user to produce attractive and useful forms for viewing and updating data. Additionally, Access includes report creation tools that make it easy to produce sophisticated reports for presenting data.

BTW
Creating Queries
Although the Simple Query Wizard is a convenient way to create straightforward queries, you will find that many of the queries you create require more control than the wizard provides. In Module 2, you will use Design view to create customized queries.

Creating Queries

Queries are simply questions, the answers to which are in the database. Access contains a powerful query feature that helps you find the answers to a wide variety of questions. Once you have examined the question you want to ask to determine the fields involved in the question, you can begin creating the query. If the query involves no special sort order, restrictions, or calculations, you can use the Simple Query Wizard.

To Use the Simple Query Wizard to Create a Query

1 CREATE FIRST TABLE | 2 ADD RECORDS | 3 PRINT CONTENTS | 4 IMPORT RECORDS
5 MODIFY SECOND TABLE | 6 CREATE QUERY | 7 CREATE FORM | 8 CREATE REPORT

The following steps use the Simple Query Wizard to create a query that PrattLast Associates might use to obtain financial information on its accounts. *Why? The Simple Query Wizard is the quickest and easiest way to create a query.* This query displays the number, name, amount paid, current due, and account manager number of all accounts.

- If the Navigation Pane is closed, click the 'Shutter Bar Open/Close Button' to open the Navigation Pane.

- Be sure the Account table is selected.

- Click Create on the ribbon to display the Create tab.

- Click the Query Wizard button (Create tab | Queries group) to display the New Query dialog box (Figure 1–53).

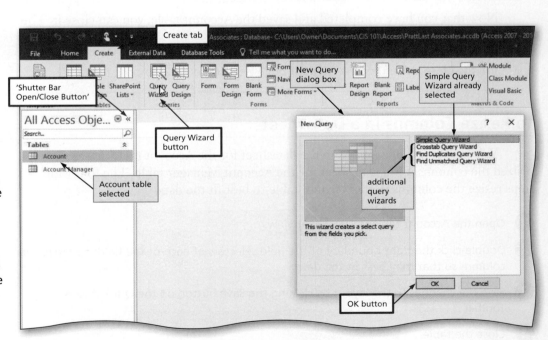

Figure 1–53

2

- Be sure Simple Query Wizard is selected, and then click the OK button (New Query dialog box) to display the Simple Query Wizard dialog box (Figure 1–54).

Q&A

What would happen if the Account Manager table were selected instead of the Account table?

The list of available fields would contain fields from the Account Manager table rather than the Account table.

If the list contained Account Manager table fields, how could I make it contain Account table fields?

Click the arrow in the Tables/Queries box, and then click the Account table in the list that appears.

Figure 1–54

3

- With the Account Number field selected, click the Add Field button to add the field to the query.

- With the Account Name field selected, click the Add Field button a second time to add the field.

- Click the Amount Paid field, and then click the Add Field button to add the field.

- In a similar fashion, add the Current Due and Account Manager Number fields (Figure 1–55).

Figure 1–55

4

- Click the Next button to move to the next screen.

- Ensure that the 'Detail (shows every field of every record)' option button is selected (Figure 1–56).

Q&A

What is the difference between Detail and Summary?

Detail shows all the records and fields. Summary only shows computations (for example, the total amount paid).

Figure 1–56

- Click the Next button to move to the next screen.

- Confirm that the title of the query is Account Query (Figure 1–57).

Q&A What should I do if the title is incorrect?
Click the box containing the title to produce an insertion point. Erase the current title and then type Account Query.

Figure 1–57

- Click the Finish button to create the query (Figure 1–58).

- Click the Close button for the Account Query to remove the query results from the screen.

Q&A If I want to use this query in the future, do I need to save the query?
Normally you would. The one exception is a query created by the wizard. The wizard automatically saves the query it creates.

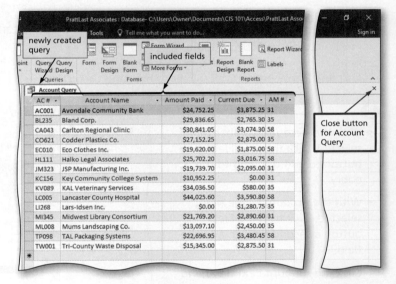

Figure 1–58

Using Queries

After you have created and saved a query, Access stores it as a database object and makes it available for use in a variety of ways:

- If you want to change the design of the query, right-click the query in the Navigation Pane and then click Design View on the shortcut menu to open the query in Design view.

- To view the results of the query from Design view, click the Run button to instruct Access to **run** the query, that is, to perform the necessary actions to produce and display the results in Datasheet view.

- To view the results of the query from the Navigation Pane, open it by right-clicking the query and clicking Open on the shortcut menu. Access automatically runs the query and displays the results in Datasheet view.

- To print the results with the query open in either Design view or Datasheet view, click File on the ribbon, click the Print tab, and then click either Print or Quick Print.

- To print the query without first opening it, be sure the query is selected in the Navigation Pane and click File on the ribbon, click the Print tab, and then click either Print or Quick Print.

You can switch between views of a query using the View button (Home tab | Views group). Clicking the arrow in the bottom of the button produces the View button menu. You then click the desired view in the menu. The two query views you will use in this module are Datasheet view (which displays the query results) and Design view (for changing the query design). You can also click the top part of the View button, in which case you will switch to the view identified by the icon on the button. For the most part, the icon on the button represents the view you want, so you can usually simply click the button.

To Use a Criterion in a Query

1 CREATE FIRST TABLE | 2 ADD RECORDS | 3 PRINT CONTENTS | 4 IMPORT RECORDS
5 MODIFY SECOND TABLE | 6 CREATE QUERY | 7 CREATE FORM | 8 CREATE REPORT

After you have determined the fields to be included in a query, you will determine whether you need to further restrict the results of the query. For example, you might want to include only those accounts managed by account manager 35, Mark Simson. In such a case, you need to enter the number 35 as a criterion for the account manager field. *Why? A criterion is a condition that the records must satisfy in order to be included in the query results.* To do so, you will open the query in Design view, enter the criterion below the appropriate field, and then view the results of the query. The following steps enter a criterion to include only the accounts of account manager 35 and then view the query results.

- Right-click the Account Query in the Navigation Pane to produce a shortcut menu (Figure 1–59).

Figure 1–59

- Click Design View on the shortcut menu to open the query in Design view (Figure 1–60).

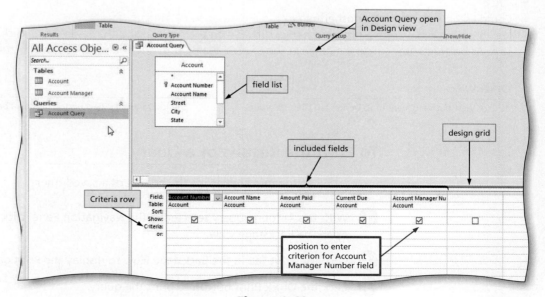

Figure 1–60

3

- Click the Criteria row in the Account Manager Number column of the grid, and then type 3 5 as the criterion (Figure 1–61).

Q&A

The Account Manager Number field is a text field. Do I need to enclose the value for a text field in quotation marks?
You could, but it is not necessary because Access inserts the quotation marks for you automatically.

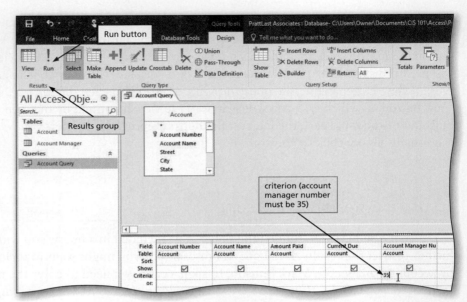

Figure 1–61

4

- Click the Run button (Query Tools Design tab | Results group) to run the query and display the results in Datasheet view (Figure 1–62).

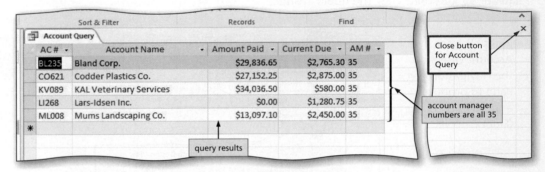

Figure 1–62

5

- Click the Close button for the Account Query to close the query.

- When asked if you want to save your changes, click the No button.

Q&A

If I saved the query, what would happen the next time I ran the query?
You would see only accounts of account manager 35.

Could I save a query with another name?
Yes. To save a query with a different name, click File on the ribbon, click the Save As tab, click Save Object As, click the Save As button, enter a new file name in the Save As dialog box, and then click the OK button (Save As dialog box).

Other Ways

1. Click View button (Query Tools Design tab | Results group)   2. Click Datasheet View button on status bar

To Print the Results of a Query

The following steps print the results of a saved query.

1 With the Account Query selected in the Navigation Pane, click File on the ribbon to open the Backstage view.

2 Click the Print tab in the Backstage view to display the Print gallery.

3 Click the Quick Print button to print the query.

Creating Forms

In Datasheet view, you can view many records at once. If there are many fields, however, only some of the fields in each record might be visible at a time. In **Form view**, where data is displayed in a form on the screen, you can usually see all the fields, but only for one record.

To Create a Form

1 CREATE FIRST TABLE | 2 ADD RECORDS | 3 PRINT CONTENTS | 4 IMPORT RECORDS

5 MODIFY SECOND TABLE | 6 CREATE QUERY | **7 CREATE FORM** | **8 CREATE REPORT**

Like a paper form, a **form** in a database is a formatted document with fields that contain data. Forms allow you to view and maintain data. Forms can also be used to print data, but reports are more commonly used for that purpose. The simplest type of form in Access is one that includes all the fields in a table stacked one above the other. The following steps use the Form button to create a form. *Why? Using the Form button is the simplest way to create this type of form. The steps use the form to view records and then save the form.*

 1

- Select the Account table in the Navigation Pane.

- If necessary, click Create on the ribbon to display the Create tab (Figure 1–63).

Figure 1–63

2

- Click the Form button (Create tab | Forms group) to create a simple form (Figure 1–64).

Q&A A Field list appeared on my screen. What should I do?
Click the 'Add Existing Fields' button (Form Layout Tools Design tab | Tools group) to remove the Field list from the screen.

Figure 1–64

3

- Click the Form View button on the Access status bar to display the form in Form view rather than Layout view.

Q&A

What is the difference between Layout view and Form view?

Layout view allows you to make changes to the look of the form. Form view is the view you use to examine or make changes to the data.

How can I tell when I am in Layout view?

Access identifies Layout view in three ways. The left side of the status bar will contain the words, Layout View; shading will appear around the outside of the selected field in the form; and the Layout View button will be selected on the right side of the status bar.

- Click the Next record button three times to move to record 4 (Figure 1–65).

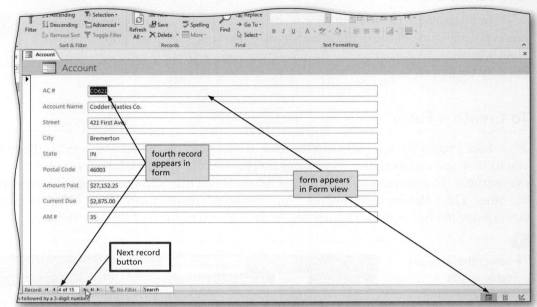

Figure 1–65

4

- Click the Save button on the Quick Access Toolbar to display the Save As dialog box (Figure 1–66).

Q&A

Do I have to click the Next record button before saving?

No. The only reason you were asked to click the button was so that you could experience navigation within the form.

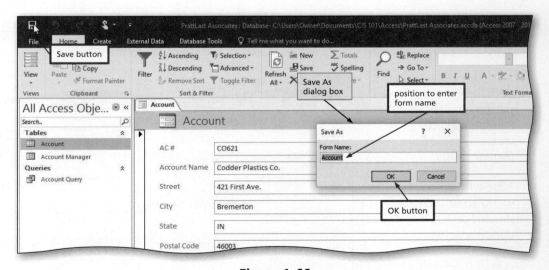

Figure 1–66

5

- Type **Account Form** as the form name, and then click the OK button to save the form.

- Click the Close button for the form to close the form.

Other Ways

1. Click View button (Form Layout Tools Design tab | Views group)

Using a Form

After you have saved a form, you can use it at any time by right-clicking the form in the Navigation Pane and then clicking Open on the shortcut menu. In addition to viewing data in the form, you can also use it to enter or update data, a process that is very similar to updating data using a datasheet. If you plan to use the form to enter or revise data, you must ensure you are viewing the form in Form view.

Break Point: If you wish to take a break, this is a good place to do so. You can exit Access now. To resume at a later time, run Access, open the database called PrattLast Associates, and continue following the steps from this location forward.

Creating and Printing Reports

PrattLast Associates wants to be able to present account financial data in a useful format. To do so, they will create the Account Financial Report shown in Figure 1–67. To create this report, you will first create a simple report containing all records. Then, you will modify the report to match the one shown in Figure 1–67.

Account Financial Report

Tuesday, September 12, 2017
7:54:24 PM

Account Number	Account Name	Amount Paid	Current Due	Account Manager Number
AC001	Avondale Community Bank	$24,752.25	$3,875.25	31
BL235	Bland Corp.	$29,836.65	$2,765.30	35
CA043	Carlton Regional Clinic	$30,841.05	$3,074.30	58
CO621	Codder Plastics Co.	$27,152.25	$2,875.00	35
EC010	Eco Clothes Inc.	$19,620.00	$1,875.00	58
HL111	Halko Legal Associates	$25,702.20	$3,016.75	58
JM323	JSP Manufacturing Inc.	$19,739.70	$2,095.00	31
KV089	KAL Veterinary Services	$34,036.50	$580.00	35
KC156	Key Community College System	$10,952.25	$0.00	31
LC005	Lancaster County Hospital	$44,025.60	$3,590.80	58
LI268	Lars-Idsen Inc.	$0.00	$1,280.75	35
MI345	Midwest Library Consortium	$21,769.20	$2,890.60	31
ML008	Mums Landscaping Co.	$13,097.10	$2,450.00	35
TP098	TAL Packaging Systems	$22,696.95	$3,480.45	58
TW001	Tri-County Waste Disposal	$15,345.00	$2,875.50	31
		$339,566.70	$36,724.70	

Figure 1–67

To Create a Report

1 CREATE FIRST TABLE | 2 ADD RECORDS | 3 PRINT CONTENTS | 4 IMPORT RECORDS
5 MODIFY SECOND TABLE | 6 CREATE QUERY | 7 CREATE FORM | **8 CREATE REPORT**

You will first create a report containing all fields. *Why? It is easiest to create a report with all the fields and then delete the fields you do not want.* The following steps create and save the initial report. They also modify the report title.

1

- Be sure the Account table is selected in the Navigation Pane.

- Click Create on the ribbon to display the Create tab (Figure 1–68).

Q&A Do I need to select the Account table prior to clicking Create on the ribbon?
You do not need to select the table at that point. You do need to select a table prior to clicking the Report button, because Access will include all the fields in whichever table or query is currently selected.

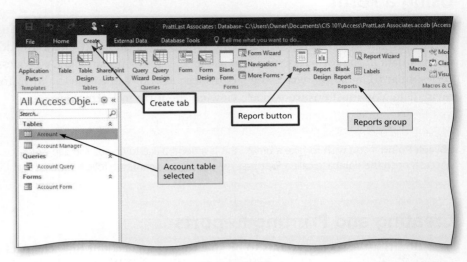

Figure 1–68

2

- Click the Report button (Create tab | Reports group) to create the report (Figure 1–69).

Q&A Why is the report title Account?
Access automatically assigns the name of the table or query as the title of the report. It also automatically includes the date and time. You can change either of these later.

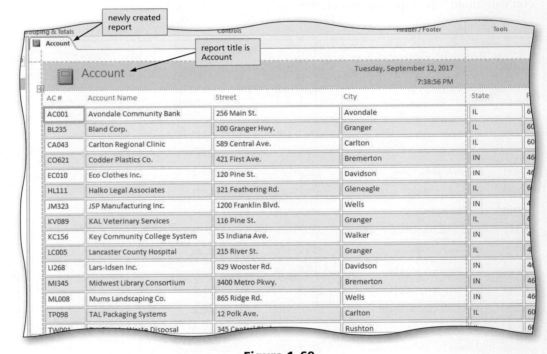

Figure 1–69

3

- Click the Save button on the Quick Access Toolbar to display the Save As dialog box, and then type Account Financial Report as the name of the report (Figure 1–70).

Figure 1–70

- Click the OK button (Save As dialog box) to save the report (Figure 1–71).

Q&A

The name of the report changed. Why did the report title not change?

The report title is assigned the same name as the report by default. Changing the name of the report does not change the report title. You can change the title at any time to anything you like.

Figure 1–71

- Close the report by clicking its Close button.

Using Layout View in a Report

Access has four different ways to view reports: Report view, Print Preview, Layout view, and Design view. Report view shows the report on the screen. Print Preview shows the report as it will appear when printed. Layout view is similar to Report view in that it shows the report on the screen, but it also allows you to make changes to the report. Layout view is usually the easiest way to make such changes. Design view also allows you to make changes, but does not show you the actual report. Design view is most useful when the changes you need to make are especially complex. In this module, you will use Layout view to modify the report.

BTW
Report Navigation
When previewing a report, you can use the Navigation buttons on the status bar to move from one page to another.

To Modify Report Column Headings and Resize Columns

1 CREATE FIRST TABLE | 2 ADD RECORDS | 3 PRINT CONTENTS | 4 IMPORT RECORDS
5 MODIFY SECOND TABLE | 6 CREATE QUERY | 7 CREATE FORM | **8 CREATE REPORT**

To make the report match the one shown in Figure 1–67, you need to change the title, remove some columns, modify the column headings, and also resize the columns. The following steps use Layout view to make the necessary modifications to the report. *Why? Working in Layout view gives you all the tools you need to make the desired modifications. You can view the results of the modifications immediately.*

- Right-click Account Financial Report in the Navigation Pane, and then click Layout View on the shortcut menu to open the report in Layout view.

- If a Field list appears, click the 'Add Existing Fields' button (Report Layout Tools Design tab | Tools group) to remove the Field list from the screen.

- Close the Navigation Pane.

- Click the report title once to select it.

- Click the report title a second time to produce an insertion point (Figure 1–72).

Figure 1–72

Q&A

My insertion point is in the middle of Account. How do I produce an insertion point at the position shown in the figure?

You can use the RIGHT ARROW key to move the insertion point to the position in the figure, or you can click the desired position.

2

- Press the SPACEBAR to insert a space, and then type `Financial Report` to complete the title.

- Click the column heading for the Street field to select it.

- Press and hold the CTRL key and then click the column headings for the City, State, and Postal Code fields to select multiple column headings.

Q&A

What happens if I do not hold down the CTRL key?

When you click another column heading, it will be the only one that is selected. To select multiple objects, you need to hold the CTRL key down for every object after the first selection.

I selected the wrong collection of objects. What should I do?

You can click somewhere else on the report so that the objects you want are not selected, and then begin the process again. Alternatively, you can repeatedly click the Undo button on the Quick Access Toolbar to undo your selections. Once you have done so, you can select the objects you want.

- Click Arrange on the ribbon to display the Report Layout Tools Arrange tab (Figure 1–73).

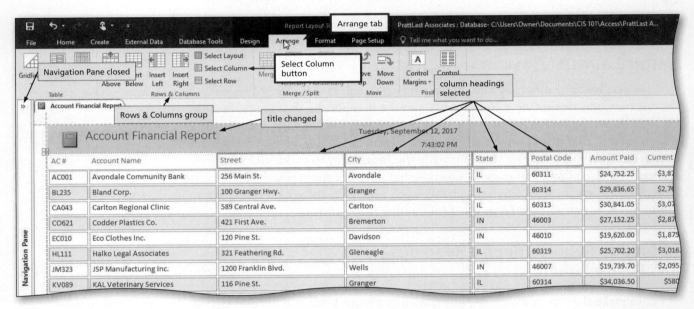

Figure 1–73

3

- Click the Select Column button (Report Layout Tools Arrange tab | Rows & Columns group) to select the entire columns corresponding to the column headings you selected in the previous step.

- Press the DELETE key to delete the selected columns.

- Click the column heading for the Account Number field twice, once to select it and the second time to produce an insertion point (Figure 1–74).

Q&A

I selected the wrong field. What should I do?

Click somewhere outside the various fields to deselect the one you have selected. Then, click the Account Number field twice.

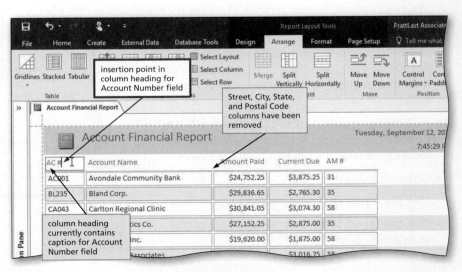

Figure 1–74

4

- Use the DELETE or BACKSPACE keys as necessary to erase the current entry, and then type `Account Number` as the new entry.

- Click the heading for the Account Manager Number field twice, erase the current entry, and then type `Account Manager Number` as the new entry.

- Click the Account Number field heading to select it, point to the lower boundary of the heading for the Account Number field so that the pointer changes to a two-headed arrow, and then drag the lower boundary to the approximate position shown in Figure 1–75 to expand the column headings.

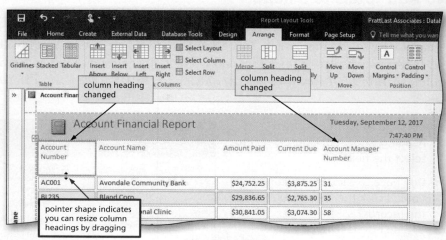

Figure 1–75

Q&A I did something wrong when I dragged and now my report looks strange. What should I do?

Click the Undo button on the Quick Access Toolbar to undo the change. Depending on the specific action you took, you might need to click it more than once.

My screen displays Account Manager Number on one line, not two. Is this a problem?

No. You will adjust the column heading in a later step.

5

- Point to the right boundary of the heading for the Account Number field so that the pointer changes to a two-headed arrow, and then drag the right boundary to the approximate position shown in Figure 1–76 to reduce the width of the column.

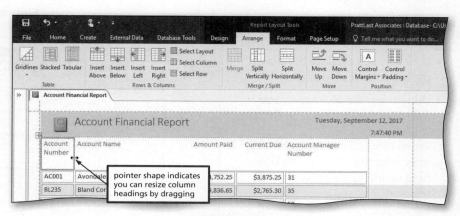

Figure 1–76

6

- Using the same technique, resize the other columns to the sizes shown in Figure 1–77.

Figure 1–77

AC 46 Access Module 1 Databases and Database Objects: An Introduction

1 CREATE FIRST TABLE | 2 ADD RECORDS | 3 PRINT CONTENTS | 4 IMPORT RECORDS
5 MODIFY SECOND TABLE | 6 CREATE QUERY | 7 CREATE FORM | **8 CREATE REPORT**

To Add Totals to a Report

The report in Figure 1–67 contains totals for the Amount Paid and Current Due columns. You can use Layout view to add these totals. Once you have added the totals, Access will calculate the appropriate values whenever you display or print the report. The following steps use Layout view to include totals for these three columns. *Why? In Layout view you can click a single button to add totals. This button sums all the values in the field.*

1

- Click the Amount Paid field heading (shown in Figure 1–77) to select the field.

Do I have to click the heading? Could I click the field on one of the records?
You do not have to click the heading. You also could click the Amount Paid field on any record.

- Click Design on the ribbon to display the Design tab.

- Click the Totals button (Report Layout Tools Design tab | Grouping & Totals group) to display the Totals menu containing a list of available calculations (Figure 1–78).

Figure 1–78

2

- Click Sum to calculate the sum of the amount of paid values.

- Using the same technique, add totals for the Current Due column.

When I clicked the Totals button after selecting the Current Due field heading, Sum was already checked. Do I still need to click Sum?
No. In fact, if you do click it, you will remove the check mark, which will remove the total from the column.

- Scroll down to the bottom of the report to verify that the totals are included. If necessary, expand the size of the total controls so they appear completely by dragging the lower boundary of the controls to the approximate position shown in Figure 1–79.

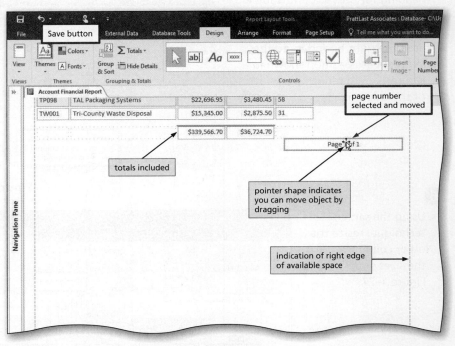

Figure 1–79

- Click the page number to select it, and then drag it to the approximate position shown in Figure 1–79.

Why did I need to move the page number?
The dotted line near the right-hand edge of the screen indicates the right-hand border of the available space on the printed page, based on whatever margins and orientation are currently selected. A portion of the page number extends beyond this border. By moving the page number, it no longer extends beyond the border.

❸

- Click the Save button on the Quick Access Toolbar to save your changes to the report layout.
- Close the report.

To Print a Report

The following steps print the report.

① Open the Navigation Pane, if necessary, confirm that the Account Financial Report is selected, and then click File on the ribbon to open the Backstage view.

② Click the Print tab in the Backstage view to display the Print gallery.

③ Click the Quick Print button to print the report.

Q&A When I print the report, I have pound signs (####) rather than numbers where the totals should be for the Amount Paid and Current Due columns. The report looked fine on the screen. How can I correct it?

The columns are not wide enough to display the complete number. Open the report in Layout view and slightly increase the width of the Amount Paid and Current Due columns by dragging the right boundary of the column headings.

How can I print multiple copies of my report?

Click File on the ribbon to open the Backstage view. Click the Print tab, click Print in the Print gallery to display the Print dialog box, increase the number in the Number of Copies box, and then click the OK button .

How can I print a range of pages rather than printing the whole report?

Click File on the ribbon to open the Backstage view. Click the Print tab, click Print in the Print gallery to display the Print dialog box, click the Pages option button in the Print Range area, enter the desired page range, and then click the OK button (Print dialog box).

Database Properties

Access helps you organize and identify your databases by using **database properties,** which are the details about a file. Database properties, also known as **metadata,** can include such information as the project author, title, or subject. **Keywords** are words or phrases that further describe the database. For example, a class name or database topic can describe the file's purpose or content.

Five different types of database properties exist, but the more common ones used in this book are standard and automatically updated properties. **Standard properties** are associated with all Microsoft Office documents and include author, title, and subject. **Automatically updated properties** include file system properties, such as the date you create or change a file, and statistics, such as the file size.

Why would you want to assign database properties to a database?

Database properties are valuable for a variety of reasons:

- Users can save time locating a particular file because they can view a file's database properties without opening the database.
- By creating consistent properties for files having similar content, users can better organize their databases.
- Some organizations require Access users to add database properties so that other employees can view details about these files.

CONSIDER THIS

To Change Database Properties

To change database properties, you would follow these steps.

① Click File on the ribbon to open the Backstage view and then, if necessary, click the Info tab in the Backstage view to display the Info gallery.

② Click the 'View and edit database properties' link in the right pane of the Info gallery to display the PrattLast Associates Properties dialog box.

Q&A | Why are some of the database properties already filled in?
The person who installed Office 2016 on your computer or network might have set or customized the properties.

③ If the property you want to change is displayed in the Properties dialog box, click the text box for the property and make the desired change. Skip the remaining steps.

④ If the property you want to change is not displayed in the Properties dialog box, click the appropriate tab so the property is displayed and then make the desired change.

⑤ Click the OK button in the Properties dialog box to save your changes and remove the dialog box from the screen.

BTW
Tabbed Documents Versus Overlapping Windows
By default, Access 2016 displays database objects in tabbed documents instead of in overlapping windows. If your database is in overlapping windows mode, click File on the ribbon, click Options in the Backstage view, click Current Database in the Access Options dialog box, and select the 'Display Document Tabs' check box and the Tabbed Documents option button.

Special Database Operations

Additional operations involved in maintaining a database are backup, recovery, compacting, and repairing.

Backup and Recovery

It is possible to damage or destroy a database. Users can enter data that is incorrect; programs that are updating the database can end abnormally during an update; a hardware problem can occur; and so on. After any such event has occurred, the database may contain invalid data or it might be totally destroyed.

Obviously, you cannot allow a situation in which data has been damaged or destroyed to go uncorrected. You must somehow return the database to a correct state. This process is called recovery; that is, you **recover** the database.

The simplest approach to recovery involves periodically making a copy of the database (called a **backup copy** or a **save copy**). This is referred to as **backing up** the database. If a problem occurs, you correct the problem by overwriting the actual database — often referred to as the **live database** — with the backup copy.

To back up the database that is currently open, you use the Back Up Database command on the Save As tab in the Backstage view. In the process, Access suggests a name that is a combination of the database name and the current date. For example, if you back up the PrattLast Associates database on October 20, 2017, Access will suggest the name, PrattLast Associates_2017-10-20. You can change this name if you desire, although it is a good idea to use this name. By doing so, it will be easy to distinguish between all the backup copies you have made to determine which is the most recent. In addition, if you discover that a critical problem occurred on October 18, 2017, you may want to go back to the most recent backup before October 18. If, for example, the database was not backed up on October 17 but was backed up on October 16, you would use PrattLast Associates_2017-10-16.

TO BACK UP A DATABASE

You would use the following steps to back up a database to a file on a hard disk, high-capacity removable disk, or other storage location.

1. Open the database to be backed up.
2. Click File on the ribbon to open the Backstage view, and then click the Save As tab.
3. With Save Database As selected in the File Types area, click 'Back Up Database' in the Save Database As area, and then click the Save As button.
4. Navigate to the desired location in the Save As box. If you do not want the name Access has suggested, enter the desired name in the File name text box.
5. Click the Save button to back up the database.

Access creates a backup copy with the desired name in the desired location. Should you ever need to recover the database using this backup copy, you can simply copy it over the live version.

Compacting and Repairing a Database

As you add more data to a database, it naturally grows larger. When you delete an object (records, tables, forms, or queries), the space previously occupied by the object does not become available for additional objects. Instead, the additional objects are given new space; that is, space that was not already allocated. To remove this empty space from the database, you must **compact** the database. The same option that compacts the database also repairs problems that might have occurred in the database.

TO COMPACT AND REPAIR A DATABASE

You would use the following steps to compact and repair a database.

1. Open the database to be compacted.
2. Click File on the ribbon to open the Backstage view, and then, if necessary, select the Info tab.
3. Click the 'Compact & Repair Database' button in the Info gallery to compact and repair the database.

The database now is the compacted form of the original.

Additional Operations

Additional special operations include opening another database, closing a database without exiting Access, and saving a database with another name. They also include deleting a table (or other object) as well as renaming an object.

When you are working in a database and you open another database, Access will automatically close the database that was previously open. Before deleting or renaming an object, you should ensure that the object has no dependent objects; that is, other objects that depend on the object you want to delete.

TO CLOSE A DATABASE WITHOUT EXITING ACCESS

You would use the following steps to close a database without exiting Access.

1. Click File on the ribbon to open the Backstage view.
2. Click Close.

CONSIDER THIS

TO SAVE A DATABASE WITH ANOTHER NAME

To save a database with another name, you would use the following steps.

1. Click File on the ribbon to open the Backstage view, and then select the Save As tab.
2. With Save Database As selected in the File Types area and Access Database selected in the Save Database As area, click the Save As button.
3. Enter a name and select a location for the new version.
4. Click the Save button.

If you want to make a backup, could you just save the database with another name?
You could certainly do that. Using the backup procedure discussed earlier is useful because doing so automatically includes the current database name and the date in the name of the file it creates.

TO DELETE A TABLE OR OTHER OBJECT IN THE DATABASE

You would use the following steps to delete a database object.

1. Right-click the object in the Navigation Pane.
2. Click Delete on the shortcut menu.
3. Click the Yes button in the Microsoft Access dialog box.

TO RENAME AN OBJECT IN THE DATABASE

You would use the following steps to rename a database object.

1. Right-click the object in the Navigation Pane.
2. Click Rename on the shortcut menu.
3. Type the new name and press the ENTER key.

To Exit Access

All the steps in this module are now complete.

1 If desired, sign out of your Microsoft account.

2 Exit Access.

BTW
Access Help
At any time while using Access, you can find answers to questions and display information about various topics through Access Help. Used properly, this form of assistance can increase your productivity and reduce your frustrations by minimizing the time you spend learning how to use Access. For instructions about Access Help and exercises that will help you gain confidence in using it, read the Office and Windows module at the beginning of this book.

BTW
Determining Database Requirements
The determination of database requirements is part of a process known as systems analysis. A systems analyst examines existing and proposed documents, and examines organizational policies to determine exactly the type of data needs the database must support.

Database Design

This section illustrates the **database design** process, that is, the process of determining the tables and fields that make up the database. It does so by showing how you would design the database for PrattLast Associates from a set of requirements. In this section, you will use commonly accepted shorthand to represent the tables and fields that make up the database as well as the primary keys for the tables. For each table, you give the name of the table followed by a set of parentheses. Within the parentheses is a list of the fields in the table separated by commas. You underline the primary key. For example,

Product (<u>Product Code</u>, Description, On Hand, Price)

represents a table called Product. The Product table contains four fields: Product Code, Description, On Hand, and Price. The Product Code field is the primary key.

Database Requirements

The PrattLast Associates database must maintain information on both accounts and account managers. The business currently keeps this data in two Word tables and two Excel workbooks, as shown in Figure 1–80. They use Word tables for address information and Excel workbooks for financial information.

- For accounts, PrattLast needs to maintain address data. It currently keeps this data in a Word table (Figure 1–80a).

- PrattLast also maintains financial data for each account. This includes the amount paid and current amount due for the account. It keeps these amounts, along with the account name and number, in the Excel worksheet shown in Figure 1–80b.

- PrattLast keeps account manager address data in a Word table, as shown in Figure 1–80c.

- Just as with accounts, it keeps financial data for account managers, including their start date, salary, and bonus rate, in a separate Excel worksheet, as shown in Figure 1–80d.

Finally, PrattLast keeps track of which accounts are assigned to which account managers. Each account is assigned to a single account manager, but each account manager might be assigned many accounts. Currently, for example, accounts AC001 (Avondale Community Bank), JM323 (JSP Manufacturing Inc.), KC156 (Key Community College System), MI345 (Midwest Library Consortium), and TW001 (Tri-County Waste Disposal) are assigned to account manager 31 (Haydee Rivera). Accounts BL235 (Bland Corp.), CO621 (Codder Plastics Co.), KV089 (KAL Veterinary Services), LI268 (Lars-Idsen Inc.), and ML008 (Mums Landscaping Co.) are assigned to account manager 35 (Mark Simson). Accounts CA043 (Carlton Regional Clinic), EC010 (Eco Clothes Inc.), HL111 (Halko Legal Associates), LC005 (Lancaster County Hospital), and TP098 (TAL Packaging Systems) are assigned to account manager 58 (Karen Murowski). PrattLast has an additional account manager, Peter Lu, whose number has been assigned as 42, but who has not yet been assigned any accounts.

BTW
Additional Data for PrattLast Associates
PrattLast could include other types of data in the database. The Account table could include data on a contact person at each organization, such as name, telephone number, and email address. The Account Manager table could include the mobile telephone number, email address, and emergency contact information for the account manager.

Account Number	Account Name	Street	City	State	Postal Code
AC001	Avondale Community Bank	256 Main St.	Avondale	IL	60311
BL235	Bland Corp.	100 Granger Hwy.	Granger	IL	60314
CA043	Carlton Regional Clinic	589 Central Ave.	Carlton	IL	60313
CO621	Codder Plastics Co.	421 First Ave.	Bremerton	IN	46003
EC010	Eco Clothes Inc.	120 Pine St.	Davidson	IN	46010
HL111	Halko Legal Associates	321 Feathering Rd.	Gleneagle	IL	60319
JM323	JSP Manufacturing Inc.	1200 Franklin Blvd.	Wells	IN	46007
KC156	Key Community College System	35 Indiana Ave.	Walker	IN	46004
KV089	KAL Veterinary Services	116 Pine St.	Granger	IL	60314
LC005	Lancaster County Hospital	215 River St.	Granger	IL	46004
LI268	Lars-Idsen Inc.	829 Wooster Rd.	Davidson	IN	46010
MI345	Midwest Library Consortium	3400 Metro Pkwy.	Bremerton	IN	46003
ML008	Mums Landscaping Co.	865 Ridge Rd.	Wells	IN	46007
TP098	TAL Packaging Systems	12 Polk Ave.	Carlton	IL	60313
TW001	Tri-County Waste Disposal	345 Central Blvd.	Rushton	IL	60321

Figure 1–80a Account Addresses

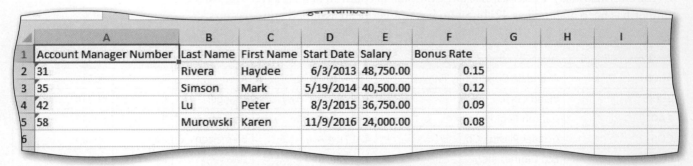

	A	B	C	D	E	F	G	H	I	J
1	Account Number	Account Name	Amount Paid	Current Due						
2	AC001	Avondale Community Bank	24,752.25	3,875.25						
3	BL235	Bland Corp.	29,836.65	2,765.30						
4	CA043	Carlton Regional Clinic	30,841.05	3,074.30						
5	CO621	Codder Plastics Co.	27,152.25	2,875.00						
6	EC010	Eco Clothes Inc.	19,620.00	1,875.00						
7	HL111	Halko Legal Associates	25,702.20	3,016.75						
8	JM323	JSP Manufacturing Inc.	19,739.70	2,095.00						
9	KV089	KAL Veterinary Services	34,036.50	580.00						
10	KC156	Key Community College System	10,952.25	0.00						
11	LC005	Lancaster County Hospital	44,025.60	3,590.80						
12	LI268	Lars-Idsen Inc.	0.00	1,280.75						
13	MI345	Midwest Library Consortium	21,769.20	2,890.60						
14	ML008	Mums Landscaping Co.	13,097.10	2,450.00						
15	TP098	TAL Packaging Systems	22,696.95	3,480.45						
16	TW001	Tri-County Waste Disposal	15,345.00	2,875.50						

Figure 1–80b Account Financial Data

Account Manager Number	Last Name	First Name	Street	City	State	Postal Code
31	Rivera	Haydee	325 Twiddy St.	Avondale	IL	60311
35	Simson	Mark	1467 Hartwell St.	Walker	IN	46004
42	Lu	Peter	5624 Murray Ave.	Davidson	IN	46007
58	Murowski	Karen	168 Truesdale Dr.	Carlton	IL	60313

Figure 1–80c Account Manager Addresses

	A	B	C	D	E	F	G	H	I
1	Account Manager Number	Last Name	First Name	Start Date	Salary	Bonus Rate			
2	31	Rivera	Haydee	6/3/2013	48,750.00	0.15			
3	35	Simson	Mark	5/19/2014	40,500.00	0.12			
4	42	Lu	Peter	8/3/2015	36,750.00	0.09			
5	58	Murowski	Karen	11/9/2016	24,000.00	0.08			
6									

Figure 1–80d Account Manager Financial Data

Database Design Process

The database design process involves several steps.

CONSIDER THIS

What is the first step in the process?
Identify the tables. Examine the requirements for the database to identify the main objects that are involved. There will be a table for each object you identify.

In a database for one organization, for example, the main objects might be departments and employees. This would require two tables: one for departments and the other for employees. In the database for another organization, the main objects might be accounts and account managers. In this case, there also would be two tables: one for accounts and the other for account managers. In still another organization's database, the main objects might be books, publishers, and authors. This database would require three tables: one for books, a second for publishers, and a third for authors.

Identifying the Tables

For the PrattLast Associates database, the main objects are accounts and account managers. This leads to two tables, which you must name. Reasonable names for these two tables are:

Account

Account Manager

After identifying the tables, what is the second step in the database design process?

Determine the primary keys. Recall that the primary key is the unique identifier for records in the table. For each table, determine the unique identifier. In a Department table, for example, the unique identifier might be the Department Code. For a Book table, the unique identifier might be the ISBN (International Standard Book Number).

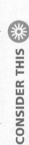

CONSIDER THIS

Determining the Primary Keys

The next step is to identify the fields that will be the unique identifiers, or primary keys. Account numbers uniquely identify accounts, and account manager numbers uniquely identify account managers. Thus, the primary key for the Account table is the account number, and the primary key for the Account Manager table is the account manager number. Reasonable names for these fields would be Account Number and Account Manager Number, respectively. Adding these primary keys to the tables gives:

Account (<u>Account Number</u>)

Account Manager (<u>Account Manager Number</u>)

What is the third step in the database design process after determining the primary keys?

Determine the additional fields. The primary key will be a field or combination of fields in a table. A table will typically contain many additional fields, each of which contains a type of data. Examine the project requirements to determine these additional fields. For example, in an Employee table, additional fields might include Employee Name, Street Address, City, State, Postal Code, Date Hired, and Salary.

CONSIDER THIS

Determining Additional Fields

After identifying the primary keys, you need to determine and name the additional fields. In addition to the account number, the Account Address Information shown in Figure 1–80a contains the account name, street, city, state, and postal code. These would be fields in the Account table. The Account Financial Information shown in Figure 1–80b also contains the account number and account name, which are already included in the Account table. The financial information also contains the amount paid and current due. Adding the amount paid and current due fields to those already identified in the Account table and assigning reasonable names gives:

Account (<u>Account Number</u>, Account Name, Street, City, State, Postal Code, Amount Paid, Current Due)

Similarly, examining the Account Manager Address Information in Figure 1–80c adds the last name, first name, street, city, state, and postal code fields to the Account Manager table. In addition to the account manager number, last name, and first name, the Account Manager Financial Information in Figure 1–80d would add the start date, salary, and bonus rate. Adding these fields to the Account Manager table and assigning reasonable names gives:

Account Manager (<u>Account Manager Number</u>, Last Name, First Name, Street, City, State, Postal Code, Start Date, Salary, Bonus Rate)

BTW

Database Design Language (DBDL)
Database Design Language (DBDL) is a commonly accepted shorthand representation for showing the structure of a relational database. You write the name of the table and then within parentheses you list all the columns in the table. If the columns continue beyond one line, indent the subsequent lines.

What happens as the fourth step, after determining additional fields?
Determine relationships between the tables. A relationship is an association between objects. In a database containing information about departments and employees, there is an association between the departments and the employees. A department is associated with all the employees in the department, and an employee is associated with the department to which he or she is assigned. Technically, you say that a department is related to all the employees in the department, and an employee is related to his or her department.

The relationship between department and employees is an example of a **one-to-many relationship** because one employee is associated with one department, but each department can be associated with many employees. The Department table would be the "one" table in the relationship. The Employee table would be the "many" table in the relationship.

When you have determined that two tables are related, follow these general guidelines:

• Identify the "one" table.

• Identify the "many" table.

• Include the primary key from the "one" table as a field in the "many" table.

Determining and Implementing Relationships between the Tables

According to the requirements, each account has one account manager, but each account manager can have many accounts. Thus, the Account Manager table is the "one" table, and the Account table is the "many" table. To implement this one-to-many relationship between account managers and accounts, add the Account Manager Number field (the primary key of the Account Manager table) to the Account table. This produces:

Account (<u>Account Number</u>, Account Name, Street, City, State, Postal Code, Amount Paid, Current Due, Account Manager Number)

Account Manager (<u>Account Manager Number</u>, Last Name, First Name, Street, City, State, Postal Code, Start Date, Salary, Bonus Rate)

After creating relationships between tables, what is the fifth step in the database design process?
Determine data types for the fields, that is, the type of data that can be stored in the field.

Assigning Data Types to the Fields

See the earlier section Determing Data Types for the Fields for a discussion of the available data types and their use in the PrattLast Associates database. That section also discusses other properties that can be assigned, such as captions, field size, and the number of decimal places.

Identifying and Removing Redundancy

Redundancy means storing the same fact in more than one place. It usually results from placing too many fields in a table — fields that really belong in separate tables — and often causes serious problems. If you had not realized there were two objects, such as accounts and account managers, you might have placed all the data in a single Account table. Figure 1–81 shows an example of a table that includes both account and account manager information. Notice that the data for a given account manager (number, name, address, and so on) occurs on more than one record. The data for rep 35, Mark Simson, is repeated in the figure. Storing this data on multiple records is an example of redundancy.

Account table

Account Number	Account Name	Street	...	Account Manager Number	Last Name	First Name
AC001	Avondale Community Bank	256 Main St.	...	31	Rivera	Haydee
BL235	Bland Corp.	100 Granger Hwy.	...	35	Simson	Mark
CA043	Carlton Regional Clinic	589 Central Ave.	...	58	Murowski	Karen
CO621	Codder Plastics Co.	421 First Ave.	...	35	Simson	Mark
EC010	Eco Clothes Inc.	120 Pine St.	...	58	Murowski	Karen
...	...	...	...	...	...	...
...	...	...	...	...	...	...

Account Manager numbers are 35

name of Account Manager 35 appears more than once

Figure 1–81

What problems does this redundancy cause?

Redundancy results in several problems, including:

1. Wasted storage space. The name of account manager 35, Mark Simson, for example, should be stored only once. Storing this information several times is wasteful.

2. More complex database updates. If, for example, Mark Simson's name is spelled incorrectly and needs to be changed in the database, his name would need to be changed in several different places.

3. Possible inconsistent data. Nothing prohibits the account manager's last name from being Simson on account BL235's record and Stimson on account CO621's record. The data would be inconsistent. In both cases, the account manager number is 35, but the last names are different.

How do you eliminate redundancy?

The solution to the problem is to place the redundant data in a separate table, one in which the data will no longer be redundant. If, for example, you place the data for account managers in a separate table (Figure 1–82), the data for each account manager will appear only once.

Account table

Account Number	Account Name	Street	...	Account Manager Number
AC001	Avondale Community Bank	256 Main St.	...	31
BL235	Bland Corp.	100 Granger Hwy.	...	35
CA043	Carlton Regional Clinic	589 Central Ave.	...	58
CO621	Codder Plastics Co.	421 First Ave.	...	35
EC010	Eco Clothes Inc.	120 Pine St.	...	58
...	...	...	...	...
...	...	...	...	...

Account Manager numbers are 35

Account Manager Table

Account Manager Number	Last Name	First Name	...
31	Rivera	Haydee	...
35	Simson	Mark	...
42	Lu	Peter	...
58	Murowski	Karen	...

name of Account Manager 35 appears only once

Figure 1–82

Notice that you need to have the account manager number in both tables. Without it, there would be no way to tell which account manager is associated with which account. The remaining account manager data, however, was removed from the Account table and placed in the Account Manager table. This new arrangement corrects the problems of redundancy in the following ways:

* Because the data for each account manager is stored only once, space is not wasted.

* Changing the name of an account manager is easy. You need to change only one row in the Account Manager table.

* Because the data for an account manager is stored only once, inconsistent data cannot occur.

Designing to omit redundancy will help you to produce good and valid database designs. You should always examine your design to see if it contains redundancy. If it does, you should decide whether you need to remove the redundancy by creating a separate table.

If you examine your design, you will see that there is one area of redundancy (see the data in Figure 1–1). Cities and states are both repeated. Every account whose postal code is 60314, for example, has Granger as the city and IL as the state. To remove this redundancy, you would create a table with the primary key Postal Code and City and State as additional fields. City and State would be removed from the Account table. Having City, State, and Postal Code in a table is very common, however, and usually you would not take such action. No other redundancy exists in your tables.

Summary

In this module you have learned to create an Access database, create tables and add records to a database, print the contents of tables, import data, create queries, create forms, create reports, and change database properties. You have also learned how to design a database.

What decisions will you need to make when creating your next database?

Use these guidelines as you complete the assignments in this module and create your own databases outside of this class.

1. Identify the tables that will be included in the database.

2. Determine the primary keys for each of the tables.

3. Determine the additional fields that should be included in each of the tables.

4. Determine relationships between the tables.

  a) Identify the "one" table.
  b) Identify the "many" table.
  c) Include the primary key of the "one" table as a field in the "many" table.

5. Determine data types for the fields in the tables.

6. Determine additional properties for fields.

  a) Determine if a caption is warranted.
  b) Determine if a description of the field is warranted.
  c) Determine field sizes.
  d) Determine formats.

7. Identify and remove any unwanted redundancy.

8. Determine a storage location for the database.

9. Determine the best method for distributing the database objects.

CONSIDER THIS

How should you submit solutions to questions in the assignments identified with a symbol?
Every assignment in this book contains one or more questions identified with a symbol. These questions require you to think beyond the assigned database. Present your solutions to the questions in the format required by your instructor. Possible formats may include one or more of these options: write the answer; create a document that contains the answer; present your answer to the class; discuss your answer in a group; record the answer as audio or video using a webcam, smartphone, or portable media player; or post answers on a blog, wiki, or website.

Apply Your Knowledge

Reinforce the skills and apply the concepts you learned in this module.

Adding a Caption, Changing a Data Type, and Creating a Query, Form, and Report

Note: To complete this assignment, you will be required to use the Data Files. Please contact your instructor for information about accessing the Data Files.

Instructions: Friendly Janitorial Services provides janitorial services to local businesses. The company uses a team-based approach and each team has a team leader or supervisor. Friendly Janitorial Services has a database that keeps track of its supervisors and its clients. Each client is assigned to a single supervisor; each supervisor may be assigned many clients. The database has two tables. The Client table contains data on the clients who use Friendly Janitorial Services. The Supervisor table contains data on the supervisors. You will add a caption, change a data type, and create a query, a form, and a report, as shown in Figure 1–83.

Perform the following tasks:
1. Run Access, open the Apply Friendly Janitorial Services database from the Data Files, and enable the content.
2. Open the Supervisor table in Datasheet view, add SU # as the caption for the Supervisor Number field, and resize all columns to best fit the data. Save the changes to the layout of the table and close the table.
3. Open the Client table in Design view and change the data type for the Supervisor Number field to Short Text. Change the field size for the field to 3 and add SU # as the caption for the Supervisor Number field. Save the changes to the table and close the table. Then, open the Client table in Datasheet view and resize all columns to best fit the data. Save the changes to the layout of the table and close the table.
4. Use the Simple Query Wizard to create a query for the Client table that contains the Client Number, Client Name, Amount Paid, Current Due, and Supervisor Number. The query is a detail query. Use the name Client Query for the query and close the query.
5. Create a simple form for the Supervisor table. Save the form and use the name Supervisor for the form. Close the form.
6. Create the report shown in Figure 1–83 for the Client table. The report includes totals for both the Amount Paid and Current Due fields. Be sure the totals appear completely. You might need to expand the size of the total controls. Move the page number so that it is within the margins. Save the report as Client Financial Report.
7. If requested by your instructor, add your last name to the title of the report, that is, change the title to Client Financial Report LastName where LastName is your actual last name.
8. Compact and repair the database.
9. Submit the revised database in the format specified by your instructor.
10. ✳ How would you change the field name of the Street field in the Client table to Address?

Continued >

Apply Your Knowledge *continued*

| Client Financial Report | | | | Tuesday, September 12, 2017 |
| | | | | 6:19:45 PM |

Client Number	Client Name	Amount Paid	Current Due	Supervisor Number
AT13	Atlas Repair	$5,400.00	$600.00	103
AZ01	AZ Auto	$9,250.00	$975.00	110
BB35	Babbage Bookkeeping	$8,820.00	$980.00	110
BL24	Blanton Shoes	$1,850.75	$210.25	120
MM01	Moss Manufacturing	$10,456.25	$1,125.00	114
PL03	Prime Legal Associates	$19,905.00	$2,245.00	110
PS67	PRIM Staffing	$4,500.00	$500.00	114
TE15	Telton-Edwards	$0.00	$700.00	120
		$129,979.20	$14,542.55	

Figure 1–83

Extend Your Knowledge

Extend the skills you learned in this module and experiment with new skills. You may need to use Help to complete the assignment.

Using a Database Template to Create an Events Database

Instructions: Access includes both desktop database templates and web-based templates. You can use a template to create a beginning database that can be modified to meet your specific needs. You will use a template to create an Events database. The database template includes sample tables, queries, forms, and reports. You will modify the database and create the Events Query shown in Figure 1–84.

Perform the following tasks:
1. Run Access.
2. Select the Desktop event management template in the template gallery and create a new database with the file name Extend Events.
3. Enable the content and close the Event List form.
4. Open the Navigation Pane and change the organization to Object Type.
5. Open the Events table in Datasheet view and delete the Attachments field in the table. The Attachments field has a paperclip as the column heading.
6. Add the Event Type field to the end of the table. Assign the Short Text data type with a field size of 15.
7. Save the changes to the Events table and close the table.
8. Use the Simple Query Wizard to create the Events Query shown in Figure 1–84. Close the query.

Figure 1–84

9. Open the Current Events report in Layout view. Delete the controls containing the current date and current time in the upper-right corner of the report. Change the title of the report to Current Events List.

10. Save the changes to the report.

11. If requested to do so by your instructor, add your first and last names to the end of the title and save the changes to the report.

12. Submit the revised database in the format specified by your instructor.

13. ❁ a. Why would you use a template instead of creating a database from scratch with just the fields you need?

b. The Attachment data type allows you to attach files to a database record. If you were using this database to keep track of events for a 4th of July celebration in a small town, what specific documents might you attach to an Events record?

Expand Your World

Create a solution, which uses cloud and web technologies, by learning and investigating on your own from general guidance.

Problem: You and two friends recently started a business that provides temporary non-medical help to individuals and families in need of assistance. You want to be able to share query results and reports, so you have decided to store the items in the cloud. You are still learning Access, so you are going to create a sample query and the report shown in Figure 1–85, export the results, and save to a cloud storage location, such as Microsoft OneDrive, Dropbox, or Google Drive.

Note: To complete this assignment, you will be required to use the Data Files. Please contact your instructor for information about accessing the Data Files.

Instructions:

1. Open the Expand Temporary Help database from the Data Files and enable the content.

2. Use the Simple Query Wizard to create a query that includes the Client Number, First Name, Last Name, Balance, and Helper Number. Save the query as Client Query.

3. Export the Client Query as an XPS document to a cloud-based storage location of your choice.

4. Create the report shown in Figure 1–85. Save the report as Client Status Report.

Continued >

Expand Your World *continued*

Client Number	Last Name	First Name	Balance	Helper Number
AB10	Autley	Francis	$55.00	203
BR16	Behrens	Alexa	$90.00	205
FF45	Ferdon			
		Libby		207
PR80	Priestly	Martin	$85.00	205
SA23	Sanders	Marya	$0.00	207
TR35	Teeter	Rich	$50.00	205
			$469.00	

Client Status Report — Tuesday, September 12, 2017 — 6:22:36 PM

Figure 1–85

5. Export the Client Status Report as a PDF document to a cloud-based storage location of your choice. You do not need to change any optimization or export settings. Do not save the export steps.

6. If requested to do so by your instructor, open the Helper table and change the last name and first name for helper 203 to your last name and your first name.

7. Submit the assignment in the format specified by your instructor.

8. ✳ Which cloud-based storage location did you use for this assignment? Why?

In the Labs

Design, create, modify, and/or use a database following the guidelines, concepts, and skills presented in this module. Labs are listed in order of increasing difficulty. Labs 1 and 2, which increase in difficulty, require you to create solutions based on what you learned in the module; Lab 3 requires you to apply your creative thinking and problem-solving skills to design and implement a solution.

Lab 1: Creating Objects for the Garden Naturally Database

Problem: Garden Naturally is a company that provides products for the organic gardening community. Sales representatives are responsible for selling to distributors, nurseries, and retail stores. The company recently decided to store its customer and sales rep data in a database. Each customer is assigned to a single sales rep, but each sales rep may be assigned many customers. The database and the Sales Rep table have been created, but the Salary YTD field needs to be added to the table. The records shown in Table 1–6 must be added to the Sales Rep table. The company plans to import the Customer table from the Excel worksheet shown in Figure 1–86. Garden Naturally would like to finish storing this data in a database and has asked you to help.

Note: To complete this assignment, you will be required to use the Data Files. Please contact your instructor for information about accessing the Data Files.

Instructions: Perform the following tasks:

1. Run Access, open the Lab 1 Garden Naturally database from the Data Files, and enable the content.

2. Open the Sales Rep table in Datasheet view and add the Salary YTD field to the end of the table. The field has the Currency data type. Assign the caption SR # to the Sales Rep Number field.

3. Add the records shown in Table 1–6.

Table 1–6 Data for Sales Rep Table

Sales Rep Number	Last Name	First Name	Street	City	State	Postal Code	Start Date	Commission Rate	Salary YTD
32	Ortiz	Gloria	982 Victoria Ln.	Chesnee	NJ	07053	9/12/2015	.05	$32,555.65
35	Sinson	Mike	45 Elm St.	Quaker	DE	19719	8/28/2017	.04	$1,500.00
29	Gupta	Rufus	678 Hillcrest Rd.	Gossett	PA	19157	6/1/2015	.06	$35,075.30
26	Jones	Pat	43 Third St.	Greer	PA	19158	5/16/2016	.05	$33,100.50

4. Resize the columns to best fit the data. Save the changes to the layout of the table.

5. Import the Lab 1–1 Customer workbook shown in Figure 1–86 into the database. The first row of the workbook contains the column headings. Customer Number is the primary key for the new table. Assign the name Customer to the table. Save the Import steps, and assign the name Import-Customer Workbook to the steps. Assign Import Customer Workbook as the description.

	A	B	C	D	E	F	G	H	I
1	Customer Number	Customer Name	Address	City	State	Postal Code	Amount Paid	Balance Due	Sales Rep Number
2	AA30	All About Gardens	47 Berton St.	Greer	PA	19158	$1,190.00	$365.00	26
3	CT02	Christmas Tree Farm	483 Cantor Rd.	Pleasantburg	NJ	07025	$2,285.50	$825.35	29
4	GG01	Garden Gnome	10 Main St.	Gossett	PA	19157	$1,300.00	$297.50	29
5	GT34	Green Thumb Growers	26 Jefferson Hwy.	Pleasantburg	NJ	07025	$3,325.45	$865.50	32
6	LH15	Lawn & Home Store	33 Maple St.	Chambers	NJ	07037	$895.00	$515.00	26
7	ML25	Mum's Landscaping	196 Lincoln Ave.	Quaker	DE	19719	$0.00	$1,805.00	29
8	OA45	Outside Architects	234 Magnolia Rd.	Gaston	DE	19723	$4,205.50	$945.00	32
9	PL10	Pat's Landscaping	22 Main St.	Chesnee	NJ	07053	$1,165.00	$180.00	26
10	PN18	Pyke Nurseries	10 Grant Blvd.	Adelphia	PA	19159	$2,465.00	$530.00	32
11	SL25	Summit Lawn Service	345 Oaktree Rd.	Chesnee	NJ	07053	$3,225.45	$675.50	26
12	TG38	TriState Growers	24 Main St.	Gaston	DE	19723	$1,075.00	$0.00	29
13	TW34	TAL Wholesalers	234 Cantor Rd.	Pleasantburg	NJ	07025	$4,125.00	$350.00	26
14	TY03	TLC Yard Care	24 Berton St.	Greer	PA	19158	$1,845.00	$689.45	29
15	YS04	Yard Shoppe	124 Elm St.	Quaker	DE	19719	$445.00	$575.00	32
16	YW01	Young's Wholesalers	5239 Lancaster Hwy.	Adelphia	PA	19156	$1,785.50	$345.60	32
17									
18									
19									
20									
21									

Figure 1–86

Continued >

In the Labs *continued*

6. Open the Customer table in Design view and make the following changes:

   a.   Change the field size for the Customer Number field to 4. Change the field size for the Customer Name field to 30. Change the field size for the Address field to 25 and the field size for the City field to 20. Change the field size for the State field to 2 and the field size for the Postal Code field to 5. Change the field size for the Sales Rep Number field to 2.

   b.   Add the caption CU # to the Customer Number field.

   c.   Add the caption SR # to the Sales Rep Number field.

7. Save the changes to the Customer table. If a Microsoft Access dialog box appears with the 'Some data may be lost' message, click the Yes button.

8. Open the Customer table in Datasheet view and resize all columns to best fit the data. Save the changes to the layout of the table.

9. Create a query using the Simple Query Wizard for the Customer table that displays the Customer Number, Customer Name, Amount Paid, Balance Due, and Sales Rep Number. Save the query as Customer Query.

Customer Financial Report				Tuesday, September 12, 2017
				6:25:09 PM
Customer Number	Customer Name	Amount Paid	Balance Due	Sales Rep Number
AA30	All About Gardens	$1,190.00	$365.00	26
CT02	Christmas Tree Farm	$2,285.50	$825.35	29
TG38	TriState Growers	$1,075.00	$0.00	29
TW34	TAL Wholesalers	$4,125.00	$350.00	26
TY03	TLC Yard Care	$1,845.00	$689.45	29
YS04	Yard Shoppe	$445.00	$575.00	32
YW01	Young's Wholesalers	$1,785.50	$345.60	32
		$29,332.40	$8,963.90	

Figure 1–87

10. Create the report shown in Figure 1–87 for the Customer table. The report should include the Customer Number, Customer Name, Amount Paid, Balance Due, and Sales Rep Number fields. Include totals for the Amount Paid and Balance Due fields. Be sure to change the column headings to those shown in Figure 1–87. Save the report as Customer Financial Report.

11. If requested to do so by your instructor, change the address for Pat Jones in the Sales Rep table to your address. If your address is longer than 20 characters, simply enter as much as you can.

12. Submit the revised database in the format specified by your instructor.

13. ❊ The Commission Rate field has a field size of Single. If you changed the field size to Integer, what values would appear in the Commission Rate column? Why?

Lab 2: **Creating the Museum Gift Shop Database**

Problem: The local science museum operates a gift shop that sells science-related items. The gift shop purchases the items from vendors that deal in science-related games, toys, and other merchandise. Currently, the information about the items and the vendors is stored in two Excel workbooks. Each item is assigned to a single vendor, but each vendor may be assigned many items. You are to create a database that will store the item and vendor information. You have already determined that you need two tables, a Vendor table and an Item table, in which to store the information.

Note: To complete this assignment, you will be required to use the Data Files. Please contact your instructor for information about accessing the Data Files.

Instructions: Perform the following tasks:

1. Use the Blank desktop database option to create a new database in which to store all objects related to the items for sale. Call the database Lab 2 Museum Gift Shop.

2. Import the Lab 1–2 Vendor Data Excel workbook into the database. The first row of the workbook contains the column headings. Vendor Code is the primary key for the new table. Assign the name Vendor to the table. Do not save the Import steps.

3. Open the Vendor table in Datasheet view. Change the field size for the Vendor Code field to 2; the field size for the Vendor Name field to 25; and the field size for the Telephone Number field to 12. Assign the caption VC to the Vendor Code field.

4. Import the Lab 1–2 Item Data Excel workbook into the database. The first row of the workbook contains the column headings. Item Number is the primary key for this table. Assign the name Item to the table. Do not save the Import steps.

5. Open the Item table in Design view. Change the field size for the Item Number field to 4. Change the field size for the Description field to 28. Add the caption Wholesale for the Wholesale Cost field, the caption Retail for the Retail Price field, and the caption VC for the vendor code. The On Hand field should be an Integer field. Be sure that the field size for the Vendor Code in the Item table is identical to the field size for the Vendor Code in the Vendor table. Save the changes to the table and close the table.

6. Open the Item table in Datasheet view and resize the columns to best fit the data. Save the changes to the layout of the table and close the table.

7. Create a query for the Item table. Include the Item Number, Description, Wholesale Cost, Retail Price, and Vendor Code. Save the query as Item Query.

8. Create a simple form for the Item table. Use the name Item for the form.

9. Create the report shown in Figure 1–88 for the Item table. Do not add any totals. Save the report as Item Status Report.

Item Status Report			Tuesday, September 12, 2017
			6:26:31 PM
Item Number	Description	On Hand	Wholesale Price
3663	Agate Bookends	4	$16.25
3673	Amazing Science Fun	8	$13.50
4553	Cosmos Uncovered	9	$8.95
4573	Crystal Growing Kit	7	$6.75
4583	Dinosaur Egg Ornament	12	$7.50

Figure 1–88

Continued >

10. If requested to do so by your instructor, change the telephone number for Atherton Wholesalers to your telephone number.

11. Submit the database in the format specified by your instructor.

12. ✹ If you had designed this database, could you have used the field name, Name, for the Vendor Name field name? If not, why not?

Lab 3: **Consider This: Your Turn**

Apply your creative thinking and problem solving skills to design and implement a solution.

Creating the Camshay Marketing Database

Note: To complete this assignment, you will be required to use the Data Files. Please contact your instructor for information about accessing the Data Files.

Part 1: Camshay Marketing Associates is a small company that specializes in data mining for marketing research and analysis. The company focuses on the service, nonprofit, and retail sectors. Camshay uses marketing analysts to work collaboratively with clients. Marketing analysts are paid a base salary and can earn incentive pay for maintaining and expanding client relationships. Based on the information in the Lab 1–3 Camshay Marketing workbook, use the concepts and techniques presented in this module to design and create a database to store the Camshay Marketing data. Change data types and field sizes as necessary. Add captions where appropriate. Create a form for the Client table and a report for the Client table similar to the Account Financial Report shown in Figure 1-67. Use the simple query wizard to create a query for the Client table that includes the Client Number, Client Name, Current Due and Marketing Analyst Number. Open the query and add a criterion to the query results to find only those clients whose amount due is $0.00 and save this modified query with a different name. Submit your assignment in the format specified by your instructor.

Part 2: You made several decisions while determining the table structures and adding data to the tables in this assignment. What method did you use to add the data to each table? Are there any other methods that would also have worked?

2 | Querying a Database

Objectives

You will have mastered the material in this module when you can:

- Create queries using Design view
- Include fields in the design grid
- Use text and numeric data in criteria
- Save a query and use the saved query
- Create and use parameter queries
- Use compound criteria in queries
- Sort data in queries

- Join tables in queries
- Create a report and a form from a query
- Export data from a query to another application
- Perform calculations and calculate statistics in queries
- Create crosstab queries
- Customize the Navigation Pane

Introduction

One of the primary benefits of using a database management system such as Access is having the ability to find answers to questions related to data stored in the database. When you pose a question to Access, or any other database management system, the question is called a query. A **query** is simply a question presented in a way that Access can process.

To find the answer to a question, you first create a corresponding query using the techniques illustrated in this module. After you have created the query, you instruct Access to run the query, that is, to perform the steps necessary to obtain the answer. Access then displays the answer in Datasheet view.

For an introduction to Windows and instructions about how to perform basic Windows tasks, read the Office and Windows module at the beginning of this book, where you can learn how to resize windows, change screen resolution, create folders, move and rename files, use Windows Help, and much more

Project — Querying a Database

Examples of questions related to the data in the PrattLast Associates database are shown in Figure 2–1.

In addition to these questions, PrattLast managers need to find information about accounts located in a specific city, but they want to enter a different city each time they ask the question. The company can use a parameter query to accomplish this task. PrattLast managers also want to summarize data in a specific way, which might involve performing calculations, and they can use a crosstab query to present the data in the desired form.

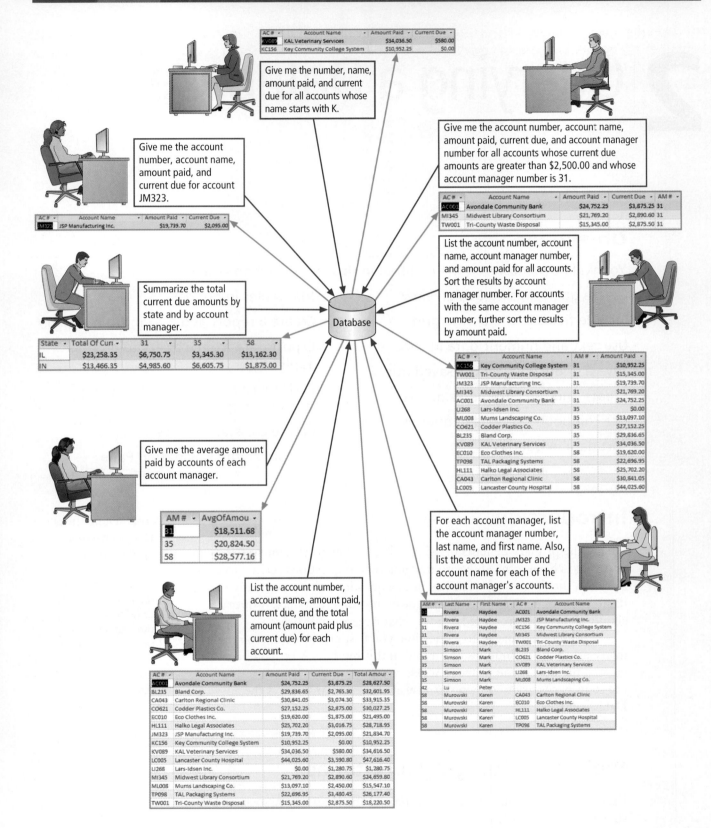

Figure 2–1

In this module, you will learn how to create and use the queries shown in Figure 2–1. The following roadmap identifies general activities you will perform as you progress through this module:

1. **CREATE QUERIES** in Design view.
2. **USE CRITERIA** in queries.
3. **SORT DATA** in queries.
4. **JOIN TABLES** in queries.
5. **EXPORT** query **RESULTS**.
6. **PERFORM CALCULATIONS** in queries.
7. **CREATE** a **CROSSTAB** query.
8. **CUSTOMIZE** the **NAVIGATION PANE**.

For an introduction to Office and instructions about how to perform basic tasks in Office apps, read the Office and Windows module at the beginning of this book, where you can learn how to run an application, use the ribbon, save a file, open a file, print a file, exit an application, use Help, and much more.

Creating Queries

As you learned in Module 1, you can use queries in Access to find answers to questions about the data contained in the database. *Note:* In this module, you will save each query example. When you use a query for another task, such as to create a form or report, you will assign a specific name to a query, for example, Manager-Account Query. In situations in which you will not use the query again, you will assign a name using a convention that includes the module number and a query number, for example, m02q01. Queries are numbered consecutively.

BTW

Select Queries

The queries you create in this module are select queries. In a select query, you retrieve data from one or more tables using criteria that you specify and display the data in a datasheet.

To Create a Query in Design View

1 CREATE QUERIES | 2 USE CRITERIA | 3 SORT DATA | 4 JOIN TABLES | 5 EXPORT RESULTS
6 PERFORM CALCULATIONS | 7 CREATE CROSSTAB | 8 CUSTOMIZE NAVIGATION PANE

In Module 1, you used the Simple Query Wizard to create a query. Most of the time, however, you will use Design view, which is the primary option for creating queries. *Why? Once you have created a new query in Design view, you have more options than with the wizard and can specify fields, criteria, sorting, calculations, and so on.* The following steps create a new query in Design view.

1

- Run Access and open the database named PrattLast Associates from your hard disk, OneDrive, or other storage location.

- Click the 'Shutter Bar Open/Close Button' to close the Navigation Pane.

- Click Create on the ribbon to display the Create tab (Figure 2–2).

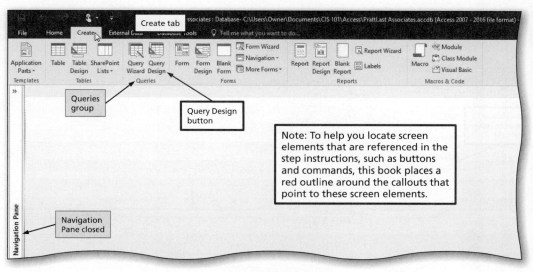

Figure 2–2

2

- Click the Query Design button (Create tab | Queries group) to create a new query (Figure 2–3).

Q&A Is it necessary to close the Navigation Pane?

No. Closing the pane gives you more room for the query, however, so it is usually a good practice.

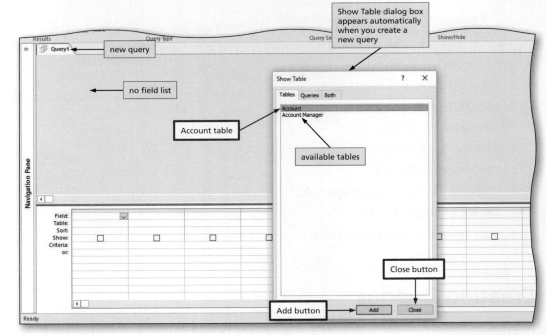

Figure 2–3

3

- Ensure the Account table (Show Table dialog box) is selected. If it is not, click the Account table to select it.
- Click the Add button to add the selected table to the query.
- Click the Close button to remove the dialog box from the screen.

Q&A What if I inadvertently add the wrong table?

Right-click the table that you added in error and click Remove Table on the shortcut menu. You also can just close the query, indicate that you do not want to save it, and then start over.

- Drag the lower edge of the field list down far enough so all fields in the table appear (Figure 2–4).

Q&A Is it essential that I resize the field list?

No. You can always scroll through the list of fields using the scroll bar. Resizing the field list so that all fields appear is usually more convenient.

Figure 2–4

Querying a Database   **Access Module 2**   **AC** 69

Access Module 2

1 CREATE QUERIES | 2 USE CRITERIA | 3 SORT DATA | 4 JOIN TABLES | 5 EXPORT RESULTS
6 PERFORM CALCULATIONS | 7 CREATE CROSSTAB | 8 CUSTOMIZE NAVIGATION PANE

To Add Fields to the Design Grid

Once you have a new query displayed in Design view, you are ready to make entries in the **design grid**, the portion of the window where you specify fields and criteria for the query. The design grid is located in the lower pane of the window. You add the fields you want included in the query to the Field row in the grid. *Why add fields to the grid? Only the fields that appear in the design grid are included in the query results.* The following step begins creating a query that PrattLast Associates might use to obtain the account number, account name, amount paid, and current due for a particular account.

1

- Double-click the Account Number field in the field list to add the field to the query.

Q&A
What if I add the wrong field? Click just above the field name in the design grid to select the column and then press the DELETE key to remove the field.

- Double-click the Account Name field in the field list to add the field to the query.

- Add the Amount Paid field to the query.

- Add the Current Due field to the query (Figure 2–5).

Q&A
What if I want to include all fields? Do I have to add each field individually?
No. Instead of adding individual fields, you can double-click the asterisk (*) to add the asterisk to the design grid. The asterisk is a shortcut indicating all fields are to be included.

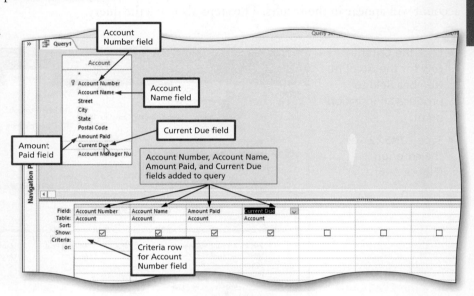

Figure 2–5

Determining Criteria

When you use queries, usually you are looking for those records that satisfy some criterion. In the simple query you created in the previous module, for example, you entered a criterion to restrict the records to those with the account manager number 35. In another query, you might want the name, amount paid, and current due amounts for the account whose number is JM323, for example, or for those accounts whose names start with the letters, La. You enter criteria in the Criteria row in the design grid below the field name to which the criterion applies. For example, to indicate that the account number must be JM323, you first must add the Account Number field to the design grid. You then would type JM323 in the Criteria row below the Account Number field.

Running the Query

After adding the appropriate fields and defining the query's criteria, you must run the query to get the results. To view the results of the query from Design view, click the Run button to instruct Access to run the query, that is, to perform the necessary actions to produce and display the results in Datasheet view.

BTW
Touch Screen Differences
The Office and Windows interfaces may vary if you are using a touch screen. For this reason, you might notice that the function or appearance of your touch screen differs slightly from this module's presentation.

BTW
Access Screen Resolution
If you are using a computer or mobile device to step through the project in this module and you want your screens to match the figures in this book, you should change your screen's resolution to 1366 x 768. For information about how to change a computer's resolution, refer to the Office and Windows module at the beginning of this book.

To Use Text Data in a Criterion

To use **text data** (data in a field whose data type is Short Text) in criteria, simply type the text in the Criteria row below the corresponding field name, just as you did in Module 1. In Access, you do not need to enclose text data in quotation marks as you do in many other database management systems. *Why? Access will enter the quotation marks automatically, so you can simply type the desired text.* The following steps finish creating a query that PrattLast Associates might use to obtain the account number, account name, amount paid, and current due amount of account JM323. These steps add the appropriate criterion so that only the desired account will appear in the results. The steps also save the query.

1
- Click the Criteria row for the Account Number field to produce an insertion point.
- Type **JM323** as the criterion (Figure 2–6).

Figure 2–6

2
- Click the Run button (Query Tools Design tab | Results group) to run the query (Figure 2–7).

Q&A
Can I also use the View button in the Results group to run the query?
Yes. You can click the View button to view the query results in Datasheet view.

Figure 2–7

3

- Click the Save button on the Quick Access Toolbar to display the Save As dialog box.

- Type `m02q01` as the name of the query (Figure 2–8).

Q&A

Can I also save from Design view?
Yes. You can save the query when you view it in Design view just as you can save it when you view query results in Datasheet view.

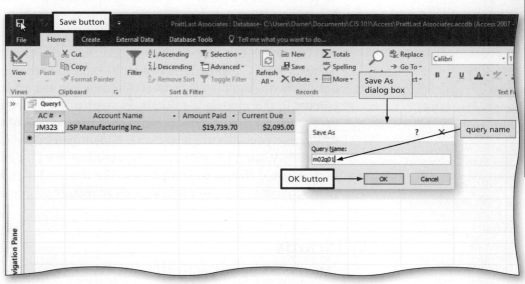

Figure 2–8

4

- Click the OK button (Save As dialog box) to save the query (Figure 2–9).

Figure 2–9

Other Ways

1. Right-click query tab, click Save on shortcut menu   2. Press CTRL+S

Using Saved Queries

After you have created and saved a query, you can use it in a variety of ways:

- To view the results of a query that is not currently open, open it by right-clicking the query in the Navigation Pane and clicking Open on the shortcut menu.

- If you want to change the design of a query that is already open, return to Design view and make the changes.

- If you want to change the design of a query that is not currently open, right-click the query in the Navigation Pane and then click Design View on the shortcut menu to open the query in Design view.

- To print the results with a query open, click File on the ribbon, click the Print tab in the Backstage view, and then click Quick Print.

BTW

The Ribbon and Screen Resolution
Access may change how the groups and buttons within the groups appear on the ribbon, depending on the computer or mobile device's screen resolution. Thus, your ribbon may look different from the ones in this book if you are using a screen resolution other than 1366 x 768.

- To print a query without first opening it, be sure the query is selected in the Navigation Pane and click File on the ribbon, click the Print tab in the Backstage view, and then click Quick Print.

- You can switch between views of a query using the View button (Home tab | Views group). Clicking the arrow at the bottom of the button produces the View button menu. You then click the desired view in the menu. The two query views you use in this module are Datasheet view (to see the results) and Design view (to change the design). You can also click the top part of the View button, in which case you will switch to the view identified by the icon on the button. In Figure 2–9, the View button displays the icon for Design view, so clicking the button would change to Design view. For the most part, the icon on the button represents the view you want, so you can usually simply click the button.

Wildcards

Microsoft Access supports wildcards. **Wildcards** are symbols that represent any character or combination of characters. One common wildcard, the **asterisk (*)**, represents any collection of characters. Another wildcard symbol is the **question mark (?)**, which represents any individual character.

What does S* represent? What does T?m represent?

S* represents the letter, S, followed by any collection of characters. A search for S* might return System, So, or Superlative. T?m represents the letter, T, followed by any single character, followed by the letter, m. A search for T?m might return the names Tim or Tom.

To Use a Wildcard

1 CREATE QUERIES | 2 USE CRITERIA | 3 SORT DATA | 4 JOIN TABLES | 5 EXPORT RESULTS
6 PERFORM CALCULATIONS | 7 CREATE CROSSTAB | 8 CUSTOMIZE NAVIGATION PANE

The following steps modify the previous query to use the asterisk wildcard so that PrattLast Associates can select only those accounts whose names begin with K. *Why? Because you do not know how many characters will follow the K, the asterisk wildcard symbol is appropriate.* The steps also save the query with a new name using the Save As command.

1

- Click the View button (Home tab | Views group), shown in Figure 2–9, to return to Design view.

- If necessary, click the Criteria row below the Account Number field to produce an insertion point.

Q&A
The text I entered now has quotation marks surrounding it. What happened?
Criteria for text data needs to be enclosed in quotation marks. You do not have to type the quotation marks; Access adds them automatically.

- Use the DELETE or BACKSPACE key as necessary to delete the current entry.

- Click the Criteria row below the Account Name field to produce an insertion point.

- Type **K*** as the criterion (Figure 2–10).

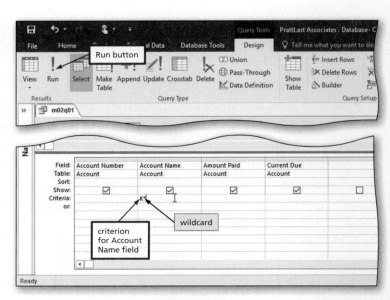

Figure 2–10

2

- Run the query by clicking the Run button (Query Tools Design tab | Results group) (Figure 2–11).

 Experiment

- Change the letter K to lowercase in the criterion and run the query to determine whether case makes a difference when entering a wildcard.

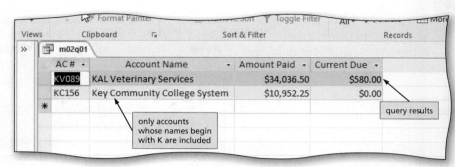

Figure 2–11

3

- Click File on the ribbon to open the Backstage view.

- Click the Save As tab in the Backstage view to display the Save As gallery.

- Click 'Save Object As' in the File Types area (Figure 2–12).

Q&A Can I just click the Save button on the Quick Access Toolbar as I did when saving the previous query? If you clicked the Save button, you

Figure 2–12

would replace the previous query with the version you just created. Because you want to save both the previous query and the new one, you need to save the new version with a different name. To do so, you must use Save Object As, which is available through the Backstage view.

4

- With Save Object As selected in the File Types gallery, click the Save As button to display the Save As dialog box.

- Erase the name of the current query and type m02q02 as the name for the saved query (Figure 2–13).

Q&A The current entry in the As text box is

Figure 2–13

Query. Could I save the query as some other type of object?
Although you usually would want to save the query as another query, you can also save it as a form or report by changing the entry in the As text box. If you do, Access would create either a simple form or a simple report for the query.

5

- Click the OK button (Save As dialog box) to save the query with the new name and close the Backstage view (Figure 2–14).

Q&A
How can I tell that the query was saved with the new name?
The new name will appear on the tab.

Figure 2–14

Other Ways

1. Click Design View button on status bar

To Use Criteria for a Field Not Included in the Results

1 CREATE QUERIES | 2 USE CRITERIA | 3 SORT DATA | 4 JOIN TABLES | 5 EXPORT RESULTS
6 PERFORM CALCULATIONS | 7 CREATE CROSSTAB | 8 CUSTOMIZE NAVIGATION PANE

In some cases, you might require criteria for a particular field that should not appear in the results of the query. For example, you may want to see the account number, account name, amount paid, and current due for all accounts located in Granger. The criteria involve the City field, but you do not want to include the City field in the results.

To enter a criterion for the City field, it must be included in the design grid. Normally, it would then appear in the results. To prevent this from happening, remove the check mark from its check box in the Show row of the grid. ***Why?*** *A check mark in the Show check box instructs Access to show the field in the result. If you remove the check mark, you can use the field in the query without displaying it in the query results.*

The following steps modify the previous query so that PrattLast Associates can select only those accounts located in Granger. PrattLast does not want the city to appear in the results, however. The steps also save the query with a new name.

1

- Click the View button (Home tab | Views group), shown in Figure 2–14, to return to Design view.

Q&A
The text I entered is now preceded by the word, Like. What happened?
Criteria that include wildcards need to be preceded by the word, Like. However, you do not have to type it; Access adds the word automatically to any criterion involving a wildcard.

- Erase the criterion in the Criteria row of the Account Name field.

- Add the City field to the query.

- Type **Granger** as the criterion for the City field (Figure 2–15).

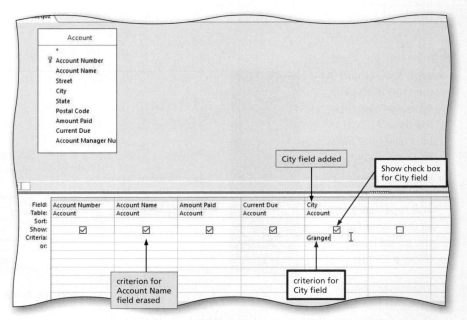

Figure 2–15

2

- Click the Show check box for the City field to remove the check mark (Figure 2–16).

Q&A Could I have removed the check mark before entering the criterion?

Yes. The order in which you perform the two operations does not matter.

Figure 2–16

3

- Run the query (Figure 2–17).

Experiment

- Click the View button to return to Design view, enter a different city name as the criterion, and run the query. Repeat this process with additional city names, including at least one city name that is not in the database. When finished, change the criterion back to Granger.

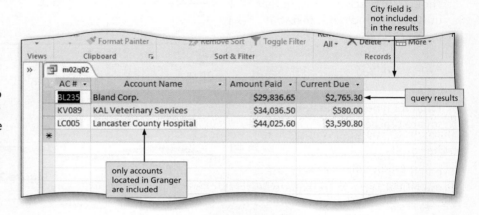

Figure 2–17

Creating a Parameter Query

If you wanted to find accounts located in Wells instead of Granger, you would either have to create a new query or modify the existing query by replacing Granger with Wells as the criterion. Rather than giving a specific criterion when you first create the query, occasionally you may want to be able to enter part of the criterion when you run the query and then have the appropriate results appear. For example, you might want a query to return the account number, account name, amount paid, and current due for all accounts in a specific city, specifying a different city each time you run the query. A user could run the query, enter Wells as the city, and then see all the accounts in Wells. Later, the user could use the same query but enter Granger as the city, and then see all the accounts in Granger.

To enable this flexibility, you create a **parameter query**, which is a query that prompts for input whenever it is used. You enter a parameter (the prompt for the user) rather than a specific value as the criterion. You create the parameter by enclosing the criterion value in square brackets. It is important that the value in the brackets does not match the name of any field. If you enter a field name in square brackets, Access assumes you want that particular field and does not prompt the user for input. To prompt the user to enter the city name as the input, you could place [Enter City] as the criterion in the City field.

BTW

Designing Queries
Before creating queries, examine the contents of the tables involved. You need to know the data type for each field and how the data for the field is stored. If a query includes a state, for example, you need to know whether state is stored as the two-character abbreviation or as the full state name.

AC 76 **Access Module 2** Querying a Database

1 CREATE QUERIES | 2 USE CRITERIA | 3 SORT DATA | 4 JOIN TABLES | 5 EXPORT RESULTS
6 PERFORM CALCULATIONS | 7 CREATE CROSSTAB | 8 CUSTOMIZE NAVIGATION PANE

To Create and View a Parameter Query

The following steps create a parameter query. *Why? The parameter query will give users at PrattLast the ability to enter a different city each time they run the query rather than having a specific city as part of the criterion in the query.* The steps also save the query with a new name.

- Return to Design view.
- Erase the current criterion in the City column, and then type **[Enter City]** as the new criterion (Figure 2–18).

Q&A

What is the purpose of the square brackets?
The square brackets indicate that the text entered is not text that the value in the column must match. Without the brackets, Access would search for records in which the city is Enter City.

What if I typed a field name in the square brackets?
Access would simply use the value in that field. To create a parameter query, you must not use a field name in the square brackets.

Figure 2–18

- Click the Run button (Query Tools Design tab | Results group) to display the Enter Parameter Value dialog box (Figure 2–19).

Figure 2–19

- Type **Wells** as the parameter value in the Enter City text box, and then click the OK button (Enter Parameter Value dialog box) to close the dialog box and view the query (Figure 2–20).

Experiment

- Try using other characters between the square brackets. In each case, run the query. When finished, change the characters between the square brackets back to Enter City.

Figure 2–20

- Click File on the ribbon to open the Backstage view.

- Click the Save As tab in the Backstage view to display the Save As gallery.

- Click 'Save Object As' in the File Types area.

- With Save Object As selected in the File Types area, click the Save As button to display the Save As dialog box.

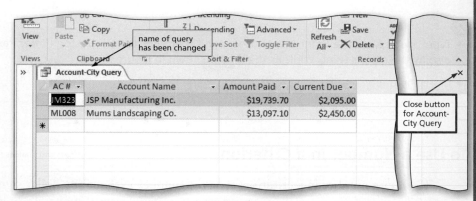

Figure 2–21

- Type `Account-City Query` as the name for the saved query.

- Click the OK button (Save As dialog box) to save the query with the new name and close the Backstage view (Figure 2–21).

- Click the Close button for the Account-City Query to close the query.

Break Point: If you wish to take a break, this is a good place to do so. You can exit Access now. To resume later, run Access, open the database called PrattLast Associates, and continue following the steps from this location forward.

To Use a Parameter Query

1 CREATE QUERIES | 2 USE CRITERIA | 3 SORT DATA | 4 JOIN TABLES | 5 EXPORT RESULTS
6 PERFORM CALCULATIONS | 7 CREATE CROSSTAB | 8 CUSTOMIZE NAVIGATION PANE

You use a parameter query like any other saved query. You can open it or you can print the query results. In either case, Access prompts you to supply a value for the parameter each time you use the query. If changes have been made to the data since the last time you ran the query, the results of the query may be different, even if you enter the same value for the parameter. *Why? In addition to the ability to enter different field values each time the parameter query is run, the query always uses the data that is currently in the table.* The following steps use the parameter query named Account-City Query.

1

- Open the Navigation Pane.

- Right-click the Account-City Query to produce a shortcut menu.

- Click Open on the shortcut menu to open the query and display the Enter Parameter Value dialog box (Figure 2–22).

Q&A

The title bar for my Navigation Pane contains Tables and Related Views rather than All Access Objects as it did in Module 1. What should I do?
Click the Navigation Pane arrow and then click 'All Access Objects'.

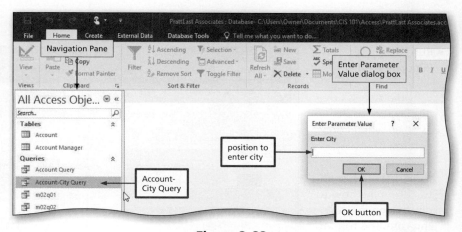

Figure 2–22

I do not have the Search bar at the top of the Navigation Pane that I had in Module 1. What should I do?
Right-click the Navigation Pane title bar arrow to display a shortcut menu, and then click Search Bar.

• Type **Wells** in the Enter City text box, and then click the OK button (Enter Parameter Value dialog box) to display the results using Wells as the city, as shown in Figure 2–21.

• Close the query.

To Use a Number in a Criterion

To enter a number in a criterion, type the number without any dollar signs or commas. *Why? If you enter a dollar sign, Access assumes you are entering text. If you enter a comma, Access considers the criterion invalid.* The following steps create a query that PrattLast Associates might use to display all accounts whose current due amount is $0. The steps also save the query with a new name.

• Close the Navigation Pane.

• Click Create on the ribbon to display the Create tab.

• Click the Query Design button (Create tab | Queries group) to create a new query.

• If necessary, click the Account table (Show Table dialog box) to select the table.

• Click the Add button to add the selected table to the query.

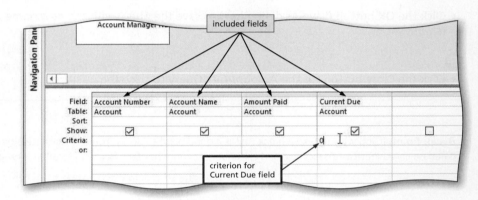

Figure 2–23

• Click the Close button to remove the dialog box from the screen.

• Drag the lower edge of the field list down far enough so all fields in the list are displayed.

• Include the Account Number, Account Name, Amount Paid, and Current Due fields in the query.

• Type **0** as the criterion for the Current Due field (Figure 2–23).

Q&A Do I need to enter a dollar sign and decimal point?
No. Access will interpret 0 as $0 because the data type for the Current Due field is currency.

• Run the query (Figure 2–24).

Q&A Why did Access display the results as $0.00 when I only entered 0?
Access uses the format for the field to determine how to display the result. In this case, the format indicated that Access should include the dollar sign, decimal point, and two decimal places.

Figure 2–24

3

- Save the query as m02q03.

Q&A How do I know when to use the Save button to save a query or use the Backstage view to perform a Save As?
If you are saving a new query, the simplest way is to use the Save button on the Quick Access Toolbar. If you are saving changes to a previously saved query but do not want to change the name, use the Save button. If you want to save a previously saved query with a new name, you must use the Backstage view and perform a Save Object As.

- Close the query.

Comparison Operators

Unless you specify otherwise, Access assumes that the criteria you enter involve equality (exact matches). In the last query, for example, you were requesting those accounts whose current due amount is equal to 0 (zero). In other situations, you might want to find a range of results; for example, you could request accounts whose current due is greater than $1,000.00. If you want a query to return something other than an exact match, you must enter the appropriate **comparison operator**. The comparison operators are > (greater than), < (less than), >= (greater than or equal to), <= (less than or equal to), and NOT (not equal to).

To Use a Comparison Operator in a Criterion

1 CREATE QUERIES | 2 USE CRITERIA | 3 SORT DATA | 4 JOIN TABLES | 5 EXPORT RESULTS
6 PERFORM CALCULATIONS | 7 CREATE CROSSTAB | 8 CUSTOMIZE NAVIGATION PANE

The following steps use the > operator to create a query that PrattLast Associates might use to find all account managers whose start date is after 1/1/2015. **Why?** *A date greater than 1/1/2015 means the date comes after 1/1/2015.* The steps also save the query with a new name.

1

- Start a new query using the Account Manager table.

- Include the Account Manager Number, Last Name, First Name, and Start Date fields.

- Type >1/01/2015 as the criterion for the Start Date field (Figure 2–25).

Q&A Why did I not have to type the leading zero in the Month portion of the date?
It is fine as you typed it. You also could have typed 01/1/2015. Some people often type the day using two digits, such as 1/01/2015. You also could have typed a leading zero for both the month and the day: 01/01/2015.

Figure 2–25

2

• Run the query (Figure 2–26).

Experiment

• Return to Design view. Try a different criterion involving a comparison operator in the Start Date field and run the query. When finished, return to Design view, enter the original criterion (>1/01/2015) in the Start Date field, and run the query.

Figure 2–26

Q&A

I returned to Design view and noticed that Access changed 1/01/2015 to #1/01/2015#. Why does the date now have number signs around it?
This is the date format in Access. You usually do not have to enter the number signs because in most cases Access will insert them automatically.

My records are in a different order. Is this a problem?
No. The important thing is which records are included in the results. You will see later in this module how you can specify the specific order you want for cases when the order is important.

Can I use the same comparison operators with text data?
Yes. Comparison operators function the same whether you use them with number fields, currency fields, date fields, or text fields. With a text field, comparison operators use alphabetical order in making the determination.

3

• Save the query as m02q04.

• Close the query.

BTW
Queries:
Query-by-Example
Query-By-Example, often referred to as QBE, was a query language first proposed in the mid-1970s. In this approach, users asked questions by filling in a table on the screen. The Access approach to queries is based on Query-By-Example.

Using Compound Criteria

Often your search data must satisfy more than one criterion. This type of criterion is called a **compound criterion** and is created using the words AND or OR.

In an **AND criterion**, each individual criterion must be true in order for the compound criterion to be true. For example, an AND criterion would allow you to find accounts that have current due amounts greater than $2,500.00 and whose account manager is manager 31.

An **OR criterion** is true if either individual criterion is true. An OR criterion would allow you to find accounts that have current due amounts greater than $2,500.00 as well as accounts whose account manager is account manager 31. In this case, any account who has a current due amount greater than $2,500.00 would be included in the answer, regardless of whether the account's account manager is account manager 31. Likewise, any account whose account manager is account manager 31 would be included, regardless of whether the account has a current due amount greater than $2,500.00.

1 CREATE QUERIES | 2 USE CRITERIA | 3 SORT DATA | 4 JOIN TABLES | 5 EXPORT RESULTS
6 PERFORM CALCULATIONS | 7 CREATE CROSSTAB | 8 CUSTOMIZE NAVIGATION PANE

To Use a Compound Criterion Involving AND

To combine criteria with AND, place the criteria on the same row of the design grid. *Why? Placing the criteria in the same row indicates that both criteria must be true in Access.* The following steps use an AND criterion to enable PrattLast to find those accounts who have a current due amount greater than $2,500.00 and whose account manager is manager 31. The steps also save the query.

- Start a new query using the Account table.

- Include the Account Number, Account Name, Amount Paid, Current Due, and Account Manager Number fields.

- Type **>2500** as the criterion for the Current Due field.

- Type **31** as the criterion for the Account Manager Number field (Figure 2–27).

Figure 2–27

- Run the query (Figure 2–28).

- Save the query as m02q05.

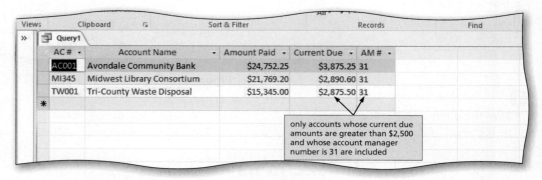

Figure 2–28

To Use a Compound Criterion Involving OR

1 CREATE QUERIES | 2 USE CRITERIA | 3 SORT DATA | 4 JOIN TABLES | 5 EXPORT RESULTS
6 PERFORM CALCULATIONS | 7 CREATE CROSSTAB | 8 CUSTOMIZE NAVIGATION PANE

To combine criteria with OR, each criterion must go on separate rows in the Criteria area of the grid. *Why? Placing criteria on separate rows indicates at least one criterion must be true in Access.* The following steps use an OR criterion to enable PrattLast to find those accounts who have a current due amount greater than $2,500.00 or whose account manager is manager 31 (or both). The steps also save the query with a new name.

- Return to Design view.

- If necessary, click the Criteria entry for the Account Manager Number field and then use the BACKSPACE key or the DELETE key to erase the entry ("31").

- Click the or row (the row below the Criteria row) for the Account Manager Number field, and then type **31** as the entry (Figure 2–29).

Figure 2–29

2

• Run the query (Figure 2–30).

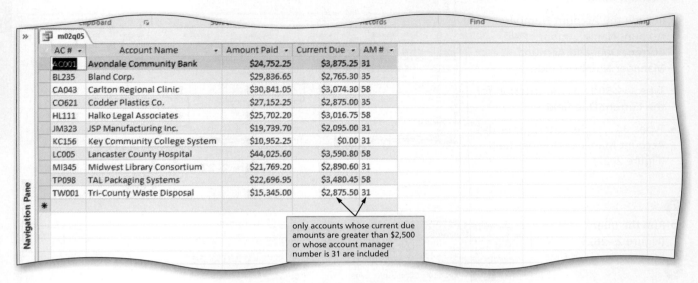

only accounts whose current due amounts are greater than $2,500 or whose account manager number is 31 are included

Figure 2–30

3

• Save the query as m02q06.

Special Criteria

You can use three special criteria in queries:

BTW

Rearranging Fields in a Query

To move a field in the design grid, click the column selector for the field to select the field and drag it to the appropriate location.

1. If you want to create a criterion involving a range of values in a single field, you can use the **AND operator**. You place the word AND between the individual conditions. For example, if you wanted to find all accounts whose amount paid is greater than or equal to $20,000.00 and less than or equal to $40,000.00, you would enter >= 20000 AND <= 40000 as the criterion in the Amount Paid column.

2. You can select values in a given range by using the **BETWEEN operator**. This is often an alternative to the AND operator. For example, to find all accounts whose amount paid is between $20,000.00 and $40,000.00, inclusive, you would enter BETWEEN 20000 AND 40000 as the criterion in the Amount Paid column. This is equivalent to entering >=20000 and <=40000.

3. You can select a list of values by using the **IN operator**. You follow the word IN with the list of values in parentheses. For example, to find accounts whose account manager number is 31 and accounts whose account manager is 35 using the IN operator, you would enter IN ("31","35") on the Criteria row in the Account Manager Number column. Unlike when you enter a simple criterion, you must enclose text values in quotation marks.

CONSIDER THIS

How would you find accounts whose account manager number is 31 or 35 without using the IN operator?

Place the number 31 in the Criteria row of the Account Manager Number column. Place the number 35 in the or row of the Account Manager Number column.

Sorting

In some queries, the order in which the records appear is irrelevant. All you need to be concerned about are the records that appear in the results. It does not matter which one is first or which one is last.

In other queries, however, the order can be very important. You may want to see the cities in which accounts are located and would like them arranged alphabetically. Perhaps you want to see the accounts listed by account manager number. Further, within all the accounts of any given account manager, you might want them to be listed by amount paid from largest amount to smallest.

To order the records in a query result in a particular way, you **sort** the records. The field or fields on which the records are sorted is called the **sort key**. If you are sorting on more than one field (such as sorting by amount paid within account manager number), the more important field (Account Manager Number) is called the **major key** (also called the **primary sort key**) and the less important field (Amount Paid) is called the **minor key** (also called the **secondary sort key**).

To sort in Microsoft Access, specify the sort order in the Sort row of the design grid below the field that is the sort key. If you specify more than one sort key, the sort key on the left will be the major sort key, and the one on the right will be the minor key.

BTW
Sorting Data in a Query
When sorting data in a query, the records in the underlying tables (the tables on which the query is based) are not actually rearranged. Instead, the DBMS determines the most efficient method of simply displaying the records in the requested order. The records in the underlying tables remain in their original order.

BTW
Clearing the Design Grid
You can also clear the design grid using the ribbon. To do so, click the Home tab, click the Advanced button to display the Advanced menu, and then click Clear Grid on the Advanced menu.

To Clear the Design Grid

1 CREATE QUERIES | 2 USE CRITERIA | 3 SORT DATA | 4 JOIN TABLES | 5 EXPORT RESULTS
6 PERFORM CALCULATIONS | 7 CREATE CROSSTAB | 8 CUSTOMIZE NAVIGATION PANE

Why? If the fields you want to include in the next query are different from those in the previous query, it is usually simpler to start with a clear grid, that is, one with no fields already in the design grid. You always can clear the entries in the design grid by closing the query and then starting over. A simpler approach to clearing the entries is to select all the entries and then press the DELETE key. The following steps return to Design view and clear the design grid.

- Return to Design view.

- Click just above the Account Number column heading in the grid to select the column.

Q&A
I clicked above the column heading, but the column is not selected. What should I do?
You did not point to the correct location. Be sure the pointer changes into a down-pointing arrow and then click again.

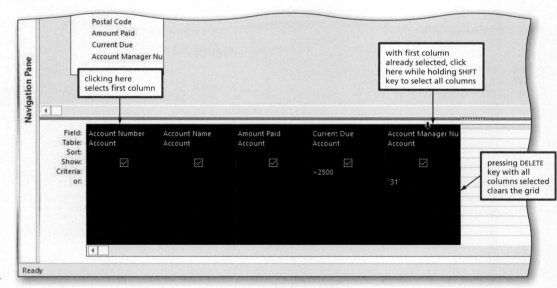

Figure 2–31

- Hold the SHIFT key down and click just above the Account Manager Number column heading to select all the columns (Figure 2–31).

- Press the DELETE key to clear the design grid.

To Sort Data in a Query

If you determine that the query results should be sorted, you will need to specify the sort key. The following steps sort the cities in the Account table by indicating that the City field is to be sorted. The steps specify Ascending sort order. *Why? When sorting text data, Ascending sort order arranges the results in alphabetical order.*

1
- Include the City field in the design grid.
- Click the Sort row in the City field column, and then click the Sort arrow to display a menu of possible sort orders (Figure 2–32).

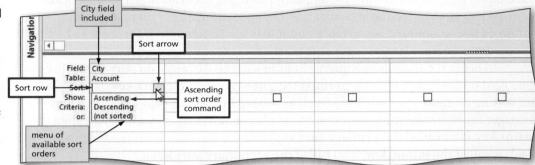

Figure 2–32

2
- Click Ascending to select the sort order (Figure 2–33).

Figure 2–33

3
- Run the query (Figure 2–34).

Experiment
- Return to Design view and change the sort order to Descending. Run the query. Return to Design view and change the sort order back to Ascending. Run the query.

Q&A
Why do some cities appear more than once?
More than one account is located in those cities.

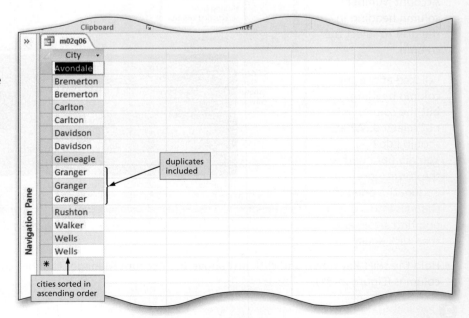

Figure 2–34

To Omit Duplicates

When you sort data, duplicates normally are included. In the query shown in Figure 2–34, for example, Bremerton appears twice. Several other cities appear multiple times as well. You eliminate duplicates using the query's property sheet. A **property sheet** is a window containing the various properties of the object. To omit duplicates, you will use the property sheet to change the Unique Values property from No to Yes.

The following steps create a query that PrattLast Associates might use to obtain a sorted list of the cities in the Account table in which each city is listed only once. *Why? Unless you wanted to know how many accounts were located in each city, the duplicates typically do not add any value.* The steps also save the query with a new name.

1

- Return to Design view.

- Click the second field (the empty field to the right of City) in the design grid to produce an insertion point.

- If necessary, click Design on the ribbon to display the Design tab.

- Click the Property Sheet button (Query Tools Design tab | Show/Hide group) to display the property sheet (Figure 2–35).

 Q&A My property sheet looks different. What should I do?
If your sheet looks different, close the property sheet and repeat this step.

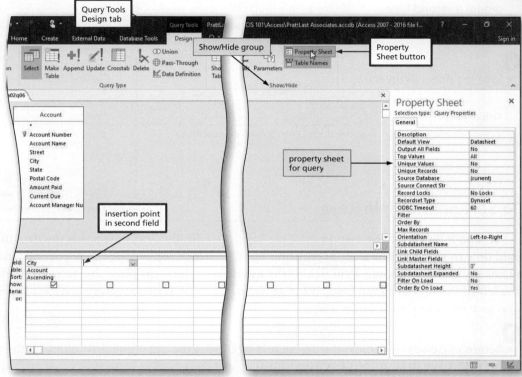

Figure 2–35

2

- Click the Unique Values property box, and then click the arrow that appears to display a list of available choices (Figure 2–36).

Figure 2–36

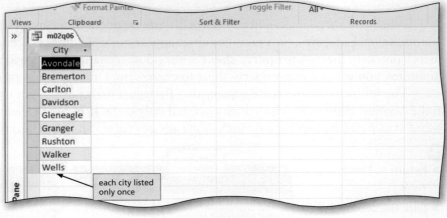

Figure 2–37

- Click Yes to indicate that the query will return unique values, which means that each value will appear only once in the query results.

- Close the Query Properties property sheet by clicking the Property Sheet button (Query Tools Design tab | Show/Hide group) a second time.

- Run the query (Figure 2–37).

- Save the query as m02q07.

Other Ways

1. Right-click second field in design grid, click Properties on shortcut menu

---

To Sort on Multiple Keys

1 CREATE QUERIES | 2 USE CRITERIA | 3 SORT DATA | 4 JOIN TABLES | 5 EXPORT RESULTS
6 PERFORM CALCULATIONS | 7 CREATE CROSSTAB | 8 CUSTOMIZE NAVIGATION PANE

The following steps sort on multiple keys. Specifically, PrattLast needs the data to be sorted by amount paid (low to high) within account manager number, which means that the Account Manager Number field is the major key and the Amount Paid field is the minor key. The steps place the Account Manager Number field to the left of the Amount Paid field. *Why? In Access, the major key must appear to the left of the minor key.* The steps also save the query with a new name.

- Return to Design view. Clear the design grid by clicking the top of the first column in the grid, and then pressing the DELETE key to clear the design grid.

- In the following order, include the Account Number, Account Name, Account Manager Number, and Amount Paid fields in the query.

- Select Ascending as the sort order for both the Account Manager Number field and the Amount Paid field (Figure 2–38).

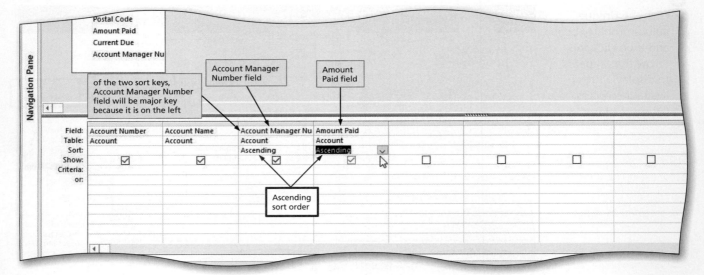

Figure 2–38

2

• Run the query (Figure 2–39).

🔍 **Experiment**

• Return to Design view and try other sort combinations for the Account Manager Number and Amount Paid fields, such as Ascending for Account Manager Number and Descending for Amount Paid. In each case, run the query to see the effect of the changes. When finished, select Ascending as the sort order for both fields.

Q&A What if the Amount Paid field is to the left of the Account Manager Number field?

It is important to remember that the major sort key must appear to the left of the minor sort key in the design grid. If you attempted to sort by amount paid within account manager number, but placed the Amount Paid field to the left of the Account Manager Number field, your results would not accurately represent the intended sort.

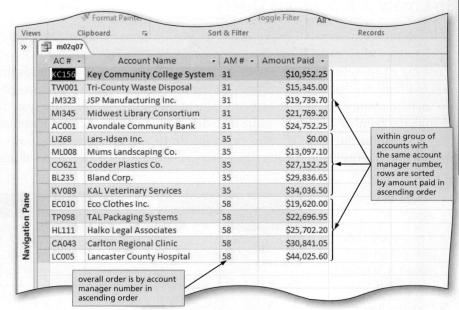

within group of accounts with the same account manager number, rows are sorted by amount paid in ascending order

overall order is by account manager number in ascending order

Figure 2–39

3

• Save the query as m02q08.

CONSIDER THIS

Is there any way to sort the records in this same order, but have the Amount Paid field appear to the left of the Account Manager Number field in the query results?

Yes. Remove the check mark from the Account Manager Number field, and then add an additional Account Manager Number field at the end of the query. The first Account Manager Number field will be used for sorting but will not appear in the results. The second will appear in the results, but will not be involved in the sorting process.

How do you approach the creation of a query that might involve sorting?

Examine the query or request to see if it contains words such as *order* or *sort*. Such words imply that the order of the query results is important. If so, you need to sort the query.

• If sorting is required, identify the field or fields on which the results are to be sorted. In the request, look for language such as *ordered by* or *sort the results by*, both of which would indicate that the specified field is a sort key.

• If using multiple sort keys, determine the major and minor keys. If you are using two sort keys, determine which one is the more important, or the major key. Look for language such as *sort by amount paid within account manager number*, which implies that the overall order is by account manager number. In this case, the Account Manager Number field would be the major sort key and the Amount Paid field would be the minor sort key.

• Determine sort order. Words such as *increasing*, *ascending*, or *low-to-high* imply Ascending order. Words such as *decreasing*, *descending*, or *high-to-low* imply Descending order. Sorting in *alphabetical order* implies Ascending order. If there were no words to imply a particular order, you would typically use Ascending.

• Examine the query or request to see if there are any special restrictions. One common restriction is to exclude duplicates. Another common restriction is to list only a certain number of records, such as the first five records.

To Create a Top-Values Query

Rather than show all the results of a query, you may want to show only a specified number of records or a percentage of records. **Why?** *You might not need to see all the records, just enough to get a general idea of the results.* Creating a **top-values query** allows you to restrict the number of records that appear. When you sort records, you can limit results to those records having the highest (descending sort) or lowest (ascending sort) values. To do so, first create a query that sorts the data in the desired order. Next, use the Return box on the Design tab to change the number of records to be included from All to the desired number or percentage.

The following steps create a query for PrattLast Associates that shows only the first five records that were included in the results of the previous query. The steps also save the resulting query with a new name.

1
- Return to Design view.
- If necessary, click Design on the ribbon to display the Design tab.
- Click the Return arrow (Query Tools Design tab | Query Setup group) to display the Return menu (Figure 2–40).

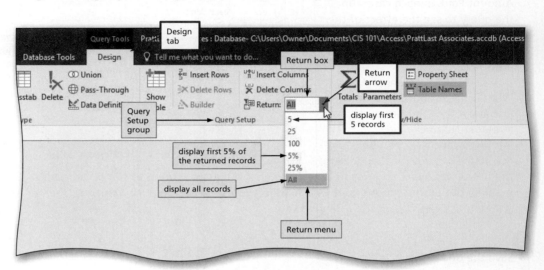

Figure 2–40

2
- Click 5 in the Return menu to specify that the query results should contain the first five rows.

Q&A
Could I have typed the 5? What about other numbers that do not appear in the list?
Yes, you could have typed the 5. For numbers not appearing in the list, you must type the number.

- Run the query (Figure 2–41).

3
- Save the query as m02q09.
- Close the query.

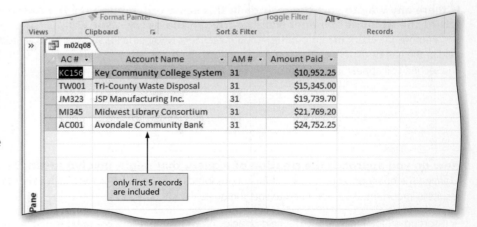

Figure 2–41

Q&A
Do I need to close the query before creating my next query?
Not necessarily. When you use a top-values query, however, it is important to change the value in the Return box back to All. If you do not change the Return value back to All, the previous value will remain in effect. Consequently, you might not get all the records you should in the next query. A good practice whenever you use a top-values query is to close the query as soon as you are done. That way, you will begin your next query from scratch, which ensures that the value is reset to All.

Joining Tables

In designing a query, you need to determine whether more than one table is required. For example, if the question being asked involves data from both the Account and Account Manager tables, then both tables are required for the query. For example, you might want a query that gives the number and name of each account (from the Account table) along with the number and name of the account's account manager (from the Account Manager table). Both the Account and Account Manager tables are required for this query. You need to **join** the tables to find records in the two tables that have identical values in matching fields (Figure 2–42). In this example, you need to find records in the Account table and the Account Manager table that have the same value in the Account Manager Number fields.

BTW
Ad Hoc Relationships
When you join tables in a query, you are creating an ad hoc relationship, that is, a relationship between tables created for a specific purpose. In Module 3, you will create general-purpose relationships using the Relationships window.

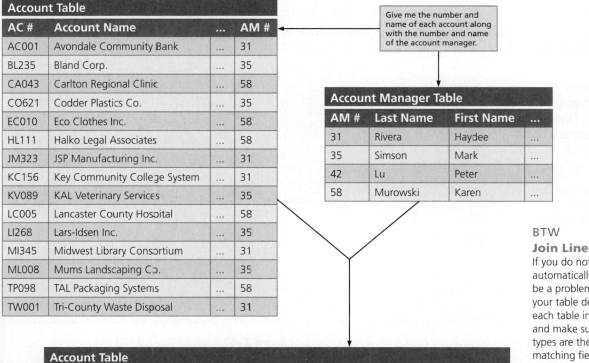

BTW
Join Line
If you do not get a join line automatically, there may be a problem with one of your table designs. Open each table in Design view and make sure that the data types are the same for the matching field in both tables and that one of the matching fields is the primary key in a table. Correct these errors and create the query again.

BTW
Join Types
The type of join that finds records from both tables that have identical values in matching fields is called an inner join. An inner join is the default join in Access. Outer joins are used to show all the records in one table as well as the common records; that is, the records that share the same value in the join field. In a left outer join, all rows from the table on the left are included. In a right outer join, all rows from the table on the right are included.

Figure 2–42

To Join Tables

If you have determined that you need to join tables, you first will bring field lists for both tables to the upper pane of the Query window while working in Design view. Access will draw a line, called a **join line**, between matching fields in the two tables, indicating that the tables are related. You then can select fields from either table. Access joins the tables automatically.

The first step is to create a new query and add the Account Manager table to the query. Then, add the Account table to the query. A join line should appear, connecting the Account Manager Number fields in the two field lists. *Why might the join line not appear? If the names of the matching fields differ from one table to the other, Access will not insert the line. You can insert it manually, however, by clicking one of the two matching fields and dragging the pointer to the other matching field.*

The following steps create a query to display information from both the Account table and the Account Manager table.

1

- Click Create on the ribbon to display the Create tab.

- Click the Query Design button (Create tab | Queries group) to create a new query.

- If necessary, click the Account Manager table (Show Table dialog box) to select the table.

- Click the Add button (Show Table dialog box) to add a field list for the Account Manager Table to the query (Figure 2–43).

Figure 2–43

2

- Click the Account table (Show Table dialog box).

- Click the Add button (Show Table dialog box) to add a field list for the Account table.

- Close the Show Table dialog box by clicking the Close button.

- Expand the size of the two field lists so all the fields in the Account Manager and Account tables appear (Figure 2–44).

Q&A I did not get a join line. What should I do?
Ensure that the names of the matching fields are the same, the data types are the same, and the matching field is the primary key in one of the two tables. If all of these factors are true and you still do not have a join line, you can produce one by pointing to a matching field and dragging to the other matching field.

Figure 2–44

❸
- In the design grid, include the Account Manager Number, Last Name, and First Name fields from the Account Manager Table as well as the Account Number and Account Name fields from the Account table.
- Select Ascending as the sort order for both the Account Manager Number field and the Account Number field (Figure 2–45).

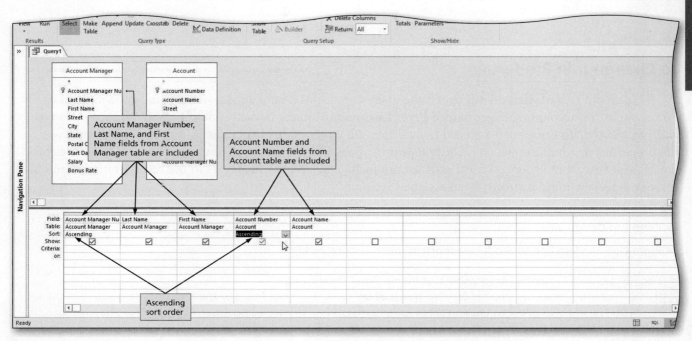

Figure 2–45

❹
- Run the query (Figure 2–46).

Figure 2–46

- Click the Save button on the Quick Access Toolbar to display the Save As dialog box.

- Type **Manager-Account Query** as the query name.

- Click the OK button (Save As dialog box) to save the query.

To Change Join Properties

1 CREATE QUERIES | 2 USE CRITERIA | 3 SORT DATA | 4 JOIN TABLES | 5 EXPORT RESULTS
6 PERFORM CALCULATIONS | 7 CREATE CROSSTAB | 8 CUSTOMIZE NAVIGATION PANE

Normally, records that do not match the query conditions do not appear in the results of a join query. For example, the account manager named Peter Lu does not appear in the results. *Why? He currently does not have any accounts.* To cause such a record to be displayed, you need to change the **join properties**, which are the properties that indicate which records appear in a join. The following steps change the join properties of the Manager-Account Query so that PrattLast can include all account managers in the results, rather than only those managers who have already been assigned accounts.

- Return to Design view.

- Right-click the join line to produce a shortcut menu (Figure 2–47).

Q&A | I do not see Join Properties on my shortcut menu. What should I do?
If Join Properties does not appear on your shortcut menu, you did not point to the appropriate portion of the join line. You will need to point to the correct (middle) portion and right-click again.

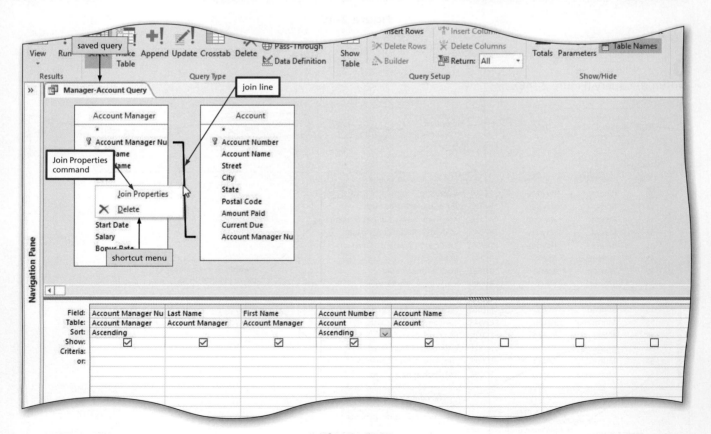

Figure 2–47

2

• Click Join Properties on the shortcut menu to display the Join Properties dialog box (Figure 2–48).

Figure 2–48

3

• Click option button 2 (Join Properties dialog box) to include all records from the Account Manager Table regardless of whether they match any accounts.

• Click the OK button (Join Properties dialog box) to modify the join properties.

• Run the query (Figure 2–49).

🔎 **Experiment**

• Return to Design view, change the Join properties, and select option button 3. Run the query to see the effect of this option. When done, return to Design view, change the join properties, and once again select option button 2.

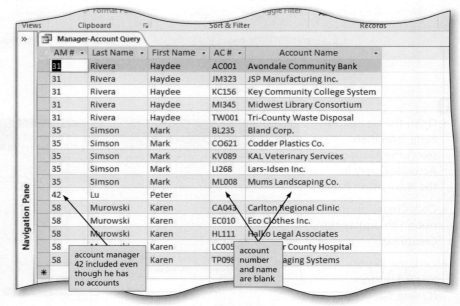

Figure 2–49

4

• Click the Save button on the Quick Access Toolbar to save the changes to the query.

• Close the Manager-Account Query.

Q&A | I see a dialog box that asks if I want to save the query. What should I do?
Click the OK button to save the query.

To Create a Report from a Query

You can use queries in the creation of reports. The report in Figure 2–50 involves data from more than one table. *Why? The Last Name and First Name fields are in the Account Manager table. The Account Number and Account Name fields are in the Account table. The Account Manager Number field is in both tables.* The easiest way to create such a report is to base it on a query that joins the two tables. The following steps use the Report Wizard and the Manager-Account Query to create the report.

Manager-Account Report

AM #	Last Name	First Name	AC #	Account Name
31	Rivera	Haydee	AC001	Avondale Community Bank
31	Rivera	Haydee	JM323	JSP Manufacturing Inc.
31	Rivera	Haydee	KC156	Key Community College System
31	Rivera	Haydee	MI345	Midwest Library Consortium
31	Rivera	Haydee	TW001	Tri-County Waste Disposal
35	Simson	Mark	BL235	Bland Corp.
35	Simson	Mark	CO621	Codder Plastics Co.
35	Simson	Mark	KV089	KAL Veterinary Services
35	Simson	Mark	LI268	Lars-Idsen Inc.
35	Simson	Mark	ML008	Mums Landscaping Co.
42	Lu	Peter		
58	Murowski	Karen	CA043	Carlton Regional Clinic
58	Murowski	Karen	EC010	Eco Clothes Inc.
58	Murowski	Karen	HL111	Halko Legal Associates
58	Murowski	Karen	LC005	Lancaster County Hospital
58	Murowski	Karen	TP098	TAL Packaging Systems

Figure 2–50

1

- Open the Navigation Pane, and then select the Manager-Account Query in the Navigation Pane.

- Click Create on the ribbon to display the Create tab.

- Click the Report Wizard button (Create tab | Reports group) to display the Report Wizard dialog box (Figure 2–51).

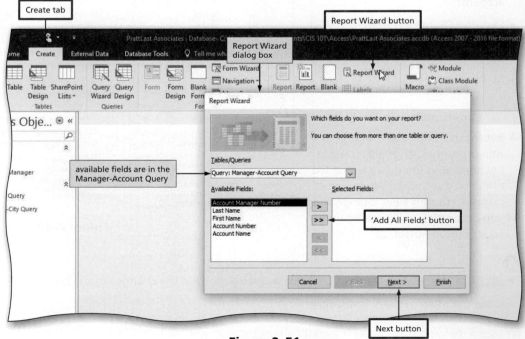

Figure 2–51

2

- Click the 'Add All Fields' button (Report Wizard dialog box) to add all the fields in the Manager-Account Query.

- Click the Next button to display the next Report Wizard screen (Figure 2–52).

Figure 2–52

3

- Because you will not specify any grouping, click the Next button in the Report Wizard dialog box to display the next Report Wizard screen.

- Because you already specified the sort order in the query, click the Next button again to display the next Report Wizard screen.

- Make sure that Tabular is selected as the Layout and Portrait is selected as the Orientation.

- Click the Next button to display the next Report Wizard screen.

- Erase the current title, and then type **Manager-Account Report** as the new title.

- Click the Finish button to produce the report (Figure 2–53).

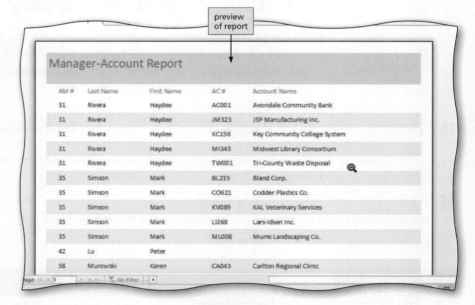

Figure 2–53

Q&A | My report is very small and does not look like the one in the figure. What should I do?
Click the pointer, which should look like a magnifying glass, anywhere in the report to magnify the report.

- Close the Manager-Account Report.

To Print a Report

The following steps print a hard copy of the report.

1 With the Manager-Account Report selected in the Navigation Pane, click File on the ribbon to open the Backstage view.

2 Click the Print tab in the Backstage view to display the Print gallery.

3 Click the Quick Print button to print the report.

How would you approach the creation of a query that might involve multiple tables?

• Examine the request to see if all the fields involved in the request are in one table. If the fields are in two (or more) tables, you need to join the tables.

• If joining is required, identify within the two tables the matching fields that have identical values. Look for the same column name in the two tables or for column names that are similar.

• Determine whether sorting is required. Queries that join tables often are used as the basis for a report. If this is the case, it may be necessary to sort the results. For example, the Manager-Account Report is based on a query that joins the Account Manager and Account tables. The query is sorted by account manager number and account number.

• Examine the request to see if there are any special restrictions. For example, the user may only want accounts whose current due amount is $0.00.

• Examine the request to see if you only want records from both tables that have identical values in matching fields. If you want to see records in one of the tables that do not have identical values in the other table, then you need to change the join properties.

Creating a Form for a Query

In the previous module, you created a form for the Account table. You can also create a form for a query. Recall that a **form** in a database is a formatted document with fields that contain data. Forms allow you to view and maintain data.

To Create a Form for a Query

1 CREATE QUERIES | 2 USE CRITERIA | 3 SORT DATA | 4 JOIN TABLES | 5 EXPORT RESULTS
6 PERFORM CALCULATIONS | 7 CREATE CROSSTAB | 8 CUSTOMIZE NAVIGATION PANE

The following steps create a form, then save the form. *Why? The form will be available for future use in viewing the data in the query.*

1

• If necessary, select the Manager-Account Query in the Navigation Pane.

• Click Create on the ribbon to display the Create tab (Figure 2–54).

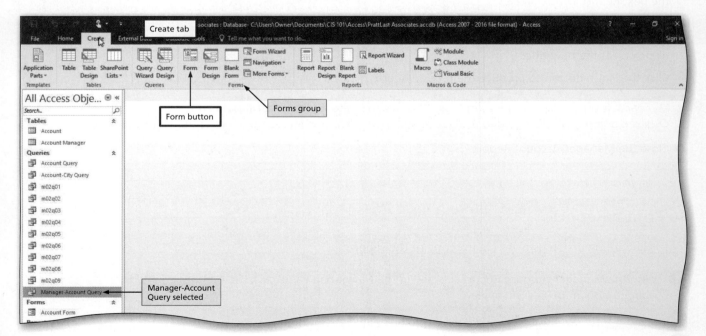

Figure 2–54

2

- Click the Form button (Create tab | Forms group) to create a simple form (Figure 2–55).

Q&A I see a field list also. What should I do?
Click the Close button for the Field List.

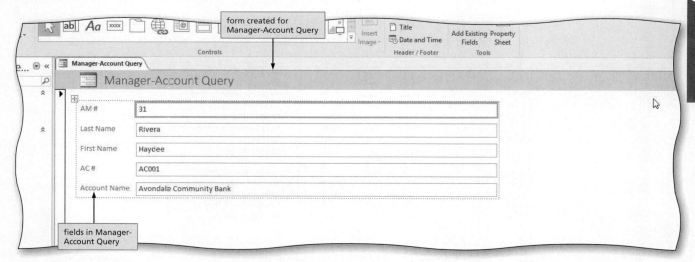

Figure 2–55

3

- Click the Save button on the Quick Access Toolbar to display the Save As dialog box.
- Type **Manager-Account Form** as the form name.
- Click the OK button to save the form.
- Click the Close button for the form to close the form.

Using a Form

After you have saved a form, you can use it at any time by right-clicking the form in the Navigation Pane and then clicking Open on the shortcut menu. If you plan to use the form to enter data, you must ensure you are viewing the form in Form view.

Break Point: If you wish to take a break, this is a good place to do so. You can exit Access now. To resume later, run Access, open the database called PrattLast Associates, and continue following the steps from this location forward.

Exporting Data From Access to Other Applications

You can **export**, or copy, tables or queries from an Access database so that another application (for example, Excel or Word) can use the data. The application that will receive the data determines the export process to be used. You can export to text files in a variety of formats. For applications to which you cannot directly export data, you often can export an appropriately formatted text file that the other application can import. Figure 2–56 shows the workbook produced by exporting the Manager-Account Query to Excel. The columns in the workbook have been resized to best fit the data.

BTW
Exporting Data
You frequently need to export data so that it can be used in other applications and by other users in an organization. For example, the Accounting department might require financial data in an Excel format to perform certain financial functions. Marketing might require a list of account names and addresses in Word or RTF format for marketing campaigns.

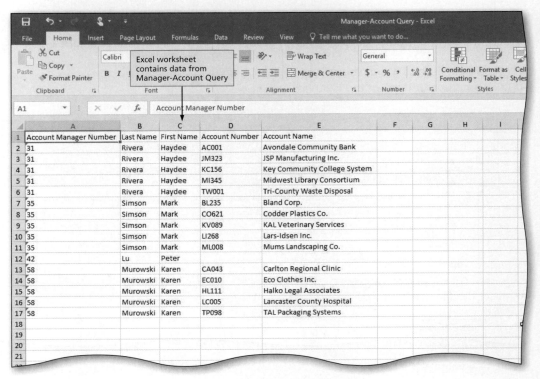

Figure 2–56

To Export Data to Excel

For PrattLast Associates to make the Manager-Account Query available to Excel users, it needs to export the data. To export data to Excel, select the table or query to be exported and then click the Excel button in the Export group on the External Data tab. The following steps export the Manager-Account Query to Excel and save the export steps. *Why save the export steps?* *By saving the export steps, you could easily repeat the export process whenever you like without going through all the steps.* You would use the saved steps to export data in the future by clicking the Saved Exports button (External Data tab | Export group) and then selecting the steps you saved.

1

- If necessary, click the Manager-Account Query in the Navigation Pane to select it.

- Click External Data on the ribbon to display the External Data tab (Figure 2–57).

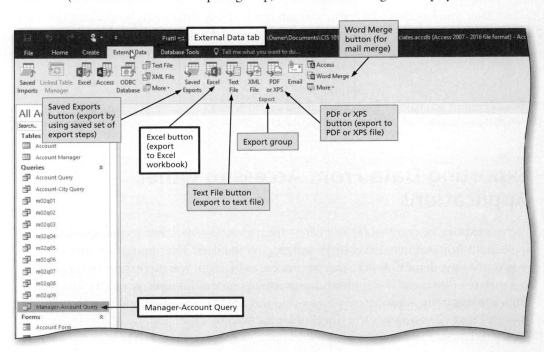

Figure 2–57

2

- Click the Excel button (External Data tab | Export group) to display the Export-Excel Spreadsheet dialog box.

- Click the Browse button (Export-Excel Spreadsheet dialog box), and then navigate to the location where you want to export the query (your hard disk, OneDrive, or other storage location).

- Confirm that the file format is Excel Workbook (*.xlsx), and the file name is Manager-Account Query, and then click the Save button (File Save dialog box) to select the file name and location (Figure 2–58).

Q&A Did I need to browse?
No. You could type the appropriate file location.

Could I change the name of the file?
You could change it. Simply replace the current file name with the one you want.

What if the file I want to export already exists?
Access will indicate that the file already exists and ask if you want to replace it. If you click the Yes button, the file you export will replace the old file. If you click the No button, you must either change the name of the export file or cancel the process.

- Click the OK button (Export-Excel Spreadsheet dialog box) to export the data (Figure 2–59).

Figure 2–58

Figure 2–59

- Click the 'Save export steps' check box (Export-Excel Spreadsheet dialog box) to display the Save Export Steps options.

- If necessary, type **Export-Manager-Account Query** in the Save as text box.

- Type **Export the Manager-Account Query without formatting** in the Description text box (Figure 2–60).

Q&A

How could I re-use the export steps?

You can use these steps to export data in the future by clicking the Saved Exports button (External Data tab | Export group) and then selecting the steps you saved.

Figure 2–60

- Click the Save Export button (Export-Excel Spreadsheet dialog box) to save the export steps.

Other Ways

1. Right-click database object in Navigation Pane, click Export.

BTW

Saving Export Steps
Because query results are based on the data in the underlying tables, a change to an underlying table would result in a new query answer. For example, if the last name for account manager 35 changed from Simson to Smith, the change would be made in the Account Manager table. If you run the Manager-Account Query again and export the query using the saved export steps, the Excel workbook would show the changed name.

TO EXPORT DATA TO WORD

It is not possible to export data from Access to the standard Word format. It is possible, however, to export the data as a rich text format (RTF) file, which Word can use. To export data from a query or table to an RTF file, you would use the following steps.

1. With the query or table to be exported selected in the Navigation Pane, click the More button (External Data tab | Export group) and then click Word on the More menu to display the Export-RTF File dialog box.

2. Navigate to the location in which to save the file and assign a file name.

3. Click the Save button, and then click the OK button to export the data.

4. Save the export steps if you want, or simply click the Close button in the Export-RTF File dialog box to close the dialog box without saving the export steps.

Text Files

You can also export Access data to text files, which can be used for a variety of purposes. Text files contain unformatted characters, including alphanumeric characters, and some special characters, such as tabs, carriage returns, and line feeds.

In **delimited files**, each record is on a separate line and the fields are separated by a special character, called the **delimiter**. Common delimiters are tabs, semicolons, commas, and spaces. You can also choose any other value that does not appear within the field contents as the delimiter. The comma-separated values (CSV) file often used in Excel is an example of a delimited file.

In **fixed-width files** the width of any field is the same on every record. For example, if the width of the first field on the first record is 12 characters, the width of the first field on every other record must also be 12 characters.

To Export Data to a Text File

When exporting data to a text file, you can choose to export the data with formatting and layout. This option preserves much of the formatting and layout in tables, queries, forms, and reports. For forms and reports, this is the only option for exporting to a text file.

If you do not need to preserve the formatting, you can choose either delimited or fixed-width as the format for the exported file. The most common option, especially if formatting is not an issue, is delimited. You can choose the delimiter. You can also choose whether to include field names on the first row. In many cases, delimiting with a comma and including the field names is a good choice.

To export data from a table or query to a comma-delimited file in which the first row contains the column headings, you would use the following steps.

1. With the query or table to be exported selected in the Navigation Pane, click the Text File button (External Data tab | Export group) to display the Export-Text File dialog box.

2. Select the name and location for the file to be created.

3. If you need to preserve formatting and layout, be sure the 'Export data with formatting and layout' check box is checked. If you do not need to preserve formatting and layout, make sure the check box is not checked. Once you have made your selection, click the OK button in the Export-Text File dialog box.

4. To create a delimited file, be sure the Delimited option button is selected in the Export Text Wizard dialog box. To create a fixed-width file, be sure the Fixed Width option button is selected. Once you have made your selection, click the Next button.

5. a. If you are exporting to a delimited file, choose the delimiter that you want to separate your fields, such as a comma. Decide whether to include field names on the first row and, if so, click the 'Include Field Names on First Row' check box. If you want to select a text qualifier, select it in the Text Qualifier list. When you have made your selections, click the Next button.

   b. If you are exporting to a fixed-width file, review the position of the vertical lines that separate your fields. If any lines are not positioned correctly, follow the directions on the screen to reposition them. When you have finished, click the Next button.

6. Click the Finish button to export the data.

7. Save the export steps if you want, or simply click the Close button in the Export-Text File dialog box to close the dialog box without saving the export steps.

Adding Criteria to a Join Query

Sometimes you will want to join tables, but you will not want to include all possible records. For example, you would like to create a report showing only those accounts whose amount paid is greater than $20,000.00. In this case, you would relate the tables and include fields just as you did before. You will also include criteria. To include only those accounts whose amount paid is more than $20,000.00, you will include >20000 as a criterion for the Amount Paid field.

BTW

Distributing a Document
Instead of printing and distributing a hard copy of a document, you can distribute the document electronically. Options include sending the document via email; posting it on cloud storage (such as OneDrive) and sharing the file with others; posting it on social media, a blog, or other website; and sharing a link associated with an online location of the document. You also can create and share a PDF or XPS image of the document, so that users can view the file in Acrobat Reader or XPS Viewer instead of in Access.

To Restrict the Records in a Join

The following steps modify the Manager-Account Query so that the results for PrattLast Associates include a criterion. ***Why?*** *PrattLast wants to include only those accounts whose amount paid is more than $20,000.00.*

- Open the Navigation Pane, if necessary, and then right-click the Manager-Account Query to produce a shortcut menu.

- Click Design View on the shortcut menu to open the Manager-Account Query in Design view.

- Close the Navigation Pane.

- Add the Amount Paid field to the query.

- Type >20000 as the criterion for the Amount Paid field (Figure 2–61).

Figure 2–61

2

- Run the query (Figure 2–62).

3

- Close the query.

- When asked if you want to save your changes, click the No button.

Q&A What would happen if I saved the changes?
The next time you used this query, you would only see accounts whose amount paid is more than $20,000.00.

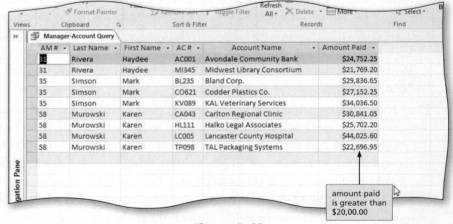

Figure 2–62

BTW
Expression Builder
Access includes a tool to help you create complex expressions. If you click Build on the shortcut menu (see Figure 2–63), Access displays the Expression Builder dialog box, which includes an expression box, operator buttons, and expression elements. You can type parts of the expression directly and paste operator buttons and expression elements into the box. You also can use functions in expressions.

Calculations

If a special calculation is required for a query, you need to determine whether the calculation is an **individual record calculation** (for example, adding the values in two fields for one record) or a **group calculation** (for example, finding the total of the values in a particular field on all the records).

PrattLast Associates might want to know the total amount (amount paid and current due) for each account. This would seem to pose a problem because the Account table does not include a field for total amount. You can calculate it, however, because the total amount is equal to the amount paid plus the current due. A field that can be computed from other fields is called a **calculated field** or a **computed field** and is not usually included in the table. Including it introduces the possibility for errors in the table. If the value in the field does not happen to match the results of the calculation, the data is inconsistent. A calculated field is an individual record calculation because each calculation only involves fields in a single record.

PrattLast might also want to calculate the average amount paid for the accounts of each account manager. That is, they may want the average for accounts of account manager 31, the average for accounts of account manager 35, and so on. This type of calculation is called a **group calculation** because each calculation involves groups of records. In this example, the accounts of account manager 31 would form one group, the accounts of account manager 35 would be a second group, and the accounts of account manager 58 would form a third group.

To Use a Calculated Field in a Query

1 CREATE QUERIES | 2 USE CRITERIA | 3 SORT DATA | 4 JOIN TABLES | 5 EXPORT RESULTS
6 PERFORM CALCULATIONS | 7 CREATE CROSSTAB | 8 CUSTOMIZE NAVIGATION PANE

If you need a calculated field in a query, you enter a name, or alias, for the calculated field, a colon, and then the calculation in one of the columns in the Field row of the design grid for the query. Any fields included in the expression must be enclosed in square brackets ([ ]). For example, for the total amount, you will type Total Amount:[Amount Paid]+[Current Due] as the expression.

You can type the expression directly into the Field row in Design view. The preferred method, however, is to select the column in the Field row and then use the Zoom command on its shortcut menu. When Access displays the Zoom dialog box, you can enter the expression. ***Why use the Zoom command?*** *You will not be able to see the entire entry in the Field row, because the space available is not large enough.*

You can use addition (+), subtraction (-), multiplication (*), or division (/) in calculations. If you have multiple calculations in an expression, you can include parentheses to indicate which calculations should be done first.

The following steps create a query that PrattLast Associates might use to obtain financial information on its accounts, including the total amount (amount paid + current due), which is a calculated field.

❶

- Create a query with a field list for the Account table.

- Add the Account Number, Account Name, Amount Paid, and Current Due fields to the query.

- Right-click the Field row in the first open column in the design grid to display a shortcut menu (Figure 2–63).

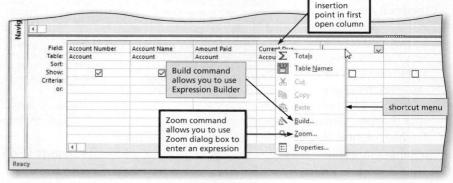

Figure 2–63

❷

- Click Zoom on the shortcut menu to display the Zoom dialog box.

- Type `Total Amount:[Amount Paid]+[Current Due]` in the Zoom dialog box (Figure 2–64).

Q&A Do I always need to put square brackets around field names?
If the field name does not contain spaces, square brackets are technically not required. It is a good practice, however, to get in the habit of using the brackets in field calculations.

Figure 2–64

3
- Click the OK button (Zoom dialog box) to enter the expression (Figure 2–65).

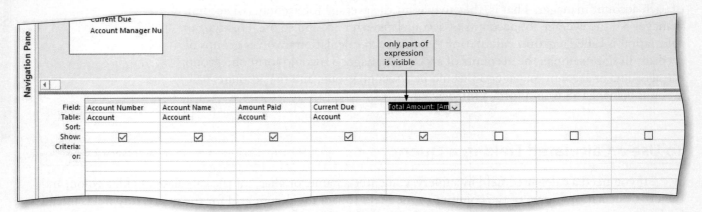

only part of expression is visible

Figure 2–65

4
- Run the query (Figure 2–66).

 Experiment

- Return to Design view and try other expressions. In at least one case, omit the Total Amount and the colon. In at least one case, intentionally misspell a field name. In each case, run the query to see the effect of your changes. When finished, reenter the original expression.

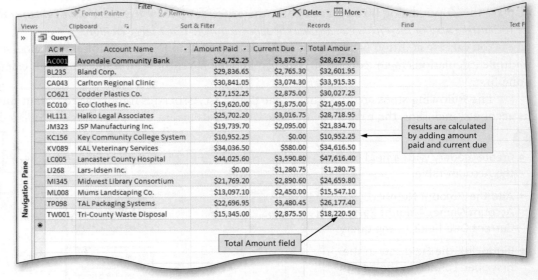

results are calculated by adding amount paid and current due

Total Amount field

Figure 2–66

Other Ways

1. Press SHIFT+F2

1 CREATE QUERIES | 2 USE CRITERIA | 3 SORT DATA | 4 JOIN TABLES | 5 EXPORT RESULTS
6 PERFORM CALCULATIONS | 7 CREATE CROSSTAB | 8 CUSTOMIZE NAVIGATION PANE

To Change a Caption

In Module 1, you changed the caption for a field in a table. When you assigned a caption, Access displayed it in datasheets and forms. If you did not assign a caption, Access displayed the field name. You can also change a caption in a query. Access will display the caption you assign in the query results. When you omitted duplicates, you used the query property sheet. When you change a caption in a query, you use the property sheet for the field. In the property sheet, you can change other properties for the field, such as the format and number of decimal places. The following steps change the caption of the Amount Paid field to Paid and the caption of the Current Due field to Due. *Why? These changes give shorter, yet very readable, column headings for the fields.* The steps also save the query with a new name.

❶

- Return to Design view.

- If necessary, click Design on the ribbon to display the Query Tools Design tab.

- Click the Amount Paid field in the design grid, and then click the Property Sheet button (Query Tools Design tab | Show/Hide group) to display the properties for the Amount Paid field.

- Click the Caption box, and then type **Paid** as the caption (Figure 2–67).

Q&A My property sheet looks different. What should I do?
Close the property sheet and repeat this step.

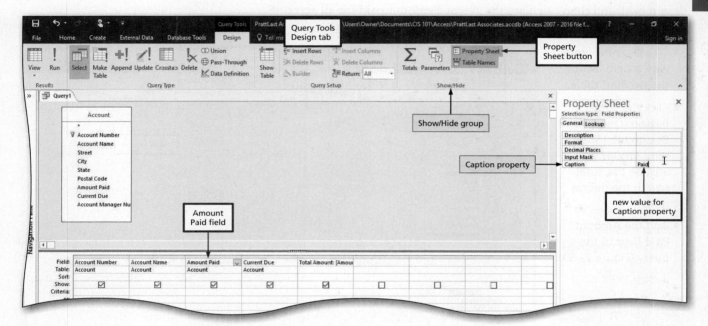

Figure 2–67

❷

- Click the Current Due field in the design grid to view its properties in the Property Sheet.

- Click the Caption box, and then type **Due** as the caption.

- Close the Property Sheet by clicking the Property Sheet button a second time.

- Run the query (Figure 2–68).

❸

- Save the query as m02q10.

- Close the query.

Figure 2–68

Other Ways

1. Right-click field in design grid, click Properties on shortcut menu

To Calculate Statistics

For group calculations, Microsoft Access supports several built-in statistics: COUNT (count of the number of records), SUM (total), AVG (average), MAX (largest value), MIN (smallest value), STDEV (standard deviation), VAR (variance), FIRST (first value), and LAST (last value). These statistics are called aggregate functions. An **aggregate function** is a function that performs some mathematical function against a group of records. To use an aggregate function in a query, you include it in the Total row in the design grid. In order to do so, you must first include the Total row by clicking the Totals button on the Design tab. *Why? The Total row usually does not appear in the grid.*

The following steps create a new query for the Account table. The steps include the Total row in the design grid, and then calculate the average amount paid for all accounts.

1

- Create a new query with a field list for the Account table.

- Click the Totals button (Query Tools Design tab | Show/Hide group) to include the Total row in the design grid.

- Add the Amount Paid field to the query (Figure 2–69).

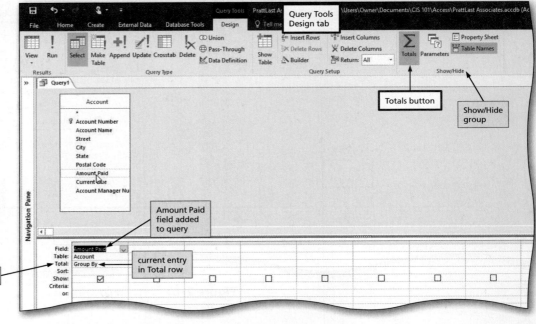

Figure 2–69

2

- Click the Total row in the Amount Paid column to display the Total arrow.

- Click the Total arrow to display the Total list (Figure 2–70).

Figure 2–70

3

- Click Avg to select the calculation that Access is to perform (Figure 2–71).

Figure 2–71

4

- Run the query (Figure 2–72).

🔎 **Experiment**

- Return to Design view and try other aggregate functions. In each case, run the query to see the effect of your selection. When finished, select Avg once again.

Figure 2–72

To Use Criteria in Calculating Statistics

1 CREATE QUERIES | 2 USE CRITERIA | 3 SORT DATA | 4 JOIN TABLES | 5 EXPORT RESULTS
6 PERFORM CALCULATIONS | **7 CREATE CROSSTAB** | 8 CUSTOMIZE NAVIGATION PANE

Why? *Sometimes calculating statistics for all the records in the table is appropriate. In other cases, however, you will need to calculate the statistics for only those records that satisfy certain criteria.* To enter a criterion in a field, first you select Where as the entry in the Total row for the field, and then enter the criterion in the Criteria row. Access uses the word, Where, to indicate that you will enter a criterion. The following steps use this technique to calculate the average amount paid for accounts of account manager 31. The steps also save the query with a new name.

1

- Return to Design view.

- Include the Account Manager Number field in the design grid.

- Click the Total row in the Account Manager Number column.

- Click the Total arrow in the Account Manager Number column to produce a Total list (Figure 2–73).

Figure 2–73

2

- Click Where to be able to enter a criterion.

- Type 31 as the criterion for the Account Manager Number field (Figure 2–74).

Figure 2–74

3

- Run the query (Figure 2–75).

4

- Save the query as m02q11.

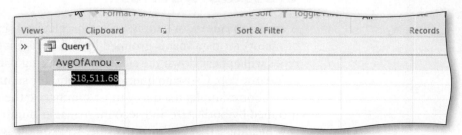

Figure 2–75

To Use Grouping

Why? Statistics are often used in combination with grouping; that is, statistics are calculated for groups of records. For example, PrattLast could calculate the average amount paid for the accounts of each account manager, which would require the average for the accounts of account manager 31, account manager 35, and so on. **Grouping** means creating groups of records that share some common characteristic. In grouping by Account Manager Number, for example, the accounts of account manager 31 would form one group, the accounts of account manager 35 would form a second, and the accounts of account manager 58 would form a third group. The calculations are then made for each group. To indicate grouping in Access, select Group By as the entry in the Total row for the field to be used for grouping.

The following steps create a query that calculates the average amount paid for the accounts of each account manager at PrattLast Associates. The steps also save the query with a new name.

- Return to Design view and clear the design grid.
- Include the Account Manager Number field in the query.
- Include the Amount Paid field in the query.
- Select Avg as the calculation in the Total row for the Amount Paid field (Figure 2–76).

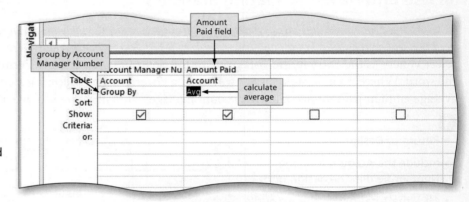

Figure 2–76

Q&A Why was it not necessary to change the entry in the Total row for the Account Manager Number field?
Group By, which is the initial entry in the Total row when you add a field, is correct. Thus, you did not need to change the entry.

- Run the query (Figure 2–77).

- Save the query as m02q12.
- Close the query.

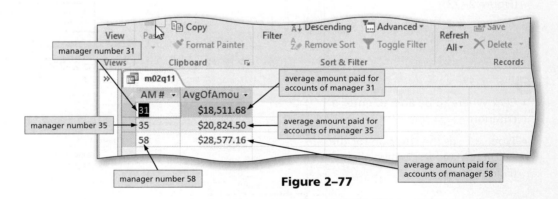

Figure 2–77

Crosstab Queries

A **crosstab query**, or simply, crosstab, calculates a statistic (for example, sum, average, or count) for data that is grouped by two different types of information. One of the types will appear down the side of the resulting datasheet, and the other will appear across the top. Crosstab queries are useful for summarizing data by category or group.

For example, if a query must summarize the sum of the current due amounts grouped by both state and account manager number, you could have states as the row headings, that is, down the side. You could have account manager numbers as the column headings, that is, across the top. The entries within the datasheet represent the total of the current due amounts. Figure 2–78 shows a crosstab in which the total of current due amounts is grouped by both state and account manager number, with states down the left side and account manager numbers across the top. For example, the entry in the row labeled IL and in the column labeled 31 represents the total of the current due amounts by all accounts of account manager 31 who are located in Illinois.

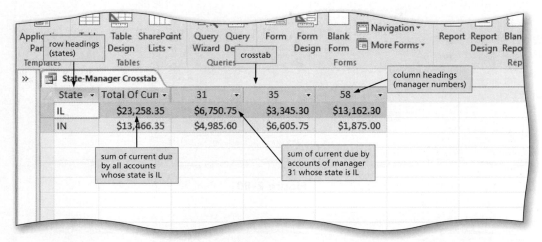

Figure 2–78

How do you know when to use a crosstab query?
If data is to be grouped by two different types of information, you can use a crosstab query. You will need to identify the two types of information. One of the types will form the row headings and the other will form the column headings in the query results.

CONSIDER THIS

To Create a Crosstab Query

1 CREATE QUERIES | 2 USE CRITERIA | 3 SORT DATA | 4 JOIN TABLES | 5 EXPORT RESULTS
6 PERFORM CALCULATIONS | 7 CREATE CROSSTAB | 8 CUSTOMIZE NAVIGATION PANE

The following steps use the Crosstab Query Wizard to create a crosstab query. *Why? PrattLast Associates wants to group data on current due amounts by two types of information: state and account manager.*

1
- Click Create on the ribbon to display the Create tab.
- Click the Query Wizard button (Create tab | Queries group) to display the New Query dialog box (Figure 2–79).

Figure 2–79

2

- Click Crosstab Query Wizard (New Query dialog box).

- Click the OK button to display the Crosstab Query Wizard dialog box (Figure 2–80).

Figure 2–80

3

- With the Tables option button selected, click Table: Account to select the Account table, and then click the Next button to display the next Crosstab Query Wizard screen.

- Click the State field, and then click the Add Field button to select the State field for row headings (Figure 2–81).

Figure 2–81

4

- Click the Next button to display the next Crosstab Query Wizard screen.

- Click the Account Manager Number field to select the field for column headings (Figure 2–82).

Figure 2–82

5

- Click the Next button to display the next Crosstab Query Wizard screen.

- Click the Current Due field to select the field for calculations.

🔎 **Experiment**

- Click other fields. For each field, examine the list of calculations that are available. When finished, click the Current Due field again.

- Click Sum to select the calculation to be performed (Figure 2–83).

Figure 2–83

Q&A

My list of functions is different. What did I do wrong?
Either you clicked the wrong field, or the Current Due field has the wrong data type. For example, if you mistakenly assigned it the Short Text data type, you would not see Sum in the list of available calculations.

6

- Click the Next button to display the next Crosstab Query Wizard screen.

- Erase the text in the name text box and type **State-Manager Crosstab** as the name of the query (Figure 2–84).

7

- If requested to do so by your instructor, name the crosstab query as FirstName LastName Crosstab where FirstName and LastName are your first and last names.

- Click the Finish button to produce the crosstab shown in Figure 2–78.

- Close the query.

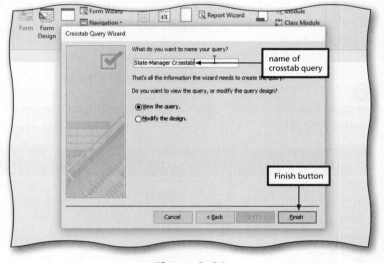

Figure 2–84

Customizing the Navigation Pane

Currently, the entries in the Navigation Pane are organized by object type. That is, all the tables are together, all the queries are together, and so on. You might want to change the way the information is organized. For example, you might want to have the Navigation Pane organized by table, with all the queries, forms, and reports associated with a particular table appearing after the name of the table. You can also use the Search bar to restrict the objects that appear to only those that have a certain collection of characters in their name. For example, if you entered the letters, Ma, only those objects containing Ma somewhere within the name will be included.

BTW

Access Help
At any time while using Access, you can find answers to questions and display information about various topics through Access Help. Used properly, this form of assistance can increase your productivity and reduce your frustrations by minimizing the time you spend learning how to use Access. For instructions about Access Help and exercises that will help you gain confidence in using it, read the Office and Windows module at the beginning of this book.

To Customize the Navigation Pane

The following steps change the organization of the Navigation Pane. They also use the Search bar to restrict the objects that appear. *Why? Using the Search bar, you can reduce the number of objects that appear in the Navigation Pane and just show the ones in which you are interested.*

1

- If necessary, click the 'Shutter Bar Open/Close Button' to open the Navigation Pane.

- Click the Navigation Pane arrow to produce the Navigation Pane menu (Figure 2–85).

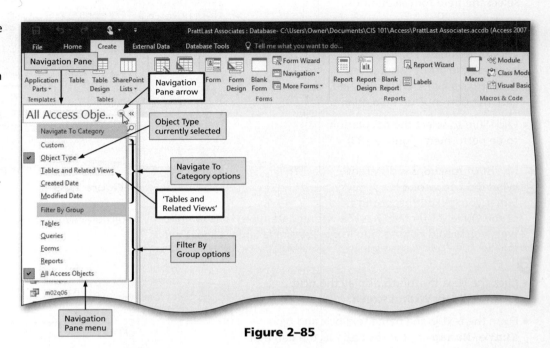

Figure 2–85

2

- Click 'Tables and Related Views' to organize the Navigation Pane by table rather than by the type of object (Figure 2–86).

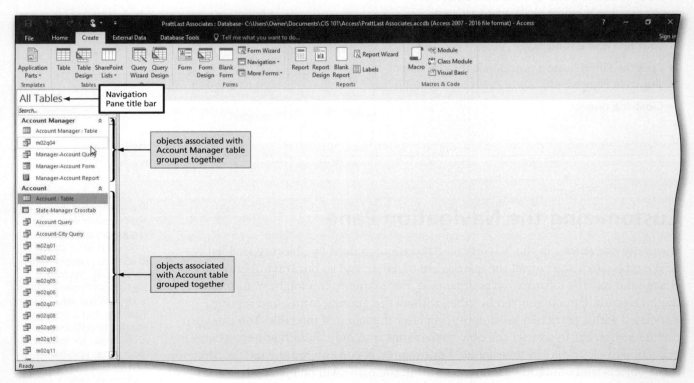

Figure 2–86

3

- Click the Navigation Pane arrow to produce the Navigation Pane menu.

- Click Object Type to once again organize the Navigation Pane by object type.

 Experiment

- Select different Navigate To Category options to see the effect of the option. With each option you select, select different Filter By Group options to see the effect of the filtering. When you have finished experimenting, select the 'Object Type Navigate To Category' option and the 'All Access Objects Filter By Group' option.

- If the Search bar does not appear, right-click the Navigation Pane and click Search Bar on the shortcut menu.

- Click in the Search box to produce an insertion point.

- Type **Ma** as the search string to restrict the objects displayed to only those containing the desired string (Figure 2–87).

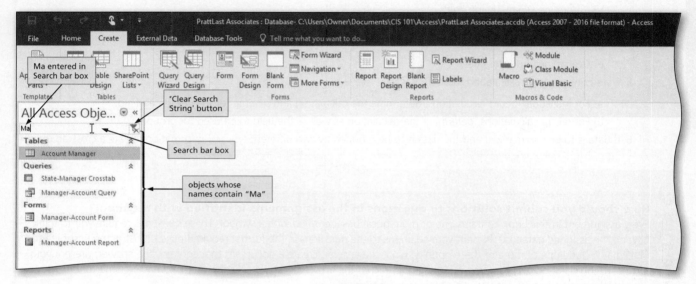

Figure 2–87

4

- Click the 'Clear Search String' button to remove the search string and redisplay all objects.

Q&A Did I have to click the button to redisplay all objects? Could I simply have erased the current string to achieve the same result?
You did not have to click the button. You could have used the DELETE or BACKSPACE keys to erase the current search string.

- If desired, sign out of your Microsoft account.

- Exit Access.

Summary

In this module you have learned to create queries, enter fields, enter criteria, use text and numeric data in queries, use wildcards, use compound criteria, create parameter queries, sort data in queries, join tables in queries, perform calculations in queries, and create crosstab queries. You also learned to create a report and a form that used a query, to export a query, and to customize the Navigation Pane.

CONSIDER THIS

What decisions will you need to make when creating queries?

Use these guidelines as you complete the assignments in this module and create your own queries outside of this class.

1. Identify the fields by examining the question or request to determine which fields from the tables in the database are involved.

2. Identify restrictions or the conditions that records must satisfy to be included in the results.

3. Determine whether special order is required.

    a) Determine the sort key(s).

    b) If using two sort keys, determine the major and minor key.

    c) Determine sort order. If there are no words to imply a particular order, you would typically use Ascending.

    d) Determine restrictions, such as excluding duplicates.

4. Determine whether more than one table is required.

    a) Determine which tables to include.

    b) Determine the matching fields.

    c) Determine whether sorting is required.

    d) Determine restrictions.

    e) Determine join properties.

5. Determine whether calculations are required.

    a) For individual record calculations, determine the calculation and a name for the calculated field.

    b) For group calculations, determine the calculation as well as the field to be used for grouping.

6. If data is to be summarized and the data is to be grouped by two different types of information, create a crosstab query.

CONSIDER THIS

How should you submit solutions to questions in the assignments identified with a symbol?

Every assignment in this book contains one or more questions identified with a symbol. These questions require you to think beyond the assigned database. Present your solutions to the questions in the format required by your instructor. Possible formats may include one or more of these options: write the answer; create a document that contains the answer; present your answer to the class; discuss your answer in a group; record the answer as audio or video using a webcam, smartphone, or portable media player; or post answers on a blog, wiki, or website.

Apply Your Knowledge

Reinforce the skills and apply the concepts you learned in this module.

Using Wildcards in a Query, Creating a Parameter Query, Joining Tables, and Creating a Report

Instructions: Run Access. Open the Apply Friendly Janitorial Services database that you modified in Apply Your Knowledge in Module 1. (If you did not complete the exercise, see your instructor for a copy of the modified database.)

Perform the following tasks:

1. Create a query for the Client table and add the Client Number, Client Name, Amount Paid, and Current Due fields to the design grid. Add a criterion to find all clients whose names start with the letter B. Run the query and then save it as Apply 2 Step 1 Query.

2. Create a query for the Client table and add the Client Number, Client Name, Amount Paid, and Supervisor Number fields to the design grid. Sort the records in descending order by Amount Paid. Add a criterion for the Supervisor Number field that allows the user to enter a different supervisor each time the query is run. Run the query and enter 114 as the supervisor number to test the query. Save the query as Apply 2 Step 2 Query.

3. Create a query for the Client table and add the Client Number, Client Name, and Current Due fields to the design grid. Add a criterion to find all clients whose current due amount is less than $500.00. Run the query and then save it as Apply 2 Step 3 Query.

4. Create a query that joins the Supervisor and Client tables. Add the Supervisor Number, Last Name, and First Name fields from the Supervisor table and the Client Number and Client Name fields from the Client table to the design grid. Sort the records in ascending order by Client Number within Supervisor Number. Run the query and save it as Supervisor-Client Query.

5. Create the report shown in Figure 2–88. The report uses the Supervisor-Client Query.

Supervisor-Client Report

SU #	Last Name	First Name	CL #	Client Name
103	Estevez	Enrique	AT13	Atlas Repair
103	Estevez	Enrique	CP03	Calder Plastics
103	Estevez	Enrique	HC17	Hill Crafts
103	Estevez	Enrique	KD15	Klean n Dri
110	Hillsdale	Rachel	AZ01	AZ Auto
110	Hillsdale	Rachel	BB35	Babbage Bookkeeping
110	Hillsdale	Rachel	CJ45	C Joe Diner
110	Hillsdale	Rachel	HN23	Hurley National Bank
110	Hillsdale	Rachel	PL03	Prime Legal Associates
114	Liu	Chou	CC25	Cramden Co.
114	Liu	Chou	MM01	Moss Manufacturing
114	Liu	Chou	PS67	PRIM Staffing
120	Short	Chris	BL24	Blanton Shoes
120	Short	Chris	KC12	Kady Regional Clinic
120	Short	Chris	TE15	Telton-Edwards

Figure 2–88

6. If requested to do so by your instructor, rename the Supervisor-Client Report in the Navigation Pane as LastName-Client Report where LastName is your last name.

7. Submit the revised database in the format specified by your instructor.

8. ☀ What criteria would you enter in the Street field if you wanted to find all clients whose businesses were on Beard?

Extend Your Knowledge

Extend the skills you learned in this module and experiment with new skills. You may need to use Help to complete the assignment.

Creating Crosstab Queries Using Criteria and Exporting a Query

Note: To complete this assignment, you will be required to use the Data Files. Please contact your instructor for information about accessing the Data Files.

Continued >

STUDENT ASSIGNMENTS

Extend Your Knowledge *continued*

Instructions: Run Access. Open the Extend TAL Maintenance database, which is located in the Data Files. TAL Maintenance is a small business that provides various outdoor maintenance services, such as painting, lawn maintenance, and parking lot re-paving, to commercial customers. The owner has created an Access database in which to store information about the customers the company serves and team leaders working for the company. You will create the crosstab query shown in Figure 2–89. You will also query the database using specified criteria and export a query.

Perform the following tasks:

1. Create the crosstab query shown in Figure 2–89. The crosstab groups the total of customers' balance by city and team leader number.

2. Create a query to find all customers who are not located in Rock Hill. Include the Customer Number, Customer Name, and Balance fields in the query results. Save the query as Extend 2 Step 2 Query.

Views	Clipboard	🖫		Sort & Filter			Reco
»	🗗 City-Team Leader Crosstab						
	City ▾	Total Of Bala ▾	26 ▾	29 ▾	32 ▾		
	Chester	$985.00	$180.00	$805.00			
	Lancaster	$3,301.60	$515.00	$1,000.50	$1,786.10		
	Rock Hill	$3,650.30	$1,790.50	$1,514.80	$345.00		
	York	$530.00			$530.00		

Figure 2–89

3. Create a query to find all team leaders whose first name is either Alex or Alix. Include the Team Leader Number, First Name, and Last Name in the query results. Save the query as Extend 2 Step 3 Query.

4. Create a query to find all customers where the team leader number is either 29 or 32 and the balance is greater than $550.00. Include the Customer Number, Customer Name, Balance, and Team Leader Number fields in the design grid in that order. Use the IN operator in your query design. Sort the results by customer number within team leader number. Save the query as Extend 2 Step 4 Query.

5. Export the City-Team Leader Crosstab as a Word file with the name City-Team Leader Crosstab.rtf and save the export steps.

6. Open the Customer table and change the balance for account C04 to $1,000.50.

7. If requested to do so by your instructor, change the customer name of customer K10 from Kathy's Books to Last Name Books where Last Name is your last name.

8. Use the saved export steps to export the City-Team Leader Crosstab again. When asked if you want to replace the existing file, click Yes.

9. Submit the revised database and the exported RTF file in the format specified by your instructor.

10. ✳ How would you create the query in Step 4 without using the IN operator?

Expand Your World

Create a solution, which uses cloud and web technologies, by learning and investigating on your own from general guidance.

Problem: You are taking a general science course and the instructor would like you to gather some weather statistics and query the statistics as part of the unit on climate change.

Instructions:

1. Examine a website that contains historical weather data, such as accuweather.com or weatherunderground.com. Select weather data for the city in which you were born for the month of January, 2014. If you cannot find your city, then select a large city near your current location.

2. Create a database that contains one table and has the following fields: Day of the month (1 through 31), Day of the week, high temperature for the day, and low temperature for the day. (*Hint:* Use the autonumber data type to record the day of the month.)

3. Create queries that do the following:

   a. Display the five days with the highest high temperature.

   b. Display the five days with lowest low temperature.

   c. Display the average high and low temperature for the entire month.

   d. Calculate the difference between the high and low temperatures for each day.

   e. Display the high and low temperatures for each day in both Fahrenheit and Celsius. (*Hint:* Use the Internet to find the conversion formula.)

4. Submit the revised database in the format specified by your instructor.

5. Use an Internet search engine to find the historical average high and low temperatures in January for your city.

6. ☀ Which websites did you use to gather data and search for the historical averages? How does the query result in Step 3c differ from the historical average?

In the Labs

Design, create, modify, and/or use a database following the guidelines, concepts, and skills presented in this module. Labs are listed in order of increasing difficulty. Labs 1 and 2, which increase in difficulty, require you to create solutions based on what you learned in the module; Lab 3 requires you to apply your creative thinking and problem solving skills to design and implement a solution.

Lab 1: Querying the Garden Naturally Database

Problem: The management of Garden Naturally has determined a number of questions it wants the database management system to answer. You must obtain the answers to these questions.

Note: Use the database modified in Lab 1 of Module 1 for this assignment, or see your instructor for information on accessing the required files.

Instructions: Perform the following tasks:

1. Run Access. Open the Lab 1 Garden Naturally database you modified in Module 1 and create a new query for the Customer table. Add the Customer Number, Customer Name, Amount Paid, Balance Due, and Sales Rep Number fields to the design grid, and restrict the query results to only those customers where the sales rep number is 29. Save the query as Lab 2-1 Step 1 Query.

2. Create a query for the Customer table that includes the Customer Number, Customer Name, and Balance Due fields for all customers located in Delaware (DE) with a balance due greater than $1,000.00. Save the query as Lab 2-1 Step 2 Query.

3. Create a query for the Customer table that includes the Customer Number, Customer Name, Address, City, and State fields for all customers located in cities that begin with Ch. Save the query as Lab 2-1 Step 3 Query.

Continued >

In the Labs *continued*

4. Create a query for the Customer table that lists all states in ascending order. Each state should appear only once. Save the query as Lab 2-1 Step 4 Query.

5. Create a query for the Customer table that allows the user to type the name of the desired city when the query is run. The query results should display the Customer Number, Customer Name, Balance Due, and Amount Paid fields in that order. Test the query by searching for those records where the customer is located in Quaker. Save the query as Lab 2-1 Step 5 Query.

6. Create a query for the Sales Rep table that includes the First Name, Last Name, and Start Date for all sales reps who started after June 1, 2015. Save the query as Lab 2-1 Step 6 Query.

7. Create a query that joins the Sales Rep and Customer tables. Include the Sales Rep Number, Last Name, and First Name from the Sales Rep table. Include the Customer Number, Customer Name, and Amount Paid from the Customer table. Sort the records in ascending order by sales rep's last name and then by customer name. All sales reps should appear in the result even if they currently have no customers. Save the query as Lab 2-1 Step 7 Query.

8. Open the Lab 2-1 Step 7 Query in Design view and remove the Sales Rep table from the query. Add the Balance Due field to the design grid. Calculate the total of the balance and amount paid amounts. Assign the alias Total Amount to the calculated field. Change the caption for the Amount Paid field to Paid and the caption for the Balance Due field to Owed. Save the query as Lab 2-1 Step 8 Query.

9. Create a query for the Customer table to display the total amount paid for sales rep 26. Save the query as Lab 2-1 Step 9 Query.

10. Create a query for the Customer table to display the average balance due for each sales rep. Save the query as Lab 2-1 Step 10 Query.

11. Create the crosstab query shown in Figure 2–90. The crosstab groups the average of customers' amount paid by state and sales rep number. Save the crosstab as State-Sales Rep Crosstab.

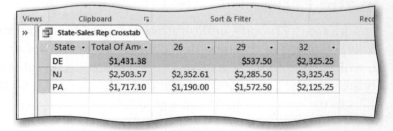

12. If requested to do so by your instructor, open the Lab 2-1 Step 1 query and change the caption for the Sales Rep Number field to your last name.

Figure 2–90

13. Submit the revised database in the format specified by your instructor.

14. ✹ How would you modify the query in Step 7 to include only sales reps that currently have customers?

Lab 2: Querying the Museum Gift Shop Database

Problem: The manager of the Museum gift shop has determined a number of questions she wants the database management system to answer. You must obtain answers to these questions.

Note: Use the database created in Lab 2 of Module 1 for this assignment or see your instructor for information on accessing the required files.

Instructions: Perform the following tasks:

1. Run Access. Open the Lab 2 Museum Gift Shop database and create a query for the Item table that includes all fields and all records in the Item table. Name the query Lab 2-2 Step 1 Query.

2. Create a query for the Item table that includes the Item Number, Description, Wholesale Cost, and Vendor Code fields for all records where the vendor code is AW. Save the query as Lab 2-2 Step 2 Query.

3. Create a query for the Item table that includes the Item Number and Description fields for all items where the description starts with G. Save the query as Lab 2-2 Step 3 Query.

4. Create a query for the Item table that includes the Item Number and Description for all items with a Wholesale Cost greater than $15.00. Save the query as Lab 2-2 Step 4 Query.

5. Create a query for the Item table that includes the Item Number, Description, and Wholesale Cost fields for all items with a Wholesale Cost between $5.00 and $10.00. Save the query as Lab 2-2 Step 5 Query.

6. Create a query for the Item table that includes the Item Number, Description, On Hand, and Wholesale Cost fields for all items where the number on hand is less than 5 and the wholesale cost is less than $15.00. Save the query as Lab 2-2 Step 6 Query.

7. Create a query for the Item table that includes the Item Number, Description, Wholesale Cost, and Vendor Code for all items that have a Wholesale Cost greater than $20.00 or a Supplier Code of SD. Save the query as Lab 2-2 Step 7 Query.

8. Create a query that joins the Vendor and the Item tables. Include the Vendor Code and Vendor Name from the Vendor table and the Item Number, Description, Wholesale Cost, and Retail Price fields from the Item table. Sort the query in ascending order by Description within Vendor Code. Save the query as Vendor-Item Query.

9. Create a form for the Vendor-Item Query. Save the form as Vendor-Item Form.

10. If requested to do so by your instructor, rename the form in the Navigation Pane as LastName-Item Form where LastName is your last name.

11. Create the report shown in Figure 2–91. The report uses the Vendor-Item Query but does not use all the fields in the query.

Vendor-Item Report

Vendor Name	Description	Wholesale	Retail
Atherton Wholesalers	Amazing Science Fun	$13.50	$24.99
Atherton Wholesalers	Crystal Growing Kit	$6.75	$12.97
Atherton Wholesalers	Discovery Dinosaurs	$12.35	$19.95
Atherton Wholesalers	Gem Nature Guide	$9.50	$14.95
Atherton Wholesalers	Onyx Jar	$7.50	$13.97
Gift Specialties	Agate Bookends	$16.25	$27.97
Gift Specialties	Dinosaur Egg Ornament	$7.50	$14.99
Gift Specialties	Fibonacci Necklace	$16.75	$29.99
Gift Specialties	Gyrobot	$27.99	$49.99
Gift Specialties	Molecule Necklace	$16.25	$29.95
Smith Distributors	Cosmos Uncovered	$8.95	$15.00
Smith Distributors	Fun with Math	$12.95	$24.95
Smith Distributors	Geek Toys Guide	$5.10	$9.99
Smith Distributors	Paper Planes	$7.10	$13.99
Smith Distributors	Slime Time	$15.35	$24.99

Figure 2–91

Continued >

In the Labs *continued*

12. Create a query for the Item table that includes the Item Number, Description, Wholesale Cost, and Retail Price. Calculate the difference between Retail Price and Wholesale Cost (Retail Price – Wholesale Cost). Assign the alias Mark Up to the calculated field. Save the query as Lab 2-2 Step 12 Query.

13. Create a query for the Item table that displays the average Wholesale Cost and the average Retail Price of all items. Save the query as Lab 2-2 Step 13 Query.

14. Create a query for the Item table that displays the Item Number, Description, On Hand, and Retail Price for the 5 items with the lowest retail price. Save the query as Lab 2-2 Step 14 Query.

15. Submit the revised database in the format specified by your instructor.

16. ✳ How could you modify the query in step 2 to find all vendors where the vendor code is AW or GS? If there is more than one way to perform this query, list all ways.

Lab 3: **Consider This: Your Turn**

Querying the Camshay Marketing Database

Instructions: Open the Lab 3 Camshay Marketing database you created in Module 1. If you did not create this database, contact your instructor for information about accessing the required files.

Part 1: Use the concepts and techniques presented in this module to create queries for the following. Save each query.

   a. Find all marketing analysts who started between June 1, 2015 and September 30, 2015. Show the marketing analyst's first name, last name, salary YTD, and incentive YTD.

   b. Find the client name and street address of all clients located in a city that starts with Bu.

   c. Find the client number, client name, amount paid and current due of all clients whose amount paid is $0.00 or whose current due is $0.00.

   d. Find the client number, client name, amount paid, current due, and total amount for all clients located in North Carolina (NC).

   e. Create a parameter query for the Client table that will allow the user to enter a different city each time the query is run. The user should see all fields in the query result.

   f. Create a crosstab query that groups the amount paid total by city and marketing analyst.

   g. Find the marketing analyst for each client. List the marketing analyst number, first name, last name, client number, client name, and current due. Sort the results by client number within marketing analyst number.

   h. Open the query you created in Step g above and restrict retrieval to only those clients whose current due amount is greater than $5,000.00.

   i. Change the organization of the Navigation Pane so that all objects associated with the Client table are grouped together and all objects associated with the Marketing Analyst are grouped together.

Submit your assignment in the format specified by your instructor.

Part 2: You made several decisions while creating the queries in this assignment, including the parameter query in Step e. What was the rationale behind your decisions? There are two ways to create the query in step e. What are they? Which one did you use?

Index